Stratification, Class, and Conflict

Irving Krauss

THE FREE PRESS
A Division of Macmillan Publishing Co., Inc.
NEW YORK

Collier Macmillan Publishers
LONDON

For L. B. and Miriam,
and to the memory of
my father, Joseph

The Free Press
A Division of Macmillan Publishing Co., Inc.
866 Third Avenue, New York, N.Y. 10022

Collier Macmillan Canada, Ltd.

Library of Congress Catalog Card Number: 75–12060

Printed in the United States of America

printing number

1 2 3 4 5 6 7 8 9 10

Library of Congress Cataloging in Publication Data

Krauss, Irving.
    Stratification, class, and conflict.

    Includes bibliographical references and index.
    1. Social classes. 2. Social conflict.
3. Social classes--United States. I. Title.
HT609.K725   301.44   75-12060
ISBN 0-02-917690-5

Copyright Acknowledgments

Contents

Introduction

All or most of us are quite aware of stratification and class since they impinge on so many aspects of our lives. Moreover, people have always acknowledged differences among themselves in wealth, prestige, and the ability to make others do what they want. Such distinctions are mentioned in the Bible, the Koran, and in the Veda scriptures; they represent part of the folklore of many peoples.[1] For example, among the Indian tribes in the area which is now Washington state and the northwestern part of Oregon there is the following tale:

> At the beginning of the world God created a certain number of men and women and gave to them the flocks that were necessary for their subsistence. Afterwards he created some others, to whom he gave nothing. When they demanded their share, God said to them, "Serve the others, and they will give you what you need." This was the origin of master and servant—in other words of nobles and common people.

And a medieval European rhyme reads:

> God hath shapen lives three;
> Boor and Knight and priest they be.

Contemporaneously, people acknowledge differences which set them off from others. Individuals may feel "one up" on their fellows because of their language or behavior, or because they belong to the "in" crowd. Others may believe that they are better or somehow superior because of certain possessions, such as fine furniture, costly jewels, Brooks Brothers clothing, Paris-designed gowns, or an expensive sports car, or because of their occupation or where they live. Such differences are reflected in everyday language, and the label "classes" and to a lesser extent "stratification" are often applied to them. Thus we hear talk about the "upper class," the "middle class," or the "lower class." People refer to others as belonging to the "white-collar class" if their occupation is clean and requires brain power over muscle power, or to the "blue collar" or "working class" if they work with their hands. Sometimes neigh-

[1] See Stanislaw Ossowski, *Class Structure in the Social Consciousness* (New York: The Free Press, 1963), pp. 19–37. The quotations that follow are from Gunnar Landtmann, *The Origin of the Inequality of the Social Classes* (London: Kegan Paul, Trench, Trubner, 1938), p. 69; and James W. Thompson, *The Middle Ages, 300–1500* (New York: Alfred A. Knopf, 1932), p. 721, respectively.

borhoods are cited in which "upper strata" people live, while in some sections of a city persons are referred to as "lower strata."

Such distinctions and the designation of classes and strata have interested many novelists who have described the life conditions which seem to generate them. For example, Sinclair Lewis in *Babbitt* examines the middle class in a presumably typical midwestern American community. Upper-class life in two widely different contexts provides the setting for the novels of Giuseppe di Lampedusa and John P. Marquand: the first, *The Leopard,* is concerned with an upper class family in Sicily in the latter half of the 19th century, and the second, *B.F.'s Daughter,* with an American upper-class family of the 1940's.

A number of classes are described in *The Thirteen* by Honoré de Balzac, who mentions "the middle classes and the proletariat"; "the patricians, the upper classes, and yet other ranks below them"; "the least intelligent classes," "aristocracy," and "upper and lower spheres of social activity, emphasized by differences in their manner of living. . . ." The American writer Theodore Dreiser in *Sister Carrie* vividly contrasts lower- and upper-class life.

George Orwell, in *The Road to Wigin Pier* describes the English upper-middle class, and deals with several criteria which affect class position. The upper middle class, he writes, is

> . . . the layer of society lying between £2,000 and £300 [sic] a year. . . . Nevertheless, the essential point about the English class-system is that it is *not* entirely explicable in terms of money. Roughly speaking it is a money-stratification, but it is also interpenetrated by a sort of shadowy caste-system. . . . A naval officer and his grocer very likely have the same income, but they are not equivalent persons and they would only be on the same side in very large issues such as a war or a general strike—possibly not even then. . . . Probably the distinguishing mark of the upper-middle class was that its traditions were not to any extent commercial, but mainly military, official, and professional.

He also writes about the working-classes and the ". . . hostility between upper and lower classes, . . ." as well as a person's ". . . stuck-up-ness and . . . accent and manners which stamp [him] as one of the boss class." The American novelist Upton Sinclair, in *The Jungle,* takes the reader to the "back of the yards" section of Chicago—the slum area behind the stockyards—and describes the poverty and hopelessness of a segment of the lower or working class. Claude Brown, in *Manchild in the Promised Land* shows the grinding poverty and social disorganization of the inner-city ghetto.

The movement from one class or stratum to another—vertical social mobility—also interests novelists, and Budd Schulberg's *What Makes Sammy Run?* depicts a case of extremely rapid upward mobility. A more ordinary instance of upward vertical movement is the subject of another of Marquand's novels, *Point of No Return,* in which mobility for the young man requires that he leave his home town, both in a physical and social sense.[2]

But if stratification and class are important only for casual observations or as subject matter for interesting novels, then we need go no further. As we show in this book, however, stratification and class permeate almost all aspects of our lives, and vitally affect what goes on in a local community as well as in a nation. Among the strata there are important differences in such things as health, possessions, educational opportunity, political activity, and social behavior. In regard to the latter, for example, who we go out with and marry are significantly associated with stratum position.

Even though many of us tend not to think in terms of class behavior—in the sense of class conflict—our discussion shows that it is as American as apple pie, that it has existed from Colonial times to the present. Moreover, such behavior is common throughout human history, and knowledge of it helps us understand current contesting between the "haves" and "have-nots," and provides benchmarks for assessing the future of stratification, class, and conflict.

Overview

This book is divided into five parts. In Part One we try to clarify the concepts of stratification and class and show how they are an elemental part of human group life. Chapter I goes into the theoretical bases and introduces the idea of social goods. Also examined are the transition from strata to classes, and the conditions which facilitate class conflict, including revolution. Strata and classes may be relatively "closed"—that is, it is extremely difficult for individuals or their children to move out of them. Or, they may be relatively "open," which means considerable social mobility. That is the topic of Chapter II. Chapter III goes into stratification in greater detail, showing how people obtain social goods; it then looks at the dimensions of income, occupation, and education. Part Two examines stratification through the life cycle. Chapters IV, V, and VI show how conditions in the different strata affect pepple's well-being, in

---

[2] Sinclair Lewis, *Babbitt* (New York: Harcourt, Brace & Co., 1922); Giuseppe di Lampedusa, *The Leopard* (New York: The New American Library, 1961); John P. Marquand, *B.F.'s Daughter* (New York: Bantam Books, 1951); Honoré de Balzac, *The Thirteen*, trans. by Ellen Marriage (New York: The Wheeler Publishing Co., 1901), pp. 153–155; Theodore Dreiser, *Sister Carrie* (New York: The New American Library, 1962; first pub. in 1900), pp. 45–47, 451; George Orwell, *The Road to Wigin Pier* (London: Victor Gollancz, Ltd., 1937), pp. 153–155; Upton Sinclair, *The Jungle* (New York: The New American Library, 1963; first pub. in 1905); Claude Brown, *Manchild in the Promised Land* (New York: The New American Library, 1965); Budd Schulberg, *What Makes Sammy Run* (New York: Modern Library, 1952), and Marquand, *Point of No Return* (Boston: Little, Brown, 1949).

terms of infancy through adolescence, youth, and adulthood and old age, respectively.

Beginning with Part Three the emphasis shifts to class. Changes in material conditions and people's perspectives, and the way they affect stratification and class behavior are studied historically. Chapter VII surveys developments in preindustrial society, and Chapter VIII deals with their impact on people's outlook. The importance of industrialization and the factors which led to the world-shaking French Revolution of 1789 and related upheavals are examined in Chapter IX. The next two chapters investigate the manner in which the material and ideational changes have influenced the concepts and theories of stratification and class; Chapter X is devoted to early writers and Chapter XI to modern writers.

Part Four examines stratification, class, and conflict in America, beginning with Colonial times and the Revolution of 1776 (Chapter XII); the triumph of the conservatives is the topic of Chapter XIII. The social and economic consequences of American industrialization are dealt with in Chapter XIV, and the attendant class conflict in XV. Chapter XVI details these phenomena in the modern period. In Part Five (Chapter XVII) we peer through our rather clouded crystal ball and try to assess what future stratification, class, and conflict will be like.

Part One

SOCIAL GOODS, STRATIFICATION, AND CLASS

Chapter I.   Social Goods, Stratification, and Class

To understand stratification and class it is important to show how they are related to human group life, and we therefore look at social interaction and roles, authority and associations, and social goods.

Relation of Stratification and Social Goods to Human Group Life

Stratification and class are an integral part of human group life. Out of social interaction, which is basic to humans' collective definitions, develop roles, a division of labor, authority, and associations. In turn people find themselves in different strata, and they may become members of opposing classes. Let us now examine some of the social processes which lead to stratification and class.

SOCIAL INTERACTION AND ROLES

The way we act is based on the meanings we attach to things, which include physical objects, specific individuals, categories of persons, institutions, ideals, and others' activities such as commands or requests. The meanings are not intrinsic but social products; it is out of our interaction with our fellows that these meanings emerge. They are the result of the interpreting and sizing up which we commonly do, as we interact with others.[1] The interpreting and sizing up is not merely an automatic application of established meanings, but rather a ". . . formative process in which the meanings are used and revised as instruments for the guidance and formation of action."[2] This process occurs because humans are able to make self-indications; we can act toward ourselves as objects—that is, we can see, in our imagination, how others might re-

[1] Herbert Blumer, *Symbolic Interactionism* (Englewood Cliffs, N.J.: Prentice-Hall, 1969), pp. 2 ff.

[2] *Ibid.*, p. 5.

spond to what we will say or do. For example, if we want to impress someone such as a job interviewer we try to imagine what would be the most appropriate clothes to wear and the best things to say. In doing this we are acting toward ourselves as objects, and are thus able to posit alternatives. This allows us to make choices and guide our behavior in the direction we think most beneficial to us. An important consequence of this is that individuals and collectivities may attach new meanings to institutions or categories of persons, and act in a manner which goes against traditional practices.

When humans interact over any period of time, shared understandings and expectations develop.[3] When the farmer and village merchant haggle, each takes the role of the other, each modifies his demands and expectations until an agreement is reached. But this is not the end of the transaction for each expects the other to live up to his end of the bargain, and so do the other farmers and merchants. The shared understandings and expectations transcend the specific individuals and become collective; they are then *collective definitions* which help guide future interactions in similar situations. The process is dynamic in that understandings are constantly being modified, and expectations are not always fulfilled, or are sometimes met differently. Yet it is necessary that most or at least a good portion of the understandings and expectations be fulfilled. If the persons involved, whether a family, business, or nation, lack reasonable certainty that their behaviors will elicit appropriate responses from others, the group is in danger of disintegrating. This does not mean that a group holds together only when there is harmony; the dynamic aspects which we mentioned above may include conflict, both between groups or within them. Also, there may be shared understandings and expectations which an overwhelming portion of the population despise, but cannot alter because of the force used by those in a superordinate position.[4]

Collective definitions affect almost all aspects of life, including how people are evaluated. Certainly personal attributes vary: some individuals are stronger, braver, harder working, smarter, or craftier than others. Similarly, there are variations in possessions and power: some persons have more money, finer clothes, or bigger houses; some are able to make others do what they wish, even though the others may not want to. These differences encourage members of the group to see themselves as superior, equal, or inferior to others; however, this is *not* the result of any intrinsic value in various attributes or possessions, but *the result of the collective definitions that develop*. Objects become defined favorably or unfavorably; for example, certain physical features, home furnishings, or

[3] See, e.g., Tamotsu Shibutani, *Society and Personality* (Englewood Cliffs, N.J.: Prentice-Hall, 1961), pp. 22–25 ff.

[4] See William J. Goode, "The Place of Force in Human Society," *American Sociological Review*, 37 (October 1972), 507–519.

occupations are seen as very desirable and others less so. Also, relative differences in power are affected in the same way.

The individual's self-conception is also influenced by group definitions. For example, those who have great wealth and power are usually viewed as superior in many ways; in turn they are likely to picture themselves as fine, smart, and noble. The person who is poor and powerless is likely to see himself as inferior intellectually and in numerous other ways. Among the effects of such differential self-conceptions is the likelihood that persons in a superordinate position will assert their rights and claims and will be accorded more privileges than they would seem entitled to. On the other hand those in a subordinate position are likely to concede more rights than may be necessary. In addition, the relative distribution of privileges over obligations is likely to be in favor of the superordinate persons.

Among the many shared expectations and understandings some are especially important. Called "roles," they facilitate interaction and the carrying out of the activities which help sustain the group.[5] They reflect what the group expects of the individual, and what he believes others expect of him. There are many different kinds of roles, including student, nurse, cowboy, friend, engineer, poet. Also, the individual plays many roles: an accountant, for example, may also be a husband, a father, a golfer, an official in a fraternal association, a member of the local Chamber of Commerce, a son, an uncle, and so on. In each role a person is expected to do a number of things and not others. It is understood that a doctor performs certain tasks and acts toward patients in a particular manner; these expectations are held by doctor and patient and by fellow doctors and others in the community.

There is likely to be a division of labor wherever coordinated activity occurs, as in the case of husband–wife, orchestra conductor–players, foreman–assembly line workers. The division of labor makes for efficiency, as individuals generally become proficient in their particular endeavors; coordination of the activities of many persons is possible, and responsibility for carrying out tasks can be fixed. It also avoids the confusion, conflict, and wasted effort which might otherwise occur. A baseball team would not perform very well if more than one player tried to be pitcher simultaneously, and exploration of outer space would be impossible without hundreds of persons, such as astronauts, scientists, and technicians who have become expert in their specialties.

Now some roles are more important than others for the effective functioning of the group: the ship captain's over the sailor's, the surgeon's over the nurse's, the teacher's over the student's. Differences in ability, training, and responsibility underlie the way the group evaluates roles and largely determine whether deference or scorn is shown toward them.

5 Shibutani, *op. cit.*, pp. 46–54.

Prestige or honor, and monetary and other rewards are associated with roles, and there are likely to be additional and better perquisites with the more important ones. In part these perquisites serve to attract a sufficient number of able candidates, who will expend the effort to fulfill the usually difficult requirements. Fewer rewards are needed for the lesser roles because less ability and training is required generally, and the amount of responsibility is more limited.[6]

It should be stressed that this is *an ideal typical description* of roles and how they are related to organized human activity. In real life there are usually many well-qualified individuals for top positions and competition among them is lively.[7] Also, people often try to increase the prestige, power, and privileges of their roles. They may try to limit access by setting up requirements which are not needed for competent performance, such as a particular ethnic background or graduation from an elite college. If the restrictions lead to a shortage of practitioners the rewards increase for the select few, even though the mass of the population may suffer. In addition, those in a role usually favor their own family and friends over strangers in filling vacant positions, and by "pulling strings" they may attempt to keep out more competent candidates.[8] Nevertheless, the abstraction or concept of roles with differential responsibilities, expectations, and rewards is a useful device for understanding how human groups are organized. It is also very helpful in analyzing stratification provided one remains aware of the problem of reification and the ideological implications. On this basis, Kingsley Davis and Wilbert E. Moore's position that there is a "functional necessity" for stratification [9] does not mean that the ablest and the best trained persons are in fact selected for the important roles, and that they conscientiously carry out their responsibilities. Rather, it is an ideal type depiction of how roles are filled, evaluated, and rewarded.

Not only do roles vary in perquisites and disadvantages, but there are also differences in power and authority.

POWER, AUTHORITY, AND ASSOCIATIONS

Most roles are likely to be complementary and mutually dependent, as in the case of airplane pilot and navigator, or sales clerk and store

[6] See Kingsley Davis and Wilbert E. Moore, "Some Principles of Stratification," *American Sociological Review*, 10 (April 1945), 242–249; and Moore, "But Some Are More Equal Than Others," *American Sociological Review*, 28 (February 1963), 13–18.

[7] Georg Simmel, *The Sociology of Georg Simmel*, ed. and trans. by Kurt H. Wolff (Glencoe, Ill.: The Free Press, 1950), pp. 75–76, 300–303.

[8] See, e.g., Melvin Tumin, "Some Principles of Stratification: A Critical Analysis," *American Sociological Review*, 18 (August 1953), 387–394; Tumin, "On Inequality," *American Sociological Review*, 28 (February 1963), 19–26; and Walter Buckley, "On Equitable Inequality," *American Sociological Review*, 28 (October 1963), 799–801.

[9] Davis and Moore, *op. cit.*, pp. 242–243.

manager. The differences in amount of power associated with roles is necessary; otherwise, the construction worker would not follow the orders of the construction crew foreman, nor would the motorist obey the signals of the traffic policeman. However, the power that goes with roles is seldom based on sheer force because of the understandings and shared expectations we mentioned earlier. Nevertheless, the differential power is authorized by the group, and is commonly called *authority*—the recognized right of persons in a given role to exercise the power associated with it. Examples are the authority of the President of the United States as commander-in-chief of the armed forces, the authority of the British parliament to levy taxes, and the authority of an employer over his employees. This does not mean that everyone or even a majority of the citizens agree to this exercise of power or that it is not constantly challenged. The authority continues as long as it is supported by the politically effective element in the society, even if it comprises only a small minority. In a negative sense the authority continues unless, or until, it is successfully overturned.

Authority is regularly challenged by individuals as they interact with those who have legitimate power; it is also contested more or less regularly by organized groups who feel disadvantaged by existing arrangements. And sometimes it is attacked through riots or similar collective behavior by unorganized masses who feel oppressed. The challenges are actually a measure of the society's health since they often arise because of changed conditions and the need for new arrangements. The reaction of authorities is also important for if it is arbitrary, capricious, or repressive it is likely to retard needed change. In addition, regular contesting helps support authority through a reassertion of the expectations upon which it is based.[10]

Authority relationships exist in many situations; however we limit ourselves to associations, such as a nation, a local community, or a factory. *Association* refers to *a formal set of relationships*, where there are a division of labor, a distribution of roles, an authority structure, superordinate-subordinate relationships, and a differential distribution of advantages and disadvantages. We are following Ralf Dahrendorf and Max Weber, who use the term *imperatively coordinated association*; however for simplicity we shall use the term "association."[11]

In an association the emphasis is on formal ties which hold a unit together, rather than personal ones such as sentiments. As regards social stratification and social class they are relevant only for individuals and

---

[10] Even challenges which take an extreme form, such as revolution, may indicate a healthy society. See Barrington Moore, Jr., *Social Origins of Dictatorship and Democracy* (Boston: Beacon Press, 1967), p. 457 and notes pp. 457–458.

[11] Cf. Ralf Dahrendorf, *Class and Class Conflict in Industrial Society* (Stanford, Calif.: Stanford University Press, 1959), pp. 138, 179–187; and Max Weber, *Max Weber: The Theory of Social and Economic Organization*, trans. by A. M. Henderson and Talcott Parsons (London: The Free Press of Glencoe, 1947), pp. 153, 324–328.

groups within such associations. These concepts lose meaning if they are used indiscriminately; for example, they do not apply to persons engaged in crowd behavior or to the family where other concepts are more appropriate. Neither are they appropriate for the many common ranking orders such as those based on beauty, athletic prowess, intelligence, or musical ability.[12]

There is an hierarchical arrangement of roles in an association, for an inherent trait is the unequal distribution of rights and obligations.[13] Not only do persons in the advantageous positions have more authority and perquisites, but they strongly influence collective definitions regarding the desirability of various objects. It is these individuals who help set the standards of the association.[14]

Superordinate-subordinate relationships continue in part because of consensus, and in part because of the wherewithal of those in a superordinate position to continue the existing favorable relationships.[15] In addition, people must "get something out of" the interactions if the structure of relationships is to be sustained. Even under conditions of exploitation, the exploited and the exploiters are to some extent mutually dependent upon one another. Even though employees may feel that their employer is taking unfair advantage of them they still need him for their jobs; similarly, the employer is dependent on his workforce to continue in business.[16]

When an association is formed, differences in authority and in the distribution of advantages and disadvantages may be accepted for a number of reasons. The mass of the population may believe that they are necessary for successful operation of the social unit. Or, those with power may be able to enforce the authority structure and the inequities that go with it because the others feel powerless to oppose them. An-

[12] Some of these could be the bases for stratification and class within the context of an association. For example, the members of a symphony orchestra may be stratified according to degree of talent.

[13] Pitirim A. Sorokin, *Social and Cultural Mobility* (Glencoe, Ill.: The Free Press, 1959 first pub. in 1927), pp. 11–16.

[14] See Simmel, "Fashion," *American Journal of Sociology*, 62 (May 1957), 541–558; and Thorstein Veblen, *The Theory of the Leisure Class* (New York: The Modern Library, 1934), pp. 163–164.

[15] Weber points out that the legal order usually enhances the power of those in the superordinate position. See Weber, *Max Weber: Essays in Sociology*, trans. by Hans H. Gerth and C. Wright Mills (New York: Oxford University Press, 1958), p. 180.

[16] See Peter M. Blau, *Exchange and Power in Social Life* (New York: John Wiley and Sons, 1961); and George C. Homans, *Social Behavior: Its Elementary Forms* (New York: Harcourt, Brace & World, 1961), pp. 30–82, 316–320. See also Simmel, *The Sociology of Georg Simmel*, pp. 181–206; and Stanislaw Ossowski, *Class Structure in the Social Consciousness* (New York: The Free Press, 1963), pp. 58–61, 90–92, 110–112.

For an interesting illustration in the case of Indian-white relationships, see Niels W. Braroe, "Reciprocal Exploitation in an Indian-White Community," *Southwestern Journal of Anthropology*, 21 (Summer 1965), 166–178.

other reason is a sacred interpretation of the situation. Whatever the justifications, the haves are encouraged to view their possessions and power as inalienable rights, and the have-nots to go along with their inferior condition. Over time tradition usually supports such differences, and people can live under great deprivation and accept their situation as the natural order of things.

In order to detail these determinants of stratification we may find the concept *social goods* useful.

SOCIAL GOODS

An aggregate of persons in an association may be interested in increasing various privileges for themselves; for example, they may want higher income or greater access to restricted neighborhoods or exclusive country clubs. Or, they may wish to deny such privileges to others. Now most writers on stratification and class discuss such interests and behaviors in terms of economic, power, or prestige dimensions. However it is too limiting to focus on a single one; [17] furthermore, the various dimensions are interrelated: it is likely that the owner or majority stockholder of a large corporation will have much wealth, power, and prestige while the unskilled worker will have little of each. It is for these reasons that we suggest an all-encompassing term, "social goods." [18] They may be conceived of, very broadly, as involving anything that people strive for. Among the many social goods are the elemental necessities such as food, clothing, and shelter, certain types of relationships,[19] and objects which have symbolic value—for example, money, jewels, works of art. Certainly some social goods are more important than others, and they may have different meanings among the various strata. For the semi-skilled factory employee size of paycheck is likely to be the most important of the social goods available; the college professor is also very much interested in income but this is weighed against other forms of social goods such as his institution's prestige.

A society's social goods are the result of collective definitions; as we pointed out above, wherever people lead a group life common expectations arise regarding what is necessary and desirable. Group definitions develop regarding these social goods; some become more valuable than others, and people strive to obtain and hold on to them. And when they

[17] See Charles H. Cooley, *Social Organization* (New York: Charles Scribner's Sons, 1929), p. 255n.; and R. H. Tawney, *Equality* (New York: Capricorn Books, 1961), pp. 52–53.

[18] Cf. David Easton, *The Political System* (New York: Alfred A. Knopf, 1965), p. 146; Harold D. Lasswell and Abraham Kaplan, *Power and Society* (New Haven, Conn.: Yale University Press, 1950), pp. 63, 72; and Pierre L. van den Berghe, "Dialectic and Functionalism: Toward a Theoretical Synthesis," *American Sociological Review*, 28 (October 1963), 701.

[19] Regarding the latter see Blau, *op. cit.*; and Homans, *op. cit.*

perceive that what they have is threatened they try to prevent others from taking them away. Although social goods exist in all human societies the *specific objects and relationships* which are valued or despised differ according to the complexity of the society and its history.

At the core of the collective defining of social goods is a degree of scarcity. This is true in a society of abundance as well as in a subsistence economy, for people must work or in some other way expend effort to obtain and hold on to social goods, especially those which have become highly valued. The scarcity may be due to limitations of an ecosystem, such as the amount of food available to a primitive tribe. Or, it may be socially induced; for example the strong may prevent the weak from owning land, even if there is plenty to go around. The standard of living—in the collective sense and in terms of a person's aspirations—is largely determined by collective attitudes. While the individuals reflect the group's definitions they have to decide if, how, and when they will seek to obtain the valued social goods. The social nature of these decisions was pointed out by Thorstein Veblen: one evaluates his own condition of life by comparing it with his neighbor's; a person sets his own standard by what his neighbor has. But when he reaches the new level he finds that his neighbor's has risen, and in order to maintain a favorable self-evaluation he must continue to strive.[20] "Keeping up with the Joneses" is a never-ending affair.

Thus to provide for sustenance and to maintain a favorable self-evaluation, most people are likely to seek those social goods which are collectively defined as necessary and desirable. However, they do not engage in this quest on equal terms since some individuals are more able than others. And even if the members of each generation started out on an equal footing, they would still end up with an unequal distribution. But each generation does not begin afresh. Society is on-going and persons are born into a world of inequality where some already have much of the social goods and others little.[21] As we will show later, particularly in Chapters IV, V, and VI, many begin the race with handicaps not of their own making.

The Persistence of Superordination-Subordination

The interaction over social goods leads to differentiation and stratification; in turn it may lead to classes. Sustained interaction results in

[20] Veblen, *op. cit.*, pp. 30–32. See also Emile Durkheim, *Suicide* (Glencoe, Ill.: The Free Press, 1960), pp. 252–254.

[21] Cf. Robert A. Dahl, *Modern Political Analysis* (Englewood Cliffs, N.J.: Prentice-Hall, 1963), p. 15.

structures of relationships: social stratification is one of them, social class another. The outcome of such interaction is twofold. First, patterns of behavior develop whereby numbers of people see themselves as superordinate or subordinate to others. Such self-conceptions are more than simply subjective evaluations, for there must be acknowledgment of differential status by others. But most important, these self-conceptions and attitudes of others are strongly influenced by differential control over social goods.[22] Second, structured relationships which include those of a superordinate-subordinate nature become institutionalized and persist for generation after generation. These relationships which involve aggregates of people who differentiate themselves from other aggregates *have as their basic foundation control over social goods.*[23]

Over time there is likely to be noticeable variance between the haves and the have-nots in life style, aspirations, attitudes, and language; even genetic differences may develop.[24] While these things help label superordinates and subordinates and thus serve as a hindrance to upward mobility, we want to again stress the importance of institutional arrangements. For the haves are likely to use their wealth, power, and prestige to change institutions in order to insure retaining or increasing their social goods. The favorable institutional arrangements are likely to persist over time and become invested with sanctity. These arrangements, together with tradition, custom, and laws perpetuate the advantages of the haves and encourage the development of an hereditary superordinate stratum. It is therefore essential that any study of stratification and class examine the historical context; we do this in later sections.

The reader may have noticed that we constantly refer to social stratification *and* social class. This is purposeful since there is an important difference. Some recent works have contributed significantly toward clarifying these two concepts and we draw heavily on them in the following section.[25] Next we examine the important difference between stratification and class and the process whereby incumbents of strata become members of classes.

[22] See Simmel, *The Sociology of Georg Simmel*, pp. 291–293.

[23] This is true of so many relationships; even those between parents and child involve control over social goods. Adults desire to retain control for as long as possible, but when they are no longer able to do so they favor its transfer to their children. The collective aspect of such individual interests can be seen in the customs, mores, and laws surrounding marriage and inheritance. Endogamy, for example, limits dispersion of wealth, and is particularly important for the more affluent families.

[24] See C. D. Darlington, "The Control of Evolution in Man," *The Eugenics Review*, 50 (October 1958), 1–9.

[25] These recent valuable critical examinations of stratification and class are Dahrendorf, *Class and Class Conflict in Industrial Society;* Ossowski, *Class Structure in the Social Consciousness;* Seymour M. Lipset and Reinhard Bendix, "Social Status and Social Structure: A Re-examination of Data and Interpretations," *British Journal of Sociology*, 2 (June and September 1951), 150–168, 230–254; and Howard Brotz, "Social Stratification and the Political Order," *American Journal of Sociology*, 64 (May 1959), 571–578.

The Distinction Between Social Stratification and Social Class

Dahrendorf emphasizes the importance of distinguishing between the two ideas. He views social stratification as a *descriptive* concept, and social class as an *analytic* one, with questions of groups and group behavior limited to the latter. Dahrendorf, who bases his work on Marx and Engels' treatment of class, but extends and improves on it, holds that

> [C]lass is always a category for purposes of the analysis of the dynamics of social conflict and its structural roots, and as such it has to be separated strictly from *stratum* as a category for purposes of describing hierarchical systems at a given point of time.[26]

Social stratification then is any ordering of society's members, using any convenient criteria such as income, education, style of life, ethnic background. In other words social stratification is merely the *description* of a population in terms of "strata," or categories of people who have similar characteristics. Also, the categories are arranged hierarchically. The categorization may be based on a people's *subjective evaluations*, how they rank themselves in relation to others; on their *reputations*, the way people who know them rank them; on *objective criteria*, such as income, education, place of residence, or on combinations of each.[27] Classes, on the other hand, are *conflict groups* which challenge the existing distribution of authority, perquisites, and other advantages in an association. First we examine stratification in detail, and then class.

SOCIAL STRATIFICATION

Whatever criteria are used for analyzing stratification, they may be viewed as social goods; thus stratification is simply a statement or description of how social goods are distributed. Valuable guidelines for depicting strata are found in Max Weber's writings.[28] We have in-

[26] Dahrendorf, *op. cit.*, p. 76. Emphasis in the original. Cf. Sorokin, *Social and Cultural Mobility*, pp. 263–278.

[27] Examples of each method are, respectively, Richard Centers, *The Psychology of Social Classes* (Princeton, N.J.: Princeton University Press, 1961); W. Lloyd Warner and Paul S. Lunt, *The Social Life of a Modern Community* (New Haven, Conn.: Yale University Press, 1941); and August B. Hollingshead, *Elmtown's Youth* (New York: Wiley and Sons, 1948), and Mollie Orshansky, "Who's Who Among the Poor: A Demographic View of Poverty," *Social Security Bulletin*, 28 (July 1965), 3–32.

[28] The remainder of the chapter draws heavily on *Max Weber: The Theory of Social and Economic Organization*, pp. 347–348, n. 27, 424–428; and *From Max Weber: Essays in Sociology*, pp. 183–194.

terpolated several of his statements in order to make a clear distinction between stratification and class, and suggest the following definition: A *social stratum* is any aggregate of persons who are similar in the possession of, or access to, social goods. In other words, the incumbents of a stratum are similar in the kinds of things they have—objects, attributes, opportunities, and so forth, which are collectively defined as desirable or undesirable. The incumbents of a stratum are also likely to have similar feelings of satisfaction or dissatisfaction regarding their condition of life.

The differences which are used in stratifying individuals or groups may be viewed statistically, and the key question is: Are the variations greater between or within the categories that are labelled strata? When using income as a criterion, "cut off" points can be determined by appropriate statistical techniques, or through inspection if the data are in tabular or graphic form. Or, if there are meaningful social categories such as primary, secondary, and college education, or white-collar and blue-collar occupations, they may be used for marking off one stratum from another. Statistical methods such as analysis of variance may be useful in analyzing as well as delimiting strata.

Any criteria may provide the basis for examining stratification; however, it is desirable to select those which are most critical for people's lives, in the context of their nation, community, or work-place. Again drawing on Weber, there are two main strata in capitalist industrial society: One is composed of aggregates of persons whose source of social goods is property or accumulated wealth. The other consists of aggregates of persons whose source of social goods is their occupation. There are, of course, numerous substrata within each major one; the first includes aggregates of persons who obtain rent from land or buildings, others who subsist on interest from loans or securities, and those whose income is from the ownership of factories or other business enterprises. Included in the second are aggregates of persons whose income comes from the sale of mental skills (e.g. scientists, college professors, bookkeepers), and those whose income is obtained through the sale of manual skills. Of the two main strata, people in the first are likely to have greater access to social goods and to possess more of them than those in the second.

Strata also exist in non-capitalist industrial society, but they are differentiated mainly by position in the authority structure and the nature of one's occupation. There are also two main strata: aggregates of persons who are high in the authority structure and aggregates who are low. Those in the first stratum are likely to possess more social goods and have greater access to them than individuals in the second. Not only are occupations also an important basis for stratification but there is a rough parallel with the way they are ranked in capitalist economies. Persons in non-manual work receive more perquisites and in terms of popular evaluation have greater prestige, in contrast to those in manual occupations or farming.[29]

Finally, a pertinent question in regard to strata is how unified they are. Weber correctly holds that the "unity" of strata is highly relative and variable, because there is overlapping for many individuals and continuous movement from one stratum to another. That is, two persons may have the same income but different amounts of education, or two individuals may be lawyers but one may work for a labor union, the other for a corporation. In addition vertical mobility is considerable in modern industrial society. Consequently when we discuss strata we are dealing with only *relatively* homogeneous categories of people.

While the incumbents of a stratum are likely to have similar life conditions and interests, by definition they are unorganized and cannot engage in concerted action. Organized attempts to alter the allocation of social goods within a community are likely to involve social classes, which are quite different phenomena. It is therefore essential in studying social stratification to realize that we are dealing with statistical categories and *not* classes, that we are examining the behavior of persons in different strata, and not class behavior.

Research on stratification rather than class is the preference of most sociologists, particularly American; what they label "social class" is likely to be some variant of stratification. Thus W. Lloyd Warner's classes—upper upper; lower upper; upper middle; lower middle; upper lower, and lower lower—are essentially a prestige ranking, based on people's reputation and modified by education, occupation, and economic criteria. For Richard Centers class is what people say it is: those studied are asked whether they belong to the upper, middle, working, or lower class. Occupational prestige is the most widely used ranking measure. Designations such as "middle class" or "working class" are based on the U.S. Census Bureau's listing of occupations, and a variant is the National Opinion Research Center's evaluation which is determined by how a nation-wide sample of adults views occupations. The emphasis on studying stratification to the neglect of class is discussed in greater detail in Chapter XI.[30]

SOCIAL CLASS

While stratification is found in almost all aggregates, collectivities, and groups, classes exist only within the context of associations. Al-

[29] See Ossowski, *op. cit.,* p. 112; M. N. Rutkevich, "Elimination of Class Differences and the Place of Non-Manual Workers in the Social Structure of Soviet Society," *Soviet Sociology,* 3 (Fall 1964), 3–13; and Alex Inkeles and Peter H. Rossi, "National Comparisons of Occupational Prestige," *American Journal of Sociology,* 61 (January 1956), 329–339.

[30] See Warner and Lunt, *op. cit.;* and Warner and associates, *Social Class in America* (New York: Harper Torchbooks, 1960); Centers, *op. cit.;* and Robert W. Hodge, Paul M.

though we suggested earlier that it is most meaningful to limit the study of stratification to people in an association, it is not critical that we do so; however in the case of social class it is *essential*. There is little value in analyzing class unless it is done within the context of a factory, a local community, a nation, or other associations. As we noted earlier, in every association there is a differential distribution of authority and social goods which is effected through roles involving superordinate-subordinate relationships. However there is also at least a *latent* conflict of interest between those in the different roles.

A consequence of this latent conflict is that the legitimacy of authority relations is always precarious: the superordinate group wishes to maintain its advantages and views the interests of the subordinate group as a threat to its right to rule. In turn, the subordinate group, in attempting to increase its advantages, challenges the status quo and thus the legitimacy of the existing authority relations.[31] For example, even though employee demands for wage increases affect the status quo only minimally, they are resisted by employers, sometimes quite strongly but rarely to an extreme degree. But when there is an attempt to infringe on what is considered management prerogatives such as decision-making by workers in the running of the business, or union access to financial records, then employers react fiercely. Similarly university administrators balk at faculty attempts to share power, school principals resist such an encroachment by teachers, and teachers react the same way when students challenge their authority. However, the existence of latent conflict does not inevitably lead to subordinate groups seeking to increase their advantage. It is necessary for these persons to define their situation as undesirable, for interests and issues to become sharpened, and for the changed perspectives to become shared.

Weber emphasizes that class is not a community, although classes emerge only on the basis of communalization. Classes are formed when an aggregate of persons defines their interests as similar to those of the others in their aggregate, and as different from and opposed to the interests of another aggregate of persons. The interests in question are based on differential control over social goods in an association. To alter control over the social goods means challenging the authority structure; to prevent change in control means supporting the existing arrangement.

The key difference between social stratification and social class is communalization; therefore class formation requires some kind of structuring which may lead to informal groups or to formal organizations. Otherwise the aggregates of persons continue to be strata, and discontent does not lead to organized attempts to change conditions.

Siegel, and Peter H. Rossi, "Occupational Prestige in the United States, 1925–1962," *American Journal of Sociology*, 70 (November 1964), 286–302. The NORC findings are discussed in Chapter III.

[31] Dahrendorf, *Class and Class Conflict in Industrial Society*, p. 176.

Yet history shows that when people are dissatisfied with the distribution of social goods, the have-nots often seek to increase their supply at the expense of the haves, and vice versa. The key question is how aggregates of persons with similar social goods become organized in order to alter or retain the existing distribution. Or, put another way, how do the incumbents of strata become members of classes?

From Strata to Classes

It is possible that over time people living under the same circumstances may begin to feel a similarity of interest with one another and that interaction among them intensifies; they start to share a common perspective and group consciousness emerges. Actions such as attempts to increase the amount of social goods available to them are now group behavior, for an aggregate has been transformed to a collectivity and thence to a group.

While specific social goods such as wages or working conditions are essential elements in class behavior, the collective definitions are also critical. Absolute deprivation may lead to discontent and frustration; however, if people blame themselves or fate class behavior is not very likely. On the other hand if collective definitions direct their antagonism toward the social structure then class formation is to be expected. A number of studies has shown that left radicalism among the lower class is associated with this situation.[32] It also encourages left radicalism among people at higher levels, such as writers, businessmen, or professionals. However, there the problem is usually not absolute deprivation, but their condition relative to others. It is this relative deprivation, Robert K. Merton suggests, that makes such people very dissatisfied with their lot.[33] For example, white-collar workers such as teachers are likely to be fairly content with rather small salaries as long as the income of persons in less prestigeful jobs is lower than theirs. But if the wage level of these persons rises and approaches the teachers', then they are likely to become quite dissatisfied.

Some very important factors in encouraging or discouraging class formation are the way the society is organized; certain life conditions; changed perspectives, which we just alluded to, and particular cultural and historical aspects. These circumstances are detailed in the following section which draws heavily on Weber.

[32] See Alejandro Portes, "On the Interpretation of Class Consciousness," *American Journal of Sociology*, 77 (September 1971), 228–244.

[33] Robert K. Merton, *Social Theory and Social Structure* (rev. ed.; Glencoe, Ill.: The Free Press, 1957), pp. 227–235.

THE ORGANIZATION OF THE SOCIETY

The economic and legal organization of the society is the first aspect to look at. Class formation is encouraged where there are highly rationalized enterprises which are organized around the goal of lowest per unit cost and maximum profit. It does not matter whether beer cans are manufactured or insurance forms processed. Profit may be money in a capitalist system or credits in a non-capitalist society. The organization of work is impersonal, and there is free labor rather than a paternalistic arrangement. Thus loss of employment becomes a strong sanction and the employer has few or no responsibilities for his employees off the job.[34] In addition, legal sanctions support the authority structure of the work enterprise, and these include the laws, courts, police, and government agencies.

Where the economic and legal organization of the society is such that the factories and other work arrangements are highly rationalized, the way goods and profits may be disposed of is also important. If the owners and managers can freely dispose of them, as under capitalism, this means that they determine their markets, prices, and wages, and decide what to do with their profit with little or no government regulation. In turn this may lead to an accumulation of wealth and control over the productive process, which may result in tremendous influence over the government and other institutions in the society.

These circumstances which are typical under industrialism, particularly the capitalist form, encourage class formation. Yet, even when they are absent or imperfectly developed as in a non-industrial situation communalization and group conflict along class lines is possible. Where the vast majority of the population are in agriculture or in other primary economic pursuits,[35] there will still be associations, authority structures, strata, group interests, and at least latent conflict. Although communalization and conflict are more likely to develop along tribal, familial, village, regional, or similar lines than in industrial society, class behavior does occur. This may be the case even in a caste or estate system, and it is worthwhile to briefly look at these two forms.

---

[34] A contrary case is Japan where most business enterprises including some of the largest are extremely paternalistic. Many retain employees during slack periods, provide housing, arrange vacations, and provide other perquisites. While this is likely to minimize class formation within the plant, there can be other foci in the society for class interest, class formation, and class conflict.

[35] See Colin Clark, *The Conditions of Economic Progress* (3rd ed.; London: Macmillan Co., 1957). Clark distinguishes among three stages of economic development: the *primary* in which agriculture, fishing, mining and lumbering predominate; the *secondary* where manufacturing is most important, and the *tertiary* which consists mainly of service industries.

CASTE AND ESTATE SOCIETY

In an ideal typical sense there are basically three forms: the caste arrangement epitomized by traditional India, the estate system as found in medieval Europe, and the class society which is common in industrial nations. In the class situation, regardless of political form, the tendency is toward impersonality and rationality. As a result employer-employee relations, the application of technology, the distribution of social goods, and the nature of the strata are more decisively affected by the market than in the caste or estate arrangements.

While the economy remains a primary influence in the latter two, stratification and behavior related to it are critically affected by social arrangements, which are underpinned by strong traditions, customs, mores, and even laws. The following are the chief characteristics of caste society: castes are hierarchically graduated with great differences in the distribution of social goods; membership is hereditary; occupation and caste go together; mobility from one caste to another is extremely rare; and there is an overriding emphasis on caste endogamy. In addition, cross-caste contact is avoided except when mutual dependence requires it. In that case the impersonal and ritual forms, which stress the superordinate-subordinate relationships, are followed. In an extreme type of caste society, such as traditional India, the desire for avoidance is more critical because of the fear of defilement. There is also strong residential segregation, and a very high association among residence, family, and occupation. Finally, there are strong proscriptions on behavior. These are deeply imbedded in the mores, which may be religiously based as in the Hinduism of India.

The agricultural economy, the predominantly village-based living arrangements, slow change, and limited opportunity encourage a traditional outlook and concern over holding on to what limited social goods one has. Scavengers may have very little, but they are at least better off than many others in a poverty-ridden society. And by fulfilling the expectations of caste psychic as well as economic security is provided. But over-attention to the deeply held secular and religious values may obscure the economic and power arrangements which give them substance. Caste includes rigid superordination-subordination in which the inequities in the distribution of social goods are maintained. While there is mutual economic dependence the advantages lie with the upper levels. In traditional India power was maintained by an absolutist sacerdotal elite and the professional priests and literati catered to them and fulfilled their needs. These arrangements helped uphold the stratification system.

There are inter- and intra-caste differences and conflict, however. On the basis of our schema they may be viewed as class differences and class conflict for they occur within the context of associations and involve contesting over the distribution of social goods. Yet one of the fascinating aspects of Indian society is the accommodative nature of the caste system. Historically it has been able to absorb invaders, migrating groups, and changes in technology and the workforce without any basic alteration in the system. In addition, there are various institutional arrangements within and among the castes which are able to regulate the conflict.[36]

The estate system in medieval Europe, particularly beginning in the 12th century, was very highly stratified, status and occupations were largely hereditary, endogamy was encouraged, especially for the higher levels, there was little mobility, and a strong set of values supported the inequitous distribution of social goods. It was much less rigid than the Indian caste system, however. While there were reciprocal benefits in the estate arrangement it was clearly one of superordination-subordination; a small, powerful class of nobles whose status was supported by law maintained strong economic subjugation of the mass of the population. Landholding provided one of the major bases for social goods in a very sluggish economy in which farming, not much more than subsistence level, predominated. The other was military prowess, advantageously maintained by the knights: nobles who had the legal right to be fully armed horse soldiers and who could afford the expense. In an era of disorder and limited political authority, martial might was the chief way of securing and increasing one's social goods, but again the advantage lay with the higher strata. The different levels of the society were linked to each other through the ties of vassalage in which men bound themselves to one another for mutual gain. The benefits were mainly for the upper levels where land ownership and the bearing of arms made reciprocal agreements meaningful. These arrangements were strongly supported by religion. Although it often helped meliorate the harsh aspects it served basically to uphold the status quo by providing justification for the inequitous system and by promising the lower strata a better life in the hereafter.

Yet there was considerable conflict over the distribution of social goods among the different levels in the hierarchy. The greater knights were embroiled with the lesser ones and this meant continual warfare;

---

[36] See J. H. Hutton, *Caste in India, Its Nature, Function and Origins* (Cambridge, Eng.: Cambridge University Press, 1946); Harold A. Gould, "Castes, Outcastes, and the Sociology of Stratification," *International Journal of Comparative Sociology*, 1 (September 1960), 220–238; and Pauline M. Kolenda, "Toward a Model of the Hindu Jajimani System," *Human Organization*, 22 (Spring 1963), 11–31. Cf. Bryce Ryan, *Caste in Modern Ceylon* (New Brunswick, N.J.: Rutgers University Press, 1953). See also John Dollard, *Caste and Class in a Southern Town* (New York: Doubleday Anchor Books, 1949); and Gerald D. Berreman, "Caste in India and the United States," *American Journal of Sociology*, 61 (September 1960), 120–127.

there was also enmity between knights and serfs and this led to peasant protests and uprisings.[37] These differences and the conflict which occurred involved class behavior. We will examine the imperatively coordinated association of the estate arrangement in greater detail in Chapter VII.

With this brief look at the caste and estate systems, we return to our investigation of the conditions which are relevant for understanding the transformation of strata into classes. The contributing factors are noted under life conditions; changes in perspectives; and historical and cultural aspects. While they are universal they have particular significance for class formation and conflict in modern society.

LIFE CONDITIONS

We must understand the circumstances of people's lives, particularly those that affect their daily needs, such as food, clothing, and shelter, as well as opportunity for additional things which are collectively defined as desirable, if we are to understand class formation. But it is not enough to simply identify the haves and have-nots, or to determine how equitable the distribution of social goods throughout the society is. Rather, it is necessary to know the extent to which there are aggregates of persons with similar backgrounds and life conditions; for example, people who engage in the same occupation, live in the same area of town, are of similar national origin or ethnic background, and remain in the same occupation throughout their lives. Now contrast them with a collection of people who are also in one type of occupation but whose residences are dispersed, who are from many different national origins and ethnic backgrounds, and who are very likely to leave one occupation for another. The first aggregate constitutes a distinct stratum while the latter does not, and, other things being equal, the former are much more prone to class formation.

Another important consideration is how much of a monopoly over the control of social goods the incumbents of a stratum have. Class formation is encouraged if those in one stratum have control over opportunities, such as access to desirable jobs, to the detriment of the incumbents of other strata. One example is a colonial situation where only those from the mother country are allowed to hold prestigious and remunerative positions while the natives are restricted to manual occupations. Another example is a small number of haves who are able to

---

[37] See Marc Bloch, *Feudal Society* (London: Routledge & Kegan Paul, 1961); Henri Pirenne, *A History of Europe* (Garden City, N.Y.: Doubleday Anchor Books, 1958), Vols. I and II; and James W. Thompson, *The Middle Ages, 300–1500* (New York: Alfred A. Knopf, 1931), pp. 205–207.

prevent the rest of the population from obtaining education, land, or other social goods.

These circumstances, particularly the similarity or dissimilarity of people's attributes, and the nature of the distribution of social goods provide the necessary background for analyzing class formation. (The important components of stratification are examined in Chapter III; life conditions among the various strata are described in Chapters IV through VI, as well as in later sections of the book. The extent to which people remain at one level, or move up or down, is discussed in the following chapter.) Yet life conditions do not determine social action but set the framework within which it occurs; they may encourage discontent, envy, unrest, and new interpretations of the situations people find themselves in.[38]

CHANGES IN PERSPECTIVE

Certain conditions encourage people to change their view of themselves and their world, to object to and challenge arrangements which they may have accepted previously. Among them is a high degree of transparency of the connections between the causes and consequences of class-inducing behavior. If the deprived can readily see who is responsible for their condition that group may soon be defined as the enemy and become the focus for the discontent. Also, the possibility of class formation is greatly increased if the incumbents of a stratum are in a situation in which communication among them is facilitated. If discontented persons cannot communicate readily with one another, it is difficult for individual discontent to become collective and therefore potentially more powerful. On the other hand if working conditions facilitate communication, as in the case of persons employed in a factory, group formation is much more likely. This was observed by Karl Marx and was the basis for his belief that industrial workers were much more likely than dispersed peasants to engage in collective action and revolutionary change.[39] However, if an aggregate of persons in the same occupation or with similar interests are in communication, yet as a group are isolated physically or socially they are likely to be much more cohesive and ag-

[38] See Blumer, *Symbolic Interactionism*, pp. 87–88. Deprivation, it should be pointed out, is neither a necessary nor sufficient condition for class behavior. Absolute deprivation can lead to riots or other forms of collective behavior; such actions can occur even where people have the necessities, and even more, but feel a strong sense of relative deprivation. Yet such behavior is not class conflict for it is unorganized; however, it may quicken the changes which lead to class formation. See Blumer, "Collective Behavior," in Alfred M. McClung, ed., *New Outline of the Principles of Sociology* (New York: Barnes & Noble, Inc., 1946), pp. 167–222, especially pp. 167–185.

[39] See Karl Marx, "The Eighteenth Brumaire of Louis Bonaparte," in Robert C. Tucker, ed., *The Marx–Engels Reader* (New York: W. W. Norton 1972), pp. 515–516.

gressive than other workers. This is true of longshoremen, miners, and lumberjacks throughout the world.[40]

Given appropriate life conditions, communication, and changed perspectives discontent may intensify to the degree that collective action occurs. Two paths are likely: one is short-range in which hostile and aggressive feelings are released through such means as rioting. It may be more or less random, for example, shopkeepers may be beaten up because of the high cost of food. Yet the authority structure remains essentially unchanged. Nevertheless, there has been some modification in outlook for the status quo has been upset, if only temporarily. The other response is long-range in that the discontent and energy are directed toward changing the authority structure; the structure itself is assaulted and its traditions and symbols disregarded or denigrated. When this occurs a major alteration of perspective is in process and a long-ranged response is facilitated by the emergence of new values and symbols, together with a set of goals which promise a better future. A coherent set of such ideas and guidelines for altering the authority structure is an *ideology*. Ideologies are "doctrines that purport to formulate the distinctive perspective of social groups. These ideologies profess to be 'true' not only in upholding certain values but in giving a correct picture of what the world is really like." [41] Usually the ideologies have easily understandable goals; moreover, they provide justification for a break with the past, offer hope to the deprived, and promise a more desirable social order. An ideology which encourages class behavior questions the status quo, suggests alternatives, and proposes means for attaining the desired ends. There are numerous examples of ideologies; among them are the doctrines of democracy, communism, and fascism which were instrumental in the class conflicts which led respectively to the American and the French Revolutions, the Russian Revolution, and the dictatorships of Hitler and Mussolini.

Yet, in addition to an ideology and other appropriate conditions, leadership and organization are necessary if there is to be significant change. Whether natural leaders who arise from the ranks or outside organizers, they help the incumbents of a stratum change their self-conceptions. The leaders also encourage group members to question the present distribution of social goods and the legitimacy of the existing authority structure, and they work out the practical means for attaining the goal. Candidates might be put up and the vote gotten out or, if the conflict is not peaceful, arms, food and other supplies raised. Successful

---

[40] See, e.g., Clark Kerr and Abraham Siegel, "The Interindustry Propensity to Strike—An International Comparison," in Arthur Kornhauser, Robert Dubin and Arthur M. Ross, eds., *Industrial Conflict* (New York: McGraw-Hill Book Co., 1946), pp. 189–212.

[41] Leonard Broom and Philip Selznick, *Sociology* (4th ed.; New York: Harper & Row, 1968), p. 256. See also Karl Mannheim, *Ideology and Utopia* (New York: Harcourt, Brace and Co., 1946), pp. 49 ff.

leadership and organization direct the released energy toward a common end and provide the mechanisms for reaching it.

While the above are important for class formation, cultural and historical conditions may help or hinder the transformation of strata into classes.

CULTURAL AND HISTORICAL ASPECTS

As we noted earlier classes are possible even in a tradition-bound agriculturally-based society. However certain cultural conditions and historical experiences which facilitate class formation are more likely to be found in modern society. Perhaps the most important is the way people typically organize to protect or further their interests. Therefore if in a particular nation or community there exist formal organizations such as trade unions, employers' associations, or revolutionary groups, the potential for strata turning into classes is greatly increased. These organizations may become a convenient base for class formation since they may furnish the needed ideology as well as organizational expertise. In addition to the formal associations, the practice regarding the formation of voluntary organizations to pursue group interests is also significant. If the organization of interest groups is prevented or made very difficult by legal or other means, class formation will be hindered; in the absence of such restrictions it will be facilitated.

The final consideration is the extent to which the nation or community has experienced class behavior. While such a history is certainly not essential it encourages subsequent class formation as a means of altering the distribution of social goods.

Whether differences in the distribution of social goods will lead to class behavior depends on the above factors, which vary in importance from one situation to another. Of special significance are agitators and ideologists for they help define the situation and provide new perspectives. Organization is also extremely important because it helps move the class toward its goal.[42] The means for attaining group goals vary, of course. They include passive resistance, legislative activity, and revolutionary behavior; but above all is the desire to change the allocation of social goods.

The factors enumerated above may be useful in two ways: First, as a general probability statement. That is, one may expect a greater likelihood of class formation and conflict in associations or communities with such conditions, in contrast to associations and communities where they are absent. Second, these factors may provide a guide for understanding situations where class formation and conflict have occurred.

[42] See Blumer, *op. cit.*, pp. 202–214.

Concrete illustrations of class formation and their analyses will be found in later sections of this book. As a preview, however, the following criteria for identifying classes are posited:

1. *An associational context.* The persons are in a social situation characterized by formal ties, wherein there are a division of labor, a distribution of roles, an authority structure, superordinate-subordinate relationships, and a differential distribution of social goods. The concept "association" describes such an arrangement.

2. *A relatively high degree of similarity in background conditions and in life chances.* The stratification of the population is a convenient guide. It is particularly important to note the degree of congruence of people's attributes and roles.

3. *A shared awareness of undesirable conditions.* There is a collective awareness of conditions of life which are defined as undesirable, and the belief that feelings of discontent and deprivation are shared by others who are living under the same circumstances.

4. *A specification of the cause of the undesirable conditions.* The feelings of discontent and antagonism regarding the undesirable conditions are directed toward another aggregate of persons who may constitute a stratum or class.

5. *Organized attempts to bring about change.* There are organized attempts to change people's perspective, to turn discontent and antagonism toward another stratum or class, and to bring about a change in the structure of anthority relations and in the distribution of social goods. Organized groups such as a political party or a revolutionary cadre may emerge at any point in the process of class formation. While they are not essential in the beginning stages, they become increasingly important during the latter ones in that they can direct activities toward specific goals. If the class action is successful the organized group may become the vehicle for institutionalization.

Let us assume that classes have formed, that the authority structure has been challenged successfully, and that there has been a redistribution of social goods: for example, a disenfranchised class obtains the right to vote, an ethnically-based class has racial or religious qualifications for office removed, or a group of unions obtains legislation favorable to employees. The success of one of the conflicting classes over the other or the accommodation of both may lead to quiescence, especially if the outcome is institutionalized. But the stability may only be apparent, or temporary. For even though there has been a change in the distribution of social goods, as soon as new interests, desires, and interpretations develop the process which leads to class conflict will begin all over again.

The conflict may be localized as in labor-management disputes, or it may involve an entire nation, as in the case of a governing class aligned against a disenfranchised proletariat. What critically affects the scale of class conflict is suggested by Dahrendorf: the extent to which the many attributes and roles persons have coincide or are disparate. That is, other things being equal, the more similar they are the greater the potential scale of class conflict. Additional considerations are how open or closed the strata and classes are, and the amount of social mobility.[43]

The above comments should not lead the reader to believe that class formation is limited to those at the lower levels. On the contrary, the *higher* the stratum the greater the likelihood that the incumbents will develop a sense of common interests and shared understandings. And being fewer in number the chances of sustained interaction with one another are much more likely. In turn this means greater communication, friendship, and intermarriage, as well as mutual aid and obligations. In addition, those at the top are usually quite aware of how precarious the legitimacy of authority relations is and that they are greatly outnumbered by the have-nots. Since a successful challenge to the authority structure is likely to alter the distribution of social goods to their disadvantage, the haves do not hesitate to act in defense of their interests.

An upper class is usually quick to use the institutional arrangements for its own benefit, and to weaken or destroy opposition whenever necessary. Challengers may be called subversives and may be denied jobs, jailed, run out of town, or worse. Or, more subtle means may be used as in the case of so-called right-to-work laws which greatly weaken unions. In the economic arena an upper class may seek to obtain more social goods through laws or administrative decisions which limit wage increases while at the same time allowing for increased profits. Or it may try to have tax laws enacted which are regressive rather than progressive.[44]

The cohesiveness of the upper class is influenced by degree of status consistency, as is true of the lower class. The greater the similarity of upper class members in nationality, religion, geographic area, schools attended, and family background, the more likely they are to have a similar outlook and act in concert. But again, as in the case of the lower class this is a probability statement: the more similar the members of the upper class are the more likely they are to stick together and vice versa. Even where backgrounds are quite similar economic competition, overly

---

[43] Dahrendorf, *Class and Class Conflict in Industrial Society*, pp. 213–218, 222–223, 315.

[44] Regressive taxation may be in the form of a "head tax" in which everyone is assessed the same amount; it may be a use tax on say each window in one's home as in medieval Europe, or it may be a sales tax which is a fixed percentage on purchases. Obviously these taxes do not take into account the ability of the individual to pay. To illustrate: A husband, wife, and two children with an income of $4,000 a year will likely spend all of it, and if the sales tax is five per cent they pay $200. A family of the same composition which spends $100,000 a year will pay sales taxes of $5,000; however that family can much more easily afford it. On the other hand progressive taxation is based on ability to pay, with higher income persons paying proportionately more than those with lesser earnings. However, as we show later, even with progressive taxation such as the graduated income tax there are many loopholes which greatly reduce the taxes of the upper strata.

ambitious persons, or family feuds may limit solidarity. However, when the class itself is threatened, for example by a rising middle class or by government trying to nationalize industry, the members usually close ranks.

Yet, the upper class faces certain problems, and the way it meets them affects its tenure. Foremost is social mobility, particularly movement into its own ranks. A strong tendency in the upper class is to award economic advantages, honors, and other benefits to its own and to recruit new members from among its children and relatives. The tendency toward in-breeding encourages parochialism and a disparagement of ambition and innovation; it also increases the likelihood that less able upper-class people will obtain important positions and opportunities while lower-class individuals with greater ability are kept out. The result is a loss of vitality and a weakening of this class, together with strong resentment from those who are denied access. If there are many able, successful, and ambitious people just below the upper class who believe they deserve entrée they may form into a class of their own and challenge the upper class. These individuals have been socially mobile, that is they have moved up the authority structure and have increased their social goods, relative to when they first started out or in regard to their parents' attainment. The blockage of their mobility may lead them to agitate for changes which will allow them in; however, if the upper class remains intransigent the demands for reform may turn into calls for revolutionary change. Such a class often tries to enlist the rest of the population by claiming that they will also benefit. If the existing arrangements block the upward mobility of those at the lowest levels, or in other ways limit their opportunity, they may join the agitation. Under these circumstances the possibility of significant reform is great; unless reform comes, the likelihood of revolution is increased.

Class formation and conflict are constant and occur at all levels; they are among the major forces for change, if not the major causes. Much of the conflict does eventually result in reforms through alteration of laws or administrative decisions; sometimes the change is accomplished by the upper class grudgingly but voluntarily giving up some of its advantages, or a middle or lower class forces enactment of reforms. Yet in these instances the basic framework of the society, including the authority structure, remains.

On the other hand there may be a fundamental upheaval if the conflict is not resolved but intensifies, and certain conditions are present. Although revolutionary change is not common, it always remains a threat. Historically there have been a number of revolutions; among them the American, the French, and the Russian which were mentioned earlier. More recent examples are the Chinese and the Cuban, as well as the numerous upheavals in which natives overthrew colonial regimes. Over the past few years there have been major disturbances in the

United States, on campuses, in inner city ghettos, and in other places, and some have been marked by considerable violence. But whether these were revolutionary or harbingers of revolution is problematical. Nevertheless, in order to understand them as well as the other upheavals it is important to outline this type of change and the circumstances under which it occurs.

THE DETERMINANTS OF REVOLUTION

The definition of revolution is this: a relatively rapid and basic change in the authority structure of an association.[45]

The conditions which are necessary for a revolution to occur have been analyzed by Crane Brinton.[46] In his excellent study he found first, that societies which undergo such an upheaval experience serious economic difficulties, yet there are rising expectations. There is a general rise in the standard of living prior to the downturn, and people become quite discontented because they are unable to obtain the social goods they feel they deserve. This was true of the English Revolution of the 1640's and the American, French, and Russian Revolutions studied by Brinton.[47]

Second, those in the authority structure lose their effectiveness. The government is in serious financial straits and unable to meet its obligations. Just prior to the French Revolution in 1789 businessmen lost faith in government securities, contractors were not paid, and government workers could not count on receiving their salaries. Also, the government becomes indecisive and unable to use its police power wisely or effectively. On the one hand brutality against peaceful protestors enrages the citizenty and wins converts to the revolutionary cause; on the other hand, failure to quell disturbances encourages more of them. In addition, people in the upper class continue to assert their rights and privileges yet fail to fulfill their responsibilities. This self-seeking and their inability to improve economic and political conditions augments the antagonism of the lower class which increasingly questions the special rights and privileges. In turn, self-doubts among members of the upper class grow until a portion rejects its old values, rights, and privileges and joins the revolutionary movement.

Third, there is great ideational change. Many intellectuals—writers, artists, musicians, actors, teachers, clergymen, and others—become extremely critical of the social order and attack it. Not only do they show

---

[45] A qualification is necessary: the protagonists are indigenous or identify with those who are indigenous. This would exclude major change which results from conquest by an outside force.

[46] Crane Brinton, *The Anatomy of Revolution* (New York: Vintage Books, 1965).

[47] *Ibid.*, p. 32. See also James C. Davies, "Toward a Theory of Revolution," *American Sociological Review*, 27 (February 1962), 5–19.

that "the emperor has no clothes" but they also depict the foibles of the members of the upper class. In addition, they describe in word, picture, and song the injustices and suffering of the lower or other oppressed classes, and they speculate on how things might be improved. They promulgate what Brinton calls the revolutionary ideal, and their disavowal of the existing order is, in his words, "the transfer of the allegiance of the intellectuals." [48] Now this transfer is no light matter; it indicates extreme dissatisfaction, ". . . a gut-deep hatred for the way things are." [49] Their attacks help people articulate feelings of discontent and encourage them to see the present situation as intolerable.

Fourth, while there is always class conflict, it intensifies and divisions grow. More and more, incumbents of strata begin to see themselves as members of a class, and hold that those who rule are responsible for their troubles. Class barriers which in the past were viewed as gates that were opened to the able and successful begin to be seen as unnatural and as means of assuring unjust privileges. In addition to widening conflict, organized class-based or class-oriented groups begin to agitate against the class in power. Interestingly, class interests are generally not openly advanced as justification for overturning existing institutional arrangements. Rather, a higher, moral purpose is put forth and the appeals include such things as establishing "life, liberty, and the pursuit of happiness"; "Liberty, Equality, and Fraternity," or a conflict-free society in which the individual can freely develop his or her potential.[50] Finally, there is widespread feeling that change is imminent.[51]

Yet Brinton cautions that many of the circumstances cited above exist under "normal" conditions.[52] There are periodic economic difficulties in all societies; all governments exhibit some inefficiency and are never completely effective, and it is not unusual for the upper class to exhibit stupidity and ineptness. And, even in normal times some of its members harbor doubts about the rightness of the power and privileges they enjoy.[53]

Nevertheless, these several factors provide benchmarks for assessing class conflict which has revolutionary potential. No precise formula is possible, however; the best we can do is suggest that when society is "high" on each of these items there is the strong likelihood that it will undergo major change. Whether it will be reformist and sufficiently accommodate the conflicting interests or whether there will be a cataclys-

---

[48] Brinton, op. cit., pp. 41–43, 46–47.

[49] Ibid., p. 47.

[50] Regarding the latter, see Marx and Friedrich Engels, "The Communist Manifesto," in Marx, Capital, The Communist Manifesto, and Other Writings, ed. by Max Eastman (New York: The Modern Library, 1932), p. 343.

[51] Brinton, op. cit., pp. 29–30, 33–36, 40–43, 46–49, 51–53, 56–58, 60, 62–64, 66 ff.

[52] Ibid., pp. 28, 42, 50.

[53] Ibid., pp. 51–52.

mic upheaval depends to a very large degree on the society's political structure and history,[54] as well as the specific factors we enumerated earlier.

Summary

Stratification and class are critical aspects of human group life. They are linked to social interaction, through which the meanings we attach to such things as institutions or categories of persons arise. Collective definitions and expectations develop regarding the business of daily life. These, and the meanings, help hold the society together. However, since people make self-indications and judge and evaluate before acting, the possibility of change is inherent in human affairs. Thus, current meanings and expectations may be modified, rejected, or replaced with new ones. Collective definitions are responsible for some personal attributes, possessions, and roles being viewed favorably, and others unfavorably; these collective definitions are the basis of stratification. Although there are obviously significant differences between the haves and the have-nots in possessions and opportunities, the collective definitions are important for understanding the placement of people into different categories, or strata, as well as for attempts to change an existing ordering.

Inherent in organized group life is a division of labor and a multiplicity of roles, with differences in authority and rewards. While authority relations exist in many situations, for the purpose of studying class we limit our interest to associations, as conceived of by Weber and Dahrendorf. The roles in associations, such as a factory, city, or nation, are hierarchically arranged, for an unequal distribution of rights and obligations is characteristic of associations. There is always a latent conflict of interest between the superordinate and subordinate roles. Superordinate-subordinate relations become institutionalized, persist over time, and are invested with sanctity, whereby tradition, custom, and laws help perpetuate the advantages of the haves over the have-nots.

Stratification, which describes categories of people who have similar characteristics, differs from classes which are conflict groups. The incumbents of strata, by definition, are unorganized and cannot engage in concerted action. While stratification is found in almost all aggregates, collectivities, and groups, classes exist only in associations. The latent interests do not inevitably lead to conflict; it occurs only under certain circumstances, when an aggregate of persons, usually in the same stratum, see their interests as similar to those of their fellows, and as different from and opposed to the interests of another aggregate of people.

[54] See Seymour M. Lipset, *Political Man* (New York: Doubleday Anchor Books, 1963).

Classes are conflict groups which contest over the allocation of social goods—income, rights, prestige, and so on—in an association.

A number of factors encourage or discourage class formation. It is encouraged where there are highly rationalized enterprises and an emphasis on profit—money in a capitalist system and its equivalent in a noncapitalist arrangement. Even in agricultural economies, as in the cases of caste and estate society, there are associations, authority structures, group interests, and class conflict. People's life conditions are also important; in addition to the nature and degree of deprivation, the more similar persons are in their attributes and backgrounds, the greater the likelihood that discontent will lead to class formation. Changed perspectives, and ideologies, help channel discontent into concerted action. Cultural and historical aspects play a part, especially whether voluntary organizations for pursuing group interests are tolerated.

Class formation is by no means limited to persons at the lower levels; actually, the higher the stratum the greater the likelihood that the incumbents will engage in class behavior. Yet class formation and class conflict are constant and occur at all levels; they are among the major forces for change. Yet the outcome of such conflict may be a reinforcement of the status quo, reform of institutional arrangements, or, in rare instances, a revolutionary reconstruction of the society.

Stratification is greatly affected by social mobility for it determines in large part how much alike the incumbents of a stratum are. And, as we noted earlier, the greater the similarity in attributes and roles the more likely it is that personal discontent will become collective, and vice versa. Social mobility is also important in class formation and conflict. If there are few or only minimal class barriers, there can be much upward movement without the basic structure of the society being altered. But if there is blockage, those who are prevented from rising—especially able, energetic, and innovative persons—may become the instigators of revolutionary change. Downward mobility also has significant consequences for the individual and society. Therefore, to adequately analyze class behavior as well as stratification it is essential to understand social mobility, which is the subject of the next chapter.

Chapter II.   Social Mobility

The amount and nature of social mobility tell us a great deal about the stratification of a given society; also, it is an essential element in understanding class formation. For example, if there is much mobility—that is, many people rising into higher strata and others descending to lower levels—then at any given time a goodly portion of the incumbents of a particular stratum are likely to be heterogeneous in background, interests, and experiences. These dissimilarities discourage group formation and collective action to bring about change. On the other hand, while very little mobility makes for stratum homogeneity, class behavior does not necessarily follow. The growth rate of the economy may be so low that there is little opportunity for anyone. Or, there may be opportunity but people are limited in how far they can rise because of social, economic, or political barriers. Finally, there are differences among and within societies in the way individuals interpret mobility and the extent to which they believe the social structure provides opportunity. In turn, these subjective factors affect aspirations and reactions to success or failure.

In this chapter we will first examine the causes of mobility, focusing on the basic nature of a society, particularly its stage of economic development. Then we will look at institutional arrangements and other structural factors which hinder or facilitate mobility. The last section will be concerned with how people react personally and collectively to mobility or its lack. The first task, however, is to distinguish between the two main forms of mobility.

The Basic Types of Mobility

There are two basic types: vertical and horizontal. Both involve change in a person's life conditions but only the former applies to alteration in control over, or access to, money, highly valued jobs, exclusive neighborhoods, or anything that is collectively defined as desirable. We called such things, in the preceding chapter, *social goods*. Vertical mobility assumes that there are collective definitions regarding social goods and that the social goods are unequally distributed. In this context a population

31

may be categorized or stratified according to their control. It further assumes that invidious distinctions among the strata are made by the respective incumbents. Finally, the differences may be viewed as being in an hierarchical ordering.

Vertical mobility then is the change or "movement" of individuals, aggregates, collectivities, and groups from one level of control over social goods to another. If there is a substantial gain in control we have upward vertical mobility; if there is a substantial loss we have downward vertical mobility. For the vast majority of the population, occupation is the most important of social goods for it is the key to control over many other forms; consequently change in occupational level is the most common indicator of vertical movement. An individual's mobility is usually measured by comparing his position with his father's or by noting changes in his own career. Thus the engineer whose father was a laborer, and the salesman whose father was a doctor, are illustrations of *inter*generational vertical mobility; the first of upward movement, the second of downward. Instances of *intra*generational mobility are the carpenter who now has his own construction business and the corporation executive who was formerly a clerk, for upward mobility. Illustrative of downward mobility are the farm owner who is now a sharecropper and the Vice President of the United States who becomes a college professor or corporation lawyer.

Horizontal mobility refers to an alteration of life conditions which does not involve change in control over social goods. While the individual moves—physically from one place to another, or figuratively in terms of work tasks—he does not rise or fall in level. Examples are the construction worker from Pennsylvania who takes the same kind of job in Illinois and the New York school teacher who accepts a similar position in the Los Angeles school system. In each case the assumption is that neither has gained or lost with regard to such things as prestige or pay; in real life, however, horizontal mobility is usually tied in with vertical movement. This is common among executives where a horizontal move is usually coupled with a step upward, as so vividly described by William F. Whyte;[1] it is also common among professionals and technical specialists who work in large organizations. Persons who progressively rise in this fashion have been called "spiralists."[2]

The combination of horizontal and vertical mobility also holds for downward movement. An academic may be forced to leave his college or university for another institution because of lack of publications, staff reductions, or friction with the department head. His department may

[1] William F. Whyte, *The Organization Man* (Garden City, N.Y.: Doubleday Anchor Books, 1956), pp. 310 ff.

[2] Stephen Edgell, "Spiralists: Their Careers and Family Lives," *British Journal of Sociology*, 21 (September 1970), 314–323.

locate the new job for him, but this lateral move is actually a demotion.[3] Even though vertical and horizontal mobility are often coupled it is useful to keep the two types separate for analytic purposes.[4]

Amount of vertical mobility is determined primarily by the number of desirable positions available; secondly by institutional arrangements which make movement easy or difficult, and thirdly by cultural factors. The latter include historical conditions, aspirations, and beliefs; however, the first two are by far the most important and it is these structural factors which we examine next.

The Economic Structure

The availability of desirable positions is determined mainly by the rate of economic expansion. A rapidly growing economy is likely to provide greater occupational and other opportunities and even if there are restrictions there will be increased mobility throughout the stratification structure. In a very slowly growing society, or one where there has been economic expansion which has since declined, there will be limited movement even without legal or social restrictions.

It is important to distinguish between an inadequate supply of desirable positions and inadequate opportunity for mobility, which make it difficult for persons to change their level. Discriminatory laws and customs, religious strictures, ethnic or sexist prejudice, and limited opportunity for education or other means of job preparation adversely affect the disadvantaged. Yet suppose there were no restrictions and there was a free exchange of persons according to ability, with the capable rising and the incompetent dropping regardless of origin. If few desirable positions were available there would still be little mobility; this is illustrated in Figure II-1, which is based on Colin Clark's ideal type of economic development.[5]

In the first, primary stage of economic development, almost everyone is in agriculture, fishing, mining, and lumbering; there are very few occupations which pay well, have prestige, and involve "clean" work. Thus there is little opportunity for mobility. If, for the sake of discussion, all the persons at the top level were to be replaced by individuals from

---

[3] See Theodore Caplow and Reece J. McGee, *The Academic Marketplace* (Garden City, N.Y.: Doubleday Anchor Books, 1965), p. 42.

[4] These concepts of mobility are basically from Pitirim A. Sorokin, *Social and Cultural Mobility* (Glencoe, Ill.: The Free Press, 1959; first pub. in 1927), the classic work on social mobility.

[5] Colin Clark, *The Conditions of Economic Progress* (3rd ed.; London: Macmillan Co., 1957).

FIGURE II-1.
Economic Development and Mobility Potential

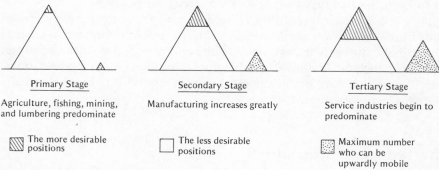

Primary Stage	Secondary Stage	Tertiary Stage
Agriculture, fishing, mining, and lumbering predominate	Manufacturing increases greatly	Service industries begin to predominate

⧄ The more desirable positions

☐ The less desirable positions

▦ Maximum number who can be upwardly mobile

Source: Adapted from Colin Clark, *The Conditions of Economic Progress* (3rd ed.; London: Macmillan & Co., Ltd., 1957).

the lower stratum very few could rise because of the proportionately small number of desirable positions. As the predominant economic base becomes manufacturing, the proportion of better occupations grows, which in turn increases potential opportunity. And, as a society moves into the tertiary, or service industry phase, the possibility of mobility increases further.

Modern society is characterized by an extensive and growing division of labor and a rapid change in occupational needs as well as in other areas of social and economic life. Among the consequences of an extensive and increasing division of labor which are significant for mobility is the breaking down of restraints on the individual. Emile Durkheim noted that as the division of labor increases people are freed from family and community bonds.[6] In addition, urbanization, which grows as the division of labor increases, provides conditions which further free people. In the city there is greater freedom to follow one's own interests because the individual is less likely to experience collective restraints.[7]

This weakening of collective restraints means that attributes over which the person has no control lessen in importance, such as being born on the wrong—or right—side of the tracks, or being a minority group member vs. belonging to the majority group. Such attributes, which are termed *ascribed*, are an accident of birth, and in non-modern society are of primary importance in the allocation of privileges and opportunities.[8] People are judged on the basis of ascribed criteria, and the possibility that an individual can improve his situation by what he achieves through his own efforts is very slim. But with industrialization and urbanization there is a growing tendency for people to succeed, or

[6] See Emile Durkheim, *The Division of Labor in Society* (Glencoe, Ill.: The Free Press, 1947), especially, pp. 291–292, 329–336.

[7] *Ibid.*, pp. 297–298.

[8] See Ralph Linton, *The Study of Man* (New York: Appleton Century, 1936), Chap. 8.

fail, on the basis of their achievement; more and more it is not "who you are" (or "who your family is") but "what you can do." [9]

The growing number of occupations provides a more widespread choice; thus persons with talent may find opportunities which would not exist for them in a society with a lesser division of labor. For other persons, the fact that there is much choice may serve to encourage them to strive for positions which appear to be more rewarding than those held by their fathers. Also, in the newer occupations there may be few or no limitations on entry, compared to the older and more established ones. [10]

The opportunity for mobility which results from individuals being freed from collective restraints, the tendency to favor achievement over ascription, and the increased variety of occupations is greatly enhanced by the growing proportion of highly-valued and better-paid positions. As the society becomes more complex and more bureaucratized, and as technology is applied to wider areas of life, there is an increase in the number of jobs with considerable responsibility. There is also an increase in the need for special skills, many of which can be developed only as a result of lengthy training. In order to attract qualified candidates to fill these positions, relatively greater rewards must be offered than for less skilled and less responsible ones. [11] This contributes to increasing the attractiveness of such positions, and by that token their status. Status refers to the rank or position in an hierarchical ordering. The ranking is the result of collectively defined criteria as to what is desirable or undesirable. While most often applied to occupations, status is also used in comparing families according to their wealth, in ranking neighborhoods or colleges, and so on. Similarly, individuals may evaluate their status in terms of other persons, and if their fortunes improve may feel a gain in their relative position, or status.

Now as the statuses of occupations rise, since the rewards increase, there may be a shortage of candidates for the less prestigeful and poorly-paid ones. This speeds the application of technology and rationalization to the lower-level positions, which in turn upgrades them and provides additional opportunity for social mobility. [12] For low-skilled and menial work employers may find it economically advantageous to recruit im-

[9] It should be emphasized that this is a *relative* shift in emphasis. Even in the most achievement-oriented society ascription remains a limitation on opportunity, while in an ascriptive society some degree of adequate performance, if not achievement, is necessary and expected. See William J. Goode, "The Protection of the Inept," *American Sociological Review*, 32 (February 1967), 5–19, especially 9–10.

[10] Everett C. Hughes, "Professions in Transition," in *Men and Their Work* (Glencoe, Ill.: The Free Press, 1958), pp. 133–135.

[11] See Kingsley Davis and Wilbert E. Moore, "Some Principles of Stratification," *American Sociological Review*, 10 (April 1945), 242–249. Note our discussion in Chapter I on the ideal type nature of Davis and Moore's formulation.

[12] See Conrad Taeuber and Irene B. Taeuber, *The Changing Population of the United States* (New York: John Wiley and Sons, 1958), p. 211.

migrants, which "pushes" natives out of such jobs. The natives feel a loss of status and move into more desirable occupations, and this increases their mobility.

Another factor which expands the number of higher-status positions is the tendency toward the "professionalization" of occupations. Pressure may be applied by those in an occupation to raise its status in their own eyes as well as in the eyes of clients and the larger public.[13] This is usually done by changing the name of the occupation, attempting to limit access through stiffer requirements such as formal education, and by codifying the responsibilities of the practitioners. In addition sanctions are provided which apply to members who violate the rules of the group. The name change attempts to create an image of the work as involving considerable responsibility and tasks which are difficult and call for great expertise. An illustration is provided by the employees who conduct tests in the laboratories of a state public health department. They successfully had the title of their occupation changed from "laboratory technician" to "medical technologist."[14] In the case of an unpleasant occupation the name change usually attempts to disguise the nature of the work. An illustration of this occurred on the sugar and pineapple planations of Hawaii where the former "rat catchers" are now called "rodent controllers."

Whatever the level of the occupation which is being recast, a demand for increased compensation and greater recognition usually follows. The result of this professionalization is not only a rise in status and pay for those in the occupation; there is also a widening of opportunity since additional higher status positions are being created. The stiffer entrance requirements are likely to include more training which usually requires additional education. In turn education becomes an increasingly important means for mobility.

The professionalization process as a way of increasing opportunity is nothing new; also, it is especially important if individual opportunity for mobility is absent. In the caste society of traditional India, which had extremely little mobility, persons would rise by improving the status of their caste. Among the steps would be a change in its name and more propitious behavior on the part of its members. The results would be approval by members of other castes, and eventually the status of the caste would rise.[15]

In modern society, where the bulk of opportunity has been the result of economic expansion, the professionalization of occupations has been of lesser importance; however, it seems likely that with increased bu-

[13] Hughes, *op. cit.*, pp. 131–138.

[14] California State Department of Public Health, divisional report (Berkeley: California State Department of Public Health, 1957, mimeographed).

[15] See J. H. Hutton, *Caste in India, Its Nature, Function and Origin* (Cambridge: Cambridge University Press, 1946), Ch. 8.

reaucratization, which is common, and a decrease in expansion, the professionalization of occupations may be used more and more as a means of mobility. Put another way, we suggest that pressures for group mobility are inversely related to opportunities for individual mobility.

The economic expansion, the growing division of labor, and the other characteristics of industrial society we discussed are responsible for increased opportunity for upward vertical mobility. Recent research has shown that there is considerable upward movement in all modern societies, particularly the more industrialized.[16] The most comprehensive analysis of mobility in the United States to date shows that there is continuing vertical movement, most of it upward.[17]

Although most of the mobility in modern societies is upward, downward movement also occurs, and we shall examine some of the consequences of both types toward the end of the chapter. There is another aspect of the structural aspects of mobility, and that is the institutional arrangements in the society which increase opportunity for some and limit it for others.

Institutional Arrangements

The nature of the formal and informal institutional arrangements facilitates or hinders mobility for persons at all levels, but particularly affects those in the lower strata. If there are no formal restrictions such as laws which designate who can own land, obtain education, enter the better occupations, or belong to "inner circles," or if there are no significant informal restrictions which have the same effect, then we may talk about an "open" society. On the other hand a society *with* such restrictions would be labeled "closed." Yet even in the most egalitarian situation where everyone has the legal opportunity to rise some will be more equal than others. Custom, accident of birth, or the simple fact that parents favor children over strangers, as was pointed out in the preceding chapter, are restrictive of general opportunity. While modern societies are much more open than earlier ones, even with the absence of legal restraints there may still be social, racial, and sexual barriers which greatly limit ascent.

An interesting illustration of contrasting institutional arrangements is provided by Ralph Turner's study of the utilization of education for mo-

[16] Seymour M. Lipset and Reinhard Bendix, *Social Mobility in Industrial Society* (Berkeley and Los Angeles: University of California Press, 1959), pp. 11–75; and S. H. Miller, "Comparative Social Mobility: A Trend Report," *Comparative Sociology*, 9 (1960), 1–5.

[17] Peter M. Blau and Otis D. Duncan, *The American Occupational Structure* (New York: John Wiley & Sons, 1967), pp. 103, 112, and Appendix J2.1.

bility in England and in the United States.[18] In a country with a long history of class distinctions, such as England, the institutional arrangements of education, including the beliefs and attitudes which sustain them, comprise a sponsored system of mobility. It receives support from the assumption that only the upper class is qualified to rule and that successful stewardship requires the embodiment of traditional manners, practices, and thinking. Only those born into circumstances which provide opportunity for learning the proper ways may be trusted to fill important roles. These views are promulgated by the upper class and accepted by many in the lower; therefore, only a number sufficient for openings in positions of leadership receive university training. The education emphasizes high culture and the producing of "gentlemen" rather than more practical studies such as technical programs. The selection of candidates for higher education is done very carefully so that only those likely to succeed are allowed in. Then every effort is made to see that the select few successfully complete their schooling; the dropout rate is very low and the graduates move into important positions in the society.[19]

Now mobility occurs through the selection of a small number of very able lower-class persons who are then sponsored, as are the upper-class students; however the sponsorship of these poor but able youngsters includes full scholarships so that the recipients do not have to work part-time. They can then devote themselves to their studies and become socialized into the ways of the upper class. Upon graduation these scholarship students also move into important positions in the society.

Turner contrasts this educational system with that of the United States which does not have the conception of a traditional ruling class. The more egalitarian belief system holds that practically anyone has the potential for leadership; thus any person who has the motivation, ability, and necessary training should be considered, regardless of social origin. Higher education, instead of being selective as in England should be open and anyone who wants to give it a try should be allowed to do so. Moreover, since there are no traditional specifications for leadership there is great stress on motivation and perseverence; the consequence is that large numbers of young people are enrolled in institutions of higher learning and mediocre work is acceptable. There are also many provisions for a second chance in order to prolong the race so as to minimize the possibility that a deserving individual will be eliminated prematurely. In other words, this educational system is a big contest with many entrants, in contrast to a sponsored arrangement.[20]

It is difficult to say whether the caliber of those who fill important roles is higher under sponsored or contest mobility. There is probably

[18] Ralph H. Turner, "Sponsored and Contest Mobility and the School System," *American Sociological Review*, 25 (December 1960), 855–867.

[19] *Ibid.*, pp. 856–857, 859, 861–862.

[20] *Ibid.*, pp. 856–858, 860–861, 863–864.

little difference except that under the sponsored system the autobiographies and memoirs of leaders may be more literate.[21] Even though the sponsored arrangement with its school ties and intermarriage may allow for greater protection of the inept, this also occurs under the contest system.[22]

It is also difficult to say whether a sponsored or a contest system leads to greater mobility into the ruling class, other things being equal; that is, assuming the same stage of economic development and rate of growth. Under the sponsored arrangement very few lower-class youth have a chance to rise so high but once selected they are guaranteed important positions; yet they have to be extremely able. There are many lower-class youngsters of lesser but still considerable ability who cannot get into this channel to the top; however, they are *more* able than many of the upper-class persons who are accepted for college and eventually move into top positions. This is not surprising for those from the better-off homes have advantages which have nothing to do with ability, but which the lower-class youths lack. These include superior pre-college schooling, familial support, favorable cultural conditions at home, and the outlook, manners, and habits which make for educational success.

Yet are these advantages and disadvantages much different under contest mobility? Even though many more from the lower levels are allowed to participate in the contest, the proportion of failures and dropouts is very high. All told, very few obtain top positions. Similarly, the children from upper-level families have the favorable circumstances which give them the advantage in the competition, not to mention getting into the prestigious universities which are the path to elite positions. The differences in life chances among the several strata will be detailed in Chapters IV, V, and VI.

Whether there is predominantly sponsored or contest mobility depends primarily on the structural conditions in the society, particularly the stage of economic development and rate of expansion, as we noted above. The institutional arrangements which come about are of course strongly influenced by historical factors and the outlook that people have. However, these influences are likely to fall by the wayside or at least be greatly modified as the structural conditions change. Thus countries such as England are beginning to move increasingly toward the contest system of education.[23]

[21] F. Musgrove observes that disciplined learning and written and verbal skills are emphasized, but at the expense of oral expression, creativity, and spontaneity of behavior. Musgrove, *Youth and the Social Order* (Bloomington, Ind.: Indiana University Press, 1965), pp. 5–6, 160. See also Turner, *op. cit.*, p. 865.

[22] See Goode, "The Protection of the Inept."

[23] See, e.g., T. B. Bottomore, *Classes in Modern Society* (New York: Pantheon Books, 1966), pp. 45–46. Bottomore states that ". . . it is probable that middle-class families have actually made greater use of the new opportunities for grammar school and university education." This is similar to the American experience, as we shall show.

The rate of economic expansion seems to be the most important of the structural conditions affecting the institutional arrangements that are significant for mobility. This appears increasingly to be the case since World War II with the growing spread of egalitarian ideas. Slow expansion favors a sponsored system as well as a closed class arrangement, while rapid expansion encourages contest mobility and an open class system. But what is the effect of economic growth on sponsored mobility, and economic decline on contest mobility?

Sponsored mobility and a closed class system are undermined by economic expansion, for then alternate channels to wealth and power become available; also, the establishment is confronted with challengers who have not been socialized into the ways of the ruling class. Since the sponsored system also requires acquiescence by the lower strata, including the belief that they are inherently inferior, increased opportunities may help change their self-conceptions and further undermine traditional class relations.

On the other hand, a contest system is undermined by a decline in economic growth, for there is then an insufficient number of the better positions, from the topmost to the lesser but still desirable ones. The latter serve as consolation awards for those who don't quite make it, and are thus important for minimizing discontent. If the general belief is that everyone should be a winner, granted there is a wide range in the prizes, then a serious decline in opportunity may result in great frustration. In a sense, even though there are still many participants the contest has been called off and there are no more prizes. Or, the rules have been made so stringent that large categories of people can no longer compete.

DISCRIMINATORY PATTERNS

Both formal and informal institutional arrangements facilitate upward mobility at all levels for some but not for others. They usually favor the rise of persons in the upper strata and hinder it for those in the lower. Such use of the laws and the police power of the state is nothing new: in the 13th century in Europe an individual who was not of noble ancestry was prohibited from being a knight or from obtaining land. This restricted the privileges that went with knighthood to nobles, but more importantly, only they could acquire land, which was the basis of wealth.[24] More recently in California, the Alien Land Law which was first passed in 1913 prevented aliens, particularly orientals, from land ownership.[25] Laws and the police power of the state have also been used

[24] See Henri Pirenne, *A History of Europe* (Garden City: N.Y.: Doubleday Anchor Books, 1958), Vol. I, p. 138.

[25] Tamotsu Shibutani and Kian M. Kwan, *Ethnic Stratification* (New York: The Macmillan Co., 1965), p. 326.

to prohibit minorities from entering the more desirable occupations, as in the ante-bellum South, Hitler's Germany, the Union of South Africa, and Rhodesia.[26]

Residential and occupational segregation of minorities or other lower-strata persons help perpetuate social distance; in turn this minimizes competition, the developing of higher aspirations, and the challenging of the status quo.[27] Whether segregation is legal and thus formal, or informal, it still has these consequences; in addition, customs and etiquette help maintain the social distance. Even where there are no laws that set job ceilings this is often done informally, as in the practice of medicine. Hospitals are likely to select interns whose ethnicity and stratum background are similar to those of the resident staff. Thus minority-group members and persons from lower-strata backgrounds are likely to be found in county hospitals and public clinics. On the other hand interns who are white, majority group members, and from middle- and upper-level homes are likely to predominate in the elite hospitals. Also, these prestigious institutions usually allow only the doctors on their staff to be permanent members and practice there; and these doctors come from the "right" medical schools and are trained in the "right type" of hospital. Since a new member must be sponsored by a colleague already on the staff this limitation on mobility is perpetuated.[28]

Restrictions on mobility through informal job ceilings have been common in most occupations. Minority-group members have been virtually excluded from the printing and construction industries, and where they have been accepted are usually relegated to the least desirable jobs.[29] Job ceilings are common for women employees and also limit mobility.[30]

BLACKS

The effects of such informal institutional arrangements become clear when the mobility rates of minority-group members are examined. In her path-breaking study of mobility, Natalie Rogoff found blacks to be greatly disadvantaged regardless of father's level. "From all occupational origins," she writes, "Negroes were absorbed into the occupational structure only at those positions which were least economically and socially rewarding." [31] Rogoff cautions that her findings may apply only to

[26] *Ibid.*, pp. 321–324.

[27] *Ibid.*, pp. 314–315.

[28] *Ibid.*, p. 327.

[29] See Philip Shabecoff, "Bethlehem Steel Ordered to Bar Racial Inequities," *New York Times* (January 17, 1973), pp. 1 ff.

[30] See Eileen Shanahan, "A.T.&T. to Grant 15,000 Back Pay in Job Inequities," *New York Times* (January 19, 1973), pp. 1 ff.

[31] Natalie Rogoff, *Recent Trends in Occupational Mobility* (Glencoe, Ill.: The Free Press, 1953), p. 108.

communities such as Indianapolis, which was the locale of her research. However, a more recent study by Peter M. Blau and Otis D. Duncan underscores the disadvantages of blacks.[32] Even when the effects of region of birth, less advantageous social origins, and lower educational attainment are statistically controlled, blacks' occupational chances are still inferior to whites'. That is, the occupational chances of blacks and whites in the North were analyzed separately from those of blacks and whites in the South, to eliminate the effects of regional differences. Also, blacks and whites with similar social origins were compared, as were blacks and whites with the same amount of education. Although the minority of black college graduates apparently do as well as their white counterparts, at all other levels of education the black fares worse. That is, whites with *less* education are at the same occupational and income level than better-educated blacks.[33] In addition, with the exception noted, educational investment by the black person does not pay off; he is likely to be in a lower-level occupation and make less money than the black with less education, who began working earlier.

WOMEN

While the discriminatory pattern is somewhat different for women, still they are less mobile than men and more poorly rewarded. The problem in interpreting the chances of women rising relative to men is complicated by criteria which are affected by historical and cultural factors. Peter Y. DeJong and associates found in a study of women in the labor force, using broad occupational categories such as professional, clerical, operative, and so on, essentially the same intergenerational mobility pattern as men.[34] However these broad categories may obscure differences in mobility, particularly in the higher status professions. For example, many females categorized as professionals are public-school teachers or nurses while their male counterparts are principals or doctors.[35]

What is clear is that there are differential rewards among all occupational levels.[36] Larry E. Sutter and Herman P. Miller found that ". . .

[32] Blau and Duncan, *The American Occupational Structure.*

[33] *Ibid.*, pp. 238–240. It is understandable, as Blau and Duncan note, that some blacks, especially underprivileged youngsters, show little motivation for education, since it is simply not very profitable for them.

[34] Peter Y. DeJong, Milton J. Brawer, and Stanley S. Robin, "Patterns of Female Intergenerational Occupational Mobility: A Comparison with Male Patterns of Intergenerational Occupational Mobility," *American Sociological Review*, 36 (December 1971), 1033–1042.

[35] *Ibid.* See also Elizabeth M. Havens and Judy Corder Tully, "Female Intergenerational Occupational Mobility: Comparisons of Patterns?" *American Sociological Review*, 37 (December 1972), 774–777; and DeJong *et al.*, "Reply to Havens and Tully," pp. 777–779.

[36] Larry E. Sutter and Herman P. Miller, "Income Differences Between Men and Career Women," *American Journal of Sociology*, 78 (January 1973), 962–974. Cf. our discussion in Chapter III.

most women were receiving 'just average' wages, regardless of training, job status, or experience. The income distribution of men, on the other hand, tends to be skewed toward higher income levels." [37] Career women—that is year-round full-time female workers who have worked all their adult lives—receive 25% less than what men make. The salaries of professional career women are 32% less than professional men's; career operatives, compared to men in the same line of work, receive 43% less.[38] When career females who have not worked all their adult lives are included the discrepancies increase, and the gap is even wider with the inclusion of part-time female workers. Then, ". . . the overall difference between the earnings of men and women was about $2,800 in annual wages in 1966 or about 38% of the wages of men." [39]

These findings are also based on broad occupational categories and therefore are subject to the same criticism as the research of DeJong and his associates. Another recent study which used much narrower job categories found even greater differences between female and male salaries. A random survey of employed persons conducted by the Survey Research Center of the University of Michigan, controlling for education, length of service, amount of supervisory responsibility, and occupational prestige, revealed the overall salary discrepancy to be 42%.[40]

Yet even these data understate the lesser chances for mobility among women, for cultural imperatives keep many out of the labor market completely and lessen the mobility chances of others who do work. Joan Huber's comment is appropriate:

> A woman is kept off the ladder for high prestige jobs because she might leave to get married or have a baby. After some years at home with her children, her skills rusted, she is easily outranked by males of the same age who have supposedly accumulated valuable occupational experience while she has been scrubbing crud from the kitchen floor and running the PTA.[41]

There is another consideration which concerns all channels of mobility, which is illustrated by sex-typed work such as public-school teaching. When conditions change and such an occupational area begins to offer more prestigious and better paid positions men begin to flow into it. When previously the jobs were less desirable some opportunity for mobility was available for women; however, as the positions grow in importance they are filled by men, further limiting opportunity for women.

---

[37] *Ibid.,* p. 973.

[38] *Ibid.,* p. 966.

[39] *Ibid.,* p. 973.

[40] Teresa Levitin, Robert P. Quinn, and Graham L. Staines, "Sex Discrimination Against the American Working Woman," *American Behavioral Scientist,* 15 (November–December 1971), 237–254.

[41] Joan Huber, "Editor's Introduction," *American Journal of Sociology,* 78 (January 1973), 765. The entire issue is devoted to reporting research on women.

Edward Gross has shown that occupations sex-typed as male have remained stable since 1900 while female occupations are being entered in growing numbers by men.[42]

Thus, as with blacks various institutional arrangements, both formal and informal, limit the mobility opportunity of women.

But, it is said, you can't keep a good man (or woman) down; this is true in the sense that extremely able and ambitious individuals, whatever their origin, will likely make their mark regardless of the economic structure or the institutional arrangements. However their chances, let alone those of people with ordinary ability or disadvantaged background, are sorely affected by the structural conditions. There are several other structural aspects that we want to consider.

Additional Structural Factors

Among the structural conditions which also affect opportunity for mobility are war and revolution; the specific nature of the economy; channels for mobility; differential fertility, and motivation.

WAR AND REVOLUTION

Any large-scale societal upheaval such as war or revolution is likely to greatly increase mobility—upward for some and downward for others. During wartime, expansion of the armed forces and battlefield casualties create a "vacuum" which is in part filled by lower-rank personnel. Civilians benefit from the expansion of the armaments industry and the generally intensified economic activity.[43] Whether this initial upward mobility continues or whether it reverses is of course related to the outcome of the war; but with victory there is usually further economic expansion and general upward mobility is likely to continue, or most people are likely to at least remain at the level they reached. Even with demobilization, most of the military personnel probably move into somewhat comparable civilian statuses. This especially holds for the higher military leaders; illustrations of this are the attainment of the Presidency by Generals George Washington, Andrew Jackson, Ulysses S. Grant, and Dwight D. Eisenhower. There is also considerable movement from military positions into industry, perhaps the best illustration being General Douglas S. MacArthur who, after being relieved of his command in

---

[42] Edward Gross, "Plus Ça Change. . . .? The Sexual Structure of Occupations Over Time," *Social Problems*, 16 (Fall 1968), 198–208.

[43] See Sorokin, *Social and Cultural Mobility*, p. 144.

Korea in 1951 became Chairman of the Board of Directors of Remington Rand, Inc.

During revolutions, ruling classes and many other high strata groups are deposed, creating openings for persons at lower levels. Even though the initial high mobility is reduced during subsequent stages of the revolution dramatic rises as well as much moderate movement are likely to persist for some time. Economic expansion which is often both a cause and consequence of revolution further adds to the upward mobility. Such increased mobility opportunity is characteristic of revolutions, particularly the modern ones—the American, French, Russian, Chinese, and Cuban.[44]

Other major upheavals such as great economic changes, rapid industrialization, or large-scale reform movements are likely to have a similar impact on mobility, although it is usually less dramatic and over a longer period of time.[45]

In discussing economic structure earlier we were dealing with a market economy in which more or less free economic forces are at play. This is an ideal type situation since in all societies there are attempts to control various aspects of the economy, with greater or lesser consequences for mobility. The maximum control occurs in totalitarian societies and with it goes a very great influence on mobility rates.

THE COMMAND ECONOMY AND MOBILITY

In a totalitarian state such as the U.S.S.R. equality-inequality are critically affected by political and economic decisions.[46] John H. Goldthorpe points out that in the Soviet system government decisions have an extremely pervasive effect on such things as wage rates, the expansion or contraction of industries and occupations, and educational opportunity. In turn, the amount of inequality and mobility are affected, and much more so than in Western industrial nations. In the West the market economy is basically responsible for the degree of social inequality; however, the government sets limits on it through subsidies to business, income and inheritance taxes, and Social Security and other programs. Although market forces have an impact in the Soviet system, they are subordinated by political control, which is consequently much more decisive in determining the degree of inequality in the society.[47] Political decisions dur-

[44] See Sorokin, *op. cit.*, pp. 143–144, 370–371, 466–467; Lipset and Bendix, *Social Mobility in Industrial Society*, pp. 33n, 282; and Alex Inkeles and Raymond A. Bauer, *The Soviet Citizen* (Cambridge, Mass.: Harvard University Press, 1959), pp. 67–100.

[45] See Sorokin, *op. cit.*, pp. 446–471, 481–485; and Lipset and Bendix, *op. cit.*, pp. 261–262.

[46] John H. Goldthorpe, "Social Stratification in Industrial Society," in Bendix and Lipset, eds., *Class, Status, and Power* (rev. ed.; New York: The Free Press, 1966), pp. 648–659.

[47] *Ibid.*, p. 657.

ing the Stalinist period increased inequality; in recent years it has been checked and in some respects reversed by new policies.[48]

Yet, once the rank order of the social structure has been set, the command economy of totalitarian societies could discourage social mobility processes.[49] Daniel Kubat found this to be the case in Czechoslovakia where there has been a decline in the great mobility that took place in 1948 as a result of nationalization of industries, ascent in the Party, and industrial expansion. Upward movement has been limited directly through administrative commands such as the leveling of income differences between manual and non-manual workers, the regulation of occupational choice, and restrictions on labor turnover. It has been limited indirectly by discrediting the social mobility ethos and emphasizing the value of workers *as workers* to Marxism, and by discouraging individual competitiveness and status symbols such as the accumulation of consumer goods.[50] However in a command economy new decisions by the regime can alter such policies and encourage social mobility processes, should it wish to.

Yet in every society, whether it is based on a market or command economy, there are particular channels for mobility; these are occupational groupings or institutional arrangements, such as government or education.[51] Not only are they paths for upward movement but they are important in a much broader sense. For some of these channels play a critical part in the economic, political, and social organization of the society in a given epoch. However as societal conditions change so does the relative importance of each.

CHANGING CHANNELS FOR MOBILITY

The several channels always provide opportunity for some individuals, but as material conditions, broader societal organization, and people's perspectives change the significance of these channels for large numbers of people also alters. In addition, the channels are affected by particular events such as war and revolution which were discussed earlier.

Pitirim A. Sorokin lists the major channels as the military; the church;

[48] *Ibid.* Goldthorpe notes that the Party may be compelled to give great consideration to popular feeling in making its decisions, it may rely more on technical and scientific expertise, and it may decentralize administration; however it maintains ultimate authority and control.

[49] Daniel Kubat, "Social Mobility in Czechoslovakia," *American Sociological Review*, 28 (April 1963), 203–212.

[50] *Ibid.*, pp. 206, 208, 209–212.

[51] See Sorokin, *Social and Cultural Mobility*, pp. 164–181; and Suzanne Keller, *Beyond the Ruling Class* (New York: Random House, 1963). See also Richard T. Morris and Raymond J. Murphy, "The Situs Dimension in Occupational Structure," *American Sociological Review*, 24 (April 1959), 231–239.

education; the government, and the political party; professional associations; wealth-making organizations, and the family. We have touched on some of them previously, but here we want to focus on changes in relative importance. The military which historically was the major channel remains important and it is the first one we will look at.

THE MILITARY

During periods of militarism or war the military is a primary channel. Among war-like primitive tribes the majority of chieftains achieve their position through the military organization; over a third of the Roman emperors were from the lowest strata and rose through the army, and this was true for almost 20% of the Emperors of Byzantium. During the warfare-ridden Middle Ages the military was a prime means of rising.[52] As feudalism declined, however, the overriding importance of the military dropped; with economic expansion and the growth of commerce and manufacturing it was superseded by wealth-making organizations.

Even with its relative decline as a channel, at least in industrial nations, the significance of the military increases during wartime and then drops with peace. Yet its importance as an integral part of industrialism should not be overlooked. The military was an essential element in the development of the Western nations for it obtained colonies which provided cheap raw materials and secured the markets in which the manufactured goods were sold. Today military expenditures are a major if not dominant part of national budgets and exert a very important economic impact throughout the society.[53] It is estimated that in the United States if the persons in the armed forces, in defense industries, and in the manufacturing and service activities affected by the first two were thrown on the job market the unemployment rate would be something like 24%. This would approximate the 25% unemployment during the depth of the Great Depression in 1932.[54] Since the infusion or withdrawal of Federal funds for the military establishment has a strong impact on the economy, civilian mobility is significantly affected. It is also affected by a nation's economic activities overseas, and the military plays a key role in that regard. In addition, the armed forces themselves are always a channel for mobility since war rather than peace is the normal state of affairs; for example, beginning with the Revolutionary War, on the average there have been three full years in which the American armed forces have been engaged in action for every full year of peace.[55]

[52] Sorokin, *op. cit.*, pp. 164–166.

[53] See Harry Magdoff, "Militarism and Imperialism," *American Economic Review*, 40 (May 1970), 237–242.

[54] *Ibid.*, p. 241.

[55] *Ibid.*, p. 237. Magdoff notes that this does not include relatively small scale activities such as the constant patrolling of some 2,000 miles of the Yangtze River in China during the early part of the century.

Even though the military remains important in industrial society, opportunity through this channel increases during wartime and decreases with peace and demobilization, as we noted above. However in less developed nations the military is likely to be the major channel both during war and peace.[56]

The Church

In the past the church was the second principal channel of vertical circulation. The significance of the Roman Catholic Church as a source of upward movement is suggested by Sorokin's study of 144 Popes which found that 19% were from the middle strata.[57] Sainthood is the ultimate in vertical mobility; Katherine and Charles H. George's analysis of the social origins of 2,489 Roman Catholic saints shows that 78% were from the upper strata, 17% from the middle, and five per cent from the lower.[58]

But the opportunity a channel such as the church provides for the disadvantaged relative to the better-off shifts as the importance of the activity changes. It is part of the same process we observed when we discussed sex-typed occupations earlier: when the work is not held in high regard it provides very little mobility, although it may be useful for the disadvantaged. Then, as it gains in importance and becomes significant they are displaced by the more advantaged who rise into the top positions.

Since a new religion is often a break with the past, it is denigrated by those in the authority structure and by the better-off citizens. Initially the low-born are attracted to it, but at this stage there is not much opportunity for mobility. If it becomes widely accepted or the state religion then some of the leaders, who are from among these early members are likely to be propelled into top positions. Once the religion is established and the church attains power, however, it is no longer the mobility channel for the lower strata that it was during its earlier expansion; now, persons from the higher levels begin to take over the important positions. Finally, as the church declines so does its significance as a channel for mobility; those from the upper strata leave and, although more people from the lower levels move into leadership positions, overall opportunity has declined.

The changes in opportunity that occur as the church goes through the periods of early growth, expansion, and finally decline is illustrated by the Roman Catholic Church. It grew initially during the first century and

[56] See Morris Janowitz, *The Military in the Political Development of New Nations* (Chicago: The University of Chicago Press, 1965), pp. 28, 49–56.

[57] Sorokin, *Social and Cultural Mobility*, p. 167.

[58] Katherine George and Charles H. George, "Roman Catholic Sainthood and Social Status," *Journal of Religion*, 35 (August 1955), 85–98.

continued to expand; its power increased greatly during the 10th and 11th centuries, and remained strong until the French Revolution at the end of the 18th century. George and George's research revealed that during the first century less than half the saints were from the upper strata while 41% were from the middle and 12% from the lower (see Table II-1). Between the second and fourth centuries almost two thirds were from the upper strata and nine per cent from the lower. The average for the next 500 years was 93% upper, six middle, and only one per cent lower. During the tenth century, the Church's most powerful period, 97% of the saints were of upper strata origin, only three per cent from the middle, and none was from the lower. The domination of the upper strata continues, although by the 16th and 17th centuries the decline is clear. By that time the proportions from the three levels are similar to those of the second to fourth centuries. During the 18th and 19th centuries only a third are upper strata, just over half are middle, and 16% are lower.

TABLE II-1. Social Origins of Roman Catholic Saints (in percentages)

| | Social Origin | | | |
Century	Upper Strata	Middle Strata	Lower Strata	Number
1st	47%	41%	12%	(83)
2nd-4th	64	28	9	(617)
5th-9th	93	6	1	(869)
10th	97	3	0	(58)
11th-12th	91	7	2	(233)
13th-15th	78	17	6	(355)
16th-17th	66	25	9	(195)
18th-19th	33	51	16	(92)

Source: Figures adapted from Katherine George and Charles H. George, "Roman Catholic Sainthood and Social Status," *Journal of Religion,* 35 (August 1955), 85-98, Table 1. Published by The University of Chicago Press.

EDUCATION

Education has always been a means of upward mobility. Where schooling is accessible to all, Sorokin writes,

. . . the school system represents a "social elevator" moving from the very bottom of a society to its top. In societies where the schools are accessible only to its higher strata, the school system represents an elevator moving only within the upper floors . . . and transporting up and down only the dwellers of these upper stories. Even in such societies, however, some individuals from the lower layers always have succeeded in slipping into the school elevator and, through it, climbing.[59]

[59] Sorokin, *op. cit.,* p. 169.

In preindustrial society the school system is like the elevator moving only within the upper floors.[60] An interesting use of education which would theoretically broaden opportunity was in conjunction with the examination system of old China. At the beginning of the medieval period (around 220 B.C. to about 1,000 A.D.), China began to develop a bureaucratic system of administration and made use of written examinations to select capable men.[61] While this undoubtedly increased opportunity there were a number of drawbacks: the needed education was classical, thus its content was far removed from the culture of the lower strata; also it required tutoring which the poor could not afford. In addition, the examination system was neither the major mode of mobility, nor the way upper strata families retained their status; the primary means were family position, wealth, influence, and military activities.[62]

It is not until industrialization that education becomes a major channel. The machine technology and the growth in commercial activities increase the need for literacy which in turn leads to more widespread schooling. As we noted earlier there is an expansion in the proportion of desirable occupations, and they require training which the schools provide. And, with more people from the lower strata becoming educated, the channel grows in importance.

This channel also serves as a testing and socializing agency. The examinations, grades, certificates, and degrees insure that those who have passed through have at least the minimum ability for the occupations they will move into. The socialization aspect of education was mentioned in the discussion on sponsored and contest mobility; however, we might add that the socialization of the lower strata into the upper occurs under contest as well as sponsored mobility. In the United States this is most true of the prestigious private universities, less so for the public institutions. The latter help socialize lower strata individuals into the ways of the middle and the upper-middle strata.

Not only is the upward movement of those who receive an education facilitated, but the educators also benefit: positions such as principal, dean, and professor gain in prestige and pay, and more such positions are created. However, as with other channels, education's importance for mobility fluctuates, and at times opportunity for the disadvantaged may become limited. In the United States, for example, the proportion of women attending college and obtaining higher degrees rose steadily from 1869 to 1920 and remained high until 1940, but between the end of World War II and 1960 there was a great decline. Only since 1960 has the

---

[60] See Gideon Sjoberg, *The Preindustrial City* (Glencoe, Ill.: The Free Press, 1960).

[61] Wolfram Eberhard, "Social Mobility and Stratification in China," in Bendix and Lipset, *Class, Status, and Power*, p. 176.

[62] See *Ibid.*, pp. 171–182.

proportion been going up; now the proportion is about what it was during 1930.[63]

Much attention will be paid to education as a means of mobility in the following chapters of this book.

THE GOVERNMENT, AND THE POLITICAL PARTY

As a society industrializes and grows in size and complexity the government provides increasing opportunity through more positions, especially the prestigious ones, and by setting up universalistic means for selecting employees. This is done in order to insure competency and avoid favoritism; but existing job-holders and others who feel threatened by the competition, and persons who will be adversely affected by the loss of patronage are likely to fight such an arrangement. This was the case in the United States where the opponents derided the proposal for a civil service system, calling it "snivel service." The Pendleton Act of 1883 which provided for appointments through competitive examinations initially covered only 14,000 out of 100,000 federal employees; today most government workers are included.[64]

Bureaucratic systems such as the civil service which emphasize appointment and promotion through universalistic criteria open the door to able persons from the lower strata, especially those from minority group backgrounds. Similar bureaucratic arrangements develop in business, at least at the middle and lower levels, also as a response to size and complexity.[65] As in the case of government, such emphases in business also increase opportunity for the lower strata.

In modern society the political party is another channel for mobility, often in conjunction with the government. Achievement may occur within the party itself and is often a prelude to moving into a high position in the government. This is true in a liberal parliamentary society as well as in a totalitarian one; in the latter however the party is much more important in regard to control over social goods. By that token it is much more significant as a channel for mobility as Kubat's study of Czechoslovakia showed.

[63] Cynthia Fuchs Epstein, *Woman's Place: Options and Limits in Professional Careers* (Berkeley and Los Angeles: University of California Press, 1971), pp. 56–60; Mabel Newcomer, *A Century of Higher Education for Women* (New York: Harper & Bros., 1959); William L. O'Neill, *Everyone Was Brave* (Chicago: Quadrangle Books, 1969), p. 305; and National Center for Educational Statistics, *Digest of Educational Statistics, 1974 Edition* (Washington, D.C.: Government Printing Office, 1975), pp. 75 and 84.

[64] See Samuel P. Hays, *The Response to Industrialism, 1885–1914* (Chicago: University of Chicago Press, 1957), p. 26.

[65] See Wilbert E. Moore, *The Conduct of the Corporation* (New York: Vintage Books, 1962), pp. 83–84, 160; and Whyte, *The Organization Man*, p. 190. Cf. Peter F. Drucker, *The Concept of the Corporation* (New York: The New American Library, 1964), p. 41.

PROFESSIONAL ASSOCIATIONS

In industrial society professional associations are very numerous, and provide opportunity for mobility. Examples are the American Medical Association and the American Bar Association; others are the American Council on Education, and the organizations of sociologists, economists, physicists, and other academics. Persons who participate in such associations make contacts and develop friendships which may be helpful for rising within their profession. Additional mobility is possible through holding office in a professional association, for the positions provide perquisites, prestige, and added opportunity for contacts and friendships. Also, moving to the top of a professional association may facilitate entry into politics and government and in turn lead to additional mobility through those channels.

Trade and business organizations and labor unions, although usually differentiated from professional associations, have the same function as regards opportunity for mobility.

WEALTH-MAKING ORGANIZATIONS

Organized activities which create wealth, such as manufacturing, banking, and oil-producing have always provided opportunity for mobility. In the later periods of Greece and Rome aristocrats were recruited principally from the successful money-makers. Even in caste society wealth leads to a rise in social status, although it may take some time. In the later Middle Ages, with economic expansion those who became wealthy soon superseded in large part the aristocracy of birth. This occurred in England where they rose to prominent positions, in addition to which they purchased titles and privileges from the Crown. A somewhat similar situation prevailed in France.[66]

The successful individual rises to a position of power and influence within the wealth-making organization. In addition, the person's wealth can lead to power and influence in other sectors, such as government and politics. For more recent times there are many illustrations of individuals whose wealth has helped them rise to important positions in government and politics: Herbert C. Hoover (mining and engineering), Edwin W. Pauley (oil), W. Averell Harriman (railroads, finance, shipbuilding), and Nelson A. Rockefeller (oil).

THE FAMILY

As with these other channels the importance of the family for mobility shifts as societal conditions change. In China prior to 1948 it played a

---

[66] Sorokin, *Social and Cultural Mobility*, pp. 175–179.

preeminent role through the clan or kinship group, and it has also been extremely important elsewhere prior to industrialization. But the concomitants of industrialization which we discussed earlier—the growth in the division of labor, greater rationalization, more formal training required for jobs, urbanization, and individuation—have had two major impacts on the traditional family. They have weakened it and reduced its role in the mobility process; moreover, the traditional extended family with its mutual obligations, geographic concentration, and parochialism is in conflict with the needs and demands of industrialization. With the decline of the kinship group, its influence and possible aid become limited.

While it appears that contemporaneously the family no longer provides the direct aid for mobility it did in traditional society, this is by no means certain. It is possible that its influence is considerable even today, but because of individualistic values in societies such as the United States this is conveniently overlooked or denied. Not only may there be much more help extended than realized, but it may be particularly important for elite mobility or where the parents have a great deal of control over social goods. An interesting illustration of the latter involves Mayor Richard J. Daley of Chicago who used his influence to channel lucrative consumer lawsuits and city insurance to firms in which his sons had an interest. The volatile mayor told his closest political associates that he saw nothing wrong in using his influence to help his sons.

> "If a man can't put his arms around his sons, then what kind of world are we living in?" Daley said at a meeting of the Cook County Democratic Central Committee.
> "I make no apologies. If I can't help my sons, they should kiss my ass," the mayor said of his critics. "There are many in this room whose fathers helped them and they became fine public officials." [67]

This is an area worthy of empirical research because if such aid is widespread it might call into question the assertion that modern society is basically universalistic while traditional society is largely particularistic. It might be that for most of the population today relatively little aid is given not because of lack of desire but rather because of lack of social goods. Consequently, indirect help such as motivation and good work habits may be the modern family's support for the mobility of its offspring.

In all societies there is at least some social mobility through marriage and in Western industrial nations it appears to be sizeable.[68] And, as non-industrial nations modernize the amount of mobility through marriage may be expected to increase. When cross-strata unions occur the

[67] "Daley Tells Friends He Sees Nothing Wrong Helping Sons," *Chicago Sun-Times* (February 15, 1973), p. 22.

[68] Lipset and Bendix, *Social Mobility in Industrial Society*, pp. 42–47.

women tend to marry men of higher rank (hypergamy) while men are much less likely to marry up (hypogamy).[69] When such marriages take place, however, they are most often between brides and grooms from adjacent strata; rarely is there marriage between extreme levels.[70]

In any event, when mobility does occur it has a significant impact on the family. For one thing, recent research has shown that with upward mobility there is a decrease in family contacts.[71] Yet while upward mobility weakens family ties they usually are not completely severed; there is evidence that contacts within the extended family are retained where there are differences in status. Also, limited aid is provided which may be helpful for upward mobility, and the familial contacts and obligations do not hinder it.[72] In the case of the downwardly mobile there are indications of an actual increase in family interaction; possibly as compensation for the descent. While family solidarity may encourage downward movement by its acceptance,[73] it could also have the opposite effect. By providing succor the family helps cushion failure which, first, may minimize the social and psychological strains. Second, family aid may help prevent further descent, and third, such help and the sympathetic understanding may encourage a state of mind which is useful in seeking out new opportunities.

While the family's role in mobility is quite different from what it was in traditional society it is still an important channel, even though the major burden is now on the nuclear family. The best way it can help its offspring rise is to provide the social-psychological conditions which facilitate educational success, and we will have much more to say about this in the following chapters.

SOME OTHER CAUSES OF MOBILITY

Additional factors which cause mobility are differential fertility and motivation. In modern society the upper strata have fewer children than the lower, and as the older generation vacates its positions there may be a shortage of candidates. This "vacuum" is then filled by some of the

[69] See discussion by Zick Rubin, "Do Americans Marry Up?" *American Sociological Review*, 33 (October 1968), 750–752.

[70] Morris Zelditch, Jr., "Family, Marriage, and Kinship," in Robert L. Faris, ed., *Handbook of Modern Sociology* (Chicago: Rand, NcNally & Co., 1964), pp. 688–690; Richard Centers, "Mate Selection and Occupational Strata," *American Journal of Sociology*, 54 (May 1949), 530–535; and John Aldous and Reuben Hill, "Social Cohesion, Lineage Type, and Intergenerational Transmission," *Social Forces*, 43 (May 1965), 471–482.

[71] Kenneth Kessin, "Social and Psychological Consequences of Intergenerational Occupational Mobility," *American Journal of Sociology*, 77 (July 1971), 1–18.

[72] Eugene Litwak, "Occupational Mobility and Extended Family Cohesion," *American Sociological Review*, 25 (February 1960), 9–21.

[73] Kessin, *op. cit.*, p. 15.

"surplus" from the lower strata.[74] The role of differential fertility will be examined in greater detail in Chapter IV.

So far we have emphasized the structural conditions that increase opportunity. Thus in modern society some upward mobility is inevitable through an increase in the number of desirable positions, the "upgrading" of occupations as a result of wider application of technology, and through professionalization. These tendencies serve to raise the status of individuals who are already a part of the workforce. In the case of young persons entering the job market, although their initial position may be low, they may soon rise to a higher level than their fathers', for, as mentioned previously, the general tendency in industrial society is to replace the lower-paid and more menial tasks with higher status positions. However, for much of this type of mobility little conscious effort on the part of the individual is required. But other mobility, particularly that involving rapid ascent and several jumps in rank, as well as movement into the well-paying and prestigeful occupations, requires some degree of conscious effort. The person must have a strong desire to rise to a more highly-valued position and be willing to exert the effort to attain it.

One of the reasons why people attempt to improve their circumstances is to maintain their self-esteem in the eyes of friends and associates, as we noted earlier.[75] The wish to improve one's situation through emulation is particularly important in a society that places a high value on consumption such as the United States, and it is becoming increasingly apparent in other industrial nations. Yet John Porter questions the universality of this trait, and the desire for mobility itself; he suggests that even in Western industrial societies they may be characteristic of the middle strata but not of the lower.[76] Nevertheless, the greater rewards that go with higher positions are an encouragement for mobility, at least for a portion of the population.[77]

It would seem that mobility aspirations are likely to increase in any society where there is a growth in opportunity; similarly one would expect that emulation as a factor in mobility would become more important as consumer goods become widespread. This has been the experience in Western societies and there are hints of it in communist nations.[78] Aspirations and emulation are less significant in the latter, however, because

[74] See Sorokin, *Social and Cultural Mobility*, p. 346; and Lipset and Bendix, *Social Mobility in Industrial Society*, p. 86.

[75] This phenomenon was observed by de Tocqueville when he travelled in America during its early years. Alexis de Tocqueville, *Democracy in America* (trans. by George Lawrence; ed. by J. P. Mayer) (Garden City, N.Y.: Doubleday Anchor Books, first pub. 1835), pp. 536–537.

[76] John Porter, "The Future of Upward Mobility," *American Sociological Review*, 33 (February 1968), 5–19. Cf. de Tocqueville, *op. cit.*, p. 636.

[77] See Davis and Moore, "*Some Principles of Stratification*," pp. 242–243.

[78] See, e.g., Milovan Djilas, *The New Class* (New York: Frederick A. Praeger, 1957), especially p. 82.

of the political control over the economy, channels for mobility, and the mass media and other forms of communication which affect people's perspectives.[79]

The role of motivation in mobility will be further considered in Chapters IV and V. In subsequent chapters we will also be interested in the consequences of mobility both for the individual and the social structure; however a few comments are in order at this point.

Some Consequences of Mobility

Social mobility has both beneficial and detrimental consequences; we will look first at how the individual is affected and then at the social structure.

MOBILITY AND THE INDIVIDUAL

Obviously the major advantage of upward movement is an increase in an individual's social goods such as income and prestige. Moreover, where there is a great deal of opportunity able persons can make use of their talent; this is probably a major reason for the apparent increase in the number of geniuses during the great mobility which usually follows revolutions and wars.

There is also likely to be greater plasticity and versatility in the behavior of those who move up. Whereas the person who remains in his occupation for a lifetime is likely to become very rigid, and develop habitual ways of thinking and acting, the mobile individual must cope with and adapt to new situations. Also, mobility involves exposure to new groups, ideas, and practices, and there is likely to be less narrow-mindedness and fewer occupational idiosyncracies.[80] In addition to obtaining a greater amount of social goods, as we noted above, the upwardly mobile individual is likely to have a more favorable self-evaluation.

On the other hand while downward movement means fewer social goods and a less favorable self-conception, in some cases there may be positive consequences. Downward mobility may lead a person to make a more realistic assessment of his goals in terms of his talents and existing opportunity. It may also encourage him to work at something which while less remunerative offers more interest and pleasure; also, greater family solidarity may be the result of the descent.

[79] See *ibid.*, especially pp. 166–167, 207, 210; Goldthorpe, "Social Stratification in Industrial Society"; and Kubat, "Social Mobility in Czechoslovakia."

[80] Sorokin, *Social and Cultural Mobility*, pp. 508–510, 512, 530.

Yet mobility also has detrimental effects. Whether an individual experiences horizontal, vertical, or "spiral" movement, and whether it is upward or downward, he changes his membership group. That is, the people he associated and interacted with, both on a personal and impersonal basis are replaced by new ones. In addition, prior to the move he begins to anticipate the expectations of the group he wishes to enter and to modify his behavior accordingly. He begins to think, dress, and in other ways act like the persons in that group, who constitute his *reference group*. This identification and behavior, or *anticipatory socialization*, leads to strains with his associates and often estrangement; yet this process facilitates entrance into the new group. It is of course possible that disenchantment with one's membership group may precede the turning to a new reference group and the anticipatory socialization; in either case mobility is facilitated. The new reference group may be a category of persons, such as those in an occupation, or an organized body, such as a political club or religious sect.[81]

Participation in voluntary organizations may be helpful for upward movement. Since members are likely to be from the higher strata, persons who join such associations may be able to make new contacts and develop new informal ties which may be useful for rising. Instrumental organizations such as a Chamber of Commerce are much more significant for mobility than expressive organizations such as religious bodies. Also important are sports teams and hobby clubs.[82]

Yet Sorokin questions the extent to which such participation is psychologically satisfying. He holds that while the mobile may belong to many voluntary associations and come in contact with numerous people, social mobility decreases intimacy and increases psychological isolation and loneliness. "In spite of his fellows and clubs," he writes, "one remains 'a stranger'; his psychological isolation persists; formal meetings and the usual 'How do you do?' 'Hello!' and community of occupation cannot always break the psychical walls which surround an individual. His loneliness remains with him."[83] He further suggests that mobility encourages individualism as well as superficiality, insensitivity, skepticism, and cynicism. There is thought to be a growth in restlessness and a hunt for pleasure, together with an increase in sensualness and a disintegration of morals.[84]

[81] For discussion of reference groups see Alice Kitt Rossi and Robert K. Merton, "Reference Group Theory and Social Mobility," in Merton and Paul F. Lazarsfeld, eds., *Continuities in Social Research* (Glencoe, Ill.: The Free Press, 1950), pp. 84–95; and Tamotsu Shibutani, "Reference Groups as Perspectives," *American Journal of Sociology*, 60 (May 1955), 562–569.

[82] See Richard F. Curtis, "Occupational Mobility and Membership in Formal Voluntary Associations: A Note on Research," *American Sociological Review*, 24 (December 1959), 848. Participation in voluntary associations is discussed in greater detail in Chapter VI.

[83] Sorokin, *op. cit.*, p. 523.

[84] *Ibid.*, pp. 510, 516–520, 522, 526, 534, 541.

We do not know to what extent this is true, or, if it is, the degree to which other conditions in industrial-urban society are responsible. Nevertheless, these conditions may lead to anomie, or "normlessness"; when difficulties or crises arise those who have no social anchor are prone to mental illness or suicide. Recent research shows a tendency toward mental disorders for both the upwardly and downwardly mobile. Robert J. Kleiner and Seymour Parker found excessive goal-striving as a cause.[85] Durkheim showed a positive association between anomie and suicide and observed that suicide increased during periods of prosperity as well as during depressions; the former being characterized by much upward and the latter by much downward movement. Recent studies bear out the higher suicide rate for both the upwardly and the downwardly mobile.[86] This is not to suggest that self-destruction is common for those who are mobile. Actually only a small portion of the total population is suicidal: the suicide rate is 11.7 per 100,000 persons. This is less than one half the death rates from automobile accidents or pneumonia—27.2 and 27.0 per 100,000 respectively.[87] Rather, the point is that theoretically the upwardly or downwardly mobile may be expected to experience more social and psychological strains than the stationary and, in extreme situations, suicide is one of the responses. The evidence is not clear-cut, however, because of the many methodological problems in the study of mobility.[88] Yet Kenneth Kessin's careful work, which we cited previously in discussing the family, finds a statistically significant association between male upward mobility and lessened primary affiliations, as well as higher levels of anxiety and psychosomatic symptoms than expected. He also found that the disruptive effects were very great where there was much upward movement, that is where the person rose two or more strata.[89]

In this section we have focused on some of the consequences of mobility for the individual. Additional research is needed on the effect of upward and downward movement, and even on what happens to those who remain stationary. For example, what social and psychological strains, if any, develop among the non-mobile when others around them

[85] Robert J. Kleiner and Seymour Parker, "Goal-Striving, Social Status, and Mental Disorder: A Research Review," *American Sociological Review*, 28 (April 1963), 189–202. See also Jerome K. Myers and Bertram H. Roberts, *Family and Class Dynamics in Mental Illness* (New York: John Wiley and Sons, 1959).

[86] Emile Durkheim, *Suicide* (Glencoe, Ill.: The Free Press, 1951), pp. 252–257; Austin L. Porterfield and Jack P. Gibbs, "Occupational Prestige and Social Mobility of Suicides in New Zealand," *American Journal of Sociology*, 66 (September 1960), 147–152; and Warren Breed, "Occupational Mobility and Suicide Among White Males," *American Sociological Review*, 28 (April 1963), 179–188.

[87] U.S. Bureau of the Census, *Statistical Abstract of the United States: 1974* (95th ed.; Washington, D.C.: Government Printing Office, 1974), p. 62.

[88] See discussion by Kessin, "Social and Psychological Consequences of Intergenerational Occupational Mobility."

[89] *Ibid.*, p. 15.

are moving up? From the available evidence it seems quite clear that certainly the upwardly mobile pay a price. But it is also likely that the cost depends on the social distance traveled, the suddenness of the movement, and on how many others are also mobile.

While we have focused on some of the individual consequences of mobility, it is also significant for the society. The social structure may be affected whether just a few persons move up or down, or whether large numbers are mobile, as we shall see in the next section.

MOBILITY AND SOCIETY

Social mobility also has both beneficial and detrimental consequences for the society. There are a number of ways in which mobility is beneficial: periods of great upward mobility are associated with economic progress, an increase in inventions and discoveries, and in intellectual life. In addition, the interchange of persons and ideas leads to new values and social movements.[90] It also results in persons becoming better acquainted with individuals in other strata which tends to reduce antagonistic feelings.[91]

Even downward movement has beneficial aspects: such mobility may mean that the less competent are being replaced by the more able, provided there are adequate testing mechanisms and equality of opportunity.[92]

One of the major effects of mobility on the society is the instability that is created. Familial and community ties may become attenuated, traditional values undermined, and existing patterns of behavior inappropriate. The normlessness and other problems we mentioned above may become extensive and weaken many aspects of the society. In part this is the result of differential expectations among the strata regarding mobility; thus middle-strata persons, in contrast to the low, anticipate upward movement and are in a better position to handle it. But when the latter, who tend to be stationary, become mobile because of economic prosperity or structural changes, they are less able to cope with the new situation. One reaction to the new stimuli is to avoid complicated theories and explanations and if collective crises arise to opt for simplistic ones such as fascism, communism, or extreme nationalism.[93]

[90] Sorokin, *Social and Cultural Mobility*, pp. 511–512, 532. Sorokin cites the cases of Ancient Greece, Rome, China, the Renaissance and the growth of Christianity and Confucianism.

[91] *Ibid.*, p. 534.

[92] See *ibid.*, p. 530; and *Goode*, "The Protection of the Inept."

[93] See Sorokin, *op. cit.*, p. 521. The socialization of lower strata persons may make it difficult for them to deal with substantial material and ideational change. See Michael Mann, "The Social Cohesion of Liberal Democracy," *American Sociological Review*, 35 (June 1970), 423–439. Implying that the above choices are detrimental depends of course on one's value

Another possibly detrimental effect may be the drawing off of the more ambitious and able in the mobility process. This may occur in the migration from countryside to city as well as in the movement of individuals from lower to higher strata. The argument is that over time those who remain at the lower levels are the residue, the least able in the society. This situation is exacerbated by the differential fertility between the higher and the lower strata: with families at the higher levels having fewer children than those at the lower, the most intelligent, competent, and ambitious underproduce children, while the least able elements overproduce. The "vacuum" at the top is then filled by people who rise from lower levels. But the newly risen repeat the upper level experience: they also fail to reproduce themselves, and soon another cohort from the lower level moves up. Thus, the argument goes, each mobile cohort is slightly less able than the previous one, and as the process continues the society becomes more enfeebled mentally and socially.[94]

One difficulty with this assertion is that it is almost impossible to test because of the long time span that would be involved, and because of downward mobility from changing economic conditions over which the individual has little control. Also, we still do not know with much certainty the importance of nature-nurture factors; yet it is quite apparent that there are substantial environmental and structural detriments to achievement. Thus a much more equitable distribution of social goods is necessary before this question can be laid to rest.

In part this controversy relates to one's concept of the "pool of talent"; is it limited or unlimited? If limited, it then follows that even with extraordinary efforts to remove social and economic barriers very few additional able would come to the fore simply because there aren't very many of them. On the other hand, if talent is widespread then removal of these restraints would unveil many more persons with ability. The position taken has implications for public policy regarding the distribution of social goods, and reflects liberal or conservative perspectives. Today, for example, an argument appears to be gaining currency that the very poor are the residue of the mobility process.[95]

Such controversies are nothing new; these issues have been debated by social theorists since ancient times, as we shall see in Chapter VIII. It was particularly during the extensive industrialization of the 19th century that the causes and consequences of mobility were articulated, with the liberal and radical writers taking an opposite position from the conservatives'. It was the contention of the liberals and radicals, write Seymour Martin Lipset and Reinhard Bendix,

---

orientation. They are undesirable in terms of the tenets of liberal parliamentary democracy which requires political moderation including the toleration of divergent viewpoints.

[94] Sorokin, *op. cit.*, pp. 495, 503–504.

[95] See, e.g., Daniel P. Moynihan, "The Schism in Black America," *The Public Interest*, 27 (Spring 1972), 3–24.

. . . that the prevailing inequality of opportunities led to a drastic underemployment of the talent available in the lower classes, and also fostered the growth of mediocrity and decadence in the middle and upper classes. The conservative counter-argument asserted that in the long run the talented would rise to the top, and that the prevailing inequality was both a necessary precondition for the development of the talent already at the top and a necessary bulwark against the dangers of rapid change.[96]

Changes in the amount of mobility and its direction have implications for political behavior since they influence people's perspectives and may lead to attempts to alter the authority structure. Obviously there is no simple cause-effect situation; the nature of the social structure affects the overall life chances of the population, and in turn they are modified by institutional arrangements, social stratum position, historical and cultural aspects, and personality and other idiosyncratic factors. These many variables influence individual responses to mobility as well as group perspectives and political behavior. Thus, if very few people are downwardly mobile and there is widespread belief that failure is due to an individual's shortcomings, the main result may be self-blame. The descent then becomes a personal problem with little effect on the social structure. On the other hand if large numbers of people are downwardly mobile, this becomes a social or societal problem and has important ramifications for group action including class behavior. It should be noted that even though mobility has disorganizing aspects, a stable social structure is compatible with a great deal of movement, and unstable structures may persist with very little mobility.[97] Also, a stable structure with very little mobility may continue for a long time without serious moves to alter the distribution of social goods.

A key factor in how people respond to the circumstances of their lives is their perspective, which is tied in with their history and culture. This perspective helps them interpret and define the situation; thus they may see the society and its arrangement of strata and classes as providing much opportunity and as benefitting those who exert themselves to rise. Or, they may see it as offering little opportunity and as failing to reward those who try. Put another way, what are people's expectations regarding the distribution of social goods and their access to them through social mobility?

Group Perspectives and Responses to Mobility

In a closed society there may be very little opportunity, much stratum homogeneity, and feelings of unity among the incumbents of the strata.

[96] Lipset and Bendix, *Social Mobility in Industrial Society*, p. 286.
[97] *Ibid.*, p. 265.

It does not necessarily follow that there will also be much antagonism and tendencies toward class formation and conflict. In such a situation limited aspirations and values which uphold the status quo may develop and even with poverty there may be little deviant behavior such as crime.[98] The lower strata may be quite unhappy with their deprivation but feel there is nothing they can do about it; at most they may tell apocryphal stories or make jokes which put the superordinates in a bad light.[99] This is one way of releasing hostility which makes it just a bit easier to put up with a life of deprivation. Another response which has the same effect is to extol the virtues of the lower strata in contrast to the undesirable qualities of those who rule.[100]

Such passivity which helps maintain the status quo may end, and quite quickly, if the deprivation increases to the extent that there is much downward mobility. Perspectives may alter rapidly and strong support may be given to radical political parties or movements. The support may be a form of individualistic aggressive reaction to alienation which the passivity may have masked. Or, it may be a collective response which has been strengthened by communication and interaction.[101]

The social order which until then had appeared to be secure—"the people (peasants; natives) seemed happy"—is now under serious challenge. Even in a closed society there is some change and opportunity and a few will succeed; however there will also be failures: the downwardly mobile, or "skidders," and the upwardly mobile who are held back. Now in an *open* system the individual holds himself responsible for lack of success, as will be discussed below. But in a closed society both the skidders and the upwardly mobile whose rise has been blocked fault the system. Joseph Lopreato and Janet Saltzman Chafetz found that the Italian skidder blames the society for his failure, for the lack of greater opportunity, and for the unjust distribution of social goods. He directs his personal frustrations, disappointment, and resentment against the existing order and is more likely to support leftist political parties than a stable worker.[102]

Even if there is some upward movement in a closed society, its rapidity and the distance that can be traveled are limited. This creates difficul-

[98] Robert K. Merton, *Social Theory and Social Structure*, (rev. ed.; Glencoe, Ill.: The Free Press, 1961), p. 147.

[99] See Gerald D. Berreman, "Caste in India and the United States," *American Sociological Review*, 66 (September 1960), 124–126.

[100] See Ferdinand Tönnies, *Community & Society* (New York: Harper Torchbooks, 1957; first publ. 1887), p. 255.

[101] See Adam Przeworski and Glaucio A. D. Soares, "Theories in Search of a Curve: A Contextual Interpretation of Left Vote," *American Political Science Review*, 65 (March 1971), 51–68.

[102] Joseph Lopreato and Janet Saltzman Chafetz, "The Political Orientation of Skidders: A Middle-Range Theory," *American Sociological Review*, 35 (June 1970), 440–451.

ties when the upwardly mobile edge near the ruling class and their further ascent is blocked by legal or customary barriers. These *nouveaux riches* become especially resentful at not receiving the social goods they believe they are entitled to: social approval, economic opportunities available to the ruling class, or entrée into the ruling circle. They turn against the institutions of society such as the government, the judiciary, the church, and against various institutional arrangements; they begin to see the existing social order as preventing them from achieving their legitimate goals and seek radical change.

Such persons whose ascent is blocked often furnish the leadership for revolutionary movements. Bitter at being kept down by the ruling class, they are frequently more educated, articulate, and experienced in leadership than the mass of the population. While they themselves are not solely responsible for radical change they are very important when economic, political, and social problems have weakened the society and strata are beginning to form into classes. They may provide necessary leadership and they may help focus discontent and organize larger numbers of people to undertake a restructuring of the social order. Since they lack a power base there is a tendency to enlist the mass. This is one of the reasons that the ideology they espouse usually contains universal appeals that stress the brotherhood of man and call for a more equitable distribution of social goods. The universalistic claims are also a means of getting around the major secular and religious traditions and values which tend to support the status quo.

Thus it is not only the skidders in a closed society who reject the social order; the upwardly mobile whose ascent has been blocked also blame the system and are likely to seek radical change.[103]

In an open society there are fewer customary restraints and few if any legal barriers to upward movement, even into the ruling class. Assuming continuing economic expansion and opportunity for mobility, it is to be expected that those who rise will tend to move away from the political orientation of their class of origin, and that they will begin to adopt the political coloration of their class of destination. A recent analysis of voting behavior in the 1952, 1956, and 1960 elections in the United States found this to be the case.[104] The study also revealed that a similar pattern is exhibited by skidders. Thus on the one hand those who are rising into the upper strata are less conservative than the stable incumbents, but more conservative than the stable lower strata. On the other hand the skidders are more leftist than the stable upper strata, but they are not as much to the left as the stable incumbents of the lower strata. Con-

[103] See Merton, *op. cit.*, pp. 156–157, 191–192; Lipset and Bendix, *Social Mobility in Industrial Society*, p. 262; Crane Brinton, *The Anatomy of Revolution* (New York: Vintage Books, 1965); and our discussion in Chapter I.

[104] James A. Barber, Jr., *Social Mobility and Voting Behavior* (Chicago: Rand McNally & Co., 1970), pp. 74–79, 256–258, 267.

sequently, both the upwardly and the downwardly mobile are a moderating influence.[105] However these findings are based on data which have been aggregated, which may hide the behavior of significant deviant groups such as ethnic minorities. The mobile who have similar racial, religious, or other attributes conceivably would be prone to greater communication and interaction than those from the majority group, and if downwardly mobile might be more leftist than the stable lower strata. However if upwardly mobile and if blocked in how far they can go they may move considerably to the left, more so than majority group members in the same situation.

Also, no society is completely insulated from economic changes which affect opportunity for mobility, be it a command economy or one which is more subject to market forces. However a capitalist society such as the United States is more prone to periods of prosperity and depression and to rapid technological and other changes, which regularly upset various sectors of the economy including the labor market.[106] Therefore even in an open society with considerable mobility there are bound to be failures; the proportion may be minimal during economic expansion and widespread in a depression. There are of course many responses which are possible: blame may be directed toward the society or the individual, and people may act to change existing arrangements or they may engage in behaviors which support them.

In open societies with considerable upward mobility, an ideology of egalitarianism, and a stress on achievement over ascription, people's image of the society is likely to include equality of opportunity as well as inequality among the strata. These views are not incompatible: they merely indicate that even though there may be differences in the distribution of social goods among the strata, anyone who is able and exerts himself can rise and enjoy the fruits of the inequality. Interestingly, this creed can exist in a non-capitalist society where there is an ideology of egalitarianism, opportunity for mobility, and the rewarding of merit, even though there are significant inequalities from one stratum to another.[107] Writing about the Soviet Union, the Polish sociologist Stanislaw Ossowski observes:

> The Socialist principle "to each according to his merits," is in harmony with the tenets of the American Creed, which holds that each man is the master of his fate, and that a man's status is fixed by an order of merit. The Socialist principle allows of the conclusion that there are unlimited opportu-

---

[105] *Ibid.*, pp. 259–260.

[106] The range in the unemployment rate in the United States since 1900 was from 0.8 per cent in 1906 to 24.9 per cent in 1933. During the past two decades the range was from 2.9 per cent in 1953 to 9.1 per cent in 1975. U.S. Bureau of the Census, *Historical Statistics of the United States, Colonial Times to 1957* (Washington, D.C.: Government Printing Office, 1961), p. 73; and U.S. Department of Labor, *Employment and Earnings,* 21 (April 1975), 19.

[107] Stanislaw Ossowski, *Class Structure in the Social Consciousness* (New York: The Free Press of Glencoe, 1963), pp. 100–118.

nities for social advancement and social demotion; this is similar to the American concept of "vertical social mobility." The arguments directed against *uravnilooka* [equalization or leveling of wages] coincide with the arguments put forward on the other side of the Atlantic by those who justify the necessity for economic inequalities in a democratic society.[108]

Given such a perspective it is not surprising that failure does not lead to support of radical politics or other means of changing existing institutional arrangements. Instead, the unsuccessful are likely to blame themselves, scale down their aspirations, withdraw, or "drop out" through the use of drugs or by isolating themselves in communes. Or, they may turn to such things as evangelical religion, child-centeredness, extensive television-watching, or compulsive involvement in sports.[109] This is the reaction in the United States, and, we suspect, is similar to a considerable degree in the Soviet Union.

Such responses help maintain existing institutional arrangements, although there is the possibility that they may unwittingly serve to undermine them. For example, if the "dropping out" is extensive enough, the functioning of the society could be affected; also religious sects or similar groups might become the basis for new political movements.

While excessive involvement in sports may be a form of withdrawal, participation may facilitate upward mobility or cushion downward movement; for the stationary it may act as a palliative. As Curtis has suggested, interest in sports provides a basis for communication between men of widely differing statuses; consequently the upwardly mobile can participate regardless of social origins.[110] Similarly, the downwardly mobile can participate even though their status has declined. For the skidders as well as for the stationary, the "circus" aspects of the magic-like world of commercialized sports helps take their minds off their problems. But it also provides all its fans with an orderly world which is hierarchically arranged and gives just rewards to those who deserve them. There is no ambiguity as to the criteria for success nor when the pinnacle is reached. Sports allows the spectator to participate vicariously in important contests where the stakes are high, the outcomes decisive, and the winners glorified. The emphasis is on the successful who receive the society's largesse, and the fan is able to identify with them. However, the real losers—the vast army of high-school and college athletes who never make it to the top—are ignored, as is the exploitation of players.[111]

---

[108] *Ibid.*, p. 114.

[109] See Merton, *Social Theory and Social Structure;* and Lipset and Bendix, *Social Mobility in Industrial Society,* p. 263.

[110] Curtis, "Occupational Mobility and Membership in Voluntary Associations," p. 848.

[111] See Paul Hoch, *Rip Off the Big Game* (Garden City, N.Y.: Doubleday Anchor Books, 1972), pp. 100–146. This otherwise good book is marred by an inverted ethnocentrism: all the problems are blamed on monopoly capitalism. While the worst abuses are undoubtedly encouraged under capitalism, the causes are much broader. They are related to trends in industrial society, and some of the problems Hoch discusses are also found in non-capitalist industrial nations.

But those who do make it are well rewarded materially and by public acclaim. Among the successful athletes are many of low social origin and their rise helps reinforce the image of equality of opportunity. Yet even though the elite of the sports and entertainment world may hobnob with heads of state or big industrialists, they have practically no power themselves.[112]

Of greater importance to the society is mobility into upper reaches of the authority structure. There is a problem which confronts every ruling class, and we will examine it in this last section.

Mobility and the Ruling Class

Whether open or closed all social orders must obtain competent recruits to fill top level positions that are essential for the functioning of the society. The competition is limited because not everyone has the ability and motivation and, in the case of the lower strata, there is the added disadvantage of poor life chances. Nevertheless there is still an excess of candidates since the positions are desirable and usually well rewarded; not only are they sought by those from the upper strata but also by a small portion from the lower. Among the latter there are likely to be some very able candidates considering the greater difficulty they have in obtaining the necessary training. Now in a completely open system theoretically there would be no problem: the less able contestants from the upper strata would move down, and their places would be taken by the better ones from the lower strata. Where there are candidates from different strata but with equal ability the selection could be made by a toss of a coin. However such a situation does not occur, for, as was discussed in Chapter I, superordinates generally seek to retain maximum control over social goods. This is particularly true of those who constitute the ruling class; one of the common methods is to try to monopolize important positions by favoring relatives, friends, and persons whose background, interests, and attitudes are similar to theirs. They seek to further minimize upward mobility by erecting legal and customary barriers.

Yet every ruling class finds itself on the horns of a dilemma—and a three-horned dilemma at that. First, there are some lower-strata candidates who are more able than those in the ruling class and their mobility would bring in new talent. Not only would this be beneficial to the society as a whole but if these individuals are properly socialized the ruling class would be strengthened. Second, monopolization leads to

---

[112] They could rise in the authority structure of the larger society via the channel of business by making wise use of their money. Or, they could do it by gaining public office, drawing on their popularity to help them get elected. Two well known examples are former Governor Ronald Reagan and the former Senator George Murphy of California.

social inbreeding with a narrowing of outlook, a dearth of innovation, and insensitivity to the needs of those outside the ruling class. Under these circumstances the ruling class may be unable to handle economic and political crises and faces the danger of being deposed either by a foreign power or by a revolt from below. Third, if there is not sufficient mobility into the ruling class the able candidates from the lower strata may become dissidents or revolutionaries because their talent is not being rewarded. Thus such mobility serves as a safety valve.

The more closed the social order, the more critical is the problem of mobility into the ruling class; but it is also a problem in an open society. Even though an open system allows more mobility into the ruling class as well as more movement into other levels there are also tendencies toward restricting access. Much political behavior involves conservatives seeking to secure positions for themselves and attempts by leftists to open them up. The former are likely to be from the higher strata, the latter from the lower; nevertheless the politics is mainly moderate and reformist. This is a function of continuing mobility, most of it upward, and people's perspectives; together they encourage the failures to blame themselves and not the system. Also, there are adequate consolation prizes for the skidders. However there is a higher level of aspiration and striving in an open society; consequently continued upward mobility at all levels, and particularly into the ruling class, is extremely important as a safety valve.

Summary

We have examined the major causes and consequences of social mobility, particularly upward and downward vertical movement. The structural conditions, especially the stage of economic development is critical in determining the overall amount of opportunity. Other structural factors such as war and revolution and changing channels for mobility affect the chances of different categories of people for rising or falling. The personal and societal consequences of mobility are also affected by structural conditions, including the growth rate of the society, and the extent to which it is open or closed.

Knowledge about the mobility in a given society provides a clearer understanding of the nature of the strata, as well as some of the circumstances under which inequality is more or less accepted, or resented to the point that people may try to do something about it. Yet there are important conceptual as well as methodological problems in the study of mobility. The distinction between stratification and class which was discussed in Chapter I is also applicable to social mobility. Mobility research which focuses on stratification is primarily descriptive, that which concentrates on class is mainly analytical. Yet each is important and complementary. Studies from the perspective of stratification emphasize rates of vertical mobility and provide us with a picture of how open or closed the society is, whether mobility is increasing or decreasing, whether upward or downward movement predominates, and the distance the mobile travel. In order to properly make inferences as to the consequences of the mobility for conflict and change, however, it is necessary to make use of the perspective of class. This might require a reordering of categories since occupational groupings, the most common measure in mobility research, are not the same as classes. Also, it would most likely call for additional information to determine whether and to what extent class behavior is involved. For example, stratification studies might detail the poorer chances of mobility for blacks as compared to whites.[113] Yet, class analysis is required to tell us whether the difference is significant for group feelings and behavior aimed at changing the status quo. For the same rate may have different consequences depending on previous rates and on group definitions; thus a low rate which is much greater than in the past may still be seen as fulfilling the American Dream and this may minimize class action to increase opportunity. Or, a consistently low rate could encourage resignation and thus also minimize class behavior. On the other hand, with the existence of communalization, ideology, and organization a low rate which is high relative to previous rates may be interpreted quite differently. It may be seen as still too low and lead to agitation to change existing institutional arrangements. Even an objectively high rate may be defined as unacceptable, given class formation.

While there has been a great deal of research on social mobility, most of it has been from the perspective of stratification and the focus has been on occupational mobility.[114] Consequently fundamental questions on the causes and consequences of mobility remain unanswered, especially the significance of mobility for social movements and change. Much of the difficulty is the result of the wrong questions being asked, but this is in large part due to the lack of conceptual clarity in the literature on stratification and class. We addressed ourselves to this issue in Chapter I and will have more to say about it in Chapter XI.

Even though stratification is a descriptive concept, it provides the information that is needed to understand the significance of various kinds of mobility and differing rates; it is also essential for any analysis of class behavior. Our next task will be to examine in detail the components of stratification.

---

[113] See, e.g., Rogoff, *Recent Trends in Occupational Mobility;* and Blau and Duncan, *The American Occupational Structure.*

[114] See, e.g., Lipset and Bendix, *Social Mobility in Industrial Society,* and the many studies they analyze, as well as the researches cited above.

Chapter III. Components of Stratification

In this chapter we are primarily interested in the basis for stratifying a society, particularly a modern industrial nation such as the United States. First we will briefly discuss how social goods are obtained and in that context some of the advantages of position. Next the dimensions of income, occupation, and education will be examined. Finally, there will be comments on the multi-dimensionality of stratification and some questions which are related to it.

One way of determining stratification seems simple enough: find out how much social goods people have. But this task is complicated because of three problems. The first is that there are different *kinds* of social goods: possessions, income, and prestige, for example. The second is that there are different *sources* of social goods: for instance, dividends from stocks and bonds, rent from real estate holdings, and income from wages. The researcher must also consider the way people evaluate working conditions: "easy" work is more desirable than "hard," "clean" than "dirty," "mental" than "manual." These considerations affect the prestige of occupations, as do the extent to which they serve the general welfare, and in other ways help maintain the society and its values.[1] The third factor is that social goods *differ* in ability to be converted into other forms of social goods: contrast the individual whose only social goods are his wages with the landlord who has rental income as well as property. Not only are these considerations significant but amount of social goods is obviously important. We will examine this aspect as well as kind, source, and convertibility shortly, but meanwhile let us consider how social goods are obtained.

Methods of Obtaining Social Goods

The individual's attributes and inheritance, the limiting or facilitating aspects of social and economic conditions, and fortuitous circumstances affect both amount of social goods and how they are obtained. Among

[1] See Robert W. Hodge, Paul M. Siegel, and Peter H. Rossi, "Occupational Prestige in the United States, 1925–1963," *American Journal of Sociology*, 70 (November 1964), 286–302.

personal attributes which are likely to have favorable consequences in the marketplace or work situation are intelligence, physical and social skills, diligence, and reliability. However, it is contingent upon the individual to apply himself: the very bright person who has poor work habits or who is unreliable limits his opportunity and the amount of social goods he accumulates. On the other hand, some unfavorable attributes may be compensated for by hard work.

Inheritance, aside from genetic factors, includes social goods as well as attitudes and patterns of behavior which are transmitted to the young. A child born into a wealthy family will be sent to the best schools, helped to obtain a desirable position, and may be expected to lead a comfortable life. Moreover, to the extent that this fortunate individual has favorable attributes, he will probably be able to increase the social goods he has inherited.

But the vast majority of persons do not inherit significant wealth; [2] for them *social* inheritance is critical: aspirations and patterns of behavior within the family which may facilitate obtaining social goods. Prime examples are the development of attitudes and work habits which make for educational and occupational success.

Other things being equal, favorable attributes, social inheritance, and hard work are the main conditions for achievement for most people. Yet special circumstances facilitate or hinder the accumulation of social goods: among them are war, economic growth or decline, special needs in the economy, and fortuitous circumstances. The latter is not important in terms of a person buying a winning lottery ticket or a gold prospector striking it rich for the likelihood of either occurring is exceedingly slim. Rather, fortuitous circumstances or "luck" are important in the sense that an individual may happen to be in the right place at the right time. For example, a piece of property a person has owned for a long time may triple in value when the zoning is changed from residential to business.

It is of course true that at least some initiative was involved: obtaining the property originally, holding on to it by paying taxes, and so on. Usually the individual expends effort through education, hard work, or through other means which allows him to take advantage of favorable circumstances. Yet luck may enter into his success: for example, there may be a sudden demand for certain products which may enrich manufacturers and merchants, as often happens in wartime. When a shortage occurs, those who are able to traffic in the scarce items are likely to profit greatly, as did some American entrepreneurs in the steel "gray market"

[2] In 1972 estate and gift taxes were $32 per capita. U.S. Bureau of the Census, *Statistical Abstract of the United States: 1974* (95th ed.; Washington, D.C.: Government Printing Office, 1974), p. 248. This indicates that the average inheritance was quite small. At the lower end of the income scale many receive no inheritance or must use their own money for funeral costs. At the other end of the scale the legacy may be considerable, especially in the case of the very rich. See Ferdinand Lundberg, *The Rich and the Super Rich* (New York: Bantam Books, 1969), pp. 155–242.

during the Korean War.[3] Others arranged contracts between manufacturers and government procurement agencies and received considerable sums of money for their services. Such persons are actually essential in complex organizations where critical functions have not been rationalized, or existing procedures are inoperative. While some simply sold expert information about government procurement needs, others were able to exert influence so that contracts were awarded to their clients.

Personal influence or "pull" is certainly not limited to the United States; it operates in all societies and may be amply rewarded, especially at the higher levels. In the Soviet Union, for example, *blat* (pronounced "blaht")—the Russian equivalent of influence or "pull," is a fundamental element in the informal management of industry. Because of breakdowns in industrial procurement where firms cannot obtain needed parts and materials through regular channels, the "supply expediter" has arisen. Called *tolkach,* literally translated as "pusher," these persons are able to arrange mutually beneficial exchanges which would not have been possible otherwise. To illustrate, exchanges might be arranged between a truck manufacturing plant that has a shortage of tires but an excess of steel, a tractor plant that needs the steel but has an oversupply of nuts and bolts, and another truck plant that is short of nuts and bolts but has an excess of tires. Since the industrial firms benefit greatly from the efforts of the *tolkach* he is generously rewarded financially and by receiving special privileges unavailable to the ordinary working man.[4]

The preceding illustrated somewhat unusual circumstances and the activities were on the borderline of legitimacy. It is a fact of life that some people are situated more advantageously than others; specifically, position in an occupational structure is associated with both expected remuneration and the opportunity to obtain additional social goods.

POSITION AND ACCESS TO SOCIAL GOODS

In general, the higher a person's occupational role the better able he is to obtain and accumulate social goods relative to someone lower in the hierarchy. In addition to the greater income and other considerations which are a part of the position, he is favorably located to learn about and take advantage of opportunities not available to others. This extra benefit, as with the activities of the American influence peddler or the Russian *tolkach* may also border on the illegal. But, by contrast, it is more likely to be viewed as acceptable.

[3] See Louis Kriesberg, "National Security and Conduct in the Steel Gray Market", *Social Forces,* 34 (March 1956), 268–277; and "Occupational Controls Among Steel Distributors," *American Journal of Sociology,* 61 (November 1955), 203–212.

[4] Joseph S. Berliner, "The Informal Organization of the Soviet Firm," *Quarterly Journal of Economics,* 66 (August 1952), 356–357.

For example, take a state or federal official. The bureaucrat comes in contact with manufacturers, lobbyists, and others who can provide favors and opportunities in exchange for receiving contracts or other business. The favors may be proffered while he is in office or after he has left government employ. It is not unusual for such an official to receive a lucrative position in a legal or business firm which has dealings with his former agency.[5] Because of his position, the official will likely gain advance information which may prove profitable for him or his friends: for instance, he may learn of an expected change in zoning regulations or of plans to establish a park, both of which will increase the value of land which can still be obtained relatively cheaply. This is what George Washington Plunkitt, the Tammany Hall political boss, called "honest graft."[6] In some communities contracts for supplies or repairs to municipal buildings and other facilities are not tendered through competitive bids but are awarded by city councils, school boards, and other agencies. Under these circumstances the businessmen who are favored reciprocate by giving officials contributions at election time or by providing other gratuities.

Persons at the upper levels frequently have opportunities to increase their social goods directly, or indirectly through benefitting activities in which they have an interest. When funds are held pending disbursement, as in the case of a state government which collects taxes or license fees, there is gain for the financial institutions which receive the accounts. The funds may be given to those banks which contributed to the candidate's election.

The trustees of some eleemosynary foundations receive substantial commissions on land and other transactions and work out favorable arrangements for friends. Oftentimes trustees are also executives or members of the board of directors in businesses which may be favored. A congressional investigation revealed recently that in Washington, D.C. federal employees' premiums for medical insurance were kept over an eight-year period in bank accounts which paid no interest to the plan. With interest, as much as $5 million could have been realized which would have allowed lower premiums. Now the treasurer of the medical plan was also the head of one of the banks which held most of the money; the board chairman of the plan was also a director of the same bank, and the head of another bank which held premium payments was also a medical plan trustee.[7]

In a large business enterprise a top executive is in a much more favorable position to accumulate social goods than the employee in the front

[5] This is quite common. See, e.g., "FCC's Cox to Become Official of Microwave Communications Firm," The Wall Street Journal (August 31, 1970), p. 12.

[6] See William L. Riordon, Plunkitt of Tammany Hall (New York: E. P. Dutton, 1963).

[7] "Blue Cross Got No Interest, Saving Millions for 4 Banks," The [Madison, Wisconsin] Capital Times (June 8, 1970), pp. 1 ff. This practice was discontinued at the end of 1967.

office, or the man on the assembly line. The executive's salary is so much larger, and his fringe benefits may include options to purchase stock at a great discount, a liberal retirement plan, an expense account, and the use of a company automobile. Clearly these fringe benefits greatly raise his income.[8] Moreover he comes in contact with influential persons in business and government where information, help, and favors may be reciprocated, with one result being that his opportunities to obtain social goods are increased.

Luck, economic inheritance, pull, influential contacts, or occupying a high position as ways of increasing one's social goods hold only for a relatively small, albeit significant part of the population. For most people, personal attributes and social inheritance are crucial. Also very important for the ordinary person is the state of the economy, for with a tight labor market opportunities become available for qualified persons who are unemployed or underemployed. Non-whites and women are affected, but so are youths and the elderly. When there is a labor shortage, as during a major war, there are even jobs for those with inadequate education, with physical or other handicaps, and for individuals who can only work part time.[9] But when the demand for labor drops not only do these "last hired-first fired" categories suffer, but the extent of the distress is inversely related to position in the occupational structure.

Regardless of how people obtain their social goods, it is necessary to have some measure of what they are worth in order to analyze stratification. Money income is one of the best measures and we now turn to this important dimension.

The Income Dimension

Every society has some medium of exchange for the distribution of social goods. In modern society, the medium is money primarily, and there is a high degree of impersonality among those who exchange the goods and services; in a highly industrialized nation such as the United States there are few if any personal ties between manufacturer and consumer, employer and employee. Consequently people's income is a very useful means of stratifying a population.

When families and unrelated individuals in the United States are ranked according to income level we find wide differences, as is to be expected. Figure III-1 reveals that 50% of the family units have incomes of

[8] Gabriel Kolko, *Wealth and Power in America* (New York: Frederick A. Praeger, 1954), pp. 17–20, 41–42, 66; and Richard M. Titmuss, *Income Distribution and Social Change* (Toronto: University of Toronto Press, 1962), pp. 169–186.

[9] Hyman P. Minsky, "The Role of Employment Policy," in Margaret S. Gordon, ed., *Poverty in America* (San Francisco: Chandler Publishing Co., 1965), pp. 175–200.

FIGURE III-1.
Percentage Distribution of Income of Families and
Unrelated Individuals, 1973

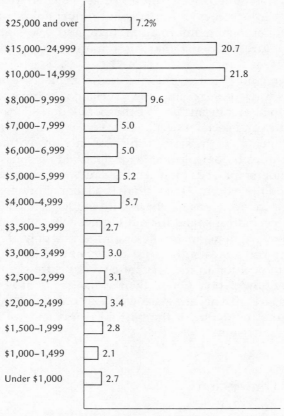

$25,000 and over	7.2%
$15,000–24,999	20.7
$10,000–14,999	21.8
$8,000–9,999	9.6
$7,000–7,999	5.0
$6,000–6,999	5.0
$5,000–5,999	5.2
$4,000–4,999	5.7
$3,500–3,999	2.7
$3,000–3,499	3.0
$2,500–2,999	3.1
$2,000–2,499	3.4
$1,500–1,999	2.8
$1,000–1,499	2.1
Under $1,000	2.7

Source: U.S. Bureau of the Census, "Money Income in 1973 of Families and
Persons in the United States," Series P-60, No. 97 (Washington, D.C.:
Government Printing Office, January 1975), p. 24.

$10,000 or higher, 31% receive between $4,000 and $9,999, and 20% have
incomes under $4,000. But if we examine those at both extremes we see
that seven per cent of the families and unrelated individuals have a
yearly income of $25,000 or more, while eight per cent earn less than
$2,000 a year.[10] Many if not most of the persons in this latter category are
at the poverty level.

[10] It should be noted that the breaks or cut-off points for dividing income into different
categories are arbitrary, and there is no set number of divisions.

THE POOR, THE RICH, AND CONVERTIBILITY OF SOCIAL GOODS

Let us briefly look at the persons below the poverty level and then at those at the other end of the income scale. The proportion of poor is determined by the revised index of the Social Security Administration. This measure attempts ". . . to specify the minimum money income required to support an average family of given composition at the lowest level consistent with the standards of living prevailing in this country." In 1973 the low-income threshold for a non-farm family of four was $4,540. This means that 4.8 million families were in a state of poverty. Approximately eight per cent of whites are poor, while 31% of blacks are in a state of poverty. Among persons of Spanish origin the percentage is 22.[11]

Large cities are characterized by poverty areas where the poor who are mostly non-whites are concentrated. Some 13% of families in central cities were below the poverty level; this breaks down to seven per cent of the whites and 29% of the blacks. Among both the rural and urban poor there are many households where a woman is the head because of desertion, separation, divorce, or death of the husband. In such homes 28% of the white families are poverty stricken while this is true of approximately 57% of the non-white families.[12]

The significance of poverty is obvious: people are unable to obtain the social goods they need, let alone the non-essentials the mass media are constantly urging everyone to buy. Lack of income also has many serious social psychological consequences for children, youths, and adults, which will be explored in the following chapters.[13]

Let us now turn to those at the other end of the scale, the top wealth-holders in the United States as defined by the U.S. Treasury Department. These are the 9,013,000 persons whose holdings, which include stocks,

[11] See Mollie Orshansky, "Counting the Poor: Another Look at the Poverty Profile," *Social Security Bulletin* (July 1965), pp. 8–10; and U.S. Bureau of the Census, "Characteristics of the Low-Income Population: 1973," Series P-60, No. 98 (Washington, D.C.: Government Printing Office, January 1975), pp. 1–2.

[12] "Characteristics of the Low-Income Population: 1973," pp. 39, 43.

[13] Much has been written about poverty. See, e.g., Michael Harrington, *The Other America: Poverty in the United States* (Baltimore: Penguin Books, 1966). First published in 1962 it was probably the single most influential document which aroused popular interest and led to a number of ameliorative programs by the government. It was important for social science, for it aided in the "rediscovery" of poverty. See also Orshansky, *op. cit.*; Jack L. Roach, "Sociological Analysis and Poverty," *American Journal of Sociology*, 71 (July 1965), 68–75; Gordon, *op. cit.*; Arthur B. Shostak and William Gomberg, *New Perspectives on Poverty* (Englewood Cliffs, N.J.: Prentice-Hall, 1965); Paul Jacobs, "Unemployment as a Way of Life," in Arthur M. Ross, ed., *Employment Policy and the Labor Market* (Berkeley and Los Angeles: University of California Press, 1965), pp. 381–398; and Jacobs, *Prelude to Riot* (New York: Vintage Books, 1967).

bonds, and real estate are worth $60,000 or more. This does *not* include income which would boost their wealth considerably.

Approximately 37% of them are worth from $60,000 up to $100,000 and another 58% from $100,000 up to $500,000. The remainder, five per cent, have holdings of $500,000 to $10,000,000 or more. This last category breaks down to 311 in the half a million up to a million bracket and 147 who are worth over one million. Most of these assets are corporate stocks, followed by real estate holdings.[14]

While many families own their own homes, wealth in the sense of large-scale real estate holdings, fixed assets such as factories, and large amounts of stocks, bonds, and savings is concentrated in relatively few hands. Sixteen per cent of the families have no money in checking or savings accounts, or in savings bonds. Of those who have, for 26% the value is under $500, while for 50% it is under $2,000.[15]

An important advantage of having assets such as stocks, bonds, and real estate, aside from income through dividends, interest, and rent is their convertibility. The owner of such assets can redeem them for cash, exchange them for other social goods, or they can serve as collateral for borrowing money. These assets can be used to increase the amount of social goods one has and they are available for an emergency. Yet the overwhelming majority of the population does not acquire wealth of any significance; consequently they have little to fall back on if they lose their jobs. Most people have only their labor to exchange for the income they need.

Income then is clearly a very important measure of stratification; for the vast majority of the population it is *the* most important dimension. It determines how well they will live, whether there will be enough food on the table, whether they will be housed in a slum or a suburb, whether they can afford to visit the dentist, whether there is enough left over for a new pair of shoes for the child.

Income differences take on additional meaning when family units are ranked by income fifths, and we examine the proportion of the aggregate family income each fifth receives (see Table III-1). Table III-1 shows that the richest 20% of the families receive 41% of the total income of all families, while the poorest 20% get only five and a half per cent of the total. A comparison of this inequitous distribution with the distributions back to 1947, shows that these relative income shares have not varied significantly in the past 26 years.[16] But income data tend to understate the

[14] *Statistical Abstract of the United States: 1974,* p. 398. The figures are for 1969.

[15] See, e.g., U.S. Bureau of the Census, *Statistical Abstract of the United States: 1965* (86th ed.; Government Printing Office, 1965), p. 349. The data on liquid assets are from *Statistical Abstract of the United States: 1974,* p. 397 and are for 1971.

[16] U.S. Bureau of the Census, "Money Income in 1973 of Families and Persons in the United States," Series P-60, No. 97 (Washington, D.C.: Government Printing Office, January 1975), p. 43.

TABLE III-1. Percentage of Aggregate Income Received in 1973 by Each Fifth of Families and Unrelated Individuals, Ranked by Income

Families Ranked by Income Fifth	Percentage of Aggregate Income Received
Highest fifth	41.1%
Fourth fifth	24.0
Third fifth	17.5
Second fifth	11.9
Lowest fifth	5.5
Total	100.0%

Source: U.S. Bureau of the Census, "Money Income in 1973 of Families and Persons in the United States," Series P-60, No. 97 (Washington, D.C.: Government Printing Office, January 1975), p. 43.

amount received by those at the upper end of the distribution. For example, the real income of top executives and others whose companies pay for liberal medical and retirement programs and provide perquisites such as automobiles is actually higher than the income figures would indicate.[17] Yet these benefits need not be and are not reported to census enumerators or to the Bureau of Internal Revenue.

When we talk about income inequality, the immediate question is, "Inequality with regard to what?" One extreme would be almost complete inequality where a tiny portion of the population receives almost all the income and the rest practically none. This might conceivably be the case in a slave economy but does not apply to other societies, certainly not to modern ones nor even to the so-called underdeveloped countries. The other extreme would be complete equality where everyone had the same income.

Thus we are interested in the *degree* of inequality (or equality) and one way to get at this is to operationalize it in terms of the actual distribution of income relative to a theoretically equal distribution. A useful device to use is the Gini Index which is a measure of income concentration. It is derived from the Lorenz curve which is obtained by plotting one set of statistics on the X axis against another set of statistics on the Y axis. The data on the X axis are the cumulative percentage of units, which may be families or individuals. Now the cumulative percentage of units on the X axis is plotted against the cumulative percentage of aggregate income accounted for by these units on the Y axis (see Figure III-2,A).

If there were no differences in income among the family or individual units then the Lorenz curve would take the form of a straight diagonal line as indicated in Figure III-2,A. The other extreme would be the case where one family or person received almost all the income with practically nothing for anyone else. In that case the area under the Lorenz

[17] See Kolko, *Wealth and Power in America;* and Titmuss, *Income Distribution and Social Change.*

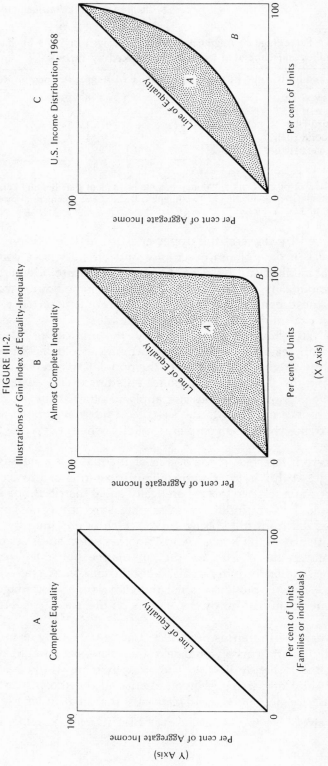

FIGURE III-2.

Illustrations of Gini Index of Equality-Inequality

A
Complete Equality

Per cent of Units
(Families or individuals)

Per cent of Aggregate Income

(Y Axis)

Line of Equality

B
Almost Complete Inequality

Per cent of Units

(X Axis)

Per cent of Aggregate Income

Line of Equality

A

B

C
U.S. Income Distribution, 1968

Per cent of Units

Per cent of Aggregate Income

Line of Equality

A

B

Source: Herman P. Miller, *Income Distribution in the United States* (a 1960 Census Monograph) (Washington, D.C.: Government Printing Office, 1966), pp. 220-221. See also Kaare Svalastoga, *Social Differentiation* New York: David McKay Co., Inc., 1965), pp. 38-39; and Hayward R. Alker, Jr., *Mathematics and Politics* (New York: The Macmillan Co., 1968).

curve would be almost near its maximum of 100 (Figure III-2,B). However the curve for the income data for the United States falls somewhere between the extremes as illustrated in Figure III-2,C.[18]

The degree of inequality for a given set of data may be computed and conveniently expressed by a figure which will be somewhere between zero and 100. This Gini Index is determined by the proportion of the total area under the diagonal that is between it and the Lorenz curve (the shaded section). The Index is designated "L," the area under the diagonal that is between it and the Lorenz curve "A," and the remainder "B." The relationship may be expressed as follows: [19]

$$L = \frac{A}{A + B} = \frac{\text{area between curve and diagonal}}{\text{area under diagonal}}$$

Whether one receives much income or little, the chances are that the person must look to his occupation to provide for the things he needs and wants. It is this important dimension which we next examine.

The Occupational Dimension

Occupations differ widely in income, wage spread, stability of employment, and prestige. One may contrast, for example, the mean yearly income for professionals with that of laborers: $16,134 vs. $8,088. But there are other differences related to wages: in some job categories there is little spread between what the highest- and the lowest-paid workers make while in others it is wide. The least dispersion between the incomes of the highest paid 25% and the lowest paid 25% within a given category is found among such occupations as mailmen and railroad conductors. Tailoring and college teaching fall in the middle while such categories as parking attendant and private household worker have the highest wage spread. Most of these occupations with the greatest spread are also among the lowest paid.[20]

---

[18] Herman P. Miller, *Income Distribution in the United States* (a 1960 Census Monograph) (Washington, D.C.: Government Printing Office, 1966), pp. 220–221. See also Kaare Svalastoga, *Social Differentiation* (New York: David McKay Co., 1965), pp. 38–39; and Hayward R. Alker, Jr., *Mathematics and Politics* (New York: Macmillan Co., 1968).

[19] Miller, *op. cit.* The following formula may be used for computing the Gini Index:

$$L = 1 - \sum_{i = i}^{K} (f_{i+1} - f_i)(y_i + y_{i+1})$$

[20] The income figures are for 1973, from "Money Income in 1973 of Families and Persons in the United States," pp. 137–138, for year-round, full-time male workers. The information on wage spread is from Miller, *op. cit.*, pp. 99–101. Although his data are for 1959 there was no change for mailmen and railroad conductors from their 1949 or 1939 posi-

The chances of being unemployed vary among occupations: in 1975 the unemployment rate among blue-collar workers was 16.8% as contrasted with 4.7% for white-collar employees.[21]

In regard to prestige, it is a common observation that it varies among the occupations. A simple test is to ask yourself in which occupation you would prefer your prospective spouse to be, and from that point of view, which you would consider undesirable. Or, you might think in terms of a prospective son- or daughter-in-law. More will be said about prestige shortly.

While there are several bases for judging occupations, income remains one of the most convenient ways of ordering them. We have noted that they differ significantly in average income and if we wish we may arrange them from those with the highest remuneration to those with the lowest. Figure III-3 rates a number of occupations on the basis of the salaries received.

Understandably income is a major consideration in the way people view different occupations since it provides the means of obtaining social goods, as we noted earlier. But as we also suggested there are other factors which enter into people's evaluations. This was taken into account by the U.S. Bureau of the Census; its occupational categories are based on the "socioeconomic groups" set up by the Bureau statistician Alba M. Edwards. Edwards believed that an occupation's social status

FIGURE III-3.
Mean Yearly Income for Males in Selected Occupations

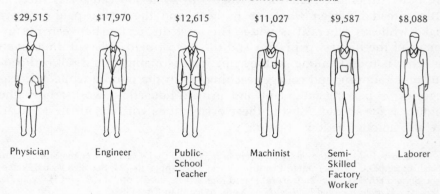

$29,515	$17,970	$12,615	$11,027	$9,587	$8,088
Physician	Engineer	Public-School Teacher	Machinist	Semi-Skilled Factory Worker	Laborer

Source: U.S. Bureau of the Census, "Money Income in 1973 of Families and Persons in the United States," Series P-60, No. 97 (Washington, D.C.: Government Printing Office, January 1975), pp. 137-138.

tions (they were among the lowest tenth in dispersion), nor was there any change during these periods for the parking attendants and household workers (who were in the highest tenth). Tailors, who were in the fifth decile, also showed no change. However the college teacher category which was in the sixth decile in 1959 was in the eighth in 1949 and in the fifth in 1939.

[21] U.S. Department of Labor, *Employment and Earnings*, 21 (April 1975), 32–33.

depended to a very large extent on the job-holders' educational level as well as on their income. His ordering, with some modifications, has been used by the Bureau of the Census since 1940.[22] The major occupational categories, together with the number of persons in them, the relative proportions of each, and the median incomes are shown in Table III-2.

These categories are useful for giving a broad outline of stratification. Thus 44% of the persons in Table III-2 are in white-collar work, 45% in blue-collar, seven per cent are in service occupations, and five per cent in farming. More detailed occupational data and information on the education, employment history, and marital status of job-holders is available from the Census Bureau and other government sources. From these data the researcher can study the various social attributes which are related to occupational stratification.

However, the broad categories contain many different kinds of occupations—for example the first one, "professional, technical, and kindred workers," includes physicians as well as musicians and draftsmen; the craftsmen grouping includes foremen. This raises questions regarding occupational prestige, especially when dealing with specific occupations, and investigators have sought to determine how they are

TABLE III-2. Major Occupational Categories of Year-Round Full-Time Male Workers and Median Yearly Income, 1973

Major Occupational Category	Number of Workers	Per Cent	Median Yearly Income
Professional, technical, and kindred workers	6,036,000	15.3%	$14,306
Managers, administrators, and proprietors, excluding farmers	6,414,000	16.2	14,519
Clerical and kindred workers	2,646,000	6.7	10,627
Sales workers	2,299,000	5.8	12,296
Craftsmen, foremen, and kindred workers	8,700,000	22.0	11,245
Operatives	7,001,000	17.7	9,503
Service workers, excluding private household	2,673,000	6.8	7,937
Laborers, excluding farm	2,013,000	5.1	8,158
Farmers and farm managers	1,330,000	3.4	6,697
Farm laborers and foremen	465,000	1.2	4,727
Total	39,577,000	100.2%	

Source: U.S. Bureau of the Census, "Money Income in 1973 of Families and Persons," Series P-60, No. 97 (Washington, D.C.: Government Printing Office, January 1975), pp. 137-138. Private household workers, who comprise less than one per cent, are excluded.

[22] See Alba M. Edwards, *Comparative Occupation Statistics for the United States, 1870 to 1940* (Washington, D.C.: Government Printing Office, 1943), p. 180.

evaluated by ordinary people. In order to find out the National Opinion Research Center of the University of Chicago interviewed a cross-sample of American adults. One of the questions asked was what makes a job excellent, and a high income was the most frequently mentioned criterion. However almost as many felt that a job should be judged in terms of its service to humanity and its necessity. Training requirements and prestige tied for third place.[23]

Those interviewed were asked to give their personal opinion of the general standing of 90 occupations by indicating whether they thought each had excellent, good, average, somewhat below average, or poor standing. On this basis United States Supreme Court Justice which received a score of 96 was rated highest while shoe shiner with a score of only 33 was rated lowest.[24] What is most interesting is that the survey was repeated in 1963 and although there were some differences, mainly in the higher prestige accorded scientific occupations, generally very few changes occurred in the 16-year period. The findings of the two surveys are shown in Table III-3. The researchers also analyzed studies of occupational ratings dating back to 1925 and found that ". . . no appreciable changes in the prestige structure of occupations have occurred in the United States in the last four decades."[25]

After reading these ratings for the United States, one may wonder how people in other countries rank occupations. Alex Inkeles and Peter H. Rossi compared prestige ratings of occupations in Great Britain, New Zealand, Germany, Japan, and Soviet Russia, and the United States, and found remarkable similarities despite the variety of sources upon which the ratings were based.[26] They believed the similarities were due mainly to common structural features of industrialized nations, and that cultural differences would not significantly affect the evaluations. They expected that in underdeveloped countries, on the other hand, there would be important variations because of cultural factors.[27] Yet Robert W. Hodge, Donald J. Treiman, and Peter H. Rossi found a high degree of similarity in occupational ratings in studies of nations varying widely in industrialization and cultural background; among them were Brazil, Canada, Indonesia, Norway, and Turkey, in addition to the countries in the ear-

[23] National Opinion Research Center, "Jobs and Occupations: A Popular Evaluation," in Reinhard Bendix and Seymour M. Lipset, eds., *Class, Status, and Power* (Glencoe, Ill.: The Free Press, 1953), p. 418. Income was cited by 18%; service to humanity and the job's necessity, 16% each, and training requirements and prestige, 14% each. The other criteria were morality and responsibility, nine per cent; intelligence and ability, nine per cent; security, three per cent; pleasantness, ease and safety of work, two per cent; and miscellaneous, ten per cent.

[24] *Ibid*, pp. 412–414.

[25] Hodge *et al.*, *"Occupational Prestige in the U.S., 1925–1963,"* p. 286.

[26] Alex Inkeles and Peter H. Rossi, "National Comparisons of Occupational Prestige," *American Journal of Sociology*, 61 (January 1956), 329–339.

[27] *Ibid.*, p. 339.

TABLE III-3. Occupational Prestige Ratings in the United States, 1963 and 1947

Occupation	1963 Survey NORC Prestige Score*	Rank	1947 Survey NORC Prestige Score*	Rank
U.S. Supreme Court justice	94	1	96	1
Physician	93	2	93	2.5
Nuclear physicist	92	3.5	86	18
Scientist	92	3.5	89	8
Government scientist	91	5.5	88	10.5
State governor	91	5.5	93	2.5
Cabinet member in the federal government	90	8	92	4.5
College professor	90	8	89	8
U.S. Representative in Congress	90	8	89	8
Chemist	89	11	86	18
Lawyer	89	11	86	18
Diplomat in the U.S. foreign service	89	11	92	4.5
Dentist	88	14	86	18
Architect	88	14	86	18
County judge	88	14	87	13
Psychologist	87	17.5	85	22
Minister	87	17.5	87	13
Member of the board of directors of a large corporation	87	17.5	86	18
Mayor of a large city	87	17.5	90	6
Priest	86	21.5	86	18
Head of a department in a state government	86	21.5	87	13
Civil engineer	86	21.5	84	23
Airline pilot	86	21.5	83	24.5
Banker	85	24.5	88	10.5
Biologist	85	24.5	81	29
Sociologist	83	26	82	26.5
Instructor in public schools	82	27.5	79	34
Captain in the regular army	82	27.5	80	31.5
Accountant for a large business	81	29.5	81	29
Public school teacher	81	29.5	78	36
Owner of a factory that employs about 100 people	80	31.5	82	26.5
Building contractor	80	31.5	79	34
Artist who paints pictures that are exhibited in galaries	78	34.5	83	24.5
Musician in a symphony orchestra	78	34.5	81	39
Author of novels	78	34.5	80	31.5
Economist	78	34.5	79	34
Official of an international labor union	77	37	75	40.5
Railroad engineer	76	39	77	37.5
Electrician	76	39	73	45
County agricultural agent	76	39	77	37.5

TABLE III-3. (Continued)

Occupation	1963 Survey NORC Prestige Score*	Rank	1947 Survey NORC Prestige Score*	Rank
Owner-operator of a printing shop	75	41.5	74	42.5
Trained machinist	75	41.5	73	45
Farm owner and operator	74	44	76	39
Undertaker	74	44	72	47
Welfare worker for a city government	74	44	73	45
Newspaper columnist	73	46	74	42.5
Policeman	72	47	67	55
Reporter on a daily newspaper	71	48	71	48
Radio announcer	70	49.5	75	40.5
Bookkeeper	70	49.5	68	51.5
Tenant farmer—one who owns livestock and machinery and manages the farm	69	51.5	68	51.5
Insurance agent	69	51.5	68	51.5
Carpenter	68	53	65	58
Manager of a small store in a city	67	54.5	69	49
A local official of a labor union	67	54.5	62	62
Mail carrier	66	57	66	57
Railroad conductor	66	57	67	55
Traveling salesman for a wholesale concern	66	57	68	51.5
Plumber	65	59	63	59.5
Automobile repairman	64	60	63	59.5
Playground director	63	62.5	67	55
Barber	63	62.5	59	66
Machine operator in a factory	63	62.5	60	64.5
Owner-operator of a lunch stand	63	62.5	62	62
Corporal in the regular army	62	65.5	60	64.5
Garage mechanic	62	65.5	62	62
Truck driver	59	67	54	71
Fisherman who owns his own boat	58	68	58	68
Clerk in a store	56	70	58	68
Milk route man	56	70	54	71
Streetcar motorman	56	70	58	68
Lumberjack	55	72.5	53	73
Restaurant cook	55	72.5	54	71
Singer in a nightclub	54	74	52	74.5
Filling station attendant	51	75	52	74.5
Dockworker	50	77.5	47	81.5
Railroad section hand	50	77.5	48	79.5
Night watchman	50	77.5	47	81.5
Coal miner	50	77.5	49	77.5
Restaurant waiter	49	80.5	48	79.5

TABLE III-3. (Continued)

Occupation	1963 Survey		1947 Survey	
	NORC Prestige Score*	Rank	NORC Prestige Score*	Rank
Taxi driver	49	80.5	49	77.5
Farm hand	48	83	50	76
Janitor	48	83	44	85.5
Bartender	48	83	44	85.5
Clothes presser in a laundry	45	85	46	83
Soda fountain clerk	44	86	45	84
Sharecropper—one who owns no livestock or equipment and does not manage farm	42	87	40	87
Garbage collector	39	88	35	88
Street sweeper	36	89	34	89
Shoe shiner	34	90	33	90

*Respondents were asked to state whether they believed each occupation had a standing of "excellent," "good," "average," "somewhat below average," or "poor." Then these arbitrary values were assigned to each rating: 100 for excellent, 80 for good, 60 for average, 40 for somewhat below average, and 20 for poor. Calculation of the numerical average of these arbitrarily assigned values for all respondents rating the occupation yielded the NORC prestige score.

Source: Adapted from Robert W. Hodge, Paul M. Siegel, and Peter H. Rossi, "Occupational Prestige in the United States, 1925-63," *American Journal of Sociology*, 70 (November 1964), 286-302. Published by The University of Chicago Press.

lier study. Although Hodge and his associates observed some differences, they felt they were due to cultural and economic development patterns. The authors emphasize that structural similarity among nations with any degree of complexity leads to similar prestige ratings of occupations.[28] This is further underlined by Robert M. Marsh in his study of occupational prestige in Taipei, Taiwan. After comparing his findings with data from Denmark and the United States he concludes that not only do societies share in a general way common institutional structures but, more importantly, a given occupation has highly similar requirements for recruitment and role functioning, and it provides similar rewards.[29]

Prestige ratings are useful to the researcher for they indicate the occupation's general standing in the eyes of the public in terms of criteria such as the following: (1) *The nature of the work:* How pleasant are the work tasks, are they physically demanding, do they call for brains or for brawn, is the work injurious to one's health? (2) *Whether the satisfactions are intrinsic or extrinsic:* Does the worker feel that his occupation is important, does it provide him with a sense of accomplishment, and does

[28] Robert W. Hodge, Donald J. Treiman, and Peter H. Rossi, "A Comparative Study of Occupational Prestige," in Bendix and Lipset, eds., *Class, Status, and Power* (2nd ed.; New York: The Free Press, 1966), pp. 309–321.

[29] Robert M. Marsh, "The Explanation of Occupational Prestige Hierarchies," *Social Forces*, 50 (December 1971), 214–222.

he invest some of his self in his occupation, or is his work almost entirely a means of obtaining money for satisfactions off the job? (3) *The working conditions:* How pleasant is the place of work, is it located in a desirable part of town, what are the co-workers like? (4) *The extent of opportunity:* What are the possibilities of accumulating wealth, or of rising in position and income, or of an advantageous transfer to a competitor, or to a higher occupational category? (5) *What other people think of the occupation:* Is it generally thought of as desirable by people one knows? How is it viewed in relation to other occupations? (6) *How difficult it is to enter the occupation:* Is the training lengthy, expensive, and difficult, are special talents and abilities required? Are there legal, social, or other barriers to entering?

Favorable conditions of work and prestige draw candidates; consequently the pay need not be as high as similar occupations which are less attractive. On the other hand, where lengthy training, difficulty of entry, and the need for special talent and ability limit competition, the likely result is either increased prestige, higher income, or both.[30] There is a tendency toward balancing off job openings and qualified candidates, for when there are too few aspirants the income or other social goods are more likely to be increased than when there are too many. And in turn, if there is a surplus of candidates fewer attractions are needed. This is only partly due to the occupational "demand" and the talent "supply." Technological development, government policies, population growth, occupational information, and access to education or other means of job preparation affect both demand and supply. In addition there are social and psychological conditions which encourage or discourage occupational aspirations. These conditions are discussed at some length in Chapters IV and V.

It is questionable whether a single prestige ranking can be applied to an entire nation. There are thousands of different types of occupations,[31] which leads to some arbitrariness in assigning ranks. Specific occupations as well as occupational categories vary in prestige regionally, by community size, and in terms of the number of women, youths, old people, and minority-group members who are typically found in the occupation. In addition there are variations in income which are related to the above factors.[32]

Nevertheless for some purposes it may be useful to stratify occupations by means of a prestige index "as if" there was a single continuum of occupational prestige. A useful index which also takes into account so-

[30] Cf. Kingsley Davis and Wilbert E. Moore, "Some Principles of Stratification," *American Sociological Review,* 10 (April 1945), 242–249.

[31] See, e.g., U.S. Department of Labor, *Dictionary of Occupational Titles* (3rd ed.; Washington, D.C.: Government Printing Office, 1965), Vols. I and II. The *Dictionary* lists 21,741 separate occupations.

[32] See Albert J. Reiss, Jr., with Otis D. Duncan, Paul K. Hatt, and Cecil C. North, *Occupations and Social Status* (New York: The Free Press of Glencoe, Inc., 1961), pp. 162–238.

cioeconomic factors was developed by Albert J. Reiss, Jr. and his associates. One advantage of their index is that it is constructed in conjunction with the Census Bureau's listing of occupations. This provides the stratification researcher a useful yardstick for determining a respondent's occupational prestige with reference to the widely used census classification system. This index has been refined by Hodge, Paul S. Siegel, and Rossi and should prove very useful to survey researchers who wish to rank occupations.[33]

While most people can probably rank the better known jobs easily, it would seem that occupational evaluation is more meaningful for the individual when it involves his own work situation. How does the junior executive evaluate his own occupation and others in his field of business, how does the nightclub singer evaluate her own job and others in the entertainment world, how does the governor in the field of politics? Several writers suggest that occupations be stratified within occupational families or situses, and Paul K. Hatt proposes the following: political, professional, business, recreation and aesthetics, agriculture, manual work, military, and service.[34]

In our discussion prestige has been linked with occupation. However prestige is also used in a more general sense to indicate a person's position or status in the community. W. Lloyd Warner and his associates, for example, had knowledgeable members of a community rank individuals and their families according to their reputation vis-à-vis with whom they associate, their institutional memberships, house type, dwelling area, and occupation. These criteria are seen as "evaluated symbols" or signs of status. The judges place the subjects into different ranks, which the researcher translates into different prestige categories, usually half a dozen. This technique is most appropriate for small communities where the judges know individuals and families well enough to rank them, either personally or by reputation; obviously it does not apply to the nation, or to large, impersonal urban concentrations. Its value even for the small community has been questioned: among other things, those who do the ranking tend to be from the higher strata. Consequently their criteria for stratification are likely to be different from those of lower-level persons.[35]

---

[33] See Reiss *et al.*, especially Appendix B. The newer version may be found in National Opinion Research Center, *National Data Program for the Social Sciences, Codebook for the Spring 1973 General Social Survey* (Chicago: National Opinion Research Center, July 1973), pp. 105–124.

[34] Paul K. Hatt in Reiss, Jr., *Occupations and Social Status*, pp. 239–258. Cf. Joel E. Gerstl and Lois K. Cohen, "Research Note: Dissensus, Situs and Egocentrism," *British Journal of Sociology*, 15 (September 1964), 254–261; and Richard T. Morris and Raymond J. Murphy, "The Situs Dimension in Occupational Structure," *American Sociological Review*, 24 (April 1959), 231–239.

[35] See W. Lloyd Warner, Marcia Meeker, and Kenneth Eells, *Social Class in America* (New York: Harper Torchbooks, 1960), especially pp. 10, 40, 86, and 176 ff. The most thorough critique of the Warner method remains Ruth Rosner Kornhauser, "The Warner Approach to Social Stratification," in Bendix and Lipset, eds., *Class, Status, and Power*, pp. 224–254.

For stratifying people in urban society, criteria which depend minimally on others' judgments would seem to be the most reliable and useful; therefore we have so far stressed income and occupation, and we considered prestige mainly in conjunction with occupation. There are additional criteria which are extremely valuable: the first one we will discuss is education.

The Educational Dimension

Education is especially important in present-day America as well as elsewhere. Increasingly a person's job opportunities are determined by his schooling, and there is a strong association between amount of education and income. If we stratify the 115,005,000 persons in the United States who are 25 years of age or older by educational attainment, we find that approximately 25% have gone to college, 52% have high-school training, 18% have between five and eight years of schooling, and four per cent have less than five years of education.[36] In Part A of Figure III-4 the per-

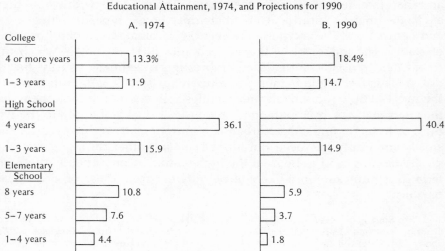

FIGURE III-4.
Percentage Distribution of Persons 25 Years or Older by
Educational Attainment, 1974, and Projections for 1990

A. 1974

B. 1990

College

4 or more years   13.3%   18.4%

1–3 years   11.9   14.7

High School

4 years   36.1   40.4

1–3 years   15.9   14.9

Elementary
School

8 years   10.8   5.9

5–7 years   7.6   3.7

1–4 years   4.4   1.8

Source: U.S. Bureau of the Census, "Educational Attainment in the United States: March 1973 and 1974," Series P-20,
No. 274 (Washington,D. C.: Government Printing Office, December 1974), p. 29 and *Statistical Abstract of the
United States: 1974* (95th ed; Washington, D.C.: Government Printing Office, 1974), p. 117.

[36] U.S. Bureau of the Census, "Educational Attainment in the United States: March 1973 and 1974," Series P-20, No. 274 (Washington, D.C.: Government Printing Office, December 1974), pp. 27, 29.

centages are broken down further by years of schooling; in Part B are the estimates for 1990. They show that by 1990 the educational level will have continued to increase; one-third of the population will have gone to college and very few will not have attended high school.

The significance of education for stratification is that it provides access to social goods. The association between education and income is revealed very dramatically when families are stratified according to amount of schooling of the head of the family (see Table III-4). Where the head has not completed elementary school 26% of these families have annual incomes of less than $4,000, and only 29% earn $10,000 or more. By contrast where the head has a BA degree only three per cent make less than $4,000 while 85% have incomes of $10,000 or more. Where the family head has done postgraduate work the proportion is even higher. Among the highest income families in Table III-4—those with $25,000 or more a year—only two in a hundred has less than elementary education, while one in three has gone to graduate school.

The disparities are cumulative; thus the lifetime earnings of men who finished elementary school are almost one quarter more than the earnings of those who didn't, or a discrepancy of $64,000. The lifetime income for men who have a high-school diploma is 40% higher than that of elementary-school graduates, or $135,000. As for the person who has completed college, the differences are much greater, in spite of the expenses which include the loss of income for several years. His lifetime earnings are 58% higher than the high-school graduate's, or $279,000 more.[37] There are several exceptions which are discussed later in this chapter.

Education itself is a source of prestige. Yet it is mainly important for stratification as a ranking measure and as a necessary condition for entering various occupations and obtaining the related income. Education, income, and occupation, are the key criteria for stratification; they provide an overall picture for a given city, region, or nation. But because of historical or other factors there may be categories of persons who have lesser access to social goods. Oftentimes their attributes, such as race or sex, are a convenient means of and justification for keeping them in a subordinate status. If there is reason to believe that there are such categories of persons then appropriate statistical measures should be used to learn the extent to which they differ from other groups. In Figure III-5 we compare the income distribution of white, black, and Spanish-origin families. We see that 57% of the black, and 41% of the Spanish-origin families have incomes under $7,000 a year, while this is true of only one-third of the white families. At the top end of the income scale only 12%

[37] U.S. Bureau of the Census, "Annual Mean Income, Lifetime Income, and Educational Attainment of Men in the United States, for Selected Years, 1956 to 1972," Series P-60, No. 92 (Washington, D.C.: Government Printing Office, March 1974), p. 22.

TABLE III-4. Percentage Distribution of Families by Income Level and Education of Family Head, 1973

Education	Income Level							
	Under $4,000	$4,000-5,999	$6,000-7,999	$8,000-9,999	$10,000-14,999	$15,000-24,999	$25,000 and over	Total
Elementary School								
Less than 8 years	26.0	19.3	15.2	10.5	16.2	10.8	2.2	100.2
8 years	14.0	15.4	13.9	12.2	23.0	17.6	3.9	100.0
High School								
1-3 years	12.4	11.1	10.9	10.9	28.2	22.1	4.6	100.2
4 years	5.8	5.9	8.0	10.4	30.7	31.0	8.0	99.8
College								
1-3 years	4.4	4.8	6.4	8.4	27.5	35.9	12.7	100.1
4 years	3.2	3.2	3.6	5.2	21.0	40.4	23.5	100.1
5 years or more	1.7	1.9	2.9	4.4	17.8	38.4	32.8	99.9

Source: U.S. Bureau of the Census, "Money Income in 1973 of Families and Persons in the United States," Series P-60, No. 97 (Washington, D.C.: Government Printing Office, January 1975), p. 77.

FIGURE III-5.
Percentage Distribution of Family Income by Race, 1972

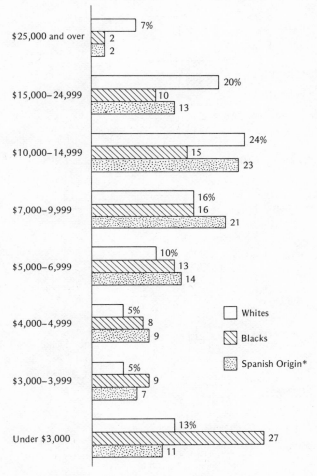

*Includes families of Mexican, Puerto Rican, and other Spanish origin.

Source: U.S. Bureau of the Census, " Money Income in 1972 of Families and Persons
in the United States," Series P-60, No.90 (Washington, D.C.: Government
Printing Office, December 1973), p. 75; and " Persons of Spanish Origin
in the United States: March 1973," Series P-20, No. 264 (May 1974), p. 26.

of black and 15% of Spanish-origin families earn $15,000 a year or more,
in contrast to 27% of white families.

When we reexamine the occupational dimension and compare blacks
and whites we find the former in the less prestigious and poorer paying
occupations (see Figure III-6).

FIGURE III-6.
Occupation of Male Family Head, by Race, 1973

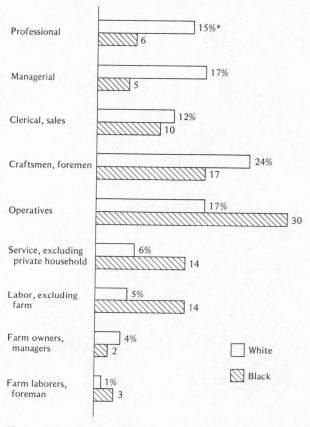

*Percentages do not total 100 because of rounding.

Source: U.S. Bureau of the Census, "Characteristics of the Low-Income
Population: 1973," Series P-60, No. 98 (Washington, D.C.: Government
Printing Office, January 1975), p. 102.

BLACKS VS. WHITES

Education, occupation, and income are linked, as we noted pre-viously; thus it is not surprising that blacks, whose median years of schooling is 10.8 compared to the whites' 12.4, are found in the lesser paid occupations. If we examine income according to educational level, however, we find that overall blacks have lower incomes than whites, even when both have the same amount of schooling (Figure III-7). But al-though relatively few blacks obtain a college education, those who do are predominantly in white-collar occupations and their income is very close

FIGURE III-7.
Education of Family Head, Total Money Income in 1973, and Race

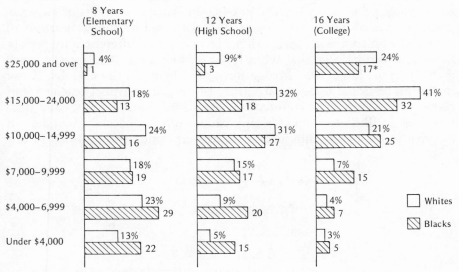

*Percentages do not total 100 because of rounding.

Source: U.S. Bureau of the Census, " Money Income in 1973 of Families and Persons in the United States, " Series P-60, No. 97 (Washington, D.C. : Government Printing Office, January 1975), pp. 80, 82.

to the whites'.[38] They are also close in terms of total family income, with 57% of the black families with a college graduate as head earning between $10,000–$24,000 a year (Figure III-7). Yet, as we pointed out in Chapter II, in general minority groups such as blacks and Spanish-origin do not receive the kind of occupational or monetary returns from their educational investment as do the whites. The same is true for women, as we also noted in the previous chapter.

FEMALES VS. MALES

In the past, sex as a criterion for stratification tended to be ignored. However there are larger numbers of women in the labor force, and for a growing proportion of families the wife's earnings are a regular and expected contribution to total income. With the decline in the birth rate [39] less time will be absorbed by caring for children and more will be available for paid work. In addition, perspectives on male-female roles are

[38] "Educational Attainment in the U.S.: March 1973 and 1974," pp. 31, 36.

[39] See U.S. Bureau of the Census, "Projections of the Population of the United States, by Age and Sex: 1972 to 2020," Series P-25, No. 493 (Washington, D.C.: Government Printing Office, December 1972).

changing and it is likely that increasingly young women will look toward regular careers in conjunction with marriage. Consequently the dimension of sex is becoming more important for stratification: first, in regard to increasing the family's social goods, and second in terms of superordination-subordination. In Figure III-8 we examine the proportion of men and women at each occupational level and the differences in median income. It can be seen that while most women are in white-collar work they are in the lower-level occupations, most being in clerical jobs. Those in the professional category are likely to be public-school teachers and nurses while their male counterparts are school administrators and doctors. Figure III-8 also shows a tiny proportion in the skilled trades, in contrast to the males, although there are substantial proportions in un-

FIGURE. III-8.
Male-Female Differences in Occupation and in Median Income, 1973

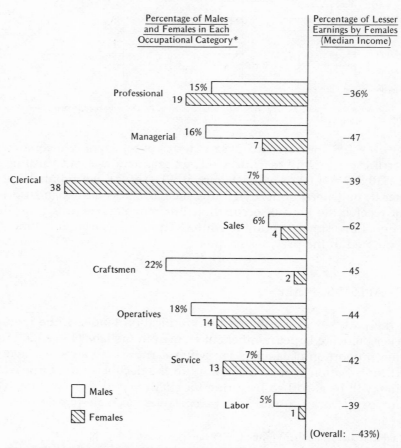

*Farming and private household work are excluded. Five per cent of the males and two per cent of the females are in these occupations.

Source: U.S. Bureau of the Census, " Money Income in 1973 of Families and Persons in the United States," Series P-60, No.97 (Washington, D.C.: Government Printing Office, January 1975), pp. 137-139.

skilled work and in service occupations. Nevertheless, women in every occupational category receive lower salaries than the men: from 36 to 62% less. These women, incidentally, are year-round full-time workers.

ETHNICITY

There are numerous other criteria that may be useful for stratification. Any dimension should be examined carefully because other factors may account for differences, sometimes more so than the dimension itself. For example, half of the American population reports English, Scottish, or Welsh; German; Irish; Italian; French; Polish, or Russian descent. The numbers range from 29.5 million with English, Scottish, or Welsh background to 2.2 million of Russian origin.[40] One might expect those of Anglo-Saxon descent, that is persons of English, Scottish, or Welsh background to rank first in occupational, educational, and income levels, given the history of the United States and the achievement of persons of such ancestry.[41] However, individuals of Russian origin are topmost; the Anglo-Saxons are second in occupational and educational status, and third in income. Persons of Polish descent are also relatively high, being third in occupational and educational levels and second in income (see Table III-5). Table III-6 shows that the differences between persons of

TABLE III-5. Ethnic Descent and Occupational, Educational, and Income Rank, 1972

Ranking According to Percentage:		
Professionals and Managers[a]	College Graduates[b]	With Family Income Over $15,000 a Year
Russian	Russian	Russian
Anglo-Saxon[c]	Anglo-Saxon[c]	Polish
Polish	Polish	Anglo-Saxon[c]
German	German	Italian
Italian	Italian	German
Irish	Irish	Irish
French	French	French
Spanish	Spanish	Spanish

[a]Males, 14 years old and over.
[b]Persons 23-34 years old.
[c]English, Scottish, and Welch.
Source: U.S. Bureau of the Census, "Characteristics of the Population by Ethnic Origin: March 1972 and 1971," Series P-20, No. 249 (Washington, D.C.: U.S. Government Printing Office, April 1973), pp. 11, 23, 24, 26.

[40] U.S. Bureau of the Census, "Characteristics of the Population by Ethnic Origin: March 1972 and 1971," Series P-20, No. 249 (Washington, D.C.: Government Printing Office, April 1973), p. 11.

[41] See E. Digby Baltzell, *The Protestant Establishment* (New York: Random House, 1964).

TABLE III-6. Selected Occupational, Educational, and Income Characteristics by Ethnic Origin, 1972

	Russian	Polish	English Scotch Welsh	German	Italian	Irish	French	Spanish
Total number (millions)	2.2	5.1	29.5	25.5	8.8	16.4	5.4	9.2
Professionals and managers[a]	55.3%	31.0%	34.8%	28.9%	27.2%	25.6%	25.5%	17.3%
College graduates[b]	51.8%	24.1%	26.3%	19.2%	16.5%	16.3%	13.2%	4.2%
Family income over $15,000	44.5%	32.7%	29.5%	27.1%	29.0%	26.8%	20.9%	10.2%

[a]Males, 14 years old and over.   [b]Persons 23–34 years old.
Source: U.S. Bureau of the Census, "Characteristics of the population by Ethnic Origin: March 1972 and 1971," Series P-20, No. 249 (Washington, D.C.: Government Printing Office, April 1973), pp. 11, 23, 24, 26.

Russian descent and individuals of Anglo-Saxon ancestry are considerable: 55% are professionals and managers compared to 35%. Fifty-two per cent have gone on from college, compared to 26%, while the percentages for family income over $15,000 a year or more are 45 and 30, respectively. It seems probable that those of Russian origin include a high proportion of Jews, whose attributes of urban residence, high achievement motivation, and emphasis on education likely explain the differences. In large part this probably also explains the ranking of the Polish cohort.[42]

OTHER FACTORS

In addition, the significance of a dimension varies from one context to another. For example, while the racial dimension is important in the United States, a researcher in Sweden would find it of little value because of the great homogeneity in that country. Of, if one were to stratify the population of Northern Ireland religion would be critical, because of the Protestant and Catholic populations. On the other hand religion would not be a meaningful dimension in Southern Ireland, which is almost entirely Catholic.

While the dimension of power is important, particularly for class, it is difficult to determine how much power individuals have since there are different kinds of power. Also much power is potential in that people often accede to the wishes of others not because of overt sanctions but because they are aware that they can be invoked. The existence of power becomes apparent in social situations where groups of people with different interests confront one another. Therefore it is more appropriate to analyze this dimension in the context of social class.

Several of the dimensions cited above will be examined at some length in the next chapter as well as in later portions of the book. Some will only be touched on, not because they are not relevant for stratification or class, but because it is necessary to be selective. That is, the researcher will learn more about stratification and class and will be more confident of his findings if he limits his analyses to those dimensions which appear to "make the most difference." It is for these reasons that we have stressed income, occupation, and education. They are most appropriate for studying stratification in modern as well as in industrializing society, and they are likely to be predictive of access to social goods for most people.

Some researchers have attempted to combine these dimensions plus

[42] See Celia Stopnicka Rosenthal, "Social Stratification of the Jewish Community in a Small Polish Town," *American Journal of Sociology*, 59 (July 1953), 1–10. For a discussion of relative opportunity for native and foreign-born whites see Peter M. Blau and Otis D. Duncan, *The American Occupational Structure* (New York: John Wiley & Sons, Inc., 1967), pp. 231–238.

others into a composite index, but by doing so the significance of each is obscured as are the relationships among them.[43] For example, a person's occupation, his income, education, house type, neighborhood, style of life, and who he associates with are interrelated. But to what extent are the dimensions listed determined by occupation, or by neighborhood, or by the status of one's associates? That is, for most persons, are not style of life, house type, residential area, associates, memberships in formal associations, power, and prestige dependent primarily on one's occupation and the income it provides? In fact Kaare Svalastoga argues that for macrosocial purposes and in industrial society occupation is so important that other dimensions may be disregarded in determining a person's overall rank.[44] It seems to us that for many if not most researches involving general populations the occupational dimension is likely to be the single most useful measure of stratificational position. However where resources permit information should be obtained on additional dimensions, such as income and education. This could provide a check on the utility of the occupational criterion, and it could also reveal the extent to which the other dimensions contribute to explaining whatever is under scrutiny. This is particularly important when persons of similar occupational background are being studied, especially when there is an indication that there may be significant inconsistencies among the dimensions.

Before concluding this chapter it is necessary to make some comments on status inconsistency and the number of strata.

Status Inconsistency

From the discussion of income, occupation, education, and other criteria it should be clear that stratification is multidimensional, even though one factor may be primary and others secondary. However the *extent* to which it is uni- or multidimensional depends on the nature of the society as well as the stratificational category being investigated. In a small, traditional society those high on one dimension are likely to be equally high on others. Thus the wealthy individual will also be in a highly evaluated occupation, will be well educated, live in the best part of town, and associate with other high status persons. Such an individual is said to be status consistent. However, in a large industrial society there is bound to be greater differentiation among its parts: there is likely to be heterogeneity in population origin and ethnicity, in interests, work activities, and in style of life. There will be less visibility and fewer "con-

[43] See, e.g., Warner et al., Social Class in America, pp. 163–185. For critical comments see Kornhauser, "The Warner Approach to Social Stratification"; and Ely Chinoy, "Research in Class Structure," Canadian Journal of Economics and Political Science, 16 (May 1950), 260.

[44] Svalastoga, Social Differentiation, p. 11. See also Natalie Rogoff, "Social Stratification in France and in the United States," American Journal of Sociology, 68 (January 1953), 353.

nections" among the dimensions. That is there will be people who have a great deal of education but do not make very much, well-off families who are not accepted in the social circles into which their economic position should provide entrée, and so on. This may be illustrated by the case of the black doctor who is high status on the educational and occupational dimensions but low status in terms of race. He is not given the deference which is usually accorded persons high on these two dimensions, and his economic opportunities will probably be limited as he is not likely to be allowed to practice in the better hospitals.[45]

There are numerous other possibilities where discrepancies exist among several dimensions: the uneducated but wealthy businessperson; the individual of noble birth who is impoverished, or the chemist or engineer with a PhD who is doing manual work because of a recession. The question is, how are the people affected by such status discrepancies?

We dealt with status inconsistency to some extent in the previous chapter when we examined the effects of social mobility. The reader may recall that mobility, especially when rapid, seemed to affect people psychologically and in terms of their political preference. There has been much research on the effects of social mobility, or status inconsistency (basically the same).[46] However, except where there has been extreme movement, the findings are contradictory due to inadequate research methods and conceptual problems. Elton F. Jackson and Richard F. Curtis suggest that the life conditions and expectations of a given stratum may be the primary determinant of attitudes and behaviors, rather than the effects of breaking old ties and making new ones, or of conflicting demands because of status inconsistency. This may be especially true where the studies are of random samples, and in countries such as the United States where because of considerable mobility status inconsistency is reasonably common.[47] Nevertheless, status inconsistency appears to be a concept well worth further investigation, particularly because of historical situations where status discrepant individuals have become sources of discontent, critics of the existing social order, and leaders in movements to change it.

[45] See Everett C. Hughes, "Dilemmas and Contradictions of Status," *American Journal of Sociology*, Vol. 50 (March 1945), 353–359.

[46] Early studies include Gerhard E. Lenski, "Status Crystallization: A Non-Vertical Dimension of Social Status," *American Sociological Review*, 19 (August 1954), 405–412; Peter M. Blau, "Social Mobility and Interpersonal Relations," *American Sociological Review*, 21 (June 1956), 290–295; and Elton F. Jackson, "Status Consistency and Symptoms of Stress," *American Sociological Review*, 27 (August 1962), 469–480. Among the more recent ones are Robert W. Kleiner and Seymour Parker, "Goal-Striving, Social Status, and Mental Disorder: A Research Review," *American Sociological Review*, 28 (April 1963), 189–203; K. Kessin, "Social and Psychological Consequences of Intergenerational Occupational Mobility," *American Sociological Review*, 77 (July 1971), 1–18; and Elton F. Jackson and Richard F. Curtis, "Effects of Vertical Mobility and Status Inconsistency: A Body of Negative Evidence," *American Sociological Review*, 37 (December 1972), 701–713.

[47] Jackson and Curtis, *op. cit.*, p. 712.

The Number of Strata

At some point a question might arise in the reader's mind as to how many strata there are. From the discussion in Chapter I the answer should be clear: there are as many strata as the investigator determines; it depends on the criteria he uses and how fine he wishes the distinctions to be. Thus if he distinguishes simply between those who work with their head and those who work with their hands there will be two strata; if he includes the distinction between non-agricultural and agricultural activities and farmers are treated separately there will be three. If one wishes to separate people into occupational categories as the U.S. Bureau of the Census does there will be ten (see Table III-2). Regarding education one could have persons with college, secondary, and elementary training or number of years of schooling. In the case of income the distinction could be between those whose earnings are "adequate," say $10,000 a year or more, and those who earn less; it could be between the "well off," perhaps the $50,000 a year or more category, and the poor— where the income is under $4,000 a year. The categories could be based on $5,000 intervals, or they could be finer: if the breaks were every thousand dollars there would be over 10,000 on the basis of the Treasury Department's top income bracket which is $10,000,000 or more.

Marx posited two strata in terms of owners of the means of production and non-owners; for certain situations he saw more. W. Lloyd Warner basically sees six strata; August B. Hollingshead lists five, and in a study in Southern California S. Stansfeld Sargent found 17.[48]

The discrepancies are due mainly to differences in approach. If one sees society as composed of strata whose incumbents have fundamentally different interests which are bound to lead to conflict, as Marx did, then, as polarization proceeds the several groupings will form into two major ones. If one is mainly concerned with the social distinctions people make with regard to whom they associate with there can be many gradations, or strata. It might be noted that among other things the number of strata varies according to the observer's position; that is, the higher the person's status the more distinctions he makes, the lower the status the fewer.[49]

The number of strata and their nature are also influenced by the research procedures. The techniques are the subjective, the reputational,

[48] See Karl Marx and Friedrich Engels, *Manifesto of the Communist Party* (New York: International Publishers, 1932); Warner, Meeker, and Eells, *op. cit.*; August B. Hollingshead, *Elmtown's Youth* (New York: John Wiley & Sons, 1949), and S. Stansfeld Sargent, "Class and Class-Consciousness in a California Town," *Social Problems*, 1 (June 1953), 22–27.

[49] Allison Davis, Burleigh B. Gardner, and Mary R. Gardner, *Deep South* (Chicago: University of Chicago Press, 1941), p. 65.

and the objective, or combinations of them. In the subjective approach respondents rank themselves; they may be asked to select among choices such as "upper class, middle class, working class, and lower class," or the question may be open-ended. The advantage of this approach is that it reveals people's perceptions regarding stratification, and even if they differ from the observer's they are nevertheless meaningful to the persons involved. The blue-collar worker who rates himself "middle class" may be socially mobile, or his children may be pushed to achieve, and his political preferences may be those of higher strata people. Also, subjective perceptions are extremely important when strata begin to form into classes.

But the subjective approach may give a distorted picture because, regardless of the category people say they belong to, most of their attitudes and behaviors are likely to reflect their particular life chances. Thus their occupation and income, for example, may be better indicators of group divisions in a community. How people rank themselves is also undoubtedly influenced by economic conditions and the opportunity structure.

The reputational approach requires that raters have sufficient knowledge about the people they are ranking; consequently this technique lends itself to studying relatively small, homogeneous communities, although it has been used to analyze the power structures of larger cities and even of the nation.

While the subjective and reputational approaches are quite valuable, especially under the circumstances noted above, we believe that objective criteria provide the most meaningful basis for examining social stratification and the most solid foundation for analyzing class formation.[50]

Summary

To understand a modern industrial society such as the United States it is necessary to learn how the advantages and disadvantages are distributed. This is observed when the population is stratified, which is done most effectively according to people's income, education, and occupation. The latter is the most significant criterion; not only is there popular agreement on the prestige of occupations, but, more importantly, they provide the wherewithal for the family's well-being, style of life, and

---

[50] For an example of the subjective approach see Richard Centers, *The Psychology of Social Classes* (Princeton, N.J.: Princeton University Press, 1961); for the reputational see W. Lloyd Warner and Associates, *Democracy in Jonesville* (New York: Harper and Row, 1949); and Floyd Hunter, *Community Power Structure: A Study of Decision-Makers* (Chapel Hill: University of North Carolina Press, 1953) and *Top Leadership, U.S.A.* (Chapel Hill: University of North Carolina Press, 1959). For illustrations of the objective approach see U.S. Bureau of the Census data, as found in Tables III-1, 2, 4, 5, and 6, above. A combination of the subjective and objective approaches is found in Centers, *loc. cit.*

children's opportunities. Yet, additional information about the distribution of these things may be revealed by other dimensions, such as income and education, as well as race and sex. The data we presented make it abundantly clear that there is considerable inequality in the distribution of social goods.

We wish to examine next some of the consequences of these inequities in terms of what they mean in everyday life. Therefore, we will look at the life conditions of the different levels of people, or strata. How do well-being and opportunity to obtain social goods, as well as related attitudes and behaviors vary among them? Put another way, how do the life chances differ among the strata?

Part Two

STRATIFICATION AND THE LIFE CYCLE

Chapter IV.   Infancy Through Adolescence

This chapter and the next two will examine the significance of stratification in terms of the life cycle of the individual: how differences in access to social goods affect persons in various strata throughout their lifetime. In the present chapter differences among the strata from birth through early life, childhood, and adolescence will be explored and the significance of institutional arrangements and social milieu will be touched on.

Since we are using data collected by others we are limited to their designations of strata, although in some cases we will combine categories where this seems desirable. Where researchers use the term "classes" to identify what we believe to be clearly strata, we have taken the liberty of substituting the term "strata." Also, we recognize that there are variations in particular aspects of life conditions within a given stratum, and even where circumstances are similar they do not have the same effect on everyone. Nevertheless our focus is on the typical case and we propose to show the importance of stratum position for various facets of people's lives. We are not interested in specific strata; rather we wish to show how conditions change, usually from favorable to unfavorable, as one goes down the strata hierarchy. Terms such as "higher strata," "lower strata," "highest stratum," and "lowest stratum" should be understood as referring to *relative differences* in life conditions, or their effects, among levels or categories of persons.

Birth and Early Life

It is commonly believed that there are more children among the lower rather than the upper strata. Vital statistics and other data show that with some exceptions this is true: when families are stratified according to income and education the relationship is inverse. That is, generally, the lower the income the larger the number of children; thus where the family income is between $3,000 and $4,999 a year there are likely to be 3.79 children, in contrast to families earning $25,000 a year or more where there are only 2.48 (Table IV-1, A). Mothers who have not completed elementary school bear 4.25 children, whereas college graduates have only 2.39 (Table IV-1, B).

TABLE IV-1. Number of Children Born to Wives 35-44 Years old, by Income, Education, and Occupation, 1974

A. Family Income	No. of Children Born	B. Education of Mother	No. of Children Born	C. Occupation of Husband	No. of Children Born
$25,000 and over	2.48	*College*		*Non-Manual*	
$15,000-24,999	2.76	4 years or more	2.39	Professional, technical	2.82
$10,000-14,999	3.07	1-3 years	2.84	Managers, officials, proprietors	2.95
$7,500-9,999	3.34	*High School*		Clerical	2.91
$5,000-7,499	3.20	4 years	2.96	Sales	2.73
$3,000-4,999	3.79	1-3 years	3.10	*Manual*	
		Elementary School		Craftsmen, foremen	3.12
		8 years	3.72	Operatives	3.29
		Less than 8 years	4.25	Service, incl. private household	3.21
				Laborers	3.61

Source: U.S. Bureau of the Census, "Fertility Expectations of American Women: June, 1974," Series P-20, No. 277 (Washington, D.C.: Government Printing Office, February 1975), pp. 35 and 40.

The picture is not as clear when families are stratified according to the occupational level of the husband, although as a whole manual families have more children than non-manual (Table IV-1, C). Part C of Table IV-1 shows that laborer families have 3.61 offspring while there are 3.12 in the craftsmen and foremen category. However the families of operatives have 3.29 children and service workers 3.21. These discrepancies may be due to the employment status of the wives, as well as to their age structure and family income. Among non-manual families those in sales have the fewest children, followed by clerical worker families. Again, the employment status and age structure of the wives may explain the discrepancies.

While in general the higher status families have the fewest children, it is interesting that in the West the reverse was true prior to industrialization. However, a strong inverse relationship became clear in the late 1800's, and long-range trends point to a narrowing of strata differences in fertility.[1] Yet this relationship between low status and many offspring persists in Western nations, and is also found in less industrialized countries of the world.

A study of 2,380 Indian couples by J. E. Rele illustrates this inverse relationship in a less industrialized nation.[2] Rele randomly selected these couples from 60 villages in one of the states of India, stratified them into four categories on the basis of caste and occupation, and ranked them hierarchically. He also took into account duration of marriage and found that in the first 15 years of married life there were few differences in fertility among the strata. However, for couples married 15 years or more the differences were substantial: in the highest stratum an average of 5.97 children were born per woman, in the next stratum 6.33, in the third 6.45, and in the lowest 7.17.

Although the lower strata have higher fertility there is a difference between the number of children born and family size, because of strata variations in survival rates. Rele found that 68.0% of the children in the top stratum survived in contrast to only 60.6% in the fourth or lowest stratum. Consequently actual family size for the Indian couples whose marriage has lasted 15 years or more is greater for the highest stratum (3.92 children), compared to the second and third (3.82 and 3.83 children respectively). But at the lowest level, in spite of the low survival rate, there are still 4.20 children per family. This reflects the very large number of children born to women in this stratum.[3]

[1] See Frank W. Notestein, "Class Differences in Fertility," *The Annals of the American Academy of Political and Social Science,* 188 (November 1936), 26–27; and Dennis H. Wrong, "Trends in class Fertility in Western Nations," *The Canadian Journal of Economics and Political Science,* 24 (May 1958), 216–229.

[2] J. E. Rele, "Fertility Differentials in India," *The Milbank Memorial Fund Quarterly,* 41 (April 1963), 183–199. See also Kingsley Davis, *The Population of India and Pakistan* (Princeton, N.J.: Princeton University Press, 1951), pp. 73–82.

[3] Figures adapted from Rele, *op. cit.,* p. 190.

There have always been differences among the strata in how long people may be expected to live. However the gap among the higher and lower levels has varied according to changes in the overall death rate. It has been estimated that from ancient times up through roughly the 19th century the average child could expect about 20 or 30 years of life. The birth rate was very high but because of poor sanitation, inadequate medical care, and nutritional deficiencies the death rate was also very high. Under these circumstances there was little difference in mortality among the strata. But beginning in the middle of the 17th century conditions improved and the overall death rate started to drop; however for the next two hundred years, from 1650 to 1850, there was a wide gap between the upper and lower strata. While there were rapid gains in life expectancy for the upper levels the increase was much slower for the lower. By the latter half of the 19th century the gap began to diminish, and today in industrial nations the average child may be expected to live approximately 70 years. Yet differences among the strata remain.[4]

There are even modern nations which show a considerable gap; for example in the United States in 1972 life expectancy among whites was 72.1 years in contrast to 65.5 years for non-whites.[5] We are viewing the whites as an upper and the non-whites as a lower stratum, which is amply justified by differences in income, occupation, and education.[6]

The lesser life expectancy among the lower strata is paralleled by higher death rates for children and mothers. Among whites there are likely to be 12.4 stillbirths per 1,000 live births, in contrast to 22.6 for non-whites. Infant deaths are much lower for whites than for non-whites: for infants under 28 days old the mortality rate per 1,000 live births is 12.3 for whites and 20.6 for non-whites. For infants less than one year of age the mortality rate per 1,000 live births is 16.3 in contrast to 29.0 (see Table IV-2).

[4] Aaron Antonovsky, "Social Class, Life Expectancy and Overall Mortality," The Milbank Memorial Fund Quarterly, 45 (April 1967).

[5] U.S. Bureau of the Census, Statistical Abstract of the United States: 1974 (95th ed.; Washington, D.C.: Government Printing Office, 1974), p. 58.

[6] Median income for white families in 1973 was $12,595 while for non-whites it was $7,269. Thirty-eight per cent of the white families were in the $15,000 or higher income bracket vs. 16% of non-whites; eight per cent of the white families earned less than $4,000 a year while this was true of 26% of the non-whites. In regard to occupation, in 1973 48% of the whites were in non-manual work in contrast to 24% of non-whites; among craftsmen and foremen 22% were white and 14% non-white, and among non-farm laborers the percentages were five and 11, respectively. As for education, in 1974 among those 25 or older the median for whites was 12.4 years of schooling and for non-whites 10.8; the percentages completing high school were 37 vs. 27, and the percentages with four or more years of college were 14 vs. five.

U.S. Bureau of the Census, "Money Income in 1973 of Families and Persons in the United States," Series P-60, No. 97 (Washington, D.C.: Government Printing Office, January 1975), p. 46; "Characteristics of the Low-Income Population: 1973," Series P-60, No. 98 (Washington, D.C.: Government Printing Office, January 1975), p. 102; and "Educational Attainment in the United States: March 1973 and 1974," Series P-20, No. 274 (Washington, D.C.: Government Printing Office, December 1974), pp. 31, 36.

TABLE IV-2. Death Rates of Young Children and Mothers, Whites vs. Non-Whites

Basis of Death	Whites	Non-Whites
Stillbirths per 1,000 live births (Fetal Death Ratio)[a]	12.4	22.6
Deaths of infants under 28 days old per 1,000 live births (Neonatal Mortality Rate)[b]	12.3	20.6
Deaths of children under 1 year of age per 1,000 live births (Infant Mortality Rate)[b]	16.3	29.0
Deaths of mothers from childbirth and complications of pregnancy per 100,000 live births (Maternal Mortality Rate)[a]	14.4	55.9

[a]1970.   [b]1972.
Source: U.S. Bureau of the Census, *Statistical Abstract of the United States: 1974* (95th ed.; Washington, D.C.: Government Printing Office, 1974), p. 60.

Similarly, the death rates of mothers from childbirth and complications of pregnancy are much higher for non-whites than for whites. On the basis of every 100,000 live births, 56 non-white mothers are likely to die in contrast to 14 white mothers (Table IV-2). Put simply, the chances of fetal or infant death are nearly twice as high for non-white babies as for white babies, and the chances of the non-white mother dying are almost four times greater.

Historically, as was noted above, when overall mortality rates drop the differences among the strata narrow. We may therefore expect to find less of a gap in many other Western industrialized nations because their rates are so much better than that of the United States. A study of infant mortality in seven nations—Denmark, England and Wales, the Netherlands, Norway, Scotland, Sweden and the United States, revealed that the American rate is indeed the highest. Some of these countries which are quite comparable as regards climate, age composition of the population, and health conditions had higher rates than the United States in the early part of the 20th century. Today, however, theirs are lower. Even though there has been a great decrease in infant deaths in the United States during the first half of this century the rate of decline has slowed since 1950, and the United States has failed to keep pace with the reductions in these other countries.[7]

Not only is the American infant mortality rate excessively high but so is its maternal death rate. This can be seen in statistics recently released by the World Health Organization: Sweden's maternal death rate in 1966

[7] U.S. National Center for Health Statistics, *International Comparison of Perinatal and Infant Mortality: The United States and Six West European Countries,* Public Health Service Publication No. 1000-Series 3-No. 6 (Washington, D.C.: Public Health Service, March 1967), especially p. 87.

was only 11.3 which contrasts to the overall American rate of 29.1 for the same year.[8]

Why are the rates so high for Americans generally, and for the lower strata in particular? Poor living conditions among a substantial portion of the population, together with inadequate medical care, are largely responsible. One of the conclusions in a study of infant and fetal mortality is that "[c]lose to 30% of the infant deaths are still attributed to factors related to identifiable environmental conditions and to conditions that may reflect quality of medical and hospital care." [9] Among the environmental factors are poor sanitation and nutritional deficiencies.[10]

These unsatisfactory conditions also leave their mark on the children who survive, a good portion of whom are underweight or premature. Mothers who are undernourished during pregnancy are likely to give birth to underweight children, who suffer a variety of physiological and behavioral deficits by the time they reach school age. A long-term British study of more than 17,000 births found that these underweight children, whose growth was retarded while in their mother's womb, are more than twice as common among mothers of low socioeconomic groups.[11]

Premature babies are more likely to be born to lower-strata women. Helen Wortis and Alfred Freedman who studied 250 extremely poor black mothers found that the great poverty of these mothers was ". . . linked with [the] increased susceptibility of their children to neurologic abnormality and mental defect." [12] As they grow older, the lower-strata youngsters are likely to be in poorer health than the higher-strata children. The former, for example, are more likely to be absent from school because of illness.[13] But despite the high mortality rates and the unfavor-

[8] "Sweden is the Safest Place to Have a Baby, U.N. Says," New York Times (March 15, 1970), p. 26; and U.S. Bureau of the Census, Statistical Abstract of the United States: 1972 (93rd ed.; Washington, D.C.: Government Printing Office, 1972), p. 57. The U.S. rate includes both whites and non-whites.

[9] U.S. National Center for Health Statistics, Infant and Prenatal Mortality in the United States, Public Health Service Publication No. 1000-Series 3-No. 4 (Washington, D.C.: Government Health Service, October 1965), p. 56.

[10] While there are difficulties in making comparisons with other countries, because of variations in registration procedures and in the compilation of vital statistics, and because of the size and diversity of the United States (see Metropolitan Life Insurance Co., Statistical Bulletin [New York: Metropolitan Life Insurance Co., December 1968], p. 5), they do not account for the unfavorable American rates. For a graphic description of the kinds of conditions responsible for the high rates see Citizens' Board of Inquiry, Hunger, U.S.A. (Boston: Beacon Press, 1968). See also "Four Special Panels Call on Nixon to Declare Hunger Emergency," New York Times (November 30, 1969), pp. 1 ff.

[11] Jane E. Brody, "Low Birth Weight Is Linked to Ills," New York Times (November 14, 1972), p. 19. See also Infant and Perinatal Mortality in the United States, p. 19.

[12] Helen Wortis and Alfred Freedman, "The Contribution of Social Environment to the Development of Premature Children," American Journal of Orthopsychiatry, 35 (January 1965), 66.

[13] U.S. National Center for Heath Statistics, Family Income in Relation to Selected Health Characteristics, United States, Public Health Service Publication No. 1000-Series 10-No. 2 (Washington, D.C.: Public Health Service, July 1963), p. 10.

able situation of the children who survive, the poor continue to have large families.

FAMILY PLANNING

The high birthrate among the lower strata has led to the common belief that these persons want large numbers of children, or that they are unconcerned about the size of their family. But this is not completely true, according to several researchers. "Contrary to popular stereotypes," Arthur B. Shostak writes, "lower class Americans want as few, or even fewer, children than do those of higher status." He points out that although the incidence of unwanted and accidental pregnancy is very high among members of the lower strata, they endorse the idea of family planning more strongly than the general population.[14] Similar attitudes were found in a study of preferred family size in Peru by J. Mayone Stycos: the lower the stratum position of the respondents, the fewer children desired. However, while these lower-strata mothers may want smaller families they reveal that they have given little previous thought to or seldom engaged in discussion about family size. They also have misconceptions about fertility believing for example that theirs is much lower than that of other women. Thus they think the number of children they have is less than the average, which is usually not true.[15]

The lack of knowledge about fertility and reliable methods of contraception, and the expense and sometimes limited availability of contraceptive devices are mainly responsible for the relatively high birth rate in the lower strata. In some cases however cultural values encourage having many children: a large number of offspring may be tied in with traditional attitudes toward the family and conceptions of masculinity and femininity. There are strong economic reasons for having many children: in rural economies they are needed to help with farm chores, and where there is manufacturing or other non-agricultural industry children's labor contributes to family income. Finally, in poor countries, having many children is a means of insuring care for the parents in their old age.

There are additional important differences among the strata regarding children, as we shall see when we examine socialization and other aspects of childhood and adolescence.

[14] Arthur B. Shostak, "Birth Control and Poverty," in Arthur B. Shostak and William Gomberg, eds., *Perspectives on Poverty* (Englewood Cliffs, N.J.: Prentice-Hall, Inc., 1965), pp. 50–51.

[15] J. Mayone Stycos, "Social Class and Preferred Family Size in Peru," *American Journal of Sociology*, 70 (May 1965), 651–658.

Childhood and Adolescence

When the infant comes into the world he has none of the social attributes we label as human: he has neither language, a self, a conscience, nor what Charles H. Cooley calls the sentiments and Kurt Riezler the passions.[16] Yet he is born into a human group whose members have these attributes and through the process of socialization he also develops them. In this process many of the interactions between parent and child are unconscious, others are deliberate; encouragement and discouragement are expressed; pride, joy, and disappointment are shown; and parents undertake specific training regimens. As the child becomes socialized he develops the various social attributes and learns the values and practices of the culture he is born into.

However socialization varies among the strata in terms of content and in its completeness. That is, words and language patterns, values, beliefs, and behaviors differ among the strata. While there may be incomplete socialization in any stratum, it is more likely to occur at the lower levels, where there is social and economic deprivation and where many children are neglected.

CHILD-REARING PRACTICES

Researchers have found differences among the strata in the content of socialization which are in part expressed in child-rearing practices. This was observed by Urie Bronfenbrenner in a survey of research on methods of child rearing from 1932 to 1957; however he noted that the practices are changing. He found that from the 1930s up to World War II parents in the lower strata were more permissive than those in the middle strata, but following World War II this was reversed. Now lower-strata fathers and mothers are more strict than middle-strata parents and they are more likely to use physical punishment to obtain compliance. By contrast in the middle-strata home, reasoning, isolation of the child, and other practices involving the threat of the loss of the parents' love are likely to be employed. The studies surveyed showed that in general parent-child relationships in middle-strata families were more acceptant and equalitarian, whereas lower-strata practices were oriented toward maintaining order and obedience.[17] Bronfenbrenner's observations are

[16] See George H. Mead, *Mind, Self and Society,* ed. by Charles W. Morris (Chicago: University of Chicago Press, 1934); Charles H. Cooley, *Human Nature and the Social Order* (New York: Charles Scribner's Sons, 1922); and Kurt Riezler, *Man Mutable and Immutable* (Chicago: Henry Regnery Co., 1950).

[17] Urie Bronfenbrenner, "Socialization and Social Class Through Space and Time," in Eleanor E. Maccoby, Theodore Newcomb and Eugene L. Hartley, eds., *Readings in Social Psychology* (New York: Henry Holt and Co., 1958), pp. 400–425. Arnold Green, in a very perceptive article ("The Middle-Class Male Child and Neurosis," *American Sociological Re-*

buttressed by those of Zena Smith Blau who studied 250 mothers during their confinement in the maternity wards of four hospitals located in different parts of Chicago.[18]

Bronfenbrenner observed that the gap between the strata appears to be narrowing, largely as a result of the child-rearing theories discussed in the mass media and often promulgated by counselors, physicians and others. Understandably, parents in any stratum who have the greatest access to such agents of change are most likely to alter their practices. In this regard, Blau also found that the more heterogeneous the members of a stratum are, the greater the disposition to adopt child-rearing practices different from their mothers'.

Yet differences persist. A secondary analysis by Glen H. Elder of data collected from 1,000 persons in the United States, Great Britain, West Germany, Italy, and Mexico contrasted "democratic family ideology," or permissiveness, with "autocratic family ideology." The findings were that among the higher strata the emphasis was democratic while among the lower it was autocratic.[19]

LANGUAGE

One of the most important aspects of the socialization process is the development of language. It is essential for adequate socialization and it is necessary for acceptable functioning in the peer group, in the school, and in one's occupation. Yet lower-strata children are much more likely to be inadequate in their handling of language than middle-strata youngsters, according to research by Martin Deutsch. He found that the lower-strata children have poor language functioning and often cannot use language as an elaborating form of communication. These deficiencies cumulate, being more marked at the fifth-grade level in school than in the first, and are directly related to the dropout problem. In suggesting the reasons for these deficiencies he cites Basil Bernstein's study of language usage among lower-strata British families where there is much less verbalization, where a child's question will likely be answered by a simple "yes" or "no," a gesture, or even a grunt. This may be the result of parents having been reared under similar circumstances, and may reflect lack of time for their offspring due to housekeeping chores, long hours of work, tiredness, or demoralization and disinterest. By contrast the superior verbal ability of the higher-strata children is due largely to the

view, 2 [February 1946], 31–41), suggests that this form of gaining compliance may be more damaging psychologically than physical punishment.

[18] Zena Smith Blau, "Class Structure, Mobility and Change in Child Rearing," *Sociometry*, 28 (June 1965), 210–219.

[19] Glen H. Elder, Jr., "Role Relations, Socio-Cultural Environments and Autocratic Family Ideology," *Sociometry*, 28 (June 1965), 173–196. Cf. Richard A. Rehberg, Walter E. Schafer, and Judie Sinclair, "Adolescent Achievement Behavior, Family Authority Structure, and Parental Socialization Practices," *American Journal of Sociology*, 75 (May 1970), 1012–1034.

greater verbalization among family members, to the time and interest devoted to the child, and even to conscious attempts to increase his vocabulary and his ability to use language. In addition upper-strata parents are likely to be more literate and their homes are likely to contain books, magazines, or other aids to language development.[20]

The lower-level child suffers not only from language inadequacy but his grammar, vocabulary, and idioms help identify him as a member of the lower strata, as do his accents and speech patterns. There are strata variations in the same national language in many societies. This is true in several European countries,[21] as well as in the Orient where grammar and word usage readily distinguish higher- and lower-strata persons. For the child such identification may limit his social contacts to lower-strata youngsters and may also adversely affect his job opportunities later on. While language differences are not so great in the United States as elsewhere, still very bad grammar and certain terms are usually associated with the lower strata.[22]

TIME ORIENTATION AND DEFERRED GRATIFICATION

As the child is socialized he develops interests and ways of behaving which will affect his life chances. One example is his time orientation and another is the extent to which he is able to defer gratification. The lower-strata child's concept of future time is quite limited: he is concerned mainly with the here and now. He finds it difficult to project himself in his imagination, very far into the future and thus set meaningful goals or see how current activities might affect him later on. Even if he has long-range goals he finds it difficult to defer immediate pleasures; he prefers to spend rather than save money and to engage in behavior which although immediately satisfying may be detrimental for his future. Thus he may go out with "the gang" while he should be doing his homework. He may put time, energy and money into an automobile. This may detract from his studies and encourage him to limit his schooling in order to begin earning money as soon as possible. Such a limited time orientation and the difficulty in deferring gratification among

[20] Martin Deutsch, "The Role of Social Class in Language Development and Cognition," *American Journal of Orthopsychiatry*, 35 (January 1965), 78–88. See also Basil Bernstein, "Language and Social Class," *British Journal of Sociology*, 11 (September 1960), 271–276.

[21] Kaare Svalastoga, *Social Differentiation* (New York: David McKay Co., 1965), p. 13.

[22] The differences are not so great as say in England where socially mobile individuals attempt to cultivate an upper-strata intonation. Variation in language usage is illustrated in the musical play, "My Fair Lady," when Professor Doolittle who is grooming Eliza to associate with upper strata persons teaches her to say "the rain in Spain" rather than "the rhyne in Sphyne." In the United States "jive talk" may serve to identify lower-strata blacks and in the State of Hawaii pidgin is an indicator of low-stratum position.

Strata language differences in the United States are not as apparent today as some years ago since many expressions of the lower strata have been popularized by contemporary writers and the mass media.

lower-strata youngsters is paralleled by their relatively low levels of educational and occupational aspirations.[23]

AMBITION

Many studies have shown that striving for success, the desire for achievement, and educational and occupational aspirations differ among the strata.[24]

The research also suggests that students from the lower strata in contrast to those from the upper strive less, have less ambition, and less of a "need" for achievement. This could lead one to believe that if only the lower strata were more ambitious, if they could somehow be "motivated," the children would then want to do well in school, and as adults would work hard to get into the better paying and more prestigious occupations. Presumably the number of poor school achievers, dropouts, unemployed, and underemployed would be reduced and there would be less personal and social disorganization. But Suzanne Keller correctly questions whether the lesser striving is due to lack of ambition; she holds that these persons realize that there are limited opportunities for the poorly educated with few skills, and that they have made a realistic adjustment to existing conditions.

It is also likely that lower-strata children will reflect parents' interests and behaviors; in turn this will discourage them from a longer time orientation, from deferring immediate gratification, and from raising their educational and occupational aspirations.[25] A recent study by Richard A. Rehberg, Walter E. Schafer, and Judie Sinclair lends support to earlier findings on the significant role that parents play in the success of the young. The importance of achievement training in socialization practices is brought out in their survey of 1,455 freshmen male high-school stu-

[23] See Lawrence L. Leshan, "Time Orientation and Social Class," *Journal of Abnormal and Social Psychology,* 47 (July 1952), 589–592; and Louis Schneider and Sverre Lysgaard, "The Deferred Gratification Pattern: A Preliminary Study," *American Sociological Review,* 18 (April 1953), 142–149. Cf. Murray A. Strauss, "Deferred Gratification, Social Class, and the Achievement Syndrome," *American Sociological Review,* 27 (June 1962), 326–335. Strauss did not find a significant association between deferment of need gratification and socioeconomic status. However his sample underrepresents the lowest socioeconomic levels. See *ibid.,* p. 328, n. 11.

[24] See Leonard Riessman, *Class in American Society* (New York: The Free Press, 1959), pp. 361–362. Studies which seek to measure achievement orientation are summarized by Joseph A. Kahl, "Some Measurements of Achievement Orientation," *American Journal of Sociology,* 70 (May 1965), 669–681.

[25] Suzanne Keller, "Sociology of Social Stratification, 1945–1955," in Hans L. Zetterberg, ed., *Sociology in the United States* (Paris: U.N.E.S.C.O., 1956), p. 116; and Keller and Marisa Zavalloni, "Ambition and Social Class: A Respecification," *Social Forces,* 43 (October 1964), 58–70. See also Allison Davis, "The Motives of the Underprivileged Worker," in William F. Whyte, ed., *Industry and Society* (New York: McGraw-Hill Book Co., 1946), pp. 84–106 and Strauss, "Deferred Gratification," p. 335.

dents in New York State. Their research also found that achievement training which encourages college aspirations is more characteristic of middle- rather than working-strata families, although the differences were not substantial.[26]

A number of investigations show that there is less stress on achievement among the lower strata; e.g., Herbert H. Hyman details how this group places relatively little emphasis on education and does not try for high-level occupations.[27] This would seem to imply that lower-level persons are not interested in "success" or in "getting ahead"; however, Ephraim H. Mizruchi, Joseph A. Kahl, and Joan Huber and William H. Form found that the success theme permeates society.[28] In addition, Mizruchi and Huber and Form observe that the lower strata actually indicate a somewhat greater belief in equality of opportunity than the middle strata.[29] Similar results are reported in a study of high-school seniors, who were asked to what extent they agree or disagree with this statement: "Anyone who wants to can rise to the top. It just takes determination and hard work." Substantially more blue-collar than white-collar students agreed; also, among blue-collar youths, those who did not expect to obtain additional education were more likely to agree than those who planned on college.[30]

While the lower strata evidence a strong, or stronger, belief in the existence of opportunity, compared to the higher strata, the latter place more emphasis on achievement. Yet the studies which indicate greater stress on achievement among higher-status students also reveal variance within the strata; they show that a substantial minority of lower-strata youngsters have high achievement orientation. More than that, a goodly number go on to college; there are children who break away from a culture of poverty, obtain higher education, and enter well-paying and prestigious occupations.[31]

[26] Rehberg et al., "Adolescent Achievement Behavior," pp. 1012–1034.

[27] Herbert H. Hyman, "The Value Systems of Different Classes: A Social Psychological Contribution to the Analysis of Stratification," in Reinhard Bendix and Seymour M. Lipset, eds., Class, Status, and Power (2nd ed.; New York: The Free Press, 1966), pp. 488–499. Similar findings are reported by Ephraim H. Mizruchi in Success and Opportunity (London: The Free Press, 1964), p. 78.

[28] Mizruchi, op. cit., pp. 82–83; Kahl, op. cit.; and Joan Huber and William H. Form, Income and Ideology (New York: The Free Press, 1973), p. 90.

[29] Mizruchi, loc. cit.; and Huber and Form, loc. cit.

[30] Irving Krauss, "Sources of Educational Aspirations Among Working-Class Youth," American Sociological Review, 29 (December 1964), 878. The study was undertaken in the San Francisco Bay area, and 537 students responded as follows: blue collar vs. white collar: strong agreement, 38 and 35%; moderate agreement, 56 and 55%; and neutral or disagreement, six and eleven per cent, respectively. Responses among the terminal blue-collar seniors compared to the college-bound were, respectively: strong agreement, 43 vs. 35%; moderate agreement, 54 vs. 58%, and neutral or disagreement, four vs. seven per cent.

[31] See Lipset and Bendix, Social Mobility in Industrial Society (Berkeley and Los Angeles: University of California Press, 1962), pp. 11–75; Bernard C. Rosen, "The Achievement Syndrome: A Psychocultural Dimension of Social Stratification," American Sociological Re-

The apparent contradictions are explained by the different meaning the several strata attach to the success goal. Huber and Form show that when belief in equality of opportunity is linked to family income, the better off the respondent the stronger the belief. This is also true in regard to belief in opportunity for higher education and for occupational mobility.[32] In addition, the symbols of success differ. The higher strata stress education as an end in itself and minimize the importance of money. On the other hand, the lower strata see education as a means toward an end, and place a higher emphasis on money.[33]

Considering the relative advantages and disadvantages among the strata, it is quite realistic that the lower-level person wants a job that provides good pay, security, and a home, and views risk-taking as dangerous; he therefore feels he had best strive for goals which, although limited, are attainable. On the other hand the upper-strata individual who already has achieved the basic minimum of material success, or whose family has, can, understandably, have high educational and occupational aspirations.[34] These contrasting perspectives are meaningful, especially for lower-strata persons who are minority group members. The reader may recall that in Chapter II we pointed out that for groups such as blacks and those of Spanish origin investment in additional education generally does not pay off.

Cultural Conditions in the Home

Among the many factors which affect a child's intellectual development, aspirations, and success in school are the cultural conditions at home. They include attitudes toward books and other reading matter, activities such as going to concerts, plays, or the zoo; in general the kinds of experiences which will either arouse the child's curiosity and broaden his world, or will limit his interests and narrow his outlook.

The child is also affected by his parents' interests: are they mainly concerned with immediate, day-to-day problems or is their range wider? Are they aware of what happens in their local community, the nation,

---

view, 21 (April 1956), 47–61; Joseph A. Kahl, "Educational and Occupational Aspirations of 'Common Man' Boys," *Harvard Educational Review,* 23 (Summer 1953), 186–203; Krauss, *op. cit.,* pp. 867–879; and Whyte, *Street Corner Society* (Chicago: University of Chicago Press, 1947), pp. 103–106.

[32] Huber and Form, *Income and Ideology,* pp. 90–92, 96.

[33] Huber and Form, *op. cit.,* pp. 84, 87; and Mizruchi, *Success and Opportunity,* pp. 72, 74–75, 79–80.

[34] Kahl, "Some Measurements of Achievement Orientation," *op. cit.;* Mizruchi, *op. cit.,* pp. 70, 74–75, and 77–78; and Huber and Form, *op. cit.,* pp. 84–87. Cf. Robert K. Merton, *Social Theory and Social Structure* (rev. ed.; Glencoe, Ill.: The Free Press, 1957), pp. 131–194; and Keller and Zavalloni, *op. cit.*

and the world? Parents' interests are reflected in what they talk about, their travels, what they read, listen to on the radio or watch on television, and in turn their behaviors influence the children. Strata differences in television watching and newspaper and magazine reading were investigated by Bradley Greenberg and Brenda Dervin. They found that lower-strata persons, in contrast to higher, spend much more time watching television, and favor entertainment over more serious programs. Greenberg and Dervin also note that lower-strata persons are less likely to read magazines or newspapers, and that their source of news is television, whereas higher-strata individuals prefer the newspaper. Interestingly, the researchers observed that low-income blacks are similar to low-income whites in television and reading preferences.[35]

Martin Deutsch in a study of factors related to school achievement reports that among approximately 400 lower-strata black children, the majority had no books at home. And although a substantial number said there were newspapers and magazines, further probing revealed that most of the magazines were comic books, *Ebony*—a picture-magazine featuring blacks, and sometimes *Life*.[36]

These data suggest that lower-strata families are likely to live in a very constricted world in a social-psychological sense. But this is also true in a physical sense: in one community, which was studied a number of years ago, the average upper-strata individual in the course of a lifetime had traveled within a radius of 1,100 miles from where he lived, in contrast to the average lower-strata person who had traveled only 145 miles.[37] And although people travel much more today, undoubtedly the relative difference remains. We might note that among the low-strata black children Deutsch studied, except for school field trips approximately 65 per cent of the youngsters had never been beyond a 25-mile radius of their homes.[38]

There are many reasons for these differences, and money is but one. While poorer families may feel that they cannot afford books or theater tickets, most are able to find sufficient funds for a television set. Television does not require literacy, concentration, or a noisefree place and may provide a welcome escape from depressing surroundings. Even if concerts or plays were free the father may be physically tired from his job or the mother exhausted from household tasks and caring for many chil-

[35] Bradley Greenberg and Brenda Dervin, "Mass Communication Among the Urban Poor," *Public Opinion Quarterly*, 34 (Summer 1970), 224–235. See also W. Lloyd Warner, *American Life: Dream and Reality* (Chicago: University of Chicago Press, 1962), p. 270.

[36] Deutsch, *Minority Group and Class Status as Related to Social and Personality Factors in Scholastic Achievement*, Monograph No. 2 (Ithaca, N.Y.: The Society for Applied Anthropology, New York State School of Industrial and Labor Relations, Cornell University, 1960), p. 4.

[37] Genevieve Knupfer, "Portrait of the Underdog," in Bendix and Lipset, eds., *Class, Status, and Power* (Glencoe, Ill.: The Free Press, 1953), pp. 225–263.

[38] Deutsch, *Minority Group and Class Status*, p. 28.

dren; there may not be appropriate clothes, or the family may fear embarrassment over not knowing how to act in such unfamiliar situations. But perhaps more important is their lack of such experiences as children, as well as lower-strata norms which exert pressures against "higher class" activities.

In dealing with factors which affect the child's intellectual development, interests, and behaviors, the physical features of the home should not be ignored. While conditions such as the number of persons in a dwelling unit, space, and quietness vary from family to family at all levels, the problem of an adequate place for study is likely to be acute for the lower-strata child. In this respect the following report in Deutsch's study is pertinent:

> In one of the experimental classes there was a boy who after school habitually went into a large closet and closed the door. . . . The [investigator] in the class meanwhile discovered that the boy left the light on in the closet. . . . When asked why he went into the closet and what he did there, the boy replied, after urging and quite hesitantly, that it was the only place he knew of to be alone, and that he usually read while he was there. In the course of the study, it was found that this child came from a home which consisted of a three-room apartment shared by 14 people. . . . [T]his child, obviously bright, was functioning on a relatively low scholastic level, and was quite embarrassed at acknowledging the fact that he read. Under questioning he explained that at home there were always some people sleeping, so he could never leave a light on and would be laughed at anyway if caught reading.[39]

The Quality of Schooling

Not only do life conditions in the upper strata encourage educational achievement while those in the lower discourage it, but the quality of the schooling varies greatly. The elementary and secondary facilities in the upper-strata areas are newer and in better condition, the teachers are more qualified, and there are more teaching aids and better laboratory facilities, in contrast to schools in lower-strata neighborhoods. The upper-level child whose home background has prepared him for educational success finds himself in a school which is pleasant, where college preparatory courses are emphasized, and where good grades are encouraged by teachers and fellow students. In addition a large proportion of the pupils plan to attend college, which reinforces such interest in the individual. The opposite is true for the lower-strata youngster.[40] There are exceptions of course, for every school is a social institution: there are

[39] *Ibid.*

[40] See James B. Conant, *Slums and Suburbs* (New York: McGraw-Hill Book Co., 1961). Conant describes slum schools which are attended by children from the lowest stratum.

schools in poor sections of a city where a dedicated staff is able to provide a good education in spite of the deleterious effects of the neighborhood and the children's home life. Sometimes this is due to traditions and expectations which developed before the neighborhood changed, when the students were drawn from higher-strata families. And in a few cities there are high quality schools such as the Bronx High School of Science and the High School of Music and Art in New York City which can be attended by any youngster who has the necessary ability.

In general, however, students are likely to go to neighborhood schools, the quality of which is directly related to the socioeconomic level of the parents. Undesirable conditions in the lower-strata institutions reflect problems of home and neighborhood. These conditions and problems are at their worst in schools where the students are not only lower strata but also members of a minority group. In a study of the public schools in the Los Angeles area, Robert Singleton and Paul Bullock found that in the black and Mexican-American neighborhoods there was *de facto* segregation, little motivation to learn, and an emphasis on vocational and industrial arts courses. There was also a great deal of student turnover and a high dropout rate.[41] The average dropout rate for the 36 high schools in the system was 11%; however, the average for the six minority-group schools was 23%.[42] Pupil turnover in the minority-group schools averaged 75%, ranging from 53 to 90%; the average in the other schools was 49%. A 90% turnover of students means that by the end of the school year there will be an almost completely different class than the one the teacher started out with, not a very good situation for learning.[43]

While the neighborhood as well as home conditions are important influences on educational careers, obviously the school itself is a key factor. The significance of different kinds of institutions is seen in Alan B. Wilson's study of the relationship between the nature of the school attended and pupils' post-high school plans. First he categorized eight high schools as "middle class" or as "working class." He did this on the basis of fathers' occupations; the social and economic characteristics of the neighborhood the students were drawn from; and by his impression of the school's "atmosphere" through personal observation of the pupils in the classrooms, halls, and playgrounds. Then he examined the post-high school plans of the middle- and lower-strata students in each type of institution. As expected a high proportion of the middle-strata children planned to attend college while a low proportion of the lower-strata youngsters had such aspirations. But Wilson also found that if lower-strata students attended a predominantly middle-strata school, a higher proportion than expected had plans to go to college. However, if middle-

[41] Robert Singleton and Paul Bullock, "Some Problems in Minority-Group Education in the Los Angeles Public Schools," *Journal of Negro Education*, 32 (Spring 1963), 137–145.

[42] *Ibid.*, pp. 138–139.

[43] *Ibid.*, pp. 139–140.

strata students went to a predominantly "working-class" school, the proportion planning on college was lower than expected.[44]

In the previous sections we described the lower-strata child's life experiences, which are unfavorable for intellectual development and the formation of attitudes and behaviors which are necessary for success in school. There is growing realization that for many youngsters what happens to them before they enter kindergarten or the first grade may sorely affect their educational future. With this in mind, one of the programs in the federal government's "war on poverty," seeks to remedy this situation. Called "Operation Head Start," it tries to provide pre-schoolers with the training, activities, and experiences which are useful for social and intellectual development, which they lack at home.

Understandably it is difficult to ameliorate the effects of these children's life conditions. Yet laudable as such attempts are, we may justifiably ask, just how successful are they? A study carried out for the Office of Economic Opportunity sought to assess the intellectual and personal development of Head Start children.[45] First, a sample of 104 Head Start centers throughout the nation was selected; then a sample of youngsters who had gone on to the first, second, and third grades was given a series of tests dealing with cognitive and affective development. Finally, tests were also administered to a matched sample in these grades who had not attended Head Start. The results showed hardly any difference between the two groups.[46] Similar findings are reported by Max Wolf, senior research sociologist at the Center for Urban Education in New York. He studied 551 pupils in four New York public schools, comparing 168 children who had participated in the Head Start program with 383 classmates who had not. Wolf found that the Head Start program enriched the child and left him with a "thirst" for knowledge. But the educational advantages gained by these pre-schoolers disappeared within six to eight months after they started regular schooling; Wolf attributed this to poor teaching and uninspired curricula. The Head Start youngsters end up more frustrated than those who were not in the program.[47]

Unfortunately the schools available to these youngsters are usually of poor quality: they are overcrowded, lack adequate facilities, have a sub-

[44] Alan B. Wilson, "Residential Segregation of Social Classes and Aspirations of High School Boys," *American Sociological Review,* 24 (September 1959), 836–845. See also John W. Meyer, "High School Effects on College Intentions," *American Journal of Sociology,* 76 (July 1970), 59–70.

[45] Westinghouse and Ohio University, "The Impact of Head Start: An Evaluation of the Effects of Head Start on Children's Cognitive and Affective Development," in Joe L. Frost and Glenn R. Hawkes, eds., *The Disadvantaged Child* (Boston: Houghton Mifflin Co., 1970), pp. 197–201. The investigation was conducted from June 1968 through May 1969 by Westinghouse Learning Corporation and Ohio University.

[46] *Ibid.,* pp. 198, 201.

[47] "Head Start Value Found Temporary," *New York Times* (October 23, 1966), pp. 1, 64. See also "Title 1: Charges That the Funds Are Misused," *New York Times* (November 30, 1969), p. E 11.

standard teaching staff which may be overworked and underpaid, and which may find it difficult to maintain student interest and discipline. In large cities such as New York the poor tend to be minority group members, and Wolf comments on the larger educational problem these children face:

> Head Start cannot substitute for the long overdue improvement of education in the elementary schools which have failed the Negro and Puerto Rican children. It can only prepare them to reap the benefits of better education when it is provided.[48]

Apparently then, until there is considerable improvement in the public-school system, piecemeal programs such as Head Start will have little long-range effect. Moreover, Federal funds for improving the quality of education among the poor have brought about very little change. The distribution formula of Title I of Public Law 89-10, the "Elementary and Secondary Education Act," [49] favors the wealthy school districts which have a few children at the poverty level rather than poor districts with large concentrations of such youngsters. A recent report by the U.S. Office of Education revealed that districts which spend a great deal on education (i.e., relative to school population) receive an average of $257 per poor child from Title I funds. These districts are usually in the better neighborhoods or in the suburbs. Districts with a moderate expenditure for education receive $142 per poor pupil, while the low-expenditure districts receive $149 per poor pupil. The latter are usually large urban school systems or those in depressed rural areas. In addition the low-expenditure districts are more likely to lack the kinds of programs and services for effective use of Title I funds, particularly for compensatory education.[50]

Not only is there variation in the quality of education among the strata, but there are also differences in curriculum content and emphasis. In the lower-strata schools critical ability is not likely to be stressed; neither is thinking at higher levels of abstraction. The educational regimen thus reinforces the limiting aspects of the home life; both the school and the home work to narrow rather than broaden the child's outlook. The opposite is true in the better suburban schools, not only because such training is assumed to be part of preparation for college, but also because the upper-level youngsters are viewed as future leaders. These contrasting practices affect the students' self-concept and the way they interpret situations they find themselves in: lower-strata children are likely to be less self-confident than upper-strata youngsters and more hesitant to

[48] "Head Start Value Found Temporary," loc. cit.

[49] See United States Statutes at Large, Vol. 79 (1965) (Washington, D.C.: Government Printing Office, 1966), pp. 27–36.

[50] See "Distribution of Aid for Poor Favors Schools in Rich Areas," Chicago Sun-Times (September 7, 1970), p. 58.

question fundamental aspects of the society. In addition lower-strata schools emphasize patriotism, uncritical acceptance of the economic and political system, and citizens' duties rather than rights. These school and home experiences contribute to the political inefficacy of lower-strata persons when they are older; [51] we will examine this subject at greater length in later chapters of this book.

In spite of these different emphases, children in all strata are made aware of how they are supposed to act toward persons and property. These expectations are held by teachers, parents, and policemen, among others, and sanctions exist for their enforcement. To the extent that the child has similar expectations and reflects them in what he does he is able to participate in the society with little difficulty. Also, he will receive praise and material rewards for such behavior. On the other hand if his values and actions differ greatly from the institutionalized expectations he is in for trouble: he can be disowned by his parents, expelled from school, arrested by the police.

One type of discrepancy between youth behavior and institutionalized expectations which may have serious consequences for society as well as for the individual involves youthful crime or other activities which are commonly labeled "juvenile delinquency."

Juvenile Delinquency

Differences in delinquency are immediately apparent; lower-strata youngsters have the highest rate.[52] While juvenile delinquency also occurs in the upper strata, apprehension by the police is less likely to result in arrest,[53] the instituting of judicial procedures, or in being sent to jail or training school. Instead the upper-strata delinquent is likely to be reprimanded and given a warning, released in the custody of his parents, or placed on probation if the case does reach the courts. Also, upper-strata parents can afford to make restitution for damage done by their children and this may limit or eliminate official action.[54] The seriousness of being committed to jail or other correctional institution cannot be overemphasized, for the child will be marked for life: many

[51] See Michael Mann, "The Social Cohesion of Liberal Democracy," *American Sociological Review*, 35 (June 1970), 423–439.

[52] See Jack L. Roach and Orville R. Gursslin, "The Lower Class, Status Frustration, and Social Disorganization," *Social Forces*, 43 (May 1965), 502.

[53] See Austin L. Porterfield, *Youth in Trouble* (Fort Worth, Texas: Leo Potishman Foundation, 1946); and Irving Piliavin and Scott Briar, "Police Encounters with Juveniles," *American Journal of Sociology*, 70 (September 1964), 206–214.

[54] See, e.g., Monrad G. Paulsen, "Juvenile Courts, Family Courts, and the Poor Man," in Jacobus TenBroek *et al.*, eds., *The Law of the Poor* (San Francisco: Chandler Publishing Co., 1966), p. 372.

doors will be closed to him and his opportunities for obtaining social goods through legitimate means may be severely limited.

Children and adolescents who are in jails, reformatories, training schools for juvenile delinquents, or in detention homes are much more likely to be from the lower strata. Using whites and non-whites as broadly representative of higher and lower strata, we find that the former are underrepresented in these institutions and the latter overrepresented. Of the 76,729 youths who were incarcerated during 1970, 61% were white and 39% non-white. Compare this with the total youth population of 55,541,000 in 1970, comprised of 86% whites and 14% non-whites.[55]

Lest any unintended inference be drawn regarding race and crime, Edward Green has convincingly shown in his study of a small industrial city that the larger number of black arrests compared to white is due to their lower-stratum characteristics rather than to race. His analysis of official police records showed that young persons, people in low income occupations, unemployed, or migrants from the South are prone to crime, regardless of their race. More blacks are arrested because they are more likely to have these characteristics; when these variables are controlled, however, the arrest rates of both groups tend to be similar and in a few instances the rates are higher for whites.[56] A. Didrick Castberg's study of variations in sentencing in Hawaii illustrates the association between stratum position and severity of punishment. He ranked offenders according to their social distance from judge and prosecutor, and found that the greater the social distance the more severe the sentence for similar crimes.[57]

In other nations, delinquency is also highest among young persons from lower-strata backgrounds. Their home situation does not lead them to develop propitious values and parents are unable to effectively intercede in their behalf. Their limited opportunity, which in part is an encouragement to delinquent acts, is further reduced once they have a police record.[58]

---

[55] *Statistical Abstract of the United States: 1974*, p. 163; and "Estimates of the Population of the United States, by Age, Sex, and Race: April 1, 1970 to July 1, 1973," Series P-25, No. 511 (Washington, D.C.: Government Printing Office, January 1974), p. 5. For purposes of comparison "youth population" includes those eight through 21 years of age.

[56] Edward Green, "Race, Social Status, and Criminal Arrest," *American Sociological Review*, 35 (June 1970), 476–490.

[57] A. Didrick Castberg, "The Ethnic Factor in Criminal Sentencing," *Western Political Quarterly*, 24 (September 1971), 425–437.

[58] See Walter D. Connor, "Juvenile Delinquency in the U.S.S.R.: Some Quantitative and Qualitative Indicators," *American Sociological Review*, 70 (April 1970), 283–297; Alexander Todorovich, "The Application of Ecological Models to the Study of Juvenile Delinquency in Belgrade," Department of Economic and Social Affairs, United Nations, *International Review of Criminal Policy*, No. 28 (1970), 64–71; Department of Economic and Social Affairs, United Nations, *Comparative Survey of Juvenile Delinquency, Part V: Middle East* (N.Y.: United Nations, 1965); and Lois B. DeFleur, "Ecological Variables in the Cross-Cultural Study of Delinquency," *Social Forces*, 45 (June 1967), 556–570.

The contrasts in children's lives which have been described reflect differences in institutional arrangements which work to the advantage of the upper levels and to the disadvantage of the lower. This was dealt with to some extent in the discussion of schooling and juvenile delinquency, but merits further comment.

Institutional Arrangements

The significance of institutional arrangements is demonstrated by neonatal, infant, and maternal mortality rates, which are strongly affected by the adequacy of medical care, as we have seen. While the lower strata are more likely to experience ill health, they are less likely to receive medical or dental care or to be covered by medical insurance.[59] As regards dental care, for example, persons in families with an income under $5,000 a year were likely to visit the dentist slightly less than once a year (.91 times annually); where the income was between $7,000 and $9,999 there were 1.4 visits per person, and for families making $15,000 and over the number of visits per person was 2.4.[60] In the United States technological advances in medicine, together with the entrepreneurial organization of medical practice have resulted in high quality, albeit expensive, care for upper- and middle-strata persons. Increasingly though, a number of lower-strata families are able to meet medical costs through private insurance programs which are often a part of the "fringe benefits" of their employment.[61] Yet there are still wide disparities between the low and high strata. Only 36.3% of persons from families making less than $3,000 a year are covered by hospital insurance. This contrasts with 78.5% of those in families whose income is between $5,000 and $6,999 and 92.3% where the family income is $10,000 or more.[62] Even where there is coverage, it is limited because of the nature of present programs. In a careful appraisal of health insurance plans in the United States Louis S. Reed and Willine Carr state:

> . . . it is clear that all existing health insurance coverages—in greater or lesser degree—fall short. Most coverages are confined to a limited range of services

[59] U.S. National Center for Health Statistics, *Medical Care, Status, and Family Income,* Public Health Service Publication No. 1000, Series 10-No. 9 (Washington, D.C.: Public Health Service, May 1964), especially pp. 5–10, 24–51.

[60] U.S. Center for National Health Statistics, "Estimated Annual Volume of Dental Visits in the United States, 1968," *Monthly Vital Statistics Report,* 18, No. 9, Supplement 2, December 18, 1969, p. 3.

[61] See Raymond Munts, *Bargaining for Health* (Madison, Wisc.: The University of Wisconsin Press, 1967) and "Trends in Voluntary Health Insurance," *Progress in Health Services* (Chicago: Health Information Foundation, The University of Chicago), 15 (January-February 1966), 1–5.

[62] U.S. National Center for Health Statistics, "Hospital and Surgical Insurance Coverage Among Persons Under 65 Years of Age in the United States, 1968," *Monthly Vital Statistics Reports,* 18, No. 11, Supplement 2, February 2, 1970, p. 2.

and often cover these only partially; benefits for various services are subject to dollar or other limitations; certain illnesses or conditions are covered only partially or may be excluded from coverage altogether. In addition, some 17 to 25% of the population under age 65 have no private health insurance.[63]

Thus adequate medical care is beyond the reach of most of the very low strata, many of whom are unemployed or work intermittently. They must rely on the charity wards of city and county hospitals, and they tend to put off seeking medical attention until illness has progressed to a serious stage.[64]

Among changes in institutional arrangements which would aid these persons, and consequently lower the death rates associated with childbirth, are greater government financial aid for the medical needs of the poor,[65] a program of national health care like that in Great Britain and many other nations,[66] more medical scholarships, and additional medical training facilities.

The way education is institutionalized adversely affects lower-strata youngsters. While the immediate problem is inadequate facilities for these children, it goes far beyond that because the members of school boards, who allocate the necessary funds, are from the higher strata. They are more sympathetic to the educational needs of these strata, and influence the selection of school personnel so that superintendents, principals, and to a lesser extent teachers, have a similar outlook. The upper-level interests and values are reflected in differential funding, among

[63] Louis S. Reed and Willine Carr, *The Benefit Structure of Private Health Insurance, 1968,* U.S. Department of Health, Education, and Welfare, Social Security Administration, Research Report No. 32 (Washington, D.C.: Government Printing Office, 1970), p. 109.

[64] In recent years there has been a considerable increase in Federal assistance through such programs as Aid to Families with Dependent Children (AFDC). Most of the programs are financed by "vendor" payments whereby the Federal government contributes funds to the states who disperse them to the needy. Except for a few basic rules conditions of eligibility for medical care are determined by the states. See "Medical Care Under Public Assistance," *Progress in Health Services* (Chicago: Health Information Foundation, The University of Chicago), 13 (January-February 1964), 1–3. In 1967 the United States Congress expanded the Comprehensive Health Planning and Services Act of 1966, providing grants to states, schools of public health, and to research and demonstration projects. On the other hand the Congress enacted, through amendments to the Social Security Act, what may only be described as punitive restrictions on welfare assistance. For example, mothers of pre-school children could be forced to take a job, and the future proportion of children under 18 years of age who could receive AFDC aid is restricted.

[65] See *Ibid.*

[66] See Richard M. Titmuss, *Essays on "The Welfare State"* (London: Unwin University Books, 1963), pp. 133–214; and United States Department of Health, Education, and Welfare, *Social Security Programs Throughout The World* (Washington, D.C.: Government Printing Office, 1964).

There appears to be a growing interest in the United States in a national program of medical care for the general population. Discussion regarding such coverage has increased in recent years and several proposals, all of which have significant sponsorship, have been put forth. See Social Security Administration, "National Health Insurance: A Comparison of Five Proposals," *Research and Statistics Note,* No. 12, 1970, July 23, 1970.

other things. In the poorer neighborhoods, inadequate physical facilities and books and supplies, plus unsympathetic, and sometime unqualified teachers limit educational opportunity; furthermore, unfavorable cultural conditions in the homes fail to compensate for the schools' shortcomings.[67] It is not surprising then that among lower-strata youths there is a high dropout rate, and that those who manage to graduate are poorly educated. As we shall show in the next chapter, inadequate education is associated with limited opportunity and unemployment, which in turn help lower the horizons and motivations of these families and their offspring.

Not only are such institutional arrangements significant for stratification, but there are also differences among the strata in social milieu which are often traceable to institutional arrangements.

Social Milieu

The social milieu, or social "climate," affects people's perspectives which in turn influences the way they act and the things they do. For example, among poor persons inadequate medical care and a high death rate help create a fatalistic outlook on life which discourages good health practices, or seeking medical attention before an illness has become serious. Also, such a perspective may encourage emphasis on the sexual aspects of life and concepts of masculinity and femininity which stress the begetting of many children. In underdeveloped countries the high birth rate of the poor may be a consequence of this; or, it may result from the belief that even a moderate-sized family requires many births because of the high death rate.

In education the expectations reflect the interests of the middle and higher strata. In the schools attended by such children, the "climate" or social milieu encourages attitudes and behaviors which contribute to their educational and occupational success. On the other hand this milieu may seem foreign to the lower-strata youngsters, they may respond inappropriately to well-meaning teachers, suffer rebuke and frustration, and be discouraged from the educational attainment they are capable of.

There are also strata differences in the social milieu regarding law enforcement, which is in large part the outcome of institutional arrangements. Lower-level persons are likely to view the police and the courts as serving the interests of the higher strata and being against their welfare because of the kinds of practices cited earlier. Such attitudes, reinforced by experiences with police who are prejudiced against lower-strata

---

[67] Martin Mayer, *The Schools* (New York: Harper & Brothers, 1961), pp. 144–145, 190. See also, "Inequities in City Schools Documented," *Chicago Daily News* (April 22, 1970), p. 50.

youths may lead some of them to identify with a delinquent subcul-ture.[68]

These are but a few of the ways that institutional arrangements and social milieu affect the incumbents of the different strata. The overall im-pact seems to be to perpetuate the status quo.

Summary

We have examined how the lives of children differ among the strata in regard to birth and survival rates, socialization, childrearing practices, time orientation and deferred gratification, ambition, cultural conditions in the home, the quality of schooling available, and juvenile delin-quency. We have also touched on institutional arrangements and social milieu. The discussion in this chapter has focused on childhood and ado-lescence; in the next chapter we will see how the young adult's life is af-fected by stratum position.

---

[68] See Albert K. Cohen, *Delinquent Boys* (Glencoe, Ill.: The Free Press, 1961); Richard A. Cloward and Lloyd E. Ohlin, *Delinquency and Opportunity* (New York: The Free Press of Glencoe, 1960), and Piliavin and Briar, "Police Encounters with Juveniles."

Chapter V.   Youth

In the preceding chapter we showed how children's life chances differed according to the stratum into which they were born. But now they are growing up and soon will begin to think about their future life, getting a job or more education, and about becoming more seriously involved with members of the opposite sex, with thoughts of, among other things, eventually marrying and settling down. At this point, is not their future in their own hands? In one sense it is, for they must make choices: humans don't automatically react to the conditions about them, but they reflect, interpret, make self-indications, and shape and give direction to their interests and behaviors. In that sense the individual is the master of his fate. But in another sense he is not; to some extent he is at the mercy of conditions over which he has little or no control. For, as we observed in the previous chapter, the lower-strata youth begins life with many disadvantages. Yet the fact that not all are high-school dropouts or delinquents, and a goodly number do go to college and subsequently enter the higher occupations underscores the importance of individual actions in the evolving of a career. Occasionally there may be fortuitous circumstances which help: the youngster may have exceptionally high intelligence, athletic ability, or special talents; or a sympathetic teacher or counselor may provide encouragement and guidance. But even for the bright person, let alone the ordinary individual, stratum position has a crucial impact, especially as regards educational success. And, increasingly, education is the key to one's occupational and income levels.

In this chapter we are primarily concerned with education and opportunity, and we will focus on amount of schooling and job and income prospects among young people from the different strata. Of course whether or not they will obtain education beyond high school has been decided much earlier: not only are there the physiological and mental deficits among lower-strata children we discussed in the previous chapter, but wittingly and unwittingly a number of critical steps have been taken. Particularly important is placement in the college preparatory or vocational tracks in junior high school, which is strongly associated with stratum position. Young people's future life chances are sorely affected by whether or not they continue their education beyond high school.

This decision is becoming increasingly important for the female as well as for the male, for there has been a steady rise in the percentage of women who work, whether single, married, widowed, or divorced. In 1947, 32% of the labor force was female; in 1975 it had reached 46%.[1] A woman without a spouse may have to work to support herself or her family; a married woman may do so to raise the family's standard of living. Or, once the children are in school, she may wish to continue or embark on a career which may have been difficult to do earlier. In any event, married women are increasingly in the labor force: in 1950 they comprised 52% of female workers, in 1960, 60%, and in 1973, 63%.[2] Whatever her reason for working, the kind of job the woman gets will largely depend on her education, as is true with the male.

Girls are much more likely than boys to complete high school; however they are less likely to enter college, or to graduate.[3] In addition, women are underemployed and underpaid, relative to males with the same amount of education, as we saw in Chapter III.

In previous years education was not as important as it is today for occupational opportunity and by that token for income, style of living, and other life conditions. Of course more doors were always open to the better educated, but the individual with very little schooling could seek out opportunities if he was sufficiently motivated. Today it is increasingly difficult for the person who has not completed high school to get any kind of decent job. For the more desirable occupations—those that pay well, offer security and prestige—a college degree is a requisite.

Let us first look at the poorly educated, the young people who drop out of high school, and see what their background and job prospects are like, compared to youths who obtain more education.

The Poorly Educated

Those youths who have failed to complete high school have effectively ruled themselves out of any chance of entering college. It is true that some might attend evening classes or junior college, or a few may finish their high-school work while in the armed forces. However, for the vast majority of dropouts there is little likelihood of completing high school and practically no possibility of college. Instead the prospects are low-paying unskilled work, a succession of jobs, intermittent employment, and early marriage and many children.

Despite the continuing emphasis on acquiring a good education, the

[1] U.S. Department of Labor, *Employment and Earnings*, 21 (April 1975), 20.

[2] U.S. Bureau of the Census, *Statistical Abstract of the United States: 1974* (95th ed.; Washington, D.C.: Government Printing Office, 1974), p. 340.

[3] U.S. Bureau of the Census, "Educational Attainment in the United States: March 1973 and 1974," Series P-20, No. 274 (Washington, D.C.: Government Printing Office, December 1974), pp. 15–16.

number of school dropouts is still considerable: in 1973, 12% of all persons between 14 and 24 years of age were neither enrolled in school nor high-school graduates.[4] The institutional arrangements of education are a major factor; some researchers such as Robert Vinter and Rosemary Sarri of the University of Michigan School of Social Work see them as the primary one. For three years Vinter and Sarri studied youngsters in Ann Arbor and in four other Michigan schools which they felt were typical of American senior high schools. Thirteen per cent of these students failed to graduate, and Vinter and Sarri emphasize that ". . . various aspects of the school system itself, rather than any qualities inherent in the students, were the chief factors causing students to leave school." They add, "all of the pupils studied were capable of completing high school and began their careers motivated to do so." The term dropout, they suggest, might often be changed to pushout.[5]

Although there are children from all strata who drop out of school, they are predominantly from the lower. Stratifying families by education we find that among the young people who are dropouts, between the ages of 14 and 24, 70% were from homes where the head had not completed high school. Where the head had a high-school diploma or had gone to college, the rates were 18 and 12%, respectively.[6] When the dropouts are stratified by race 18% are found to be black and 11% white. Furthermore, the poverty sections of large urban places contribute disproportionately: among metropolitan cities of 250,000 or more 33% of the dropouts were from poverty areas while only 12% came from non-poverty sections.[7]

While lack of education has always limited one's opportunities, the dropout problem is much more serious today. However, it should be viewed against certain long-term trends in education and the labor market.

Occupational and Educational Trends and Some of Their Consequences

The proportion of occupations which require formal education continues to grow while the proportion which calls for little schooling steadily declines. This is evident in the changing percentage of non-manual jobs,

[4] U.S. Bureau of the Census, "Social and Economic Characteristics of Students: October 1973," Series P-20, No. 272 (Washington, D.C.: Government Printing Office, November 1974), p. 16.

[5] "A Dropout Blames Schools," *New York Times* (November 24, 1966), p. 58.

[6] "Social and Economic Characteristics of Students: October 1973," p. 36.

[7] U.S. Bureau of the Census, "Characteristics of American Youth: 1972," Series P-23, No. 44 (Washington, D.C.: Government Printing Office, March 1973), p. 17.

which has been rising greatly over the years: in 1900, 18% of the work-force was in such occupations; fifty years later it was 37%, and by 1973, 46%. The biggest change has been in agriculture where the proportion of farmworkers fell from 18 to two percent. While the proportion of manual workers has gone from 45% in 1900 to 50% in 1973, unskilled work declined greatly. Whereas 13% were laborers in 1900, by 1973 the per-centage had dropped to six; during that period maids and other private household workers declined from five to two per cent. In turn, there has been an upgrading in the skilled and semi-skilled categories, the per-centages rising from 23 to 29.[8]

Paralleling these changes has been an increase in educational attain-ment: in 1940 only 14% of those 25 years of age or older had completed high school, while in 1974 the percentage was 36; by 1990 it is expected to be 40%.[9]

Youngsters who fail to complete high school are in double jeopardy: not only are there fewer positions which do not require a high-school diploma, but they must also compete for jobs with the better educated. Thus occupational choices are very limited, let alone the chances of finding a job: in 1973, among the 16- to 21-year-olds, eight per cent of the high-school graduates were unemployed in contrast to 17% of the dropouts.[10] Available work may be intermittent; as a result, the unskilled may drift from job to job. Also, long-term unemployment—that is, being out of work 15 weeks or more—is increasing among youths and hits those with insufficient education the hardest.[11] For persons with little education the prospects for long-term unemployment are particularly great if there is a business downturn or if their job is eliminated. This can be seen in Richard C. Wilcock and Walter H. Franke's analysis of the unemployment experience of workers with differing amounts of educa-tion. They studied two firms which shut down throwing practically all the employees out of work, one a manufacturing company in East Peoria, Illinois and the other a meat packing plant in Oklahoma City, Oklahoma. They write:

> The data for Oklahoma City and Peoria . . . show . . . that among the younger workers, those with at least a ninth-grade education had much less long-term unemployment than those with less schooling. For example, among workers under age 45 in Peoria, 11 per cent of those with a grade school edu-

[8] U.S. Bureau of the Census, *Historical Statistics of the United States, Colonial Times to 1957* (Washington, D.C.: Government Printing Office, 1960), p. 74; and "Money Income in 1973 of Families and Persons in the United States," Series P-60, No. 97 (Washington, D.C.: Government Printing Office, January 1975), pp. 137–138. The figures are for persons actually working, and include females as well as males.

[9] "Educational Attainment in the United States: March 1973 and 1974," p. 68; and *Sta-tistical Abstract of the United States: 1974*, p. 117.

[10] *Statistical Abstract of the United States: 1974*, p. 118.

[11] Seymour L. Wolfbein, *Employment and Unemployment in the United States* (Chicago: Science Research Associates, 1964), p. 302.

cation or less had no work *in the year* following the shut-down, compared with only 4 per cent of those with more schooling. . . . The pattern was about the same in Oklahoma City.[12]

A nationwide analysis of heads of households conducted by the University of Michigan Survey Research Center in 1961 shows very clearly the relationship between education and unemployment (see Figure V-1). Those with a grade-school education or less and those with only some high school had the most unemployment: 44 and 46% respectively. By contrast, among high-school graduates and those with some college, only

FIGURE V-1.

Unemployment Experience of Head of Household, by Amount of Education[a]

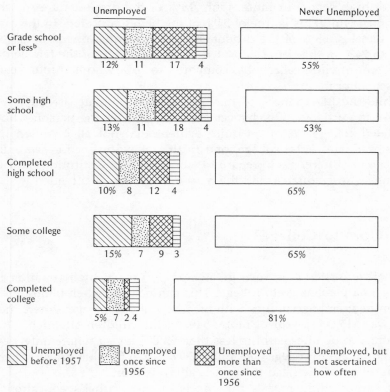

[a]Excluded are those not in the labor force, self-employed, and those whose labor force status was not known.

[b]In each category, the unemployment experience of one per cent of the cases was not known.

Source: Adapted from Eva Mueller and Jay Schmiedeskamp, *Persistent Unemployment* (Ann Arbor, Michigan: Survey Research Center, The University of Michigan, 1962), p. 16.

[12] Richard C. Wilcock and Walter H. Franke, *Unwanted Workers* (New York: The Free Press of Glencoe, 1963), p. 57. Our emphasis.

34% had been unemployed. Breadwinners who had completed college were the least likely to have been out of work: only 18%. There are also sharp differences regarding frequency. Those with some high school or less were much more prone to being unemployed more than once since 1956 in contrast to persons with more education. Furthermore only two per cent of the college graduates had been out of work more than once since 1956.

Not only is the likelihood of unemployment great for those with limited education, but, as we noted earlier, the jobs they do obtain tend to be the less desirable ones in terms of working conditions, prestige, and pay. This is further suggested by comparing the occupations of the dropouts and the graduates. Among white males, 76% of the high-school dropouts are in manual work compared to 43% of those who have four years of high school or more. Only 16% of the dropouts are in white-collar jobs, while this is true of 54% of the better educated. In the case of white females, 68% of the dropouts were in manual occupations, compared to 24% of the better-educated. Also, only 30% of the female dropouts were in white-collar jobs, compared to 76% who had four years of high school or more.[13]

While the life chances of the high-school graduate are superior to those of the dropout, life chances are better yet for the person who has completed college. Yet it is quite evident that not all qualified high-school graduates enter college, and in the following section we will examine strata differences in regard to who enrolls in institutions of higher learning, who graduates, and the nature of the school attended.

Who Goes to College?

By whatever criteria, a much greater proportion of higher- rather than lower-strata persons go to college. This can be seen when family income is examined: among families with members of college age, where the income was $15,000 a year or more, 54% of the children attended. This is in contrast to families earning less than $3,000 a year where only 13% of the children are in college (see Table V-1). When families are stratified by the education of the head the same pattern is found.[14]

An earlier study reveals the effects of both father's education and family income on the children's chances of going to college. It is not surprising, as Table V-2 shows, that such a small percentage attends

---

[13] *Statistical Abstract of the United States: 1974*, p. 118. Seven per cent of non-white male dropouts were in the non-manual category vs. 40% of those with four years of high school or more. For non-white females, only 13% of the dropouts were in white-collar work compared to 61% of the better-educated.

[14] "Social and Economic Characteristics of Students: October 1973," p. 36.

TABLE V-1. Families with Members 18-24 Years Old, by Full-Time College Attendance and Family Income, 1973

Family Income	Number of Families with 18–24 Year Olds	Percentage of Members Attending College
$15,000 and over	2,894,000	53.7%
$10,000–14,999	2,509,000	36.3
$7,500–9,999	945,000	28.9
$5,000–7,499	1,060,000	23.7
$3,000–4,999	832,000	18.0
Under $3,000	661,000	12.7
Total	8,901,000	36.7%

Source: U.S. Bureau of the Census, "Social and Economic Characteristics of Students: October 1973," Series P-20, No. 272 (Washington, D.C.: Government Printing Office, November 1974), pp. 43-44.

where the fathers have little education and low income. Neither is it surprising that a large proportion of the children of well-educated and high-income fathers goes to college. What is interesting about Table V-2 is that it shows how high income can somewhat overcome lack of education, but also that low income, even with considerable schooling, hurts the child's chances of going to college.

The importance of family income is easily understood because of the costliness of higher education, even in the public institutions which are supposed to be low-cost. In 1975 average tuition, fees, and room and board for students enrolled in public universities was $1,868 for the academic year. Thus the total for four years would come to $7,472. The yearly average for private institutions is $4,032 or $16,128 for four years.

The cost at a prestigious school such as Princeton is $5,400 a year,

TABLE V-2. College Experience of Persons 16-24, by Father's Education and Family Income

Father's Education	Family Income*	Percentage of Youths Who have Attended College
Attended college	Less than $5,000	52.3%
	$10,000 or more	88.6
Graduated from high school	Less than $5,000	41.5
	$10,000 or more	50.0
Did not graduate from high school	Less than $5,000	12.6
	$10,000 or more	40.8

*Only the top and bottom categories are included in order to simplify the table; all the categories in between were in the expected direction.
Source: U.S. Bureau of the Census, "School Enrollment of Young Adults and their Fathers: October 1960," Series P-20, No. 110 (Washington, D.C.: Government Printing Office, July 24, 1961), p. 15.

including $3,300 for tuition; the four-year total would be $21,600.[15] These amounts do not include clothing, transportation, or similar expenses; neither do they take into account the income which is lost while the young person is in school. Although it is true that most college graduates more than recoup the lost income through higher lifetime earnings, the short-run effects are more critical for the lower-strata family.

The expenses of higher education may be reduced by living at home, provided a college or university is within commuting distance; one may work part-time or during the summer, and the exceptionally able student may receive financial help through scholarships. Nevertheless, upper-strata children are overrepresented and lower-strata children under-represented in institutions of higher learning.[16]

It is not only the limited financial resources that restrict the number of lower-strata children who go to college, but also the associated unfavor-able conditions which affect the child throughout the school career. As we pointed out earlier, low-income families usually live in neigh-borhoods with inferior schools and the cultural conditions at home do not encourage interest in learning. Also, probably few of the child's peers intend to seek higher education. Dael Wolfle neatly summarizes some of the contrasts between higher- and lower-strata families:

> The occupation of a high school student's father is a good predictor of whether or not he will enter college. The socioeconomic factors which are in-dicated by the father's occupation begin early to influence a child's educa-tional progress and expectations. In some homes a child finds books, parents who value education, and many other things which point him toward college. He is expected and encouraged to do satisfactory school work and when the time for college arrives financial plans have frequently already been made. He "just naturally" goes to college.
>
> At the other extreme a child grows up in an atmosphere which is little congenial to school matters and educational ambitions. Since he normally plays with children from similar homes, such academic ambitions as he may entertain receive less support than they would if his playmates were from families which expected their children to go to college. These environmental factors work together to discourage educational ambition. As the child gets old enough to consider leaving school, financial questions arise. Not only is there less money to pay for further education, there is also frequently positive pressure to get to work in order to add to the family income.[17]

[15] *Statistical Abstract of the United States: 1974*, p. 136. The average cost of going to a public four-year college is $1,600 a year, and for a public two-year institution of higher learning it is $1,310 a year. See also Gene I. Maeroff, "Tradition No Longer Walks Prince-ton's Hallowed Halls," *New York Times* (September 15, 1973), p. 44.

[16] See, e.g., W. Lloyd Warner, Robert J. Havighurst, and Martin B. Loeb, *Who Shall be Educated?* (New York: Harper & Bros., 1944); Dael Wolfle, *America's Resources of Specialized Talent* (New York: Harper & Bros. 1954); and Raymond A. Mulligan, "Socio-Economic Background and College Enrollment," *American Sociological Review*, 16 (April 1951), 188–196. See also Table V-1, above.

[17] Wolfle, *op. cit.*, pp. 158–159.

It is not too surprising that usually the lower the stratum the poorer the student's grades and the worse he does on intelligence and other standardized tests. It is obvious that a bad scholastic record may keep any child from obtaining higher education. Yet what role do grades and intelligence play in college entrance and success among youngsters from different strata?

How Ability Affects College Entrance and Graduation

A better than ordinary level of intelligence is required for college work and it is to be expected that most entrants will be above average. This is shown by Wolfle's research. He converted intelligence test scores of high-school and college students to the Army General Classification Test (AGCT), which is centered about the average person's score of 100. Wolfle found that those who enter high school have 105 and graduates 110; for people who get into college it is 115, and for graduates 121.[18]

It might seem that lesser intelligence explains the underrepresentation of lower-strata youngsters in college, for it has been recognized for a long time that the higher the stratum the higher the intelligence test scores.[19] Now does this mean that the lower strata are inherently less intelligent than the higher, that they have less "native" ability? This question cannot be answered satisfactorily for several reasons: most pencil and paper tests of intelligence rely on verbal facility and thus favor children from the more affluent schools. Youngsters from homes in which there is considerable reading matter and where parents are interested in the child's education and can help with the schoolwork are also favored. In addition, as Kenneth W. Eells and his associates have pointed out, the tests themselves are biased in favor of middle- and upper-strata persons.[20]

Yet while intelligence scores are highly correlated with stratum posi-

[18] *Ibid.*, p. 146.

[19] See Lewis M. Terman and Maud A. Merrill, *Measuring Intelligence* (New York: Houghton Mifflin Co., 1937), p. 48. See also John B. Miner, *Intelligence in the United States* (New York: Springer Publishing Co., 1957), pp. 64–84; Scottish Council for Research in Education, *Social Implications of the 1947 Scottish Mental Health Survey* (London: University of London Press, 1953), pp. 43–46, 112, 159–160; and Jean Floud and A. H. Halsey, "Intelligence Tests, Social Class, and Selection for Secondary Schools," *British Journal of Sociology*, 8 (March 1957), 36.

[20] Kenneth W. Eells *et al.*, *Intelligence and Cultural Differences* (Chicago: University of Chicago Press, 1951).

Parental interest may help in other ways. Several experienced teachers and counselors have told us that they have observed that if an upper-strata child gets a low score on an IQ or similar test it is not unusual for the parents to complain to the school and to succeed in having the child re-take it. By contrast the lower-strata parents will not raise a fuss; more likely they won't know how their child did, or the importance of the tests.

tion, there is overlapping. That is, many lower-strata individuals have better scores than the lowest-scoring persons from the upper strata. Does this mean then that the above average lower-strata child will likely go to college while the below average upper-strata youth will not? Not quite. When lower- and upper-strata youngsters at the same intelligence levels are compared, a much higher proportion of the upper-strata youths enter college. In other words limited intelligence is less of a disadvantage to the higher- than to the lower-stratum child. This is seen in a study of college students from the Cleveland area. Among youngsters with IQ's of 115 or more who were from the upper and upper-middle strata, 89% went to college. On the other hand, among such top scorers from the lower strata only 47% entered. The same pattern holds for youths with IQ's of 100 or less: among those from the upper and upper-middle strata 83% entered college, but among those from the lower strata only 37% went.[21]

A number of researchers, while they agree that the selection process works to the disadvantage of lower-strata youths, maintain that stratification is of minor importance among those who are in college. They hold that, once admitted, intelligence and ability become primary, and as evidence they cite data which show that apparently there is little difference in the proportion of youngsters from the various strata who successfully complete their education. Such data are presented in Table V-3, which relates the experiences of more than 6,000 entrants to 41 institutions of higher learning. The percentage from different occupational backgrounds who completed college is examined according to intelligence test percentile and percentile in high-school graduating class. In the first column are the most intelligent and the most able students (those who are in the 95th percentile on each measure); in the second column are the "worst" (those in the fifth percentile). It can be seen that the probability of gradu-

TABLE V-3. Percentage of the "Best" and the "Worst" College Entrants Who Graduated from College by Father's Occupation

Father's Occupation	*"Best" College Entrants* (95th Percentile in High-School Graduating Class and in Intelligence)	*"Worst" College Entrants* (5th Percentile in High-School Graduating Class and in Intelligence)
Professional	86%	29%
Managerial	88	21
Service	97	9
Farm or farm labor	76	19
Manual labor	83	27

Source: Adapted from Dael Wolfle, "Educational Opportunity, Measured Intelligence, and Social Background," in A. H. Halsey, Jean Floud, and C. Arnold Anderson, eds., *Education, Economy, and Society* (New York: The Free Press, 1961), pp. 237-239.

[21] Reuel C. White, *Those Will Go to College* (Cleveland,: Western Reserve University Press, 1952), p. 45.

ation for a higher-strata college student, as indicated by father's occupation, is only a little greater than for a lower-strata student: 86% of the "best" students from professional homes graduated, but so did 83% of the "best" students from manual labor backgrounds. The data on the "best" college entrants from managerial, service, and farm families also do not show a clear-cut relationship between stratum position and likelihood of graduation. Table V-3 also reveals that stratum position hardly affects the graduation chances of the "worst" students: while only 29% of those from professional homes graduate, the percentage from manual-labor families is 27. There also does not seem to be a clear-cut relationship between intelligence and ability and farm background.

The general conclusion from these findings and from most earlier studies of stratification and higher education is that while very few lower-strata youngsters attend college, the ones who do have about as good a chance of graduating as those from the higher strata. The explanation is that once the student enters college, non-intellective factors are replaced by intellective ones.[22]

However the similar percentage of graduates from professional and from manual-labor backgrounds in Table V-3 may be due to the manual-labor students being a very select group; many have probably had to overcome the handicaps of poor primary and secondary schooling and unfavorable home and neighborhood conditions. This interpretation is suggested when the low intelligence–high ability graduates are compared with the high intelligence–low ability ones (Table V-4). Among the students with low intelligence and high ability, more from manual labor

TABLE V-4. Percentage of College Entrants Who Graduated According to Intelligence and Ability and Father's Occupation

Father's Occupation	Low Intelligence– High Ability College Entrants[a]	High Intelligence– Low Ability College Entrants[b]
Professional	54%	61%
Managerial	44	65
Service	50	56
Farm or farm labor	29	66
Manual labor	61	48

[a]College entrants who are in the 5th intelligence percentile but who were in the 95th percentile in their high-school graduating class.
[b]College entrants who are in the 95th intelligence percentile but who were in the 5th percentile in their high-school graduating class.
Source: Adapted from Dael Wolfle, "Educational Opportunity, Measured Intelligence, and Social Background," in A. H. Halsey, Jean Floud, and C. Arnold Anderson, eds., *Education, Economy, and Society* (New York: The Free Press, 1961), pp. 237-239.

[22] This is pointed out by Bruce K. Eckland, "Social Class and College Graduation: Some Misconceptions Corrected," *American Journal of Sociology*, 60 (July 1964), 36–37, whose research questions these assertions.

rather than from professional homes were likely to graduate. In the case of high intelligence and low ability, however, the graduates were more likely to be from a professional rather than manual-labor background.

In the absence of additional data we can only speculate: it is possible that the low intelligence–high ability manual labor students are much brighter than their IQ scores reveal because of test bias and perhaps some lack of motivation in taking them. In the case of the low intelligence–high ability children from professional homes, the low scores probably do indicate lesser intelligence. Their being in the 95th percentile in their high-school graduating class may reflect optimum home and school conditions which helped them achieve in spite of lesser intelligence.

The very poor grades of the high intelligence–low ability manual-labor students may reflect the influence of unfavorable home and school conditions, which high intelligence is unable to overcome. As for the relatively large proportion of professional children in the high intelligence–low ability category, they may not have been motivated to do as well in high school as they could have.

The importance of stratification for college is further attested to by Bruce K. Eckland's research. Eckland gathered information on the academic and social careers of 1,180 males who had enrolled in a midwestern state university in September, 1952 as full-time students. Using a five-level socioeconomic index based on father's occupation when the student was growing up, he found that 87% of the highest-strata students graduated while only 13% did not make it. But of the men from the lowest strata only 55% graduated while 45% failed to complete their college work. Eckland was also interested in how long it took to obtain a bachelor's degree since he observed that while many youths dropped out of school some returned while others stayed out permanently. He found that the students who graduated within four years were likely to be from higher-strata homes while those who took longer were from lower-strata backgrounds. Also, of the graduates from the highest strata less than a fourth had temporarily interrupted their education; by contrast almost a third from the lowest strata had previously dropped out of college.[23]

Eckland also investigated intelligence and found that, although it is an important determinant for success at each stage of the college career, strata position remains a significant influence.[24] William H. Sewell and Vimal P. Shah's study of a randomly selected cohort of Wisconsin high-school seniors covering a seven-year period supports Eckland's research. In addition it presents a more carefully controlled analysis of the relative

[23] Eckland, "Social Class and College Graduation," pp. 36–50.

[24] Eckland, "Academic Ability, Higher Education, and Occupational Mobility," *American Sociological Review*, 30 (October 1965), 735–746. See also Eldon L. Wegner and William H. Sewell, "Selection and Context as Factors Affecting the Probability of Graduation from College," *American Journal of Sociology*, 75, (January 1970), 665–679.

effects of intelligence and stratum position on college career.[25] Both were found to have direct effects on college plans, attendance, and graduation. When intelligence is controlled, socioeconomic level is significant; when socioeconomic status is controlled, intelligence is significant. For males, however the overall influence of intelligence is greater than that of socio-economic level, while the opposite holds for females. Nevertheless, the authors point out, socioeconomic status remains an important factor in the educational careers of their youth sample.[26]

It is quite clear that strata differences are significantly associated with the likelihood of entering college and graduating, and with the length of time it takes to obtain the degree. In addition, strata differences are also associated with the type of college attended.

Who Goes to What College?

Robert J. Havighurst and Bernice L. Neugarten, using a variety of sources, found that the Ivy League schools draw students overwhelmingly from the upper and upper-middle strata, those who attend the junior colleges are predominantly from the lower, while the small liberal arts colleges, the cosmopolitan universities, and the state universities fall in between in student body composition (Fig. V-2). In turn, the type of institution attended affects the person's occupational career and earnings, as shown by a U.S. Census Bureau study.[27] Colleges were ranked according to their quality on the basis of freshmen reading, comprehension, abstract reasoning, and mathematic aptitude scores. Then the background of the graduates was examined, using father's occupation as a measure of stratification. It can be seen in Table V-5 that the higher-strata student is much more likely to graduate from a high-ranked college, while the lower-strata youngster could expect to receive his degree from a low-ranked institution. In the low-ranked colleges, 42% of the graduates were from white-collar homes, while 32% came from blue-collar backgrounds. But in the high-ranked institutions, 61% had fathers who were white-collar workers, while 22% had blue-collar fathers.[28]

Granted then that there is a strong association between stratum posi-

---

[25] Sewell and Vimal P. Shah, "Socioeconomic Status, Intelligence, and the Attainment of Higher Education," *Sociology of Education*, 40 (Winter 1967), 1–23.

[26] *Ibid.*, pp. 20, 22–23. See also Wegner and Sewell, *op. cit.*

[27] U.S. Bureau of the Census, "Characteristics of Men with College Degrees: 1967," Series P-20, No. 201 (Washington, D.C.: Government Printing Office, May 21, 1970).

[28] Among graduates whose fathers were professionals, 14% received their degrees from a low-ranked college, while 23% graduated from a high-ranked institution. These figures are subsumed under white collar in Table V-5. For a more detailed breakdown see "Characteristics of Men with College Degrees: 1967," p. 22.

FIGURE V-2.
Strata Background of Students in Various Types of
Institutions of Higher Learning

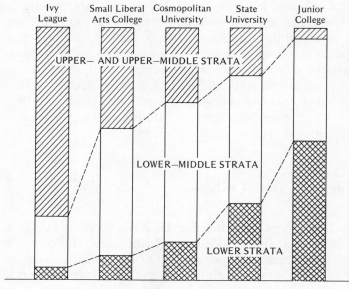

(Each bar represents 100 per cent)

Source: Adapted from Robert J. Havighurst and Bernice L. Neugarten, *Society and Education*
(3rd ed.; Boston: Allyn and Bacon, Inc., 1969), p. 107.

TABLE V-5. Father's Occupation and Rank of College Son Graduated from, 1967 (in percentages)

Father's Occupation	Rank of College Son Graduated From*		
	Low (n=1,269)	*Medium (N=3,222)*	*High (N=1,278)*
White collar	42.2%	47.9%	60.7%
Blue collar (including farm laborers)	32.4	29.7	21.8
Farm or farm manager	14.3	9.7	6.7
Other, not specified, or not reported	11.1	12.0	10.9
Total	100.0%	99.3%	100.1%

*Colleges were ranked on the basis of entering freshmen's reading comprehension, abstract reasoning, and mathematics aptitude scores.
Source: Adapted from U.S. Bureau of the Census, "Characteristics of Men with College Degrees: 1967, "Series P-20, No. 201 (Washington, D.C.: Government Printing Office, May 21, 1970), p. 22.

tion and the type of college attended, how are the graduate's life chances affected?

How Type of College Attended Affects Income and Occupation

Looking first at income, we find a strong relationship between the college's ranking and the graduate's earnings (Table V-6).

Of graduates who make less than $10,000 a year 70% are from low-ranked institutions and 41% are from high-ranked schools. Among the graduates in the $10,000–19,999 bracket, only 26% are from the low-ranked colleges while 43% are from the high-ranked institutions. As for persons earning $20,000 or over, only four per cent come from low-ranked colleges while 16% received their degrees from high-ranked schools. Of those in the topmost income bracket—$35,000 and over—there are more than ten times as many from high-ranked as from low-ranked colleges.

These findings buttress the results of an earlier study by Patricia Slater West which detailed the consequences of attending a wealthy and prestigious college. She ranked the institutions according to the size of the endowment per student, and, using data collected by *Time* in 1947, found that the wealthier the college attended the more money the student earned after graduation. Alumni from the "big three" Ivy League schools, Harvard, Princeton, and Yale made the most money, followed by those who went to other Ivy League institutions such as Columbia. After them, in descending order, were graduates of technical schools such as California Institute of Technology, eastern colleges such as Amherst, and Big Ten Midwestern schools such as Northwestern and the University of Michigan. After them, also in descending order, came the alumni of lower-ranked Midwest, New England, Middle-Atlantic, and other institutions. The differences held even when the graduates were compared job for job, grade level for grade level, major for major, and by size of city in which they settled.[29]

It might be argued that the student whose parents can afford to send him to one of the better schools would likely earn a higher income anyway because of family or other contacts, and to a large extent this is probably true. But the experience of the lower-strata youth who graduates from a wealthy and prestigeful college underscores the importance of the type of school attended: he is likely to earn more money than the

[29] Patricia Slater West, "Social Mobility Among College Graduates," in Reinhard Bendix and Seymour M. Lipset, eds., *Class, Status, and Power* (Glencoe, Ill.: The Free Press, 1953), pp. 469–477.

TABLE V-6. Earnings of Male College Graduates by Rank of College Attended, 1966 (in percentages)

Rank of College*	Number of Graduates	Yearly Earnings of Male College Graduates							
		Under $5,000	$5,000 to 6,999	$7,000 to 9,999	$10,000 to 14,999	$15,000 to 19,999	$20,000 to 34,999	$35,000 and over	Total
High	1,181,000	13.7	7.3	19.7	27.8	15.5	12.6	3.5	100.1
Medium	3,091,000	13.5	13.8	24.8	28.8	9.9	7.8	1.4	100.0
Low	1,227,000	20.0	21.8	28.0	22.3	3.9	3.8	0.3	100.1

*Colleges were ranked on the basis of entering freshmen's reading comprehension, abstract reasoning, and mathematics aptitude scores.
Source: Adapted from U.S. Bureau of the Census, "Characteristics of Men with College Degrees: 1967," Series P-20, No. 201, (Washington, D.C.: Government Printing Office, May 21, 1970), p. 23. The figures for those not reporting income and for whom rank of college attended was not available are not included.

graduate of a less wealthy and less prestigeful institution. But within each type of school, the student from a poor home will not earn as much as the graduate whose parents are better off. Using as a measure of family affluence whether the graduates had worked while in college or had been supported by their parents, West compared the incomes of the self-help and the supported students. She found that at successive stages in their careers the supported students have higher incomes: at age 30 they are already ahead of the self-help students; between 30 and 39 the differences increase, and by age 40 and over they are even greater.[30]

If young people's educational income prospects are affected by the stratum they are born into, as these studies indicate, what may we expect in the future?

Trends in College Attendance

The first thing to consider is the growing proportion of college-educated people: in 1940, ten per cent of persons 25 years of age or older had one or more years of college; by 1974, this had risen to 25%.[31] The proportion of high-school seniors who plan to go to college continues to be high. Forty-five per cent of the 3.3 million enrolled as seniors in October, 1972, said they definitely planned to attend college after graduation. Another 27% indicated that they "may" attend.[32] This interest is reflected in the growing proportion that enters college. In 1940, among persons 20 to 21 years of age who had finished high school, 30% of men and 24% of women had also completed one year of college or more. By 1974 the percentage had risen to 50 and 46, respectively.[33]

What this means is that people without a college diploma are at a disadvantage in the competition for the more desirable jobs, and their situation will worsen in the future. In addition, educational requirements for almost all occupations are constantly being raised,[34] and if present trends continue the college degree will increasingly be necessary for many jobs which now call for only a high-school diploma. This growth in degree certification introduces ascriptive criteria for it reduces

---

[30] *Ibid.*, pp. 474–477.

[31] "Educational Attainment in the United States: March 1973 and 1974," p. 68.

[32] U.S. Bureau of the Census, "College Plans of High School Seniors: October 1972," Series P-20, No. 252 (Washington, D.C.: Government Printing Office, August 1973), pp. 1, 5. The vast majority actually do attend: in 1959 and 1965 around 70% of those who planned on college were enrolled a year later, and for the 1965 cohort 77% were attending college six years after completing high school.

[33] "Educational Attainment in the United States: March 1973 and 1974," p. 5.

[34] See Randall Collins, "Functional and Conflict Theories of Educational Stratification," *American Sociological Review*, 36 (December 1971), 1003–1004.

the opportunity for advancement through work activity alone.[35] Ascription becomes additionally important to the extent that going to college, and the type of school attended reflect stratum position rather than ability.

Understandably, the recognition of the necessity of education for income and occupational benefits has encouraged more young people to seek further schooling. This has led to the expansion of educational facilities, which in turn encourages more young people to go to college. The number of institutions of higher learning rose from 1,708 in 1940 to 2,665 in 1973; however the greatest growth was in the public colleges, and in recent years this has included a great increase in the two-year schools. In 1940 only one out of every ten college students was in a junior or community college but by 1973 it was over two out of every ten. While the enrollment in four-year institutions grew four-fold during this period, the increase in the two-year schools was twelve-fold.[36]

The growth of the college population and the expansion of institutions of higher learning would make it seem that educational opportunity has increased. Is this the case?

RELATIVE OPPORTUNITY FOR HIGHER EDUCATION

Even though there are more college students and more schools, *relative* opportunity for the very low strata has actually decreased over time. It is true that the proportion of lower-strata youths in college has gone up; for example, among 18- to 24-year-olds, there was a seven per cent increase of non-white collegiates between 1960 and 1970. But although the growth for whites was eight per cent, they still comprised 26% of young people in college. This compared to 18% for the non-whites.[37] The latter-day increase in college-going reflects substantial additions from the middle strata, as well as from the upper portions of the lower strata. This, plus the fact that college attendance among the top strata continues to be very high, accounts for the lesser opportunity for those at the very bottom. William G. Spady found that compared to the sons of college-educated fathers, the *relative* chances of lower strata boys going to college or graduating have diminished over time.[38] "Paradoxically," he writes,

> while completion rates have continued to rise for all men, the probabilities of going to college, given that you finished high school, and finishing college once you entered, have decreased over time for low-status sons.[39]

[35] See Barbara Jacobson and John M. Kendrick, "Education and Mobility: From Achievement to Ascription," *American Sociological Review*, 38 (August 1973), 439–460.

[36] *Statistical Abstract of the United States: 1974*, p. 133.

[37] *Ibid.*, pp. 33, 114.

[38] William G. Spady, "Educational Mobility and Access: Growth and Paradoxes," *American Journal of Sociology*, 73 (November 1967), 273–286, especially p. 285.

[39] *Ibid.*, p. 285.

He also found that the growing importance of status differences holds when age and race are taken into account.[40]

There is another way in which the large number attending college is not an indication of expanded opportunity, and this is in terms of the chances of getting into the more prestigious institutions. The expansion of educational facilities has been mainly in the public sector, and most recently in two-year institutions, as we noted above. The increase in private colleges, especially the prestigious ones, has been relatively small compared to the growing number of college aspirants. Not only is there increased competition for admission to the better private schools, but also to the high-ranked public ones.

Eckland suggests that, with the expansion of educational opportunities and the growth of mass education, stratum position may become even more important than previously in regard to the type of college attended. One result of the larger numbers of high-school graduates entering college will be greater diversity in ability among them; another will be more highly qualified applicants than the prestigious institutions can accept. Although these high-ability applicants come from all the strata, those from the upper ones predominate since high-school grades and performance on admission tests are associated with stratum position. In addition, the selective devices the prestigious colleges and universities use favor children from the more advantageous backgrounds. Consequently these schools will increasingly admit higher-strata students.[41]

While this holds particularly for the better private institutions, the prestigious state universities are also facing a similar problem. Because of institutional arrangements private schools have much more autonomy than public ones, and if they favor the more affluent applicants this is generally considered to be within their rights. In the case of public colleges and universities it is another matter, however, and democratic ideology calls for minimizing strata-based advantages. Yet a recent attempt to make for greater equality in admissions to a large midwestern university was abandoned when it appeared that students of somewhat lower status background might benefit.

AN UNSUCCESSFUL ATTEMPT TO INCREASE EDUCATIONAL OPPORTUNITY

When there are more qualified applicants than places the simplest and most widespread practice in public institutions is to choose those with the highest test scores and the best secondary school grades. However, among the very highly qualified applicants minor variations are

[40] *Ibid.*

[41] Eckland, "Social Class and College Graduation," pp. 36–50; and Robert J. Havighurst and Bernice L. Neugarten, *Society and Education* (3rd ed.; Boston: Allyn and Bacon, 1969), pp. 113–115.

likely to reflect strata rather than ability differences. The more affluent suburban schools usually have better instructors, teaching materials, and counselling services, as well as a "climate" and peers which encourage college aspirations and academic achievement.[42] This was recognized by the admissions officers of the University of Illinois who recently found themselves with many more very-well-qualified applicants for the College of Liberal Arts and Sciences than there were places. Their experience also told them that the schools in the better-off neighborhoods were usually more liberal with grades and letters of recommendation, in order to enhance the chances of their graduates getting into a good college or university. Given these circumstances the University's solution seems eminently fair: use random selection to determine which of the very highly qualified students would be admitted.

But there was a public outcry from disappointed parents and students, members of the Board of Trustees, the Governor of the State, and even from the noted writer on education, Dael Wolfle. They all charged the University with substituting a "lottery" for merit. Its defense that variations in the qualifications were not significant, that the tests are not sufficiently refined, and that selecting only those with top grades and test scores would make for an educationally elitist institution were to no avail. The University caved in and the random selection policy was rescinded.[43]

Public as well as private institutions of higher learning are stratified in terms of prestige and quality; similarly, the rank of the public college attended affects the student's income and occupational opportunities. What, then, are the likely trends as regards stratification among both public as well as private institutions?

Trends in Higher Education Stratification

We may expect increasing stratification. The highest scoring entrants will be found in the most prestigious private schools while the students just below them will end up in the better public universities. High-school graduates with poorer grades and test scores will seek out the second

[42] See Alan B. Wilson, "Residential Segregation of Social Classes and Aspirations of High School Boys," *American Sociological Review*, 24 (December 1959), 836–845; and Irving Krauss, "Sources of Educational Aspirations Among Working-Class Youth," 29 (December 1964), 867–879.

[43] "Public Reaction May Force Illinois to Revise 'Lottery' Admissions," *The DeKalb* (Illinois) *Chronicle* (January 8, 1970), p. 3 and "UI Chancellor Explains" (December 10, 1969), p. 14; Dael Wolfle, "Chance or Human Judgment?" *Science* 172 (February 1970), 1201; and " 'Lottery' Admission U of I Policy Stopped," *The Northern* (Illinois University) *Star* (April 16, 1970), p. 8. Under the random selection plan students who were not chosen for the College of Liberal Arts and Sciences would be able to enter another college of the University.

rank state universities; those with still lower grades and test scores will opt for the state colleges, while the group with the poorest grades and test scores will enter the junior colleges.[44] There is bound to be overlapping because of personal considerations and factors such as geographical access and scholarship programs; overall, however, the likelihood is increasing that the affluent will matriculate in the more prestigious institutions while the lower strata students will end up in the less prestigious ones. In addition, since race and stratum position are associated, institutions of higher learning will increasingly become color segregated, which is already happening.[45]

We noted earlier that stratum position is associated with the length of time it takes to get the college degree and the chances of success. We may expect that with the growing diversity of the college population there will be an increase in the proportion which fails to graduate. More and more of these youngsters will be from lower-strata homes, and in many ways they will be similar to the present-day high school dropout.[46] Some state and local colleges, particularly the junior colleges, have an "open door" policy on admissions and as is to be expected also have a high attrition rate. The City University of New York has instituted open admissions, and while the number of lower-strata entrants has gone up so has the dropout rate.[47] While such an admissions policy encourages educational aspirations it also increases the possibility of failure, and some institutions try to minimize the psychic shock to the low-ability student who is unable to obtain a bachelor's degree. Burton Clark calls this the "cooling-out" function in higher education whereby through special counseling and other means the failure is encouraged to seek alternative avenues to status, to accept his limited ability, and to lower his level of ambition.[48]

While we have concentrated on educational opportunity, there are other aspects of young people's lives where stratification plays an important part. One of them is military service, to which we next turn.

[44] See Eckland, "Social Class and College Graduation."

[45] See U.S. Bureau of the Census, "Undergraduate Enrollment in 2-Year and 4-Year Colleges: October 1972," Series P-20, No. 257 (Washington, D.C.: Government Printing Office, November 1973), pp. 2, 5; and Fred E. Crossland, *Minority Access to College* (New York: Schocken Books, 1971), pp. 32–35.

[46] See Eckland, "Social Class and College Graduation," pp. 48–50.

[47] M. A. Farber, " 'Open Admissions' Begins at City University Today," *New York Times* (September 14, 1970), pp. 1 ff. and Farber, "Open-Entry Dropouts Twice Others at City U.," (November 18, 1971), p. 61.

[48] Burton R. Clark, "The 'Cooling-Out' Function in Higher Education," *American Journal of Sociology*, 65 (May 1960), 569–576.

Stratification and Military Service

James W. Davis, Jr. and Kenneth Dolbeare, in their careful analysis of the
Selective Service system, found that young men from the lower strata are
much more likely to be drafted than those from the upper. Using education as a measure of stratification they found that college men are much
less likely to go into military service than those with less schooling; for
example only 40% of all college graduates who were 26 years of age in
1964 had been in the service in contrast to 53% of men with less education. In one calendar year (1965–1966) the figures were 15% for college
graduates, 85% for the others. Of the college graduates who joined the
armed forces only two per cent were drafted; the rest joined the Reserves
or the National Guard. Official policy on deferments and the way it is
put into effect by local draft boards are responsible for such inequities.
"This pattern of deferment," Davis and Dolbeare conclude,

> confers special advantages upon those who are economically capable of quali-
> fying. Summarized and reduced to its simplest terms, it means that the
> chances of military service for a qualified low-income registrant have been 50
> per cent higher than for a similarly qualified higher income registrant. When
> the higher income man does enter the service, it is most likely to be as a
> Reservist or National Guardsman, with consequently reduced prospect of ac-
> tive duty. The liberal granting of deferments in the early 1960's had the effect
> of heightening the economic differentiation inherent in the deferment poli-
> cies themselves, and gave substantial grounds for the allegation that the
> Army—and particularly the combat forces within it—was chiefly composed of
> Negroes and low-income whites.[49]

Who shall be inducted and who shall be deferred are determined first
by Selective Service policy and second by the local draft board which is
supposed to be made up of one's neighbors. However, because of the
great variability in policy interpretations from higher levels and the wide
latitude local boards have their decisions are critical.[50] The composition
of these boards is then very important and Davis and Dolbeare found
that they are white-collar dominated, particularly by those in the professional and in the managerial, official, and proprietor categories.[51]

This overrepresentation is readily apparent in Table V-7: there are almost twice the proportion of professionals as in the United States; almost
three times as many managers, officials, and proprietors; just a shade

[49] James W. Davis, Jr., and Kenneth Dolbeare, *Little Groups of Neighbors* (Chicago: Markham Publishing Co., 1968), pp. 15–16, 125–158. The quotation is from p. 16.

[50] *Ibid.*, p. 17.

[51] *Ibid.*, pp. 57–58. Only males serve on the boards and the average board includes three
veterans, one of who was in World War I; one member under 50 years of age, and one over
70.

TABLE V-7. Occupations of Members of Local Selective Service Boards Compared with Occupations of Employed Males in the United States (in percentages)

Occupation	Local Board Members[a] (14,793)	Employed Males in the U.S.[b]
Professionals	22%	12%
Managers, officials, and proprietors	36	13
Clerical and sales workers	15	13
Blue collar workers	10	55
Farmers	17	7
Total	100%	100%

[a]These individuals constitute 94 per cent of the board members serving as of October, 1966.
[b]In 1965.
Source: Adapted from James W. Davis, Jr., and Kenneth M. Dolbeare, *Little Groups of Neighbors* (Chicago: Markham Publishing Co., 1968), p. 59; and U.S. Bureau of the Census, *Statistical Abstract of the United States: 1969* (90th ed.; Washington, D.C.: Government Printing Office, 1969), p. 222. Used by permission of the authors.

more clerical and sales workers, and more than twice the proportion of farmers. Only ten per cent of the board members are in blue-collar occupations in contrast to 55% in the general population.

There is no substantiated evidence that the decisions of local boards are biased in favor of the upper strata (that is, other than through carrying out higher level policy). Nevertheless it would be surprising indeed if their decisions did not reflect the perspectives of the more substantial members of the community.

Racially, Davis and Dolbeare found that except in Delaware blacks were drastically underrepresented.[52] In recent years, however, the proportion of black draft board members has increased greatly—seven per cent in 1966 to 13% in 1970. Yet those who avoided military service continued to be whites rather than blacks, and higher- rather than lower-strata youths; student deferment, conscientious objection, and draft-counseling worked to the advantage of the whites, particularly the more affluent. In addition, a much higher proportion of them were deferred on medical grounds.[53]

Not only are lower-strata youths, especially blacks, more likely to be drafted; the chances are greater that they will end up in the front lines,

[52] *Ibid.*

[53] Paul T. Murray, "Local Draft Board Composition and Institutional Racism," *Social Problems*, 19 (Summer 1971), 129–137. One reason that blacks and poor whites are less likely to receive medical deferments is because of their greater lack of medical care. Consequently they are not as aware of ailments, neither do they have medical records that would help sustain a claim of unfitness.

and that they will be wounded or killed. Having less education and fewer skills they are prone to be enlisted men rather than officers and in combat rather than in support operations behind the lines. Consequently, it is not surprising that while blacks made up 10.7% of the troops in Viet Nam in 1968 their combat deaths were 12.9%.[54]

A study of Detroit men who were killed, captured, or missing in action during the Korean War showed that these casualties were shared unequally among the strata. Albert J. Mayer and Thomas F. Hoult determined the economic level of the homes these men came from and found that without exception the lower the income area the higher the casualty rate. They also discovered marked differences by race: overall, the rate for non-whites was almost double that for whites.[55]

Summary

This chapter showed the relevance of stratification in the lives of young people. It focused on education, exploring several facets which affect their well-being in terms of occupation, employment, and income opportunity. We observed how life conditions in the higher strata help prepare youngsters for educational success, while those in the lower strata make educational achievement less likely. We also noted strata differences in the quality of secondary schooling available, in the chances of obtaining higher education, going to a particular type of college, and graduating. We also observed that, in spite of the growing proportion of high-school graduates in higher education, the relative chances of a poor youth entering college have actually decreased. This chapter also touched on another aspect of strata differences, which for some is a matter of life or death: the disadvantages of the lower strata in regard to military service.

In the next chapter we conclude our examination of how people's lives differ according to their strata; we concentrate on adults, and follow them through to old age.

[54] "Laird Sees Discrimination in Services Still Unsolved," *New York Times* (May 11, 1969), p. 54. In regard to differences in rank, blacks constituted 9.2% of all of the nation's servicemen yet only 3.3% were officers in the Army, 0.4% in the Navy, 0.9% in the Marine Corps, and 1.8% in the Air Force.

[55] Albert J. Mayer and Thomas F. Hoult, "Social Stratification and Combat Survival," *Social Forces*, 34 (December 1955), 155–159.

Such disadvantages in regard to military service are nothing new; J. S. Stevenson found that at the end of the 18th century lower strata persons were more likely to find themselves in the armed forces, especially the army, and to have been inducted through trickery, deceit, and kidnapping. Stevenson, "The London 'Crimp' Riots of 1794," *International Review of Social History*, 16 (1971), Part 1, 48–50. In subsequent chapters we will deal with the historical basis for stratification.

Chapter VI. Adulthood Through Old Age

We have seen how people's life chances differ according to their stratum, beginning with birth and continuing throughout childhood, adolescence, and youth. This chapter focuses on the significance of stratification for adults; we examine sexual behavior, courtship and marriage, how well people live, social participation including religious affiliation and political behavior, treatment under the law, and finally, old age.

Premarital and Extramarital Sexual Behavior

While the sex drive is necessarily strong in order to perpetuate the species, it is potentially disruptive for group relations. Consequently in all human societies this drive is regulated by customs and mores and through the institution of the family. Attitudes toward sex, type and frequency of sexual activity, and behavior in courtship and marriage vary from one society to another; [1] yet they also differ among the strata within a given society. Such differences in the United States were noted by Alfred C. Kinsey and his associates, who found for example that the lower strata are likely to begin heterosexual activities earlier than the higher. Using education as a measure of status level, by age 24, 87% of the men with eight or fewer years of schooling had had premarital sexual intercourse, compared with 82% for males with nine to 12 years of education. For those with 13 or more years it was 59%.[2] The Kinsey researchers report that, among those with only a grade-school education in two or three of the lower-level communities in which they worked, they were unable to find a solitary male who had not had sexual relations by the time he was 16 or 17 years old.[3]

Sexual behavior not only varies between the middle and the lower strata but there are considerable differences within the latter, particularly

[1] See, e.g., Stuart A. Queen, Robert W. Habenstein, and John B. Adams, *The Family in Various Cultures* (Chicago: J. B. Lippincott Co., 1961).

[2] Alfred C. Kinsey, Wardell B. Pomeroy, and Clyde E. Martin, *Sexual Behavior in the Human Male* (Philadelphia: W. B. Saunders Co., 1948), pp. 381, 550. However these figures do not reveal frequency nor do we know whether the partners were prostitutes, casual acquaintances, or fiancées.

[3] *Ibid.*, p. 381.

where there are ethnic subcultures. This is revealed by Bernard Rosenberg and Joseph Bensman's study of the sexual patterns of youths from three ethnic groups: Appalachians in Chicago, blacks in Washington, D.C., and Puerto Ricans in New York.[4] All had migrated to urban centers and were living in poverty. Rosenberg and Bensman found as much difference among these groups as between them and the middle strata. They concluded that the sexual patterns are related to general life styles and reflect the effects of ghettoization, subculture isolation, and short-range hedonism of people only recently transplanted from rural origins.[5]

Sexual relations among the lower strata are not necessarily indiscriminate or promiscuous; virginity may be valued, but for the female. Some of the lower-strata men may indeed be quite promiscuous, but for others there is a code of behavior.[6] William F. Whyte's study of Italian boys in an Eastern slum found that heterosexual relations at regular intervals were thought to be necessary for health, and also considered a means of attaining prestige. However there was a strong taboo against sex with virgins and potential mates. The preference in descending order was relations with a girl which would be exclusive for a period of time, followed by the "conquest" of a promiscuous female; the least desirable was intercourse with a prostitute.[7]

The strata also differ in regard to masturbation, pre-marital petting, and sexual behavior in marriage. Those in the lower look down on masturbation as abnormal and an infantile substitute for socio-sexual contacts.[8] Although most lower-strata boys masturbate when they become adolescents, it is limited and usually ends with the first experiences in heterosexual intercourse, which tends to be quite early.[9] While higher-status persons do not view masturbation as particularly desirable or commendable they do not see it as abnormal, nor is it completely discouraged. Among the college males interviewed in the Kinsey study, 70% stated that they depended on masturbation as their chief source of sexual outlet. Furthermore, for many higher-strata males masturbation continues after marriage whereas this is less likely among the lower.

Petting is another substitute for heterosexual intercourse which is favored by upper-level youths but considered a perversion by the lower. This preference by the higher strata is the result of setting a greater

[4] Bernard Rosenberg and Joseph Bensman, "Sexual Patterns in Three Ethnic Subcultures of an American Underclass," *Annals of the American Academy of Political and Social Science,* 376 (March 1968), 61–65.

[5] *Ibid.*

[6] Cf. Kinsey *et. al., Sexual Behavior in the Human Male,* pp. 377–383, 389.

[7] William F. Whyte, "A Slum Sex Code," *American Journal of Sociology* 49 (July 1943), 24–31.

[8] Kinsey *et al., op. cit.,* p. 375, 363–380. See also Lee Rainwater, *And the Poor Get Children* (Chicago: Quadrangle Books, 1960).

[9] Kinsey *et al., op. cit.,* p. 377. See also Clifford Kirkpatrick, *The Family as Process and Institution* (2nd ed.; New York: The Ronald Press, 1963), pp. 365–366.

premium on virginity. Where premarital intercourse does occur it is more often limited to potential marriage partners or to one's betrothed, particularly on the part of girls.

However there are indications that some of the differences among the levels are narrowing. Research by Ira L. Reiss suggests that sexual attitudes and behaviors are changing in the direction of more permissiveness among the higher strata and less among the lower, especially in the case of upwardly mobile women. Reiss holds that factors such as liberal or conservative views or religion may be more important than stratification. However his study is of attitudes toward sexual permissiveness and not behavior.[10]

Sexual relations between individuals of similar backgrounds are not likely to conflict with existing patterns of stratification. But contacts between persons of different strata are most likely to be between higher-status men and lower-status women: a college male and a "pick-up" of lower-strata background, a professional man and a prostitute, a Brahmin and a lower-caste female. This has long been recognized: writing in 1781 Martin Madan decried

> . . . men of *rank* and *fashion*, who are now turned loose on the *lower order of females*, and debauch them at *free cost*, without being under the least responsibility towards them— . . . who cause the utter ruin of *thousands*, who, under the present *system* of things, are seduced, abandoned, and destroyed, without any *remedy* whatsoever, or almost any possibility of *escape*.[11]

The more unequal the distribution of social goods probably the greater the frequency of such cross strata contacts, for differences in wealth facilitate the purchase of favors. Also, power over property, jobs, or careers may encourage exploitative relationships as in the case of master-slave, lord-peasant, intern-nurse, office manager-secretary. On the other hand, occasionally the lower-status person may be the exploiter since sexual access can be used for career advancement or other gain.[12]

When individuals from widely differing strata are involved sexually

---

[10] Ira L. Reiss, "Social Class and Premarital Sexual Permissiveness: A Re-examination," *American Sociological Review*, 30 (October 1965), 747–756. In this article Reiss points out the methodological inadequacies in the Kinsey research.

[11] Martin Madan, *Thelyphthora; Or, A Treatise on Female Ruin, In Its Causes, Effects, Consequences, Prevention and Remedy; Considered on the Basis of the Divine Law: Under the Following Heads, viz. Marriage, Whoredom and Fornication, Adultery, Polygamy, Divorce; With Many Other Incidental Matters;* . . . (London: Printed for J. Dodsley, in Pall-Mall, 1781), Vol. I, p. 404. Emphasis in the original.

[12] Because of the nature of these relationships there is very little reliable data. For some evidence see John Dollard, *Caste and Class in a Southern Town* (Garden City, N.Y.: Doubleday Anchor Books, 1949), pp. 135–160; and Clark E. Vincent, *Unmarried Mothers* (New York: The Free Press of Glencoe, 1961), pp. 8–91. See also on this Winston E. Ehrman, "Influence of Comparative Social Class of Companion Upon Premarital Heterosexual Behavior," *Marriage and Family Living*, 17 (February 1955), 48–53; and Eugene J. Kanin and David H. Howard, "Postmarital Consequences of Premarital Sex Adjustment," *American Sociological Review*, 23 (October 1958), 558.

the relationships are usually outside the pale of marriage. For if a large number of such liaisons became permanent and institutionalized then a stratification structure, whether based on wealth, occupation, ethnicity, or other considerations would be threatened with dissolution. Of course a new structure would form, but the point is that unless the society were in a state of great flux or disorganization there would likely be attempts to place sanctions on the transgressors in order to uphold the existing stratification system.

There can be a certain amount of mobility through marriage without disrupting the social structure. Yet such marriage is not the result of easy access to sexual favors: on the contrary, Glen H. Elder, Jr. found that social ascent from the working into the middle stratum was associated with the avoidance of steady dating and sexual involvement. He reports that coitus during high school was much less frequent for the mobile than the non-mobile women (ten vs. 70%) and the pattern was similar for petting.[13] However, physical attractiveness is a key factor in the upward mobility of the female from the working stratum: her chances of marrying up are greatly influenced by the exchange value of her personal resources for marriage. The woman's attractiveness and the man's higher social status is one of the oldest forms of exchange in hypergamous marriage.[14] Pitirim A. Sorokin argues that the upper strata recruit the most beautiful women and the most handsome men from the lower strata. He adds that as a consequence over time these qualities become characteristic of the upper levels.[15]

Although hypergamy occurs, marriage within the same stratum predominates, as we noted in Chapter II. In fact, in every society most of the customary expectations and rituals surrounding what we commonly call courtship encourage the association of status equals. This is not happenstance; rather, they reflect the constraints on behavior associated with any ranking order.[16] Thus stratification, the hierarchical distribution of social goods, both symbolic and material, figures in assessing the worthiness of potential mates. Yet, as James M. Beshers and his associates point out, opposing strategies come into play since each family wishes to marry its children up, but wants to prevent them from marrying down. Since the daughter's status is commonly assigned by marriage, her parents endeavor to exert control over the mate-selection process. This

[13] Glen H. Elder, Jr., "Appearance and Education in Marriage Mobility," *American Sociological Review*, 34 (August 1969), 526–527, 531.

[14] *Ibid.*, pp. 519–533, especially p. 531.

[15] Pitirim A. Sorokin, *Social and Cultural Mobility* (New York: The Free Press of Glencoe, 1959; first pub. in 1927), p. 246. This is also Darwin's argument which Sorokin cites.

Elder found that adolescent girls from the middle stratum were rated higher in attractiveness than girls from the working stratum. Elder, *op. cit.*, p. 531.

[16] See James M. Beshers, Ephraim H. Mizruchi, and Robert Perrucci, "Social Distance Strategies and Status Symbols: An Approach to the Study of Social Structure," *Sociological Quarterly*, 4 (Autumn 1963), 311–324.

can be done through appropriate socialization so that she "naturally" eliminates ineligible mates. Or, the parents can attempt to control her opportunities for contact with potential mates by the location of their home, the college they send her to, the vacation spot they choose, or by threats and sanctions. Whether done consciously or not, such strategies help support the social order; they are a part of the system of constraints that flows from the stratification arrangement we described above and in previous chapters. In turn, the constraints help perpetuate the stratification.[17]

Courtship and Marriage

In the United States and increasingly in other industrial nations courtship usually begins with somewhat casual acquaintanceships, or "dating." Personal preferences are paramount, and the ideals of romantic love provide the framework within which young people get to know each other and develop deeper attachments. One would suspect that this practice and the general freedom of association between young men and women threaten the status structure. They do; but apparently not too seriously, for the reasons we discussed above. The end result is that young people are likely to associate with, date, and marry individuals in the same stratum.[18] This is encouraged by residential propinquity, particularly when the people who live near one another are from the same stratum.[19]

Propinquity in a social sense is important in the context of college life. Many students tend to be from similar backgrounds; consequently these young people are likely to date and eventually marry other college youths. Yet while college men and women are predominantly from higher-status homes, as was shown in the previous chapter, the students in the large publicly-supported institutions of higher learning are drawn

[17] *Ibid.*, pp. 311–317.

[18] Morris Zelditch, Jr., "Family, Marriage, and Kinship," in Robert E. L. Farris, ed., *Handbook of Modern Sociology* (Chicago: Rand McNally & Co., 1964), pp. 688–690; Richard Centers, "Mate Selection and Occupational Strata," *American Journal of Sociology,* 54 (May 1949), 530–535; John Aldous and Reuben Hill, "Social Cohesion, Lineage Type, and Intergenerational Transmission," *Social Forces,* 43 (May 1965), 471–482; and Zick Rubin, "Do Americans Marry Up?" *American Sociological Review,* 33 (October 1968), 750–760.

[19] Zelditch, *op. cit.,* p. 689; Alfred C. Clarke, "An Examination of the Operation of Residential Propinquity as a Factor in Mate Selection," *American Sociological Review,* 17 (February 1952), 17–22; and Joseph R. Marches and Gus Turbeville, "The Effect of Residential Propinquity on Marriage Selection," *American Journal of Sociology,* 58 (May 1953), 592–595. However Ramsoy's study of mate selection in Oslo, Norway, did not show that neighbors tend to be social equals. She did find that similarity in occupation, and in propinquity, were highly associated with the probability of marriage, but the two were independent of each other. Natalie R. Ramsoy, "Assortative Mating and the Structure of Cities," *American Sociological Review,* 31 (December 1966), 773–786.

from many different backgrounds. Might we not expect many of these youths to associate with and marry persons from different strata? There is such a tendency, for in addition to physical nearness, personal qualities such as beauty, athletic ability, or similar intellectual interests, may result in casual acquaintanceships and more lasting attachments including marriage. However there are institutional arrangements in most colleges and universities which work to perpetuate stratification, particularly in terms of parents' stratum.

Associations such as fraternities and sororities and other organized living groups are stratified, and the ranking usually reflects the stratification in the larger community. While such groups are not as important as they were prior to the 1960's, they are still a visible part of campus life and function to perpetuate stratification. The members of the Greek societies tend to date persons from houses of similar rank, and are not likely to associate with dormitory students. The latter date among themselves, or go out with "independents," those who do not live in organized groups.

John F. Scott describes how sororities perpetuate strata differences by encouraging members to date men from similarly ranked fraternities. Various social activities and the dating, where couples are matched by representatives from the appropriate fraternity and sorority, usually take up so much of the students' out-of-class time that possibilities for undesirable contacts are limited. The ritual of "pinning" signifies a stage in between dating and engagement, similar to "going steady." The male gives his fraternity pin to the coed, and if the match is successful the result is a propitious marriage meaning, among other things, that partners are from the same stratum.[20]

Not only are those who go to college likely to be from the higher strata but there are also status differences among the public and private institutions, as was shown in the previous chapter; consequently each college or university will tend to draw students from a particular stratum. Whether students belong to a fraternity or sorority, a campus dormitory or some other organized group, or are independents, there is a very strong likelihood that they will associate with, date, and marry persons of similar background.

Such free association between young men and women, dating, and personal choice of marriage partners are by no means universal phenomena. More common throughout the world are segregation of the unmarried young, limited contact between members of the opposite sex, and careful supervision by parents or other adults. When it comes to marriage the critical decisions are made as much by the parents as by the young people concerned. In some cultures the matchmaker has become institutionalized and facilitates the selection of marriage partners. The

[20] John F. Scott, "The American College Sorority: Its Role in Class and Ethnic Endogamy," *American Sociological Review*, 30 (August 1965), 514–527.

marriage broker was common among many immigrant groups in America, and is still found elsewhere. For example, in Japan where most marriages are still arranged, the "go-between" or *nakōdo* helps families arrange desirable matches. While the feelings of the prospective bride and groom are considered, they are secondary; one of the key concerns is the status levels of the families.[21] However, in Japan as elsewhere, such considerations are most important for the upper and middle strata, less so for the lower. The latter have less to lose from an ill-considered marriage; also their choices regarding a desirable mate are more limited.[22]

One of the main reasons for arranged marriage is to insure that people who marry are from the same stratum, or to avoid marrying "down." While parents in most societies probably would not mind their child marrying "up," they wish to avoid a match with a person from a much lower level because of constraints that are part of any social order. Where strata are more clearly differentiated and there is an aristocratic tradition, as in Japan, the constraints are more pervasive. Also, the means of engaging in the strategies are likely to be more highly institutionalized, as illustrated by the *nakōdo*. Nevertheless, as we indicated previously, most persons marry within the same level.

Yet some strata are more prone toward out-marriage than others and such unions are likely to involve hypergamy. This was found by Zick Rubin in his study of marriage partners and their parents, which was based on a national sample of almost 26,000 cases. Rubin stratified the brides and grooms and their parents by occupational level and observed that the daughter of a white-collar worker was likely to marry the son of a professional or manager. By contrast, it was unusual for the daughter of a professional or manager to marry the son of a white-collar worker.[23] He also found that farmers' daughters tended to marry the sons of white-collar workers; however the daughters of white-collar workers do not marry farmers' sons. Rubin concludes that, regardless of these cases, hypergamy in the United States is minimal, and that intrastrata marriage patterns have been relatively stable from about 1920 to 1962.[24]

Not only do brides and grooms tend to come from the same strata, but the likelihood of marrying differs among the status levels. Paul C.

[21] Basil H. Chamberlain, *Things Japanese* (London: Kegan Paul, Trench, Trubner & Co., 1960), pp. 220–223; R. P. Dore, *City Life in Japan* (Berkeley and Los Angeles: University of California Press, 1958), pp. 108, 166; and Richard K. Beardsley, John W. Hall, and Robert E. Ward, *Village Japan* (Chicago: University of Chicago Press, 1959), p. 317. See also Olga Lang, *The Chinese Family and Society* (New Haven, Conn.: Yale University Press, 1946), pp. 122–125.

[22] Chamberlain, *op. cit.*, p. 223; and Dore, *op. cit.*, p. 108. See also Lang, *op. cit.*; and Siang-Feng Ko, "Marriage among the Independent Lolos of Western China," *American Journal of Sociology*, 54 (May 1949), 439.

[23] Rubin, "Do Americans Marry Up?" pp. 758–759.

[24] Rubin further holds that the assertion of earlier writers that American women tend to marry up is based on the erroneous assumption that the patterns they observed among upper- and middle-level women hold for the rest of the strata. *Ibid.*, p. 759.

Glick and Hugh Carter's study which ranked persons according to amount of education showed that the chances of marrying were much slimmer for those with limited education than for the better educated.[25] This is due in large part to the association between education and occupational and income opportunities which was discussed in the previous chapter.

For those who do marry there are significant strata differences regarding when the knot is tied and under what circumstances; sexual attitudes and behavior; and the likelihood of separation or divorce.

WAS IT A SHOTGUN WEDDING?

Understandably, with marriage, children soon begin arriving. However the likelihood of the child having been conceived before the nuptial vows were exchanged differs among the strata, according to the findings of the 1964–1966 National Natality Survey. For each of these years the Survey analyzed the average 1,008,000 legitimate first births to wives aged 15 to 44. (By definition children born in wedlock are legitimate regardless of when conception occurred.) Since the gestation period is nine months, babies born less than eight months after the date of marriage were listed as having been conceived prior to the wedding. Approximately 22% of all babies were born to women who had been married for fewer than eight months; among those between 15 and 19 years of age 42% of the births were the result of premarital conceptions.[26]

For mothers with high-school or college training there is a clear association between amount of education and when the first child was conceived (Table VI-1, A). Only eight per cent of the mothers with four or more years of college gave birth before they were married less than eight months. For those with one to three years of college the percentage is 18; for high-school graduates it is 21%, while it goes up to 32% for mothers who are high-school dropouts. In the case of elementary-school mothers the percentage is 21. When stratification is by family income, however, the relationship is direct and very strong (Table VI-1, B): where yearly income was $10,000 or over, eight per cent of the mothers had the first baby while married fewer than eight months. The percentage rises as family income goes down, so that by the under $3,000 level 37% of the mothers had such early births.

These data suggest that the shotgun wedding is more common among the lower strata and are another indication of differential cultural and

[25] Paul C. Glick and Hugh Carter, "Marriage Patterns and Educational Level," *American Sociological Review*, 23 (June 1958), 299–300.

[26] U.S. Department of Health, Education, and Welfare, National Center for Health Statistics, "Interval Between First Marriage and Legitimate First Birth, United States, 1964–1966," *Monthly Vital Statistics Report*, Vol. 18, No. 12, Supplement (March 27, 1970), p. 1.

TABLE VI-1. Interval from First Marriage to First Birth under 8 Months for Women 15 to 44, by Education and Family Income (in percentages)

A. *Education*

Elementary School	1-3 years of High School	4 years of High School	1-3 years of College	4 years or more of College	Total	(Number)
21.2	31.6	20.7	18.1	7.5	100.0	(217,728)

B. *Family Income*

Under $3,000	$3,000-4,999	$5,000-6,999	$7,000-9,999	$10,000 and over	Total	(Number)
37.5	23.3	17.6	11.5	8.2	100.1	(217,728)

Source: U.S. Department of Health, Education, and Welfare, National Center for Health Statistics, "Interval Between First Marriage and Legitimate First Birth, United States, 1964–66," *Monthly Vital Statistics Report*, Vol. 18, No. 12, Supplement (March 27, 1970), p. 3.

behaviorial patterns. However there are important economic as well as social consequences: the couples who "have to" get married also tend to be relatively young, and early marriage limits educational and income prospects.[27] In addition, couples who marry early are likely to have more children generally, and particularly if there is such early pregnancy. The parents' opportunity to obtain social goods is further limited, and the children are adversely affected, as was detailed in Chapter IV.

Sexual intercourse, whether for conceiving children or for other purposes, is of course a common expectation in marriage. Yet there are significant strata differences in attitudes and behavior patterns.

Sex: Quantitative and Qualitative Aspects

Controlling for age, heterosexual activity remains higher for married men from the lower strata than from the middle. Lower-strata families live in a more constricted world with fewer social and cultural activities, as we noted in Chapter IV. Consequently, sex probably takes up a greater portion of leisure time. Also, there is a greater emphasis on *macho*, or masculinity, and lower-strata women are more likely to comply with the sexual demands of their husbands.[28]

Middle-strata attitudes toward sex were studied by Lionel S. Lewis and Dennis Brisset, and they found a tendency to infuse sex play with a kind of work ethic. They analyzed 15 books offering advice on marital sex and observed that the counselors present sex play as work. Readers are cautioned not to treat sex frivolously; it should not be undertaken on the spur of the moment; it requires effort and determination; orgasm is seen as a final product; proper skills and techniques are essential; and a careful learning and training program are necessary.[29] These "fun-but-work" attitudes may be an additional explanation for the lower rate of marital intercourse among the middle strata. (This assumes of course that the middle strata constitute the main market for the manuals, which seems likely, and that those who read them take them seriously. There are probably certain aspects of middle strata life which lead to interest in such guides.)

Sexual hanky-panky occurs at all levels; however there are strata dif-

[27] See *ibid.*, p. 2; and Lolgene C. Coombs *et. al.*, "Premarital Pregnancy and Status Before and After Marriage," *American Journal of Sociology*, 75 (March 1970), 800–820.

[28] See, e.g., Mirra Komarovsky, *Blue-Collar Marriage* (New York: Random House, 1964), pp. 83–86; and Oscar Lewis, *La Vida: A Puerto Rican Family in the Culture of Poverty—San Juan and New York* (New York: Random House, 1966).

[29] Lionel S. Lewis and Dennis Brisset, "Sex as Work," *Social Problems*, 15 (Summer 1967), 8–18. Lewis and Brisset relate these injunctions to two antagonistic forces in American society: an emphasis on work as well as an emphasis on attaining maximum pleasure.

ferences, especially as time passes, and there are also variations in marriage stability.

EXTRAMARITAL SEX, AND MARRIAGE STABILITY

Kinsey and his associates found that as lower-level men (those with eight or fewer years of education) get older, extramarital intercourse decreases, while for the higher-level men (those with 13 or more years of education), it goes up considerably. Among lower-level males who were married in their late teens (between 16 and 20 years of age), 45% reported extramarital intercourse; however by age 50 the incidence had dropped to 19%. By contrast, among young college husbands, between 15 and 20% had engaged in intercourse outside of marriage. But by age 50 the incidence was 27%. As to frequency, among married lower-level men between the ages of 16 and 20 who strayed, extramarital intercourse occurred more than once a week but by age 55 it was just under once every two weeks. Yet philandering married college males between the ages of 16 and 30 had intercourse outside of marriage only once every two or three weeks, but by age 50 the frequency was near once a week.[30]

Yet while the chances of the marriage continuing or breaking up differ among the strata, the research shows that in general rates of marriage dissolution are inversely related to status position.[31] For example, the U.S. Census Bureau compared families earning $15,000 or more with those making less than $5,000 a year: in only 17% of the more affluent households had either partner ever been divorced, whereas this was true of 28% of the poorer families.[32] The strata differences in family stability hold not only for the United States but also for other societies which are industrialized or undergoing industrialization.[33]

---

[30] Kinsey *et. al., Sexual Behavior in the Human Male,* pp. 585–587. The authors note that there is some question as to the reliability of these data, but feel that the reports of extramarital intercourse are probably understated, particularly in the case of higher-level men.

[31] Glick and Carter, "Marriage Patterns and Educational Level," p. 297; and William J. Goode, "Family Disorganization," in Robert K. Merton and Robert A. Nisbet, eds., *Contemporary Social Problems* (New York: Harcourt, Brace & World, Inc., 1961), pp. 417–418. See also U.S. Bureau of the Census, "Social and Economic Variations in Marriage, Divorce and Remarriage: 1967," Series P-20, No. 223 (Washington, D.C.: Government Printing Office, October 7, 1971); J. Richard Udry, "Marital Instability by Race and Income Based on 1960 Census Data," *American Journal of Sociology,* 72 (May 1967), 673–674; Jessie Bernard, "Marital Stability and Patterns of Status Variables," *Journal of Marriage and the Family,* 28 (November 1966), 421–439; and Colin Gibson, "A Note on Family Breakdown in England and Wales," *British Journal of Sociology,* 22 (September 1971) 324–325.

[32] "Social and Economic Variations in Marriage, Divorce, and Remarriage: 1967," p. 2. In the families which were studied the husband was between 35 and 54 years of age.

[33] Goode, "Marital Satisfaction and Instability; A Cross-Cultural Class Analysis of Divorce Rates," *International Social Science Journal,* 14 (1962), 507–526.
While family stability is associated with life chances it is not as important as suggested

That the higher strata are less prone to divorce should not be surprising. They have the social goods the society defines as necessary and desirable and over time there is an accumulation of savings, property, and other assets. There is also an absence of the social and economic strains associated with lower strata work: unpleasant and poorly-paid jobs and frequent unemployment. In short, not only do the higher strata have the good things of life, but they have more to lose by dissolving their marriages.

The increase in extramarital sex among higher strata men as they get older may simply reflect the need for a substitute outlet on the one hand, and the desire to retain the marriage on the other. The substitute may be provided by prostitutes, call-girls, pick-ups in expensive bars, or by female work associates or employees; these men can easily afford the favors of prostitutes or call-girls, as well as convention, business, or other out-of-town trips.[34] Other substitute outlets are the massage parlor and pornography, which attract higher- rather than lower-strata clientele.[35] The massage parlor offers sexual stimulation usually short of intercourse, and pornography provides auto-eroticism which often includes masturbation. The law is likely to be more lenient toward upper-strata pornography; many erotic forms are defined as art or literature, and this has led Ned Polsky to comment that ". . . the classier the pornography the more likely it is to be permitted." [36]

The constraints against divorce that direct higher-strata males to seek substitute outlets may have a similar effect on their wives. For them, however, substitute outlets may include romantic novels, regular visits to the beauty salon, and social activities such as club work.

While sex, marriage, and family are of great importance in adult life, a man's work is of overriding significance. For, as we stressed in previous chapters, the nature of a person's occupation, whether he is employed or unemployed, and the extent to which he might be underemployed, sorely affect the well-being of the individual and his

---

by the Moynihan Report (U.S. Department of Labor, *The Negro Family: The Case for National Action* [Washington, D.C.: Government Printing Office, 1965]); rather, other aspects of stratification such as income, occupation, and education are more significant. See Reynolds Farley and Albert I. Hermalin, "Family Stability: A Comparison of Trends Between Blacks and Whites," *American Sociological Review*, 36 (February 1971), 1–17, especially pp. 14–17.

[34] Kingsley Davis ("The Sociology of Prostitution," *American Sociological Review*, 2 [October 1937], 744–755) points out how prostitution, which acts as a safety-valve, helps to maintain the institution of the family.

[35] See Albert J. Velarde and Mark Warlick, "Massage Parlors: The Sensuality Business," *Society* (November–December 1973), 63–74, especially p. 69; and Ned Polsky, *Hustlers, Beats, and Others* (Garden City, N.Y.: Doubleday Anchor Books, 1969), pp. 185, 187. However the data are not very reliable and are based mainly on hearsay and limited observation.

[36] Polsky, *op. cit.*, p. 197.
While in general lower-strata men are more likely to resort to prostitutes than to pornography, an important exception is persons in prison, most of who are from the lower strata. See *ibid.*, pp. 185, 187.

family. As we noted earlier, social origin plays a decisive role as regards education and other factors that influence the occupational career. Now let us assume that a person has landed a job; what are the prospects for future mobility? Not only does an individual's background strongly affect the kind of occupation entered, but social origin exerts a direct effect on subsequent occupational life.[37] Yet there are problems in assessing the effect of stratum background and career success. For most studies of intragenerational, as well as intergenerational opportunity use broad categories, each of which contains many diverse types of work. Even when a specific occupation such as doctor is designated, the fact that there are different levels within it is obscured. To overcome these difficulties Robert Perrucci analyzed the opportunity in one profession, studying a sample of engineering graduates.[38] Perrucci found a very strong association between an individual's status in the engineering profession and his father's occupation; he also observed that this tendency was increasing over time.[39]

Stratum position remains a critical influence throughout the life cycle; not only as regards the work career, but also in terms of how well people live, place of residence, who they associate with, and the extent to which they participate in community life.

How Well People Live

It is obvious that the higher the stratum the better the living conditions, and amount of material goods is a primary factor. However, even where lower-strata persons have the wherewithal to obtain them they are likely to end up with inferior products and services while paying higher prices. This occurs in food retailing as well as in the purchase of durable goods as the Bureau of Labor Statistics has noted. Their research found that

> stores serving low-income neighborhoods were typically small. Many were dirty and poorly kept. Since these small stores typically charge higher prices than larger stores, particularly chain stores, consumers in these areas generally face higher prices than consumers in other neighborhoods.[40]

Whether it is buying food, furniture, appliances, or personal effects, "the poor pay more," as David Caplovitz has shown.[41] He relates the case of a

[37] Peter M. Blau and Otis D. Duncan, *The American Occupational Structure* (New York: John Wiley & Sons, 1967), pp. 49 ff.

[38] Robert Perrucci, "The Significance of Intra-Occupational Mobility: Some Methodological and Theoretical Notes, Together with a Case Study of Engineers," *American Sociological Review*, 26 (December 1961), 874–883.

[39] *Ibid.*, pp. 882–883.

[40] National Commission on Food Marketing, *Organization and Competition in Food Retailing*, Technical Study No. 7 (Washington, D.C.: Government Printing Office, June 1966), p. 337.

[41] David Caplovitz, *The Poor Pay More* (New York: The Free Press, 1967).

40-year-old black housewife who bought a wristwatch for her daughter from a door-to-door salesman:

> We were both home and my daughter pleaded with me to buy the watch. So I agreed to buy it for $60. I gave him $3 down and I got a payment book in the mail. *About a month later I had the watch appraised in a 125th Street store and I found it was worth only $6.50.*[42]

Caplovitz observes that "[i]nstallment credit has . . . been the door through which the poor have entered the mass consumption society, and they, more than any other group, have been victimized by the fraud and deception that have accompanied this method of selling."[43] When cash was used, shopping behavior was usually more deliberate and sophisticated; furthermore the seller had no incentive to convince the person without money to make an expensive purchase. But with the advent of easy credit it became irrelevant whether or not the customer could afford the item since persuasive means for enforcing the installment contract are available. As a consequence lower-strata persons are likely to be subjected to high pressure sales techniques, bait-and-switch tactics, and the substitution of inferior goods. Also, since the contract is usually sold to a bank or credit agency, the seller can turn a deaf ear to customer complaints.[44] Needless to say, the high interest rates in installment buying add greatly to the cost of the goods.

The situation facing the lower strata has worsened with the widespread use of the credit card for it encourages impulse buying. Also, with the "revolving credit" feature, interest costs are less apparent than when a contract has to be negotiated for each purchase.[45] Of course not all lower-strata families qualify for credit cards, but those who do use them as a respectable means of obtaining instant credit and often pay sizable amounts of interest. For the better-off, the card is more a matter of convenience and they usually pay their debt before the finance charges are due. It is the high interest paid by the less affluent—18 per cent a year in most states—that subsidizes the credit card use by the higher strata.[46]

This system of merchandizing and installment credit is supported by institutional arrangements, principally the legal system, which we explore in a later section. There are also less formal considerations, such as lower-strata socialization and life conditions which are associated with difficulty in handling personal affairs including coping with financial

[42] *Ibid.*, p. 160. Emphasis in the original.

[43] *Ibid.*, p. xvii.

[44] *Ibid.*, pp. xvi–xvii, 140–154 ff.

[45] See Institute for Social Research, "Poor Subsidize the Rich in Use of Credit Cards, Senate Committee Is Told," *Institute for Social Research Newsletter* (Spring-Summer 1973), p. 2. See also Caplovitz, *The Poor Pay More*, pp. 66–70 ff.

[46] "Poor Subsidize the Rich in Use of Credit Cards."

matters. Given the circumstances of the lower strata, it is not surprising that they are less happy than the higher; [47] it is also quite probable that they suffer more from mental disorders.

Mental Health

The evidence on the association between stratum position and mental health is far from clear, for the research in this area is beset by many theoretical and methodological problems.[48] Yet in sum the data indicate a strong association. August B. Hollingshead and Fredrick C. Redlich, in their well-known study of New Haven, Connecticut, in 1950, found a distinct inverse relationship.[49] Almost invariably the lower strata contributed many many more patients than their proportion in the population warrants: the prevalence of psychiatric disorders per 100,000 persons in the population was 553 for the highest two strata; below them the rate was 528 for the third; 665 for the fourth, and 1,668 for the lowest.[50]

A more recent study by William A. Rushing also found a strong association between status level and the prevalence of mental illness. He ranked hospitalized males in the state of Washington according to the N.O.R.C. occupational rankings and found that the lower the job level the higher the rate: those in the topmost occupational category had a hospitalization rate of only 21 per 100,000; for the level below that it was 39; for the next one it was 49, and for the one below that 64. Yet the rate for the lowest occupational category was 270 per 100,000.[51] While many researchers have not found a clear-cut relationship between psychoneurosis and stratum position,[52] clear differences in the type of mental illness have been discovered. Persons in the higher strata tend to have

[47] Alex Inkeles, "Industrial Man: The Relationship of Status to Experience, Perception, and Value," *American Journal of Sociology*, 66 (July 1960), 13–18.

[48] See Robert J. Kleiner and Seymour Parker, "Goal-Striving, Social Status, and Mental Disorder: A Research Review," *American Sociological Review*, 28 (April 1963), 189–203; Jerome C. Manis *et. al.*, "Estimating the Prevalence of Mental Illness," *American Sociological Review*, 29 (February 1964), 84–89; and H. Warren Dunham, "Social Structures and Mental Disorders: Competing Hypotheses of Explanation," in Milbank Memorial Fund, *Round Table on Causes of Mental Disorders, Harriman, New York* (New York: Milbank Memorial Fund, 1961), pp. 249–256.

[49] August B. Hollingshead and Frederick C. Redlich, *Social Class and Mental Illness* (New York: John Wiley & Sons, 1967), pp. 249–256.

[50] *Ibid.*, pp. 210, 217. The figures are adjusted for age and sex.

[51] William A. Rushing, "Two Patterns in the Relationship Between Social Class and Mental Hospitalization," *American Sociological Review*, 34 (August 1969), 533–541, especially p. 536.

[52] See Kleiner and Parker, "Goal-Striving, Social Status, and Mental Disorder"; and Benjamin Pasamanick *et al.*, "A Survey of Mental Disease in an Urban Population: Prevalence by Race and Income," in Pasamanick, ed., *Epidemiology of Mental Disorder* (Washington, D.C.: Association for the Advancement of Science, 1959), pp. 68–69.

physiologically linked psychological problems while those in the lower are more likely to suffer from schizophrenia and total psychosis.[53] This was found to be the case by Hollingshead and Redlich, and by a number of other investigators. In addition, the mentally ill from the higher strata were likely to be treated by a private physician or in a private hospital, in contrast to a public clinic, state hospital, or veterans' hospital. Also, those from the higher strata received psychotherapy, as opposed to drugs, shock treatment, psychosurgery, or custodial care.[54]

Jerome K. Myers and Lee L. Bean conducted a ten-year follow-up study of 1,463 New Haven patients who had received hospital or clinic treatment in 1950. They found that social stratum position was clearly related to the outcome of psychiatric treatment and the way former patients had adjusted in the community. The higher the stratum level, the less likely was it that the patients were hospitalized ten years after the original study. Also, the higher-strata patients were more likely to have been treated as outpatients; however, if hospitalized the chances were that they received psychotherapy rather than drugs and custodial care. They were also discharged sooner than lower-strata patients.[55]

Those from the higher strata are well adjusted socially, and do not have employment or financial problems. By contrast, the lower the stratum the poorer the adjustment in each of these areas. For the bottom level individual and his family, mental illness is catastrophic.[56]

At the time of the original New Haven research by Hollingshead and Redlich, a companion study of 50 cases by Myers and Bertram H. Roberts also found a strong relationship between stratum position and mental illness. However, Myers and Roberts were also interested in investigating the linkage between stratum position and mental illness. They observed important strata differences in familial and community experiences, interpersonal relations, family roles, and employment and mobility opportunities. The researchers found that these life experiences were much more unfavorable for the lower- in contrast to the higher-strata individuals. Moreover, these deleterious circumstances and their resultant

[53] Hollingshead and Redlich, *Social Class and Mental Illness*, pp. 220–250; and Kleiner and Parker, *op. cit.*, pp. 193, 195–199. Further studies are needed to clarify the relationship between stratification and mental illness. While it is most likely that stratum position is inversely related to amount of mental illness it is apparent that other factors are involved. Among them may be relatve deprivation, intergenerational as well as intragenerational downward mobility, and social and subcultural conditions characteristic of lower strata life. See Dunham, "Social Structures and Mental Disorders"; John A. Clausen and Melvin L. Kohn, "Relation of Schizophrenia to the Social Structure of a Small City," in Pasamanick, ed., *op. cit.*, pp. 69–86; Thomas S. Langer and Stanley T. Michael, *Life Stress and Mental Health* (London: The Free Press of Glencoe, 1963), pp. 424–475.

[54] Hollingshead and Redlich, *op. cit.*, pp. 253–301.

[55] Jerome K. Meyers and Lee L. Bean, *A Decade Later: A Follow-Up of Social Class and Mental Illness* (New York: John Wiley & Sons, 1968), pp. 202–203.

[56] *Ibid.*, pp. 203–206.

stresses were more conducive to mental illness among the lower strata.[57]

It is most likely, as Myers and Roberts suggest, that the poorer material and social conditions among the lower strata contribute to their greater tendency toward mental illness. These conditions are underscored by where they live and by their limited participation in the life of the community.

Residence and Social Participation

Whether people reside in a small town, large city, or suburb, they are likely to live among persons of similar circumstances. Hollingshead noted that in the small community he called "Elmtown" there were neighborhoods which were clearly ranked in prestige by the town's inhabitants; the higher-strata persons lived in the better ones, and vice versa.[58]

Underlying residential differentiation is the fact that grade of dwelling, meaning type and condition of lot, condition of structure, number of rooms, and the condition and use of adjoining properties generally rises with occupational rank.[59] Interestingly, income is not the chief determinant of grade of residence for when income as well as education are controlled occupation retains its primacy. Education is more strongly associated with grade of dwelling for lower-level white-collar workers, who receive less pay than those in highly skilled blue-collar occupations. Status considerations appear to be more important for them because they spend a higher proportion of their income on housing than do blue-collar workers of comparable income. It has also been suggested that type of dwelling and neighborhood are more closely related to "permanent income" than to current income. Even though some blue-collar persons receive more pay, white collar workers anticipate a much higher income in the future and therefore acquire more expensive homes.[60]

For a long time sociologists have studied residential segregation in large cities. They have delineated zones, areas, neighborhoods, and special enclaves such as ethnic ghettoes and places frequented by artists, writers, and others. The researches show that the "better" or more prestigious residential sections of the city are overrepresented by white-collar

[57] Jerome K. Myers and Bertram H. Roberts, *Family and Class Dynamics in Mental Illness* (New York: John Wiley & Sons, 1959), pp. 247–265.

[58] August B. Hollingshead, *Elmtown's Youth* (New York: John Wiley & Sons, 1949), p. 462.

[59] Charles Tilly, "Occupational Rank and Grade of Residence in a Metropolis," *The American Journal of Sociology,* 67 (November 1961), 329.

[60] *Ibid.,* pp. 328–329.

workers with higher income and education; by contrast, people in lower-level occupations with more limited income and education are in the less desirable sections.[61] As a case in point we note Edgar M. Hoover and Raymond Vernon's analysis of different types of communities within the New York metropolitan region. They found that the inner portion of Manhattan and of parts of adjacent counties contain the mass of bottom-income unskilled manual and service workers and most of the region's "disadvantaged" in-migrants.[62] The latter are mostly blacks and Puerto Ricans who live predominantly in the slum areas. Other sections, far smaller and mainly in Manhattan, are peopled by wealthy professionals and executives who reside in expensive luxury apartments. A little farther out there are communities of lower white-collar employees as well as areas of semi-skilled industrial workers. As one gets into the suburbs the proportion of skilled relative to semi-skilled and unskilled industrial workers rises; similarly the proportion of persons in higher status white-collar occupations increases. In addition there are older upper-strata suburbs of professionals and executives.[63] Analyzing cities over time, Lee J. Haggerty observed a trend toward a direct relationship between socioeconomic status and distance from the center of the city.[64]

From a review of the literature Wilfred G. Marston concludes that there has been residential segregation by strata throughout American history. He also found that this segregation is influenced by economic as well as by immigrant and minority group status. The general pattern is to first locate near the center of the city because of limited finances. Then as the family's economic condition improves it moves outward; however there is some tendency for recent immigrants to live together even when they leave the center of the city. Although blacks also decentralize as their condition improves they remain confined to the black ghetto; for them residential segregation is more likely to be the result of racial dis-

[61] See, e.g., Robert E. Park, *Human Communities* (Glencoe, Ill.: The Free Press, 1952); and Ernest W. Burgess, "The Growth of a City: Introduction to a Research Project," *Proceedings of the American Sociological Society*, 18, (1923), 85–97; also the work of the social area analysts, particularly Eshref Shevky and Marilyn Williams, *The Social Areas of Los Angeles: Analysis and Typology* (Berkeley and Los Angeles: University of California Press, 1949); Wendell Bell, "The Social Areas of the San Francisco Bay Region," *American Sociological Review*, 18 (February 1953), 39–47; and Maurice D. Van Arsdol, Jr., Santo F. Camilleri, and Calvin F. Schmid, "The Generality of Urban Social Area Indexes," *American Sociological Review*, 23 (June 1958), 277–284. See also Otis Dudley Duncan and Beverly Duncan, "Residential Distribution and Occupational Stratification," *American Journal of Sociology*, 60 (March 1955), 493–503; Eugene S. Uyeki, "Residential Distribution and Stratification, 1950–1960," *American Journal of Sociology*, 23 (June 1958), 491–498; and Wilfred G. Marston, "Social Class as a Factor in Ethnic and Racial Segregation," *International Journal of Comparative Sociology*, 9 (January 1968), 145–153.

[62] Edgar M. Hoover and Raymond Vernon, *Anatomy of a Metropolis* (Garden City, N.Y.: Doubleday Anchor Books, 1962), p. 173. In their study they took into account the effect of job, income, and children in choice of residence.

[63] *Ibid.*, pp. 173–174.

[64] Lee J. Haggerty, "Another Look at the Burgess Hypothesis: Time as an Important Variable," *American Journal of Sociology*, 76 (May 1971), 1084–1093.

crimination rather than strata differences.[65] In fact, until 1948 it was the policy of the United States government to officially enforce discriminatory practices in housing. Homes insured by the Federal Housing Authority were *required* to include restrictive racial covenants in order to keep up property values.[66] One of the reasons non-manual workers, who are predominantly white, locate toward the outskirts is the newer and sounder housing that becomes available to them as the city grows away from the center.[67] The F.H.A.'s housing policy of low-interest loans for privately owned single dwelling units and its discriminatory practices greatly encouraged this trend.

Residential segregation according to such factors as occupation, education, and income are found not only in American cities but also in urban communities in other countries.[68]

Who people associate with and the nature of the association are affected by location and type of residence. There is much more "neighboring" in suburban communities in contrast to the inner city, but recent research indicates there is more informal contact in the city than had been believed.[69] Nevertheless clear differences are found among the strata even when modified by community type: there is more neighboring and participation in organized activities in the young executive and professional suburb than in the blue-collar suburb.[70] Stratification affects social participation in many other ways: for example, who people talk to. Erwin L. Linn found that there was a tendency to discuss local affairs with persons of similar or higher status, but not lower.[71]

Since there are considerable differences in the nature and extent of social participation among the strata, it is worthwhile to examine voluntary associations, to which we now turn.

[65] Marston, "Social Class as a Factor in Ethnic and Racial Segregation."

[66] Charles Abrams, *The City is the Frontier* (New York: Harper Colophon Books, 1967), pp. 61–63. The restrictive covenants were outlawed by the United States Supreme Court in 1948.

[67] Avery M. Guest, "Retesting the Burgess Zonal Hypothesis: The Location of White-Collar Workers," *American Journal of Sociology,* 76 (May 1971), 1094–1108.

[68] See Dennis C. McElrath, "The Social Areas of Rome: A Comparative Analysis," *American Sociological Review,* 27 (June 1962), 376–390; and Peter Collison and John Mogey, "Residence and Social Class in Oxford," *American Journal of Sociology,* 64 (May 1959), 599–605.

[69] Sylvia F. Fava, "Contrasts in Neighboring: New York City and a Suburban County," in William M. Dobriner, ed., *The Suburban Community* (New York: G. P. Putnam's Sons, 1958), pp. 124–131.

[70] See William H. Whyte, Jr., *The Organization Man* (Garden City, N.Y.: Doubleday Anchor Books, 1956), pp. 363–404; Bennet M. Berger, *Working Class Suburb* (Berkeley and Los Angeles: University of California Press, 1960), pp. 59–64; and Peter Willmott, *Class and Community,* cited in William M. Dobriner, *Class in Suburbia* (Englewood Cliffs, N.J.: Prentice-Hall, Inc., 1963), pp. 52–54.

[71] Erwin L. Linn, "Social Stratification of Discussions about Local Affairs," *American Journal of Sociology,* 72 (May 1967), 660–668.

PARTICIPATION IN VOLUNTARY ASSOCIATIONS

Actually, membership in voluntary organizations is not characteristic of the majority of Americans; yet those who do participate are likely to be from the higher strata.[72] Strata differences were observed in "Yankee City," a pseudonym for Newburyport, Massachusetts, a community of 17,000. Seventy-two per cent of the people in the highest strata belong to voluntary associations; in the next strata 61%, in the strata below that 49%, and in the lowest strata only 22%.[73] Among those who are members of organizations, the office-holders and the most active participants are likely to be from the higher strata.[74] By contrast lower-strata social participation tends to be limited to relatives or close friends. Even as regards interaction with friends it is greater among higher-status persons.[75]

There are important differences in the type of organization to which people belong: individuals from the higher levels are more likely to be members of instrumental organizations such as a community improvement association or a Chamber of Commerce.[76] It is through instrumental organizations that they are able to retain or increase the social goods they have and to exert power over the lower strata. (In that regard, recall the discussion of the draft board members in the previous chapter.) By contrast, not only are lower-status persons less likely to participate in voluntary associations, but those who do tend to belong to expressive organizations such as religious bodies.[77]

Yet the various religious organizations draw people disproportion-

[72] Charles R. Wright and Herbert H. Hyman, "Voluntary Association Memberships of American Adults: Evidence From National Sample Surveys," *American Sociological Review*, 23 (June 1958), 284–294; and "Trends in Voluntary Association Memberships of American Adults: Replication Based on Secondary Analysis of National Sample Surveys," 36 (April 1971), pp. 191–206.

[73] W. Lloyd Warner, *American Life: Dream and Reality* (Chicago: University of Chicago Press, 1964), p. 229.

[74] See, e.g., Thomas Bottomore, "Social Stratification in Voluntary Organizations," in David V. Glass, ed., *Social Mobility in Great Britain* (London: Routledge & Kegal Paul, Ltd., 1954), pp. 357–359, 368–369, 381–382; and Carol Slater, "Class Differences in Definition of Role and Membership in Voluntary Associations Among Urban Married Women," *American Journal of Sociology*, 65 (May 1960), 617.

[75] Leonard Reissman, "Class, Leisure, and Social Participation," *American Sociological Review*, 19 (February 1954), 76–84; Mirra Komarovsky, *Blue Collar Marriage*, pp. 323–324; and Robert W. Hodge and Donald J. Treiman, "Social Participation and Social Status," *American Sociological Review*, 33 (October 1968), 722–740.

[76] Alan Booth, Nicholas Babchuck, and Allen B. Knox, "Social Stratification and Membership in Instrumental-Expressive Voluntary Associations," *Sociological Quarterly*, 9 (Autumn 1968), 227–239.

[77] *Ibid.* Lower-strata persons who are in expressive organizations are also likely to belong to fraternal associations and unions. But they tend to be passive members. See Reissman, *op. cit.*; Komarovsky, *op. cit.*; and Hodge and Trieman, *op. cit.*

ately from different levels. For example, in Yankee City where only 15% of the population were in the upper and upper middle strata, these levels accounted for 43% of the Federated Church members (Presbyterian and Congregational). None of the members of the Baptist Church were upper strata, and only nine per cent were upper-middle.[78]

Gerhard Lenski's study of the Detroit area shows how religious affiliation is associated with stratum as well as with ethnic background. Of the 624 respondents who listed religious affiliation, 59% were Protestants, 37% Roman Catholic, and four per cent Jewish. Because of the area's large black population, the Protestants were divided into white and black, and the percentages of middle- and lower-strata persons in each category were examined. Forty-four per cent of the white Protestants were middle strata, as were 40% of the white Catholics; but only 13% of the black Protestants were in this category. Of the 27 Jews in the sample, 19 were middle- and only eight were lower-strata.[79]

Researches with national samples show how the several denominations differ according to members' status. For example, the Christian Scientists, Episcopal, and Congregational churches contain a relatively high proportion of upper-strata persons, while the Roman Catholic, Baptist, and Mormon draw most heavily from the lower strata.[80]

The major denominations were recently ranked according to education, occupation, and income with this result: the groups with the most education and income and in the highest status occupations were the Episcopalians, Jews, and Presbyterians; next were Methodists, Lutherans, and Roman Catholics; and last were white and black Baptists.[81] It should be noted that the rankings of religious bodies are relative and not absolute; that is, there are some lower strata persons who are members of the top-ranked denominations, and vice versa. Also, the members of the several religious groups differ in place of residence, educational achievement, and occupational composition and these factors critically affect stratum position.[82]

Church attendance and religiosity also differ among the strata, with persons from the higher levels participating more frequently.[83] However

[78] Warner, *American Life*, p. 230.

[79] Gerhard Lenski, *The Religious Factor* (Garden City, N.Y.: Doubleday Anchor Books 1963), p. 370. There are very few black Catholics and they are not included in Lenski's analyses.

[80] Herbert Schneider, *Religion in 20th Century America* (Cambridge, Mass.: Harvard University Press, 1952), p. 228.

[81] Bernard Lazerwitz, "A Comparison of Major United States Religious Groups," *Journal of the American Statistical Association*, 56 (September 1961), 568–579.

[82] Sidney Goldstein, "Socioeconomic Differentials Among Religious Groups in the United States," *American Journal of Sociology*, 74 (May 1969), 612–631; and Galan L. Gockel, "Income and Religious Affiliation: A Regression Analysis," pp. 632–647.

[83] See N. J. Demerath III, *Social Class in American Protestantism* (Chicago: Rand McNally & Co., 1965), pp. 3–4ff. Cf. Erich Goode, "Social Class and Church Participation," *American Journal of Sociology*, 72 (July 1966), 102–111.

church attendance should not be equated with religiosity. The more frequent attendance by white-collar people is related to their greater associational participation generally; to a large extent their church activity has become secularized. While blue-collar families are less active in formal church affairs their participation is more religious in character.[84]

The differences in social participation underline Genevieve Knupfer's observation, which we discussed in Chapter IV, that lower-strata families live in a very constricted social world. This has deleterious personal consequences; among them is the likelihood of a high degree of anomia, or the extent to which an individual feels distant and alienated from others.[85] Ephraim H. Mizruchi found a clear inverse association between stratum position and anomia, as well as between anomia and social participation. He suggests that because of both voluntary and involuntary processes, lower strata persons have limited access to those groups which provide a bridge between the individual and the community. Lack of confidence as well as rejection by higher-strata persons are probably responsible. Mizruchi further notes that the latent functions of participation in formal associations are ". . . the provision of a means of preventing personal demoralization through interaction: these serve as buffers against social psychological anomia." [86]

The anomia may help explain the tendency toward greater mental illness among the lower strata which was noted in a previous section. However, the limited participation also has political consequences, for some activities and organizations are instrumental in the distribution of social goods.

POLITICAL BEHAVIOR

Political behavior such as voting and participating in partisan activities and public affairs is an institutionalized means of contesting the allocation of social goods. But even with universal suffrage there are important strata differences in the degree of political involvement. An analysis of the adult population of the United States clearly shows that the higher the stratum the greater the percentage that votes. This is revealed by research on the 1972 national elections as well as by numerous other studies.[87] Among persons of voting age in the 1972 elections, 81% of the

[84] Erich Goode, op. cit., p. 111.

[85] See Ephraim H. Mizruchi, "Social Structure and Anomia in a Small City," American Sociological Review, 25 (October 1960), 645–654, especially p. 652.

[86] Ibid., pp. 653–654. The quotation is from p. 654.

[87] U.S. Bureau of the Census, "Voting and Registration in the Election of November 1972," Series P-20, No. 253 (Washington, D.C.: Government Printing Office, October 1973). See also Angus Campbell, Gerald Gurin, and Warren E. Miller, The Voter Decides (Evaston, Ill.: Row, Peterson and Co., 1954), pp. 72–73; Robert E. Lane, Political Life (New York: The Free Press, 1965), pp. 48–49; and Richard M. Scammon, "Electoral Participation," The Annals of the American Academy of Political and Social Science, 361 (May 1967), 63.

college graduates went to the polls, in contrast to 66% of the high-school graduates and 58% who had an elementary school education. Stratifying by occupation, 82% of the professionals voted while this was true of 61% of the craftsmen and 49% of the non-farm laborers. Only 42% of the farm laborers and foremen went to the polls. Using family income as an indicator of stratum position, 79% of the families earning $15,000 or more a year voted. This is in contrast to 46% where family income was under $3,000 a year.[88]

Data on all national elections going back to 1948 also show an inverse relationship between stratum position and voting: the lower the educational, occupational, and income levels, the greater the failure to vote.[89] Yet it is during national contests that the turnout is greatest. In municipal elections relatively few people vote and the strata differences are more pronounced: a much higher proportion of the voters are from the upper levels.[90]

Voting is but one form of political involvement. Lester Milbrath examined different degrees of political behavior and labelled the relatively passive ones "spectator activities" and the more active ones "gladiatorial activities." [91] The *spectator* exposes himself to political stimuli, votes, initiates a political discussion, attempts to talk another into voting a certain way, wears a campaign button, or puts a bumper sticker on his car. On the other hand the *gladiator* contributes time in a political campaign, becomes an active member of a political party, attends a caucus or a strategy meeting, solicits political funds, is a candidate, or holds a public or party office. After stratifying the respondents, Milbrath found that those from the working strata tend to participate mostly in spectator activities whereas the gladiators come from the higher strata.[92]

The association of strata position and political participation is not limited to the United States. Studies show strikingly similar patterns in Germany, Sweden, and Norway as well as in other countries for which there are data.[93]

---

[88] "Voting and Registration in the Election of November 1972," pp. 58, 103.

Among those who did not register to vote, 30% of elementary school graduates failed to do so, vs. 14% of college graduates. The figures are similar when occupation and income are considered: where family income was under $3,000 39% failed to register while this was true of 15% in the $15,000 or higher category; 40% of the laborers did not register while only 13% of the professionals failed to do so.

[89] Lane, *Political Life*. See also "Voting and Registration in the Election of November 1972," pp. 1–4.

[90] Howard D. Hamilton, "The Municipal Voter: Voting and Nonvoting in City Elections," *American Political Science Review*, 65 (December 1971), 1135–1140. Hamilton, in his study of Toledo, Ohio, found that occupation and income, but not education, were strongly associated with voter turnout.

[91] Lester W. Milbrath, *Political Participation* (Chicago: Rand McNally & Co., 1965), p. 18.

[92] Ibid., p. 117. Respondents were categorized according to the class they said they belonged to, and there were four levels: "Upper middle class;" "Average middle class;" "Upper working class," and "Average working class."

[93] Seymour M. Lipset, *Political Man* (Garden City, N.Y.: Doubleday & Co., 1960), p. 182.

Political party preference is also clearly related to status. The individual's decision to support one political party over another through voting or other means is the result of a number of factors in addition to stratification. Specific issues, candidates, national and international conditions at election time, and religious, regional, and historical considerations influence party choice. Nevertheless, "left" parties are supported by the lower strata while "right" parties are favored by the higher.[94] This is illustrated by the 1944 study of Erie County, Pennsylvania by Paul F. Lazarsfeld and his associates. Using criteria such as home, furniture, clothes, and money they placed their respondents into five ranks. It can be seen in Table VI-2 that, as one goes from the highest to the lowest, Democratic preference increases. More recent data show that although there are shifts from election to election the basic pattern remains: persons at higher status levels are likely to favor the Republican party, those at the lower levels the Democratic.[95] These left-right preferences hold in other countries, regardless of how the political parties are labeled. "On a world scale," Seymour M. Lipset writes, "the principal generalization which can be made is that parties are primarily based on either the lower classes or the middle and upper classes."[96] He points out that the United States is no exception in spite of the ideological emphasis on classlessness. Specifically,

> the Democrats from the beginning of their history have drawn more support from the lower strata of the society, while the Federalists, Whig, and Republican Parties have held the loyalties of the more priviledged groups.[97]

The basic explanation is that people collectively define their needs and in like manner decide which political groups best serve their interests. Consequently the left political orientation of the lower strata in-

TABLE VI-2. Socioeconomic Status and Political Party Preference (in percentages)

Socioeconomic Status	Political Party Preference		Number
	Republican	*Democratic*	
A Highest	71%	29%	(52)
B	68	32	(268)
C+	56	44	(561)
C−	46	54	(518)
D Lowest	35	65	(310)

Source: Adapted from Paul F. Lazarsfeld, Bernard Berelson, and Hazel Gaudet, *The People's Choice* (3rd ed.; New York: Columbia University Press, 1968), p. 19.

[94] *Ibid.*, pp. 223–228.

[95] Fred I. Greenstein, *The American Party System and the American People* (Englewood Cliffs, N.J.: Prentice-Hall, 1964), p. 24.

[96] Lipset, *Political Man*, p. 220.

[97] *Ibid.*, pp. 220–221. See also 286 ff.

cludes a conception of government as the primary agent for equitably distributing social goods. Thus lower-strata persons are less likely to object to government intervention in the economy or to welfare or other benefits, even if it means additional taxes for the higher strata. By contrast the latter argue for minimal governmental intervention and eschew policies which reduce their income or the value of their property or securities.[98] However their vociferous objections to governmental intervention is largely rhetoric for they are not adverse to obtaining public monies. Substantial subsidies for business, funds for industrial research and development, and similar benefits are actively sought and eagerly accepted.

The upper strata, as James Bryce observed, are more aware of issues which affect their interests; they have more to lose, they are less bound by sentiment, and are more prone to act.[99] As we noted previously the higher strata are more likely to vote than the lower, and they are more likely to participate in voluntary associations. The significance of these organizations is that members are part of a social network wherein they are likely to influence political outcomes, with voting one indicator of such efficacy. Participation in voluntary organizations mobilizes people to vote;[100] consequently the failure of the lower strata to participate obviates such an incentive. Even though they may belong to labor unions that kind of activity is not associated with voting; only with participation in true voluntary associations is there effective encouragement to go to the polls.[101]

The disinclination of the lower strata to be concerned with public issues or to participate politically—even though their potential is great because of their large numbers—stems from several factors. Among them is socialization which discourages critical analyses of the society and an emphasis on duties rather than rights, which we discussed in Chapter IV. Also, the conditions of life associated with being poor and uneducated discourage joining voluntary organizations or being interested in political affairs. Added to this is the seemingly limited effectiveness of a person's single vote.

Of course those lower-strata persons who are active in voluntary associations and interested in politics evidence a high degree of political participation.[102] But, such political involvement requires a sense of common

[98] See, e.g., *ibid.*, and Richard Centers, *The Psychology of Social Classes* (New York: Russell & Russell, 1961), pp. 55–73, 208.

[99] James Bryce, *The American Commonwealth* (New York: Macmillan, 1900), Vol. II, pp. 247–254.

[100] Marvin E. Olsen, "Social Participation and Voting Turnout: A Multivariate Analysis," *American Sociological Review*, 37 (June 1972), 317–332.

[101] *Ibid.*, p. 322.

[102] See Paul Burstein, "Social Structure and Individual Political Participation in Five Countries," *American Journal of Sociology*, 77 (May 1972), 1087–1110.

interests and group identity, as Marvin E. Olsen's study of Detroit and Indianapolis indicates.[103] In these cities, with socioeconomic status and age held constant blacks were found to participate more than whites. Apparently the Civil Rights movement of the 1960's gave blacks an impetus to become more active in all kinds of social and political activities; moreover, those blacks who identify as members of an ethnic community are much more active than those who do not.[104]

Such conditions are a part of the process of communalization, whereby strata form into classes, which we will examine in later chapters. However it is quite clear that under ordinary circumstances the lower the stratum the more limited the social and political participation. In turn this exacerbates the inequitous distribution of social goods which was detailed earlier in this chapter and in the preceding ones. The inequality is clearly evident not only in material things, educational and other opportunity, and political efficacy, but also in the primary means of allocating social goods, the law.

The importance of the law in a liberal parliamentary democracy such as the United States for distributing social goods was touched on in Chapter I. Subsequently, when we surveyed adolescents (Chapter IV) we observed how the administration of the laws differs according to stratum position; in the next section we look at how adults from the several strata fare.

Some Are More Equal than Others
Before the Law

Studies have shown that higher-status persons do not seem to be any more law-abiding than lower-status individuals; [105] yet the definitions of what constitute unlawful behavior vary, usually to the disadvantage of the lower strata. Moreover, where behavior is judged illegal the penalties also vary, again to the disadvantage of the lower levels. Gambling on the stock market is not a crime but a bet with the neighborhood bookmaker is; a $100 robbery may result in a ten-year jail term; a $100,000 embezzlement in a suspended sentence. The small-time criminals from the lower strata are likely to experience the wrath of the justice system; yet higher-status persons who commit crimes in the course of their occupation—what are called "white-collar crimes"—are likely to be treated

[103] Marvin E. Olsen, "Social and Political Participation of Blacks," *American Sociological Review*, 35 (August 1970), 682–696.

[104] *Ibid.*, pp. 695–696.

[105] See Edwin H. Sutherland, *White-Collar Crime* (New York: Dryden Press, 1949); and Austin L. Porterfield, *Youth in Trouble* (Fort Worth, Texas: Leo Potishman Foundation, 1946).

leniently because of differential laws and procedures.[106] Edwin H. Sutherland emphasizes the importance of the bias involved in the administration of criminal justice under laws which apply exclusively to business and the professions and which therefore involve only the upper socioeconomic class. Persons who violate laws regarding restraint of trade, advertising, or pure food and drugs are not arrested by uniformed policemen, are not often tried in criminal courts, and are not committed to prisons; their illegal behavior generally receives the attention of administrative commissions and of courts operating under civil or equity jurisdiction.[107]

Jail sentences for white-collar crimes are extremely rare. A recent exception involved the former chairman of the scandal-ridden Four Seasons Nursing Centers of America, Inc., who is a millionaire. Federal prosecutors estimated that his fraudulent stock practices had cost unwary shareholders $200 million, that he had profited personally by $10 million, and that he had $4 million hidden in a secret Delaware trust. The maximum sentence the law allows for such a crime is five years in prison and a $10,000 fine, and the prosecutors had urged "substantial punishment." The penalty? One year in prison with parole possible after only four months.[108]

The usual punishment in these cases is little more than a slap on the wrist; the result of consent agreements between the government and the accused in which they promise not to do it again. Some examples from the Securities and Exchange Commission: the managing partner of a brokerage house charged with "gross abuse of trust" and "personal misconduct" in his handling of an in-house mutual fund: a 90-day suspension from engaging in the securities business; a security analyst who was found to have "willfully violated" securities laws by inducing customers to buy stock through false and misleading statements about a company's prospects: censure; the senior vice president and general manager of the International Telephone and Telegraph Corporation, who did not contest the finding that he had sold some of his ITT stock on the basis of inside information: an order not to repeat his performance. Also, since a corporation is a legal entity, violations of the law can result in the corporation being fined while its officers and executives escape prosecution.[109]

For other types of crimes, which are likely to involve lower-strata people, the justice system is not so lenient. Let us assume that a person is arrested. The usual procedure is for the court to release the individual on bail which means that he must post a bond. This is a sum of money or other security which is forfeited if he fails to appear for trial. Often the

[106] Sutherland, *op. cit.*

[107] *Ibid.*, p. 8.

[108] Michael C. Jensen, "Leniency on White-Collar Crime Scored," *New York Times* (September 22, 1973), pp. 37 ff.

[109] *Ibid.*

money is provided by a bail bond broker whose fee is ten per cent of the amount required. Since it usually takes several months if not a year or more for cases to come to trial the bail system allows the accused to remain free until his case comes up; otherwise the waiting period would be spent in jail. There is value in the bond arrangement not only because the accused is able to continue his normal life, but also because many who are tried are found innocent, numerous cases are dismissed for lack of evidence, or the person found guilty may be given a suspended sentence. However the overcrowded court dockets and the system of release on bail work to the disadvantage of the poor person. He usually doesn't have the savings or securities which can be used as a bond; more likely he will be unable to afford the fee of a bail bond broker, especially if the court has set a relatively high bail. Then after spending say a year in jail, during which time he has lost his job and seen his family placed on welfare, his case may be dismissed or he may be found innocent.

Only in recent years have there been moves to remedy this situation. The Bail Reform Act passed by the United States Congress in 1966 provides procedures whereby most persons involved in federal offenses will not have to post bail prior to trial. And where bail is required the conditions are very lenient. Also, those convicted receive credit for all time served before trial and for any fines imposed.[110]

This law as well as recent decisions by the United States Supreme Court will increase justice for the lower strata. They provide greater protection against illegal search and seizure and prohibit the use of such evidence in court (*Mapp*, 1961); require that indigent persons accused of crime be represented by an attorney (*Gideon*, 1963); stipulate that a suspect cannot be denied a lawyer if he asks for one (*Escobedo*, 1964), and require that the police must emphatically inform a suspect of the right to counsel and cannot question him unless counsel is present (*Miranda*, 1966).[111]

Although there have been reforms in some state and local jurisdictions the inequities continue in most police and county courts; the Bail Reform Act, for example, applies only to the Federal level. It is the poor and uneducated who do not know their rights, who are unable to raise bond money, and who cannot afford a lawyer; it is they who remain in jail for substantial periods of time awaiting trial. These local jails are among the worst in the nation as regards brutality, overcrowding, poor living conditions and inadequate social, psychological, and medical services. Usually the public is unaware of the horror of these institutions until a riot breaks out.[112]

[110] American Civil Liberties Union, *New Dimensions . . . New Challenges; 46th Annual Report* (New York: American Civil Liberties Union, 1967), p. 42.

[111] *Ibid.*, pp. 37–40.

[112] For a participant-observer's account of life in a county jail see Donald Jonjack and William Braden, " 'An Absolute Hell': A Woman's Story of Jail," in Howard E. Freeman and Norman R. Kurtz, eds., *America's Troubles* (Englewood Cliffs, N.J.: Prentice-Hall, 1969), pp. 436–439.

In an experiment in one New York City precinct, persons accused of minor crimes were released on their own recognizance if the police captain felt that because of roots in the community they would appear for trial. The Vera Foundation, helped by a Ford Foundation grant, provided workers who were mostly law students. They obtained background information for the police captain and in that precinct 99% of those released returned for trial. While 48% of these persons were convicted, 52% were either acquitted or had their cases dismissed.[113]

Judicial procedures even under the most humanitarian circumstances are frightening and degrading. The accused very soon becomes aware of the mammoth institutional forces arrayed against him: the police, the grand jury, the district attorney, and the prison system. Supreme Court decisions not withstanding, the arrested is likely to be treated as though he were guilty until proven innocent. Other things being equal, the lower the stratum of the accused the worst the treatment.

While the threats and abuse may be unwitting, the courts may consciously be used to degrade and harass individuals as well as to impose concrete sanctions.[114] Recent illustrations of such use of the police and the courts in the United States involved civil rights activists and organizers of migrant farm workers in California and the Southwest. Actually, both here and abroad the police and the courts have commonly been employed against union organizers and others who seriously threaten the power of superordinates, especially when it may lead to a redistribution of social goods. The manner in which such institutional arrangements benefit the higher strata and the upper classes will be explored further in subsequent chapters.

There is another way in which the legal system works to the disadvantage of the lower strata that was touched on earlier: the enforcement of unethical and illegal practices by merchants and credit houses that deal with the poor.[115] Even where there are consumer protection laws low status persons are usually unaware of them; also, they are generally ignorant of the complex legal conditions in the contracts they sign for "easy credit." Often they do not realize that even if the merchant does not live up to his obligations they are still responsible for full payment.[116] The used car might break down after only a month's use. The sewing machine that is advertised may turn out to be practically unworkable and the customer is pressured into buying a much more expensive model. A television set which is cheaper than the customer paid for may be delivered. Or, inferior merchandise may be sold at highly inflated

---

[113] Gertrude Samuels, "A Summons Instead of an Arrest," *New York Times Magazine* (July 26, 1964), pp. 16 ff.

[114] See Robert J. Antonio, "The Processual Dimensions of Degradation Ceremonies: The Chicago Conspiracy Trial: Success or Failure?" *British Journal of Sociology*, 23 (September 1972), 287–297.

[115] See Caplovitz, *The Poor Pay More*, pp. 140–154.

[116] *Ibid.*, pp. 155, 158, 169, 190–191.

prices. Should the purchasers refuse to make a payment they are liable for the total cost of the goods, credit charges, and expenses for collecting the debt.

When a payment is missed, whatever the reason, they soon feel the force of the legal system, for in fact the courts work as a collection agency for merchants who sell to the poor. It is quite common for a person in arrears to have a judgment rendered against him without knowing anything about it, even though the law gives the consumer seven days in which to answer a summons. Earlier we cited the case of a housewife who bought a wristwatch on credit from a door-to-door salesman, and later found out that she would be paying ten times the amount it was worth. "I called up the company," she reported,

> and said *I wouldn't pay for it and they should come and get it. They told me I had to pay or they would take me to court. And I said, "fine, take me to court and I'll have the watch there."* Next thing I know about this I get a court notice of Judgment by Default from Brooklyn Municipal Court for $69 balance, $3 interest, $5 "costs by statute," $14 court costs. *The total cost of the watch was $91.*[117]

Judgments by default are quite common for lower-strata persons; they may not understand what will happen if they fail to appear in court; it may be located some distance from where they live, they may be unwilling to lose a day's work, or they may simply forget. But often they never receive the summons, for the process server may simply throw it away. In legal circles this is known as "sewer service." [118] Consequently, they learn about the merchant's or credit agency's claim only after the court notifies them that they have been judged in default. Or they may get the news when they are informed by their employer that their wages have been attached.

But even if the lower-strata person does come to court the chances of his receiving justice are not too good. For one thing, the buyer usually does not understand that when he signs the installment contract and promissory note he gives up some of his rights; nor does he realize that he makes it extremely easy for the creditor to obtain a judgment against him. These waivers exist in many states—Illinois for example—and this is the usual wording: "The undersigned . . . hereby authorize(s) irrevocably any Attorney of any Court of Record to appear for the undersigned . . . after any default and confess a judgment without process in favor of the holder hereof. . . ." [119] And these are the consequences:

> The man dressed in work clothes heard his name called in the courtroom and stepped up to the bench.

[117] *Ibid.*, p. 160. Emphasis in the original.

[118] *Ibid.*, p. 161.

[119] Joseph Reilly, "Debt Trap: Some Can't Spring It," *Chicago Sun-Times* (September 30, 1971), pp. 8 ff.

"Mr. Lopez," said the judge, "the Nadir Furniture Co. says you owe them $500. Do you agree or disagree?"

There wasn't much question about the debt, the man knew, but there were circumstances that forced him to miss a couple of payments. Surely he could explain that later.

"Yes," said the man, "$500. That's right,"

The judge glanced toward his clerk and said, "by agreement."

The man didn't understand. He stood there waiting to see what would happen next.

Then someone told him that it was all over, that he had just "agreed" to a judgment against himself, that now his debt was more than $500 because he had to pay court costs plus a fee to the lawyer who represented the company, and that the company now was empowered to freeze his bank account and property or garnishee his wages.[120]

The merchandise is usually repossessed and if the money owed cannot be obtained from a savings account or garnishment of wages, anything else of value may be seized, with the exception of items needed for living such as beds or chairs. City Marshals, as in New York, are empowered to repossess goods and on occasion may be quite rough in carrying out their duties. A Puerto Rican family bought three lamps on credit but were unable to make one of the payments. Although the amount they still owed was $32 the firm raised it to $80, and the husband relates his encounter with the representatives of the law:

The Marshal came with a policeman and *they wanted to take the TV instead of the lamps*. I wouldn't let them. *I had $36 in my pocket and when they pushed me* (I had the baby in my arms) my wallet fell out. *They grabbed the wallet and took the $36.*[121]

The preceding discussion of the laws and the way they are administered indicates again the differential distribution of social goods. In focusing on the significance of stratification for childhood, adolescence, and adulthood we have in a limited fashion tried to trace the relevance of stratification through the life course. It therefore seems fitting to end this chapter with social, medical, and economic conditions of old age as they are related to social stratification.

Some Social, Economic, and Medical Aspects of Old Age

Increasingly old age is a social problem, generated by long-range demographic and occupational trends and changes in social relationships.

[120] *Ibid.*, p. 8.

[121] Caplovitz, *The Poor Pay More*, pp. 162, 189–190. The quotation is from p. 162. Emphasis in the original.

First, life expectancy has been increasing and there are more older persons in the population. In the United States, a child born in 1900 could expect to live 47 years; by contrast the child born in 1973 had a life expectancy of 71 years.[122] In 1900 only four per cent of the population was 65 or older, but by 1972 the percentage had risen to ten.[123] Second, the proportion of older persons who work is much lower than it was in 1900: at that time 63% of males 65 or over were in the labor force, whereas in 1971 the percentage was only 26.[124]

One of the consequences of old age is low income, primarily because of withdrawal from the labor market. Whereas the national median for families in 1973 was $12,051, it was $6,425 where the head was 65 or over. The median for unrelated individuals 65 years of age or older, which includes widows and widowers, was only $4,106 for men and $2,119 for women.[125] Eleven per cent of the families with an aged head were below the poverty level; for unrelated individuals the percentage was three times as much.[126]

There is no question that such limited financial resources greatly exacerbate the problems of the aged. The first we shall look at is social isolation and mental health.

SOCIAL ISOLATION AND MENTAL HEALTH

Today the aged are not needed by the community or their family as was true in earlier times. In modern society younger persons are favored in most occupations, and family structure and community organization are such that there are few meaningful roles for the elderly.[127] With increasing age, many face greater isolation since children leave home; the

[122] U.S. National Center for Health Statistics, *Vital Statistics of the United States*, Vol. II *Life Tables*, p. 4. See also U.S. Bureau of the Census, "Some Demographic Aspects of Aging in the United States," Series P-23, No. 43 (Washington, D.C.: Government Printing Office, February 1973), p. 15.

[123] U.S. Bureau of the Census, *Historical Statistics of the U.S., Colonial Times to 1957*, (Washington, D.C.: Government Printing Office, 1961), p. 8; and "Estimates of the Population of States, By Age: July 1, 1971 and 1972," Series P-25, No. 500 (Washington, D.C.: Government Printing Office, May 1973), p. 2.

[124] *Historical Statistics of the U.S., Colonial Times to 1957*, p. 71; and "Some Demographic Aspects of Aging in the United States," p. 217. For women 65 or older there was a very small increase during this period: from nine per cent in 1900 to around ten per cent in 1971.

[125] U.S. Bureau of the Census, "Money Income in 1973 of Families and Persons in the United States," Series P-60, No. 97 (Washington, D.C.: Government Printing Office, January 1975), pp. 63, 112.

[126] U.S. Bureau of the Census, "Characteristics of the Low-Income Population: 1973," Series P-60, No. 98 (Washington, D.C.: Government Printing Office, January 1975), p. 98.

[127] See Ruth S. Cavan et al., *Personal Adjustment in Old Age* (Chicago: Science Research Associates, 1949), pp. 33–35; and Tamme Wittermans and Irving Krauss, "Structural Marginality and Social Worth," *Sociology and Social Research*, 48 (April 1964), 348–360. See also Bernard Kutner et al, *Five Hundred Over Sixty* (N.Y.: Russell Sage Foundation, 1956), pp. 77–79, 252–254.

spouse, relatives, or friends may die; the worker retires. Yet degree of isolation differs among the aged: it is likely to be considerably greater for lower- than for higher-strata persons.[128] Also, responses to the conditions making for isolation vary among the strata, as shown by Zena Smith Blau's research on the impact of widowhood and retirement on the friendships of older people.[129] Since friends are likely to be of the same age and sex, retirement or widowhood are detrimental to friendship if the friends have spouses who are still living or working. Friendship is also strained when spouses are alive but friends become widowed. The effect is the same if one's spouse still works but friends retire.

Blau found that for all the strata widowhood or retirement had adverse effects on friendship when peers' spouses were alive or still employed. However, in the upper and middle strata, friendships were retained where persons were widowed and where friends also lost their spouses. Similarly, the retired in the upper and middle strata retained their friendship with those who had also retired.

In the lower strata widowhood or retirement had consistently adverse effects on friendships, even where a person was widowed and friends were widowed, or where the individual was retired and friends were also retired. She suggests that the higher-strata persons' greater participation in social affairs in earlier years provides them with a reservoir of social activities which they can draw on in old age. By contrast the more limited participation by lower-strata individuals means that with widowhood or retirement social isolation is much more certain. In addition, their changed status is likely to be accompanied by severe economic deprivation which further limits social activities.[130]

There is some evidence that one of the consequences of social isolation in old age is a tendency toward poor mental health.[131] However, isolation by itself is not a cause, according to Marjorie Fiske Lowenthal's study of 1,200 institutionalized and non-institutionalized elderly persons. She notes that lifelong extreme isolation, what she calls alienation, does not necessarily lead to the kinds of psychiatric problems associated with the aged. For some social isolation may be a consequence rather than a cause of mental disorder; also, physical illness may be the critical antecedent to both isolation and mental illness.[132]

Yet there is evidence of a higher incidence of mental disorder, both hospitalized and non-hospitalized, among the aged than among younger

[128] See, e.g., Marjorie Fiske Lowenthal, "Social Isolation and Mental Illness in Old Age," *American Sociological Review*, 29 (February 1964), 60–61 and Kutner, *op. cit.*, pp. 110, 121.

[129] Zena Smith Blau, "Structural Constraints on Friendships in Old Age," *American Sociological Review*, 26 (June 1961), pp. 429–439. See also Kutner, *op. cit.*, pp. 101–122.

[130] *Ibid.*

[131] See, e.g., Ernest M. Gruenberg, "Community Conditions and Psychoses of the Elderly," *The American Journal of Psychiatry*, 110 (June 1954), 888–896.

[132] Lowenthal, *op. cit.*, pp. 68–70. Cf. Kutner, *op. cit.*, pp. 121–122.

persons.[133] This is not unexpected for social and economic as well as physical difficulties are likely to increase later in life. The person may be unable to cope with emotional problems or with degenerative physiological processes associated with old age, which may lead to mental disorder. Nevertheless the lower-strata aged are much more likely to have poor mental health than those from higher socioeconomic backgrounds.[134] Not only that, but there are sharp differences in the treatment of persons with senile psychosis: if they are from the upper strata they are likely to be given psychotherapy, but if from the lower they are much more apt to receive custodial care.[135]

Physical Disabilities

There is no question that physical disabilities increase with age; for example, the death rate from cancer in the United States in 1966–1967 among males 25–34 years old was 18.3 per 100,000 whereas for those 75 and over it was 1,472.1.[136] However, there are important strata differences in this death rate: the United States Public Health Service found that there is a fairly inverse gradient of cancer incidence by income category. Also, the lower the income level the more advanced the disease is likely to be when diagnosed.[137]

In a recent analysis of mortality from cancer among the policyholders of a large insurance company, two broad strata were compared. The first consisted of standard ordinary policyholders, persons drawn chiefly from "urban middle and well-to-do classes engaged in nonhazardous work." The second was composed of industrial policyholders who ". . . are mainly members of urban wage-earning families in the lower income brackets where a considerable proportion of the men are engaged in unskilled or hazardous occupational activities." [138] At every age category the death rates from cancer were greater for the lower- than for the

---

[133] See, e.g., Seymour S. Bellin and Robert H. Hardt, "Marital Status and Mental Disorders Among the Aged," *American Sociological Review,* 23 (April 1958), 155–162; Hollingshead and Redlich, *Social Class and Mental Illness,* and Langer and Michael, *Life Stress and Mental Health,* p. 77.

[134] Bellin and Hardt, *op. cit.,* p. 159; and Hollingshead and Redlich, *loc. cit.*

[135] Hollingshead and Redlich, *op. cit.,* p. 290. Among persons with senile psychosis, those in the top two strata were equally likely to receive custodial care or psychotherapy; in the middle stratum three times as many were given custodial care as psychotherapy, while for the bottom two strata custodial care was given six times as frequently as psychotherapy.

[136] Metropolitan Life Insurance Company, *Statistical Bulletin,* Vol. 48 (October 1967), p. 8. See also Vol. 49 (August 1968), pp. 2–4.

[137] Harold F. Dorn and Sidney J. Cutter, *Morbidity from Cancer in the United States,* Public Health Monograph No. 56 (Washington, D.C.: Department of Health, Education and Welfare, 1959), Part II, "Trend in Morbidity, Association with Income and Stage at Diagnosis," pp. 106, 117.

[138] Metropolitan Life Insurance Company, *op. cit.*

higher-strata policyholders.[139] This report also found that, among persons with higher income, cancer tends to be diagnosed earlier and is likely to be localized at the site of origin when discovered. An association between income and cancer was also found for lower-strata women, although their rate was less than for men. The researchers suggest that since the wives are not subjected to the hazardous working conditions of their husbands there may be personal and environmental factors which increase their incidence. They also suggested that such factors may contribute to the husbands' high rate.[140] However, it is primarily the work situation which is responsible for the high rate of cancer among lower-strata men. In addition, their families are affected through exposure to carcinogenic agents which saturate the husband's work clothes. For example, not only do persons such as asbestos workers have an exceptionally high rate of cancer, but it is also abnormally high for their wives.

The death rates from other diseases such as diabetes and cirrhosis of the liver are also higher for persons from the lower strata;[141] in fact, the lower the stratum the higher the death rate from all causes.[142]

Summary

The foregoing examination of the life course makes it abundantly clear that there is substantial variation among the strata in the distribution of social goods in infancy and adolescence, during the period of youth, and in adulthood through old age. The differences include infant mortality rates, educational and occupational opportunity, amount of income, social participation, and mental and physical well-being. In addition, we described how inequities are reinforced through institutional arrangements such as the educational, legal, and military-service systems.

Granted there are these inequities, why do they persist? We suggest three main reasons. The first is basically sociological and refers to the constraints in any organized human group, which influence people to act and think in ways which support existing institutional arrangements. This was brought out in the discussion of courtship and marriage practices which discourage cross-strata mating, which in turn help perpetu-

---

[139] *Ibid.*, pp. 9–10.

[140] *Ibid.*, p. 10.

[141] Metropolitan Life Insurance Co., *op. cit.*, Vol. 49, (August 1968), pp. 5–7 and (June 1968), pp. 4–6. See also Rushing, "Alcoholism and Suicide Rates by Status Set and Occupation," *Quarterly Journal of Studies on Alcohol*, 29 (June 1968), 399–412.

[142] Jacob Tuckman, William F. Youngman, and Garry B. Kreizman, "Occupational Level and Mortality," *Social Forces*, 43 (May 1965), 575–577. See also I. M. Moriyama and L. Guralnick, "Occupational and Social Class Differences in Mortality," in *Trends and Differentials in Mortality* (New York: Milbank Memorial Fund, 1956), pp. 61–73.

ate a stratification system. These kinds of constraints are found in most other areas of behavior, and their outcome is the same.

The second reason is largely political. The inequities are obviously advantageous to the higher strata, and they may be expected to act in ways, and hold beliefs, which support the existing distribution of social goods. Not only are they able to influence institutional arrangements to their benefit—we touched on this, and will go into greater detail later—but they also promulgate certain ideas and viewpoints which justify the way things are. What is extremely important about the outlook, or ideology, is that by and large it is accepted by the lower strata. This ideology, which we commonly call the American Dream, holds that there is equality of opportunity, and anyone who tries hard enough can get ahead. On the other hand, failure is blamed on personal inadequacies; those who don't make it have the wrong values, attitudes, and characteristics.[143] This perspective encourages people to strive so that they can partake of the largesse available at the higher levels; consequently strata differences are seen as necessary to spur people on. In this manner the beliefs lead to acceptance of the status quo, and such acceptance is strengthened by blaming the individual for failure and not the social system. The ideology is also very helpful for the competitiveness and constant expansion of industrial society; therefore it is not surprising that it is found in non-capitalist as well as capitalist countries.[144]

The success ideology shows up in many contexts; for example, it underlay the recent Federal War on Poverty which was designed to change the defeatist and cynical attitudes of the poor. These programs helped support the stratification system, for by focusing on individual inadequacies they limited questioning whether structural conditions might be responsible for such things as poverty. This avoids raising the issue as to whether people might be poor not because of lack of achievement motivation, but because of societal circumstances which keep them from obtaining education and jobs. Thus the social order is protected from disruptive criticism, in spite of the gap between the myth of equal opportunity and objective conditions.[145]

In addition, the higher strata tend to be active in all phases of organizational life. Even though this participation is costly in terms of time and money, the payoff is greater control over social goods, from the obtaining of honors to concrete benefits such as monetary ones. This makes them feel more efficacious and they are encouraged to participate and strive even more. But it also encourages them to promulgate the ideology

---

[143] Joan Huber and William H. Form, *Income and Ideology*, (New York: The Free Press, 1973), pp. 6–7 ff. and Ephraim H. Mizruchi, *Success and Opportunity* (London: The Free Press, 1964), pp. 70, 87, 89 ff.

[144] Huber and Form, *op. cit.*, p. 6–7, 157.

[145] Mizruchi, *Success and Opportunity*, p. 89; and Huber and Form, *Income and Ideology*, pp. xi–xii.

of equality of opportunity, with its stress on personal shortcomings as the explanation of failure.[146]

Now one can understand why the higher strata support the inequities and why they promote beliefs which justify the differences. But why do the lower strata accept things as they are? For it is apparent that people on the bottom are not happy with their situation. This is true even in those social orders where great inequality has been institutionalized and where the deprived show public acceptance and appropriate defferential behavior. Yet in private they exhibit strong feelings against the existing arrangements and deny their legitimacy.[147]

The third reason for the persistence of inequities is primarily sociological, although there are some political aspects. We noted earlier that the success ideology permeates the society, and that the lower strata give greater assent to it. However, in their life experiences they are faced with the gap between the myth of equal opportunity and objective conditions, and are forced to come to grips with the inability to achieve to the degree promoted by the American Dream. One response is to limit educational and occupational goals in favor of security, and a consequence is likely to be personal demoralization, which works against challenging the status quo. The fact that channels for alternative attainment, such as civic, political, or religious organizations are less available than for the higher strata exacerbates this consequence. Another outcome is conservatism, because of the fear of losing what little one has.[148] Also, the lesser integration of the lower strata with the organizational life of the community limits the benefits they could attain through the political process, and results in feelings of inefficacy which in turn often discourage even minimal participation such as voting.[149]

The belief that everyone accepts the American Dream may be a part of the ideology itself. There is evidence that the lower strata give assent when it is stated in global terms, and that their expectations and behaviors, grounded in the reality of deprivation, indicate a modification and growing disenchantment with the ideology.[150] However, deprivation, whether absolute—for example not enough food on the table—or relative—the schoolteacher makes less than the plumber—does not necessarily lead to challenging the status quo. Neither does discontent, even when it is expressed openly. For example, among the lower strata it is usually a "gut level" reaction to immediate difficulties. The response is mostly verbal and is the basis of the "populist" feelings evident among

[146] Huber and Form, *op. cit.*, p. 151.

[147] See, e.g., Gerald D. Berreman, "Caste in India and the United States," *American Journal of Sociology*, 66 (September 1960), 120–127.

[148] Mizruchi, *Success and Opportunity*, pp. 89, 109, 117–119, 121.

[149] Huber and Form, *Income and Ideology*, p. 151; and Mizruchi, *Success and Opportunity*, p. 117.

[150] Huber and Form, *op. cit.*, pp. 151, 153–154.

the lower levels; however, it ordinarily does not lead to action to alter the distribution of social goods.[151]

We are interested in analyzing what is responsible for people accepting things as they are or striving to bring about change, and this will be our interest in the remainder of the book. We will be concerned with material conditions as well as ideologies. In the next chapter we examine the history of stratification and class, for as great as the strata differences in modern society are they do not compare with those of earlier times. In most preindustrial societies there were fewer social goods overall, many more people toiled for the benefit of very few, and the differences between the have-nots and the haves were much more substantial. We will look at these differences but with particular interest in cases where lower strata, or segments of them, formed into classes and challenged the authority structure.

[151] See Michael Mann, "The Social Cohesion of Liberal Democracy," *American Sociological Review*, 35 (June 1970), 423–439.

Part Three

MATERIAL AND
IDEATIONAL CHANGE

Chapter VII. Stratification and Class in Preindustrial Society

In preindustrial society there was not only great inequality in the distribution of social goods, but it was more critical in terms of the well-being of the lower strata. If we had adequate data to study the life course as we did in the preceding chapters, we would most likely find that at every stage those toward the bottom were much worse off economically, socially, and legally than their counterparts today. Unfortunately the data are fragmentary, for, among other reasons, historians find the lives of the upper strata much more interesting than those of the lower. Nevertheless there is sufficient information to piece together what conditions were like. We will not be content with simply showing strata differences, however; we are also interested in the actions taken by numbers of people to change the allocation of social goods. The movement may involve the mass or an elite, or particular ethnic or regional groups; it may be religiously based or secular. An organized attempt to alter things may be "progressive" in that lower-status persons with new ideas, or with technical or business innovations challenge those in power who persist in doing things the old way, even though it is no longer appropriate. Or, it may be "reactionary": the ruling group, in seeking to maintain its position, prevents needed change.

There are a number of factors which contribute to such class behavior, which were outlined in Chapter I. The structural aspects of the society including its economic base and the legal system are extremely important. So are rapid economic, demographic, or political changes which alter the accommodations among the strata; conditions which facilitate the upward or downward mobility of important segments of the population; and absolute deprivation resulting in collective behavior such as riots, which lead to organized movements. Or, relative deprivation where particular strata feel they are not getting their due. A critical element seems to be how people define the situation they are in: if there are plausible explanations which justify conditions, and if these explanations are accepted, then great deprivation may continue for a long time without those who suffer trying to do anything about it. On the other hand if one section of the public has begun to question the legitimacy of the existing distribution of social goods, people may reject the justifica-

193

tion. Discontent may then become channeled into a movement for change.

Social scientists are well aware that the form a society takes, including its strata and classes, is strongly influenced by social, economic, and political conditions. But they also understand that the particular institutions, practices, and values are shaped by the history of that society. This history is made up of the thousands and thousands of everyday behaviors, most of which are probably habitual ways of coping with the immediate contingencies of life. The actions may be cumulative: old practices may gradually be replaced by new, tastes may change; the culture may "drift" until, from the vantage point of hindsight, the scholar may discover trends or the replacement of old forms by new. But history is also made up of more spectacular occurrences such as wars, revolutions, natural disasters, and major inventions and discoveries, although hindsight is often responsible for defining them as critical events.

The myriad events, both spectacular and commonplace, affect the ordering of categories of people and help shape the relations among them. Some of these occurrences are particularly important for stratification and class and they will be studied in terms of economic, demographic, and political change. The growth of trade, commerce, handicrafts, and manufacturing will be examined, as will population increase and migration, as both causes and consequences of economic expansion. In addition, political transformations will be investigated, including the emergence of the nation-state.

The alterations that took place in Western society resulted in a monetary economy; larger political units; a growing rationalism, secularism, and pragmatism in social and religious life; and conflict and upheavals which began to involve significant portions of the mass of the population. The latter occurred largely as a result of the changing conditions over a long period of time which attenuated traditional ideas, expectations, and relationships; brought into being new ruling strata which challenged and eventually replaced older ones; created a free labor force; and inspired Utopian and millenial social movements. These changes led to two important revolutions, the Industrial and the French, which significantly altered Western society in terms of economic, political and social life and later most of the rest of the world.

In order to try to understand the tremendous transformations that took place, it is useful to first look at some of the social, economic, and political aspects of preindustrial society.

Social, Economic, and Political Aspects of Life

The primary stage of economic development characterized preindustrial times. Most families lived in small agricultural villages, provided for their own needs and governed themselves through some organization of community elders.[1] The communities were economically and politically self-sufficient; conflicts and other differences were resolved within the group. This is illustrated in a small Turkish village where ". . . any small disagreement

> is settled by the help of the elders, the kin and even neighbors. . . . Besides, an official headmen [sic] of the village appointed by the people who is called "Muhtar" helps with every matter of the community. The muhtar solves matters when someone has been harmed by the killing of some of his herd or by the destroying of some of his crops etc.[2]

There was no need for recourse to a larger political entity, and the incidents mentioned above were never reported to the government.

Where there was a larger political structure it was usually meaningful for most villagers through tax collectors or pillaging soldiers, either local or from outside the area. Thus for most people their village and nearby communities constituted the world; the rest was foreboding and strange; the stranger such as the itinerant trader was accepted as long as he served the needs of the village. Many of the activities such as planting and harvesting depended on the seasons and consequently much of what people did was predictable and there was a high degree of regularity to life. These activities as well as critical events in the life cycle—birth, puberty, marriage, and death—were enveloped with ritual, involved mutual rights and obligations, and were an integral part of the closed communities. Large-scale and rapid change were not welcome, for they were likely to be catastrophic, as in the case of invasions, droughts, floods, or other calamities. Innovations in social, political, and economic arrangements were reluctantly accepted by these tradition-bound and highly superstitious people. Population growth was slow, undoubtedly reflecting limited resources.

Nevertheless change of great magnitude occurred: there was tremendous economic, political, and population expansion in the ancient world. Beginning about 8000 B.C. there had been important innovations in food production and a more efficient use of what nature had to offer.[3] Over time specialization increased and there was greater efficiency and stability in the production and distribution of food and other requirements. These were necessary conditions for the support of a larger population and it is estimated that by 6000 B.C. there were between one and five million people in the world. While for the preceding 100,000 years the increase had been one-and-a-half per cent per century, beginning around

---

[1] See Colin Clark, *The Conditions of Economic Progress* (3rd ed.; London: Macmillan, 1957).

[2] Nermin Erdentug, *A Study on the Social Structure of a Turkish Village* (Ankara: Ayyildiz; Publications of the Faculty of Languages, History and Geography, University of Ankara, No. 130, 1959), p. 54.

[3] Robert J. Braidwood, "The Agricultural Revolution," *Scientific American*, 203 (September 1960), 130–152.

6000 B.C. the rate shot up to between six and ten per cent each century. At the time of Christ the world's population was 200 to 300 million.[4]

The vast majority of the population was rural, yet there were cities. Gideon Sjoberg observes that

> it is doubtful that preindustrial cities have typically comprised more than 10 per cent of the total populations of feudal societies; in some instances the figure may be less than 5 per cent. Most people are farmers, closely tied to the land, who support themselves and a small elite through their own labor and that of a few domesticated animals.[5]

Nevertheless the preindustrial cities were important as markets and as centers of political, economic, and military power, as well as the seat of religious and cultural activities. It was also in these places that the division of labor was most advanced and stratification and classes most noticeable.

We might glance at Egypt for an illustration of occupational stratification in antiquity. According to the Greek historian Herodotus (484?–425? B.C.) the Egyptians were divided into seven distinct categories: priests, warriors, cowherds, swineherds, tradesmen, interpreters, and boatmen. The warriors devoted their whole time to military activities, and they, as well as the priests, had about nine acres of tax-free land assigned to them. There were other perquisites such as food and wine during special periods of service. Interestingly persons engaged in trade, as well as their children, were not held in very high esteem; neither were those who worked in handicrafts. Herodotus notes that the Egyptians as well as the Greeks, Thracians, Scyths, Persians, Lydians, and almost all other non-Greeks

> . . . hold the citizens who practice trades, and their children, in less repute than the rest, while they esteem as noble those who keep aloof from handicrafts, and especially honour such as are given wholly to war.[6]

Among the preindustrial civilizations, the Greek is of special interest. Although its stratification was less rigid than in the rest of the Near East there was considerable distance between the haves and the have-nots. Also, its democracy had meaning only for the free citizens.[7]

At the head of each of the early Greek city-states were clan chieftains, but eventually a noble class developed. In turn a class based on commercial and industrial wealth came into prominence and there was an amalgamation between the two. The result was a powerful governing oli-

[4] John D. Durand, "World Population: Trend and Prospects," in Philip M. Hauser, ed., *Population and World Politics* (Glencoe, Ill.: The Free Press, 1958), pp. 29–30.

[5] Gideon Sjoberg, *The Preindustrial City* (Glencoe, Ill.: The Free Press, 1960), p. 83.

[6] Herodotus, *The History of Herodotus*, trans. by George Rawlinson (London: J. M. Dent & Sons Ltd., 1945), Vol. I, pp. 200–201. The quotation is from p. 200.

[7] See Harold M. Hodges, Jr., *Social Stratification* (Cambridge, Mass.: Schenkman Publishing Co., 1964), pp. 20–22.

garchy. Below this governing oligarchy were the citizens, who also had the franchise, and next were the businessmen. Although the latter were free they could not vote. Finally there were the slaves and agricultural serfs who were unfree.[8]

Even the freedom-loving Athenians were not appalled by slavery; most slaves were war captives and enslavement was considered more humane than killing prisoners. Moreoever, the slaves were considered "barbarians," as were all non-Greeks, which was an additional justification.[9] This institution provided the economic underpinning of the society with the major benefits going to the citizens. In large part this was because of the ancient view of the purpose of productive effort, for the modern idea of increased output and consumption as ends in themselves was absent. This meant that the productive capacity was not directed toward the welfare of the mass of the population in order to improve life expectancy, for example. Rather, a great deal of energy was devoted to the creation of durable commodities such as beautiful buildings and decorations.[10] In addition, the labor of the slaves also gave the others time to cultivate the arts and attend to civic duties.

Yet there was much conflict and even revolts; often aspiring rulers enlisted the support of the lower strata and after gaining office there was some improvement in their situation. While there was continual flux, this was particularly true in Hellenistic Greece (after the conquest by Philip II of Macedon in 338 B.C.); also, there were great extremes of wealth and poverty and the condition of the lower strata worsened. By this time Greek civilization was in a state of decline.[11]

In spite of the great stratification certain aspects of the society encouraged Greeks to take a relatively objective view of themselves. Among these circumstances were the absence of a coercive state religion and an emphasis on secularism, a high degree of literacy, and a great deal of liberty. Comparisons and contrasts were encouraged by the absence of a highly centralized political organization together with a variety of governments among the city-states, as well as by widespread contact with other cultures through warfare and commerce. The latter was especially important.[12] Consequently, Greek writers analyzed their society very critically, including its system of stratification. (We shall examine their views at some length in the next chapter.)

While most communities were small there were some large cities: for example Rome in the second century A.D. contained about 200,000 peo-

---

[8] *Ibid.*, p. 21.

[9] *Ibid.*

[10] John Nef, *The Conquest of the Material World* (Cleveland: Meridian Books, 1967), p. 217.

[11] Hodges, *op. cit.*, pp. 21–22.

[12] Howard Becker and Harry E. Barnes, *Social Thought from Lore to Science* (Washington, D.C.: Harren Press, 1952), Vol. I., pp. 144–145.

ple; Baghdad prior to 1000 A.D. had a population of about 300,000. It is estimated that most of the preindustrial cities of any consequence were between 5,000 and 10,000.[13] Despite different cultures there was a strong consistency in the class structure among the preindustrial cities. An elite comprising between five and ten per cent of the population dominated both the city and society; its upper ranks contained the leaders of the governmental, religious, and educational bureaucracies. The rest were commoners, and this lower class included the lower echelons of the bureaucracies, as well as merchants, shopkeepers, artisans, and handicraft workers. Then there were the unskilled: servants, people who carried burdens, messengers, animal-drivers, ditch-diggers, and part-time and full-time farmers on the urban fringe.[14] At the very bottom were the outcastes, slaves, night-soil carriers, leather workers, butchers, barbers, midwives, prostitutes, and often businessmen and entertainers. These were people who performed necessary tasks yet were often viewed as non-human, as little more than animals. They usually had no legal rights, were segregated, and were prohibited from wearing certain items of clothing and jewelry. Moreover, "[T]he outcaste's status [was] an inherited one; his chances of entering the mainstream of feudal society [were] slight, less than those of a commoner. The lower class, along with the elite, [depreciated] intermarriage with outcastes." [15]

Sjoberg points out how having an outcaste group helps support the authority structure and insures that the elite obtains the lion's share of social goods. Slaves provide a low-cost and servile labor force, and others, who engage in despised or "defiling" tasks, are kept beyond the pale of respectability. Among them are the prostitutes, whose social isolation keeps them from disrupting the family system or normal male-female relations. The businessman is a potential threat to the status quo since he deals with people from all walks of life, both within and outside the community, and his work encourages a rational and pragmatic rather than traditional outlook. Also, if he travels or has contact with outsiders he may be exposed to new or heretical ideas and could disseminate them at home. It is for the same reasons that entertainers are also outcastes.[16]

In preindustrial society generally the many labored for the few. A small class-conscious group firmly held the reins of power and lived the good life. The distribution of social goods was extremely one-sided with the bulk of the commoners receiving very little and the outcastes hardly more than was required for subsistence.

Economic and population expansion in the ancient world continued, reaching its apogee with the Roman Empire; but by the fourth century A.D. this society was already in serious decline. Yet trade and other com-

---

[13] Sjoberg, *The Preindustrial City*, pp. 82–83.

[14] *Ibid.*, pp. 109–110, 121–122.

[15] *Ibid.*, pp. 133–135. The quotation is from p. 135.

[16] *Ibid.*, pp. 133–137.

mercial activities continued at a high level even with the transformation of the Roman provinces into Germanic kingdoms by the sixth century. It was the growth of Islam in the seventh century which cut off Europe from the Mediterranean and threw her on her own resources; the result was many centuries of economic stagnation.[17]

Population declined greatly; it is estimated that the rate of increase was now only two-and-a-half to five per cent per century, and that in 1650 there were only between 450 and 550 million people in the world.[18]

Not only was population sparse but life was still largely rural and the economy agricultural. Commerce was limited and the trade that existed was primarily to satisfy the needs of the upper strata; there was no mass market. It was not until the 19th century that population growth again became explosive.

To some extent these changes, but also other conditions which we will examine shortly, had important consequences for the way modern social structure, group relations, and ideologies have developed. We begin by turning to the Middle Ages and focus on economic conditions, feudalism, and the strata of noblemen, serfs, and bourgeois.

The Middle Ages

ECONOMIC CONDITIONS

With Europe cut off from the Mediterranean by the expansion of Islam, there was practically no intercourse with countries overseas from the eighth through the 11th centuries. As a result, Europe turned inward, commerce declined, trade was local; in essence it was a "no market" economy. That is, people produced almost entirely for their own needs and the concept of profit as a primary motivating force was absent. One indication of the general economic decline is the fact that gold coinage disappeared and was replaced by coins of lower denomination which were made of less valuable metal. By the end of the ninth century there was great diversity in coinage and in weights and measures, each territory having its own standards.[19]

Urban life declined and land became the only meaningful economic base; for many centuries wealth, social status, and political influence would be determined largely by land ownership. Political and social rela-

---

[17] See Henri Pirenne, *Medieval Cities*, trans. by Frank D. Halsey (Garden City, N.Y.: Doubleday Anchor Books, 1925), pp. 1–16.

[18] Durand, "World Population: Trend and Prospects."

[19] Pirenne, *A History of Europe* (Garden City, N.Y.: Doubleday Anchor Books, 1958), Vol. I, pp. 77, 184; and R. W. Southern, *The Making of the Middle Ages* (New Haven, Conn.: Yale University Press, 1964), p. 48.

tions were shaped by this economic situation for the landless were at the mercy of the landed and the small landowner was at the mercy of the large landowner. The weak were at the mercy of the strong, who might be rapacious landed proprietors, combinations of landowners and their soldiers, brigands, or invading armies. There was no national or religious organization which could maintain stable economic and political relations and provide for personal safety. Life revolved around the local domain and the ordinary person was dependent on the landed proprietor for the means of economic sustenance as well as for protection.

FEUDALISM

The bond which was established between the powerful and the weak was not merely an economic arrangement between a landowner and his tenant; actually a close economic, social, and political relationship developed.

> Born of the need of effective protection in a society given over to anarchy, it created between them a peculiar bond, as between superior and subordinate, which extended to the whole person, recalling in its intimacy and its closeness the family tie. The "contract of recommendation" which made its appearance from the 6th century onwards gave the protected man the name of vassal (*vassus*) or servitor, and the protector the name of ancient or seigneur (*senior*). The seigneur was pledged not only to provide for the subsistence of his vassal, but also at all times to grant him his succor and aid, and to represent him before the law. The freeman who sought protection might preserve the appearance of liberty, but in actual fact he had become a client, a *sperans*, of the *senior*.[20]

Increasingly the king granted the great landowners immunity from state interference in their domains and ceded crown land in order to retain their allegiance. Eventually economic and political power were transferred to them; by the second half of the seventh century the privileged landholder had replaced the officers of the State on his own territory and the king was little more than a figurehead.[21]

These large landowners were the aristocracy, each a power unto himself within his domain; outside his influence depended on his economic resources, his warlike proclivity, the vassals who attached themselves to him, and the alliances he made with other *seigneurs*. The practice of vassalage with its reciprocal expectations of protection, aid, and loyalty permeated the society: peasants and yeoman farmers attached themselves to larger landowners; the latter in turn attached themselves to great landholders. Underlords pledged fealty and service to overlords

[20] Pirenne, *A History of Europe*, pp. 50–51.
[21] *Ibid.*, pp. 51–52 ff.

who in turn pledged protection and other benefits. This system of juridical relationships is known as feudalism.

Although land ownership was the primary influence over political
relationships, the society was preeminently military, which reinforced
the peculiar economic and political arrangements. The overlord and his
warriors provided protection from the incursions of other *seigneurs*, from
brigands, and from invading armies, and the overlord used his military
resources to add land to his domain, plunder foreign and domestic enemies, settle blood feuds, and keep vassals in line.

While new technology often develops as a result of changed social
conditions, the latter may be severely altered by such innovation; this
was certainly the case with the European adoption of mounted warfare.
Up until the middle of the eighth century armies were raised in time of
war and consisted of freemen who were footsoldiers. In 732, on the
plains of Poitiers, Charles Martel defeated mounted Arab invaders who
had crossed the Pyrenees. Although his footsoldiers bested the Saracens,
Martel understood the advantages of the mounted soldier for stronger
and more efficient military organization and the superiority of mobility
over numbers. He undertook a radical reorganization of the military by
creating a class of mounted warriors with sufficient resources to maintain
themselves. He did this by distributing land including church holdings
to the strongest underlords; in turn each holder of such a fief was
required to be prepared with a war horse, armored equipment, and necessary training, and to do war service whenever required. The *chevalier*,
literally horse-soldier, confirmed his obligations with an oath of fidelity.
While the old army of freemen did not disappear, it became a reserve
which was used less and less. Understandably the expense required a
sizable land base which in turn severely restricted participation and led
to the development of a land-owning military elite.[22] Obviously the
peasants were no match for warriors clad in protective armor astride
their armored chargers; the peasant masses were militarily useless and
helpless.[23] By raising their own horse troops the members of the aristocracy further eroded the power of the king; thus they gained political as
well as military power.[24]

NOBLEMAN, SERF, AND BOURGEOIS

One of the most interesting and significant changes among the higher
strata was the transformation of the aristocracy into a nobility. "Aristoc-

[22] *Ibid.*, pp. 25, 54–56. See also James W. Thompson, *The Middle Ages, 300–1500* (New
York: Alfred A. Knopf, 1931), pp. 205–207.

[23] Stanislaw Andrzejewski, *Military Organization and Society* (London: Routledge &
Kegan Paul Ltd., 1954), pp. 58–59.

[24] Pirenne, *A History of Europe*, pp. 55–56.

racy" refers simply to powerful individuals who constitute a stratum or class, which is more or less open, whereas nobility means a privileged juridical category. Nobles are likely to be part of the stratum composed of the wealthy, the prestigeful, the powerful, and the high officials. However they need not be for this is a *legal* status; nobles could be in any stratum.

With this trend in medieval Europe, by the end of the tenth century the nobility was hereditary; such status did not require a fief although it presupposed economic independence.[25] Over time entry into the nobility became more and more restricted. In earlier periods a knight could confer knighthood on another individual, but eventually entry became limited only to those who had an ancestor who had performed mounted military service. Furthermore only knights had the right to bear arms, a solemn initiation ceremony developed, and the knight was exempt from taxation. Also, previously a person could become a part of the aristocracy by acquiring a fief, in addition to the possibility of being knighted; however by the 13th century this route was blocked by law. Not only did the knight have to be of noble blood but the acquisition of land by a commoner was legally prohibited.[26]

The knights came to be regarded as representative of the strongest and most efficient element in the society: the protector of the Church and all that is good. They developed a characteristic way of life which included the ideals of chivalry, tournaments, and fighting, including vendettas; but they were not expected to engage in productive labor. Although the knight now had to be a noble there were of course nobles who were not knights. While the nobility was basically the military arm, it also furnished the administrative personnel for the government; consequently it may properly be viewed as a political as well as a military force.[27]

The only other powerful institution in Western society was the Church. By the ninth century religion was a state affair; only those who belonged to Christian society could belong to public society, and religion was an essential factor in the political order. But increasingly the upper level of the Church began to resemble the nobility-military and often the positions in both hierarchies were the same or interrelated.[28] The Church was involved in many activities: it ministered to man's needs on earth, prepared him spiritually for the Heavenly Kingdom, fostered learning in the monasteries and universities, owned land and serfs and engaged in farming, was involved in political intrigues, and participated in warfare. While it upheld the existing order, the religious teachings contained ideas which eventually became the basis for questioning

[25] *Ibid.*, pp. 136–142.

[26] Pirenne, *A History of Europe*, p. 138; and James W. Thompson, *An Economic and Social History of the Middle Ages (300–1300)* (New York: The Century Co., 1928), p. 722.

[27] Pirenne, *A History of Europe*, pp. 139–142.

[28] *Ibid.*, p. 66.

the status quo and led to revolt. Vassalage and the inequitable distribution of social goods, including the hierarchical arrangement of power and privileges, were given religious support in two ways: the relationships of lord-vassal and landowner-serf were justified as part of God's order, and the idea of service—one of the key concepts of vassalage—was viewed as parallel to and part of servitude to God. On the other hand, the Christian notion that all men were equal before God contrasted with earlier views such as Aristotle's which held that subordination was the natural state for some men.[29]

Now what about the greater part of the population, the peasantry? While technically free, and in spite of the paternalism, the individual who bonded himself was clearly in a subordinate position, and, as it worked out, came increasingly under the domination and control of his lord. The relationship became more one-sided until the distinction between free and unfree peasant disappeared. Originally only slaves and their descendents were bound to the soil, but now serfdom was hereditary and by law the serf and his family were attached to the land of their lord who had the right of pursuit should anyone try to flee. The system was obviously advantageous to the *seigneur* but there were also benefits to the serf. For the lord, it provided a stable work force for the cultivation of his fields. And, since population was sparse, this insured the maximum utilization of labor and land. As for the serf, in addition to being represented before the law by his lord and obtaining aid from him when needed, he might receive money payment for his "contract of recommendation." But despite these benefits and the religious support for the system there was common contempt for serfdom. The serfs themselves did not object to their subordination but rather to the arbitrariness of the arrangement.[30]

The basic distinction was between the nobility and the peasantry. Also, church officials were often members of the nobility. (The various positions are ranked on page 204.)

The ordering was based on differences in power and eventually became recognized by the distinction of title, although this was not invariably the case. While the noble's title designated social rank, it did not necessarily indicate his power other than that which was related to the land he owned. Power was affected by the size, value, and strategic importance of one's domain; by military might; by forming allegiances with underlords or the church; and through a shrewd marriage. For example, an ambitious and unscrupulous lesser noble could build up a formidable combination of vassal lands and extend his control into the church through war, intimidation of his neighbors, and adroit marriages of his children.[31]

[29] See Southern, *The Making of the Middle Ages*, pp. 103–104, 106.

[30] Pirenne, *A History of Europe*, pp. 82–85; and Southern, *op. cit.*, pp. 103–107.

[31] Pirenne, *A History of Europe*, pp. 128–130.

Ranking of Positions in Medieval Europe

Nobility

King

Ecclesiastical princes: vassals of the Crown

Dukes and *margraves:* the largest landholders and the most powerful nobles, next to the king

Counts: large landowners

Viscounts or *vice-counts:* smaller landowners but holdings are substantial

Barons: owned smallest amount of land over which sovereignty was exercised

Chatelains: lords of a single castle

Personal Retainers: knights who were personal retainers of nobles of various ranks; they lived off their bounty and hoped someday to be given a small fief

Custodians: also landless; they stayed at home, guarded the castle and even tilled the land; these knights were a link with the lower vassals, who in turn were a link with the peasantry

Peasantry

Free serfs

(Eventually these two groups fused)

Slaves

Source: Adapted from Thompson, *An Economic and Social History of the Middle Ages,* pp. 708–710.

By the 11th century feudalism was everywhere established in Europe. Instead of singly governed states there was a swarm of principalities whose power and boundaries were ever-changing. Overlord-underlord allegiances were constantly being formed and reformed and constant internecine conflict regularly affected the fortunes of the *seigneur* and his vassals.[32]

It should be noted that initially heredity was not of overriding concern. In Western and Central Europe about the tenth and 11th centuries, although differences of birth were acknowledged, rights based on inheritance were not as important as later on. Bloc comments that

[s]ociety was not so much a gradation of castes distinguished from one another by blood, but rather a somewhat confused tangle of groups based upon relationships of dependence. [The] ties of protection and obedience were the strongest that could be conceived.[33]

[32] Thompson, *An Economic and Social History of the Middle Ages,* pp. 708–710, 712–716.

[33] Marc Bloc, *Land and Work in Medieval Europe* (New York: Harper Torchbooks, 1969), p. 64.

The picture we have given is an idealized one since feudal arrangements and practices were by no means uniform. In fact England provides a sharp contrast; by the latter half of the 11th century it developed a non-political feudalism in that the vassals of the king had no financial or juridical authority as did their counterparts on the Continent. By virtue of his conquest of England, the domain of William the Conqueror (1027?–1087) was its entire territory. His great vassals were merely his tenants and the fiefs he distributed to them were simply military tenures.

This eventually led to absolute monarchical power with the oppression of vassals, the Church, and the burgess (merchants and other inhabitants of the cities). Things came to a head under King John Lackland and led to a revolt by the great lords which was precipitated by increased taxes and a humiliating military defeat at the hands of the French. This revolt which was joined by the clergy and the burgess resulted in the *Magna Carta* in 1215, which interestingly retained the royal power but provided for a sharing of it by the great lords, the Church, and the burgess. One of the key features of this remarkable document was the principle that taxes should be voted on by the nation although this principle was not definitely recognized until the very end of the 13th century.[34]

But this increased sharing of power, and the emergence of parliamentary democracy, were of little benefit to the lower strata. Legislation which was ostensibly designed to ameliorate social problems usually worked to the advantage of the upper strata. On occasion this was due to unanticipated consequences, but often this was the intent of the laws. A case in point is the English laws which sought to cope with the problem of the poor, whose numbers were increasing because of long-range trends and more immediate economic factors. Contributing to the difficulties was the Black Death, the bubonic plague which swept Europe in the 14th century and decimated a large portion of the population. After it had abated there was still considerable social disorganization which included large numbers of people wandering throughout the countryside, seemingly at random. The loss in population created a shortage of workers and tended to drive up wages, while the wandering kept many able-bodied men unemployed and made the supply of labor unstable. In England the Statute of Laborers of 1349 attempted to control the labor supply by suppressing vagrancy. People who were physically able but without means of support were required to work for those who needed labor; however, they were paid the wage rates prevailing *prior* to the Black Death. To add to the coercion, giving alms to beggars was made illegal.

Yet the poor continued to be a problem. Changing land use and agricultural technology increased unemployment and quickened migration to the cities. The process was hastened by the Enclosure movement which

[34] See Pirenne, *A History of Europe*, pp. 237–242.

became prominent in the 16th century. Landowners enclosed their "commons," which meant that grazing areas, forests, and other land previously open to small independent farmers, squatters, and agricultural laborers were no longer available to them. Among the immediate effects were the dispossession of large numbers of rural folk, several peasant rebellions, and poverty. The long-range consequences included large-scale and more efficient agricultural enterprises, the growth of the wool raising and cottage industries, and an increase in commerce.[35] The general economic expansion hastened tendencies toward a monetary economy and national and international markets rather than local ones. These trends began to undermine feudalism. But there were some individuals who played a key part in destroying it and replacing the power of the old nobility; peacefully in some places, by bloody revolution in others. These were the *burgess* or *burghers*—the inhabitants of towns and cities, or *bourgs*—who came to be called the *bourgeoisie*. Their precursors were itinerants who began to lay the groundwork for the emergence of the bourgeoisie.

THE PRECURSORS OF THE BOURGEOISIE

Economic activities, population, and urban life had declined greatly in the fifth century in Europe. Except for the Italian commercial centers such as Venice, Pisa, and Genoa which retained their trade with the Muslim world and prospered, it wasn't until the tenth century that there was a revival. Initially, commerce began to grow: river trade increased, as did the number of armed caravans or *hanses* and ports and towns at the intersection of trade routes started to thrive. Slowly population expanded.

With this re-emergence of economic life a new stratum of people began to come into being. These were merchants who were "new men"; they were intruders, who did not fit into the established order; they were neither from the nobles nor from the clergy. For the nobility land and genealogy were important and they denigrated commercial activity; the Church was hostile for it saw a spiritual danger in it. There are few records of the ancestors of the merchants; apparently they were poor landless men who wandered about the country, working at harvest time, going on pilgrimages. They must have been resourceful, adventurous, able to speak many languages, and acquainted with different customs; but above all they were greedy for gain. These "merchant adventurers," the precursors of the bourgeoisie, were responsible for the revival of urban life in the tenth and 11th centuries.[36] In turn urbanism furthered

[35] See J. L. and Barbara Hammond, *The Village Labourer* (London: Guild Books, 1948), Vol. I; and Karl Polyani, *The Great Transformation* (Boston: Beacon Press, 1957), pp. 79–80.

[36] Pirenne, "The Stages in the Social History of Capitalism," *American Historical Review*, 19 (April 1914), 494–515.

economic growth and hastened the emergence of the strata we know today.

URBAN LIFE

Stratification in the cities of medieval Europe basically fit the pattern of the preindustrial city which was described earlier. Although the European cities varied in their characteristics regionally and over different time periods, in an ideal typical sense this was the situation: an upper stratum of the wealthy, primarily nobles and secondarily rich merchants. These were persons who controlled the municipal government, who maintained a style of life which dramatically set them apart from the lower strata. Often religious leaders were a part of this hierarchy. Below them were the artisans, small employers with their one or two journeymen. The skilled employees were the next category, and included the lower echelons of the religious and governmental structures, and peddlers. Next were the unskilled such as laborers and servants; although these occupations were humble they were still respectable, as contrasted with the lowest stratum consisting of beggars, prostitutes, and slaves.[37]

Population continued to increase until by the second half of the 11th century there was overpopulation in certain parts of Europe. The changing countryside reflected this growth with the rise of new towns and the expansion of old ones; whereas previously the traveler journeyed from monastery to monastery he now passed from town to town. The urbanization and population growth contributed to the disruption of traditional economic as well as political practices and relationships.

Clearly the preindustrial cities were important in terms of cultural change and economic activities. Relative to the countryside the concentrated populations, although small by present standards, required a much greater division of labor and much more extensive commercial activities. They encouraged a more rational and pragmatic outlook and ideational and technological innovation. The more rapid changes in fashions and the development of new tastes characteristic of urban life created new demands which craftsmen and merchants sought to fill, and the city population became a magnet for traveling merchants.

Among the consequences of city life and its attendant economic and political activities were the growth of more clearly differentiated strata, with more sharply conflicting interests than was the case in the agrarian community. The existence of an aristocratic elite, a stratum of merchants, and one of craftsmen, laborers, and farmers, set the pattern for the stratification and class relations of more modern times. In particular, the merchant group developed into the bourgeoisie who loomed so important in

[37] See Sjoberg, *The Preindustrial City*, pp. 113–123. Cf. Pirenne, *A History of Europe*, pp. 206–207.

the Industrial Revolution and the French Revolution. The merchants of the tenth and 11th centuries we term the "old bourgeoisie" for as we shall see they differed in important ways from their more modern counterparts.

THE OLD BOURGEOISIE

The interests and perceived needs of the old bourgeoisie made them an innovative force. For example the growth of urbanism resulted in a clash between feudal practices and the requirements of commercial life, and led to the development of new conceptions of the law. The bourgeoisie demanded more clearcut and rationalized procedures for the judgment of claims than was the case under seigneurally dispensed justice. They wanted law and order and punitive punishment to deter violations. Urban life was innovative in other ways as well: practicality or pragmatism, rationalism, secularism, contract, achievement, and the monetary economy were emphasized; a financial system and bookkeeping were invented, and civil and secular administration, schools, commercial and industrial regulations, and public works were established.

By the beginning of the 12th century the bourgeoisie achieved a legally privileged position; they now had juridical rights as a class, and the lines of conflict between the agricultural and commercial-industrial life began to be set. The nobility and clergy which were a homogeneous and self-conscious class represented the former; to a large extent the merchant cities with local interest and strong civic sentiment the latter.[38] But this bourgeoisie, once it gained prominence, became a regressive force for it then sought to protect its position by regulations which limited competition and new forms of enterprise. The guild system was a part of this protectionism. The early bourgeoisie, in spite of its conflict with past traditions and practices, retained the old feudal-based values and sought to live like and aspired to be viewed like the nobility.

This was the Europe of roughly the 11th and 12th centuries, where the institutional arrangements and people's behaviors were still strongly influenced by the land-based economy and the power of the military-nobility. But we can already see the beginnings of urbanism and the attenuation of old values, practices, and relationships.

Next we want to comment on several major critical events: the Crusades, the Renaissance, and the Reformation. After that we will be at the eve of the French and the Industrial Revolutions.

[38] Pirenne, *A History of Europe*, pp. 179–201.

The Significance of the Crusades, the Renaissance, and the Reformation

THE CRUSADES

Prior to the Crusades there was associated with the revitalization of economic life a growing restlessness both in spiritual values and in regard to material things. People's world view was broadening and they were beginning to break out of their constrained communal life physically as well as mentally. There was greater communication with the lands of the Mediterranean and, starting in the middle of the tenth century, there was a growing popularity of pilgrimages to Jerusalem. There were many reasons for the long journey: idealism, personal salvation, economic gain, and adventure. Although the travelers were relatively few in number they interested the churchman in the spiritual potentialities of the Holy Land, the merchant in its economic opportunities, and the knight in the possibility of a holy quest.

There had been conflicts with the Muslims for some time and by the middle of the 11th century the Christian Occident was on the offensive, engaged in wars of conquest. Although connected with these wars, the Crusades' primary motive was religious and the specific objective was to liberate the Holy Places and the Sepulchre of Christ; they were part of a manifestation of great religious fervor among Christians at the time, and the instigator and organizer of the first Crusade was the Pope. The Crusades (there were four, the first beginning in 1096 and the last in 1271) were not mass movements but rather expeditions of knights which, although based on a religious ideal, also stressed the material gains to be had. The immediate benefits were indeed economic, but accrued not to the Crusaders but to their outfitters and suppliers: the cities of Venice, Pisa, and Genoa. In addition the need for these goods and for transportation to the Holy Land built up Italian maritime commerce.

Following the Crusades there was an increase in trade with the Mediterranean lands. Not only material goods were transported into Europe, there was also a flow of ideas. As a consequence there was a growing interest in systematic thought and in logic in particular; the Greek classics were translated; scientific and medical knowledge became more readily available and began to disseminate more widely, and there was a growing internationalism among the great schools and universities.[39] In short, the Crusades served as a catalyst in the revitalization of European commerce and in the growth of urbanism; in addition they stimulated the questioning of age-old beliefs and institutional arrangements.

[39] See *ibid.*, p. 175 ff. and Southern, *The Making of the Middle Ages*, pp. 49–67.

The changing conditions helped undermine the feudal system. With the growth of cities and towns cash was increasingly being paid for goods and services, more money began to circulate, and with this came a decline in its value. The *seigneur* was particularly affected by the rise in the cost of living for his obligations toward his tenants continued to be fixed by custom while his revenues remained the same. On the other hand the cities now provided an outlet for agricultural goods and the larger landowner saw the possibilities of increasing production for this market and growing cash crops. But this was not feasible for the holder of a small fief, and by the end of the 12th century a large portion of the nobility was impoverished.[40] Also, because of the organization of agriculture and relatively primitive methods yields were low and the possibility of profit was limited. Small amounts of land, in the form of strips, were farmed;

> [s]mall plows were pulled by oxen, and hoes and rakes were plied by hand. Lime, marl and manure were used for fertilizing, but scantily. The cattle were small and thin, and after a hard winter were sometimes so weak that they had to be dragged out to pasture. . . . Diseases of cattle were rife and deadly. The principles of breeding were hardly understood.[41]

In order to increase their revenues, landowners leased their holdings to peasants or turned them into large farms. More and more peasants were able to free themselves with a money payment and serfdom began to disappear; from the beginning of the 13th century the rural population was becoming largely a population of free peasants. They were paid in cash rather than in produce and material interests became the basis for relationships between land owner and land worker. However this varied from place to place. For example free labor became common in Italy in the beginning of the 15th century, yet servitude became stronger in Germany at that time; in the Low Countries serfdom was abolished in the 16th century, while in outlying rural districts in France personal servitude was retained until the end of the 18th century. It was abolished throughout most of the rest of Europe by 1848, although Russian serfs did not gain their freedom until the 1860's.[42]

THE RENAISSANCE

As with the Crusades, the Renaissance had important social and economic consequences. Literally "rebirth," it began in 14th-century Italy

---

[40] Pirenne, *A History of Europe*, pp. 215–216.

[41] Preserved Smith, *The Social Background of the Reformation* (New York: Collier Books, 1967), p. 92.

[42] Pirenne, *A History of Europe*, pp. 220–221, 252–255; and E. J. Hobsbawm, *The Age of Revolution* (New York: The New American Library, 1962), p. 184.

and heralded a reawakening of interest in art, literature, and science. It also led to the abandonment of many of the old ways and the rapid decline of the traditional authorities which had dominated social, intellectual, and economic life.[43] The growing wealth and culture contact of the Italian trading cities were largely responsible for these changes. Nobles had abandoned warfare and were engaging in commerce, and social status became more important than juridical status. Also, men of affairs had leisure time and acquired refinement and objects of art, and a kind of mundane aristocracy arose.[44]

The intellectual revolution began at the height of economic development. The total amount of wealth increased and the idea of renunciation—the belief that denial of earthly pleasures was the highest ideal in the eyes of God—was giving way to the notion of attaining material happiness in the here and now, and for the largest number.[45] Nevertheless wealth was very unequally distributed—the nobles, great landowners, the Church, wholesale merchants, and manufacturers were the primary beneficiaries. But while the intellectual flowering continued, the economy began to decline for, with the discovery of the New World, commerce was diverted from Mediterranean to Northern European ports such as Antwerp. Consequently one may talk about the Renaissance of the North, which however predated the voyages of exploration and lasted into the middle of the 16th century. There too it was a period of renewal and of important social and economic transformations, among the most important of which was the appearance of a new class of entrepreneurs in Flanders, France, England, and in some cities in Southern Germany.[46]

THE NEW BOURGEOISIE

These entrepreneurs differed from the merchant adventurers. When the latter had prospered they entrenched themselves by securing protectionist legislation and their cities were usually able to restrict free trade and innovation.[47] The old entrepreneurs sought "liberty" within the context of their cities, and for them it meant the freedom to regulate their own economic activities; by contrast the new merchants and manufacturers sought *general* liberty in that they wished cities to be accessible to all businessmen, and they wanted to be free from all regulations so that they could manufacture and sell whatever they chose, in any manner

[43] Florence in particular experienced much culture contact. Machiavelli wrote in this city. Pirenne, *A History of Europe*, p. 227.

[44] Pirenne, *A History of Europe* (Garden City, N.Y.: Doubleday Anchor Books, 1958), Vol. II, pp. 221–235.

[45] Nef, *The Conquest of the Material World*, pp. 67–68.

[46] Pirenne, *A History of Europe*, Vol. II, pp. 235–236.

[47] See Pirenne, "The Stages in the Social History of Capitalism."

they desired. They also wished to industrialize the countryside in order to take advantage of the large rural labor supply and low wages which would allow them to compete successfully with the guilds of the cities. They were successful, and a new "free" relationship was instituted between entrepreneur and worker, but often this free labor was abused.

The new bourgeoisie was not a juridical estate as was true of its earlier counterpart. They were *parvenus,* a class of men whose status was determined by their wealth and style of life, who pointedly differentiated themselves from the petite bourgeoisie—the artisans and the small shopkeeper.

An industrial workforce made its appearance in the second half of the 15th century. Although not yet very important, the condition of these persons is significant: they were at the mercy of their employers and could not form organizations or what we would today call unions.[48] We see here the beginnings of capitalist and proletariat who were designed to play such important roles in the Industrial Revolution.

Many of these social and economic changes were instigated or furthered by the Renaissance. It also created conditions out of which arose an important religious movement, the Reformation, which in turn had important social and economic as well as political consequences.

THE REFORMATION

The ideas of the Reformation developed out of the intellectual ferment of the Renaissance and changing conditions of life.[49] The more immediate causes were the decline of the Papacy and its Italianization and public reaction to conditions within the Catholic Church. The latter included nepotism, Popes and Cardinals who consorted publicly with their mistresses and acknowledged their illegitimate children, and the practice of granting indulgences. The precipitating event was Martin Luther's (1483–1546) exposing to the public in 1517 his 97 theses against the selling of indulgences. Luther, who was a member of the faculty of theology at the University of Wittenberg, vigorously advocated his views which were a continuation of the earlier dissident theologies of John Wycliff (1324?–1384) and John Huss (1369–1415).

The Reformation attacked the notion of the Middle Ages that the world consisted of a hierarchy of distinct classes with functions, rights, and duties, and stressed the idea that worth and esteem are personal things determined by merit and not by rank. The emphasis was on individualism in that every Christian was considered a priest and a person's faith rather than good works indicated piety. People were encouraged to

[48] Pirenne, *A History of Europe,* Vol. II, pp. 247–248.
[49] See Smith, *The Social Background of the Reformation.*

read the Bible and it was translated from the Latin for that purpose. Lutheranism spread in Germany and elsewhere, appealing to the bourgeoisie as well as to the masses. It was aided by knights who were moved both by patriotism and hatred of Rome and by princes who anticipated the secularization of the ecclesiastical estates. The first land confiscations were in Sweden and Denmark, primarily for political reasons.[50]

Out of the ferment of Lutheranism came a new religious doctrine which even further emphasized individual responsibility. The work of John Calvin (1509–1564), it spread throughout the Western world within two decades. Calvinism focused on the concept of predestination which holds that God determines who shall be saved (i.e., go to Heaven after death); yet it is impossible for the individual to know whether he is among the elect. Consequently he is importuned to devote himself with all his energy to the service of God, to act "as if" he were one of the elect, to constantly seek for "signs" that he might be among the saved. He is encouraged to look within himself for such indications. Whereas Lutheranism concentrated on the religious aspect of people's lives, with less concern over temporal matters, Calvinism emphasized both. The supreme law is God's word, as revealed by Scripture; a person's whole life must be subject to this law. The Calvinist's conduct was subjected to intense scrutiny by his co-religionists as well as to constant self-examination to insure propitious thoughts and actions. Sobriety, hard work, and self-denial were emphasized; vice, idolatry, and self-indulgence were abhorred. These values, considered a part of God's design, had important implications for disciplining a workforce and for the commercial success of entrepreneurs. Thus Calvinism appealed to businessmen among others; particularly attractive to them was the fact that it was permissible to charge interest on loans, a practice prohibited under Lutheranism as well as under Catholicism.[51]

The Reformation stimulated industrialization. Not only were Church lands confiscated and exploited, but they were more productive under private as opposed to ecclesiastical control.[52]

No social movement is "pure" in the sense that it is concerned entirely with promulgating a religious ideal, establishing a particular form of government, or reforming specific aspects of society. Social, economic, and political considerations are often critical in the emergence, the spread, and the success or failure of such movements. These factors certainly existed in the Reformation as well as in the Crusades and the Renaissance, and we have barely hinted at some of them. In the case of the Reformation, let us look now at the situation of the German peasant.

[50] Nef, *The Conquest of the Material World*, p. 230.

[51] See Pirenne, *A History of Europe*, Vol. II, pp. 267–307; and Max Weber, *The Protestant Ethic and the Spirit of Capitalism*, trans. by Talcott Parsons (New York: Charles Scribner's Sons, 1958).

[52] Nef, *op. cit.*, pp. 232–233.

The condition of the German peasant had been continually deteriorating since the end of the 14th century. Serfdom was reestablished then and there were additional taxes and a multiplicity of *corvées* (i.e., obligations such as the requirement to perform labor for the lord of the manor). The *Todfall*, which came into use in southern Germany at the beginning of the 15th century, is one example of the peasants' plight. This was a death tax on the peasants by the owner of the estate on which they lived. Upon the death of a peasant the lord would take some valued possession from the bereaved, or a tax would be levied on the family. This could be calamitous because the survivors had few resources to begin with; it would be particularly disastrous where the breadwinner had died. This tax varied from five to 15% depending on area and local customs.

These unfortunate conditions worsened, and continued until the 19th century. In addition to the reestablished serfdom, the *corvées*, and the death tax, rents were raised and more time had to be spent working for the lord. Not only did the nobles increase their demands on the peasants, but they failed to fulfill their responsibilities as was expected by custom. For many peasants life become intolerable and there were agrarian revolts; however they were put down fiercely, with great bloodshed.[53]

Yet in the late 15th and early 16th centuries, in contrast to a hundred years earlier, there was prosperity for much of the society; there were great movements of discovery, colonization, invention, and economic growth.[54] But there was also much misery. Not only were the peasants suffering but the emerging industrial workforce bore the brunt of taxation, and government regulation was in the interest of the propertied classes. Wages were kept as low as feasible, the workday was set at 12 to 15 hours depending on the season; people were compelled to work and idlers were punished.[55]

Not only were the ideas of the Reformation a stimulus to business enterprise, but in the minds of many ordinary persons religious reform was connected with the possibility of a better social and economic life.

One final development, the nation-state, needs to be mentioned to complete the picture which forms the backdrop to modern society.

Emergence of the Nation-States

Imagine the Western world of the early Middle Ages: numerous economic-political units, each a world of its own and ruled by a nobleman;

---

[53] Jacob S. Schapiro, *Social Reform and the Reformation* (New York: Columbia University, Faculty of Political Science, 1909), pp. 58–59; and Pirenne, *A History of Europe*, Vol. II, pp. 283–285.

[54] Nef, *op. cit.*, p. 70.

[55] Smith, *The Social Background of the Reformation*, pp. 100, 102.

each subject to his power which was limited mainly by the influence of customary law. Since larger political units were based on the allegiances between lords and vassals the power of such units ebbed and flowed as the agreements were dissolved and new ones formed, as marriage, warfare, intrigue and political acumen affected the fortunes of the warrior-nobles. Kings were usually only figureheads, and the Church was only intermittently effective as a political unifying force.

Feudalism dominated the landscape until the tenth century; by the 12th urban centers became important, and from the middle of the 15th century there was a striking growth of monarchies. The Renaissance, the Reformation, and the entrepreneurial activities of the bourgeoisie [56] were not only important breaks with the past but were also progressive in the sense that they called forth new social, economic, and political arrangements. The persons who favored these changes usually supported the Crown while the traditional interests opposed it. For example, in the Low Countries the princes favored the new entrepreneurs as opposed to the restrictive urban guilds, and in that context encouraged the development of Antwerp which replaced Bruges; in England, from the reign of King Henry VII (1457–1509) onwards the Crown supported the enterprises of the merchant adventurers and schemes of maritime expansion; in Spain it intervened to make the discovery of the New World possible, and in France it encouraged economic expansion and protected the entrepreneurs. In turn they placed their credit and other resources at the disposal of the monarchy which made it independent of the traditional Estates.

There was a similar alliance in the case of the intellectuals since their ideas challenged the age-old ways. Thus their interests were in line with those of the monarchs and the latter, with the exception of the kings of Spain, supported intellectual as well as economic liberty. The Humanists believed they could obtain the reforms they desired only through the monarchy and the existing governments appeared to them to be the essential instrument of progress. The kings in turn benefitted from the support the intellectuals marshalled in terms of the public opinion of the time.[57] By the end of the 18th century there were powerful monarchies which were expanding both economically and in terms of population growth. They were centralizing their governments, making a science of administration, and instituting regular taxation and a system of laws. The latter is extremely important for stratification and mobility, for the legal system is a way of insuring the reward of merit.[58]

One outcome was a further weakening of the nobility, with the mon-

[56] Henceforth reference to the bourgeoisie will be to the new entrepreneurs.

[57] Pirenne, *A History of Europe*, Vol. II, pp. 321–334.

[58] Nef, *The Conquest of the Material World*, pp. 108–109. If a ruler can ignore the law, social goods can be confiscated with impunity. In Europe, the princes often did this to rich merchants.

archs obtaining much greater control over the economic and political forces of the nation. Another outcome was constant warfare among the nations, additional colonizing, and the wresting of colonies from rivals.

These changes which ushered the Western world into the modern era contained forces which would help bring about further economic and political upheavals; in particular the growth of capitalist industrialism and the emergence of revolutionary movements. In this final section let us briefly reexamine some of the important factors.

A Reexamination: Conditions and Perspectives

THE BREAKDOWN OF FEUDALISM

By the 14th century changing conditions began to reduce the utility of feudalism. Yet while the ancient form of chivalry remained, the earlier spirit and idealism of this institution was gone. The nobles, instead of becoming more cultivated as tradition required, became brutal sensualists and more materialistic. Since the oldest son inherited the family wealth, they sought other opportunities for their younger sons and monopolized the upper positions in the Church for them. In turn this made the clergy more worldly, and many knights became mercenaries. Also, the efficacy of the mounted warrior was diminishing as foot soldiers began to play a more important part in warfare and artillery came into use. People began to feel that the nobles were not justifying their military role and hence superior position; this was particularly the case in France and was exacerbated by marauding knights in the countryside. In addition kings were now ennobling their functionaries for reasons other than military chivalry, such as administrative service, outstanding learning, or in exchange for providing money for the royal treasury. Also, increasingly, administrators were being recruited from the bourgeoisie.

Yet the old privileges remained and the nobles were never hesistant to make use of them. This was noted in the case of Germany which was cited above; in England, even though their privileges were more limited the nobles were still powerful. For example, they were able to get Parliament to pass the Statute of Laborers in 1349 which restricted the wages of agricultural workers to what they were in 1347. That time was prior to the Black Death and the labor shortage which ensued.[59] Emboldened by their success they sought to reestablish their old rights which was in large part responsible for an uprising in 1384 which ended in a massacre.

The privileges of the nobility were juridical, and the feudal arrange-

[59] See Francis Fox Piven and Richard A. Cloward, *Regulating the Poor* (New York: Vintage Books, 1972), p. 36.

ment, originally based on reciprocal rights and obligations, became more and more one-sided: the noble retained the rights, the serf the obligations. Where serfs were freed humane interests were involved but probably the economic ones were more important: the free laborer was a more efficient worker, he could be hired and fired as needed, and the *seigneur* was no longer responsible for his welfare during slack periods and did not need to provide perquisites such as housing. When labor was in short supply or when the demand for produce rose, the agricultural worker benefitted. But when economic conditions worsened both the serf and the free laborer were badly off; however the free man was in much more dire straits for he was now on his own. Also he would have to compete with the other unemployed whose ranks might be swelled by demobilized mercenaries and others, and at such times begging increased greatly as did the number of wanderers who sought work. Entry into many trades was extremely difficult because of the rigid restrictions of the guilds, even when times were good, and the Church was less willing to give charity to the poor, especially when the unemployed were able bodied. The poor began to be viewed as professional vagabonds dangerous to the public peace and as professional loafers; in short as a social plague.

We see then a breakdown of the traditional values and practices of the feudal era. The domain was no longer a viable social and economic unit, the Church lost some of its religious and much of its political influence, and the power of the nobility began to transfer to the Crown. Among the factors which contributed to these changes were the increase in commercial activities, urbanization, and the growth of the bourgeoisie. But there were other circumstances which were both causes and consequences of the above transformations; they were also intimately involved with the economic expansion, the burgeoning of cities, and the emergence of merchants, industrialists, and financiers. These other factors are secularism, pragmatism, and innovation.

SECULARISM, PRAGMATISM, AND INNOVATION

As the dominial arrangement began to lose its *reason d'être*, people began to ponder the circumstances of their lives. While most persons were very devout and believed in the teachings of the Church, the religious explanations appeared to be less and less appropriate. This was especially true of the justification of the existing system of stratification with its great inequities. Questioning increased, particularly as the nobility and Church hierarchy began to merge and the Church became more worldly. Also, religious doctrine came into conflict with the needs of the expanding economy. The concept of the "just price" hindered the merchant who could make more profit by charging according to supply and demand; the prohibition of interest on loans limited the amount of venture capital available, and there were taxes and other restraints on commercial activity. Yet economic development was helped by some of the things the Church did. For example, it eventually succeeded in limiting the private wars of the knights in which crops were often destroyed and villages burned; it called for a suspension of conflicts during planting and harvesting seasons and on Fridays, Saturdays, Sundays, and Holy Days; and it urged the protection of travelers and merchants.[60]

Nevertheless the Church was interested in maintaining the traditional economic arrangements and it began to lose its hold on the merchants and the burghers whose actions and thinking were based on secular premises. Ironically it was the Crusades which stimulated the economic growth which eventually weakened the dominance of the Church.

The Crusades were also responsible for the traffic in ideas from the East; Europe was reintroduced to the classics of antiquity, and began to develop an interest in logic and science. These interests and the economic expansion encouraged a pragmatic outlook which led to a turning away from fatalism and the development of the belief that man could control his environment.[61] The secularism, the pragmatism, and the expanding economic opportunities encouraged innovation in practices, processes, and machinery. There was also innovation in the arts and in theology: note the Renaissance and the Reformation. Secularism, pragmatism, and innovation were also furthered by the intellectuals. Although they were quite removed from the mass of the population their ideas had more than a passing effect on the thinking of ordinary people, especially the notion that man alone could control his destiny.

The long-range trend, in both a physical and a mental sense, was from communalism to individualism. Considering these changes is it surprising that when conditions worsened there were unrest and upheavals?

UPRISINGS AND REVOLUTIONARY MOVEMENTS

As was discussed earlier, the nobles retained their feudal rights, increased their demands, and in other ways took advantage of their superordinate position while failing to live up to their traditional obligations. There were also other problems which adversely affected the lower strata: war and inflation, crop failures, a drop in demand for goods and services. All told the consequences were worsening conditions for the

---

[60] Thompson, *An Economic and Social History of the Middle Ages*, pp. 310, 666, 697.

[61] While I don't wish to belittle the present-day travelers to outer space, I suggest that the first voyage to the New World in the last part of the 15 century was a more courageous undertaking considering the limited technology, the ignorance, fear, and superstitions of the time.

peasantry and urban poor and uprisings by them. Many of the revolts were limited in scope; most had economic roots, some were for religious reasons. Tradition, the Church, the economy with its generally limited opportunity, and the armed might of the mounted warrior worked against revolution; when revolts did occur they were suppressed with great brutality.

During the 13th and 14th centuries there was great social unrest and revolutionary tendencies. Traditional authorities were criticized and assailed, and great masses of people who had endured or supported the power of the state were rebelling against it. Revolts occurred in Flanders between 1324 and 1328 when the participants were finally massacred; in France in 1357 (although in part the uprising was due to the sufferings from a war at the time), and in England in 1381. In Germany popular uprisings began to occur in the 16th century.[62]

In the cities which had developed industries antagonism increased between master and worker because of abuses by the employer, fluctuations in the economy with attendant lowering of wages and unemployment, and the growing subordination of the wage earner. There were many strikes and riots. In Ghent, a port city in Belgium, there was great violence and for six years the workers held their own against the prince, the nobles, and others of substance, until they were finally defeated in 1382.[63]

The peasant revolts were essentially conservative in that they sought to return to an earlier status quo. There was no attack on the social order or on the means through which social goods were distributed, but rather the complaint was that the lords were not adhering to traditional practices. The peasants resented the *additional* dues which appeared to them to be exhorbitant and arbitrary and the failure of the estate owners to uphold their end of the customary paternalistic relationship. The revolts in Germany furnish the best example of peasants engaging in great violence in order to return to an earlier, more desirable state of affairs.[64] From the perspective of the upper stratum, such evidence of peasant power threatened the existing social order, the manner in which social goods were distributed, and the amount each stratum received; this explains in large part the ferocity with which such revolts were put down.

The life conditions of the peasant and even of the small farmer today make for conservatism. Their primary interest is to have sufficient land, preferably their own, for a prosperous life for themselves and their families and they are likely to support whatever political authority promises this. The peasant revolts were obviously quite different from modern revolutions; yet they were significant in that they dramatically tore

[62] Pirenne, *A History of Europe*, Vol. II, pp. 97–109.

[63] *Ibid.*, pp. 105–106.

[64] See Schapiro, *Social Reform and the Reformation*.

asunder the social fabric. Even though the damage was only temporary these uprisings suggest an essential fragility in social order: for once people's expectations are no longer fulfilled, they are pressed by deprivation, and their experiences become collective, violent upheavals are possible in spite of traditions, values, and authority; in spite of the stability or apparent stability that existed beforehand.

However there were uprisings which were much more like modern revolutionary movements for they included ideologies which called for a new social order. For example there was the movement spawned by John Wycliffe of England whose ideas paved the way for the Reformation. He stressed that the Bible and not the institutionalized Church indicated the true religion. This religious movement became tied in with political interests, and although hampered by violent measures of the state it was not suppressed. The religious doctrines were introduced into Bohemia (now Czechoslovakia) by John Huss and the movement became associated with nationalistic passions and democratic instincts. It shook the very foundations of the Church and of Germany. Huss was martyred by being burned at the stake; the Czechs revolted. A sect called the Adamites which was founded by a Belgian weaver sought to establish the Kingdom of God on an island in the river Nezarka. The society was supposed to be like the Garden of Eden: it was communalistic, people didn't wear clothes, and behavior did not follow conventional morality. The members of this community were massacred by the authorities.[65]

There were also movements of urban workers, often religiously based, which were oriented toward visions of social transformation to some sort of communalistic society.[66]

These uprisings and movements were but prefaces to the upheaval which was to take place in France at the close of the 18th century. Preceding it was an important revolution in the New World. The significance of the American War for Independence was two-fold: its democratic ideology as well as the demonstration that a colony could overcome the resources and military might of a nation such as Great Britain. Like all revolutions there was a multiplicity of interests: nationalism, the economic benefits of independence, and the desire for liberty. The latter included the protection of individual rights and citizen participation in the governing process, although this was limited to propertyholders. The ideology of self-determination and the protection of individual rights had wide appeal and repercussions in other countries, particularly France.

The changes which were outlined in this chapter led to tremendous commercial expansion and the eventual development of industrialism: first in England and then on the Continent. The new conditions helped to further undermine the legal and customary privileges of the nobility

---

[65] Pirenne, *A History of Europe*, Vol.II, pp. 121–132.
[66] *Ibid.*, pp. 118–124.

and led to the emergence of the bourgeoisie as a growing economic and political force. They also led to the great upheaval across the Channel: the French Revolution.

Summary

Major transformations usually involve an interplay between events and ideas. While social, economic, and political changes help shape the main ideas of a period, the perspectives that develop are used to interpret what occurs. These perspectives become a basis for evaluating events and for action to bring about a desirable outcome, whether the aim is to alter conditions or to maintain the status quo. In either case the perspective or ideology of a group derives from the members' interest and helps justify behavior to support it. Therefore we may better understand some of the historical events we have discussed in this chapter by examining the relevant ideas and ideologies. This is the purpose of the next chapter. In what follows we will observe that one of the age-old concerns of humans—both ideationally and in terms of action—has been the distribution of social goods. Consequently by examining major ideologies of a period we will gain insight into some of the bases for conflict over their distribution. We will also better understand the origin of social movements which have significantly altered group relations and the fate of nations. And, as we shall see in the next chapter, ideas and doctrines which are concerned with social stratification and social class have a very long history.

Chapter VIII.　The Ideational Response

While the preceding chapter concentrated on significant economic, demographic, and political changes in preindustrial society, we could not help but pay some attention to relevant beliefs and perspectives. For the new conditions altered people's view of themselves and their world and increasingly they began to question the existing systems of stratification and class. In turn the new perspectives facilitated material and structural change. This is a never-ending process; a major difference today is its greater speed. But while the interplay between the ideational and the material is important it is necessary to examine the content of the ideas. For one thing, many current views about stratification and class are nothing new. For another, ideational and material changes seem to build on preceding situations; thus, once inequality has been seriously questioned and people have experienced greater freedom and opportunity it is very unlikely that the old institutional arrangements can be reinstituted, at least for any length of time.

We will now look at some early writers' views of stratification and class and then at the influence of the Enlightenment, followed by the ideas of the economic liberals and the Utopian socialists.

Some Early Views

Problems which are relevant today, such as inequality, opportunity for mobility, consensus and conflict, stability and change have a long history. They are discussed in the earliest writings, for the ancients sought to understand their society, the circumstances which made for a desirable life as they defined it, as well as the conditions responsible for upsetting it. We are not interested in tracing ideas back to their remote historical origin; this would be unrewarding for it is always possible to find precursors for every idea. As the maxim goes, "There is nothing which has been said which has not been said before." [1] Rather, we are interested in the historical background of our present ideas, concepts, and

---

[1] See Karl Mannheim, *Ideology and Utopia* (New York: Harcourt, Brace and Co., 1949), p. 60, n. 1.

ideologies regarding class and stratification. In looking at the early writers we shall observe that controversies over social, economic, and political differences are quite old.

PLATO AND ARISTOTLE

One of the earliest Greek writers who clearly dealt with stratification was Plato (427–347 B.C.). His theory of society [2] is organic in that it is based on the division of labor wherein each part is integrally related to the other. He sees three chief social functions: the legislative and deliberative, executed by the *rulers*, the executive which is performed by the *auxiliaries*, and the productive which is carried out by the *craftsmen*, the merchants, artisans, laborers, and farmers. In the ideal society he proposed, each order fulfills its proper tasks; in fact this is Plato's concept of justice. [3]

Plato's society is clearly stratified, the major divisions being between the *Guardians*, his term for the rulers and auxiliaries, and the productive stratum. In addition social mobility is restricted. A person's role is not based on birth or wealth, however, but on natural capabilities and training; inequality in attributes is assumed, but the educational system would bring out what people are best fitted for and positions would be assigned accordingly. In light of the continuing discussion on how social arrangements influence people to carry out their roles, [4] it is interesting to note Plato's solution. He suggests that with the proper mental and bodily training the different parts of the soul (i.e., reason and the "spirited element") will be in harmony. Thus they will be in command over the appetites which are by nature insatiably covetous. [5] Yet there is always the danger that the "spirited" part may usurp the rule of reason, and if this became widespread could lead eventually to the downfall of the ideal state. Plato is also concerned about personal interests such as the ambi-

---

[2] It should be noted that early writers often did not distinguish between the state, government, and society. The first to clearly do so was Bodin who lived in the 16th century. See Howard Becker and Harry E. Barnes, *Social Thought from Lore to Science* (Washington, D.C.: Harren Press, 1952), Vol. I, pp. 177–178.

[3] Plato, *The Republic of Plato*, trans. by Francis M. Cornford (New York: Oxford University Press, 1945), pp. 102–118, 139–140.

[4] See, e.g., Kingsley Davis and Wilbert E. Moore, "Some Principles of Stratification," *American Sociological Review*, 10 (April 1945), 242–249; Melvin M. Tumin, "Some Principles of Stratification: A Critical Analysis," *American Sociological Review*, 18 (August 1953), 387–393; Wlodzimierz Westowski, "Some Notes on the Functional Theory of Stratification," *The Polish Sociological Bulletin*, No. 3–4 (1962), 28–38; Walter Buckley, "Social Differentiation", *American Sociological Review*, 23 (August 1958), 369–375; and Davis, "The Abominable Heresy: A Reply to Dr. Buckley," *American Sociological Review*, 24 (February 1959), 82–83. The first three articles are reprinted in Reinhard Bendix and Seymour M. Lipset, eds., *Class, Status, and Power* (2nd ed.; New York: The Free Press, 1966), pp. 47–69.

[5] Plato, *op. cit.*, pp. 56–58, 129–140, 171–172.

tious man's love of honor. These he feels would be dysfunctional for both the individual and society.[6]

In Plato's ideal society the orders listed above are hierarchically ranked; yet he is concerned about the potentially disruptive consequences of a disproportionate allocation of social goods, since superordinate individuals would be able to take advantage of their position. To guard against this he suggests sanctions against anyone who uses his position to appropriate more than is due him.[7] He also proposes a communistic life for the ruling class, the Guardians, as a means of developing an ideal of service as well as preventing corruption. They are to have no private property beyond the barest necessities and no money or other social goods; their sustenance is paid for by the other citizens. The eating arrangements are communal, and dwellings and spouses are held in common. Children are reared away from parents, and parents and their offspring do not know each other. Another purpose of this plan is to breed new Guardians according to eugenic principles, and in that regard inferior children would be relegated to the lower strata. It should be emphasized that this communism applies only to the Guardians and not to the rest of the society.[8]

The communal marriage does not mean promiscuity, for the unions are very strictly regulated. Elaborate festivals are held annually, men and women are paired according to desirable mental and physical attributes, and cohabitation is limited to the period of the festival, which might last a month.[9] While inferior children are placed among the craftsmen and farmers, exceptionally able and intelligent lower-strata youngsters can be raised to the Guardian class.[10]

The problem of political power and the consequences of different types of political structures were also of great interest to Plato, and he outlined the dangers of oligarchy as well as those of democracy. Under an oligarchy wealth becomes the end in life, it accumulates in a few hands, and the rich become indolent and unable to resist pleasure or pain. This places the state in a precarious position because

> the poor man, lean and sunburnt, may find himself posted in battle beside one who, thanks to his wealth and indoor life, is panting under his burden of fat and showing every mark of distress. "Such men," he will think, "are rich because we are cowards"; and when he and his friends meet in private, the word will go round: "These men are no good: they are at our mercy." [11]

On the other hand there is great danger in democracy for the concepts of individual freedom and equality encourage the base appetites and imme-

[6] Ibid., pp. 268–270.

[7] Ibid., pp. 167–168.

[8] Ibid., pp. 155–168.

[9] Ibid., pp. 159–161.

[10] Ibid., p. 107.

[11] Ibid., p. 281.

diate gratification. As each man gives himself up to the pleasures of the moment society becomes divided into the wealthy, concerned only with amassing more wealth; a growing number of ruined spendthrifts and desperadoes; and the mass of country people working their small farms and uninterested in politics. The likely result is anarchy.

While Plato had doubts as to whether the ideal state he favored would ever exist, or for how long, he feared oligarchy more than democracy. It should be remembered though that the type of democratic government he discussed was characteristic of a small city-state such as Athens where more than half the population were slaves or resident aliens, neither of whom had civic rights.[12]

Because of Plato's stress on the harmonious functioning of constituent parts, his desire to inhibit individual ambitions which are not a part of the rights and obligations of each stratum, and his emphasis on stability rather than change, his approach is conservative. Yet one should keep in mind that the way he viewed society, the problems he saw, and the solutions he offered were affected by the conditions of his time. His work reflects political and military difficulties then facing Athens, as well as the increasing economic individualism and other interests and behaviors usually associated with urban growth. These problems were exacerbated by the Socratic emphasis on rational thought. Plato's rather rigid social order with restricted mobility was a reaction against the individuation of his time and the growing breakdown of traditional and stable codes of behavior.[13]

Aristotle (384–322 B.C.) also views society as an organic whole, in which the several parts are functionally related to each other and arise out of the division of labor. Thus he describes the several categories of work which fulfill the state's needs: farming, arts and crafts, marketing, defense, deliberative, judicial, and religious. In his discussion he posits an ideal state and argues for a superordinate-subordinate ordering of the strata into two basic divisions. The first consists of persons who bear arms, serve in the government, and are responsible for religious functions; these are the citizens, and only they are allowed to own property. The subordinate category includes those in arts and crafts, marketing, and agricultural labor, with the latter subdivided into slaves and barbarian (i.e., non-Greek) serfs.

He is concerned with another basis for division, the rich and the poor, and fears conflict when either predominates. The rich are unwilling and unable to submit to authority and are likely to rule despotically. The poor do not know how to command and must be ruled like slaves; however, should they gain power democracy of the mob is to be expected. A society of rich and poor, whether either predominates or they are evenly balanced will be in constant conflict, and whichever is vic-

[12] *Ibid.*, p. 265 ff.
[13] Becker and Barnes, *Social Thought from Lore to Science*, pp. 151–152.

torious will use political supremacy for their own ends rather than for establishing a just government.

It is for these reasons that Aristotle favors a society in which the middle stratum is large, where most of the citizens are similar in wealth; ideally, most should have a moderate and sufficient amount of property. Such conditions prevent either of the extremes from being dominant, they minimize factions and dissension, and lead to stable and good government.[14]

Many other writers addressed themselves to various aspects of social organization including what today we would call strata and classes. Tied in with this interest are discussions on the original state of man, and the conditions under which he came to lead a group life. This was more than idle speculation for underneath were divergent viewpoints regarding superordinate-subordinate relations and the rights and obligations of different strata. Even though there was great inequality in previous eras we tend to view them as tradition-bound wherein people accepted their lot in life. Yet there was a great deal of conflict in the city-states of antiquity, the medieval manors, and the early nation-states as evidenced by slave uprisings, princes vying for power, and palace revolts. Such strife is to be expected, for, as we observed in Chapter I, conflict relations are inherent in all associations.

In essence the early writers, who are often called social philosophers, were concerned about political power: how the use of force is legitimized and the limits of legitimate power, or authority. Their focus however was the upper strata, that is, the ruling elite and perhaps the stratum just below whose incumbents might rise into top positions, or at least felt they deserved the opportunity. Generally, the idea that the mass might share authority was outside their purview; only in later centuries did this become an issue. Yet the early writers' theories on the origin of society and the role of political authority paved the way for this eventuality, and it is worthwhile to look at their arguments. Important implications flow from different theories, and significant questions are raised; for example, What is the basis for authority? Why should men submit to the will of others? Is the legitimation of power otherworldly, that is, given by God or is it secular? If it is secular, is it based on the consent of the governed? If the answer is yes, should the ruler continue in office only as long as he retains the consent of those under him? And in that regard, do the governed have the right to overthrow him if he becomes a tyrant? Or does consent of the governed mean that it was given some time in the past and is irrevocable, regardless of how despotic the ruler may become?

[14] Aristotle. *The Politics of Aristotle,* trans. by Ernest Barker (New York: Oxford University Press, 1963), pp. 165–166, 180–183, 299–306.

THE BASIS FOR GOVERNMENTAL AUTHORITY

Among the early writers one of the main themes regarding the basis for governmental authority is a compact or "social contract" between the governed and the ruler. This concept is held by the school founded by Epicurus (342–270 B.C.), although the idea may be predated by the Sophists (e.g., Protagoras [c. 480–410 B.C.], Gorgias [c. 485–c.380 B.C.]), and Plato. For the social contract writers, as well as for some others, the nature of man's pre-social state is related to their theories of the origin of society and government. Among their speculations which are relevant are the following: People perceived the utility of association, and voluntarily accepted coercive authority (the Epicurians); man lived in a state of primordial innocence until the origin of private property, which resulted in lust after wealth, and coercive authority was necessary to curb such propensities (Seneca, 3 B.C.–65 A.D.). In Roman law, from the second to the sixth century A.D., legal authority was held to be based on the consent of the people, a conception which strongly influenced later social contract theorists; secular authority was held to be absolute, and it was felt that constitutions and laws were necessary to protect personal rights and civil liberties.[15]

During the Middle Ages the predominant Christian view was that government was a divine instrument for the preservation of order, political rulers derived their authority from God, and, consequently, revolution was a sin. Also, canon laws of the Church strengthened the concept of a primordial golden age followed by a "fall." In the 11th and 12th centuries there was a revival of Roman law which encouraged theories of popular sovereignty, the primacy of secular authority, and the absolute power of the state. While political authority was seen as necessary to curb the vices of mankind, tyranny on the part of the ruler was viewed as a breaking of the compact which gave him authority and justified rebellion.

The 13th century saw an increased challenging of religious authority and the espousal of popular sovereignty and representative government (principally Marsiglio de Padua [1270–1342]). During the 13th through 16th centuries controversies on the nature of political authority were engendered by the growth of monarchies, increased state power, and the beginnings of representative government. The writings of Niccolò Machiavelli (1469–1527) provide a significant contrast with the work of most of the earlier writers, for his work was primarily analytic rather than historical. Also, ethical considerations were absent from his notions of human nature and the governing process. He rejected the emphasis on

[15] Harry E. Barnes, "Ancient and Medieval Social Philosophy," in Barnes, ed., *An Introduction to the History of Sociology* (abridged ed.; Chicago: University of Chicago Press, Phoenix Books, 1966), pp. 10, 12, 14.

stability by Plato, Aristotle, and other writers; instead he held that the state originated in force and must continue to expand or perish.[16] Machiavelli's analytic approach influenced the later development of the social sciences, and he contributed to the study of stratification and class through his interest in elites and group conflict.

In the 17th and 18th centuries questions on political authority took on a new currency because of the tremendous changes that were going on: rapid commercial and industrial expansion, strained economic and political relationships, and weakening social ties. Increasingly people were critically examining their political institutions. Although some of the social contract writers of this period, notably Thomas Hobbes (1588–1679), took a conservative position the compact concept became the basis for arguments for popular sovereignty, for the right of revolution, and even for a communistic form of society.

The conservative position focused on the irrevocability of the social contract and on the preservation of private property. Hobbes insisted that regardless of the actions of the government the social contract is inviolable; once the people have given up their sovereignty they cannot get it back. This view argued for the unlimited power of the ruler, in contrast to most of the theorists who emphasized popular sovereignty and the revocability of the compact if the ruler abrogated his responsibility. The latter writers insisted that government retained its legitimacy as long as it ruled justly and for the benefit of all; should it become tyrannical, however, the contract is voided, the government no longer has the consent of the governed, and they have the right to overthrow it. (Among them were John Milton [1608–1674], Baruch Spinoza [1632–1677], John Locke [1632–1704], and Jean Jacques Rousseau [1712–1778].) An important development was Milton's individualizing of the concept of social contract, that every citizen must be a party to the compact.

Various arrangements of authority were proposed or may be inferred, and included monarchy, from absolute to limited; government by an intellectual elite, which might consist of large landowners or scientists; a capable leader to whom the people would submit and who would rule for the general welfare; and finally, cooperative-communal government. The latter was emphasized by radicals such as François Babeuf (1760–1797).[17]

The 17th- and 18th-century writers were very much concerned with the question of private property, and it was often cited as the cause of inequities and the destruction of the unfettered state of nature. Locke argued thusly but held that private property was the basis of society, that it was a "natural right," and that the role of government was, above all, to protect it.[18] These writers were interested in how to transform political

[16] *Ibid.*, pp. 16, 18, 21–23.

[17] *Ibid.*, pp. 33–37, 45.

[18] *Ibid.*, p. 41.

institutions which were increasingly out of joint with the times, yet protect private property. Most of the theorists including those who justified revolution were not in favor of far-reaching social and economic change; neither did they seek reform of the social and economic conditions under which the agricultural and industrial workers lived. Least of all did they wish the politicization of the mass of the population. By contrast the more radical writers, sometimes called the "radical utopians," urged broader political participation and held that government should severely limit private property, if not do away with it altogether.

Perhaps the conservative-radical differences can best be seen in the opposing views of Edmund Burke (1729–1797) and Tom Paine (1737–1797). Burke viewed government chiefly as an instrument for defending existing institutions and combatting social change. Maintaining that the social contract was binding and universal in scope, he bitterly assailed the interpretation which justified revolution in general and the French Revolution of 1789 in particular. Paine saw government as a necessary evil but insisted that man did not give up any natural rights when government was instituted, but that he added civil rights to them. A strong critic of monarchy, he defended the French Revolution; in fact he was one of the most ardent advocates of democracy and popular sovereignty in the late 18th century. Of special importance was his view that the minority must be protected by constitutional restraints on the majority.[19]

Although addressed primarily to the literate population, which usually meant the upper strata, these doctrines proved useful for different groups in the society. The lower strata, or those who claimed to be their spokesmen, saw in the idea of a social contract justification for a revolutionary restructuring of society which included the abolition of private property. Other groups, for example the English entrepreneurs who chafed under government restrictions, used the concept to argue for the "natural right" of private property, to oppose the monarchy, and to press for changes which would benefit their business activities.[20] Whatever their political persuasion, persons attracted to these doctrines found an ideological basis for altering the status quo, whether in a conservative or radical direction. In the long run the social contract idea was one of the important concepts which helped articulate a growing dissatisfaction with age-old social, economic, and political inequities. These new perspectives, together with certain long-range trends, led to the American, the French, and subsequent revolutions.

The above arguments and theories are indicative of the tremendous intellectual ferment of the 17th and 18th centuries which led to a repudiation of many age-old beliefs. But they also resulted in a reaction which

[19] *Ibid.*, p. 65.
[20] *Ibid.*, pp. 29–30.

sought to reinforce earlier values and stem the disruptive tendencies of the new ideas.

The Enlightenment and the Romantic–Conservative Reaction

The 17th and 18th centuries in England, France, and Germany, saw a spurt of intellectual activity which is commonly called the Enlightenment. It had its beginnings in the 15th and 16th centuries, the period of the Renaissance. The writers of the Enlightenment believed in natural laws and in the compact of mutual rights and obligations between the individual and the state, which was discussed above. They challenged the earlier conservative stress on the state as an organic unit; similarly, they challenged the medieval concept of the human group as a unified entity created and dominated by God where individual, family, church, and state were inseparable parts of society. Instead, they believed the individual was a true "person"; that is, separate from social institutions and the state. They considered the latter artificial entities created by man.

The basic idea of the Enlightenment was that human understanding is capable of comprehending the system of the world without recourse to supernatural power. And this understanding, together with the natural and intellectual sciences which were then developing, would lead to man's mastering of his world.[21]

The philosophers of the 17th century, as did earlier writers, sought the truth; but for them truth was not based on tradition and authority but on reason and observation. The truth they sought was *eternal truth*. In contrast, the aim of the later writers of this period was somewhat different; they sought to discover natural laws in the social world and used reason and empirical data toward this end. They fully expected to find scientific explanations of human behavior, in the same way that laws explaining natural and physical phenomena were being uncovered. This search together with their method laid the groundwork for the development of the social sciences.

An important value premise of many of the Enlightenment philosophers was the perfectability of the human and the belief that institutions such as the church and the state could be changed so that man's creative power would come to the fore. In their analyses nothing was sacrosanct and their theorizing often led to a hypercritical and negative stance. Their criticism of the prevailing institutions which they felt prevented

---

[21] Ernst Cassirer, "Enlightenment," *Encyclopaedia of the Social Sciences* (New York: The Macmillan Co., 1931), pp. 547–552. See also Cassirer, *The Philosophy of the Enlightenment* (Princeton, N.J.: Princeton University Press, 1951).

this flowering shaped the ideologies and thinking which helped bring about the French Revolution.

Following the revolution there was a reaction by intellectuals who had originally been opposed to the radical change or who had become appalled at the ensuing disorganization. The spokesmen of this Romantic-Conservative reaction, as it has been called, claimed that the social philosophers had caused the revolution, and criticized and attempted to repudiate their ideas. They particularly disliked the negative and critical aspects of the Enlightenment; but they also rejected its conception of a rational mechanistic universe and the idea that one could scientifically or objectively evaluate institutions. Instead they emphasized tradition and religion and felt that rights were not an abstract concept as held by the *philosophes;* rather, they existed only in definite and concrete relationships such as parent-child, master-servant, priest-parishioner, and king-subject. They argued that the institutions the Enlightenment philosophers were so critical of had developed over a long period of time to serve human needs, and strongly disagreed with the view that they might be changed abruptly. Such altering would cause a sundering of the ties that held groups together; the result would be disorganization, not an improvement in people's lot. They believed that the French Revolution provided ample evidence for this contention.

These Romantic-Conservative writers held to the organic concept of society, which reflected the Greek and medieval views discussed earlier. The Romantic-Conservative reaction stressed the importance of the group rather than the individual and emphasized order and stability, the interdependence and interrelatedness of the different parts of the society, and status and hierarchy. Human fulfillment, they felt, could best be achieved by a better integration of individuals and parts of the society, the carrying out of mutual expectations, and the upholding of tradition and religion. Thus they were in sharp contrast to the Enlightenment philosophers who believed among other things that human life could be improved by altering institutions.[22]

The secular, rational, and critical aspects of the Enlightenment; the revolutionary doctrine of the perfectability of man through institutional change; the French Revolution of 1789; and the Romantic-Conservative reaction set the stage for subsequent controversies which were of great significance for stratification and class. These include the nature of man, the operation of the social order, and the desirable society. Underlying these concerns, which are current in the social sciences today as well as in the world of politics, are two major issues: distribution of social goods, and the collateral factor, equality of opportunity.

Once these questions became secularized and then popularized a

---

[22] See discussion by Irving M. Zeitlin, *Ideology and the Development of Sociological Theory* (Englewood Cliffs, N.J.: Prentice-Hall, 1968), pp. 3–7, 36–37, 44–45.

Pandora's box was opened. How could ruling groups justify the inequities between the haves and the have-nots, which included such great differences in rights and obligations, and in political decision-making? In other words, what is the legitimate basis of authority on the one hand, and of inequality on the other? What were the answers to the poverty, the discontent, and the instability which were growing apace with the new industrialization? The ideas of the Enlightenment and those of the Romantic-Conservative reaction helped lay the foundations of contrasting ideologies, each of which proffered solutions: these were the ideologies of economic liberalism, socialism, and communism.

Economic Liberalism

The middle of the 18th century saw the founding of a school of thought called economic liberalism, which became the ideology of the English entrepreneur. It was also of great historical significance in the economic and political development of liberal democracies such as the United States and Great Britain. In France a group of writers, the Physiocrats, reacted against the prevailing mercantilism whose aim was to increase a nation's supply of gold and silver through government monopoly and other restrictions on trade, commerce, and manufacturing. The Physiocrats vigorously advocated laissez faire and individualism, held that social, political, and economic phenomena are governed by natural laws, and felt that if unlimited competition were allowed all institutions would freely adjust themselves to the natural order.[23]

According to economic liberalism the human world consisted of self-contained human atoms, each seeking to maximize his satisfactions and minimize his dissatisfactions. Locke's concept of the "natural rights" of life, liberty, and property was strongly upheld, as was the contention that government should not interfere with these rights. Economic liberalism was a secular ideology which believed that society, and man, could be perfected by the application of reason, but on the basis of individuals pursuing their own self-interest.

The views propounded by the Scottish philosopher Adam Smith (1723–1790) were largely a reaction to Protectionism. Features of the earlier mercantilism were retained; these included maintaining a favorable balance of trade whereby exports exceeded imports, promotion of the production of goods which could be exported, and restriction of imports to raw materials. In particular, foreign manufactures were kept out. But England's commerce suffered somewhat when other governments retali-

---

[23] See Barnes, "Ancient and Medieval Social Philosophy," pp. 62–63.

ated; for example, when the English prevented the importing of gold-lace from Flanders the Flemish in turn excluded British wool.[24]

Smith's key thesis was that if individuals were left alone to pursue their individual interests the result would be an increase in the wealth of nations. He discussed in great detail the social division of labor and stressed the importance of each person fulfilling his particular task for then all benefit. His interpretation of social and economic relationships was a functional one, that society was a network of these interrelations, and that the society "worked" to the extent that the many functions were carried out.

Smith believed that economic inequality was not incompatible with the natural equality of all men, or of justice. Although concerned with the plight of the industrial workers, he insisted that government should neither regulate economic activities nor engage in social reform, views which were quite compatible with the interests of the English entrepreneurs of that period. Smith's doctrines

> . . . were of a sort that fitted in admirably with the popular policy of noninterference with business. The capitalist manufacturers favored this policy, in order that they, if not their employees, might enjoy the alleged "blessings of the perfect freedom of contract." Smith's notions were . . . expanded and exploited by the middle class and by sympathetic economists like James Mill, to provide authoritative theoretical foundations for opposition to all social legislation designed to advance the interests of the industrial proletariat.[25]

His disciples included Thomas Malthus (1766–1834), David Ricardo (1772–1864), James Mill (1733–1836), John McCulloch (1789–1864), and Nassau Senior (1790–1864). With the exception of McCulloch they also eschewed social and economic reform for they held that it violated natural laws.[26]

Two of these writers deserve special mention. Malthus' theory that population increases faster than the means of subsistence was the basis for his argument against remedial social legislation. He held that such laws were undesirable because they interfered with the natural order of things, and because improving the condition of the poor would only mean a higher birth rate and then even greater poverty. Ricardo reflects this view for he also believed that legislation to increase workers' income would result in population growth with resultant misery. In addition higher pay would lower profits, reduce industrial initiative and increase unemployment. His theory of wages was based on the notion that they adjust to that level which allows the laboring class to perpetuate itself

---

[24] Arnold Toynbee, *The Industrial Revolution* (Boston: The Beacon Press, 1966), pp. 49–52.

[25] Barnes, *op. cit.*, p. 63.

[26] Becker and Barnes, *Social Thought from Lore to Science*, p. 605.

without either increasing or decreasing. He also theorized that value was determined basically by the amount of labor required in production.[27]

The doctrines of the economic liberals were very influential in the abolition of government restrictions on industry and commerce and helped initiate a period of unhampered competition. Although the most extensive development of these ideas took place in Great Britain, they also dominated the Continent during the first half of the 19th century. Their concepts provided the foundation for the modern study of economics and their writings, especially those of Smith and Ricardo, strongly influenced Marx and other socialists.

Early Communism, Social Reform, and Socialism

One of the responses to strife, social disorganization, and inequality in the distribution of social goods has been the development of visionary schemes which picture an ideal society. The emphasis in these Utopias is on what ought to be rather than what is and usually the miseries of contemporary life are absent. Instead there is happiness, people's physical and social needs are met, relations are pleasant, and the ultimate in individual and societal development is achieved. In the short run such visions do little to lift people's burdens, particularly persons in the lower strata. They may be significant in the long run, however, since they may alter man's way of looking at himself and his world, stimulate questioning of the propriety and inevitability of existing conditions, and provide goals for the future. They may also encourage and legitimize attempts at reform or social movements which seek a radical reconstruction of society.

One of the forms early schemes of the ideal society took was communism. The most outstanding examples are the communistic arrangement of the Guardians' lives in Plato's *Republic*, which was mentioned above, Sir Thomas More's *Utopia*, and Thomas Campanella's *City of the Sun*. Such proposals were sporadic, however, and there was no clear line of development among them; in fact 1,900 years passed between the *Republic* and *Utopia*; 105 years between *Utopia* and *City of the Sun*.[28]

The 18th and 19th centuries saw new Utopian proposals which were reactions to current social and economic change and the difficulties and

---

[27] *Ibid.*, p. 606.

[28] See Plato, *The Republic of Plato*; and Sir Thomas More, "Utopia" and Thomas Campanella, "City of the Sun," in Henry Morely, ed., *Ideal Commonwealths* (rev. ed.; Port Washington, N.Y.: Kennikat Press, Inc., 1968). See discussion by Emile Durkheim, *Socialism*, ed. by Alvin W. Gouldner (New York: Collier Books, 1962), p. 66; and Wilbert E. Moore, "The Utility of Utopias," *American Sociological Review*, 31 (December 1966), 772.

discontent which followed. Included were calls for the abolition of private property and greater equality in the distribution of social goods. The schemes ranged from reforms of limited aspects of the society to abolition of the state. The source of this intellectual interest and the movements which emerged was two-fold: one was the new industrialism with its problems and potentialities; the other was a history of attempts to ameliorate some of the worst aspects of the growing human misery.

One method of reform was through the state, notably in England as evidenced by the Poor Laws, the Corn Laws, and the Enclosure Acts. However the actions of local authorities, Parliament, and the Crown showed that the motivations were as much economic and political as humanitarian. "Reform" is used advisedly for some practices actually increased pauperism. Among them were successive statutes to regulate the poor culminating in 1601 with the 43rd Act of Elizabeth. This law increased the responsibility of the parish for the employment of the able-bodied and the relief of those unable to work, such as the sick, lame, and blind. Those able but unwilling to take jobs received no aid.[29]

These laws reflected a new perspective which distinguished between the reputable and the disreputable poor and showed great hostility toward the latter.[30] Previously, anyone in dire need should be helped. The view now was that to aid those who were able to work would encourage them to refuse low-paid, undersirable employment in favor of living off relief payments. The harsh laws used hunger as a goad; the able-bodied poor were forced into the labor market to take jobs even where wages were terribly low and working conditions atrocious. The alternative to starvation was the infamous workhouse, also established by law.

The higher strata made no bones about the value of hunger as motivation for a disciplined work force and as a means of keeping wages low. William Townsend, in his *Dissertation on the Poor Laws* published in 1786, comments:

> Hunger will tame the fiercest animals, it will teach decency and civility, obedience and subjection, to the most perverse. In general it is only hunger which can spur and goad [the poor] on to labor. . . . [H]unger is not only peaceable, silent, unremitting pressure, but, as the most natural motive to industry and labor, it calls forth the most powerful exertions. . . .[31]

Legislation establishing the workhouse, as well as the Poor Laws in general, was pushed by the business interests, including philanthropists. The workhouse was seen as a means of discouraging the poor from going on relief because of the stigma attached to these workplaces and the real-

[29] Karl Polyani, *The Great Transformation* (Boston: Beacon Press, 1957), p. 87.

[30] See David Matza, "The Disreputable Poor," in Bendix and Lipset, *Class, Status, and Power*, pp. 289–302.

[31] Quoted in Polyani, *op. cit.*, p. 113.

ity of their shameful conditions. "Never perhaps in all modern history," writes Karl Polyani,

> has a more ruthless act of social reform been perpetrated; it crushed multitudes of lives while merely pretending to provide a criterion of genuine destitution in the workhouse test. Psychological torture was coolly advocated and smoothly put into practice by mild philanthropists as a means of oiling the wheels of the labor mill.[32]

The chief function of relief-giving, Frances Fox Piven and Richard A. Cloward observe, is to regulate labor, especially during periods of change such as rapid modernization. The amount of relief and the form it takes are closely articulated with market conditions.[33] For example, when the problem was large numbers of undisciplined, wandering workers, laws with strong sanctions discouraged labor mobility;[34] when it became apparent that restrictions on the free circulation of labor hampered industrial development, the regulations were changed.[35]

A major justification for these laws was that poverty was the fault of the individual and not society: people are poor because they are lazy and unwilling to work; if given the opportunity, they would subsist on welfare. What a modern ring this viewpoint has! Actually, it simply reflects the entrepreneur's traditional desire for cheap labor and interest in using any means to obtain it, especially the authority of the state.[36] Ironically, such laws were supported by the economic liberals, the advocates of laissez faire.

Concern for those at the mercy of the new industrialism led to a number of ameliorative attempts, some of which arose within the Church. Historically Christianity had supported the status quo by eschewing reform through political activity and by promising rewards in the after-life. But it did have a tradition of caring for the poor. Important Catholic as well as Protestant reform movements developed which encouraged producer and consumer cooperative associations, proletarian education, and better housing for the lower strata.[37]

Other approaches for reform arose which included the Utopian socialists, the philosophical anarchists, and the advocates of state socialism. They were predecessors of Karl Marx and influenced him in im-

[32] *Ibid.*, p. 82.

[33] Frances Fox Piven and Richard A. Cloward, *Regulating the Poor* (New York: Vintage Books, 1972), pp. 3, 6–8, 31 ff.

[34] Phyllis Deane, *The First Industrial Revolution* (Cambridge: Cambridge University Press, 1965), pp. 145, 147.

[35] Paul Mantoux, *The Industrial Revolution in the Eighteenth Century* (New York: Harper Torchbooks, 1962), p. 434.

[36] Piven and Cloward, *op. cit.*, pp. 38–41, 124–177.

[37] See Polyani, *The Great Transformation*, pp. 34–49, 77–85; Becker and Barnes, *Social Thought from Lore to Science*, pp. 612–619; and Matza, "The Disreputable Poor," pp. 297–299.

portant ways. The views of the socialists and anarchists of the first half of the 19th century were a reaction against the misery of the Industrial Revolution and the ideas of romanticism, individualism, and economic liberalism. The Utopian socialists believed that human nature is primarily the product of the social environment; to remedy contemporary evils it is necessary to create better social institutions. Whereas the classical liberals considered economic life to be outside society and the concern of the individual, the Utopian socialists saw it as an integral part of the social order.

Summary

We have seen how interest in stratification and class and the related problems of inequality and opportunity for social mobility are age-old. Plato and Aristotle's analyses of social structure reflected the concerns and problems of their day. Similarly other writers of antiquity, the philosophers of the Middle Ages, and those of the 17th and 18th centuries reflected contemporary conditions.

The bases and limitations of political authority and the role of private property were argued by conservatives and radicals. The former wished to revitalize existing institutions, using as their model earlier conditions and relationships, while the latter sought a more revolutionary restructuring of society. The clash in views was most apparent during the Enlightenment and the Romantic-Conservative reaction which followed.

Growth in the scale of society, increased trade and commerce, and the beginnings of industrialization altered social, economic, and political relationships. They also brought forth new explanations, justifications, and proposals for change. The theories and schemes were primarily addressed to the literate portion of the population, which meant mainly the higher strata. Concrete steps for implementation were usually absent but the implication is clear that the necessary changes would be decided upon and put into effect by this level; more important, effective control would remain in their hands.

The heritage of intellectual thought, particularly that of the Enlightenment, together with the ineffectiveness of Utopian proposals, uprisings, and mass movements in meeting the problems of the new industrialism led eventually to a more radical approach: the theories of Karl Marx. Yet the ideas of the time were shaped by current conditions, and in turn the ideas influenced the development of the society. Similarly Marx, the Marxian writers, and those in opposition to Marx's views were also a product of their time. To better understand their work and the response to it, we pause to examine the two most important events over the past two hundred years from the perspective of stratification and class: the Industrial and the French Revolutions.

Chapter IX.   Industrialization and Revolution

The changes we examined in Chapter VII and the ideational response discussed in Chapter VIII set the stage for two momentous events: the Industrial and the French Revolutions. These two upheavals radically transformed the material conditions of the world and the relationships among different groups of people; they were also responsible for the emergence of ideologies and movements aimed at a wider distribution of social goods.

We next look at these two phenomena, called by E. J. Hobsbawm the "Dual Revolution," [1] which are most significant for understanding modern-day stratification, class, and conflict.

The Industrial Revolution

The concept of "industrial revolution" rightfully calls to mind technological change, such as the invention of the steam engine, mechanical looms that replaced hand weaving, and new methods of producing iron. It also involved a mushrooming of population, the rapid growth of cities, a great rise in trade and commerce, and alterations in social organization. In regard to the latter, of particular importance was the factory system, the development of a free labor force, and the ascendancy of an entrepreneurial class.

The term "revolution" both aids and obscures our understanding of this important phenomenon for the significant changes had begun several centuries earlier. For some time merchants had been venturing to the far corners of the earth, and the feudal system of the Middle Ages was breaking down; manufacturing was growing although much of it was still cottage industry or other small-scale activity. The economy was increasingly based on a monetary economy and there was greater opportunity to accumulate capital. The trends culminated in England toward the middle of the 18th century and with dramatic rapidity brought about a

[1] E. J. Hobsbawm, *The Age of Revolution, 1789–1848* (New York: The New American Library, 1962).

new organization of work, a more rapid pace of life, faster change, and new social, economic, and political relationships. The form of business organization was what we know as capitalism: private ownership of the means of production, profit as a motivating force, and rationalism and pragmatism in technical arrangements and social relationships.

There are several reasons why rapid industrialization first took place in England rather than on the Continent. Her naval supremacy facilitated world-wide commercial and military activities: English merchantmen covered the four corners of the earth, lands were colonized, and favorable business and military arrangements were established. Through commerce, slave trading, exploitation of colonies, piracy, and war, wealth flowed to England and she became the richest nation in the world. In addition there were large deposits of coal and iron ore plus a tremendous enthusiasm for science and engineering. A national patent system stimulated and protected inventions and new techniques. Among the landed aristocracy innovators used crop rotation and fertilizers and more rationalized and efficient methods to increase agricultural yields. The long-term displacement of rural workers helped provide the labor force for the factories and the mills, and there was a tendency toward a mass market. Other important factors included an aescetic Protestantism and the development of an entrepreneurial class. All in all, England was transformed from a feudal to a commercial-industrial society in a relatively short time; interestingly, the new riches accrued largely to the upper classes.[2]

There was greater flexibility in England for economic and political innovation than, for example, in France. English farmers and bourgeoisie were better able to meet the needs for increased consumption of necessities and luxuries and to take advantage of new opportunities. The nobility didn't have the extensive power of their counterparts on the Continent; English feudalism was much looser and weaker than the system across the Channel, and there was relative autonomy of the cities vis-à-vis the Crown. Other favorable factors were the absence of an effective self-perpetuating bureaucracy and the existence of a highly developed legal system.[3] The legal-political system tended to encourage accommodation rather than overt conflict, although a civil war was necessary to end the Crown's monopoly over trade and manufacturing and to settle other important issues.

[2] The classic work on the Industrial Revolution is Paul Mantoux, *The Industrial Revolution in the Eighteenth Century* (New York: Harper Torchbooks, 1962; first pub. in 1928). Also very useful are Arnold Toynbee, *The Industrial Revolution* (Boston: Beacon Press, 1962; first pub. in 1884); Karl Polyani, *The Great Transformation* (Boston: Beacon Press, 1957); J. L. Hammond and Barbara Hammond, *The Rise of Modern Industry* (New York: Harper Torchbooks, 1969; first pub. in 1925), and Phyllis Deane, *The First Industrial Revolution* (Cambridge: Cambridge University Press, 1965).

[3] Herman Israel, "Some Religious Factors in the Emergence of Industrial Society in England," *American Sociological Review*, 31 (October 1966), 590, 593, 595, 598.

To give a picture of the major strata at the time of industrialization is difficult because of the paucity of adequate data. However, there is a remarkable accounting of the income and occupation of the English people, compiled by Gregory King at the end of the 17th century. The data are given in Table IX-1 where they are categorized roughly by situs.[4] The single largest category is agriculture, which is not surprising, followed by manual work, the poor and the near poor. These categories account for eight out of every ten people, and include persons who are doing tolerably well, especially the freeholders, artisans, and handicraftsmen. The most affluent category consists of titled persons, and the Lords' per-capita income of £70 a year contrasts with the £4 of the laborers and servants and the £2 of the poor. The merchants and sea-traders, it can be seen, are also quite well off. The poor and the "laboring poor"—persons with a per-capita income of £4 or less—constitute almost half the population.

While the figures in Table IX-1 give us some idea of stratification at the time they do not distinguish between rural and non-rural. Also, the great spurt in industrial growth did not occur until 50 or 60 years later. Stratification around the middle of the 18th century differed considerably in the countryside as opposed to the towns and cities. The strata in the countryside were basically the landowning nobility, yeoman farmers and other agriculturalists, or peasants. Finally there were the unemployed and the poor.

In the towns and cities the owners of large factories, bankers, and rich merchants constituted the upper level of the bourgeoisie, with the small proprietors and the owners of small workshops making up the lower levels. Among the artisans and laborers the self-employed and the highly skilled were in the upper ranks, the unskilled in the lower. The unemployed and those who only occasionally found a day's work, the poor with no resources—often inhabitants of workhouses—and beggars made up the lowest stratum.

There were of course gradations within each stratum, and the bottom of one shaded off into the top of the other. In fact marginal categories which increased with changing conditions were often given special labels. An example is the gentry: smaller noble landholders and well-off yeomen with considerable amounts of land. In the case of the yeomen, not all were freeholders and the less prosperous shaded off into the peasantry. In turn the more impecunious peasants merged with the unemployed and the poor. This last category included people who might occasionally find a day's employment, the poor without resources, and beggars.[5]

[4] See Albert J. Reiss, Jr., *Occupations and Social Status* (New York: The Free Press of Glencoe, 1961), p. 254; see also pp. 45, 251, 253–256; and Richard T. Morris and Raymond J. Murphy, "The Situs Dimension in Occupational Structure," *American Sociological Review*, 24 (April 1959), 231–239.

[5] Barrington Moore, Jr., *Social Origins of Dictatorship and Democracy* (Boston: Beacon Press, 1967), p. 10.

TABLE IX-1. Situs Categorization of England, 1688

	Yearly Per-Capita Income	Number of Persons		Per-cent-age
Political and Quasi-Political				
Lords	£ 70	6,920		
Baronets	55	12,800		
Knights	50	7,800		
Esquires	45	30,000		
Gentlemen	35	96,000	153,520	3%
Office-holders, major	30	40,000		
Office-holders, minor	20	30,000	70,000	1
Business				
Larger merchants and sea-traders	50	16,000		
Smaller merchants and sea-traders	33	48,000		
Shopkeepers and trades-men	10	180,000	244,000	4
Military				
Naval Officers	20	20,000		
Army Officers	15	16,000		
Common seamen	7	150,000		
Common soldiers	7	70,000	256,000	5
Professional				
Lawyers	20	70,000		
Persons in science and liberal arts	12	80,000		
Clergymen	9	52,000	202,000	4
Agriculture				
Large freeholders	12	280,000		
Small freeholders	10	700,000		
Farmers	8	750,000	1,730,000	31
Manual work				
Artisans and handi-craftsmen	10	240,000	240,000	4
Laborers and servants	4	1,275,000	1,275,000	23
Other:				
Cottagers and paupers	2	1,300,000		
Vagrants	2	30,000	1,330,000	24
		Total	5,500,520	99%

Source: Figures adapted from Gregory King, *Natural and Political Observations and Conclusions upon the State and Condition of England,* as reprinted in Phyllis Deane, *The First Industrial Revolution* (Cambridge: Cambridge University Press, 1965), pp. 8-9.

The distribution of social goods, the ordering of men, and the relations among them were affected by several critical changes. They were the commercialization of farming; the growth of an entrepreneurial-bourgeois stratum, and the development of an industrial labor force. In the first of these changes a portion of the larger landowners became agricultural capitalists. Innovators such as Charles Townshend were interested in economic reward as well as in the application of scientific method.[6] The agricultural capitalists not only determined that free labor was more useful than the earlier arrangements, but also found that they required a smaller workforce. They ended farm tenancy, dispossessed squatters, and bought out or squeezed out small farmers. Legal and extra-legal actions were undertaken to acquire more land and to move surplus labor out of rural areas. Acreage which had been used in common for pasturage and woodlands, which had provided firewood and timber for homes, was closed off for the exclusive use of the landowner. Many persons including small independent farmers suffered for these "commons" formed an essential part of their economy. In addition property belonging to the small yeoman farmer might also be enclosed; similarly land in dispute with the lord might also be closed off. Usually the small landholder had neither the resources nor the necessary knowledge to legally contest such actions. Consequently many of these persons also became a part of the landless poor.[7]

The enclosing of commons began as early as the 12th century and proceeded slowly and sporadically, increasing significantly in the 15th and 16th centuries. The Crown sought to retain elements of the older feudal society and opposed enclosures. While it could not stop this long-range trend it retarded it, persecuting landholders through Star Chamber proceedings. Differences of land use and the organization of rural life it predicated was one of the bases of the English Civil War (1642–1646; 1648–1649) which was also called the Protestant Revolution. The royalists were pitted against the supporters of Parliament who wanted the power of the state to reside mainly in that body and who were also more commercially oriented. But more about that conflict shortly. What is important here is that with the defeat of the royalists, the main barriers to enclosures were swept away and they proceeded apace, accelerating greatly toward the end of the 18th century. It is estimated that from 1760 onwards there were some 5,000 enclosures.[8]

Not only did the commercialization of farming and the more rationalized use of labor help destroy the old patterns of land settlement and use, but they also attenuated the traditional lord-serf relationship. What was left of feudalism continued to weaken, disappearing by 1840. The peas-

---

[6] Mantoux, *The Industrial Revolution in the Eighteenth Century*, p. 160.

[7] *Ibid.*, p. 152; and Hammond and Hammond, *The Rise of Modern Industry*, pp. 84–85.

[8] Moore, *op. cit.*, p. 19; and Mantoux, *op. cit.*, pp. 152, 175.

ants suffered most from the changing nature of agricultural life for there was no longer a need for them: the traditional cultivation of strips and subsistence farming gave way to more modern methods, and fewer workers were required. Many of the young unmarrieds migrated to the towns and cities; the rest remained in the rural areas in a state of destitution.[9]

One method of dealing with the distress was the "Speenhamland system" which embodied outdoor relief. It was established in 1795 following a series of bad harvests and rising prices resulting from the enclosures and the war with France. Also, because of the Elizabethan Poor Laws many who were employed were forced to work at whatever wages they could get and many were destitute. In the previous chapter we commented on some of the justifications given for these laws; here we want to focus on their consequences. Persons in the middle and upper strata became increasingly concerned, for not only was the destitution becoming widespread, but so was the number of disturbances. Also, the events of the French Revolution were still fresh in people's minds. The concept of "income-maintenance" for the poor which is still being debated today was the essence of Speenhamland. The minimum a family needed was established, based on its size and the price of bread. If wages fell below that level supplemental payments by the authorities made up the difference. This law was favored by the landowners for they saw it as a means of keeping wages low yet retaining agricultural workers. However the effect of this system was to reduce the productivity of labor and to increase pauperism. There was no incentive for the employee to satisfy his employer for even if his earnings dropped the supplementary payments kept his income up to scale. There was also no incentive for the employer to raise wages above that minimum. Pauperization continued to grow; indolent families were being supported and wage supplements encouraged workers who had been too poor to marry to do so; and the more children they had the higher the allotment.

Speenhamland was opposed by the commercial interests because it discouraged the development of a free labor supply which was needed for the growing business and manufacturing economy. It also neutralized hunger as motivation for a disciplined work force and as a means of keeping wages low, as was mentioned in the preceding chapter.[10] Speenhamland and other forms of "outdoor" relief were eventually replaced by the "indoor" relief or workhouses of the Reform Act of 1834. This law was designed to force the unemployed to accept whatever work they could find or suffer the consequences of the infamous workhouse.[11] The Poor Laws and the economic condition of the agricultural workers and

[9] Moore, *op. cit.*, p. 27.

[10] Polyani, *The Great Transformation*, pp. 77–85, 113.

[11] *Ibid.*, p. 82.

their families quickened migration to the towns and cities. Many of the displaced became part of the growing industrial workforce.[12]

Life for the industrial workers was hardly any better: their numbers increased and they were concentrated in slums. The mass of employees began to become more homogeneous as regards occupational tasks, pay, and conditions of work. These were some of the consequences of the factory system and the growing use of machinery. But the essence of the Industrial Revolution was the separation between capital and labor, which was to the disadvantage of the worker.[13]

In the towns and cities the bourgeoisie rose in importance for there was opportunity for the hardworking and ambitious entrepreneur. Many artisans and highly skilled workers also prospered since their talents were needed in the expanding economy which was beginning to industrialize. The proportion of semi-skilled and unskilled laborers increased greatly as did the unemployed and the poor.

The rapidity and scale of technological change and new opportunities and aspirations helped unhinge traditional relationships at work and in the country, town, and city. The new conditions engendered strains and disturbances at the local as well as at the national level and the conflict involved all groups: Royalist-Parliamentarian, landowner-peasant, employer- employee, farmer-manufacturer, Establishment Churchman-Puritan, enfranchised-disenfranchised, and rich-poor; each contesting over the distribution of social goods. The conflict also took many forms, including Parliamentary legislation favoring one group over another, economic sanctions against employees, strikes and worker destruction of machines, riots by the hungry, and the use of the judicial and police powers of the state against dissidents.[14]

The system of stratification was being reshaped and with this new self-conceptions and ideologies emerged. Among the significant developments which have had an unmistakable impact on world history was the formation of an entrepreneurial class which eventually successfully challenged the preeminence of the landowning aristocracy. But perhaps just as important was the growth of a free labor force whereby ties between employers and employees were almost entirely economic and impersonal. The latter sold their labor as a commodity for whatever the market offered. Yet their fortunes were affected by employer needs, business fluctuations, and world market conditions.

As the less-skilled workforce and the laboring poor grew in size there were different responses, depending on people's perspective. Many employers and members of the government became fearful over the possibility of an uprising, especially as indications of group-consciousness

---

[12] See Hobsbawm, *The Age of Revolution*, p. 185.

[13] Mantoux, *The Industrial Revolution in the Eighteenth Century*, pp. 69, 73.

[14] *Ibid.*, pp. 78–82.

became noticeable. However the aristocracy as well as the bourgeoisie did not hesitate to seek the support of working people if this furthered their own interests. Religiously-motivated reformers saw an opportunity to save men's souls while at the same time helping to instill the docility and discipline needed in the factory and workshop. They also encouraged acceptance of existing conditions with the promise of reward in the hereafter.

Other reformers sought to ameliorate abuses by getting employees to organize into combinations or unions, and such organizations grew despite severe repression by the government. The working-class movement contained elements which were reformist, in that they sought a more equitable distribution of social goods through collective bargaining with employers, through petitions to Parliament, and by extending the franchise to the proletariat. Other elements were socialistic and sought a more fundamental reorganization of society; but they too believed their goals could be achieved within the existing political system.[15]

The response of the radicals was quite different for they saw no hope for significantly bettering the lot of the masses under capitalism. For example Friedrich Engels (1820–1895) after an extensive analysis of conditions in 1844 concluded that the prejudices and short-sightedness of the bourgeoisie, the growth in the proportion of the proletariat, their increasing pauperization, and worsening economic crises, would eventually lead to revolution. He felt that the conflict between the haves and have-nots would become more overt and widespread and that soon some simple precipitating event would ignite a conflagration.[16]

From the vantage point of history we know that in England industrialization continued to grow and there was no bloody revolution. Over the years the lot of the working-man improved and group conflict became less intensive because of a more equitable distribution of social goods including the sharing of political power. But we also know that in other countries there were revolutions and the outcomes were quite different. Hopefully the English situation will give us some insights for understanding the developments in other places; therefore we next look at the conditions which seem to have contributed significantly to industrialization and some of its consequences. In doing so we want to pay special attention to the roles of different categories of persons: the land-owning aristocracy, the entrepreneurs, the proletariat, the clergy, and government officials. We will also be interested in the relevance of ideologies, both secular and religious.

[15] See G. D. H. Cole, *A Short History of the British Working-Class Movement, 1789–1947* (London: George Allen & Unwin Ltd., 1947).

[16] Friedrich Engels, *The Condition of the Working-Class in England in 1844* (London: George Allen & Unwin Ltd., 1926; first pub. in 1892). See especially pp. 294–298.

The Beginnings of Industrialization

A number of important developments in the economic, social, and political structure of England differentiated it greatly from the nations on the Continent. Maritime supremacy, successful wars, and extensive colonizing increased the wealth of the nation, provided surplusses for investment, and brought many consumer items within the reach of larger segments of the populace. New markets were created at home and abroad and were enlarged by a rapid growth in the population, primarily as a result of a decrease in the death rate. Between 1750 and 1850 the population of Europe more than doubled.[17] Prior to 1751 in England the largest decennial population increase was three per cent. For each of the next ten-year periods it was six per cent; between 1781 and 1791 it was nine per cent, and it continued to rise until it reached 18% between 1811 and 1821. In the following decades it dropped to 12% because of heavy emigration.[18]

With population growth, the increase in commerce, and the beginnings of industrialization, the more far-seeing of the landed aristocracy took advantage of the rising demand for agricultural goods. They put additional land into cultivation, increased acreage for grazing, and made agricultural labor more efficient. They did away with the strip system and other antiquated practices and made use of improvements in animal husbandry and farming techniques. For example, it was estimated that in 1700 the net carcass of cattle was 370 pounds and that of sheep 28 pounds; by 1800 the weight for each had more than doubled. Farming technology did not advance as rapidly but in spite of poor methods England produced in 1770 an average of 25 bushels of wheat per acre in contrast to France's 18. She also exported this grain.[19]

The innovators were usually not the titled aristocrats, many of whom had expensive tastes and denigrated work, but those below the peerage. Among the former who did adapt it was most often by leasing out their land to managers and much of the impetus for change came from the large tenant farmers. The market-oriented agriculturalists included the more prosperous yeomen farmers who were in essence small capitalists, often owning estates of from 25 to 200 acres of arable land as well as up to 500 to 600 acres for grazing. They were industrious and ambitious, and the chief force behind the enclosure movement in which so many

[17] A. J. Coale and E. M. Hoover, "The Effects of Population Growth on Economic Development and the Effects of Economic Development on Population Growth," in Michael Drake, ed., *Population and Industrialization* (London: Methuen & Co., 1969), p. 15.

[18] Toynbee, *The Industrial Revolution*, pp. 60–61.

[19] *Ibid.*, pp. 16, 18.

peasants were dispossessed from the land.[20] The ranks of those seeking agricultural employment were joined by immigrants from overcrowded and economically depressed Ireland and by families from small villages whose economies were being destroyed by the agricultural revolution. In addition their numbers swelled as a result of the great population increase.[21] Yet the proportion of agricultural jobs steadily decreased: in 1811 35% of the labor force was in agricultural work, in 1821 33%, and in 1831 28%.[22]

Displaced by the changes in the agrarian economy, these people flocked to the mines, the mills, the factories, and the workshops; they became the labor force of the new industrial society. Now, who were their employers, the entrepreneurs who provided the jobs for this growing workforce?

THE ENTREPRENEURS

A few entrepreneurs were from the aristocracy, as in the case of mine-owners. These were noblemen who had coal deposits on their land and took advantage of the voracious need for coal for iron smelters, foundries, and other industrial uses. Some aristocrats got rich from renting their property and invested in the new business enterprises; however, all in all relatively few of the entrepreneurs came from the aristocracy.

Some of the individuals who established mills were initially "middle men" or brokers who sold raw materials to families of weavers in the countryside and later purchased their finished products and in turn sold them to wholesalers or shopkeepers. Other entrepreneurs came from the ranks of spinners and weavers, apprentices or artisans, or were from yeoman farmer stock. They could be almost anyone who was able to borrow a little money to set up a workshop, for success required, aside from a little capital and appropriate skills, extremely hard work. The majority however were from the middle and lower-middle strata, and to a lesser extent were workers and small farmers. Reinhard Bendix notes that social origins varied by industry: for example in cotton manufacturing probably one-third to one-half of early manufacturers had working or lower-middle strata backgrounds. Bendix found that about one-third of major industrialists in 1750–1850 were from working and small farmer homes while two-thirds were from families already established in business. He adds that the idea that the large majority of early entrepreneurs rose spectacularly from very low social origins is misleading.[23]

[20] *Ibid.*, pp. 10–11, 15, 24 ff. These yeomen are likened by Moore to the *kulaks* of late 19th-century Russia. *Op. cit.*, p. 11.

[21] Hammond and Hammond, *The Town Laborer* (London: Longmans, 1966), pp. 26–27.

[22] Toynbee, *The Industrial Revolution*, p. 61.

[23] Reinhard Bendix, *Work and Authority in Industry* (New York: John Wiley and Sons, 1956), pp. 23–25. Cf. Hammond and Hammond, *The Town Laborer*, pp. 21–23.

The ones who prospered raised themselves largely by their own efforts but probably most of those who tried failed or succeeded in establishing only small workshops or moderate-sized enterprises; understandably not more than a small proportion achieved great wealth and became "captains of industry." But whatever their social origins and the extent of their success, the entrepreneurs were caught up in the excitement over the promise of technology; they had an interest and faith in it which was in essence the ideology of a social movement.[24] They not only strove for economic gain but also for social and political recognition; they resented the prevailing aristocratic prejudices against people who engaged in commerce and industry and strongly contested the power of the aristocracy. The new businessmen sought political power not only to end what they considered unwarranted privileges of the ruling class and to establish economic policies which would benefit them; their fight was also against habitual practices and traditional views of commerce, craftsmanship, and employer-employee relations. The new ways were resisted by the workers and the older ruling groups who, in combating change, clung to images of preindustrial society.[25]

CHANGING IDEOLOGIES; RELIGIOUS AND POLITICAL CONFLICT

Traditional practices and ideologies, particularly those governing superordinate-subordinate relations began to break down with the onslaught of the new technology and the reorganization of work. This sundering was abetted by the intensification of trade and commerce, expansion of the population, growth of urbanization, and the increased impersonalization between employer and employee. Nevertheless it was generally agreed that the rich should govern and that the poor should be subordinate to them. Furthermore, it was stressed that poverty was due not to conditions but to character defects among the poor. Educational associations including Sunday Schools were established to prepare children for their low rank in society and to inculcate good work habits, humility, and submission to authority. An essential part of the evangelical preaching since the 17th century was the idea that the poor should work hard, obey their superiors, and be satisfied with subordinate status for this was God's will. Moreover, it was the duty of the higher classes to see that the lower fulfilled God's plan, and this included responsibility for their moral and physical welfare. Toward the end of the 18th century, however, the idea that people must depend on themselves gained ground. No longer did the higher classes consider themselves responsi-

[24] See Bendix, *op. cit.*, pp. 15, 29.
[25] *Ibid.*, pp. 15–16, 21–23, 30–34.

ble for the well-being of the lower; specifically, the relief of the poor was no longer the concern of the better-off and the employer was no longer responsible for the welfare of his employees.[26]

These breaks with tradition were part and parcel of the new industrialization and the changing relations between the classes. The rising business class with increasing success was challenging the older aristocracy, but in the new ordering of power and privilege the lower strata sought their due. They too were becoming self-conscious as a class: first, because of changing conditions of life and work; second, the entrepreneurial class, in their conflict with the Establishment, did not hesitate to enlist their support. They were similarly courted by the land-owning nobility. The conflict between the landowning aristocracy and the rising entrepreneurial class for economic and political supremacy also involved religious differences.

Protestantism played an important role in the emergence of industrial society in England and the fact that industrialism took a capitalistic form.[27] Protestantism became useful to the entrepreneurs for justifying their business activities and for opposing the established groups in the society. Its significance may be understood by reference to Herman Israel's study which he orients around the polarizing of English society in the 17th century.[28]

The division was basically between the Anglican-Royalists and the Puritan-Parliamentarians. The former were essentially the Establishment and its supporters, and consisted of the Crown, the Church of England, the great landowners, and the large merchants, as well as many ordinary people. The latter were traditional in their outlook and became upset over attacks against the established church. The Church of England, which remained essentially Catholic in culture, was tied in with the State, attending its services became compulsory, and Protestant-oriented clergy were purged.

The Puritan-Parliamentarians included these clergymen who formed the core of the opposition, innovative businessmen, somewhat reminiscent of the merchant-adventurers of the 12th century, and others such as progressive lawyers and farmers, and many common people. Essentially the Puritan-Parliamentarians were the dissidents who opposed the religious and economic policies of the State. The Crown viewed trade as a source of revenue for royal consumption rather than for national economic development. It sought to strengthen the entrenched, less progressive landholders and businessmen who sought only limited expansion through royal monopolies over specific items or trade routes. National-

[26] *Ibid.*, pp. 16, 63–73 ff.

[27] See Max Weber, *The Protestant Ethic and the Spirit of Capitalism*, trans. by Talcott Parsons (New York: Charles Scribner's Sons, 1958). Cf. R. H. Tawney, *Religion and the Rise of Capitalism* (New York: Penguin Books, 1947).

[28] Israel, "Some Religious Factors in the Emergence of Industrial Society."

ism also played an important part since the Puritan-Parliamentarians were strongly anti-Roman Catholic. They were opposed to the Catholic aspects of the state church and its remaining ties with Rome; moreover Roman Catholic Spain and France were England's chief foreign rivals.[29]

As can be seen, religion was inextricably intertwined with the government and the economy, and "Puritanism," according to Israel, "was the only available ideology that could effectively legitimize opposition to church and state."[30] Also, while early Protestantism had an anti-economic bias, within the context of Puritan theological demands economic involvement elicited strong approval. Both the Anglican-Royalists and the Puritan-Parliamentarians stressed social control and claimed they defended religion, liberty, and property; yet not only were their approaches different but each wished to set up a new social system, quite radical from any in England's past. The Anglican-Royalists sought absolutism and centralization, and their interest favored a quasi-peasant organization of society. On the other hand the Puritan-Parliamentarians desired a more limited monarchy with control in the hands of a continuous parliament. In addition they wanted a government which would not hinder the economic opportunity of progressive manufacturers, merchants, lawyers, and farmers. The Puritan-Parliamentarians, whose aims were proto-industrial, eventually triumphed.[31]

There were many facets to the economic, political, and religious conflict but basically it was a struggle over control of social goods. For example, as the businessmen began to gain power in Parliament they sought to pass legislation favorable to their interests, as the landowning nobility had done when they were in control. Similarly they used institutional arrangements for their own benefit whenever the opportunity arose, as did the aristocracy. Much of the legislation of the time and the use of the power of the state as embodied in the judiciary and the police was aimed at the lower strata. How, then, did they fare under industrialization, and more specifically, how were they affected by the institutional arrangements?

THE INDUSTRIAL WORKFORCE

A major question is whether the life of the laboring people improved or worsened with industrialization; but to get at the answer there must be a basis for comparison. Therefore the question more properly is, How did they fare relative to their condition prior to industrialization? Also, how did they fare under industrialization relative to other segments in the society? There are numerous difficulties in attempting to compare liv-

[29] *Ibid.*

[30] *Ibid.*, p. 591.

[31] *Ibid.*, pp. 590, 593, 595, 598.

ing standards during different time periods as industrialization progressed, let alone trying to evaluate conditions before it began. If we are concerned with the condition of the majority of the work force, then little reliable information is available. Most of the statistics on income are highly questionable because figures for money-wages are chiefly time rates for skilled artisans, and little is known about the pay of piece workers and the unskilled; nor is there adequate information about unemployment or shortened work weeks. In addition, wage level is meaningful only in terms of the prices of goods and services, and the cost-of-living figures which exist are unreliable.[32] Information on the conditions under which people lived and worked also leaves much to be desired. In evaluating their circumstances it is important to maintain perspective for many of the things attributed to the Industrial Revolution had existed earlier: long hours of work, low pay, bad working and living conditions, and the employment of children. Exploitation of subordinate by superordinate did not begin with the introduction of machinery; moreover, the cruelty and ruthlessness of many entrepreneurs should be judged against what was common in English society long before industrialization.[33] Nevertheless it is important to make some assessment of how the common people fared and many scholars and others have concerned themselves with this question.

Interestingly there are two schools of thought. The classical writers take a pessimistic view of the social effects of the Industrial Revolution, while many of the modern scholars tend to be more optimistic.[34] What does the evidence, albeit scanty, show? Hobsbawn carefully analyzes the available data and tries to estimate what conditions were like. The mortality rate fell between the 1780's and the 1810's, and began to rise until the 1840's. This important indicator is linked to the amount of income and food consumption and suggests an improvement in living standards during the first period and deterioration during the second. It is estimated that in the early 1840's about ten per cent of the people were paupers, in the 1850's the percentage was between 5.7 and 4.9 and in the 1860's it was 4.6%. Yet after the 1840's, although times were better, probably 40% were still below the poverty level. By contrast the wages of the highly skilled who comprised about 15% of the work force improved considerably, and even when times were bad they were relatively better off. The remaining 45% were somewhere in between these two groups.

In some years there would be an increase in business activities and in others a depression, although the downturns would hurt some occupa-

[32] Hobsbawm, *Labouring Men* (London: Weindenfeld and Nicolson, 1964), pp. 66–67 ff.

[33] See Mantoux, *The Industrial Revolution in the Eighteenth Century*, p. 413; Hammond and Hammond, *The Town Laborer*, p. 31; and Bendix, *Work and Authority in Industry*, p. 60. Bendix points to the personalized relations of tutelage and deference between employers and workers prior to industrialization and suggests that they were not necessarily benevolent, that personalized exploitation can be just as cruel as when it is impersonal.

[34] Hobsbawm, *Labouring Men*, p. 64.

tions and areas of the country more than others. The output and employment in the brick industry reflect some of the ups and downs of the industrial economy. There were periods of rapid expansion between 1800 and 1804 which were followed by times of slower growth from 1805 to 1814; there were then slumps during 1815–1819.[35] The unskilled and workers in the declining trades suffered the most and particular regions, cities, and towns were very severely affected. The 1826 slump is a case in point. In the hard hit sections of Lancashire, between 30 and 75% of the total population was destitute; in the woolen areas of Yorkshire the percentage was between 25 and 100, and in the textile areas of Scotland 25 to 50% of the population was impoverished. During 1841–1842, the worst depression of the century, in the city of Bolton the range of unemployment was from 36% for ironworkers to 87% for bricklayers.[36] The wide difference between the low and the high figures reflect the inadequacy of the data. It need hardly be pointed out that even the low estimates suggest terrible conditions. An estimate for London was that out of a laboring force of about four-and-a-half million one-third was fully and constantly employed, one-third was working half time, and the remaining one-third was unemployed, occasionally obtaining a day's work by displacing others. Another indicator of bad conditions during the first third of the 19th century was the increase in vagrancy: the unemployed tramping from place to place in search of work.[37]

In spite of these conditions writers such as Robert L. Heilbroner feel it is doubtful that there was a deterioration in life for the masses. Their main argument is that there had been much poverty and many social problems before the Industrial Revolution.[38] It is true that conditions were bad prior to industrialization and it is also true that in the *long run* the real income of the worker has risen considerably. Yet the available evidence indicates that after 1760 real wages declined, particularly during the period 1790–1813. Between 1790 (the year Speenhamland was put into effect) and 1840, economic conditions for the mass of the laboring force deteriorated and the average working man remained close to the subsistence level.[39]

The worker's dependence on whatever wage he could obtain, and the entrepreneur's quest for profit existed in an amoral situation. That is, with the breakdown of traditional relationships the employer no longer felt a sense of responsibility toward his workforce; he felt justified in paying as little as possible and ignoring unpleasant or unsafe circum-

[35] *Ibid.*, p. 78.

[36] *Ibid.*, pp. 70–74.

[37] *Ibid.*, pp. 78–79.

[38] Robert L. Heilbroner, *The Making of Economic Society* (Englewood Cliffs, N.J.: Prentice-Hall, 1963), p. 86.

[39] See Hobsbawm, *Labouring Men,* pp. 66, 88, 120–125; and Bendix, *Work and Authority in Industry,* p. 41.

stances. The consequence was often ghastly working conditions, as the following illustration shows. During the mid-1800's an oppressive and degrading system of clothing manufacturing developed in which small entrepreneurs or "middlemen" contracted with clothing merchants to find workers. Known as "sweaters," these entrepreneurs forced the men and women they hired to live in their houses where they were literally stripped. Half a dozen men might have only one coat among them which permitted only one to go out at a time. "But the condition of most," writes E. R. A. Seligman,

> was still more horrible. As they fell into arrears they were cooped up, six and ten at a time, in a miserable dark hole which served both as work and bed-room, and in this fetid, reeking atmosphere, half stifled and half-starved, thousands of these poor wretches endured a living death.[40]

That economic and social conditions are often tied together can be seen in the employment of children. Although there had been much child labor previously it became much more widespread, being used extensively in the cotton mills and mines. Similarly the use of female workers which also had been common expanded, primarily because they could be paid less than men and were more docile. With the husband's and wife's wages often insufficient for subsistence, and with frequent male unemployment, it became essential for parents to put their offspring to work if the family was to survive. Consequently children as young as six or seven were employed; on occasion even younger. Under one system of child labor which was not prohibited until 1816 poor youngsters were consigned to mills a considerable distance from home. They were boarded and had to remain at the factory until they were 21. The parishes to which they belonged were anxious to get rid of them:

> Regular bargains, beneficial to both parties if not to the children, who were dealt with as mere merchandise, were entered into between the spinners on the one hand and the Poor Law authorities on the other. Lots of fifty, eighty or a hundred children were supplied and sent like cattle to the factory, where they remained imprisoned for many years.[41]

Ostensibly apprentices, they were in fact a cheap labor supply. Mantoux notes that "among the weavers of the north and the south-west children worked at five or even four years old, as soon in fact as they were considered capable of attention and obedience." He adds that "far from regarding this with indignation, men at that time thought it an admirable system." [42] The average working day was around 14 hours, and in most factories 40 minutes were allowed for the only meal of the day, of which

[40] E. R. A. Seligman, *Owen and the Christian Socialists* (repr. from *Political Science Quarterly*, Vol. I, No. 1[1886]), p. 229.

[41] Mantoux, *The Industrial Revolution in the Eighteenth Century*, pp. 410–411. See also Hammond and Hammond, *The Rise of Modern Industry*, pp. 199–201.

[42] Mantoux, *op. cit.*, p. 411.

some 20 minutes were taken up in cleaning the machines. In factories which operated around the clock the children were divided into shifts and, according to an 1816 government report, "the beds never got cold." [43] Even though such long hours were prohibited by Parliament in 1831—those under 18 years were limited to 12 hours a day or 69 hours a week—the law was easily evaded.[44] Child labor continued after the abolishment of the apprentice system, although working conditions hardly changed for the youthful wage earners. They were extremely useful for picking up the waste cotton and being small could creep under the machines; probably most were "piecers" who put together broken threads in the spinning machines while others would replace bobbins, the spools upon which the thread was wound. In addition to the dust and other unhygenic conditions in the factories there was the danger from the moving machinery. In that regard, with the long hours the children became fatigued and stood the chance of being injured. Those who dozed off at their machines, or tried to steal a nap some other place would be whipped.[45] Children were widely employed in mines and were also used as chimney sweeps and in many other occupations, usually at the expense of their physical and moral well-being. To the conditions we noted above we should add frequent accidents and a discipline which was savage.[46]

The deterioration of life was not limited to the factory or to the ups and downs of the economy. Communities centering around mines, mills, and factories mushroomed; towns of antiquity, such as Manchester, Leeds, and Sheffield were overwhelmed by the Industrial Revolution. There was little concern for the health and welfare of the laboring population and many mining and to a lesser extent mill communities were "company towns." The term company town is applied to a community in which there is a single dominant industry, or if several industries exist, all are owned by the same individual or concern. In addition much or all of the rest of the physical community is similarly owned, including workers' housing, shops, and other facilities. Control usually extends to most aspects of people's lives and the company sets up conditions which increase the employees' dependency and limit their alternatives.[47] For illustrations we look at Truck and Tommy Ticket.

What was meant by Truck was that workers' wages in whole or part were in the form of food or other goods. Although Parliament passed laws prohibiting the practice, the local magistrates did not enforce them. Tommy Ticket refers to the part payment of wages with a kind of script redeemable at the shops owned by mine or mill owners, or at establishments where they had an interest or had worked out a kickback arrange-

[43] Cited in *ibid.*, p. 413.

[44] Hammond and Hammond, *The Rise of Modern Industry*, p. 202.

[45] *Ibid.*, p. 201; and Mantoux, *op. cit.*, p. 410n.

[46] Mantoux, *The Industrial Revolution in the Eighteenth Century*, pp. 410–416, 465.

[47] *Ibid.*, p. 397.

ment with the owner. Not only was the worker restricted as to where he could trade, but goods were much costlier than in other shops. This system was in force as late as 1842 in remote areas.[48]

Another consideration in trying to evaluate how the laboring population was affected by industrialization is the contrast with earlier working arrangements. Cottage industry, in spite of long hours of work and the use of child labor provided some freedom; however the draconian discipline of the factory was difficult to take because the lives of these workers had not prepared them for the restraints encountered.[49]

In addition the formal and informal institutional arrangements worked to the advantage of the entrepreneurs. The mass of the workers had little or no say in the governing of the towns and the famous English justice, which included fair treatment and a jury of one's peers, applied primarily to the upper strata. In mine and mill towns a worker might be tried on charges pressed by his employer and would be judged by that same employer who was also the magistrate. Laws prohibited workers from organizing into unions, then called combinations; yet employers were not so restricted. The Vagrancy Acts were used against agitators or anyone causing inconvenience to employer or town official. The fact that law enforcement officials were rewarded monetarily for convictions led them to make felonies out of misdemeanors, bribe witnesses, and encourage people to commit crime.[50]

The history of the Industrial Revolution is also a history of violence. Earlier, as large numbers of peasants were cut adrift because of changes in agricultural life intermittent revolts had occurred; [51] now it was the turn of the new industrial workers. In desperation they went out on strike or attacked the machines that were lowering their pay or depriving them of jobs. While there had been sporadic machine breaking earlier, a movement began in 1811 which was well-organized and skillfully directed. Its goal was to protect the framework knitters in the hosiery industry whose standard of living was being depressed by new production methods. The issue centered around the making of a cheaper kind of hose; a wider frame was being used, the rates of pay were lower, and the number of workers was being reduced. Framework knitting was still being done mainly in workers' homes but the frames belonged to the entrepreneur and the destruction of these frames, or the threat to do so, was used to intimidate offending employers. It was almost impossible to prevent this for the cottages were widely scattered.

These machine breakers were called "Luddites" because their cam-

[48] Hammond and Hammond, *The Rise of Modern Industry*, pp. 154, 175; and Mantoux, *op. cit.*, pp. 73, 76.

[49] Bendix suggests that cruelty and exploitation were probably greatest in the small shops. Bendix, *Work and Authority in Industry*, p. 26.

[50] Hammond and Hammond, *The Town Laborer*, pp. 72–87; Hammond and Hammond, *The Rise of Modern Industry*, pp. 154–155; and Mantoux, *op. cit.*, p. 450.

[51] Moore, *Social Origins of Dictatorship and Democracy*, pp. 13 and 23n.

paign including warnings and proclamations in the name of a mythical leader called "Ned Ludd" or "King Ludd" of Sherwood Forest, who was linked with the legends of Robin Hood as a friend of the poor. In the Midlands where the movement started, employers were forced to remedy some of the grievances; however it was not as successful in other places, particularly in the cotton and woolen industries. There the impact of machinery was greater and workers attacked the mills.[52] Paul Mantoux emphasizes that the Luddites' fight was not against the machine but against their employers, because of the economic consequences of the changes. This was true in other industries as well, for inevitably advances in machine production meant inferior and cheaper goods, the displacement of craftsmen, work speed-up, and less pay.[53] Nevertheless, the machine-breaking movement was of sufficient scale to arouse great alarm and the House of Parliament appointed secret committees and repressive legislation to deal with it was quickly enacted.[54]

Discontent, agitation, strikes, and riots led to the use of soldiers as a police force throughout the country by 1815. Both the militia, which was composed largely of draftees, and the volunteer soldiers, were considered unreliable; when workers struck or the poor rioted they sometimes sided with them. They were replaced by a yeomanry cavalry which was the principal auxiliary to the regular army and it was their responsibility to maintain order until regular troops arrived. This yeoman police force did not hesitate to terrorize dissenters as evidenced by what happened at Peterloo in 1819.

POLICE BRUTALITY AT PETERLOO

At St. Peter's Field, or Peterloo, on the outskirts of Manchester, a mass meeting was held to demand universal suffrage, vote by ballot, annual Parliaments, and repeal of the Corn Laws. Organized by reformers from several towns great pains were taken to keep the demonstration peaceful, and although the magistrates disliked the meeting they decided that it was not illegal. Eighty thousand assembled including women and children; people were in their Sunday clothes, flags were flying, bands were playing, speeches were planned. The main speaker, a Henry Hunt, had just started when there was a

> . . . sudden and unprovoked charge on the defenceless and unresisting crowd, for if the magistrates gave the orders, the yeomanry supplied the zeal. Hunt had scarcely begun his speech, when the yeomanry cavalry advanced brandishing their swords. Hunt told the reformers to cheer, which they did;

[52] Cole, *A Short History of the British Working-Class Movement*, pp. 41–42.
[53] Mantoux, *The Industrial Revolution in the Eighteenth Century*, pp. 401–404.
[54] Cole, *loc. cit.;* and Mantoux, *op. cit.*, pp. 406–408.

the yeomanry then rode into the crowd, which gave way for them and arrested Hunt. But this was not enough for the yeomanry, who said, "Have at their flags," and began striking wildly all round them. The magistrates then gave the order to charge. In ten minutes the field was deserted except for dead and wounded, and banners, hats, shawls, and bonnets: the strangest debris of any battlefield since the madness of Ajax. Eleven people died, two of them women, one a child, and over four hundred were wounded, one hundred and thirteen being women. Of the wounded more than a quarter were wounded by the sword.[55]

The magistrates and the yeomanry were thanked by the Government, Hunt was sent to prison for two and a half years, and three of his colleagues for one year.

SOME MOVEMENTS FOR REFORM

To change the institutional arrangements and the conditions of life was difficult. There were masters who fought for shorter hours and more humane treatment of employees; some did this themselves and also provided schools and libraries. But the overwhelming majority of workers faced the conditions we described earlier. Movements to reform the industrial system or to basically alter the distribution of social goods stood little chance of success. Agitation and petitions failed; even when employers agreed to reforms Parliament would not ratify them. But most of the employers as well as the upper classes in general were likely to oppose them, and to use the power of the state to further their own interests. An interesting case was the movement for a cooperative society advocated by Robert Owen (1771–1858).

Owen rejected the principle of profit as the organizing force in society, believing that through cooperative arrangements the problems of industrialism could be solved without sacrificing individual freedom or social solidarity. The experience at his cotton spinning mills in New Lanarck, Scotland convinced him that wages were only one factor in workers' lives. Taking over the mills in 1800, he provided short hours, job security, pleasant working and living conditions, entertainment, and education for the children and insisted on high moral standards for young and old. Even though the wages Owen paid were lower than those current in some neighboring towns his employees held him in high esteem. Productivity was very great, due no doubt to the high morale as well as to the excellent organization of his enterprise, the short hours, and rested workers.[56] However Owen's personnel practices were basically structured on the traditional relationship between master and

[55] Hammond and Hammond, *The Town Laborer*, pp. 92–98. The quotation is from p. 98.

[56] Polyani, *The Great Transformation*, pp. 167–172 and A. L. Morton, *The Life and Ideas of Robert Owen* (London: Lawrence & Wishart, 1962).

servant. Together with "affectionate tutelage," discipline was strictly enforced.[57] Yet many looked to New Lanark as the model for a new society and it attracted visitors from all over Europe and even from the United States. In the latter, New Harmony, Indiana was established on Owenite principles.

Owenism became a social movement comprising hundreds and thousands of craftsmen, laborers, and other working people. Associations were formed to support Villages of Cooperation, which was the origin of agricultural producers' cooperatives as well as other cooperative organizations. Labor Exchanges were set up, and they issued their own currency, with the idea that goods would be sold at cost. To emancipate artisans and other workers the Owenites sought to form a national trade union which would include all workers in all industries in Britain. Although they met with little success they were able to organize the construction industry on a national basis. Called the Builders' Guild, this union included the various craftsmen, and attempted to bring in architects as well as laborers. In addition Regeneration Societies were formed to propagandize for factory legislation.

The basic aim of the Owenites was industrial revolution by peaceful means and the concept of non-violent resistance was fully developed. One of the direct outcomes was the development of consumer cooperatives and the modern trade union movement. At the time, however, employers bitterly fought the organization of workers, and with the development of mass support and the beginnings of agitation there was swift repression by the state. The Owenite movement, which had visions of eventually replacing the state and making it superfluous, was unable to make the cooperative undertakings sufficiently widespread and workable. The movement was effectively destroyed by the mid-1830's as a result of internal dissension, a confusion of ideas, and the onslaught of employers and the government.[58]

Although there were such attempts at improving conditions, overall there was a depreciation of human life for the working people. Basically the higher strata regarded them as being incapable of profiting by leisure and fit only for the long discipline of factory hours. They pointed to the brutal pursuits which were popular among the masses, such as bull-baiting, cock-fighting, and brawling where men would fight almost to the death.[59]

Movements which seemed to be making an impact soon felt the force of the state, as happened to the Owenites. If people held a peaceful demonstration they were physically attacked and the leaders jailed, as at Peterloo. Or, if it seemed that a movement would have little effect it would be ignored as in the case of the Chartists.

Emerging after the failure of Owenism, Chartism was an effort to in-

[57] Bendix, *Work and Authority in Industry*, pp. 49–51.

[58] Morton, *op. cit.*, pp. 20–46.

[59] Hammond and Hammond, *The Town Laborer*, pp. 42–47, 68.

fluence the government through constitutional means to grant effective popular suffrage and other reforms. Massive numbers signed petitions to a People's Charter demanding this right, at a time when less than 15% of adult males were entitled to vote. Nevertheless their case was given short shrift by Parliament. The strong feelings aroused by the Poor Law Reform Act and the bad economic conditions of the 1840's were waning, trade was increasing as was employment, and the Chartists dispersed peacefully.[60] Polyani writes:

> Their case was not even considered by Parliament until a later date, when their application was defeated by a five-to-one majority in the House of Commons. In vain had millions of signatures been collected. In vain had the Chartists behaved as law-abiding citizens. Their Movement was ridiculed out of existence by the victors. . . . A year or two later Chartism was all but forgotten.[61]

The destruction of these movements was not lost on persons who felt that major changes in social, economic, and political conditions were necessary. It was apparent that those in superordinate positions would not relinquish any of their power unless they absolutely had to, regardless of how morally justified the requests might be. There were some reforms but they were mainly to appease the masses.[62] Industrialization had raised living standards for the upper and middle classes and they had a real fear that the discontent of the working population might lead to revolution. One response was the belief that reforms were a means of prevention, the other was severe repression. "The spirit of the times," write the Hammonds, "was embodied in the common expression, 'policing the poor.' "[63]

The great fear of violence and revolution was driven home by an occurrence on the Continent. This was the world-shaking French Revolution, to which we next turn.

The French Revolution

In France as well as in England, throughout most of Europe, and in other parts of the world there was a growing awareness of the problems and

---

[60] Polyani, *op. cit.*, pp. 172–173; Hobsbawm, *The Age of Revolution, 1789–1848*, p. 151, and Deane, *The First Industrial Revolution*, pp. 195–196. The six points of the Charter included universal manhood suffrage; vote by ballot; payment of Members of Parliament; yearly elections for Parliament; equal electoral districts; and the abolition of the property qualification for Members of Parliament. Deane, *ibid.*, p. 195.

[61] Polyani, *The Great Transformation*, p. 173.

[62] A few of the reforms had an humanitarian impetus, and some were the consequence of public reaction to brutality, as in the Peterloo incident. Even though officials attempted to disguise the facts, they were unsuccessful, because of the eye-witness accounts of independent people including a reporter for the *Times*. Hammond and Hammond, *The Town Laborer*, p. 99.

[63] *Ibid.*, pp. 42–47, 68, 101. The quotation is from p. 101.

potentialities of the masses. Increasingly the underprivileged were questioning traditional inequities in the distribution of social goods. This questioning drew on the egalitarian ideas of the social philosophers, many of which were popularized and helped form the ideologies of religious and political movements. These democratic strivings were encouraged by the French Revolution of 1789 which gave hope to the oppressed and put fear into the hearts of the privileged.

Of critical importance were the changes discussed previously, particularly in Chapters VII and VIII, which increased dislocation and discontent. The outcome was an eruption in 1789 which also triggered other upheavals on the continent. The impact of the French Revolution particularly as regards ideologies continues to be felt today; it largely initiated what de Tocqueville called "the age of equality," what Bendix calls "the age of democratic revolution." [64]

For many thousands of years great inequality was seen as inevitable, if not necessary and desirable. Occasionally philosophers and religious leaders challenged this view but their criticism was mostly theoretical. With the French Revolution of 1789, however, the problem became more concrete: not only were new groups of people demanding participation in the political process and a more equitable distribution of social goods, but increasingly there were instances of achievement of these demands. Very often the successes were measured, or only temporary; nevertheless age-old beliefs and practices were being challenged. While inequality persisted no longer would it be accepted as a given, no longer would people be willing to put up with deprivation for very long. The idea of hereditary superordination-subordination as God-given, and as a requirement for social order had been effectively destroyed by changing conditions of life and people's interpretations of them.

As was pointed out earlier, the reciprocal relationships of the different strata which previously had helped support the social order were being undermined. It is true that the institutional arrangements included great inequality in almost all respects and that many were unhappy with them, especially those in a subordinate position. Nevertheless they had been viewed as traditional and were underpinned by religion. It is also true that the peasants had to work so many days a month on their lord's land, or provide him with a proportion of their harvest, but in turn they also benefitted. They received protection from brigands or others who might harm them and the lord dispensed justice. The peasants were allowed to use the lord's pasture land for grazing livestock and the forests for fuel and for building their homes. When harvests were poor the lord might provide food or other aid. Above all, the dues of the servant toward his master were considered reasonable and the obligations of the master toward the servant were fulfilled. Undoubtedly the rela-

[64] Reinhard Bendix, "The Lower Classes and the 'Democratic Revolution,' " *Industrial Relations*, 1 (October 1961), 91–116.

tionship was basically exploitative and worked to the benefit of the lord. Because these mutual expectations could be counted on there was a dependence of one on the other; the master felt paternalistic toward his peasants whom he viewed as his "children," and they in turn could identify with him and transfer some of the prestige of his position to themselves.

But changes began to occur which broke down the mutual expectations: lords increased the dues and other demands unreasonably and no longer fulfilled their obligations. Yet significant aspects of the feudal framework remained; the concept of "estates" still prevailed and the nobility, the bourgeoisie, the church, and the peasantry had legal status. Although the political power of the French nobles was lessened they retained their superordinate status, certainly relative to the peasantry and the bourgeoisie; also, their position was supported by law. Moreover, they did not hesitate to use it to their advantage, which led many people to feel that to significantly improve the society it was necessary to do away with the old order.

The changes which were taking place throughout Europe created difficulties for the landowning aristocracy. In France, the growing power of the Crown toward the end of the 18th century reduced the political power and hence the economic opportunities of the aristocracy. This, plus the expensive conspicuous consumption of noble life, lack of thrift, and poor management of estates increased the economic distress of many landowners. Inflation had reduced the value of fixed rents and this added further to their financial difficulties. They in turn sought to obtain more money from their estates which meant higher rents and more dues from their peasants and tenant farmers.[65] The French nobles were able to use the prevailing social and political framework to squeeze more and more out of the peasants, especially with the restoration of feudal rights and dues which had fallen into neglect.[66]

With the nobles primarily interested in rights rather than obligations, the tradition of reciprocity was rapidly breaking down. Consequently the French peasants of 1789, as had the German peasants of 1525, saw their lord as a legalized robber, no longer as their leader and protector.[67]

As in England there was a growth of commerce and trade and a rise in population, with large numbers of people living in towns and cities. Similarly, there were new economic opportunities and a growing demand for agricultural goods. The response of the French landholding nobility was in sharp contrast to that of most of their English counterparts. The English, it will be recalled, changed the traditional system of agricultural economics: they incorporated smaller plots into larger rationalized

[65] Moore, *Social Origins of Dictatorship and Democracy*, pp. 41–42.

[66] *Ibid.*, pp. 53, 63.

[67] Jacob S. Schapiro, *Social Reform and the Reformation* (New York: Columbia University, Faculty of Political Science, 1909), p. 64.

operations, produced for the market, and in this manner raised their profits. But instead of consolidating their land the French nobles subdivided it further; they turned over sections to peasants for a portion of the yield which they sold for cash. Now, in order to increase their income the landowners demanded a larger share of the peasant's produce. The state aided in this oppression since the law forced delinquent tenants to pay dues in arrears and allowed clever lawyers to restore the feudal rights and dues. In the last half of the 18th century such arrangements covered from two-thirds to three-fourths of French agriculture, with single peasant families working relatively small sections of land as sharecroppers or wage laborers.[68]

Whereas in England the penetration of agriculture by commercial interests hastened the breakdown of feudalism, destroyed the peasantry, and encouraged large-scale units and production for the market, in France the outcome was quite different. Feudalism was given new life, the peasantry was retained and small sections of land were farmed; when agricultural goods were marketed it was done so indirectly. The English landholder concentrated on production and innovated in technique and management, while the Frenchman was primarily interested in exacting as much produce from his sharecroppers or wage laborers as he could. He had little concern with farming or the peasants' problems. Also, in England the fusion between some of the economic interests of town and countryside aligned the commercial farmers and the bourgeoisie against the Crown; in France however the fusion took place through the Crown and set the peasants against both the monarchy and the nobility.[69]

There were rural uprisings prior to the Revolution and it was the poorer peasants who were the most revolutionary in action and egalitarian in ideology. The wealthier peasantry was also discontented, for among other things they had de facto possession of the land yet did not own it. While many of the richer nobles were willing to make substantial concessions, the petty rural nobility was extremely reactionary.[70]

Alexis de Tocqueville, who undertook a major study of the French Revolution,[71] stressed the importance of the fact that the nobility had disregarded their obligations, while they continued to use their rights to benefit themselves. In addition to demanding more from the peasants they increased their fiscal immunities and remained a privileged closed group, with the characteristics of a caste. Also, they cut themselves off from the bourgeoisie and the peasantry, and in a sense were like a

[68] Moore, op. cit., pp. 41–43, 53–55, 65.

[69] Ibid., pp. 55, 63, 65.

[70] Ibid., pp. 73–74.

[71] Alexis de Tocqueville, The Old Regime and the French Revolution, trans. by Stuart Gilbert (Garden City, N.Y.: Doubleday Anchor Books, 1955; first pub. in 1856). De Tocqueville (1805–1859) was born of a noble family in Normandy; he was active in politics and served in the French government.

foreign body within the State. This behavior of the nobility was extremely odious to the French people which developed a great jealousy of the "upper class."

The government was becoming extremely centralized in Paris and lost touch with the common people more and more. Its actions made clear that the authority of the state as well as its institutions were being used to benefit the privileged and to oppress the peasantry.[72] As an example, note de Tocqueville's comment on the dispensation of justice:

> The government of the old régime, which in its dealings with the upper classes was so lenient and so slow to take offense, was quick to act and often harsh to a degree where members of the lower orders, peasants especially, were concerned. Of all the many records I have examined, not one mentions the arrest of bourgeois under instructions from the Intendant. Peasants, on the other hand, were constantly arrested in connection with the levies of forced labor or the militia; for begging, for misdemeanors, and countless other minor offenses. One class of the population could count on impartial tribunals, protracted hearings, and all the safeguards of publicity; the others were tried summarily by the provost, and there was no appeal.[73]

The Revolution followed many years of built-up resentment among the peasants, who had two strong passions: the hatred of inequality and the desire to live as free men. The ideology of equality and freedom stemmed from two major sources: the first was the general discontent over the maldistribution of social goods, including the privileges of the nobility and the behavior of the government; the second was the writings of the philosophers. These intellectuals who became instrumental in shaping public opinion did not participate in political affairs; they speculated on the nature of man and propounded utopias for a completely new order. Their schemes were based on abstract principles, they stressed highly generalized theories, and political realities were largely overlooked. This is understandable since there were neither free institutions nor organized and experienced political parties in France. Political thought was stifled, people were unused to studying the course of political events, they were unaware of the concept of popular movements or the concept of "the people." Rather than attacking only objectionable laws and calling for modification of the existing authority structure, the intellectuals' speculations, which gained wide popular currency, helped develop the outlook that all laws must be abolished and a completely new system of government established. They failed to take into account the practical consequences of what they proposed, but neither did the masses since they too were outside the world of political activity. They saw the philosophers' call for a new order based on equality and freedom as the solution to their troubles.[74]

[72] *Ibid.*, pp. 123–137, 203–204.
[73] *Ibid.*, p. 133.
[74] *Ibid.*, pp. 138–142, 205–208.

Yet if one wonders how the government and institutions of this powerful nation were overthrown, and so quickly and with such ferocity, it is necessary to consider only a few additional circumstances. They are the failure of the social and political structures to meet the challenge of changing conditions. Of great importance was the increase in trade and commerce, the rising importance of the merchant, and the atomization of the different groups comprising French society. Also, the close involvement of the established church with the other institutions in the society came to be seen as oppressive. In regard to changing economic conditions, France participated in the quickening of economic activity which was concomitant with the Industrial Revolution taking place on the other side of the English Channel. French merchants began to prosper and a commercial elite arose; some were from the nobility because the sovereign needed merchants, while the rest were from the bourgeoisie. In the early 1700's "elite" and "nobility" were identical, and the nobility was an aristocracy of birth; it was hereditary, had biological and racial overtones, and included the idea of military service. However the trend was away from this traditional concept and toward one based on talent, particularly a nobility of government officials and military officials, but also including persons who made special contributions to the nation, such as merchants, judges, lawyers, doctors, and engineers. Yet in spite of these moves to reward talent, between 1750 and 1789 only an average of ten merchants per year were given patents of nobility; during that 40-year period only 400 families from all categories were enobled. While wealthy merchants who lived like nobles were granted some privileges it was made quite clear that they were not nobles, and this emphasized the distinction between the upper level of the Third Estate and the traditional nobility.[75]

Others of the bourgeoisie, as well as almost anyone who dealt with or worked for the government, also became more and more discontented. The government was increasingly in financial difficulties since its revenues did not keep pace with its budget and there was great inefficiency and mismanagement. People were not sure of receiving their interest on government securities, contractors were not certain of being paid, public employees could not count on getting their paychecks. Actually there was nothing new in these delinquencies and in the past the vices of the financial system had been far more glaring. What had changed was the scope of government involvement in the economy. This involvement had grown greatly and there was an enormous increase in the number of persons having monetary dealings with the Administration or dependent on

---

[75] Marcel Reinhard, " 'Élite' and 'Nobility' in the Second Half of the 18th Century in France," in Bernard and Elinor G. Barber, eds., *European Social Class: Stability and Change* (New York: Macmillan, 1965) [reprinted from *Revue d'histoire moderne et contemporaine*, January-March, 1965], pp. 91–104. Cf. Moore, *Social Origins of Dictatorship and Democracy*, pp. 65–69.

wages directly or indirectly paid by it. This had serious consequences for that section of the community usually most adverse to violent political change: *the rentiers,* merchants, manufacturers, businessmen, and financiers. This element usually supports the existing government, whatever it may be and is essentially law-abiding even when it is opposed to the laws. This stratum became strong advocates of reform and demanded most vociferously a radical change in the entire financial administration of the country.[76]

We see here increased animosity toward the government and a growing separation of different groups in French society: nobility from bourgeoisie, bourgeoisie from peasantry, and as indicated earlier, peasantry from nobility. In addition there was a growing isolation of groups within each of these categories until there was no political anchoring. De Tocqueville observes that ". . . although the nation came to be seen as a homogeneous whole, its parts no longer held together." [77] This sundering of the fabric of society was furthered by popular disenchantment with the Established Church for it was seen as being utilized for the benefit of the privileged groups. Consequently religion was another institutional arrangement which lost its effectiveness for maintaining stability and upholding the social order.

Considering these conditions it is no wonder that France was rapidly moving toward a state of crisis toward the end of the 18th century. The centralization of the government in Paris provided a focus for the discontent and facilitated its overthrow. There were certain fortuitous factors which added to the troubles: in 1786 the government greatly reduced duties on English manufactured goods which cut off outside employment for many peasants; there was a poor harvest in 1788; a harsh winter; spring floods and storms; and a series of panics and peasant uprisings in many parts of France.[78] Yet, according to de Tocqueville, economic conditions had been improving during the last two decades of the 18th century; however he noted that this served to *increase* discontent:

> It is a singular fact that this steadily increasing prosperity, far from tranquilizing the population, everywhere promoted a spirit of unrest. The general public became more and more discontented; indeed, it was increasingly obvious that the nation was heading for revolution.[79]

These factors led to the French Revolution, beginning in 1789.[80] There were three major popular upheavals: the storming of the Bastille on July 14, 1789; the storming of the Tuileries on August 10, 1792; and the upris-

---

[76] De Tocqueville, *The Old Regime and the French Revolution,* pp. 177–179.

[77] *Ibid.,* pp. 136–137.

[78] Moore, *Social Origins of Dictatorship and Democracy,* p. 75.

[79] De Tocqueville, *The Old Regime and the French Revolution,* pp. 169–175. The quotation is from p. 175.

[80] Cf. Moore, *op. cit.,* p. 109.

ing of May 31, 1793. The latter led to the Reign of Terror and the brief rule of Robespierre.

The Revolution shocked people and governments throughout the world. However, the ferocity and outrageous acts which accompanied the destruction of the old regime are not surprising if we consider the pent-up discontent of the masses, the unhappiness and frustration of the many groups which felt talent was not being rewarded, and the growing atomization of the society. But to these must be added two more factors: the breakdown of the controls that religion, custom, and law had exercised over attitudes and behavior, and the promise of a completely new social order based on equality and freedom.

In parts of France the peasants rose up or refused to honor their feudal obligations. They gained the support of the poor in the towns, aided by the prevalence of great fear and rumors including those of an aristocratic plot. As the authority of the central government deteriorated, together with public order, some of the substantial bourgeoisie welcomed the liberal nobles into their ranks. However the less affluent distrusted them and tried to keep them out. In areas where there was panic, local defense groups of middling property owners in country and town organized for protection against brigands and bandits. These terrorists, it was rumored, were supposed to have been let loose by a scheming aristocracy. In other places there was full-scale peasant violence which frightened the bourgeoisie and aligned them with the nobility. Following the storming of the Bastille in some areas the two groups worked together to suppress the peasant uprisings.[81] In turn, these counterrevolutionary moves brought the more radical of the bourgeoisie to power. There were several attempts by conservative forces to stop the Revolution but the result was that more radical sections of the bourgeoisie came to the fore. The Revolution proceeded in surges with each conservative move followed by progressively more radical portions of the bourgeoisie gaining control. The impulse for each leftward surge came from the Paris sans-culottes, although there was active support from the provinces.[82]

THE SANS-CULOTTES

Called sans-culottes because they did not wear knee-breeches but trousers, they comprised the urban lower strata. While most critical in Paris they were also active in other larger cities. Absolute deprivation provided much of the impetus for the Parisian sans-culottes; they differed greatly from earlier groups that had attacked authority structure, how-

[81] Moore, op. cit., pp. 75–76. His source is Georges Lefebvre, Le Grande Peur de 1789 (Paris, 1932), pp. 30, 31, 56, 103–105, 109, 139, 157–158, 165–167, 246.

[82] Moore, Social Origins of Dictatorship and Democracy, pp. 76–77, 79.

ever. Previous violence such as peasant revolts was aimed at bringing back an earlier, more desirable set of conditions. By contrast, the goals of the *sans-culottes* included a new order based on direct government and popular democracy.[83] Most were illiterate, yet they were aware of Rousseau's theories of popular sovereignty; through word-of-mouth, public discussions in taverns and cafes, and soapbox orators the revolutionary ideas spread.[84] Their political goals were tied in with economic ones such as fixed food prices and greater equality. There was a strong belief in violence; in fact terroristic activity was seen as irrevocably bound to the overriding need for daily bread.[85]

In their opposition to the aristocracy they found themselves aligned with the bourgeoisie, and it was the *sans-culottes* who provided the physical force of the revolution and its leftward surges. Some of their interests were contradictory, reflecting differing backgrounds. They ranged from unemployed marginal workers to journeymen and small employers. The perspectives of the *sans-culottes* were influenced by the views of the artisans and small shopkeepers, who also made up the revolutionary vanguard.[86] More basically, however, the needs of the *sans-culottes* and the bourgeoisie were incompatible: the *sans-culottes* took their sovereign rights literally, yet bourgeois democracy held that sovereignty could be exercised only through representative government. Also, popular sovereignty and direct rule conflicted with the need for stability and efficiency that even a revolutionary government required.[87]

The strength of the *sans-culottes* depended in large part on active support from the countryside. Once their demands came into conflict with those of the property-owning peasants the support was gone and they were easily repressed. Toward the end of 1793 prices were rising, there were serious difficulties in food distribution, the economic condition of the Paris poor was deteriorating, and many of the well-to-do peasants refused to bring food to the city. By the Spring of 1795 there were severe riots and for the first time the army was used to put down a popular insurrection; with this the radical revolution was ended.[88]

RESULTS AND CONSEQUENCES

It is difficult to assess the extent of the violence because, aside from the lack of reliable statistics, conservatives tend to exaggerate the amount

[83] Albert Soboul, *The Sans-Culottes*, trans. by Remy Inglis Hall (Garden City, N.Y.: Doubleday Anchor Books, 1972), pp. 29–30, 32, 95 ff.

[84] *Ibid.*, p. 241 ff.

[85] *Ibid.*, pp. 42–43, 45.

[86] *Ibid.*, pp. 29–30, 32, 42–43.

[87] *Ibid.*, pp. 133–135, 251.

[88] *Ibid.*, pp. 70, 90–92.

while radicals are wont to minimize it. Also, how does one judge whether the number of people assaulted, massacred, and executed is large or small; similarly, the amount of property destroyed? Less than 17,000 were executed by revolutionary authorities, plus many who died in prison or under other circumstances. One estimate is that the total deaths were between 35,000 and 40,000 and, on the basis of France's population of 24,000,000, this works out to a proportion of .0016.[89] While civilized people do, or should, abhor violence there is a tendency to overlook more subtle forms of coercion, deprivation, and suffering. The death tax discussed earlier, the jailing of debtors, the "transporting" of labor organizers, preventable starvation, and other injustices differ from overt destruction in style but not in kind. Therefore, when upheavals occur as in France, it is important to try to balance the violence against the more covert injustices.[90]

The French Revolution was not a bourgeois revolution in the sense that an economically strong bourgeoisie obtained political power; the absolutism of the Crown and its policies, in contrast to the English situation, precluded this. The primary achievement of the Revolution, according to Moore, was doing away with the landed aristocracy. Feudalism was partially abolished on August 4, 1789, and the task was completed a few years later. The violent destruction of the *ancien régime*, he holds, was critical for the eventual establishment of parliamentary democracy in France. Although the *sans-culottes* were the moving force behind the radical surges, the primary beneficiaries were the peasant aristocracy and the bourgeoisie. They were not interested in democracy as such but in effective guarantees for their property. The poorer peasants benefitted hardly at all; in fact the sale of church and émigré property which was supposed to provide land for them worked to the advantage of the bourgeoisie.[91]

But the consequences of the Revolution extended far beyond France's borders, both physically and ideationally. In France the breakup of the old order brought forth a tremendous energy, pride, and hope for the future. These forces together with attacks by foreign countries raised feelings of nationalism to great heights. One outcome was the Napoleonic wars in which the spirit of the French conscripts more than made up for their poor training and lack of equipment; for 20 years the forces of the tricolor triumphed over Europe and North Africa. But perhaps as important, if not more so for the long run, was the spread of revolutionary ideas and the reaction to them. No longer would men accept inequality the way they had in the past; the radical ideology provided new perspectives and justifications for challenging the status quo, and the destruction of the *ancien régime* showed that an oppressive social order could be overthrown.

[89] Moore, *op. cit.*, pp. 103–104.
[90] See *ibid.*, p. 104.
[91] *Ibid.*, pp. 107–109.

On the other hand everywhere men of substance were repelled by the new ideas; they saw the specter of revolution stalking Europe and feared that subversive thoughts would undermine if not topple existing structures and destroy their property, their privileges, and their power. The reaction was suppression: writings and speeches which questioned the status quo were prohibited as was the organizing of workers or similar activities which sought to alter the distribution of social goods.

In summary, the hundred years from the middle of the 18th century to the middle of the 19th saw two tremendous breaks with the past. The Industrial Revolution began to alter the very face of the earth, changed the nature of work and man's condition of life, raised the standard of living of many, but lowered it for many more; it expanded the scale of society and created new political relationships. The French Revolution ended the *ancien régime:* the juridical classes were abolished, and although the church and nobility were not destroyed they were severely damaged; gradations of social status as well as economic and political alignments were deeply affected. A new status system arose, based primarily on wealth, and on what a person could do.

Of world-wide significance were the doctrines of liberty and equality which were promulgated by the French Revolution. These ideas, although never fully carried out in France, became a rallying cry for the oppressed and helped spawn many other upheavals. They included a conspiracy in England, an assassination in France, and revolts in Spain, Portugal, Russia, Belgium, Austria, and Greece. These disturbances, which took place between 1814 and 1832, were followed by outbreaks in 1848 and 1871.

The upheavals of the first period occurred against a background of economic crises and political instability which plagued post-Napoleonic Europe. Popular discontent was rife and the upper classes feared revolution. Yet by the end of the second decade of the 19th century, liberal movements for reform seemed hopeless; repressive measures were passed by all governments, among them the Six Acts in England and the Carlsbad Decrees in the Germanies. Subsequently resistance went underground and many disturbances broke out.[92] In England a plot was uncovered in which the whole Tory ministry was to be assassinated at a dinner, to be followed by seizure of the Bank of England and the setting up of a provisional government. The conspirators were apprehended in the midst of their preparations, a constable was killed, several of the leaders were executed and others were forced to leave the country.[93]

"This affair," writes Artz,

together with the supression of a political riot near Glasgow, on April 2 [1820], prejudiced the liberal cause in England and for the time seemed to jus-

[92] See Frederick B. Artz, *Reaction and Revolution, 1814–1832* (New York: Harper Torchbooks, 1963), especially p. 149.

[93] *Ibid.*, p. 150. The arms were supplied by an agent provocateur who was instrumental in formulating the plans and who then brought in the police.

tify the arbitrary measures of Lord Liverpool's Tory cabinet. The popular reform movement was crushed only to appear ten years later at the time of the agitation that preceded the reform of Parliament in 1832.[94]

In France the assassination of the nephew of the King led to a growing reaction on the part of the government which included the reestablishment of severe censorship over the press and alteration of the election laws so as to throw the balance of power to the larger landed aristocrats. The hopes of the moderate royalists that there might be a reconciliation between liberalism and the monarchy were dashed; there were now two factions, the conservative royalists and the revolutionaries.[95] A consequence of this reactionary trend was the growth of secret societies aimed at overthrowing the government. These all failed for, among other weaknesses, there had been no serious attempt to enlist the peasants or the working classes of the towns.[96]

When revolution broke out in Spain the King agreed to a Constitution. But inexperience and lack of unity among the liberals, opposition by both reactionaries and radicals, financial disruption, governmental confusion and near anarchy, and the intervention of the French helped restore the rule of the royalists. The revolutions which broke out in other European countries were also crushed, although the Greek uprising eventually succeeded.[97] The general pattern followed was agitation by liberals for parliamentary government and a constitution that contained guarantees for a free press, personal, and other freedoms. The moderates would come to power but would be unable to govern or to satisfy the demands of either the radicals or the reactionaries. Near anarchy would follow and the radicals would gain control. The existing state of confusion, economic disruption, and extreme measures by the radicals would strengthen the reactionaries who desired a return to the status quo. They were usually successful, often helped greatly by foreign intervention. The majority of the populace remained indifferent; those who did show an interest generally swung to support the side that restored order. When the King of Spain regained his throne, he proceeded with savage ferocity to stamp out liberals and revolutionaries; thousands were exiled, thousands imprisoned, and hundreds were tortured and executed. As for the populace,

> [t]he same mob which a few years before had acclaimed Riego [who had been the hero of the revolution] now shouted for the king when their former idol was dragged, with savage pomp, in a basket at an ass's tail to one of the principal squares in Madrid. There he was hanged and cut into five parts which were sent to be publicly exposed in the five towns where he was best known.[98]

[94] *Ibid.*
[95] *Ibid.*
[96] *Ibid.*, pp. 151–152.
[97] *Ibid.*, pp. 162–170. In the New World the Spanish colonies successfully revolted.
[98] *Ibid.*, p. 170.

Such was the great repression that followed crushed revolutions. The returned governments, reflecting the pressures of the ruling classes, abrogated or emasculated constitutions, suppressed liberal agitation, and used extreme force to stamp out revolutionary activity. Behind these measures was the specter of revolution which the privileged feared. Yet the threat remained; a second series of revolutions broke out in 1848, once more starting in Paris and again spreading throughout Europe.

The European Revolutions of 1848

During the 60 years between the 1789 revolution in France and the 1848 upheavals throughout Europe there had been rapid industrialization. An urban proletariat, including many poor, was developing and the rural economy was rapidly changing. Cottage industry and other rural manufacturing was declining and many lost their livelihood, yet taxes were rising. These changes resulted in a great deal of unrest, and a food crisis in 1846–1847, especially a shortage of potatoes because of disease, led to widespread hunger, a sharp rise in the mortality rate, begging, vagrancy, and food and tax riots. The main urban protest groups were the craftsmen, such as construction workers, butchers, and weavers. They were facing destruction of their traditional methods of work and were hampered from protecting them by the governments of Western Europe which were encouraging new technologies and a free labor market. Labor unions were outlawed, and craftsmen who tried to organize to retain their old practices came into direct conflict with the state. Many were attracted by the writings of the Utopian socialists such as Pierre Joseph Proudhon and Louis Blanc, whose theories reflected an ideal past of the traditional work arrangements of the artisans. While the urban poor did not provide leadership in the revolutions that broke out, they were strategically located and had the force of numbers.[99]

Many who were better off were also restive, including large and small businessmen who felt hemmed in by 18th-century restrictions. There were strong class as well as social divisions, much of them centering around the question of whether the proletariat should be given the vote. In addition there was a growing romanticism about national identity, and numerous nationalistic movements arose. In some cases they helped develop class consciousness among the lower strata, especially where positions of power and privilege were held by non-natives. But nationalism also worked to minimize class antagonism, as we shall observe shortly.[100]

[99] Peter N. Stearns, *1848: The Revolutionary Tide in Europe* (New York: W. W. Norton & Co., 1974), pp. 20, 26, 28–30, 32, 34.

[100] See Priscilla Robertson, *Revolutions of 1848: A Social History* (New York: Harper Torchbooks, 1960), pp. vii, 4–6.

A key element in the 1848 upheavals was the rising middle classes which sought political power from which they were effectively excluded. Their restiveness, the difficulties faced by the craftsmen, and the deprivation experienced by the urban and rural poor led to agitation for reforms. The usual pattern of events was first a confused period of demands and demonstrations. The government was uncertain as what to do, which helped prolong the tension. Street fighting by the lower classes soon erupted, which was followed by attempts at negotiation by liberal elements of the middle class. At this point it was apparent that a revolution was in progress. Next, the leaders of the revolution attempted to define and defend their accomplishments; however pressure for more radical concessions quickly built up. Economic conditions now worsened, in large part because of the disturbances. Further despair in the lower class was created, which again goaded it into action. The growing radicalization brought forth strong repression by the government, and it put down the revolution. This move was the result of great pressure from the property owners, who responded more quickly and forcefully to threats to their well-being than during earlier revolutions. The lower class in 1848 was much more articulate than in 1789 or 1830, which in turn more easily frightened the property owners.[101] This is understandable for increasingly segments of the lower class were beginning to associate in organized groups and engage in political demonstrations. This was particularly true of workers, who participated as readily in political as well as in economic movements. Also, the attraction of the Utopian socialists was much more than romanticism about past work arrangements; there was a growing interest in socialistic schemes which stressed equality in the distribution of social goods.[102]

THE FRENCH REVOLUTION OF 1848

The French revolution of 1848 was primarily an attempt to complete the radical phase of the revolution that began in 1789. The old order had already been destroyed; the desire now was to create a more democratic republic that would guarantee key liberties to all and enact social reforms.[103] When the Parisians revolted in 1848, France seemed prosperous; yet poverty, child labor, and unemployment existed, a poor harvest had contributed to starvation, and Paris suffered an economic depression. While political repression affected all levels it weighed more heavily on the lower; in addition the latter claimed great inequality in the apportionment of social goods and there were growing demands for a

[101] Stearns, op. cit., pp. 37–45, 69.

[102] George Rudé, The Crowd in History (New York: John Wiley & Sons, 1964), pp. 164–167.

[103] Stearns, op. cit., p. 2.

redistribution. Most republicans were socialists, favoring such things as nationalization of the railroads. Nevertheless extension of suffrage became the primary thrust for social reform because most of the population, including small and middle-sized businessmen as well as workers and peasants, were disfranchised. Out of an adult male population of 9,000,000 there were only 250,000 qualified voters—less than three per cent. The disfranchised, particularly the bourgeoisie, clamored for extension of suffrage and saw the English Reform Bill of 1832 as a model. Only those persons who paid a direct tax of 200 francs or more had the privilege, and to every proposal for reform Guizot the Prime Minister replied "Get rich; then you can vote." [104]

There was growing unrest and increasing crowd behavior; the moderates were unable to bring about the reform which would mollify the bourgeoisie nor could they contain the explosive potential of the Paris working class. Government indecision and ineptness, the banning of political protests which were in the form of public banquets, and the dismissal of the ministry of Guizot added to the confusion and excitement. The university students played an important part in the agitation; interestingly the medical and the law students were the most radical, the engineers the least.[105] The precipitating event which plunged the city into violent conflict was a massacre. In response to an isolated shot, which may have been accidental, soldiers fired into a crowd of demonstrators. The survivors' reaction was quick and bitter: they piled seventeen of the dead into a large cart and formed a funeral procession which went throughout the city.[106]

> This funeral wagon went all over Paris until dawn. Its followers knocked on the doors of poor homes and made people wake up and look at the bodies. Church bells rang out the tocsin; and people—100,000, they say—began to seize arms and build more barricades.[107]

Fighting soon broke out, King Louis Philippe abdicated, and a republican government came to power.

THE OTHER REVOLUTIONS OF 1848

The winds of revolution blew over Europe, and there were upheavals in Germany, Austria, Italy, and Hungary; all in all there were over 50 if we include the small German and the small Italian states and the provinces of the Austrian Empire. The most important revolutions were in

---

[104] Robertson, *op. cit.*, pp. 14–16. The quotation is from p. 15.

[105] *Ibid.*, pp. 30–33.

[106] Jean Sigmann, *1848*, trans. by Lovett F. Edwards (New York: Harper & Row, 1970), pp. 208–209.

[107] Robertson, *Revolutions of 1848: A Social History*, p. 33.

Austria and in the German states, for they had had no great revolution like the French.[108] But it wasn't too long before the conservative forces began to emerge. In France the promised elections took place under the broadest voting law ever seen and 82% of those eligible went to the polls. Ironically more noblemen, landlords, and ecclesiastical candidates were elected than under King Louis Philippe, and Louis Napoleon Bonaparte nephew of the late Emperor was elected President. Although a professed democrat and socialist, he eventually killed off democracy and appointed reactionary ministers to his government.[109] More immediately, the armed workers were seen as a threat to the Republican bourgeoisie, who soon managed to disarm the workers and sought to transport the unemployed to rural areas. After hostilities broke out, the superior forces of the government defeated the workers and then killed many defenseless prisoners.[110]

Within a year France's revolution had virtually collapsed, and the same was true of the others. The main causes, according to Peter N. Stearns, were the liberal mentality of the revolutionary leaders and the cleavage between them and the lower classes. The liberal bourgeoisie, he suggests, were unable to come to grips with the need to engage in violence; hence they failed to establish a sufficiently strong militia which could overcome the military force of the state. In addition, he holds, the liberal bourgeoisie were incapable of maintaining an alliance with the lower classes. For example, they were incapable of consenting to major governmental intervention in the economy for the kinds of unemployment relief so desperately needed and demanded by the lower classes. Moreover, they were wedded to the concept of private property and could not countenance socialism or any other major kind of reform which would mean its abolition. Also, while the lower classes felt agitation was essential in order to reach their goals, the liberal bourgeoisie wished to end unrest.[111]

In short order the fundamental class differences surfaced. The middle class revolutionary leaders' stirring rhetoric that promised gains to all was soon replaced by class legislation, including property qualifications for voting.[112] Nationalism also contributed to the defeat of the revolutions since it often turned the proletariat away from class conflict and directed its antagonism toward an enemy of the country instead. That national loyalty was a successful way of minimizing conflict among the

---

[108] Stearns, op. cit., p. 3. The Hungarian revolution, in contrast to the others, was not a democratic one, but part of a continuing conflict between the local aristocracy and the Hapsburg government.

[109] Robertson, op. cit., pp. 75, 76, 77–79, 83, 99–103. See also Stearns, 1848: The Revolutionary Tide in Europe, p. 234.

[110] Robertson, op. cit., pp. 85–86, 88, 94, 96.

[111] Stearns, op. cit., pp. 225–228.

[112] Ibid., p. 229.

classes was obvious to the upper levels and was pointedly noted by Karl Marx.[113]

France's third revolution occurred in 1871 following the collapse of her armies in the war against the Germans. One of the outcomes was the short-lived commune.

The Commune

With the Prussian troops on the outskirts of Paris armed workers, fearful of the monarchical tendencies of the National Assembly, and beset by unemployment and hunger, took over the city and established their own government on cooperative principles. The Paris Commune was proclaimed on March 18, 1871.[114] The governing body consisted of workers or their representatives who were chosen by universal suffrage; it combined legislative and executive functions to better serve the citizenry. It was felt that the previous separation was one of the reasons legislators and administrators worked mainly for their own interests. Moreover, Commune members and other public servants were paid workingmen's wages. Church and state were separated, education was made accessible to all, magistrates and judges were elected, working conditions were improved and plans were laid to reorganize industry. The standing army was suppressed and replaced by a National Guard made up mostly of workingmen.[115] In the eyes of its supporters the Commune was the model for decentralized, self-government in industrial centers as well as in rural areas.[116] Although the proletariat provided the main base for the Commune, it apparently had widespread support among many middle-class Parisians as well. However the Government at Versailles, aided by the German Chancellor Bismarck, attacked the city and subdued it after eight days of fighting. Close to 40,000 men, women, and children were arrested,[117] and large numbers of Commune fighters and other supporters were executed.

The several revolutions exhibit what Barrington Moore, Jr. describes as a regular pattern: first, changing conditions bring about dislocations which affect all levels, but usually the lower strata most severely. The existing institutional arrangements including the political structure are un-

[113] Karl Marx, *The Civil War in France* (New York: International Publishers, 1940), pp. 23–35.

[114] Harry W. Laidler, *History of Socialism* (New York: Thomas Y. Crowell Co., 1968), p. 156.

[115] Marx, *op. cit.*, p. 57.

[116] Greenberg holds that the importance of the Commune lies in its move toward decentralization and emphasis on local liberties and republicanism, rather than as a model for socialism. Louis M. Greenberg, *Sisters of Liberty* (Cambridge, Mass.: Harvard University Press, 1971), pp. 4–7 ff. Cf. Marx, *op. cit.*, p. 59.

[117] Greenberg, *op. cit.*, p. 339.

able to cope with the situation, resulting in increased unrest and suffering. Elements of the middle and upper strata, usually those out of power, become more and more frustrated and seek reforms which will improve their position. They are encouraged by ideas, slogans, and programs which are promulgated by intellectuals, who are also usually of middle- or upper-strata background.

Those in the middle and upper strata who are in conflict with the existing government can do very little by themselves, however: they are outside the halls of power (or if in the government are in the opposition party) and they lack the advantage of numbers. They then seek to enlist the working population because its size can provide the leverage they need. The proletariat is encouraged to take to the streets in opposition to the government and violence breaks out; it is these lower-strata persons who bear the brunt of the fighting. Soon a new government promising reform replaces the old; the workers are disarmed; reforms are enacted; institutional arrangements are improved, and stability is achieved. With the end of the fighting regular economic activities resume, the pent-up need for goods and services begins to be filled, new endeavors abound, and prosperity is likely.

Although the reforms turn out to be mainly for the benefit of the higher classes they do make the economy viable and the condition of the lower classes improves. Consequently they are placated for the time being and lose their revolutionary ardor. Also, the reestablishment of authority includes the police power which is able to keep the lower strata from effectively challenging the new status quo. In addition, a large part of the population eschews further violence and property owners wish to secure their social goods. Thus the government becomes more conservative.

As time passes existing arrangements may no longer be appropriate because of changed conditions, and elements of the society may again be out of joint. Then, unless necessary reforms are forthcoming the preceding train of events is likely to be repeated: deprived segments of the middle and higher classes demand reforms; they seek the support of the lower classes and encourage them to demonstrate or in other ways threaten the regime; pent-up feelings among the lower classes are released and violence ensues; the existing government topples, and the new one institutes reforms. Authority is reestablished, the workers are disarmed, and—although they benefit from the changes—the main advantages accrue to the middle and upper classes. Nevertheless the society, for the time being, is more viable. Thus revolutionary violence helps right conditions which are dysfunctional, and in that context the lower classes periodically do society's "dirty work" for it.[118]

[118] See Moore, *Social Origins of Dictatorship and Democracy.*
The Paris revolt of 1870 departs somewhat from the pattern in that the Commune served primarily the workers' interests. Marx labelled it communism and had it in mind when he

Summary

In broad perspective, the Industrial Revolution, first in England and then on the Continent,[119] speeded up people's detachment from traditional associations and allegiances. Increasingly they were dependent on their own resources and subject to the vagaries of a market economy. There were new opportunities and some did very well; larger numbers however were ground down. More and more the industrial proletariat and other laboring people were living under urban conditions where ready communication made the development of group consciousness easier. There had always been deprivation, both absolute and relative, but now it was no longer accepted silently; neither were fetters on liberty, great inequality in the distribution of social goods, or unjust institutional arrangements.

Not only had material conditions of life changed tremendously, but so had people's perspectives. The overthrow of the *ancien régime* in 1789 and the revolutionary conflict of the 19th century showed the essential fragility of the social order; similarly they showed the power of the lower classes, once they are aroused. Also, these revolutions helped spread ideologies which justified challenging and doing something about injustice. As we have stressed, however, the upper and middle classes are usually the primary beneficiaries of revolutionary change. And, unless they stop the forces they helped set in motion, a more radical alteration of the authority structure is likely—a situation which would be to their disadvantage but would benefit the lower levels. Therefore, the final item on the revolutionary agenda is the counterrevolution of the upper and middle classes.

With this social, economic, and political change writers and other intellectuals sought to understand its causes, consequences, and potential. We are particularly interested in social analysts who dealt with the concepts of stratification and class, for they have importantly influenced our own perpectives as well as those of contemporary sociologists and other social scientists. Therefore in the next two chapters we examine works which are significant for stratification and class: in Chapter X we focus on early writers and in Chapter XI on modern writers.

---

wrote about the "dictatorship of the proletariat." Marx, *op. cit.*, p. 61. However, as we noted above it was short lived; undoubtedly its destruction was hastened because of the conservatives' fear that this redistribution of social goods might spread.

[119] See W. O. Henderson, *The Industrial Revolution in Europe* (Chicago: Quadrangle Paperbacks, 1961).

Chapter X.   The Shaping of Perspectives: 1. Earlier Writers

In the first chapter of Part Three we examined stratification and class in preindustrial society and were interested in the changes that occurred over time. We then noted the ideational response—the attempt to make sense out of what was happening and suggest how the social order might be shaped in a more desirable way. In the preceding chapter we focused on changes that ushered in the Industrial and the French Revolutions and the stupendous transformations that resulted. Not only were material conditions greatly altered but so were people's perspectives. The events which have drastically changed social, economic, and political relationships prompted intellectuals, among others, to seek explanations and raise questions regarding the future.

No longer did the ordering of life seem as predictable as in earlier times and there were numerous prognostications and suggestions for improvement. But the first task of forecasting is to provide a meaningful base; that is, to explain things as they are. The second is to pick out relevant trends and explain what is responsible for them so that their outcome may be postulated. Only then may meaningful alternatives be posited and procedures for attaining the desired ones suggested. In short, for those interested in achieving a new ordering of life it is necessary to provide a coherent picture of the existing society, an understanding of how it works, and a program for the future.

In this chapter we examine writers who tried to make sense out of the new industrial society, explicated its problems, and speculated on its potentialities. We are particularly interested in their ideas as they apply to stratification and class. Although the writings of Charles Louis Montesquieu and Jean Jacques Rousseau were concerned with these topics, especially the work of Rousseau which focused on inequality, systematic research began late in the 18th century with the work of John Millar (1735–1801).[1] He advocated what has come to be called economic determinism, and in his *Origin of the Distinction of Ranks* (1787) held that all social relations are determined by the economic organization of society.

Researchers in a number of fields such as social medicine and de-

[1] See Donald G. MacRae, "Social Stratification, A Trend Report and Bibliography," *Current Sociology*, 2 (1953–1954), p. 9.

mography contributed indirectly to the study of stratification and class for they collected data on the different strata. Also of importance was the development of the social survey in Great Britain, from the *First Statistical Account of Scotland* in the 1790's to the work of Charles Booth. While Booth dealt with the manual working poor his study provides much information about mobility, subcultures, and attitudes in regard to stratification.[2] Understandably Europe at that time provided fertile grounds for interest in stratification and class. As we indicated in the previous chapter, change in almost all aspects of people's lives was occurring with increasing rapidity. Strains between landlords and peasants, employers and factory workers, competing business groups, and between different economic interests and the government were intensifying. Industrialization and urbanization were growing apace, traditional relationships were breaking down, and the visibility of the "laboring poor" was increasing. Radical ideas about freedom and equality appeared in the writings and discussions of intellectuals and began to permeate the lower strata. Many of the notions were reinforced by the American War for Independence, which is examined in Chapter XII. Ideas about class and class conflict were very much current in works related to the French Revolution which began in 1789. However an overt theory of stratification and class did not emerge from these writers, although Henri de Saint-Simon was somewhat of an exception.[3]

For many people life did not improve but worsened following the Industrial and the French Revolutions. Many idealists became very pessimistic and a number of writers proposed schemes which they thought would make a reality of equality, freedom, and brotherhood. Among them are François Noël Babeuf, Saint-Simon, François Fourier, Louis Blanc, and Pierre Joseph Proudhon who are labeled Utopian socialists.[4] They differed considerably from one another, some suggesting that the state regulate in detail both industrial activity and individual behavior while others proposed a system of free and voluntary cooperation. Yet they all tried to

> visualize an industrial society wherein no man would be able to live off the labor of his fellows. In general they believed with their predecessors that the institution of private property was brought about by a contract made in remote ages after the disappearance of the natural state and its communistic system of property.[5]

They held that the individual members of society could alter this social contract at any time, and that it should be modified in such a manner

---

[2] *Ibid.*, pp. 9–11.

[3] *Ibid.*, pp. 9–10.

[4] See Harry W. Laidler, *History of Socialism* (New York: Thomas Y. Crowell Co., 1968), p. 44 ff.

[5] *Ibid.*, p. 45.

that people, who are by nature good, would be free from the vicious institutions and would be able to develop according to the laws of nature. However they gave little thought to industrial realities.

> All that was necessary to do, the majority of them believed, was to present a plan for social salvation, begin to experiment on a small scale, interest powerful men in its development, and extend it to the masses. Such trifles as the state of industry and the preparedness of the masses disturbed them not at all.[6]

François Noël Babeuf

Babeuf (1760–1797) who believed in the communistic idea of absolute equality rather than equality of opportunity, was deeply involved in the French Revolution. He violently attacked the institutions of society in his newspaper, was arrested, and upon release formed a secret society aimed at overthrowing the government. It was claimed that 17,000 men were ready to join the insurrection, when Babeuf—betrayed by an informer—was arrested and ended up on the guillotine.

Babeuf held that happiness is the aim of society and this happiness consists of equality. Disobedience to this natural law is responsible for all wrongs, oppressions, and wars; furthermore, the major cause of inequality is private property. Equality would be achieved gradually, with the property of corporations and institutions nationalized. There would be no inheritance so that eventually individual property would also be nationalized. Production would be carried on by officers elected by popular vote; their pay would be the same as for the ordinary workers, and office-holding would be rotated. Political rights would be held only by people performing labor considered to be useful by the government. Education would have a very practical emphasis, and children would be taken from their parents at an early age; they would be reared together and taught the principles of communism in order to prevent the reemergence of inequality.[7]

There were a number of other Utopian socialists, but perhaps the best known was Comte Henri de Saint-Simon.

Henri de Saint-Simon

Born of a noble family which traced its ancestry from Charlemagne, Saint-Simon (1760–1825) foresaw a glorious destiny in store for him and

---

[6] *Ibid.*

[7] *Ibid.*, pp. 46–47.

instructed his valet to awaken him every morning with these words: "Arise, Monsieur le Comte, you have grand deeds to perform." [8] At age 19 he participated in the American Revolution and was decorated for gallantry in the siege of Yorktown; during the French Revolution he took the side of the Revolutionists, denouncing his title. After successfully engaging in land speculation he devoted himself to study, but in order to gain practical experience he lived every kind of life, from a wealthy entertainer to a profligate and pauper. He began his career of author and social reformer at the age of 43 and continued in it until his death. At the end, his health was broken and his money gone, and he barely eked out an existence.[9]

Saint-Simon's work antedated Karl Marx's stages of societal growth and anticipated his theory of revolution, at least in its general aspects.[10] Saint-Simon held that the new order which the French Revolution brought about showed that humans had reached the adult stage, according to his schema. Liberty was no longer an abstraction, although the problem of realizing it is economic; yet he differed with the laissez faire economists in that he thought it was important to improve the condition of the poor. He believed very strongly that all human potentialities could be fulfilled through industrialism; more than that, he held that what was most favorable to industry was most favorable to society as a whole.

Saint-Simon wanted private enterprise to remain but it would be subject to control by regulatory agencies, primarily a parliament composed of engineers, artists, scientists, and industrial producers. The first branch, 300 members chosen from among engineers and artists, would draw up plans for industrial activities. They would be evaluated by the second branch consisting of 100 mathematicians, 100 physicists, and 100 physiologists. The proposals that were determined to be feasible would be put into effect by the third branch, which would be recruited from among the heads of all sections of industry and commercial farming. The outcome of this arrangement was supposed to be equality, but not in terms of an equal distribution of social goods; it was defined by Saint-Simon as "true equality" in the sense that there were to be no special privileges. For example, there would be none through birth, the idle rich would not have any political say, property rights in the case of land would be modified to benefit the producer as well as the owner, and each person would be rewarded according to capacity and contributions.

He proposed new bases of social control. The narrow self-interest of the economic liberals, and the threat of hunger, so vividly described by William Townsend in Chapter VIII, were replaced by reason, collective interest, and knowledge of the means and ends of the system. Everyone

---

[8] *Ibid.*, pp. 49–50. The quotation is from p. 50.

[9] *Ibid.*, pp. 50–51.

[10] See Irving M. Zeitlin, *Ideology and the Development of Social Theory* (Englewood Cliffs, N.J.: Prentice-Hall, 1968), p. 65.

can fit into productive life, everyone will be able to find a place suited to his abilities; people will do what is best for them and through the simple working of individual volition order will be maintained. Consequently, coercive government will not be needed. It should be noted that the second branch of parliament, the scientists, would be responsible for education which would be in the form of a national catechism with all contrary education prohibited. Authority for Saint-Simon is the authority of science; there would be a scientifically-based moral order wherein industrialists, scientists, managers, and manual workers would share the same interests. The proposed system is an organic one based on the division of labor, and reflects his admiration for the unity of the Middle Ages; but religious leaders are replaced by scientists.

Saint-Simon also differed from the economic liberals in another way for he wished to improve the condition of the poor by rearranging the social order. Yet superordination-subordination was retained in his proposed society. If anything, the position of the "haves" against the "have-nots" is strengthened for the actual running of the industrial system would be by the entrepreneurs who would make use of the knowledge and ability of the scientists and other intellectuals. This would be a highly stratified social order; however he believed that the development of class interests would be thwarted by the new religion of science which would unify the society.[11]

Nevertheless under industrial capitalism there always lurks the possibility of anarchy and revolution, and government is seen as a necessary evil to prevent them. However, class antagonism would be quickly blotted out by the rapid progress of industrialism and the conflict between classes would be transformed into a common struggle against nature. With industrial advance the science of man which he proposed would reconcile the interests of different classes and serve as the foundation of a unified society.

Saint-Simon became the founder of modern positivism. Underlying his new science was the belief that truth was to be derived only from facts. Reasoning must be based on facts alone; facts should not be referred to reason as in the speculative sciences. Scientific analysis could uncover the laws of society and he saw progress in that light. That is, progress was an independent natural law and men were mere instruments before its omnipotent force. He felt that a scientifically-based moral order was needed for social unity and that the necessary scientific principles would be discovered in the natural laws of society.[12]

[11] See Emile Durkheim, *Socialism*, trans. by Charlotte Sattler and ed. by Alvin W. Gouldner (New York: Collier Books, 1962; written circa 1896), pp. 174–201; and E. J. Hobsbawm, *The Age of Revolution, 1789–1848* (New York: The New American Library, 1962), p. 285.

[12] Zeitlin, *Ideology and the Development of Social Theory*, pp. 59–68; and Herbert Marcuse, *Reason and Revolution* (Boston: Beacon Press, 1968), pp. 330–332.

Whereas Marx stressed differences of interest and conflict as basic features of modern group life as we shall see shortly, Saint-Simon emphasized similarity of interests and accord. While Saint-Simon also sought considerable changes in the society they were ameliorative rather than revolutionary as with Marx. For Saint-Simon, the essence of human group life is a moral bond. This bond consists of the things people believe in—what are often called "values." They are responsible for holding the society together and for people engaging in organized activities. Differences of interest and conflict, as well as individualism and rationalism are eschewed for they weaken this moral bond and are thus destructive of social order.[13]

The impact of Saint-Simon's schemes in terms of concrete and long-lasting changes in the social order was almost nil, although his ideas were instrumental for the development of sociology. His views strongly influenced other social theorists, however, and even had an impact on the more radical ones. Among the other important Utopian socialists was Saint-Simon s countryman Fourier.

François Fourier

Fourier (1772–1837) proposed an "apartment house Utopia," a cooperative community of 1,800 people, and envisioned a reconstitution of society in which there would be a world federation of such cooperatives. Private property would not be abolished, but he called for a more equitable distribution of income among labor, capital, and enterprise. Although his ideas did not profoundly affect France, a large and sympathetic following developed in America and led to the establishment of Brook Farm. Located about 10 miles from Boston, it was founded in 1841 by intellectuals who hoped to unite intellectual life with manual labor. Initially Brook Farm was seen as an embodiment of the Transcendental movement, a romantic philosophical outgrowth of Unitarianism. Most of its income came from its fine school, which attracted many pupils. But the spread of Fourier's ideas, which seemed especially relevant in light of a terrible business panic, led its members to turn it into a Fourieristic cooperative in the winter of 1843–1844. However, following vicious attacks by outsiders, which resulted in a decline in the number of students, and a disastrous fire in 1846, Brook Farm was abandoned. Other Fourieristic experiments also failed.[14]

[13] See Robert A. Nisbet, "Conservatism and Sociology," *American Journal of Sociology*, 68 (September 1952), 167–175.

[14] Howard Becker and Harry E. Barnes, *Social Thought from Lore to Science* (Washington, D.C.: Harren Press, 1952), Vol. I, p. 630 and Zoltán Haraszti, *The Idyll of Brook Farm* (Boston: The Trustees of the Public Library, 1937).

Fourier was less concerned with the addition of unearned income than Saint-Simon. Each member of the community would get a portion of the earnings of industry, with the surplus being divided as follows: five-twelfths to labor, four-twelfths to capital, and three-twelfths to talent. He distinguished between necessary, useful, and agreeable labor, with the first receiving the highest reward and the last the lowest. While he expected that different gradations in society would remain, he felt that even though there would be rich and powerful people they would be so filled with the spirit of cooperation that their presence would bring no disharmony. Finally, he believed that an experiment in communal living along his principles would be so convincing to the world that revolution would not be necessary.[15]

Harry W. Laidler writes that although

> Fourier's philosophy was fantastic at many points, he nevertheless did valuable service in calling attention to the wastes in the modern economic system, the unnecessary hardships of labor, and the need for devising some system which would make work pleasanter than it was in the France of his day. He emphasized the value of machinery in doing the work of the world. His writings had considerable influence on factory laws and sanitary reforms.[16]

There were other Utopians, like Robert Owen whom we mentioned in the previous chapter, and Blanc, at whom we look next.

Louis Blanc

At 26 Blanc (1811–1882) founded a leftist journal in which his most important socialistic writings appeared. He was active in politics, serving in the French governments of 1848 and 1871. He believed that human happiness and human development should be the goal of social effort; specifically that everyone should have the opportunity for the highest mental, moral, and physical growth. This he felt could not be achieved under the existing competitive system, and he proposed that everyone be guaranteed work through state organized national workshops. These workshops would eventually replace private ones, and after the first year worker control would be established.

Blanc realized that people differ in their abilities, but felt that each person should be in a position to fully use his capacities. However, an individual should not use his superior abilities to exploit others. Blanc rejected the reward systems of other Utopians: Saint-Simon's idea that

---

[15] Laidler, *History of Socialism*, pp. 56–59. In fact he believed the millennium was so near that he urged his followers not to invest in real estate because it would lose value as Fourierism spread.

[16] *Ibid.*, p. 60.

people should be rewarded according to the work performed; Fourier's unequal division among labor, capital, and talent, and Babeuf's belief in absolute equality. On the contrary, his view is encapsuled in the phrase he coined, "From each according to his ability, to each according to his *needs.*" [17]

Blanc was the first of the Utopian socialists to appeal to the working rather than the privileged classes to bring about a transformation of society. In this sense he is a connecting link between the Utopian and Marxist socialists.[18] There is one other writer, Proudhon, who we want to consider before moving on to Marx.

Pierre Joseph Proudhon

Proudhon (1809–1865) was born of poor parents and worked his way through school, although at 19 was forced to drop out of college. However he continued to educate himself and received an award of 1,500 francs given to promising students in literature and science. His writings attempted to prove the inequity of private property and expounded the doctrine that the amount of time a person put in on his or her work was the measure of the value of what was produced. He held that property is theft, that it is either the result of accident, such as time of arrival of those who obtained it, or the difference between the cost of labor and what the capitalist charges for the goods or services. Thus, not only is property theft but the proprietor is a thief.[19]

Proudhon ridiculed the plans of his predecessors, especially the idea of some that society could be made to adopt a ready-made plan of social reform. Also, he did not believe that a perfect state such as he proposed could be brought about overnight. To move toward his goal he urged the formation of a great national bank through which workers would be able to purchase the things they needed on a profit-free basis. Paper money in the form of checks would be issued in exchange for items that were produced. In this manner the laborer would receive the full value of his work, and in turn the things he bought would be priced at their true value. Loans without interest would also be available.

He looked toward the time when a society could operate on the basis of liberty, equality, and fraternity, when no government would be needed. In fact, he bitterly denounced all government and authority; he did not participate in the Revolution of 1848 because he believed all forms of government were bad and it didn't matter which faction won.

[17] *Ibid.*, pp. 60–64. The quotation is from p. 63. Emphasis in the original.
[18] *Ibid.*, p. 60.
[19] *Ibid.*, pp. 66–68.

His goal was anarchy and he desired a society based on absolute equality; this he felt would require the absence of government, of the control of one person over another.[20]

Even though very little of what the Utopian socialists advocated came to fruition, they had a great influence on other writers, including Marx as well as the "founders" of sociology. Marxists distinguish between their socialism and that of the Utopians, and we next examine Marx's work.

Karl Marx

A German by birth, Marx (1818–1883) first studied law but became interested in philosophy, receiving his Ph.D. at Jena in 1842. In that year he became editor of a small newspaper which became more and more radical in its demands for reforms and was suppressed in 1843. He went to Paris where he met Friedrich Engels (1820–1895) and they became lifelong associates. Engels, in addition to his collaboration with Marx, wrote a number of important works himself and helped organize revolutionary movements on the continent. The son of a wealthy textile manufacturer he was a successful businessman and his income allowed him to support Marx who was thus able to devote himself to research and writing.[21]

Much of the difficulty in assessing the work of Marx results from Marx the political advocate interfering with Marx the social scientist. The impassioned phrases and the religious fervor in much of his writings are understandable in terms of the conditions and ferment of the 19th century. It was clear that the capitalist entrepreneurs, the bourgeoisie, were prospering under the new system of production while for most of the workers life was becoming more and more miserable. They had only their labor to sell, they were dependent on the owners of the means of production for their livelihood, and they were at the mercy of business cycles and other consequences of the industrial system. Marx's doctrines were aimed at them, the "unsuccessful many." [22] Nevertheless he con-

[20] *Ibid.* Cf. p. 69. Proudhon believed that in time inequality in talent and capacities would be reduced to an inappreciable minimum, which seems unrealistic. Also, absolute equality and anarchy are inconsistent. *Ibid.*, pp. 67–69.

[21] In discussing Marx we include Engels' writings, although Marx was the prime contributor to the ideas and theories in their work.

Robert Freedman, ed., *Marxist Social Thought* (New York: Harcourt, Brace & World, 1968), provides a good introduction to Marx. Especially useful are the commends by Freedman, pp. xv–xxiii and by Jerome Balmuth, pp. xxv–xxxiv. An excellent analysis of Marx's idea of class is Reinhard Bendix and Seymour M. Lipset, "Karl Marx's Theory of Social Classes," in Bendix and Lipset, eds., *Class, Status, and Power* (2nd ed.; New York: The Free Press, 1966), pp. 6–11. For a critical appraisal of Marx's ideas in light of developments in industrial and post-industrial society see Ralf Dahrendorf, *Class and Class Conflict in Industrial Society* (Stanford, Calif.: Stanford University Press, 1959).

[22] Joseph A. Schumpeter, *Capitalism, Socialism, and Democracy* (New York: Harper & Brothers Publishers, 1950) pp. 1–8.

tributed greatly to an understanding of class and stratification. His stress on the economic dimension and his theory of institutional change, as well as his analyses of the association between the form of production in a society and its institutions, the role of capital and labor in industrial development, and the problem of alienation have influenced social scientists, historians, and economists, particularly the latter. Moreover, his theories, conjectures, and assertions, although interpreted and misinterpreted by a host of disciples have affected the political fortunes of many nations. As has been said many times, if Marx's writings were mere polemics with no substance, he would have been forgotten long ago.

Marx's endeavors have been subjected to searching examination and scholars continue to strongly criticize his theories and concepts.[23] Yet, as Joseph A. Schumpeter concludes, in Marx's works the whole is greater than any of its parts. That is, his overall contribution was the very difficult task of attempting to synthesize economic, political, and social relationships from the perspective of historical change.[24] In doing so he raised significant questions about man and society. Some disagree with the answers he gave or the way he arrived at them but, by posing the questions as he did, any serious analyst of society regardless of political orientation remains in his debt.

To understand Marx's work we must recognize, in addition to the circumstances of the times in which he lived, the part the social philosophies of the period played in the development of his thought. In this regard the Utopian socialists, the classical economists, and the "idealist philosophers" deserve special mention. Although he derided the theories of the Utopian socialists he shared with them the belief that industrialism could provide the base for the ideal society. As for the classical economists he was strongly influenced by Adam Smith and David Ricardo. But the key to Marx's concepts of historical change and materialism are found in the philosophies of Immanuel Kant (1724–1804), Georg Wilhelm Friedrich Hegel (1770–1831), and Ludwig Feuerbach (1804–1872).

INFLUENCE OF KANT, HEGEL, FEUERBACH

Kant's ideas were adapted by Hegel for the construction of his system of philosophy. Certain aspects of Hegel's work were considerably revised by Feuerbach, and in turn Marx saw in Feuerbach's writings a unique interpretation of Hegel, which became the cornerstone to his own thinking. It is worthwhile to look at some of the concepts of these philosophers who sought to understand the processes of human thought and the potentialities of reason.

[23] See, e.g., *ibid.*, p. 24 ff.
[24] *Ibid.*, pp. 41–45.

Kant was among the writers of the Romantic-Conservative reaction who challenged the general methodological assumptions of the social philosophers of the Enlightenment, and emphasized the validity of faith and intuition for understanding nature and society. He wrote that only through philosophic reflection can one understand his world and its potential, for man's behavior involves more than simple responses to external and internal stimuli. Conceptualization must occur because the human must have some categories in his mind in order to respond to stimuli in a social way. That is, there must be logical categories that we have formed which allow us to interpret and judge what we are experiencing. Otherwise the phenomenon will have no meaning for us. This rational ordering of phenomena, Kant held, is the basis for the laws of natural science; the scientist usually has some notion of what he is looking for or an understanding of the significance of what he observes.

Understanding and perception are not enough, however, since the mind seeks to uncover the totality or ultimate meaning of experience. But the problem is that "objects" or the "world" are themselves rational conceptions, or ideas. Kant suggests that if philosophical reflection shows that the world is but a concept in man's mind, it follows that everything in the world, including nature and the sciences, are rational reflections of the ideas of men.[25]

Accordingly, it would seem that man is quite limited in the extent to which his thoughts can range beyond the here and now. The philosopher realizes this restriction on reason; however, by becoming aware of the limits of the consciousness of man he becomes *self*-conscious and thus attains a clearer understanding of his world. And reason expands through such awareness of its character and limits. Herein lies the basis of what later became known as the dialectical method which is an essential part of Marx's thought; however this development required certain modifications of Kant's theory, and these were supplied by Hegel and Feuerbach.[26]

Hegel viewed reason as an immanent force that is constantly developing and becoming, rather than as an abstraction from the real; it is not something merely within the individual for analyzing phenomena. Reason for Hegel is a great cosmic force which determines the structure and development of the universe; and this conception of reason he called the Spirit, the Absolute, or finally, God.[27] Hegel added to Kant's theory the belief that higher levels of conceptualization develop as a result of a triadic series of steps in thinking; a concept is proposed, a contradictory or opposing notion is put forth, and the result of the ensuing conflict of ideas is a higher level of understanding. Hegel also put historical dimension in Kant's ideas, for he believed no set of circumstances, whether a

---

[25] Zeitlin, *Ideology and the Development of Social Theory*, p. 37.

[26] Balmuth, *op. cit.*, pp. xxviii–xxix.

[27] See Zeitlin, *op. cit.*, pp. 40, 42; and Balmuth, *op. cit.*, p. xxx.

theory, an art style, or a form of social organization can be understood without its negation, or what it is not. For the new object is necessarily different, that is, "opposite" from its predecessor; yet it is related to it because everything develops out of some other thing.

Included in Hegel's logic is the contention that everything is related to everything else; thus a change in one aspect of a set of ideas or of a society will have ramifications in other parts. There are no accidental or chance happenings; everything, including social phenomena has a cause. Also, every historical event affects social, economic, and political thinking, and in turn these thoughts affect historical events. Consequently, since every change has a cause, and since society develops in a dialectic pattern, the study of historical events can lead to an uncovering of the laws of human society.

Hegel's work had both a conservative and a radical side. On the one hand his analyses led him to the conclusion that the state is the highest order, and that one state in particular, Prussia, embodied the truth and the eternal wisdom of the spirit of God. The radical side, which greatly influenced Marx, held that the development toward freedom is not a mindless process; rather it is contingent upon consciousness and will. Also, development is in phases, and each succeeding phase realizes the potentiality of its preceding form, which is its negation. Thus there is an emerging form (thesis) which develops out of an earlier state, which is its negation (antithesis). However, this development involves conflict, out of which the final form arises (synthesis).

He sees reality as a process which involves the unification of contradictory forces, and holds that it should be shaped by reason. That is, what is "real" is not what actually exists but what exists which is in line with the standards of reason. Thus a state would not be "real" or "reasonable" if it did not correspond to the given potentialities of men: it would be real only when it did correspond to these potentialities and allowed their full development. Hegel's critical concept of reason leads him to demonstrate that a given state of affairs contains antagonisms that dissolve it into other forms, and it is this "spirit of contradicting" that is the key to his dialectic method.[28]

Yet as with Kant, Hegel's concern was basically theoretical and speculative; he dealt with man's self-awareness apart from his world of practical activities. Feuerbach's philosophy was also theoretical and speculative in his *Essence of Christianity*. He held that religion and its various aspects are idealistic projections of man's own human nature, that God is man's projection of himself, actually his ideal self. This stimulated Marx to emphasize the materialistic basis of human life, what he felt was the real world where the mind interacts with the social and physical aspects of society, where the human spirit manifests itself through action.

While Marx is indebted to these philosophers he rejected contempla-

[28] Marcuse, *op. cit.*, pp. 7–11 ff.

tive philosophy, that is philosophy for its own sake; he emphasizes the importance of using reason and knowledge of the laws of human society to change the conditions of mankind for the better.[29] Consequently in his focus on the materialistic aspect of life he underscored the importance of the human's basic need for food, shelter, and clothing. And the form of production, the means whereby people obtain the necessities, is directly related to the organization of the society, to its institutions, and to the nature of relations among individuals and groups. He also suggested that the form of production of any society is related to its level of technology and that capitalism was an inevitable development out of the preceding feudal economy which it replaced. Feudalism, in turn, had been the outcome of earlier social, economic, and political arrangements which it had replaced. Such changes occur when institutions, laws, and customs are no longer suited to new circumstances, in part because of inherent contradictions, and in part because of a false view of the world by the ruling class.

By inherent contradictions Marx meant that institutional arrangements and practices in a society may unwittingly create conditions which reduce its viability. For example, the feudal system of political ties fractionated the society and increased conflict, and the economics of feudal land tenure and the practice of strip farming limited agricultural production. As for the "false" outlook of the ruling class, its members became caught up with patterns of thought which made them blind to needed reforms. More than that, their shortsightedness encouraged actions which hastened the collapse of the system.

Under such circumstances a new stratum of persons arises whose interests and activities increasingly diverge from those in power. This new stratum is likely to contain many innovative and energetic individuals who chafe at the shortcomings and restrictions of an archaic system. Over time they become more powerful, challenge the ruling class for supremacy, and eventually become the dominant class themselves. In a sense the broad changes the rising class seek is the thesis, and the usually repressive reaction by the ruling class is the antithesis; out of this conflict arises a new set of institutional arrangements, the synthesis.

Capitalism arose in this fashion, Marx wrote. And the energies and inventiveness unleashed by the ascendency of the bourgeoisie resulted in a rapid buildup of industrialism, with its factories and ever-expanding industrial workforce. However, in its turn capitalism would be replaced as the result of a new synthesis, for the poverty of the industrial workers was growing. There were several reasons but it was principally the periodically worsening business cycles and the continual reduction in wages. The latter was caused by the capitalist's desire to maximize

---

[29] Balmuth, *op. cit.*, pp. xxix and xxxiii–xxxiv. See Sidney Hook, *From Hegel to Marx* (New York: John Day, 1936), pp. 15–76, 112, 220–307.

profits which is the basis of capital accumulation. Another problem was that the margin of profit was declining which led manufacturers to use more labor-saving machinery in order to further cut labor costs. In addition, surpluses built up because the low wages of the masses prevented them from purchasing the manufactured goods. This in turn increased business failures and threw more people out of work. Not only would a drop in demand adversely affect business and the workers, but a rise in demand would eventually have the same effect: a short period of prosperity would be followed by overproduction, and business activity and employee wages would decline.

Free competition contributed to the worsening condition of the industrial workers. For example, look at the production of linens. If the price of linen goods rose because of greater demand, manufacturers would increase production and new entrepreneurs would enter the field. Although the ensuing labor shortage would raise wages, both the shortage and the rise in wages would only be temporary since the better wages would attract many job-seekers which would soon depress the workers' pay. In turn, assuming that the demand remained constant, the increased production of linens would result in an oversupply. Then the price would drop, profit margins would get smaller, wages would be lowered, and production would be reduced and workers discharged. The enterprises of the weaker capitalists would fail and this would further increase the number of unemployed. With low prices and little profit, capital will move into more lucrative fields which may soon mean that not enough linens are being manufactured, assuming again that the demand remains constant. As a consequence prices will rise and the whole process will be repeated.

Not only do manufacturers compete with buyers but they also compete with one another; each tries to obtain as much of the market as possible by selling cheaper, offering special discounts to buyers, and so on. This competition tends to depress prices. In addition, the buyers compete with each other, which tends to drive prices up. The effect of such fluctuations is to increase the existing instability of job-holding and wage rates for the proletariat.

The rise and fall in prices of consumer goods also affects the worker, usually to his disadvantage. If prices rise and wages remain the same, his real income goes down; if prices and wages remain the same but the value of money decreases, his real income also drops. Now suppose the worker's real income goes up: wages remain the same but prices drop, or prices do not change but wages rise. His benefit is only short-lived for he finds that his wants increase, and he is soon back to where he was when his real income was lower.[30]

[30] Karl Marx, "Wage Labor and Capital," *Marx-Engels Selected Works,* Vol. I (Moscow: Foreign Language Publishing House, 1958), pp. 79–105.

In addition to economic practices that impoverish the proletariat, one may expect a growing estrangement between capitalist and worker, for with the increase in the division of labor, which is a component of capitalist production, the worker becomes alienated from his work and from himself. His job loses meaning, he is treated as an object, and begins to view himself as such. The same holds for the capitalist. He no longer has intrinsic interest in his own activity; work becomes impersonal because his concern is profit, in the same way that the worker's interest is wages and not what he does.

Not only will the capitalists, or bourgeoisie, become richer and the workers poorer but distinctions among the workers will disappear. The growing use of machines and the increase in the division of labor not only lower wages but also reduce work tasks to their simplest level. The proletariat becomes a body of minimally skilled as well as low-paid workers. In addition other categories of persons, such as small entrepreneurs or shopkeepers—the petite bourgeoisie—soon enter the ranks of the proletariat. For as the means of production become concentrated in fewer and fewer hands they are forced out of business by the large, monopoly enterprises.

Marx wrote that another contradiction inherent in capitalism was the likelihood of war. This is related to the declining rate of profit, surplus production, and monopoly control. For capitalists would see war with its conquests and colonial exploitation as a profitable way to use surplus production facilities, create additional markets, and open up new sources of raw materials. It was for these several reasons that Marx believed the condition of the proletariat could be expected to worsen and the tension between them and the bourgeoisie increase.

The communication of the feelings of deprivation and antagonism among the workers is facilitated by close proximity with fellow employees in factories and by the concentration of laboring families in the same sections of cities. While lower-strata people in peasant society also suffered, their isolation from one another hindered communication and the formation of group consciousness; thus the conditions of capitalism work to polarize the bourgeoisie and the proletariat.

Yet the ideology of the bourgeoisie prevents them from understanding capitalism's inherent contradictions and realizing that their actions are making conditions even worse; they are not interested in the widespread changes which are needed to forestall collapse and conflict. Furthermore, the ameliorative programs of Utopian socialists or "dogooders" such as charity workers only retard the revolution and prolong the misery; substantial changes cannot be expected through such efforts.

A serious problem from Marx's perspective is the fact that the proletariat is influenced by the ideas and values of the bourgeoisie; thus they have a "false" consciousness. Also, the bourgeoisie seek to set worker against worker, as is the case when different trade or ethnic groups or unemployed seek the jobs of those who are working. These attitudes and actions of the proletariat retard the inevitable process in which the ruling class, which has lost its vitality and *raison d'être*, will be replaced. Marx felt it was necessary for the proletariat to become conscious of its interest and its historic role which is to supplant the bourgeoisie; by legislative means if possible, by revolution if not. Then production and distribution can be redirected toward benefiting all, and work activities can be reordered to do away with alienation. With alienation ended and material needs assured, there will be a flowering of the human spirit.

Of course, change can be hastened by people who have already made a "correct" interpretation of the historical situation, who can help develop the true consciousness of the proletariat. These persons can also supply the necessary organizational know-how to channel the energy of the workers and direct the conflict toward the desirable end: common ownership of the means of production, and eventually communism. Once the bourgeoisie is overthrown these persons (the members of the party representing the workers) will likely have to rule for a while in order to combat the counterrevolutionaries, stamp out remaining capitalistic tendencies, and in general consolidate the revolution and pave the way for communism. Marx expected that this "dictatorship of the proletariat" would only be temporary.[31] The socialization of production however is not an end in itself: the goal is to set up conditions which will free people.

We have sketched the elements of Marx's thought which are of particular interest to us. Below we round out his major contributions which are of value for understanding stratification and class:

1. *The materialist conception of history.* Satisfaction of basic needs of food, shelter, and clothing are primary; consequently the economic element is of first consideration in trying to understand historical change and institutional forms such as the family, the means of production, and political arrangements. But economic conditions are not the sole cause of social structure and group relations; instead they help shape them, and should be analyzed from that perspective.

2. *The form of production is dependent on the level of technology and social organization.* Capitalist industrial society could not come about without necessary advances in science, manufacturing techniques, and business organization. Also required was the development of widespread trade and commerce and a free market economy with money as the medium of exchange. Of course, once industrialism has developed it can be "imported" even though a country may lack some of the conditions cited above.

3. *The form of production critically affects the circumstances of the several categories of persons in the society.* The capitalistic industrial form has

[31] Freedman, *op. cit.*

certain consequences for the owners of the means of production, the shopkeepers and other small businessmen, and the industrial workers. The capitalists, as a result of unregulated competition and the declining rate of profit, diminish in number with the large ones becoming more and more wealthy through monopoly and other practices. Political power follows economic power and these entrepreneurs eventually come to control the governing structure; their interests are reflected in the religious, artistic, and other aspects of the culture.

The growth of the factory system, the increase in the division of labor, and the use of labor-saving machines enlarges the proportion of laboring poor: the size of the minimally skilled workforce whose labor has become more dehumanized increases, as does the number of unemployed. The above conditions, together with overproduction and periodically worsening business crises divide the society into two antagonistic camps: the owners of the means of production and the workers. The petite bourgeoisie, unable to compete with the monopoly businessmen and adversely affected by other conditions created by them, are driven into the ranks of the proletariat. The polarized society is now at the brink of crisis. The proletariat becomes self-conscious, aware of its interests, and politicized; through the means most appropriate to the situation—elections, legislation, or violent conflict—the oppressors are overthrown. Thus there is a revolutionary reconstitution of society in which property is held in common, classes, class conflict, and alienation are absent, and the potentialities of the human come to fruition.

4. *The dialectic of history.* Marx's theory of history is evolutionary and deterministic. He believes that higher and higher levels of social organization are achieved as an outcome of the conflict of different groups caused by the contradictions in and devitalization of preceding forms. This was how feudal society formed out of ancient society and bourgeoisie out of feudal. Finally, capitalism gives way to communism.

Among Marxists there have been differing viewpoints regarding trends in capitalist society, how socialism would be achieved, and the extent to which communist nations embody Marx's ideas. Although there have subsequently been several schools of Marxism they basically divide on an orthodox or revisionist interpretation of his theories, and we shall examine these schools when considering the modern writers. We conclude the present discussion on Marx with some comments on his concept of class.

MARX ON CLASS

Although an essential part of Marx's work concerned class formation and conflict he did not systematize the concept of class. It was only in his last writings that he apparently began such a task but death took him before it was completed. After a few introductory paragraphs in the last chapter of the last volume of *Capital* there is this statement, appended by Engels: "Here the manuscript ends." But there is sufficient discussion on the topic throughout his writings to present his schema of class and class conflict. In the main, he holds that antagonism and differences in interests are a part of superordinate-subordinate relationships, and that the mode of production shapes the nature of the potential conflict and aligns the contesting groups. The major points of his schema are outlined below.

1. *Basic antagonism.* Throughout history the members of societies fall into two categories: the oppressors and the oppressed, or the rulers and the exploited ("Freeman and slave, patrician and plebeian, lord and serf, guild-master and journeyman. . . .").[32] Such antagonism and conflict based on it are the motive forces in history; they are the bases for social change and the emergence of higher and higher levels of civilization.

2. *Differential interests related to position in the productive process.* The differences are related to one's position in the productive process; the owners of the means of production and distribution have the advantage over the rest, and may be expected to exploit them.

3. *The mode of production determines the nature of the antagonistic groups.* In earlier epochs there were conflicts between town and country, industry and maritime commerce, citizens and slaves; however classes are found only in bourgeoisie society.[33] Factors such as income, education, or prestige are associated with class position, but they are dependent variables; the independent variable is one's position in the productive process.

4. *There are two potential classes.* The two most meaningful aggregates in bourgeois society are the owners of the means of production and the non-owners, or, the capitalists and the workers. There are other aggregates which eventually fuse into these two; large landlords become a part of the capitalist class, principally through investments in manfacturing enterprises, or by engaging in large-scale agriculture employing free labor. On the other hand, as was mentioned above, small shopkeepers, small landholders and the rest of the petite bourgeoisie lose out in the free competition and become a part of the proletariat.

5. *Conflict and class formation.* While certain conditions set the stage for the existence of classes, a class forms only as members of an aggregate become engaged in a common struggle against another class. Hence conflict plays an important role for through it group identity and a "we" and "they" feeling develop.

[32] Marx and Engels, "The Communist Manifesto," in Marx, *Capital, The Communist Manifesto, and Other Writings,* ed. by Max Eastman (New York: The Modern Library, 1932), p. 321.

[33] Cf. Dahrendorf's view that any groups at different positions in an authority structure may constitute classes (Dahrendorf, *Class and Class Conflict in Industrial Society*). This is also our approach, as discussed in Chapter I.

We may assume that the owners of the means of production, especially the large capitalists, form a class. Not only are they likely to be conscious of their interests, but the various aspects of society, government, the law, the arts, literature, and so on, reflect their ideas, are dominated by them, and serve their ends. The capitalists not only exploit the workers but they are quick to put down any attempts to challenge their power; moreover, they have control of most of the resources of society.

Among the circumstances which favor class formation are the following:

a. *Structural changes,* such as concentration of property among a few capitalists, growing deprivation of the proletariat, and the increasing polarization of the two groups.

b. *Intransigence by the ruling class.* By preventing changes which threaten its interests it allows conditions under (a) to worsen.

c. *Conditions which facilitate communication among the proletariat,* such as working and living in close proximity with other employees.

d. *The organization of "combinations," or unions.* This occurs in the early stage of class formation.

e. *Agitators and ideologists,* who are likely to be disaffected members of the bourgeoisie.

Circumstances which work against class formation, in addition to the converse of the above, are:

a. The acceptance by the proletariat of the ideas and values of the bourgeoisie, and consequently, the development of a *"false" consciousness.*

b. *Conflict among workers,* along occupational, ethnic, or other lines.

c. *A high degree of social mobility,* as for example, in industrialized nations such as the United States.

d. *Cooptation:* the ruling class allows in talented working class individuals, thus eliminating potential proletarian leaders.

6. *Class conflict.* With the formation of classes, class conflict is *political* conflict. This must be distinguished from *economic* conflict, as in the case of an attempt to get an employer to reduce the number of hours worked per day. If on the other hand the attempt is to get a legislature to require the change, then the conflict is political, and hence class conflict. The proletariat becomes a class as they become a political party. The main point is that only through political conflict can basic institutional changes be brought about.

7. *The classless society; communism.* The final class struggle will institute a new social order in which there will be commom ownership of the means of production, and the absence of classes and class conflict, alienation, and deprivation.

There are some ambiguities and weaknesses in Marxian doctrine regarding the revolution and the classless society. For example, the chain of events and the final outcome are supposed to be inevitable; yet they are to be helped along by agitators and party organizers. A far more serious defect, however, is his definition of private or bourgeois property, for class formation, class conflict, and alienation, as well as the classless nature of the ultimate stage of society, communism, depend on it. Ralf Dahrendorf and Schumpeter strongly criticize Marx's definition due to its narrowness: it does not allow for the existence of authority relations and differences in power which are part of social organization. Thus Marx avoided the sociological problem of power and authority which we would expect to find in any social system regardless of the presence or absence of private property.[34]

In present-day capitalist industrial nations ownership of the means of production, particularly in the case of large enterprises, is not individual but diffused through many stockholders. The enterprises are run by managers who are not always substantial shareholders. Yet we find antagonism and conflict between management and workers, alienation, and other problems. This suggests that the key may be authority relations and power over the distribution of social goods rather than ownership of property. Although there was a trend toward corporate ownership in Marx's time—such arrangements were called joint-stock companies—he did not realize or at least did not deal with its full significance.[35]

There were other writers who were interested in the nature of group relations in capitalist industrial society, including conflict and social control. They were very much concerned with the ramifications of the Industrial and the French Revolutions, and as with Marx their theories reflect this interest. Similarly their outlook and concepts were influenced by their philosophic-political orientations which in turn were related to how they viewed man and society. We examine below the work of a number of early scholars who were important for stratification and class theory as well as for the development of sociology: Auguste Comte, Herbert Spencer, Vilfredo Pareto, Gaetano Mosca, Emile Durkheim, and Max Weber. Some of their theories were developed as a reaction against those of Marx;[36] however most of these writers also reacted against the individualism of the economic liberals and the rationalism of the Enlightenment.[37]

[34] Dahrendorf, *op. cit.*, pp. 21, 30–31 and Schumpeter, *op. cit.*, pp. 19 ff.

[35] Dahrendorf, *op. cit.*, p. 21.

[36] See Zeitlin, *op. cit.*, pp. 321–322.

[37] Nisbet, *op. cit.*

Auguste Comte

If Saint-Simon's ideas tended to be conservative, Comte's (1798–1857) were more so. He argued that political evils were due to ideas and social manners and that a moral reorganization was necessary, not a tampering with existing institutions. Criticism of these institutions, particularly by laymen, leads to disorganization and anarchy. He believed there were invariable laws which governed natural phenomena and that resignation to them was necessary even though this meant maintenance of the status quo and the acceptance of existing evils.

Comte renounced the transcendental aspect of philosophical analysis for he saw society as basically a complex of facts governed by general laws. His positivistic approach sought to counteract the negative or destructive aspects of rationalism.[38] The study of society, he felt, should be treated like any other field of scientific investigation. He developed a system of analysis, although he plagiarized several key ideas from Saint-Simon, among them positivism.[39] This system he labelled *Sociology*.

The positivism of the Enlightenment made use of facts to show that contemporary government and society were not advancing people's happiness; thus it attacked the religious and metaphysical conceptions that were ideological supports of the *ancien régime*.[40] Comte's positivistic sociology, however, used the facts to justify the existing social order. In contrast to dialectical laws which would lead to conflict he held that positivistic laws would lead to stability.

While Comte believed it was necessary to improve the condition of the lower class, this must be done without destroying class barriers which he felt were indispensible to the economic order. Class conflict might be reduced if not eliminated through a moral reconciliation of the classes; nevertheless the imposition of a moral authority between the working classes and the leaders of society was required. He urged the nationalization of labor and the establishment of public enterprises, although they would be under the control of private industry. Difficulties and problems would work themselves out since the various components of the social order such as government operate under eternal laws; consequently readjustments would take place painlessly and automatically since these eternal laws work toward the irresistable progress of mankind. And inevitable progress would be shown by the fact that each historical level represents a higher stage of development than the past one.

---

[38] Zeitlin, *op. cit.*, pp. 73–74; Marcuse, *op. cit.*, pp. 340, 345–46; and Robert A. Nisbet, "The French Revolution and the Rise of Sociology in France," *American Journal of Sociology*, 69 (September 1943), 160–161.

[39] Zeitlin, *op. cit.*, pp. 57–58.

[40] Marcuse, *op. cit.*, pp. 341–342.

Yet, despite Comte's lip service to science his system expounded the values, sentiments, and interests of the bourgeoisie.[41]

It should be noted that eventually Comte's view of the science of sociology as grounded in a deterministic theory of inevitable historical progress changed. Yet he retained the idea of social progress and still saw sociology as a predictive science; however, he began to concentrate on the sources of solidarity and sought to understand the manner in which it came about. From Saint-Simon he absorbed the notion that society was constituted and sustained by a body of common beliefs, not by rational self-interest as championed by the laissez faire economists. Yet he brought together elements of the liberals' economic conception of society and the division of labor, and the conservatives' view of society as semi-autonomous, solidary communities. He synthesized elements of these opposing perspectives, holding that the division of labor was a basis of cooperation and solidarity. Moreover such socialized labor together with intermediate associations transformed egoism into the bases of social life, and hence, solidarity.[42]

Comte's belief in the importance of smaller associations such as the family, community, and church which mediate between the individual and the state further underscores the influence of conservative thought on his theories. He felt that neither the individual nor the state can be the base of a true social system. His concern with intermediate society helped direct sociological interest to the study of groups. "Stated briefly," Nisbet writes, "what Comte achieved was the reinstatement of the social group in social thought." [43]

Herbert Spencer

Spencer (1820–1903) saw classes as conflict groups. Although he felt they were not particularly desirable they were necessary, given the present stage of society's development. But the conditions which create them and the difficulties they are responsible for would disappear as society reached a higher stage. He set forth an elaborate exposition of the organismic theory of society, and saw progress as the automatic working of the general processes of the laws of evolution. Spencer held that organized society functions for the purposes of military expansion, then industrial development, and finally ethical improvement.

The main reason for classes, which he described as antagonistic groups following their self-interest, is individual egoism which leads to

[41] Zeitlin, *op. cit.*, pp. 76, 78; and Marcuse, *op. cit.*, pp. 346–347, 350, 354–360.

[42] David Cohen, "Comte's Changing Sociology," *American Journal of Sociology*, 71 (September 1965), 168–177.

[43] Nisbet, "The French Revolution and the Rise of Sociology," *op. cit.*, p. 161.

the egoism of the class the individuals form; thus class antagonism is based on selfishness. This, he writes, ". . . generates a joint effort to get an undue share of the aggregate proceeds of social activity." In turn this leads to similar action by other classes; "The aggressive tendency of each class, thus produced, has to be balanced by like aggressive tendencies of other classes." He saw the basic division between the ruling or regulating classes and the artisans and other workers.[44]

The selfishness and its attendent narrowmindedness which he called "class bias" dismayed him. Yet he felt society derives good from this in that each division and subdivision is kept strong enough to carry out its functions. Thus he implies that self-interest and group consciousness to further it is a necessary part of the division of labor. Although Spencer believed that unions, strikes, and other methods of constraint were unavoidable consequences of self-defense he deplored them and was against unions. His basic reason was that these organizations and their actions hurt the majority of the population. Yet he scored the "regulative classes" for undue wealth and idleness as well as for their own class bias.

Spencer felt that the evils of the society were faults of human nature and until human nature could be improved the evils would remain. Thus the antagonism the subordinated have toward their superiors is ill-founded, for if employee and employer switched places the individual who was now the employee would be antagonistic toward the employer. While he did not particularly like the fact of class subordination he felt that since it benefited the majority it was all right.

Although he believed that better forms of industrial organization were possible wherein, for example, workers would govern themselves, receive a higher share of the profits, and sell their products at lower prices, he did not think this was very likely. For the masses are generally ". . . neither sufficiently provident, nor sufficiently conscientious, nor sufficiently intelligent." [45] It is for these several reasons, he states, that ". . . the existing type of industrial organization, like the existing type of society is about as good as existing human nature allows. The evils there are in it are nothing but the evils brought round on men by their own imperfections." [46]

Spencer denied the possibility of ameliorating social problems through remedial legislation, believing that the state should not interfere in human conduct. He also cautioned those who are displeased with present conditions and want rapid change. A given social order has "fitness," otherwise it would not exist; it is probably the best for the given time and place, although this does not negate the possibility of improvement. Betterment can occur but like the maturation of the child it de-

[44] Herbert Spencer, *The Study of Sociology* (New York: D. Appleton and Co., 1916; first pub. in 1873), pp. 219–238. The quotations are from p. 220.

[45] *Ibid.*, pp. 224–227. The quotation is from p. 227.

[46] *Ibid.*, p. 229.

velops through small successive modifications. He insists that radical attempts at change cannot succeed; failure, frustration, and the harming of the social organism will result. Visionaries serve the useful function of providing stimulus for progress; yet successful change requires greatly moderated expectations with undiminished efforts. What is necessary, Spencer concludes, is the ". . . uniting of philanthropic energy with philosophic calm."[47]

Vilfredo Pareto

Pareto (1848–1923) countered Marx's conception of class struggle with the theory of elites and their circulation. He saw an elite in every branch of society but his primary interest was the governing elite, particularly the division between it and the non-elite. He was also interested in how it maintained itself, and how it kept the society viable. Pareto attacked the principles of the Enlightenment; for him "reason" was negligible if not altogether irrelevant.

The two-model society he posited—the elite and the subject class—retains its form even though there are changes in membership, with the elite of the lower class rising into the governing group. The movement occurs when the governing elite begins to degenerate and needs an infusion of new blood; it then takes in the best elements of the lower class. This not only revitalizes the ruling elite but by the cooptation helps align the interests of potential lower-class revolutionaries with those of the rulers. The circulation is continuous and thus provides a "safety valve"; it becomes critical when there is an accumulation of superior elements in the subject class and inferior elements in the elite. Then the failure to coopt is likely to lead to disturbances and revolution. One of the problems is that a decaying elite tends to avoid the use of force and tries to buy off its adversaries; if an elite is unable or unwilling to use force it will be defeated.

Pareto's concept of the good society is a highly stratified one run by the elite, that is, those who are superior. They are superior not only in ability but in the willingness to use force whenever necessary. In addition, the elite will constantly take in the best elements of the lower class. The elite-subject group arrangement is inevitable, for even if there is a revolution which deposes the ruling elite, the revolutionary leaders will become the new elite and those they govern will be the subject class.[48]

[47] *Ibid.*, pp. 362–386. The quotation is from p. 367.

[48] See Zeitlin, *op. cit.*, pp. 159–190 and T. B. Bottomore, *Elites and Society* (Harmondsworth, Middlesex, Eng.: Penguin Books, Ltd., 1966), especially pp. 48–67.

Gaetano Mosca

Mosca (1858–1941) seeks to refute Marx's concept of a ruling class by demonstrating that there is a continuous circulation of elites, and by the claim that a classless society is impossible since there must always be a small group which rules. Even under a representative system the representatives eventually become the masters and not the servants of those they are supposed to represent; this is particularly true in a large political community since only a small proportion can rule. Yet it is necessary to have a check on those in power otherwise they become despotic. The ruling minority has certain advantages over the mass: they are organized, have superior qualities, and are in control of important social forces. Also there are common values, beliefs, sentiments, and habits which are the result of the history and culture of the community; these make people receptive to the assumptions of the ruling class and help legitimize its rule. The elite doesn't simply rule by force or fraud, it represents in some sense the interests and purpose of important and influential groups in the society. In modern times the elite is intimately connected with the society through a sub-elite, a larger group such as the "new middle class" including managers, scientists, civil servants, and other white-collar workers.

Mosca argued for pluralism and cautioned against the preeminence of any single social force such as the church, large moneyed interests, or social democracy. He felt liberalism was important since freedom such as that of the press, worship, and speech were restraints on power. Also it was necessary to balance aristocratic and democratic tendencies, but particularly the latter. He was against universal suffrage, saw the mass as a common herd whose behavior is governed by sentiments and passions, and viewed human nature as base, selfish, and brutish.[49]

Emile Durkheim

Durkheim (1858–1917) was very much concerned with the problems of industrial society. Yet, although he wrote extensively on the professions,[50] he hardly dealt with class and gave inadequate attention to conflict, strife, and group divisions in social life. He was concerned with the "whole" of society and ignored problems of conflict and antagonism

[49] Zeitlin, *op. cit.*, pp. 195–215; and Bottomore, *op. cit.*, pp. 11, 48–67.

[50] See Emile Durkheim, *The Division of Labor*, trans. by George Simpson (Glencoe, Ill.: The Free Press, 1947; first pub. in 1893).

within the parts, nor did he adequately analyze the state or its coercive aspects.[51]

Durkheim conceived of society in classical conservative terms: political society, or the state, was formed by the coming together of large numbers of secondary social groups subject to the same authority. He saw society as an organic whole which was held together by moral ideas. Conflict and disorder he felt were not due to the decline of the old moral order but existed instead because there was not an appropriate new one. The "collective conscience" which characterized primitive society was now enfeebled; however the growing division of labor which gives rise to organic solidarity could provide the necessary moral basis for society.[52] Yet he assumed that the major social norms held for the total society and did not consider that they might be those of the dominant group which are imposed on the subordinate groups.[53]

He acknowledged great inequality and sought to reduce it by suggesting, for example, that inheritances be abolished. He saw the difficulties of society as basically moral and not structural, however, holding that even if inequality were eliminated there would still be problems such as anarchy. It was the growing division of labor that could lead to a higher solidarity without a fundamental reorganization of society. With moral unity and solidarity there would still be classes and strata and although conflict would not be completely eliminated it would be modified. He saw a homogeneity of interests, including those between capitalists and workers and believed it was necessary for the individual to adjust to his role or "destiny." That task, he felt, was the function of education. Durkheim despised and feared restlessness, social conflict, and anarchy and argued that a strong moral force was needed which was capable of moderating and curbing egoism and special interests. He stressed the importance of establishing a moral code for his main concern was anomie, not inequality. Consequently he emphasized "restraints" or social control and held that society is the end to be served for if it operates well then the individual benefits.

The increase in the division of labor produced negative consequences only in its pathological form. Thus, business failures showed a lack of adjustment of various functions, and class conflict was the result of a forced division of labor where the lower class was no longer satisfied with its role. The answer was for the division of labor to be based on natural capacities; occupational guilds should be established with precise rules regarding the rights and duties of workers, and the employers and employees in their respective groups should curb selfish interests and

[51] Lewis A. Coser, "Durkheim's Conservatism and Its Implications for His Sociological Theory," in Kurt H. Wolff, ed., *Emile Durkheim, 1858–1917* (Columbus: The Ohio State University Press, 1960), pp. 215–216, 221.

[52] Zeitlin, *op. cit.*, pp. 237–238, 241, 245–246, 265.

[53] Coser, *op. cit.*, p. 218.

think of the larger whole. Also, planning together with mutual understanding was necessary. The result would be a moderation of conflict and the solidarity of society would be enhanced.[54]

Durkheim's conception of human nature was also conservative: culture, civilization, and the maintenance of social order require a curbing of individual propensities and desires. Furthermore, he felt that change must be slow and should be introduced piecemeal, without destroying the fabric of society.[55] His schema, including the emphasis on the social nature of man in terms of societal integration, was a doctrine for the submission of the disadvantaged to existing inequalities.[56]

Max Weber

Like Marx, Weber (1864–1920) was primarily interested in the origin and nature of modern capitalism. Weber was very much aware of the socialistic movements in the Europe of his time, and for him Marxist socialist thought was the most important of the several schools. He followed Marxist terminology in calling the new organization of work activities "capitalism," and in part shared the Marxists' negative evaluation.[57] On the one hand, Marx emphasized material interests and conflict and instability in capitalism. He conceived of it as a concrete historical system, extending it back into its feudal past and forward in terms of its replacement by communism. On the other hand, Weber rejected the materialistic concept of history as a causal explanation of historical reality. Instead, he sought to develop a scheme of generalized analytical theory and was interested in comparative rather than simply historical information; thus he was concerned with the methodology of the social sciences. Also, unlike the Marxists he carefully distinguished between structure and process; he was primarily interested in studying the interdependence of values and other social phenomena.[58]

Nevertheless, Weber's work should not be viewed as a refutation of Marx; rather, it shows the inadequacy of some of the latter's revolutionary conclusions. In addition, Weber "rounds out" and supplements the methodology of Marx.[59] Weber held that in both the natural and social sciences "total reality" can never be grasped, for some sort of abstraction is needed in either case. This abstraction, together with the selection of problems to study and the phenomena and relationships to be analyzed, are always influenced by the values of the investigator, the

[54] Zeitlin, op. cit., pp. 245, 252–253, 258–260.

[55] Coser, op. cit., pp. 212–213, 226.

[56] Zeitlin, op. cit., p. 263.

[57] Talcott Parsons, "Max Weber 1864–1964," American Sociological Review, 30 (April 1965), 172.

[58] Ibid., pp. 172, 173, 175.

[59] Zeitlin, op. cit., pp. 111–112.

sponsors of the research, or others. Even the concept of culture is a value concept and knowledge of cultural reality is always knowledge from a particular point of view.[60]

Weber contributed greatly to understanding class, pointing out that classes are not communities but that they are formed on the basis of communalization. He linked them to the market situation, which allowed him to distinguish between class and status groups.[61] His treatment of authority relations and *Herrschaftsverband*, or imperatively coordinated associations,[62] was further explicated by Dahrendorf and provides the basis for the latter's important contribution to the analysis of class conflict.[63] Weber's cognizance of the separation of ownership and management is extremely important for class analysis in societies in which corporations are a significant form of business enterprise. This separation and his emphasis on authority relations make such analysis applicable to non-capitalist industrial societies as well.

Weber's attention to the economic and legal organization of society, the highly rational aspect of industrialism, and the amount of freedom owners and managers have in disposing of the goods produced, provide helpful guides for analyzing class behavior. In addition, he dealt with conditions relative to the accumulation of wealth and control over the productive process, which may result in tremendous influence over government and other institutions. He also distinguished between "open" and "closed" classes, observed that social mobility breaks down group solidarity, and recognized the growing importance of semi-skilled workers.

The work of Weber has been extremely influential for the contemporary analysis of stratification and class. American scholars, in particular, have found his theories much more attractive than Marx's.[64]

Summary

The writers we have examined above provide the intellectual heritage for present-day students of stratification and class; moreover, they have had an important influence in the shaping of the discipline of sociology. It is to these contemporary analysts of stratification and class that we next turn.

[60] *Ibid.*, pp. 112–115.

[61] See Weber, *From Max Weber: Essays in Sociology*, trans. and ed. by Hans H. Gerth and C. Wright Mills (New York: Oxford University Press, 1958), pp. 180–195.

[62] Weber, *Max Weber: The Theory of Social and Economic Organization*, trans. by A. M. Henderson and Parsons (London: The Free Press of Glencoe, 1947), pp. 153, 324–328.

[63] See Dahrendorf, *Class and Class Conflict in Industrial Society*. See also our discussion in Chapter I.

[64] Celia S. Heller, "Theories of Stratification," in Heller, ed., *Structured Social Inequality* (New York: The Macmillan Co., 1969), pp. 9–10. Cf. Gabriel Kolko, *The Triumph of Conservatism* (Chicago: Quadrangle Paperbacks, 1963), pp. 294–300.

Chapter XI.   The Shaping of Perspectives: 2. Modern Writers

We have looked at early writers who were important for stratification and class as well as for sociology itself. There were other influences which included the German historical school, field research in such areas as social medicine, demography, and social reform, and the development of the social survey.[1] But the writers we discussed in the preceding chapter contributed the basic perspectives for the contemporary study of stratification and class, and sociology. They were all Europeans, yet the bulk of subsequent research on stratification and class has been undertaken in the United States.

However, there was relatively little interest in these topics until the 1930's in spite of clear-cut evidence of stratification, classes, and class conflict which goes back to Colonial America, as we show in the next chapter. Also, until very recently research on stratification and class has largely ignored Karl Marx, and sociologists paid attention to only limited aspects of Max Weber. The slighting of Marx is curious considering that class interests and conflict were clearly evident not only in early America but throughout its history, particularly toward the end of the 19th century. It was not until the 1930's that he was "rediscovered," due mainly to the Great Depression, but also because of the influx of refugee scholars from Europe who were more knowledgeable about Marx.[2]

Early American Writers

The "fathers" of American sociology—William G. Sumner (1840–1910); Albion W. Small (1854–1926); Franklin H. Giddings (1855–1931); Charles H. Cooley (1864–1929); Edward A. Ross (1866–1951); and Lester F. Ward

[1] See Donald G. MacRae, "Social Stratification, A Trend Report and Bibliography," *Current Sociology*, 2 (1953–1954), pp. 7–35.

[2] Marxist writers contributed very little in terms of adding to Marx's formulations. Much effort was devoted to conflict between the orthodox and revisionist interpretations of his theories. See Harry W. Laidler, *History of Socialism* (New York: Thomas Y. Crowell, 1968), pp. 237–276; and Raymond Aron, *Main Currents in Sociological Thought* (New York: Basic Books, 1965), Vol. I, pp. 177–179.

(1841–1913)—varied in their interest in stratification and class. Most were well aware of the phenomena and a few paid attention to Marx's theories; but they were more likely to be influenced by the work of Thorstein Veblen (1857–1929).[3] An extremely forceful writer, his *Theory of the Leisure Class* as well as his other writings dealt with several aspects of stratification and class.[4]

Sumner was very much interested in class and class change. He saw the desire for property as fundamental and providing the basis for class conflict which he felt was inevitable, views which were in accordance with his strong belief in individualism and laissez faire. Although he takes only slight note of Marx some of his analyses are in agreement with Marxism: political phenomena, including government, have an economic basis; the state represents the specific interests of a class; industry must become plutocratic to survive; the middle class would disappear leaving plutocracy vs. proletariat. Sumner listed the classes in a modern democracy as the "high bourgeoisie," "the great 'middle-class' of farmers and workers," and the "hungry proletariat." Each class has its own folkways, although some folkways such as the "cult of success" are classless. Social change occurs largely through the masses who are the most important carriers of the folkways and the mores.

Small was also greatly interested in class and believed class conflict was a major dynamic of social change. He saw a basic dichotomy between the rulers and the ruled and the haves and have-nots but he posed a three-way schema: the privileged, the middle class, and the poor.[5] Even though Small was a student of Marx, and in spite of his interest in class, he contributed very little to its understanding.[6]

Giddings stressed the psychic forces in social change, and was concerned with how the "consciousness of kind" hindered class formation. Although he emphasized the significance of class for social science his work sheds little light upon the details of class phenomena.[7]

For Cooley, who studied communication as a basic aspect of the social process, class constituted a major portion of his work. He felt that there would always be classes because of the stratification of wealth and opportunity, and that there was the danger that class divisions may become hereditary. This could occur through the desire to provide for one's offspring and the development of "caste sentiments." Social mobil-

---

[3] Charles H. Page, *Class and American Sociology* (New York: Dial Press, 1940), especially pp. 25, and 249–250.

[4] See, e.g., Thorstein Veblen, *The Theory of the Leisure Class* (New York: Mentor Books, 1953, first pub. in 1899), the *Theory of Business Enterprise* (New York: New American Library, 1958), and *Absentee Ownership and Business Enterprise in Recent Times* (New York: Viking Press, 1923).

[5] Page, *op. cit.*, pp. 118–130.

[6] Louis Wirth, "Social Stratification and Social Mobility in the United States," *Current Sociology*, 2 (1953–1954), 279–284.

[7] Page, *op. cit.*, pp. 167–170, 180.

ity, therefore, was an important safeguard. Cooley studied different types of class conflict although he is not consistent in its treatment. He also examined class consciousness and felt that the upper classes possess it while the lower are exploited because they lack it. He disagreed with the Marxian idea of two opposed classes for he felt that through improved communication there would be an enlargement of consciousness and a feeling of community would develop among the conflicting classes.[8]

Ross acknowledged and dealt with classes and class conflict, holding that economic factors were fundamental bases. He noted, for example, that much racial conflict is essentially competition between economic classes, often masked by racial prejudice and hostility. Ross studied revolution and indicated that it can be eliminated only if class exploitation is ended. He opted for greater opportunity, believing that a high rate of mobility leads toward a meritocracy and also serves as a safety valve. He expected that enlightened public opinion would lead to reform and saw a trend away from rigid classes and class conflict.[9]

Attention is paid to "parasitic classes" which exploit others through various means of coercive social control; they also use symbolic means including the ceremonial. Ross dealt with class consciousness or "consciousness of kind" and saw it as an important subject matter of sociology. However, there is little on class psychology in his writings that is original; also, his analysis of class contains a number of contradictions.[10]

Ward had an intense interest in class and class change, and saw the world as class-divided, with class exploitation and conflict. He wrote that capitalists controlled the state, and differentiated between the classes that produce and the classes that do not ("accessories to production" vs. "parasites"). Ward took into account the subjective aspect of class and described what Veblen later called emulation and conspicuous consumption, and dealt with class consciousness. Yet Ward was ignorant of Marx.[11]

Charles H. Page concludes that although early sociologists in the United States were interested in class phenomena, its analysis occupied a decidedly secondary place in their work.[12]

As sociology developed into a discipline, there was decreasing interest in stratification and class. Milton M. Gordon notes that by the 1920's there was "little class research in progress, a minimum of theoretical consideration of the precise meaning of the term, and practically no recognition of the class framework as a major area of investigation."[13]

[8] *Ibid.*, pp. 189–209.

[9] *Ibid.*, pp. 215, 217, 223–225, 229, 231–234, 237.

[10] *Ibid.*, pp. 226, 233–235, 238.

[11] *Ibid.*, pp. 32–56.

[12] *Ibid.*, pp. 249–254.

[13] Milton M. Gordon, *Social Class in American Sociology* (Durham, N.C.: Duke University Press, 1958), p. 8.

This lack of concern was generally true of most other social scientists with the important exceptions of Veblen and Pitirim A. Sorokin; however, their work was largely neglected at the time.[14] Sorokin's work on social mobility [15] exhaustively examines differences among the strata, details the several types of mobility, and shows how structural conditions in the society affect their rates. While he focuses on stratification, he is aware of class formation and conflict.[16] But this book, as was true of the work of earlier writers, did not stimulate any major research.[17] All in all, Harold W. Pfautz observes, American sociology neglected stratification and class since the time of the "founding fathers." [18]

It was with the Great Depression of the 1930's when capitalism seemed at the verge of collapse that many sociologists and other scholars turned to the analysis of stratification and class.

> As the depression deepened, sociologists began to recognize widespread poverty and immobility, and they began to question the ability of private enterprise and political democracy to maintain prosperity and to minimize economic and social inequality.[19]

During the 1930's research which analyzed the power of corporations and the monopolization of industries began to make its appearance. An incisive study of stratification, class interests and conflict in a typical community ("Middletown") came out. Scholars examined the decrease in occupational mobility; ideological differences among occupational categories; growing income differentials; the breaking down of the social, economic, and political solidity of the "middle class," and the proletarianization of the labor force.[20]

---

[14] Wirth, "Social Stratification and Social Mobility in the United States," p. 280.

[15] Pitirim A. Sorokin, *Social and Cultural Mobility* (Glencoe, Ill.: The Free Press, 1959; first pub. in 1927). Some of Sorokin's contributions are examined in Chapter II, where we discuss social mobility.

[16] *Ibid.*, pp. 438–440. See also Sorokin, *Contemporary Sociological Theories* (New York: Harper Torchbooks, 1956; first pub. in 1928), pp. 525–526, 541–544.

[17] John Pease, William H. Form, and Joan Huber Rytina, "Ideological Currents in American Stratification Literature," *The American Sociologist*, 5 (May 1970), 129.

[18] Harold W. Pfautz, "The Current Literature on Social Stratification: Critique and Bibliography," *American Journal of Sociology*, 58 (January 1953), 391.

[19] Pease *et al., loc. cit.*

[20] *Ibid.* The following, cited by Pease *et al.*, are illustrative of these studies: Adolf A. Berle and Gardiner C. Means, *The Modern Corporation and Private Property* (New York: Macmillan, 1933); The Temporary National Economic Committee Reports, especially *Economic Power and Political Pressures*, Monograph No. 26 (Washington, D.C.: Government Printing Office, 1941) and *Competition and Monopoly in American Industry*, Monograph No. 21 (Washington, D.C.: Government Printing Office, 1940); Robert S. and Helen Merrell Lynd, *Middletown in Transition* (New York: Harcourt, Brace and World, 1937); Frank W. Taussig and Carl S. Joslyn, *American Business Leaders* (New York: Macmillan, 1932); Percy E. Davidson and Dewey H. Anderson, *Occupational Mobility in an American Community* (Stanford, Calif.: Stanford University Press, 1937); Anderson and Davidson, *Ballots and the Democratic Class Struggle* (Stanford, Calif.: Stanford University Press, 1943); Alfred W. Jones, *Life, Liberty, and Property* (Philadelphia: J. B. Lippincott, 1941); Lewis Corey, *The Decline of American Capitalism* (New York: Covici-Friede, 1934) and *The Crisis of the Middle Class* (New York:

W. Lloyd Warner and Post-Depression Writers

The end of the Depression was greeted by a focus on status, prestige, and esteem. The work of W. Lloyd Warner and his associates set the theme, and in the 1940's "[s]tratification was viewed not so much as a matter of economic and political inequality as a matter of difference in values and style of life." [21] Their work slighted class phenomena; conflict over the distribution of social goods—except as regards status, prestige, and esteem—is largely ignored. Thus Warner neglects the history of the communities he studied which often exhibited quite bitter economic and political conflict.[22] Also, he overgeneralizes from small communities, insisting that their concern and gossip over status distinctions and who associates with whom are just as meaningful in the large urban centers.[23] A host of critics has pointed out these shortcomings as well as others: unclear conceptualization, methodological errors, and in general quite evident biases favoring the status quo. These biases are revealed in the posing of questions, selection of informants, and interpretation of data.[24] Nevertheless Warner's work has stimulated a large amount of research on stratification in sociology and related fields. This has added to knowledge about stratification and differences in life chances among the strata. In addition, contributions have been made in such areas as research on ethnic groups and in education.[25] But in spite of this most of the research continues to ignore the power and economic dimensions of stratification. John Pease and his associates comment that

---

Covici-Friede, 1935); Alfred M. Bingham, *Insurgent America* (New York: Harper, 1935); and Goetz A. Briefs, *The Proletariat* (New York: McGraw-Hill, 1937).

[21] Pease *et al.*, "Ideological Currents in American Stratification Literature," pp. 129–130. See, e.g., W. Lloyd Warner and Paul S. Lunt, *The Social Life of a Modern Community* (New Haven, Conn.: Yale University Press, 1941); and Warner and Associates, *Democracy in Jonesville* (New York: Harper, 1949).

[22] See Stephen Thernstrom, " 'Yankee City' Revisited: The Perils of Historical Naïveté," *American Sociological Review*, 30 (April 1965), 234–242.

[23] Warner *et al.*, *Democracy in Jonesville*, pp. xiv–xv.

[24] See, e.g., C. Wright Mills, Review of *The Social Life of a Modern Community*, *American Sociological Review*, 7 (April 1942) 263–271; Harold W. Pfautz and Otis D. Duncan, "A Critical Evaluation of Warner's Work in Community Stratification," *American Sociological Review*, 15 (April 1950), 205–215; Seymour M. Lipset and Reinhard Bendix, "Social Status and Social Structure: A Re-Examination of Data and Interpretations, I," *British Journal of Sociology*, 2 (June 1951), 150–168 and "Social Status and Social Structure: A Re-Examination of Data and Interpretations, II" (September 1951), 230–254; and Ruth R. Kornhauser, "The Warner Approach to Social Stratification," in Bendix and Lipset, eds., *Class, Status, and Power* (Glencoe, Ill.: The Free Press, 1953), pp. 224–255.

[25] See, e.g., St. Claire Drake and Horace R. Cayton, *Black Metropolis* (New York: Harper Torchbooks, 1962), Vols. I and II and Bernice L. Neugarten, "Social Class Friendship Among School Children," *American Journal of Sociology*, 51 (January 1946), 305–313.

generally, American sociologists seized two things from the Warner school: a recipe for measuring . . . socio-economic status . . . and a rationale for the empirical study of social status in the small community. The study of community status that Warner pioneered has been continuous, and most of it has merely aped him.[26]

The majority of post-Depression studies in the area of stratification have been descriptive. But when researchers concern themselves with this phenomenon they usually take the functionalist point of view: stratification with its inequities is a functional necessity of all complex societies; it places people in the social structure and motivates them to carry out needed tasks. It is viewed as an integrating structural attribute of social systems and interclass relations are seen as accommodative.[27]

Since the end of World War II research on stratification and class has greatly increased. While it covers a wide range of interests and approaches these are the major trends: a refinement of occupational prestige scales; the use of national samples in survey research studies; a telling criticism of the functional theory of stratification and some clarifications and modifications; a shift from concern with prestige to power, although this was temporary; a renewed interest in social mobility; and a "rediscovery" of poverty.[28]

[26] Pease *et al., op. cit.,* p. 130.

[27] Pfautz, "The Current Literature on Social Stratification," p. 392. Examples are Kingsley Davis and Wilbert E. Moore, "Some Principles of Stratification," *American Sociological Review,* 10 (April 1945), 364–391; Talcott Parsons, "Social Classes and Class Conflict in the Light of Recent Sociological Theory," *American Economic Review,* 39 (May 1949), pp. 16–26 and Parsons, *The Social System* (Glencoe, Ill.: The Free Press, 1951), pp. 132 and 172; and W. Lloyd Warner, "A Methodological Note," in Drake and Cayton, *Black Metropolis,* Vol. II, pp. 769–872.

[28] Pease *et al.,* "Ideological Currents in American Stratification Literature," 130–132. The following are examples of these trends. *Occupational prestige:* Cecil C. North and Paul K. Hatt, "Jobs and Evaluations: A Popular Evaluation," *Opinion News,* 9 (September 1947), 3–13; Robert W. Hodge, Paul M. Siegel, and Peter H. Rossi, "Occupational Prestige in the United States: 1925–1963," in Bendix and Lipset, eds., *Class, Status, and Power* (rev. ed.; New York: The Free Press, 1966), pp. 322–334; and Hodge, Donald J. Treiman, and Rossi, "A Comparative Study of Occupational Prestige," in Bendix and Lipset, eds., *Class, Status, and Power,* rev. ed., *op. cit.,* pp. 309–321. *National samples:* Richard Centers, *The Psychology of Social Classes* (Princeton, N.J.: Princeton University Press, 1961). *Criticism of functional theory:* Melvin Tumin, "Some Principles of Stratification: A Critical Analysis," *American Sociological Review,* 18 (August 1953), 387–394; Tumin, "On Inequality," *American Sociological Review,* 28 (February 1963), 19–26; and Walter Buckley, "On Equitable Inequality," *American Sociological Review,* 28 (October 1963), 799–801. *Studies of power:* Floyd Hunter, *Community Power Structure* (Chapel Hill. N.C.: University of North Carolina Press, 1953); and C. Wright Mills, *The Power Elite* (New York: Oxford University Press, 1956). *Social mobility:* Stuart Adams, "Regional Differences in Vertical Mobility in a High Status Occupation," *American Sociological Review,* 15 (April 1950), 228–235; Natalie Rogoff, *Recent Trends in Occupational Mobility* (Glencoe, Ill.: The Free Press, 1953); W. Lloyd Warner and James C. Abegglen, *Occupational Mobility in American Business and Industry, 1928–1952* (Minneapolis, Minn.: University of Minnesota Press, 1955); Lipset and Bendix, *Social Mobility in Industrial Society* (Berkeley and Los Angeles: University of California Press, 1959); and Peter M. Blau and Otis D. Duncan, *The American Occupational Structure* (New York: John Wiley & Sons, 1967). *Poverty:* H. Brand, "Poverty in the United States," *Dissent,* 7 (Winter 1960), 334–354;

In recent years a number of writers have confronted the problem of class in contemporary society as opposed to simply studying stratification. The most important works which deal with these phenomena in a comprehensive manner are by Ralf Dahrendorf and Stanislaw Ossowski.[29] Other important writers are Theodore Geiger, C. Wright Mills, Seymour M. Lipset, and Barrington Moore, Jr.[30]

As noted earlier, the Great Depression sparked interest in stratification and class. In recent years there has been a growing awareness of their importance because of the many instances of group conflict: ghetto riots, campus violence, demonstrations against the Indochina war and against the busing of school children, as well as the activities of militant groups such as the Black Panthers, National Organization of Women, and Pro-Life, an anti-abortion organization. In addition, much international conflict involves struggles over social goods and the frameworks of stratification and class are applicable.[31]

While the present-day research is adding to our knowledge of stratification and class, there is still a serious shortcoming: conceptual clarity. One would expect that with the long history of stratification, classes, and class conflict together with more than 17 decades of sociology, there would be a high degree of consensus and precision regarding these concepts. Unfortunately we do not find this in the work of contemporary sociologists.

How Sociologists View "Social Class" and "Social Stratification"

In general—and there are some notable exceptions—there is confusion regarding the two concepts; they are used interchangeably, and there seems to be almost a studied avoidance of class analysis. American sociologists in particular tend to focus on various aspects of stratification but neglect the causes, processes, and consequences of class formation and conflict.[32] More specifically, an examination of a number of works deal-

---

and Michael Harrington, *The Other America* (New York: Macmillan, 1963). Most of these works are cited by Pease *et al., op. cit.*

[29] Ralf Dahrendorf, *Class and Class Conflict in Industrial Society* (Stanford, Calif.: Stanford University Press, 1959) and Stanislaw Ossowski, *Class Structure in the Social Consciousness,* trans. by Sheila Patterson (New York: The Free Press of Glencoe, 1963).

[30] See Theodore Geiger, "Class Society in the Melting Pot," trans. by Celia S. Heller, in Heller, ed., *Structured Social Inequality* (New York: Macmillan, 1969), pp. 91–104; Mills, *The Power Elite;* Seymour M. Lipset, *Political Man* (New York: Doubleday), 1960; and Barrington Moore, Jr., *The Social Origins of Dictatorship and Democracy* (Boston: Beacon Press, 1967).

[31] See, e.g., Irving L. Horowitz, *Three Worlds of Development* (New York: Oxford University Press, 1966).

[32] See Pease *et al.,* "Ideological Currents in American Stratification Literature."

ing with class and stratification, and several introductory textbooks in sociology reveals the following: titles notwithstanding, *social stratification* remains the primary concern; the bases for ranking vary widely among the writers, with prestige being the single most important one; the terms "social stratification" and "social class" are most often used interchangeably, and the classical or conflict concept of class is largely ignored. This lack of clarity and consensus has been observed by many writers and, as Leonard Reissman has pointed out, in general there is a tendency to use operational definitions.[33]

In spite of the considerable amount of research during the past several decades,[34] there is still confusion in the use of the concepts of strati-

---

[33] Leonard Reissman, *Class in America* (New York: The Free Press of Glencoe, 1959), p. 230.

The works on stratification and class which were examined are Bernard Barber, *Social Stratification, a Comparative Analysis of Structure and Process* (New York: Harcourt, Brace & Co., 1957); John F. Cuber and William F. Kenkel, *Social Stratification in the United States* (New York: Appleton-Century-Crofts, 1954); Dahrendorf, *op. cit.*; Gordon, *Social Class in American Sociology*; Richard F. Hamilton, *Class and Politics in the United States* (New York: John Wiley & Sons, 1972); Joseph A. Kahl, *The American Class Structure* (New York: Rinehart, 1960); Gerhard Lenski, *Power and Privilege* (New York: McGraw-Hill, 1966); Judith Matras, *Social Inequality, Stratification, and Mobility* (Englewood Cliffs, N.J.: Prentice-Hall, 1975); Kurt B. Mayer and Walter Buckley, *Class and Society* (3rd ed.; New York: Random House, 1970); Ossowski, *op. cit.*; Karre Svalastoga, *Social Differentiation* (New York: David McKay Co., 1965); Melvin M. Tumin, *Social Stratification* (Englewood Cliffs, N.J.: Prentice-Hall, 1967), and W. Lloyd Warner, Marchia Meeker, and Kenneth Eells, *Social Class in America* (New York: Harper Torchbooks, 1960).

The following introductory textbooks in sociology were also examined: Robert Bierstedt, *The Social Order* (rev. ed.; New York: McGraw-Hill, 1970), pp. 434–462; Leonard Broom and Philip Selznick, *Sociology* (5th ed.; New York: Harper & Row, 1973), pp. 162–205; William J. Chambliss and Thomas E. Ryther, *Sociology: The Discipline and Its Direction* (New York: McGraw-Hill, 1975), pp. 38–42; 59–68 ff. Ely Chinoy, *Society* (New York: Random House, 1967), pp. 168–208; Paul B. Horton and Chester L. Hunt, *Sociology* (New York: McGraw-Hill, 1972), pp. 244–275; Lenski, *Human Societies* (New York: McGraw-Hill, 1970), pp. 42–44, 361–363, 384–409, 443–445, 496; Donald Light, Jr. and Suzanne Keller, *Sociology* (New York: Alfred A. Knopf, 1975), pp. 188–223; Ritchie P. Lowry and Robert P. Rankin, *Sociology* (New York: Charles Scribner's Sons, 1972); pp. 259–309; George A. Lundberg, Clarence C. Schrag and Otto N. Larsen, *Sociology* (3rd ed.; New York: Harper & Row, 1963), pp. 329–363; James B. McKee, *Introduction to Sociology* (New York: Holt, Rinehart, and Winston, 1974), pp. 198–217; William F. Ogburn and Meyer F. Nimkoff, *Sociology* (4th ed.; Boston: Houghton Mifflin, 1964), pp. 431–469; Everett K. Wilson, *Sociology* (2nd ed.; Homewood, Ill.: The Dorsey Press, 1971), pp. 250–293; and Raymond W. Mack and John Pease, *Sociology and Social Life* (5th ed.; New York: D. Van Nostrand Co., 1973), pp. 271–306.

The unclear and interchangeable use of these concepts is by no means limited to works which address themselves to stratification and class, or to the chapters on these topics in sociology textbooks. See, e.g., James S. Coleman, *Adolescent Society* (New York: The Free Press of Glencoe, 1961); and Jean E. Floud, A. H. Halsey, and F. M. Martin, *Social Class and Educational Opportunity* (London: William Henemann Ltd., 1958), pp. 4–8, 150–151. Nor is this usage limited to sociologists. See, e.g., Frank Riessman, *The Culturally Deprived Child* (New York: Harper Bros., 1962); Patricia C. Sexton, *Education and Income* (New York: The Viking Press, 1961); and Edward P. Thompson, *The Making of the English Working Class* (New York: Random House, 1963).

[34] See, in addition to Pfautz, "The Current Literature on Social Stratification"; MacRae, "Social Stratification, a Trend Report"; Pease *et al.*, "Ideological Currents in American Stratification Literature"; and Thomas E. Lasswell, "Social Stratification: 1964–1968," *The Annals of the American Academy of Political and Social Science*, 384 (July 1969), 104–134.

fication and class and they are applied indiscriminately. Moreover, the failure to distinguish between them and the tendency to use operational definitions have in large part been responsible for the controversies among sociologists and others regarding the number and identification of classes, whether classes in American society are becoming more or less rigid, and whether the United States is becoming more or less stratified.[35]

The problem is particularly acute with regard to the concept of class.[36] Dahrendorf comments on the many definitions and concludes: "The history of the concept of class in sociology is surely one of the most extreme illustrations of the inability of sociologists to achieve a minimum of consensus even in the modest business of terminological decisions." [37] This statement which was made in 1959 is still appropriate today.

Fortunately, however, there are some writers who have contributed significantly toward clarifying these important concepts. Not only are they aware of the differences between stratification and class but they are also cognizant of the conflict aspect of classes. Several of them were cited previously: Dahrendorf, Ossowski, Geiger, Mills, and Lipset. In addition, Reinhard Bendix and Howard Brotz should be mentioned, as well as Gerhard Lenski, and Kurt B. Mayer and Walter Buckley. Among authors of introductory sociology textbooks who make the distinction between stratification and class and deal with the conflict aspect of class are Leonard Broom and Philip Selznick, William J. Chambliss and Thomas E. Ryther, Ely Chinoy, and James B. McKee. In addition, there is a growing number of Marxist critiques of sociology and modern society which may be harbingers of a new interest in the study of class from a conflict perspective.[38] Nevertheless, even though there has been progress in the

[35] See, e.g., Ely Chinoy, "Social Mobility Trends in the United States," *American Sociological Review*. 20 (April 1955), 180–186; J. O. Hertzler, "Some Tendencies Toward a Closed Class System in the United States," *Social Forces*, 30 (March 1952), 313–323; and Warner, Robert J. Havighurst and Martin Loeb, *Who Shall Be Educated?* (New York: Harper & Bros., 1944).

[36] This has been observed by researchers such as Dahrendorf, *Class and Class Conflict in Industrial Society;* Joseph A. Kahl and James A. Davis, "A Comparison of Indexes of Socio-Economic Status," *American Sociological Review*, 20 (June 1955), 317–325; Laswell, *op. cit.;* MacRae, *op. cit.;* Pfautz, *op. cit.*, pp. 393–398; and Pitirim A. Sorokin, *Society, Culture and Personality* (New York: Harper & Brothers, 1947), pp. 261–271.

[37] Dahrendorf, *op. cit.*, p. 74.

[38] See Dahrendorf, *op. cit.;* Ossowski, *op. cit.;* Lipset, *op. cit.;* Lipset and Bendix, "Social Status and Social Structure"; Bendix, *Work and Authority in Industry* (New York: John Wiley & Sons, 1956); Howard Brotz, "Social Stratification and the Social Order," *American Journal of Sociology*, 34 (May 1959), 571–578; Lenski, *op. cit.;* Mayer and Buckley, *op. cit.*, pp. 74–79, 417–428; Mills, *The Power Elite* and *White Collar* (New York: Oxford University Press, 1956); Broom and Selznick, *op. cit.;* Chambliss and Ryther, *op. cit.*, and McKee, *op. cit.*, pp. 263–266. The Marxist-oriented works include Barbara Chasin and Gerald Chasin, *Power and Ideology* (Cambridge, Mass.: Schenkman Publishing Co., 1974); Charles H. Anderson, *The Political Economy of Social Class* (Englewood Cliffs, N.J.: Prentice-Hall, 1974), and Nicos Poulantzas, *Political Power and Social Classes* (London: Sheed and Ward, 1973).

last few years, there is still little consensus regarding the concepts of stratification and class and related terminology.[39] The reasons for this situation are related to the nature of sociology's subject matter as well as to differing perspectives and approaches.

Sociology's Subject Matter

The richness and complexity of human group life make precise assessments of important aspects of behavior and the extrapolation of trends difficult. Because of social interaction, which is basic for human group life, the kinds of uniformities physicists and other scientists can count on are absent. Humans do not simply react mechanically to stimuli; they take note of others, interpret their actions, and construct alternative responses in their imagination before acting. This plus the spontaneous aspect of the self may result in only slight modifications of behavior or in novel reactions.

In addition there are many approaches in sociology and they reflect different images of man and society. Among those which are of particular pertinence to students of stratification and class are what have come to be called the conservative and the radical perspectives.

The Conservative and the Radical Perspectives

Two intellectual traditions have developed over time which have differing views on social order and the nature of man, and which have important implications for research on stratification and class.[40]

Since ancient times controversies regarding the desirable form of social structure, the relations between superordinate and subordinate groups, and in general the allocation of social goods have involved these contrasting viewpoints. One of these traditions, the *conservative perspective,* holds that inequality is both inevitable and just. It is inevitable since it is part of the division of labor; it is just because the hierarchical arrangement of roles with differential rewards is essential to attract well-qualified candidates and motivate them to carry out their responsibilities. Furthermore, there is a close association between the importance of a position and its rewards.[41] The various aspects of the society are seen as interrelated and mutually dependent; consequently the harmoni-

---

[39] Lasswell, *op. cit.,* p. 133.

[40] See Bendix and Lipset, *Class, Status, and Power,* pp. 7–12.

[41] See discussion in Chapter I and in the previous chapter.

ous functioning of the social order requires each group to know and fulfill its obligations and rights within the framework of status differences. A clearly ranked order with differential power, privilege, and prestige which are recognized and accepted by the citizenry is the mark of the good society. Furthermore, the existing ordering reflects differences in inherent capacities. The conservative viewpoint holds that the society operates most smoothly when people accept their place, fulfill the expectations of their position, and exercise the rights that go with it. On the other hand the society is undermined when individuals seek the privileges of other groups, or when groups do not fulfill their responsibilities. Illustrations of the first instance would be lower classes seeking privileges such as economic opportunities which are the monopoly of higher classes, entry into social circles from which they are kept out, suffrage, or free education. An illustration of failure to live up to responsibilities would be nobles who exercise their right of collecting dues from peasants yet do not fulfill the customary obligation of providing succor during a bad harvest or other adversity.

To avoid such dysfunctions it is necessary, according to the conservative, to emphasize traditional values and stress the mutual dependence of the different strata and other groupings, because the social bond is the essential element of human group life. This bond consists of beliefs, values, prejudices, and feelings which tie the members of a group together and facilitate organized activities. Its nemesis is differences of interest and conflict which the conservative sees as destructive of social order. Not only is the conservative opposed to rationalism, but also to individualism, for such emphasis weakens the group; instead he stresses tradition and the positive aspects of institutions such as the church, education, and the family for they provide social anchoring and give meaning to people's lives.[42] In addition, institutions help socialize the individual for his appropriate position in the stratification structure. Specific groups such as one's family, co-religionists, or workmates not only help weave the individual into the fabric of society but also provide him with psychological satisfactions and a sense of purpose. These facilitate the carrying out of the various roles and thus contribute to the efficient functioning of the society. The emphasis is on harmonious relationships among the different elements and conflict, too rapid social change, and the breakdown of group affiliations are eschewed.[43]

The *radical perspective* on the other hand holds that inequality is neither inevitable nor just. A rigidly ranked order with wide differences in poverty and wealth, where access to better positions is severely restricted by custom or law, and where statuses are inherited, is seen as stultifying for the individual as well as for the society. Such an order is viewed as particularly onerous by those at the lower levels since the obligations and

---

[42] See Robert A. Nisbet, "Conservatism and Sociology," *American Journal of Sociology*, 63 (September 1952), 167–175.

[43] See, e.g., Nisbet, *Community and Power* (New York: Oxford University Press, 1962).

rights of the different ranks are stacked in favor of the higher strata; they have most of the rights and the lower strata most of the obligations.

The good society, according to the radical, is one in which customary and legal restrictions on opportunity for mobility are absent, as are extremes of wealth and poverty. Under these circumstances there will be a more equitable distribution of social goods; moreover, this type of social order will bring out the best in people since sheer economic survival will no longer be a problem. In that regard, the radical holds that people's inherent capacities differ much less than the conservative believes, and that most differences are the result of environment rather than genetics. The radical's response to problems such as unemployment, family disorganization, or drug abuse is to change the societal conditions which are seen as primarily responsible for them. By contrast the conservative is likely to blame the individual rather than the society. The conservative's solution is to reemphasize the traditional values of family, church, state, and occupational group and to reintegrate the individual. He feels that if people would only believe in these values, do an honest day's work, and not aspire to more than their station in life entitles them there would be few social problems.

The radical perspective is a product of the Enlightenment of 17th- and 18th-century Europe which questioned the traditional beliefs of society and man's place in it, and emphasized that the old ways were not necessarily the best. Rather, everything could be improved; it stressed the perfectability of society and the human and looked for natural laws as a guide rather than traditional beliefs. Science and the process of rationality are also a product of the Enlightenment and the conservative and radical differ in regard to their worth. The radical might say "Let us study a particular social arrangement very carefully and objectively (that is, scientifically), find out what makes it tick, and if possible change it so that it works better." The conservative would likely recoil and suggest that such a dissection by itself may shatter people's beliefs and leave them at loose ends, and that it is most unlikely that age-old institutional arrangements can be improved. Furthermore, he believes that, since the various elements of the society are intricately interrelated, any serious tampering may throw the whole system out of kilter, if not destroy it.

Radicals and conservatives also differ on rationality as it applies to humans. The radical emphasizes their essential rationality, that any individual, given the facts and unfettered by undesirable aspects of society will be able to make wise choices. By contrast the conservative believes that most people particularly those in the lower strata are much less rational. Rather, they are prone to make decisions on the basis of emotion, fear, and superstition, and are easily swayed by others. This does not hold for persons in positions of authority, however, and their task is to guide, influence, and if necessary coerce those below them to act in a manner best for all. The conservative outlook leads to elitism and distrust of the mass of the population, while the radical perspective has faith in the "common man" and is likely to be wary of authorities in the government, church, and economic structure.[44]

When it comes to research, or for that matter concrete situations involving stratification and class, neat distinctions between the conservative and the radical perspectives usually cannot be made. For societies as well as their institutions contain both elements of persistence and elements of change. Consequently the investigator who has a radical approach must take into account the conservative or persisting aspects of the society; even if he dislikes them intently he must understand the institutional arrangements and the traditions, beliefs, and myths which have a strong hold on people. Otherwise he will likely not understand which aspects need alteration to achieve a particular change. He will also be at a loss to explain why many people, particularly at the lower levels, often appear to act against their interests. Similarly, the investigator with the conservative viewpoint must pay attention to the elements of change as well as to the persisting aspects. Otherwise he may construct a model of society which overemphasizes the conservative or integrative side and is unable to adequately account for conflict, let alone significant change.

While the canons of scholarship allow the researcher to use any perspective, the members of his audience are also free to be critical and to indicate preferences. Thus a study focusing on the status aspects of a social order: who associates with whom, the type furniture found in homes of different strata, or the social life of the upper levels, may be a contribution to knowledge. But one may deem as more important concern with such things as poverty, the fewer life chances of minority groups, or the alienation involved in much blue-collar work and increasingly in white-collar activities. Mills' point is well taken that scholars should pay attention to human concerns and problems and endeavor to locate them in a broader social and historical context. This will make for a better understanding of their institutional causes which in turn may help in ameliorating the difficulties.[45]

The conservative and the radical perspectives are not the only kinds of outlooks. Closely paralleling them are the contrasting approaches of consensus and conflict.

The Consensual and the Conflict Approaches

Dahrendorf notes that throughout the history of Western social thought two contrary viewpoints have sought to explain how it is that human

---

[44] See Ernest Casirir, "Enlightenment," *Encyclopaedia of the Social Sciences* (New York: Macmillan, 1931), pp. 547–552 and *The Philosophy of the Enlightenment* (Princeton, N.J.: Princeton University Press, 1951). The significance of the Enlightenment and the reaction which followed, for stratification and class, are discussed in greater detail in Chapter VIII.

[45] C. Wright Mills, *The Sociological Imagination* (New York: Oxford University Press, 1959).

societies cohere; that is, what makes them "hold together." [46] One school avers that social order results primarily from a general agreement of values, while the position of the other school is that coherence is due to force and constraint, with the domination of some and the subjugation of others. The first, the *consensual approach*, acknowledges differences of interests but sees them as subordinated to agreed-upon values. Thus most people ordinarily "toe the line," go to work, do not steal, and submit to military conscription because there is consensus in the society regarding what is right and proper. On the other hand, the *conflict approach* holds that compliance is the result of sanctions or their threat: people do not steal because getting involved with the police and the courts is quite unpleasant, they go to war mainly because of the punishment meted out to those who refuse, and they must work if they are to subsist.

Force and conflict are inherent in the organization of associations. As we observed in Chapter I, the differential distribution of authority and social goods means the existence of haves and have-nots. As we indicated previously the haves wish to hold on to and increase their social goods, while this is also the object of the have-nots. If one group benefits, however, it is likely to be at the expense of the other, and each uses whatever force it can in order to improve its situation. Yet the police power and political, economic, and other means of coercion are more readily available to the haves who use them to subjugate the have-nots.

Since society is held together by coercion and the various groups and classes employ force to gain their ends, there is constant conflict. Thus the very organization of society produces "within itself the forces that maintain it in an unending process of change." [47]

On the other hand the consensual approach not only views values as basic for cohesion but also sees society as a functionally integrated system. It is kept in equilibrium by recurring patterns of behavior which both reflect and reinforce the agreed-upon values. Conflict is neither necessary nor desirable; it is dysfunctional for the social system.

Until recent years the consensual emphasis, as epitomized by the work of Talcott Parsons,[48] has pretty much dominated sociological thinking. Yet, even though each of the two schools believes that its respective approach is most useful for analyzing society, each contains segments of the other. The notion of integration admits that there are conflicting interests among the various elements in the society which are integrated. In turn the conflict approach presupposes that the agreed-upon values are held by the memberships of the opposing groups. Also, consensus can lead to instability and conflict, for strong agreement on societal val-

---

[46] Dahrendorf, *Class and Class Conflict in Industrial Society;* p. 157.

[47] *Ibid.,* p. 159.

[48] See, e.g., Parsons, *The Social System* and *Structure and Process in Modern Societies* (Glencoe, Ill.: The Free Press, 1960).

ues can prevent adaptation to change or result in inertia. Over time this failure to adapt may precipitate the breakdown of the society. Similarly, consensus on certain norms such as extreme competition and individualistic laissez faire can lead to instability and disintegration.[49] Or, consensus that slaves, natives, or a lower class must be kept in subordination without access to social goods beyond bare necessities can lead to revolution.

On the other hand, as a number of writers have pointed out, conflict has integrative and stabilizing effects; also, it can be institutionalized and ritualized in ways that are conducive to integration.[50] This occurs when labor unions as well as employers' organizations are legal and there are mechanisms which facilitate accommodation, such as collective bargaining, mediation, conciliation, and arbitration. Dahrendorf emphasizes that both approaches are "valid" for each deals with a different aspect of society. "Using one or the other model," he writes, "is a matter of emphasis rather than of fundamental difference; and there are . . . many points at which a theory of group conflict has to have recourse to the integration theory of social structure." [51]

Yet Dahrendorf opts for the conflict emphasis, as we do. We feel that the conflict approach will tell us more about how society "works" and how change comes about. In addition, we feel that the conflict approach directs the researcher to more important investigations. That is, the struggles of large numbers of people to improve their life chances and increase their access to social goods; attempts by those who have improved their situation to prevent the newly socially mobile from reducing their social goods, as well as the social movements which seek to improve society. While the consensual elements must be taken into account, it is the conflict emphasis which will allow the researcher to make sense out of such matters as the breakdown of feudalism and the emergence of capitalist industrialism; the American, the French, and other revolutions; as well as contemporary class struggles.

Summary

The founders of sociology in the United States in general paid relatively little attention to class phenomena. What research there was on stratification and class declined in amount by the 1920's, there was little concern over theoretical questions, and the study of stratification was fa-

---

[49] Pierre L. van den Berghe, "Dialectic and Functionalism: Toward a Theoretical Synthesis," *American Sociological Review*, 28 (October 1963), 703.

[50] *Ibid.* See also Lewis A. Coser, *The Functions of Social Conflict* (Glencoe, Ill.: The Free Press, 1956).

[51] Dahrendorf, *op. cit.*, pp. 159, 163, 164. The quotation is from p. 164.

vored over class analysis. With the Great Depression there was renewed interest in these phenomena, especially class conflict; however, the bulk of the studies dealt with various aspects of stratification. In recent years there has been a revival of interest in class, yet important theoretical questions remain unresolved. This is due in part to the nature of sociology's subject matter, as well as to the differing approaches: the conservative and radical on the one hand, and the consensual and conflict on the other.

The next section examines American society whose mythology avers consensual values and equality of opportunity, and, while it acknowledges stratification denies the existence of classes. Age-old questions about the proper distribution of social goods were extant in the Colonial period, during the establishment of the United States, and ever since. There were problems arising out of industrialization and rapid change, as there had been in Europe. Spokesmen of conservative and of radical persuasions offered their contrasting interpretations and solutions, but the former drowned out the latter except for brief periods. Sociologists and other scholars focused largely on the consensual aspects of the society, as we noted above. It is unfortunate that conflict did not become a focus of study until the Great Depression, for a careful reading of American history clearly shows important strata differences from the very beginning, together with class conflict, sometimes quite intense. In Part Four we detail this stratification, class, and conflict. Chapter XII focuses on Colonial times up to the end of the Revolutionary War, while Chapter XIII deals with the conservative counterrevolution. Industrialization and its social and economic consequences are examined in Chapter XIV and reformist and radical responses to them are studied in Chapter XV. Chapter XVI presents stratification, class, and conflict in modern times.

Part Four
THE AMERICAN EXPERIENCE

Chapter XII.   Stratification, Class, and Revolution

As we observed in earlier chapters, in any organized group there is an authority structure and a differential distribution of social goods, including wealth, prestige, and opportunity. It is therefore instructive to examine in some detail a situation in which a social order emerges under circumstances which would seem to minimize stratification and classes.

The New World offered many contrasts with the Old: there was neither an hereditary aristocracy nor a history of class conflict, while there existed vast amounts of arable land and many opportunities for social mobility. Yet in terms of social goods, authority structure, group differences, and class behavior the New World was hardly any different from the Old. Not only were stratification and class differences evident from the very beginning of American civilization, but class conflict has been much more violent than elsewhere. Before focusing on these topics, let us briefly look at the continent's resources and the conditions which encouraged their exploitation.

The New Land: Resources and Their Exploitation

Picture a vast continent, sparsely inhabited with immigrants from an advanced civilization. Conditions were extremely favorable for settlement and economic expansion: North America, particularly that portion between the 30th and 48th parallels, provided rich and plentiful natural resources including extensive amounts of arable land and a mild climate. To this region of great abundance, the settlers brought a culture which stressed the exploitation of natural resources.[1]

The resources could be developed with relatively small amounts of capital, and a large and cheap labor supply was available through immigration. Also, when capital was needed it could be obtained from domestic enterprises: from the profits of merchants, plantation owners,

[1] See David M. Potter, *People of Plenty* (Chicago: University of Chicago Press, 1954).

and slave traders, and from privateering which was sometimes akin to piracy.[2] Very importantly, these domestic funds were augmented by European capital; in addition, few political barriers to economic exchange existed and there were capable entrepreneurs. The extensive expansion of canals and then railroads linked important communities and provided cheap transportation for raw materials and finished goods. The tying together of these communities and the low-cost transportation extended markets and facilitated land settlement and the exploitation of resources from the Atlantic to the Pacific. Overall, they greatly increased the economic potential of the nation. Also important were the development of rapid nationwide communications, a mass market, technological improvements, and increasing specialization and growth in the division of labor.[3] Finally, there was a great deal of government intervention in the economy through its issuing of charters, founding of development banks, and encouragement of foreign capital. The government also subsidized projects such as the Erie Canal, aided manufacturing, and made cheap land available for settlement.[4]

While there was widespread opportunity there was also considerable inequality in the distribution of social goods, and much of the contesting over them involved class conflict. It is true that there was not the pervasiveness of classes as in the Old World; a structure of feudal-like relations supported by custom, tradition, and law was absent, as was an hereditary aristrocracy. An analysis of the American experience requires examination of significant differences in interests, attitudes, and behaviors which have developed mainly from two sources: variations in economy and in the distribution of social goods, and from concepts of freedom, liberty, and equality. These ideas were European in origin, coming out of British traditions on the one hand and from the French writers on the other; but American conditions helped modify them into a unique blend.

One aspect of material and ideational differences in America is to a large extent sectional although much more than geography is involved. Another aspect concerns the contesting over social goods which leads to strata differences and class conflicts which are likely to cut across regions. We shall briefly note sectional variations in economy and outlook and consider them at greater length subsequently.

---

[2] Charles A. Beard and Mary R. Beard, *A Basic History of the United States* (New York: Doubleday, Doran, 1944), p. 43.

[3] Samuel P. Hays, *The Response to Industrialism: 1885–1914* (Chicago: The University of Chicago Press, 1965), pp. 4–11.

[4] See, e.g., Seymour M. Lipset, *The First New Nation* (New York: Basic Books, 1963), pp. 48–49, 55–57.

The Three Americas

There were three lines of economic, social, and political development in early America: the commercial North, the plantation South, and the small farmer West. While all were capitalistic in organization, each region developed contrasting perspectives and social organization.

While there were strata differences and class conflicts within each of the sections, often similarities of interest bridged geographical boundaries. Thus, for example, merchants in northern as well as southern port cities might find themselves aligned against artisans and mechanics or small farmers. There were also apparent anomalies: a part of the largely conservative planter South spawned revolutionary ideologists who espoused democratic egalitarianism and the hope of humane progress.[5] Yet despite the rhetoric of Thomas Jefferson and others, they maintained slavery.

Although the major sectional differences may be explained in large part by the nature of the respective economies, ideological influences from overseas blended with home-grown views. Out of the confluence of materialistic and ideational factors, both national and regional, there developed a social order which foreign visitors saw as unique. And, depending on their political orientation, as either progressive or regressive.

Initially, the colonies fell into two clear groups: the commercial provinces north of Maryland and the plantation provinces to the South; [6] later with further settlement the West was added. While the vast majority of the population were small farmers, sectional differences in economy and outlook were quite pervasive. However, both northerners and southerners were of similar national origin and they had the same language. Moreover, they were products of the English political tradition, holding to the ideas of liberty and equality before the law. Nevertheless, the circumstances of their lives gave somewhat different meaning to these concepts.

NEW ENGLAND

In early New England Puritanism at first very much restricted thoughts of liberty and equality; however, with the increase in entrepre-

[5] Vernon L. Parrington, *Main Currents in American Thought* (New York: Harcourt, Brace, 1954), Vol. II, "1800–1860, The Romantic Revolution in America," p. ix. He points out, in addition, that Virginia was the mother of the agrarian West. *Ibid.*, pp. 5–6. For differences in economic interests between North and South in Revolutionary America, see Arthur M. Schlesinger, *The Colonial Merchants and the American Revolution 1763–1776* (New York: Frederick Ungar Publishing Co., 1964), pp. 22–24 ff.

[6] Schlesinger, *op. cit.*

neurial activity these concepts took on a practical bent. Businessmen sought freedom from economic restrictions as did their counterparts in England, and they were also imbued with Adam Smith's doctrine of unrestricted competition and the self-regulation of the market. As the scale of the society expanded and as opportunity for worldly achievement increased the Puritan hold weakened. The Calvinistic components of Protestantism which were relevant for economic gain came to play a significant role; interestingly, Max Weber quotes from Benjamin Franklin's writings to illustrate the kinds of attitudes and behaviors which encouraged capitalistic business enterprise. "Remember," Franklin observes, "that money is of the prolific, generating nature. Money can beget money, and its offspring can beget more, and so on. . . ." He recognized the significance of borrowing for " . . . credit is money. . . ." Suggestions for self-regulation in business practices and appropriate personal habits are offered:

> Remember that *time* is money. . . . He that idly loses five shillings worth of time, loses five shillings, and might as prudently throw five shillings into the sea. . . . Remember this saying, *The good paymaster is lord of another man's purse.* He that is known to pay punctually and exactly to the time he promises, may at any time, and on any occasion, raise all the money his friends can spare.

> After industry and frugality, nothing contributes more to the raising of a young man in the world than punctuality and justice in all his dealings. . . .

> The most trifling actions that affect man's credit are to be regarded. The sound of your hammer at five in the morning, or eight at night, heard by a creditor, makes him easy six months longer; but if he sees you at a billiard table, or hears your voice at a tavern, when you should be at work, he sends for his money the next day. . . .

Weber emphasizes that what Franklin preaches is not mere business astuteness but an *ethos.*[7]

While the New Englander epitomized this ethos, it was not limited to the North; in fact, it stamped the Americans, particularly the inhabitants of the coastal trading cities as well as many of the small farmers throughout the Colonies. The outlook of the larger plantation owner and of the backwoods subsistence farmer were somewhat different, however. The large planter revealed aristocratic leanings and tended to consume a good part of his profit. The backwoodsman, pushed to marginal lands by the expansion of the plantation system and unable to compete with it, accommodated by minimal exertion and a low level of subsistence. In the North,

---

[7] Max Weber, *The Protestant Ethic and the Spirit of Capitalism,* trans. by Talcott Parsons (New York: Charles Scribner's Sons, 1958), pp. 48–51. The quotations are from Benjamin Franklin's *Necessary Hints to Those That Would Be Rich* and *Advice to a Young Tradesman,* written in 1736 and 1748 respectively. The emphases are Franklin's.

aside from Colonial administrators and English military leaders prior to the Revolution, the ruling class consisted primarily of large merchants.

THE SOUTH

In the South, with the qualification just noted, the ruling class was largely the wealthy plantation owners and some of the large merchants in the coastal cities. While the chief drafters of the Declaration of Independence were southerners, this revolutionary document was largely the product of an aristocratic elite which was strongly influenced by the Enlightenment and the *philosophes* of the Old World. The institution of slavery strongly influenced the thinking, customs, and laws of this region, moreover; where the concepts of liberty and freedom were espoused, they were meant to apply only to free whites, particularly those in the upper strata. Southern leaders were wont to suggest a parallel between their institutional arrangements and those of the ancient Greeks.

THE WEST

The West figures prominently in the development of America in terms of territorial and population expansion, as a source of radicalism, and in regard to the emergence of an agrarian mythology. There were many causes of the Westward movement: the farmer's desire for land; the activities of land speculators; the schemes of the railroads; population pressure; trade and exploitation of natural resources; and the desire to make the rest of the continent secure from foreign powers.

The "West" is often used synonomously with the "frontier" and it is in this context that agrarian radical activities may be understood. The remoteness of official government and the premium on self-help for survival promoted a spirit of independence. Thus people in frontier areas chafed at taxes and any other restrictions; it didn't matter whether they were sought by Colonial administrators or by American state or federal officials. Yet the western farmers faced a dilemma since they needed the government for protection against Indians, the building of roads and canals, and for other undertakings which were vital to their economic interests. As the continent was settled, farmers became part of a national and world-wide market which experienced periodic depressions. They then increasingly saw the government as a means of ending their distress. Radical movements with socialistic programs came out of the West and included organizations of miners, lumbermen, and others in addition to farmers.

The West is also important in regard to the development of an agrarian ideology. This "Garden Myth," according to Henry Nash Smith, was given form by Benjamin Franklin, St. John de Crevecœr, and Thomas Jefferson. The agrarian ideology, particularly as developed by Jefferson and his followers, had its sources in the work of Hesiod and Virgil and the French Physiocrats. The first two glorified the husbandman; the latter put forth the idea that agriculture was the primary source of wealth. The Garden Myth posited a simple agrarian society of equality of station, freedom, benevolence, achievement, economic and moral independence, and virtue. It praised the laborious, frugal farmer while it denigrated the artisans and mechanics of the coastal cities; the Myth also contrasted these farmers with the conniving merchants and their luxuries. It was clear that the small freeholders were the most precious part of the state.[8]

The Garden Myth included the doctrine of the safety valve which persisted up to the end of the 19th century. It held that the frontier was a haven for the excess population of the East for it provided land and opportunity. Thus urban masses could be drained off and artisans and mechanics, especially surplus labor, could return to the soil.[9] With such alternatives, the proletarianization of the Old World need not occur; thus class formation and conflict were supposed to be minimized in the new nation. These beliefs have influenced historians, social scientists, and others in spite of considerable evidence to the contrary. It is some of this evidence that we want to look at next.

Strata and Class Differences in Early America

The European settlers of the New World came from a highly stratified society of clearly recognized classes, where the wealth, power, and privileges of the ruling groups were sanctified by tradition and upheld by law. Even though vassalage was disappearing, the inequities in the distribution of social goods remained enormous. Peasants tilled small plots of land, often inefficiently because of the strip method; many were dispossessed as a result of the enclosure movement or because of the confiscatory exactions of the landowners.

Most of the people who set out for the American colonies were eager to avail themselves of the expected surfeit of social goods. Farmers were attracted by cheap land; workers, such as artisans and mechanics whose numbers were increasing with the beginnings of industrialization, were lured by the chance of a better livelihood. In addition, adventurers and younger sons of high-status families were attracted by the possibility of fame and fortune.

[8] Henry Nash Smith, *Virgin Land* (New York: Vintage Books, 1957), pp. 141–145 ff.
[9] *Ibid.*, p. 234 ff.

Although there was abundant land America was a wilderness which the settlers set out to subdue. The Europeans' background which gave them the belief in and the tools for control of the environment made them well suited for the task. Their passion for the acquisition of land and material goods furthered the rapid exploitation of the continent. Their use of the soil and other resources were in conflict with the economic and social foundations of aboriginal life and it was soon destroyed. This is not surprising for throughout history, where there have been wide differences in interests and great inequality between the contesting parties, the stronger usually subdues the weaker with little moral concern over the means. From the perspective of the settler, the Indians had to go since they couldn't be pacified though Christianization, were unwilling to become a disciplined labor force, and were decidedly in the way of economic development. They were forcibly removed from their land or cheated out of it, and treaties were ignored. Indian attacks were usually out of desperation in futile attempts to stop the encroachment of the whites. Yet the mass of the aggression was by settlers and soldiers and bloody episodes abound in the decimation of the Indians. The fact that they were racially and culturally different as well as pagans helped justify doing away with them, so that "the only good Indian is a dead Indian." They were the counterpart of contemporary non-persons: the "gooks" American forces killed in Asia. The coercion also took a more subtle form, through the relentless expropriation of hunting and gathering areas as settlement advanced.[10] The Indians who survived were herded onto reservations, usually land no one else wanted. There they were kept in subjugation through force, legal means, and economic deprivation.

Aside from the inconvenience of the Indians, the immigrants had before them a *tabula rasa*. However, strata differences and the outlines of classes were evident from the first settlement and soon wide variations in the distribution of social goods as regards land, wealth, and influence were apparent. Even though the majority of settlers were freehold farmers there were great variations in amount of property. A prime example was land controlled by the Crown which awarded vast estates or sold them cheaply to Colonial administrators and others in favor. By this means and through shrewd investment, marriage, speculation, chicanery, and corruption, enormous landholdings came into the hands of a few families.[11] There were inequities other than those based on land; merchants and other businessmen, particularly those in the seaport cities, increased their worth and influence through hard work and some of the above practices. Furthermore, the Colonial administrators, high-

[10] For a moving account of the kind of conflict and destruction that occurred, see Theodora Kroeber, *Ishi* (Berkeley and Los Angeles: University of California Press, 1961).

[11] Beard and Beard, *A Basic History of the United States*, pp. 29–30.

ranking military officers, and their rich merchant friends formed an inner circle which had access to wealth-making possibilities not available to lower levels.

Undoubtedly there were differences in ability and motivation which account for some of the variations in social goods that developed. However, the primary cause appears to be the differential privileges dispensed by the Crown, not only as regards land but also in terms of business activities. Time of arrival was also a factor; the earlier immigrants were often in a position to secure opportunities which were not available later on.[12]

The main strata in Colonial America, ranked roughly in terms of influence and wealth, were as follows: the ruling class of Colonial administrators, high-ranking military men, and wealthy merchants and large plantation owners. Just below them were merchants of considerable means and smaller yet substantial plantation owners, then lawyers, physicians, and clergymen. Next were small farmers, small shopkeepers, artisans, mechanics, and laborers, and at the bottom, indentured servants and slaves.[13]

The Revolution of course removed the Colonial rulers; yet the structure of stratification and class remained but with a new ruling group replacing the old. Jackson T. Main provides a picture of the strata differences as well as the tendencies toward group antagonisms and class formation; however, he also points to the conditions which minimized these tendencies. Main emphasizes that economic life in Revolutionary America was primarily agricultural: most of the population were farmers and property-holding differentiated the strata. The majority of the Northern whites were small farmers operating at a subsistence level, unable to afford a slave or hired hand. In the South much more of the farming was commercial, and there were many slaves.[14]

Yet there were considerable regional and rural-urban differences. On

[12] Time of arrival has been a primary factor in the dominant position of the United States' upper class, what Baltzell calls the Protestant Establishment. See E. Digby Baltzell, *The Protestant Establishment* (New York: Random House, 1964). This advantage can also be seen in modern urban communities. Cressey and Ford have shown how the rise in status of recent foreign immigrants and their descendents, as measured by their movement from the central to the outer sections of the city, is associated with time of arrival. See Paul F. Cressey, "Population Succession in Chicago: 1898–1930," *American Journal of Sociology*, 44 (July 1938), 59–69; and Richard G. Ford, "Population Succession in Chicago," *American Journal of Sociology*, 56 (September 1950), 156–160.

[13] See Beard and Beard, *op. cit.*, pp. 58–60; Bernard Bailyn, *The New England Merchants in the Seventeenth Century* (New York: Harper Torchbooks, 1955), pp. 168–197; and Jackson T. Main, "The Class Structure of Revolutionary America," in Reinhard Bendix and Seymour M. Lipset, eds., *Class, Status, and Power* (rev. ed.; New York: The Free Press, 1966), pp. 111–121. See also Main, *The Social Structure of Revolutionary America* (Princeton, N.J.: Princeton University Press, 1965).

[14] Main, "The Class Structure of Revolutionary America," especially pp. 113 and 116. "Subsistence level" does not imply poverty; rather, it refers to the absence of surplus agriculture or cash crops.

the frontier, land was cheap and in those places where there was little speculation between three-quarters and four-fifths of the population owned property. Very few were rich. However, the picture was quite different in the speculative frontier areas where a limited number held most of the property; in some counties a very small proportion of the population owned most of the land, up to 70% in some cases.[15] The greatest inequities were in the South which will be examined in greater detail shortly.

In the bigger towns there were large numbers of wealthy persons and many poor laborers. Although most of the inhabitants had some property, over half of it was owned by the richest ten per cent. In Boston, for example, 57% of the wealth was owned by the most affluent ten per cent.[16]

In the smaller towns from two-thirds to three-fourths of the inhabitants were in a middle stratum of small property holders. However, between 35 and 40% of the real property was in the hands of the top ten per cent of the wealthy. On the other extreme were hired hands, indentured servants and, in the South, slaves.

A composite picture of the nation shows that ten per cent were large landowners or rich merchants who owned nearly half the wealth of the country; between 50 and 55% were small property holders, mostly small farmers. This middle stratum included a small number of artisans, professionals, shopkeepers, and others. An additional 20% were indentured servants, hired hands, or other workers, with the remainder slaves. Thus, depending on the region, somewhere between one-fifth to one-third of the population were dependent laborers.[17] The difference in social goods between them and the wealthy was very great: not only did they lack property but the annual income of the rich was 50 times what the laborers received.[18]

An analysis of probate records for some 4,000 estates provides a rough idea of how personal wealth was distributed (Table XII-1). It can be seen that the merchants were the best off. Next were the doctors, ministers, traders and shopkeepers, and farmers. The worst off were the artisans, teachers, and laborers; the latter were the poorest. Even though these percentages are approximations, they show quite clearly that most of the wealth was in the hands of the merchants: 27% had estates worth £2,000 or more compared to eight per cent for doctors, seven for ministers, and four per cent each for small businessmen and farmers. By contrast, 98% of the laborers had estates of between £1 to £99, 60% of the teachers fell into this bottom category, as did half the artisans.

---

[15] *Ibid.*, pp. 112–113.
[16] *Ibid.*, pp. 113, 115–116.
[17] *Ibid.*, p. 116.
[18] *Ibid.*, pp. 116–117.

TABLE XII-1. Distribution of Personal Property in 4,000 Estates in Revolutionary America* (in percentages)

Size of Estate	Laborers	Teachers	Artisans	Doctors	Ministers	Traders and Shopkeepers	Farmers	Merchants
£ 2,000 and over	0%	0%	0%	8%	7%	4%	4%	27%
£ 500 – 1,999	0	0	10	22	18	20	20	29
£ 100 – 499	2	40	40	50	50	56	45	35
£ 1 – 99	98	60	50	20	25	20	30	9
Total	100%	100%	100%	100%	100%	100%	99%	100%

*Figures adapted from Jackson T. Main, *The Social Structure of Revolutionary America* (Princeton, N.J.: Princeton University Press, 1965), p. 113. Copyright © 1965 by Princeton University Press; reprinted by permission. Main notes that the percentages are only approximate because the sample is not large enough, and because the currencies differed from colony to colony. Furthermore, the figures are in currency and not sterling and they do *not* include real estate.

There were other inequities such as property qualifications for voting, which meant that more than half the population was not enfranchised. There were other restrictions such as primogeniture and entail; however in practice they had little impact. The laws on primogeniture required that the eldest son inherit the entire estate, and entails prevented a person from selling his land or even giving it away. The purpose of primogeniture and entail, which were common in medieval Europe, was twofold: to insure a stable society by keeping land in the same families generation after generation, and to keep property from being subdivided among many heirs.[19]

Pre-Revolutionary Class Behavior

Competition over social goods, such as land and other forms of wealth, and variations in political participation often led to class behavior. This is illustrated by the conflict between discontented farmers and the ruling class. The farmers' difficulties reflected traditional agrarian problems: the underrepresentation of rural interests in general as well as the desire for more land. Although North America is a vast continent there were limits on the amount of land that was arable, inexpensive, and safe from marauding Indians.

From earliest times there were periods of rural discontent and instances of farmers acting in concert, to the point of taking up arms. In the wilderness areas of Virginia their demands for protection and equal rights in colonial legislatures led to a rebellion in 1676 under the leadership of Nathaniel Bacon. It was a long struggle which the Governor put down by desperate measures. In the spring and summer of 1766 the "Great Rebellion"—an uprising of large landlords as well as small farmers—was put down only through the calling out of troops.[20] Hardly five years prior to the American Revolution there was an uprising in North Carolina. The turbulent spirit of the backwoodsmen and their vigorous means of redressing grievances led them to take up arms in protest against excessive taxes, dishonest sheriffs, and extortionate fees by the government. The British put down the rebellion which was called the "Regulator War," and executed a number of the leaders.[21]

The rural elements were likely to protest any restrictions placed upon them by the central authority as in the case of the federal government's

[19] J. Franklin Jameson, *The American Revolution Considered as a Social Movement* (Boston: Beacon Press, 1956), pp. 36–38; and Elisha P. Douglass, *Rebels and Democrats* (Chicago: Quadrangle Books, 1965), pp. 299–303.

[20] Beard and Beard, *A Basic History of the United States,* pp. 53–55.

[21] John S. Bassett, "The Regulators of North Carolina," *Annual Report of the American Historical Society, 1894* (Washington, D.C.: Government Printing Office, 1895), pp. 141–212.

efforts in 1794 to collect an excise tax on whiskey. Disturbances broke out and although the rioters were relatively few in number President Washington called out 13,000 soldiers to put them down.[22]

These uprisings espoused ideas of liberty and freedom as justification. They sought laissez faire or non-interference by government; also, they cited the natural rights of man, ideas they adopted from the French writers. The nature of this ideology differentiates the uprisings from the German peasant revolts of the 15th century or the machine-breaking of the Luddites. The earlier disturbances were romantic and reactionary in that they sought return to an earlier, idealized social order. By contrast the American uprisings sought new arrangements involving a more equitable distribution of social goods; in that sense they were revolutionary. And to the extent that they espoused equalitarianism they put fear into the hearts of the more substantial elements.

In spite of the tumultuous history of early America, the large number of property holders, the many economic opportunities and the high level of comfort, the dispersal of the population, and the difficulties of communication worked against the development of a continuing or institutionalized class conflict.[23] Even though the ruling class sought to restrict opportunity to its own members the stratification structure was quite fluid. Thus Main estimates that among the whites the proportion of poor who remained poor probably didn't exceed five per cent.[24] He writes:

> Beggars were almost unknown; paupers were few; and the poor people were provided for. Even slaves and servants were guaranteed a minimum livelihood, while most people lived well above the subsistence level. Finally, all but the slaves could look forward to a better future.[25]

But as time went on the gap between the rich and the poor widened as a result of the commercial expansion in the North, land speculation, an increase in the number of white indentured servants, and the use of slave labor in the South. In addition, property qualifications for voting and officeholding and control of local governments by Colonial aristocracies often gave wider scope to specific grievances. The latent resentment encouraged demands for political democracy, especially after the ending of British authority.[26] But, as we shall subsequently see, political equality was strongly opposed by the leaders of the Revolution.

This pattern of nascent class formation and conflict continued after the Revolution. Thus in 1786 a band of debt-burdened Massachusetts farmers tried to redress their grievances by taking up arms. Led by Dan-

[22] Ibid., pp. 144, 168.

[23] Douglass, Rebels and Democrats, p. 4; and Main, "The Class Structure of Revolutionary America," p. 117.

[24] Main, op. cit., p. 117.

[25] Ibid., p. 121. One should include Indians in the last sentence.

[26] Douglass, op. cit., pp. 3–4.

iel Shays who had been a captain in the Revolutionary army the rebellion was put down with difficulty and some bloodshed. Yet popular sympathies with the uprising were so strong that the state officials did not dare to execute Shays or his followers.[27]

Many writers have held that an important factor in the egalitarian values of American society was the absence of a traditional aristocracy.[28] Yet there were clearly tendencies in that direction after as well as prior to the Revolution.[29] There are obvious attractions to being part of a small, select group at the top of the authority structure. Not only are those with fewer social goods kept out but there are social, economic, and political advantages for the small circle. During the Colonial period and after the Revolution, conditions were favorable for the formation of aristocracies in the commercial cities of the North as well as on the plantations of the South. Given the opportunity, and since there seems to be a propensity for those in the upper strata to form exclusive circles, it is important to understand what led to such developments and why an Old World type aristocracy did not succeed.

ARISTOCRATIC TENDENCIES

In spite of the leveling influences of the frontier and social mobility which was probably quite extensive, economic ties and the Colonial government structure encouraged the formation of an aristocracy. The imposed hierarchical arrangement placed the Colonial administrators on top, and they, high-ranking military officers, large landowners, and wealthy merchant families with excellent connections in England, constituted a "first circle" of privilege and prestige. These ruling circles were found in Boston, New York, and Philadelphia as well as in the South. The "in" groups received favored treatment as regards the awarding of contracts and other opportunities for increasing their wealth. They were also influential in political affairs which provided additional economic advantages. These individuals and their families subscribed to the notion that they were among the elect; they distinguished themselves from what they saw as the baser elements—the small farmers, small shopkeepers, peddlers, mechanics, laborers, and indentured servants. Moreover, they drew a line between themselves and substantial merchants

[27] Beard and Beard, *op. cit.*, p. 122.

[28] See e.g. Lipset, *The First New Nation*, pp. 58–59.

[29] See Bailyn, *The New England Merchants in the Seventeenth Century*; Schlesinger, *The Colonial Merchants and the American Revolution*, especially pp. 27–28; Beard and Beard, *A Basic History of the United States*, especially pp. 49–51; Dixon Wecter, *The Saga of American Society* (New York: Charles Scribner's Sons, 1937); Baltzell, *The Protestant Establishment*; Douglass, *Rebels and Democrats*; and Cleveland Amory, *The Proper Bostonians* (New York: E. P. Dutton, 1947).

who were outside the ruling group even though many of those excluded were important businessmen with considerable wealth.

Members of the ruling class circulated in the same social circles and developed personal and familial as well as business ties. They viewed themselves as the New World aristocracy, taking England as their model. Some had blood ties with the nobility of the mother country but many more did not and sought to substitute money and propitious marriage for the genealogy their progenitors had failed to provide. Their lavish social functions included imitation royal courts in the Colonial capitals; their style of life involved expensive mansions, raiments of fine woolens, silks, and laces, and numerous servants; they had affection for the seasoned culture of Britain in contrast to the boorish customs of frontier America. The social affairs, the life style, and the manners and pretensions which were similar to those of the British aristocracy helped tighten the strong economic and political bonds between England and her colonies.[30]

The Colonial aristocracy and its supporters saw social, economic, and political security in a patrician and inherited order which was tied to the greater British society. They urged conformity and felt that the ordinary people should submit to government by gentlemen, an arrangement which conservatives such as the Anglican clergyman Jonathan Boucher believed was devised by God. "Obedience to Government," he preached, "is every man's duty, because it is every man's interest, but it is particularly incumbent on Christians, because it is enjoined by the positive commands of God." He added that even if the government is less liberal than is reasonable, "still it is our duty not to disturb the peace of the community, by becoming refractory and rebellious subjects, and *resisting the ordinances of God.*" [31]

CHALLENGING THE AUTHORITY STRUCTURE

Understandably, those in the "inner circle" favored the status quo and their apologists tried to justify their rule. But the justifications became more and more difficult to sustain. Even though the colonists had many grievances, objectively they were not very serious; more important was the growing conflict of interests between mother country and colony, especially as they involved the substantial merchants just below the ruling class. Paralleling these circumstances was a reexamination of people's perspectives, engendered by the ideas of the intellectuals and the exhortations of the radicals among them. The intellectuals' specula-

[30] See Bailyn, *op. cit.*; Schlesinger, *op. cit.*, especially pp. 27–28; and Beard and Beard, *op. cit.*, especially pp. 49–51.

[31] Quoted in Beard and Beard, *A Basic History of the United States*, p. 52. The emphasis is in the original.

tions on the ideal form of government in part reflected the thinking of the Enlightenment; however, their discussions and writings also reflected the belief that alteration of the authority structure was imminent. Whether England would retain control or whether the Colonies would be independent, many saw the possibility of creating a more perfect society. Increasingly the idea of great change was "in the air."

Also significant was the widening belief that British authority could be challenged successfully. This was the result of the history of uprisings mentioned earlier; even though they were failures militarily, they were the first holes in the dike. The Regulator incident had its greatest impact outside the locality where it occurred; lurid accounts of the struggle of the oppressed North Carolinians appeared in newspapers in other colonies, particularly in Pennsylvania and Massachusetts. This uprising was especially important for it set people to thinking of armed rebellion, and it showed the essential weakness of the British army in hostile territory.[32]

It is difficult if not impossible to determine when a revolution begins —it is part of a social movement which grows as it gains adherents, defines an ideology, and challenges the authority structure with increasing frequency and intensity. As for the basic cause of a revolution, its determination is made all the more difficult by whether or not historians and others favored it. That is, those opposed to a given upheaval hold that organized malcontents upset a well-functioning society to the point where it begins to break down and the troublemakers gain control. On the other hand those who are favorable toward a revolution find that it was the outcome of popular discontent with institutional arrangements, and that the upheaval itself was a spontaneous uprising to throw off the oppressors. But the truth involves both facets: there is growing discontent *and* organized groups. Initially they are composed chiefly of the scheming malcontents, but soon moderates are attracted and the latter also form additional organizations. These often take the form of pressure groups or business associations.[33] The several groups, radical as well as moderate, help shape the ideology and provide organized opposition.

In Colonial America radicals as well as moderates played key roles. Radical writers such as Tom Paine helped stir up popular discontent and helped focus it on the need to end British rule. His writings were addressed to the ordinary person and promised a society based on equal rights. Paine cited scripture in denouncing monarchy in general, and the King of England in particular. This King ". . . hath little more to do than to make war and give away places; which, in plain terms, is to empoverish the nation. . . . Of more worth is one honest man to society, and in the sight of God, than all the crowned ruffians that ever lived." He in-

[32] Bassett, "The Regulators of North Carolina," pp. 208, 211.

[33] Crane Brinton, *The Anatomy of Revolution* (New York: Vintage Books, 1965), pp. 72, 79–80, 84–86.

sisted there was no advantage whatsoever for reconciliation with Great Britain; on the contrary, ". . . the injuries and disadvantages which we sustain by that connection, are without number; and our duty to mankind at large, as well as to ourselves, instruct us to renounce the alliance. . . ." [34] Paine stresses that the hope for freedom lies in the New World, and he appeals to his readers with these stirring words:

> O! ye that love mankind! Ye that dare oppose not only the tyranny but the tyrant, stand forth! Every spot of the old world is overrun with oppression. Freedom hath been hunted round the Globe. Asia and Africa have long expelled her. Europe regards her like a stranger, and England hath given her warning to depart. O! receive the fugitive, and prepare in time an asylum for mankind. [35]

Douglass comments on the significance of Paine's widely read *Common Sense:*

> [It] was a breath of fresh air to a propaganda literature which was beginning to suffocate on legalisms. The educated might be impressed by Dickinson's and Dulany's briefs for an equitable division of taxing power between colonies and mother country and by Jefferson's and Wilson's theory that the alleged expatriation of the colonists justified their claim for autonomy, but argument on this level could have little meaning for the man on the street or at the plow. Everyone, however, could understand Paine's contention that America was an independent continent temporarily held in subjection by a vicious despot who derived his authority from a no less vicious system of government. [36]

It is estimated that about 300,000 people read *Common Sense,* which would mean about ten per cent of the population at the time. [37]

The radicals organized the "Sons of Liberty" to combat the Stamp Act and met both openly and secretly to promote opposition to the Crown. They maintained a kind of "Holy Inquisition" on business dealings and individual activities in order to discourage trade with the British as well as Loyalist sympathies. And whenever they deemed it ncesssary they engaged in acts of violence. The Committees of Correspondence, formed originally as private pressure groups were skillfully manipulated into a radical position by Samuel Adams. Yet moderates also organized: thus in 1763 the merchants of Boston formed a "Society for Encouraging Trade and Commerce with the Province of Massachusetts Bay." Accounts of the group's activities were sent to merchants in the other colonies, [38] and unwittingly they became the agents of revolution.

---

[34] Howard Fast, *The Selected Works of Tom Paine and Citizen Tom Paine* (New York: The Modern Library, 1945). The quotations are from "Common Sense," pp. 18, 21.

[35] *Ibid.,* p. 31.

[36] Douglass, *Rebels and Democrats,* p. 13.

[37] Fast, *op. cit.,* p. 40.

[38] Brinton, *op. cit.,* pp. 84–85.

Merchant and Mob

The British policies of the 1760's particularly affected the substantial merchants outside the ruling class and they spoke out vehemently against them. Not only did their opposition influence people in the lower strata, but, more important, these merchants actively sought their support. Moreover, they encouraged mass demonstrations and other forms of collective protest against the authorities. The conflict escalated until separation from Britain was inevitable. This was ironic, for two reasons: In the first place the Americans escaped the injurious restraints of mercantilist theory; whatever burdens they suffered as colonies were counterbalanced by corresponding benefits. The basis of the merchant's prosperity, and in turn that of the petty shopkeepers, sailmakers, coopers, carpenters, and others who were dependent on them was Britain's maintenance of its empire. In addition, the Colonies were given favored treatment by the Crown in many ways and most of the trade restrictions worked to the advantage of the colonists. For example, the requirement that goods be conveyed in British or Colonial bottoms was lucrative for American shipbuilders, suppliers, and sailors. Also, British wares were cheaper and of better quality than those produced elsewhere, and some non-English goods actually cost less in the Colonies than in England. Furthermore, British merchants extended excellent credit, particularly in regard to long-term loans.[39] In that regard, Arthur M. Schlesinger suggests that the contrastingly slow development of Canada under French rule was the result of the short-term credit granted by French merchants.[40]

The primary interest of the merchants who played this critical role in bringing about separation was economic; they had little concern for theoretical rights. More than that, they were repelled by the ideology of radicals such as Tom Paine. Their opposition to British control waxed and waned with economic conditions. They took advantage of the laws which aided them and openly violated those that were restrictive, engaging in extensive smuggling for example. When trade policies were favorable they were conciliatory; or when business was good in spite of British restrictions their ardor for opposition cooled. Thus the merchant boycott of English goods broke down during the period of Colonial prosperity between 1770 and 1773.[41]

Merchant agitation against Great Britain after 1763 sought to reestablish the favorable conditions that Parliament was whittling away; they were hurt the most by the new laws and administrative changes, plus an

[39] Schlesinger, *The Colonial Merchants and the American Revolution*, pp. 15–20, 28–30.
[40] *Ibid.*, p. 30.
[41] *Ibid.*, pp. 17, 78, 91, 100, 215–240, 594.

economic depression. Their active agitation is not surprising considering that their improving economic fortunes suffered a sudden setback. Rising expectations play an important part in all revolutionary change, and the merchants were experiencing that intolerable gap between what people expect and what they get.[42] But their objective was reform, not rebellion. Nevertheless, they were instrumental in developing an identity of interests among businessmen throughout the colonies and began to affect the larger population.

Initially the manual workers, the small shopkeepers, and others who made up the "ordinary people" did not have a sense of common interests; neither did they perceive of themselves as being in opposition to another group. Institutional arrangements were such that for the most part they could not vote, and they were unaware of the potential they possessed in terms of numbers.[43] They were aroused by the merchant-instigated agitation, however, and the "rougher elements" and the unemployed in the seaports readily responded to the merchants' leadership. It was primarily these people of the coastal towns and groups of workmen, such as members of The Sons of Liberty, who engaged in violence. Often trouble was started by irresponsible youths as was the case in the disturbance which led to the Boston Massacre. Mob violence became more frequent following that incident.[44] Mob behavior was quite common, even prior to 1760. Yet the mobs were usually moderate, purposeful, and responsible. Popular uprisings were often considered a constant and even necessary element of free government; the mob was an extralegal arm of the community, to redress grievances. Since mobs were a permanent entity in Colonial America, the task of the revolutionary leaders was to give them direction.[45]

But the radicals lacked a compelling issue which might put the opposition on a broader basis. It was still largely limited to the merchants and many of the inhabitants of the seaport towns, particularly those of the commercial colonies of the North. The British government's awarding of a monopoly in tea to the East India Company provided such an issue, and the violence of the Boston merchants and their confederates in dumping the tea into the harbor advertised it very effectively. Ironically, the American consumer would have paid less for his tea under the East India Company monopoly because middlemen's profits would have been eliminated. Thus, it was the merchants who would lose out; hence their opposition. Nevertheless, the coercive laws of Parliament, incidents such

[42] See Brinton, *The Anatomy of Revolution*, p. 32; and James C. Davies, "Toward a Theory of Revolution," *American Sociological Review*, 27 (February 1962), 5–19.

[43] See Schlesinger, *op. cit.*, p. 28.

[44] *Ibid.*, pp. 63–66, 72, 91–92, 180–181.

[45] Pauline Maier, "Popular Uprisings and Civil Authority in Eighteenth-Century America," *William and Mary Quarterly*, 27 (January 1970), 5–15, 24–25, 28, 35. Such mobs were common in 17th and 18th century England. *Ibid.*, pp. 15–17.

as tea dumping, boycotts of British goods, open defiance of regulations, and the repressive actions of Colonial administrators brought about a polarization of forces. Among the merchants, some became converts to radicalism while others sided with the British.[46]

While the merchants were motivated primarily by economic considerations, this was not invariably the case; individual temperament and commitment to the ideals of liberty and freedom led some to act against their own self-interest.[47] In fact, recent historians believe that the association between stratum position and being pro- or anti-revolution was not as strong as earlier writers contended.[48] Yet there were two discernible themes, one egalitarian and the other conservative. The outcome of the conflict between their respective adherents significantly shaped the political structure of the new nation.

Summary

The New World had neither an hereditary aristocracy as in the Old, nor a history of class conflict; yet there were significant strata differences and class behavior. There were aristocratic tendencies among those in the topmost level who formed an inner circle of prestige and privilege. The smaller yet substantial merchants who were excluded—the near ruling class—were especially affected by the British commercial policies of the 1760's, and became a key element in the agitation that led to revolution. They aroused the ordinary people and encouraged violence against the British. The merchants' actions, in conjunction with radical ideologists and agitators, and previous violent conflicts, particularly in the frontier areas, were instrumental in bringing about the American Revolution.

Yet the major significance of the Revolution from the perspective of stratification and class is threefold: The first aspect was the near-ruling class enlisting the support of a larger portion of the population for its own ends. The second was its inability to control the force it unleashed, which led to extremes of radicalism most of the members of that class opposed. The third was the way the conservatives triumphed in the end, which is the topic of the next chapter.

[46] Schlesinger, *The Colonial Merchants and the American Revolution*, pp. 254–255, 283, 306, 309, 319 ff.

[47] *Ibid.*, pp. 377, 377n.

[48] See Richard B. Morris, *The American Revolution Reconsidered* (New York: Harper & Row, 1967).

Chapter XIII.   The Conservative Counterrevolution

Class behavior, as we have stressed, takes place within an organized entity, or association. There is an authority structure with a differential distribution of social goods, such as wealth, income, prestige, and opportunity. Contesting groups, in seeking to alter the distribution, try to modify the structure. Not only do the contestants marshal whatever resources they can, but they espouse ideologies which justify their actions. In pre-revolutionary America, as we saw, conflict revolved primarily around the Colonial authority structure; yet, conceivably, following its destruction it could have been replaced with separate associations. Each of the 13 former colonies could have had its own authority structure, with a loose federation tying them together. There were practical considerations which argued against this: primarily, the need to mobilize resources on a national basis to fight the war, and afterward to keep the nation viable. There were ideological reasons, the desire of some intellectuals to establish a new social order in which ideas of the Englightenment might be fulfilled. But there were also strong economic pressures which argued for an authority structure that would emphasize national over regional and local interests. These pressures reflected changes beginning prior to the Revolution. The great profits from the shipping industry, for example, became an important source of domestic investment capital. The mobilization of such capital, plus other economic forces, set the stage for the emergence of a political framework,[1] which, first, helped rally various interests around the cause for separation from Great Britain, and second, provided the organizational basis for nationhood. The type of association that would be established, it would seem to follow, would be one with an authority structure that would be strong and national. However, the allocation of social goods was a key element in the conflict over what the new authority structure would be like.

Even with the ouster of the British fundamental differences in the distribution of social goods remained, as did viewpoints regarding the

---

[1] John J. McCuskar, "Sources of Investment Capital in the Colonial Shipping Industry," *Historical Methods Newsletter*, 5 (December 1971), 22–23.

proper allocation. Consequently the form the new government would take became a critical decision. The two likely possibilities were either semi-independent states as provided for under the Articles of Confederation or a strong, central federal government. A weak arrangement would mean that local groups such as small farmers would have a major voice and would be able to influence legislatures to issue paper money, limit land taxes, avoid duties on imports, and in other ways aid the debtor class. State governments were more open to egalitarian tendencies and were not overly interested in the sanctity of private property, particularly the capital of merchants, manufacturers, financiers, and shippers.

A strong government, on the other hand, would mean protection of property rights, collection of debts—both private and public, restriction of foreign competition, a common and stable currency, and a greater voice for urban businessmen. The different outlooks as they related to the adoption of the Constitution may be understood by considering several opposing interests: among property-holders, landowners were aligned against those whose capital was based on trade, commerce, manufacturing, and finance; another distinction was between debtors and creditors. The landowners consisted mostly of yeomen farmers and a small proportion of manorial lords, as along the bank of the Hudson River in New York and the slaveowning planters of the South. The small farmers, especially those back from the seacoast, were quite homogeneous in circumstances and strongly conscious of identical interests in the several states. Their indebtedness, antagonism toward seaboard groups, and suffering at the hands of land speculators led them to oppose the adoption of the Constitution. The manorial landholders who constituted the dominant class in New York during the time of the Revolution and the adoption of the Constitution were also opposed, but because their vast lands would be taxed. On the other hand the southern slaveholders, many who had personal wealth from other sources, favored a strong government. They saw it as insurance against a slave revolt that the local police and the state militia might not be able to put down.[2]

There was a strong association between being a farmer and debtor on the one hand and being a businessman and creditor on the other. In the case of the creditors, government securities potentially worth about $60,000,000 were in the hands of American citizens in the spring of 1787. Issued during the Revolution, the value of these notes had dropped during the unstable period which followed. Prior to the movement to replace the Articles of Confederation their selling price was one-sixth to one-tenth of their original worth; in some instances it was as low as 1/20th of their face value.[3]

---

[2] Charles A. Beard, *An Economic Interpretation of the Constitution of the United States* (New York: The Free Press, 1968), pp. 29–30, 31 ff. Cf. Richard B. Morris, *The American Revolution Reconsidered* (New York: Harper and Row, 1967), especially pp. 144–147.

[3] Beard, *op. cit.*, pp. 34–35.

Charles A. Beard calls attention to economic considerations in the adoption of the United States Constitution, and the way things were stacked in favor of the haves. The selection of delegates to the Constitutional Convention insured that conservatives rather than radicals would be chosen for it was done through the state legislatures and not by the electorate. As a result, the delegates represented the monied interests; none represented the farmers or mechanics. Of the 55 delegates, at least 83% would be directly and personally affected by the outcome. One way they would benefit economically from the adoption of the Constitution is indicated by the following: 75% held public paper with a face value from just a few dollars to more than $100,000. Of these delegates who would gain handsomely through government redemption, approximately four out of every ten were minor holders of securities from a few dollars up to $5,000; about six out of every ten owned notes valued at $5,000 or more.[4] The financial interests, merchants and manufacturers, and land speculators were the most powerful forces in Revolutionary America. Alexander Hamilton acutely saw that without them there was no chance for a federal union; so, policies were shaped to retain their support.[5] With the adoption of the Constitution and the sound financial system which it made possible, those who held securities, Beard estimates, gained at least $40,000,000.[6]

This is not to suggest that there was a conspiracy by the haves to do in the have-nots, nor that the economic motive was primary in whether people supported or opposed the Constitution. Nevertheless, what one has to gain or lose economically is an important influence on one's political outlook. The conflicting interests had a strong economic basis, and they reflected contrasting ideologies which each of the political parties espoused.

Federalists and Republican-Democrats

The Federalists represented the business interests who wanted a strong central government with limited participation and elaborate safeguards against the popular will, the caprices of officeholders, and the coalition of factions. The Jeffersonian Republican-Democrats spoke for the small farmers, the backwoodsmen, and the lower strata of the cities; the people who were most likely to be oppressed by the institutional arrangements of government. The Federalists strongly feared egalitarianism and popular control: the former they associated with the dividing up of property

[4] *Ibid.*, pp. 17, 63–65, 149–151.
[5] *Ibid.*, pp. 31, 102.
[6] *Ibid.*, pp. 34–35.

and the latter with mobocracy. They wished to avoid tyranny by the majority as well as by the minority, yet they felt that the businessmen were the most competent individuals to serve as the elected representatives of the people.[7] Hamilton argued that representation by all segments of the population was Utopian nonsense; it was impractical and unnecessary. If the better people were elected they not only would take into account the interests of the different elements of the population, but they would be better able to defend them. Thus he wrote, ". . . the influence and weight and superior acquirements of the merchants render them more equal to a contest with any spirit which might happen to infuse itself into the public councils. . . ."[8]

The Federalists believed that since self-interest and class conflict cannot be prevented the only way to avoid tyranny or anarchy, yet retain freedom, was for the government to institutionalize and regulate the conflict. This would be accomplished by indirect representation and by a system of checks and balances among the several branches of the government, and furthered by a large enough population. Predating sociological theories on the relevance of numbers, James Madison postulated that the larger the size the greater the differentiation; hence, there would be a greater number of interests which legislators would have to take into account and accommodate. This would encourage compromise and consideration of the common good.

But "common good" was defined from the perspective of the more substantial portion of the population who feared egalitarianism and wanted a strong central government in which property rights would be secure. Their sentiments are quite apparent in a letter by General Henry Knox to George Washington. Referring to Shays' Rebellion he wrote:

> The people who are the insurgents have never paid any, or but very little taxes—But they see the weakness of government; they feel at once their own poverty, compared with the opulent, and their own force, and they are determined to make use of the latter, in order to remedy the former. Their creed is "That the property of the United States has been protected from the confiscations of Britain by the joint exertions of all, and therefore ought to be the common property of all. And he that attempts opposition to this creed is an enemy to equity and justice, and ought to be swept from the face of the earth." In a word, they are determined to annihilate all debts, public and private, and have agrarian Laws, which are easily affected by means of unfunded paper money which shall be a tender in all cases whatever. . . .[9]

He feared that there would be a "formidable rebellion against reason, the principle of all government, and the very name of liberty. This dreadful

---

[7] See Alexander Hamilton, No. 35, *The Federalist Papers* (New York: The New American Library, 1961), pp. 214–217 and James Madison, No. 10, *ibid.*, pp. 77–84. See also Charles A. Beard and Mary R. Beard, *A Basic History of the United States* (New York: Doubleday, Doran, 1944), p. 165 ff.

[8] Hamilton, *op. cit.*, pp. 214–215.

[9] Quoted in Beard, *op. cit.*, pp. 58–59.

situation," he continues, "has alarmed every man of principle and property in New England. . . . Our government must be braced, changed, or altered to secure our lives and property." [10]

The people for whom the Jeffersonian Republican-Democrats were the spokesmen saw the Federalist proposals as a double-edged sword: as a means of benefitting the better-off in the distribution of social goods and thwarting their own needs and wishes. Moreover, there was no guarantee in the new Constitution for such freedoms as speech, assembly, religion, and the press. It is no wonder that from their point of view independence meant the replacement of one ruling class by another. Interestingly, there was the distinct possibility that the new American government would become a constitutional monarchy for there were many Americans, particularly among the upper strata, who believed that was the only way to have stability. In fact, a few officers in the Revolutionary army strongly urged the establishment of a one-man military dictatorship. Even though the monarchists preferred a true aristocracy of blood and lineage as existed in nations overseas, they were willing to accept an "aristocracy of wealth and talent." Yet, they were unsuccessful, primarily because of Washington's refusal to accept a crown; nor did an aristocracy of wealth and talent attain supreme power. [11]

Seymour M. Lipset discusses instability in newly emerging nations and the role that the armed forces often play. Usually stability is achieved through a military dictatorship; however, in early America, he notes, one of the factors working against this outcome was the weakness of the army. It was relatively small, there were state militias, and there was no military class. [12] In fact, during the seven years of war only approximately one out of every sixteen men of fighting age served in either the Continental Army or the state militias. In 1776 when the armed forces were at their peak the proportion rose, but even then it was only about one out of every eight. [13]

The instability and confusion following the Revolution and the many conflicts that took place greatly endangered the fledgling government. Its initial survival was largely due to compromises by the spokesmen for the different classes and by the leaders of political factions, to Washington's charisma, his dedication to republican principles, his refusal to use the President's office for his own purposes, and to the physical isolation of America. Another important factor was the inability of any one group to muster sufficient force to make its will supreme. [14]

[10] *Ibid.*, p. 59.

[11] Beard and Beard, *op. cit.*, pp. 119, 138–139.

[12] Seymour M. Lipset, *The First New Nation* (New York: Basic Books, 1963), p. 93.

[13] J. Franklin Jameson, *The American Revolution Considered as a Social Movement* (Boston: Beacon Press, 1956), pp. 45, 48. By contrast, during World War II about four out of every five eligible males saw service. U.S. Bureau of the Census, *Historical Statistics of the United States, Colonial Times to 1957* (Washington, D.C.: Government Printing Office, 1960), p. 10.

[14] Jameson, *op. cit.*, pp. 16–23.

The Founding Fathers had the opportunity to establish a new governmental arrangement, or at least one that was in line with the modernizing of political institutions in Europe at the time. The Americans reflected the political ideas of Tudor England which they brought with them; they adhered to these old notions which were already outmoded overseas and made them the touchstone of the American system. The American reverence of law as something fixed, which may be modified but basically should not be changed, is a traditional outlook; it was being abandoned in Europe as it was gaining credence on this side of the Atlantic. The pluralistic concept, which is at the base of the separation of powers, reflects the medieval separation of Estates. While in England Parliament was gaining in power at the expense of the King, in the United States the Presidency was designed in the image of a constitutional monarch in spite of popular disavowals to the contrary and the absence of a crown.[15] Although the antiquated political form America adopted did not significantly hinder modernization and the extension of the franchise, they occurred *in spite of it* because of very favorable social and economic conditions. By contrast, in Europe modernization has been preceded by a more modern polity. Because of these circumstances, Samuel P. Huntington doubts whether the American model is appropriate for developing nations since one of their major problems is the existence of such antiquated political arrangements. What they actually need, he holds, is a more unified system.[16]

Thus the Founding Fathers lost the opportunity to design an American government which would have incorporated the modern European developments. In a more modern system, Congress would have been preeminent and popularly elected, and laws would be viewed not as something sanctified but as man-made, to be changed as soon as needs changed. One can only speculate as to whether such an arrangement would have meant more political freedom, greater citizen participation, and a more equitable distribution of social goods. The growing power of the Presidency and the tremendous size and influence of the military in contemporary America, as well as the absence of social legislation which has become commonplace in other Western democracies may very well be due to this failure.

Democracy in the sense of wider distribution of social goods including popular sovereignty made little progress as a whole during the Revolution and for years afterward. There were several reasons: in peacetime, as well as during the war, the government was inefficient and economically weak, which limited what it could do; even if it had sought radical reforms it very likely would have been unable to carry them out. In addition, the dis-

[15] Samuel P. Huntington, *Political Order in Changing Societies* (New Haven, Conn.: Yale University Press, 1969), pp. 93–139. See especially pp. 114–115. This is ironic considering Washington's refusal to be crowned.

[16] *Ibid.*

persal of the population and poor communications further limited government effectiveness.

As for the ideologists, even the more "left" among them, such as Thomas Jefferson, were conservative in many respects. Certainly his legislative actions revealed the endorsement of political equality and popular checks on government; but he feared that popular representation would mean an elective despotism. Though Jefferson was against an hereditary aristocracy he wanted an aristocracy of talent into which the most able would rise. This would be the ideal arrangement from his point of view and he believed that the government should be responsible for keeping the channels open.

Upon the conclusion of the war and the formation of the new nation, the Jeffersonian Republican-Democrats went along with the conservatives in emphasizing stability over democracy. They did this in order to bring forth a government that would not be still-born and even radicals such as Tom Paine supported conservative state constitutions for this reason. The great failure of the radicals was that, although they had been successful in arousing popular opinion, they had no concrete means for achieving their goals; they lacked a workable plan for putting into effect what were many meritorious ideas.

Additional reasons for the failure of egalitarian democracy were considerable social mobility and agrarian interests. The agitation for radical reform usually lacked effective leadership because of the opportunities for mobility which drained off leaders from the lower strata. Also, the vast majority of farmers, whether rich or poor, often had similar interests. Finally, the general availability of cheap land lessened pressures for reform.[17]

Thus the main accomplishment of the Revolution was the deposing of the British. The failure of the radical element to follow through and the conditions cited above which discouraged reform worked to the advantage of the business interests. It was the conservatives, including the merchants who had favored the war, the ones who had been lukewarm, and those who had secretly hoped for a British victory who were triumphant in the end. "When the war closed," Arthur M. Schlesinger writes,

. . . they had a mournful satisfaction . . . of finding their worst fears confirmed in the inefficient government which the revolutionary leaders established and in the enfeebled state of American commerce and business at home and abroad. In the troubled years that followed the merchants of the country, regardless of their antecedents, drew together in an effort to found a government which would safeguard the interests of their class. Thus, once more united, the mercantile interests became a potent factor in the conservative counter-revolution that led to the establishment of the United States Constitution.[18]

[17] Elisha P. Douglass, *Rebels and Democrats* (Chicago: Quadrangle Paperbacks, 1965), pp. 307–319.

[18] Arthur M. Schlesinger, *The Colonial Merchants and the American Revolution in 1763–1776* (New York: Frederick Ungar Publishing Co., 1964), pp. 605–606.

The concept "counterrevolution" should not be viewed as depicting a plot to undo a revolution, to bring back the old order. Rather, it refers to a common element in rapid social change: a reemergence of conservative perspectives which are submerged during agitation and upheaval. The conservatism reflects the interests of groups who are likely to have relatively more social goods which they wish to secure. But the conservatism also reflects the interests of others, including revolutionary leaders, who now desire the stability which a viable government requires. It is in this sense that we discuss counterrevolution.

Counterrevolution

The circumstances that led to conservative institutional arrangements such as the United States Constitution and the government based on it are understandable. Not many people had a burning desire for revolution, as indicated by the small proportion of eligible males who took up arms. The interest of the businessmen waxed and waned according to what was advantageous for their profits. This was particularly true of the large merchants who comprised the near-ruling class; some of them favored conciliation with Great Britain right up to the war, especially when they realized that their dominance would be threatened by popular sovereignty and other radical demands.

If only segments of the population were interested in independence, fewer still wanted democracy. Yet, the intellectuals who became the leaders of the revolution put forth some rather radical appeals; among them were a nation based on natural rights, freedom, and a revocable social compact. How do we account for this since the intellectuals were basically conservative, as we noted earlier? The explanation is quite simple: their propaganda espoused populism since their main source of power was the masses. The promise of a wider distribution of the social goods appealed to the middle as well as to the lower strata and soon brought a significant portion of the population around to the idea of separation and a new nation. Lipset notes that the intellectuals play this important role in nation-building, and, although they appeal to the masses, they are not necessarily democratic.[19]

In the case of the American Revolution, as is true today among new nations struggling for freedom, the masses are "used"; they are aroused by promises which cannot or will not be fulfilled. As we have seen, their aspirations are raised in order to make change seem desirable and violence is encouraged as a means of destroying the old regime. Even the conservatives will use the masses to bring pressure against existing authority and, as we have observed, encourage mob violence when it suits

[19] Lipset, *The First New Nation*, pp. 66–68.

their purpose. Under such circumstances they publicly defend it even though they have great disdain for the common people; those who denounced the Stamp Act riots were told: "It was indeed a very improper way of acting, but may *not the agonies of minds not quite so polished as your own* be in measure excused?" [20] Even the radicals showed disdain for the lower strata who participated in mob behavior. Samuel Adams described effigy burnings and riots as "joys of the Evening among the lower Sort, which, however innocent, are sometimes noisy." [21]

With the ending of British rule, however, the conservatives' apparent tolerant attitude toward lawlessness underwent a transformation; they now feared the possibility of anarchy in the confusion of the Revolution. The reestablishment of the courts is an interesting case in point. Both the members of the near-ruling class and many ordinary people had opposed the judicial system when it had worked against their interests. With the Revolution there was popular resistance to reestablishing the courts; in some places, debtors used their absence to prevent collection of the money they owed.

"The responsibilities of government," Elisha P. Douglass observes, "gave the Whigs a new appreciation of the necessity for order, authority, and subordination. The radicals had been turned out; therefore, good patriots should settle down and show a proper respect for authority." [22] With the adoption of the Constitution and the desire for stability, the once common uprisings, often considered a constant and even necessary element of free government, were no longer tolerated. This was part of the movement to minimize the role of the people at large. [23]

Class and other conflicts continued unabated during the formative years. There were many attempts to weaken the government and authoritarian tendencies appeared; an illustration was the overreaction to the Whiskey Rebellion (1794) and the enactment of the Alien and Sedition Acts (1798). [24] Nevertheless, the liberal parliamentary republic survived and gained legitimacy. This was aided by a number of critical factors in addition to those cited previously. The members of the intellectual elite which had conceived of the idea of nationality were committed to the survival of the government and many were now in positions of authority. Individuals, such as John Adams and Alexander Hamilton, restrained personal conflicts in favor of supporting a viable government. Also, because of the common goal and the exigencies of the political situ-

[20] John Dickinson, *Political Writings*, 2 Vols. (Wilmington, 1801), Vol. I, p. 128, quoted in Douglass, *op. cit.*, p. 18. Emphasis in the original.

[21] Harry A. Cushing, ed., *The Writings of Samuel Adams*, 4 Vols. (New York, 1904–1908), Vol. III, p. 244. Quoted in Douglass, *op. cit.*, p. 18.

[22] Douglass, *Rebels and Democrats*, pp. 19–20. The quotation is from p. 18.

[23] Pauline Maier, "Popular Uprisings and Civil Authority in Eighteenth-Century America," *William and Mary Quarterly*, 27 (January 1970), 35.

[24] Beard and Beard, *A Basic History of the United States*, p. 168.

ation, the conservatives, who held power, realized that they had to work within a society with equalitarian ideals. Many of their actions, including the redistribution of the land of the Tories who had fled or been hounded out of the colonies helped to institutionalize democracy.[25] In addition, Washington's refusal to run for a third term led to the election of the Jeffersonian Democrat-Republicans and resulted in a peaceful change of government. While they were in office, the Constitution was amended to include a Bill of Rights which reduced the fears and hostility of the left and of many ordinary citizens. This Administration also ended entails and primogeniture. The fact that Jefferson did not retaliate against the Federalists when his party was in office and his refusal to run for a third term further helped strengthen democratic institutions.[26]

The adoption of the Constitution and the continuation of the government in spite of many difficulties and setbacks established sufficient stability for economic growth. This was further encouraged by the government honoring debts, maintaining financial stability, issuing charters, providing subsidies, and setting high tariffs. Some segments benefitted greatly, especially the large plantation owners and the wealthy merchants who replaced the Colonial aristocracy.

The ascendancy of the leading landholders and businessmen of Massachusetts furnishes an interesting case. It is particularly relevant because of this group's influence on the fortunes of the new republic, at least well into the 19th century. Composed of a small number of families, it furnished the nucleus of the later Federalist party, the party of the conservatives. The members of this group, which included the families of John Adams, Theosophilus Parsons, John Lowell, and George Cabot, formed a clique, intermarried, and managed to control a sizable portion of the mercantile and financial wealth of Massachusetts. A few of the families held control and monopolized elective offices in the villages, but most settled in Boston, some purchasing the homes of dispossessed aristocrats.[27] They formed a "first circle" and were distinguishable, aside from their wealth, by their manners and clothing; they considered themselves the "better people" and fashioned the policies of the Commonwealth for nearly half a century. The legal system, the press, and the clergy provided strong support for the ruling group. These Brahmins had great influence among the judiciary and most of the important newspapers of Massachusetts identified with them. Also, traditional religion was still important and they were helped by the Congregational clergy who followed the then widespread practice of using the pulpit, especially

[25] Lipset, *op. cit.*, pp. 21, 27, 44, 66–68, 88.

[26] Beard and Beard, *op. cit.*, pp. 168–172.

[27] Norman Jacobson, "Class and Ideology in Revolutionary America," in Reinhard Bendix and Seymour M. Lipset, eds., *Class, Status, and Power* (Glencoe, Ill.: The Free Press, 1959), pp. 547–554. See also Jameson, *The American Revolution Considered as a Social Movement*, pp. 16–17.

on Thanksgiving, Fast days, and Election days, for extremely strong partisan political speeches. Moreover, the clergy preached submission, patience, frugality, industry, and humility and urged the poor to submit to the stewardship of the wealthy.[28] Thus, as Norman Jacobson points out, the merchants and others who formed the inner circle had a more stabilized and regularized base than if they had to depend entirely on the fickleness of the electorate.[29]

Yet, they faced the classical problem of every new ruling group: the legitimation of power. How could they justify to the citizenry their replacement of the Colonial aristocracy? To do so they emphasized their superiority vis-à-vis the common people and promulgated criteria for successful rule which narrowed the field to themselves. Thus they argued that birth, wealth, education, and leisure were still required for the competent exercise of power, that only the gentlemen-politician with a background of practical business experience was able to formulate social policy. Given such requirements, obviously few outside the ruling circle could qualify. From their perspective, the choice was clear: they were the truly meritorious, industrious, and well-informed while the bulk of the people sorely lacked wisdom, firmness, consistency, and perseverance. They saw the latter as " 'worthless' poor and ignorant drones." While they believed that a few such as yeomen farmers might become worthy and useful citizens, they insisted that ability with plow and dung-fork was no criterion for the higher positions. In short, the multitudes of the poor, ignorant, and vulgar should defer to their betters who were the more respectable and substantial classes in society.[30]

These claims were buttressed by the stress on utility. Not only were the members of the ruling class supposed to be superior to the ordinary citizen in birth, wealth, education, and leisure, but they stressed that they were also *practical men*; they argued that their inherent qualities for ruling were sharpened by their involvement in the world of business. Yet these views contributed to their downfall. By 1840, the nation had come into the "era of the log cabin" and those who sought political power could no longer openly show cynical disdain for the common man. Even more important, the common man now applied his own yardstick of utility and decided that the New England Brahmins were no longer useful.[31] Thus ended the reign of this ruling group, although it remained influential. In any event, 50 years of economic and political domination is not such a bad score.

If the new nation benefitted the upper levels, what about the lower—the small farmers, laborers, and mechanics? Relative to the others, the common people gained little from the Revolution and the new govern-

[28] Jacobson, *op. cit.*, pp. 549, 552.
[29] *Ibid.*, p. 549.
[30] *Ibid.*
[31] *Ibid.*, pp. 550–554.

ment. Creditors were now backed by the judicial authority of the American government instead of the Crown and commercial interests were as little concerned with the plight of the small farmer or of the urban working people as in the days of the colonies. While more land was made available, much of it and often the best fell into the hands of speculators. If small farmers or others of the lower strata stepped out of line the force of the new government was brought to bear on them; on the other hand, the Congress, the state legislatures, and the Supreme Court usually supported the business interests even when their activities were unethical and sometimes outright dishonest. One of the most notorious cases of chicanery and bribery involving state officials was the Yazoo land companies' speculations. The state legislature of Georgia sold vast tracts of land in the Yazoo River region to private companies in 1789. Subsequently, Georgia refused to yield title when offered payment in its own currency which was then worthless. In 1795, as a result of bribery, the legislature passed the Yazoo Act which allowed four new companies to buy even larger amounts of land. A new legislature was elected in 1796 and repudiated the sales. But in 1810, the United States Supreme Court held that the speculators' land claims were valid and they later received $4,000,000 from Congress. The Court reasoned that although the land sale legislation was obtained through fraud it was still a binding contract. Thus, morality lost out to the sanctity of contract when it favored vested interests.[32] The Supreme Court's ruling in favor of the speculators set the stage for the subsequent conservative interpretations of the Constitution.

The stratum that gained least from the new government consisted of the slaves. They were considered to have many of the obligations of other humans but none of their rights.

THREE-FIFTHS OF A PERSON

During deliberations over the ratification of the Constitution, the slave became a critical issue. Although the first draft of the proposed constitution condemned the King of England for maintaining slavery, the clause was later deleted because the delegates intended to keep slavery here.[33] Ironically, England abolished the slave trade in 1807 and in 1833 enacted legislation to end all slavery.

While legally the slave was a chattel as was a cow or a horse, it was also acknowledged that he had human judgment and was held morally responsible for his actions. Thus, he could be punished for stealing, killing, rebelling, or running away. He was human but at the same time

[32] See C. Peter Magrath, *Yazoo* (Providence, R.I.: Brown University Press, 1966).

[33] John H. Franklin, "The Future of Negro History," *The University of Chicago Magazine*, 62 (January–February 1970), 15–21.

less than human. In determining the basis for representation for the House of Representatives the southerners stressed the slaves' human aspects and demanded that they be counted with the rest of the population. The southern delegates engaged in this sophistry since obviously such a determination would mean more southern representatives. Northerners argued that since the slave was a chattel he should not be counted at all. The compromise was that the slave would be considered the equivalent of three-fifths of a non-slave.[34] Through this accommodation the Founding Fathers helped perpetuate this servitude for more than seven decades.

The institution of slavery is not the only significant aspect of stratification in the South. The region contained forces for both equality and inequality; it also contained forces for freedom as well as for repression. These anomalies become understandable when we next examine stratification and class in this region.

Stratification and Class in the South

The South was a highly stratified society; not only were there great differences between the large and small farmers, but there was an almost impenetrable barrier between whites and blacks. Yet, as we noted in the previous chapter, this region furnished a high proportion of the leaders and much of the ideology for the Revolution, including concepts of equality and the natural rights of man. Overall, however, the heritage of the South is one of inequality supported by custom, the economy, and law. Southerners have also made use of the Jeffersonian ideology which favors weak central government in ways that Jefferson probably would have frowned upon: to support inequality and deny liberty.

While there are several sources of the South's great inequality in the distribution of social goods and its penchant for aristocracy, it is necessary to look first at its economy. The slave-based, commercial farming-plantation agriculture, which was the primary source of wealth, had certain consequences: clear-cut superordinate-subordinate relationships and a considerable amount of leisure for the planter class. In turn, these conditions encouraged aristocratic self-conceptions and the larger plantation owners took on many of the attitudes, behaviors, and trappings of the aristocracies of the Old World.

During the Colonial period, the larger plantation owner was heavily in debt to his factor, the agent who sold his cotton on commission, and to British merchants. In part this was because of his consumption and wastefulness as a gentlemen farmer; the other reason was the marketing

[34] Madison, *The Federalist Papers*, No. 54, pp. 336–341.

system itself. This debtor-creditor situation was a very important consideration in his favoring separation from Great Britain. There was a great dislike of the factors which was due mainly to their being creditors and secondarily because they were considered "foreigners." They were natives of Scotland and had the reputation of being shrewd, hard businessmen. The extent of planter indebtedness may be gleaned from the claims in the Treaties of 1783 and 1794 and the Convention of 1802. British claims against the commercial provinces were £218,000, which in large part was for compensation of loyalist property; on the other hand, claims against the plantation provinces were £3,869,000 which were primarily to repay debts.[35]

The idea that every plantation owner was an aristocratic gentleman who possessed feelings of *noblesse oblige* is strictly a myth, however. This myth was fostered largely by conditions endemic to the South and its development, but it was also a reaction to the disorganizing tendencies of the new industrialism of the Northeast and England. It also reflected the Romantic-Conservative reaction following the French Revolution.[36] But there were great differences in wealth, style of life, and interests among the several strata. In the main, class formation and conflict did not occur and the following discussion explores the reasons.

The economy of the South made extensive use of slave labor, the slaves comprising around 35% of the population in 1790.[37] Considered chattels, the owner's responsibility was based on economic considerations: how to maximize his investment. Social distance was enforced and although there was repugnance of intimate contact there were important exceptions: black cooks, servants, and nursemaids were used in the master's home and sexual contact was not infrequent although only white male–black female relations were sanctioned.

Inequality in sexual access is a characteristic of stratification. It follows that the greater the difference in control over social goods, the greater the advantage higher strata persons have over lower as regards sexual favors. Even where there is not too much inequality among the strata, those in the upper levels are able to employ money or other things of value; where the differences are extreme as in a slave system, the upper strata have almost complete control over social goods, including the bodies and even the lives of the slaves. Theoretically upper level females are in an advantageous position to obtain the favors of lower strata males. However male chauvinism is nothing new: abhorrence and severe punishment surrounded black male–white female contacts. The

[35] Schlesinger, *The Colonial Merchants and the American Revolution*, pp. 35–36, 38–39, 504–535, 591; and Beard, *An Economic Interpretation of the Constitution of the United States*, p. 39n.

[36] See W. J. Cash, *The Mind of the South* (Garden City, N.Y.: Doubleday Anchor Books, 1941).

[37] *Historical Statistics of the United States, Colonial Times to 1957*, pp. 11–12.

observations of writers such as Gunnar Myrdal and John Dollard suggest that even today the fear many whites have of such contacts helps shape race relations wherever there are sizeable numbers of blacks.[38]

This not to imply that all white southerners were Simon Legrees nor that human kindness did not occur. The manumission of household slaves suggests the existence of sympathetic understanding; also, slaves could purchase their freedom and this occurred.[39] However, the proportion of slaves who gained freedom was very small, the percentage of free blacks in 1790 being only a fraction over four per cent. Of these, less than one per cent resided in the South; almost all the rest were in the Northeast. Probably most of the freed slaves left the South, for emigration was often a condition of emancipation. In 1860, the year before the Civil War began, almost six per cent of the southern blacks were free; nationwide, the total was a little more than ten per cent.[40] The idea that the black was inherently inferior and thus not suited to freedom was not limited to the South; this view was held by Jefferson, Lincoln, and others.[41] While persons such as Washington and Jefferson were aware of the moral issue of slavery, they argued against it for practical reasons; they felt that such a large slave population was incompatible with a democratic society.

The democratic ideas that came out of the South to a large extent reflected frontier interests. Prior to the Revolution and for some time afterward most of Virginia was largely frontier and the Mississippi Valley was primarily a wasteland. Jeffersonian democracy represented small peasant interests and the individualism of the frontier as well as the ideas of the French writers. Although the English philosopher John Locke defended the status quo, his writings were also influential. His description of how the social compact was formed together with his favoring of popular sovereignty constituted the framework of a democratic philosophy.[42]

One outcome of these ideas and the spirit of independence fostered by frontier life was that these small farmers not only refused to pay taxes to the Crown, they refused to pay any taxes at all. Changes in the economy increased strata differences. While the frontier of the South was still being subdued up to 1840, the plantation system became important around 1800 and was fully developed by the 1820's.[43] Large-scale cultiva-

---

[38] Gunnar Myrdal, *An American Dilemma* (New York: Harper & Bros., 1944), Vol. I, pp. 586–589; and John Dollard, *Caste and Class in a Southern Town* (Garden City, N.Y.: Doubleday Anchor Books, 1949), pp. 163, 165, 170–171.

[39] Tamotsu Shibutani and Kian M. Kwan, *Ethnic Stratification* (New York: Macmillan, 1965), pp. 268, 353.

[40] *Historical Statistics of the United States, Colonial Times to 1957*, pp. 11–12.

[41] See, e.g., Alan P. Grimes, *Equality in America* (New York: Oxford University Press, 1965), p. 48.

[42] Cash, *The Mind of the South*, pp. 22–23; and Douglass, *Rebels and Democrats*, pp. 10–11.

[43] Cash, *op. cit.*, p. 22.

tion was encouraged by the invention, in 1793, of the cotton gin which separated the cotton fibers from the seeds efficiently and economically. The great demand for cotton by British and New England mills spurred interest in such a device. If Eli Whitney had not invented it, undoubtedly someone else would have.

With the plantation system strata differences among the white population became sharper. At the apex was the planter elite which had large amounts of land and many slaves and considerable economic, political, and social influence. Next were yeoman farmers with only a few slaves and those with none. Below them were the subsistence level farmers, variously labelled "poor whites" or "white trash." Finally, there were the slaves who constituted the bottom category.

There was a great deal of snobbishness with pride in the possession of land and slaves and contempt for those without them. This was emphasized by the *nouveaux riches* who became the large plantation owners as the Civil War approached. They viewed themselves as aristocrats and were very much concerned with social distinctions; they gave the appearance of superior refinement through style of living and claims of noble birth, although genealogies were forged where necessary. The South was aware of and thought in terms of Big Men and Little Men with strict reference to property, power, and claims to gentility.[44] These distinctions were apparent to all; they were stressed by the upper strata and acknowledged by the lower. Yet, the economic interests of the yeoman farmers, as well as those of the poor whites, were opposed to those of the large plantation owners. For one thing, the extension of the cotton economy gobbled up desirable acreage, boxed in the smaller farmers, and pushed the poor whites back to the marginal lands.[45]

That there was a strong potential for class behavior is shown by the conflict between the yeoman farmers and the slave-owning interests in a number of places, particularly Virginia. These smaller farmers fought a losing battle against the extension of slavery for they could not compete against the system. This largely explains the two nearly successful attempts to abolish slavery by the Virginia legislature.[46]

As the plantation economy became more firmly established so did the differences in the distribution of social goods. One would think that the smaller farmers would realize the difference of interest between themselves and the larger plantation owners and that the system of slavery tended to enslave them as well as the blacks. Yet there were a number of factors which minimized class formation and conflict among whites. The first was that the plantation elite exercised political control and the yeo-

[44] Cash, *op. cit.*, pp. 47, 75–77, 134.

[45] Cash, *op. cit.*, pp. 35–36. See Paul Lewison, *Race, Class, and Party* (New York: Grosset & Dunlap, 1965), pp. 6, 50 ff.

[46] Cash, *op. cit.*, p. 73.

man farmers followed their leadership.[47] The second factor applies to the poor whites. They were outside the agricultural economy of the South, living mainly at a subsistence level in the backwater areas; [48] consequently they mattered little economically or politically. The third factor was that the maintenance of slavery provided among other things status for the whites: no matter how low-down, shiftless, or ignorant they might be, the existence of the slave stratum gave them a feeling of superiority. Regardless of their condition the whites saw themselves as a part of the master class.[49]

There were additional factors which, although subsidiary, were significant. Most of the whites had common origins and there was considerable intermarriage of persons of different strata levels, particularly in the early years. There was opportunity on the frontier with many rags-to-riches sagas; thus, social mobility withdrew the rebellious. Also, the frontier aspect of Southern life encouraged friendliness, visiting, and mutual aid and thus muted somewhat the tendencies toward snobbishness and class distinctions. Thus, the smaller farmer usually saw the larger one as an old friend or kinsman rather than as an exploiter and antagonist. And the poor whites, although living at a subsistence level, were able to grow what they needed without too much effort; they were left alone and felt that their condition was tolerable and would not worsen. Also, the development of class consciousness was further hindered by the romanticism and hedonistic spirit that developed in the South. The planter elite justified slavery on economic and even humanitarian grounds, and drew upon the writings of Auguste Comte; they saw the South with its slavery as developing the ideal society.[50] Finally, as abolitionist sentiment in the North increased and as the Civil War approached, loyalty to the South solidified all the strata among the whites and antagonism was directed toward the Yankee North. One of the internal consequences of war is usually to minimize class antagonisms, as the European conflicts of 1848 so clearly showed. From a Marxian perspective, the lower class whites were a class *an sich*.

If there is any question as to why the slaves did not revolt it may be disposed of very quickly; the economic and political power of the planter elite together with local and national laws, the judiciary, and law enforcement officials insured the perpetuation of the system of domination. In addition, extra-legal means were frequently employed. Thus, both the formal and informal institutional arrangements supported this extreme form of stratification and made it almost impossible for the slaves to oppose it. Yet, there was constant and bitter opposition to slavery: there

[47] Barrington Moore, Jr., *The Social Origins of Dictatorship and Democracy* (Boston: Beacon Press, 1966), p. 116.

[48] *Ibid.*

[49] Cash, *The Mind of the South*, p. 47.

[50] *Ibid.*, pp. 49, 51, 59–61, 64, 74–75, 77, 98.

were some revolts which were brutally put down; more common was malingering and to a lesser extent running away. Frantz Fanon points out that where the superordinates have complete control malingering, apparent laziness, and a lack of comprehension are about the only forms of protest available to a subjugated people.[51]

Another factor which helped perpetuate the status quo was the white southerner's tendency toward violence, which included fighting, dueling, and lynching. W. J. Cash notes that from 1840 to 1860 over 300 persons are said to have been hanged or burned by mobs and that less than ten per cent were blacks.[52] It wasn't until the period of 1882 to 1903 that lynching became predominantly racial. Probably what hindered this development during slavery was the reluctance to destroy one's valuable property.[53] In any event, the white southerner's violent behavior, often following minimal provocation, was not lost upon the slaves.

Finally, the remoteness of the plantation and the feudal-like control by the owner helped keep the slaves from contact with persons who might seek to spread dissent or organize revolt.[54]

The factors we have enumerated above worked against class formation among the whites, even though the range in the possession of social goods was tremendous. They also prevented a successful uprising by the blacks. Yet, widespread conflict which focused on the issue of slavery did come and led to the destruction of this institution. The future of American democracy required that this conflict—the Civil War—take place; its importance was moral and political as well as economic.

The Necessary Conflict

Barrington Moore, Jr., emphasizes that there was no basic antagonism between the southern and the northern economies as is sometimes averred. Their interests were complementary to one another: the manufacturer needed the cotton and other agricultural products of the South while the plantation owner required the North's manufactured goods. In addition, much of the southern income was spent in the North for plantation needs, consumer items, on holidays, and so forth. As for the West,

---

[51] Frantz Fanon, *The Wretched of the Earth* (New York: Grove Press, 1968). See also Frederick L. Olmsted, *The Cotton Kingdom* (New York: The Modern Library, 1969; first pub. in 1861).

[52] Cash, *op. cit.*, p. 56.

[53] See *ibid.*, p. 123, and Hugh D. Graham and Ted R. Gurr, eds., *Violence in America: Historical and Comparative Perspective* (New York: Bantam Books, 1969), p. 791.

[54] There was abolitionist sentiment in the South: more than 100 out of the 130 abolitionist societies established by Benjamin Lundy, the forerunner of William Lloyd Garrison, were in the South. These 100 organizations contained four-fifths of the total membership. Cash, *op. cit.*, p. 73.

the South purchased its food from that region. Moreover, southern plantation agriculture was a critical element in the industrial development of the nation. Between 1815 and 1860 the cotton trade exercised a decisive influence on American economic expansion; up until about 1830 it was the most important cause of the growth of manufacturing. During the 1840's, even though it no longer dominated the economy it still remained important. In contrast to some other nations American agriculture was not a fetter on industrial development; rather, it helped promote it. There was a convergence rather than a conflict of interest between northern manufacturers and southern plantation owners; moreover, northern businessmen did not seem eager for war with the South.[55]

Thus Moore argues, and with great plausability, that on strictly *economic grounds* accommodation was possible with no need for the Civil War. However, slavery was an obstacle to political and social democracy in the United States; had there been such an accommodation, slavery would have become entrenched and it would have adversely affected the nature of the industrial system. In 19th century Germany there was an accommodation between the Prussian manufacturers and the Junker landholders; the result being that the German peasants were enslaved. In the United States, quite a few forces pushed in the direction of an alignment between northern industrialists and southern plantation owners against slaves, small farmers, and industrial workers.[56] The key was the retention of slavery, and its proponents were seeking to expand it. Such an alignment would have meant that the ideals and the concept of democracy itself would have been further eroded. While plantation agriculture, itself a capitalist enterprise, was no obstacle to capitalist industrialism, it was an obstacle to a *democratic form* of industrial capitalism. It was from this perspective that slavery had to be destroyed and the Civil War was necessary to do it. The basic question was whether the machinery of the federal government should be used to support a free or an unfree society.[57]

The precipitating issues were whether the Western territories would be admitted to the Union as slave or free states and whether tariffs would be high or low. The South as well as the West wanted them low as is usually the case with agriculturalists. Low tariffs mean that imported manufactured goods are cheaper; also, the foreign competition holds down the price of domestic manufactures. On the other hand the North wanted high duties in order to keep out foreign competition. This would expand manufacturing, provide more jobs, raise prices, and increase profits.

As for the extension of slavery into the new states, the South's inter-

[55] Moore, *The Social Origins of Dictatorship and Democracy*, pp. 112, 116, 118–119, 121, 124–125.

[56] *Ibid.*, pp. 131, 147.

[57] *Ibid.*, pp. 112, 136, 151–153.

est was political as well as economic. The growing demand for cotton plus wasteful and destructive planting practices required large acreages. If the new states were slave this land would become available to planters; also, it would mean additional southern representatives in Congress who could use their voting power to lower tariffs and to further extend slavery.[58] Northern manufacturing interests were also opposed to free states since this would increase homesteading and they wished to stem the loss of their labor supply. The West of course wanted new states to be free because its farmers also desired cheap land. In addition, free-state Congressmen would be expected to vote for low tariffs.

The differences between the northern business interests and the western farmers were resolved by a compromise: the new states would be free, which benefitted the West. In turn, the western Congressmen agreed to high tariffs, which satisfied the northern manufacturers. But this solution was untenable to the South. Its political power would be reduced and the higher tariffs would mean increased costs for manufactured goods with the possibility of retaliatory foreign duties on cotton. More than that, slavery would eventually be doomed. The compromise meant that the Civil War was inevitable.[59]

With the war, loyalty to the Confederacy checked any tendencies toward class formation among the whites. On the other hand the gulf between the whites and blacks widened, primarily because of the fear of black revolts.[60]

In the North, the war was also divisive. Long-standing economic and social grievances were exacerbated: in part because many northerners were sympathetic to the South, but also because the advance of industrialism had sharpened strata differences and increased tendencies toward class behavior. Antagonism between the haves and the have-nots increased and most openly in the case of the draft. This law whose provisions benefitted the upper strata led to a great amount of violence and bloodshed.

"I Didn't Raise My [Rich] Son to Be a Soldier"

That the lower strata are more likely to be drafted than the higher is nothing new as we showed in Chapter V. The Union Conscription Act of 1863 grossly discriminated against the poor: any man drafted could be exempted if he provided an acceptable substitute or paid the government

---

[58] Lewison, *Race, Class, and Party*, p. 14.

[59] Moore, *op. cit.*, p. 130.

[60] See Lewison, *op. cit.*, pp. 5 and ff.

$300. Widely unpopular, the legislation provoked nation-wide disturbances with the most serious being in New York City. There, class antagonism, labor unrest, religious and ethnic tensions, and the violence of street gangs and volunteer firemen made this the ". . . most brutal of all civil upheavals [and] cost a greater number of lives than any other incident of domestic violence in American History." [61] The rioting began on July 13, 1863, and lasted for four days. A tremendous mob consisting to a large extent of Irish laborers overpowered the police and soldiers, seized weapons from an armory, set fire to buildings, and robbed and looted. Numbering in the thousands, the mob fought pitched battles with the police and the militia, using cannons as well as rifles and pistols. First the draft headquarters was destroyed, then wealthy homes were attacked.

But this was also a race riot: anti-black feelings had arisen from job competition and as a result of fears instilled by the Democrats. Irish immigrants had been displacing blacks from longshore and other manual work and blacks often could find no employment other than strikebreaking, which frequently led to violence. In addition, Democrats told white workers that the free slaves would come North and take their jobs away. At the same time, they predicted that other blacks would go on welfare and the whites would have to pay taxes to support them. The mob also attacked abolitionists but vented most of their fury on the blacks. Many were shot, beaten to death, or hanged; black homes were burned as was a black orphanage. A contemporary account describes the fate of William Jones, a black:

> A crowd of rioters in Clarkston Street, in pursuit of a negro, who in self-defence had fired on some rowdies, met an inoffensive colored man returning from a bakery with a loaf of bread under his arm. They instantly set upon and beat him and, after nearly killing him, hung him to a lamp-post. His body was left suspended for several hours. A fire was made underneath him, and he was literally roasting as he hung, the mob reveling in their demoniac act. . . .[62]

Order was not restored until troops were rushed from the battlefront. The number of casualties is uncertain because of unreported deaths, secret burials, and victims who were thrown in the the rivers and drowned. Probably at least 300 people were killed and the total number

[61] Richard Hofstadter and Michael Wallace, eds., *American Violence, A Documentary History* (New York: Vintage Books, 1971), p. 211.

The draft riots also illustrate the tendency for upheavals to occur when rising expectations have been dealt a sudden setback. The workmen in New York, who could not afford to buy their way out of military service, had been enjoying wartime prosperity. They were greatly frustrated by the threat of being drafted as well as by inflation. See James C. Davies, "Toward a Theory of Revolution," *American Sociological Review*, 27 (February 1962), 5–19.

[62] Hofstadter and Wallace, *op. cit.*, pp. 211–212 and 217. The quotation is from p. 217 and the original source is David Barnes, *The Draft Riots in New York* (New York: Baker & Goodwin, 1863).

killed or wounded may have been as high as 1,200. Property damage was estimated at between $1,500,000 and $2,000,000. The next year the law was changed so that only conscientious objectors could buy their way out of the draft.[63]

Class Divisions in the South

It should not be thought that class antagonisms were limited to the North, however. There were also strong class feelings in the South in spite of the general solidarity of the whites against the blacks. For one thing, the better off could also purchase their way out of military service. For another, the small farmer felt that he suffered more than the large plantation owner. The Confederate tax, when it could be collected, took one-tenth of one's produce; yet, land and slaves were not directly taxed. These circumstances gave rise to the expression "a rich man's war and a poor man's fight." [64] Although there had always been conflicts between the haves and have-nots, they were exacerbated by the war, especially in border states such as western Virginia, Kentucky, and Tennessee. In these places there were radical movements following the defeat of the Southern forces: Unionist parties were formed which showed their strong resentment against their former social and economic superiors. They passed many resolutions and ordinances against the large planters in which they sought to seize the former plantations and divide them into small farms. They required drastic loyalty oaths of jurors and attorneys and drove from office and disenfranchised those who had aided the Confederacy.[65] This legacy of class conflict is reflected in present-day political behavior in West Virginia.[66]

The Lack of Revolutionary Change

A major upheaval provides the opportunity for revolutionary change, such as a lower stratum gaining power, as well as for a significant redis-

[63] Hofstadter and Wallace, *op. cit.*, p. 212.

[64] Lewison, *op. cit.*, 26.

[65] *Ibid.*, pp. 17–24.

[66] Gerald W. Johnson found that the more radical counties of Virginia, which became West Virginia, have always had a high degree of voter turnout in presidential elections in contrast to Virginia and other border states and to the southern states as a whole. Although students of political participation find a positive relationship between turnout and socio-economic status, West Virginia is low in socioeconomic status yet it continues to have one of the highest turnout percentages in the United States. Johnson suggests that the historical situation together with the political organization of the lower socioeconomic groups are responsible. Gerald W. Johnson, "Research Note on Political Correlates of Voter Participation: A Deviant Case Analysis," *The American Political Science Review*, 65 (September 1971), 768–776.

tribution of social goods. In many ways this was the case with the French Revolution of 1789 and was true to a lesser degree of the English Puritan Revolution. In each conflict the split within the ruling class enabled radical tendencies from the lower strata to come to the surface. Yet this did not occur in America.[67] Given the magnitude of an internal conflict such as the Civil War, the nature of the opposing interests, and the sense of unequal sacrifices by the lower strata in the South as well as in the North, why was there no revolutionary change?

Moore holds that a fundamental restructuring did not occur because class divisions in the American cities were nowhere near as great as in Europe, the western lands provided a safety valve, and there was a lack of a revolutionary impulse from the slaves in spite of some sporadic outbreaks. Interestingly, the only radical impulse that had any significant potential came from northern capitalists. After the war, a group known as the Radical Republicans, led by Thaddeus Stevens, wished to destroy the old institutions of the South and rebuild them in the image of the democratic North. They wanted to confiscate the plantations, divide the land among the blacks, and provide them with minimal economic security and political rights, including the right to vote.[68]

But the North could not stomach an outright attack on private property, even if it was the property of the defeated rebels. In the absence of a redistribution of land, the plantation system recovered; the former slaves became sharecroppers and tenants. They soon found themselves indebted to the local merchant who advanced them groceries and supplies. This merchant was usually the plantation owner and he required that they buy only from him and often at inflated prices. In this manner the political fetters were replaced by economic bondage.

The possibility of significant political and economic change toward equality in the South was ended by the coming to power of southern businessmen who formed an alliance with their northern counterparts. The end of revolutionary movements such as Unionist parties in the South and the Radical Republicans in the North was insured by the compromise in the disputed Hayes-Tilden election of 1876. Southern support in Congress was thrown to Hayes, and in turn the last remaining Federal troops were withdrawn from the former Confederate states.[69]

The Reemergence of White Supremacy

Thus, there was no longer any question of the return of white supremacy. It was enforced not only by economic means but also through seg-

---

[67] Moore, *The Social Origins of Dictatorship and Democracy*, p. 141.

[68] *Ibid.*, pp. 141–146.

[69] *Ibid.*, pp. 147–148; and Lewison, *Race, Class, and Party.*

regation laws and disenfranchisement of the blacks. Although Congress had passed civil rights legislation, the Supreme Court in 1883 declared the Civil Rights Act of 1875 unconstitutional; in 1896, in *Plessy vs. Ferguson*, the Court upheld the practice of "separate but equal" facilities. Thus social discrimination became legal; "Jim Crow" practices now had the full support of the law. The threat of altering the authority structure through political participation by blacks continued to unite the whites regardless of strata. Through legal and quasi-legal means and violence the blacks were effectively disenfranchised.[70]

Inequality in treatment of black persons and in their access to social goods became entrenched. While the Northern victory in the Civil War meant that the machinery of the government would no longer be available to uphold slavery, the most extreme form of stratification, it would continue to support discriminatory social, economic, and political practices.

What was the gain from this war, so costly both in human suffering and money? Somewhere around half a million soldiers from both sides were killed with hundreds of thousands wounded or maimed for life; and these figures do not include civilian casualties. A conservative estimate is that the total financial cost was over ten billion dollars.[71] The main accomplishment of the war was the preservation of the Union and the destruction of the legal basis of slavery. However, white employer now replaced white master and, because of discriminatory laws and economic bondage, a rigidly ordered superordination-subordination relationship remained. Yet, the Northern victory meant that the industrial-political order which had been developing would likely continue to be in the form of a capitalist, liberal, parliamentary democracy. Under these circumstances the forces of industrialization and urbanization, which tend to undermine rigid stratification systems, would have a good chance of weakening the economic, and eventually the political, controls of the whites over the blacks. In addition, these forces increase the possibility of greater equality of access to all forms of social goods.

[70] See Lewison, *op. cit.*, p. 194.

[71] Beard and Beard, *A Basic History of the United States*, p. 280. The number of Federal deaths in battle was 140,414. With 2,213,363 men under arms this means approximately 65 deaths per thousand. Confederate casualties are believed by Beard and Beard to have been 258,000 including other than battlefield deaths. On the basis of the Beards' figure of 1,300,000 in the Southern forces (the estimates range from 600,000 to 1,500,000), the ratio is 198 per thousand. If we use their calculations of 359,528 Union casualties, which include deaths off the battlefield, and 2,898,304 men under arms, then the Northern rate rises to 124 per thousand. U.S. Bureau of the Census, *Statistical Abstract of the United States: 1971*. (92nd ed.; Washington, D.C.: Government Printing Office, 1971), p. 251; and Beard and Beard, *loc. cit.*

Summary

The formation and growth of the American nation reveals great conflict over the distribution of social goods. The emergence of a strong national authority structure was encouraged by certain economic and political trends. Yet the circumstances leading to it illustrate the constraints inherent in a social order. The desire for stability and the reining in of the more rambunctious among the lower levels did not emanate solely from the higher strata. Many ordinary citizens and even the radicals wanted a stable and workable government. It is in this context that we examined the conservative counterrevolution. That conservative tendencies surface after an upheaval should not be surprising; it is simply that they are likely to be submerged during the revolutionary period. Constraining the forces of violence which helped a revolution succeed is more than just an expression of conservative tendencies; it also illustrates the fact that the mass is "used" in bringing about major change. Its aspirations are raised, often by those among the higher strata who yearn for change, and they are encouraged to engage in violence, as mob members or soldiers. But with the new order those in the higher strata, to secure their property or other social goods, understandably wish to end the equalizing tendencies of the revolution.

These constraints of social order sometimes make the ruling class blind to serious inequities in the distribution of social goods, and the class formation which may follow. Unchecked, this may lead to a new upheaval. In early America these circumstances were recognized, as evidenced by the instituting of the Bill of Rights. Also, not using the power of office to destroy opponents kept access to social goods more open, which helped develop the practice of mediating conflicting claims. This way of handling class differences encourages accommodating opposing groups while retaining the basic economic and political structure. Yet great inequities among the strata persisted, the authority structure was used to benefit special interests, as in the Yazoo scandal, and the most extreme form of stratification—slavery—was reinforced.While there were clear differences in economic and political interests between the higher and lower strata Southern whites, the latter were a class *an sich*—against itself, to use Karl Marx's term. For they threw in their lot with the higher strata whites, in opposition to the blacks. The Civil War solidified this tendency.

The Civil War was America's second revolutionary upheaval; it denied slavery the support of the federal authority structure, and it voided the possibility of an accommodation between northern manufacturers and southern plantation owners. Such an accommodation would have been a strong deterrent to political and social democracy. This is suggested by the experience of the Prussian manufacturers and Junker land-holders working against the German peasants.[72] The Civil War presented an opportunity for a more equitable restructuring of the South, but the radical impulse to do so was thwarted by constraints in the American social order: the fear that tampering with the southerner's property might undermine the property rights of others. In consequence, great subordination reappeared, but in a new guise; legal bondage was replaced by new social, political, and economic fetters.

In broad sweep, the outcome spanning the two upheavals was a viable nation espousing the ideals of egalitarianism but exhibiting considerable inequities among the strata. Nevertheless, the possibility of a wider distribution was enhanced by the growing industrialism and urbanism. While they had been increasing in the South, their major advances were in the North. It is to the post-Civil War growth of these two phenomena and their impact on stratification and class that we turn next.

---

[72] See Moore, *The Social Origins of Dictatorship and Democracy*, pp. 112, 131, 136–137, 151–153.

Chapter XIV. Industrialism and "Creative Destruction"

Industrial and urban growth is associated with increased opportunity, and in the long-run a rising standard of living. But there are also dislocations as old forms give way to new ones, and those who become the new labor force are the most severely affected. With industrialism, social relations and political arrangements are altered as the government becomes increasingly involved in the distribution of social goods. It becomes a major source of benefits, through direct subsidies or regulating economic and other activities. As regulator, it can attempt to restrict particular entrepreneurial practices for the general welfare, or its policy can be laissez faire. In that event the power of groups outside the government is enhanced.

Industrial Growth

The post-Civil War period saw tremendous industrial expansion and increased urbanization, together with the emergence of an industrial proletariat, wider strata differences, and greater class conflict. While manufacturing existed in prerevolutionary America it had been on a very limited scale, often cottage industry or small undertakings in towns. As we noted previously, England discouraged American manufacturing for she wished to export her own goods to the colonies; also, they were cheaper and the quality better. After the War for Independence, however, English products were cut off, giving local entrepreneurs the opportunity to fill the gap. In addition, American commerce and manufacturing received a strong impetus from the economic boom that followed the war.

That business and political interests go hand in hand was shown earlier, in the discussion on the conditions which led to the Revolutionary War and the establishment of the United States Constitution. With independence, many segments wanted an increase in the power of the national government, but the main pressure was from merchants and other commercial interests; federalism was good for business.[1]

[1] J. Franklin Jameson, *The American Revolution Considered as a Social Movement* (Boston: Beacon Press, 1956; first pub. in 1926), pp. 50, 61, 71.

Several critical aspects in the economic development of America helped shape expectations and institutional arrangements which are still very important today. They also set the stage for the strata differences and the type of class behavior which have become characteristic of American society. The following discussion must be seen against the background of a wealth of natural resources which was commented on earlier. The first consideration is the tremendous population growth: large families were encouraged by favorable economic conditions and the farmer's need for additional hands. The population increase stimulated the need for cheap textiles, footwear, farm implements, nails, and glass; in turn the demand for such goods meant a labor shortage which encouraged immigration. Workers were needed not only for the factories but also to dig the canals and build the railroads to transport manufactured products in one direction and farm produce in the other. The immigrants further increased the market for such goods. As railroads and people pushed west, as villages grew into towns and towns into cities, continued expansion seemed to be the order of things; in addition, there was much opportunity and considerable social mobility. The prevalent feeling was one of optimism and individualism: anyone could succeed and a person's achievement was seen as the result of ability and hard work.[2] In spite of the emphasis on individualism there was a tremendous amount of government intervention in the economy: national and local bodies provided funds and other aids to spur economic development; entrepreneurs eagerly sought and gladly accepted this help. Charters were issued to business enterprises, development banks were established, projects such as the Erie Canal were undertaken, and foreign investments were encouraged.[3]

Industrialism increased substantially in the early 1800's and by the time of the Civil War there had been extensive economic expansion and growth. For example, by 1840 capital invested in manufacturing was $250,000,000; by 1860 it had risen to one billion dollars. During that period the number of spindles in cotton manufacturing increased from two and a half million to nearly five and a quarter million. In 1840 300,000 bales of cotton were consumed as opposed 1,000,000 in 1860. Imports rose from $4.66 per capita in 1843–1846 to $10.47 in 1856–1860 and exports went up from $5.22 to $10.47 per capita. There were only 2,818 miles of railroad track in 1840; 20 years later there were 30,635 miles. And as for the number of industrial employees, the total went from 72,000 to 122,000.[4]

[2] Thomas C. Cochran and William Miller, *The Age of Enterprise* (rev. ed.; New York: Harper Torchbooks, 1961), pp. 12–13.

[3] Seymour M. Lipset, *The First New Nation* (New York: Basic Books, 1963), pp. 48–49, 55, 56–57.

[4] Norman Ware, *The Industrial Worker, 1840–1860* (Chicago: Quadrangle Books, 1964; first pub. in 1924), pp. 2–3.

There was a new orientation in business during the 1840's and 1850's with novel attitudes toward profit-making, property, and labor. Even though profits had always motivated entrepreneurs, in part the producing of goods and the providing of services had been an end in itself. That is, the emphasis had been on earning a livelihood and the entreprenuer's activities were tied in a personal way to the community's needs. In addition, new inventions, techniques, and enterprises had brought recognition, particularly as they helped community needs. But now profit was the primary emphasis: the innovator gave way to the profit-seeker who stressed restrictive market agreements, price-fixing and other monopolistic practices, and the manipulation of securities.[5]

The growth in the scale of business activities, the spread of the limited liability corporation, and the widespread use of paper currency, promissory notes, mortgages, stocks, bonds, and land warrants facilitated and encouraged manipulation and speculation. Corporations were able to raise the capital needed for large-scale undertakings such as railroads and steel mills. Much of the business dealings involved buying, trading, and selling *rights* to property, which at the time of the transaction might not yet exist as in the case of a new enterprise or agricultural futures. The premium was now on money wealth rather than on land wealth.[6] These circumstances and the growing use of machines encouraged impersonality and calculability in business activities. Relations between management and labor were greatly affected and social distance between employer and employee increased. This was obvious to those who tended the machines; however, they could only vaguely understand the new social and economic developments which were responsible.

The industrial worker was caught up in changing relationships which critically affected his life chances; while there were gains for him there were also many abuses and he was unable to come to grips with the new system.[7] In general life worsened for the industrial worker in the first half of the 19th century, not only in terms of comfort but also in loss of status and independence. Although not actively opposed to machinery he protested against the way it was introduced and the discipline of the factory system; in addition he resented the new capitalists who had acquired their wealth not as producers but as merchants in foreign and domestic trade.[8]

Between 1840 and 1860 the condition of the industrial workers rapidly deteriorated. For most there was no rise in wages over living costs; where there were increases in real income it was mostly by certain

[5] Cochran and Miller, *op. cit.*, p. 53. See also Thorstein Veblen, *The Theory of Business Enterprise* (New York: The New American Library, 1958; first pub. in 1904), p. 87 ff.

[6] Cochran and Miller, *op. cit.*, pp. 53, 72–75.

[7] See Samuel B. Hays, *The Response to Industrialism: 1885–1914* (Chicago: The University of Chicago Press, 1965), pp. 32–37.

[8] Ware, *op. cit.*, pp. x–xi.

skilled groups. The pay of the semi-skilled, or operatives declined in terms of the cost of living; in general the industrial worker lost ground absolutely during that first decade and relatively during the second.

For the nation as a whole there was prosperity between 1840 and 1860 except for some minor depressions. There were high profits, high dividends on investments, and the cost of production declined. Yet prices were maintained and profits increased. Wages, however, fell or remained stationary.[9] The periodic depressions occurring in 1840–1842, 1848, 1853–1854, and 1857,[10] no doubt affected industrial workers more than other segments of the population. Their total stock of social goods was lower and thus they were closer to the margin. Moreover they had few alternatives in contrast to farmers who could still obtain sustenance from the soil or businessmen whose capital was transferable. Increasingly many of the industrial workers lived in crowded urban places where poverty was quite apparent, as in sections of New York City. An investigation by the chief of police in 1850 found that one in 20 lived in cellars, and the very poor averaged six people to a room up to a maximum of 20.[11]

Those in smaller manufacturing cities and factory towns fared no better. The Holyoke, Massachusetts, Board of Health reported in 1856:

Many families were huddled into low, damp and filthy cellars, and others in attics which were but little if any better, with scarcely a particle of what might be called air to sustain life. And it is only a small wonder (to say nothing of health) that life can dwell in such apartments.[12]

Yet who spoke up for the industrial laborer? During the first part of the century the real voice and spirit of the workers could be found only in labor papers and in the resolutions of newly-formed labor organizations. Horace Greeley, editor of the New York *Daily Tribune* has erroneously been called the industrial workman's champion. Although his sympathy was unquestionably real it was for the downtrodden, not for those who wished to stand up for their rights. "Much of his advice to the worker," writes Norman Ware, "could be briefly stated: 'Don't strike. Don't drink. Save your money and start in business for yourself.' "[13] He saw labor and management interests as similar, which reflected the prevailing view of the higher strata and of most of the reformers of the time. The idea that the interests might be antagonistic was slow in growing, although this was understood by union organizers and many work-

[9] *Ibid.*, pp. xii, 6, 9.

[10] *Ibid.*, p. 2.

[11] *Ibid.*, p. 15.

[12] Cochran and Miller, *The Age of Enterprise*, p. 64. The quotation is from Constance M. Green, *Holyoke, Massachusetts* (New Haven, Conn.: Yale University Press, 1939), p. 43, cited in Cochran and Miller, *loc. cit.*

[13] Ware, *The Industrial Worker*, pp. 22–23, 22n.

ers. Labor editors such as Fletcher expressed the conflict view, and in class-conscious terms: "There is at this very moment," he wrote in 1845,

> a great strife between capital and labor and capital is fast gaining the mastery—the gradual abasement of the working men and women of this country abundantly sustains this position. . . . The combined, incorporated, and protected capital can starve out the workers.[14]

O. A. Bronson, one of the few reformers of the time who held that the interests of capital and labor were antagonistic, believed that labor-management conflict could lead to strikes with the use of great force. "If a general war should break out," he wrote,

> it will resolve itself into a social war. . . . between the aristocracy and the democracy, between the people and their masters. . . . Already does it lower on the horizon. . . . But if the war comes it will not be brought about by the reformers, but by the conservatives in order to keep the people out of their rights.[15]

The mid-19th century, as we noted earlier, was a period of revolutions throughout Europe. On this side of the Atlantic, the upheavals provided encouragement to those concerned with the plight of the American industrial worker; they expected that great change was in the offing. They believed that liberal sentiment was increasing everywhere and that the times were auspicious for the cause of human rights; in addition, the Free-Soil and the ten-hour work day movements were growing in strength. But there was no change. The energy which had vitalized reform movements was diverted by the slavery struggle, the conquest of the continent, and by the discovery of gold in California. The latter underscored a new spirit of acquisitiveness that was not confined to any one stratum. Self interest and individual struggle rather than collective action received new emphasis.[16]

Spurred on by the Civil War, industrialization expanded considerably during the war years and afterward it grew very rapidly. One measure of the growth is bituminous coal production which was two-thirds greater in 1865 than in 1860, and then increased 17-fold between 1865 and 1900. During this latter period cotton consumption went up 15 times and the production of steel rails grew 17.5 times.[17] This industrial development required a large labor force which was provided through natural population increase and immigration. The latter was encouraged by manufacturers and other entrepreneurs including land speculators who offered

---

[14] *Ibid.*, p. 23. The quotation is from *Voice of Industry*, October 9, 1845, cited in Ware, *ibid.*

[15] Ware, *op. cit.*, p. 24. The quotation is from the *Boston Quarterly Review* (October, 1840), p. 508, cited in Ware, *ibid.*

[16] Ware, *op. cit.*, pp. 24–25.

[17] U.S. Bureau of the Census, *Historical Statistics of the United States, Colonial Times to 1957* (Washington, D.C.: Government Printing Office, 1960), pp. 355, 416, 417.

the migrants cheap land. The population growth was tremendous: the 35,701,000 people in 1865 grew to 76,094,000 in 1900, an increase of more than two times.[18] Immigration was responsible for a relatively large portion of this growth: between 1865 and 1900 more than 13,500,000 foreigners reached American shores. Prior to 1880 most were from northwestern Europe but from then on large numbers began to come from central, eastern, and southern Europe.[19]

Cities grew rapidly, reflecting both the immigration and the changing job market. The urban population which was a little over six million in 1860 rose to just over 30 million in 1900, almost a five-fold increase. This meant that whereas in 1860 only four out of every ten Americans lived in an urban place, by 1900 it was almost seven out of every ten.[20] Not only did population growth add to the needed labor force, but, as we noted above, it also created new markets for agricultural and manufactured products. Similarly the settlement of the West opened a large market.

By the time of World War I the United States was an industrial nation with an increasing portion of the labor force in the factories, mines, and mills. But it is not only the change in work locale which is significant; there were important changes in social relationships and in the nature of work.

WORK AND LABOR DISCIPLINE

Industrialism requires a disciplined and motivated labor force, a problem all developing countries face. The potential workforce is usually rural with interests, attitudes, and behaviors that are often ill-suited to the needs of manufacturing or commercial agriculture. The way this problem is met is largely through coercion, as we observed in the case of slavery.

Coercion in shaping up a labor force is common the world over: in England there were the Enclosure Acts and the Poor Laws; in Asia, long-term indentured contracts by colonial employers with penal sanctions for nonfulfillment; in Africa, a "head tax" or "hut tax," with natives receiving cash only through wage employment; in Latin America, peonage; in the U.S.S.R., forced collectivization of agriculture and slave labor camps, primarily during the Stalin era.[21] In the United States considerable coercion characterized the "padrone" arrangement among Greek and Italian immigrants, and the contract labor system, even though neither was extensively used. Under the "padrone" relationship boys were imported

[18] *Ibid.*, p. 7.
[19] *Ibid.*, pp. 56–57.
[20] *Ibid.*, p. 14.
[21] Harold L. Wilensky and Charles N. Lebeaux, *Industrial Society and Social Welfare* (New York: The Free Press, 1965), pp. 50–51.

and worked under conditions suggesting feudal serfdom; under the contract labor law enacted by Congress in 1864 indentured laborers were employed in ways which also had feudal aspects. Even though the law was repealed in 1868 the practice continued although the extent is not known.[22] In Hawaii, however, the contract system was widely used on the sugar and pineapple plantations and was very coercive.[23]

Persuasion may precede coercion in committing people to lifelong membership in the industrial workforce; that is, the initial emphasis may be on the carrot rather than the stick. Thus seemingly high pay and the prospects of regular wages may encourage people to enter the factory or the mill. Also, there is often great exaggeration of opportunities by labor recruiters. In any event, as migrants cut themselves off from other prospects, raise families, and go into debt they become increasingly dependent on this wage system, which in practice is coercive. Except for periods of prosperity and labor shortage loss of job or reduction in wages are a constant threat, as are the possibilities of illness or injury which may prevent one from working.

Further Development

The economic development of the nation included the commercialization of farming. The growth of the plantation system in the South was noted earlier; in the rest of the nation the demise of the self-sufficient farmer was quite evident by the first third of the 19th century. Although this cannot be dated precisely, commerical farming predominated in Ohio around 1830, in Indiana, Illinois, and Michigan around 1850, and in the Northwest by 1860.[24]

With the growing importance of manufacturing, commerce, finance, as well as commercial farming, new networks of influence and communication developed. While the town meeting and county courthouse politics were useful for settling local issues, increasingly the important decisions were being made at the regional and national levels. In addition, a new class of persons, enriched by the profits of manufacturing, commerce, finance, land sales, and commercial agriculture was extending its influence over the economy and the nation as a whole. Political and economic power are usually closely intertwined, and these businessmen took advantage of every opportunity to further their interests. Consequently, the years between the end of the Civil War and World War I are not only important as the period of intense economic development; this period also stands out in terms of tremendous waste of natural re-

[22] *Ibid.*, pp. 53–54.

[23] See Lawrence H. Fuchs, *Hawaii Pono* (New York: Harcourt, Brace, 1961).

[24] Richard Hofstadter, *The Age of Reform* (New York: Alfred A. Knopf, 1955), p. 39.

sources, the upsetting of ecological balances, and general destruction of the environment.[25] It further stands out as a period of tremendous speculation and dishonesty. Illegal rebates on shipping charges were common, as was the manipulation of securities. Whole legislatures were bribed and there were innumerable instances of businessmen and politicians involved in graft and corruption. Government jobs were commonly used for patronage and financial support.[26]

THE MANIPULATIVE SIDE OF INDUSTRIAL GROWTH

Not only did industrial growth proceed rapidly but so did monopolistic practices and the concentration of ownership and control of the most important elements of the economy. Industrial pools and combinations were evident in the 1880's; by 1890 there were 100 associations in such areas as whiskey, beef, sugar, nails, and electrical appliances. The Sherman Anti-Trust Act of 1890 was at most an inconvenience; it did not check this movement.[27]

The basic reason for these illegal arrangements was to maintain or increase profits. Secondly, they eliminated cutthroat competition, and thirdly they helped rationalize production and distribution and made them more efficient. (In regard to rationalization and efficiency, they are from the perspective of large-scale enterprises. For example, from the viewpoint of the customer the local meat market which provides the precise cut of meat desired and advances credit may be a more rational and efficient enterprise than the large "chain" store which does not offer such services.) In addition, the growing size of markets, both domestic and foreign, and the increased scale of business activities meant that large amounts of money were at stake: fortunes could be made by keeping prices high, driving out competitors, dividing markets, obtaining favorable shipping rates, or by securing exclusive contracts with local or national government. With little or no government regulation the ever present opportunity and temptation for corruption was often taken advantage of. For example, several companies were consolidated into the American Sugar Refining Company in 1887, and in the importation of sugar, $2,500,000 in taxes went uncollected over a number of years because of collusion with customs officials and "short weights." Even without dishonesty the profitability of the sugar monopoly can be seen in its being able to maintain a high profit margin regardless of growing conditions. Thus the American Sugar Refining Company was able to pay its

[25] This should be placed in proper perspective, however, for the amount of unsettled land and unused resources was still very great.

[26] Hays, *The Response to Industrialism*, pp. 17–24.

[27] Matthew Josephson, *The Robber Barons* (New York: Harcourt, Brace & World, 1962), p. 381.

stockholders dividends of nine per cent in 1892; 22% in 1893, and 12% during 1894–1899.[28]

Charles Coffin, president of General Electric, recommended to George Westinghouse that they both raise the cost of street lamps from $6 to $8. In response to Westinghouse's observation that $6 gave a fair manufacturing profit, Coffin indicated that it cost about $2 a lamp in payment to aldermen and some other government officials. "Thus," writes Matthew Josephson,

> in the new electrical industry the cost of political privilege came to be calculated with exact science. But in the field of public utilities, in the organizing of street-car lines, lighting and gas companies for the industrial cities of the country, the pace of exploitation was even more frenzied, while the barter of eternal franchises owned by the people was carried out with gargantuan cozenage and fraudulence.[29]

Such practices take advantage of situations which require economic development of a specific need, where the suppliers have a distinct advantage. It has been termed "honest graft," a practice described by George Washington Plunkitt as "I seen my opportunities and I took 'em." [30] Fraud, bribery, and other illegal methods were commonly involved in these practices.

The limited liability corporation provided the vehicle for consolidating virtually every industry in the country, and for manipulation and corruption on a fantastic scale. The typical procedure in forming a trust was as follows: a promoter would incorporate a brand-new business with a stated amount of capital, with the intent to combine material purchasing, manufacturing, distribution, and sales under one corporation. He would then form a syndicate of bankers or "underwriters" who would furnish cash or credit to buy up the scattered properties. With this done the market value of the stock sold by the corporation could be multiplied many times. Thus, when the American Tobacco Company was set up $10,000,000 in public stock was issued. The amount was subsequently raised to $70,000,000, and when the company was changed into a New Jersey corporation it was recapitalized at $180,000,000.[31]

In this manner large fortunes were made with relatively small investments. It is believed that the initial outlay in promoting the tobacco trust and capturing its stock was only $50,000. The National Steel Company which was worth $27,000,000 was capitalized at more than twice that amount—$59,000,000; the American Steel Hoop Company's money investment was $14,000,000 yet it issued $33,000,000 in securities.[32]

[28] Ibid.

[29] Ibid., pp. 384–385. The quotation is from p. 385.

[30] William L. Riordon, Plunkitt of Tammany Hall (New York: E. P. Dutton, 1963), p. 3.

[31] Josephson op. cit., p. 387.

[32] Ibid., pp. 387–388.

Despite the extent of the money manipulation and the power of these combines, this was small potatoes compared to the trusts after the turn of the century. By 1904, 395 corporations controlled nearly two-fifths of the capital in American manufacturing. Two well-known examples of the gigantic trusts, both extremely wealthy and powerful, were in the oil and steel industries. By 1904 John D. Rockefeller's Standard Oil Company controlled about 85% of the domestic petroleum business and 90% of the export trade; at the turn of the century J. P. Morgan's "Billion Dollar Trust," U. S. Steel, had tangible property worth $682,000,000 and was capitalized at $1,321,000,000. There were also holding companies and extensive interlocking directorates. The Federal Trade Commission estimated that through these means the House of Morgan controlled one quarter of America's total corporate assets.[33]

This practice of stock "watering" or inflating provided enormous gain for promoters and company directors. In setting up the U.S. Steel Corporation, Morgan underwrote and offered for sale $303,000,000 in mortgage bonds, $510,000,000 in preferred stocks, and $508,000,000 in common shares. Yet two-thirds of the preferred stock and all of the common had nothing backing them except the name or "good will" of the corporation. The total promotional costs for launching the Steel Trust was $150,000,000. Who ultimately paid for them? "Promotion costs plus 'good will,'" writes Josephson, "would be imbedded forever in the capital structure of the steel industry, exacting immense fixed charges annually upon the whole community in the shape of interest payments and dividends."[34] In order to make these payments, the profit margin, and in turn the price of steel, would resolutely be kept as high as possible. As an example, steel-rail quotations were held stationary for 13 years. "The wonder of it," Josephson continues,

> was that the toil of nearly 200,000 nonunion laborers working twelve hours a day would support this burden; the wonder of it was that the country, growing by leaps and bounds, needing steel in a thousand forms, would willingly pay toll to the bankers who commanded this key industry without owning it.[35]

Given the exploitation of workers, the bilking of the public, and the many illegal acts, to what extent were these "captains of industry" crooks? In the sense that they violated legal statutes they were criminals, and in fact there were many prosecutions.[36] But such behavior, or "white-collar crime," does not indicate that there is any greater criminality among the higher strata than the lower, as Edwin H. Sutherland

[33] Hays, *The Response to Industrialism*, pp. 23–24, 50, 55; and Josephson, *The Robber Barons*, p. 429.

[34] Josephson, *op. cit.*, p. 429.

[35] *Ibid.*

[36] See Edwin H. Sutherland, *White Collar Crime* (New York: The Dryden Press, 1949).

noted. First, the financiers and industrialists, in contrast to ordinary persons, were in a position to take advantage of opportunities through legal or illegal means. Second, their lawbreaking may be understood in part as responses to changed social situations in which earlier standards and practices seemed inappropriate; that is, attitudes, procedures, and statutes based on agrarian needs, small scale manufacturing, and concepts of free trade. These did not apply to the wider markets, growing demand, and machine production which created the opportunity for tremendous gain. On the other hand unrestricted competition limited profits, created chaos, and even destroyed industrial, marketing, and financial ventures; consequently the entrepreneurs acted to eliminate this disruptive element. Similarly, governmental regulations which favored competition and in other ways restricted business activities were fought by legal actions and if that did not work they were gotten around by illegal means; mostly they were circumvented or ignored. Another factor encouraging such criminal behavior is the attitude of one's fellows, and the associates of the businessmen defined such behavior as favorable.[37]

Also, different standards are applied to upper and lower strata crime. C. Wright Mills comments wryly that in terms of prevailing business practice and differential opportunity "[i]t is better . . . to take one dime from each of ten million people at the point of a corporation than $100,000 from each of ten banks at the point of a gun. It is also safer." [38] In addition, many in the middle strata, and those in the lower who could afford to speculate were caught up in the financial frenzy, at least during periods of prosperity. This helped mute any outcries against the shenanigans since much of the public had a piece of the action, or at least thought they did. But the moral corruption was only one aspect; the other was that unfettered capitalist industrialism was legitimated by many ordinary people who felt that they had a stake in the system. They saw themselves as being aligned with the interests of the capitalists for they were in effect partners in crime.

Yet in spite of the criminal behaviors these capitalists may also be viewed as innovators, and as "progressive" in terms of economic development; the country had not been faced before with the conditions to which they responded. For the new industrialism, as with major social change generally, requires the breaking down of old institutional arrangements. In this process of destruction new forms are created.

Creative Destruction

The term "creative destruction" is applied by Joseph A. Schumpeter to the development of American industrial capitalism at the turn of the

[37] Ibid., pp. 252–255.
[38] C. Wright Mills, The Power Elite (New York: Oxford University Press, 1956), p. 95.

century.[39] For capitalism is an evolutionary process in which there are incessant revolutions, a view also held by Marx. These revolutions usually follow the development of new markets or new processes. Schumpeter writes that the opening up of new markets, whether foreign or domestic, as well as the organizational development from the craft shop and factory to such concerns as United States Steel

> illustrate the . . . process of industrial mutation—if I may use that biological term—that incessantly revolutionizes the economic structure *from within*, incessantly destroying the old one, incessantly creating a new one. This process of Creative Destruction is the essential fact about capitalism. It is what capitalism consists in and what every capitalist concern has got to live in.[40]

Yet what about the monopolistic practices and the exploitation of labor which were cited earlier?

Schumpeter holds that the various monopolistic practices furthered rapid industrialization and raised the general standard of living, rather than the opposite. He points out that these practices actually reduced inefficiency in production and that output increased continuously since the 1890's. Similarly, the living standard of the mass, in terms of the number of hours that have to be worked in order to buy various items, has continued to rise. Moreover, the monopolistic activities of the American capitalists drove out inefficient producers and created sufficient stability to realize the potential of new processes and markets. As for excess profits, they provided money for new investments. In addition, Schumpeter believes, with monopolies prices are not higher, *other things being equal*. This qualification is important because such discussions are usually based on the assumption of free market conditions with perfect competition, which do not exist. Also, his general thesis is that the practices of these large capitalistic industries were beneficial in the long run, in spite of short run dislocations, unnecessary business failures, recessions, and unemployment.[41]

There regularly occur throughout history periods of tremendous change in which many old institutions and beliefs are radically altered. Many factors contribute but the economic seem to be the most important. During such times new social types who are able to take advantage of the opportunities come into prominence; they strive ahead boldly and create a new social order. Over time they or their heirs become the basis of a new aristocracy; they enjoy the wealth, deference, and honor of their position. Sometimes they relax, but even if they remain energetic their

---

[39] Joseph A. Schumpeter, *Capitalism, Socialism and Democracy* (New York: Harper Torchbooks, 1962), pp. 81–86.

[40] *Ibid.*, p. 83. Emphasis in the original.

[41] *Ibid.*, pp. 81, 89, 100–101, 108. Schumpeter notes the importance of steady growth to minimize dislocations and the undesirability of the destruction of efficient but young enterprises because of temporary market conditions. Also, although he does inveigh against indiscriminate government "trust-busting" he is not opposed to regulation provided it is carefully considered. *Ibid.*, pp. 90–91, 90n.

attitudes and ventures are in tune with the conditions they helped establish: they no longer fit the changing situation of new needs and potentialities. In turn they are replaced by new social types who now move ahead to again establish a new order and more or less destroy the old. Henri Pirenne observes that this pattern was noticeable as early as the latter part of the 11th century. He writes that the innovative capitalists

> . . . have at the beginning been nothing else than parvenus brought into action by the transformations of society, embarrassed neither by custom nor by routine, having nothing to lose and therefore the bolder in their race toward profit. But soon the energy relaxes. The descendents of the new rich wish to preserve the situation which they have acquired. . . .[42]

It had been usual that the innovator's children added little to the fortune, and that his grandchildren concentrated on spending it; as Schumpeter notes, "from shirtsleeves to shirtsleeves in three generations." [43]

There are many instances of this generational pattern, and cases in which the fortune is dissipated by the second generation. The fortune established by Thomas Hancock prior to the Revolutionary War is a case in point. His nephew John inherited it—half a million dollars, which was a huge amount in those days—and through high living managed to spend it within ten years after the Revolution. Cleveland Amory observes that as King of Boston society John Hancock

> . . . lived on a social scale that included the wearing of solid gold buttons and the snubbing of George Washington. But when he died in 1793 he left no will at all, and even his house, Beacon Hill's famed Hancock House, once the pride of Yankee Society, was unable to ride the storm.[44]

Yet in recent times when immense fortunes such as those of Astor, Carnegie, Vanderbilt, and Rockefeller are created they tend to persist or increase, because of the professionalization of management, investment counselors, and special tax benefits. The latter include political pay-offs and such devices as family trusts. Even if the fortunes do decline somewhat over time, or are eclipsed by the wealth of new capitalists the families remain powerful because of the sheer magnitude of their accumulation. They remain influential as regards political parties, government, and style of life. In a liberal parliamentary democracy the rich are a source of campaign funds and thus influence candidates and platforms. In truth they influence the government, even if the party or the candidates they back do not win, for other avenues are open to them. For example, through local or regional levels pressure can be exerted on

[42] Henri Pirenne, "The Stages in The Social History of Capitalism," *American Historical Review*, 19 (April 1914), 515.

[43] Schumpeter, *Imperialism and Social Classes* (New York: Augustus M. Kelley, 1951), p. 169.

[44] Cleveland Amory, *The Proper Bostonians* (New York: E. P. Dutton, 1947), p. 38.

Congress, administrators, and judges so that favorable decisions are rendered.

The important point is that even when legislation which seeks to reduce the economic or other power of such individuals or their businesses is passed, the money they control and the politicians and government officials who are beholden to them help blunt the attack. Through compromise some of their power is reduced, but the basic structure remains the same. That is, institutional arrangements may be modified, tax advantages reduced, and certain business practices sharply curtailed. Yet the concerns remain in private hands, tax loopholes are found, and new practices are worked out. The privileged continue to hold a disproportionate share of social goods, be they political influence, wealth, or income.

Differential Benefits

That there was tremendous inequality in the distribution of wealth when the great fortunes were made may be inferred from income data. Unfortunately they are not at all reliable prior to 1913 and even then they are not complete. Furthermore even then they show only income and not total wealth. Nevertheless, in 1917 one per cent of the population received 15% of the total income. Over the years the percentage of income this stratum received fluctuated but never dropped below 12%; in 1929 it was 15%. If we look at the income of the highest five per cent category, these persons obtained 25% of the total income in 1917. There was some but not much fluctuation in succeeding years, and in 1929 their percentage was 26.[45]

While we know that in 1917 one out of every 100 people was receiving about 15% of the total income, and that five out of every 100 took in a quarter of the total, we don't have such detailed information for the rest of the population, especially for those on the bottom. We can only infer that there was maldistribution all along the line. What it was probably like is suggested by these 1929 figures for each 20% of the population, or each income fifth: considerably more than one half the total family income was received by the top income fifth; a little more than 19% was received by the next income fifth; approximately 14% was obtained by the next income fifth, while the two lowest income fifths *together* received only 12.5% of the total.[46]

The figures that are available are shown in Table XIV-1, which also gives a breakdown of the income of the top five per cent.

[45] *Historical Statistics of the United States, Colonial Times to 1957*, p. 167.
[46] *Ibid.*, p. 166.

TABLE XIV-1. Family Personal Income Received by Each Fifth, and Top Five Per Cent, of Families and Unattached Individuals, 1929

Income		Percentage
Highest Income Fifth	{Top 5 per cent	30.0%*
	{Remaining 15 per cent	24.4
Second Income Fifth		19.3
Third Income Fifth		13.8
Fourth Income Fifth and Lowest Income Fifth		12.5
	Total	100.0%

*The difference between this figure and the one cited earlier in our discussion is due to different bases used by the Census Bureau in compiling the data.
Source: U.S. Bureau of the Census, *Historical Statistics of the United States, Colonial Times to 1957* (Washington, D.C.: Government Printing Office, 1960), p. 166.

Needless to say, the captains of industry and their lieutenants lived well. Yet these parvenus were snubbed by the high society of America—the old rich who often were not as wealthy but who had social position and recognition. The parvenus set out to emulate them, and their activities and life style are graphically described by Dixon Wecter.[47] There were persons at all levels who obtained vicarious enjoyment from this opulence, and those who had pretensions to society or were socially mobile furnished the market for the many etiquette books that were published at the time. The *Bazar Book of Decorum* (1870) advised: "When you salute a lady or gentleman to whom you wish to show particular respect, in the street, you should take your hat entirely off and cause it to describe a circle of at least ninety degrees from its original resting place." *The Manual of Social and Business Forms* (1887) warned against bad manners such as "Eats with his mouth too full;" "Drinks from the saucer, and laps with his tongue the last drop from the plate," and "Scratches her head and is frequently unnecessarily getting up from the table." Other guides such as *Manners that Win* (1880); *The P.G., or, Perfect Gentleman* (1887), and *Success in Society* (1888) were clearly intended to help the ambitious parvenu.[48]

The results of the "creative destruction" were benefiting one segment of the society, principally the higher strata and to a lesser degree the highly skilled portion of the workforce. But what about the lower strata, especially the industrial workers and the farmers?

"Creative Destruction" Reexamined

As we noted earlier, Schumpeter contends that despite the dislocations and deprivations which occur with important change, as during the

[47] Dixon Wecter, *The Saga of American Society* (New York: Charles Scribner's Sons, 1937).

[48] *Ibid.*, pp. 177–179.

emergence of large-scale industrial capitalism, the population benefits in the long run. But the problem is that men and women live in the short run. As we observed in Chapter I the vast majority of people have only their labor to sell and depend on their paychecks for the things they need for themselves and their families. Consequently, insufficient income, whatever the cause, means not enough food on the table, squalid living conditions and other deprivations, even though living standards are rising for the upper levels and will improve for everyone in 20 or 30 years.

The large-scale industrial growth produced great riches, but side by side with them were harsh working conditions. The workday was long—12 hours in the steel mills, for example—and the employees had very little protection or say regarding their conditions of work. In addition there was an appalling injury rate especially in industries such as steel. There was also great squalor particularly in the large cities. In New York, near the turn of the century, it was estimated that a family needed a minimum annual income of $700; yet one-third to one-fourth of factory workers earned about $500 a year.[49]

The most degraded of the workers were found in the boarding and lodging cellars. Not only were they characterized by the lowest standard of living but the inhabitants were stratified according to what they could afford. Those who paid 37½¢ per week for board and lodging slept on loose straw on the floor and ate at the "first table." This was the highest category. Next were those who paid 18¾¢ a week: they slept on the bare floor and sat at the "second table." The weekly charge for persons in the lowest category was 9¢ and they ate at the "third table." These individuals also slept on the bare floor but were turned out if 18¾¢ lodgers were available.[50]

The food in these hostelries was obtained by children who were sent out to beg or by professional beggar women who contracted with the proprietors. All the baskets of food would be brought in at a certain hour and dumped on the table. Those in the "first class" dined first and they were followed by the second-level boarders; the third category ate what remained. These conditions held for the worst-off urban industrial workers; the standard of living for the skilled mechanics was much higher.[51] But they too were affected when business slowed down.

Economic instability including periods of prosperity followed by recessions and depressions, overproduction and then unemployment, and business failures added to the industrial workers' woes. The way they were affected may be illustrated by Chicago in 1893 where there was widespread factory unemployment. While tourists were still flocking to the city's World Columbian Exposition, wages were being cut between 10 and 20%. Relief measures were inadequate and there were demon-

---

[49] Patrick Renshaw, *The Wobblies* (New York: Doubleday Anchor Books, 1968), p. 24.

[50] Ware, *The Industrial Worker*, pp. 15–17.

[51] *Ibid.* The New York slums were quite profitable: a return of 100% on their value was not at all uncommon.

strations by the unemployed who denounced the rulers of the society.[52] A reporter described how the unemployed slept: On one pier 500 men lay under the open sky; 250 were crowded into a building on the excursion dock while others lay on the dock itself. Numbers of men slept in such places as alleys, vacant lots, hallways, wagons, and the viaducts and rights of way of the elevated trains. Thousands found cheap lodgings in cellars which they shared with vermin. In the City Hall sleeping mechanics, sailors, ship engineers and mates covered practically every inch of floor space in the halls and on the stairs.[53]

Yet the authority structure continued to operate primarily for the benefit of the upper strata—the large property holders, industrialists, and financiers. By and large, the national and local governments, the laws, the judiciary, and the police seemed to serve their interests. There were few aspects of American life that did not feel the impact of corporate power. The cities were dominated by business interests[54] and increasingly workers came to depend on large enterprises for jobs. The growth of industrial capitalism very much affected the rural population as well. The change from local to national and international markets and financial and technological innovations encouraged large-scale "factory" farms. Many family operations could no longer compete against them, especially with the manipulation of the money market and shipping rates. Inability to borrow sufficient money at low interest to finance the season's planting critically hurt the small farmer; so did the railroads' discriminatory shipping charges.

Generally, neither the small farmer nor the laborer received redress or protection from the government, and the reasons are quite simple. In the first place the institutional arrangements in a society, especially the legal system, are commonly such as to benefit the upper levels. In the second place the tremendous economic and political power of the corporate giants so strongly influenced the legislative and judicial systems that there were few restraints over their actions. "Law!" exclaimed Cornelius Vanderbilt the railroad magnate, "What do I care about law? H'aint I got the power?" [55] Consequently, not only was anti-trust legislation ineffective against them but other attempts at restraints were overturned by judicial decisions.

Corporate power permeated the law and the courts which benefitted them handsomely. The dogma of natural rights and individual liberty, which was current in 19th-century America and well into the 20th was helpful as justification. Influential judges and the leaders of the American

[52] Chester M. Destler, *American Radicalism, 1865–1901* (Chicago: Quadrangle Books, 1966), p. 177.

[53] *Ibid.*, pp. 177, 179.

[54] Scott Greer, *Governing the Metropolis* (New York: John Wiley & Sons, 1962), p. 63.

[55] Renshaw, *op. cit.*, p. 24; and Hays, *The Response to Industrialism*, p. 55. The quotation is from Renshaw, *loc. cit.*

bar reduced to a minimum the police power of the federal and state courts and imposed judicial-made restraints upon the legal power. For example, Congress was prevented from putting into effect a federal income tax law, the Interstate Commerce Commission was emasculated, and anti-trust suits were regularly thrown out of court.[56] This pattern of favoring vested interests was nothing new; it had been set much earlier by the Supreme Court's decision in the famous Yazoo land fraud which was mentioned in Chapter XIII.

While the new capitalists benefited from the institutional arrangements and judicial interpretations they helped subvert what social legislation there was. A case in point is the vaunted Homestead Act, which was a failure. Not only was it badly and improperly administered but it also led to tremendous land speculation, and immense tracts of land were given to the railroads.[57]

Yet while the new capitalists opposed factory regulation, welfare, or other help for workers and farmers they did not hesitate to use the government for their own ends. This double standard is brought out by an observer of the period. He comments that the

> . . . magnates of industry . . . have not merely looked to the government to assist their enterprises, they have taken possession of it. Hat in hand, they have begged with such importunity that the law-making power, federal, state, and municipal, seems to have been looked upon as a private preserve. Yet these [magnates who have] . . . reduced it to a political art and method, never fail to raise the alarm when the humbler classes ask legislative aid of city or state.[58]

Under such circumstances protest movements may be expected. In a preindustrial situation they are likely to emerge as social banditry or millenarian movements which are essentially rural, or they may take the form of urban mobs or labor sects.[59] These responses are less likely in the industrial situation, although as we shall see there were some aspects of them in America.

The responses fell mainly into two categories: Utopian and protest. The former included a romantic element and the latter radical and reformist social movements.

Utopian Response to Creative Destruction

The Utopians were romantic in that they rejected the growing industrialism and urbanism. Their way of coming to grips with these changes

[56] Destler, *op. cit.*, p. 23.
[57] Hofstadter, *The Age of Reform*, pp. 54–55.
[58] John G. Brooks, *The Social Unrest* (London: Macmillan, 1903), pp. 46–47.
[59] E. J. Hobsbawm, *Primitive Rebels* (New York: W. W. Norton, 1959).

was to establish communal societies which would have an agrarian base, although a few did engage in manufacturing. They were Utopian in that they sought to establish a form of economy and social organization in which the burdens would be shared by all and stratification would be minimized or done away with. Most had a religious foundation and their members sought to return to true religion, modeled on the Early Church in which the faithful had lived the common life as brethren.[60] Apparently a very strong commitment to the communal goals of selflessness, a community of goods, and work in common, toward the end of achieving a just society was necessary. Such a commitment need not be religiously based; yet the communes with non-institutionalized religion or just "moral principles" were short-lived. The successful ones were organized on patriarchical principles with competent and strong leaders who often were charismatic.[61]

The commune model was one of great equality, minimal stratification, and considerable mobility. In addition each male member played a significant part in the distribution of social goods and in the critical decisions of the commune. The women were usually second class citizens in the authority structure. But they were in a much better situation in contrast to the society at large at that time. The observations of Charles Nordhoff who visited the major communes in the 1870's indicated equality in the distribution of social goods. He reported that there was sufficient and nourishing food for all, adequate clothing and lodgings, with basically no distinction in their distribution. This equality was helped no doubt by the simplicity of wants that was emphasized, and by the economic surplus group cooperation created. Industriousness, considerable self-sufficiency, and good business management, which included purchasing supplies at wholesale helped create this surplus. While part of it was reinvested in the common undertaking a portion was used up by providing each person with an equal share of social goods.[62] Thus was achieved what most societies have been unable or unwilling to accomplish. By contrast, most including the modern ones consist of two worlds: the haves and the have-nots.

The main basis for stratification, aside from the lower status of the women, devolved around the top leaders who were appointed and were likely to hold their positions for life. In the Amana and Shaker communes they were selected by the highest religious authority and seldom changed. They had almost complete authority, limited only by the requirements that they manage so as to preserve harmony and act within the general regulations of the association. While this type of leadership arrangement meant some stratification in many of the communes, the

[60] Franklin H. Littell, "Prefatory Essay," in Charles Nordhoff, *The Communistic Societies of the United States* (New York: Shocken Books, 1965; first pub. in 1875), pp. xv–xix.

[61] *Ibid.*, p. xx.

[62] See Nordhoff, *op. cit.*, pp. 390–392, 394, 397–398, 400–402.

next level of leadership, which was responsible for civil or temporal affairs which included finances, was much more democratic in personnel selection and decision-making. In the case of the Amana communes the male members annually chose 13 trustees who in turn selected the president. This body could act only with the unanimous consent of the members. The trustees lived in different villages but exercised no authority as individuals. In the villages the work arrangements and the keeping of accounts were the responsibility of the foremen and the "elders." The latter were a numerous body; not necessarily old, they were presumably men of deep piety and spirituality who were selected by inspiration and presided at religious assemblies. Servants were not permitted in this relatively egalitarian community; neither did anyone work for anyone else. However at planting time and harvest time needed workers would be hired from the outside.[63]

Among commune members there was apparently little or no alienation from work; neither was it hard, and the workshops were comfortable and well cared for. Nordhoff writes that in the successful communes such as the Amana the members worked industriously but not exhaustingly. Yet people labored for the common good; thus all efforts were considered of value and all work provided social recognition. On the other hand the industriousness, wise management, and cooperative efforts provided enough surplus so that exhausting labor was not required.[64] Moreover, the practice was that each person contributed to his ability and received according to his need.

A critical aspect of the communes was the subordination of the individual to the group, and social control was maintained by common understandings covering the customs and mores. Deviant behavior was minimized through collective criticism such as the "Confession of sins to the elders" among the Shakers, the *untersuchung* or inquiry into members' sins and spiritual condition among the Amana, and the mutual self-criticism of the Oneida Perfectionists.[65]

There were also secular communes but they were largely unsuccessful. As may be recalled from Chapter IX, Robert Owen the industrialist hoped that his New Lanark would encourage reform of the abuses of the English Industrial Revolution. He also established a secular commune in New Harmony, Indiana in 1825 as a model for the rest of the society. However, his idiosyncrasies and conflict among members over the form the organization should take led to its breaking up in 1828.[66]

Brook Farm, near Boston, which was discussed in Chapter X, was originally set up by a group of New England intellectuals in an attempt to unite intellectual life with manual labor. However, its members found

---

[63] Nordhoff, *op. cit.*, pp. 37, 394.

[64] *Ibid.*, p. 400.

[65] *Ibid.*, pp. 289–299, 393.

[66] See Ware, *The Industrial Worker*, p. 166.

Charles Fourier's ideas attractive, and it was converted to a Fourieristic cooperative, or Phalanx.[67]

Fourierism was a middle-class movement which attached itself to the worker agitation of the period, often to the latter's detriment. Its purpose was to reorganize society, especially industry, for it objected to a growing industrial feudalism that was replacing the old feudalism. Fourier and his followers sought to prevent class war and revolution which they saw as the outcome of contemporary trends. Their answer, in essence, was to make industry efficient and pleasant. Greeley's support of the movement reflected a conservative's attempt to avoid the dangers of the new industrialism as well as to head off a working class revolution.

The Phalanxes failed within a few years, the longest one lasting 11. There were basically two reasons for the failure: The first, as noted by Ware, was that unfortunately ". . . business men were not then ready to make industry 'attractive.' Labor was cheap and plentiful, and the only ones who interested themselves in the matter were intellectuals and some workers." The second reason was that the ideology reflected European middle-class fears of working-class revolution, a fear generally not shared by Americans; in fact, Fourierism was too conservative for America.[68]

To what extent was the commune an alternative to the disruptive industrialism? Even though most eventually failed, a good number were successful, and a few lasted for a long time. Nordhoff noted 72 successful ones in 1874, and all told there were about 5,000 people living in such communities in 13 states.[69] The successful communes were religious; also many of their members were immigrants and ethnic ties provided a bond which would be expected to weaken in succeeding generations. But the total commitment required, the generally strong religiosity, and the asceticism made them unattractive to most people.

Yet these were the first successful attempts in modern times to offer an alternative to the new industrialism. The communes provided a degree of equality which was unmatched in the larger society, where a few received the lion's share of social goods while many more obtained little beyond subsistence. It has only been in recent years that there has been a resurgence of this interest—in the kibbutzim in Israel and in several places in the United States. In any event the communal idea was not seen as the solution by the majority of the population at the turn of the century. Grudgingly, bitterly, most accepted the new industrialism for they felt they were at the mercy of this "creative destruction."

[67] *Ibid.*, pp. 164–175. See our discussion of Fourier in Chapter X.

[68] *Ibid.*, pp. 167, 169. The quotation is from p. 169.

[69] *Ibid.*, pp. 385–386. Fifty-eight of the 72 communes were Shakers.

Summary

Part and parcel of the rapid industrialization during the first half of the 19th century was a rapid increase in the scale of business activity, the corporate form, the widespread use of machinery, and rationalization of production. These developments also reflected new entrepreneurial perspectives. Previously, although profit was of great interest, producing goods and providing services for the community was an end in itself; but now profit became the primary emphasis. This encouraged business expansion, but it also encouraged and justified speculation, monopolistic practices, dishonesty, concentration of ownership, and the growth of great fortunes. Among the consequences was the widespread use of the national and local authority structures for corporate interests. In spite of the popular emphasis on individualism there had always been much government involvement with business; however, this was furthered immensely by the large corporations and holding companies' control over vital elements of the economy, and by their great influence over politicians, government officials, and sometimes whole legislatures. Corporate power also permeated the law and the courts. It was during this period that the modern corporation, with its amoral perspective, took shape.[70]

Such major alterations in the economy, Schumpeter observes, are a recurrent feature of capitalism. Old forms are destroyed and are replaced with ones more appropriate to the new conditions. Terming this process "creative destruction," he notes that it also benefits the lower strata because in the long run their standard of living rises.[71] This is true; as we emphasized, however, people also live in the short run. The changes also affected relationships among the strata, especially an increase in social distance between employer and employee. More and more, workers became objects, to be turned into a disciplined labor force. While there were government subsidies and other benefits for business, no aid was provided for the small farmer or laborer. During the first half of the 19th century life worsened for the industrial worker; overall, there was great inequity in the distribution of social goods.

As the scale of business activity grows, national and local authority structures become increasingly important for they are able to proffer benefits or sanctions. Hence, widespread business involvement with government is to be expected. Also, in an ideal typical sense, the larger community cannot count on the corporation acting in a socially responsi-

---

[70] We are not using "amoral" in a pejorative sense, but simply to indicate that the purpose of the corporation is to engage in profitable operations.

[71] Schumpeter, *Capitalism, Socialism and Democracy*, pp. 81–86.

ble manner; consequently, legal controls are necessary. This in turn leads to further business involvement in the political process to avoid restraints on its activities, social welfare legislation, or anything that may interfere with profits.

One of the outcomes of "creative destruction" is similar to what occurs in revolutionary change. In the latter the lower strata are "used" during the changeover to a new social order. They are most likely to suffer disproportionately, while the major gains go to other strata. During "creative destruction" the lower strata are also "used." Workers whose temperament or skills are no longer appropriate are discarded, while those employed in the new impersonal situations are subject to the vagaries of the marketplace. They no longer have available the help that more paternalistic employers might provide, nor are there government welfare measures. Small farmers who cannot compete in regional and national markets are also discarded; many become part of the new industrial workforce, most likely in the lowest skilled and lowest paid positions.

Under these circumstances protest usually occurs. However, movements which challenge the distribution of social goods, which seek to alter the authority structure, must cope with popular ideologies that oppose collective action. Such movements are also hindered by the strong business influence in the executive, legislative, and judicial components of government. This influence, together with the ideologies, make reform, let alone basic change, extremely difficult. Nevertheless, the more articulate and at times the most desperate protested. While the objections were largely ineffective, a few led to important social movements, some reformist and a few revolutionary. In the next chapter we detail the attempts to overcome the consequences of the "creative destruction."

Chapter XV. Reformist and Radical Responses to "Creative Destruction"

Widespread change, especially where there are considerable dislocations and inequities in the distribution of social goods, is likely to be accompanied by class-based protest movements. One of the bases for incumbents of strata forming into classes is a serious decline in the well-being of numbers of people, particularly when other groups appear to be benefitting. In the new industrialism there was deprivation in several of the strata and differences between the haves and the have-nots were increasing. These factors, plus deliberate actions such as the manipulation of money and railroad rates, as well as periodic depressions, helped engender a whole host of protest movements beginning in the second half of the 19th century. Among them were Locofoco, Greenback, Henry George, Granger, Populist, Progressive, Communist, and Socialist. There were also reformist labor movements such as the American Federation of Labor and the Congress of Industrial Organizations, and radical ones such as the International Workers of the World.[1]

Early Protest Movements

Many reform movements began in the eastern part of the United States and some appealed to both the rural and the urban deprived. The Locofocoism which had originated in the Jacksonian era was transplanted to the Middle West in the 1840's and the 1850's and agitated against the trusts, particularly the railroad monopolies and their exploitation. But the influence of this movement which also stressed free trade was not limited to the Midwest.[2]

The name "Locofocos" resulted from an intra-party conflict in Tammany Hall in 1835 in which a faction of radical Democrats bitterly fought

[1] See Harry W. Laidler, *History of Socialism* (New York: Thomas Y. Crowell, 1968).

[2] Charles M. Destler, *American Radicalism, 1865–1901* (Chicago: Quadrangle Books, 1966), p. 3.

the party organization. They were opposed to its control by those reflecting the interests of the privileged classes; they were against bankers and banking in particular, sought reform of the city government, and in other ways reflected the concerns of the working class. At a Tammany Hall nominating meeting this faction had voted down the organization's choice, after which the gas lights were turned off plunging the hall into darkness. But from the light of matches and candles they were able to continue; the matches they used were called "locofocs," hence the name.[3]

The Greenbackers sought inflation to aid in paying debts and this appealed to farmers; their program to end financial manipulation and usury and to establish a national bank was also attractive to wage earners.

THE PLIGHT OF THE FARMERS

The difficulties of the farmers led to widespread agitation and attempts at structural change. One of the chief problems was that the institutional arrangements, particularly the financial system and tariffs on foreign manufactured goods protected the manufacturing and related commercial interests. But the farmer was at the mercy of a "free" market which could easily be depressed by foreign surplusses. He was also at the mercy of the banker who lent him money for seeds and implements, the railroad which shipped his crops, and the middleman who purchased them.[4]

It was the grinding burden of debt that intensified strata differences and led to class formation and conflict. In borrowing money for seeds and implements, a mortgage on the farm provided the necessary security. If the farmer received a good price after the harvest, if the interest rates had been reasonable, and if money was still worth as much as when he had obtained his loan, then he would be able to repay it. Or at least keep up the interest payments. However, increasingly during the last two decades of the 19th century, farm prices were low and interest rates very high—between 20 and 25%. The farmer was also hurt by the dollar's changing value; when he had borrowed, it was worth more than when he sold his crops. Creating further difficulties was the inelasticity and shortage of money. When the crops were being sold there was a great demand on the money in circulation but there was not enough currency available to pay the prices the farmer wanted. Being unable to hold

[3] Arthur M. Schlesinger, Jr., *The Age of Jackson* (Boston: Little, Brown, 1945). Many Locofocos later supported the Barnburners, another radical wing of the Democratic party, who wished to destroy the corporations and their abuses. After 1848 some Barnburners returned to the Democratic party while others joined the Free-Soilers which became a part of the new Republican party.

[4] John D. Hicks, *The Populist Revolt* (Lincoln, Neb.: University of Nebraska Press, 1959), p. 74 ff.

on to his crops because of their perishable nature, he was forced to take whatever money he could get. Thus he not only received fewer dollars but they were deflated dollars, which works to the benefit of the lender.

After the crops were sold, however, and the farmer went to buy new farm implements or things that he or his family needed, prices rose! Once the crop-selling period was over and the abnormal demand for currency dropped, more was available; with more money available, its value declined. These inflated dollars meant that the farmer had to pay higher prices for his purchases. Not only did the creditors, the middlemen, and the railroads benefit at his expense; Wall Street speculators and others made enormous profits by buying heavily when prices were low and selling when they were high.[5]

The economic consequence of these conditions, plus a heavy tax burden, was that many farmers were unable to keep up their interest payments, let alone repay the loan. Then the mortgage holder foreclosed and the farmer was likely to lose all his property. "In the late eighties and the early nineties," John D. Hicks writes,

> foreclosures came thick and fast. Kansas doubtless suffered most on this account, for from 1889 to 1893 over eleven thousand farm mortgages were foreclosed in this state, and in some counties as much as ninety per cent of the farm lands passed into the ownership of the loan companies.[6]

Agrarian Protest

The social consequences were collective resentment and class formation. Many farmers saw themselves as an exploited group, being taken advantage of by an entrepreneurial-financial-commercial capitalist class primarily in the eastern part of the United States. Commentaries of the time clearly point up the antagonism. The farmers believed that the big businesses, the trusts, and the monopolies joined with the railroads and when necessary with the politicians ". . . to hold the people's hands and pick their pockets."[7] They believed that the eastern capitalists had conspired ". . . to levy tribute upon the productive energies of West and South," and that they had turned the American freeman into ". . . a tenant at will, or a dependent upon the tender mercies of the soulless corporations and of absentee landlords."[8] Class differences are expressed in this turn-of-the-century poem:

[5] Hicks, *op. cit.*, pp. 86–92.

[6] *Ibid.*, p. 84.

[7] *The Farmer's Alliance*, September 30, 1890. Quoted in Hicks, *op. cit.*, p. 78.

[8] Smythe, in *Review of Reviews*, Vol. 10, p. 44 and Goodloe, in *The Forum*, Vol. 10, p. 355. Quoted in Hicks, *op. cit.*, p. 81.

There are ninety and nine who live and die
In want, and hunger, and cold,
That one may live in luxury,
And be wrapped in a silken fold.
The ninety and nine in hovels bare,
The one in a palace with riches rare.

* * *

And the one owns cities, and houses and lands,
And the ninety and nine have empty hands.[9]

The protest movements of the farmers must be understood against the tremendous changes that were taking place. Up to about 1870 there was generally a broad diffusion of wealth, status, and power. The small merchant or manufacturer, lawyer, and editor were persons of local eminence. It was after the Civil War that nationwide sources of power and prestige emerged, wealth became concentrated, and the new rich bypassed the smaller businessmen and the "old" middle class.[10] Also, the frontier was being closed; no longer was it available as a safety valve, no longer could the deprived flee to new land in the West.[11] It was at this time that several groups were founded which organized into the "people's" or Populist movement.

The Populist Movement

The Populists were the first political movement to seriously confront the problems created by industrialism and to insist that the federal government has responsibility for the common weal. While the movement had romantic aspects, it had inherited the tradition of Jacksonian democracy, and stressed the natural harmony of interests among the productive classes. These people—urban workers as well as farmers—must unite against the plutocrats, the nonproductive capitalist exploiters.[12] The basic propositions of the Populists were first that the government must restrain the selfish tendencies of those who profit at the expense of the poor and the needy, and second that the people and not the plutocrats must control the government. To achieve the first they called for government ownership of the railroads, government control of money, and low interest loans; to attain the second they sought the Australian (secret) ballot, direct elections, especially of senators, the initiative, referendum, and recall. They also favored female suffrage.[13]

[9] *Alliance*, July 31, 1889. Quoted in Hicks, *op. cit.*, pp. 81–82.

[10] See Richard Hofstadter, *The Age of Reform* (New York: Alfred A. Knopf, 1955), pp. 135–137; and C. Wright Mills, *White Collar* (New York: Oxford University Press, 1959).

[11] Hicks, *op. cit.*, p. 405. See Frederick Jackson Turner, *The Frontier in American History* (New York: Henry Holt, 1920).

[12] Hofstadter, *op. cit.*, pp. 61–65.

[13] Hicks, *The Populist Revolt*, pp. 405–407.

Although the Populists' program was collectivist, it was not socialist either in purpose or spirit.[14] Nevertheless their proposals seemed radical indeed; however they were designed basically to reform the existing order and over time legislation was passed which ended or minimized almost all the abuses they had fought against.

Yet what about the class conscious statements in their platforms, pamphlets, and newspapers, a few of which were cited earlier? Undoubtedly some were simply rhetoric and others expressed the feelings of great deprivation; nevertheless the Populists contained the potential for a more radical or revolutionary movement. Yet, although they were successful in a number of state and local elections they failed to gain national political power. In the election of 1892 they polled more than 1,000,000 votes; but, even though they appealed to labor they did not get its support in the great industrial regions. For example, in Pennsylvania the Populist candidate received less than one per cent of the vote and the same was true in Massachusetts.[15] The next four years saw business panic, strikes, unemployment, depression, and worsening economic distress. The Populists and their sympathizers capitalized on these conditions to capture the Democratic Party convention in 1896 and nominated William Jennings Bryan. This convention, write Charles A. and Mary R. Beard, totally ". . . vibrated with revolutionary fervor." [16] The platform that was adopted denounced the Supreme Court which had invalidated the income tax law the previous year; it also demanded that the Court be reconstructed so that the burden of taxation would be made more equitable with wealth bearing its due share. Bryan's opponent was the Republican candidate William McKinley who had been picked by Marcus A. Hanna, an industrial magnate.[17]

"The battle between Bryan and McKinley," write Beard and Beard,

> was accompanied by censorious charges and teroristic threats, aroused the country from coast to coast, as it had not been moved since 1860. Bryan defended his cause and his followers against what he called "English toadies and the pampered minions of corporate rapacity." His party, he declared, represented "the masses of the people, the great industrial and producing masses of the people . . . the men who plow and plant, who fatten herds, who toil in ships, who fell forests, and delve in mines . . . who produce the wealth of the republic, who bear the heaviest burdens in time of peace; who are ready always to give their lifeblood for their country's flag." [18]

McKinley countered that Republicans "would squarely face this 'sudden, dangerous, and revolutionary assault upon law and order and upon

[14] Destler, *American Radicalism*, pp. 17–24.

[15] Charles A. Beard and Mary R. Beard, *A Basic History of the United States* (New York: Doubleday, Doran, 1944), pp. 332–333.

[16] *Ibid.*, p. 334.

[17] *Ibid.*

[18] *Ibid.*, p. 335.

those to whom is confided by the Constitution and the laws the authority to uphold and maintain them.' " The editor of the New York *Tribune* assured his readers that Bryanism had sprung from "the assiduous culture of the basest passions of the least worthy members of the community." [19]

Although the vote was close, McKinley won, 7,000,000 to 6,500,000. Thus Populism with its revolutionary potential was thwarted. Its failure was in large part the inability of small farmers and the urban proletariat to forge a common bond, for they defined their interests differently. The workers feared that the inflation the farmers wanted would harm them by raising prices; in turn they favored high tariffs which would protect their jobs against foreign-made goods.[20]

Never in the history of the United States had such a large potentially revolutionary movement existed. Other movements which gained considerable support were basically romantic, as was true to some extent of the Progressives or strictly reformist, as in the case of the New Deal. Truly radical or revolutionary movements were very small and unable to attract anything like a mass following. A strong individualistic strain remained and although on occasion Americans might band together for the common good it was a kind of practical collectivism, for limited or short-run objectives. The aim was not to do away with inequality but rather to increase opportunity; the desire was not for equality in any communal or socialistic sense, rather it was for greater equality of opportunity. To achieve this people increasingly began to turn to the government.

Government as Reform Agent

Looking to the government for redress was not unreasonable since the principle of the state as an agent of reform had already been established; this was one of the outcomes of the Granger agitation to regulate the railroads. Led by Illinois in 1871–1873 some states had begun to set up such regulatory agencies.[21]

These attempts to cope with economic and political crises were home-grown responses and largely pragmatic. In the Old World, programs for reform were more ideologically based, and the Marxian socialist movement was one of the important ones which made its way across the seas.

[19] *Ibid.*

[20] Samuel P. Hays, *The Response to Industrialism: 1885–1914* (Chicago: The University of Chicago Press, 1965), pp. 44–45.

[21] Destler, *American Radicalism,* pp. 9–11. It is interesting that there was a strong eastern influence in this: for example, the theory upon which the regulating was based was first championed by a New Yorker who had been educated at Harvard. *Ibid.*

The Granger movement, a predecessor of the Populists, was founded in 1867 and expanded rapidly following the panic of 1873. It captured several Midwest state legislatures, reaching its high point in 1875.

Marxian Socialism

Marxian Socialism came to the United States with the arrival of numbers of German revolutionaries, following the unsuccessful uprisings of 1830 and 1848. But several things limited their effectiveness. First, they were beset by ideological conflict over such questions as whether they should participate in politics or trade union activities, and whether a socialist state would be expected to wither away immediately or eventually. Second, the American workers were interested in more practical policies such as those of Samuel Gompers which focused on wages and working conditions. In addition, the Marxists became involved in the anti-slavery movement and the Civil War.[22] And finally, they were foreigners propounding an alien creed.

There were two indigenous movements which attracted some interest, that of Henry George, and the socialists. The followers of Henry George urged land reform and indicted the existing business system. His writings appealed to natural rights and offered an alternative to Marxian Socialism; they promised social justice while preserving individualism. George propounded his ideas not only through his writings but also through agitation, principally in San Francisco and Oakland, California. His work greatly influenced the labor movement of the time.[23]

The emergence of an American born socialist movement was influenced by the 1888 novel *Looking Backward* by Edward Bellamy. In it the hero lies down for a quick nap only to awaken 100 years later in 2000 A.D., and proceeds to describe the Utopian society that has developed. The book which pictures among other things communal living and eating arrangements and a labor army in which each person serves for a limited period of time sold over 1,000,000 copies in a few years.[24] This novel offered an antidote to the destruction and demoralization of industrialism and led to socialistic movements in the United States. It appealed to many Americans who were socially conscious but would have nothing to do with foreign and doctrinaire theories such as Marxism. The movements sought to establish Utopian communities and use them as a base for gaining political power, but they came to naught.[25]

Socialistic ideas derived from American Utopian writers such as Bellamy and to some extent from Marxist thought, strongly influenced the Populists and later movements. Marxist organizations which reappeared

---

[22] Laidler, *History of Socialism*, p. 577; and Patrick Renshaw, *The Wobblies* (New York: Doubleday Anchor Books, 1968), pp. 17–18, 20.

[23] Destler, *op. cit.*, p. 13. See Henry George, *Progress and Poverty* (New York: Robert Schalkenbach Foundation, 1962).

[24] Edward Bellamy, *Looking Backward* (New York: Houghton Mifflin, 1966).

[25] See Selig Perlman and Philip Taft, *History of Labor in the United States, 1896–1932* (New York: Macmillan, 1935), pp. 224–226.

after the Civil War at times had impressive memberships, garnered size-able numbers of votes, and occasionally elected some local candidates. Yet the ideological conflicts which plagued the Marxists prior to the Civil War continued and led to many splinter groups and much infighting. The critical problem was how to act in regard to the growing number of industrial and other workers and the burgeoning labor movements. Those influenced by the German socialist Ferdinand Lassalle sought the establishment of workingmen's cooperatives with state aid, emphasized the similarity of interests between farmers and industrial workers, and urged the elimination of middlemen so that workers could afford to pay farmers a fair price.[26] As the socialistic movements continued to grow they took the position that basic changes could best be attained by the ideas of Socialism, and political activities should be supportive toward this end. They were encouraged by the growing unionization, even though the goals were primarily to improve wages and working condi-tions. The opposing viewpoint, as stressed by the forceful Daniel De-Leon, head of the Socialist Labor Party, insisted that political organiza-tion was the primary reason for participation in labor unions, that organized labor could provide the base for revolutionary change. This position was diametrically opposed to the "bread and butter" unionism of Samuel Gompers and the American Federation of Labor; they accepted the capitalist system and worked within it to give a greater share of the surplus to the workers. Great invective was used by the DeLeonites in attacking these "pure and simple trade union" leaders who they called "labor fakers." [27] In addition, much energy was spent on internal rifts within the Socialist Labor Party, on conflict between its followers and groups which split off from it, and in the attempts of the DeLeonites to take over other organizations.

While these battles were going on in the East, socialist movements which would eventually become the Socialist Party were forging ahead in the Midwest. Formed in 1901, the Socialist Party was an amalgam of diverse elements: "opportunistic" socialists who favored immediate de-mands and municipal ownership and reform; the "impossibilists" who ignored immediate demands but wanted a clear-cut revolutionary pro-gram for overthrowing capitalism; reformers who were not socialists but wished to support a party of protest, and "middle of the road" Populists. Although the "impossibilists" were very vocal, from the beginning the party was controlled by those who favored immediate demands and re-forms.[28] The Socialist Party grew steadily in membership and influence between 1901 and 1912. There were 15,975 dues-paying members in 1903; by 1912 the number had risen to 118,045. The party's candidate, Eugene V. Debs, received 402,400 votes in the presidential election of

[26] Laidler, op. cit., pp. 578–579.

[27] Ibid., pp. 578–581.

[28] Perlman and Taft, op. cit., p. 282; and Laidler, op. cit., pp. 587–588.

1904 and 897,011 in the 1908 election. In 1912 the party claimed over a thousand public officials who were dues-paying members. They included 56 mayors, over 300 aldermen, a number of state legislators, and one congressman. Milwaukee, Wisconsin was controlled by the socialists, as were a number of smaller cities. The party had considerable influence in the trade unions, and the socialist point of view was presented in a flood of books, novels, plays, pamphlets, poems, daily newspapers, and socialist schools which served as educational centers for the movement.[29]

World War I heralded the decline of the party for it was unalterably opposed to the war and urged the workers of all countries not to support their governments in such undertakings. The party recommended opposition to all capitalistic wars and urged demonstrations, petitions, and legislation against militarism, industrial conscription, press and mail censorship, and restrictions on free speech, assemblage, and organization. It opposed arbitration and fought for the right to strike. Party headquarters were raided, its press suppressed, and many socialists were arrested; membership fell from the 1912 high of 118,045 to 82,344 in 1918.[30]

While the Socialist Party reflected the interests and aspirations of a sizeable portion of the population it could not overcome the power of the two-party system on the national level. Neither could it overcome the basic conservatism of the population as a whole. Also, as in the case of the European wars of nationalism in the middle of the 19th century, Americans quickly forgot about the need for reform as they rallied around the flag.

World War I ends the first period of American capitalist industrialism. This capitalism created vast riches and material goods which were shared unequally; it monopolized the major aspects of the economy, and basically controlled the political life. It is understandable then that except for a number of local victories the protest movements were unsuccessful; while eventually many of their reforms were enacted, they failed as political movements. This is most significant, for only through a powerful political movement did there seem to be the possibility of any basic alteration in the nature of capitalist industrialism. That is, changes such as government ownership of banks, railroads, the telegraph system, and the large industrial enterprises. Certainly regulation of utilities, limitation of hours of work, protection for factory workers, and similar reforms which were enacted were highly desirable; these were also meaningful in the everyday lives of substantial numbers of the middle and lower strata. Yet these reforms did not alter the basis of capitalism. Neither did government regulation of business between the turn of the century and the first world war, even the legislation which came out of the Progressive movement.

[29] Laidler, *History of Socialism*, pp. 588.

[30] *Ibid.*, p. 591.

Reforming and Strengthening Capitalism

The rhetoric of the time suggested a crucial struggle between the anti- and pro-business interests, and that government regulation would mean the victory of human as opposed to property rights. But this was not the case: *First,* much of the legislation was wanted by business in order to insure stability. This is highly beneficial for planning and regularizing production and markets; it is important for regular profits and the long-term success of the enterprise. As a matter of fact, many of the bills which became federal law were *proposed by business interests.* Not only did they want to reduce cutthroat competition and in other ways increase stability but they also wished to forestall action by the states. There the tendencies were more radical, reflecting the protest movements of the Populists, socialists, and others. Also, the protesters might be more likely to gain political control of some state legislatures rather than the national. It was much easier to fight such moves by concentrating on one legislature, the national; moreover, not only was it controlled by business interests but often there was outright collusion between financiers and industrialists and Congressmen and government officials.

Second, regardless of the government restrictions, even when they "hurt"—as in the case of the railroads—the basic premises of capitalism were accepted. Thus there was no fundamental change; if anything, the regulations in the long run embedded capitalism more firmly. And *third,* the bond between government and business was strengthened immensely. One of the most significant outcomes of the Progressive period was the emergence of *political capitalism,* which continues until this day.[31] The significance of political capitalism for the present and future of stratification and class will be discussed in the concluding chapter of this book.

Among the movements which sought to cope with capitalist industrialism the most long-lasting has been the labor movement. It has involved relatively large numbers of people, occasionally engaged in protest, and in particular situations showed revolutionary potential.

The Labor Movement

The changing conditions of work, alteration of traditional relationships, and the tying of the local economy to the national and international provide the background for the emergence of the modern labor movement.

[31] Gabriel Kolko, *The Triumph of Conservatism* (Chicago: Quadrangle Books, 1967).

Dissatisfaction and the desire for a better way of life on the one hand, and the desire for protection from the vagaries of the economy and the arbitrariness of the employer on the other, provided the motive force. Organizational expertise was supplied by labor organizers, sometimes socialists or reformers; they helped direct the feelings and fears of those who had only their labor to sell into specific movements.[32]

While organizations of workers existed prior to industrialization they were basically craft guilds composed of persons who combined the functions of laborer, master, and merchant. They organized to limit the number of legal craftsmen, regulate the quality of work, and maintain customary prices.[33] There was little conflict of interests among the members. Although the apprentice was in the bottom stratum within this organization, and was undoubtedly exploited by his master, he could reasonably expect to eventually become a master himself.

The beginning of the 19th century saw a growing differentiation between employers and employees and the breaking down of customary relationships. Employers took advantage of this, especially as regarded the apprenticeship regulations; they utilized the competition of "illegal" men in order to lower wages and increase the hours of work. In turn the workers organized to protect the apprenticeship system and the closed shop, engaging in strikes to enforce their demands. Locked out by the employers and thrown on their own resources, the organizations of workers established legal defense funds, insurance, and sickness and death benefits for their members.[34]

That the early unions took the craft form is understandable since employees' associations develop in relation to the organizational basis of the employer.[35] The larger political structure also affects the nature of the unions as well as labor-management relations. Thus where political control severely limits class formation and class conflict, as in the Soviet Union, grievances tend to be handled through informal means. Where the labor movement is the adjunct of a political party conflicts tend to move into the larger political arena. And where the unions are part of a revolutionary or nationalistic movement political motivations play a large part in strikes and other labor-management conflict.[36] In the United States there are minimal hindrances to class behavior because of the political structure; therefore labor-management conflict may be expected to be out in the open. As none of the major parties appeals only to labor,

[32] See Herbert Blumer, "Collective Behavior," in Alfred McClung Lee, ed., *New Outline of the Principles of Sociology* (New York: Barnes & Noble, 1946), pp. 199–202.

[33] Robert F. Hoxie, *Trade Unionism in the United States* (New York: D. Appleton, 1921), p. 78. There were early attempts to develop workers' cooperatives but they were given up. Perlman and Taft, *History of Labor in the United States,* p. 623.

[34] Hoxie, *Trade Unionism in the United States,* pp. 79–80.

[35] *Ibid.,* p. 80.

[36] Neil J. Smelser, *The Sociology of Economic Life* (Englewood Cliffs, N.J.: Prentice-Hall, 1963), p. 49.

disputes are not normally settled in the political arena. Also, since American unions are not part of revolutionary or nationalistic movements strikes and related conflict are likely to be based on economic rather than political issues. It is mainly for these reasons that the American labor movement is basically job-oriented, nonpolitical, and only minimally class conscious. Yet American unions have always existed in a hostile environment and historical circumstances and the intransigence of employers have helped shape a movement which is prone to violence and at times has exhibited revolutionary potential. From its beginning and at least up to the second world war the paramount concern of the American labor movement has been to maintain its existence. This is in contrast to the English situation: while those employers continue to oppose unions on specific demands they accepted unionism before the end of the 19th century. "But," write Selig Perlman and Philip Taft,

> to American employers unionism has always remained the invader and usurper to be expelled at the first opportunity. American employers were endowed by America's history with a will to power unrivaled in other countries. American employers were steeled in their opposition to unionism and at the same time enabled to make that opposition effective by the extraordinary strength of the institution of private property. . . . For, unionism however conservative its objectives, is still a campaign against the absolute rights of the private property of the employer.[37]

A basic difference is that the United States, in contrast to England, has always had a significant stratum of small property holders. In spite of the closing of the frontier in the last decade of the 19th century and the advent of large-scale industrial enterprises, small farmers and small businessmen abounded. In spite of depressions and mass bankruptcies and the very high failure rate of the small undertakings, new contestants would always come forth. Since some did succeed, and the opportunity to keep trying remained, this substantial stratum of small entrepreneurs persisted and helped shield the business system from assault. Thus, when the judiciary supported property rights as opposed to unionism they spoke for the majority of the population as well as for the large businessmen.[38]

The persistence of small property holding together with considerable opportunity for mobility are the chief factors minimizing class feelings in the United States. While there is substantial occupational inheritance among the lower strata there is enough movement upward to prevent the formation of a permanent lower stratum. The fact that some do rise, even though the distance is not great, is destructive of those subjective feelings which encourage class consciousness. Also minimizing class consciousness was the extraordinary ethnic heterogeneity of American

[37] Perlman and Taft, op. cit., p. 621.
[38] Ibid., pp. 621–622.

labor.[39] An additional reason is the lack of an hereditary aristocracy as in Europe, although this is of secondary importance.

Even where the differences between employees and employers were very great in terms of the authority structure and the distribution of social goods, the laboring stratum saw the situation as basically economic. That is, the political aspect was minimized because universal male suffrage was not an issue when unions became important. This was in contrast to other countries where workingmen were still denied the franchise when their labor movements began.[40] Thus America lacked a meaningful ideological basis for a politically radical labor movement. While the conflicts which did arise had a revolutionary potential in terms of their intensity and magnitude, they had little immediate impact on the social structure even though they did eventually lead to reforms. Once specific conflicts were over and employees either achieved some gains or were defeated, things returned pretty much to their former state. Even where union leaders were ideologically radical—we noted earlier the influence of socialists in the labor movement—the unions were basically "bread and butter" oriented. As we observed, they sought better wages and working conditions—a larger cut of the economic pie—rather than a basic reorganization of the society. This was true of many of the crusades of the farmers and others who attacked the capitalist system when economic deprivation spurred them to organize; they were just as prone to castigate labor for seeking to prevent wage cuts or for going out on strike.[41]

With the growth of a national market, labor organizations also developed on a national scale. However businessmen continued to bitterly fight collective bargaining and union recognition; [42] they resisted any attempts to modify the authority structure or the distribution of social goods and insisted on their right to absolute control. They further insisted that existing arrangements were just if not beneficient to the workers and believed that if the latter were dissatisfied outside agitators were responsible. The following expresses the sentiments of the employers and their spokesmen as regards labor organizers:

> [These unions leaders are] a professional set of agitators, organizers, and walking delegates who roam all over the country as agents for some combination, who are vampires that live and fatten on the honest labor of the coal miners of the country, and who are busybodies, creating dissatisfaction among a class of people who are quite well disposed, and who do not want to be disturbed by the unceasing agitation of this class of people.[43]

[39] *Ibid.*, p. 622.

[40] *Ibid.*

[41] *Ibid.*

[42] See Hays, *The Response to Industrialism,* pp. 53, 64–67, 68–69; and Perlman and Taft, *History of Labor in the United States.*

[43] John G. Brooks, *The Social Unrest* (London: Macmillan, 1903), p. 34.

However this was no employer but a judge, Judge Jackson of West Virginia. Business engaged in an open shop campaign in order to destroy labor unions and used such devices as "scientific management" as propounded by Frederick W. Taylor. This was a means of strengthening management's hand and weakening unionization.[44]

Nevertheless, employees organized to protect their jobs and improve their conditions of work and there was a tremendous growth in union membership: from 447,000 in 1897 to 2,140,000 by 1910. This was nearly a five-fold increase while the number of gainfully employed during this period rose only by two-thirds.[45] Yet the preeminent task of American unions, Perlman and Taft emphasize, was to stay alive.[46]

Struggle for Survival

The growing differentiation between employers and employees, the development of an industrial proletariat, the intransigence of employers, and the lack of institutionalized means for resolving disputes led to many work stoppages. Between 1890 and 1900 they averaged over 1,600 a year,[47] and there was great violence on both sides. Employers used lockouts, blacklisting, industrial spies, and sometimes armed forces they obtained from the Pinkerton organization or hired independently. In turn workers engaged in strikes, sabotage, intimidation and other forms of collective action.

Of all the industrial nations of the world the United States has the most bloody and violent labor history. There are hardly any industries or sections of the country in which violent confrontations have not occurred. Yet most often they arose during labor disputes and in specific situations, such as pickets and sympathizers attempting to prevent strikebreakers from reopening a struck plant or trying to keep raw materials from entering or finished products from being taken out. The conflicting parties usually included company guards, police, or even National Guardsmen who were used to prevent interference with plant operation.[48]

Sometimes the violence was caused by company guards, by the police who were usually strongly influenced by or under the control of manage-

[44] See Reinhard Bendix, *Work and Authority in Industry* (New York: John Wiley & Sons, 1956), p. 265.

[45] U.S. Bureau of the Census, *Historical Statistics of the United States, Colonial Times to 1957* (Washington, D.C.: Government Printing Office, 1960), pp. 72, 99.

[46] Perlman and Taft, *op. cit.*, p. 621 ff.

[47] U.S. Bureau of the Census, *op. cit.*, pp. 98–99.

[48] Philip Taft and Philip Ross, "American Labor Violence: Its Causes, Character, and Outcome," in Hugh D. Graham and Ted R. Gurr, eds., *Violence in America: Historical and Comparative Perspectives* (New York: Bantam Books, 1969), pp. 281–282, 380–381.

ment, or by National Guard or federal troops. At times the violence was initiated by strikers or sympathizers but it was usually in response to provocative management or police actions. However these were often exacerbated by conditions which encouraged collective behavior. The violence arose primarily when people's livelihood was threatened, as when there were wage cuts or large-scale layoffs. Anti-union actions which were seen as threatening jobs were also causes: when management refused to honor a union agreement, fired workers identified as union organizers, or refused to rehire those who had gone out on strike.[49]

Picture this situation: wages are cut and workers strike in protest; management refuses to bargain but instead announces that those who walked out are fired; non-strikers, sometimes newly-arrived immigrants or persons from out of town, are brought in. Company guards or the police shepherd the non-strikers through the picket lines, and they also protect those bringing in raw materials and taking out the finished products. Successful operation means that wages will remain cut; it also means that strikers no longer have jobs. Also the plant is now being picketed (unless a court has issued an injunction which is quite common). Nevertheless outside there are many strikers and sympathizers who are milling around, and the company guards, police, or troops add to the tension. Any interference with the operation of the plant is usually dealt with quickly and often brutally. Usually the first brick is thrown by a striker; thus the violence is usually started by the worker side, although in a number of instances there is suspicion that such violence was initiated by an *agent provocateur* in the pay of the company.

While the strikes and the attendant violence were almost always blamed by the public on labor the coercion by management was largely ignored. That is, the actions of employers, judges, and others were also a kind of brutality against the workers although it was less blatant than physical acts. Moreover such coercion, plus the physical kind as carried on by company guards or local police subservient to management was perfectly legal and morally justified. Private property was sacrosanct, there were no laws which required union recognition upon majority vote, collective bargaining, or living up to union-management agreements. The laissez faire ideology and stress on individualism provided justification for anti-union actions. The plant owner of the time felt morally correct if not impelled to prevent the organizing of his workforce or, if there was a union, to destroy it.[50] Some even held that the existing authority structure and distribution of social goods were underwritten by the Almighty. During a violent anthracite strike in 1902 a local photographer sent a letter to President Baer, head of the major coal company, appealing to him as a Christian to settle with the miners. Baer replied:

[49] *Ibid.,* pp. 281–282, 380–382.
[50] Bendix, *Work and Authority in Industry,* pp. 267–274.

I see you are evidently biased in your religious views in favor of the right of the workingman to control a business in which he has no other interest than to secure fair wages for the work he does. I beg of you not to be discouraged. The rights and interests of the laboring man will be protected and cared for, not by the labor agitators, but by the Christian men to whom God in His infinite wisdom, has given control of the property interests of the country.[51]

This attitude should be seen against the contradictory perspectives of the time: on the one hand many Americans cherished the illusion that class divisions did not exist; on the other hand differences in life chances and conflict were rationalized through Social Darwinism. Charles Darwin's theory was popularized and held that evolution occurs through a process of natural selection, a struggle for existence in which the more capable survive and the less fit perish. Translated into societal processes by writers such as Herbert Spencer and John Fiske, the theory emphasized free economic competition. Thus the successful were those who survived the struggle while the poor were the less able. Moreover, it was believed that poverty was a necessary evil and any attempts to abolish it would interfere with nature's law and hinder the success of the more capable. But, what about slums, long hours of work, and low living standards? They could be ignored, the Social Darwinists argued, for they were the sacrifices society had to pay for its own larger and more permanent good.[52]

Yet it was increasingly difficult to ignore such conditions as well as the widening differences between rich and poor, employers and employees, urban and rural workers, and native Americans and immigrants. Nevertheless there was a tendency to explain complex economic and social problems in terms of private and public morality. Thus poverty was supposed to arise from immorality and character defect and the poor were urged to be honest, thrifty, and sober. This explanation was applied to other areas as well. For example, corrupt urban government was attributed to dishonest officials and businessmen rather than to the difficulties of shaping an effective community amid rapid change. Consequently the sporadic "clean government" campaigns invariably failed for they were unable to provide solutions to the major problems of social adjustment and community organization that the cities faced.[53] This is analogous to current campaigns to eliminate drug addiction by doing away with drug pushers.

These perspectives help explain public reaction to labor-management strife. Given the minority position of organized labor the public could be an important source of political pressure and thus was a force to be reckoned with. The public might show sympathy for the underdog and

[51] *Independent*, August 28, 1902, p. 2043. Cited in Perlman and Taft, *History of Labor in the United States*, p. 43.

[52] Hays, *The Response to Industrialism*, p. 39.

[53] *Ibid*.

initially support strikers when they were clearly being treated unfairly, as when peaceful pickets were killed by company guards, policemen, or soldiers, when employers drastically reduced wages, used the blacklist, replaced native workers with immigrants, or brought in armed strike-breakers. The unhealthy and unsafe mines and mills, the deplorable living conditions outside, and the ways the employee's life was controlled sometimes struck a sympathetic chord. An illustration of control was the employer-owned housing which meant that the worker would be evicted if he defied management; another was the company store. Often called the "pluck-me store," it sold goods which were higher-priced and shoddier than in other retail establishments; in addition employees were required to patronize it and in some places they were paid in script which was redeemable only in the company store. During labor-management disputes credit would be withheld. This form of employer domination was similar to what the English workers experienced under Truck and Tommy Ticket, which we described in Chapter IX.

Apparently what much if not most of the public believed was that great differences among the strata were inevitable, that they were a part of the natural order of things in which the adventurous and risktakers should be rewarded handsomely. After all, they built the industries, created the jobs, and moved the country forward. As for the employees, they should work hard and not complain; rather, they should appreciate the fact that were it not for the entrepreneur they would not have a job. Moreover, although workers were needed, as a stratum they were defined as a less desirable element. Those who had the gumption could save their money and start a business of their own, or make their fortune in the West; the people who continued to toil in the mines and the mills were obviously the less fit. Yet this viewpoint included the assumption of equality of opportunity, that anyone who really wanted to get ahead could. Consequently obvious interference with opportunity was decried and great unfairness, as was noted above, was sometimes seen in that light. However, the public was fickle; it was quick to side with management if there was violence, economic loss, inconvenience, inflammatory newspaper articles and editorials, or the fear of radicals and subversion. Even where the initial response to labor disputes was sympathy to the strikers people turned against them, particularly when there was violence.[54] Regardless of who initiated it the strikers were usually blamed, and this was encouraged by most of the big city newspapers, the majority of which were anti-labor. Hostility to strikes and labor agitation was strong in the middle and upper strata, particularly within the business community. However, many religious bodies also showed great hostility; the Protestant religious press was bloodthirsty in its reaction.[55] For

[54] Taft and Ross, "American Labor Violence," pp. 382–383, 387.
[55] Hofstadter, *The Age of Reform*, p. 150.

example, this is what the *Independent*, a Congregational journal, had to say about violence:

> If the club of the policeman, knocking out the brains of the rioter, will answer, then well and good; but if it does not promptly meet the exigency, then bullets and bayonets, canister and grape . . . constitute the one remedy. . . . Napoleon was right when he said the way to deal with a mob is to exterminate it.[56]

We will cite only a few of the more important labor-management conflicts since this history has been well detailed elsewhere.[57] Actually most of the relations between labor and management have been peaceful. The reasons for our focus on violent confrontations are that under such circumstances issues tend to be sharpened and opposing interests are often laid bare.[58] Furthermore, the outcome, be it accommodation, victory, or defeat often tells us much more about the opposing interests than the rhetoric of biased contestants or outsiders.

Continuing Strife

Among the important confrontations were the Carnegie Steel and the Pullman Sleeping Car strikes, the disputes in the bituminous and anthracite coal mining areas, the conflict in the Western mines, and the activities of the International Workers of the World, or "Wobblies." All of these events were at the turn of the century—from the Carnegie strike in 1892 to the IWW activities which were important up to World War I. However, the pattern for these confrontations had been set a decade and a half earlier, particularly during 1877 which Robert V. Bruce aptly calls the "year of violence." [59] There was a severe depression: it began in 1873 and by the middle 1870's as many as 25% of the labor force, if not more, was unemployed.[60] For those lucky enough to be working wages were being cut and many were living at a subsistence level.

A *New York Sun* reporter gave an example of the earnings of a Delaware, Lackawanna & Western Coal Company miner. His monthly wage was $28.40, out of which he had to pay $9.40 for blasting powder, oil, and other working materials. The remainder went to support himself, his wife, their three children, and his 74-year-old father. The meals were mostly of starchy foods; there had been no beef in the house for six months. Other examples were a laborer with a family of five who had

[56] Quoted in Robert V. Bruce, *1877: Year of Violence* (Chicago: Quadrangle Books, 1970), p. 313.

[57] See, e.g., Perlman and Taft, *op. cit.* and Taft and Ross, *op. cit.*

[58] See Louis Coser, *The Functions of Social Conflict* (New York: The Free Press, 1956).

[59] Bruce, *op. cit.*

[60] *Ibid.*, pp. 19–20.

averaged $14 a month; another miner averaged $18 a month with which he provided for his wife, six children, and a dependent mother.[61] "For those who did not succeed," Bruce notes, "the 'pluck-me stores' had recently put in an undertaking service and a coffin department at not much more than regular prices." [62]

With the hard times unions were smashed; perhaps more important than the legal harassment and blacklisting was the fact that scores of men were available to take the place of every job-holder. By 1876 union membership had plummeted with only one in a hundred workers unionized. The year of 1877 saw a series of strikes in a number of areas but principally in railroading and mining. They were strikes of desperation and great violence; men fought to prevent wage cuts or being fired, or if there was a strike being replaced by strikebreakers. Clashes with strikebreakers, the police, company guards, and the militia occurred; meetings and demonstrations sometimes turned into bloody attacks by the police, and there were also riots for food.[63]

By the fall of 1877 the "Great Strike" was over; the railroads were running again, the Trainmen's Union had been destroyed. However, on balance the workmen gained: on many of the railroads pay was raised and the universality of the strike prevented reprisals except in a few instances. Most important the strike ended wage-cutting. This also put a floor under prices which helped break the spiral of deflation and depression.[64]

There were several long-run consequences that stand out: among them was the crystallization of two divergent management philosophies on how to deal with labor. One view was that workers were not simply objects, and that such things as morale were important. Thus in some plants relief and insurance plans, employee medical care, and other morale-building programs were instituted. This paternalistic concept was in contrast to the ironed fist approach which probably was the predominant view. An illustration of the latter was the Coal and Iron police which were hired by several of the Pennsylvania railroads. Extremely effective during the Great Strike, by 1902 they had largely replaced the regular police in Pennsylvania in industrial disputes.[65] These two perspectives were harbingers of what C. Wright Mills has termed sophisticated and conservative managers in contemporary American business.[66]

That the institutional arrangements which comprise the policing function of the state were controlled by the business strata was quite evident: if the companies didn't have their own police force the local consta-

---

[61] *Ibid.*, p. 294.

[62] *Ibid.*

[63] *Ibid.*, p. 17 ff.

[64] *Ibid.*, pp. 307–309.

[65] *Ibid.*, pp. 304–305.

[66] C. Wright Mills, *The New Men of Power* (New York: Harcourt, Brace, 1948), pp. 23–27.

bles who were usually beholden to them were at their beck and call; to a large extent this was also true of the state as well as the federal militia. Similarly, the judiciary served the business interests. While those responsible for police violence got off with a slap on the wrist, if even that, punishment of strikers who had damaged company property or who participated in riots or other disturbances was swift and often severe. Thus police and posse members charged with murder were acquitted while strikers and rioters were likely to be jailed. Another flagrant misuse of the judicial power was the standing injunctions issued against strikers and enforced by the Army. Such injunctions did not require a jury trial.[67]

One of the aftermaths of the Great Strike was the growing awareness of the nation-wide aspects of economic and political affairs and interest grew in some kind of federal regulation of the railroads. Labor realized the need for a national organization and the Knights of Labor grew to 700,000 in eight years. Another consequence was the greater political activism of workers, and "workingmen's parties" sprang up in many cities. The Workers' Party of the United States had some successes; a Communist organization, it reconstituted itself into the Socialist Labor Party. In addition labor and Greenback elements formed the Greenback-Labor Party. However, these movements which challenged the power of the middle and upper classes were cut short by the Red scare of 1877; similarly the Knights of Labor were destroyed by the public hysteria after the Haymarket Riot in 1886 in which the bomb-throwing had been provoked by the police.[68]

Fear over the growing control of the economic and political life of the country by nation-wide business interests was expressed by former President Rutherford B. Hayes. The first President to use federal troops in a labor dispute, his comments nearly a decade after the Great Strike remind one of President Dwight D. Eisenhower's concern over the growing military-industrial complex after he left office.

> Hayes had begun asking himself strange questions. "Shall the railroads govern the country, or shall the people govern the railroads. . . . This is a government of the people by the people, and for the people no longer. It is a government of corporations, by corporations, and for corporations, how is this?" And he came to the conclusion that "the governmental policy should be to prevent the accumulation of vast fortunes; and monopolies, so dangerous in control, should be held firmly in the grip of the people." [69]

These fears became more widespread and led to the passage in 1894 of the Sherman Anti-Trust Act. As we noted earlier this legislation was

---

[67] Bruce, *1877: Year of Violence*, pp. 307–309.
[68] *Ibid.*, pp. 315–318.
[69] *Ibid.*, p. 320.

ineffective in curbing the trusts; its first great triumph, however, was the jailing of the socialist Eugene V. Debs.[70]

The growing domination by the industrialists and their subjugation of workers continued, and there were large-scale and violent strikes.

HOMESTEAD

In 1892 a reduction of wages by H. C. Frick, the manager of the Carnegie steel works at Homestead, Pennsylvania led to a widespread and violent strike. The entire labor force went out and in turn Frick recruited some 300 guards from the Pinkerton detective agency, sending them in by night on river barges. The strikers were waiting for them, and in the battle which took place as they attempted to land, nine workers and three Pinkerton guards were killed. After 13 hours the Pinkertons surrendered. Subsequently, strikebreakers were brought in under the protection of the National Guard of Pennsylvania and production resumed. After dragging on for several months the strike ended in complete defeat with only a few of the strikers being rehired. The union, the Amalgamated Association of Iron, Steel, and Tin Workers which was an affiliate of the American Federation of Labor suffered an almost fatal blow. One of the initial problems of the steel union was that it restricted its membership to skilled workers and failed to recruit the growing numbers of unskilled. The depression of 1893–1897 further weakened it, as did the consolidations which formed the United States Steel Company, the largest industrial concern in the world. Not only was the union in a very weak position against this corporate giant, but the introduction of new processes lessened the need for the skilled workers who were eligible for membership. United States Steel opposed the extension of unionism and its defeat of a general strike in 1901 meant the virtual end of unionism in that industry for over three decades.[71]

PULLMAN

Another instance of large-scale labor-management violence was the famous Pullman Sleeping Car strike of 1894. Workers were incensed by injunctions issued against the leaders of the American Railway Union by the U.S. District Court in Chicago and became even more aroused with

[70] *Ibid.*

[71] Henry Pelling, *American Labor* (Chicago: The University of Chicago Press, 1960), pp. 97–99. It wasn't until 1937, with the encouragement of the New Deal's Wagner Act, that the steel industry was organized. The large steel companies, in contrast to earlier times, did not vigorously oppose unionization. See Joseph G. Rayback, *A History of American Labor* (New York: Macmillan, 1959), p. 351.

the sending in of federal troops. Their arrival precipitated extensive rioting and great destruction of railroad property. This was largely the result of pent-up bitterness against the railroads and the national government with its transparent subservience to eastern money interests; specifically, the open alliance between the White House, the United States District Court, and the General Managers Association. Also contributing were the hostility of the commandant of the troops and the anti-labor bias of the bulk of the Chicago press.[72]

To these several causes of violence must be added another one: The propensity for conflict in certain occupations over others. As Clark Kerr and Abraham Siegel have observed, there is greater likelihood where there is much homogeneity among workers, isolation from the general community, and where the working and living conditions encourage cohesion.[73] They found that mining had a high propensity, as did the maritime and longshore industries. Kerr and Siegel suggest that the unpleasant, unskilled, and seasonal nature of these activities attract tough and combative workers, which further adds to the potential for conflict.[74] We might add that these industries are also characterized by tough and combative management which often finds itself in cutthroat competition with similar firms. These are the factors which encourage class formation and conflict, as we noted in Chapter I.

While such conditions were found in railroading to a large extent, they were even more characteristic of bituminous mining at the turn of the century.

THE COAL MINES

Coal mining was a small enterprise activity in which cutthroat competition had reduced prices. Wages were lowered since there was no counter influence because of the union defeat in 1894. Also, Slavs and Italians who accepted lower wages were replacing the English-speaking miners. In addition, the workers were further angered by the company store, the exorbitant cost of powder, the compulsory doctor's fees with no choice of physician, and management dishonesty in paying for the coal mined. In that regard, the miner was paid by the carload and would be docked for impurities in the coal. He was also required to have a perpendicularly filled coal car rather than a rounded one, as had been the practice. Other abuses included short-weighing.[75] With the wage reduc-

[72] Destler, *American Radicalism*, pp. 177–180.

[73] Clark Kerr and Abraham Siegel, "The Interindustry Propensity to Strike—an International Comparison," in Arthur Kornhauser, Robert Dubin, and Arthur M. Ross, eds., *Industrial Conflict* (New York: McGraw-Hill, 1954), p. 195.

[74] *Ibid.*

[75] Perlman and Taft, *History of Labor in the United States*, pp. 20–35.

tions reaching 20% the miners struck, over 100,000 leaving the pits during the first four days.

There was a great deal of public support because of the miners' plight and the peaceful nature of the strike, and it was a success. It was a great victory in which a demoralized union which had previously been defeated challenged powerful national interests which depended on the coal. The miners' success also worked to the advantage of management as it stabilized prices and regularized labor relations in much of the industry. However, some employers retained an aggressive stance, as in the case of the Pana and the Virden Coal Companies which refused to negotiate and imported armed strikebreakers.[76]

In the anthracite fields the union had also been defeated previously. Not only had there been unsuccessful strikes but the existence of many ethnic groups often with great antipathies for one another made organization almost impossible. Working and living conditions were similar to those in the soft coal areas and there had been several wage reductions because of falling coal prices. The companies were extremely powerful; many of the mines had been acquired by the railroads which dominated the area and they used the police power as a weapon against the strikers. For example, in 1897 the miners at Latimer, Pennsylvania struck against the exactions of the company store. They put forth a set of demands and began picketing; yet 3,000 miners peacefully marching from Hazelton to Latimer to join in the picketing

> were met on the road by the sheriff and his deputies and ordered to disperse. The marchers failed to obey instantly. An order to fire was given, and the deputies emptied their weapons into the ranks of the unresisting paraders. Nineteen of the marchers lost their lives, and 40 were seriously wounded. Not a single weapon was found on the dead and wounded, many of whom were shot in the back while seeking to obey the sheriff's order. No overt act had been committed by the paraders, and the militia was called out to prevent further bloodshed. The sheriff and his deputies were subsequently tried for murder, but the jury failed to agree.[77]

The strike in the anthracite mines spread rapidly and shortly after it began 80% of the workers were out. This showed widespread support since only 8,000 of the 142,000 anthracite miners belonged to the United Mine Workers union. The support was amazing, given the polyglot population which was mentioned earlier. As soon as the strike seemed imminent, the United Mine Workers sent in a large force of organizers who succeeded in welding the heterogeneous and unorganized miners into a disciplined group. The strike was very successful, in large part because of favorable public sentiment. This was the result of the leadership of John Mitchell, President of the UMW who was able to avoid vio-

[76] *Ibid.*, pp. 21–29.
[77] *Ibid.*, pp. 31–33. The quotation is from p. 33.

lence by the strikers and presented a conciliatory attitude. The key was his appeal to fair play rather than to class interest.

By contrast the strike of 1902 had a great deal of violence. Brutally treated by the coal operators, the strikers responded in kind which escalated the conflict. In turn, this led to the use of the police power by the state. The militia was called in not only to protect the companies' property but also in an attempt to get coal mining resumed as supplies were dwindling throughout the nation. In spite of the presence of troops violence continued, and a summary by the *New York Tribune* showed that 14 persons had been killed; 42 severely injured; 16 had been shot from ambush; one lynching had been attempted; and there were 67 cases of aggravated assault. One house had been dynamited and 12 had been burned; ten other buildings had been burned, as well as three coal washeries and three stockades. Four bridges had been dynamited; six railroad trains were wrecked with nine attempted wrecks, in addition to which seven trains were attacked. Finally, there had been 69 riots and 14 strikes in schools against teachers whose fathers or brothers continued to work.[78]

Mitchell's conciliatory attitude contrasted with the coal operators'. Under President Theodore Roosevelt's urging Mitchell agreed to order a return to work provided that an investigative commission were appointed, with its decision to be binding on both parties. The coal operators rejected Mitchell's proposal, denounced the United Mine Workers as a lawless body, and charged that the mass of the miners were being coerced to strike. In addition, the owners claimed they could operate the mines if given sufficient military protection, and the Governor sent the entire National Guard of Pennsylvania into the strike area; however, their presence failed to increase coal production. The strikers voted almost unanimously to continue the strike until their demands were met, which refuted the claims of the employers that the union was forcing the miners to strike against their wishes. A Presidential commission to arbitrate the dispute was finally agreed upon by the operators and it awarded a number of gains to the union. It also condemned the use of the police for the benefit of management and criticized the employment of children in the mines. Yet the commission would not treat the union as a responsible partner in the industrial authority structure for it refused union recognition.[79]

Perlman and Taft emphasize the significance of John Mitchell's conservatism, conciliatory attitude, and his fear of arousing the American

[78] *New York Tribune*, September 30, 1902, cited in Perlman and Taft, *op. cit.*, p. 44.

[79] Perlman and Taft, *op. cit.*, pp. 44–47.

The coal owners agreed to a Presidential commission after Theodore Roosevelt had held a conference with J. P. Morgan. However, the employers accepted on the condition that no labor leader or ex-labor leader would be appointed. Nevertheless the President included the director of the Interstate Commerce Commission who had been the head of the Conductors' Brotherhood. He was appointed as a "sociologist." *Ibid.*, p. 46.

community's latent anti-labor feelings. They believed that public support was essential for labor union success, especially in vital public utilities.[80] This support is not as essential today with unionism more widespread and the labor organizations much stronger. Nevertheless, it remains important since only a minority of working people are unionized.

As we noted previously, the primary aim of American unions had been to maintain themselves in the face of hostile employers and the latent anti-labor feelings of much of the public. That staying alive was a real problem was seen in the cases of the railroad, steel, and coal unions; it was true in the craft as well as in the industrial labor organizations. The major energy had been devoted to fighting for job rights fixed under collective bargaining, and this is a basic reason why the American labor movement has been job-oriented rather than a force for fundamental change. The espousal of revolutionary causes was rejected for experience showed that this could lead to suppression by mob action. Or, labor might feel the force of the police power, ordered by public officials who readily responded to hysterical public opinion.[81] There were similar reactions when violence occurred which, rightly or wrongly, was usually blamed on the unions.

As the nation became more industrialized and urbanized, strata of employees and employers increasingly saw their interests as opposed to each other as they contested over the distribution of social goods, formed into classes, and engaged in class conflict. This conflict ranged from peaceful strikes to violent affairs which on occasion involved much of the nation. In the labor disputes we described above revolutionary rhetoric on the part of the workers began to be heard even though hindsight reveals that many of the goals such as nationalization of the railroads were reformist. Yet it should be kept in mind that there was much group solidarity born out of common struggles; ideologies which stressed human rights over property rights were current, and there were strong antagonisms toward industrialists, financiers, and public officials. It should also be remembered that the labor leaders, some of whom had radical backgrounds, had organizational expertise, a critical element in a social movement. While the potential for revolutionary change was there, such change was thwarted by suppression or settlement of the conflicts.

This labor-management strife was class conflict, according to Dahrendorf's theory. That is, in the sense that they were contests over the distribution of social goods by self-conscious groups in the authority structure of the work situation. However we would not call it revolutionary class conflict for the reasons stated above. Yet such conflict did occur in the western mines, and we next examine an important aspect of the American West which is never portrayed on television or in the movies.

[80] *Ibid.*, pp. 47–48.
[81] See *ibid.*, pp. 624–625.

The Wild (Class Conscious) West

"The violent industrial struggles in the mining regions of the West during the quarter century after 1890," write Perlman and Taft, "show a picture of class war as conceived by Marx." [82] The alignment was labor in one camp and employers in the other, with government a football between the two. This was due to the absence of middle groups such as farmers or merchants who did not settle the area until later. The pattern of conflict in the gold, silver, and lead mines of Idaho and Colorado was as follows: The operators attempt to cut wages because of falling prices or the introduction of labor-saving machinery. To prevent this the workers organize into the Western Federation of Miners. In turn the mine owners organize and generally present a united front against the union. Wages are then cut, the miners go out on strike, and the owners bring in strikebreakers. The strikers try to prevent them from taking their jobs, often at the point of a gun. The mine owners arm the strikebreakers and use the local police force and gun-toting company guards to keep the mines open. The mining community is now an armed camp and tempers are short on both sides. The shooting of a miner by a company guard leads to retaliation by the miners: the guards and company property are attacked, a mill is dynamited. Those sympathetic to the mine owners form an armed Citizens' Alliance and the sheriff deputizes the armed strikebreakers. The Citizens' Alliance and the strikebreakers attack the union miners and pitched battles ensue. The National Guard or federal troops are sent in to restore order. They also safeguard the company property, protect the strikebreakers, and disarm and arrest the strikers who are herded into "bull pens," held without trial and maltreated, or deported out of the state. Eventually most of the charges against the miners are dropped for lack of evidence, or if convicted the cases are thrown out after appeal. In a few instances a compromise between the union and the owners is reached and the miners go back to work; more often the mines are reopened but union members are not rehired. Those taken on must sign a loyalty oath to the company, affirm that the union is a criminal conspiracy and promise not to join it. In addition, they must provide a detailed history of their work experience so that union members or anyone with such sympathies can be ferreted out. The information is circulated among the operators and thus the union miners are effectively blacklisted and kept from working in these mines. [83]

Theoretically, the authority structure of the state is supposed to be neutral. Those responsible for enforcing the law are expected to be impartial; they are supposed to protect the rights of all groups in the com-

[82] *Ibid.*, p. 169.
[83] *Ibid.*, pp. 169–213.

munity. This should hold for all levels of government: the mayor, the governor, and the President on the one hand and the sheriff, the state National Guard, and the federal militia on the other. Where the government was neutral, as in the Cripple Creek strike of 1894 (the Governor had been elected as a Populist), it acted as mediator between union and management and affected a compromise.[84]

However, more often the government favored the mine owners, helped break the strikes, and enforced the open shop. Local authorities who were known to be sympathetic to the strikers would be forced to resign and would be replaced by officials who were likely to be company employees. The police power of the state, at the local, state, and national levels could be expected to do the bidding of the mine owners and the National Guard and the federal troops were extremely important in that regard. The militia usually acted as conquerors in enemy territory and under martial law would set up a military dictatorship. For example, "[I]n one of the mines the pumpmen had left their jobs in defense of the union shop. A Lieutenant went to the miners' hall and gave them five minutes to go to work voluntarily or be driven at the point of the bayonet." This was in Coer d'Alene, Idaho. In Victor, Colorado the militia raided the local newspaper and arrested the entire workforce following an editorial sympathetic to the union. After martial law was declared in the Telluride District the military established censorship over telephone and telegraph lines.[85] This type of behavior was in addition to the notorious bull pens and deportations which were mentioned earlier.

Clearly, the government was not neutral. Granted, the state has an obligation to prevent violence; nevertheless it used its police power to further the interests of the mine owners and against those of the striking miners. The judiciary was also used against the miners and in essence condoned illegal actions, as in the case of those charged with the bomb assassination of Governor Frank Stuenenberg of Idaho in 1905. He had been elected as a Populist eight years earlier largely as a result of the miners' vote. However, they considered him a traitor; he had been in office during the riots of 1899 and had declared martial law and was responsible for the mass arrests and detention of miners. After the confessed assassin claimed that the union had plotted the Governor's death, three leaders of the union were arrested and then *kidnapped* so that they might be returned to Colorado. The case stirred up the socialist and labor movements throughout the nation, and they rallied to the defense. Speakers at protest meetings and writers in the labor press continuously asked why legal processes had not been followed if these men were guilty beyond a reasonable doubt. They were in fact acquitted.[86]

[84] *Ibid.*, pp. 173, 189.

[85] *Ibid.*, pp. 186, 199, 205. The quotation is from p. 199.

[86] *Ibid.*, pp. 210–213. One of the defense witnesses who had been an employee of the Pinkerton Detective Agency produced reports which showed that their undercover agents in the miners' union had always counseled violence. *Ibid.*, p. 212.

Not only was this class conflict extremely violent and of great magnitude, but the opposing interests extended beyond the Western mines, drawing in the business community on the one hand and the labor movement and those sympathetic to it on the other. However the economic resources of the mine owners and the police power of the state were able to defeat the strikers in almost every case. Yet, in spite of the intensity and magnitude of the conflict the goals of the Western Federation of Miners were basically reformist. Aside from the desire to improve wages and working conditions there was interest in modifying the authority structure; in particular there was the wish to break down the overriding sanctity of private property that prevailed at the time, and to make working people a partner in industrial enterprises through collective bargaining. Nevertheless, the capitalistic arrangement was accepted. By contrast, the stated purpose of one very large union was the revolutionary transformation of the society.

The Bindle Stiffs

In addition to its revolutionary goals, the International Workers of the World differed from the other unions in another important way. Whereas the skilled workers were organized by the latter, the Wobblies spoke for the downtrodden of the labor force. These were the migrant agricultural workers and the lumbermen; these were the "bindle stiffs," who went from job to job carrying their bedroll or "bindle" on their backs. The effective life span of the IWW was from 1905 to 1924.[87] Unlike the Knights of Labor or the American Federation of Labor the IWW advocated direct action and sabotage; yet it was virtually free of violence.[88] Many of its founders including "Wild Bill" Haywood, Thomas J. Haggerty, and William E. Trautman desired a socialist state run by the workers. They believed that the working class could achieve power through a general strike in which the factories would be seized and the employers locked out. So did many of its members, but probably the majority had more limited goals centering on better pay and working conditions.

The membership rarely exceeded 100,000 at any one time although a total of as many as 1,000,000 had been in its ranks.[89]

Despite its advocacy of direct action, and having leaders and members who were professed revolutionaries, almost all of its strikes

[87] See Renshaw, *The Wobblies*, p. 2 ff. The origin of the nickname is unknown. One explanation is the "wobble saw" used in lumber mills; another is the instability of the organization.

[88] Taft and Ross, "American Labor Violence," p. 285.

[89] Renshaw, *op. cit.*, p. 40.

were peaceful. Even its attempts to organize itinerant workers—its "free speech" fights—involved passive resistance. Where violence occurred it was primarily caused by employers, the police, or vigilante mobs. Employers and the middle and upper classes of the communities in which the IWW tried to operate were enraged at their activities and fearful of their ideology. Between 1909 and 1912 this union concentrated on the West, seeking to improve the conditions of the migratory workers.

Usually in the communities where laborers were recruited the men would gather each morning and an employer's agent would choose from among them. The agent would encourage competition for the available jobs in order to drive down wages or would require kick-backs from those who were hired. IWW representatives would appear at these "shape ups" and make speeches denouncing the practices and urge the men to join together in order to protect their interests. In consequence of these activities—in which they were exercising their Constitutional rights of free speech—IWW members were jailed, beaten up, or tarred and feathered. When this happened Wobblies from far and wide would arrive, filling up the local jails, and generally inundating the town. In most cases the organizers would be released; in some instances the troops were called out.[90]

Two of the bloodiest episodes in the history of the organization occurred in Everett and Centralia, Washington; in each the IWW was the victim. Attacks on them were made by armed citizens and the authorities; yet the violence they were held responsible for was in response to these attacks.[91]

Nevertheless the IWW continued to organize those industries and the low-skilled workers spurned by the AF of L; it wasn't until the 1930's with the formation of the Congress of Industrial Organizations (CIO) that active recruitment of this segment of the labor force was again undertaken.

Continued IWW organizing success led to greater stability and to a degree of reformism in that it entered into collective bargaining agreements with employers it had earlier scorned. As it became more secure it also formed alliances with the socialists, the AF of L, the foreign language federations, and women's emancipation and birth control groups.[92] Patrick Renshaw holds that the Wobblies might have become the permanent spokesmen for the semi-skilled and unskilled workers had it not been for World War I and its drastic consequences for radical and socialist groups.[93]

One might conjecture that had the IWW remained a viable organization it might have quickened the movement toward greater consideration

[90] *Ibid.*, pp. 89–90 ff.

[91] Taft and Ross, *op. cit.*, p. 287.

[92] Renshaw, *op. cit.*, pp. 141–142.

[93] *Ibid.*, p. 142.

of human rights as opposed to property rights; in conjunction with the socialists it might have hastened reform legislation. Whether it would have been able to achieve its revolutionary goals, either through one big strike or in the legislative halls seems highly problematical. Yet it might very well have been a critical element in bringing about a wider distribution of social goods generally, and in particular improving the life conditions of the lower strata. But this is all speculation, for the upper classes saw in the IWW the danger of such a redistribution and used every means they could master, legal as well as illegal to destroy it. They were aided by the anti-labor sentiment of small businessmen and the conservative press. Consequently, in the minds of many ordinary citizens the IWW stood for bomb-throwers, foreign revolutionaries, agitators who upset formerly peaceful employer-employee relationships, hoboes and bums, and free love.

America's entry into World War I provided a convenient justification for using the full power of the state against them as well as against other radical organizations. The war also encouraged attacks by citizen groups.

> . . . the IWW was persistently hounded and persecuted during the war, by the judiciary at both the state and Federal level, and by self-appointed vigilante groups formed during the wave of xenophobia and war hysteria which swept the country after America entered the European conflict in 1917.[94]

Charged with sabotage and conspiracy to obstruct the war, 101 IWW leaders underwent a five-month trial under Judge Kenesaw Mountain Landis who later became the Baseball Commissioner. All the defendants were found guilty and long sentences and heavy fines were given out. While most of the IWW leaders were opposed to the war, for they saw it instigated by and for the capitalists, the organization had not taken an official position on the matter. It was clear that the authority structure of the state was being used to attack unpopular beliefs and in that sense the case is reminiscent of recent trials of leaders of movements against the Indochina War. Also, the government's move to destroy the IWW under the guise of patriotism was encouraged by the business community which would be happy to be rid of the organization's union activities.

There were many instances where employers and members of communities in which there were labor disputes took the law into their own hands. One of the most notorious occurred in the Arizona copper mines where the IWW led strikes against wage cuts while war-time profits were soaring. The Copper Trust and the local newspapers denounced the IWW as being pro-German, and in July 1917 members of the Bisbee Loyalty League rounded up some 1,200 Wobblies, tried them in a "kangaroo court," herded them into a cattle train, and transported them to the New Mexico desert. They were kept there without food or water for 36 hours,

[94] *Ibid.*

then they were beaten up and sent to a Federal stockade. There they were held without charge for three months before being released.[95]

An investigation by President Woodrow Wilson found that the strike had not been seditious, and although 21 leaders of the Bisbee Loyalty League were later indicted by a Federal jury none was convicted. The inadequacy of the evidence used to convict the leaders of the IWW, and the prejudicial effect of war time patriotism were eventually recognized, for by the end of 1923 the last of the IWW prisoners had been released. There had been an amnesty campaign which included many liberals, left wingers, and others. Senator William E. Borah joined in the campaign to free the prisoners, even though he had no sympathy for the IWW. In fact, he had prosecuted one of the leaders, William Hayward in Boise, Idaho in 1907. Borah maintained that there had been no evidence to "justify a conviction. . . . In other words . . . they were convicted under the compelling influence of the passions and fears which accompany wars." [96] It must have been small comfort for the IWW leaders to know that they had been convicted on insufficient evidence and because of strong wartime feelings, for by 1923 the IWW was all but dead. The trial in particular, as well as the intimidation, harrassment, physical violence, and legal coercion had destroyed the organization. Contributing to its demise was intense factional conflict.

In spite of its stated syndicalist goals, which included the abolition of the wage system, worker control of production, participatory government rather than a parliamentary system, and the achievement of power through a mass strike, it was never a revolutionary threat. Also, it is highly doubtful that the leaders took their revolutionary language too seriously. Although the IWW was a revolutionary agitational body in its early years, after 1912 it became increasingly conservative in its methods, playing the role of a hard-bargaining industrial union.[97] Nevertheless it was seen as a serious and immediate threat by the upper classes who trembled at the thought of a revolution in America as had just occurred in Russia.

The anti-radicalism of the 1920's hurt other left-wing organizations as well as the IWW. In addition to the Russian Revolution many strikes in America and a number of terrorist acts added to the climate of fear. Among them were several bombings and the discovery in post offices throughout the country of 36 bombs addressed to prominent persons. The most destructive incident occurred on September 16, 1920: a bomb went off in Wall Street, outside the House of Morgan, killing 34 people and injuring more than 220. The Attorney General, A. Mitchell Palmer, who had been responsible for wholesale arrests and deportations of radi-

[95] *Ibid.*, pp. 187–188; and Perlman and Taft, *History of Labor in the United States*, pp. 398–400.

[96] Renshaw, *The Wobblies*, pp. 188, 208, 209. The quotation is from p. 208.

[97] *Ibid.*, p. 216.

cals and immigrants claimed it was part of a plot to overthrow capital-ism,[98] which added to the hysteria and repression.

The fear of violence was only second to the fear of alteration of the au-thority structure with a change in the distribution of social goods. Large-scale violence was characteristic of early labor-management relations in the United States, as we noted earlier. This violence, which prominent businessmen and politicians, many clergymen, and the mass media claimed was the beginning of bloody revolution exercised many ordinary citizens. Thus, when such conflict occurred it usually worked to the ad-vantage of the employer, regardless of who was responsible. In many in-stances community sentiment was initially favorable to the strikers for often the inequities and injustices were blatant; yet with the advent of violence sympathy with the strikers was replaced by the desire to attain peace by any means, with little regard for the merits of the issues in-volved.[99]

But the overriding fear was basic change. Understandably the upper class was opposed for it saw any reallocation of social goods as occurring at its expense. And, having easy access to or control over political and economic resources it used them to the utmost to fight any movement which seemed a threat. As for the lower class, even though organizations such as the Populists or the IWW had wide followings they never at-tracted anywhere near a majority of the population. Therefore, the posi-tion of the middle class became critical. But enough of these people were either apathetic or sided with the upper class to deny success to the movements for change. The ideology of individualism, anti-labor sen-timent, the image of reformers as foreign revolutionaries, and the fact that many Americans were small property holders and feared that they might lose what little they had effectively allowed power to remain in the hands of the upper class. The mass media which was controlled by the upper class or mirrored its interests whipped up strong feelings against major reform. In addition, with much of the country still rural, the basic conservatism of small communities also played a part.

Summary

The "creative destruction" of capitalism leads to increased riches and material goods, but they are shared unequally. The inequities and dislo-cations engendered by the change encourage class formation and class-based protest movements. The persons who do not fit into the new or-

[98] See Hofstadter and Michael Wallace, eds., *American Violence* (New York: Vintage Books, 1971), pp. 430–433.

[99] Taft and Ross, "American Labor Violence," pp. 282–283.

dering are faced with absolute deprivation; even many who become part of the new arrangements suffer with the ups and downs of the economy, as market conditions change. Others experience relative deprivation. Ideologies aimed at greater equality arise, and they are in conflict with conservative perspectives which uphold the status quo. The conservative ideologies deny that there are great inequities in the distribution of social goods, and hold that what differences exist are due to individual variations in ability and effort. The conservative outlook also denies that there are class divisions, and where there are such tendencies believes that foreign agitators are responsible.

When, under worsening social and economic conditions, institutional arrangements become the focus of protest vigorous movements are likely to arise. These include agrarian as well as labor movements, each seeking to modify the authority structure and reallocate the distribution of social goods. However, each of these movements is likely to reflect conflicting needs making cooperation, which would lead to greater power, difficult. In addition, left protesters face great obstacles in trying to win over a substantial portion of the middle strata. Among them, in addition to conservative ideologies, are small propertyholders' fears that with major change they will lose what little they have, and repugnance of violence.

The preeminence of large business in the economy and in political life, and its strong influence in the judicial and police systems make basic change unlikely. At most the protest movements bring about reforms, which are beneficial for the lower strata and many others. But, rather than undermining the basic premises of capitalism, the reforms serve to embed them more firmly. Some, especially those involving regulation of business by the government, further cement the bond between them.

It is therefore not surprising that revolutionary movements made little headway in America. Although over the long run there has been considerable reform through legislation, the basic structure of capitalism, parliamentary government, and substantial differences between the haves and the have-nots remain. The depressions and dislocations which are endemic in a free market economy continued, as did protest movements which arose in reaction to them. The nature of modern social, economic, and political problems, and reformist and radical responses to them, are the concern of the next chapter.

Chapter XVI.   Modern Times

We have seen that industrialization brought with it new relationships between employer and employee and new meaning to stratification and class. Industrialization also increased the riches of the nation but not all strata benefitted equally; capitalist industrialism also meant greater ups and downs in the economy. During periods of deprivation, we observed, numerous class-based movements emerged and there was considerable violence. At times, the possibility of revolutionary conflict seemed real.

While revolution does not necessarily mean violence it is usually associated with it, for the state is likely to respond in this manner to serious challenges to the authority structure. When institutional arrangements are no longer functioning adequately widespread protest by the deprived engenders tremendous fear in the upper classes. Under normal circumstances protest can be accommodated or ignored, with minimal effect on the social structure. However, during troubled times agitation by any substantial number is seen as a grave threat by the upper classes who begin to imagine the possibility of being overwhelmed by the mass of the population. After all, the upper classes are outnumbered by the lower and since the value system and the threat of economic loss no longer serve to keep them "in their place" what is to prevent the have-nots from taking away the social goods from the haves?

To forestall basic change some reforms are usually instituted which may do away with some of the worst abuses, or at least make life more tolerable. But the only sure preventive is coercion by the state and the legal and police powers are used to the utmost for this purpose. As long as the state can maintain its monopoly on the use of force,[1] and as long as it does not hesitate to do so, revolution can be prevented. The usual pattern is the carrot and the stick: amelioration on the one hand and the mailed fist on the other, as was demonstrated in England during the Napoleonic Wars, and in the United States during its period of rapid industrialization. However, neither repression nor amelioration is sufficient to

[1] See Max Weber, *From Max Weber: Essays in Sociology*, trans. by Hans H. Gerth and C. Wright Mills (New York: Oxford University Press, 1946), p. 78.

explain lack of revolution. The chances of it occurring are extremely high if a substantial portion of a population is convinced of its need, and if proponents include such groups as intellectuals, numbers of business people and other "solid citizens," plus a sizeable stratum which has become organized, such as industrial workers, students, or peasants. Should these conditions exist, reforms may simply raise aspirations and increase the desire for more drastic change. Repression, by creating martyrs and arousing the sympathy of the uncommitted may lead more of the population to support or at least not oppose revolution. And at some point portions of the police and militia may become unreliable or join the revolutionary movement.

In asking what convinces people that major change is necessary, we refer to the discussion in the earlier part of the book. As we observed, a stratum may suffer great deprivation in terms of objective conditions, yet the incumbents may fight among themselves, say along ethnic lines, or, instead of blaming the social structure may be convinced that their difficulties are the result of personal failure. There is also a tendency to hold the beliefs and outlook of the higher strata. This is the case for persons in the middle levels, particularly individuals who have some property or are upwardly mobile; however, it is also true for many in the lower strata. Not only are these ideologies ever-present—in the mass media, for example—but they are reinforced in the socialization of lower strata children, at home and in school. Their socialization stresses obligations over rights and encourages acceptance of the status quo; and, in conjunction with such things as lack of participation in the organizational life of the community, results in political inefficacy. These factors inhibit class formation. On the other hand, a nation such as the United States does have conditions which are favorable for class behavior: impersonal ties between employer and employees; organizations, such as labor unions; equalitarian ideologies; a history of protest movements, and considerable differences in the distribution of social goods. In addition, there are regular ups and downs in the economy in which substantial numbers suffer deprivation.

These conditions have been characteristic of industrial America. So has the pattern of amelioration and force in dealing with protest, especially when there seems to be the possibility of significant alteration of the authority structure. We want to pay special attention to the Great Depression which is a case study of the likelihood of revolutionary change in America. As we shall see the government was quick to use violence during this period as it had done earlier in the Whiskey Rebellion, in Shays' Rebellion, and against the railroad workers, the miners, and the IWW. Yet there was great deprivation and discontent, radical organizations and activities, class conscious protests, and violence; there was also the widespread fear of revolution, probably like that on the eve of the French Revolution.

The Great Depression

On the surface the 1920's was a time of dazzling prosperity; yet the largess was not shared by all. As for the industrial workers, the technological advances and rising productivity went mainly into profits rather than real wages. In fact, for many the result was technological unemployment, which was particularly a problem for those over 40. Not only was the distribution of income and wealth inequitable but it grew more distorted.[2] Income stratification during the earlier Depression years shows the bulk of the population toward the bottom (Fig. XVI-1). Granted, money at that time was worth more; however, the distribution of total income of families and unrelated individuals by income fifths reveals much greater inequity than today. The reader may recall from Chapter III that in 1973 the two bottom fifths received 17% of the total income; this compares with 1929 when the income share of the lowest two fifths was 13%. However, in 1973 the top income fifth received 41% of the total income, whereas in 1929 it was 54%. The extent of the maldistribution can be seen when the income share of the top five per cent is compared for 1973 and 1929: in the current period it is 16%, in the earlier one it was 30%.[3]

The farmers did not partake of the prosperity, and with the Depression many lost their farms and became renters, sharecroppers, itinerant laborers, or migrated to the cities. Those who held on to them found they could not afford to harvest or sell their produce because of the great drop in prices; they therefore kept their goods off the market in an attempt to raise prices. Thus while a growing number of people had insufficient food, crops were being plowed under, produce was being burned, milk dumped, and livestock slaughtered.

What are those out of work to do? Most of the umemployed eked out an existence by reducing their food intake, wearing clothes until they fell apart, and by moving in with relatives. The worst-off begged, went from mission to mission, or stole; they lived in flophouses or shanty towns which were dubbed "Hoovervilles," or slept in parks or wherever they could find a place to lay their heads. Disposed farmers migrated to the cities, while some urban unemployed returned to rural areas. Others went from city to city looking for work and many became part of a large group for which transiency was now a way of life.[4]

[2] Irving Bernstein, *The Lean Years* (Baltimore, Md.: Penguin Books, 1960), p. 506.

[3] U.S. Bureau of the Census, "Money Income in 1973 of Families and Persons in the United States," Series P-60, No. 97 (Washington, D.C.: Government Printing Office, January 1975), p. 43; and *Historical Statistics of the United States, Colonial Times to 1957* (Washington, D.C.: Government Printing Office, 1960), p. 166.

[4] See David A. Shannon, ed., *The Great Depression* (Englewood Cliffs, N.J.: Prentice-Hall, 1960).

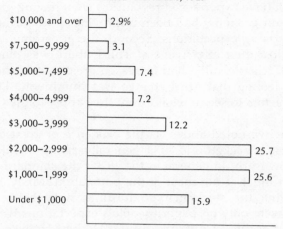

FIGURE XVI-1.
Percentage Distribution of Income of Families and
Unrelated Individuals, 1929

$10,000 and over   2.9%

$7,500–9,999   3.1

$5,000–7,499   7.4

$4,000–4,999   7.2

$3,000–3,999   12.2

$2,000–2,999   25.7

$1,000–1,999   25.6

Under $1,000   15.9

Source: U.S. Bureau of the Census, *Historical Statistics of the United States,
Colonial Times to 1957* (Washington, D.C.: Government Printing
Office, 1960), p. 165.

Family relations suffered, especially where the male was unable to fulfill the role of breadwinner.[5] Young people with no prospect of a job were increasingly a burden to their families and many became nomads, wandering from one end of the country to the other. There were other responses, such as self-help schemes, greater religious involvement, and resignation and despair. But there were also protests and demonstrations, most of them violent. The widespread deprivation, general unrest, and class antagonism made the possibility of revolutionary conflict real.

The social and political forces which were generated during the Great Depression were responsible for important changes which have significantly affected the society. But there was no revolution: there were no sudden changes in the social structure, particularly in regard to the ruling class or in the distribution of social goods. It may be worthwhile to restate our definition of revolution which was first discussed in Chapter I: *A relatively rapid and basic change in the authority structure of an association, where the protagonists are indigenous or identify with those who are indigenous.* The last point, it will be recalled, is necessary in order to rule out such change when an association is taken over by an outside force. This definition applies to violent revolutions such as the French, the American, and the Russian, as well as to non-violent ones such as the English.

[5] Mirra Komarovsky, *The Unemployed Man and His Family* (New York: Dryden Press, 1940).

For a revolution to occur it is necessary to have certain conditions, as we noted earlier. Crane Brinton, it will be recalled, found that, first, societies which have experienced revolution were having great economic difficulties. Their economy had been improving, however, and one consequence was rising expectations. Second, the government and the ruling class had lost their effectiveness. Third, there was much ideational change. Fourth, class conflict had increased greatly. And fifth, there was a widespread feeling that great change was imminent.[6] Let us look at each of these factors to see to what extent they apply to the Great Depression.

The first, as we noted above, is the existence of great economic difficulties against a background of a generally rising standard of living prior to the downturn. In general in the 1920's the standard of living had been rising for much if not most of the population. Many ordinary people were playing the stock market; fortunes were being made, even though many were only on paper; people's expectations were rising and there was great optimism over the future. Herbert Hoover, in his presidential acceptance speech of August 11, 1928 remarked that

> [we] in America today are nearer to the final triumph over poverty than ever before in the history of any land. The poorhouse is vanishing from among us. . . . We shall soon . . . be in sight of the day when poverty will be banished from this nation.[7]

Yet it was just a little more than a year before the good times came to a sudden halt, beginning with the stock market crash on "Black Thursday"—October 25, 1919. The collapse of American finance and with it much of the country's business was made clear on "Tragic Tuesday," five days later. Inflated stocks were being offered at any price, with no buyers; paper fortunes as well as real ones were wiped out overnight; loans were called in, mortgages foreclosed, banks failed, businesses went bankrupt, and unemployment soared.[8]

By March of 1930 between 3,200,000 and 4,000,000 had lost their jobs; a year later the number out of work had doubled; unemployment had increased 50% by the following year, and it reached a peak in 1933 with an estimated 15,000,000 jobless. By 1936 it had declined to between 5,378,000 and 8,145,000 but rose to between 9,000,000 and 11,000,000 in March of 1938.[9] This meant that by 1931 almost one out of every six members of the civilian labor force was out of work, and during 1933, the peak year, it was *one out of every four*. Even though the rate began to

---

[6] Crane Brinton, *The Anatomy of Revolution* (New York: Vintage Books, 1965).

[7] Herbert Hoover, *The New Day* (Palo Alto, Calif.: Stanford University Press, 1928), p. 16. Quoted in Bernstein, *op. cit.*, p. 247.

[8] See Shannon, *op. cit.*

[9] Paul Webbink, "Unemployment in the United States, 1930–1940," *Papers and Proceedings of the American Economic Association*, 30 (February 1941), pp. 250–251, in Shannon, *op. cit.*, pp. 6–7.

decline it rose again so that in 1938 one out of every five was unemployed.[10]

For the fortunate who had jobs pay rates fell, the number of hours worked declined, and many were employed only part-time. In 1929 the United States Steel Corporation had 224,980 full-time workers; by 1930 they dropped to 211,055; by 1931 the total was 53,619, and in 1932 there were only 18,938. By 1933 there were *no* full-time employees, just 112,000 part-time workers, or approximately half the number of regular employees in 1929.[11] The joblessness varied among industries and from place to place. The automobile, textile, and coal mining industries were in a virtual state of collapse. For example, in Toledo, Ohio, the number of employees at the Willys-Overland automobile company plummeted from 28,000 in March of 1929 to 4,000 by January 1930. The local Merchants and Manufacturers Association estimated that from 30 to 40% of the city's male labor force of 75,000 was out of work. In Detroit, the Ford Motor Company's payroll of 128,142 in March 1929 had dwindled to 37,000 by April of 1933. In the textile industry almost half of New England's 280,000 millhands were jobless with many others working only part time. In Lowell, Massachusetts two-thirds of the labor force was idle, and every third store was vacant. The Metropolitan Life Insurance Company reported that as of December 1930 almost 24% of its more than 356,000 industrial policyholders were out of work. Conditions were especially bad in the coal fields where operators cut wages with impunity because of the oversupply of labor.[12]

Even though white-collar as well as blue-collar workers suffered, unemployment was distributed unevenly among the strata; the lower the level the worse the situation. The unskilled were the hardest hit, next were the skilled, and then the clerical; managerial employees suffered the least.[13] In 1930 about four per cent of the office and sales people were out of work compared with over ten per cent of the skilled and semi-skilled and about 13% of the urban unskilled. By 1937, when the worst was already over, about 11% of the white-collar workers were unemployed or on public emergency jobs compared with 16 to 27% of the urban wage workers.[14]

Blacks were in worse straits than whites, and the large cities which contained many low-paid manual workers, many of them blacks, were worse off than small cities. There was a great deal of malnutrition and actual cases of starvation. In 1931 the New York City hospitals reported 95 such cases; there were numerous instances in the coal areas, where there

---

[10] *Historical Statistics of the United States, Colonial Times to 1957,* p. 73.

[11] Bernstein, *The Lean Years,* p. 507.

[12] *Ibid.,* pp. 254–256, 361.

[13] *Ibid.,* p. 257.

[14] C. Wright Mills, *White Collar* (New York: Oxford University Press, 1959), p. 281.

was tremendous poverty, as well as much malnutrition and a rise in the incidence of tuberculosis and bleeding dysentery.[15]

Considering the poor state of vital statistics at the time there was undoubtedly much more malnutrition, and probably more starvation than officially reported. Moreover, malnutrition and poor living conditions most likely made people susceptible to various diseases and contributed to a higher death rate from other causes.

Our judgment is that the first condition for revolution was fulfilled: a severe economic crisis following a period of general rise in the standard of living, together with rising expectations. The next question is how the government and the ruling class react to such a situation.

Local government was in a financial crisis; it was unable to handle the large relief load and in cities such as Chicago, teachers and some other public employees went unpaid, or were paid in script. Local governments quickly found that their tax base was inadequate, and with many people unemployed and businesses failing tax delinquencies increased greatly. By the fall of 1931 public as well as private relief was bankrupt in practically every city of the United States.[16]

The federal government, despite a drop in revenues, remained strong and was in a position to help. The magnitude of the social and economic problems clearly called for action on a nation-wide scale; however, this would require a decidedly leftward shift which would be a drastic break with tradition. While government intervention in the economy was nothing new it had been, as we noted earlier, primarily to serve business interests. What would be new would be extending such aid for the mass of the population. Yet the Republican administration of Hoover, together with conservative Democrats sought to keep the federal government from helping. These officials and legislators saw relief as an undesirable "dole" and government intervention to cope with the problems created by the crisis as "socialistic."

While both federal and local government failed to provide the desperately needed relief money or funds for regular public services which were badly strained, they made effective use of the police power. It is true, there were instances where the police looked the other way when there were petty violations of the law—homeless sleeping in deserted houses or in the parks or the hungry pilfering food. However, when put to the test they enforced the orders of public officials and, as we shall see shortly, of the ruling class. This was particularly true of the National Guard and the federal soldiers.

As for the ruling class, its financial leaders tried to stem the crisis but were unable to. The best they could do was to put on a public front that things were not as bad as they seemed, and insist that in any event the crisis was only temporary.

[15] Bernstein, *op. cit.*, pp. 329, 331, 364.
[16] *Ibid.*, p. 301.

"In the very midst of the [stock market] collapse," *The New York Times* reported,

> five of the country's most influential bankers hurried to the office of J. P. Morgan & Co., and after a brief conference gave out word that they believe the foundations of the market to be sound, that the market smash has been caused by technical rather than fundamental considerations, and that many sound stocks are selling too low.[17]

This was the line taken throughout the Depression, especially by the financiers who were largely responsible for the crisis through their promotion and manipulation of watered stock, monopolistic practices, graft, and other illegal activities.

Business spokesmen such as Roger W. Babson suggested that unemployment was not a social but an individual problem: anyone who tried hard enough and used sufficient ingenuity could certainly find a job. The federal government which was closely tied in with the ruling class also attempted to minimize the difficulties, beamed optimism, and told the public that prosperity was just around the corner. President Hoover even misrepresented vital statistics data to claim that the nation was in better health than during prosperity![18]

During the early years of the Depression the government, both local and national, did little of a concrete nature to ameliorate conditions. This was also true of the ruling class. However, although the latter controlled most of the country's wealth the economic collapse was beyond their ability to do anything about it. While people became disenchanted with the ruling class, and many blamed the large financiers and the industrial capitalists, it apparently did not reach the stage where a substantial portion of prominent citizens were openly and conspicuously questioning the tenets of capitalism. Even though members of the ruling class suffered great losses, there was not the disintegration which occurred prior to say the French Revolution. While self-doubts were expressed,[19] there was not the desertion to the ranks of the underdogs.

It seems then that although the ruling class was weakened it was able to survive and remain influential. Also, the federal government was still viable, and even though it failed to act it had the necessary resources or could obtain them through taxes, the sale of securities, or deficit financ-

[17] "Worst Stock Crash Stemmed by Banks," *New York Times* (October 25, 1929), in Shannon, *The Great Depression*, p. 2. The five bankers were Charles E. Mitchell, Chairman of the National City Bank; Albert Wiggin, Chairman of the Chase National Bank; William Potter, President of the Guaranty Trust Company; Seward Prosser, Chairman of the Bankers Trust Company; and Thomas W. Lamont, senior partner of J. P. Morgan & Co.

[18] The claim was based on demographic trends in which long-term forces were lowering the mortality rate. Furthermore, the data were averages and did not take into account the situation of the different strata. See Bernstein, *The Lean Years*, p. 330.

[19] See, e.g., Frank A. Vanderlip, "What About the Banks?" *The Saturday Evening Post*, 205 (November 5, 1932), 3–4 in Shannon, *op. cit.*, pp. 73–75. Vanderlip was the former President of the National City Bank of New York. For the reaction of smaller businessmen see *ibid.*, pp. 75–86.

ing. Moreover, its lack of hesitancy in using the police power to quell disturbances underscored its viability in the eyes of much of the public.

We are next interested in the extent of ideational change. With the Stock Market debacle, bank failures, business bankruptcies, home and farm foreclosures, and unemployment few people were unaware that something was seriously wrong. However, government officials, the leaders of the ruling class, and the spokesmen for the business community continually tried to minimize the difficulties, as we noted above. This was also true of most of the mass media, especially the newspapers; however, the selective reporting and optimistic editorials were overshadowed by the sheer volume of bad news. Furthermore, the unemployed and those on a short work week didn't have to study the newspapers to learn about the economic situation. Much of the writings and other works of the intellectuals served to articulate people's discontent and helped make them aware of how widespread the social and economic problems were.

The first step in the turning of a stratum into a class is to help the individual clearly express his feelings of discontent and make him realize that many others have the same problem. This helps to shift the blame from the self to the society; the individual is more likely to think that there is something wrong with the social order rather than with himself. Excerpts from the poem below by Florence Converse, entitled "Breadline," not only elicit sympathy for the deprived and give a universal quality to the suffering, but also deal with the explosive potential of the deprivation:

> What's the meaning of this queue,
> Tailing down the avenue,
> Full of eyes that will not meet
> The other eyes that throng the street . . .
>   * * *
> To see a living line of men
> As long as round the block, and then
> As long again? . . .
>   * * *
> What's the meaning in these faces
> Modern industry displaces,
> Emptying the factory
> To set the men so tidily
> Along the pavement in a row?
>   * * *
> Idle, shamed, and underfed,
> Waiting for his dole of bread,
> What if he should find his head
> A candle of the Holy Ghost?
> A dim and starveling spark, at most,
> But yet a spark? It needs but one.

> A spark can creep, a spark can run;
> Suddenly a spark can wink
> And send us down destruction's brink. . . .[20]

Most intellectuals became highly critical and plays, novels, and other works dealt with problems of the Depression and attacked existing institutional arrangements. Many intellectuals joined radical causes and many others were sympathetic; there was clearly the beginnings of the transfer of allegiance. However, this process was not sufficiently widespread or advanced to make it a significant element for revolution. There were four main reasons for this: first, a market for non-critical artistic and literary productions; second, government employment of intellectuals in artists' and writers' projects under the New Deal; third, harassment of radicals, and fourth, the larger problem of the intellectual in America. In addition, there was no full development of a revolutionary ideal.

There were many artists, playwrights, novelists, songwriters and others whose productive efforts might earn them the label of intellectual. However, they were not critical of the society; in fact their work was romantic and reactionary. They stressed return to earlier, more pleasant times in song (for example, "Happy Days are Here Again") and in other artistic endeavors, and emphasized that love overcomes all problems (for example the movie, "Ziegfeld Follies"). Especially significant was the movie industry which provided the circuses that helped keep people's minds off their troubles. In addition, the soap operas, pulp magazines, and the mass media in general looked backward and stressed traditional values and romantic love. They also offered vicarious participation in a more affluent life. Among the persons responsible for these productions were highly intelligent, creative and articulate individuals, men and women who had the capacity to be true, that is critical, intellectuals. However, we label them pseudo-intellectuals because of their non-critical stance. Undoubtedly their work helped discourage political interest and a political solution to the Depression.

The fact that there was a market for their skills kept most of them from becoming critical and radical, for a decent paycheck is a strong deterrent. There was also an army of others whose efforts were devoted to commercial art, hack novels, the pulps, or to the less creative aspects of movie making, radio production, publishing, and similar endeavors. These were persons of lesser ability, who fall into Russell Lynes' "middle brow" and "low brow" categories,[21] but also included are potential intellectuals who had no other opportunity for employment. It is of course true that with mass education and literacy, a concomitant of industrialization, the market for middle brow and low brow productions increases tremendously. In turn it offers financial rewards and popularity

[20] Florence Converse, "Bread Line," *The Atlantic Monthly* (January 1932), 55–56.
[21] Russell Lynes, *The Tastemakers* (New York: Harper & Brothers, 1955).

for intellectuals and pseudo-intellectuals who emphasize the traditional values and whose work is "upbeat." Consequently, these persons also are not likely to become a force for social criticism.

A second factor that minimized the transfer of the allegiance of the intellectuals was the New Deal's artists' and writers' projects. Among the hundreds of artists, writers, musicians, and others who were paid to produce plays, give musical performances, paint murals in public buildings, and employ their talents in other ways that might benefit the public, were many intellectuals and potential intellectuals. Even though many of them remained very critical, their paychecks, even though very meager, undoubtedly prevented them from developing that "gut-deep" antagonism to the existing order that precedes revolution.

Another reason the intellectuals did not play the role they might have, given the social and economic conditions of the Great Depression was their harassment by the government. Conservative businessmen, labor leaders, legislators, and government officials often blamed them for stirring up discontent, and working directly or indirectly with subversive elements, mostly foreign agents, who were out to destroy the American way of life. It is true that communists often led the protests, and if they did not instigate riots were certainly pleased when the police bloodied heads. However, the failures of the capitalist system—particularly unemployment—were almost completely ignored as the basic causes of the discontent and demonstrations. In the spring of 1930 the House of Representatives passed a resolution by a vote of 210 to 18 to set up what later became known as the House Committee on Un-American Activities. Introduced by Republican Hamilton Fish of New York and backed by the AF of L, its purpose was to ferret out and if possible deport the troublemakers. The lopsided Congressional vote indicated marked popular support for this harassment, which was a continuation of the attacks on radicals during and after World War I, the Palmer Raids, the exaggeration of the terror of the Russian Revolution, and the associating of radicalism with godless Communism. Any basic criticism of the institutional arrangements could be and often was labelled "unpatriotic" by members of the ruling class and the press. And, as is well known the House Committee on Un-American Activities zeroed in on politically active intellectuals. But even without the harassment it is questionable whether radicalism would have gotten very far, for reasons which will be discussed shortly. Nevertheless, the impact of the Committee was to intimidate intellectuals and to mute criticism.

But it was more than simply harassment. Except for the period in which America gained its independence intellectuals have had little effect on major economic and political change. This is due to historical conditions which are rooted in the concept of egalitarianism and to the absence of a true conservative tradition. It is only where there is a history of inequality and a conservative tradition that the intellectual has a position of importance and is influential as regards new ideas and change. Under these circumstances the intellectuals are responsible for "high culture" for which the upper class is the consumer. The intellectuals associate with the higher echelons, and since in such societies the superiority and authority of the upper classes are stressed, the intellectuals share in some of their prestige. Furthermore, the illiterate masses are made to feel incompetent to deal with significant economic, political, or religious questions and are encouraged to accept things on authority, including ideas. In such societies change is likely to be instigated by people at the higher levels and the intellectuals, being in or close to the "halls of power," are likely to be influential. For example, it is questionable whether Luther would have been so successful had he lived in an age of equality and there had not been the princes and great territorial magnates who listened to him.[22] Even in societies with a conservative tradition which have become democratic the intellectuals remain important.

De Tocqueville comments on this situation:

> It is not simply that in democracies confidence in the superior knowledge of certain individuals has been weakened. . . . [T]he general idea that any man whosoever can attain an intellectual superiority beyond the reach of the rest is soon cast in doubt.[23]

Even if someone such as an intellectual proposed a new political or economic theory, let alone a revolutionary ideal, it would be very difficult to interest people in it. Again, de Tocqueville's observation is pertinent:

> I think it is an arduous undertaking to excite the enthusiasm of a democratic nation for any theory which does not have a visible, direct, and immediate bearing on the occupations of their daily life.[24]

On the other hand, in a society which stresses egalitarianism, pragmatism guides people's behavior and there is little interest in ideas and speculations. In addition, since it is believed that basically each individual is as good as any other it follows that the opinion of one person is just as worthwhile as that of the next. Not only does the intellectual fail to command much more attention than anyone else but people even question the very basis of intellectualism. Consequently there is no special place for the intellectual in American society. Also, since intellectuals in America espouse the heritage of egalitarian society, and their work appeals to the mass, they have difficulty in asserting their claims for special treatment.[25] More important, they have difficulty in getting people to listen to them.

[22] See Alexis de Tocqueville, *Democracy in America* (Garden City, N.Y.: Doubleday Anchor Books, 1969; first pub. in 1848), p. 642.

[23] *Ibid.*, p. 641.

[24] *Ibid.*, p. 642.

[25] See Seymour M. Lipset, *Political Man* (New York: Doubleday, 1960), pp. 344–345.

Finally, although there was great disenchantment among many intellectuals there was no transfer of allegiance. All told, they did not have a significant impact in moving the country toward revolution, in spite of the great increase in class conflict.

While all strata experienced a decreased standard of living during the Depression the lower levels suffered the most, particularly the semi-skilled and the unskilled, as we noted above. The responses were in terms of class behavior; it was almost immediate on the part of the upper class and developed more slowly in the case of the lower. The upper classes at first tried to pooh-pooh the economic crisis and throughout the Depression sought to minimize it. They insisted it was temporary, that basically the economy was healthy. This response reflected self-interest; they felt that presenting an optimistic front would mollify the lower strata and discourage them from taking any action. Also, by not admitting its severity they were on stronger grounds in opposing government intervention for relief or jobs. There were economic as well as ideological reasons for their opposition: government aid would mean higher taxes. Responding to these interests the Republican administration did practically nothing to alleviate the deprivation people were experiencing.

The lower class responded in a number of ways, as we noted earlier: among them were self-help schemes, greater religious involvement, and resignation and despair. A portion of the lower class engaged in collective action, however, some spontaneous and some organized.

Lower Class Riots and Demonstrations

Riots occurred on breadlines and people broke into grocery stores; by 1932 organized looting of food was a national phenomenon. A thin line separated legal from illegal self-help, and desperate workers repeatedly took the law into their own hands. Most of these incidents remain unrecorded for the press often refused to print such news for fear of encouraging similar action.[26] While much of the violence by the unemployed was spontaneous, there were cases where it was calculated. For example, this writer has talked to several people who lived in working-class neighborhoods in Chicago during the Depression who helped dynamite homes which had been foreclosed by the banks.

The collective behavior that occurred was clearly class based: those involved were mainly manual workers, particularly the less skilled and the unskilled; they lived in the poorer sections of town; they were unemployed, and they were suffering from absolute deprivation. Their physical location and idleness provided opportunity to associate more with

[26] Bernstein, *The Lean Years*, pp. 422–423.

one another and discuss mutual woes. There were also political organizations around with ready-made ideologies, propaganda mechanisms, and organizational expertise. These were principally the Socialist and the Communist parties, various smaller splinter groups, and remnants of the IWW. That there were riots is not surprising; what is surprising is that there were not more of them. The reasons for the relatively small number, aside from the mass media's reluctance to report them, will be gone into shortly. In any event, aside from the local riots and looting for food there were planned demonstrations aimed at dramatizing the plight of the unemployed and getting the authorities to do something about the situation. There were also social movements with programs that proposed solutions to the problems of the times.

Most of the demonstrations of the unemployed were organized by radicals, who saw the economic collapse as a golden opportunity to enlist the proletariat. The first attempts were by the socialists who were largely unsuccessful.[27] Of course the Socialist Party had been greatly weakened by the earlier struggle, which had led to the formation of the Communist Party, by the government and citizen persecution during the World War I period, and by the Palmer Raids and anti-radical hysteria of the 1920's. The IWW, the reader will recall, was destroyed during World War I. As for the labor unions, they were greatly weakened by the Depression; but even if they hadn't been they still eschewed direct political involvement. The Democratic Party, which traditionally is identified with the interests of the lower strata, worked for success in the voting booth.

The Communist Party on the other hand was ready to go into the streets and agitate among the unemployed, with the idea of setting in motion a revolution against capitalism. Thus, because of the inability of the others to organize the victims of the Depression the communists, by default, became the major group which sought to channel discontent into political action. Not only did the communists see the Depression as providing a golden opportunity for organizing the proletariat, but this was the "third period" of international Communism wherein Communist parties all over the world adopted ultrarevolutionary tactics. This was an outcome of the conflict between the Stalin and the Trotsky factions in the Soviet Union: the former believed in strengthening Russia first as a means of advancing Communism; the latter emphasized world revolution. In order to undercut Trotsky, Stalin moved sharply to the left on this issue and ordered the worldwide Communist movement to undertake ultrarevolutionary activities;[28] the Communist Party of the United States dutifully obeyed. Although it had only limited success, it organized demonstrations and was quick to try to take over spontaneous movements or protests instigated by other groups.

[27] Arthur M. Schlesinger, Jr., *The Crisis of the Old Order* (Boston: Houghton Mifflin, 1957), pp. 206–208, 219–223.

[28] Bernstein, *op. cit.*, p. 426; and Schlesinger, *op. cit.*, p. 217.

Most of the demonstrations followed a pattern. Initially they were peaceful until set upon by the police. This is shown in the following cases which also suggest the extent of the unrest throughout the country: On February 11, 1930, 3,000 unemployed men, incited by communist speakers, attempted to storm the Cleveland City Hall but dispersed after the police threatened to turn fire hoses on them; on February 15, 250 people who marched to City Hall in Philadelphia and demanded an interview with the Mayor were driven off by the police; on February 22, mounted police armed with nightsticks dispersed 1,200 jobless men and women who marched upon the municipal government in Chicago, in view of thousands in the windows of Loop office buildings; on February 26 the police used tear gas to break up a crowd of 3,000 in front of the Los Angeles City Hall, and a week later the police dispersed a demonstration of unemployed at the New York City Hall using brutal tactics.[29]

One of the most violent demonstrations occurred on March 7, 1932 in Dearborn, Michigan. The Detroit area was seething with labor unrest, with much of it directed at Henry Ford. A crowd of 3,000 marched from downtown Detroit to Dearborn. The leaders were communists, and the plan was to present a set of demands to the Ford management, which included among other things: jobs, a seven-hour day, the end of the speedup, rest periods, no discrimination against blacks, free medical care at the Ford Hospital, and the elimination of the company's spying and police operation.

When the marchers reached the Dearborn city limits their way was blocked by a force of 30 to 40 policemen. They had ties to the Ford management and were most likely beholden to it; the Dearborn mayor was a distant cousin of Henry Ford and owned a Ford agency, while the chief of police was a former Ford detective on the company payroll. The police first used tear gas and then began firing point-blank at the demonstrators with pistols and a machine gun. Four marchers were killed and at least 50 seriously wounded; a *New York Times* reporter was shot in the hand.[30]

Not all the demonstrations were organized by communists or other radicals. A very large one was put together by a Pittsburgh priest, James R. Cox, who led 12,000 Pennsylvanians to the nation's capitol on January 7, 1932. The demonstration was well-received; was peaceful, petitions for public works, federal relief, and higher taxes on the rich were presented to officials, and a wreath was laid on the Tomb of the Unknown Soldier.[31]

Yet the most impressive demonstration involved the Bonus Army, composed of World War I veterans who demanded the money that had been promised by Congress. Legislation had been passed in 1924 giving

[29] Bernstein, *op. cit.*, pp. 426–427.

[30] *Ibid.*, pp. 432–434. See also Schlesinger, *op. cit.*, pp. 255–256.

[31] Bernstein, *op. cit.*, p. 432.

each veteran an adjusted service certificate, based on the number of days spent in uniform. It was like an insurance policy; for example, if cashed in 1925 the former serviceman might receive $400, whereas if held until 1945 it would likely be worth $1,000. This was the only asset many veterans had and with the Depression they needed the money right away; however, there were no funds to pay them. Representative Wright Patman of Texas introduced a bill in 1932 to provide for immediate payment at full maturity value. Even though there was little chance of its passage, and President Hoover would most likely veto such legislation, it set in motion a mass movement to Washington, most of it spontaneous. It began in Oregon in mid-May when 300 veterans set out for the nation's capitol, calling themselves the "Bonus Expeditionary Force"—a play on "American Expeditionary Force" which had been sent to Europe during the first world war. Soon a flood of ex-servicemen began to descend on the city—all in all some 23,000. Many people were sympathetic to their demands and helped house and feed them on their journey. Many businesses and individuals contributed money and services while the B.E.F. was in Washington, and the government allowed the veterans to stay in some old buildings which were vacant.

Although the House passed the Patman Bill it was overwhelmingly defeated by the Senate 62–18. However, the Bonus Army remained and tension rose. Even though the B.E.F. was a manifestation of transient joblessness which came into being because of inadequate relief measures, President Hoover saw it as a potential insurrection and called in federal troops to evacuate them. The operation was under the command of General Douglas MacArthur; his aide was Major Dwight D. Eisenhower, and one of his officers was George S. Patton, Jr. Four companies of infantrymen, four troops of cavalry, a mounted machine gun squadron, and six tanks were positioned. MacArthur's soldiers used tear gas to clear the old buildings, and set them on fire.

> MacArthur then sent his forces across the Anacostia bridge. Thousands of veterans, their wives, and children fled before the advancing soldiers. The troops attacked with tear gas and set fire to a number of huts. There was virtually no resistance . . . and the military operation was carried out swiftly and efficiently.[32]

Yet two veterans were shot to death; two children were seriously injured, one fatally; an additional dozen or so people were injured, including veterans, bystanders, and policemen, and about 1,000 persons were tear gassed.[33]

---

[32] *Ibid.*, pp. 437–454. The quotation is from p. 453. See also Schlesinger, *op. cit.*, pp. 256–265.

[33] Bernstein, *The Lean Years*, p. 453.

Organizing the Proletariat

While the demonstrations and violence made the biggest headlines, attempts to organize the unemployed received little public notice. The approaches took two forms: one focused on the political aspect and the other emphasized self-help. Radicals believed that by organizing the jobless to agitate for public works and relief they would not only improve conditions for the proletariat but they would also further the development of class consciousness. This, together with organization, would help politicize the lower strata which they saw as an essential step for revolutionary change. The socialists were the first to try to set up councils of unemployed in each city. However, except for Chicago they were unsuccessful, and even there they tended to attract teachers, lawyers, social workers, and preachers but very few blue-collar people. This was true elsewhere. Also, not only did they fail to gain a following among the proletariat, whether employed or unemployed, but they were torn by internal dissension.[34]

On the other hand, the communists were much more successful. They set up councils of unemployed in the major cities and among other things fought evictions. In Chicago they organized what were called the "black bugs." When a black family was evicted a battalion of these black communists would march through the street, up to the house, and reinstall the family and its belongings. After these demonstrations a street meeting would be held and the communist line preached. These meetings inevitably led to police intervention and bleeding heads. During one eviction riot three blacks were killed by the police which led Mayor Anton Cermack to order landlords to stop evictions.[35]

Organizing the unemployed to help one another appealed to a good number of people as a means of ameliorating the economic crisis. Beginning in 1931 in Washington state unemployed leagues sprang up, and their primary emphasis was self-help. They arranged to use idle fishing boats, harvest unmarketable farm products and barter skills for needed goods; they also sought to provide relief and employment. Similar groups were organized in other parts of the nation and they met with varying degrees of success; however, there was little they could do about the causes of the Depression, and they did not have the resources for relief or jobs. Hence, most collapsed.[36]

While there was much class conflict during the Great Depression the behavior of the lower class did not move in the direction of revolutionary

[34] *Ibid.*, pp. 425–426; and Schlesinger, *The Crisis of the Old Order*, pp. 219–220.

[35] Bernstein, *op. cit.*, p. 428.

[36] *Ibid.*, pp. 416–421.

change. In spite of the discontent and demonstrations radical groups such as the socialists and communists were unable to interest the unemployed in revolution. Where they succeeded in organizing them it was for the short run aims of relief and jobs. The socialists and communists also made few inroads into the trade unions; the latter's attempt to take over the Bonus Army failed miserably; their special appeal to the blacks was unsuccessful—a saying among them was "it's bad enough to be black without being Red."

In the Presidential election of 1932 Socialist Party candidate Norman Thomas received only 881,951 votes, a little more than two per cent of the total cast; William Z. Foster, the Communist Party's choice, obtained a meager 102,785, or considerably less than one per cent.[37]

One of the consequences of the protests of the early 1930's was that the problem of unemployment was dramatized and could no longer be ignored. One of the outcomes was the strengthening of the forces seeking to provide relief and jobs,[38] which meant reformism.

Reform Yes, Revolution No

Clearly very few of the lower class supported revolutionary change as proposed by the radicals, and some of the reasons for this are inherent in the historical background of the United States. The ideology of private property remained very strong in spite of the objective conditions of great inequality in property holding, and the foreclosures of farms, businesses, and homes.

Any frontal attack on private property, even if directed at the wealthy, engenders fear: not only because of the reluctance to consider basic change which de Tocqueville observed, but also because of the belief that personal possessions and opportunity would be affected. Radical rhetoric, vulgar interpretations of socialism, and propaganda by conservatives linked revolutionary change with the abolition of private property down to the smallest personal holding. For many, redistribution of wealth was interpreted as confiscation of what few social goods people still retained for the benefit of the impecunious. But this fear of losing what little one had is only a partial answer; apparently a strong belief remained that ordinary people, or their children, still had the possibility of becoming property holders.

In addition, the belief that there was still opportunity for upward vertical mobility remained. Despite objective conditions to the contrary,

[37] *Ibid.*, pp. 434–435, 447; and *Historical Statistics of the United States, Colonial Timer to 1957*, p. 682.

[38] Bernstein, *op. cit.*, p. 427.

including much downward movement, the American dream was not completely given up. Also, because of the New Deal the severe deprivation of the early period of the Depression did not last long enough to convince people of a *permanent* decline in opportunity. It should be remembered that many of the lower strata were immigrants or second-generation Americans and probably still better off than their peers in the Old Country. Moreover, as we noted earlier radical change was tainted with being foreign, un-American, violent, and godless. The latter is particularly important because of the strong position against "godless Communism" of the Roman Catholic and fundamentalist Protestant churches, to which many lower class people belong. Finally, in general the American worker was exhausted; free enterprise provided no jobs; the government did not help, and there was little the unions could do. They were weak to begin with and the joblessness sapped their remaining strength. People were discouraged and many blamed themselves.[39]

However, although the supporters of radical change were very few, numbers alone do not tell us very much. In social movements, as in the formation of public opinion, opposing minorities seek to sway enough of the uncommitted middle for ordinarily most of the population is apathetic or only mildly concerned about issues. The usual pattern is for an energetic minority to try to convince a significant portion of the middle of the rightness of their position. They need not win over the majority, nor need they completely convince those who react favorably. What is required is simply a shift all along the line: a portion of those who had been mildly interested become strongly interested; a portion of those who had been apathetic became mildly interested; a portion of those who had been mildly opposed become neutral or apathetic, and a portion of those strongly antagonistic become only mildly opposed. If a significant portion of the population becomes receptive to widespread change and there are no institutional means to bring it about, the regime is in danger of being overthrown. And this may occur much more suddenly than anyone expects for usually minor incidents and crises are now commonplace. Collective feelings may intensify for a number of reasons, among them is unwise action on the part of the government, particularly if it is interpreted as being grossly unfair or if martyrs are created. Under these circumstances a small scale insurrection, the setting up of barricades, or mob action such as riots may start a conflagration which will topple the government. By now the police and militia are unable to prevent this for if the general shift in viewpoint has occurred, portions of the officers and men are also likely to have altered their perspectives. Consequently as a body the police or the militia are no longer reliable. In

[39] Louis Adamic, *My America* (New York: Harper & Brothers, 1938), pp. 283–284; and Robert S. Lynd and Helen Merrell Lynd, *Middletown in Transition* (New York: Harcourt, Brace, 1937), pp. 26ff.

fact some may go over to the revolutionary side, others may desert, and the rest may fight only halfheartedly.

During the Great Depression, it wasn't that there were relatively few radicals that was important, but that they were unable to make enough people receptive to their views. And it is possible that their efforts to organize the unemployed were misdirected, for the history of previous upheavals shows that the revolutionary thrust comes from the more substantial portion of the population—the American equivalent would be the Rotarians, Lions, and Kiwanis.[40]

But not only was the more substantial part of the American population insufficiently hateful of existing institutional arrangements, but another important element was missing: a group just below the ruling class suffering great relative deprivation and feeling that its opportunity was being blocked by an entrenched ruling class. Such a segment is critical for, in the words of Brinton,

> [t]he strongest feelings seem generated in the bosoms of men—and women— who have made money, or at least who have enough to live on, and who contemplate bitterly the imperfections of a socially privileged aristocracy.[41]

In addition to these intense feelings, such a group, as we observed earlier, helps instigate a revolution by speaking out and furnishing leaders as well as members for the revolutionary movement. To make their cause universal—for if it remains a special interest group the chances of success are limited—they seek to enlist the support of the lower classes. The latter provide two important benefits, in addition to broadening the base of the movement: numbers, and muscle.

Even though conditions during the 1930's were not quite ripe for revolution the potential was there. The widespread unemployment, absolute deprivation, radical movements, organizing of the jobless, demonstrations, and violence made many people believe an upheaval was coming. "Fear of a revolution," Shannon writes,

> was very widespread during the last several months of President Hoover's administration, and much of the politics of the period can be understood fully only by viewing political events against the background of anxiety about violent revolt. The vigor with which the army dispersed the Bonus Expeditionary Force from Washington in the summer of 1932, for example, had its roots in revolutionary fear.[42]

[40] See Brinton, *The Anatomy of Revolution*, pp. 92–120. Brinton analyzed the membership of the Jacobin clubs which served as centers of revolutionary activity in France and found it to be roughly 60% middle class, 30% working class, and 10% peasants. *Ibid.*, pp. 96–97. The activists in the American Revolution were also drawn from the more affluent portion of the population.

[41] *Ibid.*, p. 251.

[42] Shannon, *The Great Depression*, p. 111.

Thus it was "in the air," and this collective feeling, as we noted earlier, is one of the prerequisites to revolution.

Yet, one of the major reasons it did not occur was because there were institutional means for changing the government. The Hoover administration could be deposed via the ballot box, and this would also remove or reduce the influence of that part of the ruling class which supported him.

THROWING THE RASCALS OUT

The elections during the Great Depression brought out large numbers of lower strata voters and there was a strong swing to the Democrats. Class interests were clearly shown in the returns; for example in 1932 and 1936 those countries worst hit by the depression were the most strongly pro-Roosevelt. There was also clear evidence that the more people experienced unemployment the less conservative they became, which is also true of other countries such as Great Britain, France, and Germany.[43] The swing to the Democrats was basically a vote for jobs and social security. Roosevelt had a plurality of over 7,000,000 receiving almost six out of every ten votes cast and a Democratic Congress was elected. Groups which had favored the Republicans turned toward the Democrats; there was strong farmer support for Roosevelt, and the blacks switched from their traditional support of the G.O.P.[44]

But for new programs to be carried out change in government is not enough; as Lipset has pointed out there must be a smooth and effective transfer of power. The "outs" must allow the new administration to govern without disrupting it; in turn the new government must allow the "outs" to criticize it and to work toward reelection without sanctions being imposed on them.[45] If peaceful transfer of power has been the practice in the past, especially when there have been major differences between the political parties or when there have been crises, it is very likely that this precedent will be continued.[46]

Since it was possible to "throw the rascals out," and since it was reasonable to expect that the new administration which promised to end the economic crisis would be able to govern effectively, there seemed to be no need for revolution. At least since the Civil War there has been ample precedent for such changeover, as we observed in the previous chapter.

Harry W. Laidler suggests that to bring about revolutionary change in the United States by violent overthrow of the government would proba-

[43] Lipset, *Political Man*, pp. 247–248.

[44] *Historical Statistics of the United States, Colonial Times to 1957*, p. 682; and Bernstein, *The Lean Years*, pp. 508–511.

[45] Lipset, *op. cit.*

[46] *Ibid.*

bly necessitate a larger majority than an electoral victory would require. But what if fundamental change which occurred through the electoral process was met by armed resistance by the former ruling class? Laidler feels that there would likely be enough popular sentiment to overcome it.[47] Furthermore, there have been many major alterations which have been peaceful; this has been true in England, slavery was peacefully eliminated in many countries, as was serfdom in Prussia and Russia, and during the 1920's and 1930's there were labor, socialist, and fascist changeovers without violent revolt.[48]

The election of Roosevelt and the Democratic Congress was a strong move to the left; the federal government had a clear mandate to provide work, relief, unemployment insurance, and old age pensions.[49] Not only did those in dire straits benefit from the reforms, but a trend toward greater equality was started.

SPREADING SOCIAL GOODS

Over the long run the distribution of social goods, particularly income, has changed toward greater equality, and median income has been going up. While there are still extremes in wealth, as we showed in Chapter III, there is a large middle group which is fairly well off. In 1952 only 17% of the families were earning $6,000 a year or more; by 1973 this was true of 69% of the families. Median family income almost tripled during this period, going from $3,435 to $9,930.[50] There has been a substantial rise in real income, and the problems many families face today are not whether they can buy a car, but whether it will be new or used; not whether their child will attend college but will it be a private or a public institution. Figure XVI-2 shows the great change that has occurred over the past two decades in income distribution.

Not only has income gone up but so have the levels of education and occupational status. Between 1940 and 1974 among those 25 years of age or older, median school years completed have risen from 8.6 to 12.3.[51] In this age group, presently, 11% have completed grade school, 36% have high-school diplomas, and 13% have four or more years of higher education. The trend toward increased schooling is revealed by the attainment of a younger age group, those between 22 and 24: only five per cent

[47] Harry W. Laidler, *History of Socialism* (New York: Thomas Y. Crowell, 1968), p. 450.

[48] *Ibid.*, pp. 452–454.

[49] See Bernstein, *op. cit.*, p. 506.

[50] "Money Income in 1973 of Families and Persons in the United States," p. 24, 170. The figures are in constant dollars, which takes inflation into account.

[51] U.S. Bureau of the Census, "Educational Attainment in the United States: March 1973 and 1974," Series P-20, No. 274 (Washington, D.C.: Government Printing Office, December 1974), p. 68.

FIGURE XVI-2.
Percentage Distribution of Income of Families and
Unrelated Individuals, in Current Dollars, 1952 and 1973

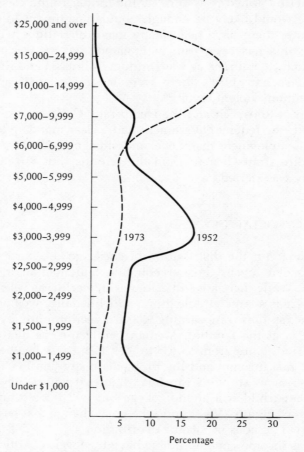

Source: U.S. Bureau of the Census, "Money Income in 1973 of Families and Persons
in the United States," Series P-60, No. 97 (Washington, D.C.: Government
Printing Office, January 1975), p. 24.

have not gone beyond elementary school, and 12% are high school
dropouts, but 41% have high school diplomas, while 43% have at least
some college (see Table XVI-1).

Educational attainment is associated with social mobility, and there is
continuing upward movement in the United States as well as in other industrialized nations.[52]

[52] Peter M. Blau and Otis D. Duncan, *The American Occupational Structure* (New York:
John Wiley & Sons, 1967), pp. 103, 112, and Appendix J2.10; Seymour M. Lipset and
Reinhard Bendix, *Social Mobility in Industrial Society* (Berkeley and Los Angeles: University
of California Press, 1959), pp. 11–75; and S. H. Miller, "Comparative Social Mobility: A
Trend Report," *Comparative Sociology*, 9 (1960), 1–5.

TABLE XVI-1. Years of School Completed, by Selected Age Groups, 1974 (in percentages)

Years of School Completed	Age Group	
	25 years and older	22-24 years
Elementary school		
0 - 4 years	4.4%	.6%
5 - 7 "	7.6	1.8
8 "	10.8	2.1
High school		
1 - 3 years	15.9	11.7
4 "	36.1	41.3
College		
1 - 3 years	11.9	25.9
4 years or more	13.3	16.6
Total	99.9%	100.0%

Source: U.S. Bureau of the Census, "Educational Attainment in the United States: March 1973 and 1974," Series P-20, No. 274 (Washington, D.C.: Government Printing Office, December 1974, p. 15.

Increasing numbers of persons are in white-collar occupations, while blue-collar employment has remained about the same, and farm workers have declined very much. This is clearly seen in Table XVI-2 which compares the major occupational groups of employed males for 1950 and 1974. This table shows that the overall increase in white-collar workers was from 32% to 41%, with the biggest growth being in the professional

TABLE XVI-2. Employed Males by Major Occupational Group, 1950 and 1974 (in percentages)

Major Occupational Groups	1950	1974
White-collar workers		
Professional & technical	6.4%	14.0%
Managers, officals and proprietors	12.9	13.9
Clerical workers	7.2	6.5
Salesworkers	5.6	6.1
Blue-collar workers		
Craftsman & foremen	17.7	21.0
Operatives	20.9	18.1
Nonfarm laborers	8.1	7.2
Service workers	6.4	8.2
Farmers and Farmworkers	14.7	5.0
Total	99.9%	100.0%

Source: U.S. Bureau of the Census, *Statistical Abstract of the United States:1974* (95th ed.; Washington, D.C.: Government Printing Office, 1974), p. 350.

and technical category which more than doubled. The biggest change was in the farm worker category which dropped by almost two-thirds. These occupational changes reflect long range shifts in the labor force, from an initial concentration in primary industries, such as agriculture, lumbering, and mining to secondary ones such as manufacturing, and finally to tertiary in which service industries predominate.[53] Table XVI-3 shows this shift: 14% of the workforce was in primary industries in 1950 in contrast to five per cent in 1974. Thirty-four per cent were in secondary industries in 1950 whereas this was true of 29% in 1974. And, while 52% were in tertiary industries in 1950 this sector accounted for 66% in 1974.

The increases in family income, educational attainment, and occupational status mean a labor force quite different from the impoverished proletariat Marx predicted. While there are still people living in poverty, they represent a minority of the population; the majority is quite well off. Even though the unemployment rate is substantial, most people have jobs and are making good wages. Also, the amount of social mobility has essentially remained the same over the past several decades.[54] Although the situation of migrant farm laborers and some others is undesirable, they make up a relatively small segment of the labor force. Most people

TABLE XVI-3. Labor Force in Primary, Secondary, and Tertiary Industries, 1950 and 1974 (in percentages)

Industry Group	Employed Persons	
	1950	1974
Primary industries		
Agriculture	12.2%	4.0%
Mining	1.8	.8
	14.0	4.8
Secondary industries		
Manufacturing	29.6	24.8
Construction	4.6	4.4
	34.2	29.2
Tertiary industries		
Wholesale and retail trade	18.2	20.5
Government	11.7	17.8
Services	10.5	16.6
Transportation & public utilities	7.8	5.8
Finance, insurance & real estate	3.7	5.2
	51.9	65.9
Total	100.1	99.9

Source: U.S. Bureau of the Census, *Statistical Abstract of the United States:1974* (95th ed.) (Washington, D.C.: Government Printing Office, 1974), pp. 336, 345.

[53] See discussion in Chapter III.
[54] See Blau and Duncan, *op. cit.*

work under pleasant or at least tolerable conditions. And the nature of work is changing, with a decline in those jobs which required great physical labor to pursuits calling for mental activities and interpersonal skills. Although still far from generous, Social Security, Medicare, unemployment insurance, workmen's compensation, and other welfare measures have increased the real income of the lower strata and have minimized absolute deprivation. The deprivation that most people experience today is *relative* deprivation, as we suggested above. While there are still ups and downs in the economy, they are much more moderate compared to earlier years. The limited government planning, federal monetary and fiscal controls, as well as social welfare measures such as unemployment insurance have so far been able to prevent downturns from becoming major depressions such as that of the 1930's. An unanswered question, however, is the extent to which the recession of the mid-1970's will worsen or whether economic conditions will improve. While the current rate of unemployment is high, it is unevenly distributed among the strata; unemployment is not generally a problem among persons at the upper or middle levels.[55]

Full Stomachs Make Moderates

As long as most people are relatively well off economically class feelings are minimal and there is moderation in politics; when change is necessary the reformist route is the one likely to be taken. The outcome of the 1930's was certain political patterns which persist today. The Democrats have become the majority party: from 1900 to 1932 there had been 24 years of Republican presidents versus eight of Democratic, while between 1932 and 1974 Democratic presidents were in office for 28 years while there were Republican presidents for 18. The Democrats have also retained almost continual control of both houses of Congress: of the 21 sessions between 1933 and 1973, 19 were Democratic and only two Republican.

In the popular mind the Democrats continue to be seen as the party of the ordinary person and the Republicans as party of the wealthy and the higher classes; the proportion voting Democratic continues to increase as one goes down the strata,[56] and in local elections people in the professional, managerial, and business occupations support the Republicans while those in sales, clerical, and manual work vote Democratic. While

[55] The unemployment rate among white-collar workers is 4.5%, whereas among blue-collar workers it is 14.4%. U.S. Department of Labor, *Employment and Earnings*, Vol. 21, No. 10, April, 1975, pp. 32–33.

[56] See Lipset, *Political Man*, pp. 303–313. The exception is those in the professions from which the intellectuals are drawn. *Ibid.*, pp. 337–341.

ethnicity and historical factors affect voting patterns, among religious groups in general the higher the status of the denomination the greater the likelihood of voting Republican. Also, Anglo-Saxons and Protestants are more likely to be Republican than persons of other backgrounds.[57] In addition to blacks, minority groups such as persons of Spanish origin continue to favor the Democratic party.

Not only do the lower strata have the franchise but their needs can be fulfilled through the Democratic Party and this further encourages moderation in political behavior. In addition, since there is considerable shifting in loyalty, as well as failure to go to the polls, a party must obtain a substantial number of votes from those normally in the other camp to be victorious. Consequently the Republicans need to attract Democratic voters; therefore their program cannot be too far to the right. On the other hand, since the Democratic Party has to attract Republican votes it's program cannot be too far to the left.[58] Both tend toward the middle of the road and play down ideological issues. Not to do this is to court electoral disaster, as illustrated by the Goldwater and McGovern debacles.

Moderation in political behavior and reformism is further encouraged by the growing number of voters who profess loyalty to neither party, those who call themselves "Independents." A recent Gallup poll (1974) found that one out of every three adults interviewed classified themselves in this manner, while 44% considered themselves Democrats and 23% Republicans. Two years earlier 29% said they were Independents, 43% Democrats, and 28% Republicans.[59] This poll also shows that persons in the higher status occupations are more likely to identify with the Republican party, whereas those who call themselves Democrats are in the lower level occupations. However, a substantial portion of manual workers classify themselves as Republicans while the opposite holds for those in the professions and business. Moreover, each occupational group contributes a very high proportion of Independents. (See Table XVI-4.)

This mandate for moderation also affects the Presidency. When a Republican president is elected he shifts to the left of his party's leadership for they represent the more conservative elements. The powerful Republican Congressmen, especially those with seniority, are likely to come from "safe," that is very conservative, districts. The Democratic Party leadership also tends to be more conservative than the rank-and-file for the Congressional leaders with seniority are likely to be from the South. Now when there is a Republican president and a Democratic Congress, the Democrats shift to the right. This shifting not only makes

[57] *Ibid.*, pp. 303–313.

[58] See *ibid.*, p. 326.

[59] *Gallup Opinion Index*, Report No. 112, October, 1974, pp. 26–28.

TABLE XVI-4. Occupational Group and Party Identification (1974)* (in percentages)

	Party Identification			
Occupational Group	Republican	Democratic	Independent	Total
Professional and business	28%	34%	38%	100%
Clerical and sales	24	39	37	100
Manual	18	48	34	100

*A total of 12,430 adults 18 and older in eight successive national surveys between March and June, 1974 was interviewed.
Source: Adapted from *Gallup Opinion Index*, Report No. 112, October, 1974, p. 28.

for moderation in politics, but often makes the policies of the two parties seem indistinguishable.[60] Also, since each party tries to take away voters from the other, as well as to persuade Independents, both tend to focus on immediate problems and pragmatic solutions rather than to deal with fundamental questions or radical alternatives. The emphasis on the immediate and the pragmatic is further encouraged by the nature of the politician. Since the broadening of the franchise in the 1820's and the 1830's America's political parties have been controlled by professional politicians whose major concern is to win elections and remain in office.[61]

Finally, labor-management conflict, which since the Civil War has been the single most important cause of violent class behavior, has become institutionalized. Beginning with the Wagner Act and anti-injunction measures of the 1930's, a whole host of legislation has eliminated the worst abuses of the industrial system and established mechanisms such as the National Labor Relations Board which regulate conflict. One of the best illustrations of this development is the change in labor-management relations in the copper industry. There was a history of extreme violence, as in the Bisbee incident which was mentioned in Chapter XV. Conflict continues but in the form of hard but peaceful bargaining. The change began with the New Deal for unions were then able to organize the major copper companies. Subsequently rival unions merged, eliminating conflict between them including the raiding of one another's memberships. In order to solidify its position vis-à-vis the employers, the main union combined for bargaining purposes 27 lesser unions, four trades councils, and a railroad system federation. But coordinated bargaining, which gives local units added strength in dealing with industry negotiators, was achieved only after a lengthy strike. Beginning in 1967 it lasted up to a year in some plants. At the height of the walkout 50,000 workers were on strike, including 30,000 in the Rocky Mountain states which were formerly centers of bitter and open warfare during

[60] Lipset, *op. cit.*, p. 328.
[61] *Ibid.*, p. 319.

labor disputes. Yet the strike was conducted peacefully and without serious incidents.[62] Similarly, violence in labor-management relations in all other industries has greatly diminished, and what occurs tends to be accidental and random.[63]

Summary

The deprivation and protest movements of the Great Depression led to important reforms but no basic alteration of the authority structure. Yet many of the necessary conditions for revolutionary change existed: great economic difficulties following a period of rising expectations; loss in effectiveness of the government and a weakening of the ruling class; disenchantment by the intellectuals; violent class conflict; and a widespread feeling that change was imminent. Nevertheless, these conditions were not sufficiently severe, although this judgment is aided by hindsight.

The economic difficulties were extremely great and widespread, and local and federal government lost much of its effectiveness. However, the federal government was able to provide enough economic resources to prevent total collapse as well as to ameliorate the worst conditions. While the ruling class was weakened, it survived and continued to be influential, thus remaining a significant force against basic change. The intellectuals were extremely critical yet their disenchantment was not complete, in part because there was some market for their productions. The federal government helped greatly with its artists and writers' projects; on the other hand its harassment of leftists, particularly radical intellectuals, limited their effectiveness. Also, because of the emphasis on egalitarianism American intellectuals are not held in as high regard as in many other countries, nor are they looked to for leadership.

Although there was widespread class behavior and much violence significant segments of the strata could not be organized for revolution. The lower strata eschewed basic change; many feared that with a redistribution of wealth they would lose all. The American Dream remained. Not only did belief in the possibility of upward mobility persist but among many there was also self-blame for the dire circumstances they found themselves in. There was no group near the ruling class that felt antagonistic toward those who ruled, as was true in France during the *ancien régime* or in Colonial America. Also, there were no significant segments of the middle strata who were so disenchanted with the authority structure that they were open to basic change.

[62] Philip Taft, "The Bisbee Deportation," *Labor History*, 13 (Winter 1972), 3–40.

[63] Philip Taft and Philip Ross, "American Labor Violence: Its Causes, Character, and Outcome," in Hugh D. Graham and Ted R. Gurr, eds., *Violence in America: Historical and Comparative Perspectives* (New York: Bantam Books, 1969), p. 386.

Working for moderation and reformism are the two-party system and the fact that for electoral success the Republicans must attract a substantial number of votes from the lower strata, and the Democrats from the higher. The programs of the New Deal and the slight improvement of economic conditions gave hope for the future, and with World War II there was a revitalization of the economy. Better times and patriotism discouraged tampering with the authority structure. Also working against basic change has been a long-range trend toward a wider distribution of social goods, including income, education, and better paid and more prestigeful jobs. In addition, there continues to be moderate social mobility, most of it upward. Finally, class conflict involving labor and management, the single most important source of violent class behavior, has become institutionalized with symbolic replacing violent conflict.

The experiences of this period emphasize the utility of amelioration and repression in minimizing the likelihood that protest will lead to revolutionary change. Continuing belief in the success ideology, as discussed previously, hinders protest, let alone basic alteration of the authority structure. This is particularly significant as regards the lower strata, for their home and school socialization additionally reinforces acceptance of existing arrangements.

Given the widening distribution of social goods among the strata, and the factors which minimize violent class behavior and encourage moderate politics, what may we expect in the future? That is, do we foresee overall happiness among the incumbents of the several strata, minimal class conflict, and lack of violence? And, when change becomes necessary, will it be strictly reformist? To try to answer these questions is the major task of the final chapter, to which we now turn.

Part Five

THE FUTURE OF
STRATIFICATION, CLASS,
AND CONFLICT

Chapter XVII.   Trends and Prospects

We certainly expect strata differences and class conflict to continue for they are integral parts of organized human life. We have shown their pervasiveness throughout history as well as contemporaneously. Before commenting on future patterns of stratification and class behavior it is worthwhile to restate the perspective which has guided our work.

The Bases of Stratification

Stratification is based first on collective definitions regarding desirable attributes and possessions, what we called social goods. Its second basis is certain relationships found in all human groups: superordination-subordination and the institutional patterns related to it which have developed over time. Among them are a division of labor, a distribution of roles, and a concomitant differential distribution of authority. The latter is extremely important, for location in the authority structure provides advantages for obtaining and holding on to social goods.

Human groups are held together both by consensus and coercion; those at the apex of the authority structure play a key role in defining the folkways and mores and usually have the power to enforce them. They employ moral persuasion and various degrees of coercion including, on occasion, extreme violence. Their power may be used for the benefit of the society; but there is a tendency to serve their individual, familial, and group interests to the disadvantage of those with fewer social goods and less authority.

We may simply describe the various categories, arranged hierarchically for convenience. In this ordering incumbents who have most of what is collectively defined as desirable are on top and those with the least are on the bottom. This description is *stratification*. In that fashion, a stratum is any aggregate of persons with similar life chances. An important point is that the people in a stratum are not organized: they may be very much aware of how they differ from or are oppressed by those in another stratum; nevertheless they are a social category. When people in a stratum begin to organize to change the distribution of social goods, then class behavior is involved.

The Bases of Class and Class Conflict

A class consists of people who have similar life chances, are organized to a greater or lesser degree, and collectively attempt to change the existing distribution of social goods. Class behavior occurs *only* in associations—formally organized groups, what Weber and Dahrendorf call "imperatively coordinated associations." [1] The association, which may be a factory, a community, or a nation has an authority structure, and formal ties and not sentiments knit the members together. There is a differential distribution of authority which is effected through roles involving superordinate-subordinate relationships, and there is at least a latent conflict of interest between those in the different roles. Classes form when the individuals who compose these aggregates feel their interests are similar to their fellow members', and opposed to the interests of another aggregate in the association. The alignment of the camps follows the superordination-subordination in the association. And, since authority positions are dichotomous, there will be only two conflict groups in a given association. Labor vs. management and colonial administrators vs. natives are examples of class conflict groups. Once such groups have organized their contesting brings about structural change. [2]

Certain factors affect class formation: the nature of the work enterprise; people's life conditions; the existence of leaders, ideologies, and organizations; and cultural conditions. The amount of social mobility is also important, for the greater the upward and downward movement the more dissimilar are the incumbents of a stratum, and the greater the difficulty of forming a common bond. Upward movement may serve as a safety valve; on the other hand, if ascent to the very top is blocked great antagonism may develop and lead to class conflict as happened in France of the *ancien régime* and in Colonial America.

While class conflict is endemic to human group life, in every society ways are devised for dealing with it. Among them are regulation, accommodation, and suppression. Regulation is likely to occur in traditional society, where the church or village elders may insure that the rights and responsibilities of the various groups are fulfilled. Yet, even though there are wide differences between the haves and have-nots, and the strong take advantage of the weak, it is not done arbitrarily or capriciously. Accommodation is common in industrial society, especially an advanced one where there is parliamentary democracy. While there is class con-

---

[1] Max Weber, *The Theory of Social and Economic Organization*, trans. by A. M. Henderson and Talcott Parsons (New York: The Free Press, 1947), pp. 153, 324–328; and Ralf Dahrendorf, *Class and Class Conflict in Industrial Society* (Stanford, Calif.: Stanford University Press, 1959), pp. 179–187.

[2] Dahrendorf, *op. cit.*, pp. 172–173, 204, 210, 213.

flict, there are institutional arrangements which reduce the degree. Examples are the legislative and judicial systems, and in the case of labor-management conflict collective bargaining, conciliation, mediation, and arbitration. Suppression, which may occur in any type of society, may be effective for a considerable period of time; but the conflict may remain below the surface until a seemingly minor incident brings forth a great deal of violence.

Violence exists on a continuum, the class warfare of Marx being one extreme. But the key to violence is whether or not conflict groups share in the authority or are excluded from it. The amount of violence decreases when conflict groups are permitted and are allowed to organize; it goes up when the groups are neither permitted nor allowed to organize. When absolute deprivation is added to the latter situation, a great deal of violence is possible. Intensity of violence, which varies independently with amount, is related to degree of involvement—how much of the self is invested in the struggle. Intensity as well as amount is affected by whether or not conflict behavior is legitimate. Intensity is also related to whether group members' attributes and backgrounds are similar or different; it is much greater when the former is the case. Relative deprivation however increases intensity rather than degree.[3]

Past, Present, and Future

Regardless of a society's past or present situation, class formation and conflict may be expected to continue. For, as we suggested above, with authority structure, distribution of roles, and differential allocation of social goods there is always latent conflict. Under appropriate circumstances it becomes overt. Moreover, the legitimacy of authority relations is always precarious: superordinate groups are constantly seeking to maintain their advantages while subordinate groups try to improve their lot. Yet the structure of the society influences the strata arrangement and shapes the kind of class behavior that occurs. This can be seen in the contrast between traditional society on the one hand and transitional and industrial society on the other.

TRADITIONAL SOCIETY

There was great variation from place to place in the magnitude of strata differences and accessibility to important positions. Nevertheless,

---

[3] Dahrendorf, *op. cit.*, pp. 211–215, 218; and Robert K. Merton, *Social Theory and Social Structure* (rev. ed.; New York: The Free Press, 1957), pp. 227–229, 235–236.

industry, luck, and good weather played a major part in determining people's fortunes, and there was probably a fair degree of equality as regards rising in the authority structure.[4] Also, there were often personal and familial ties which cut across the various levels and muted tendencies toward class formation. While classes existed they were probably barely organized and antagonism between them was largely latent. Yet the apparent absence of class conflict does not mean that the primary community was a paradise for lower status persons. Richard Dewey has suggested that ". . . whereas high social visibility plus high status adds up to a genuinely satisfactory way of life, high visibility added to mediocre or low social status results in a social situation that falls far short of satisfaction."[5]

In this form of society traditional support of the authority structure is emphasized and the lower class tends to accept the status quo. Lower class persons see their subordinate situation as an act of God and they extol the special skills they have and the virtues of their class, virtues which they claim are absent in the dominating class.[6]

The particular form of stratification and class in a society reflects its history, particularly economic conditions. Two important cases are the feudal and the caste arrangements. The feudal ordering which characterized Europe of the Middle Ages was a society of great superordination-subordination. While the feudal bond formally specified mutual obligations, in practice it worked out to extreme domination by the powerful over the weak.[7] The coercion of the economic situation and of the sword,[8] plus the traditions and justifications promulgated by the church and by the peasants themselves kept this lower class in its place. The lower class acquiescence was withdrawn only under conditions of absolute deprivation, as in the case of the peasant uprisings in 16th-century Germany. These revolts were extremely violent and bloody. Yet what happened was overshadowed by the violence and brutality of the upper class in suppressing them.[9]

Next to slavery, the most extreme form of stratification is the caste system, which is enveloped by strong traditions, religion, and consensus. It might seem that these characteristics would keep classes from forming and engaging in conflict. But one cannot overlook the highly co-

[4] Gerhard Lenski, *Power and Privilege* (New York: McGraw-Hill, 1966), pp. 94–98.

[5] Richard Dewey, "The Neighborhood, Urban Ecology, and City Planners," *American Sociological Review*, 15 (August 1950), 503–507.

[6] Ferdinand Tönnies, *Community and Society*, trans. and ed. by Charles P. Loomis (New York: Harper Torchbooks, 1963), p. 255.

[7] Henri Pirenne, *A History of Europe* (Garden City, N.Y.: Doubleday Anchor Books, 1958), Vol. I, pp. 50–51 ff.

[8] Stanislaw Andrzejewski, *Military Organization and Society* (London: Routledge & Kegan Paul, 1954), pp. 58–59.

[9] Jacob S. Schapiro, *Social Reform and the Reformation* (New York: Columbia University, Faculty of Political Science, 1909), pp. 58–59; and Pirenne, *op. cit.*, Vol. II, pp. 283–285.

ercive aspect of dire economic conditions as they are spelled out in the class relationships of employer-employee and landlord-tenant. While most accounts of caste—which are from upper-class perspectives—acknowledge wide differences in life chances, they imply acceptance by the lower levels. Yet the few probings we have of the life as seen from the bottom suggest strong animosities, and by implication, intense class feelings.[10]

Both the feudal and caste orders were rural-oriented; yet there were some cities during the traditional and transitional periods. These too were highly stratified and a wide gulf separated a powerful ruling class from the commoners. While traditions had a strong hold, the economic and police power of the upper class underlay them. The religious teachings were very important in justifying the existing authority structure and in supporting the traditions which helped give it legitimacy.[11]

In this and in the previous cases the lower classes may not have been happy with their situation, but there was little they could do about it. I think we are justified in saying that in traditional society the lower class "knew its place."

TRANSITIONAL AND INDUSTRIAL SOCIETY

The growth of industrialism led to changing patterns of stratification which were accompanied by new relationships, ideologies, and social movements. Beginning in England around the middle of the 18th century, industrialism spread to the Continent as well as to the American Colonies. While the total amount of social goods expanded, their distribution was unequal. Some strata benefitted: the property holders, entrepreneurs, financiers, white-collar, and skilled workers. However, their affluence was at the expense of the dispossessed agricultural laborers and the unskilled of town and city. Whenever old forms of social organization begin to break down, the traditions, justifications, and reciprocal relationships weaken. Consequently restraints on group animosities and on class conflict also weaken. Given a growing consistency of statuses, and since new forms of regulation have not yet developed, class conflict is likely to be widespread and quite intense. This was the case in industrializing England where the lower class suffered because of the one-sided distribution of authority and absolute deprivation, as well as from social and personal disorganization due to the living and working condi-

---

[10] Gerald D. Berreman, "Caste in India and the United States," *American Journal of Sociology*, 66 (September 1960), 120–127.

[11] Gideon Sjoberg, *The Preindustrial City* (Glencoe, Ill.: The Free Press, 1960), pp. 108–114, 220–222.

tions.[12] There was great instability; economic expansion was regularly followed by retraction, labor shortages by surplusses, with related unemployment, inflation by deflation, and rises in real income were followed by declines. There were also overproduction as well as underproduction and widespread manipulation of money and markets.

The formal and informal institutional arrangements worked to the great advantage of the upper class. While employers organized, workers were prohibited from doing so; also, the Vagrancy Acts were used against agitators or anyone causing inconvenience to employer or town official.[13] Peaceful protest was either ignored or savagely repressed.[14] Similar conditions characterized the growth of industrialization in America. But the similarities diverge principally in terms of management behavior and violence. The intransigence of American employers, in contrast to their British counterparts has given the United States the most violent labor history in the world.

The new industrialism and the changes which led to it encouraged new perspectives, particularly the questioning of traditional justifications of inequality. These ideas, whose heritage is the Enlightenment, were used to justify the American Revolution. The successful expulsion of the British excited people throughout the Western world who sought greater liberty and equality in their own lands. The social and economic changes, the questioning of traditional concepts, and the American experience helped bring about the French Revolution of 1789. The overthrow of the *ancien régime* ushered in the age of democratic revolutions.[15] In this new era subordinate groups no longer passively accept what they consider to be an unfair distribution of social goods; they increasingly heed ideologists who promise a better life, and are more prone to participate in social movements to change the status quo. In short, the incumbents of a lower stratum are much more likely to form into a class and engage in conflict with the class they define as oppressing them. The new perspectives and the conditions of life led to widespread, intense, and violent class conflict during the growth of industrialization. Clearly, in this transitional period the members of the lower class no longer "knew their place." While some upper-class persons worked for reform, the vast majority, together with the authorities, felt the overriding necessity was to "police the poor." [16]

[12] Friedrich Engels, *The Condition of the Working Class in England in 1844* (London: George Allen and Unwin, 1920); E. J. Hobsbawm, *Labouring Men* (London: Weidenfield and Nicolson, 1964), pp. 66–67 ff.; and J. L. Hammond and Barbara Hammond, *The Town Laborer* (London: Longmans, 1966).

[13] Hammond and Hammond, *op. cit.*, pp. 72–78.

[14] G. D. H. Cole, *A Short History of the British Working-Class Movement* (London: George Allen and Unwin, 1947), pp. 92–98.

[15] See Alexis de Tocqueville, *Democracy in America*, trans. by George Lawrence and ed. by J. P. Mayer (Garden City, N.Y.: Doubleday Anchor Books, 1969; first pub. in 1848), pp. 13 ff.

[16] Hammond and Hammond, *op. cit.*, 42–47, 68, 101.

The growing size of the lower class, as epitomized by the industrial proletariat, its refusal to accept absolute deprivation, and its increasing restlessness over relative deprivation put fear into the hearts of upper-class people. While they continued to support the policing, they acceded to reforms in order to prevent revolution. Also, rising groups whose opportunities were blocked sought the support of the lower class in order to achieve their ends. The payoff for this was reform of some of the worst abuses of the industrial system and extension of the franchise. The growing importance of the lower class in the authority structure has meant a continued movement to the left by governments with any kind of popular base. There has been a wider distribution of social goods particularly through governmental welfare programs such as unemployment insurance and Social Security. There has also been a considerable increase in real income through higher wages. While in the short run the lower strata suffered greatly, in the long run industrialization has meant a greater amount of social goods and a more equitable distribution. Reformist rather than radical change has become common, and much class conflict has become institutionalized; also, the amount of conflict has decreased, especially violent confrontations. What then, may we expect for the future as regards stratification, class, and conflict?

Current Trends

At present, in spite of the long-range trend of wider distribution of social goods, inequities remain; the movement toward greater equality in income has stopped, and a substantial portion of the population still lives in a state of poverty. After commenting on these points, we ask why this is the case, and in seeking answers we consider the actions of special interest groups; corporate power and its ramifications for stratification and class; the lack of public concern; and aspects of socialization which minimize lower strata protest. Finally, we investigate several segments of the population as potential sources of increased class conflict.

INEQUALITY REMAINS

Chapters IV through VI which examined stratification through the life cycle revealed that considerable inequality in the distribution of social goods remains. The fetal death rate and the neonatal, infant, and maternal mortality rates continue to be shockingly high for those at the lower levels. Also, underweight and premature infants are more likely to be born to lower strata mothers. Children from the lower strata receive poorer education, and they have the highest juvenile delinquency rate; as youths, they are much less likely to complete high school or go to college. Institutional arrangements are such that persons at the lower levels receive inadequate medical care and are at a disadvantage when involved with the police and judicial systems. Lower strata individuals are more likely to be unemployed, and out of work for longer periods. In wartime they are more likely to be drafted, sent to the front, and killed or wounded.

There is greater family instability among the lower strata, and their chances for being hospitalized for mental health problems are higher, especially for schizophrenia and total psychosis. They are more likely to have inadequate housing, live in slums, receive fewer public services, and be sold shoddy goods or be taken advantage of in other ways by unscrupulous merchants. They participate little in voluntary organizations, nor are they active in politics. Finally, old age is much more trying; not only do the lower strata elderly have greater difficulty in making ends meet, but they are more likely to suffer from social isolation, have a higher incidence of mental and physical disabilities, and a lower life expectancy.

It would appear that the continuing rise in median income would eventually do away with these inequities. But there has hardly been any improvement in the income share of those on the bottom.

THE MALDISTRIBUTION OF INCOME CONTINUES

Since 1929 there has been a decline in the proportion of total income the richest 20% of families and unrelated individuals receive. While their share has gone down, from 54 to 41%, they are still quite well off. The change has mainly benefitted the next fifth and the middle fifth, from 19 to 24% and from 14 to 18% respectively. But the current income shares of the second fifth, 12%, and of the lowest fifth, six per cent, have hardly improved at all.[17] The trend toward a more equitable distribution of income ended during the post-World War II period. A comparison of the current shares received by each income fifth with the distribution in 1947 shows that there has been no significant change.[18]

The small proportion of total income received by the bottom two fifths, especially the lowest, may be looked at in another way. On the basis of yearly earnings, 23% of families and unrelated individuals receive less than $4,000 annually. If we exclude the unrelated individuals, then we find that 13% of the families still make less than $4,000 a year. This means 6,943,000 families.[19]

[17] U.S. Bureau of the Census, "Money Income in 1973 of Families and Persons in the United States," Series P-60, No. 97 (Washington, D.C.: Government Printing Office, January 1975), p. 43; and Herman P. Miller, *Rich Man, Poor Man* (New York: The New American Library, 1964), p. 52.

[18] "Money Income in 1973 of Families and Persons in the U.S.," *loc. cit.*

[19] U.S. Bureau of the Census, "Illustrative Projections of Money Income Size Distributions for Families and Unrelated Individuals," Series P-23, No. 47 (Washington, D.C.: Government Printing Office, February 1974), p. 11.

Now what of the future? On the assumption that the income shares will remain the same and that there will be moderate growth of the economy, it is expected that median income will almost double by 1990; moreover, only five per cent of the families will have annual incomes under $4,000. Also, whereas 25% of families made over $15,000 a year in 1971, the percentage in this category is expected to rise to 61. Table XVII-1 shows the projections for the several income categories.

TABLE XVII-1. Family Income for 1971 with Projections for 1980 and 1990 in Constant 1971 Dollars* (in percentages)

Income Intervals	1971	1980	1990
$25,000 and over	5.3%	11.9%	27.7%
$15,000-24,999	19.5	29.3	33.7
$10,000-14,999	26.9	24.8	16.9
$4,000-9,999	35.2	25.5	16.9
Under $4,000	13.0	8.6	4.9
Total	99.9%	100.1%	100.1%
Median Income	$10,281	$13,259	$18,122

*The projections assume a moderate growth rate in the economy of 3 per cent annually.
Source: U.S. Bureau of the Census, "Illustrative Projections of Money Income Size Distributions for Families and Unrelated Individuals," Series P-23, No. 47 (Washington, D.C.: Government Printing Office, February 1974), p. 2.

Since these figures take inflation into account they indicate considerable growth in real income. Does this mean then that the future lower strata will be relatively well off and contented? Not very likely, for as Marx and others observed a long time ago, the nature of an industrial society is such that as income rises so do people's wants. Thus, even though income will go up so will the minimum acceptable standard of living. And, rather than leading to contentment, feelings of relative deprivation may be expected to increase. Also the deprivation, whether relative or tending toward absolute affects some segments more severely, particularly groups such as blacks and the elderly. And, for reasons we shall discuss shortly, such groups are potential instigators of considerable class conflict.

Why Continued Poverty?

An obvious reason why people remain in a state of poverty is lack of social goods; insufficient money to obtain the things they need. The main causes are also readily apparent: unemployment and underemployment due to insufficient education and lack of skills required for the growing proportion of technical jobs; skills which become obsolete because of technological change; discrimination; failure to create sufficient jobs to match population growth; [20] and a slack labor market.[21]

The causes of inadequate education were discussed in Chapters IV and V: lower strata youths find themselves in homes and neighborhoods which provide little encouragement for education; they attend poor schools and tend to drop out or are "pushed out" by curricula which have little meaning for them. Government funds to improve these schools have been inadequate, and special programs such as Head Start have failed, primarily because the schools themselves have not been improved. Because of technological change people whose skills become obsolete are no longer needed, and this is a special problem for the older worker. Retraining programs have had little impact because of their small scale, but more importantly, because there has been no way of insuring jobs for the retrained. These problems create additional difficulties for minorities—"the last hired and the first fired"—and they particularly feel the effects of a slack labor market.

Ostensibly, social welfare such as unemployment insurance, Social Security, Workmen's Compensation, and welfare aid should provide for those who are out of work or unemployable. They provide some help but are either woefully inadequate or only take care of short-term needs. Unemployment insurance is only for a limited period, a portion of the labor force is not covered, and it does not apply to persons who have not yet held a job. As for Social Security, the payments are so low that the elderly who depend on them are in the poverty category. Whereas 23% of all families and unrelated individuals earn less than $4,000 a year, this is true of 54% of those 65 or older.[22] If Sweden can provide its retired with two-thirds of what they earned during their highest paid years,[23] certainly a nation such as the United States should be able to. There are built-in inequities in the Social Security law which not only hurt the lower strata but anyone who works for a living. Designed to keep those over 65 off the labor market, if more than a minimum income is earned, Social Security payments are reduced accordingly. But people whose income is from rents, dividends, interest, sale of property, or other capital gains are not penalized.

For those injured on the job, Workmen's Compensation programs are inadequate and inequitable, according to a recent report to Congress by the National Commission on State Workmen's Compensation Laws. Basically, coverage is too narrow and payments are too low. Also, 15% of the labor force is not protected, including those who need it most: non-union, low-wage workers, such as agricultural laborers, domestics, and

[20] See Gunnar Myrdal, *Challenge to Affluence* (New York: Vintage Books, 1965).

[21] Hyman P. Minsky, "The Role of Employment Policy," in Margaret S. Gordon, ed., *Poverty in America* (San Francisco: Chandler Publishing Co., 1965), pp. 175–200.

[22] "Illustrative Projections of Money Income Size Distributions for Families and Unrelated Individuals," p. 11.

[23] Myrdal, *op. cit.*, p. 62.

employees of small firms. Many states limit the duration of the benefits and the total amount, and in some states not all work-related diseases are covered.[24] Job-related disabilities are a major problem since each year one out of every ten workers is injured, killed, or succumbs to an occupational disease. The U.S. Public Health Service estimates that

> prolonged on-the-job exposure to toxic chemicals, dusts, noise, heat, cold, radiation and other industrial conditions each year results in the death of at least 100,000 workers and the development of disabling occupational diseases in 390,000 more.[25]

This is in spite of the existence of the Department of Labor's Occupational Safety and Health Administration, and the Occupational Safety and Health Act passed in 1971, which established the National Institute for Occupational Safety and Health. These agencies are under-funded and unable to survey industrial health problems, conduct needed research, or develop standards for known and potential occupational hazards. For example, the Labor Department has only 600 federal inspectors and hygienists for canvassing nearly five million workplaces. At the current rate of investigation it would take the inspectors 200 years to visit each place once. Similarly, the N.I.O.S.H. is currently unable, because of lack of funds and personnel, to develop standards for over 14,000 chemical and physical agents to which workers are exposed. Here is another example: industry introduces some 400 new chemicals each year, most of which are untested as to possible long-term effects on employees who handle them. Furthermore, federal standards that do exist are usually extremely lenient, as in the case of vinyl chloride. The present federal standard for maximum exposure to this chemical which causes fatal liver cancer is ten times higher than the minimum adopted by industry many years ago; it is infinitely higher than the zero exposure level labor union and university scientists recommend.[26]

There are other social welfare measures which are of some help to the lower strata but probably do more good for administrators, middlemen, and investors. Housing policy is an excellent illustration. We mentioned previously how control of the Federal Housing Administration was taken over by people who deal in real estate and, as a result, the federal government enforced restrictive racial covenants. While the F.H.A. program did aid middle-income people, it was a special boon to the real estate and home-building industry. Yet, not only was little done for the poor but the program encouraged suburban development and urban sprawl, and contributed to the problem of the decaying inner cities. In spite of

[24] "A Critical Report on Workers' Compensation," *San Francisco Chronicle* (July 31, 1972), pp. 1 ff.

[25] Jane E. Brody, "Many Workers Still Face Health Peril Despite Law," *New York Times* (March 4, 1974), pp. 1 ff.

[26] *Ibid.*

government aid there is still inadequate housing. According to the Joint Center for Urban Studies of M.I.T. and Harvard, today one out of every 20 households in the United States is substandard, over-crowded, or the rent is excessively high.[27] Federally subsidized housing for the poor has been one attempt to ameliorate the situation. However, as much as half the subsidy funds never reach the families for whom the program is designed; instead, this money goes for federal and local administrative expenses, real estate dealers' fees, land speculators' profits, lending institutions' interest, and title and insurance companies' costs.[28]

In many respects the most inhuman of the social welfare measures is aid to the needy. A recent report by the Department of Health, Education, and Welfare cited inequity, inadequacy, and inefficiency, and condemned "the existing conglomeration of income supplement programs as hopelessly disjointed, often functioning at cross-purposes and failing to help those most in need." [29] These are some of the problems: aid for dependent children is not given if there is a male head of the household, which encourages men to leave their families; aid is reduced if one is employed, which discourages working; plus inefficiency and red tape.[30] But in addition the welfare system works to degrade the recipients, for essentially they are viewed as having no productive usefulness. This stratum, Piven and Cloward observe, ". . . is not treated with indifference, but with contempt. Its degradation at the hands of relief officials serves to celebrate the virtue of all work, and deters actual or potential workers from seeking aid." [31]

As we have said before, the many reforms which were introduced to meet pressing societal needs have had many beneficial effects. However, they often fall far short of people's needs and have serious flaws. Why is it that ameliorative measures so often seem to have a catch to them?

"Catch-22" Reform

When old forms no longer satisfy people's needs and/or expectations, movements for change are likely. We have shown that in the United States, except for the Revolution and the Civil War, the changes have been reformist. However they never seemed to go as far as the propo-

---

[27] Joseph P. Fried, "13 Million Families Are Held 'Housing-Deprived'," *New York Times* (December 12, 1973), p. 64.

[28] *Ibid.*

[29] "HEW Report, Harsh Attack on Programs for the Poor," *San Francisco Chronicle* (July 15, 1974), p. 1 ff.

[30] *Ibid.* See also Frances Fox Piven and Richard A. Cloward, *Regulating the Poor* (New York: Vintage Books, 1971).

[31] Piven and Cloward, *op. cit.*, p. 165.

nents wished; more than that, they have often been subverted. The main reasons are the nature of capitalist industrialism and the acquiescence of the larger public.

UP FOR GRABS

In a capitalist industrial society with a liberal parliamentary political form, as in the United States, organized groups regularly contest over the distribution of social goods. In a basically unplanned society without a collective means of determining how social goods should be distributed, the strongest win out. Essentially, everything is up for grabs. The only limitation, aside from government sanctions which are minimal, is the existence of a number of competing groups, which often balance each other off, sometimes by several combining forces. Social scientists have used the concept *pluralism* to describe this situation. As an ideal type the system works through a balancing of the power of competing but over-lapping groups, including business, labor, religious, ethnic, and regional. There are two main approaches among social scientists: one views government as the arena in which the contesting occurs and where differences are resolved; the other sees the conflicting groups operating and balancing outside government, with the latter acting as an umpire.[32] Actually both approaches help explain the economic and political behavior of the important groups whose actions and decisions have a significant effect on the society. Conflict and accommodation or destruction take place within government, as in the case of a manufacturers' association and a farmers' group fighting over tariff legislation, or pro- and anti-military groups battling over the ending of the draft. In the above instances the locus is the government, for it is the official association which has the legitimate power to make these kinds of decisions. But associations also exist outside government, which acts as an umpire over their contesting. One example is General Motors, others are the Farm Bureau Federation, the AFL-CIO, the American Medical Association. Conflict occurs within each, as factions try to alter the distribution of social goods over which the association has control. There is also conflict, accommodation, and destruction between such groups, and they take place outside the government; corporations compete for markets, a farm workers' union struggles with a growers' association, organized environmentalists and home builders fight over land use.

[32] See discussion by William E. Connolly, "The Challenge to Pluralist Theory," in Connolly, ed., *The Bias of Pluralism* (New York: Lieber-Atherton, 1973), pp. 3–34, especially pp. 3, 8–13. The first approach is typified by the work of Robert Dahl (see *Who Governs?* [New Haven: Yale University Press, 1961] and *Pluralist Democracy in the United States: Conflict and Consent* [Chicago: Rand McNally, 1967]). The second is represented by Adolf A. Berle (see his *Power Without Property* [New York: Harcourt, Brace and World, 1959]).

The choice of battleground—whether the conflict is to take place within the government arena or outside—is simply a matter of strategy. If protagonists believe they will be successful through laws or administrative decisions they will go to the government; on the other hand they will conduct their fight outside if that seems the best way to accomplish their ends. Often both are used; for example, management tries to destroy a union through hiring strikebreakers and uses the government to provide police or an injunction against the strikers. Or, automobile manufacturers compete with each other for buyers of small cars while at the same time trying to get the government to restrict such imports. At the turn of the century the trusts not only monopolized industries and markets but also bribed whole state legislatures in order to obtain favorable laws and administrative decisions.

Today the government is becoming more and more important as a means of obtaining social goods. This is the result of its extensive intervention in economic life and in the society as a whole, a trend which was spurred on by the Progressive movement and then accelerated greatly, especially beginning with the New Deal. Consequently powerful groups increasingly make use of the official authority structure for their own ends.

TWO FEET IN THE DOOR

The powerful groups, which Keller calls the strategic elites,[33] are intimately involved in all aspects of the governmental process; many freely dispense money and other aids to candidates who may be counted on to further the groups' interests; and lobbying, the offering of favors, or threats of sanctions take place in the legislative halls. The courts are used to fight undesirable laws, and various emoluments encourage favorable decisions by administrators. Finally, regulatory agencies are staffed by persons with close ties to the bodies being regulated. In a modern industrial society such as the United States, the group composed of the large corporations is the most important, and we shall concentrate on it.

The modern corporation—known as the "joint stock company" in the early days of industrial capitalism—is a highly rationalized association whose primary goal is profit. It is "soulless" in the sense that ownership is usually dispersed; legally, assuming the absence of criminal acts, no individual is accountable for its success or failure. The managers are employees and are usually not the major stockholders, and the dynamics of corporate life impel them, in the quest for increased profits, to expand their operations, widen their markets, and minimize their competition. There is a countertendency however which is a component of their

[33] Suzanne Keller, *Beyond the Ruling Class* (New York: Random House, 1963).

highly rationalized nature; it is the desire to operate in as highly stable an environment as is compatible with the profit goal. In the past this led to monopolistic practices aimed at regulating competition, and legislation such as the Sherman Anti-Trust Act has been largely ineffective, as we mentioned before. Government regulation, which was instituted during the Progressive movement and the New Deal has managed to minimize some of the worst practices of the past. As we noted above and in Chapter III, however, regulatory agencies are commonly staffed by people from the industries they are required to regulate.

While the public interest is not completely forgotten, the practice is regulation which is conducive to business stability. When organized groups help shape public opinion so that demands for ameliorating corporate behavior cannot be ignored, the regulatory agencies most often side with the businesses involved. Or, they accommodate them by delaying or watering down any changes. This is illustrated by the experience of a consumers' advocate group which discovered that the airlines regularly overcharge for connecting flights. The Civil Aeronautics Board investigated but in such a way that it minimized the problem; yet it found overcharging which if projected to the number of passengers each year would amount to around $13 million annually. The penalty for such violations? $25,000 in fines; however the CAB merely recommended that the airlines train their ticket agents better and make better use of their computers in quoting fares. The reaction of the organization which conducted the original inquiry underlines the regulatory problem:

> The CAB's tepid response is a gross violation of the public trust. It is in line with the whole history of the CAB's warm cooperation with the airlines and cold neglect for the public. Moreover, it's not the cure for airline abuses; it's the reason those abuses still exist.[34]

Another case in point is automobile safety, which is the purview of the National Highway Traffic Safety Administration. Presumably this agency would fight hard to see that motor vehicles are built to be as safe as possible. Yet its efforts are often directed to protecting the auto industry from requirements which would raise their costs.[35] The shameful record of mine disasters is primarily due to lack of enforcement of mine safety requirements by both federal and state bodies.

In the case of state regulatory bodies, the problems are similar to those at the federal level: the members of state agencies usually have just as close ties to the industries they are supposed to oversee for the public good. In almost all states, regulation of public utilities is nominal; rate increases are usually granted with minimal investigation of the merits of the requests. Industries which are vital to local economies are treated very leniently.

---

[34] "CAB Speaks Softly but Wields No Stick," *Consumer Reports* (November 1972), p. 692.
[35] See e.g., "Marks of Negligence in Handling a Hazard," *Consumer Reports, ibid.*

Basically then, government regulation of business has not accomplished what the Populists, and to a lesser extent the Progressives, hoped for: an industrial capitalism sufficiently controlled by the people to insure an equitable distribution of social goods, and to prevent the concentration of economic and political power in fewer and fewer hands. Instead regulation, particularly by the federal government, has served to take the rough edges off business practices and in the long run entrench the corporation more firmly. Over the years, through mergers and concentration they have grown in size as well as in economic and political power. It is rare that any political candidate who opposes major corporate interests is ever successful. Where there are exceptions, they are usually due to the existence of competing interest groups. Even when a state legislator or Congressman is ideologically opposed to a dominant business, the fact that his constituents are likely to depend on it for their paychecks helps modify his opposition. What is more likely, however, is that the legislator, regardless of party, will support the dominant economic interest, be it through high farm prices, sugar quotas, restricting foreign oil imports, or subsidies to local industry.

The high cost of election campaigns increases the corporation's influence over candidate selection and election issues, and increases the likelihood of substantial payoffs in return for campaign contributions. The close tie-in carries over to the operation of the government itself, as was mentioned earlier. Its significance is not so much the scandals or special arrangements such as the wheat sale to Russia in 1974, or some of the events involved in the 1972 presidential election, such as the ITT fracas, the milk producers' campaign contributions followed by a hike in milk prices, or the airline, shipbuilding, and other corporations' illegal political contributions. Rather, the intimate involvement of the corporations in the electoral and governing process works out so that decisions tend to be made from the perspective of what is good for business, and big business at that. A case in point is the imposition of wage and price controls in the early 1970's: little interest was shown in regulating profits, and the basic regulation was of wages. By holding them down, and also prohibiting raises which ordinarily would have gone into effect, business reaped windfall profits. Also, as was discussed in the preceding chapter, national economic policy goes along with an unemployment rate of five per cent or higher. That this translates into several million people without jobs is apparently of little concern. That high interest rates mean that many in the lower strata cannot afford to purchase a home is of little matter; the fact that inner cities continue to deteriorate, that the reduction of government funds is creating a crisis for higher education, that programs for social needs are being cut back seem unimportant. What seems to matter is the reduction of expenditures in order to try to achieve some mythical "balanced budget." This goal is questionable for the family and national budgets are two entirely different animals. Actually, such arguments may be specious, a smokescreen to cover the fact that the social goods over which the federal government has control are much more generously distributed to business.

Capitalist industrialism has raised the standard of living, and continues to produce ever greater quantities of consumer items. Yet, in addition to the inequities in the distribution of social goods which we mentioned above, the emphasis is on private use; consequently the public sector continues to suffer. The rationale of business enterprise requires it to strive for larger markets and greater profits with little or no attention to social needs. Social planning, increased taxes for social programs, or anything which interferes with its activities are usually fought.[36]

By its very nature the corporation is amoral and irresponsible; corporate morality and responsibility come primarily from the laws. The pressure for profit encourages rationality and efficiency with minimal consideration of the social costs to employees, consumers, or the public at large.[37] This imperative leads business enterprise to use any institution for its own ends if it can. One illustration is higher education, whose discoveries in science, technology, and other areas are applied by business, or scholars work on projects of direct applicability. Its research grants or donations to schools of engineering or agriculture help shape the scientist's and other scholar's research interests. Even the public funding of such schools, as well as the special units which directly apply the results of scientific and other scholarly endeavors reflects the commercial influence.

Present-day large-scale agriculture provides an illustration of some of the consequences of the pressure for profit, rationality, and efficiency together with the disregard of social costs. It also shows the involvement of higher education through the establishment of a complex of colleges of agriculture, state agricultural experiment stations, and the agricultural extension service.[38] Jim Hightower points out that this complex

> has been eager to work with farm machinery manufacturers and well-capitalized farming operations to mechanize all agricultural labor, but it has accepted no responsibility for the farm laborer who is put out of work by the machine. It has worked hand-in-hand with seed companies to develop high

[36] See, e.g., "Ban on Dumping of Cyanide Is Fought," *New York Times* (December 25, 1974), p. 19.

[37] In a non-capitalist industrial society the pressures may be in the form of maximizing "credits" or the meeting or surpassing of production quotas. However decisions which affect stratification are mainly political, even though they are affected by market forces. In a capitalist country the decisions are influenced primarily by the economic considerations. See John H. Goldthorpe, "Social Stratification in Industrial Society," in Reinhard Bendix and Seymour M. Lipset, eds., *Class, Status, and Power* (rev. ed.; New York: The Free Press, 1966), pp. 655 ff. and our discussion in Chapter II.

[38] These were established by the Morrill Act of 1862, the Hatch Act of 1887, and the Smith-Lever Act of 1914, respectively.

yield seed strains, but it has not noticed that rural America is yielding up practically all of its young people. It has been available day and night to help non-farming corporations develop schemes of vertical integration, while offering independent family farmers little more comfort than "adapt or die." It has devoted hours to the creation of adequate water systems for fruit and vegetable processors and canners, but 30,000 rural communities still have no central water systems. It has tampered with the gene structure of tomatoes, strawberries, asparagus and other foods to prepare them for the steel grasp of mechanical harvesters, but it has sat still while the American food supply has been laced with carcinogenic substances.[39]

The same situation holds for large manufacturing and related operations. Yet their actions as well as those of corporate agriculture are within the law; however, the pressure for profit together with the many impersonal contexts of the market encourage cutting corners, minimizing quality, building in obsolescence, seeking special favors from government officials, and other behaviors, many of which stop just short of being illegal. The temptations are great because mass production and large-scale marketing mean that a minor change may be translated into hundreds of thousands of dollars. Thus reducing the size of a candy bar one-tenth of an ounce, or using sheet steel for automobiles which is one ten-thousandths of an inch thinner lower costs and raise profit margins. Since government actions affect the balance sheet, business representatives constantly try to lobby for favorable decisions. A common way of rewarding the public official is through a campaign contribution as was suggested above; another is by promising a job after the person leaves office. But because the stakes are high, the line between legal and illegal behavior is quite frequently overlooked. This is illustrated by the recent case of a United States senator who accepted an allegedly unlawful gratuity from the lobbyist for a large mail-order firm to influence his vote on postal rate legislation. During the trial it was revealed that each one-cent rise in third class postage rates would cost the concern one million dollars a year.[40]

It would hardly seem necessary to resort to extra-legal means since the laws, especially those dealing with taxation, offer big business so many opportunities to increase profits. Philip M. Stern's description of the tax laws, in his aptly titled *The Rape of the Taxpayer*,[41] suggests that these laws were written in some corporate board room and not in the U.S. Congress. There are numerous tax preferences or "loopholes" which include the oil depletion allowance, capital gains taxed at one half the rate of salary income, rapid depreciation, and tax-free municipal and

[39] Jim Hightower, "Hard Tomatoes, Hard Times: Failure of the Land Grant College Complex," *Society* (November–December 1972), 10–11.

[40] Anthony Ripley, "Brewster Guilty of Accepting Gratuity," *New York Times* (November 18, 1972), p. 1 ff.

[41] Philip M. Stern, *The Rape of the Taxpayer* (New York: Vintage Books, 1973).

state bonds.[42] As a consequence nine corporate giants that earned 650 million dollars in profits in 1970 and 1971 paid no taxes. Among them were Continental Oil whose 1971 profits were $109,030,000 and U.S. Steel with profits of $109,491,000 in 1970. While most businesses pay taxes the laws work out so that the larger ones are able to reduce them substantially. Thus in 1971 the taxes for ITT which had a net profit of $413,858,000 before taxes were five per cent; Standard Oil of California paid only 1.6% on its before-taxes earnings of $855,692,000.[43] Loopholes also allow a portion of the upper strata to pay zero taxes: this was true for 1,235 families who earned over $100,000 in 1969 and the percentage has been increasing rapidly, as Table XVII-2 shows. What this means is that the burden falls on the middle and lower strata; for example, a laborer whose annual wages are $7,373 pays federal taxes of $1,131, or 16%.[44]

It is readily apparent that corporate business is intimately involved in the governmental process and benefits handsomely from it, at the expense of small business and the middle and lower strata. But what about countervailing forces, such as organized labor, the many voluntary associations, and the voters?

THE WEAKNESS OF COUNTERVAILING FORCES

Neither organized labor, professional associations, consumer groups, nor other voluntary associations are any match for the corporations in terms of money, which can be used for economic or political purposes. Nor are they any match in terms of involvement in the elective process and government. None has the resources that the large corporations readily deploy: extensive legal staffs and economic and other experts; well-heeled and skillful public relations units; and influence over the

TABLE XVII-2. Number of Families Who Paid No Taxes in 1960 and 1969

| | Number of Families Who Paid No Taxes | |
Family Income	1960	1969
Over $1,000,000	11	56
From $500,000 up to $1,000,000	23	117
From $100,000 up to $500,000	174	1,062
Total	208	1,235

Source: Figures adapted from Philip M. Stern, *The Rape of the Taxpayer* (New York: Vintage Books, 1973), p. 14. Copyright © 1973 by Random House, Inc.

[42] *Ibid.*, pp. 21, 27, 93–118, 228–251.

[43] *Ibid.*, pp. 17, 18, 209.

[44] *Ibid.*, pp. 16–17. Also, these taxes are withheld from wages, and lose interest. *Ibid.*, pp. 18, 23, 346, 375. In the above illustration the worker is actually out an additional $39; this is what he would receive if the $94 monthly withholding were placed in a savings account earning six per cent yearly, compounded monthly.

mass media, particularly through advertising.[45] But perhaps more important is the power of the corporation elite to chart its own course and to affect the economy. Corporate managers often can determine prices as they see fit, and usually charge what the market will bear. Top management determines the distribution of profits between the company and stockholders, with little or no interference from the latter. While wages are subject to collective bargaining, this process simply maintains the status quo, for increases just about keep pace with the cost of living. Also, the share of a corporation's income going into wages remains about the same over the years. The corporation elite decides when to invest in new capital equipment, processes, and products; it decides on the kinds and number of jobs there will be, where plants and offices will be located, and, in that regard, what parts of the country will prosper and which will stagnate.[46] Hacker observes that

> [i]nstead of government planning there is planning by an elite that is accountable to no outside agency. Its decisions set the order of priorities on national growth, technological innovation, and ultimately the values and behavior of human lives.[47]

There are close ties among those who compose the topmost levels of corporations. Not only are interlocking directorates widespread,[48] but there are also familial, school, and social ties among the business, government, and military elites whose decisions critically affect the society.[49] These people determine the fortunes of the society; descriptively, they are a ruling stratum. But to what extent are they a class?

RULING STRATUM OR RULING CLASS?

While it is acknowledged that there are powerful decision makers in the society, and that they may be categorized as an elite, there is debate on whether or not they act in concert: do they work together as a class, or is it just happenstance that on occasion their decisions support one an-

---

[45] The perspectives of media owners and editors are similar to those of the large corporations and the upper strata. I do not recall a newspaper, mass circulation magazine, or television station ever siding with strikers against management, although this must have happened.

[46] Andrew Hacker, "Power to Do What?" in Connolly, The Bias of Pluralism, pp. 70–73.

[47] Ibid., p. 73.

[48] See C. Wright Mills, The Power Elite (New York: Oxford University Press, 1959), p. 123, 123 n. See also Louis D. Brandeis, Other People's Money (Washington, D.C.: National Home Library Foundation, 1933), pp. 21–22, 35–58.

[49] Mills, op. cit.; G. William Domhoff, Who Rules America? (Englewood Cliffs, N.J.: Prentice-Hall, 1967); Ferdinand Lundberg, The Rich and the Super-Rich (New York: Bantam Books, 1969); and America's Sixty Families (New York: Vanguard Press, 1937).

other? [50] Drawing on Keller's thesis [51] allows us to formulate the problem as follows: we know that there are groups in the society which have an important impact on the distribution of social goods, that each may be depicted in terms of an hierarchical ordering. The influential elite at the apex of each may or may not be a ruling class for that situs. However, the basic question is whether these elites act in a veto capacity or as a ruling class. In schematic form, does diagram A or B in Figure XVII-1 depict the true state of affairs? Keller holds that in earlier times the several elites formed a ruling class, but that today they are separated by competing interests, geography, different origins, and other factors, so that they are essentially veto groups. Yet each conception is an extreme polar type and of necessity exaggerated. In earlier times the probability was high that the behavior of ruling elites very frequently approximated Type B. But we know from history that there were often disagreements and conflicts and a failure to act in concert when there were compelling reasons to do so; the scale of the society was smaller, it was more transparent, and the

FIGURE XVII-1.

Schematic Representation of Major Situses and Elite Behavior

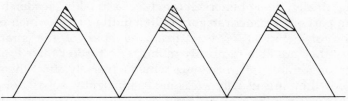

A. Under conditions which pose little or no threat to superordination and decisive control over distribution of social goods

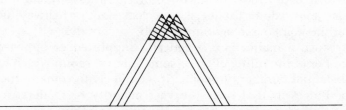

B. Under conditions which pose a great threat to superordination and decisive control over distribution of social good

[50] See G. William Domhoff and Hoyt B. Ballard, eds., C. *Wright Mills and the Power Elite* (Boston: Beacon Press, 1969); and Marc Pilisuk and Thomas Hayden, "Is there a Military-Industrial Complex Which Prevents Peace?: Consensus and Countervailing Power in Pluralistic Systems," in Connolly, *The Bias of Pluralism*, pp. 123–155.

[51] See Keller, *Beyond The Ruling Class.*

possible alternatives for given actions seemed fairly predictable. (It is also likely that our image of earlier ruling classes is influenced by historical distance; that is, we may imagine greater unity among a ruling class in the medieval or early industrial society than existed.) Now, in the modern period, the ruling elites at times are separate, as in diagram A. However, upon a major threat to their welfare they coalesce as in diagram B. If this is the situation, then what may we expect in regard to the possibility of any fundamental change? That is, change which would critically affect the preeminence of the major ruling elites.

These elites, who compose the ruling stratum, are much more likely to form a class when their interests are affected, in contrast to the lower strata. For the upper strata in general are much more prone to social participation including politics, as we noted earlier. Also, because of their economic activities and political involvement they are likely to be aware of the interconnections among the economic, political, and social spheres. Consequently, the ways of holding on to or increasing their social goods are apparent to them and they have the expertise and technical means to accomplish these ends. Also, the large amount of social goods they have is an incentive to remain alert to any threat to reduce them. And finally, being better educated, used to taking leadership roles, and being part of a smaller category of like individuals—which is simply a function of being at or very near the apex of the stratification hierarchy—they are able to readily mobilize to further their interests. If legislation or administrative changes which adversely affect them cannot be scuttled, they are usually weakened sufficiently so as not to be a threat. This is done through an army of lawyers, economists and other experts, and lobbyists. They swing into action, supported by personal contacts in government which have been cultivated previously, and with the help of accommodating officials and Congressmen are usually successful. Much if not most of these occurrences never come into public view; deals are made in the legislative cloakroom or hallway, over cocktails, or at the golf course or country club.

Unless such a matter is energetically supported or opposed by another member of the ruling elite, or some interest group which can mobilize a substantial number of people, it is unlikely to come to the public's attention. But even if it does the vast majority of readers or viewers usually pay little attention. Those in the upper stratum are well aware of what is going on, however, particularly the things which affect their interests, as we mentioned above. These are the people who read *The New York Times, The Wall Street Journal,* and more specialized publications. Such concern drops off rapidly as one moves down to the middle stratum, and is almost nonexistent in the lower. Paralleling this falloff is the rise in interest in entertainment and the frivolous. Aside from such things as sports there is little concern with events outside their daily lives, and familial and friendship activities take up most of their nonworking time.[52] Yet they are not completely unaware of economic and political matters which affect them; in fact their response to situations which have a direct impact on their welfare has the potential for being quite radical and violent. This is one of the main reasons revolutionary movements are able to recruit people from the lower strata. The response is a gut reaction, however, and not an intellectual decision; moreover, it is a reaction with an extremely limited perspective which, in the absence of a revolutionary movement, is likely to have minimal impact and not seriously challenge the status quo.

It is the contrasting life experiences of the several strata, which were examined in Chapters IV, V, and VI, which are responsible for the differing responses to important issues. For the lower strata the experiences amount to socialization for inefficacy.

SOCIALIZATION FOR INEFFICACY

We previously observed that lower strata socialization discourages the kind of critical thinking that allows one to place immediate experiences in a broader or abstract framework. In an extremely perceptive article Michael Mann points out that because of home and school experiences lower stratum persons are ill-equipped to relate something of immediate concern to a broader economic or political context.[53] Consequently, the reaction to unemployment, inability to obtain adequate housing, or other social problems is self-blame, Populist feelings which amount to little more than "letting off steam," alienation, or withdrawal, which may include the use of alcohol or drugs. Mann shows how lower strata education results in confused political values which contain a conservative bias. He cites studies of schools and textbooks in the United States and Great Britain which find that they cultivate patriotism, a benevolent image of authority, and the harmonious nature of political life. The emphasis is on what the social, economic, and political aspects of the society are supposed to be rather than what they are really like, and responsibilities are stressed over rights. While the conflictual elements of politics are dealt with in upper strata schools, however, they are kept out of the lower strata classroom. The lower strata's simplistic view of the social world as the "rich" and the "poor," their lack of knowledge of the political process, and their indoctrination of nationalistic and authority values limit their interest in basic economic or political questions. Even if adequately presented by the mass media, it seems very unlikely that they would pay attention to them.

It is for these reasons that the mass of the population, despite having

[52] See Richard Hoggart, *The Uses of Literacy* (New York: Oxford University Press, 1970).

[53] Michael Mann, "The Social Cohesion of Liberal Democracy," *American Sociological Review*, 35 (June 1970), 423–439.

the franchise, is rarely a countervailing force to the ruling class. With this in mind, we now speculate on the future of stratification, class, and conflict.

The Future of Stratification, Class, and Conflict

To expect absolute or near-equality so that there are no differences in the life chances of the population seems unlikely. The very nature of social differentiation, the fact that people are born with different attributes, and the collective process surrounding the distribution of social goods work against equality. What is important are the *extent* of the differences and the *institutional arrangements* through which the distribution may be altered. The thesis by Clark Kerr and others that there is an inherent tendency in industrial society toward greater equality and opportunity [54] has been successfully challenged.[55]

As we noted earlier, the trend toward a more equal distribution of income pretty much ended during the late 1940's. Unless there are radical changes in people's perspectives or successful humanistic political movements, the extremes we now find in stratification will remain: a relatively small proportion of very rich at one end of the scale, while the largest segment, the middle stratum, will be quite well off. At the other extreme will be a small yet substantial proportion of poor. This lower stratum will continue to be composed predominantly of the unskilled, the inadequately educated, and minority group members, as well as the elderly and the disabled. Because of the demands of machine technology and the needs of capitalist enterprise there is increasingly no place for these persons. They are structurally marginal; some provide a labor reserve when there is a sudden economic expansion, but ordinarily these are the underemployed and unemployed, who exist through an occasional paycheck, help from family or friends, Social Security, or welfare payments, or through other means such as crime.[56]

Thus there are residues of deprived who in a sense have nothing to lose but their chains. It is from them that we may expect increased agitation and collective behavior such as demonstrations and riots and on occasion class conflict. The likelihood of widespread violent class conflict is

[54] Clark Kerr, John T. Dunlop, Frederick H. Harbison, and Charles A. Meyers, *Industrialism and Industrial Man* (Cambridge, Mass.: Harvard University Press, 1960).

[55] Goldthorpe, "Social Stratification in Industrial Society"; and Myrdal, *Challenge to Affluence.*

[56] For a discussion of structural marginality see Tamme Wittermans and Irving Krauss, "Structural Marginality and Social Worth," *Sociology and Social Research,* 48 (April 1964), 348–360.

slim, however, because of the relatively small number in absolute deprivation and the resources the state can command to prevent such violence. For the state in a modern industrial society is able to afford reform as well as to invoke sufficient negative sanctions. This latter ability has been amply demonstrated through the use of the courts, and police and militia violence against radical movements and agitation.

As an industrial society becomes more mature, relative rather than absolute deprivation becomes a critical element as regards class formation. Any segment may find itself in this situation but presently minority groups are particularly affected. In earlier chapters we showed how persons of Spanish origin and blacks were relatively worse off than their white counterparts. Education, we observed, did not bring the promised rewards,[57] and increasingly some middle and many lower strata whites may be affected in a similar manner. Occupational and educational trends which we outlined previously may begin to add to a sense of relative deprivation among these persons. For, with education becoming more widespread it no longer serves as a major indicator of social status, particularly as the correlation between years of schooling and occupation and income decreases. This is particularly true for youths who attend the junior and community colleges, and the second and lesser rank state institutions of higher learning. The widespread availability of higher education in one sense increases opportunity, as was noted earlier. The chances of talent and ability being recognized is probably greater than previously when lack of educational opportunity kept many youngsters with great potential out of school. Today, some of the most able of the students from less affluent backgrounds will probably rise into the professions and a few will move into the top echelons of business and government. But what about the rest of the large number of middle and lower strata youths who are of average ability and intelligence? In the past, semi-professional and other middle-level white-collar occupations were available to them. Today, however, the growing number of these educated persons together with the failure of the job market to expand sufficiently is leading to underemployment and in some cases unemployment.[58] If the economy grows very slowly or hardly at all then opportunity for mobility from expansion of the economy will obviously decline, and for many a greater sense of relative deprivation may develop.

Even if the economy expanded as in the past, if there is to be significantly greater equality in the distribution of social goods as well as in-

---

[57] Blau and Duncan observe that "[a]lthough educated Negroes achieve occupations superior to those of the less educated, the more education a nonwhite man acquires the further his occupational status falls behind that of whites with comparable education." Peter M. Blau and Otis D. Duncan, *The American Occupational Structure* (New York: John Wiley & Sons, 1967), p. 211.

[58] As one illustration, opportunity for elementary and secondary school teaching which had always been a prime means of mobility for the children from blue-collar and lower level white-collar families is decreasing rapidly.

creased opportunity for the lower strata, the major means is through altering the institutional arrangements. Reform of taxes on income, wealth, and inheritance would be needed, as would the allocation of funds for public needs to raise the quality of life and provide jobs and other socially beneficial pursuits for the lower stratum. In addition, it would be necessary to have substantial social and economic planning to stabilize economic demand at a level at which it would be possible to have full employment.

Yet the history of the United States, particularly its capitalist heritage and the extant popular myths about individualism and the sanctity of private property makes anything but minimal and piecemeal change extremely difficult. More important, however, is the great power of the corporations and their tie-in with the government and most other aspects of economic and political life. Widespread class conflict which seriously threatened the existing institutional arrangements, particularly the concept of private property, would be put down vigorously. It is this tie-in which, among other things, makes it extremely difficult if not impossible to achieve major reforms such as a significant reallocation of social goods, meaningful social planning, or any change that would basically alter corporate control over their own activities. Should there be such a threat, the corporate ruling elite can count on the ruling elites of most other segments of the society for support, as we suggested above. Under such circumstances the several elites coalesce; the ruling stratum becomes a class and is able to fight such attempts. Because of their socialization for inefficacy the mass of the population fails to use its numbers as a force for its own benefit.

It is because of these several considerations that we do not foresee revolutionary change in a mature capitalist industrial society such as the United States. Rather, we expect only occasional class conflict of any magnitude, and only sporadic violence in the contesting over the distribution of social goods. What makes this likely, in addition to the reasons cited above, is the fact that the larger portion of the population is relatively well off and there is a wider distribution of authority than during the earlier period of industrialization. In addition, class conflict is legitimized as are organizations for that purpose, and there are institutional arrangements which try to regulate it. As a result the extensive and violent class conflict associated with early industrialization has decreased. For example, Sheldon G. Levy found that violent protest in the United States has declined over a 150-year period. While the data show that even in recent times industrial class conflict is far from being completely regulated, it is in sharp contrast to what amounted to open warfare in the early strikes and other labor disputes.[59]

[59] Sheldon G. Levy, "A 150-Year Study of Political Violence in the United States," in Hugh D. Graham and Ted. R. Gurr, eds., *Violence in America* (New York: Bantam Books, 1969), pp. 84–100.

In most industries today very intense class conflict and violence are infrequent in spite of the impression we might get from the mass media. Perhaps it is because the peaceful settlement of a dispute, like the happy marriage, does not make headlines. In some areas of occupational life, however, there does seem to be an increase in class conflict: it is no longer uncommon to read about teachers, policemen, firemen, and other government workers being out on strike. Does this presage a dramatic reversal or is it simply a little bump on a declining trend line? Probably the latter for what we have here is a failure to legitimize class conflict in the public sector and some attempts to suppress rather than regulate it. It seems to me that in a sense we are in a transitional period in the public sector, and that there will eventually be a movement toward legitimation and regulation rather than suppression.

However there is another area, that of race relations, where conflict seems to be increasing in intensity if not in violence. But again we face the question of a short range flareup as opposed to a longer trend. Since one of our major interests is class behavior, one might properly ask whether we should be considering racial conflict at all. Well, a good part of it is class conflict insofar as the authority structure is able to allocate resources; specifically in terms of occupational, educational, and residential opportunity. In regard to occupations, the keys are first the nature of restrictions on access, and second, how slack or tight the labor market is.[60] As for education, there is continual contesting over the distribution of funds, with the schools in better neighborhoods or suburbs usually winning out.[61]

The third aspect concerns residential opportunity. The process of invasion and succession characteristic of the larger American cities has always had a class basis although this has usually been overshadowed by ethnic differences. In the past, although there have been violent confrontations, by and large class conflict has been avoided by the whites fleeing to the suburbs. However, the ecological process is a continuing one and it is likely that there will be a great deal of conflict as this invasion and succession increases, especially when the suburbs can no longer expand; outwardly it will be racial, but basically it will be class conflict.

Summary

Throughout recorded human history there have been stratification, and class conflict, and because of the nature of organized group life we may

---

[60] Minsky, "The Role of Employment Policy"; and Barry J. Schiller, "Stratified Opportunities: The Essence of the 'Vicious Circle'," *American Journal of Sociology*, 76 (November 1970), 426–442.

[61] See James B. Conant, *Slums and Suburbs* (New York: McGraw-Hill, 1961); and James S. Coleman *et al.*, *Equality and Educational Opportunity* (Washington, D.C.: Government Printing Office, 1966).

expect their continuance. Certain aspects of superordination-subordination have changed, however: initially the poor were kept subservient not only by the power of the ruling class, but also by their acceptance of traditions, values, and beliefs which justified the status quo. In short, the poor "knew their place." But with widespread economic, political, and social change, particularly the development of a market economy, the cash nexus, and industrialization, the social bond between superordinates and subordinates weakened. Paternalism gave way to free labor and the emergence of an industrial proletariat, a portion of which suffered considerable absolute deprivation. Subsequently, because of these conditions as well as the rise of ideologies which questioned inequality the poor began to object; they no longer "knew their place." Because of the growing size and restlessness of the proletariat, the upper classes felt it necessary to "police the poor," while at the same time they introduced reforms. In modern times the lower class does not "know its place." By contrast, however, it is no longer official policy to police the poor, although this is what most law enforcement amounts to, especially calls for "law and order." Nevertheless, as a *whole* the lower class is passive; it does not take full advantage of citizenship rights and it acquiesces in a minimal sharing of authority.

Given these circumstances, we believe that in industrial societies general class conflict will continue to decline to a minimal level, although there will be regular flareups. But they are not likely to be widespread, intensive, and violent. Where there is great intensity and violence, the conflict will likely involve special segments of the population which suffer absolute deprivation or intolerable relative deprivation. Overall we expect decreased industrial class conflict; there is likely to be a rise in racially-based class conflict, however. An unknown factor is the state of the economy for expansion means increased opportunity, especially for upward social mobility which tends to minimize class formation; class behavior is likely to increase when the economy is unable to meet job and other demands. Yet the most critical element in future stratification and class conflict is the extent to which the subordinates will insist on a greater share of authority and other social goods, and the extent to which the superordinates will be willing to give up a part of what they have.

Name Index

Subject Index

Applied Forest Tree Improvement

Applied Forest Tree Improvement

Bruce Zobel
John Talbert
North Carolina State University

John Wiley & Sons
New York   Chichester   Brisbane   Toronto   Singapore

Library of Congress Cataloging in Publication Data:

Zobel, Bruce, 1920–
    Applied forest tree improvement.

    Includes bibliographical references and index.
    1. Trees—Breeding. 2. Forest genetics. I. Talbert,
John. II. Title.

SD399.5.Z62   1984   634.9'5   83-21912
ISBN 0-471-09682-2

Printed in the United States of America

10 9 8 7 6 5 4 3 2 1

This book is dedicated to Dr. C. Syrach-Larsen.

Among the numerous pioneers in tree improvement, one of the most outstanding was C. Syrach-Larsen. His vision and "missionary zeal" gave the needed impetus to have tree improvement accepted as a useful tool in operational forestry. (Photo of Dr. Syrach-Larsen in his younger years through courtesy of Dr. Bent Søegaard, Director of the Arboretum at Hørsholm, Denmark).

Shown are stages in a tree improvement program. To the left is a 34-year-old selected loblolly pine tree that has many of the desired characteristics of a parent tree. To the right (above) is a mature grafted seed orchard of pine, now in full production. The results from a tree improvement program are shown in the 16-year-old progeny test (lower right) in which growth, tree form, disease resistance, wood qualities, and adaptability have been improved.

Preface

There has been a tremendous increase of interest recently in tree improvement and the use of genetics in forest management. Applied tree improvement activities began in earnest during the 1950s. There is now a considerable amount of information and research data available that makes efficient planning and operation of tree improvement programs possible.

The objective of our book is to consolidate and summarize the concepts that are necessary for useful and efficient operational tree improvement programs. This book will concentrate on the biological and the practical, rather than on the more theoretical and statistical aspects, even though basic statistical concepts that are vital to breeding and selection programs will be presented. The book is based on more than 30 years' experience with large applied tree improvement programs. It will emphasize why and how certain things should or should not be done. Much of the information presented comes from background that was obtained from the large cooperative tree improvement programs in the southeastern United States, and many of the examples used in the book will involve pines, although the hardwoods will receive considerable coverage. Because the authors have had experience in programs in countries in South America and Central America, the West Coast of the United States and Canada, the northeastern United States, Australia, New Zealand, and Europe, the book will have a global coverage. Because of the rapidly expanding use of exotic species in intensive forest management, there is much emphasis in the book on exotics in the tropical and subtropical regions as well as in the temperate zones.

The book has an emphasis on young tree improvement programs. It does not deal with specifics or minutiae but covers the general concepts and principles necessary to manipulate and use forest tree populations in operational tree improvement programs. The concepts discussed are applicable to most forest tree species throughout the world; when feasible, specific examples are used to clarify the concepts. Because the greatest gains from the use of genetics in forestry will be from plantation programs, artificial regeneration will be stressed, but not to the exclusion of programs using natural regeneration.

The book has been written for three different audiences.

1. **Students**   This book will be of special value to new and beginning students who wish to know how to develop a tree improvement program. It will also be of particular interest to advanced students who have forgotten, or who never knew, the basic biological concepts and economic considerations that are necessary for success in applied tree improvement. Introductory courses in genetics and statistics would be helpful but are not mandatory for a basic understanding of the concepts presented in the book.

2. **Personnel of tree improvement programs**   Many programs for improving forest trees are carried out by persons with limited formal training in genetics. Although many of them are doing an excellent job, both their interest and efficiency will be greatly improved by an understanding of

genetic principles and a knowledge of how to manipulate genetic variation to achieve the greatest gains. Although the book is written in a format that is useful to students, it will also be readily understandable to persons without formal training in genetics.

3. **Forest management personnel**   Although managerial foresters deal with the whole range of activities, from regeneration through harvesting, tree improvement is often a vital and large part of their activities. Management foresters do not want to become specialists in tree improvement, but they need to know enough to use tree improvement wisely. Some major errors have been made by forest managers who were ignorant of, or who overlooked, tree improvement principles. This book will enable them to obtain an overview of important concepts in tree improvement quickly that will help them coordinate their operations.

In rapidly developing fields such as tree improvement and forest genetics, a textbook is often out of date before it is published. We have tried to avoid this problem by emphasizing the biological basis of concepts that are fundamental to forest tree populations and their manipulation, while avoiding a concentration on the rapidly evolving and changing techniques and methodologies. The book emphasizes both practical and applied aspects; thus, economic considerations are either stated briefly or implied throughout most of the presentation. The book will be useful to anyone interested in improving forest tree growth, quality, adaptability, and pest resistance. It is of value for all stages of tree improvement programs, but it is of special importance to those who are just beginning this area of endeavor.

Pertinent references will be used throughout the text, but there will be no attempt to cite all available literature; to do so would make the book unwieldy and difficult to read.

Bruce Zobel
John Talbert

Acknowledgments

The authors greatly appreciate the extensive help obtained in preparing our book *Applied Forest Tree Improvement.* Many persons edited various chapters, made suggestions, and supplied photographs. To each of these we owe a debt of gratitude. Those who have contributed to the success of the book are listed alphabetically. It is unfortunate that the contribution of each cannot be personally recognized.

However, one reviewer deserves special mention. Dr. Ted Miller, professor emeritus of the School of Forestry at North Carolina State University, reviewed every chapter. He knows several languages, and he especially helped with the spelling, accent marks, and the use of foreign titles that are listed. Dr. Miller's help was invaluable.

Following is an alphabetical listing of many of those who contributed to the development of the book.

NAME	ORGANIZATION	LOCATION
Jim Barker	International Paper Company	Tuxedo Park, New York
Walt Beineke	Purdue University	Lafayette, Indiana
Floyd Bridgwater	U.S. Forest Service	Raleigh, North Carolina
Arno Brune	Federal University of Minas Gerais	Vicosa, Minas Gerais, Brazil
Rollie Burdon	Forest Research Institute	Rotorua, New Zealand
Jeff Burley	Oxford University	Oxford, England
Cheryl Busby	Graduate student, North Carolina State University	Raleigh, North Carolina
Roger Blair	Potlach Corp.	Lewiston, Idaho
Mike Carson	Forest Research Institute	Rotorua, New Zealand
Susan Carson	Forest Research Institute	Rotorua, New Zealand
Donald Cole	Consultant	Raleigh, North Carolina
Ellis Cowling	School of Forest Resources, North Carolina State University	Raleigh, North Carolina
Bill Critchfield	U.S. Forest Service	Berkeley, California
Gary DeBarr	U.S. Forest Service	Athens, Georgia

NAME	ORGANIZATION	LOCATION
Wade Dorsey	Graduate student, North Carolina State University	Raleigh, North Carolina
Keith Dorman	U.S. Forest Service, retired	Asheville, North Carolina
Jack Duffield	Professor emeritus, North Carolina State University	Shelton, Washington
Dean Einspahr	Institute of Paper Chemistry	Appleton, Wisconsin
Carlyle Franklin	School of Forest Resources, North Carolina State University	Raleigh, North Carolina
Carlos Gallegos	A.I.D. Washington, D.C.	Mobile, Alabama
Bill Gladstone	Weyerhaeuser Timber Company	Tacoma, Washington
Max Hagman	Forest Research Institute	Marsala, Finland
J. B. Jett	School of Forest Resources, North Carolina State University	Raleigh, North Carolina
Hyun Kang	U.S. Forest Service	Rhinelander, Wisconsin
Lauri Karki	Foundation for Forest Tree Breeding	Helsinki, Finland
Bob Kellison	School of Forest Resources, North Carolina State University	Raleigh, North Carolina
Bill Ladrach	Cartón de Colombia	Cali, Colombia
Gladys Ladrach	Translator	Cali, Colombia
Clem Lambeth	Weyerhaeuser Company	Hot Springs, Arkansas
Bill Libby	University of California	Berkeley, California
Bill Lowe	Texas Forest Service	College Station, Texas

NAME	ORGANIZATION	LOCATION
Steve McKeand	School of Forest Resources, North Carolina State University	Raleigh, North Carolina
Kris Morgenstern	University of New Brunswick	Fredericton, New Brunswick, Canada
Garth Nikles	Queensland Forest Service	Brisbane, Queensland, Australia
Ron Pearson	School of Forest Resources, North Carolina State University	Raleigh, North Carolina
B. Phillion	Ministry of Natural Resources	Orono, Canada
Dick Porterfield	Champion Papers	Stamford, Connecticut
Harry Powers	U.S. Forest Service	Macon, Georgia
Lindsay Pryor	Consultant	Canberra, Australia
Pamela Puryear	Librarian, North Carolina State University	Raleigh, North Carolina
Diane Roddy	Prince Albert Pulp Company	Prince Albert, Saskatchewan, Canada
Marie Rauter	Ministry of Natural Resources	Toronto, Canada
Leroy Saylor	School of Forest Resources, North Carolina State University	Raleigh, North Carolina
Earl Sluder	U.S. Forest Service	Macon, Georgia
Dan Struve	Ohio State University	Columbus, Ohio
Richard Sniezko	Graduate Student, North Carolina State University	Raleigh, North Carolina
Per Stahl	Swedish Forest Service	Falun, Sweden
Bent Søegaard	Arboretum	Hørsholm, Denmark
Oscar Sziklai	University of British Columbia	Vancouver, British Columbia, Canada

NAME	ORGANIZATION	LOCATION
Hans van Buijtenen	Texas Forest Service	College Station, Texas
Bob Weir	School of Forest Resources, North Carolina State University	Raleigh, North Carolina
Ozzie Wells	U.S. Forest Service	Gulfport, Mississippi
Tim White	International Paper Company	Lebanon, Oregon
Peter Wood	Commonwealth Forest Institute	Oxford, England
Marvin Zoerb	Union Camp Corporation	Savannah, Georgia

B. Z.
J. T.

Contents

Applied Forest
Tree Improvement

CHAPTER 1

General Concepts
of Tree Improvement

WHAT IS TREE IMPROVEMENT?
WHERE AND WHEN SHOULD TREE IMPROVEMENT BE USED?
ESSENTIALS OF A TREE IMPROVEMENT PROGRAM
THE IMPORTANCE OF TIME
BREEDING OBJECTIVES
ADVANTAGES AND LIMITATIONS OF TREE IMPROVEMENT
GENOTYPE AND PHENOTYPE
TERMS COMMONLY USED IN TREE IMPROVEMENT
REFERENCES AND PUBLICATIONS
Some Books of Special Interest to Tree Improvers
Magazines That Include Articles of Special Interest to Tree Improvers
Proceedings and Symposia of Special Interest to Tree Improvement
Proceedings of Meetings Held
Periodically for Which Addresses May Vary
LITERATURE CITED

Historically, foresters generally did not view trees as typical plants having systems of heredity similar to all other living organisms. Genetic variability was ignored, and it was somehow felt that a tree's development depended only upon the environment in which it was grown. It has only been in relatively recent years that there has been a general recognition that *forest tree parentage is important* and that changes and improvements in tree growth and quality can be brought about through breeding and parental control. Forest tree improvement activities were undertaken seriously on an operational scale only after this was recognized.

A whole book could be written about the fascinating steps in the development of tree improvement and about the contributions made by the early pioneers. Several publications deal with the history of forest genetics, both overall and locally. Examples are Ohba (1979), Toda (1980), and Wright (1981). No attempt will be made in this book to completely cover the historical development or even to mention all of the pioneers, who had much faith and foresight in doing such a radical thing as applying genetic principles to improve forest trees. Even though most forest genetics research is rather recent, some was done centuries ago. Perhaps the most striking early activities were in Japan. These have been abstracted in two volumes by Toda (1970, 1974). His references relating to tree improvement date to the seventeenth century. While helping Toda edit these books into acceptable English, it was evident to the senior author that foresters are today rediscovering a large number of concepts that were known or suspected hundreds of years ago.

A few of the pioneers in forest genetics are listed in Table 1.1, which is a portion of a table originally entitled "Chronology of Forest Genetics" that was prepared by Sziklai (1981).

Some excellent ideas on the use of genetics in forestry were suggested by the earlier workers, although many of the publications contained mostly generalized concepts and ideas. Examples of some early writings in the United States are Austin (1927), Leopold (1929), Schreiner (1935), and Righter (1946). These, along with publications such as the one by Richens (1945), contributed to tree improvement by making foresters cognizant of the fact that parentage is important in forest trees and can be manipulated to help in forest management.

A major contribution by the early workers was that they observed and cataloged patterns of variation in commercially important tree species. In this way, they achieved familiarity with the various species, which is an absolute essential to the success of any breeding program. The early activities resulted in only limited amounts of firm evidence regarding the possible improvements, but by drawing on methods employed in plant and animal breeding the early workers were able to make some very good estimates about potential gains in forest trees. Therefore, when the forest industry finally became interested in developing large programs of applied genetics in the early 1950s, it had little proof of the returns that would be obtained to justify the investments that had been made, but it did have some reasonably useful projections on which plans could be based.

The success of the first large programs was due primarily to good intuition about how the important forest tree characteristics would respond to genetic

TABLE 1.1.
Some of the Early Forest Geneticists and Their Areas of Interest[a]

1717 Bradley (England)	Importance of seed origin
1760 Duhamel de Monceau (France)	Inheritance: oak
1761 Koehlreuter (Germany)	Hybridization
1787 Bursdorf (Germany)	Plantation for seed production
1840 Marrier de Boisdhyver (France)	Vegetative propagation
1840 de Vilmorin (France)	Fir hybrids
1845 Klotzsch (Berlin)	Intraspecific hybrids: oak, elm, and alder
1904 Cieslar (Austria)	Provenances: larch and oak
1905 Engler (Switzerland)	Elevation differences of species: fir, pine, spruce, larch and maple
1905 Dengler (Germany)	Provenance tests: fir and spruce
1906 Andersson (Sweden)	Vegetation propagation
1907 Sudworth, Pinchot (U.S.A.)	Breeding nut and other forest trees
1908 Oppermann (Denmark)	Straightness: beech and oak
1909 Johannsen (Sweden)	Elite stands
1909 Sylven (Sweden)	Self-pollination: Norway spruce
1912 Zederbauer (Austria)	Crown form: Austrian pine
1918 Sylven (Sweden)	Seed orchards
1922 Fabricius (Austria)	Plantation for seed production
1923 Oppermann (Denmark)	Seedling seed orchards
1924 Schreiner (U.S.A.)	Poplar breeding
1928 Burger (Switzerland)	Pine selection
1928 Bates (U.S.A.)	Seed orchards
1930 Larsen S. (Denmark)	Controlled pollination: larch
1930 Heikinheimo and M. Larsen (Finland)	Curly grain: birch
1930 Nilsson-Ehle, Sylven, Johnsson, Linquist (Sweden)	Pine and aspen breeding
1935 Nilsson-Ehle (Sweden)	Triploid aspen

[a]After Sziklai (1981).

manipulation. This point can be illustrated by the results that were achieved by including wood properties in some initial breeding programs of several pine species in the southeastern United States. Essentially nothing was known about the inheritance of wood specific gravity, the most important wood quality. However, the patterns of natural variation of specific gravity were well known (Figure 1.1). These indicated that significant gains might be made through a selection and breeding program, although there was no available proof. Based on these patterns, wood-specific gravity was included as a major characteristic in some tree improvement programs. It is now clear that including that trait in the breeding program was helpful both biologically and economically because specific gravity, which greatly influences the yield and quality of wood products, has proved to be controlled strongly enough by genetics so that it will respond well to a

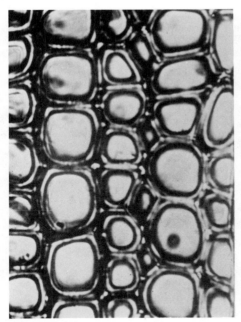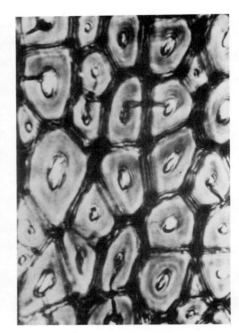

FIGURE 1.1

Variability among trees of the same age growing adjacent on the same site is shown by wall thickness of two *Eucalyptus grandis* trees. Wall thickness affects specific gravity, which is reasonably strongly inherited, enabling the development of trees with either high or low-wood specific gravities.

selection program. If characteristics of importance but of unknown inheritance, such as wood specific gravity, had not responded well to breeding, the entire program of genetic manipulation of forest trees on a large scale probably would have faltered.

A major emphasis on *applied* tree improvement developed rapidly in the early 1950s in a number of countries throughout the world. There are dozens of references that could be cited. However, for the sake of simplicity a few are indicated in Table 1.2 to give the reader an idea about the international scope of activities in tree improvement during this period. There was a literal explosion of activities, including both applied and fundamental aspects of forest genetics, and many new programs were established. Note that even though tree improvement started in many countries throughout the world about the same time, there have been great differences from country to country about how vigorously the programs were followed up.

It is of interest how three different incidents triggered the establishment of large, well-organized, and adequately financed tree improvement programs in the southeastern United States over 30 years ago. The first was the publication in 1948 of a book on forest genetics by Bertil Lindquist of the Göteborg Botanical Garden in Sweden. The book was translated into English and was circulated widely among

TABLE 1.2.
A Sampling of Authors Who Published on Applied Tree Improvement and Forest Genetic Activities During the 1950s

Author	Date	Country	Type of Article
Barner	1952	Denmark	General tree breeding
Bouvarel	1957	France	General tree improvement
Buchholz	1953	Russia (Germany)	Review of Soviet activities
Duffield	1956	U.S.A.	Breeding approaches
Fielding	1953	Australia	Variation studies
Fischer	1954	Germany	General tree breeding
Greeley	1952	U.S.A.	History of Institute of Forest Genetics
Haley	1957	Australia	Status of tree breeding in Queensland
Heimburger	1958	Canada	General tree breeding
Hellinga	1958	Indonesia	General tree improvement
Hyun	1958	Korea	General tree breeding
Johnsson	1949	Sweden	Results of breeding
Langner	1954	Germany	General tree breeding
Larsen	1951	World (Denmark)	General tree breeding
Matthews	1953	Great Britain	General tree breeding
Pauley	1954	U.S.A.	General tree breeding
Perry and Wang	1958	U.S.A.	Value of genetically improved seed
Rao	1951	India	General tree improvement
Schreiner	1950	U.S.A.	General tree breeding
Thulin	1957	New Zealand	General tree breeding
Toyama	1954	Japan	General tree breeding
Wright	1953	U.S.A.	General tree breeding
Zobel	1952	U.S.A.	Improving wood quality

Note. See Literature Cited for complete references.

foresters in the southern United States. It was written in a manner that caught the interest of foresters, and from it many obtained their first insights into the use of genetics in forest trees. In his book *Forest Tree Breeding in the World,* Toda (1974) makes reference to Lindquist's lectures in Japan in 1952 and their strong influence on the senior foresters in that country.

Another major influence was a series of lectures on crop breeding given in Texas by Åke Gustafsson of the Royal College of Forestry in Stockholm. In one lecture on forest genetics he predicted that trees would respond to genetic manipulation and urged that tree breeding be incorporated into silviculture. The third influence was a series of articles on tree breeding that were published by a newspaper in Texas as a result of Gustafsson's lectures. The articles resulted in a public campaign to raise money for a program of tree improvement. On behalf of the Texas Forest Service and with the participation of 14 forest industries, Bruce Zobel organized such a program in 1951. The working territory included Texas,

Louisiana, and Arkansas. The major initial task was to convince foresters that the interaction of the environment and genetics and not the environment alone, determine the growth, form, and adaptability of a tree.

After a slow beginning, enthusiasm for forest genetics grew to such an extent in certain areas that some people considered it a cure for most of forestry's ills. Since then, tree improvement has gained its proper perspective as a powerful tool of the forest manager, and it is successful in relation to the degree that it is employed in conjunction with good forest management practices.

WHAT IS TREE IMPROVEMENT?

In order to understand what tree improvement is, it is necessary to know three terms and their development and relationship to each other. Although some authors, such as Toda (1974), equate the three terms, most scientists differentiate between *forest tree breeding, forest genetics,* and *forest tree improvement.* Activities that are restricted to genetic studies of forest trees are termed *forest genetics;* here, the objective is to determine the genetic relationships among trees and species. An example of a forest genetic activity is the attempt to determine crossability patterns among species within a genus. The crosses are made to determine relationships, but otherwise they have no special breeding objective. The next term is *forest tree breeding,* in which activities are geared to solve some specific problem or to produce a specially desired product. An example of such directed breeding is the development of pest-resistant strains of trees or breeding trees that possess specially desired wood. The third term, *forest tree improvement,* is applied when control of parentage is combined with other forest management activities, such as site preparation or fertilization, to improve the overall yields and quality of products from forestlands.

Tree improvement is effective only when it consists of the combination of *all* silvicultural and tree-breeding skills of the forester to grow the most valuable forest products as quickly as possible and as inexpensively as possible. It consists of a "marriage" of silviculture and tree parentage to obtain the greatest overall returns (Figure 1.2). Stated simply, tree improvement is an additional tool of silviculture that deals with the kind and genetic makeup of the trees used in forest operations.

It has taken foresters a long time—much too long—to recognize that intensive forest management activities, such as site preparation or fertilization, never will yield maximum returns unless the genetically best trees are also used. Conversely, in recent years, foresters have learned from bitter experience that no matter how excellent trees may be genetically, maximum production cannot be achieved unless good forest management practices are used along with the improved plants. This concept of combining forest management with parentage is now quite widely accepted as tree improvement, but unfortunately there still are some who do not recognize this most critical relationship.

Tree improvement activities have sometimes developed without a suitable knowledge of the necessary genetic principles. Basic information is now becoming

FIGURE 1.2

Tree improvement can only be successful when combined with intensive
silviculture, such as the bedding prior to planting shown in southern Brazil.
The combination of good culture and good genetic stock makes possible
optimum timber production.

available more rapidly than in the past, but there still is a major gap that needs to
be filled. An inspiration for those who have been involved with tree improvement
from the start is that in most forested areas in the world, tree improvement is
currently included as an essential part of forest management operations. No
longer is tree improvement considered an impractical academic exercise that
requires special treatment and financing but contributes little to the income from
forest land. Most forestry organizations now handle tree improvement as a
regular part of silviculture. After a slow start and years of intensive propaganda to
make tree improvement accepted by the forestry profession, a reversal in attitude
took place, and for a time in the late 1950s and 60s tree improvement specialists
found themselves in the unusual position of having to deemphasize the genetic
approach because some people were "carried away" by its supposed potential and

value. For a time, tree improvement was treated as a utopian activity that would solve all forestry problems. Luckily, tree improvement is now realistically considered to be an essential tool of silviculture.

There is nothing mysterious or difficult about tree improvement. It consists mostly of the use of common sense in forest management, looked at from the "point of view" of the basic biological organism—the tree. It is concerned with how trees vary and how this variation can be utilized to improve forest productivity. Although some people have the impression that a good tree improver must have some special training and possess certain mystical powers, this is not the case.

All beginning tree improvement programs rely on and consist of the following:

1. A determination of the species, or geographic sources within a species, that should be used in a given area.
2. A determination of the amount, kind, and causes of variability within the species.
3. A packaging of the desired qualities into improved individuals, such as to develop trees with combinations of desired characteristics (Figure 1.3).
4. Mass producing improved individuals for reforestation purposes.
5. Developing and maintaining a genetic base population broad enough for needs in advanced generations.

In some instances, step 1 may have been completed before intensive tree improvement programs are initiated. In others, considerable time, money, and skill may be required to complete step 1. This first step must be done well before steps 2 to 5 can be really effective. There is a danger, however, that an organization may become so involved with testing species and sources that all available resources are used in this phase of a tree improvement program. In our opinion, an overemphasis on species and provenance testing by some organizations has become a most serious stumbling block to their making maximum progress in the total tree improvement activity.

The five steps essentially outline what is needed for the development of any tree improvement program, and although they may make the scope of activities clear, they do not indicate the time and effort required to develop each of them properly. The outline may appear to be simple, but getting the job done is not easy, and it requires a great deal of skill, common sense, time, and money. For example, with the southern pines (where the first step on species determination was not a major activity), the senior author has spent over 30 years of intensive effort trying to satisfy steps 2 through 5.

Nature has created the variation needed for use in a tree improvement program (Figure 1.4). The tree improver's major job is to be able to recognize the variability, isolate it, package it in a desired tree, and multiply it. As results are obtained and advanced generations of improved trees are developed, a much more sophisticated and scientifically based approach than that used initially will

FIGURE 1.3

The yellow poplar tree shown represents a "package" of good characteristics in a single individual. The tree has desirable limbs, good form, fast growth, and desirable wood.

FIGURE 1.4

Natural stands of forest trees show great variability as is indicated by differences in branch habit among eastern white pines (*Pinus strobus*). The tree improver must first recognize and then use the variability related to the genetic makeup of the tree.

be necessary to maintain and increase variability and to take full advantage of the natural variation found in trees growing and unimproved forests.

In tree improvement programs using hybridization and/or vegetative propagation, the principles previously listed will still hold, although their order of importance may vary. In truth, all methods of tree improvement require that all five steps must be followed. The special advantage with a vegetative propagation program is that once a suitable "package" has been located, or developed through breeding, it can be reproduced rapidly many times, and the propagules are essentially the same genetically as the desired parent tree (Figure 1.5). Vegetative propagation allows quick and large gains because all types of genetic variation can be captured. (This will be described in later chapters.) When seed reproduction is used, only a portion of the genetic variation of the trees used as parents will be passed on to the progeny. Hybridization has an advantage because it enables the creation of something entirely different by recombining the variability produced in nature into a new "package," the hybrid tree. Thus, it may be possible through hybridization to create a plant with characteristics for difficult environments, pest resistance, or specially desired products.

One aspect of a tree improvement operation that is of great importance, but that is not usually mentioned in a textbook, is a vague thing called *intuition* or *feel*. Many of the earlier phases of a program were very often intuitive. The user could not always explain exactly why certain things were done or why they worked. Such an intuitive approach cannot be taught, but it does begin with a working knowledge of the species on which the improvement is to be done. Many of the younger and more highly technically trained scientists scoff at the importance of an intuitive approach, but it is valuable and successful. Any really new, large-scale

FIGURE 1.5

A vegetatively reproduced stand of radiata pine (*P. radiata*) in Australia is shown. Note the great similarity among the trees, all of which came from the same "donor" tree. There is a strong trend toward more use of vegetative propagation in forestry that will yield great gains and good uniformity.

operational program must initially rely on this vague "green thumb" approach as part of its methods if it is to quickly achieve its goals; this is true because usually only a limited amount of fundamental data are available. Some of the more successful tree improvers state that they "think or feel like the tree," and the resultant intuitive actions, often aided by experience, frequently prove to be the correct ones.

WHERE AND WHEN SHOULD TREE IMPROVEMENT BE USED?

The contributions that tree improvement can make to growth, quality, pest resistance, and adaptability of forest stands are greater under some conditions than under others. Obviously, large-scale, aggressive planting programs are most conducive to the use of genetic improvement. Tree improvement is more difficult to justify economically when forests are regenerated naturally. The basic fact remains, though, that all forest management activities can profit from using tree improvement concepts. If this is not done, forest managers can only partially achieve their objectives. Forest trees are plants with responses controlled by the environment and by genetics, like all other organisms. The result obtained from any forest management operation will be determined both by the genetic makeup of the tree and by its interaction with the environment in which it grows. Tree improvement should play a significant role in forest management any time the production of high volumes of good quality timber is the principal management objective. The most intensive tree improvement efforts will be made where stands are regenerated artificially at least once every few rotations. It is in these cases that the greatest gains can be obtained from tree improvement.

The *objective* of *intensive tree farming* can be stated simply as the *production of the desired-quality timber in maximum amounts in the shortest period of time at a reasonable cost.* This objective is simpler to state than it is to achieve, of course, but in the past three decades tree improvement has played an increasingly important role in helping to achieve it by increasing forest productivity and reducing the time needed to harvest. Tree improvement can be used to help accomplish many management objectives to overcome problems, but this will not be done without some adverse reactions. For example, the harvest age of trees can be reduced through genetic selection for growth rate, but the reduction may lead to significant changes in wood quality, harvesting costs, and regeneration costs. A major job of the tree breeder is also to help overcome problems that arise from intensive forest management. There are essentially three lines of attack that the tree improver can use to increase timber production: (1) Breeding can be accomplished for improved yields and quality on the more productive forested areas; (2) trees can be developed that will grow satisfactorily on land that is currently submarginal and noneconomic for timber production; and (3) strains of forest trees can be developed that are more suitable for specialized products or uses. The first approach has been widely utilized for several tree species, and dramatic results have been obtained. Many persons only associate tree improvement and the use of genetics with yield and quality improvement.

The development of trees especially suitable for marginal sites is long term in nature, but it will result in substantial benefits as pressures for forestland use intensify. Competition for land is increasing, which is forcing forestry operations from the more productive sites to areas that were previously considered to be marginal or useless for timber production. As a result, large amounts of genetically improved seeds are needed quickly that are specifically developed to grow on the vast forest areas that are currently marginal or submarginal for economic forest or agricultural production. The current emphasis in tree improvement is toward breeding for adaptability to marginal sites, in addition to improving trees for better products or better growth on forest sites that are suitable for forest production. Potential gains from breeding for adaptability to marginal sites are great, and huge areas of such land are available for forestry use. However, forest managers and tree breeders must be constantly alert to the basic biological constraints to the productive potential on a given area of land. High production will not be obtained from deficient soils, no matter how good the trees are genetically.

One of the more serious errors being made by some forest geneticists is to predict ever-increasing gains from the use of genetics without suitable consideration of the absolutely essential accompanying better forest management practices. As do all organisms, trees respond to the "law of limiting factors." Today, the most important limiting factor to increased forest yields often is the genetic potential of the plants being used. However, as genetically improved stock becomes more generally available, other factors necessary for good tree growth, such as limited moisture, excess moisture, or limited nutrients, will still limit tree growth no matter how excellent the genetic potential of the trees may be. It is not possible to obtain continued large gains from genetics without correcting whatever factor or factors in the environment may presently be, or may become, limiting. Thus, predictions of gains of several hundred percent from the use of genetics are misleading if the commensurate improvement of forest management methodology is not undertaken concurrently. The idea held by some persons that improved trees can be planted in the grass, brush, or briars with little care and still grow outstandingly well is totally unrealistic.

Tree improvement without commensurate intensive forestry is generally of marginal value, and there must be a union between the two if maximum gains from either are to be achieved. This combination of genetics and culture has been shown many times to be essential in agriculture. For example, the old open-pollinated strains of corn did not take full advantage of intensive culture and fertilization. Conversely, the highly genetically improved corn varieties will not produce anywhere close to their potential without intensive management. Trees react in the same way; the total genetic potential can only be exploited if the trees are grown in the best environments.

There are essentially two ways to ameliorate conditions limiting forest productivity. First, the forester can help to reduce the limiting factors of the environment through use of better forest management techniques and silviculture. This has been, and for a long time will continue to be, the easiest and most common method used to increase forest productivity. However, as forestry operations are driven from the better lands that are needed for agriculture, the second option of developing strains of trees to overcome severely limiting environmental factors will become increasingly important. This type of breeding has already made some forestry operations profitable on land that had been considered marginal or submarginal for economical forest production.

It is frequently possible to overcome a limiting factor by breeding. For example, drought-tolerant (Brix, 1959; Bey, 1974), water-tolerant (Zobel, 1957; Hosner and Boyce, 1962; Heth and Kramer, 1975), or cold-tolerant (Dietrichson, 1961; Schönbach, 1961; Parker, 1963; Sakai and Okada, 1971; and many others) strains can be developed to overcome moisture imbalance or excess cold. It is possible to breed trees that can tolerate low levels of nutrients, thus partially overcoming the limitation of nutrient deficiency (Lacaze, 1963; Goddard et al., 1976; Roberds et al., 1976; McCormick and Steiner, 1978). In the northern coniferous forests where a deficiency in nitrogen is severe, improving growth through fertilization is generally accepted as a better option than breeding for trees that can grow with a lesser nutrient supply. A large part of the decision about whether to breed tolerant trees or take corrective action by supplying nutrients depends on the costs and availability of fertilizers. Occasional trees grow well on soils deficient in micronutrients such as boron (Figure 1.6). A number of appar-

FIGURE 1.6

Shown is a radiata pine (*P. radiata*) growing on a boron-deficient site in southcentral Chile. Note the health and vigor of the tree when compared to the veritable bushes surrounding it that result from a boron deficiency. Sometimes it is possible to use such trees to develop a new strain that is more tolerant to some deficiency in the environment.

ently boron-deficiency-tolerant radiata pine trees have been found indicating the possibility of developing a special strain to grow on the nutrient-deficient soils. Success will depend on the extent and kind of genetic variation in boron tolerance as well as the relative returns and costs of fertilizing versus developing a nutrient-tolerant strain of trees. Breeding for adaptability and pest resistance has proven to be feasible, and soon millions of hectares will be converted to productive forests on lands formerly considered to be nonproductive (Batzer, 1961; Goddard et al., 1975; Zobel and Zoerb, 1977; and numerous others).

It is essential, therefore, to remember that when production has not been hampered by limiting factors of the environment, greater yields of better-quality products will result from tree improvement. For many situations where the environment is limiting, such as drought or cold, the most effective approach is to develop trees that have greater tolerance to the limiting factors when it is not possible economically to overcome the deficiencies through forest management actions.

ESSENTIALS OF A TREE IMPROVEMENT PROGRAM

There are two aspects to any successful tree improvement program. The first relates to obtaining an immediate gain of desired products as rapidly and as efficiently as possible. This is achieved by intensively applying genetic principles to operational forestry programs that will result in better-quality, better-adapted, and higher-yielding tree crops. Maximum gains are achieved by the use of a few of the very best genetic parents to supply planting stock for operational programs. A benefit of a tree improvement program that is often not recognized is the production of large and regular seed crops that are suitable for the forest operations. Lack of suitable seed is one of the greatest deterrents to forestry.

The second aspect of a tree improvement program is concerned with the long-term need to provide the broad genetic base that is essential for continued progress over many generations. Although not emphasized in some current programs, the long-term aspect of tree improvement is of great importance.

All tree improvement programs must have an *operational* (production) and a *developmental* (research) phase. The two are closely linked, yet they require different approaches and philosophies. The two phases are roughly outlined in Figure 1.7; the solid boxes indicate operational activities for large-scale planting programs. The developmental, or research, phases are necessary for a successful long-range program. As the programs mature, the operational activities become increasingly dependent on continued progress in the developmental area. Therefore, to be successful, a tree improvement program must have the *developmental aspects initiated at an early stage* in the program, along with the operational activities. Too often, the developmental activities are not begun until later years because of the press of work in operations and, as a result, a gap develops in plant materials and information necessary for advanced breeding.

The operational phase produces quick economic gains from tree improvement and is the most easily understood and obvious to the general public and to forest managers. This phase consists of obtaining improved planting stock as quickly and efficiently as possible and with as much genetic improvement as possible. *Time* is of the essence, and often initial gains are only partially as large as the biological potential. Modest gains are often accepted in order to obtain improvement quickly. Although there is an inevitable time lag between the investment and returns on the investment in the operational phase, this lag is small compared to the time required for the payoff from the developmental phase.

The main objective of the developmental phase is to obtain and retain a broad genetic base and to combine desired characteristics into suitable trees that will be valuable for future generations. No program can be better than the base of genetic material upon which it is founded, and although the developmental phase takes considerable time to yield useful results, the provision of the skill and money required to maintain it is mandatory. A large number of tree improvement

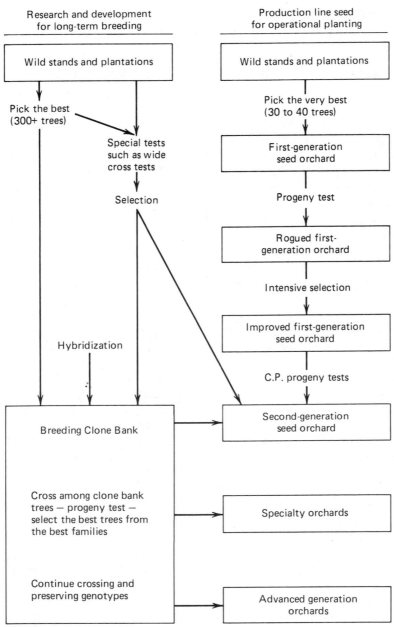

Research and development
for long-term breeding

Production line seed
for operational planting

Wild stands and plantations

Wild stands and plantations

Pick the best
(300+ trees)

Special tests
such as wide
cross tests

Selection

Pick the very best
(30 to 40 trees)

First-generation
seed orchard

Progeny test

Rogued first-
generation orchard

Intensive selection

Improved first-generation
seed orchard

C.P. progeny tests

Hybridization

Breeding Clone Bank

Second-generation
seed orchard

Cross among clone bank
trees — progeny test —
select the best trees from
the best families

Specialty orchards

Continue crossing and
preserving genotypes

Advanced generation
orchards

FIGURE 1.7

Tree improvement programs consist of two main lines of endeavor, the operational phase and developmental phase, as indicated. The quality of the breeding clone bank will determine long-term success; gains from the production seed orchards determine immediate success.

programs ignore the developmental or research aspects. Such programs will eventually come to a dead end. Because of the complexity and cost, the research or developmental work is ideally suited to a cooperative approach where several organizations jointly fund the work and share the results.

Some laymen, and even some foresters, are not aware of the need for the continuing long-range aspect of tree improvement and the necessity for active support of the developmental phase. Tree improvement work is never completed, and actions and success 10, 20, or 30 years from now are determined by the quality of the developmental phase that is established early. Many persons think that all tree improvement consists of is the location of trees with good phenotypes and manipulating them to produce large quantities of seeds. Nothing could be further from the truth. Continual improvement is always required. The operational portion of the program really touches only the surface of the total skill, cost, and energy required for a successful long-range tree improvement program. Problems and needs that arise in keeping a well-balanced program have been emphasized by Namkoong et al. (1980.

It is sad but true that the forest industry has been one of the most backward of the major industries in supporting biological research on forest trees. There seems to be an absolute distrust and suspicion of the words *fundamental* or *basic research,* and activity tagged in this way is often not encouraged and not funded. We have found, however, that substitution of the words *supportive research* has done wonders for acceptance by administrators in the forest industry. The idea that certain actions are necessary to obtain the basic information that will enable the operational program to continue to progress is usually received with no objections when it is called *supportive* research.

No matter what words are used—*fundamental, basic,* or *supportive*—information is needed if tree improvement programs are to be successful. Perhaps more than in any other discipline, the tree improver often does things on an operational scale before there is proof that they will work, or how much gain will be obtained. In a field like forestry, one cannot wait for all the answers, or even a good part of them, before taking action to make forestland more productive. Although this magnifies the danger of mistakes, the success of such empirical actions has been quite evident in newly begun tree improvement programs and has resulted in a tremendous improvement in forest productivity. A knowledge of the species and its variation in addition to a good bit of intuition enables rapid progress to be made with minimal basic knowledge. However, as tree improvement moves into advanced generations, much more scientific information will be needed for orderly and rapid development. Thus, the emphasis on supportive research needs to be increased.

THE IMPORTANCE OF TIME

One of the most important considerations in an active, ongoing tree improvement program is TIME (Zobel, 1978). It takes years to do the necessary selection, breeding, and testing to obtain the desired improvements. When an organization is planting large areas annually, each year that unimproved, rather than improved, stock is used represents a loss in future revenues. Therefore, operational programs are under great pressures to produce early returns. For example, members of the North Carolina State University–Industry Tree Improvement Cooperative were planting about 500,000 acres (200,000 ha) of pine each year when the tree improvement program was started. The urgency to engender as much improvement as possible as quickly as possible was great. Pressures for early improvements meant that all efforts had to be taken to obtain gain quickly, even if it required the use of some shortcuts.

In all applied tree improvement programs the time needs must be balanced against possible gains in both the short and long term; the key objective is to *obtain maximim gains per unit time*. For most forest trees, the generation time is long because of long-rotation ages and the 10 to 20 years required before abundant flowering occurs. To accrue the greatest gains in the shortest time through selective breeding, there must be a quick turnover of generations that are combined with some meaningful selection pressures in each generation. A most critical factor is the necessity for an assessment at a young age of such important characteristics as growth rate, adaptability, pest resistance, and tree form. Currently, for most species it generally is not satisfactory to assess growth parameters before about half-rotation (harvest) age, although certain form, pest resistance, wood, and adaptability characteristics can be accurately assessed earlier. In operational forestry, the rotation age can vary from as short as 6 to 8 years for the eucalypts, to 80 years or more for western U.S., northern U.S., Canadian, and northern European species. The southern pines, which are usually considered to be fast growing, are usually harvested at 20 to 35 years of age; therefore, 10- to 15-year assessments are feasible. On the surface, it would appear that a meaningful tree improvement program that will yield useful gains in a reasonable time would not be feasible, considering the restrictions caused by a lack of early flowering and an early assessment of growth. However, good progress has been made.

Although long-generation times are a major disadvantage in forest tree breeding, certain shortcuts have been developed. A good example of a most successful shortcut is illustrated by the seed orchard programs. Without the pressures and urgency of time, the best scientific method to establish a seed orchard that will yield maximum gains is to evaluate thoroughly the offspring of the select parents through progeny testing followed by the establishment of the production seed orchard from which improved seed will be obtained. Although eventually giving the greatest gain, this method entails several years' delay during the period required to make the tests, which can be up to one-half rotation age for some characteristics. Such a large loss of time before improved trees are established in orchards and seed are available cannot be accepted when seed are needed immediately for large-scale planting programs. To partially offset such a time loss, the shortcut usually taken in seed orchard programs is one in which good phenotypes are selected and are immediately established in the orchard before their genotypic worth has been determined. The grafted trees are established at a closer spacing than is ultimately desired, with the knowledge that some of the phenotypes will, in fact, not be good genotypes and therefore must ultimately be removed from the orchard. At the time (or shortly thereafter) of orchard establishment with the best phenotypes, progeny tests are initiated to determine the genetic worth of the parents used in the initial seed orchard. After progeny data are available, the orchard can then be rogued of the undesirable parents. This results in an orchard as good genetically as if it had been established after the parent trees were progeny tested. During the 10- to 20-year testing period, seed for planting have been obtained from the orchard that are considerably improved over wild seed, although they are not as good as those from proven parents. However, the added value of the partially improved seed to the forest management operation is large.

The concept of the value of time is indicated in Figure 1.8. Note that smaller but earlier gains are obtained when the orchard is established with parents chosen only on their appearance than when the parental genetic quality is known. These gains will increase as progeny test data are obtained, and roguing is done in the seed orchard. If the testing is properly designed, the genetic gain from both types of programs will be about the same following progeny assessment. This is illustrated in Figure 1.8. It is the shaded area in the first rectangle that indicates gain that is additional to that at some later time following progeny testing, which is shown by the nonshaded area. In programs in which there are small pressures for

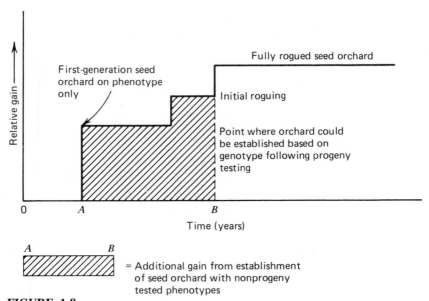

FIGURE 1.8

Time is all important in an operational tree improvement program associated with a large planting program. Shortcuts, such as establishing untested phenotypes in the seed orchard, may be taken to give early gains (AB). These are an addition to greater gains that are obtained after progeny test data are available.

immediate planting on a large scale, the prospective parents should be tested with respect to their genetic worth before the production orchards are established.

Although covered in detail elsewhere, a current major feature of tree improvement programs is to produce the *same amount and quality of product in less time at a reasonable cost* rather than to *produce more at a given time*. This objective of reducing time to harvest is now of prime importance in many tree improvement programs, and it will result in large monetary gains to the forest manager.

BREEDING OBJECTIVES

Although many aspects of tree improvement that are related to gains and genetic control will be covered in detail in later chapters, it is nevertheless necessary at this point to have some concept of those issues that will determine which approach to a tree improvement program should be used. Tree improvement specialists strive to improve the forest both for better yields and better quality (Zobel, 1974). Along with better forest management practices and the reduction of time to achieve specific goals, gains in tree improvement are determined by the intensity of inheritance and how well manipulated is the variation that is present in the population with which one is working.

There is little that the tree improver can do to change the inheritance pattern for a given characteristic; it is generally well established. The tree improver can, however, capture more of the genetic variation that is present in a population by suitable manipulation of the environment. The tree improver's best tool to increase gains is to use the existing variation to its fullest and to help develop additional variability when needed.

In order to obtain the best possible gains from tree improvement, it is necessary to understand the nature of wild populations, how they have developed, and how their variability can be used. A complete discussion and understanding of this subject encompassing the essence of the fields of speciation and evolution is too advanced for this volume, although some of the simpler concepts will be covered in several chapters. The important item to remember is that *forest trees* are mostly *wild populations that are not yet greatly changed by the action of people.* This gives the tree improver an outstanding opportunity to make improvements.

The differences within and among wild tree populations have developed naturally over many eons. But with proper management, intensity of selection, and suitable breeding systems people can bring about desired changes very rapidly. Prior to 1950, the senior author was strongly urged by a very well-known silviculturist not to pursue the field of tree improvement. His reason was "if nature has not been able to produce desirable trees in eons, how do you think you can make any useful changes in your lifetime?" He had no real knowledge of the forces that shape populations or why and how these work. What is most important, he had no concept of the pressures that people can apply to forest populations and individuals to cause rapid changes and to alter them in the desired direction. Although not totally intended, one of our major effects on changing forest trees, especially in areas like Europe and Japan, has resulted from widespread movement and the ultimate mixing of different geographic sources within a species.

Methods that can be used to change trees and the realized improvement arising from them vary with different characteristics. Because of the nature of the genetic patterns that influence the inheritance for most characteristics of forest trees, only part of the genetic variation that exists within a population can be utilized, especially when regeneration using seed is employed. Thus, progenies obtained for operational planting from a tree improvement program are only partially as good on the average as the combination of the parents from which they came. When vegetative propagation is feasible, gains that are realized may be greater, but even then, some of the desired parental characteristics are not obtained in the progenies because of the interaction of genotypes with the environment. There is always the desired goal of perfection, but this is rarely achieved. The practical approach is to come as close to the ideal as possible with a reasonable and justifiable expenditure of time and energy.

An understanding of the practical versus ideal goals is of special importance for pest *resistance,* the term generally used when breeding to reduce diseases or insects. Complete resistance or immunity to pests seldom can be obtained. What is hoped for is enough resistance or tolerance to enable growing a profitable crop of trees. A good example is the very bad fusiform rust disease on southern pines (*Cronartium quercum f. sp. fusiforme*) in the southeastern United States. Tree improvement organizations will be quite satisfied if the disease incidence can be reduced from the very high level now found in some operational plantations to about 15 or 20% infection. This amount of rust infection will have only a slight effect on the yield and quality of products from the forest. The cost, time, and effort to reduce infection further are not warranted economically. Emphasis in the program can then be directed to improving characteristics that will give a greater response.

A similar situation applies to such things as straightness of tree bole or to essentially all adaptability characteristics. We have been able to improve tree straightness in loblolly pine (*Pinus taeda*) enough to produce high-quality products in one generation of intensive selection. Even though a small additional improvement in straightness can be obtained with continued breeding, it is not worth the additional time and effort to place intensive selection pressures on this characteristic.

When breeding for adaptability characteristics, the objective is to gain maximum tolerance to adverse environmental factors. One will never find trees that are totally resistant to drought, cold, or excess moisture. However, one should strive to obtain trees that can better tolerate severe droughts, or colder weather, or that will grow reasonably well in other adverse environments.

It is necessary for the reader to remember always that the objective of a tree improvement program is to obtain trees that will be closer to the desired state than those that are currently available. The situation of diminishing returns is encountered as increased efforts come to the point where they yield a lesser amount of improvement per "unit effort" (Figure 1.9). A well-designed tree improvement program will have as its achievement objective the production of the greatest

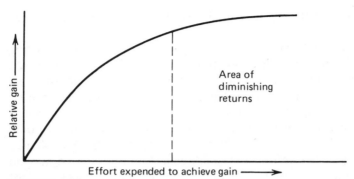

FIGURE 1.9

The law of diminishing returns is fundamental in tree improvement. As one gets closer and closer to the ideal, the cost and effort becomes greater for each added unit of gain. There comes the time when breeding for additional gains is not warranted by the time and effort involved (see Chapter 14 on economics).

amount of improvement that will still yield profitable returns. The problem is to determine when returns on the investment diminish to an extent that additional efforts for improvement are not warranted.

The most *important* and *exciting part of tree improvement* is that *it is usually possible to breed for improved economic characteristics while at the same time to maintain or broaden the genetic base for adaptability and pest resistance.* This is also true for changing product requirements. This is possible because very few of the important characteristics of forest trees are strongly correlated genetically. For example, one can develop disease resistance in either straight trees or crooked trees. Drought-resistant trees can either have high- or low-specific-gravity wood.

ADVANTAGES AND LIMITATIONS OF TREE IMPROVEMENT

Although this book will deal with the advantages and limitations of tree improvement in depth in later chapters, it is worthwhile to list here a few of the more important items in order to help the understanding of people interested in tree improvement.

One major advantage of genetic improvements in forest trees is that once a change is obtained, it can be kept over a number of generations. When improvements are made through silviculture (fertilization, for example), they will need to be done one or more times at each rotation. This quality of the "permanence" of genetic improvements over several rotations makes them very appealing economically, even though the initial cost of developing desired trees may be considerable. The advantage will be somewhat reduced when environments, pests, or markets change, so that the genetic material is no longer suitable.

Another major advantage of tree management is that the genetic material that is developed can be kept essentially intact for an indefinite time through methods of vegetative propagation. Many outcrossing annuals require continued replacement through producing new seeds because seeds lose viability after a few years in storage. Every new crop will differ somewhat from that of the parents because of genetic recombinations. Also, the cost and effort of producing new seed crops every few years is large. However, for forest trees, the desired genotype can be kept indefinitely in the form of grafts or cuttings.

Some difficulties associated with working with large long-lived plants are obvious. The size of the trees creates problems in measurement, crossing, and especially in seed collection. Another item related to size is finding suitable areas necessary for "storage" of desired genetic material and for testing. Many trees do not flower at a young age, thus making a quick breeding program difficult. To add to the problem of slow generation time, juvenile–mature correlations, especially for growth characteristics, often are not satisfactory. This requires the maintenance of tests for a considerable number of years before the growth rate potential of a given genotype can be assessed accurately. The poor juvenile-to-mature correlations for growth result from the fact that different trees posess different growth curves. Some are fast starters that mature quickly, followed by a growth slowdown, whereas others are slow starters that grow at a constant rate over a long period of time and eventually overtake the fast starters.

Availability of seed with the known or desired genetic background is a frequent problem. Even when sufficient seed is available, there is a very difficult situation with respect to the size and configuration of test plots. Because of great environmental variability within a short distance in forestland, rather small plots are desired for uniformity. However, when plots are too small, not enough trees are represented to obtain reliable results because most trees are quite variable, one from another, even within closely related groups. Such variability necessitates the use of a number of individuals to accurately categorize a genetic grouping, thus requiring a considerable area in which to make the tests.

A lack of knowledge about what will be desired in the future can be a major deterrent to a tree improvement program. For example, will high- or low-specific-gravity wood be desired 30 years from now? Decisions must be made early with respect to future requirements, and once made, the type of tree produced must be used even though it may no longer be the ideal. This dictates a cautious or conservative approach to making decisions in tree improvement. Fads must be avoided, but if gains are to be obtained, early decisions must be made about long-term forestry objectives. Uniformity of products and the characteristics of tolerance to pests and adverse environments are uniformly desired, but other tree properties of form and wood qualities are not so easy to predict relative to future needs.

One problem that was severe in the early years, which is much improved now but nevertheless is still with us, is the attitude of foresters themselves. Training in forestry has tended to emphasize that the reasons trees differ one from another are due to the differing environments in which they grow. There was little recognition that some of the differences that occur among individuals in a forest are the result of differing parentages. The idea that trees are plants and therefore will respond to genetic manipulation like other plants was not understood at all by early foresters. This past block about the use of genetics in forestry now seems to be rapidly disappearing.

A major problem in the development of tree improvement programs is the permanence of organizations and movements of peoples. Tree improvement is a long-term process and as such, it must have good permanent records that are handed on from person to person. This often has not been the case. Records are sometimes poorly kept or not kept at all, and valuable information moves on with the personnel who leave. Often, the new person is a highly trained specialist who wants to do "his thing"; therefore, the old studies that were inherited suffer because they are only of passing interest to the new person. The loss and wastage caused by poor records and constant personnel changes cannot be overemphasized. Although not based on available data, the senior author estimates that at least 50% of the forest research that has been started never comes to the desired fruition because of a lack of care, loss of records, or the movements of key persons. This is even more serious in the developing countries that have few trained local staff members and where heavy use is made of short-term visiting experts.

As stated previously, one advantage of forest tree improvement, often not thoroughly recognized, is that most forest stands have great genetic variability and have not been greatly changed by the actions of people. There are exceptions, of course, but generally poor or dysgenic selection has not been intensive enough, or it has gone on long enough to cause a permanent degradation in the genetic constitution of a population. It is true that the ratio of desired trees may have been reduced, but the good genes and gene complexes are still present in the forest so that the tree improver can use them if sufficient effort is made to locate them. The problem sometimes encountered is that the tree characteristics desired by the silviculturist may differ somewhat from those developed over time through natural selection in wild forests. But generally, the tree improver has enough variation from wild stands to enable good gains to be achieved. This is especially true for adaptability characteristics.

GENOTYPE AND PHENOTYPE

Although they are widely used by many persons in publications and conversations, two important terms that must be clearly understood are *phenotype* and *genotype*. All concepts in tree improvement are dependent on knowing what a genotype and phenotype is.

The *phenotype is the tree we see*. It is influenced by the genetic potential of the tree and by the environment in which the tree is growing, including the managerial history of the site. The phenotype is often indicated by the simple formula $P = G + E$ (phenotype = genotype + environment). The pheonotype of the tree is what we measure and what we work with.

The *genotype is the genetic potential of the tree*. It cannot be seen directly, and it can only be determined through well-designed tests. The genotype is determined by the genes that reside in chromosomes in the nucleus of every cell in the tree. *The sum total of nongenetic factors that affect the growth and reproduction of trees is called the environment.* It is a very general and catchall term applied to soils, moisture, weather, and often also to the influence of pests and sometimes to the interference of people.

The *basic fact is that one cannot say anything definite about the genetic worth of a tree just by looking at it,* that is, from its phenotype (Figure 1.3). One is never sure whether the characteristics observed are primarily determined by the environment in which the tree is growing or by the genetic control from the genotype of the tree. Both will interact to affect the tree's phenotype. The objective of the tree improver is to package the better genes into improved genotypes and then to manipulate the environment so that this genotype will react in a positive way to produce the most desirable phenotype.

If we can say nothing definite about the genetics of a tree from its phenotype, how then does one proceed to determine genetic superiority in a tree improvement program? Because the genotype is a component of the phenotype, it is related to the genetic potential of the tree; therefore, if good phenotypes are selected, improved genotypes will often result. Once the general relationship between the phenotype and genotype is known, it will then be possible to make some assumptions about the genetic value of a tree, just from observing its phenotype. For example, it is known that the straightness of the tree (phenotype) and its genetic potential for straightness are correlated, so that predictions can be made with some confidence that straighter trees will be obtained if straight trees are used as parents.

The concepts of *genotype* and *phenotype* are so simple that there may be doubt about the need for the preceding discussion. Yet these concepts are widely misunderstood by many persons who, for example, feel that if a tall tree at a given age is used as a parent, then its progenies should all be as tall as the parent at the same age. Many people do not separate the genetic and environmental causes that contribute to tree height. Progeny of the tall trees will grow to a size that is dependent upon the environment and the genetic potential for height passed from parent to offspring.

TERMS COMMONLY USED IN TREE IMPROVEMENT

In this book, there will be no special glossary or definitions for terms used in tree improvement work. The most important terms will be defined when they are encountered in the specific subject matter area to which they belong. If exact definitions are required, they can be obtained from any one of a number of biological texts or glossaries, such as those by Richens (1945), King (1968), Ford-Robertson (1971), Snyder (1972), and Lamontagne and Corriveau (1973).

There are a few general terms that will constantly be encountered throughout the text that must be understood right from the beginning. These are defined very simply as follows.

Progeny   The trees produced from the seed of a parent tree are called its progeny. *Progeny tests* are established to determine the genetic worth of the parent trees or for determination of other genetic characteristics. Sometimes, a test of the vegetative propagules from a given donor is referred to as a progeny test, but usually it is called a *clonal test*.

Population   This term is very loosely used by workers in the field of tree improvement. In this text, the term *population* will be used in a general way to designate a community of interbreeding individuals. No degree of relationship is assumed. The word *stand* is often used synonymously with population; at other times, *stand* refers to a group of trees of special interest within a population.

Race   Groups of populations that generally interbreed with one another and that intergrade more or loss continuously are referred to as *races*. Many kinds of races are recognized, such as edaphic, climatic, elevational, and so forth.

Family   Individuals that are more closely related to each other than to other individuals in a population are called a *family*. Generally, the term *family* is used to denote groups of individuals who have one or both parents in common. As used in this book, the term *family* does not refer to a taxonomic category except when it is specifically indicated.

Siblings   A group of individuals within a family are referred to as *siblings;* the group of related individuals when only one parent is common is called a *half-sib family;* when both parents are common, they constitute a *full-sib family*. An *open-pollinated family* is one in which one parent is common and the other parent(s) are unknown.

Rotation age   The age at which a stand of trees is to be harvested is called the *rotation age*.

Seed orchard   An area where superior phenotypes or genotypes are established and managed intensively and entirely for seed production is referred to as a *seed orchard*.

REFERENCES AND PUBLICATIONS

There are a large number of publications that deal directly with, or are related to tree improvement. Only a few of the most important of these can be listed in this book. The authors have over 10,000 references in their personal libraries, and these are certainly not complete. Contrary to the practice in most books, some of the older references will be listed along with the new ones, because in some areas the most interesting and definitive work was done some years ago.

In any chapter, there will not be space to list all pertinent references to the subject covered. The interested reader will need to pursue the subject to the depth he or she desires. To aid in this activity, the best and most comprehensive references available have been listed. A reader who wishes to go further into a subject should look at the references listed and follow up on other pertinent references, especially those in the newest publications. Commonly, students and foresters ask, "How do I proceed to become better informed in subject X?" One answer is to use references from new publications to find older ones that may be pertinent. Although most foresters do not develop exhaustive libraries, they must keep lists of key references. Every personal library should include the most important periodicals, especially for those working in isolated areas. *Expenses for books and magazines are as legitimate to the forester as are costs of field equipment, tools, and vehicles.*

As computers become more widely used, the literature can be accessed through bibliographic data bases, many of which are the computer-readable counterparts of printed indexes. These data bases are termed *bibliographic* because searches result in a list of references, or a bibliography. Among the files useful for searching tree improvement topics are the FORESTRY ABSTRACTS subfile of the CAB data base, which is the computer equivalent of the printed FORESTRY ABSTRACTS, produced by the Commonwealth Agricultural Bureaux (CAB) in England; AGRICOLA, the computer counterpart of the BIBLIOGRAPHY OF AGRICULTURE, produced by the U.S. National Agriculture Library; and BIOSIS, the computer-readable equivalent of BIOLOGICAL ABSTRACTS, BIOLOGICAL ABSTRACTS/REPORTS, REVIEWS, MEETINGS, and BIORESEARCH INDEX, which is supplied by BioSciences Information Service in Philadelphia. Files containing information on soil science, chemistry, hydrology, tree improvement, and other topics pertinent to forestry are available. Coverage in many data bases is international, and it usually includes journal articles, books, translations, and technical reports. Occasionally, these and patents may also be included. Generally, computerized bibliographic files index the printed literature from the 1960s to the present.

Data base searches can be tailored to the individual user's needs, using genus and species, language of publication, date, and geography. Computerized searching also offers the capacity for scanning article titles and abstracts for relevant terms, a procedure that is very time consuming when done by hand. Computerized searches are particularly useful for topics that are too comprehensive or complex to be found easily when searched for manually. They are helpful when speed is desirable, and they are valuable in locations where printed indexes may be inaccessible.

Computerized search of the literature is available in most countries of the world. Although it is possible for the "end user" to conduct the search, users often obtain the service through intermediaries, such as libraries, information centers, or private information brokers. These agencies maintain the equipment needed for searching, they hire staff members trained to manipulate the files effectively, and, if they do not mount the data bases themselves, they will establish accounts with data base vendors. Those who are uncertain of the identity of agencies offering computerized searching in their areas can obtain this information from the national libraries in their respective countries.

Listed here are the addresses of the major American commercial data base vendors, all of whom offer service outside the United States. These corporations are not search intermediaries; however, the addresses are given for the benefit of institutions interested in establishing accounts.

LOCKHEED INFORMATION SERVICES, INC.
3460 Hillview Avenue
Palo Alto, California 94304
(405) 858–3785
(800) 982–5838 within California
(800) 227–1927 within the continental United States
TELEX 334499 (DIALOG)
TWX 910/339–9221

SDC SEARCH SERVICE
2500 Colorado Avenue
Santa Monica, California 90406
(800) 352–6689 within California
(800) 421–7229 within the continental United States
TELEX 65–2358
TWX 910/343–6443

BIBLIOGRAPHIC RETRIEVAL SERVICES, INC. (BRS)
1200 Route 7
Latham, New York 12110
(800) 833–4707 within the continental United States
(518) 783–7251 within New York state and Canada; call collect
TWX 710/444–4965

Although long lists of references have not been cited in the text, the most pertinent references have been available to the reader who is interested in pursuing a specific subject. Some good references have undoubtedly been missed, and we apologize for their omission; most notably, some publications in languages other than English may have been overlooked. The reference material in the book will be handled in four different ways:

1. Literature that is directly cited in a chapter will be listed alphabetically at the end of each chapter as "Literature Cited."

2. The following section contains a list of books on tree improvement or on closely related subjects. General textbooks, such as those on botany or dendrology, have not been listed, with the exception of a few that are of specific, direct interest to tree improvement professionals.

3. A list of journals that carry articles of interest in tree improvement appears in another of the following sections. Addresses are shown for readers who wish to subscribe to some specific journal; those that are particularly suitable for tropical areas are indicated with a footnote.

4. Another section contains an incomplete list of some important proceedings or symposia. Addresses are shown, when it is feasible to do so. The addresses of periodic meetings, such as tree improvement conferences, change with the place where the meeting was held. Therefore, no addresses will be shown for this type of publication. Some proceedings and symposia are not numbered, and therefore they are most difficult to index. However, outstanding information is available from them and they should be consulted whenever possible. Of key importance is the fact that many publications do not fall within the category of *refereed publications*. Therefore, they may not be listed in abstracts or computer reference lists.

In an effort to make the references in the following sections as comprehensive as possible, the initial lists of publications were sent to other workers in the area of tree improvement and to libraries, asking them to supply missing information. The good response is greatly appreciated.

SOME BOOKS OF SPECIAL INTEREST TO TREE IMPROVERS

Burley, J., and Styles, B. T. 1976. *Tropical Trees—Variation, Breeding and Conservation.* Commonwealth Forestry Institute. Academic Press, New York.

Burley, J., and Wood, P. J. 1976. *A Manual on Species and Provenance Research with Particular Reference to the Tropics.* Department of Forestry, CFI, University of Oxford, Oxford, England.

Dobzhansky, T. 1951. *Genetics and the Origin of Species.* Columbia University Press, New York.

Dorman, K. W. 1976. *The Genetics and Breeding of Southern Pines,* Agriculture Handbook No. 471. USDA, U.S. Forest Service, Washington, D.C.

Enescu, V. 1972. *Ameliorarea arborilor Partea Generala.* Editura "Ceres," Bucharest, Rumania.

Enescu, V. 1975. *Ameliorarea Principal elor Specii Forestiere.* Editura "Ceres," Bucharest, Rumania.

Falconer, D. S. 1960. *Introduction to Quantitative Genetics.* Ronald Press, New York.

Faulkner, R. 1975. "Seed Orchards." Forestry Commission Bulletin No. 54, Her Majesty's Stationary Office, London.

Goldschmitt, R. B. 1952. *Understanding Heredity: An Introduction to Genetics.* John Wiley & Sons, New York.

Hedlin, A. F., Yates, H. O., Lovar, D. C., Ebel, B. H., Koerber, T. W., and Merkel, E. P. 1980. *Cone and Seed Insects of North American Conifers.* USDA, U.S. Forest Service, Washington, D.C. (also Universidad Autónoma de Chapingo, Chapingo, Mexico—Environment Canada, Canadian Forestry Service, Ottawa, Canada).

Khosla, P. K. (Ed.). 1981 *Advances in Forest Genetics*. Ambika Publications, New Delhi, India.

Mettler, L. E., and Gregg, S. G. 1969. *Population Genetics and Evolution*. Prentice-Hall, Inc., Englewood Cliffs, N.J.

Namkoong, G. 1979. "Introduction to Quantitative Genetics in Forestry." Technical Bulletin No. 1588., U.S. Forest Service, Washington, D.C.

Snedecor, G. 1981. *Statistical Methods*. Iowa State College Press, Ames.

Srb, A. M., Owen, R. D., and Edgar, R. S. 1965. *General Genetics*. W. H. Freeman and Co., San Francisco/London.

Stebbins, G. L. 1950. *Variation and Evolution in Plants*. Columbia University Press, New York.

Stern, K., and Roche, L. 1974. *Genetics of Forest Ecosystems*. Springer-Verlag, New York.

Stonecypher, R. W., Zobel, B. J., and Blair, R. L. 1973. "Inheritance Patterns of Loblolly Pine from a Nonselected Natural Population." Agricultural Experimental Station Technical Bulletin No. 220, North Carolina State University, Raleigh.

Sziklai, O., and Katompa, T. 1981. *Erdészeti Növény-Nemesítés [Forest Tree Improvement]*. Mezögazdasagi Kiado, Budapest, Hungary.

Thielges, B. A. (Ed.). 1975. "Forest Tree Improvement—The Third Decade." 24th Annual Forestry Symposium, Louisiana State University, Baton Rouge.

Toda, R. (Ed.). 1974. *Forest Tree Breeding in the World*. Government Forest Experiment Station, Meguro, Tokyo, Japan (27 authors).

Toda, R. 1979. *Forest Genetics Up-to-Date*. Noorin Syuppan Co., Ltd., Tokyo Japan.

Wright, J. W. 1976. *Introduction to Forest Genetics*. Academic Press, New York.

Magazines That Include Articles
of Special Interest to Tree Improvers

Magazine	Address
AFOCEL	Association Foret-Cellulose, 164 Boulevard Haussman, 75008, Paris, France
Australian Forest Research	CSIRO (Commonwealth Scientific and Industrial Research Organization), P.O. Box 89, East Melbourne, Victoria 3002, Australia

(*continued*)

Magazine	Address
Biotropica[a]	Association for Tropical Biology, Inc., Washington State University Press, Pullman, Washington 99163 ORDERS TO: Clifford Evans, Secretary-Treasurer, c/o Anthropology-MNH 368, Smithsonian Institution, Washington, D.C. 20560
Bois et Forets des Tropiques[a]	Centre Technique Forestier Tropical, 45 bis, Ave. de la Belle Gabrielle, 94130 Nogent-sur-Marne, France
Boletim de Pesquisa Forestal[a]	EMBRAPA, Unidade Regional da Pesquisa Florestal Centro-Sul, Caixa Postal 3319, 80,000 Curitiba, Brazil
Brazil Florestal[a]	IBDF. Ministerio da Agricultura, Institute Brasileiro de Desenvolvimento Florestal, Brasilia, Brazil
Bulletin of Forestry and Forest Products Research Institute	Forestry and Forest Products Research Institute, P.O. Box 16, Tsukuba Norin Kenkyu, Danchi-nal, Ibavaki, 305, Japan
Bulletin Recherche Agronomic, Gembloux	Station de recherches des Eaux et Forets, Groenendaal—Hoeilaart, Belgium
Canadian Journal of Forest Research	National Research Council of Canada, Ottawa K1AOR6, Canada
Commonwealth Forestry Review[a]	The Commonwealth Forestry Association, c/o CFI, South Parks Road, Oxford OX1 3RB, England
Forest Ecology and Management[a]	Forest Ecology and Management, P.O. Box 330, 1000 AH, Amsterdam, The Netherlands
Forest Farmer	P.O. Box 95385, 4 Executive Park East, N.E., Atlanta, Georgia 30347
Forest Products Journal	2801 Marshall Court, Madison, Wisconsin 53705
Forest Science	Society of American Foresters, 5400 Grosvenor Lane, Washington, D.C. 20014
Forestry Abstracts[a]	Commonwealth Agricultural Bureaux, Farnham House, Farnham Royal Slough SL2 3BN, England

(*continued*)

Magazine	Address
Indian Forester[a]	Forest Research Institute and Colleges, P.O. New Forest, Dehra Dun, India
IPEF (Institute de Pesquisas e Estudos Florestais, Brasil)[a]	Instituto de Pesquisas e Estudos Florestais, Caixa Postal 9, Escola Superior de Agricultura, Piracicaba, Sao Paulo, Brazil
Journal of Forestry	Society of American Foresters, 5400 Grosvenor Lane, Washington, D.C. 20014
New Zealand Journal of Forestry Science[a]	Forest Research Institute, Private Bag, Rotorua, New Zealand
Research Report of the Institute of Forest Genetics	Institute of Forest Genetics, Suwon, Korea
Rapporter, Institutionen för Skogsproduktion	Sveriges Lantbruksuniversitet, Department of Forest Yield Research, S-770 73 Garpenberg, Sweden
Rapporter och uppsatser	Sveriges Lantbruksuniversitet, Department of Forest Genetics, S-770 73 Garpenberg, Sweden
Revista Arvore[a]	Comissao Editorial da *Revista Arvore,* Sociedade de Investigacoes Florestais, Universidade Federal de Vicosa, 36.570 Vicõsa, Minas Gerais, Brazil
Silvae Genetica[a]	Institut für Forstgenetik und Forstpflanzenzüchtung, Grosshandsdorf 2, Schmalenbeck, Federal Republic of Germany
South African Forestry Journal [*Suidafrikaanse Bosboutydskrif*][a]	South African Forestry Association, 62 Lugan Road, Johannesburg 2193, South Africa
Southern Journal of Applied Forestry	Society of American Foresters, 5400 Grosvenor Lane, Washington, D.C. 20014
Studia Forestalia Suecia	Sveriges Lantbruksuniversitet, Ultunabiblioteket, S-750 07 Uppsala, Sweden
Sveriges Skogsvårdsförbunds Tidskrift	Sveriges Skogsrardsföband, Box 273, S-18252 Djursholm, Sweden
Tappi	Technical Association of Pulp and Paper Industry, One Dunwoody Park, Atlanta, Georgia 30338

(*continued*)

Magazine	Address
Tree Planters Notes	U.S. Forest Service, Washington, D.C. 20250
Turrialba: Revista Interamericana de Ciencias Agricolas[a]	Instituto Interamericano de Ciencias Agricolas de la OEA Secretariado, Apartado 55, Coronado, San José, Costa Rica
Unasylva: International Journal of Forestry and Forest Products[a]	Food and Agriculture Organization of the United Nations, Forestry Department, Distribution and Sales Section, Via delle Terme di Caracalla, 00100 Rome, Italy *Note:* Distributed in the United States by UNIPUB, 345 Park Avenue South, New York, New York 10010
Wood Science and Technology	Springer-Verlag, 175 Fifth Avenue, New York, New York 10010

[a]Publications that are particularly suitable for tropical forestry.

Proceedings and Symposia
of Special Interest to Tree Improvement

Title	Country	Date	Organization or Publication
"Die Früdiagnose in der Züchtung and Züchtungsforschung"	Germany	1957	Der Zuchter, Springer-Verlag, Berlin (collection of papers)
"IX International Botanical Congress" (Vol. II)	Canada	1959	Proc. Montreal, University of Toronto Press
"Forest Genetics Workshop"	U.S.A.	1962	Proc. Southern Forest Tree Improvement Committee, Macon, Georgia.
"The Influence of Environment and Genetics on Pulpwood Quality"	U.S.A.	1962	Annotated Bibliography, Technical Association of Pulp and Paper Industry, TAPPI Monograph Series, No. 24, Atlanta, Georgia
"Genetics Today"	The Netherlands	1963	Proc. XI, International Congress on Genetics, The Hague
"Statistical Genetics and Plant Breeding"	U.S.A.	1963	Pub. No. 982, National Academy of Science, National Research Council, Washington, D.C. 62300
"Conference on Forest-Tree Genetics, Selection and Seed Production"	Russia	1969	Synopses of Reports (translated from Russian for USDA and National Science Foundation)

(continued)

Title	Country	Date	Organization of Publication
"Twelve Selected Articles" (translated from Russian)	Russia	1969	Botanicheskii, Zhurnal, from U.S. Dept. Commerce and USDA and National Science Foundation
"Quantitative Genetics"	U.S.A.	1970	2d Meeting of Working Group on Quantitative Genetics, IUFRO, Raleigh, North Carolina. Published by U.S. Forest Service, New Orleans, Louisiana
"Seminar on Forest Genetics and Forest Fertilization"	Canada	1970	Proc. Pulp and Paper Research Institute of Canada, Montreal, Canada
"Effect of Growth Acceleration"	U.S.A.	1971	Symposium, University of Wisconsin, Madison, Wisconsin
"Biology of Rust Resistance in Forest Trees"	U.S.A.	1972	Proc. NATO–IUFRO, Advanced Study Institute (USDA Miscel. Pub. No. 1221)
"Working Party on Progeny Testing"	U.S.A.	1972	IUFRO Proc., Georgia Forest Research Council, Macon, Georgia
"Selection and Breeding to Improve Some Tropical Conifers" (Vols. I and II; 15th IUFRO Congress)	U.S.A.	1972	Commonwealth Forestry Institute, Oxford, England, and Department of Forestry, Queensland, Australia
"Tropical Provenance and Progeny Research and International Cooperation"	Kenya and Australia	1973	Commonwealth Forestry Institute, Oxford, England
"Population and Ecological Genetics: Breeding Theory and Progeny Testing"	Sweden	1974	Proc., Department of Forest Genetics, Royal College of Forestry, S-104 05, Stockholm, Sweden
"Advanced Generation Breeding"	France	1976	Proc. IUFRO, Bordeaux, INRA, Laboratoire d' Amélioration des Conifères, 33610 Cestas, France
"Forest Genetic Resources"	Sweden	1976	Royal College of Forestry, Stockholm, Sweden
"Management of Fusiform Rust in Southern Pines"	U.S.A.	1977	South. Forest Disease and Insect Research Council, University of Florida, Gainesville
"Vegetative Propagation of Forest Trees—Physiology and Practice	Sweden	1977	Symp., The Institute of Forestry Improvement and Department of Genetics, College of Forestry, Uppsala, Sweden
"Progress and Problems of Genetic Improvement of Tropical Forest Trees" (Vols. I and II)	Australia	1978	Commonwealth Forestry Institute, Oxford, England

(continued)

Title	Country	Data	Organization of Publication
"Tree Improvement Symposium"	Canada	1979	Ontario Ministry of Natural Resources and Great Lakes Forest Research Center, Toronto, Ontario (COJFRC Symp. Proc. O-P-7)
"Effects of Air Pollutants on Mediterranean and Temperate Forest Ecosystems"	U.S.A.	1980	U.S. Forest Service, Riverside, California
"Genetic Improvement and Productivity of Fast-Growing Trees"	Brazil	1980	IUFRO Symposium and Workshop, São Paulo, Brazil
"The Forest Imperative"	Canada	1980	Proc. Canadian Forestry Congress, Toronto (The Pulp and Paper Industry of Canada)
"Workshop on the Genetics of Host–Parasite Interactions in Forestry"	Wageningen	1980	Proc. several international organizations

Proceedings of Meetings Held Periodically for Which Addresses Vary

Southern Forest Tree Improvement Conferences

Biology Workshops (sponsored by the Society of American Foresters)

Lake States Forest Genetics Conferences

North-Central Tree Improvement Conferences

Central States Forest Tree Improvement Conferences

Northeastern Forest Tree Improvement Conferences

Canadian Tree Improvement Association in Canada (Committee on Forest Tree Breeding in Canada)

First, Second, and Third World Consultations on Forest Tree Breeding held in Stockholm, Washington, D.C., and Canberra, Australia, respectively

LITERATURE CITED

Austin, L. 1927. A new enterprise in forest tree breeding. *Jour. For.* **25**(8):977–993.

Barner, H. 1952. Skovtraeföraed lingens muligheder (possibilities in forest tree breeding). *Dan. Skovfören. Tidsskr.* **37**:62–79.

Batzer, H. O. 1961. "Jack Pine from Lake States Seed Sources Differ in

Susceptibility to Attack by the White Pine Weevil." Technical Note No. 595, Lake States Forestry Experimental Station.

Bey, C. F. 1974. "Drought Hardiness Tests of Black Walnut Seedlings as Related to Field Performance." Proc. 9th Central States For. Tree Impr. Conf., Ames, Iowa, pp. 138–144.

Bouvarel, P. 1957. Génétique forestière et amélioration des arbres forestiers [Forest genetics and the improvement of forest trees]. *Bull. Soc. Bot. Fr.* **104**(7–8): 552–586.

Brix, H. 1959. "Some Aspects of Drought Resistance in Loblolly Pine Seedlings." Ph.D. thesis, Texas A&M College, College Station.

Buchholz, E. 1953. Neuen sowjetische Arbeiten über Forstpflanzenzüchtung and forstliche Samenkunde [Recent Soviet work in forest tree breeding and seed collection]. *Z. Forstgenet.* **2**(3):65–70.

Dietrichson, J. 1961. Breeding for frost resistance. *Sil. Gen.* **10**(6):172–179.

Duffield, J. W. 1956. Genetics and exotics. *Jour. For.* **54**(1):780.

Fischer, F. 1954. Forstliche Pflanzenzüchtung als ein Mittel zur Steigerung des Waldertrages (Tree breeding as a means of increasing forest yields). *Schweiz. Z. Forstwes.* **105**(3–4):165–183.

Ford-Robertson, F. C. 1971. *Terminology of Forest Science, Technology Practice and Products,* The Multilingual Forestry Terminology Series No. 1. Society of American Forestry, Washington, D.C.

Goddard, R. E., Schmidt, R. A., and Vande Linde, F. 1975. "Immediate Gains in Fusiform Rust Resistance in Slash Pine from Rogued Seed Production Areas in Severely Infected Plantations." Proc. 13th South. For. Tree Impr. Conf., Raleigh, N.C., pp. 197–203.

Goddard, R. E., Zobel, B. J., and Hollis, C. A. 1976. "Response of *Pinus taeda* and *Pinus elliottii* to Varied Nutrition." Proc Conf. on *Physiol Genetics* and Tree Breeding, Edinburg Scotland, pp. 449–462.

Greeley, W. B. 1952. Blood will tell. *Am. For.* **58**(9):18–19, 28.

Haley, C. 1957. "The Present Status of Tree Breeding Work in Queensland." Seventh British Comm. For. Conf., Queensland For. Department.

Heimburger, C. 1958. Forest tree breeding in Canada. *Gen. Soc. Can.* **3**(1):41–49.

Hellinga, G. 1958. "On Forest Tree Improvement in Indonesia." Proc. 12th IUFRO Congress, Oxford, England, Vol. 1(11), pp. 395–397.

Heth, D., and Kramer, P. J. 1975. Drought tolerance of pine seedlings under various climatic conditions. *For. Sci.* **21**(1):72–82.

Hosner, J. F., and Boyce, S. G. 1962. Tolerance to water saturated soil of various bottomland hardwoods. *For. Sci.* **8**(2):180–186.

Hyun, S. K. 1958. "Forest Tree Breeding in Korea." Proc. 12th IUFRO Congress, Oxford, England, Vol. I(11), pp. 375–385.

Johnsson, H. 1949. "Experiences and Results of 10 Years Breeding Experiments at the Swedish Forest Tree Breeding Association." Proc. 3rd World For. Cong., Vol. 3, pp. 126–130.

King, R. C. 1968. *Dictionary of Genetics.* Oxford University Press, New York.

Lacaze, M. 1963. "The Resistance of *Eucalyptus* Trees to Active Limestone in the soil." Proc. World Consul. on For. Gen. and Tree Impr. 4/8, Stockholm, Sweden.

Lamontagne, Y., and Corriveau, A. G. 1973. *Glossaire des termes techniques utilisés en amélioration des arbres forestiers.* Ministere des Terres et foréts, Quebec, Canada.

Langner, W. 1954. Die Entwicklung der Forst—genetik und Forstpflanzenzüchtung in Deutschland (the development of forest genetics and forest tree breeding in Germany). *Z. Forstgenetik* **3**:55–60.

Larsen, C. S. 1951. Advances in forest genetics. *Unasylva* **5**(1):15–19.

Leopold, A. J. 1929. Some thoughts on forest genetics. *Jour. For.* **27**:708–713.

Lindquist, B. 1948. *Forstgenetik in der Schwedischen Waldbaupraxis (Forest Genetics in Swedish Forestry Practice).* Neumann Verlag, Radebeul/Berlin.

Matthews, J. D. 1953. Forest tree breeding in Britain. *Forstgenet* **2**(3):59–65.

McCormick, L. H., and Steiner, K. C. 1978. Variation in aluminum tolerance among six genera of trees. *For. Sci.* **24**(1):565–568.

Namkoong, G. Barnes, R. D., and Burley, J. 1980. "A Philosophy of Breeding Strategy for Tropical Forest Trees." Tropical Forest Paper No. 16, Comm. For. Inst., Oxford, England.

Ohba, K. 1979. Forest tree breeding in Japan. *JARQ* **13**(2):138–144.

Parker, J. 1963. Cold resistance in woody plants. *Bot. Rev.* **29**(2):123–201.

Perry, T. O., and Wang, C. W. 1958. The value of genetically superior seed. *Jour. For.* **56**(1):843–845.

Rao, H. S. 1951. Genetics and forest tree improvement. *Indian For.* **77**:635–647.

Richens, R. H. 1945. "Forest Tree Breeding and Genetics." Imperial Agr. Bureaux, Joint Pub. No. 8, Imp. Bur. Plant Breed. and Gen. Imp. For. Bur., Oxford, England.

Righter, F. I. 1946. New perspectives in forest tree breeding. *Science* **104**(2688):1–3.

Roberds, J. H., Namkoong, G., and Davey, C. B. 1976. Family variation in growth response of loblolly pine to fertilizing with urea. *For. Sci.* **22**(3):291–299.

Sakai, A., and Okada, S. 1971. Freezing resistance of conifers. *Sil. Gen.* **20**(3):53–100.

Schönback, H. 1961. The variation of frost resistance in homegrown stands of Douglas fir. *Rec. Adv. Botany* **2**(14):1604–1606.

Schreiner, E. J. 1935. Possibilities of improving pulping characteristics of pulp-woods by controlled hybridization of forest trees. *Paper Trade Jour. C*, 105–109.

Schreiner, E. J. 1950. Genetics in relation to forestry. *Jour. For.* **48**(1):33–38.

Snyder. E. B. 1972. *Glossary for Forest Tree Improvement Workers*. U.S. Forest Service, Southern Forestry Experimental Station, New Orleans, La.

Sziklai, O. 1981. "Present and Future Research Requirements." Seminar, Tree Improvement in the Interior of British Columbia, Prince George, British Columbia, Canada.

Thulin, I. J. 1957. "Application of Tree Breeding to New Zealand Forestry." Technical Paper No. 22, Forest Research Institute, New Zealand Forest Service.

Toda, R. 1970. *Abstracts of Japanese Literature in Forest Genetics and Related Fields*, Vol I-A. Noorin Syuppan Co., Ltd., Shinbashi, Tokyo, Japan. (2156 refs. before 1930) 1972; Vol. I-B, pp. 363–918 (refs. 2157 to 5385), 1931–1945.

Toda, R. 1974. "Forest Tree Breeding in the World." Bull. Govt. Forest Experiment Station, Meguro, Tokyo, Japan.

Toda, R. 1980. An outline of the history of forest genetics. In *Advances in Forest Genetics*. Ambika Publications, New Delhi, India.

Toyama, S. 1954. "Studies on Breeding for Forest Trees." Bull. Govt. Forest Experimental Station, Meguro, Tokyo, Report 24, pp. 56–269.

Wright, J. W. 1953. A survey of forest genetics research. *Jour. For.* **51**(5):330–333.

Wright, J. W. 1981. "A Quarter Century of Progress in Tree Improvement in the Northeast." 27th Northeast. For. Tree Impr. Conf., Burlington, Vt. pp. 6–15.

Zobel, B. J. 1952. The genetic approach for improving wood qualities of the southern pines. *Jour. For. Prod. Res. Soc.* **2**(2):45–47.

Zobel, B. J. 1957. Progeny testing for drought resistance and wood properties. *Der Zuchter H.,* 95–96.

Zobel, B. J. 1974. "Increasing Productivity of Forest Lands through Better Trees," S. J. Hall Lectureship, University of California, Berkeley.

Zobel, B. J. 1978. "Progress in Breeding Forest Trees—The Problem of Time." 27th Ann. Sess. Nat. Poultry Breed. Roundtable, Kansas City, Mo., pp. 18–29.

Zobel, B. J., and Zoerb, M. 1977. "Reducing Fusiform Rust in Plantations through Control of the Seed Source." Symposium on Management of Fusiform Rust in Southern Pines, South. For. Dis. and Insect Res. Coun., Gainesville, Fla., pp. 98–109.

CHAPTER 2

Variation and its Use

SOME BASIC GENETIC CONCEPTS
General
Cells and Chromosomes
Mitosis and Meiosis
Genes and Alleles—Gene Action
CAUSES AND KINDS OF VARIABILITY
General
Environmental Variation
Genetic Variability
Mating Systems
Polyploidy
Genotype x Environment Interaction
VARIATION IN NATURAL STANDS
Introduction
Geographic (or Provenance) Variation
Variability among Sites
Differences among Stands within Sites
Tree Differences within a Stand
Variation within a Tree
Summary of Natural Variation
DETECTING VARIATION IN PEDIGREE STANDS
MAINTENANCE AND USE OF VARIATION
General
Forces That Shape Variation
Mutations
Gene Flow (Gene Migration)
Selection
Genetic Drift
VARIATION CAUSED BY MAN
LITERATURE CITED

Without sufficient genetic variability of the correct types for traits that are of economic interest, an attempt to use genetics to improve forest trees will be unsuccessful or a failure. Therefore, the first thing to do when starting a tree improvement program is to determine the amount, cause, and nature of the variation that is present in the species of interest and to learn how to use it. Activities related to assessing variation take much of the tree improver's time, and they require continued and intensive effort. The fact that variation does exist among species, races, and individuals within species is generally not too difficult to prove, but the determination of its causes can be very time consuming and costly. A difficult but essential task is to discover what portion of the variation is genetically controlled so that a determination can be made about how best to exploit it in a tree improvement program to produce better forests with higher-quality products (Figure 2.1; see also Figure 1.4).

Foresters are lucky in this instance because tree populations are generally genetically variable. They must be so in order to survive, grow, and reproduce under the differing conditions and numerous environments that are encountered during a single generation and over generations (Antonovics, 1971; Nienstaedt, 1975). The value of this "gift" of great variability in forest trees is often underestimated. The proper kind of genetically controlled variation provides the needed conditions for a tree improvement program, giving the necessary tools for large, quick gains from the use of genetics in forestry. As compared to agricultural crops, forest tree populations have been little influenced by human activities until now. Tree breeders are working essentially with wild populations that contain the genes and gene complexes needed for breeding programs. It is a fact that most *forest tree species possess greater variability* than species of other organisms; it is reported to be almost double that of other plants (Hamerick et al., 1979). Forest tree improvers therefore possess a huge advantage by being able to draw on this variability in their breeding programs. However, it places a great responsibility on the breeder to maintain and enhance the great store of variation for future use, a subject that will later be dealt with in some detail.

SOME BASIC GENETIC CONCEPTS

General

Trees are the largest and are among the most complex organisms in a world with millions of diverse life forms. Despite the tremendous diversity that exists in nature, however, certain basic mechanisms of inheritance are common to all species, including forest trees. Although this book is not meant to serve as a genetics text, a brief review of a few basic concepts and their effects on variation will be helpful in understanding the tree improvement principles presented in subsequent chapters. The message to be gained is that genetic processes are ordered, and in many instances they are predictable. Tree improvers must appreciate this fact and use it in their programs if they are to be successful. Detailed

FIGURE 2.1

Great variability commonly occurs within a species. Shown are two loblolly pines in an area subjected to fume damage. One tree has been killed by fumes; the other appears to be growing normally. When such variation has a genetic basis, it can be used to develop strains of trees of special value and use.

explanations of inheritance mechanisms can be found in genetics textbooks, such as those by Srb et al. (1965), Gardner (1984), Grant (1975), or Strickberger (1976).

Cells and Chromosomes

Like all organisms, trees are composed of cells. There are numerous types of cells in trees, but all living plant cells have in common a *cell wall*, a *cytoplasm*, and a *nucleus* (Figure 2.2). The nucleus is of special interest genetically because it

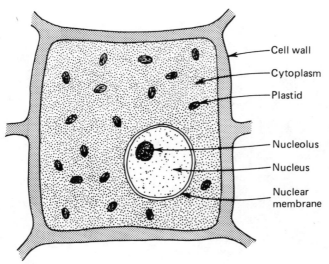

FIGURE 2.2

This schematic drawing of a cell indicates the integral parts of a
cell that consists of (1) a surrounding wall; (2) the cytoplasm; (3)
plastids, which are small bodies in the cytoplasm that aid cell
function and reproduction; (4) the nucleus, which contains most
of the material that affects inheritance; (5) a membrane around
the nucleus; and (6) a nucleolus, which apparently controls
cellular activity.

contains the *chromosomes,* which harbor most of the genetic information necessary for the growth and development of the tree. Chromosome numbers are
usually constant in number in every vegetative (somatic) cell of an organism, in all
populations of a species, and in most instances, in every individual of a species.
Chemically, chromosomes are composed of deoxyribonucleic acid (DNA), which
is the source of genetic information, and a protein sheath. Genes, which are the
functional units of inheritance, occur in a linear arrangement along the DNA
molecule in each chromosome. The location of a gene on a chromosome is said to
be a *gene locus.* Genes occurring on the same chromosomes are said to be *linked*
or to be in the same *linkage group.*

During most phases of a cell's growth and development, chromosomes exist as
long, threadlike structures that are difficult to observe except with the most
powerful microscopes. Just prior to cell division, chromosomes contract into
rodlike structures that are observable under light microscopes and are usually
countable. Species of trees differ widely in the number of chromosomes found in
their nuclei. For example, all normal members of the genus *Pinus* have 24
chromosomes, whereas redwood (*Sequoia sempervirens*) has the rare number of

66 chromosomes in its vegetative cells (Figure 2.3); Douglas fir (*Pseudotsuga menziesii*) has 26 chromosomes. Generally, the conifers have a few large chromosomes (although there are rare exceptions like redwood), whereas the angiosperms tend to have higher numbers of smaller chromosomes. As examples, American sycamore (*Platanus occidentalis*) has 42 chromosomes, whereas members of the *Eucalyptus* genus have a relatively low number of 20 to 22 somatic chromosomes. In some species, the number of chromosomes varies, depending on the population that is being sampled. In paper birch (*Betula papyrifera*), for example, chromosome numbers range from 56 in variety *cordifolia* to 84 in variety *occidentalis*. The chromosome numbers of most cultivated species are listed by Darlington and Janaki Ammal (1947); for conifers, by Koshoo (1961); and for hardwoods, by Wright (1976). The chromosome number for some selected tree species are shown in Table 2.1.

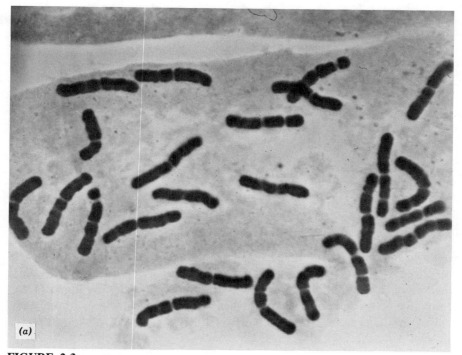

(a)

FIGURE 2.3

(a) Pines have 24 chromosomes as shown in the aceto-carmine preparations from the root tip of *P. taeda*. (b) (on next page) Occasionally, conifers are polyploid as shown by the 66 chromosomes from a cell of *Sequoia sempervirens*. (Photos courtesy of L. C. Saylor, North Carolina State University.)

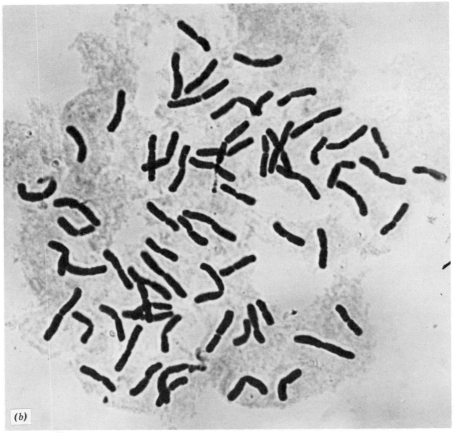

(b)

FIGURE 2.3 (*continued*)

Mitosis and Meiosis

Trees grow and reproduce by cell extension and cell division. When reproduction occurs through the normal sexual cycle, each individual begins as a single-celled zygote, which is formed in a process known as *fertilization* by the union of two reproductive cells (gametes), each of which has only half the usual number of chromosomes. One gamete is an egg cell from the female parent, and the other is a sperm cell from the male parent. Each gamete contributes one set of chromosomes and genes to the newly formed zygote. Since the zygote has two sets of chromosomes, it is said to be *diploid* (or 2n). The gametes are *haploid* (1n) because they each carry only one chromosome set, that is, one of each type of chromosome. The two chromosome sets in the zygote that carry the same genes are homologous and carry genes that affect the same function. Therefore, each gene locus is represented twice in the zygote, once on a chromosome from one parent and again in the homologous chromosome from the other parent.

TABLE 2.1
Varying Chromosome numbers of Trees.

Gymnosperms		Angiosperms	
Genus	**Somatic Chromosome No.**	**Genus**	**Somatic Chromosome No.**
Abies	24	Acadia	26 (52)
Araucaria	26	Acer	26 (and variable)
Cedrus	24	Albizzia	26 (and variable)
Chamaecyparis	22	Alnus	28 (and variable)
Cryptomeria	22	Betula	28 (2n)
Cunninghamia	22	Carya	32
Cupressus	22	Castanea	24
Cycas	22 (24)	Diospyros	30 (60)
Ginkgo	24	Eucalyptus	22 (24)
Juniperus	22 (44)	Fagus	24
Larix	24	Ficus	26

These are expressed either as the basic n number or the somatic number, which is usually double the n number. Some trees are polyploid and have more than $2n$ chromosomes. The gymnosperms often have small somatic numbers (22, 24, or 26,) whereas the angiosperms frequently have much higher numbers. Only a few of the forest tree genera can be shown. Chromosome values were obtained from a number of sources in the literature.

One of the unique properties of DNA is its ability to replicate itself. This is the key to the mechanism of inheritance, which allows a parent to pass along his or her genetic potential to his or her progeny. DNA also carries genetic information intact from one cell to the next as a tree grows.

Vegetative growth in a tree occurs throughout its lifetime. A mature tree contains billions of cells, all of which are direct descendants of the zygote formed at fertilization and each of which carries the same genetic information. Cells divide in all phases except the reproductive phase by means of a process called *mitosis*. Mitotic cells division begins with the replication of DNA, and therefore with a temporary doubling of chromosome numbers in the parent cell. The chromosomes then shorten into the rodlike structures described previously, and one copy of each chromosome moves to the opposite ends of the parent cell. The cell then builds a wall between them that results in two daughter cells, each with its own cell wall, cytoplasm, nucleus, and full complement of chromosomes. As trees grow and mature, numerous types of cells are formed, each with a special function and morphology, but the genetic information contained in the nucleus of each cell is identical to that in the original zygotic cell. The reason for cell and tissue differentiation is that certain sets of genes are activated in one type of cell, whereas other genes are active in other cell types.

Sexual reproduction is made possible through a process known as *meiosis*. Meiosis actually involves two cell divisions, and it results in the reduction of the chromosomes from the $2n$ number in the parent to $1n$ in the gametic (reproductive) cells (Figure 2.4). The meiotic process begins with DNA replication. Homologous chromosomes then pair. Duplication is evident at this point, and it is followed by an arrangement of the chromosomes in an orderly fashion in the center of the cell. During the time in which homologous chromosomes (*homologues*) are paired, an exchange of genetic material can occur through what is termed *crossing over*. When this happens, the chromosomes break in equivalent positions and exchange chromosome segments. This exchange of genetic material by means of crossing over is an important occurence because it serves to break up linked groups of genes, and this results in new combinations of genes and thus variation in the population. Following pairing and crossing over, one member of each homologous pair of chromosomes moves to opposite ends of the cell in a random manner so that each end contains mixtures of maternal and paternal chromosomes. A wall usually develops between the ends, and the first cell division then results in the formation of two daughter cells. Following this division, chromosomes line up again in the center of each of the two daughter cells. The two replicates of each chromosome that were formed at the beginning of meiosis then move to opposite ends of the cells, and cell division by means of a new wall occurs again. The result is that four gametic cells have formed, each with one set ($1n$) of chromosomes (see Figure 2.4). When the $1n$ gametes (usually from different parents) come together in fertilization, the resultant zygote will be diploid (n), and it will contain the same number of chromosomes as it parents but with a new combination of genes, half from one parent and half from the other.

Genes and Alleles—Gene Action

Genes can be thought of as the functional units of inheritance. Each gene may be represented in the population by one, two, or more alternate forms. Each of the alternate forms for a given gene is called an *allele*. Alleles carry the genetic potential for different expressions of the same trait. For example, an allele at a gene locus that influences leaf size (allele A) might code for long leaves, whereas another allele of the same gene (allele a) might code for shorter leaves. An analogy could be made between alleles and different kinds of pickup trucks. A number of companies manufacture pickup trucks. All are pickup trucks, and they have the same function, even though each one is a bit different in appearance. Similarly, all alleles for one gene locus serve the same function, but they may cause a different expression of the same trait.

Each gene locus is represented twice in a diploid cell, once on each of the two homologous chromosomes. Therefore, if more than one allele exists for a gene locus in the population, an individual tree may have two of the same alleles or two different alleles that govern the expression of the particular trait that is influenced by that locus. If we continue with the hypothetical example of leaf size, an individual could possess two alleles for large leaves (AA), which would make it *homozygous* for that gene locus; it would be referred to as a *homozygote*. Similarly, an individual could be homozygous for the allele that codes for smaller leaves (aa). Alternatively, the tree could be *heterozygous*, which means that it

Interphase		Nucleus appears homogeneous; chromosomes appear as long, loosely coiled threads; period of chromosome duplication.
Prophase I		Chromosomes shorten; homologous chromosomes come together and pair; duplication becomes evident.
Metaphase I	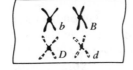	Chromosome pairs shift from haphazard arrangements to an orderly position in the equatorial region.
Anaphase I	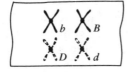	Pairs separate with one of each kind of chromosome moving to opposite ends of cell; distribution of members of any given pair is random.
Telophase I	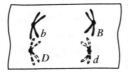	Cell wall is generally formed (an Interphase II stage may or may not occur).
Metaphase II	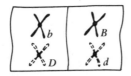	Chromosomes in each new cell again line up in equatorial region.
Anaphase II	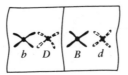	Sister chromatids separate and move to opposite ends of cells.
Telophase II	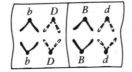	Cell walls form; each of the four cells (gametes) have half the original number of chromosomes with one of each kind.

FIGURE 2.4

Sexual reproduction takes place through the process called meiosis. It involves two cell divisions and results in a reduction of the chromosomes from the 2*n* number in the parent to 1*n* in the reproductive cell (gamete). See telophase II.

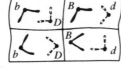

possesses the two different alleles (*A* and *a*) for leaf size. This type of individual is referred to as a *heterozygote*.

When individuals are homozygous for a trait, expression of that trait is set and straightforward. An individual with two alleles for large leaves (*AA*) will always produce large leaves if the environment is suitable. In other words, it will be a large-leaved phenotype. The phenotype of the heterozygous genotype *Aa*, however, is not so predictable. Its appearance will depend upon the interaction of the two alleles at the locus for leaf size. However, if one allele shows at least *partial dominance* over the other, the phenotype will be governed more by the dominant allele. When *complete dominance* is present, the expression of the trait is governed solely by the dominant allele. When allele *A* is completely dominant over allele *a*, then the *AA* and *Aa* genotypes will produce the same phenotypes. In the latter situation, allele *a* is said to be *recessive,* and its effects on the phenotype are observed only when the genotype is a homozygote for that allele. These various types of gene action are shown diagramatically in Figure 2.5.

Genotypes of progenies that are produced when two parents are crossed depend upon the type of gametes produced by each parent. An *AA* genotype would produce only *A* gametes, whereas an *aa* individual will produce only gametes with an *a* genetic constitution. Heterozygous genotypes (*Aa*) would

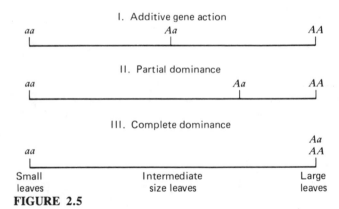

FIGURE 2.5

Effects of allelic interaction on phenotypic expression of the leaf size trait are shown when the trait is governed by a single gene locus. (I) Additive gene action. The phenotype of the heterozygote (*Aa*) is midway between the phenotypes of the two homozygotes (*AA* and *aa*). (II) Partial dominance. The phenotype of the heterozygote (*Aa*) is influenced more by one allele than the other, but both alleles have some effect on the phenotype. (III) Complete dominance. The phenotype of the heterozygote is the same as that of the homozygote for the dominant allele.

produce both *A* and *a* types of gametes. The array of genotypes that can be found in the progeny produced by a cross of two *Aa* individuals can be shown as follows:

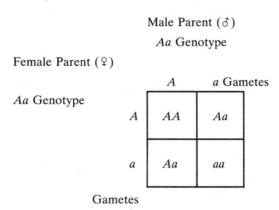

Male Parent (♂)

Aa Genotype

Female Parent (♀)

Aa Genotype

	A	*a* Gametes
A	*AA*	*Aa*
a	*Aa*	*aa*

Gametes

Genotypes of the progeny produced by this cross are shown in the box. They occur in the following ratio:

$$1AA:2\ Aa:1\ aa$$

Other possibilities for crossing two parents exist as follows:

$$AA \times aa \rightarrow \text{all } Aa \text{ progeny}$$
$$AA \times AA \rightarrow \text{all } AA \text{ progeny}$$
$$aa \times aa \rightarrow \text{all } aa \text{ progeny}$$
$$AA \times Aa \rightarrow 50\% \ AA \text{ progeny}, 50\% \ Aa \text{ progeny}$$
$$aa \times Aa \rightarrow 50\% \ aa \text{ progeny}, 50\% \ Aa \text{ progeny}$$

The expression of any particular trait may be governed by one, two, or many gene loci. In the hypothetical leaf size example, the leaf was influenced by only one gene locus. When one or only a few genes influence a trait, those genes are said to be *major genes* or to have major effects. However, a most important concept is that *most economic traits* in forest trees are *influenced by many genes,* each of which has a small effect on the trait. Therefore, tree breeders are rarely concerned with a particular gene locus, but, rather, they work with the understanding that the characteristic represents the culmination of the effects of many genes. Under this concept, each gene has only a small effect on the phenotype, and the effects of the environment are usually large. Special techniques have been developed by geneticists to deal with traits that are influenced by many genes. These are called *quantitative characteristics.* A discussion of quantitative characteristics is presented in detail in Chapter 4.

In subsequent sections of this chapter as well as in later chapters, there will be an emphasis on observing and measuring variation within and among forest trees. Traits will be described largely as they result from the effects of many genes on a tree's appearance, and rarely will reference be made to individual gene loci; sometimes the term *gene complex* is used. It is important to remember, though, that regardless of the number of loci influencing a particular trait, inheritance at any one locus is governed by the same principles that were presented previously for the hypothetical leaf size example.

CAUSES AND KINDS OF VARIABILITY

General

Basically, all differences among trees are the result of three things: the differing environments in which the trees are growing, the genetic differences among trees, and the interactions between the tree genotypes and the environments in which they grow. Some genetic variations are predictable and useful, whereas other types are random and are more difficult for the tree breeder to use.

In forest trees, a number of categories of variation exist that can be broadly grouped into species, geographic sources (provenances), stands, sites, individual trees, and the variability within individual trees (Zobel et al., 1960b). Everyone is aware of differences among species, and this need not be discussed further. However, knowledge of the relative importance of the other categories of variation is mandatory if a tree improvement program is to be successful. For example, it has been found for characteristics related to survival and adaptability (such as cold hardiness) that geographic variation is often the most important, whereas for economic characteristics, which are not so obviously related to fitness (such as stem straightness or wood specific gravity), individual tree variability is generally the greatest.

A key point, which is often overlooked, is that a study of variation of natural stands or plantations in which parentage is unknown *tells one nothing about the genetic control* of the characteristic involved. All one sees and measures in the forest is the *phenotype* of the tree. It is not possible to assess which portion of the differences among trees, stands, or provenances are genetically or environmentally controlled without actually making genetic tests. Inferences certainly can be made that are based on the magnitude and pattern of variation, but proof of genetic control requires genetic tests in which the parentage is known. The expensive and time-consuming activity of genetic testing is the key to a determination of the kind and control of variability that exists in a species, and thus to making continued and maximum progress in tree improvement activities.

Environmental Variation

Environmental variation is understood by most foresters, and its management is the basis of most silvicultural activities. Some environmental factors that influence tree growth can be controlled and manipulated, whereas others cannot. Things such as stocking levels and tree-to-tree competition can be handled by controlling plant spacing or by thinning. Within limits, nutrient deficiencies can be adjusted by fertilization, and soil moisture can be changed by drainage. Soil texture cannot generally be altered, but site preparation can change the soil structure to a considerable extent. Operations such as subsoiling are sometimes useful to create an environment for better root development and tree growth. Site preparation and herbicides are commonly used to reduce competition that, if left unchecked, will reduce or limit tree growth. Other environmental variables, such as rainfall, temperature, wind action, soil depth, aspect, and many other segments of a tree's environment, can be little influenced by humans, but all of these forces influence the phenotype of the tree. Variation among trees caused by environmental differences cannot be used in a breeding program and is often not even predictable. However, environmental forces are the greatest cause of variability in some characteristics, especially those related to growth. Form and quality may also be strongly affected by environmental differences, but, generally, the quality characteristics in forest trees tend to be more highly inherited and less influenced by the environment than are growth characteristics.

Although foresters generally cannot easily control the environment, it is frequently possible to develop strains of trees that will grow satisfactorily under adverse environmental conditions. In fact, about the only method the forester possesses to overcome adverse temperature, rainfall, wind action, pests, or other strong environmental influences is to create strains of trees through breeding or to use those found in nature that are more tolerant to the adverse factors.

Genetic Variability

Genetic variability is complex, but if its magnitude and type are known and if it is well used, genetic variation can be manipulated to obtain good gains in some tree characteristics. Genetic variation can be generally divided into *additive* and *nonadditive* components so that genetic variance = additive variance + nonadditive variance. In simple terms, the additive variance is due to the cumulative effects of alleles at all gene loci influencing a trait. Nonadditive genetic variance can be divided into two types. *Dominance* variance is due to interaction of specific alleles at a gene locus, whereas *epistasis* variance is due to interactions among gene loci. (These concepts will be developed more fully in Chapter 4.) For now, it is sufficient to know that the additive portion is the one of value in population improvement programs. Nonadditive variation can be exploited only by use of other, more specialized production programs that involve making specific crosses or using vegetative propagation for the commercial production of planting stock. In most tree improvement programs, the nonadditive types of genetic variability have generally been given little attention, because the additive portion of genetic variance is easier to utilize.

Most characteristics of economic importance in forest trees are under some degree of additive genetic control. This is fortunate because additive variance can be successfully used in simple selection systems such as those that are most suitable to new tree improvement programs. Characteristics such as wood specific gravity, bole straightness, and other quality characteristics of trees have stronger additive variance components than do growth characteristics. Although growth traits are controlled to some degree by additive genetic effects, they also have considerable nonadditive variance associated with them. Therefore, any selection program must include testing the progeny of selected phenotypes to determine the actual genetic worth of the tree. The response to selection of characteristics with considerable nonadditive variance, such as growth, is generally less satisfactory than for the quality characteristics that are usually under strong additive genetic control (Stonecypher et al., 1973).

Although not yet thoroughly quantified, it appears that most adaptability characteristics are strongly inherited in an additive manner. Thus, excellent gains have been made in developing strains of trees that will grow suitably on marginal or submarginal sites by selecting those individuals that grow best there and then using seed from them to reforest similar areas. Pest resistance involves both additive and nonadditive variance, depending on the pest and the tree species involved, but, generally, good gains are possible through selection programs that use the additive portion of the genetic variation.

There is little that the tree improver can do in the short term to improve the amount or kind of genetic variance available for use. The initial challenge to the tree improver is to determine the magnitude and kind of variance present from natural or unimproved populations and then to use it wisely. By better control of the environment, it is possible to capture and use more of the genetic variance. This results when intensive forest management is teamed with genetic manipulation of the trees.

Mating Systems

The type of crossing system within a species has a major effect upon the variation pattern. *Outcrossing* systems, which are common in most forest tree species, usually produce highly variable (heterozygous) genetic populations. In outcrossing systems, different genotypes cross successfully with each other, and little successful crossing takes place between male and female structures of the same plant, or with closely related individuals. When pollen from a tree or a given genotype pollinates flowers on itself, the term *selfing* is applied. This also applies to pollinations resulting among ramets of the same clone. Even though the ramets (grafts, rooted cuttings, etc.) are different plants, they are genetically identical. Thus, if pollen flies from one ramet of a particular clone to another ramet of the same clone, it is the same as pollination between flowers of the same tree. This concept is of key importance in clonal seed orchards, requiring extreme care so as not to establish ramets of the same clone too close together.

Most of this book deals with outcrossing mating systems; therefore, they will not be discussed further here. It is sufficient to state that the outcrossing breeding system maintains a high degree of genetic variation: Related matings reduce genetic diversity. Foresters are most fortunate in that most important tree species are outcrossers, making it easy to maintain the variation needed for simple selection and breeding programs. However, some related matings do occur in many forest trees, and they are discussed in greater detail below because of their great effect on genetic diversity (Orr-Ewing, 1976; Allen and Owens, 1972; Eldridge, 1977).

Vigor often is greatly reduced when related matings occur; it is a kind of reverse hybrid vigor. Related matings can occur within the same tree, among ramets of related clones, or among related trees. Relatedness is common in natural forest stands. It is for this reason that in most programs only one tree per stand is selected for use in operational seed orchards. Many degrees of relatedness can occur. Too little is known of the effects of sibling, cousin, or other types of related matings in forest trees, but their adverse effects are well recognized in agricultural crops. Numerous studies have been started to clarify the situation of relatedness of forest trees. Those that have been completed (Franklin, 1971; Orr-Ewing, 1976; Libby et al., 1981) all show that matings between close relatives have some adverse result and should be avoided. One of the most common effects is a reduction in seed set, although Andersson et al. (1974) found none when full- and half-sibs were mated. There is abundant knowledge about the adverse effects of selfing, the most severe form of related matings. Almost always, seed set and germination are reduced (Diekert, 1964). When viable seedlings are obtained, they often have reduced growth rates that can continue to advanced ages (Eriksson et al., 1973) (Figure 2.6).

The importance of related matings is increasing dramatically as forest tree breeding programs move into advanced generations. This will be discussed more

FIGURE 2.6

When selfing occurs, such adverse reactions as low-seed set or reduced growth rate often result. Shown are three rows of loblolly pine all having the same mother. The two outside rows resulted from pollinations by nonrelated fathers, whereas the center row was derived from pollinations using pollen from the "mother tree" itself; that is, it is a self.

fully in later chapters, but it is mentioned here in relation to the effects on variation patterns. Outstanding individual trees from good general combiners are found in every seed orchard with the result that many of the best progeny chosen for advanced generation breeding have one or both parents in common. Until the effects of related matings are known, the breeder cannot know in the advanced generation breeding program whether to use poorer, but nonrelated individuals in seed orchards or whether occasional full-sib or half-sib selections from a superoutstanding progeny can be used even though some inbreeding depression may result. The question is how much gain is sacrificed when sib relatives are allowed to mate in seed orchards.

Relatedness is common in natural populations, often occurring in neighborhood patterns (Coles and Fowler, 1976). It is particularly common in areas where abandoned fields have been populated from a very few parents that were growing along fences, near houses or roads or along areas too wet to be farmed (Figure 2.7). Most of the forests in the Piedmont area of the southern United States arose in this manner. Many have been logged two or three times, with the amount of relatedness increasing with each logging. In hardwoods that regenerate by root sprouts, such as the aspens (*Populus*) or sweetgums (*Liquidambar*), all individuals in a stand may have identical genotypes, the most extreme form of relatedness. One can assume that some degree of relatedness will exist among close neighbors within a natural stand of trees. Therefore, the only safe approach is to do as

FIGURE 2.7

Relatedness is common in natural stands of forest trees. As an example, old fields are frequently populated with trees from a very few residual parents along fences or around buildings. Among the forces that can change the variation within population is one called *genetic drift*. It can operate only in small populations. Whether it is important in forestry is debated, but the conditions required for a small population are common in stands arising from abandoned agricultural fields.

suggested in the subsequent chapter on seed orchards: Do not put more than one tree from a given stand into a single-seed orchard.

The extreme form of related matings (selfing) occurs in many species, both conifers and hardwoods (Barnes, 1964; Gabriel, 1967; Franklin, 1971; Orr-Ewing, 1976; and many others). Selfing can have a number of different results as has been indicated by the wide experience of the authors with *Pinus taeda,* and as others have found with other species like *Pinus radiata* (Bannister, 1965). Results from selfing can vary greatly by individual species and mother trees within a species. Some common results are the following:

1. No sound seed are formed.

2. Seed are formed but they will not germinate.

3. Seed germinate but the seedlings are abnormal and often will survive only a short time before they die.

4. Seedlings will survive, but they will be small, weak, often yellow in color, and grow slowly. Some of these can be recognized and removed in the nursery prior to field planting.

5. Seedlings grow more slowly than do normal trees, but they are not poor enough to be observed easily and culled in the nursery bed. This result is quite common and is most dangerous because the selfed trees will be outplanted and survive in plantations, but they will produce much less wood than would be obtained from outcrossed seedlings.

6. Seedlings grow as well, or sometimes even better, than outcrosses; selfed trees that grow as well as outcrosses are rare.

The use of inbred lines, later to be outcrossed, has been suggested as a breeding system. This method is widely used in agriculture where inbred lines are produced later to be outcrossed. The outcrossing restores the vigor lost when the inbred lines are developed and, what is most important, it results in populations that are very uniform. Because the number of selfs of forest trees that grow well enough so that they reproduce and can later be outcrossed is small, large numbers of genotypes are lost in a selfed breeding program resulting in a drastically reduced breeding populations.

In breeding in forest trees with its resulting reduction in variability is being studied in several species. Sniezko (1982), working with nearly 100 flowering selfs of loblolly pine, made crosses between inbreds and noninbreds, inbreds × inbreds, and he also selfed inbreds. He found great difficulty in obtaining a good enough seed set to allow for further tests. Working with foliage color in jack pine (*Pinus banksiana*), Rudolph (1980) found that selfing S_1 (S refers to generations of selfing) families increased homozygosity, resulting in smaller intrafamily variation. When selfs were outcrossed ($S_1 \times S_1$), he found heterosis and full recovery from the inbreeding depression. Although some of Rudolph's results were similar to those of Sniezko (who also reported that inbreeding depression in loblolly pine increases into the second generation), they differed in that Sniezko found that outcrosses among selfs failed to equal the performances between their parents. Thus, the hoped-for restored vigor from crossing selfs was not obtained.

Some species self poorly or not at all. Examples are sycamore and sweetgum (Boyce and Kaeiser, 1961; Schmitt and Perry, 1964; Beland and Jones, 1967). Other species, like *Pinus resinosa,* seem to be unaffected by selfing (Fowler, 1964). No general statement regarding the amount or ease of selfing can be made for forest trees, because they vary widely. Obviously, selfing is no problem in dioecious species.

Some researchers, such as Franklin (1969), have concluded that an inbreeding–outcrossing breeding system is not practical in a forest tree improvement program because of the low seed set of the inbreds, the low vigor of the inbreds, and the resultant drastic reduction in the size of the breeding population.

Polyploidy

The number of sets of chromosomes a tree has is termed *ploidy,* and it can greatly affect the variability pattern within and among species. Usually, each parent contributes one set of chromosomes ($1n$) to the progeny, so the tree has two sets of chromosomes and is called *diploid* ($2n$). Sometimes species, or individuals within species, have more than the usual sets of chromosomes; these are called *polyploids.* The subject of polyploids—their causes and results—are fascinating. [This has been well covered for forest trees in a chapter in Wright's (1976) book.] Polyploid breeding has been suggested as a tree improvement tool by persons such as Gustafsson (1960). Generally, success has been limited. A discussion of the kinds and causes of polyploids is not suitable for this beginning text, but it will be summarized as follows:

1. Polyploidy is more common in hardwoods than in conifers. The poplars (Zufa, 1969), alders (*Alnus*), birches (*Betula*), ashes, (*Fraxinus*) and numerous other groups have polyploid members; it is estimated that one third of the hardwoods are polyploid derivatives (Chiba, 1968). Polyploid hardwoods, such as the triploid aspens, have attracted considerable attention as fast growers, and research programs have been developing more triploids (Sarvas, 1958; Benson and Einspahr, 1967). Generally, the polyploid hardwoods are no better than the diploids, although there are some exceptions, such as in *Alnus* (Johnsson, 1950). Usually, an intensive search will locate diploids as good as the polyploids. The best-known polyploid conifer is redwood (*Sequoia sempervirens*), which is hexaploid; that is, it has 66 chromosomes rather than $2n = 22$ (see Figure 2.3). Other polyploid conifers have been reported as having outstanding properties, like the triploid larch (*Larix*), but generally, as in the pines, the polyploid conifers usually are deformed runts, with deformed roots (Hyun, 1954; Mergen, 1958).

2. Polyploidy can complicate a tree-breeding program, depending on its type and cause. Inheritance patterns can be very complex and difficult to manipulate. Creation of polyploids by controlled crosses is quite possible in some species, but often this does not produce viable plants in others. Development of haploid plants ($1n$) has been suggested as a breeding tool, but the success to date with most species of trees has been limited (Stettler, 1966).

3. The best way to use good polyploids is by means of vegetative propagation where sexual reproduction and the resultant genetic recombination are not required. In the plant kingdom, it has been observed that many polyploids easily propagate vegetatively and that some polyploid species seem to have lost the ability to propagate by seed.

4. At the present time, polyploid breeding is of limited value in forest tree improvement but as methods to develop them are improved, and especially as methods of vegetative propagation become more refined, polyploids will very likely play an increasing role in forest tree breeding.

Genotype × Environment Interaction

A condition that is of key importance in studying variation is commonly referred to as *genotype × environment interactions*. The term is used to describe the situation *where there is a change in the performance ranking of given genotypes when grown in different environments*. Such interaction must be known if maximum progress in breeding is to be obtained. Too frequently in tree improvement, a group of families are tested in a single environment, and their performance is then extrapolated to other environments, when in fact their relative performance might have been different when grown under other conditions. The trademark and challenge of forestry is the necessity to grow trees in a variety of environments, some of which are greatly different from others.

It is essential not to confuse true genotype × environment interactions as defined with a simple response to environmental differences, where the relative ranking among the families tested remains essentially the same even though the average performances of families in the different environments vary greatly. For example, it is usual to find that the average height of Family A might be 65 ft (19.5 m) in one area and only 55 ft (16.8 m) in another whereas Family B is 70 ft (21.1 m) in the first area and 62 ft (18.8 m) in the second. The differences in height between the same families in the two differing environments are only growth responses to different environments, but there is no meaningful genotype × environment interaction because the relative performances of families A and B do not change in the two environments. A common error is to refer to performance differences from site to site as genotype × environment interaction.

Strong genotype × environment interactions are more likely to occur when environments differ widely. As forestry operations become more intensive and as the productive forestland base decreases, there is need to establish plantations on sites that formerly were considered marginal or submarginal for satisfactory tree growth. This results in offsite planting in environments that are grossly different from those to which the species is best adapted. Even in normal forestry environments, peoples' activities and attempts to improve forestland productivity through intensive management usually create a different and quite often artificial habitat that is considerably different from the one in which the original forest was growing. A major concern now becoming generally recognized is how the best species, sources, or even the best individual genetic selections that have been obtained will perform when grown in the different environments (Squillace, 1970;

Matheson, 1974; Zobel and Kellison, 1978). Expressed another way, knowledge is needed about how stable a given genotype is when grown in quite different environments (Hanson, 1970).

A detailed treatment of genotype × environment interaction will be presented in Chapter 8.

VARIATION IN NATURAL STANDS

Introduction

Foresters are exceptionally fortunate to usually work with an undisturbed pool of high natural variability that has developed over eons (Perry, 1978). Intensive studies of variation within species are necessary for tree improvement programs to be successful. Many have already been made, such as on the loblolly pine by Thor (1961), on Virginia pine (*Pinus virginiana*) by Lamb (1973), Barnes et al. (1977) and others on *Pinus caribaea,* and by Yeatman (1967) on jack pine. (*f. banksiana*)

A determination of the amount and kind of variability present within a species is a large job and must be done carefully. There is no one "correct" way to assess the variability patterns within natural stands, but time and experience have shown that employment of a *nested sampling procedure* is very good.

The nested sampling method consists of determining variability within a species among varying groupings from large ones through ever smaller ones to individuals and within individuals. In forest trees it generally consists of determining the variation present in the following categories:

1. Geographic (provenance) variation

2. Sites within provenances

3. Stands within sites

4. Individual trees within stands

5. Within trees (when applicable)

A study of natural variation of a given species should first determine what geographic differences are present and then the variation that might be present within the lesser categories. A knowledge of where the bulk of the variation exists can indicate much about the development of a specific characteristic and how it might best be used in a breeding program. It must be emphasized that because the genetic and environmental components of variation cannot be separated by a study of natural stands, *no definitive conclusions about degree of inheritance of any characteristics can be made* from nested sampling studies.

Geographic (or Provenance) Variation

Geographic variation will be discussed in detail in Chapter 3; therefore, it will only be mentioned here. Genetically controlled geographic differences are often large, especially for traits related to adaptability. The differences can be of key importance, and the success of any tree improvement program depends upon knowledge and use of geographic variation within the species of interest. Geographic differences within species often are not easy to define, and boundaries usually are not clear-cut, unless there is a definite environmental separation. Therefore, the determination of what constitutes a geographic source is often one of judgment and opinion.

Variability among Sites

A given provenance can sometimes contain quite large differences related to differing sites; frequently, these are not genetically fixed and only represent the effects of varied environments on the growth and development of the forest. For example, trees of a given provenance that grow like shrubs on the sand dunes facing the sea where there are constant winds may grow normally when planted inland. Whether the scrubby sand dune trees are actually genetically different from the taller inland trees can only be determined through tests made on both sites.

In general, studies of pines have shown that site differences contribute only a small amount to the total genetic variation compared to other causes of genetic variation. However, site differences within a provenance are large and common enough so that they must be considered important when natural populations are sampled, even though they usually turn out to be environmentally rather than genetically, caused.

Differences among Stands within Sites

Sometimes stands of trees within a given site differ; usually the genetic differences are relatively small, but sometimes unexplained pockets of variation are found (Ledig and Fryer, 1971). This is especially true for form characteristics, which usually differ very little genetically for trees on any common site. Forces of natural selection that can cause differentiation from stand to stand are small. Sometimes stand-to-stand variation results from an accident of sampling caused by small population sizes. Usually, stand-to-stand differences within a site are of such little importance that they can be ignored, but this is not always true, especially when humans have intervened by changing populations through selective cutting, thinning, or other forest management activities. It is common, for example, to find stands of straight trees growing near stands of crooked trees, the difference having been caused by past pole and piling operations that left only crooked trees for parents in the exploited stand.

Tree Differences within a Stand

Individual trees of a species often vary a great deal from one another even when growing in the same stand. This is the major type of genetic variation the geneticist uses in a selection and breeding program. Many individual tree differences, especially quality traits such as form and adaptability, are strongly controlled genetically. It is amazing how two trees can be the same age, grow side by side with their roots intertwined, and still be so different in form, wood qualities, pest resistance, and even in growth patterns (Figure 2.8).

(a)

FIGURE 2.8

Genetic differences from tree to tree within a species can be large and are the major source of variation used by the tree breeder. Illustrated are two types of variation. (*a*) Individual differences are shown for progeny from select and wild standard pine in Finland. (*b*) The

(b)

(*continued*)

spruce variant shown for possible use as a parent tree is straight, narrow crowned, thin branched, and rapidly grown. (Photos courtesy of Lauri Kärki, Foundation for Forest Tree Breeding and Max Hagman, Forest Research Institute, Finland.)

In general, most economic characteristics of special value in forest trees have a large amount of individual tree variability that will be available to the tree breeder. This is true even for characteristics that are complex. An occasional tree species, such as *Pinus resinosa* (red pine), will show only a small amount of tree-to-tree genetic variation (Fowler and Morris, 1977), but these cases are the exception rather than the rule.

Variation within a Tree

Within a tree, variability can occur only for some characteristics. A tree is only so tall or has only one diameter at breast height (dbh); therefore, no within-tree variation for height or dbh can exist. But for other characteristics, considerable within-tree differences can occur. For example, wood specific gravity in the southern pines shows considerable differences, depending upon the height in the tree at which the wood sample is taken (Zobel et al., 1960a). Great within-tree differences occur for foliage characteristics, as, for example, in sun and shade leaves on the same tree (Figure 2.9). Within-tree variation is important where it occurs, because it influences the types of measurements and the positions where measurements must be taken to obtain statistically sound assessments of the real tree-to-tree differences.

Summary of Natural Variation

In general, provenance variation and tree-to-tree differences account for the bulk of the genetic variation found within a tree species growing in natural stands; these two variants may account for nearly 90% of all the variation observed. Wood specific gravity and cold resistance estimates for loblolly pine show the approximate distribution of the total variation (genetic plus environmental) for two very different types of characteristics.

Type of Variation	Wood Specific Gravity (%)	Cold Tolerance
Provenance (geographic)	15	70
Site	5	0
Stand	0	0
Tree to tree	70	30
Within tree	10	0

Because genetic tests have shown that for many characteristics much of the tree-to-tree variation is genetically controlled, good gains can be achieved from a selection and breeding program that concentrates on tree-to-tree differences.

It is essential to emphasize again that a study of variation in natural stands can give no proof of the intensity of genetic control of a characteristic because, in such a study, one cannot separate the effects of environment and genetics or their interactions. But the patterns of variation in natural stands can give good indications of possible genetic gains. To cite one example: Nothing was known about the inheritance of wood specific gravity of loblolly pine when intensive tree improvement programs were first started for the species. An intensive nested sampling study showed that the bulk of the variation in wood specific gravity was from tree to tree within a provenance. Despite some differences among geographic locations, nearly the same magnitude of individual tree variation was found at all geographic locations. This consistent individual tree variation in the north and south, on the coast and inland, and on sandy and on clay soils hinted

(a)

FIGURE 2.9

It is essential to recognize within-tree variation when sampling. There is no within-tree variation for characteristics like height, but there are great differences for things like leaves. Shown is the variation between sun (a) and shade leaves (b) (on next page) of *Quercus macrocarpa* from Michigan; both are taken from the same tree. (Photo courtesy of R. Braham, North Carolina State University, Raleigh, North Carolina.)

(b)

FIGURE 2.9 (continued)

that there was a broad and probably reasonably strong genetic control of wood specific gravity of individual trees. Based on this assumption, wood was included as a major characteristic in the operational loblolly pine tree improvement programs. It was relatively costly but, happily, later research showed that wood specific gravity was indeed strongly genetically controlled in such a manner that excellent gains could be made through selection.

DETECTING VARIATION IN PEDIGREE STANDS

Methods to assess variability in stands of trees with known and recorded pedigrees, such as half-sib or full-sib families, are essentially the same as for wild stands, but much more information is available from the analyses. In contrast to wild stands of unknown pedigree where only the total (or phenotypic) variation related to provenance, site, stand, and tree can be determined, one can assess the relative importance and contribution of the environmental and of the genetic variance in pedigree stands. From this information, it is then possible to obtain an assessment of the genetic value of the parents involved.

If the pedigree includes information on both the mother and father trees, it is then possible to divide the genetic variability into its component parts of additive and nonadditive variance and even to assess different types of nonadditive variance. Details of this breakdown become rather complex statistically, and they are handled in the special field called *quantitative genetics*. A later chapter in this book will deal with quantitative genetics in a simplified manner; more exhaustive treatments are covered by such persons as Falconer (1960) and Namkoong (1979). Calculations dealing with quantitative genetics in forest trees have been made by several authors; one of the better of these studies is by Stonecypher et al. (1973) for loblolly pine.

The question is often raised whether different provenances within a species can be treated as having a pedigree that can be assessed in a way that is similar to families in the calculation of variances. This is sometimes done, but it requires some differences in the interpretation and use of the values obtained.

In summary, phenotypic variation can be divided into its genetic and environmental components only when pedigree stands are available. The degree of separation of the genetic variation depends on the mating design used. This will be discussed in more detail in Chapter 8.

MAINTENANCE AND USE OF VARIATION

General

Although the subject will be dealt with in later chapters, it should be mentioned here that one absolute necessity in a tree improvement program is to maintain and increase genetic variability within the forest tree populations being used. Unless properly applied, an intensive selection program will reduce variability for the characteristics involved. Indeed, the objective of genetic manipulations in forestry is to produce more quickly the desired products with greater uniformity. All successful breeding programs will change gene frequencies; if this does not happen, the program will fail.

Most forest tree species contain great variability for such economically important characteristics as tree straightness or wood specific gravity, for such adaptability as tolerance to cold or drought, and for resistance to diseases or insects and for growth (Figure 2.10). As clearly stated previously, a major strength of tree improvement is that most characteristics of value to the tree breeder are complex and are essentially inherited independently, so it is possible to "tailor make" trees with the desired combination of characteristics. But continued development in

FIGURE 2.10

Shown is a mutant form of white pine; compare it with the size and characteristics of normal white pine of the same age growing adjacent to it. Mutants sometimes can have great value. The pine here would seem excellent for a Christmas tree, but it would have to be propagated vegetatively because most mutants do not produce viable seed.

later generations is not possible unless the variability in the breeding population is maintained, and this is no easy job. Maintaining and even increasing variability is a key objective of the developmental, or research, phase of a tree improvement program.

Forces That Shape Genetic Variation

All the variation in wild stands has occurred as the result of natural forces. It is available for use by the forester if it can be recognized and packaged into individual trees in the form of improved genotypes. The ultimate source of all variability is mutations, but other strong forces are at work to either increase or decrease variation within a stand. In addition to the variability found in natural stands, humans can interfere and help create either new variability or bring together genotypes to create new and useful genetic combinations.

Although variation in our forests today is primarily the result of natural forces over which the forester has little control, it is essential that these forces are understood. They determine the amount and kind of genetic variation found among and within populations. These forces form the basis for the specialized area of *speciation* and *evolution,* subjects on which many books have been written. [A few of the most lucid and easily understood are those by Stebbins (1950, 1977) and Grant (1975).]

In the most simplified terms, variability in natural stands is caused by four main forces, two that increase variation and two that decrease it. The forces in nature working to increase variation are *mutation* and *gene flow;* those that reduce it are *natural selection* and *genetic drift.* The forces at work are illustrated schematically in Figure 2.11.

Mutations Mutations are the ultimate source of variation. A *mutation* is a heritable change in the genetic constitution of an organism, usually at the level of a gene. Since the total genetic makeup of a tree (its *genotype*) is determined by the action and interactions of thousands of genic and allelic combinations, mutations can occur somewhere in an organism with considerable frequency, but this will not happen often for any specific gene or gene complex or for a given tree characteristic. Although talking about frequency of mutations really amounts to nothing more than an academic exercise, because they vary greatly by species and loci within species, a general figure often quoted is 1 in 10,000 to 1 in 100,000 genes. When one considers that trees have tens of thousands of genes, it is not unusual for a single tree to have several mutations. Most are recessive and have little effect on the phenotype of the tree.

Mutations occur more or less randomly. Most mutations are deleterious, and many are eliminated from the population. Through time, forces of evolution have made most populations well adapted to their environments, with genes and gene complexes in the population that are the most suitable for growth and reproduction. The chance that a random mutation would improve such a well-coordinated system is very small.

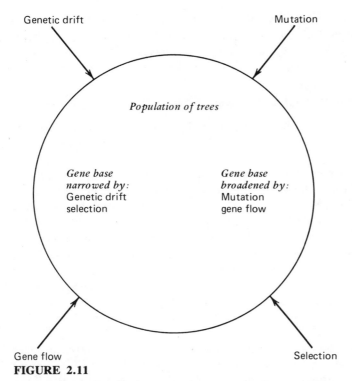

Genetic drift

Mutation

Population of trees

*Gene base
narrowed by:*
Genetic drift
selection

*Gene base
broadened by:*
Mutation
gene flow

Gene flow

Selection

FIGURE 2.11

There are a number of forces that alter the variation pattern
within a population. It is increased by mutation and gene flow
and reduced by natural selection and genetic drift. These are
indicated by the schematic drawing.

Some mutations are retained in the population, even though they are deleterious, because they are of the recessive type and are not recognizable or detectable
unless in the homozygous form. The value of this kind of mutation may not be
known. It may only become significant at a much later date when different forces
affect the environment and the formerly useless mutation may actually make the
tree more fit to grow and/or reproduce. These recessive or neutral mutations do
not normally disrupt an integrated genetic system like a dominant one would.
Therefore, they can be carried along in the population for many generations.
Although mutations may be rare and small, they will produce variation that can
possibly make a tree more adaptable as environments change.

Gene Flow (Gene Migration)   The other action within a population that increases
variation is called *gene flow;* it is the migration of alleles from one population or
species into another where they may be absent or at a different frequency. Gene

flow can result from several causes, but the most common is movement of pollen or seed. Occasionally, gene flow or gene transfer takes place on the species level through a process called *introgression* that sometimes occurs between two species after hybridization (Anderson, 1949). The hybridization brings together two dissimilar parental genetic complexes, thus creating a "new" genotype. This new organism may not be well adapted to compete with the parental species, but sometimes it will find an environmental "niche" that is especially suitable and that enables the new genotype to grow and reproduce. Because the new genotype is rare, or one of a kind, it will usually exchange genes with one of the parents to produce a backcross to one of the parental species. After this process occurs several times, the resulting population of trees can look very similar to the original parent species, although they will contain some genes or gene complexes that have been transferred from the one parental species to the other.

We can utilize the concept of gene flow in breeding programs (Sluder, 1969). For example, *Pinus Jeffreyi* is a well-formed species that is susceptible to the pine reproduction weevil. *Pinus Coulteri,* on the other hand, has poorer form but because of its thicker bark, it is resistant to the weevil. If we create a *P. Coulteri* × *P. Jeffreyi* hybrid and then backcross to *P. Jeffreyi* several times and select the most desired individuals, a tree that is similar to Jeffrey pine can be produced that still carries considerable weevil resistance. The gene complex for thicker bark would have been transferred from Coulter to Jeffrey pine.

Gene flow can be important in natural populations, and will cause distinct changes in patterns of variation. Gene flow in conjunction with recombination is the immediate source of increased variation patterns in many populations, even though the ultimate source of variation was mutation.

Selection *Natural selection* is a strong force that usually reduces variability (Mason and Langenheim, 1961). Because it determines which trees will grow and reproduce, it has a directional (nonrandom) effect on the genetic makeup of trees in a population. Natural selection favors the fittest; that is, those trees with gene combinations that make them best suited to grow and reproduce in a given environment. Natural selection preserves and results in an increase in the number of those genotypes most suited to a specific environment. Although normally a process that reduces variability, natural selection can actually preserve or increase variation if selection favors the heterozygotes. Whether natural selection works to favor heterozygotes (which would maintain variability) or homozygotes (which would decrease variability) is currently a topic of considerable debate (see, for example, Lewinton, 1974), although most geneticists think that selection works to decrease variation by favoring the best alleles in a homozygous condition.

It is often difficult to assess the effects of selection because so many factors are involved in determining which tree will be best fitted to grow and reproduce. Each fitness characteristic has its own selective value, and the adaptations created by one factor may either positively or adversely affect others. In general, natural selection is considered to be a powerful force to reduce variability within a population in a given direction.

Genetic Drift *Genetic drift* is a complex mechanism that operates through chance fluctuations (not fluctuations caused by selection pressures) in allele frequencies within a population. It is essentially a sampling phenomenon in which the gene frequencies in the progeny populations deviate by chance from those found in the parent populations. Such populations are almost always small and have a tendency toward fixation or loss of an allele that affects a characteristic. Thus, genetic drift tends toward reducing variation by fixing or losing alleles.

Genetic drift is nondirectional and tends to create "disorder." Which genes or alleles are fixed or lost is strictly a matter of chance. Although the theory of genetic drift is plausible, its operation is difficult to prove with long-lived trees, and many reasons can be cited why it cannot be a factor in the natural variation of forest trees. But despite these objections, some natural stands show variation patterns that could be the result of genetic drift if it was operating. Genetic drift is usually of consequence in small breeding populations of perhaps 25 or fewer individuals, a situation that frequently occurs in forestry due to natural catastrophies or man's influence (see Figure 2.7).

VARIATION CAUSED BY MAN

In addition to the normal variation patterns that occur in natural populations, many changes in the variation pattern in forest trees can be caused by human beings. Such things as dysgenic selection, where the best trees are removed and the poor trees are left to reproduce, or a selection method in which only the best are left, will ultimately cause a shift in gene frequencies, and thus in variation patterns. Our actions can cause a very rapid change in variability when we apply intensive selection and breeding practices.

Because the major objective of tree breeding is to change the percentage of certain characteristics in a desired direction within a population, the bulk of this book deals with variation caused by human beings or by our activities to change variation. As breeding programs progress, it will be essential for the tree improver to purposely increase variability. There are a number of options that can be followed to do this when natural variability becomes too limited for a breeding program. The first is to make sure that all variability within a species is known. Wide crosses may be made within species to bring together genotypes that could never occur under natural conditions. Interspecific hybrids and back crosses can be produced to develop new genetic combinations. Finally, programs to increase variation by means of mutations may ultimately be possible. The objective of all the above options is to assure that enough genetic variation exists so that productive breeding programs can be pursued.

The key point to remember is that our activities can cause large changes in variance relatively rapidly, either in a positive or in a negative way. Thus, it is possible through our efforts to make the large and quick genetic gains that are needed to keep tree improvement programs solid.

LITERATURE CITED

Allen, G. S., and Owens, J. N. 1972. "The Life History of Douglas-Fir." Canadian Forest Service, Ottawa Cat. No. Fo. 42-4972.

Anderson, E. 1949. *Introgressive Hybridization.* John Wiley & Sons, New York.

Andersson, E., Jansson, R., and Lindgren, D. 1974. Some results from second generation crossings involving inbreeding in Norway spruce (*P. abies*). *Sil. Gen.* **23**(1–3):34–43.

Antonovics, J. 1971. The effects of a heterogeneous environment on the genetics of natural populations. *Am. Sci.* **59**(5):593–595.

Bannister, M. H. 1965. "Variation in the Breeding System of *Pinus radiata.*" New Zealand Forest Service Report No. 145. *In The Genetics of Colonizing Species,* Asilomar Symposium, Pacific Grove, Calif., pp. 353–374.

Barnes, B. V. 1964. "Self- and Cross-Pollination of Western White Pine: A Comparison of the Height Growth of Progeny." U.S. Forest Service Research Note INT-22.

Barnes, R. D., Woodend, J. J., Schweppenhauser, M. A., and Mullen, L. J. 1977. Variation in diameter growth and wood density in six-year-old provenance trials of *Pinus caribaea* on five sites in Rhodesia. *Sil. Gen.* **26**(5–6):163–167.

Beland, J. W., and Jones, L. 1967. "Self-Incompatability in Sycamores." Proc. 9th Conf. For. Tree Impr., Knoxville, Tenn., pp. 56–58.

Benson, M. K., and Einspahr, D. W. 1967. Early growth of diploid, triploid and tetraploid hybrid aspen. *For. Sci.* **13**(2):150–155.

Boyce, S., and Kaeiser, M. 1961. "Why Yellow Poplar Seeds Have Low Viability." USDA, Central States Forestry Experiment Station Technical Paper 186.

Chiba, S. 1968. "Studies on Tree Improvement by Means of Artificial Hybridization and Polyploidy in *Alnus* and *Populas* Species." Bull. Oji. Inst. For. Tree Impr., Hokkaido, Japan.

Coles, J. F., and Fowler, D. P. 1976. Inbreeding in neighboring trees in two white spruce populations. *Sil. Gen.* **25**(1):29–34.

Darlington, C. D., and Janaki Ammal, E. K. 1955. *Chromosome Atlas of Flowering Plants.* George Allen & Unwin, Ltd., London, England.

Diekert, H. 1964. Einige untersuchungen zur selbststerilität und inzucht bei fichte und larche [Some investigations on self sterility and inbreeding in spruce and larch]. *Sil. Gen.* **13**(3):77–86.

Eldridge, K. G. 1977. "Genetic Improvement of Eucalypts." 3rd World Cons. For. Tree Breed., Canberra, Australia.

Eriksson, G., Schelander, B., and Åkebrand, V. 1973. Inbreeding depression in an experimental plantation of *Picea abies*. *Hereditas* **73**:185–194.

Falconer, D. S. 1960. *Introduction to Quantitative Genetics*. Ronald Press, New York.

Franklin, E. C. 1969. "Inbreeding as a Means of Genetic Improvement of Loblolly Pine." Proc. 10th South. Conf. For. Tree Impr., Houston, Tex., pp. 107–115.

Franklin, E. C. 1971. Estimates of frequency of natural selfing and of inbreeding coefficients in loblolly pine. *Sil. Gen.* **20**:(5–6):141, 224.

Fowler, D. P. 1964. Effects of inbreeding in red pine, *Pinus resinosa. Sil. Gen.* **13**(6):170–177.

Fowler, D. P., and Morris, R. W. 1977. Genetic diversity in red pine; evidence for low genetic heterozygosity. *Can. Jour. For. Res.* **7**(2):343–347.

Gabriel, W. J. 1967. Reproductive behavior in sugar maple; self-compatibility, cross-compatibility, agamospermy and agamocarpy. *Sil. Gen.* **16**(5–6): 165–168.

Gardner, E. J. and Snustad, D. P. *Principles of Genetics,* 7th ed. John Wiley & Sons, N.Y. 1984.

Grant, V. 1975. *Genetics of Flowering Plants*. Columbia University Press, New York.

Gustafsson, Å. 1960. "Polyploidy and Mutagenesis in Forest Tree Breeding." Proc. 5th World For. Conf., Vol. 2, pp. 793–805.

Hamerick, J. L., Metton, J. B., and Linhart, Y. B. 1979. "Levels of Genetic Variation in Trees: Influence of Life History Characteristics." Proc. Symp. on Isozymes of N. Amer. For. Trees, Berkeley, Calif., pp. 35–41.

Hanson, W. 1970. "Genotypic Stability." 2nd Mtg., Work. Group on Quant. Gen. IUFRO, Sect. 22, Raleigh, N.C., pp. 37–48.

Hyun, S. K. 1954. Induction of polyploidy in pines by means of colchicine treatment. *Teit. Forestgen. Forstpflan* 3(2)25–33.

Johnsson, H. 1950. On the C_0 and C_1 generations in *Alnus glutinosa. Hereditas* **36**:205–219.

Khoshoo, T. N. 1961. Chromosome numbers in gymnosperms. *Sil. Gen.* **10**(1): 1–9.

Lamb, A. F. A. 1973. *Pinus caribaea,* Vol. I, *Fast Growing Timber Trees of the Lowland Tropics,* Oxford University Press, Oxford.

Ledig, F. T., and Fryer, J. H. 1971. A pocket of variability in *Pinus rigida. Evolution* **26**(2):259–266.

Lewinton, R. C. 1974. *The Genetic Basis of Evolutionary Change*. Columbia University Press, New York.

Libby, W. J., McCutchen, B. G., and Millar, C. I. 1981. Inbreeding depression in selfs of redwood *Sil. Gen.* **30**(1):15–24.

Mason, H. L., and Langenheim, J. H. 1961. Natural selection as an ecological concept. *Ecology* **42**(1):158–165.

Matheson, A. 1974. "Genotype–Environment Interactions, and Regions for Breeding." 4th Mtg., Res. Comm. of the Australian For. Council, Res. Working Group No. 1, Gambier, South Australia.

Mergen, F. 1958. Natural polyploidy in slash pine. *For. Sci.* **4**(4):283–295.

Namkoong, G. 1979. "Introduction to Quantitative Genetics in Forestry," Tech. Bull. No. 1588, U.S. Forest Service.

Nienstaedt, H. 1975. "Adaptive Variation-Manifestations in Tree Species and Uses in Forest Management and Tree Improvement." Proc. 15th Can. Tree Impr. Assoc., Part 2, pp. 11–23.

Orr-Ewing, A. L. 1976. Inbreeding Douglas fir to the S₃ generation. *Sil. Gen.* **25**(5–6):179–183.

Perry, D. A. 1978. "Variation between and within Tree Species." IUFRO, Proc. Ecology of Even-Aged Forest Plantations, pp. 71–98.

Rudolph, T. D. 1980. Autumn foliage color variation among inbred Jack pine families. *Sil. Gen.* **29**(5–6):177–183.

Sarvas, R. 1958. Kaksi Triploidista Haapaa Ja Koivia (two triploid aspens and two triploid birches). *Commun. Inst. Forest. Fenn.* **49**(7):1–25.

Schmitt, D., and Perry, T. O. 1964. Self-sterility in sweetgum. *For. Sci.* **10**(3):302–305.

Sluder, E. R. 1969. "Gene Flow Patterns in Forest Tree Species and Implications for Tree Breeding." 2nd World Consul. on For. Tree Breed., Washington, D.C., pp. 7–16.

Sniezko, R. 1982. "Inbreeding in Loblolly Pine." Ph.D. thesis, North Carolina State University, Raleigh.

Squillace, A. 1970. "Genotype–Environment Interactions in Forest Trees." 2nd Mtg., Working Group on Quant. Gen. IUFRO, Sect. 22, Raleigh, N.C., pp. 49–61.

Srb, A. M., Owen, R. D., and Edgar, R. S. 1965. *General Genetics*. W. H. Freeman, San Francisco.

Stebbins, G. L. 1950. *Variation and Evolution in Plants*. Columbia University Press, New York:

Stebbins, G. L. 1977. *Processes of Organic Evolution,* 3rd ed. Prentice-Hall, Englewood Cliffs, N.J.

Stettler, R. F. 1966. "The Potential Role of Haploid Sporophytes in Forest Genetics Research." Sexto Congreso Forestal Mundial, Madrid, Spain.

Stonecypher, R. W., Zobel, B. J., and Blair, R. L. 1973. "Inheritance Patterns of Loblolly Pine from Nonselected Natural Populations." Agricultural Experimental Station Technical Bulletin No. 220, North Carolina State University, Raleigh.

Strickberger, M. W. 1976. *Genetics*. Macmillan, New York.

Thor, E. 1961. "Variation Patterns in Natural Stands of Loblolly Pine. 6th South. Conf. For. Tree Impr., Gainesville, Fl. pp. 25–44.

Wright, J. W. 1976. *Introduction to Forest Genetics*. Academic Press, New York.

Yeatman, C W. 1967. Biogeography of jack pine. *Can. Jour. Bot.* **45**:2201–2211.

Zobel, B., Henson, F., and Webb, C. 1960a. Estimates of certain wood properties of loblolly and slash pine trees from breast-height sampling. *For. Sci.* **6**(2):155–162.

Zobel, B. J., Thorbjornsen, E., and Henson, F. 1960b. Geographic site and individual tree variation in wood properties of loblolly pine. *Sil. Gen.* **9**(6):149–158.

Zobel, B. J., and Kellison, R. C. 1978. "The Importance of Genotype × Environment Interaction in Forest Management." 8th World For. Cong., Jakarta, Indonesia.

Zufa, L. 1969. "Polyploidy Induction in Poplars." Proc. 11th Meet. Comm. For. Tree Breed. in Canada, Part 2, pp. 169–174.

CHAPTER 3

Provenance, Seed Source, and Exotics

THE IMPORTANCE OF SOURCE OF
SEED IN TREE IMPROVEMENT PROGRAMS

Success in the establishment and productivity of forest tree plantations is determined largely by the species used and the source of seed within species (Larsen, 1954; Callaham, 1964; Lacaze, 1978). The need to use the best-adapted source of seed was recognized in the early years as being important by such persons as Tozawa (1924), Wakeley (1954), and Langlet (1967). No matter how sophisticated the breeding techniques, the *largest, cheapest, and fastest gains in most forest tree improvement programs can be made by assuring the use of the proper species and seed sources within species* (Figure 3.1). This chapter will deal with the use and manipulation of seed sources within species, especially as they are used for planting exotics.

The best information available in the tree improvement field relates to seed sources. Many studies on this subject were started a number of years ago. In some species, much is now known about which are poor and which are good seed sources. Much effort, energy, cost, and thought have been expended on seed source studies. The most successful tree improvement programs are those in which the proper seed sources and provenances are used. The losses from using the wrong source can be great and even disastrous.

Many studies on provenance and seed sources have been made or are currently underway (Wright and Baldwin, 1957; Wakeley and Bercaw, 1965; Wells and Wakeley, 1970; Burley and Nikles, 1973a; Lacaze, 1977). In some countries, almost all the tree improvement effort has been expended on determining the best species and sources within species. However, even with the amount of effort already expended, ignorance about the best sources to use is still widespread for many species. When source information is available, the *reliability* and *availability* of the desired source of seed needs to be determined. As Anderson (1966) put it, "A reliable provenance would be one producing a decent forest crop with 90% probability rather than an outstanding crop 50% of the time. An available provenance is one from which seed are readily and economically available as needed."

The literature on exotics and source of seed is voluminous, and only a few references can be cited in this book. Summary publications such as those by Langlet (1938), Burley and Nikles (1972, 1973b), Dorman (1975), Nikles et al. (1978), and Persson (1980) list many study results and describe the techniques used in provenance breeding and testing. Many publications not listed include different species throughout the world.

A book could be written outlining the history and development of provenance activities in the European countries, Australia, South Africa, and numerous other areas. However, it would serve no useful purpose to discuss all of the studies in detail. Lessons have been learned about how difficult it is to define seed or planting zones in areas with complex physiographies. Some general rules on what should and should not be done have been developed. For example, the need for representative sampling to obtain seed to test sources properly is no longer

FIGURE 3.1

Attention to seed source is essential for the best success in forestry. The largest and quickest gains possible in tree improvement can be obtained from use of the proper source. The difference by source is illustrated for a 2-year-old loblolly pine in Zimbabwe (Rhodesia). The row behind the man is an inland source of *P. taeda,* and the large row in front of the man is a southern coastal plain source.

questioned. Another major finding is that no single rule can be applied to all species on all areas.

One example of source studies that we know best is the southwide seed source study of the four major pine species in the southern United States. Based on European results and experience, limited seed source studies were begun in the southern United States shortly after the turn of the century. The first results on *Pinus taeda,* reported by Wakeley (1954), were so striking that much larger assessments were then initiated. Alerted to the importance of seed source, foresters quit shipping seed indiscriminately for long distances and made it a rule to obtain seed from as close to the intended planting site as possible. Several major tree improvement programs were organized around 1950, and use of the proper seed source was a major basis for their development (Figure 3.2).

One result of the larger studies showed that in the southern part of the area, some outside sources performed better in growth characteristics than did the local source (Wells and Wakeley, 1966). An important finding was that loblolly pine from part of its natural range was more resistant to fusiform rust (*Cronartium quercum f. sp. fusiforme*) than were other species. This information is now being utilized in areas with a high rust potential up to 1000 mi (1600 km) east of the indigenous range of the resistant material (Wells, 1971). In the northern part of its range, the local sources of loblolly pine were found to be best, and tree improvement programs rely on this information. The idea that the coastal sources grew more rapidly than those from the interior Piedmont was confirmed, and now this information is utilized in large planting programs. The general rule is to use the local seed source until tests have shown the utility and suitability and advantage of nonlocal sources.

FIGURE 3.2

The large "southwide seed-source study" in the southern United States has produced some outstanding results and gives proof of the value of using the proper seed source. Shown is one of the plantings in Arkansas. The larger group of 25-year-old trees on the right are from the fast-growing *P. taeda* source from coastal South Carolina; the smaller group of trees to the left are of Oklahoma origin. There was more than 2 m difference in height that was accompanied by dramatic diameter differences. (Photo courtesy of O. O. Wells, U.S. Forest Service, Gulfport, Mississippi).

Decisions about which is the best source should not be made until extensive testing has been carried out for the greater part of the rotation age. The gains to be achieved by moving sources must be weighed against the risks involved, and this requires a period of testing that will yield reliable results. One of the most common problems related to provenance testing is to have a good initial performance that is followed by a later slowdown, lack of vigor, or even death. Once sufficient information is available, breeding zones can be identified within which tree improvement programs should operate.

In no area of forestry is the need for international cooperation stronger than in provenance testing. In fact, this has occurred on a very wide scale. Some very large international seed source tests have been made in such species as *Pinus silvestris, P. caribaea, Pseudotsuga menziesii, Picea abies, Picea sitkensis, Populus species, Tectona grandis,* the *Eucalyptus* species, and many others. Some of these studies are huge, containing hundreds of sources. Many of the studies are now old enough so that reliable results are available.

The very extensive and expensive seed source studies have been made possible by the cooperation among governments and industries. The international organizations like IUFRO (International Union of Forest Research Organizations) and FAO of the United Nations have been especially helpful. Specific groups like the CFI (Commonwealth Forestry Institute) in Oxford, England, have been instrumental in organizing numerous large-scale tests. Many governmental organizations, such as Queensland, Australia, have spearheaded international studies. Coalitions of industries and governments, like the CAMCORE Cooperative (Central America and Mexico Coniferous Resources Cooperative) have had a major influence on international seed collection and testing.

Although more work is always needed, activities in provenance testing have been most satisfying and the results most rewarding. For any tree improvement program, it is essential to obtain information about the best source of seed as soon as possible. Genetic gains from conventional tree breeding are determined or restricted by the quality of the geographic race or seed source used (Squillace, 1966). The ideal is to undertake an intensive tree improvement program only after the best geographic source is known (see Figure 3.2). In practice, this is often not possible, but good gains can still be made if proper land race development is followed, even though the original provenance used may be suboptimal.

TERMS RELATED TO SOURCE OF SEED

Terms such as *adapted, exotic, provenance, geographic source, geographic race, seed source,* and *land race* are standard for the tree improver. They are now coming to be used routinely in forestry circles, so their meanings must be clearly understood. The following definitions and illustrations are intended to simplify the very confused group of terms that have been related to exotics and seed sources.

Adapted   The term *adapted* refers to how well trees are physiologically suited for high survival, good growth, and resistance to pests and adverse environments. For exotics, it refers to how well the trees will perform in their new environments. These may differ greatly from those found in the indigenous range of the species or seed source. *Adaptation* commonly refers to the tree's performance over a full rotation in the new environment.

Exotic   The term *exotic* can be defined in several ways, but for the sake of simplicity, the following is useful: "An exotic forest tree is one grown outside its natural range." For example, ponderosa pine (*Pinus ponderosa*) from the western United States is an exotic when grown in the eastern United States; *Eucalyptus* and radiata pine are exotics when grown in Chile. Some persons restrict the term *exotic* to trees grown outside certain geographic or governmental boundaries, but the preferred usage is as shown here.

In the previous chapter, the major types of natural variation described for forest trees were those related to provenance, geographic source, or geographic race. These terms are similar, and they *are* used interchangeably and usually mean the same thing. A fourth term, *seed source,* appears to be similar but has an important and different meaning that must be recognized and should not be used synonymously with the other three.

1.   **Provenance, geographic source, or geographic race**   These denote the original geographic area from which seed or other propagules were obtained (Callaham, 1964; Jones and Burley, 1973). If, for example, seed of *Eucalyptus grandis* were obtained from Coff's Harbour, New South Wales, Australia, and grown in Zimbabwe, they would be classified as the Coff's Harbour provenance (or geographic source or geographic race).

2.   **Seed source**   If seed from the trees grown in Zimbabwe were harvested and planted in Brazil, they would be referred to as the Zimbabwe seed source and the Coff's Harbour provenance. The term *origin* is used by Barner (1966) in the same way as *seed source.* When the difference between provenance and seed source is not recognized, large and costly planting errors can be made. *Seed source* will be used very specifically throughout this book, whereas provenance, geographic source, and geographic race will be used interchangeably.

Destructions of source of seed that are finer than provenance and seed source are commonly employed. There is often a perplexing proliferation of terms such as *altitudinal race, climatic race, physiological race, physiographic race, edaphic race,* and many others. All of these are used in the literature to describe within-species variation and are referred to as *races.* Not only are these terms confusing in themselves, but they are often further mixed with such words as *variety, strain, ecotype,* and *cline.* What follows is an attempt to recognize and to simplify terms that are encountered.

Racial Variation

As mentioned in the discussion on provenance, geographic source and geographic race are synonymous. Barner (1966) discusses the concept of race; he feels the term *race* should be used only when natural populations are described. Races develop in response to evolutionary forces, such as natural selection, that vary in different parts of the natural range of a species. Populations thus developed will show large-to-small differences when grown together in a uniform environment. This is racial variation. Since provenance, geographic source, and geographic race have the same definition, the comprehensive descriptions of races in forest trees prepared by Wakeley[1] are most useful. Some of his descriptions are paraphrased as follows.

1. A geographic race is a subdivision of a species, differing in ways that can be demonstrated by observation and experiment from another race or races within the same species.
2. A geographic race has evolved within the species of which it is a part through the process of natural selection, and the individuals making up the race are related by descent from a common ancestor or group of related ancestors.
3. The characteristics that distinguish a race are genetically controlled; that is, they are heritable in the ordinary process of reproduction.
4. As the name implies, a geographic race occurs naturally in a fairly well-defined environment to which it normally is well adapted as a result of natural selection and has the ability to survive and reproduce in that environment.

From these four statements, Wakeley defined a *geographic race as a subdivision of a species consisting of genetically similar individuals, related by common descent, and occupying a particular territory to which it has become adapted through natural selection.*

If the specific territory or environment to which the race is adapted is a distinct altitudinal or climatic zone or soil province, it may be referred to as an *altitudinal, climatic,* or *edaphic race* rather than the more general term, *geographic race.* But differences in soil or altitude or even in climate usually do not account in total for the specific characteristics of a race. For example, a particular race may result from migration of plants from some mountain mass to a coastal site that has been recently uplifted from the sea, so that the characteristics of the race can be determined by rates of migration, or barriers to migration, as well as by extremes of heat, cold, drought, or other characteristics of the environment. In such

---

[1]Wakeley, P. C. 1959. In "Proceedings of Forest Genetics Short Course," North Carolina State University, Raleigh, June 1959 (unpublished mimeo).

instances, the general term *geographic race* is more appropriate than altitudinal, adaphic, or other specific race categories.

Geographic races occur most often in species that have a wide natural range and so encompass a large range of environments (Figure 3.3). They are determined by differences in latitude, altitude, rainfall patterns, or other environmental conditions that expose the trees to considerable variation in temperature, moisture, soil, day length, or any number of other environmental variables (Holzer, 1965). Most forest species have distinct geographic races. The species that contain the largest racial divergence afford the best opportunity for genetic gains through provenance selection, but they also are the ones with which the tree improver must use the greatest caution to assure that proper sources are identified for use. It is not unusual for differences to be less between species than between races within a given species that occurs over widely differing environments. This is seen for a number of genera, such as the pines in Mexico, where sometimes the differences between high- and low-elevation material can be greater within a species than between two species growing on similar environments at similar elevations.

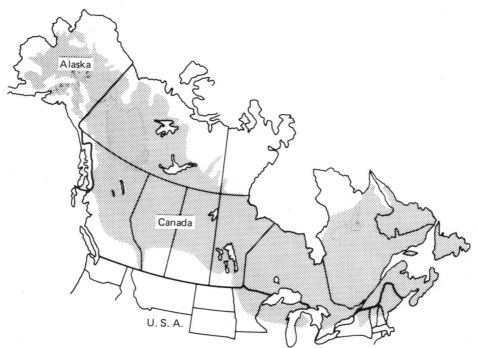

FIGURE 3.3

Geographic races almost always develop in species that have very wide geographic ranges, as is shown here for white spruce (*Picea glauca*). The diverse provenances encountered enable the tree improver to find strains of trees that are the most adapted to the area in which planting will be done.

When two species occupy the same or similar ranges, races may develop within them that are quite alike physiologically. Most high-latitude sources grow slowly, but have better tree form with straight stems and smaller limbs than those from lower latitudes. In addition, they can withstand cold weather that would kill or injure trees adapted to lower latitudes. These three characteristics of slow growth, good form, and good resistance to cold are common to most high-elevation and latitude sources, regardless of the species.

Often a determination of the boundaries of a geographic race is difficult. The gradation can be abrupt and clear where there are gaps in the species range (such as separation by deserts or mountains), or they can be gradual in cases in which the species occurs continuously from south to north or from low to high elevations. When variation is continuous, the distinction among geographic races becomes one of judgment or viewpoint (Langlet, 1959a; Farmer and Barnett, 1972); this is the most common situation. The definition of what exactly constitutes a race is not the important item; what is important is *an understanding of the patterns of variation and how this knowledge can be used* in a tree improvement program.

Characteristics that determine different races *are more frequently* physiological than morphological (Langlet, 1936). This means that racial determination based on phenotype alone without intensive testing will often be inaccurate. The need for testing is of primary importance because the physiological characteristics usually are related to survival, growth, and reproduction. Thus, they are key items in determining which geographic race of a species should be used in an operational planting program. This need is especially great when seed are moved long distances. Changing environments can cause unusual growth patterns, such as "foxtailing" of several pine species when grown in tropical environments. The foxtail produces no limbs; this situation can vary from only for a few years to the lifetime of the tree (Woods et al., 1979; Whyte et al., 1980). The ultimate proof of suitability of a source as an exotic and whether it will have such characteristics as foxtailing must be based on test results.

Although individuals within a race are somewhat similar from past heritage or selection pressures, they are by no means genetically identical. Usually, great individual differences in genotype and often in phenotype occur among trees within each race. This heterogeneity enables individual tree selection within sources to be used effectively. For example, there are differing genotypes that will produce either straight or crooked trees in the higher latitudes as well as in the lower latitudes.

Clines and Ecotypes

A whole series of categories have been proposed and used to describe patterns of genetic variation. Among these, the most important are the *ecotype* and the *cline,* which are very briefly discussed in this chapter. The terms are most widely used in the fields normally referred to as *speciation* and *evolution,* which are a whole "science" unto themselves. Many books and articles have been written in which these concepts have been discussed, for example, Turreson (1922), Stebbins (1950), Mettler and Gregg (1969), Grant (1971), and Endler (1977). Speciation and evolution are complex and often controversial subjects, and this book is no place for a detailed discussion of them. Yet, because ecotype and cline are so commonly used, an attempt will be made to define them clearly as they apply to forest trees.

An *ecotype* is a group of plants of similar genotype that occupy a specific ecological niche. In forestry, the ecotype is sometimes used synonymously with race but usually consists of a smaller discrete population. Frequently, ecotypes are not distinguishable by morphological characteristics and can only be separated by physiological differences, which are usually related to survival capabilities (Rehfeldt, 1979). The concept of ecotype was suggested by Turreson (1922) who defined it as a "genotypical response of a species to a particular habitat." The whole concept is based upon the adaptability to a specific environment. Gregor (1944) compared the environment to a sieve that sorts out the genotypes that are best able to survive.

Cline was first defined by Huxley (1938) as "a gradient in a measurable characteristic." Most people add the following to this: "which follows an environmental gradient." A cline, by definition, is based on a single characteristic that has continuous variation; it may or may not be genetically fixed (Figure 3.4). There may be a whole series of clines for different characteristics within a given population. Recognition of clines in tree improvement is very important, and such things as drought or cold resistance usually follow a clinal pattern. Since *clines* refer to a given characteristic and not to the entire genetic constitution of a population, the concept of *ecotype* would have more utility to the tree breeder. However, because ecotypes and clines both occur in nature, a successful breeder needs to understand both of them.

The *ecotype* and *cline* concepts have widespread utility in forestry. Because of the commonly observed continuous type of geographic variation, ecotypic differentiation is difficult to observe. It was to point out that ecotypes are discreet and separate that Langlet (1959a) wrote "a cline or not a cline." The key characteristic in understanding ecotypes is that they are the adaptation of *whole genotypes* or *gene complexes* to *specific environments*. They are not just expressions of single characters, and they are distinct one from another (they do not intergrade). Although they are not called *ecotypes,* we use something similar when developing land races that are adaptable to extremes of environments, such as very dry, wet, or cold habitats.

Table 3.1 was developed to aid in comparison of the two terms.

WHERE RACES ARE DEVELOPED BEST

It is of importance to recognize the conditions in which differing races are most likely to be found or developed.

1. *Species with very wide ranges over diverse environments* usually have the greatest racial development. Those species that span continents, or that grow over very wide latitudinal or altitudinal ranges contribute the most useful

FIGURE 3.4

Wood specific gravity indicates well the gradual change in a characteristic in conjunction with an environmental gradient. For example, there is a clinal change in wood specific gravity of loblolly pine from high values in the southern coastal plain to low values in the northern areas. There is also an abrupt pattern from the higher-specific-gravity coastal sources to the lower-gravity inland values, as is indicated on the map.

TABLE 3.1.
Comparison of Clines and Ecotypes

	Cline	Ecotype
Number of characteristics	One	Many (the genotype or gene complex)
Pattern	Continuous	Distinct populations
Genetics	May or may not be genetically controlled	Genetically controlled
Cause	Follows environmental gradient	Adaptation to specific environment
Use	Descriptive	Descriptive and as breeding unit, similar to race

races. The differences may be visible morphologically (Figure 3.5), or they may only be distinguished on the basis of physiological characteristics that are detected by testing. Usually, morphological and physiological differences both occur, but the physiological differences, which often are of the most importance to the tree improver because they affect survival and growth, sometimes develop without visible differences among trees. Thus, cold-, drought-, or moisture-tolerant races may develop within a species, even

FIGURE 3.5

Many species show anatomical variation with geographic source. Shown are leaves of *Liriodendron tulipifera* from differing sources. The extreme, nonlobed form at bottom left is commonly associated with coastal, acid soils. (Photo courtesy of Bob Kellison, North Carolina State University.)

though the trees appear to be similar phenotypically. Examples of wide-ranging species with great racial development are *Pseudotsuga menziesii, Pinus banksiana, Pinus silvestris, Eucalyptus camaludulensis, Pinus caribaea* (where varieties are recognized), *Pinus oocarpa* (where both varieties and new species are debated), *Tectona grandis, Pinus taeda,* and many others (Figure 3.6). Only a few wide-ranging species do not have strong racial development. For example, it has been suggested that the very widespread aspen (*Populus tremuloides*) has limited geographic variability throughout its range when compared to most species. There are not enough data from truly in-depth provenance studies of aspen to support or refute the statement that this species has limited racial development.

2. *Species growing in a wide altitudinal range* commonly develop races, and often changes are such that one species will intergrade into another with no break that is evident between the two. This appears to occur in Australia where *Eucalyptus regnans* in the lower elevations seems to intergrade into *E. delegatensis* in the higher regions. There are many examples of such intergradation in the Mexican and Central American pines, where different species grow at different elevations with no distinct divisions between them

FIGURE 3.6

Country with severe and rapidly changing environments is ideal for the development of differing races. Shown is a view in Guatemala, where trees are growing in dry, poor sites as well as in excellent forest conditions at higher elevations. Much racial development occurs in this area.

(Caballero, 1966). Racial differences are often recognized, such as those that occur in *Pinus oocarpa* or Douglas fir where some persons feel the current races should be given subspecific or specific taxonomic ranking. Within-species differences for survival and growth that are attributable to geographic variation can be very large, such as those for yellow poplar (*Liriodendron tulipifera*) (Kellison, 1967). A well-documented example is the altitudinal races that were developed in the pines in the Sierra Nevada mountains in California (Callaham and Liddicoet, 1961).

3. *Species that grow in regions of greatly diverse* soils, soil moisture, or slope and aspect (Squillace and Silen, 1962) can develop very distinct racial differences. A good example of extremely differing soil environments that are close together are the granitic and serpentine soils in the Sierra Nevada of California; this is also true for the greatly differing environments on the western and eastern sides of the Cascade Mountain Range in Oregon. Here, in relatively short distances, natural selection caused by the differing soil and climatic environments has resulted in racial differences within species.

Where to Select

A serious problem facing the tree improver working with indigenous species is whether to use local or outside sources of seed. There is a natural attraction to prefer outside sources, and this often results in the use of exotics. However, the safest method is to use the local source until an outside source has been proven better (Krygier, 1958). Frequently, the local source turns out to be best (Long 1980), and sometimes source seems to make little difference (Talbert et al., 1980). There are also examples when an outside source proves to be superior (Nam-koong, 1969). Using the local source until tests have proven that something else is better is admittedly a conservative approach, but it helps avoid large-scale losses that might occur if the nonindigenous population is poorly adapted to its new environment.

An ongoing argument is whether one should select from the center or fringe of the species range (Figure 3.7). Discussions of this kind that often involve the so-called *center of origin* of a species (Stebbins, 1950), or the *gene center theory* of Vavilov (1926), indicate that the richest genetic pool is present in these areas. There can be no completely correct answer to the question about where to select; therefore, the stock sentence "it depends" must be employed. If one is seeking a population of trees for introduction into some specific or extreme environment, then the fringe populations will often be best if the environments in which they are growing resemble those where the exotics will be planted. They may have limited total variability but may possess specially needed adaptability. If one is going to plant the introduced trees in a nonextreme environment and wishes for the maximum genetic variability, then it is best to select from the center of the range where genetic variation usually is the greatest. This problem has been addressed by Muller (1959) and van Buijtenen and Stern (1967).

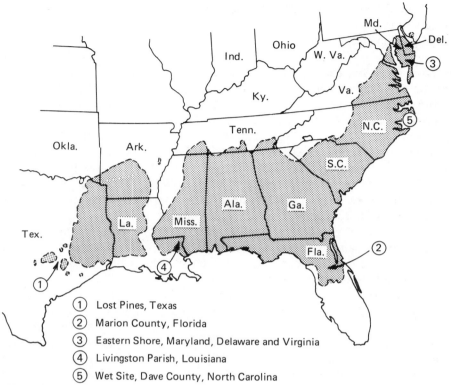

① Lost Pines, Texas
② Marion County, Florida
③ Eastern Shore, Maryland, Delaware and Virginia
④ Livingston Parish, Louisiana
⑤ Wet Site, Dave County, North Carolina

FIGURE 3.7

Shown is the natural range of loblolly pine (*P. taeda*). There are many "outlier" populations such as the lost pines in Texas and the wet-site loblolly in Dare County, North Carolina, that apparently are quite different genetically from the general species. Controversy exists about how much selection should be practiced in the outlier areas.

The Land Race Concept

The concept of a *land race* is a simple and is of key importance when working with provenances planted outside their normal environments (Marsh, 1969; Pellate, 1969). A *land race* is *a population of individuals that has become adapted* to a specific *environment in which it has been planted*. The steps involved in land race development consist of planting the trees in the new environment, letting nature sort them out according to their adaptability through natural selection. This is followed by choosing the best of the naturally selected trees and then using them as a source of seed to replant the area. This can be done after a single generation, but the best land races occur after several generations of growth and selection in the new environment. The group of best-adapted individuals with desirable growth and form are collectively referred to as a *land race*. In reality, one could also call the fittest individuals from indigenous stands a land race, but common usage and understanding of the term land race has limited it to the best trees of suitable provenances of species following testing when used as exotics.

Why Land Races Are Important   When one moves a species or provenance into an exotic environment, it rarely is fully adapted to the new environment, and sometimes it is quite poorly adapted. As individuals of the exotic grow in the new environment, the most well adapted will survive and perform the best (Figure 3.8). When the best trees are selected for use as a source of propagules for planting or for the next generation, either through seed or vegetative propagation, the performance of the new forest will often be from moderately to greatly better than the original stand from which the trees were chosen. This depends upon the quality of the original trees, the selection intensity, population size, breadth of its genetic base, and the severity of the new environment. It is not unusual for a land race, even from only a moderately well-adapted source, to outperform any other provenance of the same species that is planted directly in the exotic environment. This indicates that selection can be very effective within a broadly based, large, moderately well-adapted population.

Use of land races can be the easiest and best way of making quick and large genetic gains in exotic forestry. There are numerous examples in which land races have performed well above the level expected or hoped for, and *almost always* they perform better than any newly imported sources of the species. For example, Owino (1977) found that for *P. patula* and *Cupressus lusitanica* the advanced "land race" selections were highly superior. For northwestern Europe, Edwards (1963) stated that great advances can be made when seed of exotic species can be collected from stands of plus trees growing in the exotic environment. Distinction between native and exotic species may then disappear.

Previously established plantations of the species desired are the first thing to look for when starting a large program involving exotics. When such exist, occasionally outstanding individuals may be found (see Figure 3.8), even though the plantations may be rather poor overall. Seed from these individuals can be used in operational plantings, while seed orchards are being established and further introductions and tests are being made. If applied intensively, the land race approach will lead to the development of new strains of a species with great utility in the new environments. For example, in the southern United States, a cold-hardy strain of eucalypt is being developed by planting the exotic *Eucalyptus*

FIGURE 3.8

Occasional individuals in exotic plantings grow exceptionally well compared to the average of the plantation. Shown is an outstanding 7-year-old *P. caribaea* growing on the very severe sites of the Guyano llanos in the Orinoco Basin of Venezuela. A group of such trees is used to establish a land race that is better suited to the new environment than the population used for the original planting.

viminalis, selecting the best of the trees that survive the severe cold, and bringing these together as a seed source to grow *Eucalyptus* in a region where it previously could not be grown operationally (Hunt and Zobel, 1978).

When land races are developed in one region, they often will also be useful in other, similar regions (Nikles and Burley, 1977). Too often this source of material has been overlooked for exotic plantings. A good example of a broad usage is the apparent good adaptability of the greatly improved land race *P. caribaea var. hondurensis* developed in Queensland, Australia. The land race in Queensland has performed very well in Fiji, New Caledonia, parts of Brazil, Zambia, and in other countries.[2]

In summary, land race development is most feasible when the following conditions are met:

1. The original provenance is reasonably well adapted to the environment in which it will be planted. This can be helped by a careful consideration of climatic similarities between the exotic environment and the one where the provenance was developed.

2. The populations from which the land race trees will be selected must have a broad genetic base. Usually, several hundred parent trees should contribute seed to the plantation from which the land race selections are to be made.

3. The plantations from which selections will be made should be reasonably large, generally on the order of 400 ha (1000 acres) or more. This is not always possible, but small plantations do not have enough trees to give a reasonably high-selection intensity.

4. Enough local plus trees need to be selected to form the land race. As few as 30 can be used for a production seed orchard, but 200 to 300 or more will be needed for the developmental program. Smaller populations will soon lead to trouble from related matings and will restrict the genetic base needed for advanced generation development.

5. The selection system used to choose parents for the land race must be well devised and rigorous to assure the choice of only the very most outstanding trees.

The Stress Theory

The stress theory is of great importance because trees planted as exotics are usually not well adapted to new site; therefore, they will be growing under stress. If there is a problem with adaptation, some of the poorly adapted trees may die immediately, but the rest will grow normally until they come under a period of extreme stress caused by severe environmental fluctuations or pest attack. At that time, many trees will develop leader and branch dieback or perhaps even die, and only those that are well adapted will survive and grow normally (Figure 3.9). It is

---

[2]Personal communication, Garth Nikles, Queensland Forest Service, Brisbane, Australia.

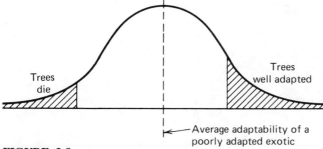

FIGURE 3.9

How well a tree can tolerate stress is the key to whether geographic races or species will grow well in an area. A *land race* is made up of those individuals that will best tolerate stress, as shown diagramatically by a population of exotics planted on a severe site.

these few best-adapted individuals that should be used to develop the land race with the assumption that most are superior genotypes and that their phenotypic superiority is not due primarily to an accidentally favorable environment.

Everywhere throughout the world where trees are planted on stress environments, such as the *llanos* (grasslands) of the Orinoco Basin in Colombia and Venezuela, dieback may occur in one form or another at some time in the life of the stand (Figure 3.10). Stress increases following drought, or as the trees become larger and come into severe competition with one another for available moisture. Dieback is a response to stress, and after the stress situation is alleviated the trees that have not died will recover to some extent. When stressed again, the trees will go through the same cycle, and the amount of deformity and death will increase with each cycle unless this situation is modified by silvicultural practices such as thinning. This reduces the stress and removes the poorly adapted individuals. *Thinning* is a major way of avoiding damaging stress in exotic plantations until a proper land race can be developed. The key to working with exotics is to develop a land race that grows better under stress than does the plantation from the original introduction.

EXOTIC FORESTRY

Exotic species are used when the local indigeous forests cannot, or do not, produce the desired quantity and quality of forest products. In countries that have very few species available, such as in northern Europe, exotics fill a special need (Edwards, 1963). In the tropics, there is often a great desire for coniferous timbers, because the indigenous forests frequently do not contain this type of wood. To fill the need, exotic plantations have been widely used. Many exotics are

FIGURE 3.10

When exotics are planted, some individuals will not be suited to the new (exotic) environment. When stress occurs, they will die or become deformed. Shown are damaged *P. caribaea* in the llanos of Venezuela following a prolonged drought. Other neighboring trees have developed and grown well despite the dry weather.

planted in the grasslands in tropical areas, such as in the llanos of the Orinoco Basin of Venezuela and Colombia and in central East Africa. Large plantations of exotics are also established in scrub forests, such as in the state of Minas Gerais, Brazil, or in large areas in Colombia and Chile. Many other regions, such as Australia, New Zealand, India, Indonesia, and the Middle East, use exotics much of the time. In many areas, especially in the Southern Hemisphere, there is no option except to use exotic conifers because no suitable indigenous species exist (Zobel, 1961, 1964, 1979).

It is important to note again that the use of a proper provenance is one key to having a successful program with exotics. Provenance differences that exist within the natural range of a species often become more evident when a species is grown as an exotic. One of many examples is for *P. taeda* in southern Brazil (Shimuzu and Higa, 1981). Exotic forestry is very widespread in tropical areas, both in naturally forested and grassland ecosystems. Tropical hardwood forests are so variable, nonuniform, and difficult to manage ecologically that, on suitable sites, foresters generally prefer to use exotic species that are more uniform, easier to handle, and whose products are known and accepted. Some of the tropical hardwoods have magnificent wood, but usually the most-desired species are slow growing and hard to manage in plantations. Currently knowledge is generally lacking about how they should be handled. Foresters are often trained to handle the exotic species and feel comfortable with them. Because exotics grow at a rapid rate, they are commonly chosen as the heart of an economically viable forestry enterprise in tropical areas. Despite the past bias toward exotics, it is likely that certain indigenous species from the tropics will become more widely used while foresters learn to manage them, learn their biology and the value of their wood, and are able to develop suitable markets (Figure 3.11).

One serious problem related to plantation management of nonindigenous tropical species that often makes an intelligent tree improvement program impossible is a great lack of knowledge about the soils in the tropical regions. The idea that all tropical soils are fragile and that they are unsuited to forest management has been grossly overemphasized, and it has led to efforts to develop new strains of trees that really are not needed. The statements about the amount of the very intractable lateritic soils in the tropics have been especially misleading. Where these types of soils do occur, they must be absolutely avoided for exotic plantations. However as Sanchez and Buol (1975) state in "Soils of the Tropics & the

FIGURE 3.11

There has been an overemphasis on growing exotics in the tropics because foresters know how to grow them, seed are available, and their woods are known. Often such information is lacking for indigenous species. But some species indigenous to the tropical areas, such as this *Toona ciliata* growing in Brazil, has great potential. Foresters need to learn more about these species.

World Food Crisis" less than 10% of the forest soils in the tropics are laterites. They report the following values for different tropical areas.

Location	Percentage of lateritic soils
Tropical America	2
Central Brazil	5
Indian Subcontinent (tropical)	7
Tropical Africa	11
Sub-Saharan West Africa	15

Sanchez and Buol (1975) state that "on the basis of these and other estimates, we venture that the total area of the tropics in which laterite may be found close to the soil surface is in the order of 7%." They conclude with the observation that soils in the tropics are essentially similar to those in such temperate regions as the Piedmont of the southern United States. As such, tree improvement activities are suitable and are not too difficult. Based on our experience in the tropics in South America, it appears that about 50% of the tropical forest area is suitable to support plantation forestry with few soil problems or adverse ecological impacts. The areas on which plantations are to be considered should be surveyed with respect to soil types, and then actual suitable areas must be handled correctly. Ideally, tropical forestry in the future will consist of natural regeneration on the more fragile soils; on the more operable sites some plantations will be established using indigenous species, the rest will use exotics. Tree improvement allocations to these different types of management will vary, depending on soil types and wood needs. It is certain, however, that much more information is needed to plan allocations most appropriately.

Planting of exotics in tropical areas is now mainly in the grasslands or scrub forestlands, especially in South America. This is not done because those lands are better or more productive. In fact, they are often marginal for forest production, and the soils are often inferior, either structurally or chemically or in their moisture relations. Some consist of deep droughty sands, whereas others have heavy textured soils that are difficult to manage. Quite frequently, phosporous is deficient, and sometimes a lack of other elements like boron or copper limit tree growth. All of these pose a major challenge to the tree improver to find the genetically best-adapted trees. Yet these sites are chosen for much of the exotic tropical forest plantings that are now being established because of the following factors:

1.   They are usually easy to handle. Site preparation is simple and inexpensive, and competition from regrowth is limited. Converting a tropical hardwood forest to a plantation is a formidable and very expensive job, both in

removing the trees from the planting site and from the need to release the planted trees from regrowth forests.

2. They can be directly converted to plantations without the need to use, or dispose of, the wood in the indigenous forest. Markets for tropical hardwoods are limited, and even when markets exist, only a part of the wood can be economically utilized; also, the remaining wood must be disposed of at a considerable expense. It is unconscionable to destroy the wood in tropical forests, and yet it is often not feasible to use it economically under current utilization standards. The result is that the most productive tropical hardwood forest sites are often bypassed for plantation establishment.

3. The land is available and much of it is not suitable for agriculture.

Use of exotics in the northern forest regions, such as in northern Europe, is also widespread. The usual movement of species is from the West Coast of North America to Europe and Asia. Such magnificent species as Douglas fir (*Pseudotsuga menziesii*), Sitka spruce (*Picea sitchensis*), the pines, hemlocks, and larches have been and are now widely being used as exotics. One of the species being used on a large scale in northern Sweden in the last few years is lodgepole pine (*P. contorta*), where it is performing better than the indigenous species (Hagner, 1979) (Figure 3.12). The species has been used as an exotic in Scotland and Ireland for many years. Generally, movement of forest tree species from Europe to North America as exotics has not been successful. There are not many exotic forest tree species that grow well in the northeastern United States, although species such as Norway spruce (*Picea abies*) and larch have potential (Carter et al., 1981). In areas such as the southern and the western United States, which contain numerous valuable species, exotics are rarely of much value (Zobel et al., 1956).

A long list of species that have been successfully used as exotics could be made, but this would serve no purpose. It is important to realize how wide the choices are; for example, poplars in the Middle East, willows (*Salix*) in Argentina, teak (*Tectona grandis*) in Indonesia, and tropical pines in many countries. The most successful and widely used conifer has been *P. radiata;* in the tropics, *P. caribaea* and *P. oocarpa* are being used extensively. *Eucalyptus* species are the most widely used exotic hardwoods and, in fact, they are the most widely planted exotic forest tree, with huge areas having been established in South America, Africa, and many other regions.

Exotics are sometimes used in quite unlikely areas; an example is *P. taeda* that grows at high elevations in Colombia (Ladrach, 1980). Only a few of the many seed sources of loblolly pine that have been tried are suitable for the wet, high elevations, and cool sites in this tropical area. It would be an advantage if one could easily predict what will be a successful exotic based upon its performance in its indigenous range. Unfortunately, it is not yet always possible to do this with sufficient reliability. In most cases, it is only after tests have indicated wide adaptability, fast growth, and usable wood properties that one can be certain

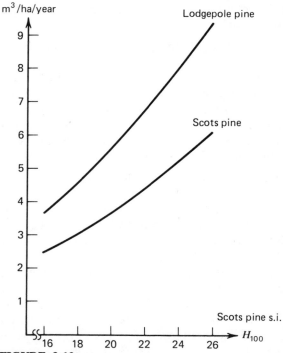

FIGURE 3.12

Sometimes an exotic species will outproduce indigenous species. This is shown for lodgepole pine (*P. contorta*) compared to Scots pine (*P. silvestris*) in northern Sweden. (Graph courtesy of Per Stahl, Swedish Forest Service, data from College of Forestry.)

about what species and sources will actually be successful exotics. The ability to predict performance in new environments is progressively improving because it is based on experience and the results of many previously established studies.

Occasionally, exotics are espoused as being of outstanding value; a recent one, which is often called the miracle tree, is *Leucaena* (Anonymous, 1978; Brewbaker and Hutton, 1979). This tree has received much publicity, but only time will prove its true value. Many trees that are proposed as exotics fail, but one seldom hears about them. In fact, only a small proportion of trees that have been tried or recommended for exotics is successful.

The advantages that exotics may present to the forester can be briefly summarized as follows:

1. More wood of greater uniformity and desirability can be produced quickly. Coniferous-type wood, which is scarce in the tropics, can be grown.

2. Rotation ages may be shortened and can be as low as 5 or 6 years for some eucalypts. This result in a large economic advantage in the cost of wood

production. Many indigenous species in the tropics are slow growing, although some, such as *Gmelina,* grow very rapidly.

3. Exotics are suited to intensive management and plantation culture, and silvicultural methods are known. Many indigenous species cannot yet be grown successfully in plantations because seeds are not available, methodology is not known, or the biology of the species is such that pure stands will not grow satisfactorily.

4. The wood quality produced by exotics and its utility are known. Many of the tropical hardwood species have wood that is unknown on the market or is technologically difficult to manufacture, even though it may be of high quality.

5. Frequently, extensive study, including genetic improvement, has been done on the exotic species, and improved genotypes are available to use directly in operational planting. Such use has great potential, but must be done cautiously until the value of the improved trees has been proven in the new environment.

6. The biology of reproduction in the exotics is known. Ignorance about the biology of tropical hardwoods is often great; sometimes, it is not even known how to collect and store seed, or what is the mode of pollination of the species.

Problems with Exotics

There will always be problems encountered when using exotic species; these can occur in many ways when poorly adapted species or unsuitable seed sources or provenances are planted on a given area. For example, pest attacks can occur immediately or be delayed for many years. It is essential that the forest manager and tree improver realize that pest problems will eventually occur, and plans must be made to cope with these. *But pest attacks will occur.* The production of an exotic in its early years should never be used to estimate future production. Problems with exotics may manifest themselves in several ways.

1. *Immediate failure of the plantation.* Losses of this type are obvious and do not need further discussion. A surprising number of such complete failures do occur, but one rarely hears about them, and they are almost never reported in published articles.

2. *Delayed failure* is a common problem and can occur in one of many forms that can be categorized as follows:

   a. There is good survival and growth in the early years, but the trees never develop into a useful forest. This often occurs when high-elevation of high-latitude sources are planted at low elevations or low latitudes or when trees from a Mediterranean climate are planted in a Continental climate. For example, many of the poplar hybrids developed for the northeastern United States have been planted in the southeastern area of the United States. During the first 2 or 3 years these trees grow at an amazing rate, but after 10 years many trees are dead and often those still alive have lost vigor, the leaves are small, tops and limbs die back, and the trees literally "fall apart." Another good example of delayed failure occurs when *Eucalyptus* is planted on lands with a heavy subsoil layer a few centimeters from the surface. The trees grow well for 1 or 2 years, then they develop top dieback, and in 4 or 5 years no effective forest stand still remains. This problem of delayed failure causes severe loss, but the mistake is usually recognized soon enough to prevent continued, long-term planting of the wrong source.

b. *There is good survival and growth rate but the wood is not suitable* (Kellison, 1981; Zobel, 1981). There are many examples of the problem of undesirable wood from exotics, especially when temperature species are planted in tropical or subtropical areas. One occurs in South Africa where in some parts of the coastal area, *Pinus caribaea* produces very low-specific-gravity wood that is not desirable either for paper or for solid wood products (Falkenhagen, 1979) (Figure 3.13). In this same

FIGURE 3.13

When trees are grown as exotics, their wood quality may vary greatly from that produced in the original environment from where the exotic was taken. Shown is a stand of *P. caribaea* from the warm low area of South Africa, which had excellent growth. However, the wood quality was quite inferior to the species in its indigenous range. Trees in this photograph had an unusually low specific gravity and an absence of summerwood, producing a wood undesirable for many products.

general forest region, *P. elliottii* produces wood with such a high density that it is also undesirable for many products. One of the most costly and common errors made when seed sources are moved or exotics are used is to plant large plantations before the quality of the wood that will be produced has been determined. The problems with wood from exotics is described more fully in Chapter 12.

c. The exotic *trees show initial good survival and growth, but there is a delayed attack by pests or adverse environmental conditions* that ultimately destroys the value of the forest. This common and very costly cause of loss is most disheartening; it is similar to item 2a, but is more long term. Many examples could be given, but perhaps the worst is the destruction of pine by the disease *Dothistroma* that is most destructive when the trees are about 5 years of age. Most of the radiata pine plantations in Brazil and central East and central South Africa have been damaged or destroyed by this disease, and damage occurs in many other areas, such as New Zealand and Chile. *P. radiata* should never be planted in a climate that has wet and warm summers because *Dothistroma* flourishes under those conditions. Another example of delayed damage is the planting of *P. caribaea* from the Guatemala source on the deep sands in Venezuela. The trees grow satisfactorily for several years, but when drought stress occurs, many trees develop a dieback of the leaders and branches, and often the whole tree dies (see Figure 3.10). Another graphic example occurs when the well-recognized Florida source of *P. taeda* is planted in northern latitudes. The trees may grow well and normally for several years, and generally they will significantly outgrow the indigenous pine sources. But when certain cold weather sequences occur, the physiology of the plant is upset so that the trees lose dominance, and the leader and branches grow in a sinuous way so that the growth of the trees is slowed and the trees become very deformed. There are innumerable examples of late decline in such hardwoods as *Eucalyptus, Populus, Gmelina, Platanus,* and other genera. One example in Minas Gerais, Brasil, is particularly worrisome. There, an unknown pest or combination of pests attacks one source of *E. grandis,* but does less harm to others. Damage does not occur until the second or third year after outplanting; then the trees develop small, yellow-white leaves, many leaves fall off, branch dieback occurs, and sometimes the trees die.

3. A major problem with exotics can be a *continued substandard performance* resulting in low production. This is a major problem with some exotics and causes the greatest losses from planting species or provenances offsite. Such losses are subtle and cannot be assessed without a comparison with the suitable sources and the best species. Often, losses can amount to 50% or more of the productive potential of the site. Unfortunately, the forester is often quite unaware of the loss because there is nothing to compare with the

planted trees. If this kind of loss is not detected, inferior sources may be used on a large scale in plantations. A good example of the subtle loss is the use of the Piedmont source of *P. taeda* in the coastal plain. Yields from the Piedmont trees will be small compared to those where the proper loblolly coastal plain source has been used. Several countries have planted large acreages with the Piedmont source of loblolly pine, not fully aware that their forests are producing 30 to 50% less than if the correct coastal plain source had been used (see Figure 3.1). *Eucalyptus* is especially sensitive to a reduced growth pattern, and there are numerous examples in Colombia, Venezuela, Brazil, Africa, and elsewhere where growth of *Eucalyptus* is much below standard because the wrong sources and species have been used in large operational programs.

4. *Growth is unsatisfactory* due to a *shortage or absence of suitable mycorrhizae.* This has been a major problem with some exotic plantings, especially in the tropics, but the importance of mycorrhizae is now generally recognized. Often the soils of the exotic environment are marginal for survival and the growth of mycorrhizal fungi.

The question needs to be asked why poor sources or wrong species are used in exotic forestry programs. The reasons are many, but some of the most important are the following:

1. **Ignorance** Geographic differences are not well known for many species. Despite the fact that numerous studies on variation have been and are still being made, only a limited amount of information is available for some species. When a program to grow exotics has been funded and action must be taken, the only thing to do is to use one's best judgment while tests that are underway to determine the best sources are maturing. Perhaps the greatest error in determining which species to use is the lack of knowledge about provenances within the species of interest. It is common for the wrong seed source to be selected to represent a certain species. When planted, the trees do not perform well, and as a result, the whole species is tagged as being of no value for the area. Prime examples of the use of inadequate source information or poor sources resulting in rejection of the species are *P. taeda* in subtropical areas, *P. oocarpa* in the tropics, and *Eucalyptus* in many places throughout the world. Ignorance tends to build upon itself, and some of the most costly decisions made in the entire field of forestry are due to obtaining a handful of seed of a given species from an unknown source, testing it, and using the results to formulate rigid policies about which species can or cannot be used.

2. **Dishonesty or lack of concern** It is a terrible thing, but too often seed are not of the quality or from the source from which they were supposed to be, because the supplier, and sometimes the buyer, did not care. Horror stories about buying and relabeling seed to fit an order, "salting" a good source with

poor-quality seed, and of deliberately mislabeling could be told at length. Luckily, this is becoming less common but is still a problem for some species like the tropical pines, especially where there is a seed shortage. The major cause of lack of concern is a result of the attitude that *seed is seed* and that it will not make much difference if the seed used do not exactly fit those requested. It is not unusual to find even mixtures of species in lots supposedly obtained from a given source of a desired species. The problem really is that many foresters and seed dealers simply are ignorant of or do not believe in the importance of differences in source of seed within a species. Whatever the reason, it is essential that *anyone obtaining seed from a special source* should make sure it is as labeled. Many organizations send their own personnel to the collection area to assure themselves of obtaining the desired seed. Greed also causes a part of the problem. Whole indigenous sources have been destroyed by collectors who cut the trees or hacked them to pieces with machetes because someone was offering a good price for the seed. Certification of forest tree seed, as discussed elsewhere, is a partial solution of the problem.

3. **The proper source of a species is not available**   In rapidly expanding planting programs, the best seed sources are often not available; this is one of the major stumbling blocks in the currently aggressive tropical and subtropical forestry operations. Seed is in such short supply that costs have skyrocketed, and some organizations have become so desperate that they will buy and use seed from literally any source available. Sometimes they even use the wrong species. Lack of seed from a suitable source is almost always a major problem when indigenous tropical hardwood species are used. Too often a less desirable source is chosen to fill a specific regeneration quota. Sometimes it is impossible to obtain the desired seed. In this situation, great care must be taken to obtain the next best source, and to avoid planting just any kind of trees to fill the area.

4. **Costs**   It is unbelievable, but in many instances a few cents or dollars difference per kilogram of seed become the decisive factor about whether the best source or an inferior one is used. It is known, for example, that the Piedmont source of *P. taeda* is not suitable in subtropical areas. However, seed of this source are abundant and cheap, and thousands of kilograms of it have been purchased to plant in subtropical areas simply because the Piedmont seed are less costly than the correct coastal plain source. Actually, when prorated against total plantation costs, seed costs are an infinitesimal part of the outlay to establish a plantation. Doubling or tripling seed costs will have essentially no effect on the per-hectare costs of plantation establishment.

It is a *basic fact of exotic forestry* that pest damage usually will occur; it may happen quickly after planting or may be delayed many years before it comes. Problems with pests are worse when offsite plantings are made. All exotic plantings are offsite, and some, such as those in the dry grasslands in the tropics, are extremely so.

There are three categories of pests that attack exotics. These are as follows:

1. The insect or disease is a pest on the exotic *in its natural range,* and somehow follows the exotic to its new planting area. A good example of this type of pest is *Dothistroma* on radiata pine. This disease is little more than a nuisance on radiata in its native range in California, which has cool, dry summers. However, the disease becomes a killer when it attacks radiata pine planted in areas that have warm, wet summers.

2. The pest is indigenous to the area where the exotic is planted. It may take years, but ultimately some pests will adapt to the exotic. A good example of such a pest is the cypress defoliator *Glena bisulca* in Colombia. The insect is found endemically on the indigenous hardwoods and did not seriously attack the *Cupressus lusitanica* for many years. Now, it is potentially a very serious pest. Attacks by indigenous pests seem to be the most common types that damage exotics. One example is leaf-eating beetles that commonly attack *Eucalyptus* in many regions.

3. An exotic pest, which is not from the original area of the exotic, may adapt to the exotic tree species. A reported example of this is *Sirex* on radiata pine in New Zealand and Australia, where the imported *Sirex* has adapted to the imported radiata pine.

Donor and Receptor Areas

When we deal with exotics, it is convenient for purposes of reference to speak of *donor* and *receptor* countries or areas. The donors are those areas such as Central America, Mexico, and western North America which are rich in species that have great value in the receptor countries where the material will be planted (Figure 3.14). Frequently, the donor countries are not themselves major timber-producing regions, but this does not always hold true. Examples are Mexico and western North America. The receptor countries are poor in the kinds of trees desired, or they do not have them at all; examples are Australia and Africa for pines, and South America, Africa, and many other regions for eucalypts and pines.

CHOOSING SPECIES AND PROVENANCES

How does one decide which species or sources should be obtained from a donor country to test in a receptor country? If this question could be easily answered, much labor, time, and large quantities of money could be saved. The theory for success of a transfer is quite simple; match the environment of the donor species or provenance with the one where the plantation will be established. Many helpful methods have been suggested, such as the zoning of northeastern Brazil, by

FIGURE 3.14

Species from donor countries, like those in Central America and Mexico, are widely used in exotic plantings in the tropical regions. Shown is a fine Mexican pine from which seed are being collected to test in South America.

Golfari and Caser (1977) who made a search for similar regions in countries rich in the desired species. But the decision is not that simple because rapid screening of environments is only the first step. However, some general rules can be given for choosing likely species to use in new environments. Suitability for survival, growth, and wood qualities are the key items to look for when choosing suitable material to grow in a receptor country. The ability to reproduce in the new environment is desirable but is not essential in plantation forestry if seeds can be obtained from seed orchards or seed stands that are established elsewhere. For example, *P. caribaea* will grow very well in some lowland areas near the equator, but here the species often does not produce abundant seed, therefore, it must be produced elsewhere.

In forestry, weather data are usually not available either for the donor area or for the area where new planting is to be done. Thus, matching of environments can be most difficult. When information is available, it usually is for yearly averages, although rarely, monthly or weekly averages or even daily figures have been recorded. Gross average conditions can be most misleading when making a decision about the best source to plant. Natural selection *does not operate on averages; it operates on the extremes.* It may be the 1 day in the 1 year of the plantation's life that will result in death or injury from something like cold weather. Alternatively, it may be the one dry period out of 50 years that will kill from drought. The *important aspects* in deciding about the use of *provenances* or species are things that are *unusual, extreme,* or that have *large fluctuations.* Because extremes do not occur yearly, but perhaps only once or twice during the lifetime of a given plantation, meaningful testing of the suitability of species and provenances cannot really result until the trees have grown for a full rotation. Sometimes that length of time is not even enough. For example, a "50-year freeze" may occur only once in several rotations. Even a knowledge of extremes is not sufficient. The key is the *sequence prior to or following the extremes;* for example, if cold weather occurs gradually, so the plants have a chance to harden off, results will be greatly different than if a severe cold spell immediately follows a period of warm weather.

There is always an urgent need for information about which provenance or species is suitable for use, and decisions are commonly made after only a few years of testing. The problem of too short a test period is especially critical for such exotics as *Eucalyptus* in Brazil or *P. oocarpa* in Colombia (Figure 3.15). However,

FIGURE 3.15

Tests must be of a sufficiently long duration to give the trees a chance to express their characteristics. Shown is a stand of slash pine (*P. elliottii*) grown near the equator in South America. Initial growth appeared to be normal, but later all the trees developed severe sweep; the cause was not root binding.

it can also be critical for species within their natural ranges. For example, one of the most important current questions in the southeastern United States, now that seed orchards are in full production and excess seed are available, is how far can the seed from a given orchard be moved safely for use in operational plantings? There is no immediate answer to this problem other than to apply experience with wild seed of the same origin, combined with common sense (Langlet, 1967; Rohmeder, 1959). However, for long-term answers, tests need to be made (Wells and Wakeley, 1966).

There are many rules that have been suggested as a guide to movement of provenances or species, but most fit only specific situations. A few board generalizations that can be made are as follows:

1. Do not move provenances *from a Mediterranean to a continental climate;* it is somewhat safer to move seed from continental to maritime areas. The seasonal periods of moisture and temperature are so different that rarely will a source developed where there are cool, wet winters and warm (hot), dry summers do well where rain fall is uniform year round, or where the cool seasons are dry and the warm periods are wet (Kiellander, 1960). Failures are common when species are moved between areas with winter rains to those with winter drought and between areas with summer rains to those that have summer drought (Hillis and Brown, 1978). It sometimes is satisfactory to move trees from areas with extreme seasons to those with uniform year-around rainfall, but quite often this is not successful.

2. Do not move trees from areas of *uniform climates with small fluctuations* in rain fall and temperature to those with *severe and large fluctuations* in these factors, even though the annual averages and extremes may be similar. Many plants require preconditioning before they can tolerate extreme environments, and without this preparation period they are susceptible to damage. For example, the climate in the southeastern United States is one of the most difficult for exotic trees because of random wet and dry spells and particularly because temperatures can fluctuate from 80°F (27°C) in 1 day to15°F (-8°C) the same night. It is not uncommon to have several days of 80°F temperature in midwinter that is followed immediately by several days when the temperature will drop below 10°F (-12°C). Few plants can tolerate such large fluctuations, although with proper preconditioning they can easily withstand the absolute temperature extremes. Cold-hardy species that can normally stand temperatures as low as -30°F (-34°C), if they have been properly and gradually preconditioned, will often freeze at 10°F (-12°C) following a warm spell. Species, such as many of the eucalypts, are particularly sensitive to environmental extremes because they never seem to have a real dormancy. Such species start growth during warm spells, and then are killed or damaged when cold weather follows. Because of the large fluctuations in environment in the southeastern United States, most exotics have proven to be complete failures there (Zobel et al., 1956).

3. *Do not move high-elevation or high-latitude sources to low elevations or low latitudes,* or the reverse. However, high-elevation provenances from low

latitudes can often be moved successfully to lower elevations at higher latitudes and vice versa. High-latitude and high-elevation sources are usually slow growing but of good form, whereas lower-elevation and low-latitude sources have faster-growing trees with heavy limbs and crooked boles. As for all rules, this one does not always hold; for example, the inland and upland provenances of *P. caribaea v. hondurensis* tend to be larger limbed and more crooked than those from the coastal region that are straight and have better form.[3] The major question is *how far* seed can be moved without too much risk. Usually, the interest is in movement from lower elevations to higher elevations or from lower latitudes to higher in order to increase the growth rate. But with such moves, adaptability problems can occur, and a major decision must be made about whether the *gain* from the move is great enough to justify the *risk* from initially poorer adaptability. Once a large and broadly based population is established, land race development can begin.

4.   Do not plant trees originating on *basic soils* on *acid soils* or vice versa. This rule also often holds for soil types, such as clay to sand or sand to clay. Some geographic races have a very high adaptability and will grow on a number of sites and soils; and example is *P. caribaea v. hondurensis* and *P. radiata*. But other races or species show very limited adaptability to differing soil environments, such as several of the best species of *Eucalyptus* and *P. oocarpa* (Figure 3.16).

No matter how carefully one may choose or match environments, the final answer regarding suitability of an exotic or provenance can only be obtained through testing. There are many subtle interactions between environment and trees that will determine the success or failure of a plantation. These often cannot be accurately predicted. Sometimes, as for some *Eucalyptus,* the species seems to have a very narrow range of adaptability in its indigenous range but grows well under many diverse environments when used as an exotic, probably because the factors that limit the natural distribution are not present in the new environment. Species like *P. radiata* come from a narrow environmental range but grow well under a wide range of environments. Most species like *P. taeda* or *Pseudotsuga menziessii* grow naturally in many different environments; therefore, the overall species has a wide range of adaptability. However, each provenance has a somewhat more narrow range of adaptability.

WHAT SHOULD BE DONE IF THE PROPER SOURCE IS NOT AVAILABLE OR IS NOT KNOWN?

The preceding question is a widespread and standard problem that must be faced by all operational organizations. Despite the ideal objective of only making small plantings while studies are underway to determine needs regarding the proper

---

[3]Personal communication, Garth Nikles, Queensland Forest Service, Australia.

FIGURE 3.16

Moving exotics without previous testing sometimes has bizarre results. Shown is a test of one source of *P. oocarpa* in Colombia that was totally unsuited to this new exotic environment. Other sources of *P. oocarpa* grow well in this same environment, and they are used operationally. Testing of sources before operational planting will prevent possible disasters.

species and provenances, the general situation, especially in the developing countries, is to go from essentially no operational forestry program to a large-scale one in just a few years. Tests to determine the proper species and sources for current planting are not available and often are not completed until the second generation of planting on a given site. Without test results as a guide, decisions are difficult to make, and some mistakes will be made. However, quick establishment of plantations is of key importance. Therefore, most forestry programs proceed with the minimal information necessary to properly guide the forester. When this situation occurs, the following procedures should be followed:

1. *Match the environment* of the potential exotic species or provenance and the new environment to be planted as closely as possible. Usually, suitable data to do this are not available, so one must make as intelligent an estimate as possible. As emphasized in the section on choosing species or provenances, the extremes and sequences of temperature, moisture, soils, or other environmental factors must be compared, not just the normal or average conditions. Often extremes are not recorded, especially in the tropical regions. Therefore, one may have to rely on the general knowledge of persons living in the area.

2. *Use common sense and experience.* The best experience is to have seen or worked with similar environmental conditions elsewhere. With knowledge of the species involved, one can make a good estimate of what will grow best on

an area being considered for use. Most of the early plantings in the tropical and subtropical areas, and in severe environments elsewhere, have been made in this way. Sometimes mistakes are made! This is inevitable, but it is absolutely amazing how close the opinions of an experienced and alert forester will be with respect to what later tests indicate are best. The *key to success* in making such recommendations is *close observation, knowing the species* being considered for use, and having a *good knowledge of the environment.*

Frequently, a situation occurs when a political decision has been made that a forestry planting program will be immediately initiated on a large scale. When this is done, the forester must do the best possible even when seed of the best species or sources are not available. There is no option but to act, and a planting program will be initiated whether or not the forester feels it is a wise decision. If one can find plantations of the desired species in the area, a land race should be immediately developed, even if the original seed source is not the best. At the same time, a series of species and provenance studies should be initiated as soon as possible (Burley and Nikles, 1972, 1973a, b; Nikles et al., 1978). These will provide the needed information and plant material necessary to develop a base for future selections. The overriding concern is time and the need for immediate action. Many programs have been scrapped because planting was delayed with the excuse that suitable seed were not available. Making operational plantings before proper information or proven plant materials are available will result in inefficiency. This is a penalty that must be absorbed to accommodate the political pressures and time needs. *Any* type of *crash program* is *inefficient,* and this is especially severe in forestry. When faced with establishing a crash program because of needs and political considerations, drastic failures can be avoided when one draws on all the experience and common sense available and applies them when making the initial recommendations.

How Far Can Seed Be Moved?

Tree improvement specialists are constantly being asked about how far it is safe to move seed. There are many answers and many formulas that have been proposed. Rules have been made for certain species, such as "it is safe to move seed 1000 ft (300 m) in elevation of 100 mi (160 km) in latitude." Wiersma (1963) uses the rule that displacement of 1° latitude is equivalent to a 100-m elevation difference; in a recent progress report of the Inland Empire Tree Improvement Program, Rehfeldt (1980) suggests that seed for reforestation of ponderosa pine in southern Idaho may be transferred about 230 m (750 ft) in elevation, 0.7° in latitude, and 1.2° in longitude. In another report, Rehfeldt (1979) states that there is no limit on elevation, latitude, or longitude that seed of white pine (*P. monticola*) can be moved in northern Idaho. In the southeastern United States, Wakeley (1963) summarized seed movement, giving cautions about the distances that are safe.

In reality, no general rule on seed movement can be made because it differs for each species and location. However, some general guidelines appear to be useful. One of these is that a wide seed transfer is safer near the center of a species range than near its edge. Thus, much more care must be taken in seed movement when species boundaries are approached (Wells and Wakeley, 1966). Also, in areas where environmental gradients are steep, such as in boreal Canada, movement of seed must be very restricted, and the well-adapted indigenous species will become more useful.

SUMMARY—STEPS SUGGESTED TO SELECT EXOTICS OR PROVENANCES

1. Make a decision about the objective of the plantings and the products desired. Then, determine the category of trees (for example, pines or hardwoods) that will best fulfill the objective.

2. Obtain all information possible, from the literature and from plantations or from tests that may be available. This informational phase should include visiting areas with similar environments and species to those that will be used for establishing plantations.

3. Survey the area for any plantations of the desired species that may be available. Immediately develop land races from these plantations for use as an immediate source of seed, unless the provenances of the plantation are obviously very unsuitable.

4. Make a systematic investigation through planting trials of potential species and provenances to determine their growth and variation patterns. Obtain seed from the best trees from these plantings to use as a good land race. Obtain improved stock through additional testing and seed orchard establishment to develop a permanent seed supply for operational planting. Choice of species or provenances to test must be made by using common sense, experience, and through matching environmental extremes and sequences.

5. Operationally, use seed from the initial land race or best potential provenance while better material is being developed through a tree improvement program.

LITERATURE CITED

Anderson, K. F. 1966. Economic Evaluation of Results from Provenance Trials. Seminar, For. Seed and Tree Impr., FAO and Danish Board of Tech. Coop. with Devl. Countries, Rome.

Anonymous. 1978. Leucaena: The miracle tree. *Africa* **86**:75.

Barner, H. 1966. "Classification of Seed Sources." Seminar, For. Seed and Tree Impr., FAO and Danish Board of Tech. Coop. with Devel. Countries, Rome.

Brewbaker, J. L., and Hutton, E. M. 1979. Leucaena—versatile tropical tree legume. In *New Agricultural Crops,* pp. 207–259. American Association for the Advancement of Science Press, Boulder, Colo.

Burley, J., and Nikles, D. G. 1972. *Selection and Breeding to Improve Some Tropical Conifers,* Vol. I. Commonwealth Forestry Institute, Oxford, England, and Department of Forestry, Queensland, Australia.

Burley, J., and Nikles, D. G. 1973a. "Tropical Provenance and Progeny Research and International Cooperation." Proc., Joint Workshop IUFRO in Nairobi, Kenya, Commonwealth Forestry Institute, Oxford, England.

Burley, J., and Nikles, D. G. 1973b. *Selection and Breeding to Improve Some Tropical Conifers,* Vol. II. Commonwealth Forestry Institute, Oxford, England, and Department of Forestry, Queensland, Australia.

Caballero, M. 1966. "Comparative Study of Two Species of Mexican Pine (*Pinus pseudostrobus* and *P. montezumae*) Based on Seed and Seedling Characteristics." M.S. thesis, North Carolina State University, Raleigh.

Callaham, R. Z., and Liddicoet, A. R. 1961. Altitudinal variation at 20 years in ponderosa and Jeffrey pines. *Jour. For.* **59**(11):814–820.

Callaham, R. Z. 1964. Provenance research: Investigation of genetic diversity associated with geography. *Unasylva* **18**(2–3):73–74, 40–50.

Carter, C. K., Canavera, D., and Caron, P. 1981. "Early Growth of Exotic Larches at Three Locations in Maine." Coop. For. Res. Unit, Res. Note No. 8, University of Maine, Orono.

Dorman, K. W. 1975. *The Genetics and Breeding of Southern Pines.* USDA Agriculture Handbook No. 471, pp. 173–175.

Edwards, M. W. 1963. "The Use of Exotic Trees in Increasing Production with Particular Reference to Northwestern Europe." World Cons. on For. Gen. and Tree Impr., Stockholm, Sweden.

Endler, J. A. 1977. *Geographic Variation, Speciation and Clines.* Princeton University Press, Princeton, N.J.

Falkenhagen, E. R. 1979. "Provenance Variation in Growth, Timber and Pulp Properties of *Pinus caribaea* in South Africa. Bull. 39, South African For. Res. Ins., Dept. of For., Pretoria.

Farmer, A. E., and Barnett, P.E. 1972. Altitudinal variation in seed characteristics of black cherry in the southern Appalachians. *For. Sci.* **18**(2):169–175.

Golfari, L., and Caser, R. L. 1977. "Zoneamento ecológico da região florestal [Ecological Zoning of the Northeastern Region for Experimental Forestry]." PRODEPEF, Technical Bulletin no. 10.

Grant, V. 1971. *Plant Speciation.* Columbia University Press, New York.

Gregor, J. W. 1944. The ecotype. *Biol. Rev.* **19**:20–30.

Hagner, S. 1979. Optimum productivity—a silviculturist's view. In *Forest Plantations—The Shape of the Future,* pp. 49–68. Weyerhaeuser Science Symposium, Tacoma, Wash.

Hillis, W. E., and Brown, A. G. 1978. *Eucalypts for Wood Production.* Griffin Press Ltd., Adelaide, Australia.

Holzer, K. 1965. "Standardization of Methods for Provenance Research and Testing." IUFRO Kongress, München, Germany, Vol. III (22), pp. 672–718.

Hunt, R., and Zobel, B. 1978. Frost-hardy *Eucalyptus* grow well in the southeast. *South. Jour. Appl. For.* 2(1):6–10.

Huxley, J. S. 1938. Clines: an auxiliary taxonomic principle. *Nature* 143:219.

Jones, N., and Burley, J. 1973. Seed certification, provenance nomenclature and genetic history in forestry. *Sil. Gen.* 22:53–92.

Kellison, R. C. 1967. "A Geographic Variation Study of Yellow Poplar (*Liriodendron tulipifera*) within North Carolina." Technical Report no. 33, North Carolina State University, School of Forest Resources.

Kellison, R. K. 1981. "Characteristics Affecting Quality of Timber from Plantations, Their Determination and Scope for Modification." World Forestry Congress, Tokyo, Japan.

Kiellander, C. L. 1960. Swedish spruce and continental spruce [Svensk gran och Kontinentgran]. Föreningen Skogsträdsförädling, F.S. Information No. 3.

Krygier, J. T. 1958. "Survival and Growth of Thirteen Tree Species in Coastal Oregon." Res. Paper No. 26, Pacific Northwest Forestry and Range Experimental Station, Portland, Ore.

Lacaze, J. F. 1977. "Advances in Species and Provenance Selection." 3rd World Cons. on For. Tree Breeding, Canberra, Australia.

Lacaze, J. F. 1978. Advances in species and provenance selection. *Unasylva* 30(119–120):17–20.

Ladrach, W. E. 1980. "Variability in the Growth of *P. taeda in* Colombia Due to Provenance." Investigation Forestal, Carton de Colombia.

Langlet, O. 1936. Studien uber die physiologische Variabilität der Kiefer und deren Zusammenhang mit dem Klima, Beiträge zur Kenntnis Ökotypen von *Pinus silvestris. Medd. Statens Skogsförsöksanstalt.* 29:219–470.

Langlet, O. 1938. Proveniensförsök med olika trädslag [provenance tests with various wood species]. *Särtryck Svenska Skogsvårdsföreningens Tidskrift.* I–II:255–278.

Langlet, O. 1959a. A cline or not a cline—a question of Scots pine. *Sil. Gen.* 8(1):13–22.

Langlet, O. 1959b. Polsk gran för Sverige [Polish seed for Sweden]. *Särtryck Skogen* 5:1–4.

Langlet, O. 1967. "Regional Intra-specific Variousness." IUFRO Congress, München, Germany, Vol. III(22), pp. 435–458.

Larsen, C. S. 1954. "Provenance Testing and Forest Tree Breeding." Proc. 11th Cong. IUFRO, Rome, pp. 467–473.

Long, E. M. 1980. Texas and Louisiana loblolly pine study confirms importance of local seed sources. *South. Jour. Appl. For.* **4**(3):127–131.

Marsh, E. K. 1969. "Selecting Adapted Races of Introduced Species." 2nd World Cons. For. Tree Breed., Washington, D.C., pp. 1249–1261.

Mettler, L. E., and Gregg, T. G. 1969. *Population Genetics and Evolution.* Prentice-Hall, Englewood Cliffs, N.J.

Muller, H. J. 1959. The prospects of genetic change. *Am. Sci.* **47**(4):551–561.

Namkoong, G. 1969. "Nonoptimality of Local Races." 10th South. Conf. on For. Tree Impr., Houston, Tex., pp. 149–153.

Nikles, D. G., and Burley, G. 1977. "International Cooperation in Breeding Tropical Pines." 3rd World Cons. For. Tree Breed., Canberra, Australia.

Nikles, D. G., Burley, J., and Barnes, R. D. 1978. "Progress and Problems of Genetic Improvement in Tropical Forest Trees." Proc. Joint Workshop in Brisbane, Australia, Vol. 1., Commonwealth Forestry Institute, Oxford University, England.

Owino, F. 1977. "Selection of Species and Provenances for Afforestation in East Africa." 3rd World Cons. on For. Tree Breed., Canberra, Australia.

Pellate, E. De Vecchi. 1969. "Evolution and Importance of Land Races in Breeding." 2nd World Cons. For. Tree Breed, Washington, D.C., pp. 1263–1278.

Persson, A. 1980. "*Pinus contorta* as an Exotic Species." Swedish Un. of Ag. Sciences, Dept. For. Gen. Research Notes, Garpenberg, Sweden.

Rehfeldt, G. E. 1979. Ecotypic differentiation in populations of *Pinus monticola* in north Idaho—Myth or reality? *Am. Natur.* **114**:627–636.

Rehfeldt, G. E. 1980. "Genetic Gains from Tree Improvement of Ponderosa Pine in Southern Idaho. U.S. Forest Service Research Paper Int-263, Ogden, Utah.

Rohmeder, E. 1959. Beispiele für die Überlegenheit fremder Provenienzen über die heimische Standorstrasse bei den Baumarten *Pinus silvestris* und *Picea abies* (examples of the superiority of foreign provenances over the native races in the species *Pinus silvestris* and *Picea abies*). *Sonderdruck Allgemeine Forstzeitschr.* **43**:1–5.

Sanchez, P. A., and Buol, S. W. 1975. Soils of the tropics and the world food crises. *Science* **188**:598–603.

Shimuzu, J. Y., and Higa, A. R. 1981. Racial variation of *Pinus taeda* in Southern Brazil up to 6 years of age. *Bol. Pesquisa Flor.* **2**:1–26.

Squillace, A. E., and Silen, R. R. 1962. Racial variation in ponderosa pine. *For. Sci. Mon.* **2**.

Squillace, A. N. 1966. Geographic variation in slash pine. *For. Sci. Mon.* **10**.

Stebbins, G. L. 1950. *Variation and Evolution in Plants*. Columbia University Press, New York.

Talbert, J., White, G., and Webb, C. 1980. Analysis of a Virginia pine seed source trial in the interior South. *South Jour. Appl. For.* **4**(3):153–156.

Tozawa, M. 1924. Necessity of provenance test and the urgent need of a test plantation network. *Jour. Korean For. Assoc.* **22**:1–5.

Turresson, G. 1922. The species and variety as ecological units. *Hereditas* **3**:100–113.

van Buijtenen, J. P., and Stern, K. 1967. "Marginal Populations and Provenance Research." IUFRO Kongress, München, Germany, Vol. III(22), pp. 319–331.

Vavilov, N. I. 1926. Studies on the origin of cultivated plants. *Appl. Bot. Plant Breed.* (*Leningrad*) **16**(2):1–248.

Wakeley, P. C. 1954. The relation of geographic race to forest tree improvement. *Jour. For.* **52**(9):653.

Wakeley, P. C. 1963. "How Far Can Seed be Moved?" Proc. 7th South. Conf. on For. Tree Impr., Gulfport, Miss., Pub. No. 23, pp. 38–43.

Wakeley, P. C., and Bercaw, T. E. 1965. Loblolly pine provenance test at age 35. *Jour. For.* **63**(3):168–174.

Wells, O. O., and Wakeley, P. C. 1966. Geographic variation in survival, growth and fusiform-rust infection of planted loblolly pine. *For. Sci. Mono.* **11**.

Wells, O. O., and Wakeley, P. C. 1970. Variation in longleaf pine from several geographic sources. *For. Sci.* **16**(1):28–42.

Wells, O. O. 1971. "Provenance Research and Fusiform Rust in the Southern United States," 4th N. Amer. For. Biol. Workshop, Syracuse, N.Y., pp. 23–28.

Whyte, A. G. D., Adams, P̄., and McEwen, S. E. 1980. "Size and Stem Characteristics of Foxtails Compared with *P. caribaea* v. *hondurensis* of Normal Habit." IUFRO, Division 5 Conference, Oxford, England, p. 59.

Wiersma, J. H. 1963. A new method of dealing with results of provenance tests. *Sil. Gen.* **12**(6):200–205.

Woods, F. W., Vincent, L. W., Moschler, W. W., and Core, H. A. 1979. Height, diameter and specific gravity of "foxtail" trees of *Pinus caribaea. For. Prod. Jour.* **29**(5):43–44.

Wright, J. W., and Baldwin, H. I. 1957. The 1938 International Union Scotch pine provenance test in New Hampshire. *Sil. Gen.* **6**(1):2–14.

Zobel, B. J., Campbell, T. E., Cech, F. C., and Goddard, R. E. 1956. "Survival and Growth of Native and Exotic Pines, Including Hybrid Pines, in Western Louisiana and East Texas." Research Note 17, Texas Forest Service.

Zobel, B. J. 1961. "Pines in the Tropics and Sub-tropics." Proc. IUFRO, 13th Congress, Vienna, Austria, Vol. 1(22/10), pp. 1–9.

Zobel, B. J. 1964. Pines of southeastern U.S., Bahamas and Mexico and their use in Brazil. *Silvi. São Paulo* **3**(3):303–310.

Zobel, B.J. 1979. Florestas baseadas em exoticas (forestry based on exotics). *Bol. Tec.* **2**(3):22–30.

Zobel, B. J. 1981. Wood quality from fast grown plantations. *Tappi* **64**(1):71–74.

CHAPTER 4

Quantitative Aspects of Forest Tree Improvement

The first three chapters of this book have been largely concerned with the variation that occurs in forest tree populations and how it can be used. It has been shown that variation almost always has both a genetic and an environmental component, and that genetic tests are necessary to separate genetic and environmental influences. A major task of the forest geneticist is to obtain estimates of the genetic and environmental components and to determine how each can best be manipulated. Such estimates are crucial to tree improvement programs, and to a large degree, they will determine the efficiency of a selection and breeding program. The successful forest tree improver must have a working knowledge of various aspects of forest management and silviculture. Added to this, he or she must also have an understanding of basic genetic principles and how they are applied in tree improvement. This chapter will cover some general details of the mechanisms of inheritance in forest trees, concepts that are crucial to the development of a selection and breeding program.

GENETICAL AND STATISTICAL CONSIDERATIONS

It was emphasized in Chapter 2 that genetic variation that occurs in living organisms is inherited in a way that is common to all species. Much of the basic genetic research that elucidated the mechanisms of heredity was done with such organisms as garden peas, fruit flies, mice, and corn. Most of the early studies involved genes with major effects; that is, the expression of the trait was controlled by one or two gene loci that had a profound effect on the phenotype. Phenotypes could be classified into distinct categories, such as tall or short or brown or white, and there was rarely any overlap between them. These are defined as *qualitative* traits. The classic experiments conducted by Gregor Mendel on the garden pea (*Pisum sativum*) dealt with traits inherited in a qualitative manner, and they were the basis for the science of genetics (Strickberger, 1976). Principles derived from Mendel's experiments are included in nearly all introductory biology classes. There are many other examples of traits involving major gene effects in addition to peas. Some of the most familiar of those are eye color (i.e., blue eyed vs. brown eyed) and the A, B, and O blood groups in humans.

Very few economic traits in forest trees are inherited in a pattern that can be attributed to the effects of major genes. Most major gene effects in trees are evident when dealing with selfing, which increases levels of homozygosity for rare recessive alleles. For example, selfing studies with loblolly pine and several other conifers revealed a number of recessive alleles that produced seedlings with several unusual phenotypes (Franklin, 1968, 1970). Occasionally, an economically important trait of forest trees is influenced by genes with major effects, especially for pest resistance. One example is the inheritance of resistance of sugar pine (*P. lambertiana*) to blister rust (*Cronartium ribicola*) (Kinloch and Byler, 1981).

Almost all important traits in forest trees are influenced by several or many gene loci, each of which has a relatively small effect on the phenotype. This results in a large array of genotypes for traits influenced by many genes if there is genetic variation at the influential gene loci. When environmental effects are added to this array, a continuem of phenotypes results. An important aspect of this type of inheritance is that individuals cannot generally be placed into distinct groups. Characteristics of this sort that vary continuously are said to be *quantitative* or metric traits. These are best dealt with through *measurements* on numbers of progenies of different parents. It is important to recognize that many traits that are measured as "all-or-none" characteristics, such as presence or absence of disease symptoms, are actually influenced by multiple gene loci and are quantitative characteristics; therefore, they must be treated as such.

During the past half century, a special branch of genetics called *quantitative genetics* has been developed to deal with characteristics that are inherited quantitatively and show continuous variation. Concepts developed by quantitative geneticists form much of the basis for many plant and animal breeding programs in existence today, including forest tree improvement programs. They differ from concepts developed for qualitative traits in that they *involve large numbers of progenies* (simple ratios cannot be observed) and measurements. It is not possible to fully cover the field of quantitative genetics in one or two chapters. Indeed, that is not the purpose of this book. However, to understand tree improvement it is necessary to acquire an understanding of its concepts. In the following sections the more basic and pertinent aspects of quantitative genetics that are of primary importance to tree improvement programs will be discussed. A more complete coverage of the principles of quantitative genetics can be found in texts, such as those by Kempthorne (1957), Falconer (1960), and Becker (1975). Thorough coverage of the relationship of quantitative genetics to forest trees can be found in Namkoong's monograph (1979).

Statistical Concepts

The study and manipulation of quantitative characteristics is essentially one involving the inheritance of measurements that are analyzed using statistical techniques. For example, if tree height is the trait of interest, the tree improver begins assessment by measuring heights on large numbers of trees, either in natural stands, plantations from wild seed, or pedigreed genetic tests. Once these height–measurement data are accumulated, they are analyzed through the use of statistics.

The tree improvement specialist must have a working knowledge of statistical methods to make decisions about tree populations and how they will respond to selection and breeding. Both graduate and undergraduate training programs in forest genetics involve statistics. Although some individuals are reluctant to become involved in statistical analyses, these are not really too difficult. Also, excellent textbooks are available that provide both an introductory and advanced treatment of statistical methods (e.g., Cochran and Cox, 1957; Steel and Torrie, 1960; Snedecor and Cochran, 1967; Sokal and Rohlf, 1969; Neter and Wasserman, 1974). The statistical concepts presented in this chapter are as simplified as possible, and will already be familiar to some readers. They form the foundation for much quantitative genetics theory, and are essential for a successful selection and breeding program.

The term *population* has been used numerous times in previous chapters. In the statistical sense, a population refers to the entire group of individuals, items, or scores from which a sample is drawn. This supplements the biological definition of a population given in Chapter 1 as *a community of interbreeding individuals*. A population may be described in several ways; terms used to describe it are called *parameters*. Usually the population being studied is much too large to allow measurement of every individual in it. For example, there might be interest in the population consisting of all loblolly pine growing on the Coastal Plain of North Carolina. If specific gravity was the trait of interest, it would not be possible to measure this characteristic on every tree in the population. Therefore, to obtain an estimate of the population parameter specific gravity, samples must be obtained from the population from which analyses and inferences about the population are made. Descriptions of a population based upon samples obtained from it are estimates of the population's parameters. As successive samples are taken, they will usually be somewhat different due to sampling chance. A large number of statistical methods have been developed that will guide the researcher or practitioner in deciding if the sample obtained provides a sufficiently precise estimate of the population parameter of interest.

The most common and useful parameter used to describe a population is the *population mean*, or the average of the individuals that make up the population. Symbolically, the population mean is expressed as

$$\bar{X} = \frac{\Sigma X_i}{n}$$

where $\bar{X}$ = mean, Σ = sum of, X_i = individual observations, and n = number of observations. Simply stated, the population mean is the sum of the individual observations divided by the number of observations. A mean can be computed for any characteristic for which measurements are taken or scores are given.

Although the mean is a most useful and widely used statistic, it indicates nothing about the *distribution* of the individuals within the population. In other words, one can tell nothing about the *variation* that exists in the population just by computing the mean. The amount and pattern of variation is of vital importance in the analysis and use of information from a population. Variation patterns or distributions often are easily visualized when pictured graphically by plotting the frequency in which a measurement occurs on the vertical or Y axis against the range in values in the horizontal or X axis. This is illustrated in Figure 4.1, which shows the distribution of sampled trees having different specific gravities within a population of loblolly pine. Numerous types of distributions can occur biologically in populations, but the one most often encountered is the "normal" distribution (see Figure 4.2).

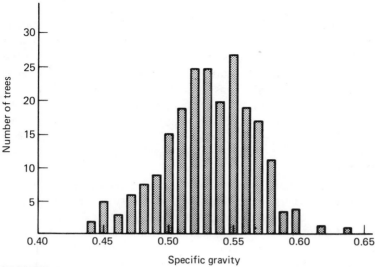

FIGURE 4.1

Variation in wood specific gravity in a loblolly pine population is illustrated. Trees sampled had the same age and were growing on land of the same general site class. The X, or horizontal, axis denotes specific gravity values, whereas the Y, or vertical, axis gives the number of trees that have a given specific gravity value. The distribution of wood specific gravity values approximates a "normal" distribution (see text).

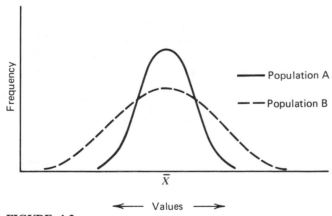

FIGURE 4.2

An example of two populations with different variances is shown. Although the mean is the same in both instances, individuals in Population B are more widely distributed than those in Population A. Therefore, Population B has a greater variance.

In a normal distribution, the measurement or score most frequently observed is an intermediate value that is equal to the population mean when the distribution is exactly "normal." Measurements or scores that differ from the mean occur with decreasing frequency the farther one proceeds from the mean. Most quantitative genetics theory assumes a normal distribution of measurements from a population. Although exactly normal distributions often do not occur, the observations usually approximate a normal distribution closely enough so that the assumption of a normal distribution is valid for analytical purposes. When other distributions occur, methods are often available to transform the measurements so that they more nearly resemble a normal distribution; then standard analyses can be used (Snedecor and Cochran, 1967).

Normal distributions are found for many characteristics in trees, especially for height and other growth factors. Sometimes, actual measurements cannot be made, but subjective scores are used to describe tree phenotypes. As an example, tree straightness may be judged on a 1-to-5 scale. A tree of average straightness would be given a score of 3, with scores of 1 or 5 given only to the straightest or most crooked individuals. Such scores are often treated as if they resemble a normal distribution.

The parameter most often used to describe the spread of individuals within a population is the *variance,* which is computed in the following manner:

$$\sigma^2 = \frac{\Sigma(X_i - \bar{X})^2}{n - 1}$$

where σ^2 = variance, X = mean, Σ = sum of, X_1 = individual observations, and n = number of observations. The *variance* is the sum of squares of the deviations of individuals from the mean divided by one less than the total number of observations. The term $(n - 1)$ in the denominator defines what is commonly referred to as the number of *degrees of freedom* for the variance estimate. A large variance occurs when individual values are widely dispersed, whereas a smaller variance results when the distribution around the mean is narrow (Figure 4.2).

Another useful population parameter is the *standard deviation,* which is simply the square root of the variance. Computationally, the standard deviation can be expressed as

$$\sigma = \sqrt{\sigma^2} = \sqrt{\frac{\Sigma(X_i - \bar{X})^2}{n - 1}}$$

The standard deviation is expressed in the same units of measurement as the mean of the population and is a very useful tool for describing the dispersion of individual values. When measurements are distributed in a normal fashion, approximately 67% of the observations will fall within one standard deviation on either side of the mean, and 95% of the observations will be within two standard

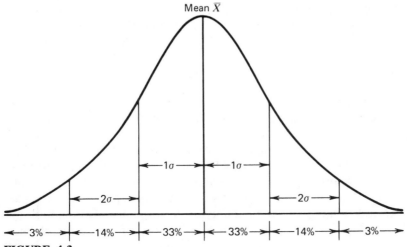

Mean $\bar{X}$

$-1\sigma-$ $-1\sigma-$

$-2\sigma-$ $-2\sigma-$

$-3\%-$ $-14\%-$ $-33\%-$ $-33\%-$ $-14\%-$ $-3\%-$

FIGURE 4.3

Illustrated is a summary of population parameters—the normal distribution, the population mean, a standard deviation, and the proportion of values within the indicated number of standard deviations from the mean.

deviations of the mean. A diagramatic illustration of a normal curve showing mean and standard deviations is given in Figure 4.3.

Populations are often described by their mean and standard deviation, or, symbolically as follows:

$$\bar{X} \pm \sigma$$

For example, if the heights of trees in a genetic test were described by the terms 14 ± 2 m, it would indicate that average tree height in the plantation was 14 m and that the standard deviation was 2 m (the variance would be 4 m). If heights in the test were normally distributed, about 67% of the trees would be between $+1$ and -1 standard deviations of the mean or between 12 and 16 m tall.

Although the mean and the variance, or standard deviations, are the statistical parameters most often used to describe a population, they do not describe modes of inheritance or the proportion of the variation that is genetic in origin. The observed or estimated variance must therefore be separated into its genetic and environmental components. Computation of these components involves partitioning the phenotypic values into genetic and environmental sources of variation.

Genetic Values

The selection phase of an applied tree improvement program has as its objective the choice of the best genotypes to use as parents for the production of improved planting stock and as a base for future breeding activities. We know that nothing certain can be said about a tree's genotype from its appearance, or phenotype, because it is influenced both by its genetic potential and the quality of the environment in which the tree is growing. In simple terms,

$$P = G + E, \text{ or phenotype} = \text{genotype} + \text{environment.}$$

The best way to tell if a parent tree is of superior genetic quality is to compare the performance of its offspring against the offspring of the other parent trees. These progeny trials are designed to separate genetic from environmental differences by giving all progenies a similar environment in which to grow. Thus, if Parent A has taller offspring than Parent B in similar environments, and these differences can be confirmed statistically, Parent A is said to produce *genetically superior* progeny. A major effort in most tree improvement programs is directed toward testing and ranking selected phenotypes for their genetic qualities.

The genetic values of parents are expressed in terms of *combining abilities*. There are two types of combining abilities of special interest to the tree breeder, and these will be explained by use of the following example.

Assume that eight trees have been selected and that it is desired to determine their genetic worth. Four of the trees are chosen as male parents, and the other four will serve as female parents. Each male is mated to each female, and the offspring are established in a progeny test. After several years in the field, the progenies are assessed. The average performance of each cross is measured in units of volume, as is presented in the following two-way table. Also indicated is the average performance of the progeny of each parent, and the overall test mean.

Female parents	Male parents				Progeny means
	1	**2**	**3**	**4**	
5	9	17	12	14	13
6	10	16	12	10	12
7	11	20	10	15	14
8	14	15	6	17	12
Progeny means	11	17	10	14	Test mean 13

Note that the average performance of the progeny of the specific cross 5 × 1 is 9 volume units, whereas the average performance of the offspring of all crosses with parent 5 is 13 units. The test mean, or the average performance of all trees growing in the test, is 13 units.

General combining ability (GCA) is defined as the average performance of the progeny of an individual when it is mated to a number of other individuals in the population (Falconer, 1960). Although general combining abilities may be expressed in absolute units, it is usually more convenient and meaningful to express them as deviations from the overall mean. Thus, a parent with GCA of 0 has an average general combining ability. A positive GCA indicates a parent that produces above-average progeny, whereas a parent with a negative GCA produces progeny that perform below average for the population.

The preceding table can be used to calculate general combining abilities for each of the parents. For example, the GCA of male Parent 2 would be calculated as

$$\text{GCA}_2 = \text{mean of parent 2} - \text{test mean}$$
$$= 17 - 13 = +4$$

Parent 2 therefore has a general ability (GCA_2) for volume of $+4$ units. Other general combining abilities would be calculated in the same way. For example, general combining ability for Parent 4 is $+1$ volume units, whereas GCA of Parent 3 is -3 units.

The *breeding value* of an individual is defind as *twice* its general combining ability. The difference between breeding value and general combining ability is largely conceptual in nature. Breeding values are meaningful because the parent in question contributes only half of the genes to his or her offspring, the other half coming from other members of the population. The breeding value of Parent 2 would be calculated as

$$2\,(\text{GCA}_2) = 2 \times (4) = 8$$

Specific combining ability (SCA) is a term that refers to the average performance of the progeny of a *cross* between two specific parents that are different from what would be expected on the basis of their general combining abilities alone. It can be either negative or positive. Specific combining ability *always* refers to a specific cross, and *never* to a particular parent by itself.

Specific combining ability for the cross between Parents 3 and 6 (a cross value of 12) would be calculated as follows:

1. Calculate general combining abilities for both parents.
$$\text{GCA}_3 = -3;\ \text{GCA}_6 = -1$$
2. The general combining abilities are added to the population mean giving the anticipated value of the cross 3×6 based upon general combining abilities.
$$\text{Anticipated value} = \text{test mean} + \text{GCA}_3 + \text{GCA}_6$$
$$= 13 + (-3) + (-1) = 9$$
3. Subtract the value calculated in (2) from the observed value of the cross. The result is the specific combining ability.
$$\text{SCA}_{6 \times 3} = \text{observed value} - \text{anticipated value}$$
$$= 12 - 9 = +3$$

This means that cross 6×3 is performing 3 volume units better than would be expected based on the GCA's of Parents 3 and 6.

It must be stressed that *nothing* can be said about the utility of a cross based solely on its specific combining ability. Because SCA is a deviation from what is expected based on general combining abilities, a cross may have a positive SCA but still not be a good performer relative to other crosses, as in the example given with Parents 6 and 3. The cross has an SCA $= +3$, but its average performance of 12 is still below the population mean of 13 because of the poor general combining abilities of the two parents involved. It should be stressed here that GCA, breeding value, and SCA are trait-specific descriptions of a parent's or cross's genetic value. For example, a parent could have an above-average GCA for volume and at the same time, a below-average GCA for wood specific gravity.

The two types of combining abilities are a reflection of different types of interactions between alleles at the gene loci. General combining ability represents an average performance of the progeny of a parent when it is crossed to many other parents. It is therefore a reflection of the parent's *additive genetic value*; that is, it reflects that portion of its genotype for a specific trait that the parent may transmit to its progeny, regardless of which other parent is involved in the cross. It represents the additive type of gene action discussed in Chapter 2. Parents who are known to have a high GCA for a trait are said to be *good general combiners*, but they are not always desirable. One can have a high GCA for disease susceptibility, for crooked tree boles, or other undesired characteristics.

Because it represents an additive effect that can be predicted, general combining ability is sometimes thought of as the "dependable" portion of a tree's genetic constitution. It is the type of combining ability that is utilized in forest tree seed orchards that are composed of many parents. The improved performance of the planting stock derived from the orchard is due to the accumulation of favorable alleles that have an additive genetic effect on the phenotypes of the trees derived from the orchard.

The specific combining ability shown by a given cross is a reflection of the interaction of the two alleles at the gene loci influencing that trait (dominance gene action) and interactions between alleles at different gene loci influencing the trait, or epistatic gene action. As discussed in Chapter 2, these two types of genetic effects are usually referred to as nonadditive genetic effects. SCA can usully be attributed in large part to the dominance type of gene action. Since specific combining ability occurs because of interactions between specific alleles, or between gene loci, its value cannot be predicted from the phenotypes of the parents before the cross is made. It cannot be utilized in a seed orchard program involving many parents because open pollination results in many different combinations of alleles across gene loci.

There are two major ways to make use of specific combining ability in a tree improvement program. One is to use vegetative propagation to produce commercial quantities of planting stock that are genetically identical to the tree from which they were taken. In vegetative propagation, the genetic makeup of the parent is passed along intact, and the specific combinations of alleles at all gene loci are preserved. The second way to utilize specific combining ablty is to make crosses to mass-produce seed from specified parental combinations; this can be done by control pollinations or by methods such as two-clone seed orchards. Both of these methods, especially vegetative propagation (Chapter 10) have been used with some species to produce improved planting stock. For most species, though, costs and technological difficulties associated with use of SCA have made general combining ability the major focus of operational tree improvement programs.

Types of Genetic Variation

Variation in tree populations can be partitioned into genetic and environmental components. The simple model described previously for individual tree values can be extended to apply to variation encountered in a *population* of individuals. If an individual phenotype is described as

$$P = G + E$$

then variation can be stated as

phenotypic variation = genetic variation + environmental variation

or

$$\sigma_P^2 = \sigma_G^2 + \sigma_E^2$$

Genetic values (σ_G^2) are influenced by both additive and nonadditive effects. Genetic variation can therefore be partitioned into additive and nonadditive components. Symbolically,

$$\sigma_G^2 = \sigma_A^2 + \sigma_{NA}^2$$

The model of phenotypic variation can therefore be extended to read

$$\sigma_P^2 = \sigma_A^2 + \sigma_{NA}^2 + \sigma_E^2$$

The additive genetic variance (σ_A^2) arises from differences among parents in general combining ability and is simply the variance of breeding values (breeding value = $2 \cdot$ GCA) in the population. Nonadditive variance (σ_{NA}^2) is the result of specific combining ability effects. The variance of specific combining abilities in a noninbred population can be shown to be equal to $\frac{1}{4}\sigma_{NA}^2$.

Most tree improvement programs are aimed at selecting parents with high general combining abilities or high breeding values. In these instances, the additive variance is the "type" of genetic variation that is utilized to produce improved propagules. Successful use of nonadditive variance depends upon vegetative propagation or using specific crosses.

Heritability

The concept of heritability is one of the most important and most used in quantitative genetics. *Heritability* values express the proportion of variation in the population that is attributable to genetic differences among individuals. It is therefore a ratio indicating the degree to which parents pass their characteristics along to their offspring. Heritability is of key importance in estimating gains that can be obtained from selection programs. The discussion here will focus on individual-tree heritability. Another type of heritability estimate, the heritability of family means, will be discussed in the chapter on genetic testing (Chapter 8).

Two types of individual-tree heritabilities are important in applied tree improvement. *Broad-sense heritability* (H^2) is defined as the ratio of total genetic variation in a population to the phenotypic variation, or

$$H^2 = \frac{\sigma_G^2}{\sigma_P^2} = \frac{\sigma_A^2 + \sigma_{NA}^2}{\sigma_A^2 + \sigma_{NA}^2 + \sigma_E^2}$$

Broad-sense heritability can range from 0 to 1. A lower limit of 0 would occur if *none* of the variation in a population was attributable to genetics. If *all* variation was due to genetics, then broad-sense heritability would be equal to 1. Broad-sense heritability has a limited application in tree improvement and is of primary use when both the additive and nonadditive variation can be transferred from parent to offspring, such as when vegetative propagation is used.

Narrow-sense heritability is the ratio of additive genetic variance to total variance. Symbolically,

$$h^2 = \frac{\sigma_A^2}{\sigma_P^2} = \frac{\sigma_A^2}{\sigma_A^2 + \sigma_{NA}^2 + \sigma_E^2}$$

The lower limit for narrow-sense heritability is also 0 (no additive variance), and the upper limit is 1 (no environmental or nonadditive variance). Narrow-sense heritability is *never* greater than broad-sense heritability; if all the genetic variance is of the additive type, narrow- and broad-sense heritabilities are equal. Most heritability estimates given in the forest genetics literature are for narrow-sense heritability, because most tree improvement programs today are aimed at improving general combining ability and thus utilize only the additive portion of the genetic variance. This will undoubtedly change as vegetative propagation methods and economical methods of producing specific crosses, such as supplemental mass pollination, become available, but as of today, narrow-sense heritabilities are of the most use to tree breeders.

An important but often overlooked aspect of heritability estimates is that they apply only to a particular population growing in a particular environment at a particular point in time. For example, estimates of heritability for a group of trees grown in a greenhouse would not be appropriate for the same trees growing in a field environment. Height in the greenhouse may not be influenced by exactly the same genes as height in the field. Even if the two traits were the same, though, estimates of h^2 obtained in the greenhouse will usually be higher than those from the field, because there is less environmental variation in the greenhouse. As can be seen in the formula for h^2, changes in the environmental variance component (σ_E^2) in the denominator will have a direct effect on the h^2 ratio. Because of the influence of the environment on the heritability ratio, the h^2 estimates for a given characteristic in a species in one geographic area probably will not be the same as those found in another region. The heritability values of a given characteristic in a population often change with age when the environment changes and when the genetic control of the characteristic changes as the trees mature. The degree of change with age has been debated, but there is now an accumulating body of evidence that suggests that heritabilities do change markedly, and perhaps in a predictable fashion, as test plantations grow and develop (Namkoong et al., 1972; Namkoong and Conkle, 1976; Franklin, 1979).

The most widely used technique in forest genetics to estimate heritability is to grow progeny from a group of parents or crosses together in the same genetic test plantation. Heritability estimates are then derived from the relative performance of the progenies within and between parent trees. Breeding schemes and experimental designs that can be used to estimate the necessary variances and heritabilities are discussed in Chapter 8. Another method of estimating heritabilities is through parent–offspring regression techniques (Falconer, 1960).

Narrow-sense heritability estimates for height, wood specific gravity, and form traits for a number of species are shown in Table 4.1. There is obviously much variation in the degree to which traits are under additive genetic control. Some characteristics, like wood specific gravity, appear to be strongly controlled genetically regardless of the species and are uniform over somewhat different environments. Other traits, like height growth, are under a lesser degree of genetic control and are strongly influenced by the environment in which the trees are grown.

Even in large experiments with many families, heritabilities are not estimated without error. All h^2 estimates should be thought of as being figures that give a general idea of the strength of inheritance. For example, a heritability of 0.15 should not be thought of as being much different than a heritability of 0.20. The imprecision of many heritability estimates can be seen in Table 4.1, where the heritability of black walnut height at age 8 was listed as $h^2 = 1.25$. Earlier discussion indicated that heritability cannot be greater than one; hence the $h^2 = 1.25$ value is an overestimate. Absolute estimates of heritability are needed for many purposes, such as in gain estimation, where h^2 is an integral part of the gain formula. However, the main value of the heritability concept to the tree breeder is to indicate the general strength of genetic control and the best approach for use in tree improvement programs. Despite its usefulness, one should always keep in mind that heritability is not an invariant value fixed to a population. Heritability itself is a variable ratio and is subject to changes. Therefore, whenever heritability is used in determining the amount of genetic gain or breeding strategies, values should be qualified with a statement that the confidence level is less than 100%

The basic and key point about heritability is that it is a ratio between genetic and phenotypic variances; thus, it is not a fixed value for a given characteristic of a given species. Estimates of heritability are not estimated without error; therefore the ratios obtained are only a relative indication of genetic control and should not be interpreted as absolute or invarient values.

TABLE 4.1

Individual Tree Narrow-Sense Heritability Estimates in Forest Trees

Trait	Heritability	Reference
Height		
Douglas fir	0.10–0.30	Campbell (1972)
Loblolly pine	.44	Matziras and Zobel (1973)
Loblolly pine	0.14–0.26	Stonecypher et al. (1973)
Slash pine	0.03–0.37	Barber (1964)
Longleaf pine Age 5	0.18	Snyder and Namkoong (1978)
Age 7	0.12	Snyder and Namkoong (1978)
Yellow poplar	0.42–0.84	Kellison (1970)
Black walnut Age 1	0.55	McKeand (1978)
Age 8	1.25	McKeand (1978)
Sweetgum Age 2	0.25	Ferguson and Cooper (1977)
Age 11	0.08	Ferguson and Cooper (1977)
Wood Specific Gravity		
Loblolly pine	0.76–0.87	Goggans (1961)
Loblolly pine	0.41	Chuntanaparb (1973)
Scots pine	0.46–0.56	Personn (1972)
Slash pine	0.50	Goddard and Cole (1966)
Eucalyptus deglupta	0.44	Davidson (1972)
Eucalyptus viminalis	0.55	Otegbye and Kellison (1980)
Form		
Loblolly pine—stem		
straightness	0.14–0.21	Stonecypher et al. (1973)
Loblolly pine—crown		
form	0.08–0.09	Stonecypher et al. (1973)
Slash pine—pruning		
height	0.36–0.64	Barber (1964)
Douglas fir—stockiness	0.26	Silen (1978)

Note. Heritability estimates vary with species, populations within species, age, and characteristics assessed.

QUANTITATIVE GENETICS AND SELECTION

Introduction

The primary objective of an applied tree improvement program is to change the frequency of desired alleles that influence important tree characteristics in such a way that the improved plants are superior in performance to unimproved material. The way of accomplishing this is through the process of *selection,* which can be defined as "choosing individuals with desired qualities to serve as parents for the next generation." Although selection can be a major tool for studying the way traits are inherited, in applied tree improvement programs selection is primarily used for the improvement of economically important characteristics. The following sections are developed with this in mind.

If selection is to be effective, there must be a genetic variation in the population. As shown before, for most tree improvement activities it is the additive portion of the genetic variation that is readily usable for manipulation by the tree breeder. Selection that is based on utilization of the additive variance works by increasing the frequencies of favorable alleles. The additive effects of these alleles are observed in the improved performance of progeny produced by the breeding program or in seed orchards.

The practice of selection in tree improvement is both a science and an artistic skill that must be developed by the tree improver. It will be the main subject of the next chapter in this book, in which selection will be discussed in detail as it relates to specific phases of tree improvement operations. The following paragraphs will introduce the genetic principles associated with selection activities.

Selection and Genetic Gain

Selection is based upon the principle that the average genetic value of selected individuals will be better than the average value of individuals in the population as a whole. For metric or quantitative traits, gain from selection is usually measured as a change in the population mean. The improvement that can potentially be made from selection for a characteristic is a function of the heritability of the trait, and the variation for the trait that exists in the population.

The importance of heritability in determining the response to selection was stressed earlier. A high heritability indicates that much of the variation for a given characteristic observed in the population is genetic in origin, and that the breeder has a high probability to choose parents that are good genetically by selecting those that have desirable phenotypes.

The total amount of variation for a trait is equally as important as heritability in determining gain that can be made from selection, but it is often overlooked by persons involved in tree improvement activities. The total, or phenotypic, variation is important because of its influence on the *selection differential*. Symbolized by *S*, selection differential is defined as "the average phenotypic value of the selected individuals, expressed as a deviation from the population mean." If there is much phenotypic variation for a given characteristic, then the selection differential can be large, whereas if the total variation is minimal, then the selection differential must be small. The selection differential is pictured graphically in Figure 4.4.

The hatched area in Figure 4.4 represents individuals that have been selected; that is, those that are to be used as parents to produce the next generation of progeny. The selection differential, or *S*, is the difference between the mean of the selected individuals $(\bar{X}_s)$ and the population mean $(\bar{X})$. Symbolically,

$$S = \bar{X}_s - \bar{X}$$

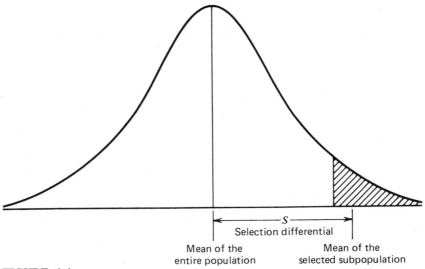

FIGURE 4.4

The selection differential is indicated as the difference between the mean of the entire population and the mean of the selected subpopulation.

When individuals are selected based only on their phenotypic values without information on relatives, response to selection can be estimated by the following formula:

genetic gain = narrow-sense heritability × selection differential

or

$$G = h^2 S$$

From the preceding formula, it is obvious that the progenies from selected parents can be no better than the mean of the selected parents and are usually much less. There are two reasons for this.

1. Usually, only a portion of the superiority of selected parents is due to genetics. The remainder is due to the environment. Superiority caused by environment cannot be passed on from parent to offspring. For example, a selected parent may have been superior to its neighbors because it was growing in a slightly better microhabitat.

2. In population improvement programs where many selected parents are mated together, only the additive genetic variance can be utilized. This is the reason why the narrow-sense heritability is utilized in the preceding equa-

tion. Even if all the variation observed was genetic in origin (no environmental variance), gain would be equal to selection differential only if all the variation was additive and none was of the nonadditive type; that is, $h^2 = 1$.

The tree breeder can influence gain from selection in essentially two ways. First, the base population can be managed so as to maximize heritability by the use of uniform sites and control of the environment. This is one of the primary factors involved in site selection and experimental design for genetic testing and will be discussed in more detail in Chapter 8. Once a population is established in a given environment, however, there is little the breeder can do to increase heritability. As a practical matter, the greatest opportunity to improve gain from selection is to increase the selection differential. This is how tree improvement programs have obtained gains by selection of trees from natural stands. Heritability values for natural stands of trees are usually low, especially for growth traits, because of extreme environmental variation, including competition, but individual trees are greatly different from one another and selection differential can be high.

The selection differential that the breeder uses is dependent upon two factors. One is the proportion of individuals in the population that are selected; that is, the intensity with which selection is done. The other factor is the phenotypic standard deviation, which, as we have seen, is a description of the variation in the population and is expressed in the same units as the population mean. Many breeders prefer to express response to selection or gain by the formula

$$G = ih^2\sigma_p$$

where

$$i = \text{intensity of selection}$$
$$h^2 = \text{heritability}$$
$$\sigma_p = \text{phenotypic standard deviation}$$

This formula indicates that both selection intensity and phenotypic variation influence gains that can be made.

A comparison of the two formulas for selection response shows that

$$G = h^2 S = ih^2\sigma_p$$

Therefore, $S = i\sigma_p$, and $i = S/\sigma_p$

The selection intensity, or i, measures how many standard deviations the mean of the individuals that were selected exceeds the mean of the base population. For example, a selection differential (S) of 10 indicates that the mean of the selected population is 10 units better than the mean of the whole population. If the phenotypic standard deviation (σ_p) is equal to 5, then $i = S/\sigma_p = 2$, and the mean of the selected population is two phenotypic standard deviations better than the mean of the whole population. Because of the characteristics of the normal distribution, the equation $G = ih^2\sigma_p$ is a convenient way to calculate genetic gain. If the breeder knows the phenotypic standard deviation and the intended selection intensity, a response to selection can be predicted before selections are ever made. Alternatively, selection intensity can be varied to determine how many individuals must be chosen to obtain a certain desired gain. Selection intensity is related to the proportion of individuals in the population that are selected. If this proportion is known, it can be calculated directly from that value. Calculation of selection intensity involves a more in-depth knowledge of statistics than has been presented in this text; the procedure involves a determination of areas under the normal curve presented in Figure 4.4. When the population from which selections are to be made consists of only a few individuals, selection intensities will be lower for any given proportion saved. Selection intensities for several different levels of selection and population sizes are indicated in Table 4.2. Complete tables of selection intensities for populations of differing sizes can be found in Becker (1975).

In summary, response to selection for a given trait is determined by two factors: the heritability of the trait and the selection differential that is used. The tree improvement specialist must manage his or her population in such a way that both of these are large enough to give a useful gain from selection.

Selection Methods

There are several different selection methods available to the breeder, depending upon the types of information available. The selection systems commonly used in natural stands and unimproved plantations are discussed in detail in the next

TABLE 4.2

Approximate Selection Intensities (i) for Populations of Various Sizes and Proportions Selected

Proportion Selected	Population Size				
	20	50	200	200	Infinite
0.01	—	—	2.51	2.58	2.66
0.05	1.80	1.99	2.02	2.04	2.06
0.10	1.64	1.70	1.73	1.74	1.76
0.20	1.33	1.37	1.39	1.39	1.40
0.30	1.11	1.14	1.15	1.15	1.16
0.40	0.93	0.95	0.96	0.96	0.97
0.50	0.77	0.79	0.79	0.79	0.80
0.60	0.62	0.63	0.64	0.64	0.64
0.70	0.48	0.49	0.49	0.50	0.50
0.80	0.33	0.34	0.35	0.35	0.35
0.90	0.18	0.19	0.19	0.19	0.20

Note. For a given proportion selected, selection intensity increases with population size.

chapter, and methods used in advanced generations where pedigrees are known are discussed in Chapter 13. The basis for both selection procedures is introduced in the following sections.

Mass Selection   *Mass selection involves choosing individuals solely on the basis of their phenotypes, without regard to any information about performance of ancestors, siblings, offspring, or other relatives.* Mass selection works best for highly heritable traits, where the phenotype is a good reflection of the genotype. It is the only type of selection that can be used in natural stands or in plantations where tree parentage is unknown. Mass selection is rarely used when pedigrees are known, as in advanced-generation genetic tests, because more gain can be obtained using other methods. The terms *mass selection* and *individual selection* are used synonymously in this text.

Family Selection   *Family selection involves the choice of entire families on the basis of their average phenotypic values.* There is no selection of individuals within families, and individual-tree values are used only to compute family means. Family selection works best with traits of low heritability, where individual phenotypes are not a good reflection of genotypes. When family averages are based upon large numbers of individuals, environmental variance tends to be reduced, and family averages become good estimates of average genetic values. Family selection by itself is rarely used in forestry, even with traits of low heritability because more gain can be obtained from other methods that include family selection as a *part* of the method. Family selection may also lead to increased rates of inbreeding because entire families are discarded, thus reducing the genetic base of the population.

Sib Selection   *This is a form of selection in which individuals are chosen on the basis of the performance of their siblings and not on their own performance.* When family sizes are large, it is very similar to family selection. Sib selection is rarely used in forestry but may be applicable when destructive sampling must be used to make measurements, and it is not feasible to preserve genotypes by grafting or other techniques before sampling begins.

Progeny Testing   *Progeny testing involves selection of parent trees based upon the performance of their progeny.* It can be a very precise selection method, because it allows direct estimation of breeding values to use in the selection process. This is what occurs when parents from a seed orchard are progeny tested, and orchards are then rogued of parents that prove to be poor genetically. Progeny testing is not generally the initial form of selection for most breeding programs. Initial selection by progeny testing considerably lengthens the generation interval, which means a critical loss in time. As mentioned in previous chapters, the goal of tree improvement should be to achieve the maximum amount of gain per unit time. Other forms of selection are usually more efficient in accomplishing this goal.

Within-Family Selection   *Here individuals are chosen on the basis of their deviation from the family mean, and family values per se are given no weight when selections are made.* Of all the selections methods, this one gives rise to the slowest rate of inbreeding, which is a major problem in most programs. In practice, family selection is rarely used in tree improvement because large increments of gain can be obtained from selection on family values. Thus, the family and within-family methods are almost always combined.

Family Plus Within-Family Selection   *This two-stage method involves selection on families followed by selection of individuals within families.* It works well with low heritabilities, and is a predominant form of selection used in most advanced generation tree improvement programs. It consists of choosing the best families along with the best individuals in them. A refinement of this method is *combined selection* where *an index is computed that rates all individuals based upon their family value combined with their individual phenotypic values.* Coefficients or weights used in the index equation depend upon the heritability of the trait, with more weight given to the family average for traits with low heritabilities, and with more weight given to the individual when heritability of the trait is high.

Selection for Several Traits

Most tree improvement programs are geared toward the improvement of several traits at the same time. This requires that information developed on several characteristics be included in the selection procedure. How best to do this is one of the major areas of research in tree improvement today. Any of the methods discussed previously could be utilized to develop information on individual traits, but that information must be manipulated to develop a multitrait selection scheme. Essentially three systems have been developed that pertain to multitrait selection.

Tandem Selection   When tandem selection is used, breeding is for one trait at a time until a desired level of improvement is made for that trait. After the desired improvement has been obtained in the first, and usually most important, trait (this may take more than one generation), selection and breeding efforts are then concentrated on other traits. This method of improving several traits in tandem is rarely used because of the pressure of time and the need to improve several traits simultaneously. The primary use of tandem selection is when one trait is of overriding importance, such as disease resistance, or when tropical or subtropical species are introduced into cold envirnments and cold hardiness must be improved before other commercially important traits can be considered.

Independent Culling   Independent culling is a method of multitrait selection that involves setting minimum values for each trait of interest. Individuals must

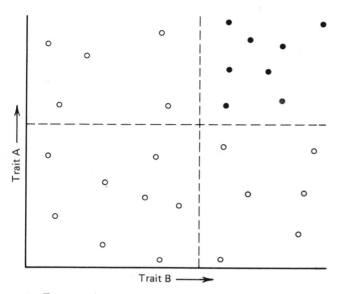

● = Trees saved
○ = Trees culled
FIGURE 4.5

The independent culling method of selection is illustrated as it would be applied for two traits. Only those individuals that meet minimum standards for both traits are saved.

meet these minimum criteria if they are to be retained. Independent culling is shown graphically in Figure 4.5. It is a very widely used form of multitrait selection in forest tree improvement.

Selection Index   The selection index is a form of multitrait selection that combines information on all traits of interest into a single index. This enables the breeder to assign a total score to each individual. In addition to genetic information, it attaches economic weights to each of the characteristics under consideration. In its most complete and complex form, a selection index combines family plus individual information for all traits into one index. Index values for individuals are derived through a multiple regression equation in which the coefficients depend on the heritabilities, the correlation among traits, and the economic weights of each trait. Theoretically, the selection index method of multitrait selection can be shown to give the greatest total genetic gain for all traits combined. A major problem, however, is to have or to determine the appropriate economic weights. Derivation of the correct economic weights is still a major stumbling block to a more widespread appliction of this most useful form of multitrait selection in forest tree improvement. Use of selection indexes where economic weights are grossly incorrect can lead to very inefficient selection programs.

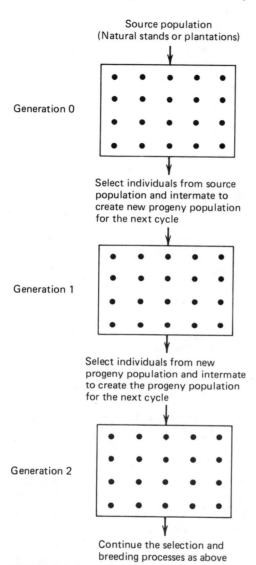

FIGURE 4.6

Illustrated is simple recurrent selection that forms the basis for many tree improvement programs. A successful recurrent selection system will result in genetic gain for many generations of improvement.

Recurrent Selection

Most tree improvement programs are designed to provide continued gain through each of many cycles of improvement. The selection methods discussed before have centered on improvement that can be obtained in one generation, but they are also applicable to programs that involve many generations. The selection procedure that involves many cycles of selection and breeding is known as *recurrent selection*. A number of recurrent selection schemes have been devised by plant and animal breeders in order to utilize variation in general combining ability, and, in some cases, specific combining ability. The system most often used in forest tree improvement is known as simple recurrent selection, which is shown diagramatically in Figure 4.6. With this system, improvement programs begin by selecting trees in natural stands or in unimproved plantations based upon their phenotypic values. Selected trees are then mated, and their progenies are established in such a way that they can be used as a source of selection for the second generation of improvement. In most instances, second-generation selections are made on the basis of family and individual values. These selections are then mated, creating a new progeny generation that can be used as a source of selections for the next generation. The system is one that repeats itself. Selections are made in a base population, mated in some fashion, and the resultant progenies serve as a population for the next generation of improvement.

Recurrent selection programs will be discussed more fully in Chapter 13. For now, it is important for the reader to realize that when many cycles of improvement are envisioned, extreme care must be taken at the outset of the program to ensure that genetic resources are available to make the recurrent selection program successful. The tree improver must have the following two goals in mind when beginning an applied tree improvement program:

1. Obtaining as much gain as possible as quickly as possible through selection and production of improved seed.
2. Maintaining a genetic base that is large and diverse enough to allow successful improvement programs to continue for many generations.

LITERATURE CITED

Barber, J. C. 1964. "Inherent Variation among Slash Pine Progenies at the Ida Cason Calloway Foundation." USDA, U.S. Forest Service Research Paper SE-10, Southeastern For. Expt. Sta.

Becker, W. A. 1975. *Manual of Quantitative Genetics*. Student Book Corporation, Washington State University, Pullman.

Campbell, K. 1972. Genetic variability in juvenile height-growth of Douglas-fir. *Sil. Gen.* **21**:126–129.

Chuntanaparb, L. 1973. "Inheritance of Wood and Growth Characteristics and Their Relationship in Loblolly Pine (*Pinus taeda* L.)." Ph.D. thesis, Department of Forestry, North Carolina State University, Raleigh.

Cochran, W. G., and Cox, G. M. 1957. *Experimental Design.* John Wiley & Sons, Inc., New York.

Davidson, J. 1973. "Natural Variation in *Eucalyptus deglupta* and Its Effect on Choice of Criteria for Selection in a Tree Improvement Program." Papua New Guinea, Trop. For. Res. Note no. SR-2.

Falconer, D. S. 1960. *Introduction to Quantitative Genetics.* Ronald Press, New York.

Ferguson, R. B., and Cooper, D. T. 1977. "Sweetgum Variation Changes with Time." 14th South. For. Tree Impr. Conf., Gainesville, Fla., pp. 194–200.

Franklin, E. C. 1968. "Artificial Self-pollination and Natural Inbreeding... *Pinus taeda* L. Ph.D. thesis, Department of Forestry, North Carolina State University, Raleigh.

Franklin, E. C. 1970. "Survey of Mutant Forms and Inbreeding Depression in Species of the Family *Pinaceae.*" USDA, U.S. Forest Service Research Paper SE-61, Southeastern Forest Experimental Station.

Franklin, E. C. 1979. Model relating levels of genetic variance to stand development of four North American conifers. *Sil. Gen.* **28**:207–212.

Goddard, R. E., and Cole, D. E. 1966. Variation in wood production of six-year-old progenies of select slash pines. *Tappi* **43**:359–362.

Goggans, J. F. 1961. "The Interplay of Environment and Heredity as Factors Controlling Wood Properties in Conifers: With Special Emphasis on Their Effects on Specific Gravity." Technical Report No. 11, North Carolina State University, Raleigh.

Kellison, R. C. 1970. "Phenotypic and Genotype Variation of Yellow-Poplar (*Liriodendron tulipifera*)." Ph.D. thesis, Department of Forestry, North Carolina State University, Raleigh.

Kempthorne, O. 1957. *Introduction to Genetic Statistics.* Iowa State University Press, Ames.

Kinloch, B. B., and Byler, J. W. 1981. Relative effectiveness and stability of different resistance mechanisms to white pine blister rust in sugar pine. *Phytopathology* **71**:386–391.

Matziras, D. I., and Zobel, B. J. 1973. Inheritance and correlations of juvenile characteristics in loblolly pine (*Pinus taeda* L.) *Sil. Gen.* **22**:38–44.

McKeand, S. E. 1978. "Analysis of half-Sib Progeny Tests of Black Walnut." M.S. thesis, Department of Forestry and Natural Resources, Purdue University, Lafayette, Ind.

Namkoong, G. 1979. "Introduction to Quantitative Genetics in Forestry," USDA, U.S. Forest Service Technical Bulletin No. 1588.

Namkoong, G., and Conkle, M. T. 1976. Time trends in genetic control of height growth in ponderosa pine. *For. Sci.* **22**:2–12.

Namkoong, G., Usanis, R. A., and Silen, R. R. 1972. Age-related variation in genetic control of height growth in Douglas-fir. *Theor. Appl. Gen.* **42**:151–159.

Neter, J., and Wasserman, W. 1974. *Applied Linear Statistical Models.* Richard D, Irwin, Inc., Homewood, Ill.

Otegbye, G. O., and Kellison, R. C. 1980. Genetics of wood and bark characteristics of *Eucalyptus viminalis. Sil. Gen.* **29**:27–31.

Personn, A. 1972. "Studies on the Basic Density in Mother Trees and Progenies of Pine." Studia Forestalia Suecia No. Nr 96.

Silen, R. R. 1978. "Genetics of Douglas-fir." USDA, U.S. Forest Service Research Paper WO-35.

Snedecor, G. W., and Cochran, W. G. 1967. *Statistical Methods.* Iowa State University Press, Ames.

Snyder, E. B., and Namkoong, G. 1978. "Inheritance in a Diallel Crossing Experiment with Longleaf Pine." USDA, U.S. Forestry Service Research Paper SO-140, Southern Forest Experiment Station.

Sokal, R. R., and Rohlf, F. J. 1969. *Biometry.* W. H. Freeman, San Francisco.

Steel, R. G. D., and Torrie, J. H. 1960. *Principles and Procedures of Statistics.* McGraw-Hill, New York.

Stonecypher, R. W., Zobel, B. J., and Blair, R. 1973. "Inheritance Patterns of Loblolly Pines from a Nonselected Natural Population." Technical Bulletin No. 224, North Carolina Agricultural Experiment Station.

Strickberger, W. 1976. *Genetics.* Macmillan, New York.

CHAPTER 5

Selection in Natural Stands and Unimproved Plantations

The objective of a selection program is to obtain significant amounts of genetic gain as quickly and inexpensively as possible, while at the same time maintaining a broad genetic base to ensure future gains. All methods of selection in an applied tree improvement program are based on the same general principle; that is, choose the most desirable individuals for use as parents in breeding and production programs. As was discussed in the previous chapter, the selection method that is used will depend on the information and plant materials that are available and on the goals of the program. The testing is done as soon as possible but is often still underway when the first use is made of the improved material.

Selection is a key part of all applied tree improvement programs. The gains can be no greater than the quality of the parents used, and the way to obtain the best parents is through intensive selection. Because this activity comes at the start of the program, many organizations become alarmed at selection costs. Although they may appear to be large, actually they generally account for a minor part of the total costs of tree improvement. Estimates from various programs range from 5% (Porterfield et al., 1975) to 11% (van Buijtenen and Saitta, 1972) to 30% (Reilly and Nikles, 1977). Selection is normally the first step in a tree improvement program and will determine how much gain will be obtained, both in the first and succeeding generations. Doing a poor job of selection to reduce initial costs certainly cannot be justified.

A number of selection methods are available to the tree improver. The one chosen for any particular program depends upon the types of genetic variations in the population, whether pedigree information exists, and the degree of urgency in establishing production seed orchards. Selection methods used for trees from stands where there is no pedigree information are almost always different than those from genetic tests where parentages are known. This chapter will concentrate on selection methods that are applicable to natural stands or unimproved plantations. Methods of selection used where pedigree information exists, as in genetic tests, will be covered only briefly in relation to beginning tree improvement programs. More thorough discussion of methods will be discussed in Chaper 13, which covers advanced-generation tree improvement.

The great variation within the important traits of most forest trees and their reasonably strong general combining ability allows a good chance for gain by selecting desired phenotypes (Figure 5.1). The best selections are then used in seed orchards, allowing favorable genic combinations to interact and produce progeny with a larger proportion of the desired characteristics. In most species, a considerable improvement in bole straightness, disease resistance, wood quality, and adaptability to adverse environments or tolerance to pests can be rapidly obtained by selecting and allowing cross-fertilization among the very best trees, as has been reported by Giertych (1967), Zsuffa (1975), Butcher (1977), and literally hundreds of others.

Of the several methods available to make gains quickly and inexpensively in a beginning tree improvement program, *individual (mass) selection* of trees is the most used and is generally the most satisfactory (Figure 5.2). It is widely applied in the initial stages of tree improvement programs and is suitable for many species.

FIGURE 5.1

Shown is an outstandingly good red maple tree (*Acer rubrum*) selected for use in a hardwood tree improvement program. Rarely does this species develop trees with small crowns and straight boles.

Occasionally, where there is little urgency for production of improved propagules for reforestation, and when time permits establishment of genetic tests, such methods as progeny test selection or family and within-family selection may be used to establish initial seed orchards. Because of its overwhelming importance in most beginning tree improvement programs, mass selection will be given the most extensive coverage in this chapter.

DEFINITIONS

To help avoid the confusion in terminology that is generally evident when selection is discussed, the following terms are defined in reference to a selection program.

1. **Candidate tree** A tree that has been selected for grading because of its desirable phenotypic qualities but that has not yet been graded or tested.
2. **Select, superior, or plus tree** A tree that has been recommended for production or breeding orchard use following grading. It has a superior phenotype for growth, form, wood quality, or other desired characteristics

FIGURE 5.2

Most tree improvement programs start with the selection of
outstanding phenotypes in wild stands or plantations. Shown is
a good loblolly pine used in a seed orchard program.

and appears to be adaptable. It has not yet been tested for its genetic worth,
although the chances of its having a good genotype are high for characteristics with a reasonable heritability.

3. **Elite tree**   A term reserved for selected trees that have proven to be
    genetically superior by means of progeny testing. An elite tree is the
    "winner" from a selection program and is the kind of tree that is most desired
    for use in mass production of seeds or vegetative propagules.

4. **Comparison or check trees**   Trees that are located in the same stand, are of
    nearly the same age, are growing on the same or better site as the select tree
    and against which the select tree is graded. Trees chosen as comparison trees

are the best in the stand, with characteristics similar to "crop" trees that would be chosen in a silvicultural operation.

5. **Advanced-generation selection** A tree selected from genetic tests of crosses among parents from the previous generation. Some form of family and within-family selection is usually used to choose advanced-generation selections.

WHEN SHOULD INDIVIDUAL SELECTION BE USED?

Individual or mass selection works best for those characteristics that have a high narrow-sense heritability. Obviously, it is the only method that can be used to select trees in stands where pedigrees are unknown. To be most successful, mass selection should be used in stands that have a large proportion of good trees and that have not been subjected to logging operations in which the best trees have been removed (Figure 5.3). Examples of characteristics showing relatively high heritabilities are wood specific gravity, resin yields in pine, and most adaptability

FIGURE 5.3

Mass- or individual-tree selection should be made in good stands that have not been high graded, such as the loblolly pine stand shown.

characteristics. Straightness of tree bole and disease resistance are intermediate, whereas for most characteristics related to growth, individual selection is less effective because of low heritability (Shelbourne et al., 1972). For some characters with very low narrow-sense heritability, such as cellulose yield in loblolly pine, individual selection may not be a suitable method to make gains (Zobel et al., 1966; Jett et al., 1977).

Gain from an individual tree selection program can be indicated as G = heritability × selection differential, or $G = h^2S$. Heritability is generally quite constant for a given characteristic at a given age in a given environment, and the tree breeder can not do much to improve it other than to create an environment that is more suitable for the tree to express its genetic potential. However, the selection differential can be manipulated (within limits) by the tree breeder by varying the intensity with which selection is applied. As explained in Chapter 4, a major objective is to increase the selection differential that, in turn, increases genetic gain (see Figure 5.4).

As selection intensity is increased, a point of diminishing returns is reached when gains become less per unit increase in selection intensity (Shelbourne, 1970). However, the intensity of selection used in operational programs is usually less than optimal. For example, in the North Carolina State University–Industry Tree Improvement Cooperative, which used a relatively intensive selection system for pine in the first generation, the selection intensity could have been increased by three times, yielding greater genetic gains but with still the desired return on the investment (Porterfield et al., 1975).

It is essential to reemphasize that an individual selection program is based solely on the phenotype of the tree. For most characteristics, individual selection should be followed by progeny testing to determine if the selected tree is in fact genetically superior; this is especially true for traits with low heritabilities. Van Buijtenen and Saitta (1971) found that individual selection was very effective to the extent that the greatest value of the genetic tests was to serve as a source from which to select for advanced generations. For characteristics that have a high heritability and large amounts of variations, one can be sure that gains from a careful selection program will be reasonable. This was true for loblolly pine (*P. taeda*) where progeny from parents intensively selected for straight boles in the first generation were straight enough so that this characteristic was not emphasized in the following generations (see Figure 5.4). Although the trees could be straightened more by additional selection, the increased economic value from this small improvement would be minimal; this enabled placing more emphasis on other characteristics.

SELECTING SUPERIOR TREES

The techniques used in tree improvement to find and select superior trees depend on the types of stands in which selections are to be made. Numerous references exist on selection techniques for various species and stand types (Langner, 1960;

(a)   *(b)*

FIGURE 5.4

Characteristics with a high heritability respond well to selection. Shown is a progeny from a cross of two straight loblolly pine parents *(a)* and from two crooked parents *(b)*. Response to straightness selection was so good in this species in the first generation that straightness was given less emphasis in advanced generations.

Wright, 1960; Vidakavic, 1965; Morgenstern et al., 1975). There are many references related to selecting conifers, such as those by Cook (1957), Walters et al. (1960), and Andersson (1963). Numerous suggestions hae also been made for selecting hardwoods. These trees differ considerably for each species or condition (Eldridge, 1966; Clausen and Godman, 1967; Beineke and Low, 1969; Pederick, 1970; Bey et al., 1971; Schreiner, 1972).

   A determination of the best selection techniques depends on several factors, including species characteristics, past history, the present condition of the forest, variability and inheritance pattern of important characteristics, and objectives of the particular tree improvement program. There are two major kinds of forest stands, each of which require differing first-generation selection systems.

1. Even-aged wild stands or plantations from unimproved seed where the parentage of the trees is unknown.
2. Uneven-aged, scattered, or sprouting species where the parentage is not known. These include stands with species growing intermixed where check trees are not available.

Selection techniques for each of these kinds of forest stands will be discussed now.

Selecting from Even-Aged Stands

Individual selection works best when good even-aged stands of the proper age are available (see Figure 5.3). This allows efficient comparisons to be made among selected trees and checks. Individual tree selection is best in even-aged natural stands composed primarily of one species or in plantations. This is by far the most common method of first-generation selection and has been applied worldwide (Figure 5.5).

FIGURE 5.5

Selection of outstanding trees from plantations is very successful and has been widely used throughout the world. Shown is an outstanding *P. radiata* selected for use in a New Zealand seed orchard.

There are several advantages to selecting in even-aged stands rather than in uneven-aged or mixed stands when practicing individual tree selection. First, the breeder can be sure that age will not differ greatly among trees, and that relative expressions of growth, form, disease tolerance, and adaptability will not be confounded with age effects. Second, trees are growing under competitive situations similar to those that will be encountered when improved trees are established in commercial plantations. Also, it is in these types of stands where the "comparison tree" system of selection can be used that trees considered for selection are graded against the best trees in the stand. All of these factors work to increase selection differential, and this results in greater gain.

Generally, plantations are preferable to natural stands in selection efforts if plantations of suitable seed source are available (Figure 5.6). In plantations, all trees are exactly the same age. In natural stands, even slight differences in age cause differential competition that can result in large differences in volume and form within the stand. It is known, for instance, that in densely stocked pine stands, a difference of one or two years in age among neighboring trees will usually result in the younger trees's never becoming dominant or codominant trees in the stand. An additional advantge of selection in plantations is that spacing among trees is more uniform. Competition is in essence an environmental force that affects the tree's phenotype. When competition is equalized, heritabilities are raised.

General guides for locating select individuals in even-aged natural stands and plantations follow. These guides have been very useful in choosing superior trees in first-generation tree improvement programs.

1. The search should be concentrated on stands and plantations that are average or better in growth, pruning, straightness, branch angle, and other characteristics of interest. An occasionally acceptable tree may be found in a poor stand but this is rare, and search efforts are more efficient when they are carried out in good stands. Outstanding stands of trees are sometimes referred to as *plus stands*.

2. Stands and plantations in which candidate trees are sought should be located on the same variety of sites where plantations from improved seed will ultimately be established. This is true unless there is evidence that sites have no effect on the performance of the genotype. If the majority of an organization's landholding are on average sites, then the majority of selections should come from such sites. *There should never be a concentration of selections from the very highest site lands,* if the plantations are to be established on average or poor sites.

3. When selections are made from plantations, information about the suitability of the seed source used in the planting should be obtained. Selections should not be made from stands planted with seeds from areas known to be poorly adapted to the area where planting will be done.

4. In older stands, the search effort should be confined to trees that have an age range of no more than 10 to 15 years younger or older than the projected

FIGURE 5.6

Selecting trees from plantations, as shown for slash pine, is relatively easy, and good trees can be obtained compared to wild stands because all trees are of the same age and were established at about equal spacings. Care must be taken that the trees used are from the correct seed source.

rotation age of the plantations that are to be established. For species that are harvested at an early age, the trees must be old enough to have shown their potential. For tropical pines, the stands need to be a minimum of 10 to 12 years old before they exhibit development that enables efficient selection, whereas in the same areas some eucalypts as young as 3 years of age can be easily selected if very short rotations are used.

5. Selections should be made from stands that are as pure in species composition as possible. Differential growth rates among species can severely

complicate selection through differential competition if the stand has a sizable component of two or more species.

6. Stands must be avoided that have been logged for poles or piling or that have been otherwise high graded or thinned from above. If the stand has been thinned from below, or if it has suffered fire damage, allow crown competition to be reestablished before selections are made. Stands that are mechanically thinned or thinned in a truly silvicultural manner are suitable for an individual selection program.

7. The minimum size of a stand or plantation in which a candidate can be located is immaterial. If the stand is large enough to locate a good candidate tree and to allow choosing comparison trees, then it is large enough to search for select trees.

8. Preferably only one select tree should be accepted from any one small natural stand to reduce the possibility of obtaining candidate trees that are close relatives. This restriction does not apply to selecting in plantations.

9. Although it is highly desirable for candidate trees to exhibit a heavy flower or cone crop, these characteristics are generally not given much emphasis. This is particularly true in young and dense stands where many trees show no sign of flowering because of insufficient light on their crowns to stimulate flower production. Usually, these will flower heavily in the seed orchard environment.

10. Once the decision has been made to look over an area for candidate trees, a thorough, systematic search should be made. Experience has shown that excellent trees are often missed when a stand is searched haphazardly. Experience has also shown that select trees are generally found only by people who are specifically looking for them. Although an occasionally acceptable tree is located during routine woods work, this is the exception. The only efficient way to locate candidate trees is to be specifically on a selection mission.

11. A comparison or check tree selection system should be used when feasible. This helps to account for environmental differences within stands and permits more efficient and objective selection of superior trees. A method of evaluating candidate trees without the use of check trees was suggested by Robinson and van Buijtenen (1971), but usually the use of check trees is desirable.

Selection in Uneven-Aged, Mixed Species, or Stands of Sprout Origin

Forest stands are quite frequently not of types allowing use of the individual selection program that was just described for even-aged stands. There are several reasons for this: (1) Stands may be truly uneven aged; (2) the desired species may be so scattered that comparison (check) trees are not available; (3) the species may be a vigorous sprouter and trees growing near the candidate tree can be on a common root system and have the same genotype; and (4) the stand is composed of mixed species.

The comparison tree system does not work when trees are growing in all-aged stands. Since growth curves within a species vary with age, it is not suitable to use ratios such as height or diameter growth per unit time for comparison purposes. In addition, the form of the tree often changes drastically with age. Therefore, even-quality characteristics cannot be compared among trees of different ages from uneven-aged stands. Rarely are truly all-aged stands of either conifers or hardwoods common under natural conditions outside of the tropical forests. Many foresters make the mistake of assuming that stands containing trees of varied sizes are all aged. The major exception to this generalization that forests are usually even-aged is when stands have been manipulated by humans into an all-aged condition by selective cutting. Even within the true uneven-aged stands, there is a tendency for a storied age class to be present.

Trees sometimes grow in *mixed stands* with relatively few individuals of a given species found in a specific area. This condition is most common for hardwoods. A comparison tree selection system will not work in this case because the scattered individuals of a species are growing under different environments. This is by far the most common situation that requires a grading system other than the standard comparison tree method (Pitcher and Dorn, 1966).

The importance and frequency of relatedness among trees from stands of *sprout origin* is often not understood. Usually, sprouts from a single tree are limited to those individuals that are adjacent to the tree, but, sometimes, sprouts from a common root system can be quite extensive. There are records of aspen stands (*Populus tremuloides*) as large as 40 acres (16 ha) having a common root system (Baker, 1925). When stands of sprout origin are large enough and of sufficient genetic diversity to enable use of a comparison tree system, the check trees must be carefully chosen so they will not be related to the candidate tree. This is sometimes difficult to do accurately.

Stands composed partially of sprouts and partially of seedlings also pose the problem of growth differential between trees from sprout and seedling origin. Initially, sprouts usually grow much faster than seedlings because of the established root system and stored food. However, sprouts often culminate growth at a younger age than do seedlings. After a few years, it commonly becomes impossible to distinguish sprouts from seedlings, but selection results will not be good if the two types of trees are mixed.

Although they are not sprout stands, occasionally trees form root grafts that can also make tree selection difficult (Yli-vakkuri, 1953; Bormann, 1966; Schultz and Woods, 1967; Eis, 1972). The result of root grafting usually is that the large tree benefits at the expense of the small tree by taking nutrients from the small tree with which it shares a common root system. This serves to inflate the superiority of the larger tree and is an environmental effect that cannot be captured through selection.

The Regression Selection System

The most useful method of tree grading for the uneven-aged or mixed-species-type stands described previously is the *regression system*. This requires the development of tables relating the characteristic of interest to tree age. The regression method is of particular value for growth characteristics because quality characteristics can often be determined on the basis of the phenotype of the candidate tree alone without need for comparison trees.

A regression selection system is built by sampling a number of trees for a desired characteristic, such as volume growth on a given site, and then plotting them against age (Figure 5.7). It is of key importance that different regressions are developed for different sites. A reliable regression curve for height or volume can be made with about 50 trees, if there is a reasonable age-class distribution. Once the curve has been developed, the regression is used as follows:

1. A candidate tree is chosen, based on the judgment of the selector and measured for the characteristics desired, such as height or volume.

2. The trait is plotted on the regression graph using the proper age and site. If the candidate tree falls at some defined distance above the regression line, it is acceptable and the higher above, the more desirable it becomes (Figure 5.7). When the value of the characteristic falls below the acceptable level, the tree is rejected.

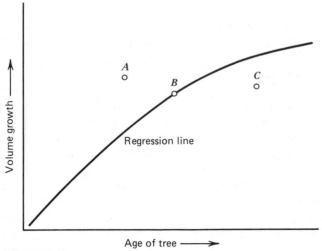

FIGURE 5.7

The regression system of selection is particularly suitable for all aged- or mixed-species stands. It consists of developing a curve of production (growth is illustrated) for different ages of trees on a given site. Candidate Tree A falls above the curve, therefore, it has the desired growth for its age. Tree B is average, therefore, its use depends on other characteristics, whereas Tree C has inferior growth for its age and should not be used. The regression line should be based on at least 50 trees if the age spread is considerable.

Although the regression system works well, it requires considerable preliminary work. To complicate the situation, some species, especially the wet-site diffuse-porous hardwoods, do not have discernable growth rings, thus making age difficult to assess. When this occurs, and if the history or age of stand establishment is not known (which is the usual situation), a reasonable estimate of age can often be made if ring-porous trees are growing intermixed in the stand. These can be used to determine the age of the stand. As an example, tupelo gum (*Nyssa aquatica*) usually has indistinguishable growth rings. Often growing adjacent to it is green ash (*Fraxinus pennsylvanica*) that produces easily determinable rings. The age of the ash is then applied to the candidate tupelo gum tree with reasonable accuracy because it is known that such stands are usually even aged. A major exception is some tropical forests that have developed in a truly all-aged condition.

The regression system is more difficult to use than the comparison tree method, but there is no doubt that it will become more commonly employed as hardwood tree improvement becomes more widely practiced.

The Mother Tree System

When there is no immediate urgency to obtain large amounts of improved seed, the mother tree system of selection may be best. It consists of locating "good" trees that are usually not as good as select trees in the comparison tree or regression systems. Then, one must obtain seed from these and establish seedlings in genetic tests. After this, either the best parent trees or the best trees of the best families can be used in a vegetative orchard. If suitably laid out, the progeny test may be thinned to create a seedling seed orchard.

The main disadvantage of the mother tree system is that time is lost before commercial quantities of seed are needed for planting programs. The testing must be carried on for a long period, approaching at least one-half rotation age if growth is to be reasonably assessed before the seed orchard can be established. This method has been used extensively for hardwoods for which planting programs are small and seed are not immediately needed. It also works very well for species that are grown on very short rotations, such as the eucalypts. If the *interim seedling orchard* concept is used, time to seed production can be shortened, but potential gain will be reduced because of the smaller selection differential from the seedling orchard as compared with the vegetative orchard. The mother tree system may also be best in seriously high-graded stands where few good phenotypes are available. It may also be best for characteristics such as disease resistance that often can only be determined through testing.

The Subjective Grading System

Some persons who are familiar with a species feel that an acceptable job of selection can be done based only on the judgment of the grader about what constitutes a good tree. This is certainly possible, but the grader must *know the species* immediately and must be as unbiased as possible. This system is used successfully but has also failed. The tendency, when the subjective system is used, is to spend less time seeking the candidate trees, thus choosing less outstanding trees with smaller selection differentials. This results in less gain. The subjective grading system is frequently used for hardwoods but is successful only if the grader is exerienced and dedicated to finding the best trees possible.

TRAITS DESIRED FOR SELECTION: DEVELOPING A GRADING SYSTEM

Two factors are of paramount importance when developing a grading scheme for the selection of superior trees. First, the trait under consideration should be under at least *moderately strong genetic control*. Second, the trait *must have considerable economic value*. Regardless of the magnitude of either of these factors, a characteristic is of little use in a selection program when either the genetic control or economic value is too low. For example, if a characteristic such as needle length of leaf size were under strong genetic control, it would have little value in a commercial tree improvement program. This would be the case if trees with long needles or large leaves yielded no greater amount of the desired products than did those with small leaves or needles. The numerical value allocated to each chracteristic in a tree-grading process is determined by weighting the heritability of the characteristic against its economic worth. For example, bole straightness usually is considered more important than limb size because of its stronger genetic control as well as its greater economic worth.

Growth rate is nearly always the *key characteristic* in a selection program (Bouvarel, 1966; van Buijtenen, 1969), but other characteristics are usually also important. In areas, such as the southeastern United States where the environment is favorable for tree growth, the major initial objective for first-generation orchards often is to improve quality characteristics with only a modest attempt to increase growth rate. This priority of quality characteristics over volume should be used when selections are from wild, unmanaged stands where heritability for growth is low. In advanced-generation tree improvement or in plantations where selections come from more uniform stands of the same age and equal spacing, the heritability for growth rate will be larger, and a greater concentration on improvement of volume growth should be made.

Most first-generation selection programs have a *"threshold"* value for each characteristic, below which no tree is accepted for an operational orchard no matter how excellent the rest of the tree's characteristics might be. Trees that have one marginally acceptable characeristic are often held in breeding clone banks for possible later use.

It is not appropriate to produce a list of characteristics for which selection should be done because these will vary with species, the product desired, and the objectives of each program. However, to illustrate the kinds of characteristics sometimes used and their weighting, a modification of the selection method used for the first generation in the North Carolina State–Industry Tree Improvement Cooperative is shown in Table 5.1. Note the differential weights given for different characteristics. Not shown are the "all-or-none" characteristics, such as

TABLE 5.1
Select Tree Grading Sheet for Conifers[a]

Organization _____   Tree Number _____

Location _____   Species _____

Grader _____   Plantation _____ Natural _____

Date _____   Age _____

Five Best Crop (Comparison) Trees[b]   **Selected Tree Score**

	Ht.	DBH	Vol.	Age
1				
2				
3				
4				
5				
Total				
Average				

1. Height _____
2. Volume _____
3. Crown _____
4. Straightness _____
5. Pruning ability _____
6. Branch diameter _____
7. Branch angle _____
Total Score _____

Select Tree (s)   Average Crop Tree (c)   **Remarks**

Vol. _____

Ht. _____

DBH _____

Wood _____

Specific Gravity _____

1. *Height Superiority*

Less than 10%	0 points
10–11%	1 point
12–13%	2 points
14–15%	3 points
16–17%	4 points
18–19%	5 points
20%	6 points
Over 20%	7 points

2. *Volume*—formula: Vs/Vc; s = select; c = check—Average of 5. Select tree is given one point for each 10% excess in volume over the checks.

3. *Crown*—judged subjectively from the standpoint of the individual select tree as compared to the five checks and scored as follows:

    a. Based on conformation, density of foliage, dominance, and crown radius 0 to 5 points depending on superiority.

4. *Straightness*—judged subjectively for the individual select tree and not compared to the checks. No tree accepted with excess spiral, any crook in two planes, or a crook in

TABLE 5.1 (*continued*)

one plane that will not allow a line from merchantable top to stump to stay within the confines of the bole. Scored subjectively allowing 0 to 5 points, the number of points dependent upon the relative straightness of the individual.

5. *Pruning ability*—ability of select tree to shed its lower limbs (dead and alive) as compared to checks: If similar to the checks, it receives 0 points; above the checks, 1 to 3 points, depending on superiority. Pruning ability is judged subjectively by comparing the select tree with each of the checks.

6. *Branch diameter* is judged subjectively—select versus checks. If branch diameter is average, 0 points are given; 1 or 2 points for branches smaller than checks.

7. *Branch angle* is also judged subjectively. When branch angle is average, 0 points are given; if angle is flat, 1 or 2 points are awarded.

If any of the preceding seven categories is poorer than the checks, points are deducted by the same scale as they are added when the select tree is superior to the checks. A tree with a minus score in one characteristic is usually not acceptable except under certain special conditions.

Specific gravity is handled separately. No points as such are given for specific gravity, because the desires of each organization differ. The value of a tree for specific gravity is judged by two criteria:
1. Comparison of the select tree with its five check trees. This gives an indication of the tree's wood quality when compared to trees growing under the same environmental conditions.
2. Comparison of the select tree with the regional average for that particular species and organization.

[a]This is a revision of Form S-2 used by the N. C. State–Industry Cooperative Tree Improvement Program.
[b]Ht., height; DBH, diameter breast height; vol., volume; age is the age of each individual tree.

presence or absence of disease or insect damage. Also not shown is a grade for wood specific gravity. In the first-generation system used by the North Carolina State Cooperative the weight placed on specific gravity was determined by each organization, depending on its own product. This was done because some desired high gravities and others low gravities, whereas still others preferred trees with intermediate gravities. Adaptability is also not included in the grade sheets due to the fact that it is automatically taken into account because trees are selected and tested in the same areas in which they will be planted. The assumption was made that healthy, vigorous trees in natural stands are well adapted to the environment in which they are growing. A somewhat different grading system is needed for hardwoods. A method of reporting selections in hardwoods has been described by Pitcher and Dorn (1966).

The general tendency is to *include too many characteristics* in a selection system. The more things that must be graded, the more difficult it becomes to find suitable trees. The objective of tree selection and grading is to emphasize the few most important characteristics, such as volume production, bole quality, adaptability, and pest resistance. The lesser characteristics that are assessed should be kept above an acceptable level, but selection intensities need not be as great. The objective is to give the greatest weight to characteristics that have the best combination of economic importance and heritability and to give less weight to other characteristics. No tree is used that has a characteristic that falls below the level of acceptability.

The main objective of a grading system is to force the grader to look critically at the tree. The grade given does not represent the final decision about whether a tree will be used forever in the improved seed orchard. This decision is finally arrived at after progeny testing. All efforts to obtain the best phenotypes should be taken, but some mistakes will be made. The method described in Table 5.1 was used at North Carolina State University to select phenotypes for immediate use in first-generation seed orchards. This was followed by progeny testing and roguing of the undesirable genotypes to upgrade the genetic quality of the first-generation orchards.

The grading system shown in Table 5.1 is relatively simple to use and is one version of the comparison tree system discussed earlier. It works as follows:

1. Once the decision has been made to grade a tree, the five best crop trees in the stand in which the candidate tree is located are chosen as comparison or check trees. They, like the candidate tree, must have a dominant or codominant crown position and must be growing under conditions of competition that are similar to the candidate tree. The comparison trees are chosen for desirable characteristics in much the same way as the candidate tree. It is helful to consider the checks as crop trees that would be retained if the grader could leave the five best trees in the stand and not including the candidate tree. Comparison trees can occur at varying distances from the candidate tree, but they are selected on a site and under an environment similar to that of the candidate tree. If the candidate tree is located on a relatively uniform site, an attempt is made to locate the comparison trees in a circle around it. If suitable trees are not available in a circle, one or all of the comparison trees can be chosen in any sector of the circle. When the candidate tree is located on sloping terrain, the comparison trees should be selected on approximately the same contour as the candidate. In cases where this is not possible, the comparison trees should be located on the downhill or better side of the candidate to ensure that it is never compared to trees growing on a poorer site.

   The candidate tree is awarded points for each characteristic shown on the grading form, based on the importance of the character and relationship of the candidate tree to the five comparison, or check, trees. Height and diameter are actually measured for the candidate and the comparison trees.

Crown conformation, pruning ability, branch angle, and branch diameter are subjectively scored by visually comparing the characteristics of the candidate and the comparison trees. Straightness and disease or insect infection are subjectively scored on the candidate tree *only* and are not judged in relation to the comparison trees. Thus, a tree must meet a given level of straightness if it is to be graded, no matter how crooked or straight the check trees may be. In even-aged natural stands, the candidate tree is automatically rejected if it is more than three years older than the average of the five comparison trees; conversely, it is awarded points if it is more than 2 years younger than the average of the comparison trees.

2. No tree is accepted if it is infected by serious diseases or insects. In the southern pines, rejection of some of the very best trees results when they are infected by fusiform rust. The disease is genetically controlled strongly enough to make good gains by selecting only nondiseased trees for use in seed orchards, if infection levels are high (Goddard et al., 1975).

3. An ll-mm bark-to-bark increment core is extracted from the candidate tree at the time of grading to be used for wood analysis. A large core, approximately 11 mm in diameter, is necessary for the determination of tracheid lengths in conifers, but smaller cores will be satisfactory for fiber length in hardwoods.

The question arises about the feasibility of using the same scoring or grading system for different species. Although the same system is used quite frequently, there is a differing emphasis for different characteristics. For example, some pines will be graded more rigorously for prunability than will others, and some will be graded more severely for straightness of bole. Different grading sheets with different weightings usually need to be developed for hardwoods, especially to include the characteristics of epicormic branching and leader dominance.

It should be stressed that the grading system discussed here was developed only for use with pine in the North Carolina State Tree Improvement Cooperative and is shown only as an example of a comparison-tree grading system. Other tree improvement programs, including some that deal with the same species as the North Carolina State Cooperatives, employ somewhat different systems, which the organizations feel are best for their particular circumstances. The bottom line is that each organization must develop systems that fit into its own genetic, environmental, and economic constraints.

INDIRECT SELECTION

For some characteristics, it has been found that it is easier to use indirect selection rather than selecting directly for a specific character. This approach is especially valuable for forest trees because of their long life span and large size. Development of techniques to select at very young ages for performance at rotation age would result in a much shorter generation interval and greater genetic gain per unit of time and would speed up the tree improvement efforts greatly.

In forest trees, selection for most growth characteristics at older ages based on the performance of very young trees has not proven to be feasible generally. The problem relates primarily to the difficulty of obtaining good juvenile–mature correlations as described in Chapter 1. There it was stressed that assessment for growth characteristics should not be made before about one-half rotation age in natural stands or in plantations. Assessments of growth may be feasible at 6 to 10 years of age in genetic tests, when the normal rotation age is 25 years or more (Lambreth, 1980). The determination of seedling characteristics that would be used to make growth predictions for older trees would be very useful, as has been stressed by Kozlowski (1961). However, most tests to predict future growth based on gross or net photosynthesis have generally given poor results for both seed sources (Gordon and Gatherum, 1967) and for families (Burkhalter et al., 1967; Ledig and Perry, 1969; Ledig, 1974). Better methods of predicting growth at young ages will undoubtedly be developed, and much research is now being expended in this effort (Shimizu et al., 1976). A determination of reasonably accurate methods to assess the growth of mature individuals from seedling characteristics is one of the most urgent needs in research in tree improvement.

A second problem related to indirect selection is the relative genetic independence among most characteristics of forest trees. For indirect selection to be effective, the two characteristics being compared must be closely correlated. Such correlation seems to be relatively low for many traits of forest trees.

Some indirect selection methods have been tried for pest resistance with only indifferent success (Lewis, 1973; Rockwood, 1973; von Weissenberg, 1973; Wilkinson, 1980). All researchers reported that both the pests and physiological characteristics used for indirect selection were reasonably and strongly controlled genetically but were not sufficiently correlated to be effective in an indirect selection method.

As the scientific information on forest biology expands, indirect selection may well become feasible for certain traits. But, as of now, this is largely in the area of research and is not usable on a large scale.

LITERATURE CITED

Andersson, E. 1963. "Directions for Selection of Plus Trees and Phenotype Control; *Pinus silvestris* and *Picea abies.*" World Cons. on For. Gen. and Tree Impr., Section 9.

Baker, F. S. 1925. "Aspen in the Central Rocky Mountain Region." USDA Bulletin 1291, Washington, D.C.

Beineke, W. F., and Low, W. J. 1969. "A Selection System for Superior Black Walnut Trees and Other Hardwoods. Proc. 10th South. Conf. of For. Tree Impr., Houston, pp. 27–33.

Bey, C. F., Hawker, N. L., and Roth, P. L. 1971. "Selecting Trees for Growth and Form in Young Black Walnut Plantations." 11th Conf. on South. For. Tree Impr., Atlanta, Ga.

Bormann, F. H. 1966. The structure, function and ecological significance of root grafts in *Pinus strobus. Ecol. Mono.* **36**(1):1–26.

Bouvarel, P. 1966. "Economic Factors in the Choice of a Method of Forest Tree Breeding." Sexto Congreso Forestal Mundial, Madrid.

Burkhalter, A. P., Robertson, C. F., and Reiner, M. 1967. "Variation in Photosynthesis and Respiration in Southern Pines." Ga. For. Res. Paper 46, Macon, Ga.

Butcher, T. B. 1977. "Gains from *Pinus pinaster* Improvement Program in Western Australia. 3rd World Consul. on For. Tree Breed., Canberra, Australia.

Clausen, K. E., and Godman, R. M. 1967. "Selecting Superior Yellow Birch Trees." North Central Forest Experimental Station Research Paper NC-20.

Cook, D. B. 1957. "Criteria for Judging "Plus" Larch Trees." Proc. 7th Northwestern For. Tree Impr. Conf., Burlington, Vt., pp. 40–42.

Eis, S. 1972. Root grafts and their silvicultural implications. *Can. Jour. For. Res.* **2**:111–120.

Eldridge, K. G. 1966. Genetic improvement of *Eucalyptus regnans* by selection of parent trees. *Appita* **19**(6):133–138.

Giertych, M. 1967. Genetic gain and methods of forest tree seed production. *Sylvan* **110**(11):59–64.

Goddard, R. E., Schmidt, R. A., and Vande Linde, F. 1975. Effect of differential selection pressure on fusiform rust resistance in phenotypic selections of slash pine. *Phytopathology.* **65**(3):336–338.

Gordon, J. C., and Gatherum, G. E. 1967. "Photosynthesis and Growth of Selected Scotch Pine Seed Sources." 8th Lake States For. Tree Impr. Conf., pp. 20–23.

Jett, J. B., Weir, R. J., and Barker, J. A. 1977. "The Inheritance of Cellulose in Loblolly Pine." TAPPI For. Biol. Comm. Meet., Madison, Wisc.

Kozlowski, T. T. 1961. "Challenges in Forest Production—Physiological Implications." 50th Anniversary of the State University College of Forestry, Syracuse, N.Y.

Lambeth, C. C. 1980. Juvenile-mature correlations in Pinaceae, and their implications for early selection. *For. Sci.* **26**:571–580.

Langner, W. 1960. "Improvement through Individual Tree Selection and Testing Seed Stand, and Clonal Seed Orchards." 5th World For. Cong., Seattle, Wash.

Ledig, F. T., and Perry, T. O. 1969. Net assimilation rate and growth in loblolly pine seedlings. *For. Sci.* **15**(4):431–438.

Ledig, F. T. 1974. "Photosynthetic Capacity: Developing a Criterion for the Early Selection of Rapidly Growing Trees." Bull. No. 1985, Champion International Corp. Lectureships, pp. 19–39.

Lewis, R. 1973. "Quantitative Assessment and Possible Biochemical Indicators of Variation in Resistance to Fusiform Rust in Loblolly Pine." Ph.D. thesis, North Carolina State University, Raleigh.

Morgenstern, E., K., Holst, M. J., Teich, A. H., and Yeatman, C. W. 1975. "Plus-Tree Selection—Review and Outlook." Department of Environment, Canadian Forest Service, Pub. No. 1347, Ottawa, Canada.

Pederick, L. A. 1970. "Selection Criteria." Proc. 2nd Mtg. Beerwah, Queensland, Australia.

Pitcher, J. A., and Dorn, D. E. 1966. "A New Form for Reporting Hardwood Superior Tree Candidates." Proc. 5th Central States For. Tree Impr., Wooster, Ohio, pp. 7–12.

Porterfield, R. L., Zobel, B. J., and Ledig, F. T. 1975. Evaluating the efficiency of tree improvement programs. *Sil. Gen.* **24**(2–3):33–34.

Reilly, J. J., and Nikles, D. G. 1977. "Analysing Benefits and Costs of Tree Improvement: *Pinus caribaea*." 3rd World Cons. For. Tree Breed., Canberra, Australia.

Robinson, J. F., and van Buijtenen, J. P. 1971. "Tree Grading without the Use of Check Trees." Proc. 11th Conf. on South. For. Tree Impr., Atlanta, Ga., pp. 207–211.

Rockwood, D. 1973. Monoterpene-fusiform rust relationships in loblolly pine. *Phytopathology* **63**(5):551–553.

Schreiner, E. J. 1972. "Procedures for Selection of Hybrid Poplar Clones for Commercial Trials in the Northeastern Region." Proc. 19th Northeastern For. Tree Impr. Conf., Orono, Me., pp. 108–116.

Schultz, R. P., and Woods, F. W. 1967. The frequency and implications of intraspecific root-grafting in loblolly pine. *For. Sci.* **13**(3):226–239.

Shelbourne, C. J. A. 1970. "Breeding Strategy." Research Work Group No. 1, Res. Comm. of the Aust. For. Council, Proc. 2nd Mtg., Beerwah, Australia.

Shelbourne, C. J. A., Thulin, I. J., and Scott, R. H. M. 1972. "Variation, Inheritance and Correlation amongst Growth, Morphological and Wood Characters in Radiata Pine." Forestry Research Institute, Genetics and Tree Improvement Report No. 61, New Zealand Forest Service, Rotorua, New Zealand.

Shimuzu, J. Y., Pitcher, J. A., and Fishwick, R. W. 1976. Early selection of superior phenotypes in *Pinus elliottii. PRODEPEF,* Brazil.

van Buijtenen, J. P. 1969. "Progress and Problems in Forest Tree Selection." Proc. 10th South. Conf. on For. Tree Impr., Houston, Tex., pp. 17–26.

van Buijtenen, J. P., and Saitta, W. W. 1972. Linear programming applied to the economic analysis of forest tree improvement. *Jour. For.* **70**:164–167.

Vidakovic, M. 1965. "Selection of Plus Trees." Sumarski List, Internacionalni simpozij, IUFRO, Zagreb, pp. 7–20.

von Weissenberg, K. 1973. Indirect selection for resistance to fusiform rust in loblolly pine. *Acta For. Fenn.* **134** 1–46.

Walters, J., Soos, J., and Haddock, P. G. The Selection of Plus Trees on the University of British Columbia Research Forest, Haney, British Columbia." Research Paper No. 33, University of British Columbia, Vancouver, Canada.

Wilkinson, R. C. 1980. Relationship between cortical monoterpenes and susceptibility of Eastern white pine to white-pine weevil attack. *For. Sci.* **26**(4):581–589.

Wright, J. W. 1960. "Individual Tree Selection in Forest Genetics." Proc. 4th Lakes States For. Tree Imp. Conf. Stat. Paper No. 81, Lake States Forestry Experimental Station, pp. 25–44.

Yli-vakkuri, P. 1953. Tutkimuksia puient valisista elimillisista juuriyteyksista mannikoissa [Studies of organic root-grafts between trees in *Pinus sylvestris* stands]. *Acta For. Fenn.* **60**(3):1–117.

Zobel, B. J., Stonecypher, R., Brown C., and Kellison, R. C. 1966. Variation and inheritance of cellulose in the southern pines. *Tappi* **49**(9):383–387.

Zsuffa, L. 1975. Broad sense heritability values and possible genetic gains in clonal selection of *P. grifithii* x *P. strobus*. *Sil. Gen.* **25**(4):85–88.

CHAPTER 6

Seed Production and Seed Orchards

The applied aspect of tree improvement consists of the development of improved trees followed by mass production of the improved stock. No program will be successful until both have been achieved. Too often, improvement of forest trees is obtained without sufficient concern about how the improved material is to be reproduced and used on an operational scale. The better trees can be multiplied through seed regeneration or by vegetative propagation. (Vegetative propagation is covered in Chapter 10; this chapter will concentrate on the production of improved seed for operational planting, although there will be reference to seed production for breeding or developmental activities.)

All tree improvement programs must have seed production at some stage of their development if continued gains are to be achieved. This is true even for programs using vegetative propagules for large-scale operational planting; seed is needed for the development of outstanding trees from which vegetative propagules can be obtained.

Organizations with extensive planting programs need large quantities of improved seed immediately. The approach followed in the circumstances of immediate need will be somewhat different from that in which the need for seed for operational planting is still sometime in the future. Even when results from the breeding program may not be used until some years in the future, it is essential to set aside or establish areas for seed production early.

The first and most difficult problem related to seed production for an operational program is to determine the amount of seed needed. In young programs, this estimate must often by made without a good knowledge of the seed-producing capacity of the species or how to manage or treat trees for greater seed production or even how to handle the seed in storage and in later germination. This problem of seed production and handling is especially critical for many tropical and subtropical species for which very little biological information is currently available. Information on the characteristics of many types of seeds for genera and species in the more temperate areas of the world is available in the European literature. Also, much is known about seeds of a number of Asian species. Especially well known are the characteristics of seed of species used in exotic forestry programs in South America, Australia, Africa, and elsewhere. In the United States, the U.S. Forest Service publication "Seeds of Woody Plants in the United States," which was edited by Schopmeyer in 1974, is comprehensive. We know of no similar publication that covers seed of tropical tree species.

Plans for seed production should exceed currently known requirements. Often overlooked in assessing needs for a given program is the continuing trend toward shorter rotations and continued expansion of forest area under management that results in the use of greater quantities of seed than were initially required. Of key importance is the fact that a buffer must be calculated for loss or failure of production of seed. A normal, effective, and conservative method is to assume that good seed crops will not be obtained every year. In addition, all organizations should keep at least a 3-year supply of seed in storage (when storage is possible). The prudent approach is to plan to produce an amount of seed that at least is 30% greater than is currently needed.

There is no method of seed production that is suitable for all species and all conditions. A number of good summaries of differing systems have been developed and published. Two of these, which are for temperate species, are those of Thielges (1975) and Faulkner (1975).

MEETING IMMEDIATE SEED NEEDS

There are several methods that can be used to obtain genetically improved seed for immediate planting. These are usually interim in nature in that they are used only until the more permanent seed orchard becomes available. Often seed from the interim procedures will not yield large-volume gains, although they sometimes greatly improve tree quality and pest resistance, and they can ensure good adaptability. Too often, the short-term methods of obtaining improved seed are ignored, and nothing is done to take advantage of the potential genetic gain until the longer-term seed orchards have been developed.

Seed from Individually Good Phenotypes

If seed is needed immediately for an operational program, one viable approach is to choose outstanding phenotypes from natural stands or plantations, mark the trees, and collect seed from them (Figure 6.1). Collection from the good trees is usually done during a logging operation or ahead of the logging crews. In the latter case, the selected trees may be felled and seeds collected when they ripen. The cut trees are then salvaged when the logging operations come to them. In some instances, the marked trees are climbed for seed collection in stands where logging is not planned.

Seed from good phenotypes in which the male is not known and is unselected will usually yield only limited volume improvement because of the low heritability for growth in most species. The very best individuals from natural stands are well adapted to the areas where they are growing. If trees are selected from plantations of native or exotic species, a land race will result that will be more adapted to the plantation site than to the original plantation. Improved adaptability alone usually makes collection from individual trees worthwhile. In most species, certain quality characteristics like stem straightness, and to some extent limb quality, will also be improved. When a change in wood specific gravity is desired, considerable improvement will occur by choice of the correct parents. If disease or insects are serious problems, a good degree of tolerance often can be achieved when seed are collected from healthy trees that are selected from stands that are heavily infected.

Many persons feel that the method of collecting seed from individually good phenotypes is not worth the effort. Although only one parent has the known desired characteristics, if selection is modestly rigid, the cumulative gains, especially for adaptability, will usually repay the effort. When planned ahead and if collections are made only when there is a reasonable seed crop on the desired

FIGURE 6.1

The first step in making genetic improvement is to select good trees from good stands, such as this *P. radiata* plantation in Chile, and to collect seed from them for operational planting. The better phenotypes are marked and cut just before or during a logging operation when the seed are ripe; therefore, seed can be taken from the best trees that had been marked. Gains will be mostly in improved form and better adaptability.

phenotypes, the cost of seed from individually felled trees is not much higher than standard seed collection. Costs will be somewhat more when trees must be climbed. The number of trees selected for seed collection per unit area will vary with species, quality of stands, availability of stands, and selection intensity. Usually, however, not many more than 5 to 10 trees per acre (12–25 trees per ha) will be of suitable quality to use for seed collection.

Seed from Good Stands

Although the gains are not well documented and the method is little discussed, a number of organizations use the practice of making mass seed collections only from the very best stands; these are sometimes referred to as *plus stands* (Faulkner, 1962). The types of gains are generally like those outlined previously for individual tree selections, although the magnitude of gains may be less because of less intensive selection. The method of collecting from plus stands is a worthwhile practice to follow when the individual tree method cannot be used. Seed will be cheaper to obtain with this method, but collecting from one or a few good stands will yield bulked seedlots with a higher degree of relatedness than seedlots collected from individual trees growing in many different stands.

Seed Production Areas

Seed production areas, also called *seed stands,* are quite widely used in young programs, especially for exotic species. Seed production areas have only limited application for those organizations with advanced tree improvement programs. In seed production areas, the poor phenotypes are rogued from the stand and the good trees are left to intermate. Eventually, seed are collected from them (Andersson, 1963; Dyer, 1964). Seed production areas are rarely progeny tested; therefore, both of the parents are selected only on their phenotypic qualities. Based on a number of tests, only limited genetic improvement for volume growth has been found for pine seed production areas in the southern United States (LaFarge and Kraus, 1981). However, growth improvement has been reasonably good from a number of seed production areas from plantations of exotic species, including pines and *Eucalyptus.* In this instance a land race results when good phenotypes are used as parents.

Because of the considerable value of seed production areas to new programs using exotic species, they will be treated in some detail in this chapter. It must be emphasized that seed production areas are generally used as interim sources of seed in forest tree improvement and that they are phased out as better genetic seed becomes available from seed orchards. Seed production areas have greater utility in a number of tropical and subtropical countries.

Seed production areas have three attributes that are vitally important. These are as follows:

1. Seed collected will have better genetic qualities than seed from commercial collections, especially in adaptability, bole and crown characteristics, and pest resistance.

2. When seed production areas are established in natural stands (and in some plantations), the geographic origins of the parent trees are known, thus yielding seed from a suitable source. This is not true for many exotic plantations, but selection of the best individuals in an exotic plantation will result in the development of a land race.

3. Seed production areas are reliable sources of well-adapted seed at modest cost. Assurance of seed supply is becoming of ever-increasing importance, especially in rapidly expanding plantation programs that are using species suitable to tropical or subtropical conditions.

Specifications for a Seed Production Area The best natural stands or plantations that are near full stocking are used for the development of seed production areas. There are no specific age limitations, other than the fact that the stand must be old enough to produce seed, and the individual trees must have sufficient crown surface areas so that they can produce large seed crops. For the southern pines, stands between 20 and 40 years of age are acceptable for use as seed production areas, whereas 10 to 20 years is a good age for *P. caribaea* and *P. oocarpa* (it can be 3 to 4 years for some eucalypts). Usually, seed production areas should contain a minimum of 10 acres (4 ha) in size because managing small stands is inefficient, and the danger from contamination from outside pollen is great. Exceptions to the 10-acre minimum are when only limited amounts of seed from a species are required or for species with very heavy seed production, such as sycamore (*Platanus occidentalis*). Other exceptions are some eucalypts where a couple of acres will supply all the seed needed.

For collection efficiency and to assure adequate cross-pollination, it is usually best if 50 seed trees of acceptable phenotype per acre (125/ha) can be retained, although the optimum number of "leave" trees will depend on tree size and selection intensity. It is sometimes impossible to obtain 50 good trees per acre. However, an area with 20 to 30 seed trees per acre (50 to 75/ha) after thinning is considered to be stocked well enough for operational use. Economic and biological considerations generally dictate that if less than 10 to 12 trees per acre (25/ha) cannot be retained after roguing has been completed, the potential seed production area should not be used. A very real danger for some species on certain sites is "windthrow" that is caused by opening up the stand too much.

Stands that look good for a seed production area based on a casual inspection are often found to be quite unsuitable when they are closely checked. Usually, there are very few stands of the correct age and location with sufficient good trees to ensure the minimum number of trees per unit area. When the stand chosen is judged to be suitable for seed production, it must also be situated so that it can be cleaned and managed for optimum seed production.

Selection of Trees for a Seed Production Area   Desired attributes of the trees left in a seed production area are similar to, but less rigorous than, the qualifications required for a select tree to be used in an intensive tree improvement program. Both because of their growth and seed-producing potential, only trees in the dominant and codominant crown classes are considered for retention. The seed production area tree must have a high level of vigor, be straight, have desirable limb form and pruning, and be free from insects and diseases. No tree below the desired standard should be left, regardless of spacing. Trees exhibiting the potential for good cone production are given preference, although the evidence of past seed production is not essential if the trees have been growing in a tightly closed stand. Excellent seed crops are often produced after heavy thinning by trees that exhibited little seed production prior to thinning (Figure 6.2). However, it is necessary that stands be thinned at a young enough age so that the trees retained will have crowns that are large enough and healthy enough to produce large seed crops.

It is essential that the crowns of the crop trees be released to full sunlight on at least three sides if good seed production is to be realized. When several good phenotypes occur in a group, enough of them must be removed so that the remaining ones will receive enough light to respond to the release. In spots where

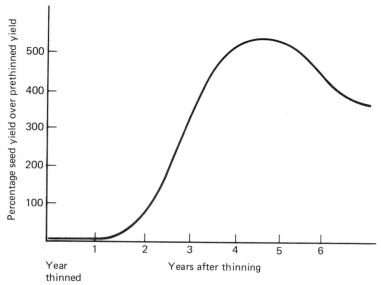

FIGURE 6.2

Full-seed production in a seed production area is delayed for 3 to 4 years after thinning. The amount of seed available following release is shown above for a loblolly pine seed production area. After the sixth year, the seed yield drops off because the stimulation from release disappears.

the only trees available are inferior phenotypes, *all trees must be removed,* even if this results in a fairly large opening in the stand. Also, even if seeds were not collected from the inferior trees that might be left to fill space, the value of the seed crop will be reduced because of contamination with the pollen from the inferior tree.

For most species, an isolation zone or pollen dilution zone should completely surround the seed production area. It is virtually impossible to eliminate completely all contaminating pollen; the purpose of the dilution zone is to reduce it to negligible amounts. Because of wind dynamics and the "dumping" effect of wind currents when they encounter an open area, it is usually best that pollen dilution zones be left unplanted or maintained in low-growing annual or perennial species. If trees are to be grown in the dilution zone, they must be of a species that does not generally hybridize with those in the seed production area.

Thinning the Seed Production Area   Timing and caution are of the utmost importance when removing undesirable phenotypes from seed production areas. Timing is important because it determines the year when the seed production area will produce the first commercial crop, and also because of its possible effect on pests that might appear following thinning. Usually, heavy cone crops of pine are not obtained until the fourth or fifth year after thinning the stand, because of the time required for development of a large, vigorous crown (see Figure 6.2).

Extreme care in conducting the actual thinning operation is important because damage to the remaining trees can result in a degeneration of trees left as seed producers. Careless thinning is a most common cause of trouble when seed production areas are used.

Management of Seed Production Areas   After thinning, it is necessary to remove the logging residue and to reduce the material left on the forest floor. Removing the residue allows for easier access into the area for management activities, reduces the potential dangers from pests and gives a measure of safety from "wildfires." If the seed production area is to be operated efficiently, vegetative material under the seed trees must be controlled. The forest floor will then become relatively open, allowing for easier access for management and cone-harvesting operations.

For permanent seed production areas, fertilization is commonly used in conjunction with the opening of the stand by thinning to induce heavy flower and cone crops. The increase in tree vigor resulting from thinning and fertilization enables the development of heavier and denser crowns that will produce additional male and female primordia.

Pesticide sprays to control cone and seed insects can be applied both aerially and from the ground. Efforts to control pests are sometimes not totally successful because of the difficulty of getting good spray coverage on large trees and because of the difficulty of timing the sprays to coincide with insect infestations. Spraying is expensive, and, coupled with the uncertain success, it is often not considered to be economical, although some insecticides have very effectively controlled certain cone and seed insects in pine, especially when applied aerially.

Harvesting Seed from a Seed Production Area   Seed production areas can be classified into *temporary* and *semipermanent* types; the type used will be dependent upon the need for seed and the extent of good stands. A *temporary* area is established and managed so that when a heavy cone crop is obtained, the seed trees are felled to harvest the seed, cones, or fruit. This method can be used where stands acceptable as seed production areas are numerous, so that new seed production areas can be established to replace the older ones when they are harvested.

The *semipermanent* seed production area is operated on the principle that several crops will be harvested following the response to initial thinning before the seed production area trees are felled. It is necessary, from an economical perspective, to determine the sound seed yield per tree. Each crop tree should be roughly inventoried from the ground to determine if a sufficient quantity of seed is available to warrant collection. The best procedure is to scan a specified sector of the crown through field glasses, and then to extrapolate the total number of cones or fruit on the tree from the number observed in the sector. Usually less than half of the cones or fruit present within the tree's crown can be observed from the ground, but specific rules need to be developed for each species.

Collecting cones and fruits from semipermanent seed production areas is more expensive than collecting from temporary ones. Most organizations prefer to hire professional climbers because of their proficiency, although for some species, mechanical tree shakers are very effective. Some damage to the crown of the tree is inevitable during harvesting operations, but heavy damage will reduce seed crops materially in future years. Specifications regarding the method of getting into the crown, the amount of damage to the crown that can be tolerated, the availability of climbing crews when the cones or fruits are ready for harvest are essentials that should be agreed upon and included in the seed collection contract when it is written.

Seed from Proven Sources

One of the most common methods of obtaining large quantities of seed quickly is to go back to the original source or provenance that has been tested earlier and that has proven to be suitable. This can be a great success or an equally great failure. If the source information is correct and is indeed the same as reported for the initial successful planting, the method works well. Much depends on the integrity of the seed supplier and how accurately the sources are matched. Many "horror stories" can be told of second collections that were purportedly from the same area that produced a successful introduction but which was totally different in reality and produced quite worthless stands of trees. The only completely safe rule to follow, if operational quantities of seed are to be obtained based upon earlier successful introductions, is for an organization to send its own personnel to assure that the collections really are made from the desired quality of trees from the correct area.

LONG-TERM SEED NEEDS—SEED ORCHARDS

The standard method of producing genetically improved seed in operational quantities is to use the seed orchard approach (Andersson, 1960). Of the many definitions for seed orchards, two are given here. A *seed orchard* is an area where "seed are mass produced to obtain the greatest genetic gain as quickly and inexpensively as possible" (Zobel et al., 1958; Zobel and McElwee, 1964). Feilberg and Soegaard (1975) use the following definition: "A seed orchard is a plantation of selected clones or progenies which is isolated or managed to avoid or reduce pollination from outside sources, and managed to produce frequent, abundant, and easily harvested crops of seed" (Figure 6.3). Seed orchards are not always solely for genetic improvement of specific characteristics but can be used to produce quantities of seed that are adapted to a specific planting location (Gerdes, 1959; Nanson, 1972). The seed orchard definitions given here apply specifically to situations in which seed are needed immediately for large operational planting programs (Figure 6.4). The objectives and methodology of seed orchard estab-

FIGURE 6.3

The objective of a seed orchard is to produce maximum amounts of seed with as much genetic improvement as quickly and as efficiently as possible. To do this large crops are needed. The orchard is managed to produce the maximum number of seed. Shown on top are female strobili on a pine tree; on the bottom are mature pine cones.

FIGURE 6.4

Shown are two seed orchards. (*a*) shows a young *P. silvestris* orchard in Sweden, (*b*) shows a producing loblolly pine orchard in the southern United States.

lishment may be modified when seed are not needed for immediate use but where there is a perceived future need for seed.

When there is an urgent need for large quantities of seed because large planting programs are involved, shortcuts must be employed to obtain seed as soon as possible, even though some genetic gain may initially be sacrificed. The method showing how this is done was detailed in the section "The Importance of Time" in Chapter 1. The method consists of initially establishing orchards based only on the phenotype of the parent trees and then later roguing out the poor genotypes from the orchard based on progeny test results rather than waiting to establish an orchard only with parents that have already been tested for their genetic worth.

Seed orchards are usually established with a number of assumptions that are not fully correct. Chief among these is that flowering and pollen exchange among genotypes in the orchard will be uniform and equal. In reality, this is rarely the case. Some genotypes or clones produce many more flowers or pollen than others, and time of flowering is such that certain genotypes rarely ever mate because they flower out of synchronization (Barnes and Mullin, 1974; Beers, 1974).

The utility of seed orchards has been widely documented for many kinds of benefits. Orchards have produced meaningful gains in disease resistance, growth, wood qualities, adaptability, and in tree form.

Types of Production Seed Orchards

There are numerous kinds of seed orchards, but they generally fit into one of two broad categories. *Vegetative orchards* are those established through use of such vegetative propagules as grafts, cuttings, tissue culture plantlets, or other methods. Vegetative orchards are the most common type used operationally. The other general type is called a *seedling seed orchard*. These are established by planting seedlings followed by a later roguing that will remove the poorest trees, generally leaving the best trees of the best families for seed production.

There has been much discussion about the best types of seed orchards to use. Sides have been taken, often inflexibly. Discussion was so animated during the early 1960s that a special issue of *Silvae Genetica* was published (Toda, 1964), which was edited by R. Toda of Japan. The special issue contained articles on the pros and cons of the two types of orchards. Since then, many articles have been published that champion one of the two types of orchards. The simple fact is that there are situations in which either type of orchard may be particularly well suited. It is most important, however, to make the decision about which kind of orchard to use that is based on the pros and cons that will be listed later; some of these are given in some detail to help the reader make better judgments about which type of seed orchard is best for a particular situation (Barber and Dorman, 1964).

Under certain conditions, a genetic test plantation can be converted into a seedling seed orchard, thus fulfilling both the testing and seed production functions at one time. When this is possible, the advantage and efficiency of the seedling orchard is evident. This advantage was initially overemphasized, and many exceptions are now recognized in which both activities cannot be accomplished on the same site. One consideration is that genetic tests should be planted on lands that are typical of those that are to be reforested with improved trees; these lands may not be conducive to good seed production or efficient orchard management (Kellison, 1971). As an example, if the progeny are tested in a swampy area or at a high elevation, the seed orchard function also cannot be followed.

Management criteria will differ for genetic tests and seedling seed orchards. If a tree is to produce heavy cone crops, it must have its crown fully developed and be in full sunlight. On the other hand, a suitable progeny assessment of growth can be made only after the trees have grown long enough to assess how they will grow when competition is strong. Therefore, the final choice of the best individuals from the best families cannot be made until that time. However, if one waits for competition before thinning for seed production, the crowns of the residual trees will be so reduced that seed production will be seriously impaired and costs of collection will be greatly increased. If thinning is done at a suitably young age so that full crown development, and thus heavy seed production, is achieved, the efficiency of the selection phase can be increased greatly. When the trees are planted at initially wide spacings to produce well-developed crowns, the progeny test function is impaired.

A partial solution to this dilemma is to establish several tests of the same families simultaneously in different areas. One can be managed for eventual seed production (i.e., wide spacing, intensive culture); the other tests are used strictly to assess family performance. The seedling seed orchard is then rogued of poor families, based upon their performances in tests designed for that purpose. A disadvantage of this alternative is that only family selection can be efficiently practiced in the orchard. Individual trees cannot be accurately assessed because they have been managed for the purpose of seed production, not for the assessment of their timber-producing characteristics. For crops where early decisions about superiority are possible before competition and for very short rotations, such as for Christmas trees, the seedling seed orchard approach is quite satisfactory. Many different designs and schemes have been worked out to take advantage of the *seedling orchard* concept. Among these are Klein (1974), Riemenschneider (1977), and Cameron and Kube (1980).

Most vegetative orchards have been established by grafting. Quite frequently, incompatibility between scion and stock develops, with resultant sick or dead grafts (Figure 6.5). For some species, such as Douglas fir, incompatibility has been a serious problem, and very heavy losses have been encountered. Such species as loblolly pine have about 20% graft incompatibility, which creates problems but can be tolerated. Most tree improvers have simply accepted this amount of incompatibility and have worked around it.

Methods have been developed to assess graft incompatibility early and to try to avoid it (Slee and Spidy, 1970; Copes, 1973a, 1981; McKinley, 1975). Currently, some vegetative orchards are being established using rooted cuttings in several

FIGURE 6.5

Shown is a typical incompatible pine graft. The graft union is abnormal, the needles are short, the tree lacks vigor, but flowers heavily. It will soon die. Incompatibility can occur almost immediately after grafting, or it can be delayed, as shown, and seriously affect trees that are 20 years or more in age.

conifer and hardwood species, such as spruce and the eucalypts. In the future it is also possible that tissue culture plantlets may be used. These types of vegetative propagation avoid graft incompatibility, but root deformation and imbalance and flowering problems sometimes develop. If severe problems are encountered with the health of vegetatively propagated orchards, then *seedling orchards* have a *clear superiority*.

The magnitude of genetic gains obtainable from the two different types of seed orchards has been debated. There are many qualifications that can be made, such as whether open-pollinated or control-pollinated seed are used for the genetic tests and seedling orchards, and which generations of improvement are being compared. If seed used for the seedling orchard are from selected parents, there will be a generation of difference between clonal and seedling orchards. If a seedling seed orchard is established as a joint test and orchard, both family and within-family selection are possible. If the progeny test is separate from the seedling orchard, then the roguing of the seedling orchard is based almost entirely on family performance.

A seedling orchard has a larger number of parents involved than the 30 to 50 that are commonly used in a vegetative orchard, thus giving it a broader genetic base. However, the selection differential is less than that for the more intensively selected parents used in the vegetative orchard. Perhaps what is the most important fact of all, but which is often not considered, is that an outstanding genotype will appear only once in a seedling seed orchard, whereas it can appear many times in many orchards when reproduced vegetatively.

Testing of each parent used in a vegetative orchard is mandatory for later roguing of poor parents. Roguing can significantly increase the genetic gain from a given orchard by removing the genotypes that have poor characteristics, such as disease susceptibility or poor growth. Testing in seedling seed orchards is not done by individuals but on a family basis, and one never can pinpoint the occasionally outstanding good general combiner parent.

The age at which seed production on seedlings and grafts occurs is highly important. Seedling orchards are very suitable for species like most *Eucalyptus,* black spruce (*Picea mariana*), the early flowering pines, and many hardwoods that produce seed at a young age. For species that have flowering delayed for 10 to 20 years, the vegetative orchard is usually best, because grafts tend to retain the physiological age of the parents from which the scions were taken, and early flowering results when grafts are made from scions from mature individuals. When young material is needed to obtain satisfactory rooting, flowering is sometimes delayed several years longer from cuttings than from grafts from mature parents. The advantage of early flower production on grafts from species that have delayed flowering is a major advantage to the vegetative approach when selections have been made from reproductively mature trees.

Until other information is available, related matings must always be avoided in all types of orchards. The danger of selfing is considerably enhanced in a vegetative orchard if the ramets of a given clone are not well separated (see Figure 2.6). Using only a few clones in the orchard makes this problem more severe, because it is not possible usually to keep a suitable separation in a vegetative orchard with less than 10 clones (van Buijtenen, 1981). In seedling orchards, selfing can occur only on the individual tree, which is what happens on the individual graft in a vegetative orchard. Great care must be taken to have related families properly spaced to avoid mating among relatives; this is a frequent oversight in seedling seed orchards.

One advantage often claimed for vegetative orchards is that they can be placed in a location that is most suitable for efficient operation, or in a climate proven to be suitable for early, heavy, and dependable seed production. This capability is now increasingly being used, even to the extent of establishing seed orchards from Northern Hemisphere species in the Southern Hemisphere to produce seeds for use in the northern areas. Seedling orchards can also be established to take advantage of such an improved flower productivity, but the dual testing and seed production function is then lost, and only family information can be exploited to rogue the seedling orchard.

Seed Orchard "Generations"

Seed orchards are commonly categorized by generation; that is, first-, second-, or more advanced-generation orchards depending upon how many cycles of improvement they represent. No matter what kind of orchard is established, pedigree records must be kept to minimize deleterious related matings and to help ensure use of only the best genetic types. The *first-generation orchard* usually results from selection from natural stands or unimproved plantations, most often by using individual tree selection methods. The pedigrees of the parent trees are usually not known. First-generation orchards are improved by roguing; that is, by removing the less desirable genotypes as determined by progeny testing. The removal of trees for spacing or health reasons in seed orchards is simply a thinning operation, not a genetic roguing. Because a first-generation orchard is started with parents whose genetic worth is unknown, the orchards are usually established at a close spacing to allow roguing of the poor genotypes and still leave a fully productive seed orchard area. often 50% or more of the initially established clones will be removed. If the orchard is established at the desired ultimate spacing and then rogued, there will be large gaps resulting in inefficiency in seed production and often in poor seed yield and quality because of reduced cross-pollination.

There is a type of orchard that is now commonly, but erroneously, referred to as a *1.5-generation orchard*. It consists of taking the very best genotypes (best general combiners) from a number of orchards of similar geographic backgrounds and bringing them together into a new, greatly improved first-generation orchard. This common method for combining the very best, which results in excellent genetic gains, has been described by the senior author as a *1.5 generation* to emphasize that the orchard will produce greatly improved seed because it is composed of only the very best genotypes. The orchards are *not 1.5 generation:* They are only greatly improved *first*-generation orchards.

Seed Orchard Location, Establishment, Size, and Management

Many things must be considered when establishing a seed orchard. Location, size, type of orchard, and management are all of vital importance; these will be discussed later. If each has not been properly considered, an orchard may fail completely or be inefficient. A basic rule in orchard establishment is to plan ahead; 2 to 3 years' preplanning for initial establishment is necessary, and a planning period of many years is required for the total orchard complex. There have been many publications relating to the various phases of the development and management of seed orchards. Some of these are Miyake and Okibe (1967), Chapman (1968), and Sprague et al. (1978). Most information that is available is for conifer orchards, although a few publications (e.g., Taft, 1968; Churchwell, 1972; Dorn and Auchmoody, 1974) deal with hardwoods.

Location A crucial early decision relates to the location of the seed orchard. Accessibility, potential labor supply, soil texture and fertility, air drainage, water supply, geographic location, isolation, insects, disease, and destructive animal problems must all be considered. Of key importance (but unfortunately determined only after a long experience) is whether the environment of an area favors the production of flowers. A major consideration when an orchard site is chosen is whether it is an area where seed production will be reliable from year to year. Another important consideration is how soon the orchard will come into commercial seed production. Many sites will ultimately produce seed, but the environment of some sites may be particularly good for early and heavy flowering. Some of the great differences in flowering and seed production potential can be predicted, whereas other differences occur for unknown or rather obscure reasons. The decision about where an orchard will be established must also be influenced by the risk involved from adverse environmental factors by the financial considerations of the organization that is involved.

Often overlooked is the public relations' value of a seed orchard. Therefore, within the biological and economic considerations that are related to orchard locations, attention should be given to the accessibility and value of the orchard with respect to public relations. One of the most certain and most effective methods of obtaining support for a tree improvement program is to have a well-established, well-kept, and well-planned seed orchard that is easily accessible to those who are involved in the allocation of financial resources.

Another major consideration in location of seed orchards relates to the possible loss or alternate usage of the seed orchard land for roads, airports, dams, supermarkets, pipelines, and so forth. This may sound trivial but it is not; a whole list of stories could be cited in which programs were stopped because the seed orchard area was needed and was taken over for other purposes.

The most efficient orchard is one that is close to headquarters, with equipment and manpower that are centralized and readily available. With proper planning and with sufficient personnel, seed orchards associated with nurseries work well. A concentration of a group of orchards in a single location is efficient but increases the risk of a heavy or complete loss due to natural catastrophes such as tornados, hurricanes, hail, or ice storms (Figure 6.6). Scattered, small orchards reduce the risk of total loss but involve more expensive establishment and operational costs (Vande Linde, 1969). The decision whether to increase security by having several scattered orchards or to have larger, concentrated, and more efficient ones with a higher risk of a major loss must be made before a program starts. Most organizations have chosen the concentrated approach. When this is done, they establish their orchard clones in separate clone banks so that the desired genotypes will not be lost in case of a catastrophe to the operational orchard.

Soils, Topography, and Geography   The appropriate soil type for a seed orchard will vary with species. In general, the orchard site should be average in fertility. It is recognized that poor sites are unsuitable for seed orchards, but reasons for the poor seed production often observed on highly fertile sites are not as well understood. They may be the result of freeze damage to the reproductive structures due to the fact that the trees do not harden off or because the resting bud may not form soon enough for proper reproductive development to be initiated before cold weather (Greenwood, 1981). Finally, they may begin growth too early in the season. Good sites often need an extended time for the orchard to become suitable for commercial seed production because of heavy vegetative and poor reproductive growth. Orchard productivity can be partially manipulated by fertilization and sometimes by irrigation, but very fertile, moist sites do not leave the orchard manager the management options that are available on a less fertile site.

Frequently, orchard success or failure can be directly related to the physical properties of the soil as they affect operating conditions. Abandoned agricultural fields have generally proven to be good seed orchard sites. When seed orchards cannot be established on flat terrain, gently sloping land that is suitable for operating equipment should be sought. In cold regions, the orchard aspect should usually face toward the equator and to the west to obtain maximum light and warmth, especially during the critical flowering season. There are, however, always exceptions with different areas and species that require cool, humid conditions for the best flowering. In several parts of the world, especially those in cooler climates, the method of temperature sums is used to assess the suitability of an area to produce reproductive structures.

An orchard must be located where there is good air drainage, especially in areas where frosts occur. The orchard should also be protected from high winds in the more exposed areas (Dyson and Freeman, 1968) (see Figure 6.6). It is desirable that the orchard be close to a water source because of a possible need for sprays, irrigation, and fire protection. An orchard should not be located in the coldest part of the species range, and it *should never* be established outside the natural range of the species without prior testing. Flowering can be erratic and losses from extreme environmental conditions are common. This does not mean that orchard locations outside the range cannot be excellent. Orchards can be put south (or north in the Southern Hemisphere) of the species range (Gansel, 1973; Schmidtling, 1978; Gallegos, 1981). Excellent seed from the pines in the south-

FIGURE 6.6

Orchards must be located to be as free as possible from damage by environmental factors. Shown (*a*) is a seed orchard that had been badly damaged by an ice storm. (*b*) shows everything that was left of a mature, fully producing seed orchard following destruction by a tornado.

eastern United States are being produced in South Africa and Zimbabwe. Moving orchards can be profitable but *should be done only after tests have shown that normal fruit and seed are produced* in the new environment. In the southeastern United States, experience has shown that the geographic area around Savannah, Georgia, produces consistently good loblolly pinecone crops with the result that a number of operational seed orchards have been concentrated there.

As a rule of thumb, the orchard should be located first in the main portion of the geographic range of the species for which the orchard was established. In some locations with extreme environments, such as cold areas, seed crops may be obtained periodically, but they will be less frequent, and a high proportion of immature or nonviable seed are sometimes produced. For hardwoods as well as pines, freeze damage to the flowers is common. In no circumstances should an orchard be established in a recognized ice belt or in regions that have extreme fluctuations in temperature or rainfall. Precautions should be taken to avoid the location of an orchard in areas where the incidence of pests, such as seed and cone insects, or diseases are known to be serious or where the population densities of deer, voles, rabbits, or other destructive animals are high. This includes our activities. Orchards should be located where the danger of loss to housing roads, power lines, or other developmental activities of humans are minimal.

Pollen Dilution Zones   An orchard must be protected from contamination by outside pollen. Although most tree improvement workers set the width of a dilution zone, an absolute minimum for pine at 400 ft (122 m) and preferably 500 ft (152 m), it is recognized that these distances are insufficient for complete isolation (Wang et al., 1960; Squillace, 1967; McElwee, 1970). Foreign pollen will still be found in an orchard with a dilution zone of this size, but studies have shown that the bulk of the pollen from outside sources will be dissipated within the dilution zone. The considerations for the maintenance of dilution zones outlined for seed production areas also apply here. Economic losses from pollen contamination can be considerable, and despite large costs, proper maintenance of dilution zones is almost always worthwhile (Sniezko, 1981). Dilution zones are most critical for advanced-generation orchards because of the greater potential loss of genetic gain, and hence profitability from pollen contamination.

Effective pollen dispersion distances of hardwoods are not yet well documented; therefore, the wise approach is to keep hardwood seed orchards as distantly separated from contaminating pollen sources as possible. The distance pollen can be transported by insects from entomophylous species is not known, but it undoubtedly varies greatly by insect and species.

Dilution zones should always be maintained between orchards from different physiographic regions and between advanced-generation and early-generation orchards. Many species, even some in the same genus, do not need to be isolated from each other because they flower at different times, or they will not cross. This is common in the pines. Such information about crossbility is badly needed for all important species, especially for those pollinated by insects. An orchard should be blocked as much as possible to permit maximum cross-pollination among members of the orchard and to reduce edge effects. It is best to orient the long axis of the orchard with the direction of the prevailing wind at the time of pollen dispersal if a rectangular configuration is used.

Seed Orchard Size   The appropriate orchard size is determined by the number of seed needed; a good coverage of methods to do this for the southern pines was the colloquium on seed orchards edited by Kraus (1974). To be certain that enough seed will be available, production capacity in excess of anticipated needs is usually developed. The actual size of the orchard needed will vary by species, location of the orchard, availability of seed from other sources, and seed needs and costs. As an example, most organizations do not consider an orchard of southern pines operational unless it is at least 5 acres (2 ha) in size. In terms of regeneration needs, if planting is to be the method used, it is not usually considered to be feasible to establish a seed orchard complex for southern pine (with a 25-year rotation age) for a forest area smaller than about 150,000 acres (60,000 ha), or an annual planting of 6000 acres (2400 ha). Small landholders usually can obtain improved seed more economically by purchase from the government or from other private organizations. Because many seed orchard costs are not directly related to orchard size, the costs per unit of seed produced will decrease when the size of the orchard is increased.

Contrary to the preceding rule, smaller orchards for specialty purposes are often established as part of a larger orchard complex. Under most circumstances, with species where long rotations are used, a minimum planting program of at least 1000 acres (400 ha) per year must be underway to justify a full-fledged seed orchard program. The rules related to size for conifers often are not suitable for hardwoods. For example, genera such as sycamore (*Platanus*) or *Eucalyptus* produce large numbers of viable seed per parent seed tree, and all the seed needed can be produced in a very small area. If enough clones are to be included in order to minimize related matings by having a suitably large genetic base, at least 1 acre (0.4 ha) of orchard is usually needed.

The most difficult stage in planning a seed orchard is making a good estimate of the number of seedlings that can be produced from a mature seed orchard of a given size. For species with unknown flowering habits, the orchard planner must make an "intelligent guess." The number of cones or fruits, or even the number of seeds produced, are not a good guide. The only real criterion is the *number of plantable seedlings that will be obtained per unit area* of seed orchard. For example, Bramlett (1974) devised a system to determine seed potential and seed efficiency; that is, how many actually useful seeds are obtained relative to the potential per cone. When this and the number of cones are known, the seed yields can be estimated quite accurately. Methods of analyzing cones and seeds have been outlined by Bramlett et al. (1977). Therefore, to estimate the needed size of a seed orchard realistically, it is necessary to know the number of cones or fruits, the number of viable seed per unit area of the orchard as well as the seed-to-seedling ratio that will be obtained in the nursery.

The nursery practices that are used will strongly influence how many plantable seedlings will be obtained from a given area of seed orchard. When calculating seedling yields per unit weight of seed, it is essential to consider that seeds from a fertilized seed orchard are often larger, more vigorous, have better germination, and often have more seed per seed-bearing structure than do those from wild stands that develop under a minimal nutrient status and without insect control.

Determining proper orchard size is difficult and the needed area may vary by two- or threefold, depending on the management given to the orchard. In *Pinus taeda,* for example, seed yields were more than doubled when control of seed-destroying insects was achieved (DeBarr, 1971, 1978). In fact, the economics of seed orchards can be greatly affected by the level of seed production and the additional value from an added amount of seed per unit area of the seed orchard (Beers, 1974; Weir, 1975).

Clonal Dispersal in Seed Orchards   For species that are wind pollinated, orchards should be designed in such a way that a minimum of relatedness will result from crossing among the parents, and so that parent trees will have an opportunity to mate freely with each other. These ideal objectives are easy to define but they hard to achieve, especially to assure a minimum of related matings and selfing (Lindgren, 1974). There are reports of high levels of selfing in orchards, but with proper spacing of the ramets of the clones, it can be kept to a modest and acceptable level. As one example, Moran et al. (1980) found 90% outcrossed seed, based on 3 years' assessment of a radiata pine seed orchard.

For vegetative orchards, the original number of clones that are used should be enough to ensure a suitably broad genetic base after roguing has been completed. Most first-generation vegetative seed orchards have been established with 25 to 40 clones. If selected correctly, this number should be sufficient to provide a suitable genetic base for operational planting. After testing and roguing, this number may be reduced to 20 or fewer clones. For planning purposes, the conservative approach is to assume that about half the clones will be rogued from the seed orchard following testing (Figure 6.7). It is essential to recognize that the operational seed production function cannot be efficiently combined with the clone bank or breeding functions. Many errors have been made trying to combine these functions, and orchards have been established with 300 to 400 clones, with the assertion that these many clones are needed in the breeding program. Large numbers of clones are needed in the breeding population, but gains from production orchards with too many clones will be seriously restricted because of a low selection differential.

The necessity for separating the clones in a seed orchard to prevent problems caused by related matings and the rate of inbreeding must be understood (Stern, 1959). Although it varies greatly by species, many forest trees, such as *Liriodendron tulipifera,* are rather highly self-compatible. Only a few, such as *Liquidambar styraciflua* and *Platanus occidentalis,* are known to be reasonably self-incompatible (Schmitt and Perry, 1964; Taft, 1966; Beland and Jones, 1967). Some genera, like *Eucalyptus,* contain some species that self easily and some that do not. In many forest tree species self-compatibility is the rule; when selfing occurs there is a greatly reduced seed germination and often a dramatic loss in growth (Barnes, 1964; Diekert, 1964; Sorenson and Miles, 1974; Franklin, 1969.

FIGURE 6.7

After progeny testing has indicated the parents with the most desired genotypes, seed orchards are rogued of the undesirable genetic material. Shown is a young seed orchard with its first roguing.

Consequently, ramet dispersal in orchards of self-compatible species is an extremely critical factor in orchard establishment. Clonal dispersion can be particularly difficult for some hardwoods (this will be discussed later in this chapter).

A myriad of designs for vegetative seed orchards have been worked out, which range from the trial-and-error type to sophisticated computer designs. Systematic seed orchard layouts have the advantage of simplicity in establishment, and they allow easy movement from one ramet of a clone to another. They can cause problems when genetic roguing is done, because good trees do not occur systematically in the seed orchard; that is, there is no assurance that good- and poor-performing parents will not be established in groups in the orchard by chance. When this happens, wide openings will occur in the orchard following roguing, and some good genotypes will need to be removed, strictly for proper spacing. The key to determining the proper number of desired individuals is an orchard is to have enough to allow for roguing the poorer genotypes, to have the desired spacing, to maximize seed production by having enough good trees to have adequate pollination, and to ensure for a minimum of relatedness.

A good seed orchard design must have flexibility for the improvement of the genetic quality of the orchard by roguing as well as to minimize the potentials for inbreeding. Enough trees must be established in the orchard to permit several roguings and still leave enough trees for seed production. Each clone should be represented by approximately equal frequencies per unit area. Also of importance is to avoid "repetitive neighborhoods" in which the same clonal pattern is repeated several times. When this is not done, clusters of good or poor clones can be located together, thus making it most difficult to do a good job of roguing. Also, when repetitive neighborhoods are used, certain clones tend to pollinate their neighbors, and the proper within-orchard mixture is not achieved.

The preceding criteria were used to develop a design for second-generation loblolly pine seed orchards in the North Carolina State University–Industry Tree Improvement Cooperative. It was recommended to start with 145 trees per acre (338 trees per ha), remove 35% of the remaining trees at each of four roguings, and ultimately to rogue 60 to 70% of the clones and to maintain a distance of 90 ft (28 m) between ramets of the some clone or related individuals. To achieve the foregoing, not less than 30 nor more than 40 clones are recommended for use. Roguing, as recommended, results in 10 to 12 clones left with a stocking of 36 to 60 trees per acre (80 to 150 trees per ha). In actuality, about 25 trees per acre (63 trees per ha) would probably make up the final orchard. Although the preceding recommendations are for one species, loblolly pine, they do give an indication of the methods used in designing a seed orchard. It is impossible to list and describe all the varied designs that have been suggested for establishing seed orchards, but a few differing types are listed as follows:

1. Goddard (1964) described some ideas about the genetic distribution in a seedling orchard following selection both within and among families.
2. Giertych (1965) early developed a systematic layout for orchards.
3. Burrows (1966) developed a theoretical model of clonal dispersion to give the greatest possible gains.
4. Van Buijtenen (1971) described the theory and practice of orchard designs for the southern pines.
5. Klein (1974) developed a special design for a jack pine seedling seed orchard.
6. Gerdes (1959) covered possible methods to use for Douglas fir, a species that has several difficult problems, especially with graft incompatibility.
7. Hatcher and Weir (1981) discussed the advanced-generation design used by the North Carolina State–Industry Tree Improvement Cooperative.

No matter what design is chosen, it must assure that related matings are minimized, and it should enhance random pollination. An orchard that is established incorrectly or carelessly becomes a horror to rogue. Instead of upgrading the genetic quality of the trees in the seed orchard, all the roguing accomplishes is to remove related individuals that are too closely spaced. *Much genetic gain is lost by poor orchard designs or sloppy planting in which a reasonably good design is not followed.*

Seed Orchard Management   Much of the advantage of a tree improvement program is lost if the seed orchards do not produce seed to their maximum potential. It certainly is beneficial to use genetically superior genotypes that are phenologically synchronized to assure cross-pollination and to use those that are inherently heavy seed producers to obtain maximum seed production. It is of equal importance, however, to understand the environmental factors and management practices that enhance seed production. An orchard that is suffering from a soil-nutrient deficiency, soil compaction, or overcrowding will not produce seed to its potential, regardless of the inherent superiority of the stock contained therein.

Seed orchard management is extremely complex. Proper procedures will vary according to the species, location of the orchard, and conditions encountered from one year to another within the same orchard. All that will be covered in this short section is a general discussion of a few of the most important items. Special articles have been published relating to the management or orchards of hardwoods (Churchwell, 1972) and for pine (Fielding, 1964; Swofford, 1968; van Buijtenen, 1968).

Soil Management   Soil *texture* (i.e., the proportion of sand, silt, and clay) is essentially unchangeable through manipulation, and as a result, the quality of the soil is one of the most important considerations in the establishment of the orchard. Soil texture has an influence on the moisture- and nutrient-holding capacity, compactibility, erodibility, and other soil characteristics. The soil texture most desired will vary with species, although most species are similar to loblolly pine, where there is evidence that a sandy loam overlying a friable subsoil, such as sandy clay, is conducive to flowering (Gallegos, 1978). Regardless of the soil texture, normal operating traffic in the seed orchards may change soil *structure* (i.e., how the sand, silt, and clay are aggregated), usually in an undesirable direction. Such activities cause formation of compaction layers ("hardpans") (compaction is worse in the clays). These pans are frequently responsible for a general decline in the vigor and seed production of the orchard and, if left uncorrected, they can result in outright death of the trees from root-penetration problems, drainage problems, and from excess concentration of salts on the pan where the roots are concentrated. The most obvious symptoms of decline in the health of orchard trees that are caused by a pan are a rounding and thinning of the crowns, shortening and poor coloration of foliage, a flattening or "fluting" of the bole of the rootstock portion of the grafts, and the emergence of the tops of large roots on the soil surface (Figure 6.8). Some of these symptoms are also indicators of graft incompatibility and may be misinterpreted as such. Incompatibility is strongly clonal, whereas general decline, because of hardpan problems, usually affects all clones to some extent. However, both can be related, and symptoms of incompatibility will appear much more rapidly under the stress conditions that result from soil compaction.

Subsoiling in established orchards helps alleviate conditions of soil compaction and associated pans (Gregory, 1975; Gregory and Davey, 1977) (Figure 6.9). It severs surface roots, resulting in greater root proliferation to greater depths, and it reduces surface water runoff, thereby improving soil moisture in the seed

FIGURE 6.8

When the soil is compacted or hardpans are present, grafts in the seed orchard often grow poorly, break down or die, (*a*). When subsoiled, the large surface roots are severed, and then reproduce a whole matrix of small feeder roots as shown (*b*) where subsoiling had been done 2 years previously.

orchard. Recent studies show that in some cases subsoiling improves flower production as well as plant development and vigor (Gregory and Davey, 1977). It may also help prevent damage by diseases that spread by root grafts through severance of the roots that would be used by the disease for movement.

The normal procedure is to subsoil on two sides of the tree in 1 year. About 2 years later the process is repeated at right angles to the original direction. It is absolutely essential that a coulter (rolling cutter) precede the subsoiler (see Figure 6.9) so that the surface roots are severed and not torn loose at the root collar of the tree. Usually, the subsoiling operation is done just prior to floral initiation. Subsoiling prior to orchard establishment is *strongly* recommended for all new orchards and is considered essential on land that was formerly cultivated or pastured, which usually will have problems of soil compaction and plow-pan formation. Initial subsoiling should be done in a grid pattern corresponding with the intended planting location of the graft. It is important to understand,

(b)

FIGURE 6.8 (*continued*)

however, that subsoiling in an established seed orchard should be done upon perscription to alleviate detrimental soil conditions and should not be applied as a "blanket" treatment in all orchards.

Surface of the Orchard   Much attention must be given to the surface of the seed orchard. Efficiency and speed of operation are increased with well-prepared smooth surfaces. In some instances, the requirement for a good orchard surface will necessitate filling and leveling and the establishment of a sod cover prior to orchard establishment. However, it is essential that good soil characteristics be maintained or restored in areas that have been altered.

The orchard floor should be protected from wind and water erosion, and the soil's organic matter should be maintained at adequate levels for proper nutrient

FIGURE 6.9

Seed orchards must be intensively managed. One most common treatment is subsoiling; a subsoiler is shown. Seed orchards must be managed for what they are; intensively operated orchards.

and water relations. These objectives can be met through the establishment and maintenance of a good sod cover that will reduce soil compaction resulting from traffic in the orchard. It will also greatly enhance trafficability during inclement weather. Sometimes a sod cover is disadvantageous when mice or voles are prevalent; when this is the case, sod should be kept away from the immediate vicinity of the tree (about 1 m). Although native or naturalized grasses will eventually colonize a new seed orchard, it usually is advisable to sow a sod cover to protect the soil from erosion and compaction (Bengston and Goddard, 1966; Schultz et al., 1975).

Frequent mowing of the sod and weeds in seed orchards favors sod maintenance and allows for the best use of fertilizers by recycling the nutrients to the trees. Grasses and herbaceous material rapidly utilize the fertilizers during the early part of the growing season; if not mowed while in a succulent stage, recycling of the nutrients may be delayed considerably. Mowing during the latter part of the growing season is done to control vegetation, to alleviate fire hazards, and to facilitate cone or seed collection. Fire is fatal to thin-barked grafts, and several seed orchards have been destroyed by only a light burn. Even burning under controlled conditions has resulted in serious damage to the grafts. Grazing the grass in the seed orchard has been suggested, but this should never be done because of the resultant compaction and injury to the orchard trees.

Orchard Fertilization   Based upon soil analyses or in some instances foliar analyses, soil amendments are applied when needed to maintain plant vigor and to promote flowering. Fertilization, particularly applications of nitrogen and phosphorus, has promoted flowering for nearly every species for which trials have been established, especially for various hardwoods (Steinbrenner et al., 1960; Webster, 1971; Jett and Finger, 1973; Greenwood, 1977; Hattemer et al., 1977).

Soil acidity (pH) is of key importance and has a direct effect on many reactions in the soil and on the behavior of soil organisms and plant roots. The optimum pH will vary with species; for most conifers the desired range is 5.5 to 6.5. When the acidity drops below 5.2 or rises above 6.5 for the pines, corrective action should be taken. For some hardwoods, the desired pH is higher and for a few conifers much lower values can be tolerated. In seed orchards, the objective is to have the pH at the desired level, not at just what can be tolerated.

Lime is commonly used to raise a low pH and an acid-forming fertilizer such as ammonium sulfate or ammonium nitrate is commonly used to reduce pH. Elemental sulfur will also lower the soil pH when it is oxidized to sulfate. The orchard manager must adequately and representatively sample the orchard to assure the correct fertilizer prescription. It cannot be overemphasized that *the information obtained through testing is no better than the samples upon which it is based.* Large uniform areas of the orchard up to 5 acres (2 ha) in size may be represented by one composite sample. However, separate samples should be obtained from every area that is distinguishably different from other areas as a result of topography, soil structure, moisture, or native vegetation. The 0- to 6-in. (15-cm) analyses are usually taken from the upper zone, but in addition, the 15; to 21-in. (38.1- to 53.2-cm) zone is occasionally investigated for physical properties in newly established orchards. The condition of the subsoil where anchor roots of the tree are commonly found is important relative to the drainage, fertility, and workability of an area. During the early years of the orchard, it is recommended that nutrient samples be taken annually. Once apparently satisfactory nurient levels have been stabilized as a result of repeated applications of lime and fertilizer, biennial sampling will often suffice.

The amounts of lime and fertilizer suggested for use in a seed orchard are based on the age of trees, species, geographical location, and soil type, and no single application is suitable to all. However, as a general guide, the following minimum fertility standards have been outlined by Davey (1981) for loblolly pine:

Calcium	400	lb/acre	(400 kg/ha)
Magnesium	50	lb/acre	(50 kg/ha)
Potassium	80	80 lb/acre	(80 kg/ha)
Phosphorus	40	lb/acre	(40 kg/ha)
pH	5.5		—

The timing of fertilization application is critical if satisfactory results are to be obtained (Schmidtling, 1972). It should be applied just before the initiation of floral buds if immediate, increased flowering is to result. Fertilizers also help keep the trees healthy and to grow to a large size, resulting in more reproductive bud locations. Usually, seed orchards are fertilized for maximum growth and vigor when young; the application is changed to favor flowering at a later date.

Irrigation   The installation of an irrigation system is expensive, and the question often posed is, "Is it worth it?" On the basis of increased seed production alone, the answer seemed at first to be doubtful; however, new tests make irrigation look increasingly attractive (see Figure 6.9). when increased success of establishing orchard trees, fire protection, more rapid development of trees, better sod cover, and increased seed production are combined, irrigation now appears to be a good investment for some species (Grigsby, 1966). In one loblolly pine orchard, irrigation as well as fertilization was responsible for an approximate 30% increase in seed production over the fertilizer-only area and for a 100% increase over the area that did not receive irrigation or fertilizer (Harcharik, 1981). In droughty years, irrigation may mean the difference between a poor or a good seed crop (Dewers and Moehring, 1970; Long et al., 1974; Gregory et al., 1976).

It has been found from experience that irrigation sometimes delays flower and fruit as well as cone maturity and increases pollen production; it has been used effectively to prevent freezing of flowers during critical periods. It has also been used in Douglas fir orchards to delay maximum strobilus receptivity until after maximum flight of the pollen in surrounding stands (Fashler and Devitt, 1980).

Like fertilization, irrigation is used at young ages in seed orchards to maintain optimal growth and vigor. To accomplish this, irrigation is used at any time during the year when the soil is dry enough to warrant it. As the trees come into flowering, the timing of irrigation appears to become very critical. There is some indication that southern pine trees should be under moisture stress during the period prior to the initiation of reproductive structures (Harcharik, 1981). The actual timing of stress and irrigation is still not clear for most species.

If the decision is made to install an irrigation system, it is important to have proper equipment to determine when and how much to irrigate. Tensiometers of some type are usually used for this purpose; they are simple to install and easy to calibrate and read. They allow the orchard manager to irrigate without guesswork and thus represent an economic savings.

Pest Problems   Any time seed orchards are established, pests in one or another form will become evident. Pests are different for each species and in each geographic area, so there is no point in listing and discussing them in more than a general way. Pests in seed orchards can be divided into those that attack the flowers, fruits, cones, and seeds, those that attack the tree foliage, bark, and limbs, and those that attack the roots. They vary from insects to diseases to animals, birds, and even to human beings.

Since pests often attack after an orchard has been established for some years, their most important effect is often overlooked. As Bergman (1968) and others have emphasized so strongly, the economic returns from tree improvement are closely tied to the amount of seed produced per unit area of seed orchard. In southern pine orchards, for example, DeBarr (1971) and others have shown a dramatic increase in the value of seed orchards resulting when seed losses were reduced through use of effective systemic insecticides (Table 6.1) (Figure 6.10).

The value of pest control was graphically illustrated by Weir (1975) who showed that the sizes of the potential losses from pests destroying seed-orchard seed were greater than the economic value of the timber destroyed by the very destructive southern pine beetle. A *major factor determining whether a seed orchard is economically feasible or not depends upon the success of control of orchard pests.*

Many methods have been developed to control pests in seed orchards, varying from manual removal, shooting or trapping, spraying, and using chemicals. By far the greatest damage to seed orchards is done by insects; their control is not easy. They vary from small insects and diseases that attack flowers, fruits, and cones (DeBarr and Williams, 1971; Miller and Bramlett, 1978; Hedlin et al., 1980; Cameron, 1981) through those that kill and destroy the whole tree. Insects can often be controlled by systemics; that is, chemicals that are taken into the plant that repels or kills the insect when it eats the foliage, cambium, or reproductive structures (Koerber, 1978; Neel et al., 1978). The methodology of systemic usage is being developed rapidly and may also hold promise for control of some fungal infections. In some cases, spraying can be the most effective method of insect control. The use of spraying is being developed, using both fixed-wing aircraft and helicopters.

The most insidious seed orchard pests are the seed, fruit, and cone destroyers. Some of them have been known for many years, but nothing was done to control them because they were considered to be of little importance and of nuisance value only. They can become of major importance in seed orchards, and their control can spell the difference between success and failure.

This short section on orchard pests in no way indicates their great importance.

TABLE 6.1
Available Pesticides for Preventing Losses to Genetically Improved Seed

Treatment	Percentage Sound Seed	Percentage Germination	Dead Cones by Coneworm	Conelets Surviving May–August	Sound Seed per Cone
Furadan	86	97	12	95	72
Guthion	79	99	17	89	78
Control	74	100	20	92	59

Note Shown are the results of a study designed to assess the utility of the pesticides Furadan and Guthion for controlling coneworm (*Dioryctria* sp.) losses in a loblolly pine seed orchard. Results are only for protection in the second year of development (data courtesy Union Camp Corporation).

FIGURE 6.10

Great damage is done by cone- and seed-destroying insects. (*a*) shows a seed bug *Leptoglosus corculus* on a loblolly pine cone. It punctures the developing seeds and destroys them (*b*) shows the dramatic effect on seed per cone from control of insects. (Photos courtesy Gary DeBarr, U.S. Forest Service, Athens, Ga.)

To the seed orchard manager and for the efficiency of a tree improvement program, they are a key problem. When losses from adverse or unusual environments are added to losses from pests, keeping the orchards healthy and fully productive is indeed a challenge.

Other Management Methods to Increase Flowering   There are numerous actions that can be taken to speed up or improve seed production (Hertmuller and Melchior, 1960); two are mentioned here, as follows.

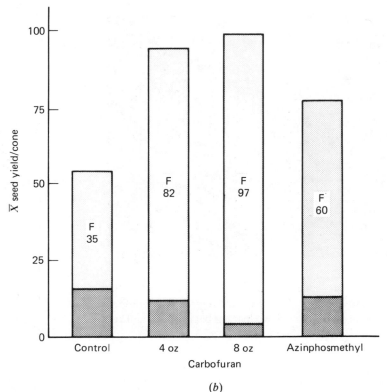

FIGURE 6.10 *(continued)*

Partial girdling of the stem often will result in increased flower and cone crops (Bower and Smith, 1961; Melchior, 1961; Hansbrough and Merrifield, 1963). Although partial girdling works, either as a girdle or a band, it is a severe method that is not usually recommended for orchards that are to be kept for long time periods. It is very useful to obtain heavy seed crops from isolated trees that will be used only temporarily.

Top pruning to keep tree height down and to make seed collection easier has been widely discussed and tried, but with indifferent success (Figure 6.11). It is also used in the hope of keeping the trees low for ease of control pollination. Generally, seed crops from top-pruned trees, compared to normal trees, vary from little or no reduction (Gansel, 1977) to as much as one half on pines (van Buijtenen and Brown, 1962; Copes, 1973b) and to much more for genera like *Abies* that bear most cones at the top of the tree. Although still being tried, top pruning is not a generally accepted seed orchard management method for most species. A problem is that the limbs below the severed portion tend to curve up to make a new top or a multiple top. This can be partially prevented by intensive

FIGURE 6.11

Topping trees to enable easy cone collection and seed orchard operation has been tried in many areas but only extensively used in southern Africa. Shown is a slash pine seed orchard that has been topped and kept low in South Africa.

measures such as tying down the upturning branch (Toda et al., 1963; van der Sijde, 1969). Shaping to increase flower buds on resulting new shoots has been tried with some success (Shibata, 1968).

Seed Orchard Records

The importance of maintaining good records on the seed orchard cannot be overemphasized. The records provide a history of the orchard upon which present and future recommendations are based. They identify the genetic material contained therein, and they reduce the possibility of errors. Of great importance is the fact that they provide a record of what environments and management practices have influenced the orchard, how these were handled, and what the results were.

Basically, two types of records are needed: (1) those related to the orchard as a unit and (2) those related to individual trees or clones within the orchard. A minimal set of information for the orchard as a unit would include the following:

A. Fertilization and liming
    1. Type—formulation
    2. Rates
    3. Date of application
    4. Method of application—broadcast or single tree, ground or aerial

B. Irrigation (if applicable)
   1. Dates required, tensiometer readings
   2. Amount and timing

C. Subsoiling—date, depth, direction

D. Insect and disease control
   1. Material used for control
   2. Rates used
   3. Method of application
   4. Date of application
   5. Effectiveness

E. Pruning
   1. Date
   2. Type

F. Roguing or thinning
   1. Date
   2. Clones and trees removed—trees remaining
   3. Type of cut (silvicultural and/or genetic)

G. Conditions—unusual environmental and biological phenomena. Dates and actions taken should be kept for the following:
   1. Ice storms
   2. Drought
   3. Late frosts
   4. Floods or extraheavy rain
   5. Unusual winds

Complete weather records greatly facilitate seed orchard management. A weather station should be maintained at each orchard to obtain precipitation, relative humidity, temperature, wind velocity, and wind direction. A maximum–minimum thermometer is of great benefit. Many organizations prefer to have additional hygrothermographs, anemometers, and other equipment.

The preceding records provide a general framework of the orchard that can be referred to in order to see what has happened, what was done to rectify any damage done, and how successful was the action taken. Of immediate use, such records can help to explain why there are small seed crops or why seed germinationis below par and can even be used to help predict seed crops. They provide the necessary general framework of knowledge that will ensure that the management of the orchard is done correctly in order to obtain maximum returns from the tree improvement program. Management practices such as fertilization, subsoiling, and irrigation must be done at a specific time and in a specific way to obtain the greatest benefits.

Clonal or individual tree records are more detailed and provide a history of every tree in the orchard; such detailed records are often not kept by new orchard managers because their utility and need is often not appreciated until operations for advanced-generation seed orchards are undertaken. As improved first-generation orchards are established, detailed clonal information becomes essential for the selection of trees and clones to use. It is of no benefit to include a genetically superior clone in an orchard if it does not produce flowers or fertile seeds. Of even more immediate importance in vegetative seed orchards, the clonal records, combined with progeny test results, provide the basis for the roguing and consequent upgrading of first- and advanced-generation orchards. Detailed clonal records on flowering and cone or fruit maturity dates also greatly facilitate control-pollination and cone-collection operations. Minimal records for each clone in a vegetative orchard should include the following:

A. Method and date of propagation

B. Degree of incompatibility

C. Flowering
   1. Age when started (males, females)
   2. Heaviness of males and females
   3. Dates of pollen shed and female receptivity

D. Cone, fruit, and seed production
   1. Seed production (light, medium, heavy)
   2. Date of cone or fruit maturity
   3. Average number of seeds per cone or fruit
   4. Soundness of seed
   5. Germinability

E. Particular susceptibility of seed, cone, or fruit to insects and diseases

F. Specialty handling of individual ramets within a clone
   1. Problems such as abnormal growth, abnormal cone, or fruit development, abortion, and so forth
   2. Special fertilizing or subsoiling for fluted bark

The preceding suggested record system is minimal, but it will provide the essential information for an operational vegetative seed orchard. Along with a good record system, it is necessary that the ramets and trees in the orchard are positively identified and labeled. An accurate and convenient labeling system will greatly facilitate orchard operations such as making control pollinations and cone collecting. Individual trees should be marked with permanent and easily readable tags. A good map of the orchard showing the exact location and identification of each tree in the orchard is essential for operations and to reidentify plants from which the identification may have been lost.

Species with Special Orchard Problems

The bulk of the discussion on seed production has dealt with *wind-pollinated species* in which the pollen is transported from one individual to another in the air.

These were mainly *monoecious* species, which means that both sexes are on the same tree. The emphasis has been on this group of trees because they are the most common in economically important forest trees and because we have the best information about how to handle and control seed production in wind-pollinated species.

There are two major types of breeding and pollination systems that cause special problems in orchard design. These are for *dioecious species* where the two sexes are on different trees and for species in which the pollen is transported by insects (*entomophilous species*) rather than by the wind.

Designs for orchards of dioecious species basically consist of pollinators (males) who are surrounded by a group of females. The problem relates to how many females should be arranged around the males. There is, of course, no danger from selfing, although there is danger from other types of related matings. The best design must be determined for each species. Problems in a tree improvement program using dioecious species usually are about tree selection, because the sex of the tree usually cannot be determined until it flowers. This sometimes results in an excess of males relative to females, as was found for green ash (*Fraxinus pennsylvanica*) (Talbert and Heeren, 1979). This problem is magnified if the males are better formed or have better growth than the females, as has been hypothesized for several dioecious species. Nevertheless, obtaining a good genetic balance for a seed orchard is difficult in dioecious species such as ash (Talbert and Heeren, 1979). Dioecious species are common in hardwoods, especially in the tropical species. They also exist in gymnosperms, for example, in some *Cupressaceae* and in genera like *Ginkgo*.

The most difficult groups of species to work with are the insect-pollinated species (Figure 6.12). Some are pollinated both by wind and insects, such as some eucalypts, whereas others, including *Liriodendron*, are strictly insect pollinated. The latter group tends to have large, sticky pollen that is difficult to collect, store, and work with. Although it is very incompletely understood, it is evident that many of the tropical hardwoods are insect pollinated, some with very specialized pollination systems.

Designs suitable for seed orchards are entomophilous species are a puzzle, and it is not possible to recommend any one system. Everything depends on the insect and its habits. For example, Taft (1961) found that bees did not randomly range throughout a yellow poplar seed orchard, but they tended to concentrate on one tree at a time. Most bees from a hive would feed on one tree; then they would go to another. This results in flying from flower to flower on a single tree, and the main outcome is selfing. Schemes have been tried to overcome this problem with yellow poplar by grafting several clones on one rootstock so that the insects would go from clone to clone on a single tree and thus effect cross-pollination. But this has not worked well, because of the differential growth rate of the different clones that are grafted onto the common rootstock. Also tried was the agricultural practice of having traps in front of the beehive containing the desired pollen or mix of pollens through which the bees walked as they left the hive and thus caused

FIGURE 6.12

Seed orchard designs for some hardwoods are complex. For example, a really suitable design has not been found for insect-pollinated species, such as the *Liriodendron tulipifera* (*a*). Dioecious species also require special designs for efficient seed production. Such problems are particularly acute in the tropical hardwoods. For hardwood species, such as *Liquidambar styraciflua* (*b*), which are wind pollinated, the normal conifer seed orchard designs are suitable.

control pollination. This has worked well for certain horticultural crops, but often in tree species the pollen is so sticky, so hard to collect, and has such a short period of viability that the trap method is most difficult to apply.

The most difficult of all would be dioecious, entomophilous species, but there are no known seed orchards composed of such species. At the present time, it can be said for the insect-pollinated species that it is not yet known how to handle them efficiently in a forest tree seed orchard situation.

RESEARCH SEED ORCHARDS—CLONE BANKS

Most orchard descriptions are for operational seed orchards whose objective is to produce large quantities of seed for production plantings. The clone bank, breeding orchard or research seed orchard, is also of great importance and is essential for long-term programs (Figure 6.13). These are used to preserve and test large numbers of genotypes, not to produce massive quantities of seed for operational planting. The objectives and operations of the research orchards are

(b)

FIGURE 6.12 (*continued*)

described in Chapter 1. These types of orchards are mentioned here only to point out that they may be considered to be seed orchards but must be handled somewhat differently than the production orchards that have been described in detail before.

The question is always asked, "How many trees within a species are necessary as a basis for a breeding orchard?" The stock answer is "the more the better." Realistically, however, some persons feel that 200 nonrelated individuals will form a suitable base; however, most calculations have shown that 300 to 400 would be more appropriate. Many programs have 400 or more different genotypes as an objective.

A few items in which the breeding orchards differ from production orchards are summarized as follows:

1. Related individuals can be placed together, if efficiency of establishment and ease in movement from one ramet of a clone to another is desired for controlled pollinations. Planting in this manner means that testing by open-pollinated seed collected from the clone bank is impossible because there will be related matings and selfs.

2. Pollen dilution zones are not required if open-pollinated seed are not to be used.

3. No less than three, nor generally more than six, ramets of the same clone or closely related individuals need to be maintained.

4. The breeding orchard can be placed wherever the trees will grow best and produce seed. It can often be established close to research headquarters for ease of operation. Usually, a breeding orchard is put in a location that is different from the production orchard as an added insurance against destruction or loss of genotypes by weather extremes or other catastrophes. Many organizations exchange plant materials for breeding orchards to assure greater safety. Representatives of each genotype of interest are put into the breeding orchard.

5. The research orchard must be managed well enough to keep it healthy so it will produce seed. This implies intensive management similar to that used in production seed orchards. *Records and labeling* must be kept up to date to prevent loss or mixing of identities or pedigrees.

FIGURE 6.13

Breeding orchards have the function of the conservation of genetic material for use in the breeding program and for advanced generations. Shown is a hardwood clone bank that contains several clones of several different species that are being held for use in future breeding programs.

Breeding orchards or clone banks need a broad genetic base to avoid inbreeding in future generations and to preserve genes and genotypes that might be useful as the tree improvement program develops. They serve as a base for later and more advanced tree improvement. In contrast, the production orchards have as their objective the production of large quantities of seed with the maximum genetic gain from the very best clones. Too often the breeding orchard is given only minimal care. The production seed orchard is essentially a "dead end" insofar as being a major basis for future generations of breeding; the function of genetic conservation and breeding is carried out in the breeding orchard.

SEED CERTIFICATION

Ever since applied tree improvement became accepted, there has been increased interest and considerable emphasis toward certifying seed as has been done so successfully for agricultural crops. Seed certification in forestry is not new. As early as 1903, Doi reported on regulations for collecting and marketing *Cryptomeria* seed in Japan. Some recent certification plans have been put into practice, but there is no uniformity among the various methods. It seems that most people think that seed certification is a good idea. In a survey in the United States, 97% of the respondents favored seed certification. Of these, 93% wanted seed certification to be voluntary and not rigidly legislated (Horning, 1961; Cech et al., 1962). Most wanted a certification program to be administered by local groups that would have the legal authority to set standards, although Horning (1961), Rohmeder (1961), and Mathews (1964) felt that an international certification program was essential.

There are many meanings for seed certification and labeling, as have been discussed by Barber et al. (1962) and Barber (1969). The details of the various uses and methods of certification are not necessary to pursue in this book. However, certification requires a general supervision over the collection and handling of forest tree seeds in a uniform and consistent manner, and great care is needed (Barber, 1969; Barner and Koster, 1976). There is a tendency to emphasize the special importance of seed certification for the tropical and subtropical areas where exotics are used (Banks and Barrett, 1973), but it is also necessary for cool-weather areas where exotics are widely planted, such as in Europe and Canada (Presch and Stevenson, 1976).

Questions are often raised as to whether or not seed certification is really needed. It is becoming clear that with seed shortages, the great need for exotics, and the advent of genetically improved seed, that uniform and simple certification procedures are desirable. Many persons understand certification to mean what is correctly termed *labeling* in which the seed size, purity, germination, and other information about the seed is given. Others consider that there should be a minimum of *source certification;* that is, to have an accurate description of where the seed were obtained and, hopefully, from what quality of parent trees. Source certification is vital to all exotic forestry, and lack of such information has caused great frustration and losses in forestry throughout the world. To some foresters, *seed certification* means a statement about the *genetic quality* of the seed; this should be the ultimate certification goal. Quality certification is increasing as progeny tests mature and data become available on genetic performance. Quality certification is the most difficult of all because it depends on so many factors of product, size, crossing and test design, method of assessment, age, and other items. It is so complex that there may never be a consensus about just what should be required.

Regardless of definitions, the key to any type of forest tree seed certification program is to assure that the purchaser knows what is being bought. The objective of certification is not to legislate what can be sold; it is to make certain that the buyer receives what is being paid for. Certification methods are certain to multiply, both regionally and internationally. The real need is to avoid rigid and dictatorial certification schemes, while at the same time fulfilling the objective of assurance of genetic quality to the buyer.

LITERATURE CITED

Andersson, E. 1960. Froplantagen I Skogsbrukets Tjänst [Seed orchards in Swedish forestry] Sätryck ur Kungl. *Skogs-och Lantbruksakademiens Tidskrift* **99**(1–2):65–87.

Andersson, E. 1963. "Seed Stands and Seed Orchards in the Breeding of Conifers. 1st World Consul. on For. Gen. and Tree Impr., Stockholm, Sweden.

Banks, P. F., and Barrett, R. L. 1973. "Exotic Forest Tree Seed in Rhodesia." IUFRO, Symposium on Seed Processing, Bergen, Norway, Vol. II, pp. 1–8.

Barber, J. D., Callahan, R. Z., Wakeley, P. C., and Rudolf, P. O. 1962. More on tree seed certification and legislation. *Jour. For.* **60**(5):349–350, 352.

Barber, J. D., and Dorman, K. W. 1964. Clonal or seedling seed orchards? *Sil. Gen.* **13**(1–2):11–17.

Barber, J. D. 1969. "Control of Genetic Identity of Forest Reproductive Materials." 2nd World Consul. For. Tree Breed., Washington, D.C., pp. 7–16.

Barner, H., and Koster, R. 1976. "Terminology and Definitions to Be Used in Certification Schemes for Forest Reproductive Materials." XVI IUFRO World Congress, Oslo, Norway.

Barnes, B. V. 1964. "Self and Cross-pollination of Western White Pine: A Comparison of Height Growth of Progeny." U.S. Forest Service Research Note INT-22, pp. 1–3.

Barnes, R. D., and Mullin, L. J. 1974. "Flowering Phenology and Productivity in Clonal Seed Orchards of *Pinus patula, P. elliottii, P. taeda* and *P. kesiya* in Rhodesia." Forestry Research Paper No. 3, Rhodesia For. Comm.

Beers, W. L. 1974. "Industry's Analysis of Operational Problems and Research in Increasing Cone and Seed Yields." Colloquim: Seed Yields from Southern Pine Orchards, *Macon, Ga., pp. 86–96.*

Beland, J. W., and Jones, L. 1967. "Self-Incompatibility in Sycamore." 9th South. Conf. on For. Tree Impr., pp. 56–58.

Bengston, G. W., and Goddard, R. E. 1966. "Establishment, Culture and Protection of Slash and Loblolly Pine Seed Orchards. Some Tentative Recommendations. Proc. Southeast. Area For. Nur. Conf., Columbia, S.C., pp. 47–63.

Bergman, A. 1968. "Variation in Flowering and Its Effect on Seed Cost—A Study of Seed Orchards of Loblolly Pine." Technical Report No. 38, School of Forest Resources, North Carolina State University, Raleigh.

Bower, D. R., and Smith, J. L. 1961. "Partial Girdling Multiplies Shortleaf Cones." South. For. Notes No. 132, U.S. Forestry Service.

Bramlett, D. L. 1974. "Seed Potential and Seed Efficiency." Colloquium: Seed Yields from Southern Pine Seed Orchards, Macon, Ga., pp. 1–7.

Bramlett, D. L., Belcher, E. W., DeBarr, G. L., Hertel, G. D., Karrfalt, R. P., Lantz, C. W., Miller, T., Ware, K. D., and Yates, H. O. 1977. "Cone analysis of southern pines—A guidebook." Technical Report SE-13, U.S. Forestry Service.

Burrows, P. M. 1966. *A Theoretical Model for the Establishment of Seed Orchards from Plus Trees.* Biometrics Team, Agricultural Research Council of Central Africa, Southern Rhodesia.

Cameron, J. N., and Kube, P. D. 1980. "Management of Seedling Seed Orchards of *Eucalyptus regnans*—Selection, Strategy and Flowering Studies." Workshop on Gen. Impr. and Prod. of Fast Growing Trees, São Pedro, São Paulo, Brazil.

Cameron, R. S. 1981. "Toward Insect Pest Management in Southern Pine Seed Orchards." Texas Forest Service, Pub. No. 126.

Chapman, W. L. 1968. "Ideas Regarding Seed Orchard Management." Proc. Southeastern Area For. Nur. Conf., Stone Mountain, Ga., pp. 131–139.

Cech, F. C., Barber, J. C., and Zobel, B. J. 1962. Comments on "Who wants tree seed certification and why?" *Jour. For.* **60**(3):208–210.

Copes, D. L. 1973a. Genetics of graft rejection in Douglas fir. *Can. Jour. For. Res.* **4**(2):186–192.

Copes, D. L. 1973b. Effect of annual leader pruning on cone production and crown development of grafted Douglas fir. *Sil. Gen.* 22(5–6):167–173.

Copes, D. L. 1981. "Selection and Propagation of Highly Graft-Compatible Douglas-Fir Rootstocks—A Case History." U.S. Forest Service Research Note PNW 376.

Churchwell, B. 1972. "Hardwood Seed Orchard Management." Proc. Southeastern Area Nur. Conf., Greenville, Miss., pp. 84–87.

Davey, C. B. 1981. Seed orchard soil management. In *Tree Improvement Short Course,* North Carolina State University–Industry Cooperative Tree Improvement Program, School of Forest Resources, Raleigh, pp. 90–95.

DeBarr, G. L. 1971. "The Value of Insect Control in Seed Orchards: Some Economic and Biological Considerations." 11th Conf. South. For. Tree Impr., Atlanta, Ga., pp. 178–185.

DeBarr, G. L., and Williams J. A. 1971. "Nonlethal Thrips Damage to Slash Pine Flowers Reduces Seed Yields." U.S. Forest Service Research Note SE-160.

DeBarr, G. L. 1978. "Importance of the Seedbugs *Leptoglossus corculus* and *Tetyra bipunctata* and Their Control in Southern Pine Seed Orchards. Proc. Symposium on Flowering and Seed Development in Trees, Mississippi State University, pp. 330–341.

Dewers, R. R., and Moehring, D. M. 1970. Effect of soil water stress on initiation of ovulate primordia in loblolly pine. *For. Sci.* **16**(2):219–221.

Diekert, H. 1964. Einige Untersuchungen zur Selbsterilität und Inzucht bei Fichte und Lärche [Some investigations on self-sterility and inbreeding in spruce and larch]. *Sil. Gen.* **13**(3):77–86.

Doi, H. 1903. The enactment of the regulations on collection and marketing of *Cryptomeria* and hinoki cypress seeds. *Dainippion Saurin Kaihoo* [*Bull. Jap. For. Assoc.* **252**:37–42]. From *Abstr. Jap. Liter.* **1**(A), 1970.

Dorn, D. E., and Auchmoody, L. R. 1974. "Effects of Fertilization on Vegetative Growth and Early Flowering and Fruiting of Seed Orchard Black Cherry." 21st Northeast. Tree Impr. Conf., University of New Brunswick, pp. 6–18.

Dyer, W. G. 1964. "Seed Orchards and Seed Production Areas in Ontario." Proc. 9th Meeting of Comm. For. Tree Breeding in Canada, Part II, pp. 23–28.

Dyson, W. G., and Freeman, G. H. 1968. Seed orchard designs for sites with a constant prevailing wind. *Sil. Gen.* **17**(1):12–15.

Fashler, A. M. K., and Devitt, W. J. B. 1980. A practical solution to Douglas-fir seed orchard pollen contamination. *For. Chron.* **56**:237–241.

Faulkner, R. 1962. Seed stands in Britain and their better management. *Quart. Jour. For.* **56**(1):8–22.

Faulkner, R. 1975. "Seed Orchards." Forestry Comm. Bull. No. 54, Her Majesty's Stationary Office, London.

Feilberg, L., and Soegaard, B. 1975. "Historical Review of Seed Orchards." Forestry Comm. Bull. No. 54. Her Majesty's Stationary Office, London.

Fielding, J. M. 1964. Notes on a Monterey pine seed orchard on Tallaganda State Forest in New South Wales. *Aust. For.* **28**(3):203–206.

Franklin, E. C. 1969. "Inbreeding Depression in Metrical Traits of Loblolly Pine (*P. taeda*) as a Result of Self-pollination." Technical Report 40, School of Forest Resources, North Carolina State University, Raleigh.

Gallegos, C. M. 1978. "Criteria for Selecting Loblolly Pine (*Pinus taeda L.*) Seed Orchard Sites in the Southeastern United States." Proc. Symposium on Flowering and Seed Development in Trees, Mississippi State University, pp. 163–176.

Gallegos, C. M. 1981. "Flowering and Seed Production of *Pinus caribaea* var. *Hondurensis* (Results of a World-Wide Survey)." Symposium on General Improvement and Production of Fast-Growing Species, São Pedro, São Paulo, Brazil.

Gansel, C. R. 1973. "Should Slash Pine Seed Orchards Be Moved South for Early Flowering?" 12th South. For. Tree Impr. Conf., Baton Rouge, La., pp. 310–316.

Gansel, C. R. 1977. "Crown Shaping in a Slash Pine Seed Orchard." 14th South. For. Tree Impr. Conf., Gainesville, Fla., pp. 141–151.

Gerdes, B. C. 1959. "Some Thoughts on Douglas-Fir Seed Orchards and Their Establishment." Proc., Society American Forestry, San Francisco, Calif.

Giertych, M. M. 1965. Systematic lay-outs for seed orchards. *Sil. Gen.* **14**(3):91–94.

Goddard, R. E. 1964. Tree distribution in a seedling seed orchard following between and within family selection. *Sil. Gen.* **13**(1–2):17–21.

Greenwood, M. S. 1977. "Seed Orchard Fertilization: Optimizing Time and Rate of Ammonium Nitrate Application for Grafted Loblolly Pine" 14th South. For. Tree Imp. Conf., Gainesville, Fla., pp. 164–169.

Greenwood, M. S. 1981. Reproductive development in loblolly pine. II. The effect of age, gibberellin plus water stress and out-of-phase dormancy on long shoot growth behavior. *Am. Jour. Bot.* **68**(9):1184–1190.

Gregory, J. D. 1975. "Subsoiling to Stimulate Flowering and Cone Production and Ameliorate Soil Conditions in Loblolly Pine (*Pinus taeda*) Seed Orchards." Ph.D. thesis, North Carolina State University, Raleigh.

Gregory, J. D., and Davey, C. B. 1977. Subsoiling to stimulate flowering and cone production in a loblolly pine seed orchard. *South. Jour. Appl. For.* **1**(2):20–23.

Gregory, J. D., Guiness, W. M., and Davey, C. B. 1976. *Fertilization and Irrigation Stimulate Flowering and Seed Production in a Loblolly Pine Seed Orchard.* Soil Science Society of America, Houston, Tex.

Grigsby, H. 1966. "Irrigation and Fertilization of Seed Orchards." West Reg. Nur. Conf., Hot Springs, Ark., pp. 1–18.

Hansbrough, T., and Merrifield, R. G. 1963. "The Influence of Partial Girdling on Cone and Seed Production of Loblolly Pine." Louisiana State University Forestry Notes No. 52.

Harcharik, D. A. 1981. "The Timing and Economics of Irrigation in Loblolly Pine Seed Orchards." Ph.D. thesis, North Carolina State University, Raleigh.

Hatcher, A., and Weir, R. J. 1981. "Decision and Layout of Advanced Generation Seed Orchards." 16th South. For. Tree Impr. Conf., Blacksburg, Va., pp. 205–212.

Hattemer, H. H., Andersson, E., and Tamm, C. O. 1977. Effects of spacing and fertilization on four grafted clones of Scots pine. *Stud. For. Suec.* **141**:1–31.

Hedlin, A. F., Yates, H. O., Lovar, D. C., Ebel, B. H., Koerber, T. W., and Merkel, E. P. 1980. *Cone and Seed Insects of North American Conifers.* Canadian Forestry Service, Ottawa.

Hertmuller, H. H., and Melchior, G. H. 1960. Über die blühfördernde Wirkung des Wurzelschnitts, des Zweigkrümmens und des Strangulation auf japanischer Lärche (*Larix leptolepis*) [On the flower-promoting effects of root pruning, bending of branches and strangulation in Jap. larch]. *Sil. Gen.* **9**(3):65–72.

Horning, W. H. 1961. Society of American Foresters' report on a study of seed certification conducted by the committee on Forest Tree Improvement. *Jour. For.* **59**(9):656–661.

Jett, J. B., and Finger, G. 1973. "Stimulation of Flowering in Sweetgum." 12th South. For. Tree Impr. Conf., Baton Rouge, La., pp. 111–117.

Kellison, R. C. 1971. "Seed Orchard Management." 11th Congress on South. For. Tree Impr., Atlanta, Ga., pp. 166–172.

Klein, J. T. 1974. "A Jack Pine Seedling Seed Orchard Plantation of Unusual Design." 21st Northeast. For. Tree Impr. Conf., Fredricton, New Brunswick, pp. 55–65.

Koerber, T. W. 1978. "Tests of Bole Injected Systemic Insecticides for Control of Douglas-fir Cone Insects." Proc. Symposium on Flowering and Seed Development in Trees, Mississippi State University, pp. 323–329.

Kraus, J. 1974. "Seed Yield from Southern Pine Seed Orchards." Colloquium: Yield from Southern Pine Seed Orchards, Macon, Ga., pp. 1–100.

LaFarge, T., and Kraus, J. F. 1981. "Comparison of Progeny of a Loblolly Pine Seed Production Area with Progeny of Plus Tree Selections." 16th South. For. Tree Impr. Conf., Blacksburg, Va., pp. 302–310.

Lindgren, D. 1974. "Aspects on Suitable Number of Clones in a Seed Orchard." IUFRO Meeting, Stockholm, pp. 293–305.

Long, E. M., van Buijtenen J. P., and Robinson, J. F. 1974. "Cultural Practices in Southern Pine Seed Orchards." Colloquium: Seed Yield from Southern Pine Seed Orchards, Macon, Ga., pp. 73–85.

Mathews, J. D. 1964. Seed production and seed certification. *Unasylva* **18**(2–3):73–74, 104–118.

McElwee, R. L. 1970. "Radioactive Tracer Techniques for Pine Pollen Flight Studies and an Analysis of Short-Range Pollen Behavior." Ph.D. thesis, School of Forest Resources, North Carolina State University, Raleigh.

McKinley, C. R. 1975. "Growth of Loblolly Scion Material on Rootstocks of Known Genetic Origin." 13th South. For. Tree Imp. Conf., Raleigh, N.C., pp. 230–233.

Melchior, G. H. 1961. Versuche zur Ringelungsmethodik an Propflingen der europaischen Lärche (*Larix decidua*) und der japanischen Lärche (*Larix leptolepis*) [Experiments with girdling of grafts of European and Japanese larch]. *Sil. Gen.* **10**(4):107–109.

Miller, T., and Bramlett, D. L. 1978. "Damage to Reproductive Structures of Slash Pine by Two Seed-Borne Pathogens: *Diplodia gossypina* and *Fusarium monoliforme* var. *subglutinans*." Symposium on Flowering and Seed Development in Trees, Mississippi State University, pp. 347–356.

Miyake, N., and Okibe, A. 1967. Fundamental studies on seed gardens (orchards) of Japanese pine. 5. Effects of some fertilizers on the growth and cone crops of Akamatsu (*P. densiflora*). *Bull. Shimane Agr. Coll.* **15A-2**:101–112.

Moran, G. F., Bell, J. C., and Matheson, A. C. 1980. The genetic structure and levels of inbreeding in a *P. radiata* seed orchard. *Sil. Gen.* **29**(5–6):190–193.

Nanson, A. 1972. The provenance seedling seed orchard. *Sil. Gen.* **21**(6):243–248.

Neel, W. W., DeBarr, G. L., and Lambert, W. E. 1978. "Variability of Seedbug Damage to Pine Seed Following Different Methods of Applying Carbofuran Granules to a Slash Pine Seed Orchard." Symposium on Flowering and Seed Development in Trees, Mississippi State University, pp. 314–322.

Presch, R. F., and Stevenson, R. E. 1976. "Certification of Source-Identified Canadian Tree Seed under the O.E.C.D. Scheme." Can. For. Ser. For. Tech. Rept. No. 19.

Riemenschneider, D. E. 1977. "The Genetic and Economic Effect of Preliminary Cutting in the Seedling Orchard." Proc. 13th Lake States For. Tree Imp. Conf., St. Paul, Minn., (U.S. Forestry Service Technical Report NC-50, pp. 81–91.

Rohmeder, E. 1961. Probleme und Vorschläge internationaler Zertification des forstlichen Saatgutes [Problems and suggestions for an international certification of forest seed]. *Sonderdruck* **30**(9):253–255; **31**(8):219–221.

Schmidtling, R. C. 1972. "Importance of Fertilizer Timing on Flower Induction in Loblolly Pine." 2nd N. Amer. For. Biol. Workshop, Society of American Foresters, Oregon State University.

Schmidtling, R. C. 1978. "Southern Loblolly Pine Seed Orchards Produce More

Cone and Seed Than Do Northern Orchards." Symposium on Flowering and Seed Development in Trees, Mississippi State University, pp. 177–186.

Schmitt, D. M., and Perry, T. O. 1964. Self-sterility in sweetgum. *For. Sci.* **10**:302–305.

Schopmeyer, C. S. (Ed.). 1974. *Seeds of Woody Plants in the United States*, Agricultural Handbook No. 450. U.S. Forest Service, Washington, D.C.

Schultz, R. P., Wells, C. G., and Bengtson, G. W. 1975. "Soil and Tree Responses to Intensive Culture in a Slash Pine Clonal Orchard: 12 Year Results." U.S. Forest Service Research Paper SE-129.

Shibata, M. 1968. "Studies on Pruning and Shaping of Grafts in Seed Orchards." Trans. of 79th Mtg. Jap. For. Soc.

Slee, M. W., and Spidy, T. 1970. The incidence of graft incompatibility with related stock in *P. caribaea* v. *Hondurensis*. *Sil. Gen.* **19**(5–6):184–187.

Sniezko, R. A. 1981. "Genetic and Economic Consequences of Pollen Contamination in Seed Orchards." Proc. Southern Forest Tree Improvement Conf., Blacksburg, Va., pp. 225–233.

Sorenson, F. C., and Miles, R. S. 1974. Self-pollination effects on Douglas fir and ponderosa pine seeds and seedlings. *Sil. Gen.* **23**(5):135–138.

Sprague, J., Jett, J. B., and Zobel, B. 1978. "The Management of Southern Pine Seed Orchards to Increase Seed Production." Symposium on Flowering and Seed Development in Trees, Mississippi State University, pp. 145–162.

Squillace, A. E. 1967. Effectiveness of 400-foot isolation around a slash pine seed orchard. *Jour. For.* **65**(11):823–824.

Steinbrenner, E. C., Duffield, J. W., and Campbell, R. K. 1960. Increased cone production of young Douglas-fir following nitrogen and phosphorus fertilization. *Jour. For.* **58**(2):105–110.

Stern, K. 1959. The rate of inbreeding within the progenies of seed orchards. *Sil. Gen.* **8**(2):37–68.

Swofford, T. F. 1968. "Seed Orchard Management." Southeast. Area For. Nur. Conf., Stone Mountain, Ga., pp. 83–89.

Taft, K. A. 1961. "The Effect of Controlled Pollination and Honeybees on Seed Quality in Yellow Poplar (*Liriodendron tulipifera*) as Assessed by X-ray Photographs," Technical Report 13, School of Forestry, North Carolina State University, Raleigh.

Taft, K. A. 1966. "Cross and Self-Incompatibility and Natural Selfing in Yellow Poplar (*Liriodendron tulipifera*)." 6th World For. Cong., Madrid, Spain, pp. 1–11.

Taft, K. A. 1968. "Hardwood Seed Orchard Management." Southeastern Area For. Nur. Conf., Stone Mountain, Ga., pp. 90–91.

Talbert, J. T., and Heeren, R. D. 1979. Sex differences in green ash. *South. Jour. App. For.* **3**(4):173–174.

Thielges, B. 1975. "Forest Tree Improvement, the Third Decade." 24th Annual For. Symp., Louisiana State University, Baton Rouge, La.

Toda, R., Akasi, T., and Kikuti, H. 1963. Preventing upward curving of limbs of topped seed-trees by growth substance treatment. *Jour. Jap. For. Soc.* **45**(7):227–230.

Toda, R. 1964. Special issue of *Silvae Genetica* **13**(1) on vegetative and seedling seed orchards.

van Buijtenen, J. P., and Brown, C. L. 1962. "The Effect of Crown Pruning on Strobile Production of Loblolly Pine." For. Gen. Workshop, Macon, Ga.

van Buijtenen, J. P. 1968. "Seed Orchard Management." Proc. Southeastern Area For. Nur. Conf., Stone Mountain, Ga., pp. 123–127.

van Buijtenen, J. P. 1971. "Seed Orchard Design—Theory and Practice." 11th Conf. South. For. Tree Impr., Atlanta, Ga., pp. 197–206.

van Buijtenen, J. P. 1981. "Advanced Generation Tree Improvement." 18th Canadian Tree Impr. Assoc. Meet., Duncan, British Columbia," pp. 1–15.

Vande Linde, F. 1969. "Some Practical Aspects of Seed Orchard Management in the South." Proc. 10th South. Conf. For. Tree Impr., Houston, Tex., pp. 199–204.

van der Sijde, H. A. 1969. "Bending of Trees as a Standard Practice in Pine Seed Orchard Management in South Africa." 2nd World Cons. For. Tree Breed., Washington, D.C."

Wang, C.-W., Perry, T. O., and Johnson, A. G. 1960. Pollen dispersion of slash pine (*P. elliottii*) with special reference to seed orchard management. *Sil. Gen.* **9**(3):78–86.

Webster, S. 1971. "Nutrition of Seed Orchard Pine in Virginia." Ph.D. thesis, North Carolina State University, Raleigh.

Weir, R. J. 1975. "Cone and Seed Insects—Southern Pine Beetle: A Contrasting Impact on Forest Productivity." 13th South. For. Tree Impr. Conf., Raleigh, N.C., pp. 182–192.

Zobel, B. J., Barber, J., Brown, C. L., and Perry, T. O. 1958. Seed orchards; their concept and management. *Jour. For.* **56**:815–825.

Zobel, B. J., and McElwee, R. L. 1964. Seed orchards for the production of genetically improved seed. *Sil. Gen.* **13**(1–2):4–11.

CHAPTER 7

Use of Tree Improvement in Natural Forests and in Stand Improvement

The best way to effectively use the genetic differences among trees is through a plantation program. However, genetic manipulation can also be beneficial when forests are regenerated naturally. Also, it is of importance in such intermediate stand treatments as thinning, pruning, and fertilization. This is fortunate, because the bulk of the forests throughout the world are now, and will continue, to be managed by using natural regeneration techniques.

Tree improvement principles can be used quite profitably both in regeneration of natural stands and in certain forest management activities that are applied to previously established stands. Although gains from the use of genetics will be less than when applied to a planting program, they can be obtained quickly because *the genetic manipulation can be applied immediately*. This is of great importance both in temperate climates and in the mixed species forests in the tropics and subtropics. In the efforts to use genetics in natural forests, most of the emphasis has been on the regeneration phase, and the real value of genetic manipulation in other aspects of silviculture has not been generally understood. In fact, even without serious genetic considerations, many of the best silvicultural practices have the effect of improving the genetic structure of the trees that are left to grow.

This chapter will cover some of the difficulties that are involved and some of the gains that can be made when applying genetic principles to natural regeneration or to previously established stands of trees. There is minimal research information that can be cited, because little has been done in this area, and economic studies are almost totally lacking. However, a knowledge of inheritance patterns and an idea of the economic worth of the characteristics involved will enable some realistic projections to be made.

NATURAL REGENERATION

Although most forest species are regenerated by seed, vegetative systems of regeneration, such as by root sprouts and stump sprouts, are also common, especially in the hardwoods. Vegetative reproduction also occurs in some conifers; two examples are redwood (*Sequoia sempervirens*) and *Cryptomeria*. It is easier to genetically manipulate natural stands when regeneration from selected seed trees can be employed. Complications arise when species sprout or have seeds that remain viable on the forest floor for many years.

Seed Regeneration

When seed trees or shelterwood systems of regeneration are used (as with the pines), genetic gain can be obtained by leaving the best trees as seed producers. The most important gain occurs because the progeny produced are well adapted to the site. Additionally, quality characteristics such as tree form can be improved by leaving the best phenotypes to produce seed, because these traits are usually highly heritable. Volume gains will be small, because growth characeristics are under only moderately additive genetic control, and most natural regeneration systems do not allow selection intensities great enough in the original stands to achieve substantial gains in growth. Resistance to many pests, such as fusiform rust in the southern pines, will be considerably improved. Goddard et al. (1975a) found that progeny from disease-free seed trees in stands heavily infected with fusiform rust produced seedlings that were considerably more disease resistant than those from the overall population.

When the best trees are removed, leaving the inferior ones to produce seed for the next generation, *dysgenic selection* will result. The most adverse cutting method within a species in even-aged stands is the *diameter limit cut* in which all trees over a given size are removed and the small diameter trees are left to grow and reproduce the stand (Trimble, 1971). The *diameter limit cut* is a type of dysgenic selection that is widely practiced throughout the world and results in succeeding generations of poorer-quality, slower-growing stands. A major dysgenic stand treatment occurs when special harvests are made to obtain certain high-value tree stems, such as poles or piling, or when the very best quality sawtimber trees are removed. An especially bad dysgenic practice occurs when only certain species are harvested, leaving the undesired species to occupy the site (Figure 7.1).

Even though there is now abundant proof that many of the poor-quality trees in even-aged stands are genetically inferior, some forest managers still claim that the lower-value and poor-quality trees can be left in a seed tree harvest or a shelterwood system because they can produce the needed quantities of seed to regenerate the site. Such trees are usually large crowned and frequently have been damaged by pests or adverse environments. Forest managers are understandably reluctant to leave high-quality and thus high-value trees because of the fear of loss from lightening, insects, or windthrow. The decision about which trees to leave as seed producers in natural regeneration systems is often made on the basis of their present value; this results in the most valuable trees being removed, leaving the crooked, deformed, and often, the diseased individuals.

Obviously, trees left to produce seed must have crown sizes large enough to produce sufficient quantities of seed. If trees are selected on growth characteristics as well as quality traits and occupy a dominant position in the stand canopy, their crowns will be of sufficient size and vigor to produce the seed needed.

Since such characteristics as disease resistance or straightness of tree bole are strongly inherited, a few generations of dysgenic selection can result in "minus-type" stands. Such a result is evident in the great increase in crookedness in the regeneration from stands that have been continuously harvested for poles or piling that removes the straightest trees. It has been stated that after many generations of continued removal of the best trees from a stand of *Pinus silvestris* in Germany, the initially good stand has degenerated to a forest of multistemmed bushes today.

One of the *most common misconceptions* by both foresters and laymen throughout the world is that *stands containing trees of various sizes will be uneven aged;* that is, trees of many different ages are growing intermixed. Generally, natural stands of both conifers and hardwoods are even aged, even though they

FIGURE 7.1

Throughout the world there is a reduction in the quality of forests because certain desirable species are preferentially logged, leaving less desirable trees. This practice is illustrated for Canada (*a*) where the conifers are removed leaving aspen residuals and sprouts. A similar situation is shown in the southern United States (*b*) where all pines have been removed, leaving low-quality hardwoods to claim the site.

contain trees of different sizes, or at most, they consist of two or three discrete age classes (Figure 7.2). When human beings selectively cut only a portion of the stand or when an overmature tropical hardwood stand is breaking up, truly uneven-aged stands may result; this also happens in the very tolerant temperate species such as beech (*Fagus*) and maple (*Acer*). The fallacy of considering stands with trees of different sizes as uneven aged has resulted in dysgenic selection in many areas of the world. The largest trees are harvested, with the incorrect assumption that the smaller trees are younger and are therefore genetically as good as the harvested trees. In even-aged stands, however, the smaller trees are the ones of poorest vigor and are more likely to be poorer genotypes, although differences may be accentuated as the result of competition. In these instances, harvesting only the larger and better trees is nothing more than a diameter limit cut in an even-aged stand.

One kind of seed regeneration that gives problems to the tree improver occurs in species whose seed can be stored in the forest floor for long periods of time. Leaving seed trees under these conditions is a waste of time, although it is done regularly. For example, seed of yellow poplar (*Liriodendron tulipifera*) can stay viable in the forest floor for many years (Clark and Boyce, 1964). Yet, there are

FIGURE 7.2

A common error is to assume that natural stands containing trees of all sizes are also all aged. This rarely is the case; most natural forest stands outside the tropics are even aged but all sized. This is true for both conifers or for hardwood stands such as the one illustrated.

laws in some states requiring that yellow poplars of a given size be left as seed trees to regenerate the area. Often, regeneration is very profuse with several hundred thousand seeds per hectare germinating. Most of these come from seed that had been stored in the forest duff for many years. Leaving high-quality seed trees does very little or nothing to improve the genetic quality of the new stand.

Dysgenic selection must be viewed in its true perspective. Despite removal of the best phenotypes, one or two generations of dysgenic selection will not result in future stands that are totally genetically degraded. Forest trees are very heterozygous, and after gene segregation and recombination some good genotypes will occur even in stands that have been heavily dysgenically selected for a few generations. The number of good trees from such a stand will be reduced, but in natural regeneration, in which perhaps only 1 out of 30 to 50 trees initially established will grow to constitute the dominant stand, the poorer-growing, noncompetitive, pest-susceptible genotypes will tend to be eliminated, and the resultant stand can be of satisfactory quality.

The ability of trees of poor phenotypic quality to produce good, young stands was used in an attempt to discredit the early forest genetic efforts. For example, many of the magnificent longleaf pine (*P. palustris*) stands in the southeastern United States were severely logged of all good trees, leaving only inferior, deformed individuals. Pole-sized reproduction from these stands was sometimes of high quality; these nice stands were pointed to with great enthusiasm by some foresters as evidence that selecting the good trees and leaving the poor trees to regenerate an area did not have a dysgenic effect on the new stand. This was correct for the firs generation after high grading, where regeneration was commonly 30,000 to 100,000 stems per hectare. With the onset of competition, the number of trees was reduced to 1000 to 2000 of the best-growing stems per hectare, and these trees were of acceptable quality. However, if dysgenic selection is practiced for several generations, stand quality will be seriously diminished.

The effect of even one generation of dysgenic selection can be quite severe when seed are collected from inferior phenotypes and planted in nurseries for use in plantation programs. Under these conditions, nearly all seed have a chance to become established in plantations and to grow in the forest. Seedlings are fertilized, sprayed, and protected in the nursery and grown at spacings such that all trees, no matter how good or poor they are genetically, have a chance to grow and develop to a plantable size. Then, the seedlings are planted in the forest on site-prepared areas at wide spacings so they have little early competition. When competition from brush becomes too great, herbicides or mechanical methods are often used to release the planted trees. The good care of the young trees in the nursery and in the forests enables many genetically weak or inferior trees to survive that would be lost under a natural regeneration system in which competition is severe. Through nursery and plantation practices, people have developed a system that is very effective in preserving the weaker genotypes.

One of the most serious types of dysgenic selection is the harvesting of desired species from mixed stands, leaving only the undesired species (Figure 7.3). Vast changes in land productivity and timber quality have resulted and are still being

FIGURE 7.3

The best individuals of the best species are often logged from hardwood stands. Low-quality trees, such as the one shown, are often left to grow and to reproduce the new stand. The poor-quality residual trees occupy a lot of space but produce very little value.

produced by this policy. Such species-specific harvesting is almost universal. It is especially bad in the tropics, in the northeastern part of the United States, in central and eastern Canada and in the southern United States where there is a massive conversion from coniferous or mixed conifer hardwood forests to largely slow-growing, low-quality hardwood forests. Selection of certain key species is dictated by silviculture, policy, and harvesting: It must be considered here because of its effect on the genetic quality of the resultant stands. Selective-species harvesting is rarely considered in genetic terms, but in reality, the impact on the genetic constitution of the forest stand is tremendous; it is nearly as effective in causing gene complex losses as is clearcutting and converting forests to uses other than growing trees.

Selective-species logging is a classical and most serious problem in the tropical hardwood forests where only a few species of greatest value are removed. There is no easy solution to this problem. Although definitive results from long-term studies are generally lacking, observation indicates that a huge change in species frequencies, and consequently in gene complexes, is the result of this most common but adverse harvest system in the mixed tropical hardwoods. Genetic and economic losses from selective-species logging in the tropics is very severe because usually the species removed are the faster-growing, dominant, and intolerant species; these do not regenerate well following partial logging. Not only are good individual tree genotypes being lost, but whole species and gene complexes are being endangered.

Contrary to the general opinion, losses of good trees and whole species similar to the situation in the tropics are also occurring in the more temperate regions. As an example, about half the forest land in the southeastern United States contains primarily hardwood forests, most of which are composed of a mixture of valuable species. Too frequently these are selectively logged (dysgenically logged) of the best trees of the best species, resulting in massive loss of valuable gene complexes (Figure 7.3). As one example, in southern Alabama there was a species mix of cherrybark oak (*Quercus falcata* var. *pagodaefolia*), green ash (*Fraxinus pennsylvanica*) and hackberry (*Celtis occidentalis*), and other low-quality species. During logging, essentially all cherrybark oaks were removed as were all green ashes of merchantable quality. As a result, 20 years after logging, these once-beautiful mixed forests are now primarily composed of hackberry and low-quality hardwoods, including poor-quality ash. Cherrybark oak has essentially been removed from the forest, or only the poorest phenotypes are left. The result is the near loss of an outstanding species from the forest stand.

Another cause of adverse genetic change occurs when forests are broken up into farmland, leaving small scattered stands of trees that are separated by fields. This results in small, isolated breeding units in which inbreeding may occur; this result will be a degrading of the residual forest. Added to this is the usual practice of high grading the best trees from the farm woodlots. Forests of this scattered type are common throughout the tropics and in areas such as the small woodlots in the midwestern hardwood areas in the United States. In an assessment of black walnut, Beineke (1972) summarized the situation as follows: "By relying on natural regeneration in black walnut from scattered high-graded remnants in wood lots, small isolated breeding populations are developing . . . low vigor, slow growing, disease prone and poorly formed black walnut trees probably are being produced.''

Although shifting agriculture, such as occurs in tropical and subtropical areas, is hardly a method of forest regeneration, it has the same effect because most of the farms are abandoned, often are grazed for a time, and eventually revert back into trees. Shifting agriculture is a severe cause for dysgenic selection in tropical areas. Usually, the abandoned farms are colonized by very fast-growing but poor-quality pioneer trees that can survive on the degraded soils with little humus and poor moisture regimes that are no longer suitable for the desired species. It is of special interest to assess the difference in colonizers between adjacent plots of abandoned farmland and a clear cut from the forest where the forest floor was left essentially intact.

Regeneration in Sprouting Species

Many species of hardwoods have sprouting as their major method of regeneration (see Figure 7.2). For example, in cutover forests, sweetgum (*Liquidambar styraciflua*) often has over 90% of its regeneration from stump or root sprouts. In general, the use of genetic principles in sprout-regenerated forest stands becomes very limited because genetic improvement will not occur when regeneration arises from sprouts from trees that are already established. Often, little can be done to improve the genetics of such stands other than later selective thinning. The small understory suppressed trees destroyed in the logging operation usually sprout more profusely than do those from the dominant overstory.

Sprouting species are especially difficult to manipulate in stands that have been badly degraded by previous selective logging. Following the selection harvest, the high-quality phenotypes that have been cut may sprout, but they are suppressed by the poor-quality trees remaining in the overstory and eventually die, or if they survive, they do not become part of the dominant stand. Any later attempt to regenerate the high-quality trees through removal of the remaining low-value trees will usually be met with failure, because the new stand will be composed largely of sprouts from the low-value trees. The only hope for genetic improvement in badly degraded sprout-regenerating stands is to destroy the sprouts, plant with good trees of the desired species, and then use sprouts from those good stumps for the following generations. This is a practice that is possible only when good silviculture is used and the desired species can be planted with reasonable success.

GENETIC IMPROVEMENT IN PREVIOUSLY ESTABLISHED STANDS

Gains from tree improvement through its incorporation into intermediate silvicultural stand treatments has been greatly overlooked. The potential is great, and the incorporation of genetic principles into management activities is the fastest way of obtaining a significant amount of genetic improvement. Other than in regeneration activities, which automatically include harvesting, the best place to apply genetics in silviculture is in thinning, pruning, and less directly, in fertilizer operations. Thinning especially lends itself to the use of genetics.

Thinning

The most common error in forestry throughout the world is to establish, or leave, forest stands in an overdense or overstocked condition. Growing space is one of the major limiting factors in tree growth, and the genetic potential of a tree can never be realized fully when it is growing in an overstocked stand. Therefore, the silvicultural action of thinning is an essential tool if the full genetic benefits are to be obtained from improved strains of trees. There will always be argument about what are the proper spacings for different species, but the important thing is that the tree is free enough to grow in order to express its potential (Maki, 1969; Hofmann, 1974; Beck, 1975).

Aside from controlling spacing and competition, thinning can have other results that aid in forest management programs.

1. **Species control can be obtained**   Often, naturally regenerated forests contain large numbers of trees of undesirable species that take up needed growing space. A thinning operation can change the species composition in the desired direction (Roberge, 1975; McGarity, 1977). As one example, an organization in eastern Canada desired birch. The natural regeneration contained less than 20% birch, but following thinning over, 60% of the remaining forest consisted of birch. Similar, desirable species changes can be obtained in naturally regenerated conifer stands, especially in increasing the numbers of conifers over hardwoods or in increasing desired genera, such as spruce, over the less desired fir.

2. **Better trees can be left**   Thinning affords the opportunity to upgrade the quality of the residual stand above that of the original stand (Wahlenberg, 1952; Smith, 1967; Trimble, 1973; Little, 1974; Erdmann et al., 1975). The forester needs to know which characteristics can be changed by thinning and which are genetically set. For example, certain types of spiral twists in the tree bole are strongly inherited, and no thinning will help spirality in the remaining trees, although it can be directed toward leaving the straightest trees. Bole sweep is environmentally caused by uneven crowding, and therefore thinning can help alleviate this problem. Ramicorn branching is strongly inherited, and trees with this defect should be removed in thinning. Water sprouting and epicormic branching will occur differentially within certain hardwood species, and a knowledge of species susceptibility to sprouting and what conditions stimulate sprouting is essential as a guide to thinning (Kormanik, 1966; Books and Tubbs, 1970; Della-Bianca, 1973). Knowledge of the degree of resistance to insects and diseases should play a major role in guiding a thinning program.

Thinning of sprout clumps in hardwoods will become of increasing importance as forest practices become more intensive and shorter rotations with sprouting species are used (Bowersox and Ward, 1972). The genetics of coppicing is known, and the response to thinning of sprout clumps can be strongly specific (Beck, 1977) and individually controlled (Webb and Belanger, 1979).

Precommercial thinning of natural stands requires good genetic knowledge of which characteristics will respond and which will not. Quite often, the thinning is done too early, and the "winner" trees that are left may turn out to be "losers" some years later (Williams, 1974; Della-Bianca, 1975; Griswold, 1979). Such things as bole straightness in young trees are sufficiently correlated genetically with mature performance so that they can be judged early, but this is not true for growth rate. As better genetic stock becomes available, the need for precommercial thinning to improve quality traits will be diminished, and wider spacings will be used in plantations.

Thinning from below, or removing the smaller, less-vigorous trees, is acceptable to the geneticist, whereas thinning from above, or especially a thinning that removes only the best trees (as for poles or piling), is never acceptable either for continued growth of the stand or for regeneration. The comment is often made that removing the dominant trees leaves the intermediate and suppressed trees free to grow, but often the smaller trees are inherently slow growers and never respond satisfactorily to release. Certainly, the smaller, poor-quality trees should never be left to regenerate a new stand.

Pruning

Although there is less opportunity to use genetic principles in a pruning program than in thinning, the choice of trees to be pruned is important (Brown, 1965). A knowledge of the inheritance of bole form, limb characteristics, and growth rate is essential in choosing the trees that will bring the greatest return from pruning (Polge, 1969). For some species, like *P. patula,* a knowledge of limb conformation of individual trees and their reaction following pruning can be most useful (Harris, 1963; Minckler, 1967; Olischlager, 1969; Beineke, 1977). The key to all pruning is to time the operation so the selected trees will really be the dominants at harvest time. It is essential to prune only those individuals that are inherently fast growers and, as such, will retain their dominance within the stand.

Fertilization

A knowledge of fertilizer response by species is essential. Such information will not be available for natural stands or from plantations from randomly collected seed, but it can be most useful for plantations from seed orchards. Some species, like *P. taeda,* show little genotype × fertilizer interaction, so there usually is not a large differential response to fertilizers (Matziris and Zobel, 1976). Other species, like *P. elliottii,* often show large family-response differences to fertilization (Goddard et al., 1975b). When this occurs, it makes no sense to plant large acreages of plantations that do not respond to fertilization (or that may even react negatively to fertilization), and then to fertilize them as a standard operational procedure. Gains are possible by determining fertilizer response and then using the responders where fertilization will be used operationally. Family × fertilizer interactions have not been studied extensively in hardwoods, but because they often respond dramatically to small environmental changes, the potential for such interactions is great.

Another use of genetics that is related to fertilizers and nutrients is to use sources that are somewht tolerant to nutrient deficiencies. For example, in Chile, individual trees of *P. radiata* are occasionally found that grow very well in soils that are very deficient in boron and, there are indications that these trees can tolerate lower than normal levels of this substance. Studies have shown also that there is a differential tolerance to phosphate deficiencies (Burdon, 1969).

Fertilizer × genotype interaction will be covered more fully in the chapter dealing with genotype × environment interaction. It is sufficient to say that the differential genetic responses to fertiizers are great enough so that most forestry programs will not be completely successful without taking them into account, although outside the species and source levels this information cannot be well used in natural forests or plantations with unknown genetic backgrounds.

SUMMARY

The genetic approach has considerable potential in naturally regenerated forest stands when it is applied to the establishment of the new stand and follow-up silvicultural treatment. The most gain can be achieved through proper thinning. One major problem is that it is difficult to quantify the gains and to pinpoint economic results from various activities. As time progresses, the use of genetic principles in natural regeneration will be of considerably greater value than is currently believed; this is especially true in managing the tropical hardwoods. Similar use of genetic principles will be made in improvement of plantations established from seed of unknown genetic sources. Much of the gain will not be improvement as such, but it will be prevention of losses by practices such as dysgenic selection or selective logging.

LITERATURE CITED

Beck, D. E. 1975. "Board-Foot and Diameter Growth of Yellow-Poplar after Thinning." U.S. Forest Service Research Paper SE-123.

Beck, D. E. 1977. "Growth and Development of Thinned versus Unthinned Yellow-Poplar Sprout Clumps." U.S. Forest Service Research Paper SE-173.

Beineke, W. F. 1972. "Recent Changes in the Population Structure of Black Walnut." 8th Central States For. Tree Impr. Conf., Columbia, Mo., pp. 43–46.

Beineke, W. F. 1977. Corrective pruning of black walnut for timber form. *For. Nat. Res.* **76**:1–5.

Books, D. J., and Tubbs, C. H. 1970. "Relation of Light to Epicormic Sprouting in Sugar Maple." U.S. Forest Service Research Note NC-93.

Bowersox, T. W., and Ward, W. W. 1972. Long-term response of yellow-poplar to improvement cuttings. *Jour. For.* **70**(8):479–481.

Brown, G. S. 1965. The yield of clearwood from pruning: Some results with radiata pine. *Common For. Rev.* **44**(3):197–221.

Burdon, R. 1969. "Clonal Replication Trial in *Pinus Radiata.*" Forest Research Institute, New Zealand Forest Service, Wellington, New Zealand.

Clark, F. B., and Boyce, S. G. 1964. Yellow poplar seed remains viable in the forest letter. *Jour. For.* **62**:564–567.

Della-Bianca, L. 1973. Screening some stand variables for post-thinning effect on epicormic sprouting in evenaged yellow-poplar. *For. Sci.* **18**(2):155–158.

Della-Bianca, L. 1975. "Precommercial Thinning in Sapling Hardwood Stands." 3rd Annual Hardwood Symp., Cashiers, N.C., pp. 129–133.

Erdmann, G. G., Godman, R. M., and Oberg, R. R. 1975. "Crown Release Accelerates Diameter Growth and Crown Development of Yellow Birch Saplings." U.S. Forest Service Research Paper NC-117.

Goddard, R. E., Schmidt, R. A., and Vande Linde, F. 1975a. Effect of differential selection pressure on fusiform rust resistance in phenotypic selections of slash pine. *Phytopathology* **65**(3):336–338.

Goddard, R., Zobel, B., and Hollis, C. 1975b. "Response of Southern Pines to Varied Nutrition." Physiological Genetics Conference, Edinburgh, Scotland, Tree Physiology and Yield Improvement, pp. 449–462.

Griswold, H. C. 1979. "An Analysis of Precommercial Thinning After Ten Growing Seasons." Research Note No. 75, Georgia Kraft Co., Rome, Ga.

Harris, J. M. 1963. "The Effect of Pruning on Resinification of Knots in Radiata Pine. New Zealand Forest Research Note No. 34.

Hofman, J. G. 1974. "Thinning in Short Rotation Plantation Forests—Will It Come to Pass? 1974 Annual Meeting, TAPPI, pp. 189–193.

Kormanik, P. P. 1966. "Epicormic Branching and Sprouting in Hardwoods; a New Look at an Old Problem." Symposium on Hardwoods of the Piedmont and Coastal Plain, Georgia Forest Research Council, Macon, Ga., pp. 21–24.

Little, N. G. 1974. "Analysis of Pre-commercial Thinning." Georgia Kraft Co., Research Note No. 44, Rome, Ga.

Maki, T. E. 1969. "Major Considerations in Thinning Southern Pines." IUFRO Conference, Stockholm, Sweden.

Matziris, D., and Zobel, B. 1976. Effects of fertilization on growth and quality characteristics of loblolly pine. *For. Ecol. Management* **1**(1):21–30.

McGarity, R. W. 1977. "Ten-Year Results of Thinning and Clearcutting in a Muck Swamp Timber Type." International Paper Co. Technical Report No. 58.

Minckler, L. S. 1967. Release and pruning can improve growth and quality of white oak. *Jour. For.* **65**(9):654.

Olischlager, K. 1969. "Studies on the Increase in Value of Spruce After Pruning." Universität zu Göttingen in Hann., Münden, Germany.

Polge, H. 1969. Densité de plantation et élagage de branches vivantes—ou pourquoi, quand et comment élaguer? [Density of planting and pruning of live branches—or why, when and how to prune]. *Silviculture* **21**:451–465.

Roberge, M. R. 1975. Effect of thinning on the production of high-quality wood in a Quebec northern hardwood stand. *Can. Jour. For. Res.* **5**(1):139–145.

Smith, L. F. 1967. "Effects of Spacing and Site on the Growth and Yield of Planted Slash Pine." U.s. Forest Service Research Note SO-63.

Trimble, G. R. 1971. "Diameter Limit Cutting in Appalachian Hardwoods: Boon or Bane?" U.S. Forest Service Research Paper NE-208.

Trimble, G. R. 1973. "Response to Crop-Tree Release by 7-Year-Old Stems of Yellow-Poplar and Black Cherry." U.S. Forest Service Research Paper NO-253.

Wahlenberg, W. G. 1952. Thinning yellow-poplar in second-growth upland hardwood stands. *Jour. For.* **50**(9):671–676.

Webb, C. D., and Belanger, R. P. 1979. "Inheritance of Sprout Growth in American Sycamore (*Platanus occidentalis*)." 15th South. For. Tree Imp. Conf., State College, Miss., pp. 171–175.

Williams, R. A. 1974. "Precommercial Thinning." Symp. on Management of Young Pines, Alexandria, La., pp. 72–74.

CHAPTER 8

Genetic Testing Programs

MATING DESIGNS

Incomplete Pedigree Designs

Open-Pollinated Mating

Polycross (Pollen Mix) Designs

Complete Pedigree Designs

Nested Design

Factorial Design

Single-Pair Mating

Full Diallel

Half Diallel

Partial Diallel

Multiple-Population Systems

EXPERIMENTAL DESIGNS

Types of Plots

Distribution of Plots

Completely Random Design

Randomized Complete-Block Design

Other Designs

Testing Procedures

Choosing Test Sites

Replication and Plot Layout

Nursery Procedures

Site Preparation

Documentation

Test Maintenance

Thinning

ANALYSIS OF GENETIC TESTS

The Analysis of Variance

Nature of the Analysis

Individual-Tree Heritability Calculations

Family Heritability

Heritability from Parent–Offspring Regression

Genetic Correlations

GENOTYPE X ENVIRONMENT INTERACTION

Impacts of *GE* **Interaction**

Species and Provenance Interaction

Family and Clone x Environment Interaction

Interaction and Forest Management

LITERATURE CITED

Trees chosen for use in seed orchards or for breeding purposes are usually selected because they appear to be superior; that is, they have a good phenotype. Once trees are selected, their genetic worth is tested by mating them in some fashion, and the offspring are then established in genetic tests. Genetic testing is mandatory for any aggressive and successful tree improvement program. It lays the foundation for genetic decisions involving management of seed orchards and provides the material and information that will be the basis for advanced-generation tree improvement efforts. It is essential, therefore, that extreme care be taken to insure that the genetic testing program is designed and implemented so that maximum gains can be achieved in both the short and long term. Genetic testing is one of the most expensive aspects of a tree improvement program, but the profitability of tree improvement efforts will be directly related to the quality of the genetic testing program.

There can be several different objectives of genetic testing, but it must be emphasized that no one testing design will be the best to meet all objectives. Therefore, care must be taken to use the proper design; this can only be done when the objectives of the testing program are clear. Objectives of genetic testing include the following:

1. **Progeny testing**   The best way to evaluate the genetic worth of selected parents is to grow their progeny in a way that allows estimation of the parental breeding values. This enables one to separate parents whose phenotypic superiority may have resulted from growing in a good environment from those that are superior because they have a good genotype. If the parents who are progeny tested have already been established in production seed orchards, the undesirable ones can be removed from the orchard by roguing. Dramatic genetic differences often appear among progeny from different parents. For example, the slow-growing and fast-growing *Eucalyptus grandis* progeny shown in Figure 8.1 both have parents that were selected because they had superior phenotypes. However, they obviously had different genotypes.

2. **Estimation of variance components and heritability**   The choice of which traits to emphasize in a tree improvement program is highly dependent upon the degree of their inheritance. Such a choice can only be made when the tree breeder has assessed the relative contribution of genetics and of environment to the total variation. Only after this is known is it possible to devise the most efficient method of selection and breeding.

3. **Production of a base population for the following generations of selection and breeding**   Perhaps the most important function of the genetic test in the long term is that it provides a source of material from which selections for the following generation can be obtained. The opportunity for improvement in advanced-generation seed orchards is dependent on the types of mating and

FIGURE 8.1

Radical family differences often appear in genetic tests when the parents are progeny tested. The slow-growing *Eucalyptus grandis* family on the left and the fast-growing family on the right both come from phenotypically superior parents. This progeny test resulted in the parent of the slow-growing family's being removed from the breeding program.

testing schemes followed in earlier generations. It is not possible to develop a long-term tree improvement program without suitable, well-planned genetic tests.

4. **Demonstration or estimation of genetic gain** The profitability of a tree improvement program depends upon the tree breeder's ability to create populations that have better characteristics than did the unimproved populations. The only way to assess accurately the progress made in a tree improvement program is to compare the relative performance of the improved and unimproved stock in the same test.

No single genetic testing scheme will be best to satisfy all of the preceding objectives. The ideal is to design tests specifically to accomplish one objective; however, because of cost and manpower restrictions, it is often necessary to try to satisfy several objectives in the same test. This presents a real challenge to the tree breeder. The design used should be most successful for the most important function of the test, but as much information as possible will be obtained for the other functions. Careful consideration of the objectives of testing, their relative importance, and the most suitable design require the most sophisticated skills of the tree breeder in developing an efficient tree improvement program.

Once the objectives of a testing program have been defined, two additional major decisions must be made. These are the choice of the mating design that is to be used to create the progeny population and the experimental design that is to be employed when the test is established in the field. In general, the mating design will determine the *type* of information that will be derived from the testing program, and the field test design will determine the *quality* of information that is obtained.

This chapter will cover various types of mating and field test designs used in tree improvement; certain concepts of methods used to analyze the tests will also be introduced. Additionally, because of its importance to any testing program, the nature and importance of genotype–environment interaction will be covered in some detail. In actuality, genotype–environment interactions are pertinent to several chapters in this book, but their relevance to the design and implementation of genetic tests makes presentation of this topic especially relevant here.

MATING DESIGNS

Numerous mating designs have been proposed for forest trees. These have been discussed in detail by several authors, including Burdon and Shelbourne (1971) and van Buijtenen (1976). For convenience, mating designs can be divided into two general classes: (1) *incomplete pedigree designs*, in which only one parent is known for any given progeny, and (2) *complete pedigree designs*, in which both parents are known to the breeder.

Incomplete Pedigree Designs

Open-Pollinated Mating   The easiest and least expensive means of creating a progeny population is to use open- or wind-pollinated offspring from selected parents. The method is simple, consisting of collecting open-pollinated seed from the parent trees that are to be tested. Seed may be collected from parent trees growing in natural stands or plantations and can also come from genetic tests, or from genotypes established in a seed orchard.

Open-pollinated seed are useful in fulfilling several breeding objectives. They can serve a progeny-testing function by giving estimates of parental general combining ability that is necessary to rogue genetically poor parents from production seed orchards. If seed orchard parents are to be progeny tested using open-pollinated seed from seed collected in the orchard, it is best not to collect seed until the orchard is in heavy seed production. Pollination patterns characteristic of young seed orchards are often very different from those of a fully productive orchard because at a young age only a few clones produce most of the pollen; therefore seed collected from young orchards may have only a limited number of pollen parents. In fact, observation of several loblolly pine seed orchard managers has indicated that in young orchards about 80% of the seed is produced by 20% of the clones, and it is only after 10 to 12 years that a somewhat more equal distribution occurs. Estimates of breeding values using open-pollinated progenies from young orchards will be biased when nonrandom pollination patterns exist. For example, if only one clone in the orchard was producing all of the pollen, estimates of the general combining abilities of the parents being tested would be totally confounded with the specific combining abilities of crosses between those parents and the single pollen parent. Several examples could be cited of nonuniform seed production. For example, Bergman (1968) reported, for one seed orchard, that 50% of the seed produced had one of the clones in the orchard as either the male or female parent.

Open-pollinated tests can also provide estimates of additive genetic variance and heritability values for the population being tested. Because only one parent is known, estimates of nonadditive genetic variance cannot be obtained.

Open-pollinated tests are of limited utility for future generations of selection. If progeny are grown from seed collected in the seed orchard, the breeder will not know whether the individuals selected were related through a common male parent. The risk of inbreeding when selections from such tests are used in advanced-generation seed orchards is a severe limitation to using the open-pollinated design. Advanced-generation selection can be made from tests involving open-pollinated progeny if seed was collected from widely spaced trees growing in natural stands or unimproved plantations, without fear that selections are related through a common male parentage. However, a drawback to use of this kind of open-pollinated material is that the pollen parent is unselected, which lowers gain from selection efforts.

Polycross (Pollen Mix) Designs   In a polycross design, each female parent is crossed with a mix of pollen from a number of male parents. Generally, a considerable number of pollens are included in the mix to insure that female parents are pollinated by a representative sample of other parents. Several variations of the polycross design have been proposed (Burdon and Shelbourne, 1971).

Like the open-pollinated design, the polycross design can be used to efficiently estimate additive genetic variances, heritabilities, and breeding values of the female parents involved. However, because the male parent's identity is unknown, estimates of nonadditive variance and specific combining abilities are not possible. Also, there is considerable danger that the estimates of breeding values obtained may be biased due to nonrandom pollination by the pollens included in the mix. Research is needed to determine if this bias is large enough to appreciably affect breeding value estimates. As with the open-pollinated design, selection efforts using a pollen mix are usually limited because the male parent is unknown, and the proportion of outstanding trees may be very largely biased in favor of one or two good general combiners that occurred by chance in the pollen mix.

Complete Pedigree Designs

For any mating design, the maximum number of unrelated families that can be created is one half the total number of parents in the breeding population, assuming that all parents are unrelated. Only when equal numbers of parents are used as males and as females are the maximum number of unrelated families created. When crosses are shown, the convention is to list the female parent first.

Nested Design   The *nested design*, which is also known as the *hierarchial mating design*, is a scheme in which groups of parents of one sex (in the case of monoecious species, sex is "designated") are mated to members of the other sex (Figure 8.2). Therefore, the progeny are composed of full-sib famiies that have both parents in common, and half sibs that have one parent in common.

The nested design has been used extensively in agricultural crops. In forest trees, the best example of its use is the Loblolly Pine Heritability Study, which was established jointly by the International Paper Company, the National Science Foundation, the National Institutes of Health, and North Carolina State University to determine inheritance patterns in an unimproved loblolly pine population. A summary of results from the study through its first ten years has been given by Stonecypher et al. (1973).

Use of the nested design allows the tree breeder to estimate both additive and nonadditive genetic variances and heritabilities; this is the test objective that is best served by the design. It has some disadvantages, however. As shown in Figure 8.2, estimates of general combining ability can be obtained only for

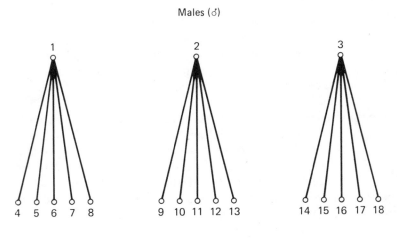

Males (♂)

Females (♀)

FIGURE 8.2

The nested, or hierarchial, mating design is a control-pollinated design that has been used in forest trees. In the diagram, Males 1, 2, and 3 are used as the rarer sex, and each is mated to four different female parents.

members of the rarer sex, because members of the more common sex are used in only a single cross. The number of unrelated selections that can be made among the progenies is limited by the number of parents used as the rarer sex.

Factorial Design   The *factorial design* is one in which members of one sex (in case of monoecious species, sex is "designated") are crossed in all combinations with several members of the other sex (Figure 8.3). The most common way this design has been employed in forestry is when four to six parents are designated as testers and crossed to all other parents in the population being tested. The factorial design is therefore also known as the *tester design*.

The factorial design is very useful for progeny-testing purposes, since breeding values can be estimated for all genotypes in the population being tested. It also allows a reasonable estimation of variance components and heritabilities. Specific combining ability can also be estimated for the actual crosses that are made. A disadvantage of the tester design is that the number of unrelated progeny that can serve as parents for the next generation is limited by the number of parents used as testers. If five testers were used (as in Figure 8.3) only five unrelated families can be produced, regardless of the number of parents used in the crossing program.

A derivation of the factorial mating scheme is the *disconnected factorial design*. With this approach, the breeding population is divided into several sets of parents,

	Male parents (♂)				
	1	2	3	4	5
6	X	X	X	X	X
7	X	X	X	X	X
8	X	X	X	X	X
9	X	X	X	X	X
10	X	X	X	X	X
11	X	X	X	X	X
12	X	X	X	X	X
13	X	X	X	X	X

Female parents (♀)

An X indicates crosses required.

FIGURE 8.3

With the factorial mating design, parents of one sex are crossed to several members of other sex. The factorial design is sometimes called the *tester design* when, as shown, a few members of one sex are designated as testers and are crossed to all other parents in the population.

and a factorial mating design is employed within each set. For example, the 18 parents shown in Figure 8.3 could be divided into three groups of six parents and factorials involving three parents as males and three parents as females could be used in each group. This is shown diagramatically in Figure 8.4. Disconnected diallels have the advantage of maximizing (if equal numbers of males and females are used) the number of unrelated families that are created while maintaining at acceptable levels the number of crosses that must be made. Therefore, the disconnected factorial is an appropriate mating design if selection is the primary objective of testing. It is not as efficient as the tester design for progeny testing because individuals in different sets are mated to different parents, and estimates of general combining ability will be biased to the extent that the genetic quality of parents differs from set to set. This becomes less of a problem as more parents are included in each set.

Single-Pair Mating   With the *single-pair mating* scheme, each parent is mated to one other member of the population (Figure 8.5); this creates the maximum number of unrelated families in each generation with a minimum number of crosses. Its use allows maintenance of a large, effective population size.

Single-pair matings are not suitable for roguing seed orchards. Since each parent is involved in only one cross, it is not possible to estimate general

| | Male parents (δ) | | | | | | | | |
	1	2	3	4	5	6	7	8	9
10	X	X	X						
11	X	X	X						
12	X	X	X						
13				X	X	X			
14				X	X	X			
15				X	X	X			
16							X	X	X
17							X	X	X
18							X	X	X

Female parents ($\female$)

An X indicates crosses required.

FIGURE 8.4

In the disconnected factorial mating design, the breeding population is divided into small sets, and factorial matings are used in each set. Shown are three disconnected factorials that might be used for a breeding population of 18 parents.

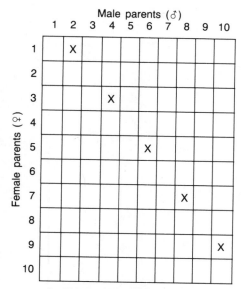

Male parents (♂)

Female parents (♀)

An X indicates crosses required.

FIGURE 8.5

The single-pair mating scheme requires that each parent be mated to one other parent in the population. In the diagram, 10 parents have been mated in single-pair fashion, requiring five crosses. In the example shown, it is assumed that the species is monoecious and that parents can be used as either males or females in the crossing scheme.

combining ability that is needed as the basis for roguing. Similarly, the design cannot be used to estimate additive and nonadditive variances. If general combining abilities of the parents involved have previously been estimated in other types of genetic tests, single-pair matings with genetically proven parents will be useful in a breeding program to produce populations for advanced-generation selection.

Full Diallel   The most comprehensive mating system available is the *full diallel* in which each parent is crossed to all others in every combination, including reciprocal crosses. *Reciprocal crosses* are two matings involving two parents in which, in the first mating, the first parent is used as a female, the second as the male; whereas in the reciprocal cross, the second parent is used as a female and the first parent is used as a male. Reciprocal crosses can be diagrammed as $A ♀ \times B ♂, B ♀ \times A ♂$. A full diallel involving 10 parents is shown in Figure 8.6.

The full diallel will yield information on general combining ability of all parents, specific combining ability of all crosses, and variance component infor-

Male parents (♂)

Female parents (♀)	1	2	3	4	5	6	7	8	9	10
1	X	X	X	X	X	X	X	X	X	X
2	X	X	X	X	X	X	X	X	X	X
3	X	X	X	X	X	X	X	X	X	X
4	X	X	X	X	X	X	X	X	X	X
5	X	X	X	X	X	X	X	X	X	X
6	X	X	X	X	X	X	X	X	X	X
7	X	X	X	X	X	X	X	X	X	X
8	X	X	X	X	X	X	X	X	X	X
9	X	X	X	X	X	X	X	X	X	X
10	X	X	X	X	X	X	X	X	X	X

An X indicates crosses required.

FIGURE 8.6

The full-diallel crossing scheme requires that all parents be crossed to each other in every combination, including selfs. The 10-parent full diallel shown requires 100 crosses.

mation; it also creates the maximum number of unrelated families available for future selection. Thus, it might appear to be the ideal mating design. However, a major disadvantage of the full diallel is that the large number of crosses reuired makes it expensive and time consuming, especially when large numbers of parents are involved. Furthermore, there often are not enough reproductive structures available to carry out a full diallel. For example, a full diallel involving $n = 10$ parents (as in Figure 8.6) would require $n^2 = 10^2 = 100$ separate crosses. A full diallel involving 200 parents, which is a more realistic breeding population size, would require 40,000 crosses. As a result, several modifications of the full-diallel system have been proposed that are planned to decrease the numbers of crosses required but also to maintain many of the desirable attributes of the full diallel. Obviously, diallels can not be used with dioecious species because the design requires that individuals be used as both male and female parents.

Half Diallel *Half diallels* are similar in design to full diallels, except that reciprocal crosses (and usually selfs) are not made. A half diallel involving 10 parents, excluding selfs, would require the crosses shown above the diagonal line in Figure 8.6.

Half diallels yield nearly as much information as full diallels but at less than half the cost and effort. However, a large number of crosses are still required for half diallels when many parents are involved. In a 200-parent half diallel, excluding selfs, $n(n - 1)/2 = 19{,}900$ crosses would be required. As a result, large half diallels are rarely used in tree improvement programs other than for studies that are very basic in nature.

Partial Diallel   Several other most useful modifications of the diallel have been developed; these are usually called *partial diallels*. One type of partial diallel, named the *sytematic or progressive mating scheme* by Wright (1976), is shown in Figure 8.7. With this design, crosses are made that fall in particular diagonals.

Male parents (♂)

♀ \ ♂	1	2	3	4	5	6	7	8	9	10	11	12	13	14	15	16	17	18
1		X	X					X	X	X							X	X
2			X	X					X	X	X							X
3				X	X					X	X	X						
4					X	X					X	X	X					
5						X	X					X	X	X				
6							X	X					X	X	X			
7								X	X					X	X	X		
8									X	X					X	X	X	
9										X	X					X	X	X
10	X										X	X					X	X
11	X	X										X	X					X
12	X	X	X										X	X				
13		X	X	X										X	X			
14			X	X	X										X	X		
15				X	X	X										X	X	
16					X	X	X										X	X
17						X	X	X										X
18							X	X	X									

Female parents (♀)

An X indicates crosses required.

FIGURE 8.7

A systematic or progressive diallel is a modification of a full diallel in which crosses are made that fall on particular diagonals. A systematic diallel with 18 parents involving each parent in 10 crosses is illustrated.

Diagonals are chosen so that no one parent is involved in more than a few crosses. This design has many of the advantages of a full diallel or half diallel in that it creates the maximum number of unrelated crosses, allows estimates of general combining ability for each parent, estimates of additive and nonadditive variances, and estimates of specific combining ability for a part of the possible combinations.

A second type of diallel modification is the *disconnected diallel* scheme, which

Male parents (♂)

	1	2	3	4	5	6	7	8	9	10	11	12	13	14	15	16	17	18
1		X	X	X	X	X												
2			X	X	X	X												
3				X	X	X												
4					X	X												
5						X												
6																		
7								X	X	X	X	X						
8									X	X	X	X						
9										X	X	X						
10											X	X						
11												X						
12																		
13														X	X	X	X	X
14															X	X	X	X
15																X	X	X
16																	X	X
17																		X
18																		

Female parents (♀)

An X indicates crosses required.

FIGURE 8.8

The disconnected-diallel mating scheme is a modification of the full diallel scheme in which the population is divided into groups and diallel or half-diallel matings are done in each group. The three six-parent disconnected half diallels shown would require 45 crosses.

is shown in Figure 8.8. With this design, parents are divided into small 5 to 10 tree groups, and diallel or half-diallel matings are done within each group. For example, in Figure 8.8, the 18-parent breeding population has been divided into three groups of six individuals, and each group of six parents has mated in half diallels, excluding selfs. The disconnected diallel maintains most of the advantages of more complete diallels but greatly reduces the number of crosses required. For example, a full diallel using 18 parents requires $n^2 = 18^2 = 324$ crosses; a half diallel, excluding selfs, with the same parents, would involve $n(n-1)/2 = 153$ crosses. The three six-parent disconnected half diallels involve $n(n-1)/2 = (6 \times 5)/2 = 15$ crosses per diallel, or $3 \times 15 = 45$ crosses for the entire 18-parent population.

Multiple-Population Systems

One type of breeding scheme that is increasing in popularity among tree breeders is that of multiple-population breeding. This is actually not a mating scheme per se, because it can involve one or several of the mating schemes discussed previously. With the multiple-population design, a large breeding population is divided into a number of smaller breeding groups. Crossing is done only within each group, and crosses are never made between individuals in different groups other than in production seed orchards. Once established, breeding groups maintain their genetic integrity and selected individuals always remain in the same breeding groups, regardless of whether they are first-, second-, or more advanced-generation selections. Inbreeding quickly becomes commonplace within groups because of the small group sizes. Breeding groups usually contain up to 25 individuals. Specific mating designs within groups can be chosen to meet the needs and constraints of the breeder.

One use of multiple population breeding is "sublining," a system designed to permanently avoid inbreeding in production seed orchards (van Buijtenen, 1976; Burudono et al., 1977; Namkoong, 1977). With this system, numerous small breeding groups are formed. Although inbreeding soon occurs within groups, production seed orchards are established that use only the best individual from each breeding group. To assure a suitable genetic base for the orchard, a number of groups are required. Using only one tree from each group in the production orchard assures outcrossing to produce the commercial seed crop.

Sublining breeding systems have been developed for several important tree species, including black walnut (McKeand, 1982) and loblolly pine (van Buijtenen and Lowe, 1979). An example of the sublining breeding scheme proposed for black walnut that involves 16 breeding groups, each with 25 parents, is shown in Figure 8.9. There are several problems involved with using sublining. First is the difficulty of selecting the best individual tree from within each group since varied amounts of related matings have occurred. Also, the inbred trees used in the production seed orchard of some species may be slow growing and produce few reproductive structures.

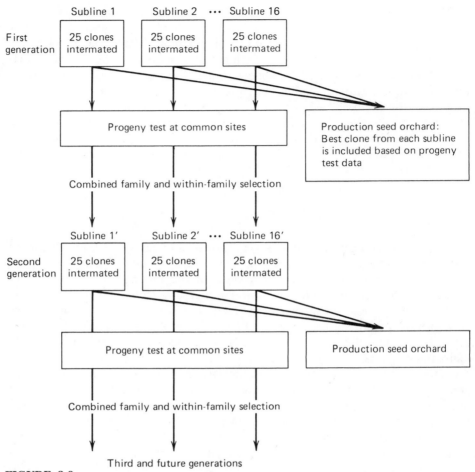

FIGURE 8.9

Sublining has been proposed as a breeding system for several forest tree species. The scheme shown for black walnut involves 16 sublines, each of which is composed of 25 clones. (from McKeand, 1982).

EXPERIMENTAL DESIGNS

Once the desired progeny have been created, the next step in genetic testing is to establish the seedlots in the nursery, greenhouse, or field so that genetic and environmental effects on progeny performance can be assessed. Many different types of experimental designs are available for use by the forest tree breeder. However, only those that are in wide use and are relatively efficient on a large scale under field conditions will be discussed here. Excellent sources of information on design and analysis of experiments can be found in basic statistical textbooks, such as those by Cochran and Cox (1957), Steel and Torrie (1960), and Snedecor and Cochran (1967). Although the following discussion will center mainly on testing of seedlots in which one or both parents are known, the same general considerations apply to provenance testing and even to species trials.

Types of Plots

A *plot* can be defined as a group of trees of a single family, provenance, or species that vary in size from one to several hundred trees that are treated as a unit in a tree-breeding experiment. In most experiments, trees within a plot are planted adjacent to one another; that is, they are planted contiguously. More than one, and usually several, plots of a given seedlot must be planted in an experiment to estimate genetic and environmental effects on progeny performance.

Plot shapes vary, depending on the goals and resources of the researcher. They may consist of single trees, rows of trees, or square or rectangular blocks of trees. When differences among provenances or species are being tested, it is usually best when large block plots are used, because in this way competitive effects between species or provenances that will not be planted together operationally can be minimized. Large block plots allow seedlots that may differ widely in growth rates to fully express their genetic potential without being suppressed by others throughout the length of the experiment. If large differences in growth patterns exist and single-tree or row plots are used, seedlots that are the largest and most vigorous when tree-to-tree competition begins in the test may suppress and eventually even kill adjacent, less vigorous seedlots, and the freely growing seedlots will develop with minimal competition. This results in exaggerated differences among seedlots when the slower-starting one has no chance to express its genetic potential. In the hypothetical situation shown in Figure 8.10, use of row or single-tree plots might make it appear that Species A would be the best at rotation age because it is larger when competition started than the initially slower-growing Species B that would actually be larger at rotation age if it was not suppressed. When the goal is to measure yield of genetic entries per unit area, large-block plots are the only types to use, regardless of whether or not the seedlots are species, provenances, open-, or control-pollinated families, or clones. When block plots are used, the outside row of trees in each plot is usually considered a border row, and measurements are made only on the interior trees. The rule to follow is to use block plots for tests of materials that will be grown together operationally. For example, rarely would provenances (or species) be interplanted; they would be used as discreet units, whereas seedlings from individual clones from a seed orchard would normally be planted together.

Row plots are commonly used to test genetic differences among open- or control-pollinated families. In some instances, single-tree plots are used; statistically, single-tree plots often are the most efficient types of plots. However, when single-tree plots are used, death of even a single tree can severely complicate the statistical analysis. Additionally, if each tree is not labeled in the field, errors of

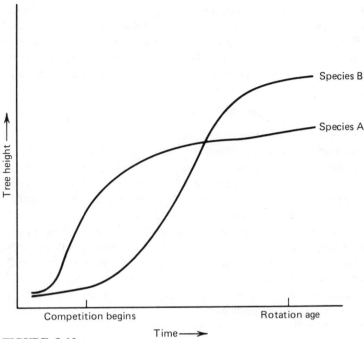

FIGURE 8.10

Block plots are preferred in tree improvement experiments when large differences in growth curves exist among the seedlots being tested. In the hypothetical situation shown, Species A and Species B have quite different growth curves. Use of single-tree or row plots in a test of these two species might result in Species A's being erroneously declared the winner at rotation age because it entered competition with a growth advantage over Species B. Species B would not have had the opportunity to express its genetic potential.

identification are often made that can ruin an entire experiment. Single-tree plots are most appropriate in situations in which each tree is given much care, and in which measurements are taken before competition and subsequent mortality begins, as for example, in Christmas tree studies.

Distribution of Plots

Several different methods have been developed to best distribute plots in an experiment; only a few have found common usage in forestry.

Completely Random Design   In a *completely random design,* two or more plots of the seedlots to be tested are distributed at random throughout the test area. It is important that the seedlots be distributed at random so that each seedlot can encounter the range of environmental conditions on the test site. Completely random designs are easy to analyze statistically, and they work well when the test area is very uniform. Because test sites for forest trees are rarely uniform, most tree breeders prefer the randomized complete-block design (that is discussed next) over completely random designs.

Randomized Complete-Block Design   Each family or seedlot is represented by a single plot in a test subunit called a *replication* or *block,* when a *randomized complete-block design* is used. Several replications are established for each test, with the plots being randomly distributed within each replication. The purposes of blocking are to adjust for different environmental conditions on the test site statistically, and to ensure that members of a seedlot are exposed to the full range of environments within the test area. Differences that occur among replications indicate the degree of environmental variation and can be adjusted for statistically so that the genetic differences can be assessed.

Randomized complete-block designs are used more frequently than any other type of design in tree improvement work. Installation of tests using this design are relatively straightforward, and analysis is relatively simple. Statistical precision is greater than for the completely random design because environmental differences (differences among blocks) can be separated from effects due to family and within-family genetic variation.

Other Designs   Several other test designs are used by tree breeders that are more precise statistically, but they are not easy to implement, maintain, and analyze in field situations where controls are difficut. These more sophisticated designs are generally used in special situations, such as in nursery beds, greenhouses, or in special experiments. In a *latin square* design, the test site is divided into rows and columns, and one plot of each seedlot is planted in each row and in each column. In *balanced incomplete-block designs* or *lattice designs,* replications of equal size are established, but each replication contains fewer than the total number of seedlots involved in the test. The major benefit of incomplete-block designs is a reduction in replication size, which makes the test more precise because of reduction in environmental variation within replications. Loss of trees and plots is particularly difficult to handle in the sophisticated tests.

One type of sophisticated design that deserves special mention is the *split-plot design* that is often employed when it is necessary to test two or more types of seedlots in one test (for example, provenances and families within provenances). It is also used where environmental treatments are to be superimposed on the experiment (e.g., to determine if families respond differently to fertilizer treatments). In a split-plot design, the treatment or seedlot type that requires large areas (fertilizer treatments or provenances) are established in major plots that are randomly distributed in each replication. Within each major plot, subplots of each family or other sources of genetic variation are planted—again in random distribution. Split-plot designs are generally not difficult to install or analyze when only two or three factors are to be tested.

Testing Procedures

Regardless of the type of experimental design used, the success of a genetic test depends to a great extent on the breeder's ability to properly install the test in the field and to keep it intact throughout the life of the experiment. Many of the factors involved in proper field installation are as much an art as a science and are often nonstatistical in nature. Even though an experimental design is potentially statistically precise, if it is improperly installed or maintained, results will not be satisfactory. There is no way to adjust for a poorly installed test. In field forestry experiments, losses of individual trees and sometimes parts or whole plots are not unusual. The many years during which the experiments must be kept and the environmental or pest catastrophes that can occur, all result in tests that rarely come to completion as established.

There are a number of factors involved that will ensure proper test installation and maintenance. Because most genetic tests employ randomized complete-block designs, the discussion that follows will concentrate on proper use of that design.

Choosing Test Sites   An elementary but very important rule in choosing test locations is that genetic tests should be located on sites that are representative of the lands that are to be reforested with the improved planting stock that is being assessed. For example, if a large majority of the land to be planted is of an organic soil type, it would not be suitable to plant genetic tests on mineral soils that might be more easily accessible. Rare site types and unusual environments should be avoided as test sites, unless the improved seedlings or vegetative propagules are to be grown on such sites in the operational program.

It is impossible to find sites for genetic testing that have no environmental variation. However, since the purpose of a genetic test is to distinguish between performance that is caused by genetic and environmental factors, tests should be established on land that is as uniform as possible within replication with respect to topography, drainage, and soil factors. Differences between replications can be handled statistically, but there is no way to separate genetic differences from environmentally caused variation within a replication.

One of the most common errors is to choose and prepare a test site that is too small or that has a shape that will not accommodate the test. Untold frustrations occur when it is time to plant to find then that the test will not fit on the land available. The experimentor should be sure to precalculate the amount of area needed. This includes borders, roads, and fire breaks. Also, the experimenter should make a trial to see whether or not the test fits. Preferably, this should be done both in the office and in the field. If the topography of the site is nonuniform, extra land may be needed so that replications can be properly located.

Replication and Plot Layout   A general rule for layout of randomized complete-block designs is that replications should be oriented so that their long axis is perpendicular to the environmental gradient. The progeny plots (family row plots) should be oriented so that their long axis is parallel to the environmental gradient. The objective is to minimize environmental variation within each replication and to have each family sample what environmental variation does exist within the replication. For example, if a test is to be established in sloping terrain and family row plots are to be used, there should be a minimum amount of elevation change within each replication, and family row plots should run up and down the hill (Figure 8.11). When poorly drained test sites have been ditched, family rows should run perpendicular to the drainage ditches. On bedded sites, family rows should run across beds, and they should be perpendicular to windrows when these are present.

Abrupt, isolated site changes in an area allocated for a replication can often be avoided by splitting the replication or through the use of filler rows. For example, if a small gully runs through a replication, filler rows, which are not measured, should be planted in the gully and in areas immediately surrounding the gully. Although small "splits" in replications are occasionally acceptable, it is absolutely mandatory that all sections of a replication be planted on similar sites as near to one another as possible. Examples of correct and incorrect ways to split replications are shown in Figure 8.12

The number of replications to be used in a test depends on the variability of the plant material being tested, the uniformity of the test site, the precision needed for evaluating seedlot differences, the amount of plant material that is available for the test, and the size of the plots. The question is often raised whether it is better to have more replications with small plots, or fewer replications with larger plots.

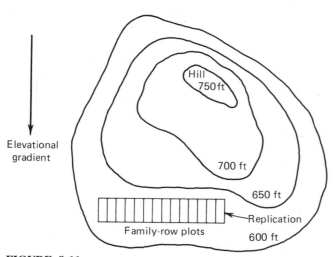

FIGURE 8.11

A generalized scheme for genetic test layout where a randomized complete-block design is used on sloping terrain is shown. The replication extends lengthwise along the contour, or across the elevational gradient. Family-row plots extend along the elevational gradient.

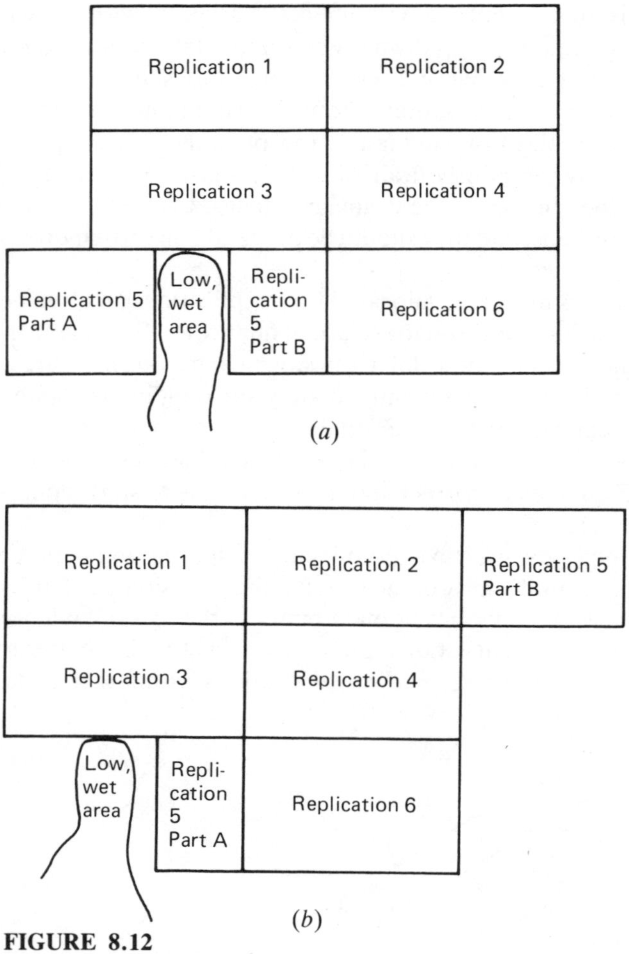

FIGURE 8.12

Sometimes replications must be "split" to avoid isolated extreme environmental conditions. Shown are correct (a) and incorrect (b) ways to split replications. The rule is to establish sections of replications as near to one another as possible.

Cost of establishment, uniformity of the site, and other factors affect this decision. Commonly, the number of replications is too small and plots are too large. In most instances, 4 to 6 replications are adequate if sites are reasonably uniform. Not much additional information is gained by using more than 10 replications. When there is a question, the choice should be to use smaller plots with more replications. Rarely are less than 3 replications acceptable. The success of a field plot layout does not depend so much on its size but on the uniformity of the environment within a replication and on how well the plots sample the environment within the replication.

Nursery Procedures Successful field establishment of genetic tests depends upon the production of quality plants. Maximum care must be used to insure that hardy trees are produced for outplanting. All testlots must be exposed to the same uniform growing conditions in the nursery or greenhouse. If a randomized complete-block design is to be used, it is best that the test be sown in the nursery or greenhouse in the same manner that it will be planted in the field. Then it should be planted in the field using the same pattern. This method is especially useful when measurements are to be made at young ages in the field because environmental effects associated with plant production in the nursery or greenhouse then will show up largely as replication (environmental) effects in the field and will not confound estimates of genetic differences among seedlots. Differences in seedlots that are caused by large environmental effects in the nursery can persist for a number of years in the field, and these differences make genetic tests imprecise. Most organizations that do not take measurements at early years in the field do not replicate in the nursery if nursery beds are uniform. This is because the small nursery-caused differences will disappear by the time when later measurements are made.

It is mandatory that genetic tests be fully documented when they are being grown for field establishment; this documentation includes a map of the nursery bed or greenhouse layout. The plot locations need to be indicated accurately and referenced to a specific starting point. It is amazing how often poor nursery monumentation is made and later lost; for example, using a pen marker on wooden stakes will lead to disaster. Loss of seedlot identity will require remaking the crosses with a resultant serious loss of time, money, and badly needed information. What is most usual is that the seed orchard will require roguing at the time of the earliest progeny measurement. To delay this measurement can seriously reduce the value of the tree improvement program.

Site Preparation Site preparation prescriptions will vary depending upon geographic areas, species, and the organization establishing the test. In all instances, it should maximize test area uniformity, seedling survival, and insure adequate tree growth following establishment. It is highly important to get the seedlings established and growing well so that correct answers can be obtained from the tests as soon as possible. Site preparation and care should be similar to that used operationally; however, extra care is sometimes justified to obtain earlier results, although experiments should be made to determine if family ranks change when the extra care is given to the test.

Documentation Each genetic test should be permanently monumented with stakes and tags in the field, and maps should be made of the field layout and kept in two separate locations for safety. It is essential to indicate where measurements start; that is, which end of the row, or which corner of the block. Overlooking this simple rule has caused confusion about, or actual loss of, many experiments. The maps showing replications and family identities will be a part of an establishment report that should also include access routes and the general location of the test. In addition, it should include the date, weather, site preparation, planting condition, planting method used, and anything else that might affect the survival and growth of the test plantation. Checks in the field should be made periodically, especially before measurement, to ensure that the test is still fully monumented. Numerous errors can result during measurement of tests because of poor field monumentation and lack of field maps. There are even instances in which vandals removed the tags, or even worse, in which they actually switched tags. Monumentation and documentation must be done carefully.

Test Maintenance   Close attention must be paid to genetic tests after planting if they are to survive and yield accurate information. What is too often done is that tests cannot be planted and then neglected until measurement time arrives. Tests should be monitored closely after planting to ensure that seedlings are not threatened by competition and to ensure that volunteer seedlings or sprouts of the same species that are being tested have been removed. Pest control is essential. This ranges from the periodic application of pesticides to fencing in cases in which animals like deer, elk, or cattle are a problem. One certain fact is that a dead or deformed seedling can give no information on the genetic growth potential or quality of the test material. It is obvious, of course, that if the test is to determine resistance to insects or diseases, then control measures should not be applied.

Thinning   Thinning practices for genetic tests will vary, depending upon initial spacing, age of final assessment, the objectives of testing, and the thinning practices used in operational plantations. In cases in which thinning is a planned silvicultural treatment, special test designs have been developed to accommodate this test treatment (Libby and Cockerham, 1981).

ANALYSIS OF GENETIC TESTS

Choice and implementation of the appropriate mating and experimental designs are only the first steps in a genetic testing program. The value of the tests to a tree improvement program depends upon proper analysis and interpretation of the measurements obtained. Genetic test analyses usually are relatively straight forward and require only a very basic knowledge of statistics. When mating or experimental designs are complex, or when tests become extremely unbalanced, analysis may then require an in-depth knowledge of statistics, data processing, and much experience. In this book, only the most basic concepts are covered. Those who wish to follow genetic analyses in more detail are referred to quantitative genetics and breedinig texts, such as those by Becker (1975), Falconer (1960), or Hallauer and Miranda (1981).

The Analysis of Variance

Nature of the Analysis   Most genetic experiments are analyzed by what is known as an analysis of variance, which is a statistical method by which the total variation in an experiment can be partitioned into different sources. In a genetics experi-

TABLE 8.1

An Analysis of Variance for a Half-Sib Genetic Test Planted in a Randomized Complete-Block Design[a]

Source of Variation	Degrees of Freedom	Mean Squares	Expected Mean Squares
Replications	$R-1$	MS_4	$\sigma_W^2 + T\sigma_{RF}^2 + TF\sigma_R^2$
Families	$F-1$	MS_3	$\sigma_W^2 + T\sigma_{RF}^2 + TR\sigma_F^2$
Families × replications	$(F-1)(R-1)$	MS_2	$\sigma_W^2 + T\sigma_{RF}^2$
Trees within plots	$RF(T-1)$	MS_1	σ_W^2

[a]F, R, and T refer to the number of families, replications, and trees per family-replication plot. σ_W^2, σ_{RF}^2, and σ_F^2 and σ_R^2 are the within-plot, replication × family, family, and replication variance components, respectively.

ment, an analysis of variance allows the tree breeder to partition the observed variation into genetic and environmental components, and when suitable, to assess their interactions.

A simple analysis of variance that is appropriate for an experiment involving open-pollinated families or families representing a polycross mating scheme that are planted in the field in a randomized complete-block design is shown in Table 8.1. Several terms used in analysis of variance warrant explanation. The term *source of variation* is self-explanatory; it simply denotes which part of the total test variation is being accounted for in that line of the analysis. *Degree of freedom* indicates the number of independently variable classes, whereas *mean squares* for any particular source denotes all of the variation that has contributed to the observed differences for that effect. The term *expected mean squares* denotes relative contributions of each type of variance to each mean square. For example, in Table 8.1 the family mean square is composed of variations from trees within plots, interactions of replications and families as well as family variation. The mean squares are used to test for the statistical significance of an effect, but further manipulation of the analysis is needed to estimate the variance components for within-plot (σ_W^2) replication × family (σ_{RF}^2), family (σ_F^2), and replication (σ_R^2). The component σ_W^2 is estimated directly from the mean square for trees within plots, MS_1. The variance component for the interaction of replications shown by mean squares in Table 8.1 and families (σ_{RF}^2) can be estimated from the within-plots mean square MS_1 and from the replications × families mean square MS_2 in the following way:

$$\sigma_{RF}^2 = \frac{MS_2 - MS_1}{T} = \frac{(\sigma_W^2 + T\sigma_{RF}^2) - \sigma_W^2}{T}$$

The family component of variance is estimated from the family mean square MS_3 and the replication × family mean square MS_2:

$$\sigma_F^2 = \frac{MS_3 - MS_2}{TP} = \frac{(\sigma_W^2 + T\sigma_{RF}^2 + TP\sigma_F^2) - (\sigma_W^2 + T\sigma_{RF}^2)}{TP}$$

The component of variance for replications (σ_R^2) would be estimated in the same way. These variance components may be used to calculate heritabilities; this will be discussed in the next two sections.

The coefficients T, R, and F (denoting number of trees/plot, number of replications, and number of families) that appear in the expected mean squares can be arranged in simple multiplicative fashion only if the data are completely balanced; that is, all families occur in all replications, and the same number of trees occur in each plot. If data are unbalanced, the coefficients for the expected mean squares will change somewhat. If only a few trees are missing, the change may not be large enough to cause concern, although this depends on the distribution of missing trees. For example, loss of entire plots is a matter of some concern, and it complicates the analysis.

An analysis of variance for a test using a factorial mating design with randomized complete-block field design is given in Table 8.2. It is assumed that there is a completely balanced set of data. Variance components are derived in the same manner as for the half-sib family test. Sources of variation due to females and male families (with variance components σ_F^2 and σ_M^2, respectively) are equivalent to half-sib families (σ_F^2 in Table 8.1). It is important to emphasize again that the coefficients for the expected mean squares hold only if data are completely balanced, that is, all males are crossed to all females, there are no plots missing, and all plots have the same number of measurable trees. In reality, this is often not the case, especially for the more complicated mating designs. Where data are considerably unbalanced, complicated techniques must be used to derive the coefficients for the expected mean squares. Methods of hand calculation can be found in many advanced statistical tests. Many organizations now have computers with the capability of easily making the complex calculations.

Analyses of variance for other mating designs are in most respects similar to the ones for half-sib family tests (open-pollinated or polycross mating designs) and tests utilizing factorial mating schemes. It should be obvious from the preceding discussion of the two designs that complex mating designs require more complicated analytical techniques. When computers are available, the complexity of

TABLE 8.2
An Analysis of Variance of a Test Employing a Factorial Mating Design and a Randomized Complete-Block Field Design[a]

Source	Degrees of Freedom	Mean Squares	Expected Mean Square EMS
Replications	$R1$		
Males	M-1	MS_5	$\sigma_W^2 + T\sigma_{MFR}^2 + TS\sigma_M^2 + TSF\sigma_M^2$
Females	F-1	MS_4	$\sigma_W^2 + T\sigma_{MFR}^2 + TS\sigma_{MF}^2 + TSM\sigma_F^2$
Males × females	$(F$-1$)(M$-1$)$	MS_3	$\sigma_W^2 + T\sigma_{MFR}^2 + TS\sigma_{MF}^2$
Pooled error	$(FM$-1$)(R$-1$)$	MS_2	$\sigma_W^2 + T\sigma_{MFR}^2$
Within plots	FMR $(T$-1$)$	MS_1	σ_W^2

[a]Pooled error represents variance due to replication × males, replications × females, and replications × males × females.

the analysis required should rarely be a limiting factor in the choice of a mating design. Rather, the constraints reside in the objectives of the breeder, and the need to proceed with the breeding and testing program as rapidly and efficiently as possible.

Analyses for other mating schemes have not been discussed here. An excellent reference that details results of an experiment using the nested mating scheme can be found in Stonecypher et al. (1973). An example of use of the diallel mating scheme is the work with longleaf pine (*Pinus palustris*) by Snyder and Namkoong (1978).

Individual-Tree Heritability Calculations   Variance components such as those derived from the analysis shown in Table 8.1 can be used to estimate heritability. This involves equating the *statistical* components of variance to their *genetic* counterparts, such as the components for additive genetic variance (σ_A^2), nonadditive genetic variance (σ_{NA}^2), and phenotypic variance (σ_P^2).

For the analysis in Table 8.1, where half-sib families are being tested, the family component of variances (σ_F^2) is equal to one fourth of the additive genetic variance (σ_A^2). With the testing scheme used in this example, the phenotypic variance (σ_P^2) is estimated by the sum of the within-plot variance component (σ_W^2), the replication × family variance component (σ_{RF}^2), and the family component (σ_F^2). Symbolically,

$$\sigma_P^2 = \sigma_W^2 + \sigma_{RF}^2 + \sigma_F^2$$

Individual-tree narrow-sense heritability, the ratio of additive genetic variance to phenotypic variance, is calculated as

$$h^2 = \frac{\sigma_A^2}{\sigma_p^2} = \frac{4\sigma_F^2}{\sigma_W^2 + \sigma_{RF}^2 + \sigma_F^2}$$

Knowledge of the genetic meaning of the family component σ_F^2 allows one to interpret the meaning of the other components. The component σ_{RF}^2 results from the failure of families to behave the same way relative to each other in different replications, and σ_W^2 is composed of the remainder of the genetic variation plus environmental variation within plots. Thus,

$$\sigma_W^2 = 3/4\sigma_A^2 + \sigma_{NA}^2 + \sigma_E^2$$

where

$$\sigma_A^2 = \text{additive genetic variance}$$
$$\sigma_{NA}^2 = \text{nonadditive genetic variance}$$
$$\sigma_E^2 = \text{environmental variance}$$

The mating design used for the example in Table 8.1 cannot be used to calculate *broad-sense heritability* (H^2), the ratio of all of the genetic variation to the phenotypic variation, because none of the statistical components of variance given an estimate of the nonadditive genetic variance σ^2_{NA}.

The component $\sigma^2_F = 1/4\ \sigma^2_A$ holds for the example in Table 8.1, only if the families were half sibs. If the families had been unrelated full-sib families, the family component σ^2_F would equal one half the additive variance plus one fourth the nonadditive variation ($\sigma^2_F = 1/2\ \sigma^2_A + 1/4\sigma^2_{NA}$). Therefore, in the nonadditive variance was of importance for a particular trait, there would be no way to estimate narrow-sense heritability from a test utiizing a single-pair mating scheme because the estimate of additive genetic variation would be confounded with that of the nonadditive genetic variance.

For the factorial mating design analysis presented in Table 8.2, the variance component for males and females (σ^2_M and σ^2_F)are equal to one fourth of the additive genetic variance. With this mating scheme, the variance component σ^2_{FM} estimates one quarter of the nonadditive variance. Narrow-sense individual tree heritability can be calculated as

$$h^2 = \frac{2(\sigma^2_F + \sigma^2_M)}{\sigma^2_M + \sigma^2_F + \sigma^2_{MF} + \sigma^2_{MFR} + \sigma^2_{OW}}$$

Since the variance component σ^2_{FM} gives an estimate of the nonadditive variance, this mating design can be used to estimate broad-sense heritability (H^2), the ratio of all of the genetic variation to phenotypic variation. This is calculated as

$$H^2 = \frac{\sigma^2_G}{\sigma^2_P} = \frac{2(\sigma^2_F + \sigma^2_m) + 4\sigma^2_{MF}}{\sigma^2_m + \sigma^2_F + \sigma^2_{MF} + \sigma^2_S + \sigma^2_W}$$

Family Heritability   In addition to individual-tree heritability, tree breeders are often concerned with heritabilities of family means, which become important when selection can be practiced on families as well as on individuals, as is done in advanced-generation tree improvement when selections are made from genetic tests. These may be calculated directly from the components of variance and a knowledge of numbers of trees per plot, replications, and families. For example, the heritability of family means for the half-sib test example given in Table 8.1 would be calculated as

$$h^2_F = \frac{\sigma^2_F}{\dfrac{\sigma^2_W}{TR} + \dfrac{\sigma^2_{FR}}{T} + \sigma^2_F}$$

Variance components and coefficients are as defined in Table 8.1. Family heritabilities are usually higher than individual tree heritabilities because they are based on averages estimated with a sample of many progenies. The effects of environmental factors within the test are thus averaged out for the family mean.

Heritability from Parent–Offspring Regression   There are other methods of calculating heritabilities in addition to sib analysis. When measurements have been made on both parents and progeny, it is possible to calculate heritability for a trait through regression techniques that relate progeny performance to parental values. Essentially, regression is a statistical technique that fits a line relating two groups of variables. The regression equation may be written as

$$Y = bX + e$$

where

Y = average of progeny values
b = regression coefficient (slope of line)
X = parent value
e = error (lack of fit of values to the line)

The regression coefficient b may be estimated as

where
$$b = \frac{\Sigma(X_i - \bar{X})(Y_i - \bar{Y})}{\Sigma(X_i - \bar{X})^2}$$

X_i = individual parent values
$\bar{X}$ = average of parental values
Y_i = progeny family averages
$\bar{Y}$ = average of all progeny

Where half-sib families are involved (i.e., measurements have been made on only one parent), the coefficient b is equal to one half the narrow-sense heritability. When full-sib families are measured, and progeny values are regressed on the average value of the two parents (midparent value), then b equals narrow-sense heritability.

Heritabilities estimated with parent–offspring regression techniques are usually much lower than those estimated through sib analyses of genetic tests. There are at least two possible reasons for this. First, parents of the progeny often do not occur in a uniform environment but are scattered throughout very large, environmentally variable stands, or they may be growing in many different stands. This is especially true when selected parents have been obtained from many different areas. The environmental variation affecting the parent trees lowers heritability. Second, measurements usually occur on parents and progeny of different ages; this will lower heritability if the traits that are being measured are most variable on trees of differing ages. Traits that are under very strong genetic control and are slightly influenced by local environments, such as wood specific gravity, may show similar heritabilities regardless of the method of estimation.

Genetic Correlations

Genetic correlations among traits are useful and of interest to tree improvers because they indicate the degree to which one trait will change as a result of a change in another trait. Conversely, they play a role in determining the degree to which indirect selection, or selection for one trait in the hopes of improving another trait, will be successful.

Analyses similar to those in Tables 8.1 and 8.2 can be used to estimate genetic correlations among traits. The major departure is that, rather than computing an analysis of *variance*, an analysis of *covariance* is performed. This involves calculating mean cross products rather than mean squares. Subsequently, the mean cross products are used to determine the components of covariance. For completely balanced data, the coefficients for the expected mean cross products are exactly the same as those for the expected mean squares. Genetic correlations may be estimated as

$$r_G = \frac{\sigma_{F_{XY}}}{\sqrt{\sigma_{F_Y}^2}\,\sqrt{\sigma_{F_X}^2}}$$

where

$$r_G = \text{genetic correlation}$$
$$\sigma_{F_{XY}} = \text{half-sib component of covariance for traits } X \text{ and } Y$$
$$\sigma_{F_X}^2 = \text{half-sib component of variance for trait } X$$
$$\sigma_{F_Y}^2 = \text{half-sib component of variance for trait } Y$$

GENOTYPE × ENVIRONMENT INTERACTION

A special concern in tree improvement and genetic testing relates to genotype × environment interaction. Simply defined, *genotype × environment interaction* means that the relative performance of clones, families, provenances, or species differ when they are grown in different environments. This may involve an actual change in rank, which is the most important type of interaction to the tree breeder or may simply involve a change in variation from one environment to the other, with no change in rank. A graphical presentation of genotype × environment interaction involving rank changes is shown in Figure 8.13, where Family 1 is the better performer in Environment A, while Family 2 is the superior family in Environment B.

Considerable variability can result in a genetic testing program when there is an interaction because genotypes respond differently to differing environments. It is

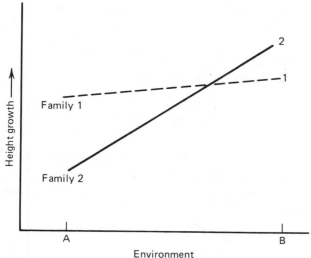

FIGURE 8.13

Genotype × environment interaction occurs when genotypes rank differently relative to one another in different
environments. In the hypothetical situation shown above,
Family 1 is the better grower in Environment A; in Environment B there is a change of rank, and Family 2 becomes
superior.

a complicating factor that must be recognized and used. It can be of great benefit
when maximum gains are desired in specific environments, but the interaction can
become a formidable barrier when broadly adapted strains suited to several
different environments are sought.

Genotype × environment interaction may be expressed symbolically by an
extension of the model relating phenotypic performance to genetic and environmental effects. The model is extended to read

$$P = G + E + GE$$

where

P = phenotypic value
G = the genetic effect
E = an environmental effect
GE = an effect due to genotype × environment interaction

The *only* way to account for the GE interaction effect is to plant genetic tests in
more than one environment. When tests are established in one location, the

interaction term is *hidden* in the genetic (G) effect. This has two major consequences if there is appreciable GE interaction.

1. Heritability may be overestimated. The appropriate formula for narrow-sense heritability when tests are planted at multiple locations is

$$h^2 = \frac{\sigma_A^2}{\sigma_p^2} \qquad \frac{\sigma_A^2}{\sigma_A^2 + \sigma_{NA}^2 + \sigma_{GE} + \sigma_E^2}$$

where

σ_{GE}^2 = variance due to genotype × environment interaction and other variance components are as defined in earlier sections of this chapter

However, in the presence of GE interaction and with information from only one environment, we have

$$h^2 = \frac{(\sigma_A^2 + \sigma_{GE}^2{}^2)}{\sigma_A^2 + \sigma_{NA}^2 + \sigma_{GE}^2 + \sigma_E^2}$$

The variance components for additive genetic variance and GE interaction are confounded and cannot be separated when tests are established in only one location. This will result in an overestimation of gain from selection when the improved material is planted in a nontest environment.

2. Suboptimal genotypes may be used in environments that are different from the test environment if the GE interaction results in rank changes. This is because the genotypes chosen as *best* in the test environment are not the best genotypes to use in other environments. The end result will be less genetic gain in the nontest environment.

Because of the possible presence of GE interaction, it is always advisable, and sometimes mandatory, that genetic tests be established in multiple environments. Environments may consist of different locations, different years, or different site preparation or management treatments.

Two methods of reducing genotype × environment interaction have been employed in breeding programs. One alternative is to stratify areas within a breeding region into subregions with similar environmental conditions. Similarities can be determined from such macroenvironmental factors as temperature regimes, physiographic provinces, or soils or may be indicated by experience and the performances of the genotypes themselves. Different breeding programs are then conducted for each subregion.

Stratification of environments can be useful when breeding programs cover large areas, but it is inefficient when the subregions become too small. In addition, stratification is not effective for unpredictable environmental factors such as large year-to-year climatic changes. Tree breeders are thus often faced with a significant GE interaction within subregions.

A second alternative is to select for genotypes that perform well and that show little interaction over a wide variety of environmental conditions. This approach has received much attention from breeders in recent years, and several different statistics estimating general adaptability (stability) have been developed (Finlay and Wilkinson, 1963; Eberhardt and Russell, 1966) that have been used in tree improvement programs. For example, Morgenstern and Teich (1969) used genotypic stability parameters in an investigation of genotype × environment interaction of jack pine provenances. Stability parameters can often be used in conjunction with environmental stratification to reduce genotype × environment interactions within subregions.

There will be no attempt to deal with the statistical aspects of *GE* interactions here. Appropriate statistical methods to analyze experiments planted at multiple locations are an extension of the methods given in the previous section and may be found in the work of Cochran and Cox (1950). Subsequent discussion of *GE* interactions will focus on the general impact of *GE* interactions in tree improvement and forest management activities.

Impacts of *GE* Interaction

For most large-scale tree improvement programs, the major objective is to develop widely adapted strains of trees that can be used over many environments. This requires genotypes that perform well in different environments. When ignored, large production losses in operational forestry can result from *GE* interaction. Losses may be of two types: death and reduced growth or quality. The former is easily recognized, but it often requires close observation to assess the importance of the latter. It must be emphasized that genotypes may interact for both growth and quality characteristics. Quality aspects are sometimes given little attention, but in some instances they can be more interactive than growth traits.

There are many causes for interaction, but it is generally conceded that most of them are more closely related to edaphic than to climatic factors (Shelbourne, 1972; Goddard, 1977), unless very little geographic areas are being considered, or where climatic variables change appreciably over short distances, as in mountainous terrain. Large genetic or environmental differences do not always result in genotype × environment interaction. For example, none was found for 3-year height growth or fusiform rust resistance in slash pine (Squillace, 1969), whereas Wright (1973) reported genetic and site effects to be stronger than genotype–site interaction in 8- to 12-year-old provenance and progeny tests of 11 forest tree species in the north central United States.

Species and Provenance Interaction

Many examples of the effect of interaction resulting in growth loss and quality for species and provenances have been cited by Binet (1963), King (1965), and others. Much of the genetic effort in forestry has been concerned with the determination of gross genotype × environment interactions, and several books could be written on the results, showing the wide adaptability of some seed sources and the required specific environmental conditions for others (Suassuna, 1977). A classic example of the interaction effect at the population level was shown by Fuentes (1971) who collected seeds of loblolly pine from both wet and dry sites and backplanted the resultant seedlings in both site conditions. He found a strong interaction for both tree diameter and height between planting site and seed source.

Determination of the environmental conditions to which a seed source is adapted *is the first essential step* if a forestry program is to be successful. Identification of an adapted strain for the test area does not completely solve the problem, because there is still the danger of *offsite* planting as a forestry program expands to include different sites. Much of the importance of genotype × environment interaction on a species or a source within-species level has been covered in the earlier disussions on seed source and provenance, and it will not be repeated here. But it *is absolutely necessary to assess the adaptability and possible interaction of any species and source in the environments in which they will be grown.*

Family and Clone × Environment Interaction

Family or clone × environment interaction has been documented within a number of species. Burdon (1971) found a very striking cone × site interaction for frequency of branch clusters, stem crookedness, and tree vigor in *P. radiata*. This mainly reflected the inability of certain clones to perform well in soils that were low in phosphorus. The danger of using families of *P. radiata* indiscriminately in production forestry has been illustrated by Fielding (1968), based on his research results that showed the failure of the progeny of one of the parents tested on dry sites but good performance of the same progeny on good sites. For the same species, Pederick (1972) found that one of 28 families had much more interaction in survival and growth than did the others. No interaction among progenies of slash and loblolly pines were found for fusiform rust and test location, but a strong one was found for crown form (Kraus, 1970). In a larger geographic area encompassing the area where Kraus worked, Powers and Zobel (1978) reported a family interaction with rust resistance.

It is obvious that the genotype × environment response is difficult to assess. There may be a significant interaction for growth, whereas there is none for form—or there may be one for adaptability and little for growth when the tree survives. For example, an occasional genotype of the most southern source of loblolly pine from Florida survives and grows very well under severe conditions of drought in Texas, whereas overall survival of the families from that source is only 5 to 10% of the local Texas families. The trees from the Florida source that *do* survive under Texas conditions grow more rapidly than the local Texas race, thus maintaining the same relative growth pattern as they do when the two sources are planted in Florida.

Problems of the practicing forester are compounded when there is genotype × environment interaction of both pest and host, such as that which occurs with fusiform rust resistance in slash and loblolly pines. It is known that there is genetic variation within both the rust and pine host and that both interact with the environment. Selected slash pine families have been identified as having good growth performances throughout a broad geographic area. In a section of that area, the tested trees may have good resistance to fusiform rust, but they may be highly susceptible to the disease at another location. Some selected families of loblolly pine respond similarly to slash pine in growth and disease resistance, but others seem to be resistant wherever the species is grown. It appears that a genotype × disease interaction is evident within loblolly pine.

Some characteristics, such as wood specific gravity, do not show much genotype × environment interaction on a family or individual level. Often, the average values change dramatically with environment, but the individual high- or low-gravity genotypes maintain their relative position regardless of the average. Changes of wood specific gravity caused by environmental differences are evident for loblolly pine, but the changes are small and ranking by families is essentially constant (Chutanaparb, 1973). However, the wood properties of families of other species are far less stable than that of the southern pines when they are planted in an exotic environment. Although such species as *P. caribaea* from Honduras generally have their wood drastically altered when grown in differing environments, not all individuals respond in the same way to the changed conditions. This difference in interaction will enable the development of trees of this species that have usable wood for sites where most trees produce a low-value product.

Interaction and Forest Management

Humans change the environment drastically when intensive forest management practices are employed. Often overlooked is the fact that the new environment may not be well suited to the type of trees that were growing on the original site. Of more concern, however, is the fact that the changed environment of the improved site may not be suited to the genetically improved stock that was developed to grow on the unimproved site.

Fertilization greatly affects the environment and more is known about the genotype × fertilizer interaction than about other management interactions (Goddard et al., 1975; Matziris and Zobel, 1976; Roberds et al., 1976). Interactions are generally lacking when fertilizers are applied at nominal rates, but whether a reaction will occur is highly dependent upon species and family. Slash pine appears to have a greater genotype × fertilizer interaction than does loblolly pine (Goddard et al., 1975). Interaction appears to be greater with nitrogen than with phosphorus fertilization, but definite phosphorus × family interactions have been reported for both slash and radiata pine (Shelbourne, 1972; Jahromi et al., 1976). Burdon (1971) found that most of the clone × site interactions for vigor in *P. radiata* arise from clonal differences in their ability to tolerate low available phosphorus and that soil fertility is more likely to account for site effect than is climate.

It was initially suspected that it might be necessary to develop special seed orchards with clones that are particularly responsive to fertilization and others that would contain genotypes that were most suited to grow without fertilization. To determine the validity of this assumption, three of the six replications of each of the early progeny tests in the North Carolina State Cooperative were fertilized. Results obtained 8 years after test establishment showed that most of the clones that performed best with fertilization also performed best when grown without supplemental nutrients. The major difference was that the poorer-growing clones responded somewhat more to fertilizers than did those that grew fastest without fertilizers. However, rankings did not change.

Considerable interaction appears to be present with differing hardwood genotypes, but it is hard to classify. Growth of planted hardwoods without fertilization (except on the very best sites) is generally so poor that family differentiation is essentially meaningless. On sites too poor to be considered normally for hardwood planting in the southern United States, an occasional family will grow quite well when fertilized, whereas most other families have completely unacceptable growth rates.

An area in need of intensive study is the interaction of genotypes with site preparation, cultivation, or in the tropical areas, cleaning. The results indicate that with increasing intensity of site preparation and cultural measures there is greater fusiform rust incidence on loblolly and slash pines (Miller, 1977). However, it is uncertain whether there is interaction between inherently rapid tree growth and fusiform rust infection. Experience indicates that interactions between tree growth and intensity of site preparation will be greater with hardwoods than with pines, but this has not been quantified.

Experience gained from 4000 acres of genetic tests of the southern pines shows that moderate site preparation and test maintenance do not change the relative family rankings. That finding has resulted in the intensified care of genetic tests, so that reliable measurements of family performance can be obtained several years earlier than those without the intensive care.

One of the greatest needs in operational forest mangement is to determine the magnitude of the interaction of genetically improved families with site preparation, cultivation, or both. When intensive site preparation is used, is followed by cultivation, and especially when fertilization is also applied, the potential for meaningful interactions is greatly increased. Such tests are complex and expensive, but the effects of interaction can be so important that great effort needs to be made to determine its presence.

Perhaps the most serious error in forest management is to ignore genotype × environment interaction. It makes little sense, for example, to plant a genotype that does not respond to fertilization in an operation where fertilization is standard. It is economically indefensible to plant a family on land that has been intensively site prepared if it does not respond favorably. On a more gross basis, it is absolutely essential to use species or sources within species that are suitable to the new environment when exotic plantations are established. To ignore the potential effect of genotype × environment interaction often spells disaster in operational forest management.

LITERATURE CITED

Becker, W. A. 1975. *Manual of Quantitative Genetics*. Student Book Corporation, Washington State University, Pullman, Wash.

Bergman, A. 1968. "Variation in Flowering and Its Effect on Seed Cost— A Study in Seed Orchards of Loblolly Pine." Tech. Rept. 38, School of For. Res., North Carolina State University, Raleigh.

Binet, F. 1963. An instance of interaction of genotype and environment at the population level. *Gen. Today* **1**:1–47.

Burdon, R. 1971. Clonal repeatabilities and clone-site interactions in *Pinus radiata. Sil. Gen.* **20**(1–2):33–39.

Burdon, R. D., and Shelbourne, C. J. A. 1971. Breeding populations for recurrent selection: Conflicts and possible solutions. *N. Z. Jour. For. Sci.* **1**:174–193.

Burdon, R. D., Shelbourne, C. J. A., and Wilcox, M. D. 1977. "Advanced-Generation Strategies." 3rd World Cons. on For. Tree Breed, Canberra, Australia.

Chuntanaparb, L. 1973. "Inheritance of Wood and Growth Characteristics and Their Relationships in Loblolly Pine (*Pinus taeda*)." Ph.D. Thesis, School of Forest Resources, North Carolina State University, Raleigh.

Cochran, W. G., and Cox, G. M. 1950. *Experimental Designs*. John Wiley & Sons, New York.

Eberhart, S. A., and Russell, W. A. 1966. Stability parameters for comparing varieties. *Crop. Sci.* **6**:36–40.

Falconer, D. S. 1960. *Introduction to Quantitative Genetics*. Ronald Press, New York.

Fielding, J. 1968. Genotype-site interaction in *Pinus radiata. Newsletter* **1**:14–15. (Research Working Group No. 1, Res. Comm., Aust. For Council.)

Finlay, K. W., and Wilkinson, G. N. 1963. The analysis of adaptation in a planting breeding programme. *Aust. J. Agri. Res.* **14**:742–754.

Fuentes, J. 1971. "Interaction Between Planting Site and Seed Source of Loblolly Pine." 7th World For. Cong., Buenos Aires, Argentina.

Goddard, R. 1977. "Genotype × Environment Interaction in Slash Pine." 3rd World Cons. on For. Tree Breeding, Canberra, Australia.

Goddard, R., Zobel, B., and Hollis, C. 1975. Response of southern pines to varied nutrition. In *Tree Physiology and Yield Improvement* (M. G. A. Cannell and F. L. Last, eds), pp. 449–462. Academic Press, New York.

Hallauer, A. R., and Miranda, J. B. 1981. *Quantitative Genetics in Maize Breeding*. Iowa State University Press, Ames.

Jahromi, S., Smith, W., and Goddard, R. 1976. Genotype-×-fertilizer interactions in slash pine: Variation in phosphate (33_p) incorporation. *For. Sci.* **22**:21–30.

King, J. 1965. Seed source-×-environment interactions in Scotch pines. *Sil. Gen.* **14**:141–148.

Kraus, J. 1970 "Progeny-×-Planting Location Interactions in Five-Year-Old Slash and Loblolly Pine Tests in Georgia." 1st North American For. Biol. Workshop, Michigan State University, East Lansing.

Libby, W. J. and Cockerham, C. C. 1981. Random non-contiguous plots in interlocking field design layouts. *Sil. Gen.* **29**:183–190.

Matziris, D., and Zobel, B. 1976. Effects of fertilization on growth and quality characteristics of loblolly pine. *For. Ecol. Man* **1**:21–30.

McKeand, S. E. 1982. Sublining for half-sib breeding populations for forest trees. *Sil. Gen.* **29**(1):14–17.

Miller, T. 1977. "Fusiform Rust Management Strategies in Concept: Site Preparation." Proc. Management of Fusiform Rust in Southern Pines Symp., University of Florida, Gainsville, pp. 110–115.

Morgenstern, E. K., and Teich, A. H. 1969. Phenotypic stability of height growth of jack pine provenances. *Can. J. Genet. Cytol.* **11**:110–117.

Namkoong, G. 1977. "Choosing Strategies for the Future." 3rd World Consul. on For. Tree Breeding, Canberra, Australia.

Pederick, L. A. 1972. "Genotype–Environment Interactions Calculated for Height Growth of Young *radiata* Pine Families at Three Locations." 3rd Mtg. Res. Comm. of the Australian For. Council, Mt. Gambier, South Australia.

Powers, H., and Zobel, B. 1978. Progeny of specific loblolly pine clones vary in fusiform rust resistance according to seed orchard of origin. *For. Sci.* **24**(2):227–230.

Roberds, J., Namkoong, G., and Davey, C. 1976. Family variation in growth response of loblolly pine to fertilizing with urea. *For. Sci.* **22**(3):291–299.

Shelbourne, C. 1972. "Genotype-Environment Interaction, Its Study and Its Implications in Forest Tree Improvement." IUFRO Genetics–SABRAO Joint Symposia, Tokyo.

Snedecor, G. W., and Cochran, W. G. 1967. *Statistical Methods*. Iowa State University Press, Ames.

Snyder, E. B., and Namkoong, G. 1978. "Inheritance in a Diallel Crossing Experiment with Longleaf Pine." U.S. Forest Service Research Paper 50-140, Southern Forest Experiment Station.

Squillace, A. 1969. Field experiences on the kinds and sizes of genotype–environment interaction. *Sil. Gen.* **18**:195–197.

Steel, R. G. D., and Torrie, J. H. 1960. *Principles and Procedures of Statistics*. McGraw-Hill, New York.

Stonecypher, R. W., Zobel, B. J., and Blair, R. L. 1973. "Inheritance Patterns of Loblolly Pines from a Nonselected Natural Population." Tech. Bull. No. 220, North Carolina State University, Raleigh.

Suassuna, J. 1977. A cultura do Pinus—uma perspectiva e uma preocupacao [The culture of pine—A perspective and a concern]. *Brazil. Flor.* **29**(8):27–36.

van Buijtenen, J. P. 1976. "Mating Designs." Proc. IUFRO Joint Meeting Genetic Working Parties on Advanced-Generation Breeding, Bordeaux, France, pp. 11–20.

van Buijtenen, J. P., and Lowe, W. J. 1979. "The Use of Breeding Groups in Advanced-Generation Breeding." Proc. 15th Southern For. Tree Imp. Conf., Starkville, Miss., pp. 59–65.

Wright, J. 1973. Genotype–environment interaction in the north-central United States. *For. Sci.* **19**:113–123.

Wright, J. W. 1976. *Inrodution to Forest Genetics*. Academic Press, New York.

CHAPTER 9

Selection and Breeding for Resistance to Diseases, Insects, and Adverse Environments

One of the most important objectives of tree improvement is to reduce damage by disease and inspect pests and to produce strains of trees that are particularly well suited to grow in adverse environments. Success can spell the difference between profitable forestry or failure to produce an economically viable crop. No matter what benefits might result from tree improvement, only limited returns can be obtained from forest operations unless the trees produced are free to develop without excessive damage or mortality caused by pests or severe environments.

In pathology and in entomology, strong and sometimes controversial stands have been taken with respect to the use of the words *tolerance, resistance,* and *immunity*. In this book the word *resistance* will be used to indicate the ability of trees to grow and develop normally even when attacked by pests or when subjected to adverse environments. The word *tolerance* is preferred by some because many people assume that resistance indicates a total lack of damage. However, the latter is properly called *immunity*. There is no expectation of breeding immune strains of trees that *will not* be affected at all by pests or adverse environments; only trees can be developed that can tolerate pests so that they will be more productive. Some pathologists use the term *tolerance* to indicate specifically the degree to which a tree can grow with a pest or in an adverse environment and still retain its economic value.

As forestry becomes more intensive and as requirements for agricultural products increase, foresters are finding their operations shifted from the best sites to areas that currently are marginal or submarginal for growing economic crops of trees. If forestry is to expand—even if it is to hold its own—trees must be profitably grown on some sites that formerly were considered to be so poor that they were of little value for forest production. Many forest geneticists are now concentrating more on developing trees that are suitable for marginal sites than on the improvement of trees that are already adapted to grow on good sites.

When combined with good forest management, breeding for resistance to disease and insect pests and for better adaptability to adverse environments has proven to be very feasible, and some remarkable achievements already have been recorded. For example, the whole cost of large-scale breeding programs in the southern pine region of the United States will probably be recovered from increased production resulting from selection and breeding for resistance to just one disease—fusiform rust (*Cronartium quercum f. sp. fusiforme*). This development will enable the successful management of pines on many millions of acres on sites on which disease is so prevalent that they previously were not profitable for pine forestry operations.

Disease and insect pests are always a problem in forest enterprises. As forest management becomes more intensive, losses will appear to become more prevalent. This *apparent increase* is partially the result of closer observation by the forester as well as a greater concern about pests and their effects on intensive forest management. In this situation, disease and insect pest attacks that were formerly overlooked or were considered to be minor nuisances suddenly become important. A good example is the impact of spider mites on the southern pines. In the past, this pest was hardly noticed in natural stands or plantations, but now it is considered to be serious on grafts in seed orchards and to some extent on young trees in genetic tests.

Sometimes the apparently greater incidence of pests is a *real* increase resulting from more intensive forest management. A good example is fusiform rust on *P. taeda;* this disease becomes progressively more serious when forest management practices such as site preparation are intensified or when nitrogen fertilizers are used (Miller, 1977).

Another reason for an increase in pests under intensive forest management is the establishment of trees with restricted genotypes over large contiguous areas. Although this concern is sometimes overemphasized, it is important in tree improvement programs. Large plantings of a single species do not present a serious hazard or loss unless the genotypes used are so uniform that a true monoculture results. This danger was emphasized by Heybroek (1980) who showed the advantages of mixing genotypes to discourage pest attack. The mixing of genotypes should be done consciously but can only be effective after much knowledge has been obtained about both the host and the parasite. There is a special danger of damage by pests when vegetative propagules of restricted genetic backgrounds are used for operational planting. Vegetative propagation in itself is not hazardous if a broad enough genetic base is assured through the use of several different genotypes.

The true amount of genetic diversity in forest trees is generally underestimated. Tree populations are almost always highly heterogeneous genetically, both among stands and trees within stands. Recent studies have indicated that forest trees have the greatest variability of all plants (Conkle, 1979) or, in fact, of any organism. Much tolerance to pests and adverse conditions would be expected, because a tree is perennial and must survive many years and reproduce under varied growing conditions and pest attacks within a year and from year to year. Even though a forest may be established with all the individuals originating from a few parents from a seed orchard, the heterozygosity of the parent trees and genetic recombinations will result in a heterogeneous stand of trees.

Tree species differ greatly in their abilities to withstand differing pests or environments. Even the ramets of a clone of a vegetatively reproduced plantation (where each individual has the same genotype) may contain several resistance genes. The danger from clonal plantings of the same genotype occurs because all ramets of the clone will have the same set of resistance genes. When these are overcome or exceeded, catastrophic losses can result because then all individuals within the plantation are susceptible to the pest or severe environment.

In an intensive tree improvement program, as in all forestry activities, there is *always* a trade-off between *the gain achievable and the risk encountered to obtain greater gains.* This is especially evident when pests or adverse environments are involved. Decisions must constantly be made that are relative to the option of obtaining greater gain from the use of better trees along with more intensive management of the forests, or the use of similar genotypes, and the possibly increased danger of pest attacks or loss to adverse environments. Only when resistant (or tolerant) strains of trees are used, can forestry come close to the optimal production of desired products and thus make its full contribution to society. Full realization of gains from the use of resistant trees can only occur if forest management and tree improvement activities are synchronized with pest control. This type of activity is particularly crucial for the success of exotic forestry.

In forest trees there is more latitude with respect to how much genetic uniformity can be tolerated to obtain greater gains that is also relative to the possible greater danger of losses from pests or adverse environments than in most crops. This is because of the opportunity for the geneticist to breed for narrowing the genetic base for economic characteristics, while at the same time broadening it for adaptability and pest resistance. This is possible because the genetic systems controlling these characteristics are usually independent. For example, it is feasible to develop straight trees that are tolerant to cold, drought, or to excess moisture. The opportunity to combine the two types of characteristics independently is a great boon to the forest tree improver.

There usually is considerable genetic resistance to most pests and adverse environments in forest trees, although some problems are much easier to breed against than are others. Zsuffa (1975) feels that the use of genetics is a powerful tool for controlling forest tree diseases and insects. He points out that most genetic studies have been directed toward the host trees, but that the genetics of the pest should also be studied. A good example is in fusiform rust on loblolly and slash pines about which Dinus et al. (1975) have discussed the differences in breeding strategies that are made necessary by variability in the pathogen. There are instances when the host species shows limited variability, such as for red pine (*P. resinosa*); the value of breeding for pest resistance in this species has been questioned (Nicholls, 1979).

The subjects of pest resistance and greater adaptability to adverse environments are huge and complex. Several books and numerous symposia have been produced that were related to each. In this chapter, it will be possible to cite a few of the many studies and breeding achievements. Because of its importance, more effort is being expended each year on pest tolerance (resistance) or on the adaptability aspects of tree improvement. There is no question about the importance and need for breeding for resistance to pests and adverse environments in forest trees (Zobel, 1980b).

ENEMIES OF THE FOREST—GENERAL CONCEPTS

Introduction

There are many kinds of forest enemies, ranging from insects and diseases to man. For convenience, they will be divided into the four categories of *diseases, insects environmental,* and *miscellaneous. Miscellaneous* includes all types of things, such as animals, parasites, mistletoe, and so forth. Some problems encountered in forest management for which resistance can be developed do not fit neatly into any category; that is, they do harm as part of the environment but are usually caused *artificially,* frequently by people. Their effects and damage patterns may be similar to those caused by pests; therefore, breeding can be done for greater adaptability and resistance to them. Air pollution and acid rain are examples of this category of pseudopest. It is evident that the preceding is an arbitrary and not totally acceptable categorization but will be helpful in discussing enemies of the forest.

The fear has been expressed that "pests will defeat us" and if action is taken to develop resistance, the situation will only become worse; some persons feel it would be best to do nothing. Such negative attitudes are misguided because any forest, managed or not, will be attcked by pests that must be controlled in one way or another if optimal yields are to be obtained. Like any crop, when intensive forestry is applied, "new" pests are found or suddenly become important, often not really because they are new, but because they had not been closely observed previously. Intensive site preparation, cultivation, thinning, and fertilization sometimes do result in trees becoming more pest susceptible, but other times the opposite result occurs in which intensively cultivated trees become more pest resistant. A good example of the latter is pine bark beetles; the healthy, well-tended stands are more resistant to insects than are the offsite, the overaged, or the overdense forests.

THE NEED FOR RESISTANT TREES

Any breeding program with forest trees is long term and expensive. Why, therefore, should one spend a lot of time and money on controlling pests through developing resistance rather than using silvicultural, chemical, or natural predator controls? Whether or not breeding for pest resistance should be done depends upon the availability and suitability of other methods of pest control.

The concept will be illustrated later, using fusiform rust and *Fomes* as examples. One would not generally try to develop a pine to be resistant to fusiform rust in the nursery; fungicide sprays are so simple, successful, and economical in the nursery that spraying is the preferred control. But in forest plantations the rust cannot be successfully controlled using chemicals. It has been suggested that actions such as reducing the alternate host can be applied and may be helpful (Squillace and Wilhite, 1977); no known practical or safe method is available, however, for efficient control of the oak host in large forest plantings. Therefore, if fusiform rust on pine is to be controlled successfully in large plantations, the only feasible method is to breed for resistance. The pine host shows large variability in susceptibility to the disease, and inheritance of resistance is of such a magnitude that it is relatively easy to develop useful resistant strains (Kinloch and Zoerb, 1971). The pest also varies genetically, but although this complicates the problem of breeding for resistance, it still appears to be possible to make good gains.

Let us continue with the fusiform rust example. The improved silvicultural methods of better site preparation, fertilization, and cultivation currently used to improve tree growth and yield in the southern pines are all conducive to increased rust infection (Miller, 1977). The need for fusiform rust control and thus resistance breeding has increased as forest management has become "better." Many persons are convinced that without the use of genetically resistant species or strains in the "hot spot" rust areas in the southeastern United States the potentially greater growth resulting from improved forest management will be more than offset by the greater losses from the increased fusiform rust attack that results from intensive forest management.

In contrast to fusiform rust, *Fomes anosus* root rot[1] appears to be an importrant widespread pest against which breeding for resistance will not be easy or of much value. Although some progress has been made in breeding for resistance to this fungus, the major control mechanisms are through silvicultural and species manipulation For example, *Fomes* has generally been kept under reasonable control by good silviculture and stand management, including the use of borax and competing fungi on the cut stump and thinning during the time of reduced spore flight.

Although the development of resistant strains is expensive and takes special skills and much time, it has the advantage that, once obtained, resistance is relatively permanent, and more resistance can be added. The long-term cost of disease management is usually less with breeding than it is with direct controls because costs of the latter reoccur frequently, sometimes several times throughout one rotation. A good example is *Dothistroma* on radiata pine. Several studies have indicated that there is a reasonable resistance to the disease (Carson, 1977). Despite this, some organizations have chosen to control *Dothistroma* by spraying with a copper fungicide during the most susceptible period of the plantation's life, rather than to include resistance to the pest in breeding programs. If only one generation of planting is considered, there is no doubt that resistance breeding would be less efficient than sprays for *Dothistroma* control. For several generations, however, this probably is not so. Resistance breeding is currently being reconsidered.

BREEDING FOR PEST RESISTANCE

No tree breeder expects to eliminate totally losses due to diseases, insects, or to environmental factors. The *objective is to reduce damage to a tolerable level.* Some foresters speak about producing trees that are immune to pests, a goal that is usually not achievable and usually not even desirable, as will be explained later. What is wanted are trees that can live with the pest and still produce a quality product that approaches the maximum yield under the given site and climatic conditions involved.

---

[1]This is now known as *Heterobasidium annosum*.

One reason that is sometimes given against breeding for resistance in forest trees is that more virulent strains may soon evolve that can overcome the resistance of the previously resistant trees. This concern arises because insect- or disease-causing organisms are also genetically variable and subject to selection. A change in the genetic structure of the trees being used could result in selection for increased virulence in the pest.

The potential for development of supervirulent strains is a real and serious consideration but has often been overemphasized. Because of several outstanding examples of pests overcoming resistance, like rusts on wheat, the attitude often is that overcoming forest tree resistance by new or virulent strains of the pest will be a regular, rapid, and normal occurrence. An experimental demonstration of this possibility for fusiform rust on slash pine has been provided by Snow and Griggs (1980). They took rust spores from seven families that were moderately resistant to fusiform rust on slash pine, and after passage through the alternate oak host they placed them back on the same seven families. One rust source proved to be more virulent on one family than the general rust for the area, but no rust source was more virulent on all families.

In a study on loblolly pine, Powers et al. (1978) did not find much increased virulence when rust spores were obtained from infected individuals from the tolerant families. In a study by Carson (1982), considerably increased virulence was found on the resistant families from which spores were obtained. In addition, the greater virulence extended to other resistant families. However, Walkinshaw and Bey (1981), working on slash pine, found that some isolates from random galls were as virulent as isolates derived from galls on a resistant family. Hattemer (1972) states that the danger of damage from more virulent strains can be greatly reduced in long-lived, heterozygous forest trees when proper precautions are taken and when resistance is obtained from a number of genes rather than a few.

The development of more virulent pests would be more critical to the forester if management methods and the kind of trees planted on a given site remained static over consecutive rotations—with the same genetic stock's being used for succeeding generations of plantations. But forest tree improvement is not static and has a special advantage because of the long rotation ages. This enables *succeeding crops to be genetically different from the previous crop* planted on a given site. The trees planted later on a given site should be more genetically improved and therefore will be different from those that had been planted there previously, if progressive breeding programs are being followed. During the period required for the crop to mature, new and improved strains of trees usually will have been developed, although this potential is less with shorter rotations. Therefore, the fear of a supervirulent pest evolving directly from the first crop to destroy succeeding crops is a concern, but is not likely to occur when aggressive development programs are pursued. The adaptation to resistant strains and evolving of pests commonly happens on some annual crops in which the same genotypes are used, cycle after cycle. Much breeding effort is concerned with overcoming the increased virulence. Specially effective is the use of multilines that combines resistant genes into the crop. This should not occur as frequently or quickly on long-lived perennials, if an active, ongoing breeding program is underway, so that the new planting stock will differ from that originally planted in a given area.

A major danger is that once virulent strains of the pest have developed, they may spread rapidly in the managed forest. Such rapid development of the pest is more likely when the forest has a uniformly high resistance than when some individuals are still susceptible. When both types of trees are present, the tendency toward maintaining a natural equilibrium is increased, thus reducing the pressure for establishment of mutants. Totally resistant (immune) trees will rarely be developed because of the biological, time, and cost restraints involved. Thus, the most desirable goal for the breeder is resistance rather than immunity.

If optimal gains through tree improvement are to be obtained, a reduced genetic base for the economically important characteristics may result. On the surface, this would appear to develop in the direction of a monoculture that would be ideal for the spread of pests. But greater pest attacks will not occur if care is taken in the development of the tree improvement program. As mentioned previously, but reemphasized here, it is most fortunate that in forest trees, almost all the economically important traits, such as tree straightness or wood quality, are genetically independent from the characteristics of resistance to pests or adverse environments. In general, the most important concept is that *one can breed for economic characteristics such as straightness or wood qualities, while at the same time one can breed for broad adaptability to pests and adverse environments.* This is not known, or is overlooked by many foresters and laymen. With few exceptions, these two sets of characteristics are controlled by multiple genes and usually are inherited independently from one another and thus are not strongly correlated.

Often, the magnitude and complexity of controls required in forest stands, whether they be chemical or biological, make it impossible to use anything efficiently other than a genetic resistance breeding program (Figure 9.1). Biological control is also a desirable option, but as of this date, with a few exceptions, successful large-scale biological control of forest pests is not currently a method that is useful on a commercial scale. However, in forest trees the success of biological control of pests is of the greatest importance and will enable foresters to avoid or decrease dependence on chemical methods of pest management.

PESTS AND INTENSIVE FOREST MANAGEMENT

As forest management becomes more intensive, foresters must adapt to and reduce the increased pest attacks. The high costs of intensive management and the high potential value of the products make it mandatory to prevent pests from seriousy reducing the volume and quality, and thus the value of the forest products that are grown. It is not possible to live with the pests or "let the pests have their share." Historically, growing forest trees has yielded a low return on the investment, and pest attacks can easily turn what would otherwise be a profitble venture into a losing enterprise. As the demand for forest products becoms greater, it is of paramount importance to society to have each forested acre more productive

FIGURE 9.1

Certain pests can only be controlled through use of genetic methods. A good example is fusiform rust in southern pine plantations; shown is a stand in which more than 50% have been destroyed by the disease. There is no known silvicultural control that is *economically suitable* for this disease in forest conditions, although it is very satisfactorily controlled in the nursery by sprays.

because land on which forest trees can be grown for wood products is becoming less available. Because the best forest lands are being taken for agriculture, forest operations are shifting toward the more marginal sites, resulting in the trees' being grown under greater stress. They then become more susceptible to pest attack, and this further increases the need for pest resistance.

As has been mentioned previously, certain pests are increased by activities such as fertilization, site preparation, or thining. Also, the biological and physical changes in the environment resulting from short-rotation forestry can alter the forest's susceptibility to pests (McNabb et al., 1980). McNabb and co-workers emphasize the importance of stand density and have coined the term *spatial resistance* to deal with changes in the susceptibility of different stands to pests.

PESTS AND EXOTICS

The relationship between pests and exotics was briefly discussed in Chapter 3. Because of the importance and complexity of this subject, it will be explored in greater depth here.

Exotics are generally planted as large blocks of single species, with the seed for the plantings sometimes being from either restricted souces or from small numbers of parents. In almost all instances, the exotic is not well adapted to its new environment. The result is that frequently the trees in the new forests are growing under considerable stress. Much flagrant offsite planting has been done with exotics and is still being done, especially with some *P. radiata, P. caribaea,* and certain *Eucalyptus* plantings. These outstanding forest trees have often been placed in quite unsuitable environments, making them more susceptible to pests.

As stated in Chapter 3, there are not too many "absolutes" in biology, but *one that comes the closest to certainty is that exotic plantations will be attacked by pests of one kind or another.* The situation is especially insidious because the exotic often grows well while it is pest free in its early years in the new environment. Too often this leads to euphoria and false projections about its production potentials (Martinsson, 1979). But it never fails—it may take 2 years or it may take 10—but pests of some type, often very destructive ones, will become established in exotic plantations. A recognition of the potential of exotic planting's being seriously affected by pests is critical to those involved in exotic forestry. Many times pest attacks will result from the severe stresses caused by conditions that often occur where exotics are grown. The poor physiological condition of the exotic trees in these conditions enhances the spread and damage by pests that previously may have been unknown or that were considered to be of only minor importance or a nuisance.

It is of great concern for the future of healthy and profitable forests to recognize the magnitude and seriousness of losses from pest attacks on exotic forest tree plantings. Massive programs have failed from such pest attacks; examples are the large *P. radiata* plantations destroyed by *Dothistroma* in several regions of the world, including Brazil, Zimbabwe (Rhodesia), and east central Africa. The loss of confidence in forestry that has occurred as a result of destruction by this disease could have been prevented, and millions of dollars could have been saved if those who established the exotic *P. radiata* had heeded the advice of a few pathologists who warned that *Dothistroma* probably would become severe in these radiata pine plantations planted in regions where there are warm and moist summers. Many persons have been puzzled about how *Dothistroma,* which is found on *P. radiata* in its indigenous range in California (where the disease is considered to be primarily a nuisance), has managed to become established in such widely separated regions throughout the world. The important fact, however, is that *Dothistroma has spread* to these areas, or was already there but not recognized, and there is no reason to believe it will not also spread to other areas having environments that are suitable for development of the disease.

Sometimes the pest is harmful, not because it kills the exotic, but because it deforms the tree, making it of value only for low-quality products. A good example of this is the so-called cypress stem canker on *Cupressus* planted in Colombia, Kenya, and other areas. Stem deformation is so severe that the only suitable use for the tree is for fiber products, and the good-quality solid-wood products for which many of the plantations were established cannot be produced.

HOW TO BREED AGAINST PESTS

There is no simple answer about how to proceed in a breeding program against pests, and no general program can be outlined. The choice of method depends on the kind of pest, on the variability of the host, the variability of the pest, and their interactions. Whatever choice is made, genetic diversity within the tree population must be maintained, because populations without diversity are poor risks, with danger of major losses (Schmidt, 1978). A knowledge of the following is necessary to construct a breeding program against pests:

1. The economic worth of the host.
2. The potential economic losses from the pest.
3. The biology and genetic variation within the host species.
4. The biology and genetic variation of the pest.
5. The interaction of the environment with tolerance of the host and virulence of the pest (Nelson, 1980).
6. The interactions between the pest and the host.

The preceding information is just a start. The difficult problem about which breeding method to use has had much thought given to it (Borlaug, 1966; Gerhold et al., 1966).

The concept of *integrated pest management* is simple but most difficult to achieve in silviculture (Waters and Cowling, 1976). This integrated approach is becoming routine with other organisms but has been used too infrequently in forestry. To apply integrated pest management, which certainly must be the final goal, the pest and host populations and the environment must be looked at as a dynamic ecosystem. Models have been developed that will allow the bringing together of the many variables in a way that most efficiently manages pests. A major objective of the tree breeder, along with the pathologists, entomologists, and economists should be to help uncover the information necessary for a successful integrated pest management program.

Part of pest management relates to deployment of the tolerant stock, such as where the resistant trees should be used and how intensively they should be used. These questions, along with how much diversity is needed, must all be addressed once resistant trees have been developed. Too often the emphasis is on developing the tolerant material with little thought about how best to use it.

SELECTING RESISTANT TREES

Although the same general principles apply in selecting trees to use in a pest resistance breeding program as for those involving other characteristics, there are several special concepts that must be kept in mind.

The most important of these is that selection of trees must be made in badly infected stands if results from mass selection are to be successful. If trees are chosen in a forest stand that has only been lightly attacked, the chance of an "escape" is very great. An *escape* is a tree that has been very lightly attacked or not attacked by the pest. When such trees are chosen, the breeding program will fail because the progeny of the selected trees often do not show special resistance. It is this situation that has resulted in the attitude by some that breeding for pest resistance is not successful. It generally will be the most successful the more severely the stand has been attacked by the pest. Put another way, selection intensity for mass selection efforts is greatest if disease-free individuals are chosen in heavily infected stands.

Another important consideration is the age of the trees screened for desirable pest-resistant characteristics. Susceptibility to pest attack sometimes changes greatly with the age of the host, because resistance genes have been turned on or off, resulting in morphological or physiological changes with age that make the tree more susceptible or resistant. The age restriction is of particular importance when working with those pests to which trees are susceptible only at older ages; for example, some of the bark beetles rarely attack young trees.

A third important consideration that applies when selections are to be made in genetic tests is to place the genetic tests so that the trees are subjected to at least moderate levels of attack by the pest. If this is not done, family and individual tree separations will not be good, and results from the tests will be inconclusive or of no value. It has been shown with several species of trees and pests that the greatest discrimination among families can be obtained if there is an intermediate amount of infection in the test. This is in contrast to situations when mass selection is to be practiced in which the greatest gain may be obtained by selection in highly infected stands.

DISEASES

General

What is a disease? There are many differing definitions. For example, Ford-Robertson (1971) defines *disease* as "harmful deviation from normal functioning of physiologicl processes generally pathogenic in origin." Webster (see Webster and McKechnie, 1980) uses "any departure from health" or "a particular destructive process in the body with a specific cause and characteristic symptoms," among a number of other definitions. Disease is not easy to define simply. For purposes of this volume, the definition of disease will be "abnormal physiology of an organism that has a specific cause." It will be immediately clear that in using this definition, air pollution and similar agents cause diseases along with fungi, algae, viruses, or other agents that are usually considered to be the causative agents for disease. However, air pollution and other related environmental causes of "disease" will be treated separately in this chapter.

Many books have been written about disease resistance in forest trees; generally, these refer to fungal organisms. Breeding for resistance to diseases is the most difficult aspect of breeding forest trees (Heimberger, 1962). Stern (1972) stresses the importance of the coevolution of host and parasite and how natural selection may lead to a balance between these. Since breeding can upset the balance, this factor must be considered in estimating genetic gain. To complicate the situation, diseases like blister rust on white pines or fusiform rust on the southern pines have alternate hosts, so the tree breeder must work with a complex genetic system involving both the host(s) and the parasite (Day, 1972). Although great gains have been made in breeding for resistance to diseases of forest trees, the basic biological foundations are usually poorly known. This fact, of course, does not negate the ability to produce and use disease-resistant trees, but it does make advanced-generation breeding methodology very difficult.

Genetically, most disease resistance in forest trees is complex, and it is not determined by a simple Mendelian dominant–recessive system. Fusiform rust and white pine blister rust are examples in which tolerance may be inherited through a complex, quantitative system (Bingham, 1963; Blair 1970). One good example of a simply inherited resistance was for *Thuja*. As reported by Soegaard (1969), the disease is controlled by one pair of dominant and recessive genes. The genetic complexity of many host–parasite systems with the frequently added problem of alternate hosts makes breeding for disease resistance unusually difficult.

Comparisons are often made between the relative difficulty of breeding for resistance against disease and against insects. Most breeders prefer working with diseases because the pest organism is usually less mobile and usually does not exhibit the wild fluctuations in population numbers that are common with insects. Artificial inoculation of a disease on the host plant often is easier to achieve than is the forced feeding of an insect. Overall, testing for resistance to insects is complicated. Diseases usually are present as *endemic* populations (i.e., they are at a normal, balanced level), so they are always present in the forest and are available to work with. Often, populations of insects go through extreme cycles in which they are *epidemic* (i.e., a buildup, often rapid, to highly abnormal and generally injurious levels). This is followed by periods in which the insect becomes so scarce that it becomes difficult to work with. Of course, the preceding is not a generality; diseases also go through endemic and epidemic cycles. However, the general experience of most tree improvement workers is that, all things being equal, the chances of successfully breeding for resistance will be greater with most diseases than with most insects.

Breeding Disease-Resistant Trees

Despite the difficulties, breeding for disease resistance has progressed well, and there have been some remarkable improvements, such as in *Albizzia* to *Fusarium* (Toole and Hepting, 1949), or pine to fusiform rust (Zobel, 1980a). Some poor results have been obtained when trees that were not infected (escapes) have been considered to be resistant because of microclimatic or other factors (Riker and

Patton, 1961). The importance of the effects of the interaction of environment and the disease has been stressed by Schreiner (1963) and many others. He illustrates these effects on clones in the genus *Populus,* which he considers to be one of the most disease-prone genera in forestry but one in which large gains in resistance will be possible.

Generally, those diseases whose symtoms are easily observed and that occur early in the life of the tree are the easiest to use in a breeding program (Heimburger, 1962). These include the rusts, the canker and gall diseases, and most leaf diseases (Bingham, 1963). Those diseases that are not easily visible or that are not evident until the tree reaches an advanced age are hard to breed against. Root diseases and heart rot organisms fit into this category. For example, it is much easier to breed for resistance to a leaf disease such as *Melampsora* rust (Schreiner, 1959; Chiba, 1964), or for a canker disease such as *Cronartium quercum f. sp. fusiforme* (fusiform rust) (Zobel, 1980a) than for a disease like *Fomes annosus* (Dimitri and Frohlich, 1971; Kuhlman, 1972).

Such authors as Callaham (1966) recognize that there is pseudoresistance as well as true genetic or inherent resistance. The former refers to the apparent resistance of potentially susceptible plants that may be caused by age, environment, cultural conditions, or other factors. Both must be clearly distinguished if a resistance breeding program is to be successful. It is also important to develop resistance that is effective over several developmental stages of the host rather than for only one.

There are many types of resistance, ranking from resistance at the species level to resistance of individual trees within families. Differences among species are well recognized (Powers, 1975), but the magnitude of differences in resistance among sources within species has also been great. For example, Stephen (1973) found great differences in susceptibility to *Rhadbocline pseudotsugae* among sources of Douglas fir with the southern sources often being the most susceptible. Geographic variation in the needle cast disease of jack pine was considerable (King and Nienstaedt, 1965), and 29 different sources of jack pine showed great differences in resistance to needle cast disease and stem rusts (Martinsson, 1980). In numerous studies on the southern pines in the United States, geographic trends of resistance to fusiform rust have been found (for example, Wells and Switzer, 1975). Thielges and Adams (1975) also reported large differences in *Melampsora* rust resistance among provenances of cottonwood. For Scots pine in Norway, Dietrichson (1968) was able to find geographic differences with the northern sources being more tolerant of *Scleroderis*; he could also relate disease resistance to cold resistance. Trees that were more frost resistant were also less susceptible to disease because of the high dry matter content of their foliage, early growth cessation, and initially rapid shoot elongation. Similar geographic patterns in resistance to the canker disease of sycamore were found (Coggeshall et al., 1981). In addition to family differences, Coggeshall and coworkers found the southern sources of sycamore to be the most resistant.

Most studies on disease resistance have been made for families as well as for individual trees within families. The literature on this is voluminous. In his summary paper, Bjorkman (1964) states that the general combining ability for disease resistance for many diseases of forest trees is high. High general combining ability was reported for fusiform rust resistance by Kinloch and Kellman (1965), Blair (1970), and several others (Figure 9.2). Even for the root disease *Phytophthora cinnamoni*, which seems to affect many genera of trees throughout the world, there appears to be genetic variation in resistance. For example, Bryan (1965) found good evidence for inheritance of tolerance to little leaf disease in shortleaf pine that is caused by *Phytophthora*. He found that certain mother trees produced outstanding resistant progeny. Similar results were found for parents used to form aspen hybrids, in which some parents produced progeny that were very resistant to Hypoxylon canker (Einspahr et al., 1979). In loblolly pine, Powers and Zobel (1978) reported that resistance to fusiform rust varied considerably from progeny from one seed orchard to another. Most of the difference was related to resistance of the specific clones used within the orchards, although some was related to differences in geograhic origin of seed orchard clones. Most reported results on disease resistance have been on the basis of overall family performance. Filer and Randall (1978), for example, found that families of sweetgum varied from 7 to 74% in resistance to *Botryosphaeria ribis*.

Experience has shown that, especially for the rust and canker diseases, breeding for resistance by selecting within the wild populations has been generally successful (Figure 9.3), although there have been specific failures in breeding for disease resistance, such as for American chestnut blight. Nearly a half century of selection and hybridization have resulted in very little improvement in the chestnut genus (MacDonald et al., 1962). The potentials of improvement through use of variants (hypovirulent strains) that will destroy the capacity of the virulent strain of the pathogen have been described for chestnut blight (Horsfall and Cowling, 1980). The potentials are exciting.

Hybrid development has been used successfully to produce tolerant trees in the chestnuts. One of many successes using hybrids has been the shortleaf × loblolly crosses and backcrosses against fusiform rust. LaFarge and Kraus (1980) and others have found that the desired resistance can be maintained along with desired growth and form by choice of parents and backcrossing. The approach for using hybridization to develop disease resistance in individuals has been detailed by Powers and Duncan (1976).

Although forced attacks under artificial environments give useful information about resistance, they are often more severe than would normally occur by pests in the forest, and assessment of results must take this into account (Callaham, 1966; Dinus, 1969). The simplest kind of forced attack is to use methods of screening in the laboratory or greenhouse. This has been done on a large scale for fusiform rust, and it has been described by Phelps (1977). Artificial screening is justified when a suitable correlation can be established between laboratory and field performance. Methods of inoculation, incubation, testing, and analysis can all be crucial in relating test results to field results. For example, Walkinshaw et al. (1980) greatly improved the correlation of laboratory to field infections by changing the method in which fusiform rust was assessed and scored.

FIGURE 9.2

Inheritance of resistance to diseases is often strong by individuals. Shown (*b*) is a row of trees from fusiform-resistant parents; (*a*) shows a row from fusiform-susceptible parents. These two rows of trees were growing adjacent to one another.

What Causes Disease Resistance?

One could hardly ask a question that would have more answers than "What causes disease resistance?" A main problem is that often more than one type of resistance is present in a poulation of a given species. This compelxity and the difficulties posed to the breeder have been mentioned by Miller et al. (1976). The ideal is to combine all, or several, kinds of resistance into a single tree, but forest tree breeding has not developed to the stage of determining how much or how easily this can be done.

There are many differing ideas that have been offered to explain why trees differ from one another in disease resistance. These have been summarized by Hare (1966) in a review article on the physiology of resistance to fungal diseases. He made three general classifications that are (1) exclusions; (2) growth restriction after entry by methods such as "walling off"; and (3) destruction of the pathogen after entry. Hare makes the rather strong point that *exclusion* probably is of limited importance and that the pathogen usually enters both the susceptible and nonsusceptible tissue. He suggests that what happens after entry will determine the seriousness of the disease. Specific possible mechanisms for resistance have been mentioned by Bjorkman (1964); these include the moisture content of the host tissue, the nutrient status of the plant, the pH, the osmotic pressure

FIGURE 9.2 (*continued*)

within the cell, and other factors. To this can be added the presence or absence of resin acids, phenols, or other substances within the plant that might be toxic to the fungus (Forrest, 1980). A much-discussed resistance method is walling off the diseased tissue by the formation of a wound periderm or cork cells, which is triggered by the balance of auxin content and kinins (Boyer, 1966). The structure of the leaf and stomatal surface also can influence disease resistance. For example, Patton and Spear (1980) reported that wax on the needles hinders infection by white pine blister rust along with inhibitory substances in the stomatal subcham-

FIGURE 9.3

The diseases most easily worked with in resistance breeding are the rust and canker diseases, which are typified by the galls of fusiform rust illustrated. Symptoms are easy to see, are usually observable early, and a large genetic component of resistance is frequently evident.

ber. Elgersma (1980) reports that internal-wood anatomical features restrict the spread of Dutch elm disease.

The terpenes (or terpenoid compounds) often appear to give resistance to disease (Bridgen and Hanover, 1980). The resin acids and monoterpenes seem to be very effective. An area in which only recent progress is evident is the possible resistance to certain wood rotting and root rot organisms. This appears to result from a compartmentalization, a walling-off of the infected tissues from the healthy tissues (Shigo, 1980). Considerable genetic variability in resistance to root rot appears to be present among trees (Ladeitschikova, 1980).

One type of resistance that has puzzled foresters for many years is recovery from disease after infection. Although the mechanisms, which are often related to compartmentalization, are imperfectly known, many foresters recognize that trees sometimes recover after disease. Several authors, such as Boyer (1964; for white pine blister rust), claim that recovery from disease has a genetic basis; certain families recover much better than others. We definitely agree with this concept and have watched trees badly infected with fusiform rust recover, heal over the diseased area, and grow to a normal life span.

Gains from Resistance Breeding

No matter what the mechanisms of resistance are, the results from breeding for resistance to diseases are that useful strains of forest trees are now becoming available on a large scale. For example, many seed orchards have been established with fusiform rust-tolerant parents by the North Carolina State–Industry Tree Improvement Cooperative. Seed are available in large quantities with many thousands of hectares being planted in the disease "hot spots" in the southern United States. Other organizations are doing the same thing. Another example is the very successful breeding against several leaf diseases in the poplars (Chiba, 1964; Einspahr et al., 1979; and many others).

Space does not permit us to outline all the gains achieved by breeding for disease resistance. Large areas of forestland, which were formerly considered to be marginal or submarginal, have been made into economic forests by use of disease-resistant trees (Zobel et al., 1971; Zobel and Zoerb, 1977) (Figure 9.4).

FIGURE 9.4

Shown are two rows of loblolly pine progeny from different parents in a clonal seed orchard. The row on the left from one clone has been very heavily attacked by fusiform rust, whereas the one on the right has been only lightly infected. Such great genetic differences enable a profitable forest enterprise even where the disease incidence is large.

Predicted and achieved gains have been significant and of great economic value (Bingham, 1967; Porterfield, 1973; Rockwood and Goddard, 1973; and many others). *Breeding* for *disease resistance* is *economically profitable* and a *necessity* for *most tree improvement programs* (Zobel, 1980b).

INSECTS

General

Although damage to forest trees by insects is sometimes catastrophic, much less progress has been made in developing insect-resistant strains of forest trees than has been achieved for diseases. There are many reasons for this, among which are the mobility of the insect, the lack of ability to predict where and when an attack will occur, lack of knowledge of genetics of the insect, lack of knowledge about what causes resistance, and in some instances, lack of ability to produce "forced attacks" as needed for controlled genetic studies (Connola and Belskafuer, 1976). Furthermore, some insects can be relatively easily controlled silviculturally, and some attack at only one phase in the life cycle of the host. Epidemic insect buildups can be very rapid and are highly dependent on environmental fluctuations.

Despite the preceding, genetic gains can be made in developing resistance to insects, and much more research and study is needed in this area. A good example is the recent report by Trial (1980) in which he made an in-depth assessment of the history of attacks by the spruce budworm (*Choristoneura fumiferana*), a member of one of the most destructive groups of insects in forestry. This insect has caused huge losses in forestry and has affected the future and fate of communities, companies, and even governments. Little breeding for resistance to spruce budworm has been attempted (Figure 9.5).

Somehow the idea has developed that resistance of forest trees to insects is not great and that other methods of control should be the only ones used. This is puzzling, and we do not generally agree with that concept. In his report, Soegaard (1964) makes it clear that both conifers and broad-leaved forest trees have shown considerable resistance to insect attacks. Attempts are being made to determine this, even for the very difficult bark beetles (Waring and Pitman, 1980). Henson et al. (1970), using resistance to sawflies (*Neodeprion*) as an example, are of the opinion that trees can be bred with comparatively low susceptibility to insect damage. Generally, this can be accomplished along with selection for growth and form. In our opinion, the use of chemical sprays should be viewed as an interim method of keeping the forest intact until resistant strains and–or biological control of the insects have been achieved. This is because of the potentially deleterious effects of pesticides on the environment. Some insects appear to be so general in their feeding habits that it will be difficult to breed for resistance. For example, the gypsy moth (*Lymantria dispar* or *Porthetria dispar*) eats foliage from all but a few species of hardwoods and even eats conifers during epidemics.

FIGURE 9.5

It is difficult to breed for resistance to some pests. Damage to spruce and fir by the spruce budworm in Newfoundland, Canada, is shown. Little resistance breeding has been attempted, although some trees are less severely attacked than are others.

Generally, three types of resistance to insects can be recognized: (1) *nonpreference,* in which the insect is not attracted to, or is repelled from, feeding and ovipositing on a tree; (2) *antibiosis,* in which the insect is killed, injured, or prevented from completing its normal life cycle after feeding on a tree; and (3) *tolerance,* in which the tree recovers from insect attack by a population approximately equal to that that will damage a normal susceptible tree (Gerhold, 1962). In their bulletin, Henson et al. (1970) proposed the term *susceptibility* as a measure of how much the tree will be attacked by the insect and *vulnerability* as a measure of how much damage will be done by the insect.

Many reasons have been given for resistance to insects. One of the most common is the amount and quality of the resin production; it has been suggested that some trees "pitch out" the attacking beetles. Some resin vapors are toxic to the insect, or they inhibit feeding of adult beetles. Trees within a species can have greatly variable resins (Smith, 1966). Physical factors, such as bark thickness, also seem to be important as do many other kinds of factors. Waring and Pitman (1980) hypothesized that the amount of carbohydrate reserves in the host controls host resistance in bark beetles. They feel that tree vigor is related to carbohydrate production and thus affects beetle resistance.

One group of insects that causes very heavy damage to the tree improvement effort is the group that attacks seeds, cones, and flowers. These can be harmful for natural regeneration and devastating for seed orchards. Even though genetic variation is very evident among clones (Sartor and Neel, 1971), a breeding program for tolerance to insects solely for seed orchards is not a feasible alternative because other methods can be used to control the insects more efficiently in this special situation. Areas are small and seed orchards are very intensively managed and isolated. Much work has already been done in insect control for seed orchards, usually by use of *systemic* insecticides that are combined with good management. The systemics enter the tissues of the tree, and the insect is either killed or repelled by the chemicals that have been established in the plant tissues. If applied correctly, the systemic has little adverse effect on the general environment. Very intensive studies have been made on the use of systemics in seed orchards with some outstanding results (Drew and Wylie, 1980; van Buijtenen, 1981).

Resistance to Insects

Variation in susceptibility to insects has been known and recognized for numerous species of trees. For example, in two major groups of pines, differences in damage were found when the trees were attacked by shoot moths (*Rhyacionia*). These insects were widespread, they occur on many species, and they are persistent pests that cause much damage and loss of quality. Some species have been found that show some resistance (Holst, 1963).

Just as for diseases, resistance to insects can be related to individual families or the geographic origins of the host tree. For example, Batzer reported in 1961 great differences in white pine weevil attack, depending on the geographic source of jack pine; the indigenous source was the least damaged. Considerable work has been accomplished on resistance to white pine weevil (Gerhold, 1962; Garrett, 1970), but the results have been variable. For example, Connola and Belskafuer (1976) have emphasized that lightly weeviled trees may be heavily weeviled in other environments, especially under caging experiments. However, some usable resistance has been found; one of several studies reporting this is that of Heimburger and Sullivan (1972). Even the extensive tip moth and webworm attacks on slash and loblolly pine showed some differences with source of seed (Hertel and Benjamin, 1975).

Resistance on an individual-tree basis is perhaps the most important in control of insect damage, although only limited studies have been done on this aspect of resistance to insects. Work has been published on resistance to white pine weevil (Garrett, 1970), but the results have not been conclusive. Heimburger (1963) and Connola and Belskafuer (1976) have emphasized the great effect of environment in selecting and testing for individual-tree resistance. Success was reported in selecting black pines (*P. thunbergii*) whose progeny showed many scars but a low rate of gall formation when attacked by the pine gall midge. This insect, which is found in many regions of the world, does not injure certain tree genotypes.

The aphids are another group of serious insects that cause widespread damage. On Douglas fir, Meinartowicz and Szmidt (1978) found populations infected from 0 to 94%, with those sources of Douglas fir from east of the Cascade Mountains being most resistant. They concluded that the differences appear to be under genetic control.

Not all studies on insect resistance have been on conifers. Good work has been accomplished on the poplars; additionally, differences in susceptibility among willows to the cottonweed leaf beetle (*Chrysomela scripta*) have been reported by Randall (1971). Studies have shown that black locust (*Robinia pseudoacacia*) trees have exhibited variability in resistance to the locust borer (*Cullene robiniae*) (Soegaard, 1964).

Insects are particularly destructive to some tropical hardwoods. Luckily, resistance has sometimes been found, such as that against the shoot borer *Hypsipla* in *Toona cileata* (Grijpoma, 1976). Much study is needed in this area because insects, both the leafeaters and shoot borers, are a major problem when tropical hardwoods are grown in plantations. Differences in insect resistance among species and sources within species are evident in the eucalypts, but only a limited amount of work has been done on individual-tree resistance to beetles and larvae that so commonly attack members of this genus. One of the great needs in tree improvement is to obtain better information on breeding for resistance to insects.

Just as for diseases, both the hosts for insects and the insects themselves vary genetically. For example, Stock et al. (1979) found genetic differences between *Dendroctonus pseudotsugae* from Idaho and coastal Oregon. Apparently, very destructive races have been formed. In the white pine weevil, Heimburger (1963) states that "the weevil is genetically a very versatile organism." It attacks several widely different species of pine, spruce, and other species. The host–insect interactions can be very important, as has been reported for *Carya* by Harris (1980).

One group of pests that do widespread damage in the tropical and subtropical regions are the leaf-cutting ants. As far as we know, no resistance testing has been carried out with respect to the leaf cutters, although the ants have definite species preferences. It is possible that selection and breeding for tolerance to ant attack could be helpful. In Venezuela, it has been noticed that within the species *P. caribaea,* the ants prefer and first defoliate those trees with finer needles; they attack the trees with heavy needles last. The problem that faces breeding for tolerance to ant attack is that when food becomes scarce, the ants seem to feed on anything that is green, and they would probably also destroy the resistant trees, even though the attack might be delayed or lessened by a resistant strain of trees.

MISCELLANEOUS PESTS

General

There are a host of pests other than diseases and insects that attack forest trees. Some of these have been studied sufficiently to show that genetic resistance by the host is present, whereas others show no resistance at all. It was mentioned earlier that humans often can be considered to be severe pests. We do not like to say "something can't be done," but the nearest thing to impossibility is to develop resistance in forest trees to people as pests. The "people problem" has strong social and economic as well as biological foundations. However, the subject of humans as pests will not be considered here. Damage by them can be great, but control is most difficult.

The other pests will be briefly listed and referenced with statements about the potential for resistance breeding. Some pests that appear to be of minor importance at the present time could become of major importance as forestry becomes more intensive and human population pressures become greater.

Some Different Pests

A newly recognized and somewhat frightening loss has been caused by wood nematodes, especially in Japan. Ohba (1980) reports heavy losses caused by nematodes but found enough resistant trees to begin a breeding program and the early results are encouraging.

Another pest that causes extensive damage is mistletoe. Foresters commonly associate it with poor sites and overaged stands, but it sometimes is very frequent in young stands. When mistletoe attacks plantations, it can have a very adverse effect. Several studies have been made on the resistance potential to this pest. Persons such as Roth (1978) have found some resistance to mistletoe in conifers, although it is not as great as the resistance to many other pests. Frochot et al. (1978) have reported considerable species difference in poplars that are resistant to attack by mistletoe. They found, for example, that *P. trichocarpa* is very susceptible and *P. nigra* is quite resistant. Intermediate types between the two had intermediate infections. Hawksworth and Wiens (1966) have reported on witches broom and hosts for members of the genus *Phoradendron*. Different patterns occur within and between host and parasite species, but it is most difficult to determine if true resistance is present.

In addition to mistletoe, other parasitic plants cause trouble. However, no studies are known relative to resistance against these insidious plants. They are mentioned here, however, becuse of their effect on tree improvement that is related to progeny testing. If not recognized, they can seriously disrupt progeny testing, and even cause incorrect selection because trees that are not parasitized grow much faster than those that are. If the tree is noninfected because it is resistant, that would be fine, but often the nonparasitized trees are merely escapes, and this will cause the selection process to be imprecise in choosing trees with genetic superiority. There are several groups of parasitic weeds that infect forest trees. Two examples are *Agalinis purpurea*, parasitic on sycamore, sweet-gum, and loblolly pine (Musselman et al., 1978), and *Seymeria cassioedes*, on pines in the southeastern United States (Fitzgerald et al., 1977).

Animals frequently become serious pests. Bear, deer, elk, rabbits, and "mountain beaver" in the western United States and elsewhere can be most destructive to young forests (Marquis, 1974). Little resistance breeding has been done for these, except against deer and rabbits (Radwan, 1972). It is evident that certain families are greatly preferred over others; also, nursery-grown seedlings are usually much preferred over naturally regenerated seedlings. No serious breeding for animal tolerance has been done because control has been sought by reducing the animal populations or by the use of repellants. One breeding scheme that would help reduce animal depredations would be to develop trees that start growth rapidly so that they could grow quickly out the animal damage zone. This characteristic has been used as a criterion for selection in a number of tree-breeding programs.

One type of damage that is difficult to categorize as a pest results when a tree species "poisons" the growth environment, either for itself or for other species (Fisher, 1980). The term used to describe this phenomenon is *allelopathy* that is defined as "the influence of plants, other than microorganisms, upon each other, arising from the products of their metabolism." A simpler definition is given in Webster (Webster and McKetchnie, 1980). Allelopathy is "the reputed influence of one living plant upon another due to secretion of toxic substances." Some species poison the environment; therefore they cannot be grown in pure plantations or with other species. Allelopathy is suspected among tropical forest tree species; the most well-known species in the temperate area is *Juglans nigra* (walnut) (Gabriel, 1975), which produces the toxic substance *juglone*. When, for example, pines are planted where walnuts are grown, they often die or are stunted; similar allelopathic tendencies have been reported for cherrybark oak (DeBell, 1971). Many species, such as those of the genus *Eucalyptus* and even some pines, appear to have allelopathic effects because of changes they cause in the environment. Many weed species are allelopathic, resulting in more excessive damage than that caused by simple competition. No within-species breeding programs have been initiated to overcome allelopathy, although choice of species and how they will be grown often depends on a knowledge of allelopathy. Some of the barriers to growing some tropical hardwoods in pure plantations may be of allelopathic origin.

AIR POLLUTION AND ACID RAIN

General

Most plants obtain a part of their essential nutrients from the air: carbon dioxide for photosynthesis, nitrogen and sulfur for synthesis of proteins, oxygen for respiration, and many of the major and minor mineral elements (Witwer and Bukowac, 1969). Uptake of nutrients from the atmosphere is especially important in forests, because nutrients from other sources are scarce and fertilization is still an infrequent management practice.

But these uptake processes also make plants susceptible to injury by air pollutants. Most toxic substances occur as gases or fine aerosol particles (smoke or smog) that diffuse readily through the open stomata of trees and kill the leaves. In some areas, especially around metal smelters, damage can be severe, and no forests will grow until resistant trees are available, or until the source of pollution is decreased.

Air pollutants can cause death, deformation, or growth loss. Some of these effects are very obvious (Berry, 1961). The most insidious, widespread, and overall serious loss is from a reduction in growth. This is often not noticed by foresters and is accepted without question.

In some parts of the world, resistance of forest trees to air pollutants has been studied, and enough variation in resistance to air pollutants is available to permit selection and breeding of more tolerant individuals, strains, or even species. But such breeding is difficult and tricky and has not been followed with suitable vigor. Most of the emphasis has been on decreasing the sources of pollution rather than on developing trees that will grow normally in polluted air.

Fume Damage

Many different chemicals are released into the atmosphere by factories, automobiles, volcanoes, and many other sources. Many different gases can damage forests; the most prevalant and damaging are ozone, sulfur dioxide, nitrogen oxide, and the fluorides, but a host of others are sometimes involved. Losses, especially in growth, are increasing, and when one estimates the area of forestland affected by air pollution, the amount of loss of forest products is staggering (Figure 9.6). The loss in one species (*P. ponderosa*) was reported by Cobb et al. (1970). They emphasized not only the direct loss to pollutants but the secondary problems from diseases and insects that attack the pollutant-weakened trees.

Many publications have dealt with breeding for resistance to air pollutants; one example is Patton (1981) who reported on the effects of ozone and sulfur dioxide on the growth and wood of poplar hybrids. The subject has been dealt with in a symposium (Bialobok 1980), and interest in breeding for resistance to air pollutants seems to be increasing. Bialobok criticizes the simple mass-selection approach, and states that the genetic basis for resistance to air pollution must be better understood.

Breeding for resistance to air pollutants is just as complicated as is breeding for disease resistance. Trees resistant to ozone may be susceptible to sulfur dioxide or vice versa. Trees that are resistant to both ozone and sulfur dioxide separately may succumb or be injured when subjected to both of them together. Whether and how much trees are affected depends on age, time of year, and the physiological condition of the tree (Berry, 1973). There is no area of forest tree breeding in which greater emphasis is needed. Strains of trees with reasonable tolerance to air pollutants are needed in many parts of the world.

Acid Rain

Another possible threat to forest trees is acid rain; the word *possible* is used because the evidence about the balance between beneficial and harmful effects of acidic and acidifying materials in the air is still not clear. Sulfur and nitrogen oxides are toxic gases. They can kill individual trees or whole forests, but when

FIGURE 9.6

Fume damage can be severe, as shown below (left) where the resistant trees are still healthy, the sensitive ones are dead. Often the results from fume damage are a loss in growth. Shown is a row from a sensitive parent that has grown only half as much as a resistant family row behind it. When grown in a clean environment, both families grew at the same rate.

some substances are transported over long distances, they are transformed chemically in the moist air to sulfuric and nitric acids. These acids can be deposited on soils and trees. In water solution the acids dissociate (break up) into ions—H^+, NH_4^+, NO_3^-, and SO_4^{2-}—that are sometimes injurious and sometimes beneficial for plants, depending on their nutrient status, concentration, and the physiological condition of the trees.

The question of the effects of acid rain on forests is so new, the variability among forest trees and soils is so great, and the growth responses are so long term that the actual effects on forest growth have not yet been quantified (Cowling, 1979; Cowling and Davey, 1981; Hornbeck, 1981).

Several different mechanisms of adverse effects caused by acid rain have been suggested (Tamm and Cowling, 1977). Some of these ideas have been verified by experiments—but always in greenhouse or field tests with simulated acid rain. These tests show that acid rain *can* damage forest trees under some conditions, but no direct evidence has yet shown that acid rain *does* damage forests.

The ideas that have been put forward include the following: erosion of protective waxes on leaves (Shriner, 1976) and killing of feeder roots by acid-mobilized aluminum (Ulrich et al., 1980), both of which would predispose trees to drought. Ozone damage has been shown to be greater in plants that also receive simulated acid rain than in plants with normal rain. Older needles on loblolly pine turn brown prematurely when exposed to the simulated acid rain of pH 3.2 (Shriner, 1976). Leaching of nutrients from foliage and from soils by simulated acid rain has been discussed by Wood and Bormann (1974).

No selection or breeding work has yet been done to determine the resistance to acid rain. Once the major mechanisms of acid rain damage have been demonstrated, it should be possible to find and use variation in resistance in the same way as with other "pests."

Some authors (Lee and Weber, 1979) feel that acid rain effects will be most severe at the regeneration stage in the life of the forest. They found that seed germination on the forest floor was much reduced by acid rain for some species and that root development of the seedlings was inhibited.

Breeding for aspects of nutrient deficiencies like those that would result from acid rain has been tried and has been successful (van Buijtenen and Isbell, 1970). The solution is to have source control of this pollutant so the situation will not continue to worsen. A limit will be reached beyond which breeding can no longer assure reasonable health and growth of trees established on soils changed by acid rain. This is an area needing intensive and urgent research.

ADVERSE ENVIRONMENTS

Perhaps the most successful of all tree-breeding efforts has been to produce trees that are better suited to adverse environments. As the human population expands, the need for more land to grow food crops will continue to increase greatly. There is already a growing trend to convert the best forest sites to agricultural uses. As the need for more forest products becomes greater, one way to produce more wood is to grow trees economically on sites that are now considered to be marginal or submarginal for forest production.

Adverse environments may be caused by conditions that are too dry, too wet, too hot, or too cold for normal tree growth. Adverse environments may be caused by such other factors as nutrient-deficient soils, hard wind, or excess salts in the soil. All of these have been encountered in tree improvement efforts and considerable success has been achieved in breeding for resistance to them. For example, Monk and Wiebe (1961) found tolerance differences to salts in woody ornamental plants. Although no breeding has been done on an individual-tree basis, tolerance of various sources within species to wind and ice damage is sometimes striking (Kerr, 1972; Williston, 1974). It is not uncommon in seed orchards that have been damaged by ice to find a few clones that are much more severely damaged than the others.

Great gains from tree improvement have been obtained from cold- and drought-resistance breeding. There are numerous publications listing results for both conifers and hardwoods. For example, Kriebel (1963) was able to select drought-tolerant strains of sugar maple whereas van Buijtenen et al. (1976) reported upon drought-hardy pines. Drought-hardy strains of forest trees are relatively common. Drought resistance occurs both by species and by individuals within species. Much gain can be obtained through provenance selection (Ferrell and Woodward, 1966); this is true for most "adverse environment" characteristics and is usually the first approach to be followed after species have been chosen for use in adverse environments.

Cold tolerance is a most important characteristic and one that has had a great breeding emphasis. For example, in Douglas fir, Szöny and Nagy (1968) have reported on the relationship between frost resistance and growth. A key characteristic in expanding the range of *Eucalyptus* is to develop cold-tolerant strains (Boden, 1958; Hunt and Zobel, 1978). Some excellent work has been done on juvenile selection of the eucalypts to frost resistance (Marien, 1980). The ability to withstand cold is of great value in the species tha grow in cold climates, and much work has also been done in this area, some of it many years ago (Bates, 1930). Great progress has been made in breeding for cold resistance in the Scandanavian countries. As one of many examples, Schummann and Hoffman (1968) tested 1-year-old spruce seedlings for frost resistance, and a number of workers report a good correlation between the dry-matter content of the needles and cold resistance. Sometimes little genetic variation is found, such as for radiata pine where no differences in cold tolerance by stand origin were found (Hood and Libby, 1980).

If one is to breed intelligently for resistance to something such as drought, it is important to know the possible causes for resistance. In their report, van Buijtenen et al. (1976) found that drought resistance was determined by only a few avoidance-of-tolerance mechanisms. They listed the avoidance mechanisms as follows:

1. Stomatal control with the drought-hardy seedlings transpiring rapidly when water was available but conserving water under stress. (A similar pattern has been reported for some species of *Eucalyptus*.)

2. Root morphology with the drought-hardy trees having deeper, more fibrous root systems.

3. Needle morphology in which the drought-hardy trees have smaller, deeper stomatal pits.

4. Number of stomata per unit needle length.

The physiological effects of drought and flooding are often similar, with flooding causing poor root development that then makes trees less efficient in nutrient and water uptake so that they become very susceptible when droughts do occur (Kormanik and McAlpine, 1971). Just as for flooding and drought, the physiology of resistance to cold and to drought also seems to be similar. This has been discussed by Shirley (1937), Pisek and Larcher (1954), and Schönback et al. (1966).

Although many more pages could be written about resistance to adverse environments, little more needs to be said here to make clear the gains to be obtained from breeding trees that are suitable for such conditions. This activity is of vital importance, and it is an integral part of developing land races. Much of the effort of the tree improver in the future will be expended on intensified breeding for resistance to adverse environments. The applied phases of the breeding efforts have far outstripped the needed fundamental information. Without continued progress in *both* the applied and fundamental phases of this type of breeding, forestry will not progress in the future as much as it should.

LITERATURE CITED

Bates, C. G. 1930. The frost hardiness of geographic strains of Norway pine. *Jour. For.* **29**:327–333.

Batzer, H. O. 1961, "Jack Pine from Lake States Seed Sources Differ in Susceptibilitiy to Attack by the White-Pine Weevil." Technical Note, Lake States Forest Experiment Station No. 595.

Berry, C. R. 1961. "White Pine Emergence Tipburn, A Physiogenic Disturbance." U.S. Forest Forest Service, Southeastern Experiment Station Paper No. 130.

Berry, C. R. 1973. The differential sensitivity of eastern white pine to three types of air pollution. *Can. Jour. For. Res.* **3**(4):543–547.

Bialobok, S. 1980. "Forest Genetics and Air Pollution Stress." Symp. Effects of Air Pollutants on Mediterranean and Temperate Forest Ecosystems, Riverside, Calif., pp. 100–102.

Bingham, R. T. 1963. "Problems and Progress in Improvement of Rust Resistance of North American Trees." First World Con. For. Gen. and Tree Impr., Stockholm, Sweden.

Bingham, R. T. 1967. "Economical and Reliable Estimates of General Combining Ability for Blister Rust Resistance Obtained with Mixed-Pollen Crosses." U.S. Forest Service Research Note INT-60.

Bjorkman, E. 1964. Breeding for resistance to disease in forest trees. *Unasylva* **18**(2–3):73–81.

Blair, R. L. 1970. "Quantitative Inheritance of Resistance to Fusiform Rust in Loblolly Pine." Ph.D. thesis, North Carolina State University, Raleigh.

Boden, R. W. 1958. Differential frost resistance within one *Eucalyptus* species. *Aust. J. Sci.* **2**(3):84–86.

Borlaug, N. E. 1966. Basic concepts which influence the choice of methods for use in breeding for disease resistance in cross-pollinated and self-pollinated crop plants. In *Breeding Pest-Resistant Trees,* pp. 327–348, Pergamon Press, Oxford, England.

Boyer, M. G. 1964. "The Incidence of Apparent Recovery from Blister Rust in White Pine Seedlings from Resistant Parents." 9th Comm. For. Tree Breed. in Canada, Part II.

Boyer, M. G. 1966. Auxin in relation to stem resistance in white pine blister rust. In *Breeding Pest-Resistant Trees*, pp. 179–184, NATO and NSF Adv. Study Inst. on Gen. Impr. for Dis. and Insect Res. of For. Trees, Pergamon Press, Oxford, England.

Bridgen, M. R., and Hanover, J. W. 1980. "Biochemical Aspects in Resistance Breeding. Indirect Selection of Pest Resistance Using Terpenoid Compounds." Workshop on Genetics of Host–Parasite Inter. in For., Wageningen, Holland.

Bryan, W. C. 1965. "Testing Shortleaf Pine Seedlings for Resistance to Infection by *Phytophthora cinnamomi.*" U.S. Forest Service Research Note SE-50.

Callaham, R. Z. 1966. "Tree Breeding for Pest Resistance." Sexto Congresso Forestal Mundial, Madrid.

Carson, M. J. 1977. "Breeding for Resistance to *Dothistroma pini.* Breeding *Pinus radiata.*" IUFRO Working Party Newsletter No. 1., pp. 2–4.

Carson, M. 1982. "Breeding for Resistance to Fusiform Rust in Loblolly Pine." Ph.D. thesis, North Carolina State University, Raleigh.

Chiba, O. 1964. "Studies on the Variation and Susceptibility and the Nature of Resistance of Poplars to the Leaf Rust Caused by *Melampsora laricipopulina.*" Bull. Govt. For. Expt. Stat., Japan, No. 166, pp. 85–157.

Cobb, F. W., and Stark, R. W. 1970. Decline and mortality of smog-injured ponderosa pine. *Jour. For.* **68**(3):147–149.

Coggeshall, M. V., Land, S. B., Ammon, V. D., Cooper, D. T., and McCracken, F. I. 1981. Genetic variation in resistance to canker disease of young American sycamore. *Plant Dis.* **65**(2):140–142.

Conkle, M. T. 1979. "Amount and Distribution of Isozyme Variation in Various Conifer Species. 17th Meet. Can. For. Tree Assoc., Gander, Newfoundland, pp. 109–117.

Connola, D., and Belskafuer, K. 1976. "Large Outdoor Cage Tests with eastern white pine being tested in field plots for white pine weevil resistance." Proc. 23rd Northeast. For. Tree Impr. Conf., State College, Pa., pp 56–64.

Cowling, E. B. 1979. Effects of acid precipitation and atmospheric deposition on terrestrial vegetation. *Environ. Prof.* **1**:293–301.

Cowling, E. B., and Davey, C. B. 1981. Acid precipitation: Basic principles and ecological consequences. *Pulp Pap.* August:182–185.

Day, P. R. 1972. "The Genetics of Rust Fungi. Biol. of Rust Resis. in For. Trees." NATO-IUFRO Adv. Study Inst. on Gen. Impr. for Dis. and Insect Res. of For. Trees, pp. 3–17.

DeBell, D. S. 1971. Phytotoxic effects of cherrybark oak. *For. Sci.* **17**(2):180–185.

Dietrichson, J. 1968. Provenance and Resistance to *Scleroderris lagerbergii* (*Crumenula abietina*). The International Scots Pine Prov. Expt. of 1938 at Matrand. Rep. *Norw. For. Res. Inst.*, No. 92 **25**(6):398–410. (Meddelelser fra Det Norske Skogforsøksvesen nr 92 **25**(6):398–410.)

Dimitri, V. L., and Frohlich, H. J. 1971. Some questions for resistance breeding with red rot of spruce caused by *Fomes annosus. Sil. Gen.* **20**(5–6):184–191.

Dinus, R. J. 1969. "Testing Slash Pine for Rust Resistance in Artificial and Natural Conditions." Proc. 10th South. For. Tree Impr. Conf., Houston, Tex., pp. 98–106.

Dinus, R. J., Snow, G. A., Kais, A. G., and Walkinshaw, C. H. 1975. "Variabiliity of *Cronartium fusiforme* Affects Resistance Breeding Strategies." Proc. 13th South. For. Tree Imp. Conf., Raleigh, N.C., pp. 193–196.

Drew, L. K., and Wylie, F. R. 1980. "Tree Injection with Systemic Insecticide to Control Leaf-Eating and Sap Sucking insects." Advisory Leaflet No. 13, Dept. For., Queensland, Australia.

Einspahr, D. W., Wyckoff, G. W., and Harder, M. L. 1979." *Hypoxylon* Resistance in Aspen and Aspen Hybrids," Proc. 1st North Cent. Tree Imp. Conf., Madison, Wis., pp. 114–122.

Elgersma, D. M. 1980. "Resistance Mechanisms of Elms to Dutch Elm Disease." Workshop Gen. Host–Parasite Interactions in For. Wageningen, Holland.

Ferrell, W. K., and Woodard, E. S. 1966. Effects of seed origin on drought resistance of Douglas-fir (*Pseudotsuga menziesii*). *Ecology* **43**(3):499–502.

Filer, T. H., and Randall, W. K. 1978. Resistance of twenty-one sweetgum families to *Botryosphaeria ribis. Plant Dis. Rptr.* **62**(1):38–39.

Fisher, R. F. 1980. Allelopathy: A potential cause of regeneration failure. *Jour. For.* **78**(6):346–348.

Fitzgerald, C. H., Schultz, R. C., Forston, J. C., and Terrell, S. 1977. Effects of *Seymeria cassioides* infestation on pine seedling and sapling growth. *South. Jour. App. For.* **1**(4):26–30.

Ford-Robertson, F. C. 1971. *Terminology of Forest Science Technology Practice and Products*. The Multilingual Forestry Terminology Series No. 1, Soc. Amer. For., Washington, D.C.

Forrest, G. I. 1980. "Preliminary Work on the Relation between Resistance to *Fomes annosus* and the Monoterpene Composition of Sitka Spruce Resin." Workshop Gen. of Host–Parasite Interaction in For., Wageningen, Holland.

Frochot, H., Pitsch, M., and Wharlen, L. 1978. "Susceptibility Differences of Mistletoe (*Viscum album*) to Some Poplar Clones (*Populus* sp.)." Congrès des Sociétés Savantes, Nancy, France, pp. 371–380.

Gabriel, W. J. 1975. Allelopathic effects of black walnut on white birches. *Jour. For.* **73**(4):234–237.

Garrett, P. W. 1970. "Early Evidence of Weevil Resistance in Some Clones and Hybrids of White Pine." U.S. Forest Service Research Note NE-117.

Gerhold, H. D. 1962. "Testing White Pines for Weevil Resistance." 9th Northeast. For. Tree Impr. Conf., Syracuse, N.Y., pp. 44–53.

Gerhold, H. D., Schreiner, E. J., Dermott, R. E., and Winieski, J. A. 1966. *Breeding Pest-Resistant Trees*. Pergamon Press, Oxford, England.

Grijpoma, P. 1976. Resistance of *Meliaceae* against the shoot borer *Hypsipyla* with particular reference to *Toona ciliata* var. *australis*. *Tropical Trees,* No. 2:69–77.

Hare, R. C. 1966. Physiology of resistance to fungal diseases in plants. *Bot. Rev.* **32**(2):95–137.

Harris, M. K. 1980. "Genes for Resistance to Insects, Emphasizinig Host–Parasite Interactions." Workshop Gen. of Host–Parasite Inter. in For., Wageningen, Holland.

Hattemer, H. H. 1972. Persistence of rust resistance. In *Biol. of Rust Res. in For. Trees.*, NATO–IUFRO Advanced Study Institute, pp. 561–569.

Hawksworth, F. G., and Wiens, D. 1966. Observations on witches-broom formation, autoparasitism, and new hosts in *Phoradendron. Madrono* **18**(7):218–224.

Henson, W. R., O'Neil, L. C., and Mergen, F. 1970. "Natural Variation in Susceptibility of *Pinus* to *Neodiprion* Sawflies as a Basis for Development of a Breeding Program for Resistant trees." Yale Univ. Bull. No. 78.

Heimburger, C. 1962. Breeding for disease resistance in forest trees. *For. Chron.* **38**(3):356–362.

Heimburger, C. C. 1963. "The Breeding of White Pine for Resistance to Weevil." 1st World Cons. For. Gen. and Tree Impr., Stockholm, Sweden.

Heimburger, C. C., and Sullivan, C. R. 1972. Screening of *Haploxylon* pines for resistance to the white pine weevil. II. *Pinus strobus* and other species and hybrids grafted on white pine. *Sil. Gen.* **21**(6):210–215.

Hertel, G. D., and Benjamin, D. M. 1975. "Tip Moth and Webworm Attacks in Southern Pine Seed Source Plantations." U.S. Forest Service Research Note SE–221.

Heybroek, H. M. 1980. "Monoculture versus Mixture: Interactions Between Susceptible and Resistant Trees in a Mixed Stand." Workshop Gen. of Host–Parasite Inter. in For., Wageningen, Holland.

Holst, M. 1963. "Breeding Resistance in Pines to *Rhyaciona* Moths." 1st World Cons. For. Gen. and Tree Impr., Stockholm, Sweden.

Hood, J. W., and Libby, W. J. 1980. A clonal study of intraspecific variability in radiata pine. I. Cold and animal damage. *Aust. For. Res.* **10**:9–20.

Hornbeck, J. W. 1981. Acid rain—facts and fallacies. *Jour. For.* **79**(7):438–443.

Horsfall, J. G., and Cowling, E. B. 1980. *Plant Disease.* Academic Press, New York.

Hunt, R., and Zobel, B. 1978. Frost hardy eucalypts grow well in the southeast. *South. Jour. Appl. For.* **2**(1):6–10.

Kerr, E. 1972. Trees that resist hurricanes. *Prog. Farmer* (March 1972):628.

King, J. P., and Nienstaedt, H. 1965. Variation in needle cast susceptibility among 29 jack pine seed sources. *Sil. Gen.* **14**(6):194–198.

Kinloch, B. B., and Kelman, A. 1965. Relative susceptibility to fusiform rust of progeny lines from rust-infected and noninfested loblolly pines. *Plant Dis. Reptr.* **49**(10):872–874.

Kinloch, B. B., and M. H. Zoerb. 1971. "Genetic Variation in Resistance to Fusiform Rust Among Selected Parent Clones of Loblolly Pine and Their Offspring." Proc. 11th South. For. Tree Impr. Conf., Atlanta, Ga., pp. 76–80.

Kormanik, P. P., and McAlpine, R. G. 1971. The Response of Three Random Clones of Yellow-Poplar to Simulated Drought and Flooding." 11th Conf. on South. For. Tree Impr., Atlanta, Ga., pp. 18–19.

Kriebel, H. B. 1963. "Selection for Drought Resistance in Sugar Maple." 1st World Cons. on For Gen. and Tree Impr., Stockholm, Sweden.

Kuhlman, E. G. 1972. "Susceptibility of Loblolly and Slash Pine Progeny to *Fomes annosus*." U.s. Forest Service Research Note SE 176.

Ladeitschikova, E. I. 1980. "Biochemical Aspects of Resistance to Root Rot in Scots Pine." Workshop Gen. of Host–Parasite Inter. in For., Wageningen, Holland.

LaFarge, T., and Kraus, J. F. 1980. A progeny test of (shortleaf × loblolly) × loblolly hybrids to produce rapid-growing hybrids resistant to fusiform rust. *Sil. Gen.* **29**(5–6):197–200.

Lee, J. J., and Weber, D. E. 1979. The effect of simulated acid rain on seedling emergence and growth of eleven woody species. *For. Sci.* **25**(3):393–398.

MacDonald, R. D., Thor, E., and Andes, J. O. 1962. "American Chestnut Breeding Program at the University of Tennessee." 53rd Ann. Meet. North. Nut Growers Assoc., Purdue, Ind.

Marien, J. N. 1980. Juvenile selection of frost resistant *Eucalyptus. AFOCEL*, pp. 225–253.

Marquis, D. A. 1974. "The Impact of Deer Browsing on Allegheny Hardwood Regeneration." U.S. Forest Service Research Paper NE-308.

Martinsson, O. 1979. "Breeding Strategy in Relation to Disease Resistance in Introduced Forest Trees. Sveriges Lantbruksuniversitet, Inter. Rep. NR3.

Martinnson, O. 1980. Stem rusts in lodgepole pine provenance trials. *Sil. Gen.* **29**(1):23–26.

McNabb, H. S., Hall, R. B., and Ostry, M. 1980. "Biological and Physical Modifications of the Environment in Short Rotation Tree Crops and the Resulting Effect upon the Host–Parasite Interactions." Workshop Gen. of Host–Parasite Inter. in For., Wageningen, Holland.

Meinartowicz, L. E., and Szmidt, A. 1978. Investigations into the resistance of Douglas fir (*Pseudotsuga menziesii*) populations to the Douglas fir woolly aphid (*Gilletteella cooleyi*). *Sil. Gen.* **27**(2):59–62.

Miller, T. 1977. "Fusiform Rust Management Strategy in Concept: Site Preparation." Symp. Management of Fusiform Rust in Southern Pines, South. For. Dis. and Insect Res. Coun., Gainesville, Fla., pp. 110–115.

Miller, T., Cowling, E. B., Powers, H. R., and Blalock, T. E. 1976. Types of resistance and compatibility in slash pine seedlings infected by *Cronartium fusiforme. Phytopathology.* **66**1229–1235.

Monk, R. W., and Wiebe, H. H. 1961. Salt tolerance and protoplasmic salt hardiness of various woody and herbaceous ornamental plants. *Plant Physiol.* **36**(4):478–482.

Musselman, L. J., Harris, C. S., and Mann, W. F. *Agalinis purpurea*: A parasitic weed on sycamore, sweetgum and loblolly pine. *Tree Plant. Notes,* Fall edition, 1978, pp. 24–25.

Nelson, R. R. 1980. "Host–parasite Interactions and Genetics on the Individual Plant Level. Strategy of Breeding for Disease Resistance." Workshop Gen. of Host–Parasite Inter. in For., Wageningen, Holland.

Nicholls, T. H. 1979. "Dangers of Red Pine Monoculture." Proc. 1st North-Central Tree Imp. Conf., Madison, Wis., pp. 104–108.

Ohba, K. 1980. "Breeding of Pines for Resistance to Wood Nematodes (*Bursaphelenchus lignicolus*)." Workshop Gen. of Host–Parasite Inter. in For., Wageningen, Holland.

Patton, R. L. 1981. "Effects of Ozone and Sulfur Dioxide on Height and Stem Specific Gravity of *Populus* Hybrids." U.S. Forest Service Research Paper NE 471.

Patton, R. F., and Spear, R. N. 1980. "Stomatal Influences on White Pine Blister Rust Infection." Proc. IUFRO Work. Group, Rusts of Hard Pines, Florence, Italy, pp. 1–7.

Phelps, W. R. 1977. Screening center for fusiform rust. *For. Farmer* **36**(3):11–14.

Pisek, A., and Larcher, W. 1954. Zusammenhang gewischen Austrock-nungsresistenz und Frost-härte bei Immergrünen [Relationship between drought resistance and frost hardiness in evergreens]. *Protoplasma* **44**(1):30–46.

Porterfield, R. L. 1973. "Predicted and Potential Gains from Tree Improvement

Programs—A Goal-Programming Analysis of Program Efficiency." Ph.D. thesis, Yale University, New Haven, Conn.

Powers, H. R. 1975. Relative susceptibility of five southern pines to *Cronartium fusiforme*. *Plant Dis. Rep.* **59**(4):312–314.

Powers, H. R., and Duncan, H. J. 1976. Increasing fusiform resistance by intraspecific hybridization. *For. Sci.* **22**(3):267–268.

Powers, H. R., Jr., Matthews, F. R., and Dwinell, L. D. 1978. The potential for increased virulence of *Cronartium fusiforme* on resistant loblolly pine. *Phytopathology* **68**:808–810.

Powers, H. R., and Zobel, B. J. 1978. Progeny of specific loblolly pine clones vary in fusiform rust resistance according to seed orchard of origin. *For. Sci.* **24**(2):227–230.

Radwan, M. A. 1972. Differences between Douglas-fir genotypes in relation to browsing preference by black-tailed deer. *Can. Jour. For. Res.* **2**(3): 250–255.

Randall, W. K. 1971. "Differences Among Willows in Susceptibility to Cottonwood Leaf Beetle." 11th Conf. South. For. Tree Impr., Atlanta, Ga.

Riker, A. J., and Patton, R. F. 1961. Breeding trees for disease resistance. *Recent Adv. Bot.* **2**(14):1687–1691.

Rockwood, D. L., and Goddard, R. E. 1973. "Predicted Gains for Fusiform Rust Resistance in Slash Pine." Proc. 12th South. For. Tree Impr. Conf., Baton Rouge, La., pp. 31–37.

Roth, L. R. 1978. "Genetic Control of Dwarf Mistletoe." Symp. Mistletoe Control Through Forest Management, Pacific Southwest Forest and Range Experiment Station General Technical Report PSW-31.1, pp. 69–72.

Sartor, G. F. and Neel, W. W. 1971. "Variable Susceptibility to *Dioryctria amatella* Among Pines in Clonal Seed Orchards." Proc. 11th Conf. South. For. Tree Imp., Atlanta, Ga., pp. 91–94.

Schmidt, R. A. 1978. "Diseases in Forest Ecosystems: The Importance of Functional Diversity." In *Plant Disease—An Advanced Treatise,* Vol. II, *How Disease develops in Poulations,* pp. 287–315.

Schönback, H., Bellman, E., and Schumann, W. 1966. Die Jugendwuchsleistung, Düre—und Frostresistenz verschiedener provenienzen der japanischen Lärche (*Larix leptolepis*) [Early growth and resistance to drought and frost in provenances of Japanese larch]. *Sil. Gen.* **15**(5/6):141–147.

Schreiner, E. J. 1959. "Rating poplars for *Melampsora* Leaf Rust Infection." U.S. Forest Service, Northeastern Forest Experiment Station, Forest Research Note No. 90.

Schreiner, E. J. 1963. "Improvement of Disease Resistance in *Populus*." 1st World Con. on For. Gen. and Tree Impr., Stockholm, Sweden.

Schummann, W., and Hoffman, K. 1968. Routine testing of frost resistance of 1-year-old spruce seedlings. *Arch. Forstw.* **16**(6/9):701–705.

Shigo, A. L. 1980. "Trees Resistant to Spread of Decay Associated with Wounds." Workshop Gen. Host–Parasite Inter. in For., Wageningen, Holland.

Shirley, H. L. 1937. The relation of drought and cold resistance to source of seed stock. *Minn. Hortic., pp. 1–2.*

Shriner, D. S. 1976. "Effects of Simulated Rain Acidified with Sulfur Acid on Host–Parasite Interactions." Proc. 1st Symp. on Acid Precipitation and the Forest Ecosystem., U.S. Forest Service General Technical Report NE-23, pp. 919–925.

Smith, R. H. 1966. "Resin Quality as a Factor in the Resistance of Pines to Bark Beetles." *Breeding Resistant Trees.* NATO and NSF Advanced Study Institute, Pennsylvania State University, pp. 189–196.

Snow, G. A., and Griggs, M. M. 1980. "Relative Virulence of *Cronartium quercuum f. sp. fusiforme* from Seven Resistant Families of Slash Pine." Proc. IUFRO Work. Group, Rusts of Hard Pines, Florence, Italy, pp. 13–16.

Söegaard, B. 1964. Breeding for resistance to insect attack in forest trees. *Unasylva* **18**(2–3):82–88.

Söegaard, B. 1969."Resistance Studies in *Thuja.*" *Soertryk Det forstlige Forsoegsvoesen Danmark beretning* **245**(31).

Squillace, A. E., and Wilhite, L. P. 1977. "Influence of Oak Abundance and Distribution on Fusiform Rust." Symp. Management of Fusiform Rust in the Southern Pines, Gainesville, Fla., pp. 59–70.

Stephen, B. R. 1973. Über Anfalligkeit und Resistenz von Douglasien Herkunften gegenüber *Rhadbdocline pseudotsugae* [Susceptibility and resistance of Douglas-fir provenances to *Rhabdocline pseudotsugae*]. *Sil. Gen.* **22**(5–6):149–153.

Stern, K. 1972. "The Theoretical Basis of Rust Resistance Testing—Concept of Genetic Gain in Breeding Resistant Trees." Biol. of Rust Res. in For. Trees, Proc. NATO–IUFRO Advanced Study Institute, pp. 299–311.

Stock, M. W., Pitman, G. B., and Guenther, J. D. 1979. Genetic differences between Douglas-fir beetles (*Dendroctonus pseudotsugae*) from Idaho and Coastal Oregon. *Ann. Entomolog. Soc. Amer., pp. 394–397.*

Szöny, L., and Nagy, I. 1968. Klimaresistenz Photsynthese und Stoff Production [Frost resistance and growth of Douglas fir]. *Sonderdruck Tagungsberichte,* No. 100:65–67.

Tamm, C. O., and Cowling, E. B. 1977. Acid precipitation and forest vegetation. *Water, Air Soil Pollu.* **7**:503–511.

Thielges, B. A., and Adams, J. C. 1975. Genetic variation and heritability of Melampsora leaf rust resistance in eastern cottonwood. *For. Sci.* **21**(3):278–282.

Trial, H. 1980. A cartographic history of the spruce budworm in Quebec, Maine and New Brunswick. *Maine For. Rev.* **13**:1–52.

Toole, E. R., and Hepting, G. H. 1949. Selection and propagation of *Albizzia* for resistance to *Fusarium* wilt. *Phytopathology* **39**(1):63–70.

Ulrich, B., Mayer, B., and Khanna, P. K. 1980. Chemical changes due to acid precipitation in a loess derived soil in central Europe. *Soil Sci.* **130**:193–199.

van Buijtenen, J. P., and Isbell, R. 1970. "Differential Response of Loblolly Pine Families to a Series of Nutrient Levels. 1st North Amer. For. Biol. Workshop, Michigan State University, East Lansing.

van Buijtenen, J. P., Bilan, V., and Zimmerman, R. H. 1976. Morpho-physiological characteristics related to drought resistance in *Pinus taeda*. In *Tree Physiology and Yield Improvement*, pp. 349–359. Academic Press, New York.

van Buijtenen, J. P. 1981. Insecticides for seed orchards—a case study in applied research. *South. Jour. Appl. For.* **5**(1):33–37.

Walkinshaw, C. H., Dell, T. R., and Hubbard, S. D. 1980. "Predicting Field Performance of Slash Pine Families from Inoculated Greenhouse Seedlings." U.S. Forest Service, Southern Forest Experiment Station Research Paper SO-160.

Walkinshaw, C., and Bey, C. 1981. Reaction of field resistant slash pines to selected isolates of *Cronartium quercuum* f. sp. *fusiforme*. *Phytopathology*. **71**:1090–1092.

Waring, R. H., and Pitman, G. B. 1980. "A Simple Model of Host Resistance to Bark Beetles." For. Res. Lab. Research Note 65, Oregon State University, School of Forestry.

Waters, W. E., and Cowling, E. B. 1976. Integrated forest pest management. A silvicultural necessity. *Integ. Pest Mgt.,* pp. 149–177.

Webster, N., and McKechnie, J. L. 1980. *Webster's New Twentieth Century Dictionary—Unabridged Second Edition.* William Collins Publishers, Inc.

Wells, O. O., and Switzer, G. L. 1975. "Selecting Populations of Loblolly Pine for Rust Resistance and Fast Growth." 13th South. For. Tree Imp. Conf., Raleigh, North Carolina, pp. 37–44.

Williston, H. L. 1974. Managing pines in the ice-storm belt. *Jour. For.* **72**:580–582.

Witwer, S. H., and Buckovac, M. J. 1969. The uptake of nutrients through leaf surfaces. In *Handbuch der Pflanzenernährung und Dungung.,* pp. 235–261. Springer-Verlag, New York.

Wood, T., and Bormann, F. H. 1974. The effects of an artificial acid mist upon the growth of *Betula alleghaniensis*. *Environ Pollut.* **7**:259–268.

Zobel, B. J. 1980a. "Developing Fusiform-Resistant Trees in the Southeastern United States." Workshop Gen. of Host–Parasite Inter. in For., Wageningen, Holland.

Zobel, B. J. 1980b. "The World's Need for Pest-Resistant Forest Trees." Workshop Gen. of Host–Parasite Inter. in For., Wageningen, Holland.

Zobel, B., Blair, R., and Zoerb, M. 1971. Using research data—disease resistance. *Jour. For.* **69**(8):486–489.

Zobel, B. J., and Zoerb, M. 1977 "Reducing Fusiform Rust in Plantations Through Control of the Seed Souce." Symp. Man. of Fusiform Rust in Southern Pines, South For. Dis. and Insect. Res. Coun., Gainesville, Fla., pp. 98–109.

Zsuffa, L. 1975. "Some Problems and Aspects of Breeding for Pest Resistance." 2nd World Consul. on For. Dis. and Insects, India, special paper.

Chapter 10

Vegetative Propagation

The use of vegetative propagation is rapidly increasing and is of vital importance to tree improvement. It always has been widely used for the preservation of genotypes in clone banks and for clonal seed orchard establishment. Currently there is an explosion of interest in using vegetative propagation in operational planting programs.

Vegetative propagation has been used successfully for several centuries by horticulturists, and much can be learned from them. The older horticultural practices as well as the new methodology are being increasingly applied in tree improvement programs (Toda, 1974; Rauter and Hood, 1980; Zobel, 1981). Actually, vegetative propagation has been employed in forestry for more than 100 years. There are records in the literature of using rooted cuttings of *Cryptomeria japonica* for planting during the nineteenth and twentieth centuries (Ono, 1882; Kanoo, 1919). Methods of rooting were developed much before that time, and commercial planting of cuttings has been standard practice for this species for many years. However, aside from a few genera like *Populus, Salix,* and *Cryptomeria,* vegetative propagation has not been used extensively in operational forest-planting programs.

This chapter will emphasize the status, value, and use of vegetative propagation in seed production and gene preservation, along with its use and potential in operational forest regeneration programs. Propagation methodology as such will not be covered in detail because it is now being rapidly developed. Much of this development has occurred during the past 5 years. Operational use of vegetative propagation is so new that there still are many questions about how best to employ it, but good progress is being made with southern pines (van Buijtenen et al., 1975), spruce (Birot and Nepveu, 1979; Rauter, 1979), radiata pine (Thulin and Faulds, 1968), *Eucalyptus* (Campinhos and Ikemori, 1980; Destremau et al., 1980) as well as with several other species. Some of the new studies and techniques have not yet been reported. Two helpful references are the series of papers that dealt with various aspects of vegetative propagation published by the Institute for Forest Improvement in Uppsala, Sweden (Anonymous, 1977) and *Micropropagation d'Arbres Forestiers* (Anonymous, 1979).

USES OF VEGETATIVE PROPAGATION

Vegetative propagation has many uses in forestry. These can be summarized as follows: (1) preservation of genotypes through use of clone banks; (2) multiplication of desired genotypes for special uses such as in seed orchards or breeding orchards; (3) evaluation of genotypes and their interaction with the environment through clonal testing; and (4) capture of maximum genetic gains when used for regeneration in operational planting programs.

Some persons prefer to separate the uses of vegetative propagation into research and operational (production) phases. These may be outlined as follows.

A. Research uses for vegetative propagation

1. Genetic evaluation of plant material, including genotype × environment interaction studies and estimating environmental and genetic correlations, such as juvenile and mature manifestations of the same characteristic.

2. Determine the magnitude and control of common environmental or C effects that are prevalent in some species.

3. Preserve genotypes and gene complexes in clone banks and arboreta for scientific purposes and for possible later use in operational programs.

4. Bring valuable plants to a centralized area, such as to a laboratory or greenhouse for intensive study and breeding.

5. Speed up the reproductive cycle for accelerated breeding and testing.

6. For nongenetic studies, to reduce genetic variability (or to obtain the information to handle it statistically) in experiments that will reduce "error variation."

B. Production (operational) uses of vegetative propagation

1. Develop seed orchards for operational seed production.

2. Use vegetative propagules directly in operational plantings.

The use of vegetative propagation in forestry will be increasing; it has become one of the most important tools of the tree improvement forester.

Except for a few genera, it is easier to apply regeneration through seed rather than to develop vegetative propagules. Yet, the effort toward vegetative propagation is being strongly sponsored in tree improvement (Fielding, 1963; Thulin, 1969; Libby, 1977; Campinhos and Ikemori, 1980). At present, tests about the comparative performance of vegetative propagules and seedlings are generally inadequate, although some studies list similarities and differences between rooted cuttings and seedlings in growth rate and form (Fielding, 1970; Sweet, 1972; Sweet and Wells, 1974; Roulund, 1978b; Jiang, 1982).

A complete and technical explanation about why vegetative propagation is desired for operational planting would be long, detailed, and complex. Simplified, the advantages of vegetative propagation are the following: (1) the potential to capture greater genetic gain; (2) the potential to obtain greater uniformity of the tree crop than is possible through seed regeneration; and (3) under some situations, the opportunity to speed up results from tree improvement activities.

Genetic variation is partitioned broadly into additive and nonadditive components. When seed regeneration is used, only the additive portion of the genetic variation can be manipulated by the tree improver, unless special efforts such as control pollinations to mass-produce desired seedlots or two-clone orchards are employed. For some characteristics, gains using seed regeneration will be large, but for others that contain significant amounts of nonadditive variance, such as certain growth characteristics, gains through seed production will only be a small portion of the potential that would be possible when vegetative propagation is used (Fielding, 1970). In general terms, the use of vegetative propagation makes it possible to *capture and transfer to the new tree* all of the genetic potential from the donor tree (Figure 10.1). For characteristics such as volume growth that have low narrow-sense heritabilities, it appears posible to more than double short-term genetic gain in many species by using vegetative propagules rather than seed regeneration.

Another advantage of vegetative propagation is the rapidity with which the desired genetic qualities of selected trees can be utilized. It is not necessary to wait for seed production before producing propagules for operational planting. As soon as tests of a tree have proven it to be a good genotype, it can be used directly in operational reforestation by employing vegetative propagation. This is especially true for the easy-to-root species like some in the genus *Populus* in which cuttings from older trees can be readily rooted. However, cuttings from physiologically mature trees of many species are difficult or impossible to root, as will be described later. In sprouting species, such as the eucalypts, the stump sprouts are physiologically juvenile; therefore, they root as juvenile material. However, it takes time to develop a "sprout nursery" that is necessary to produce the number

FIGURE 10.1

Shown are grafts of three greatly differing limb types of radiata pine in Zimbabwe. Any of the types desired could be used operationally when vegetative propagation methods are perfected. These grafts are used to illustrate how well different characteristics will be transferred to the new tree.

of cuttings needed for operational planting and, even under the best of conditions, it takes several years to develop the stock plants needed to supply the cuttings. For more difficult rooters, it is sometimes necessary to undertake expensive and involved procedures to enhance rooting ability. In many species, rooting ability can be maintained to keep the trees in a juvenile stage through methods such as hedging (Libby et al., 1972; van Buijtenen et al., 1975).

If vegetative propagules that grow well with good form at a reasonable cost can be produced, genetic gains and uniformity of growtth and wood properties will be greatly enhanced. Vegetative propagation should produce forests with the greatest possible uniformity in size, quality, and wood properties. Variability among trees is a major problem in forestry; use of vegetative reproduction will greatly help to overcome this difficulty.

METHODS OF VEGETATIVE PROPAGATION

There are many types of vegetative propagation (Hartman and Kester, 1983). However, this book on tree improvement will not cover them in detail. Several publications, such as those of Dormling et al. (1976) and Garner (1979), summarize the methodology. Several vegetative propagation methods have been developed especially for use in forestry.

The current emphasis on operational plantings has been on the use of rooted cuttings. Grafting is usually employed to preserve trees in clone banks or for seed orchards in which the objective is large-scale seed production. The newest vegetative propagation method that is receiving a lot of attention and publicity is tissue culture. Although considerble development is still necessary to make tissue culture operational (Durzan and Campbell, 1974; Zobel, 1977), it has considerable potential (McKeand, 1981).

It is important to have a broad understanding of the use, value, and problems of the different methods of vegetative propagation that are being used. Arguments always arise about which are best for regeneration programs. The only answer is to make comparative studies of them under similar, controlled conditions. Comparisons of vegetative propagules with seedlings for growth and form characteristics have been made by Copes (1977), Roulund (1978a, 1978b), and Birot and Nepveu (1979). Sometimes, grafts have more rapid initial growth than rooted cuttings or seedlings. Even when rooted cuttings and seedlings grow at the same rate, form can be quite different, with the cuttings usually having less taper, less butt swell, smaller limbs, and thinner bark (Libby and Hood, 1976). Generally, cuttings grow more slowly than seedlings. However, much depends on the age of the donor tree, how complete the root system of the rooted cutting is, and how the two were handled prior to outplanting.

There are a few terms used in relation to the different methods of vegetative propagation that are now used regularly in forestry and must be understood. The donor tree, the one from which the vegetative propagules have been taken, is called the *ortet*. Individual propagules from an ortet, or from other propagules from the ortet, are each called a *ramet*. The sum of the propagules arising from one ortet is referred to as a group as a *clone*. In forestry, these terms are being used loosely. As an example, it is common to refer to a grafted tree in a seed orchard as being clone ×. In fact, the grafted tree is a ramet of clone ×, which was originally obtained from ortet ×.

Grafts

Grafting has been used from the earliest times and is still used on a large scale to preserve and multiply desired genotypes (Dimpflmeier, 1954; Bouvarel, 1960). It is a basic tool for the horticulturist and has been used widely in forestry for clone preservation and seed orchard establishment. Methods of grafting are numerous; these are covered in many texts, among which are Hartmann and Kester (1983), Dorman (1976), Garner (1979), and documents such as that by Struve (1981). It is sometimes immaterial which method of grafting is used, although special methods have been developed for the very difficult conditions in field grafting in forestry where the environment cannot be controlled (Hoffmann, 1957; Webb, 1961). Some species, especially certain hardwoods, do not graft as easily as most conifers, and adjustments to the usual methods must be made to obtain a reasonable degree of sucess (Hatmaker and Taft, 1966). This is especially true for some oak species (*Quercus*), although seed orchards of oaks have been established (Enkova and Lylov, 1960; Farmer, 1981). Grafting in walnut has been widely developed, as has been explained by Beineke and Todhunter (1980).

Often, it is not poor grafting technique that results in failure, but rather the poor care given the scion or rootstock before or during grafting or in release following grafting. (The *scion* is the piece grafted that has been obtained from the ortet; the *rootstock* is the plant on which the graft is made.) Many more grafts are killed by poor management than by incorrect grafting per se. Methods worked out for the southern pines, where grafting success has climbed from "mediocre" to above 90%, have been described by Dorman (1976).

A major problem with grafting is incompatibility between the stock and the scion (Hong, 1975). Because incompatibility is strongly clonal, it has a major effect on tree improvement programs through loss of clones, especially in such species as Douglas fir (Duffield and Wheat, 1964). Nearly all species show incompatibility to some extent (see Burgess, 1973, for eucalypts). For most species it is an inconvenience, but one can work around it. For example, about 20% of the grafts made in loblolly pine seed orchards show some degree of incompatibility. Loss of whole clones can be a serious result when the lost clone happens to be one of the best genotypes. A series of studies has been made about the cause and possible control of incompatibility (Corte, 1968; Copes, 1969, 1970; Lantz, 1973; Slee and Spidy, 1970; McKinley, 1975). Good results have been obtained in overcoming or avoiding graft incompatibility in species like Douglas fir (Copes, 1981). Graft incompatibility is a problem that must be circumvented as much as possible, or avoided entirely by use of other methods of vegetative propagation. Only rarely is graft incompatibility so serious that it makes a program inoperative.

There are several different types of incompatibility, each with differing symptoms, that can be recognized with experience and careful observation. The most common incompatibility symptom is a swelling above the point of grafting and a *scion overgrowth* of the rootstock caused by blockage of the phloem; this is commonly referred to as a *saddle overgrowth* (Figures 10.2 and 10.3). Saddle overgrowth sometimes appears during the first or second year following grafting in pines, but often it does not become evident until the fourth or fifth year, or even later. Foliage abnormalities are usually evident before the actual overgrowth can be seen with the needles or leaves, including those of the current year, usually being small with brown tips. In most conifers, abundant resin exudation is evident

FIGURE 10.2

Although graft incompatibility is best known for the pines and Douglas fir, it occurs in most species. Shown is an incompatible *Eucalyptus* in Minas Gerais, Brazil, with the dramatic swelling, or saddle overgrowth, above the graft. Incompatibility is so severe in a few species that it precludes an efficient use of grafts for seed orchard use.

FIGURE 10.3

Typical incompatibility is shown for loblolly pine. There is a saddle overgrowth above the graft union (*a*). Often the union at point of graft is poor as is shown by the peeled specimen (*b*). It should be noted that the roots of the graft were below the knot.

on the foliage. The needles in pines often group themselves parallel to the branch and become sparse, giving the tree a distinctive abnormal appearance. Often there is an accompanying general yellowing or graying of the foliage. One almost certain sign of incompatibility, which is accompanied by the abnormal foliage, is the presence of excessively heavy flower production. In loblolly and slash pines, a 1- or 2-year-old graft that produces abundant male flowers is usually incompatible, although this is not necessarily true for early flowering species such as Virginia pine. The saddle-type incompatibility is strongly clonal, and it usually results in the death of the grafted tree within a few years. Among individual clones, from very few to as many as 100% of the ramets may show incompatibility.

Death of large grafts with *no overgrowth* appears to result from a different type of incompatibility. This form is less common and can appear on all ramets of a single clone throughout an orchard at about the same time. Affected trees die rapidly, particularly in association with extreme environmental conditions such as heat and drought. Like the overgrowth type, damage is quite clonal, and it is not unusual for nearly every graft of the affected clone to die.

In some pines an unusual cambial growth exists (usually restricted to the understock) that results in incompatibility with bark ridges and dead zones, a condition that is usually referred to as *fluted bark*. The cause of this abnormality is not known. A pathological condition has been suspected, as have been deficiencies or excesses in nutrients, but these have never been confirmed. Adverse soil conditions seemed to be a causative factor because damage appears to be most

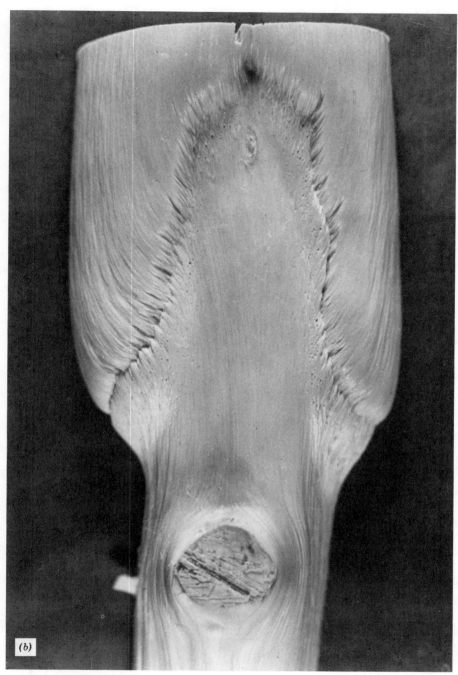

(b)

FIGURE 10.3 (*continued*)

prevalent on heavy clay soils, showing up most frequently following severe droughts. Deep, drastic subsoiling and heavy nitrogen fertilizaton has helped to correct, or at least arrest, the fluted bark condition in several pine orchards. Fluted bark has a clonal tendency that is related to the scion used (even though the abnormality is in the understock), but the tendency is not so strong clonally as are the most standard incompatibilities. Infected trees have leader dieback, with sparse, graying, or yellow foliage that sheds early; the needles of the pines are strongly appressed to the branches. Such trees may live for many years and, while alive, produce exceedingly heavy seed crops. Seeds produced on incompatible grafts often are weak or are not viable.

Rooted Cuttings

The method of vegetative propagation that is currently being developed most rapidly is *rooted cuttings*. This technique has been in use for some species for a long time (Ozawa, 1904). Methods and techniques are many, and information about them can be obtained from the books previously mentioned in the section on grafting and from numerous articles such as the following: Yim (1962), Wheat (1964), Hare (1970), Brix and Barker (1971), Hinesley and Blazich (1981), and Pousujja (1981). The rapid developments in just the past few years in the eucalypts (Franclet, 1963; Hartney, 1980; Laplace and Quillet, 1980) show what can be done to develop and use rooted cuttings in a short time (Figure 10.4). Progress with the eucalypts may well indicate what might happen in many other species. It is only a matter of time before several of the principal conifers (Cameron, 1968) and some hardwoods will be planted operationally as rooted cuttings, but much technological development is still needed for most species. As an example, great progress is being made on spruce (Rauter, 1979).

A major deterrent to using rooted cuttings is their dependency on age. Young trees will often root readily, but the same trees may be almost impossible to root when they become older. This is particularly frustrating to the tree improver who works with proven desirable genotypes. When the trees are left to grow long enough to prove their genetic worth, it is then often too late to root them. As mentioned previously, there are indications that trees that are vegetatively propagated from older individuals will grow more slowly than those taken from younger trees (Talbert et al., 1982).

Another major restriction to the use of rooted cuttings from older trees is that the propagules sometimes do not grow into a normal tree form; this concept is covered in a later section in this chapter on *abnormal growth*.

A deterrent to making maximum gains using rooted cuttings in operational planting is the very large clonal variability in rooting ability; this is especially strong in older individuals. Variation in rooting ability often dictates what trees are available to the research or applied program (Hyun, 1967; Shelbourne and Thulin, 1974; Kleinschmit and Schmidt, 1977). Clonal variation in rooting occurs, no matter what method is employed. The percentage of clones that propagate satisfactorily is so vital and sometimes so low that it is difficult to keep a sufficiently broad genetic base, and in some species so few parent trees respond well enough to rooting that an initially broad genetic potential may be reduced to an alarming degree. If one selects or develops 100 outstanding trees but only 10 of these root well enough to use operationally, the effectiveness of the tree improvement program will be greatly limited. Improved techniques will help to some extent, but losses of large numbers of otherwise excellent genotypes are one of the most serious obstacles to the operational use of rooted cuttings. Satisfactory rooting percentages will vary with species and the needs of the organization involved. As an example, for *Eucalyptus* in Aracruz, Brazil, a 75% rooting is considered minimal for use in the planting program (*Campinhos and Ikemori, 1980*).

There is no question that the use of rooted cuttings will become operational on a large scale in forestry; the actual time will depend on how quickly methodology is perfected. The key to success is the development of methods to bypass age, growth, and form problems. The hope is that researchers will learn to treat proven older trees so that they revert to the juvenile condition. In some species, mostly confined to the hardwoods, the sprouts formed following cutting or injuring the tree are juvenile; therefore, the age problem is bypassed. The ability to sprout and thus root as juvenile material is used on a large scale in some eucalypts.

Rooting Needle Fascicles

The method of taking needle fascicles of pine and rooting them has been used for a long time (Zak and McAlpine, 1957; Hoffman and Kummerov, 1966). A moderate amount of work has been done in the intervening years, as has been summarized by Girovard (1971), and interest has grown recently (Struve, 1980). Initially, rooting of needle fascicles was sometimes successful, but shoots often did not develop normally. With more knowledge and better use of chemicals and hormones, this problem has become less severe, and balanced plants can be produced.

The original idea that appealed so greatly to tree improvement workers was the opportunity to get a large number of propagules from an individual tree. Prospects appear good now, but it is too early to predict how successful the use of needle fascicles will be on an operational scale. The objective of increasing numbers is still of importance, but current interest has centered on being able to produce vegetative propagules from needle fascicles with juvenile characteristics from older trees that have already proven their genetic worth.

Air Layers

The process of air layering is one in which roots are generated on an intact branch by girdling, which is usually accompanied by hormone application (Kadambi and Dabral, 1954; Hoekstra, 1957; Chonard and Parrot, 1958). A similar process that occurs naturally in some species is called *layering*; this is when roots are formed on branches that touch or become buried in the soil (Cooper, 1911).

Air layering has several uses. One is to produce propagules directly that are needed to establish seed orchards and thus avoiding graft incompatibility (Barnes,

(a)

FIGURE 10.4

The stages in rooting cuttings of *Eucalyptus* in Espirito Santo, Brazil, are shown. Sprouts from a stump that will be used for cuttings (*a*). A rooted cutting ready for field planting (*b*). A commercial planting of rooted cuttings that have been in the field for several months (*c*). (Photos courtesy Aracruz Florestal, Espirito Santo, Brazil.)

1969). It is quite satisfactory for some species in which needs for rooted propagules are small. It is also sometimes used as an intermediate method to obtain roots for species in which rooted cutting success is marginal. This is done to *P. caribaea* in Venezuela. The air layers are detached after callus information and rooted in conventional beds with a good degree of success.

Tissue and Organ Culture

Tissue culture is the newest and currently the most publicized of the vegetative propagation methods. Because the method is developing so very rapidly, any discussion will soon be out of date. Tissue culture has great potential, but it must

FIGURE 10.4 (*Continued*)

be viewed realistically (Rediske, 1976; Zobel, 1977; Sommer and Brown, 1979; Bonga, 1980). For example, the uniformity of individuals within clones of identical genetic makeup are sometimes quite dissimilar, often showing as much variability as seedlings from individual seeds from a given tree. Also, it is difficult to move the plantlets from the environment in which they are formed so they will grow normally under the uncontrolled forest conditions. Using current methods, tissue culture plantlets are expensive because of the multiple handling that is now required. With time, however, new technology should reduce this problem.

A number of books and articles have been written about tissue culture production (see Mott, 1981, for a review and references). The major concerns with tissue culture are now being vigorously studied, and it is clear that much more research and development are needed before propagation by tissue culture will be satisfactory for operational use (Kelly, 1978; Leach, 1979; Amerson et al., 1981). It is especially important to produce plantlets that are essentially uniform within a clone before tissue culture will be of value for operational plantings. This is the case because plant uniformity is one of the major attractions of vegetative propagation.

The best immediate use for tissue culture will be as a research tool and as a rapid method of utilizing improved genetic stock (McKeand, 1981). Whether tissue culture plantlets will be important for operational planting depends on the "unknowns" listed previously. After the methodology is better developed, including transfer to field conditions, then uniformity will undoubtedly increase. Once that happens, the major job will be to make the system cost-effective. Utility of tissue culture plantlets will depend on their relative growth and form compared to other kinds of vegetative propagules and seedlings. To be of most value, it will be necessary to produce plantlets from older, previously tested, and proven trees.

ABNORMAL GROWTH

Plagiotropic and Orthotropic Response

A major problem that occurs when working with vegetative propagules is that genetically identical propagules often grow differently, depending on their origin on the original plant and the age of the donor when the propagule is taken. *Plagiotropic growth* refers to the situation in which a vegetative propagule *does not assume tree form* but continues to grow like a branch. *Orthotropic* means the propagule assumes an upright or normal tree form. Causes for propagules growing differently, even though they are "genetically identical," are many and will only be mentioned here briefly. They involve age, location on the tree, and other environmental effects. The differential in growth and development when plagiotropism is present is very frustrating. The common idea that cuttings from a tree are genetically identical and therefore they should grow alike is misleading. The cuttings *are* identical in the sense that they have the same genotype. Obviously, some genes are more effective than others, or they may be "turned on" or "turned off" by the environment, age, and position within the parent plant or by outside treatment; this will in turn affect the physiology of the tree. As a result, propagules sometimes do not grow in the same pattern, or they may not have the same tree form, even though they are genetically identical. Plagiotropic growth is common in such genera as *Abies, Picea, Araucaria,* and *Sequoia,* and it is found to a lesser extent in *Pseudotsuga.* Plagiotropism is not common in *Pinus* or in most hardwoods.

The Effect of Age and Location Where Propagules Are Obtained

The major problems in operational (and research) uses of vegetative propagules relate to the effect of the age (Ducci and Locci, 1978) and location of the propagule from the parent plant and its ability to grow as a tree.

Age differences are highly important. As Franclet (1979) has written, "There is a progressive loss with age of the aptitude for vegetative propagation." Physiologically mature tissue has a lower rooting percentage, takes longer to initiate roots, and develops fewer roots than does physiologically juvenile material. In addition, plagiotropic growth often occurs.

The term *cyclophysis* is sometimes applied to age effects and *topophysis* to location on origin effects. These are serious problems in some species (Jang et al., 1980), but studies indicate that solutions may become available. Although many physiologists consider them to be related (often using the term *topophysis*), Corriveau (1974) and Olesen (1978) consider cyclophsis and topophysis as two separate processes. Olesen defines them as follows: (1) *cyclophysis* is the process of maturation of the apical meristem; and (2) *topophysis* is the phenomenon that occurs when scions, buddings, and rooted cuttings maintain for some time the branchlike growth habit (plagiotropic growth) they had as shoots on the ortet. A third cause of variation is *periphysis,* which refers to locations in different environments, such as shade and sun shoots on an individual tree.

Although the concepts of cyclophysis and topophysis are widely recognized (Naes-Schmidt and Soegaard, 1960; Wright, 1976; Land, 1977), their effects are not always understood. They include not only growth variation but also unseen physiological and morphological changes. It is clear that problems with topophysis can be reduced and the use of vegetative propagation increased if juvenile material can be used or if rejuvenation from the mature to the juvenile stage can be accomplished. Juvenile material tends to assume orthotropic growth habits much more readily than mature material.

Methods of developing juvenility (Franclet, 1979) or maintaining juvenility by methods such as hedging (Libby et al., 1972; Libby and Hood, 1976; Brix and van Driessche, 1977) are essential to further developments for operational planting of vegetative propagules (Figure 10.5). The utility of root sprouts or sprouts from adventitious buds in developing juvenility is known, but only a few studies have been done on pines that sprout Santamour, 1965). This may have a major value if these sprouts have juvenile characteristics like the eucalypts, because several of the most important tropical pine species do sprout rather profusely. In some

FIGURE 10.5

To overcome or bypass the poor rooting and often poor form on cuttings from old trees, the method hedging is being developed. It consists of trimming the tree and keeping it low. This is shown for radiata pine in New Zealand. Cuttings from the hedged plants tend to maintain their young physiological age. (Photo courtesy of Mike Wilcox, Forest Research Institute, New Zealand.)

species, such as red maple (*Acer rubrum*), rooted cuttings obtained from grafts respond as though they are juvenile, even though the original graft came from an old tree.[1] This ability of cuttings taken from grafts to root readily is a great advantage in some hardwood species, especially those that do not sprout from the stump.

Rejuvenation of mature clones sometimes occurs during the tissue culture process. This phenomenon could become of great value once it is better understood and more reliable. Cell culture, leading to embryoids that can be coated and treated like seeds, though not yet well developed or operational, could be a most

[1]Personal communication from Dr. Dan Struve, Horticulture Department, Ohio State University, Columbus.

important contribution to the use of vegetative propagation in forestry. With current technology, systems involved with the mass production of rooted cuttings of loblolly pine would be easier to devise if rejuvenation of mature genotypes was possible (Foster et al., 1981). An example is that needle fascicles of loblolly pine cultured *in vitro* often form adventitious buds in the basal region of the fascicles at the juncture of the needles (Mehra-Palta et al., 1977). It is highly probable that these are in fact juvenile buds and can be cultured, using the techniques of Mott and Amerson (1981) to produce shoots and roots. As pointed out by Lyrene (1981), reversion from mature to juvenile characteristics may be a general phenomenon of tissue culture.

Although loss of rooting potential and sexual maturity tend to occur at about the same age, they do not appear to be strongly related to each other. Sexual maturity is usually retained following vegetative propagation, whether or not a juvenile state for rooting occurs. It is sometimes possible, especially in hardwoods, to induce good rooting from heavily flowering, vegetatively produced trees.

In many trees, especially the hardwoods, there is a "cone of juvenility" near the base of the tree that retains juvenility (de Muckadell, 1954). This can be observed on *Quercus* and *Fagus* at the time of leaf fall, when the lower leaves in the juvenile area are retained longer than are the mature leaves higher up. Cuttings taken from this area are much easier to root than those taken from the branches in the mature area of the tree.

VEGETATIVE PROPAGATION AND TREE IMPROVEMENT

Vegetative propagation is used for species in the genera *Populus, Salix, Eucalyptus, Cryptomeria, Sequoia, Picea,* and a few others. Methods for the first four genera are known and fully operational, while that for *Picea* is becoming used more widely (Figure 10.6). The major criticism of current programs is not in methodology of vegetative propagation per se but in the lack of ongoing breeding programs to produce better trees for the vegetative regeneration program. Although some organizations have genetic improvement programs combined with their vegetative regeneration, most do not. Many merely select within natural stands or plantations or produce F_1 hybrids from which to choose superior genotypes. Hybrids are usually little better than the parents used, and a genetics program to improve the parents before new hybrids are made is essential for long-term gain if hybrids are to be utilized in tree improvement programs using vegetative propagation.

With the exception of *Cryptomeria* in Japan, the vegetative propagation programs with most conifers are just getting started. Good initial gains will be possible by using outstanding genotypes from current stands, but this is not enough, and new and improved trees need to be developed. It is not recommended that a lot of time and money be spent on developing sophisticated

FIGURE 10.6

Great improvements in wood quality, growth, and uniformity are possible with rooted cuttings. Shown are 3-year-old plantations of *Eucalyptus* at Aracruz Florestal in Brazil. Trees are about 65 ft tall (20.2 m) and uniform in height by clone (*a*). Note how uniform in diameter each 3-year-old tree from 1 clone is (*b*).

vegetative propagation techniques unless there is a parallel intensive genetic improvement program.

The use of vegetative propagules has a special place in forestry; it should be used for high-value products or on sites where there is a special need. For example, if a certain kind of wood is desired, it can often be supplied by vegetative propagules, even though it may be necessary to restrict the genetic base to fill this special need. Many eucalypts have interlocked grain or wood that is under internal stresses that cause splitting when the trees are felled. Occasional trees are straight grained without internal stress and make fine high-quality plywood or furniture. The few clones with suitable wood can be used to supply the special need for *Eucalyptus* with high-quality wood. Often, disease-free trees produce disease-free rooted cuttings; a prime example is *Diaporthe cubensis* on *Eucalyptus* in Brazil. The same special usage of vegetative propagules could be made to produce trees with other special, uniform, or otherwise desirable qualities (see Figure 10.6).

Although not generally operational, studies on rooting cuttings for some quality hardwoods in the southeastern United States have been done on sweetgum (*Liquidamber styraciflua*) by Brown and McAlpine (1964); on black walnut (*Juglans nigra*) by Carpenter (1975); on black cherry *(Prunus serotina)* by Farmer and Basemann (1975); on sugar maple (*Acer saccharum*) by Gabriel et al. (1961); and on yellow poplar (*Liriodendron tulipifera*) by McAlpine and Kormanik (1972). Several of the authors mentioned feel that vegetative propagation in hardwoods can be developed operationally, and there is no doubt of its value for the species with high-quality woods, such as in some of the tropical hardwoods (Lee and Rao, 1980).

OPERATIONAL USE OF VEGETATIVE PROPAGATION

All kinds of genetic advantages as well as problems could be listed that are relative to the operational use of vegetative propagation. If one brings all considerations to a common denominator, they add up to "gain versus risk;" that is, how much extra gain can be achieved through vegetative propagation while still retaining an acceptable level of risk? This basic question is widely argued, but conclusions are rare because of differing emphases on the relative risks by the various investigators and sometimes because of a lack of knowledge about achievable gains. It is not important to come to a concensus. What is important is to be aware of the gains and risks and to make a conscious decision about their relative importance before an operational vegetative-propagation program is undertaken. The decision is not simply one of biology but includes operations and policy. Thus, the silviculturist, forest manager, and administrator must all share in any decision that is made.

The first concern that is always raised is that of the danger of planting large acreages with the same or similar genotypes. Many persons decry planting large acreages of trees of the same species, which to them represents a dangerous monoculture, no matter how variable the genotypes are that are planted (Anderson, 1975). This very real problem is often blown out of perspective when it is being argued. On the other hand, some persons cite agriculture and its widespread use of crops with very narrow genetic bases with outstanding success to society as reasons why there should be little objection. (Monocultures are covered in the following section.)

A common mistake made by some foresters is to assume that members of a clone will be adapted only to a narrow range of environmental conditions. Although clones are usually less broadly adapted than mixtures of full- or half-sibs and even though each member of a clone has the same genotype, the individual genotype can possess a considerable ability for adaptation to differing pests or to adverse environments. It is possible to select clones that possess greater adaptability than that possessed by the average seedling. A forest tree needs great adaptability merely to survive and to reproduce. The danger for planting large areas with a single clone arises when the adaptability of the clonal genotype is exceeded by adverse conditions. The result will then be that *all* trees of the clone will be subject to injury in the adverse environment. Trees seem to be less well buffered to attacks by pests than to weather extremes, especially to pests that have come from outside the natural range of the tree species.

How Many Clones Should Be Used?

The problem of what is a suitable clone number for extensive field planting is always of importance, but it is especially true when vegetative propagules are used. There is no absolute answer, although a good estimate can be made that is based on experience and knowledge of the variation in the species used. The question again relates to "gain versus risk," that is, how can one achieve the greatest improvements by selecting only the best clones while staying within acceptable limits of the danger of destructive losses in the forest? Usually, biologists are timid and they sacrifice too much gain to be certain they take little risk, whereas financially oriented people often emphasize gain to the point of real danger from destruction by pests or adverse environments. Realistically, some risk is always involved in any breeding program, but when one knows the species well the risk can be kept low.

The important question relating to how many clones are necessary to assure reasonable safety and to make optimal gain is usually answered as, "It all depends on rotation age, on intensity of forest management, on genetic variability of the species and clones involved, the likely risks and the acceptable loss levels" (Libby, 1981). But this answer needs to be defined better. It is unlikely that hundreds of clones would be required, as the more cautious advise, and there is no question that a single clone, as has been suggested by a few specialists, will not be safe. As a generalized guide, Libby's (1981) recommendation that 7 to 30 clones be used would appear to be a safe and reasonable number.

In an area in South America in which Zobel is involved, about 600 outstanding clones of *Eucalyptus* have been selected. The trees are fast growing and variable with a 6- to 8-year rotation. It was found (Zobel et al., 1982) that the best 100 clones could nearly double the gain, compared to the situation if all 600 clones had been used. The area has six different districts, some of which have quite different environments. The best 15 clones to be used in each district are being determined by testing. The same clones were not best in all environments, and it was found that about a total of 50 clones was needed. For the eucalypts, with their variability and short rotations of 5 to 6 years, there is no unusual danger by using the best 15 clones in each environment.

Generally, the more severe the stress a given species or provenance may face (i.e., they are poorly adapted to the environment), the greater the number of clones that should be used. There are special conditions, such as severe insect or disease areas or very severe environments, in which very few clones may be justified. This is because only a few that have the needed qualities are available. This short-term and rather risky strategy becomes necessary when only those few that will survive such things as freezing weather or disease must be used if the forest is to be productive.

Before vegetatively propagated clones are used for operational regeneration, they need to be tested in all the major environments of the proposed planting area. Ultimately, all the potentially good clones need to be tested on each different site. The best clones for each soil site area should then be used to reforest the area. Not all clones will be suitable for all sites. Because of site × genotype interaction, different clones will often be used on different planting sites. Overlooking this refinement, as is too often done, can lead to significant losses or even to disaster.

How Should the Clones Be Deployed?

Closely related to the number of clones that should be used is their deployment; that is, should they be planted randomly and intermixed, or should they be planted in small blocks of pure clones? This was argued as early as 1918 by Hirasiro, who felt mixtures of clones were the best.

The immediate reaction of most specialists is that clones should be planted in mixture. They argue that mixtures will be better safeguards against pest attack and spread, and thus they will provide some measure of insurance for success of the plantings. This is true for root diseases, but it is not necessarily so for airborne diseases and many insects. Leaf diseases or canker diseases carried by windborne spores seem to spread about equally rapidly in pure or mixed-species stands. Some persons argue against the superiority of multiclonal plantings. For example, the analysis of Libby (1981) indicates that mosaics of monoclonal plantings may be the best strategy. What follows are some arguments that have been given in favor of block planting.

1. Each clone tends to have a different growth curve and developmental pattern. Some clones will never be able to develop properly in mixture and will be severely suppressed by competition from other faster-starting clones.

At the very least there will be differences in size and quality of trees in the intermixed plantings, reducing one of the greatest advantages from vegetative propagation, that is, greater uniformity.

2. Planting and "nursery" operations are much simplified when planting is done by blocks.

3. Wood uniformity among trees is maximum within a block of trees from the same clone. The time will probably come when trees of different blocks will be used for special products, such as plywood or sawtimber.

4. If a really serious problem develops within a given clone, a whole block can be harvested and replaced to keep the forest in maximum productivity. Even if it was possible to salvage an individual clone in mixtures, it could not be replaced, and the result would be a forest with low stocking. Generally, salvage from mixtures is not economically feasible, and often the salvage operation causes more damge to the residuals than the net return from the salvage operation.

Although opinions about clonal distribution have changed over the years, most of the published literature indicates a preference for multiclonal mixtures. This controversy must be settled through trials rather than by the expression of opinions. However, some large operations are currently following the approach of maximizing gains by block plantings. For species with reasonable variability and short-rotation ages, the recommendations have been for 10- to 20-ha monoclonal blocks of vegetatively propagated material. Many persons feel these are too large; however, anything much smaller than 10 ha becomes inefficient to operate as a unit. With more experience, this recommendation may well change, but with what is now known it appears that 10- to 20-ha blocks are about right.

Special Considerations in the Use of Vegetative Propagation

A great danger in using vegetative propagation is to assess the worth of the "parent" tree at too young an age, or to assess the value of the cuttings or plantlets before they have had a chance to show their worth. This is especially true for growth characteristics. The time frame for testing vegetative propagules should be little different from that of seedling genetic tests. Time can be shortened, however, if the clones are from families that have already been progeny tested. Although there are occasional reports of good juvenile–mature correlations for volume growth, most of the literature for most species indicates that a reliable estimate of mature performance of individual genotypes cannot be obtained until about one-half rotation age (Wakeley, 1971; Franklin, 1979). Lambeth (1979) feels that for a 30-year rotation, an assessment at 6 to 8 years of age is the most economical time to select. This is not the place to argue this most important concept, but those who have had widespread experience with a number of species *over a long period of time* are disturbed about bad decisions that are currently being made from too early assessments regarding the genetic superiority of trees used in vegetative propagation programs. From the production standpoint, there is such an advantage in having physiologically young material, but foresters too often assume that if the tree is superior when very young it will still be superior at rotation age. This enables them to vegetatively propagate young material. A too-early assessment probably is the most serious error being made when vegetative propagation is used operationally. The error is not easily observed, no matter what the rotation age, although it is more evident under long-rotation conditions.

Although it is evident to biologists that a good phenotype may or may not produce a good plant when it is vegetatively propagated, many persons assume that a good-looking tree will automatically produce good cuttings or other propagules. Many organizations do not even make tests, and they assume that propagules from a good-looking parent will produce good trees.

Rarely has any consideration been given in the clonal use of forest trees to "within-clone" variation that may show up after several generations of propagation. This is common in horticulture, showing up as decreased rooting ability, form and growth degradation, or reduction in flowering. These can result from such things as virus infections, unexplainable internal physiological changes, or simply by root deformation (Figure 10.7). The horticulturists have observed such

FIGURE 10.7

Sometimes lack of uniformity within clones is caused by root deformation that is a result from the handling of the propagules in containers. Results of such deformation are shown on the roots of a grafted tree.

clonal degradation to be common; they establish "foundation stocks" where true-to-type pest-free plants are maintained. Foresters must be on the alert for such late-appearing within-clone variabilities as well as for occasional somatic mutations that do occur. These can be especially dangerous in seed orchards in which many ramets are produced from a given graft.

Another general concept that must be considered with respect to vegetative propagation is the cost of vegetative propagules versus seedlings. Usually, vegetative propagules are much more expensive to produce and are more difficult to establish than are seedlings. As methods are developed and experience is gained, costs of vegetative propagules can be reduced greatly (Kleinschmit and Schmidt, 1977) and even be no greater than seedlings (Campinhos and Ikemori, 1980). Cost comparisons alone are really not useful because one must weigh the added gains against the costs. Often, a considerable additional cost per planted tree becomes insignificant when assessed on a cost-per-acre and gain-per-acre basis. For example, just a couple of percentage points of improvement resulting from using the better cuttings can often more than justify a doubling or tripling of cost of the propagules established in the field.

RESTRICTING THE GENETIC BASE AND MONOCULTURE

Although the subject of the breadth of the gene base has been touched on in many places in this book, perhaps the most suitable time to discuss it is in relation to vegetative propagation, because genetic restriction can be at its most extreme in this area.

What Is Monoculture?

There is much misunderstanding about the meaning of monoculture and its potentials and problems. There is no universally accepted understanding of what monoculture means. Basically, the very broad definition in Webster,[2] "cultivation of a single crop or product without using the land for other purposes," must be accepted. This definition has been altered by some biologists as follows: "growing extensive areas of plants that are closely related genetically." The important question related to the biological definition is, How close is closely related? For example, Glasgow (1975) interprets monoculture as raising even-aged stands of one or a very limited number of species in blocks large enough to have a significant ecological impact. On the other hand, Feret (1975) feels that planting a single species does not necessarily predicate monoculture; it all depends on how uniform the species is. The understanding of monoculture by many tree improvers is as follows: "extensive plantings of similar genotypes of forest trees that are

---

[2]*Webster's New Twentieth Century Dictionary.* Unabridged 2nd ed., 1980.

homogeneous enough so that the dangers from pests or environmental extremes become too great a risk."

Using Webster's definition of monoculture as being a single crop or product carries no connotation of *good* or *bad* and is not closely tied to genetic uniformity. Therefore, growing sawtimber on a given area of land would constitute a monoculture, even if more than one species was involved. In fact, most of the biologists' or foresters' special definitions that relate to a restriction of the gene base really refer to the intensity of silviculture on land management being used, not to monoculture as it was originally defined. According to Webster's definition, nearly every forest tree plantation would be a monoculture, neither inherently good nor bad.

Whether or not the term *monoculture* is used, the tree improver must be concerned about the increase in risk resulting from reducing the genetic base in forest plantations. The variability of the base population from which the trees have been obtained is highly important. For example, plantings from most seed orchards in which selections have been restricted to one per stand have a broad gene base for adaptability and are not as restricted genetically as collections from a few individual trees from a single stand. The most extreme form of gene base reduction is the establishment of large monoclonal plantings that has both great advantages and dangers in forestry. In truth, arguments about what constitutes a monoculture are useless. It is the status of the gene base that is important (Zobel, 1972). According to Webster, even-aged management can be called a monoculture, but whether or not it is a risk depends on the heterogeneity of the gene base involved.

A question that is often raised is whether true monocultures occur in nature. Using Webster's definition, they are usual, whereas in the biological sense they are rare. Monoculturelike populations may be prevalent in some species like *P. resinosa* that seem to have a very restricted gene base (Fowler, 1961). Restricted gene bases certainly occur in some of the sprouting species, such as the aspens (*Populus* sp.), where rather extensive areas can be populated with all the trees being the same clone, growing on the same root system (Baker, 1934).

Restricting the Genetic Base

The idea of growing forest trees with relatively similar genotypes over large areas is a cause of considerable concern among foresters (Tucker, 1975). It is interesting how many of the same people will look over an agricultural field with millions of plants of nearly identical genotypes and not feel much concern. Part of the reason for this difference is the relative ease with which environments can be manipulated and controlled in the two situations. Compared with forestry, environmental manipulation is much easier, more flexible, and economically justifiable in agriculture, making it possible to control those factors that can cause catastrophic losses of similar genotypes. As forest management is intensified, the forester will move in the same general direction of greater environmental control. But no matter how well people try to manage the environment in forestry, nature will usually prevail, and stressful conditions will always be encountered for the tree crop. When the planted trees have similar genotypes, as when only a few clones are used, a catastrophic loss can occur, resulting in many years of cumulative productivity loss if the trees are not yet old enough to salvage. When a catastrophe occurs in agriculture and the crop is damaged or lost, adjustments can be made and the farmer can start again the next season. The agriculturist usually grows a crop for only a short period during the year in which the environment is optimal for crop development. But in forestry the plants must survive for many years throughout all seasons, giving a much greater chance for an unusual happenstance to damage or destroy the tree crop. Also, it takes much longer for a forester to locate, develop, and use new genetic material.

If the genetic base in forestry is narrowed, the possibility for losses will become greater. Although yields are enhanced, the forester must come to grips with the following question: How much risk of death or loss of yield or quality can be tolerated for a given amount of additional product uniformity, volume, or quality? This complex question will be answered differently by different people and organizations; a major point to be stressed is that such a decision will be easier if proper attention has been paid to keeping the genetic makeup of the forest trees used in regeneration broad enough to avoid or reduce losses.

An example of restricting the gene base and its ramifications in an operational forestry program were mentioned in the discussion related to vegetative propagation. But the problem also arises with the use of seeds. For example, one large company in the southeastern United States plants seedlings by mother tree blocks. This company collects seeds by mother tree, grows seedlings in the nursery by mother tree, and outplants in 20-ha blocks by mother tree for all of its approximately 12,000 ha per year planting program. The program started with about 40 seed orchard parents; when in short supply, seed were collected from the best 30 clones. As seed became more abundant, the total annual acreage was planted with seed from fewer clones until now they use the seven best open-pollinated families. Such planting of seed from seed orchards by clone (mother tree) appears to be most successful after 6 years and has shown some obvious advantages. Many arguments have been offered both in favor and against this degree of genetic restriction. It is a major problem that will be faced by all programs as improved seed become plentiful. The question is how much risk is involved to obtain the additional gain resulting from restricting the number of clones in the seed orchard in order to use only the best to obtain maximum gain.

Dangers of a Restricted Genetic Base

Two categories of problems can result from an interaction of an adverse environmental condition or pest attack and a restricted genetic base. The first is death or severe damage; this is easily understood and recognized. Indeed, most persons equate the adverse effects of gene restriction only in such grossly observable terms when death results. The second kind of adverse effect results in a reduction in growth and vigor; this often goes unnoticed, except by the keen observer, but can be of considerably more importance than outright kill. Assessment of this kind of damage is exceptionally difficult. Often, the loss is ignored or even accepted with the general comment that "I'd rather have unhealthy Species X than healthy Species Y because X still produces more volume." The insidious aspect of planting trees with poor adaptability is that the blame is often placed on a secondary causative factor, such as insects or fungal infection, rather than on the primary cause, which is poor adaptability of the plant to the environment.

Extreme care must be taken not to equate problems arising from using the wrong species or the wrong geographic source of a species to losses from genetic restriction related to monoculture. Use of the wrong species or geographic source can be avoided with proper understanding and care. Problems such as those resulting from using Monterey pine in the southeastern United States or in central Brazil were caused by a lack of species adaptability, not because of the common belief that the trees were planted as a "monoculture." Likewise, poor growth or even death of an eastern source of douglas fir planted in the western Cascade Mountain range of Washington should fall under the category of *carelessness* but not be blamed on the adverse effects of monoculture. The trees would have grown no better if they had been mixed with other seed sources. *The concern with so-called monoculture* by the tree improver must be *related to the dangers from reducing the genetic potential of an otherwise well-adapted species that may result from a tree-breeding program and development of improved strains.*

The danger from growing restricted genotypes of forest trees over large acreages hardly needs to be documented. Disasters from using certain *Cryptomeria* or *Populus* clones have been both of the dramatic and insidious types. Kills of large stands have occasionally occurred, whereas decline of stands wth resultant slowdown in growth caused by changing environments or attack by pests have been quite common. Examples of troubles in sexually propagated stands have been less commonly documented, probably because most are of the insidious type; however, losses are more widespread than is usually recognized. The difficult job is to assess accurately whether the death or decline is simply a result of offsite planting or has been caused by a narrowed genetic base.

How Much Can the Genetic Base Be Reduced?

The most severe restriction of the genetic base occurs with vegetative propagation, a situation in which one or a few superior genotypes is planted over large acreages. It is not unusual to find members of one clone destroyed or damaged by diseases, insects, cold, or drought while another apparently similar clone remains healthy. Few foresters will argue about the danger of using a single clone, and warnings against such a practice have been sounded for many years.

Reduction of the gene base may also be a problem with sexually propagated trees. The real problem facing the forester working with sexually propagated trees is to determine what constitutes a "too restricted genetic base" that can become "too great a risk." Is it necessary to leave mediocre or "less than the best" parents in a seed orchard to achieve a broader genetic base? For example, if 12 of 20 pine clones are really outstanding, and the rest produce only moderately good progeny, is it safe to remove the inferior 8? Should 2-clone orchards be used for special problem areas? Answers to these questions are not yet available, and decisions must be based on a knowledge of the variation within the species and how this will affect the response of a plantation to adverse environments or pests.

There is another complication in defining the size of the genetic base that is needed. In many species, the response to pests or environmental extremes often changes with tree age, and the response by young trees can be very misleading with respect to the response of the same trees with advancing age. A tree must survive and grow through a complete life cycle to be a successful member of a population. There is danger in advertently breeding a strain of trees that are quite adaptable for most of the strain's life span but not for one specific life stage. Wide experience indicates this can be serious in the juvenile period, but we have less information on the potential loss of growth or death at a later period in life. Just because a planting may grow well for the first few years is no guarantee that it will continue to do so.

Based on observation and extensive progeny tests over many years with many species both in the temperate and tropical areas, it is evident that fears of disaster due to the narrowing of the genetic base and planting forest trees in monocultures have been overemphasized—at least for the first two cycles of breeding. Tree improvers cannot quickly reduce the genetic base for complex, multigene characters that are common to forest trees. But in advanced generations and/or use of vegetative propagation, the possible adverse effect of restricted genotypic plantings will increase.

Although it will vary by species, we feel that first-generation production seed orchards of *Pinus taeda* can be reduced to as low as six cross-pollinating clones with only minimal danger from monocultural problems. This differs dramatically from the commonly expressed idea that a dangerous monoculture automatically results from plantations using a single species.

The job of tree breeder is to keep the adaptive base broad enough so that catastrophic damage will not occur. This requires planning several generations ahead and, in certain circumstances, sacrificing some immediate gain for long-term adaptability. Production seed orchards should be looked at essentially as being "dead end," that is, the genetic base may be reduced so that it is still safe for field planting but does not retain enough variability for future generations of an ongoing breeding program. It is essential that production orchards be paired with the developmental orchards or research clone banks in which many genotypes are held and crossed to serve as a broad base from which future production orchards will be drawn. Development and maintenance of proper research clone banks require a lot of money and effort and real skill.

Great care needs to be taken in invoking the horrors of a too restricted genetic base, but it can be a horror if ignored; the tree improver must always be cognizant of the potential gains and dangers from restricting the genetic base.

LITERATURE CITED

Amerson, H. V., McKeand, S. E., and Mott, R. L. 1981. "Tissue Culture and Greenhouse Practices for the Production of Loblolly Pine Plantlets." 16th South. For. Tree Impr. Conf., Blacksburg, Va., pp. 168–175.

Anderson, W. C. 1975. "Some Economics of Monoculture." Pine Monoculture in the South. Workshop of the South. Forest Economics Workers, Biloxi, Miss.

Anonymous. 1977. Proc. Symp. *Vegetative propagation of forest trees—physiology and practice.* The Inst. for For. Impr. and the Dept. of For. Gen., College of Forestry, the Swedish University of Agricultural Sciences, Uppsala, Sweden.

Anonymous. 1979. *Micropropagation d'Arbres Forestiers. AFOCEL,* No. 12, Assoc. Foret-Cellulose, Paris, France.

Baker, F. S. 1934. *Theory and Practice of Silviculture.* McGraw-Hill, New York.

Barnes, R. D. 1969. A method of air-layering for overcoming graft incompatibility problems in pine breeding programs. *Rhodesia Sci. News* 3(4):102–107.

Beineke, W. F., and Todhunter, M. N. 1980. "Grafting Black Walnut," For. and Nat. Res. FNR-105, Purdue University, West Lafayette, Ind.

Birot, Y., and Nepveu, G. 1979. Clonal variability and ortet–ramet correlations in a population of spruce. *Sil. Gen.* 28(2–3):34–47.

Bonga, J. M. 1980. Plant propagation through tissue culture, emphasizing woody species. In *Plant Cell Cultures: Results and Pespectives,* pp. 253–264. Elsevier /North-Holland, Amsterdam.

Bouvarel, P. 1960. Les vieux pino laricio greffes de la foret de Fontainebleau [The old Corsican pine grafts in the forest of Fontainebleau]. *Sil. Gen.* 9(2):43–44.

Brix, H., and Barker, H. 1971. Trials in rooting Douglas fir cuttings by a paired cutting technique. *Can. Jour. For. Res.* 1(2):120–125.

Brix, H., and van Driessche, R. 1977. Use of rooted cuttings in reforestation. Brit. Col. For. Ser. and Can. For. Ser. Joint Report.

Brown, C. L., and McAlpine, R. G. 1964. "Propagation of Sweetgum from Root Cuttings." Ga. For. Res. Paper 24, Ga. For. Res. Coun., Macon, Ga.

Burgess, I. P. 1973. Vegetative propagation of *Eucalyptus grandis. N.Z. Jour. For. Sci.* 4(2):181–184.

Cameron, R. J. 1968. The propagation of *Pinus radiata* by cuttings. *N.Z. Jour. For. Sci.* 13(1):78–89.

Campinhos, E., and Ikemori, Y. K. 1980. "Mass Production of *Eucalyptus* spp. by Rooting Cuttings," IUFRO Symposium: Genetic Improvement and Productivity of Fast-Growing Trees, São Pedro, São Paulo, Brazil.

Carpenter, S. C. 1975. Rooting black walnut cuttings with Ethephon. *Tree Planters' Notes* 25(2):31–34.

Copes, D. L. 1969. "External Detection of Incompatible Douglas-fir grafts." Proc. Inter. Plant Propagators Soc. Annual Meeting, pp. 97–102.

Copes, D. L. 1970. Double grafts in Douglas fir. *For. Sci.* 16(2):249.

Copes, D. L. 1977. Comparative leader growth of Douglas fir grafts, cuttings and seedlings. *Tree Planters' Notes* 27(3):13–16.

Copes, D. L. 1981. "Selection and propagation of highly Graft-Compatible Douglas fir rootstocks—A Case History." U.S. Forest Service Research Note PNW-376. Pacific Northwest Forest and Range Experiment Station, Portland, Ore.

Corriveau, A. G. 1974. "The Clonal Performance of Loblolly and Virginia Pines: A Reflection of Their Breeding Value." Ph.D. thesis, North Carolina State University, Raleigh.

Corte, R. 1968. Note sur l'incompatibilité de greffe chez les coniferes [Note on graft incompatibility in conifers]. *Sil. Gen.* 17(4):121–130.

de Muckadell, M. S. 1954. Juvenile stages in woody plants. *Phys. Plant.* 7:782–796.

Destremau, D. X., Marien, J. N., and Boulay, M. 1980. "Selection et multiplication vegetative d'hybride d'eucalyptus resistant au froid." IUFRO Symposium: Genetic Improvement and Productivity of Fast-Growing Trees, São Pedro, São Paulo, Brazil.

Dimpflmeier, R. 1954. Propfungen an Waldbäumen durch Prof. Dr. Hendrick Mayr vor 55 bis 60 jahren [Grafting of forest trees by Dr. Mayr 55 to 60 years ago]. *Z. Forstgen. Forstpflanz.* 3:122–125.

Dorman, K. W. 1976. *The Genetics of Breeding Southern Pines.* USDA, U.S. Forest Service, Agricultural Handbook No. 471, Washinton, D.C.

Dormling, I. C., Ehrenberg, D., and Lundgren, D. 1976. "Vegetative Propagation and Tissue Culture [Vegetativ Förökning ch Vavnadskultur]." 16th IUFRO For. Cong., Oslo, Norway, No. 22.

Ducci, F., and Locci, A. 1978. Prove de radicazione di tales provenienti da piante mature di *Pseudotsuga menziesii* [Research on rooting scions from old trees of *Pseudotsuga menziesii*]. *Ann. Ist. Sper. Silvicol.* IX:37–70.

Duffield, J. W., and Wheat, J. G. 1964. Graft failure in douglas fir. *Jour. For.* 62(3):185–186.

Durzan, D. J., and Campbell, R. A. 1974. Prospects for the mass production of improved stock of forest trees by cell and tissue culture. *Can. Jour. For. Res.* 42(2):151–174.

Enkova, E. I., and Lylov, G. I. 1960. The use of grafting in the creation of oak seed orchards. *Lesn. Hoz.* **12**(6):34–36.

Farmer, R. E. 1981. Variation in seed yield of white oak. *For. Sci.* **27**(2):377–380.

Farmer, R. E., and Besemann, K. D. 1975. Rooting cuttings from physiologically mature black cherry. *Sil. Gen.* **23**(4):104–105.

Feret, P. P. 1975. "Biological Significance and Problems of Pine Monoculture." Pine Monoculture in the South. Workshop of the Southern Forest Economics Workers, Biloxi, Miss.

Fielding, J. M. 1963. "The Possibility of Using Cuttings for the Establishment of Commercial Plantations of Monterey Pine." 1st World Consul. on For. Gen. and Tree Impr., Stockholm, Sweden.

Fielding, J. M. 1970. Trees grown from cuttings compared with trees grown from seed (*P. radiata*). *Sil. Gen.* **19**(2–3):54–63.

Foster, G. S., Bridgwater, F. E., and McKeand, S. E. 1981. "Mass Vegetative Propagation of Loblolly Pine—A Reevaluation of Direction." Proc. 16th SFRIC, pp. 311–319.

Fowler, D. P. 1964. Effects of inbreeding in red pine, *Pinus resinosa. Sil. Gen.* **13**(6):170–177.

Franclet, A. 1963. "Improvement of *Eucalyptus* Reforestation Areas by Vegetative Multiplication." 1st World Consul. on For. Gen. and Tree Impr., Stockholm, Sweden.

Franclet, A. 1979. "Micropropagation of Forest Trees—Rejuvenation of Mature Trees in Vegetative Propagation." *AFOCEL,* No. 12, pp. 3–18. Assoc. Foret-Cellulose, France.

Franklin, E. C. 1979. Model relating level of genetic variance to stand development of four North American conifers. *Sil. Gen.* **28**(5–6):207–212.

Gabriel, W. J., Marvin, J. W., and Taylor, F. H. 1961. "Rooting Greenwood Cuttings of Sugar Maple—Effect of Clone and Medium." Sta. Papu. No. 144, Northeast Forestry Experimental Station, U.S. Forest Service, Upper Darby, Pa.

Garner, R. J. 1979. *The Grafter's Handbook.* Oxford University Press, New York.

Girovard, R. M. 1971. "Vegetative Propagation of Pines by Means of Needle Fascicles—a Literature Review." Centre de Recherche Forestière des Laurentides, Quebec Region, Quebec. Info. Report No. Q-X-23, Canadian Forest Service.

Glasgow, L. L. 1975. "Public Attitudes towards Monoculture." Pine Monoculture in the South, Workshop of the Southern Forest Economics Workers, Biloxi, Miss.

Hare, R. C. 1970. "Factors Promoting Rooting of Pine Cuttings." 1st North American For. Biol. Workshop, Michigan State University, East Lansing.

Hartman, H. T., and Kester, D. E. 1983. *Plant Propagation: Principles and Practices*. Second Edition Prentice-Hall, Englewood Cliffs, N.J.

Hartney, V. J. 1980. Vegetative propagation in the eucalypts. *Aust. For. Res.* **10**(3):191–211.

Hatmaker, J. F., and Taft, K. A. 1966. Successful hardwood grafting. *Tree Planters' Notes* **79**:14–18.

Hinesley, L. E., and Blazich, F. A. 1981. Influence of postseverance treatments on the rooting capacity of Fraser fir stem cuttings. *Can. Jour. For. Res.* **11**(2):316–323.

Hirasiro, M. 1918. A proposal to grow seedlings and cuttings of *Cryptomeria* in thorough mixture. In *Abstracts of Japanese Literature in Forest Genetics and Related Fields* (R. Toda, ed.), Vol. I, Part A, p. 163. Noorin Syuppan Co., Ltd., Tokyo, Japan.

Hoekstra, P. E. 1957. Air layering of slash pine. *For. Sci.* **3**(4):344–349.

Hoffman, C. A., and Kummerov, J. 1966. Anatomische Beobachtungen zur Bewurzelung der Kurztriebe von *Pinus radiata* [Anatomic observations on the rooting of short shoots of *Pinus radiata*]. *Sil. Gen.* **15**(2):35–38.

Hoffman, K. 1957. Freilandsommerpfropfungen mit Nadelhölzern [Summer field grafting of conifers]. *Forst Jagd* **7**(5):202–203.

Hong, S. O. 1975. "Vegetative Propagation of Plant Material for Seed Orchards with Special reference to Graft-Incompatibility Problems." For. Comm. Bull. 54. Britain, HMS:38–48.

Hyun, S. K. 1967. "Physiological Differences among Trees with Respect to Rooting." IUFRO Congress (Munich), **III**(22):168–190.

Jang, S. S., Kim, J. H., and Lee, K. J. 1980. "Rooting Characteristics of Cuttings and Effect of Topophysis on the Rooting of *Pinus thunbergii*." Res. Rept. Inst. For. Gen. No. 16, Korea, pp. 41–48.

Jiang, I. B. 1982. "Growth and Form of Seedlings and Juvenile Rooted Cuttings of *Sequoia sempervirens* and *Sequoiadendron giganteum*." M.S. thesis, School of Forestry, University of California, Berkeley.

Kadambi, K., and Dabral, S. 1954. Air layering in forestry practice. *Indian Forester* **80**:721–724.

Kanoo, K. 1919. An outline of forestation by *Cryptomeria* cuttings in Obi, Miyazaki prefecture. In *Abstracts of Japanese Literature in Forest Genetics and Related Fields* (R. Toda, ed.), Vol. I, Part A, p. 113. Noorin Syoppin Co., Ltd., Tokyo, Japan.

Kelly, C. W. 1978. "Intra-clonal Variation in Tissue Cultured Loblolly Pine (*P. taeda*)." M.S. thesis, School of Forestry Research, North Carolina State University, Raleigh.

Kleinschmit, J., and Schmidt, J. 1977. "Experience with *Picea abies* Cuttings in Germany and Problems Connected with Large-Scale Application." Symposium: vegetative Propagation of Forest Trees—Physiology and Practice, Uppsala, Sweden, pp. 65–86.

Lambeth, C. C. 1979. "Interaction of Douglas-Fir Full Sib Families with Field and Phytotron Environments." Ph.D. thesis, North Carolina State University, School of Forest Resources, Raleigh.

Land, S. B. 1977. "Vegetative Propagation of Mature Sycamore." Proc. 14th South. For. Tree Impr. Conf., Gainesville, Fla., pp. 186–193.

Lantz, C. 1973. "Survey of Graft Incompatibility in Loblolly Pine." Proc. 12th South. For. Tree Impr. Conf., pp. 79–85.

Laplace, Y., and Quillet, G. 1980. "Sylviculture intensive pour matériel végétal amélioré [Intensive silviculture for rooted cuttings]." IUFRO Symposium: Genetic Improvement and Productivity of Fast-Growing Trees, São Pedro, São Paulo, Brazil, pp. 1–8.

Leach, G. N. 1979. Growth in soil of plantlets produced by tissue culture. *Tappi* **62**(4):59–61.

Lee, S. K., and Rao, A. N. 1980. Tissue culture of certain tropical trees. In *Plant Cell Cultures: Results and Perspectives*, pp. 305–311. Elsevier/North-Holland, Amsterdam.

Libby, W. J. 1977. "Rooted Cuttings in Production Forests." 14th South. For. Tree Impr. Conf., Gainesville, Fla., pp. 13–27.

Libby, W. J. 1981. "What Is a Safe Number of Clones per Plantation?" Proc. IUFRO Meeting on Genetics of Host–Pest Interaction, Wageningen.

Libby, W. J., and Hood, J. V. 1976. Juvenility in hedged radiata pine. *Acta Hortic.* **56**:91–98.

Libby, W. J., Brown, A. G., and Fielding, J. M. 1972. Effects of hedging radiata pine on production, rooting and early growth of cuttings. *N.Z. Jour. For. Sci.* **2**(2):263–283.

Lyrene, P. M. 1981. Juvenility and production of fast-rooting cuttings from blueberry shoot cultures. *J. Am. Soc. Hort. Sci.* **106**:396–398.

McAlpine, R. G., and Kormanik, P. P. 1972. "Rooting Yellow-Poplar Cuttings from Girdled Trees," USDA. U.S. Forest Service Research Note SE-180.

McKinley, C. R. 1975. "Growth of Loblolly Scion Material on Rootstocks of Known Genetic Origin. 13th South. For. Tree Impr. Conf., Raleigh, N.C., pp. 230–233.

McKeand, S. E. 1981. "Loblolly Pine Tissue Culture: Present and Future Uses in Southern Forestry," Tech. Report No. 64, North Carolina State University, School of Forest Resources.

Mehra-Palta, A., Smeltzer, R. H., and Mott, R. L. 1977. "Hormonal Control of Included Organogensis from Excised Plant Parts of Loblolly Pine (*Pinus taeda* L.)." Tappi For. Bio. Wood Chem. Conf., Chicago, Ill., pp. 15–20.

Mott, R. L. 1981. Trees. In *Cloning of Agricultural Plants via in Vitro Techniques* (B. V. Conger, ed.), pp. 217–254. CRC Press, Boca Raton, Fla.

Mott, R. L., and Amerson, H. V. 1981. "A Tissue Culture Process for the Clonal Production of Loblolly Pine Plantlets," North Carolina Agr. Res. Service Tech. Bull. No. 271.

Naes-Schmidt, K., and Soegaard, B. 1960. Podehojdens indflydelse pa podekvistens vaékstrytme og form [The influence of the grafting height on the development of the scion]. *Soertryk Det forstlige Forsogvaesen Danmark* **26**:315–324.

Olesen, P. O. 1978. On cyclophysis and topophysis. *Sil. Gen.* **27**(5):173–178.

Ono, M. 1882. Which grow faster, seedlings or cuttings in the case of *Cryptomeria* or hinoki cypress? In *Abstracts of Japanese Literature in Forest Genetics and Related Fields*, (R. Toda, ed), Vol. I, Part A, p. 22. Noorin Syuppin Co., Ltd., Tokyo, Japan.

Pousujja, R. 1981. "Potentials and Gains of a Breeding Program, Using Vegetative Propagation Compared to Conventional Systems." Ph.D. thesis, North Carolina State University, Raleigh.

Rauter, M. 1977. "Collection of Spruce Cuttings for Vegetative Propagation," For. Res. Note No. 11, Ministry of Natural Resources, Ontario, Canada.

Rauter, M. 1979. "Spruce Cutting Propagation in Canada. Breeding Norway Spruce, Norway Spruce Provenances." IUFRO, Div. 2, Bucharest, Rumania.

Rauter, R. M., and Hood, J. V. 1980. "Uses for Rooted Cuttings in Tree Improvement Programs." 18th Can. Tree Imp. Conf., Duncan, British Columbia.

Rediske, J. H. 1976. "Tissue Culture and Forestry." Proc. 4th Amer. For. Biol. Workshop, pp. 165–178.

Roulund, H. 1973. "The Effect of Cyclophysis and Topophysis on the Rooting Ability of Norway Spruce Cuttings." Forest Tree Improvement No. 5, Arboretet, Hørsholm, Akademisk Forlag.

Roulund, H. 1978a. "Stem Form of Cuttings Related to Age and Position of Scions (*Picea abies*)." Forest Tree Improvement No. 13, Arboretet Hørsholm, Akademisk Forlag.

Roulund, H. 1978b. A comparison of seedlings and clonal cuttings of Sitka spruce (*Picea sitchensis*). *Sil. Gen.* **27**(3–4):104–108.

Santamour, F. S. 1965. Rooting of pitch pine stump sprouts. *Tree Planters' Notes,* No. 70, pp. 7–8.

Shelbourne, C. J. A., and Thulin, I. J. 1974. Early results from a clonal selection and testing program with radiata pine. *N.Z. Jour. For. Sci.* **4**(2):387–398.

Slee, M. U., and Spidy, T. 1970. The incidence of graft incompatibility with related stock in *P. caribaea hondurensis*. *Sil. Gen.* **19**(5–6):184–187.

Sommer, H. E., and Brown, C. L. 1979. Application of tissue culture to forest tree improvement. In *Plant Cell and Tissue Culture: Principles and Applica-*

tions W. R. Sharp, P. O. Larson, E. F. Paddock, and V. Raghaven, (eds.), pp. 461–491. Ohio State Univ. Press, Columbus.

Struve, D. K. 1980. "Vegetative Propagation of *Pinus strobus* by Needle Fascicles and Stem Cuttings." Ph.D. thesis, North Carolina State University, Raleigh.

Struve, D. K. 1981. *Conifer Grafting Manual* (Mimeo). Depatment of Horticulture, Ohio State University, Columbus.

Sweet, G. B. 1972. "Effect of maturation on the Growth and Form of Vegetative Propagules." 2nd North American Biol. Workshop, Corvallis, Ore., Society of American Forestry.

Sweet, G. B., and Wells, L. G. 1974. Comparison of the growth of vegetative propagules and seedlings of *Pinus radiata. N.Z. Jour. For. Sci.* **4**(2):399–409.

Talbert, J. T., Wilson, R. A., and Weir, R. J. 1982. "Utility of First Generation Pollen Parents in Young Second Generation Loblolly Pine Seed Orchards." 7th North American For. Biol. Workshop, Lexington, Ky.

Thulin, I. J. 1969. "Breeding of *Pinus radiata* through Seed Improvement and Clonal Afforestation." 2nd World Consul. on For. Tree Breeding, Washington, D.C.

Thulin, I. J., and Faulds, T. 1968. The use of cuttings in breeding and afforestation of *Pinus radiata. N.Z. Jour. For.* **13**(1):66–77.

Toda, R. 1974. Vegetative propagation in relation to Japanese forest tree improvement. *N.Z. Jour. For. Sci.* **4**(2):410–417.

Tucker, R. E. 1975. "Monoculture in Industrial Southern Forestry." Pine Monoculture in the South, Workshop of the Southern Forest Economics Workers, Biloxi, Miss.

van Buijtenen, J. P., Toliver, J., Bower, R., and Wendel, M. 1975. Mass production of loblolly and slash pine cuttings. *Tree Planters' Notes* **25**(2):4, 26.

Wakeley, P. C. 1971. Relation of thirtieth year to earlier dimensions of southern pines. *For. Sci.* **17**(2):200–209.

Webb, C. D. 1961. "Field Grafting Loblolly Pine," Tech. Rept. No. 10, School of Forest Resources, North Carolina State University, Raleigh.

Wheat, J. G. 1964. Rooting of cuttings from mature Douglas fir. *For. Sci.* **10**(3):319–320.

Wright, J. W. 1976. *Introduction to Forest Genetics.* Academic Press, New York.

Yim, K. B. 1962. "Physiological Studies on Rooting of Pitch Pine (*Pinus rigida*) Cuttings," Res. Report No. 2., Inst. For. Gen., Forest Experimental Station, Suwon, Korea.

Zak, B., and McAlpine, R. G. 1957. "Rooting of Shortleaf and Slash Pine Needle Bundles." Research Note No. 112, Southeastern Forest Experimental Station.

Zobel, B. J. 1972. "Genetic Implications of Monoculture." 2nd North Amer. For. Biol. Workshop, Oregon State University, Corvallis.

Zobel, B. J. 1977. Tissue culture (as seen by a plant breeder). *Tappi* **61**(1):13–15.

Zobel, B. J. 1981. "Vegetative Propagation in Forest Management Operations." Proc. 16th South. For. Tree Imp. Comm. Meet., Blacksburg, Va., pp. 149–159.

Zobel, B., Campinhos, E., and Ikemori, Y. 1982. "Selecting and Breeding for Wood Uniformity," Proc. TAPPI Research and Development Meeting, Ashville, N.C., pp. 159–168.

CHAPTER 11

Hybrids in Tree Improvement

There has been controversy in the tree improvement area of study between those researchers who favor the hybrid approach to developing better trees and others who feel that tree improvement efforts could be better expended in other areas. Hybrids have the distinct advantage in that the tree breeder can create something different that may not occur in nature. Hybridiztion can produce new combinations of genes (Piatnitsky, 1960), but Wagner (1969) has emphasized that the parental species of the hybrids establish the poles of diversity, and hybrids only fill in the gap in variation that lies between the two poles. He has stated that nothing "new" is created and that hybridization only counteracts the extremes in characteristics produced by the evolutionary forces of mutation, selection, and genetic drift. By developing hybrids, however, the breeder can bring together desirable characteristics of the parents and "tailor make" trees that are not otherwise available in nature. The potential of hybridization was early recognized by such persons as Stockwell and Righter (1947), Righter (1955), and Duffield and Snyder (1958).

There has been a series of reviews on hybrid forest trees; for example, those for the genus *Pinus* by Critchfield (1975) and Little and Righter (1965), for *Quercus* by Palmer (1948), for *Picea* by Wright (1964), and for *Juniperus* by Hall (1952).

Despite the advantages and potential value of hybrids that are recognized by most tree improvers, they generally have been used only sparingly in operational forest regeneration. The key to success in the future use of most hybrids will be the degree to which vegetative propagation can be used operationally. Obtaining seeds of hybrids is usually difficult and expensive; therefore, their mass production using seed has been successful in only a few instances. One noticeable success has been the pitch × loblolly pine hybrid in Korea (Hyun, 1976). Hybrids have been used most extensively in species relatively easy to reproduce vegetatively, such as the poplars and willows (Stout et al., 1927; Hunziker, 1958; Schreiner, 1965). A number of scientists have urged a broader use of hybrids in tree improvement (Lester, 1973; Schmitt, 1973; Fowler, 1978). Their use is rapidly expanding as better techniques are developed, and hybrid programs such as the one for *Eucalyptus* in Brazil (Campinhos, 1980) have shown great promise (see Figure 10.6). Although production of hybrids among forest trees is considered by some to be a new activity, hybrid forest trees were recognized a long time ago (Tanaka, 1882).

WHAT IS A HYBRID?

Two of the most popular and often misused terms in forestry are *hybrid* and *hybrid vigor*. Definitions are not exact, and the word *hybrid* is used to describe several different types of crosses. To most foresters a *hybrid* is a cross between two species. To some tree improvers, the word *hybrid* also includes crosses between different geographic races within a species (Scamoni, 1950; Nilsson, 1963; Wright, 1964; Howcroft, 1974). Many botanists and agricultural crop breeders carry the definition of hybrid further to include crosses between any two unlike genotypes;

this is similar to the definition by Snyder (1972) who wrote that "a hybrid is the offspring of genetically different parents." If this definition is used, nearly every cross made between forest trees would produce a hybrid. In this book the word *hybrid* generally refers to crosses between species. However, it is not incorrect to apply "hybrid" to intraspecific crosses, such as between races, or even to crosses among two different genotypes in the same population.

Hybrids are sometimes given a "mystical value" with respect to growth and quality by people who do not understand the genetics of hybrid formation. For example, hybrids are frequently made and tested using the most convenient trees from the parental species; sometimes the major criterion for use as a parent is the ease with which a tree can be climbed. Hybrids inherit the characteristics of their parents. Therefore, if hybridization is to successfully produce improved growth, form, or pest resistance, the individual parents must be carefully chosen to provide the desired characteristics. Some persons believe that only the best and desirable characteristics of the parental species will be evident in the hybrid, but the worst characteristics of each parent can also appear in the hybrid progeny. Differences in hybrids have been reported to depend upon the particular parental combinations that happened to be used (Eifler, 1960). Ways to assure good parental combinations have been discussed by Conkle (1969) and Chaperon (1979). Often, the first crosses between species have been made on garden, park, or arboretum trees either by accidental open pollination or by controlled pollination. In either instance, the number and variability of the parental trees used in the crosses are small.

Usually, the hybrid has characteristics intermediate between its parents (Figure 11.1). Occasionally, however, the hybrid will strongly carry a desired characteristic of one parent and not show intermediacy. For example, the Coulter × Jeffrey pine hybrid (*Pinus coulteri* × *Pinus jeffreyi*) carries resistance to the pine reproduction weevil that the Coulter pine parent possesses (Miller,

FIGURE 11.1

Shown are mature cones of *P. coulteri, P. jeffreyi,* and the natural hybrids between the two. Note the intermediacy in size and conformation of cone scales of the mature cones, with Jeffrey pine at the left, Coulter pine at the right, and the hybrid in the center.

FIGURE 11.2

Sometimes hybrids are outstanding. Shown is a natural hybrid on the lands of Aracruz Florestal in Brazil with outstanding growth and form. This tree, 7 years old, can be used in the vegetative propagation program.

1950), although the hybrid is generally intermediate otherwise (Zobel, 1951a). Similarly, the loblolly × shortleaf pine hybrid is nearly resistant to fusiform rust, which is similar to the shortleaf parent, even though the cross is otherwise intermediate.

Sometimes hybrid crosses result in rare individuals that have characteristics outside the range of the parental species. Such individuals can be quite remarkable and have great potential value, especially when vegetative propagation can exploit the unusual and desirble genotypes (Figure 11.2).

HYBRID VIGOR (HETEROSIS)

The appeal of hybrids in forestry includes the potential to bring together unlike genotypes to create genetic combinations different from the parental species that may have some special value for growth or desired product. There is also the possibility of the presence of what is called *hybrid vigor*. Some persons assume all hybrids will display *hybrid vigor,* and this phenomenon is often used as the major reason why hybrids should be included in tree improvement programs. However, hybrid vigor may or may not occur in crosses between unlike forest tree genotypes.

What is *hybrid vigor*, or as it is often called, *heterosis*? Like many terms, there is no single definition that is acceptable to all. Many people define it as a growth superiority in which the hybrid exceeds that of both parents (Györfey, 1960), but others define hybrid vigor as being an increase over the mean of the parents (Snyder, 1972). Heterosis usually relates to traits of size (most often height), but it also includes yield or general thriftiness. Some persons apply the term *hybrid vigor* when the hybrid excels in *any* measurable characteristic such as wood qualities or cold hardiness or the ability to withstand pests, and not necessarily for size alone. A commonly observed result of hybridization is precocity in flowering of the cross relative to the parents; this also can be called a kind of hybrid vigor (Venkatesh and Sharma, 1976). In this book, the term *hybrid vigor* will normally refer to a size superiority over both parents, but it is essential to understand that the term may be properly used for things other than size. It is beyond the scope of this book to cover the causes and probable causes of heterosis. This is a very complex subject, but a good discussion can be found in the literature, for example, the study by Jinks and Jones (1958).

In conifers, hybrid vigor is not evident from the seeds. In his article in 1945, Buchholz made it clear that embryos of pine hybrids can grow faster, but the seeds cannot be larger than those of the female parent. He states that "the mega-gametophyte is formed before fertilization of the egg. The seed of a pine is fully grown and has reached its ultimate size at time of fertilization—there can be no enlarging effect on seed size due to the activity of the contained embryo."

There is considerable argument about the extent and importance of hybrid vigor in forestry. The general feeling has been that hybrid vigor usually is not present in meaningful amounts in forest trees (van Buijtenen, 1969). Fowler (1978) stated that "heterosis or hybrid vigor in species and provenance hybrids is the exception rather than the rule." He explained this partially as being the result of crossing highly adapted parental species that may produce hybrids that are less well adapted to the habitats where the parents are growing. For pines, Little and Somes (1951) reported little exceptional vigor in hybrids involving pitch pine, which is similar to hybrids in many other species. However, there have been a number of reports of hybrid vigor in the poplars and willows (Stout et al., 1927; Pauley, 1956; Schreiner, 1965; Chiba, 1968). More recently, significant superior vigor in hybrids has been reported in *Eucalyptus* (Chaperon, 1976; Venkatesh and Vekshasya, 1977; Camphinos, 1980), in larch (Keiding, 1962; Miller and Thulin, 1967; Wang, 1971), in spruce (Hoffmann and Kleinschmitt, 1979), and in larch intraspecific hybrids (Nilsson, 1963). With time and more complete crossing and study, significant and useful hybrid vigor in forest trees may well be found, but as of now, it must be considered only moderately important except in a few genera or for a few specific crosses. Hybrids have historically had more value as a source of new combinations of genes than for extra vigor, but this could well change as more becomes known.

One must be very careful in the assessment of hybrid vigor because time and location are most important. Hybrids can express vigor at one stage in their development while showing none at other stages or under certain environmental conditions and not under others (Johnson, 1955). This sometimes becomes very complex such as is the case for *Pinus sondereggeri*, the cross between loblolly and longleaf pine (Chapman, 1922; Namkoong, 1963). In the nursery bed the hybrid is often considerably taller and huskier than either parent. After outplanting, the loblolly usually outgrows the hybrid and longleaf pine until perhaps the fortieth year when the longleaf may become the largest. With such a pattern can one then say that the hybrid *P. sondereggeri* has hybrid vigor?

Another problem in the definition of hybrid vigor occurs when the hybrid is planted in a habitat in which only it and one parent can survive and grow but in which the other parent may not grow well or may even die. Such a situation occurs with the pitch × loblolly pine hybrid (Little and Trew, 1976). When grown on cold, poor sites the hybrid pine does well and often surpasses the pitch pine, whereas the loblolly parent is killed or is severely stunted by cold. The question has been raised whether the pitch × loblolly pine does have hybrid vigor under this condition. According to the definition followed in this book it does, because it is outperforming both parents.

NATURAL HYBRIDS

Many hybrid combinations occur naturally. Quite frequently these are over-looked and are considered to be variants of one of the parental species. Such hybrids can be very difficult to determine, especially when the parents are quite similar. Sometimes hybrids are easy to distinguish because of their intermediacy between two greatly differing species; a prime example of this is the *P. coulteri × P. jeffreyi* hybrid (Zobel, 1951a). Hybrids quite often appear when species are grown as exotics (Marien and Thibout, 1978), and especially when they are grown in arboreta where species that never occur together in nature are brought together so that gene exchange is possible. A classic example of this type of situation involves *Eucalyptus* in the arboretum at Rio Claro, Brazil, from which numerous hybrids have arisen (Brune and Zobel, 1981).

The more intensively one studies natural populations of forest trees, the more hybrids are found. But care needs to be taken; just because a tree differs considerably from its "type" species does not mean that it is necessarily a hybrid. The most difficult job in working with hybrids is to delineate between them and normal variants within a species (Figure 11.3). Often the F_1 hybrids (first cross or first filial generation as it is called) are not too difficult to distinguish, but as one encounters F_2 (crosses between F_1 hybrids), F_3, and other hybrid combinations, the job of distinguishing between hybrids and variants within a species becomes most difficult. To add to the confusion, often the hybrids cross back to the parental species (called *backcrosses* and designated as B_1, B_2, etc.), creating a group of intergrading individuals, and it becomes nearly impossible to determine accurately whether the individuals are hybrids, backcrosses, or species variants.

When two species that are growing together hybridize freely and backcross, a population known as a *hybrid swarm* is produced in which many combinations are

FIGURE 11.3

Natural hybrids are rather common in some species, and the more intensively species are studied, the more hybrids that are found. They must be considered in tree improvement programs; some are excellent. The *P. tadea* × *P. serotina* hybrid graft illustrated was selected as *P. taeda* and put into the seed orchard. It flowered out of synchronization with the other clones and had to be removed, even though its progeny were excellent.

formed with few apparent barriers being evident. Hybrid swarms have been studied under natural conditions by several investigators. For example, Namkoong (1963) did this for *Pinus sondereggeri,* (the loblolly × longleaf cross), Hardin (1957) for *Aesculus,* Kirkpatrick (1971) and Clifford (1954) for *Eucalyptus,* and Hall (1952) for *Juniperus.* The most intensive studies of natural hybridization have been for the oaks (*Quercus*). A few of the published articles are the following: McMinn et al. (1949), Muller (1952), Chisman (1955), Tucker (1959),

Bray (1960), and Burk (1962). Hybridization in the oaks has occurred so frequently that some persons feel that for some groups of related species there is an almost total intergradation and that species categorization means little. Intensive studies have also been made within the genus *Eucalpytus* by such persons as Pryor (1951, 1976) and Clifford (1954). Certain species in this genus hybridize freely, and the number of species varies greatly, depending upon whether one is a taxonomic "splitter" or "lumper." The pines in Mexico and Central America are a major group of species in which hybridization in natural stands is of key importance (Figure 11.4). It is not uncommon to find one species at the bottom of a mountain that gradually changes and intergrades as one goes higher up the mountain until it is called another species. There are no distinct breaks in variation between the two species. Some workers prefer to break such groups of interrelated and intergrading species into *complexes* that contain one to several species that frequently hybridize.

Introgression (also called *introgressive hybridization*) may be defined as the limited spread of genetic material from one species into another species as the result of hybridization that is followed by repeated backcrossing of the hybrid and its progeny to one or both of the parental species. Thus, the result of introgression

FIGURE 11.4

An area known for extensive hybridization and introgression is in Mexico and Central America. The area shown (*a*) in Nuevo León, Mexico, has very diverse environments, with trees growing on isolated mountain peaks. Pine stands, such as the one shown in Guatemala (*b*,) often are essentially hybrid swarms with all degrees of speciation, hybridization, and backcrossing.

is that in some cases of genes one species are eventually incorporated into the gene pool of another. Through introgression, an occasional individual or population of a desirable species may be found that possesses certain good characteristics from a generally less desirable species. For example, the rust resistance of the western loblolly pine populations could well be the result of introgression with shortleaf pine A similar result is obtained from an intensive breeding program in which the desired character(s) of one species are incorporated into another by hybridization and subsequent backcrossing. The general feeling among tree improvers is that introgression has a major effect on population structure and thus upon selection and breeding efforts. The subject of *introgression* has been well covered by Anderson (1968) in his book entitled *Introgressive Hybridization* and by Mettler and Gregg (1969).

Regardless of the long-term effects on evolution and speciation, hybridization

(b)

FIGURE 11.4 (*Continued*)

has created an excellent pool of genetic variability that the plant breeder needs to recognize, assess, and use. Too often this source of variability in forest trees has been overlooked.

Where Natural Hybrids Occur

Hybrids are most often found in geographically disturbed areas, such as mountainous or volcanic regions (see Figure 11.4). Such disturbed regions are particularly prevalent in Central America, where hybridization in both conifers and hardwoods is common. Large changes in the environment occur within short distances, thus affording the opportunity for species mixing and for hybrid establishment. Similar results occur when the habitat has been disturbed through the activities of people.

More hybrids are produced in nature than are ever found growing in natural settings because their seeds do not germinate and grow to maturity. Usually the species found growing on an area are well adapted to their environments so any hybrids produced have little or no selective advantage and in many instances would be at a disadvantage for survival, growth, and reproduction. But when the habitat is very diverse and has been changed naturally or altered by human beings, an "environmental niche" is often available that is ideally suited to the hybrid and in which it will flourish. This has been referred to as "hybridization of the habitat" by Anderson (1948) and usually is a prerequisite for the large-scale establishment of hybrids or their derivatives. All kinds of environmental upsets, such as frequent or very severe burning that affects the soil or logging with heavy equipment that drastically disturbs the soil, will result in a disturbed and potential hybrid habitat. Slash-and-burn farming, which is associated with shifting agriculture in the tropics, has undoubtedly produced many "hybrid habitats." Zobel has observed a small valley in the Sierra Nevada of California that formerly contained predominantly ponderosa pine (*P. ponderosa*) but that now has a considerable proportion of ponderosa × Jeffrey pine hybrids following logging and several severe fires. Sometimes the impact on the habitat is so extensive that it enables the establishment of a hybrid swarm (Chapman, 1922; Namkoong, 1963). Whole counties in Louisiana and North Carolina contain hybrid swarms of *P. sondereggeri* (*P. palustris* × *P. taeda*) following severe and continued disturbance of the sites through farming, grazing, and burning. Some trees have developed into the so-called "Erambert's hybrid" that is made up of several species, although Schmidtling and Scarborough (1968) feel it is primarily longleaf × loblolly.

Serious mistakes have been made in assessing whether two species can hybridize in natural populations. Frequently, hybrids may be formed, but they do not have a chance to become established because the environment is more suitable to one or both parental species. The only real way to tell if hybrids are being produced is to collect seeds from trees in the suspected area of hybridization and then grow them under controlled conditions. Such an assessment must be done on a large scale because the number of hybrids formed can vary from a few (less than 1%) to a relatively large percentage. For example, in areas where loblolly pine and longleaf pine grow sympatrically (i.e., occur together), individual *P. palustris* trees can be found whose seed contain no longleaf × loblolly (*P. sondereggeri*) hybrids, whereas other trees may produce well over 75% hybrids. Based on seedling production in large nurseries, where the parental species are sympatric, loblolly × longleaf hybrid seed are formed at a 5 to 15% rate even though usually only a very few hybrids grow to maturity in naturally regenerated forests.

If one hopes to find or study hybrid trees growing in wild populations, sampling should be done where there are a fair number of both parental species growing intermixed in the stand. If one species is predominant, seed collections should be made from the rare species. One should also look for forest sites that have been severely disturbed and that will enable the hybrids to become established. In undisturbed stands, one often observes what Pryor (1978) found for *Eucalyptus,* where the occurrence of interspecific hybrids was common. Hybrids were growing at stand junctions, but their progenies were limited, and they did not invade the parental stands. It is amazing how often natural hybrids will be found if searched for in disturbed or intermediate habitats. A basic necessity for working with natural hybrids is to have a complete knowledge of the characteristics of both parental species so that a hybrid can be recognized.

What are the barriers to the formation of natural hybrids when the parental species are not separated geographically and can produce hybrids artificially? The most common barrier is the time of flowering. Many otherwise compatible crosses do not occur in nature because the flowering times of the parents do not overlap. A prime example of this is *P. taeda* × *P. echinata*. Receptivity of conelets and pollen release are often 3 weeks apart between these two species, and normally receptivity of the female strobili of loblolly pine is completed long before shortleaf pollen is shed. Yet, despite this apparent isolating time barrier, hybrids do occur (Zobel, 1953). In certain years the receptive period and time of pollen shed of the two species may overlap somewhat as the result of unusual weather, which is usually a cold, wet spring. Sometimes, insects affect the male strobili of shortleaf trees, causing early pollen maturity with pollen shed 2 or 3 weeks before what is normal. Similarly, insect attack may kill the resting bud of loblolly and cause a new bud to arise in the spring from which the female strobilus will emerge. These late females are sometimes receptive in synchronization with shortleaf pollen shed. Similar happenings also occur in other species as have been reported for aspen (*Populus*) by Einspahr and Joranson (1960).

Determination of Natural Hybrids

Before one can determine whether a tree is a hybrid, it is essential to know the limits of the variation of the parental species. This sounds easy but is often most difficult and requires an extensive assessment of "pure" stands of the species. It is the word *pure* where the problem lies. How is a pure species to be defined? Even in cases not affected by crossing with other species, most species have geographic races that have developed through differential selection under different environments. It is not possible to travel to dissimilar environments to study a species and assume that the same characteristics will be found when the species is growing in a different geographic area. Therefore, the limits of variation of the parental species must be determined in the area near to where the hybrid grows.

Even more confusing and hard to handle in a determination of whether a species is pure or not is to ascertain whether it is carrying genes from another species as a result of past hybridization and introgression. For example, *P. taeda* hybridizes with *P. echinata, P. palustris, P. elliottii, P. rigida, P. serotina,* and perhaps with other species. Because of this, it is not possible to define what pure *P. taeda* really is; everywhere throughout its range, this "promiscuous" species hybridizes and carries genes in it from one to several other species. Under conditions in which parental species are not pure, hybrid determination becomes most difficult, and very sophisticated methodology is required (Smouse and Saylor, 1973; Saylor and Kang, 1973). On the other hand, the study of the *P. coulteri* × *P. jeffreyi* hybrid was relatively simple in that it was not difficult to find "pure" parental populations, and the hybrid was intermediate between two quite different species (Zobel, 1951a).

Many methods have been developed to assess natural hybrids, but details are beyond the scope of this volume. They vary from the simple system of Anderson's "hybrid index" (Anderson, 1953) to very complex methods of canonical analyses (Smouse and Saylor, 1973) and other sophisticated statistical methods, such as the one developed by Namkoong (1963). The more different and discrete the species are, the easier it is to determine hybridity and the more suitable are the simple methods, such as Anderson's "hybrid index." When species are similar and the characteristics of the hybrids strongly overlap within the range of variation of the pure species, the more complex statistical methodology is required.

In the past, most hybrid determinations in forest trees have been made using morphological and anatomical characteristics, usually based on foliage and seeds or other reproductive structures (Mergen, 1959; Schütt and Hattemer, 1959). Occasionally wood differences have been employed, but usually wood anatomy has not been too useful. In recent years, certain chemical and enzymatic methods have been developed to determine hybridity more precisely. In the pines, characteristics of the resins have been used effectively for many years (Zobel, 1951b; Mirov, 1967). Some of the other methods reported are vapor-phase chromatography to study resins (Bannister et al., 1959), paper chromatography, and flavenoid compounds (Riemenschneider and Mohn, 1975). Feret (1972) used peroxidase isoenzymes to study elm (*Ulmus*) hybrids, and isoenzymes have become a favored tool for taxonomic studies. Electrophoretic methods have been greatly improved, enabling better studies of hybridization, and positive results have been reported by many researchers. In *Fraxinus,* Santamour (1981) used flavenoids and coumarines to identify hybrids. Serological techniques were used by Moritz (1957).

Recent work that combines anatomical, morphological, and chemical methods as well as known crossability patterns is making the determination of hybridity in natural stands a much more exact undertaking. The best tool of all is to have some certified artificial hybrids between the species involved that can be used as a standard against which the putative hybrids can be judged. Unfortunately, such known and certified hybrids are often not available, but when they are, the job of determining natural hybridity becomes much simplified.

The Value of Natural Hybrids to the Tree Improver

Other than in a few genera like *Eucalyptus, Salix,* and *Populus,* in which vegetative propagation can be readily used, natural hybrids have not been widely planted on an operational scale. Hybrids do have great value for the tree improver as a source of variation for breeding programs. As vegetative methods are improved, hybrids will become more widely used..

It is extremely important for the forest geneticist and tree improver to recognize that hybridization frequently does occur naturally in forest trees and that although the crossing patterns may pose real problems from a taxonomic standpoint, the results of hybridization are invaluable for tree-breeding programs because a large number of greatly differing genotypes have been created from which the breeder can select. Skill and intensive testing are required to sort out the most useful gene combinations available from natural hybridization.

The importance of hybridization in the processes of speciation and evolution has been widely discussed and argued by such persons as Anderson (1953) and Stebbins (1959, 1969). Smouse and Saylor (1973) made an in-depth analysis of the pitch pine (*P. rigida*), pond pine (*P. serotina*), and loblolly pine (*P. taeda*) hybridization patterns and the effect of these on speciation.

It would serve no purpose to make a long list of natural hybrids that occur, but they are found in many genera in addition to those listed previously. For example, yellow birch (*Betula alleghaniensis*) and paper birch (*Betula papyrifera*) hybridize (Barnes et al., 1974) as do the aspens (Pauley, 1956) and a number of other hardwoods and conifers.

ARTIFICIAL HYBRIDS

Natural hybrids can be used in applied tree improvement programs, but usually this is rather a hit-or-miss approach. If hybrids are to be considered seriously in a breeding program, artificial hybrids should be developed from suitably good individuals from the parental species. What is of great importance is that artificial hybridization can bring together species and individuals that would not otherwise have an opportunity to cross. It enables the production of genotypes that incorporate desired characteristics from two species into a single individual or group of individuals (Diller and Clapper, 1969).

Making Artificial Hybrids

Making artificial hybrids is often not easy. Frequently, the techniques used must be developed and even after they have been perfected, a common result is that low yields of viable seeds are obtained. When crosses are made between distantly related species, viable seeds are sometimes never obtained, or if a few sound seed are obtained, they will often not germinate satisfactorily. Occasionally, use of special methods, such as excision of the embryo or removing the seed coat, makes the production of viable plants possible. This method was used to produce viable *P. lambertiana* × *P. armandii* seedlings (Stone and Duffield, 1950). In addition to having erratic germination, seeds of artificial hybrids are often small and sometimes lack vigor when they germinate.

The difficulties of obtaining seed of hybrids vary greatly by species and genus. For example, in genera such as *Quercus* (oaks), only one seed per pollinated flower can be obtained, whereas for other species (*Pinus, Platanus, Populus*), dozens or hundreds of viable seeds may be obtained from the pollination bag. The most desirable and economical method of propagation to mass produce hybrid plants will depend on the ease with which viable hybrid seed may be obtained or the ease of vegetative propagation. For example, in the oaks, vegetative propagation of some form would be necessary to mass-produce hybrid plants economically. In those species where large quantities of viable hybrid seed may be obtained more easily, mass pollination techniques may eventually be developed. For hybrids with special high values, standard control hand pollination may be possible to obtain plantable amounts of seed.

The major obstacle to the widespread use of hybrids in operational forestry has been the inability to mass-produce them easily and economically. In some instances, this has been partially overcome where labor is cheap, such as in Korea where control pollinations to produce the hybrid *P. taeda* × *P. rigida* have been done by hand on a mass scale (Hyun, 1976). Attempts have been made to produce hybrids using supplemental mass-pollination techniques for a number of species (Hadders, 1977; Bridgwater and Trew, 1981). This method distributes large quantities of pollen from one of the desired species to the receptive female structures of the other. Many different kinds of hand- and mass-pollination methods have been tried, sometimes sucessfully, sometimes with marginal success. For example, in tests employing mass pollination to produce the longleaf- × loblolly pine hybrid, success by individual mother tree has ranged from essentially no hybrids being produced to as many as 85% hybrids. Attempts to isolate large groups of flowers in tentlike structures and then to mass pollinate within this isolation zone have not been successful.

A method used successfully to produce hybrid *Eucalyptus* in Florida and in Brazil consists of establishing an orchard of one species within which individuals of another species are planted and from which hybrid seed will be collected (Campinhos, 1980; Dvorak, 1981). The individuals from which seeds are collected must be relatively or completely self-incompatible. The method also works well for dioecious species where interplanting species that flower in synchrony and are compatible has resulted in an easy production of large amounts of hybrid seed.

As mentioned several times before, problems in mass-producing hybrids can be overcome for a number of genera through the use of vegetative propagation. After hybrids are produced, tested, and selected, the most outstanding trees can then be propagated vegetatively on a large scale for production planting. This method has been used for decades for poplar and willow, and more recently it has been used operationally for *Eucalyptus* hybrids (Chaperon, 1976; Campinhos, 1980). Many millions of hybrid trees are now being planted using vegetative propagation.

Often, hybrids are difficult to produce because methods of crossing have not been sufficiently well developed. Reproductive structures of forest trees are very fragile, and careless methods can result in failure or very low seed yields. Before successful hybridization can be accomplished, intensive study of the reproductive system of the species involved is required. An excellent example is the very exhaustsive compilation of information about pines in the *Pollen Management Handbook*.[1] When such summaries on the methods of pollination and fertilization are obtained for different species, much better crossing success will result.

What Hybrids Can Be Made?   Everyone knows how difficult it is to produce hybrids from distantly related species. However, closely related species sometimes will not cross easily, even though this has been tried many times (Eklund, 1943). There are many reasons given for incompatibilities resulting in failure of seed production (McWilliam, 1958; Saylor and Smith, 1966; Krugman, 1970). These reasons sometimes are morphological or anatomical (Kriebel, 1972); this is especially true for some of the tropical hardwoods with very specialized reproductive systems. Barriers may also be chemical or physiological. Unexplained results are common; for example, two individuals from two different species may hybridize freely, whereas two other individuals from the same species may not produce viable seed. It is common to have problems with reciprocal crosses in which the hybrid can be made easily in one direction but with difficulty or not at all for the reciprocal cross with the same parents.

Hybrids quite often can be made in one environment and not in another. The literature contains numerous statements about the lack of crossability between two species based on a few trials, sometimes with only one tree of a species from an arboretum or greenhouse with an environment that is different from that where either parent grows naturally. Conclusions based on such restricted crossing are not necessarily valid, because if a greater number of trees of the two species are tried or if the crosses are made under more normal environments, efforts are often successful then. Lists of crosses that cannot be made must be carefully assessed with knowledge of how many parents hav been used or where the crosses have been tried or the conditions under which germination of the seed obtained was made. It is not unusual to obtain sound seed that appear normal but still will not germinate.

It would require a book to list all the successes and failures in producing hybrids, and such a list would soon be out of date. More combinations are constantly being found (Fowler, 1978), and there is the need to intensify and in particular to systematize the crossing data. This is emphasized strongly by Nikles

---

[1]U.S. Department of Agriculture Handbook No. 587. (C. Franklin, ed.). U.S. Forest Service, Washington, D.C.

FIGURE 11.5

A most useful hybrid is the one used in Queensland, Australia, to plant on excessively wet sites. The cross between *P. caribea* v. *hondurensis* and *P. elliottii* is much superior to either parent tree on the wet problem sites. The hybrid was produced by the Queensland Forest Service.

(1981) who has successfully produced a *P. caribaea* × *P. elliottii* hybrid that has grown well on wet sites that were not suited to either parent (Figure 11.5). The tendency is to emphasize hybridization in temperate species, but much good work has been done among some tropical species such as mahogany (*Swietenia*) (Whitmore and Hinojosa, 1977).

Wide Crosses   Usually, the more distant the relationship, the more unlikely it is that a cross will produce viable seeds. However, sometimes unusual and seemingly unlikely wide crosses can be made. In the pines, no known successful crosses have been made between the two major categories of the *Haploxylon* (soft) and the *Diploxylon* (hard) pines. The genus *Pinus* is divided into different subdivisions by several authors (e.g., Martínez, 1948; Duffield, 1952; Little and Critchfield, 1969), and usually crosses cannot be made between subdivisions. There are exceptions, however, such as the *P. elliottii* × *P. clausa* crosses made by Saylor and Koenig (1967). The more trials that are made, the more intergroup crosses there are that seem to be possible. Other genera are also divided into major categories, as in *Eucalyptus*. Extensive crossing trials have been made, and some wide crosses have been successful, but generally successful crossing is restricted to groupings within genera. Crosses between species that are widely separated geographically (Santamour, 1972) are often successful; it is surprising how often species that have been separated for thousands of years by hundreds or thousands of kilometers cross with little difficulty.

Sometimes closely related species will not hybridize. In *Pinus*, the western hard pines will not cross with the eastern hard pines. For example, *P. taeda* and *P. ponderosa* have not been successfully crossed. *Pinus resinosa* (red or Norway pine) is noted for its inability to cross with other closely related members of the genus. In an attempt to see just what might be possible, a whole group of closely and more distantly related species of pine was crossed using *P. taeda* as the female parent. Seed and seedlings were obtained from some rather unexpected species combinations, and the putative hybrids are being tested in the field (Williford et al., 1977). These wide crosses have not yet been confirmed at older ages.

Hybrids sometimes can be made between very distantly related species and in a few instances even between genera. The most well known of these is the Leyland cypress, which is a cross between *Cupressus macrocarpa* and *Chamaecyparis nootkatensis* (Jackson and Dallimore, 1926). This hybrid grows well, and there have been suggestions that it would have value for operational forestry uses. In an attempt to reinterpret existing taxa as being of hybrid origin, crosses have been hypothesized between *Tsuga* and *Picea* (Campo-Duplan and Gaussen, 1949; Vabre-Durrieu, 1954). Undoubtedly, other very wide crosses within and even between genera will be made in the years ahead as technology improves and greater efforts are made. Obviously, the intergeneric nature of hybrids depends on the definition of the genera involved. For example, in the *Rosaceae,* where the taxonomic status keeps changing, many intergeneric hybrids have been recognized.

Crossing Hybrids and Hybrid Breakdown

Some hybrid individuals are spectacular, with the result that there is a strong desire to use them. The best and simplest method of obtaining large numbers of good hybrid propagules is to locate good parental combinations, multiply the parents by grafting or rooting, and use these to create large quantities of proven quality F_1 trees. But the drawback of such a method is the difficulty of making the crosses and producing the vegetative propagules (Figure 11.6). Too often hybrid programs are based only on F_1 genotypes from the original wild or unimproved populations. Continued progress requires producing hybrids from advanced-generation parent trees.

A major question relates to how occasional outstanding F_1 hybrid individuals can be used in advanced-generation breeding. One suggested method is to use the hybrids ($F_1 \times F_1$) to produce F_2 seed; seed orchards have been established using such good F_1 parents. This is an exceedingly dangerous practice because the F_2 progeny will vary across the whole range from one parent through the intermediate hybrids to the other parent. This phenomenon is the result of genetic

FIGURE 11.6

A difficulty with working with hybrids is making the controlled crosses. (Shown are pine yearlings of a pine cross.) It is difficult to mass-produce hybrid seed by controlled crossing; the best use of hybrids occurs when vegetative propagation can be used to mass-produce the desirable hybrids.

recombination that creates parental genotypes at some gene loci. A very common and basic result is that nonuniformity will be found in the F_2 progeny and later (F_3, F_4, etc.) generations. Despite this biological fact of segregation, F_1 seed orchards have been recommended by persons such as Hyun (1976) and Nikles (1981) who reported they did not find the expected segregation in the F_2. Certainly, hybrid seed orchards should never be made using F_1 individuals *until* tests have proven that the trees produced have the desired uniformity. There is an ongoing argument by some geneticists who say that since more trees are planted per unit area in forestry than can reach maturity and since thinning may be planned, it therefore is not serious if some inferior individuals are planted. This may be true for the final harvest of crop trees, but the forester certainly wants to get the most from a thinning operation. The general trend is to widen spacing as more uniform, improved trees become available. However, this requires that a high proportion of desirable trees be planted.

An outstanding example of hybrid breakdown, combined with the adverse effects of related matings, is the so-called Brazilian source of *Eucalyptus grandis* (Brune and Zobel, 1981). A number of species were planted in the arboretum at Rio Claro in São Paulo, Brazil, and these hybridized freely. Seeds were collected and operationally planted from the best *E. grandis* trees in the arboretum. The progeny grew very well, and seed were collected from these plantations for additional planting. After using this method to obtain seed for a number of generations, the quality of trees degenerated, with unwanted species, hybrids, and dwarfs appearing. In some plantations, as many as 5 to 15% of the trees never grew into a satisfactory tree form. Stands from these seeds are very nonuniform and have low productivity. In these same stands there is an occasional superoutstanding individual with remarkable form and growth (see Figure 11.2). Some appear to be hybrids and some are similar to the parent species. Because of the unknown parentage and relatedness, these can only be used directly in operational planting through vegetative propagation. They can also be used by letting them cross, testing them, and then using the very best of the progeny through vegetative propagation. If a hybrid program is to be efficient and successful, it is essential to avoid coming to the point of hybrid breakdown and relatedness that was attained in the Brazilian source of *E. grandis*.

One of the best methods for the use of hybrids is to cross them back to outstanding individuals of one of the parental species. When done correctly, backcrossing will enable the transference of the desired characteristic into the best parental species. For example, the *P. coulteri* × *P. jeffreyi* cross is quite resistant to the pine reproduction weevil. Jeffrey pine is relatively slow growing, of good form, but very sensitive to the weevil. Coulter pine is a fast grower but of relatively poor form. Backcrossing the relatively fast-growing and insect-resistant hybrid back to the best Jeffrey pine parents and making the proper selections will result in a faster-growing, better-formed tree than the F_1 hybrid. The backcross hybrid will look more like Jeffrey pine and will also be more weevil resistant.

Future Hybrid Research

The potentials and the research left to do in forest tree hybridization are indicated in Table 11.1 (from Critchfield, 1975), which shows the number of species and the number of hybrid combinations that have been made in the genus *Pinus*. When the number of potential combinations of pines possible (4500) is compared to those successfully made (95), it is evident how much is left to do in a genus on which so much effort has already been expended. Critchfield (1975) states that "because of the economic importance of many pines, species hybridization has been more fully explored in this genus than in most other plant genera." It is true that much has already been learned. For example, some pines, like *P. pinea,* have not been sucessfully crossed with other species; others, like *P. resinosa,* have crossed with difficulty, and still others, such as *P. taeda,* cross relatively easily with a large number of species. For the spruces, another genus on which considerable hybridization work has been done, Kleinschmitt (1979) states that only 156 species crosses have been made of the 1260 possible. He found some spruce hybrids to be quite outstanding. It is sufficient to say that the possibilities for making hybrids among forest trees have only been touched.

TABLE 11.1
Successful Interspecific Hybridizations within and Between Subsections of *Pinus*[a]

Subsections(s)[b]	Number of Species	Estimated Number of Hybrid Combinations
Cembrae (white pines)	5	1
Cembrae × *Strobi*		2
Strobi (white pines)	14–15	18
Cembroides (pinyon pines)	8	6
Balfourianae (foxtail pines)	2–3	2
Sylvestres (Eurasian hard pines)	19	19
Australes (southern and Caribbean hard pines)	11	15
Australes × *Contortae*		2
Contortae (small-cone pines)	4	2
Sabinianae (big-cone pines)	3	2
Sabinianae × *Ponderosa*		2
Ponderosae (western and Mexican hard pines)	13–15	16
Ponderosae × *Oocarpae*		2
Oocarpae (closed-cone pines)	7	6

[a]From Critchfield, (1975).

[b]The eight species in the other five subsections have no verified interspecific hybrids.

HYBRID NOMENCLATURE

In the past, a number of hybrids were given names and specific rank, especially in the genus *Populus* in which a whole new and sometimes confusing nomenclature has been developed. This has also been done for some pines, such as for *Pinus sondereggeri* (loblolly × longleaf pines) or *Pinus attenuradiata* (Monterey × knob-cone pine) or the so-called Erambert hybrid (a cross possibly involving several southern pines), whose parents have not been accurately defined. It is evident that the practice of giving specific rank or new names to every hybrid forest tree would lead to chaos. The acceptable methods of naming hybrids are outlined in the *International Code of Botanical Nomenclature* adopted by the Twelfth International Botanical Congress in Leningrad, USSR (Stafleu et al., 1978).

One method is to use a "collective" name preceded by an X sign, such as *P.* X *sondereggeri* or *P.* X *attenuradiata*. Publication of these must follow the international code for validity. This is an option generally used for hybrids of natural origin. Another is to utilize a formula such as *P. attenuata* X *radiata*, using the names of the parental species. The names may be alphabetically arranged, or if parentage is known, the female parent should be listed first. The third method, which is not totally satisfactory, is to use cultivar names. These cannot be Latin or Latin combinations but may be combinations of the common names. They must be published with a description (in English), and it is recommended that a type be designated and placed in an herbarium. The cultivar name begins with a capital letter and is either placed in single quotation marks or is preceded by "cv." The name could be something like the following: *P.* (*coulteri* X *jeffreyi*) = 'Jeffcoult' or P. cv. Jeffcoult. Obviously, this method could lead to hybrid names that have little relation to the names of the parents and could result in confusion unless extreme care is taken.

A compromise for control crosses may be to use code numbers, always keeping a record of the parentage of the trees used to make the cross. The most important criterion is to keep accurate records in such a manner that one can quickly determine the makeup of the cross rather than be saddled with learning a lot of meaningless new specific names (or numbers), many of which are most difficult to pronounce or spell and which give no clue to the origin of the hybrid involved. Use of code numbers becomes more efficient when computer facilities are available, but code numbers are not descriptive except for those who made the hybrids.

J. W. Duffield[2] suggests tht natural hybrids need not be named; after a hybrid has been produced artificially, it becomes a cultivated plant, subject to the rules used for cultivated plants. As Pryor (1965) says, when discussing this major problem in the eucalypts, "some binomials have been based on hybrid type specimens and these, since they purport to describe species, must be discarded because hybrids cannot be equated with species. Thus in the literature there are some fifty or so binomials which cannot be names of valid species." Natural hybrids will be handled differently than man-produced hybrids (Little, 1960). This is typified by a recent letter from J. Perry[3] who raises the question about when is it suitable to call a tree a hybrid: Is a study of the phenotype sufficient, or does one have to rear and test offspring? The area of hybrid nomenclature in forest trees is difficult and needs to be clarified.

THE FUTURE OF HYBRIDS IN APPLIED TREE IMPROVEMENT

As mentioned previously, the chief restrictions to the use of hybrids have been the following: (1) the inability to mass produce them from seed; (2) the lack of suitable methods to produce hybrids vegetatively on a mass scale for operational planting; and (3) the inability to carry on advanced breeding programs with F_1 plants because they do not produce F_2's that are uniform enough for operational planting. Because of these restrictions, hybrids in tree improvement have generally been considered as oddities, toys, or something to develop that might someday have value. Fortunately, some of the objections have been overcome or will soon be overcome (Denison and Franklin, 1975; Matthews and Bramlett, 1981), resulting in the rapid operational use of hybrids like what was done many years ago for the poplars (Stout et al., 1927). Hybridization of forest trees is just now arriving on the tree improvement scene as an important improvement

[2]Personal communication.
[3]Personal communication.

method. As techniques are better developed and understood, there will be an explosive use of hybrids in operational forestry.

Before the use of hybrids can reach its optimum, a general realization of the biological fact must come about to the effect that the *goodness of a hybrid depends on the goodness of parents*. This means that a hybridization program must include a breeding program for the parental species to improve them to be used later as parents of new and improved hybrids. This need has been largely overlooked in current hybridization programs in which all the effort has gone into crossing species without a parallel program to produce better parents to make new crosses. A few programs have followed this pattern; for example, the rapidly moving *Eucalyptus* program referred to by Campinhos (1980) will develop several generations of improved parental trees to be used for future crossing for hybrid production. Lack of parental improvement will make a number of hybrid programs less effective than they should be.

Why do tree improvers have such enthusiasm about the future importance of hybrids? This attitude generally is due to the new methodology now being developed that will enable the vegetative reproduction of desired hybrids. Most workers are not too optimistic about an economic mass production of hybrid seeds, although such methods as mass pollination, which was described previously, are making this somewhat more feasible. But when vegetative propagation becomes feasible, a whole new world is opened up. For example, if $F_1 \times F_1$ do not produce uniform F_2 progeny, the occasional chance combination "super F_2" can be used. Further progress of the program will then depend both on improvement of parental species, which is followed by hybridization along with crossing among hybrids and choosing the occasional outstanding offspring. Even if seed yields are very low, which is a problem with some hybrids, enough seed will be produced to grow progeny from which to select for vegetative propagation.

Most people look for improvement in morphological characteristics in hybrids. But the greatest gains may well be in physiological characteristics that are related to adaptability. For example, Eriksson et al. (1978) have stated that "by selection of suitable parents interprovenance crosses can be used to produce hybrids with desired photoperiodic characteristics and temperature requirements." Improvements in cold hardiness, drought hardiness, and the ability to withstand nutrient deficiencies are possible through hybrid improvement efforts. One of the most lucrative areas is in the field of pest resistance, in which the hybrid or its derivative may carry the desired resistance (Miller, 1950; Sluder, 1970; LaFarge and Kraus, 1980, and many others). The advantage of hybridization is that it is possible to develop something that is entirely different from what exists in nature by the proper choice of parents.

As a hybrid breeding program progresses, it becomes possible through backcrossing to move a desired trait from an otherwise less desired species into a more desirable one. This has been done by LaFarge and Kraus (1980) who were able, by backcrossing the loblolly × shortleaf pine hybrid to the loblolly parent, to obtain trees that were equal to or better in growth than the parent loblolly pine but that carried considerably more resistance to fusiform rust than loblolly pine.

The potential for the use of hybrids in forest tree improvement is only now becoming recognized and usable. In the future, programs must operate in this area more seriously than they have in the past.

LITERATURE CITED

Anderson, E. 1948. Hybridization of the habitat. *Evolution* **2**:1–9.

Anderson, E. 1953. Introgressive hybridization. *Biol. Rev.* **28**:280–307.

Anderson, E. 1968. *Introgressive Hybridization.* Hafner, Co. New York.

Bannister, M. H., Brewerton, H. V., and McDonald, I. R. 1959. Vapour-phase chromatography in a study of hybridism in Pinus. *Svensk Papp. Tidn.* **62**(16):567–573.

Barnes, B. V., Dancik, B. B., and Sharik, T. L. 1974. Natural hybridization of yellow birch and paper birch. *For. Sci.* **20**(3):215–221.

Bray, J. R. 1960. A note on hybridization between *Quercus macrocarpa* and *Quercus bicolor* in Wisconsin. *Can. Jour. Bot.* **38**(5):701–704.

Bridgwater, F. E., and Trew, I. F. 1981. Supplemental mass pollination. In *Pollen Management Handbook,* (Carlyle Franklin, ed.) pp. 52–57. U.S. Forest Service Agricultural Handbook No. 587, Washington, D.C.

Brune, A., and Zobel, B. J. 1981. Genetic base populations, gene pools and breeding populations for Eucalyptus in Brazil. *Sil. Gen.* **30**(4–5):146–149.

Buchholz, J. T. 1945. Embryological aspects of hybrid vigor in pines. *Science* **102**(2641):135–142.

Burk, C. J. 1962. An evaluation of three hybrid-containing oak populations on the North Carolina outer banks. *Jour. Elisha Mitchell Soc.* **78**(1):18–21.

Campinhos, E. 1980. More wood of better quality through intensive silviculture with rapid growth improved Brazilian *Eucalyptus. Tappi* **63**(11):145–147.

Campo-Duplan, M., and Gaussen, H. 1949. Sur quatre hybrids de genres chez les Abietineae. *Bull. Soc. Hist. Nat. Toulouse* **84**(1/2):105–109.

Chaperon, H. 1976. "Amélioration génétique des Eucalyptus hybrides au Congo Brazzaville [Production of hybrid eucalypts in Brazzaville, Congo]." 3rd World Cons. For. Tree Breed., Canberra, Australia.

Chaperon, H. 1979. Nouvelles perspectives D'Amélioration génétique induites par le bouturage du pin maritime [New prospects of genetic breeding through vegetative propagation of *Pinus pinaster*]. In Assoc. Foret-Cellulose (AFOCEL) Annual Report, 1979, Paris, France, pp. 31–53.

Chapman, H. H. 1922. A new hybrid pine. *Jour. For.* **20**(7):729–734.

Chiba, S. 1968. "Heterosis in Forest Tree Breeding." 9th Symp. Jap. Soc. of Breed. Tech. Note No. 69.

Chisman, H. H. 1955. The natural hybrid oaks of Pennsylvania. *Res. Pap. Pa. State For. Sch.* **22**:1–4.

Clifford, H. T. 1954. Analysis of suscepted hybrid swarms in Eucalyptus. *Heredity* **8**(3):259–269.

Conkle, M. T. 1969. Hybrid population development and statistics. *Sil. Gen.* **18**(5–6):197.

Critchfield, W. B. 1975. "Interspecific Hybridization in *Pinus*.: A Summary Review." Proc. 14th Mtg. Can. Tree Impr. Assoc., pp. 99–105.

Denison, H. P. and Franklin, E. C. 1975. **Pollen management.** I *Seed Orchards* (A. Faulkner, ed.) Forestry Commission Bulletin No. 54, London, England, pp. 92–100.

Duffield, J. W. 1952. Relationships and species hybridization in the genus *Pinus*. *A. Forstgen. Forstpflanz.* **1**(4):93–99.

Duffield, J. W., and Snyder, E. B. 1958. Benefits from hybridizing American forest tree species. *Jour. For.* **56**(11):809–815.

Dvorak, W. 1981. "*Eucalyptus robusta*: A Case Study of an Advanced Generation Hardwood Breeding Program in Southern Florida." M.S. thesis, School of Forest Research, North Carolina State University, Raleigh.

Eifler, I. 1960. Untersuchungen zur individuellen Bedingtheit des Kreuzungserfolges zwischen *Betula pendula* und *Betula pubescens* [The individual results of crosses between *B. pendula* and *B. pubescens*]. *Sil. Gen.* **9**(6):159–165.

Einspahr, D. W., and Joranson, P. N. 1960. Late flowering in aspen and its relation to naturally occurring hybrids. *For. Sci.* **6**(3):221–224.

Eklund, C. 1943. Species crosses within the genera *Abies, Pseudotsuga, Larix, Pinus* and *Chamaecyparis,* belonging to the family Pinaceae. *Svensk Papp. Tidn.* **46**:55–61, 101–105, 130–133.

Eriksson, G., Ekberg, I., Dormling, I., and Matern, B. 1978. Inheritance of bud flushing in *Picea abies. Theor. Appl. Gen.* **52**:3–19.

Feret, P. P. 1972. Peroxidase isoenzyme variation in interspecific elm hybrids. *Can. Jour. For. Res.* **2**(3):254–270.

Fowler, D. P. 1978. Population improvement and hybridization. *Unasylva* **30** (119–120):21–26.

Györfey, B. 1960. Hybrid vigor in forest trees and the genetic explanation of heterosis. *Erdeszeti Kut.* **56**(1/3):327–340.

Hadders, G. 1977. "Experiments with Supplemental Mass Pollination in Seed Orchards of Scots Pine (*Pinus sylvestris*)." 3rd World Cons. on For. Tree Breed., Canberra, Australia.

Hall, M. T. 1952. Variation and hybridization in junipers. *Ann. Missouri Bot. Gar.* **39**(1):1–64.

Hardin, J. W. 1957. Studies in the Hippocastanaceae. IV. Hybridization in *Aesculus. Rhodora* **59**(704):185–203.

Hoffman, D., and Kleinschmitt, J. 1979. "An Utilization Program for Spruce Provenance and Species Hybrids." IUFRO Norway Spruce Meeting, Bucharest.

Howcroft, N. H. 1974. "A racial hybrid of *Pinus merkusii,*" Trop. For. Res. Note SR28, Papua, New Guinea.

Hunziker, J. H. 1958. Estudios citogeneticos in *Salix humboldtiana* y en sauces hibridos triploides cultivados en la Argentina [Cytogenetic studies of *S. humboldtiana* and triploid hybrid willows cultivated in Argentina]. *Rev. Invest. Agríc.* **12**(2):155–171.

Hyun, S. K. 1976. Interspecific hybridization in pines with special reference to *P. rigida* × *taeda*. *Sil. Gen.* **25**(5–6):188–191.

Jackson, B., and Dallimore, W. 1926. A new hybrid conifer, *Cupressus Leylandi* (between *Cupressus macrocarpa* and *Chamaecyparis nootkatensis*). *Bull. Miscel. Info.* **3**:113–116.

Jinks, J. L., and Jones, R. M. 1958. Estimation of the components of heterosis. *Genetics* **43**(2):223–234.

Johnson, A. G. 1955. "Southern Pine Hybrids, Natural and Artificial." 3rd South. Conf. For. Tree Impr., New Orleans, La., pp. 63–67.

Keiding, H. 1962. Krydsningsfrodighed Hos Laerk [Hybrid vigor in larch]. *Dans. Skovforen. Tidsskr.* **47**:139–157.

Kirkpatrick, J. B. 1971. A probable hybrid swarm in *Eucalyptus*. *Sil. Gen.* **20**(5–6):157–159.

Kleinschmitt, J. 1979. "Present Knowledge in Spruce Provenance and Species Hybridization Potential." IUFRO Norway Spruce Meeting, Bucharest.

Kriebel, H. B. 1972. Embryo development and hybridity barriers in the white pines (Section Strobus). *Sil. Gen.* **21**(1–2):39–44.

Krugman, L. 1970. "Incompatibility and Inviability Systems among Some Western North American Pines." Proc. Sex. Repro. Forest Trees, IUFRO, Sect. 22, Finland, Part 2.

LaFarge, T., and Kraus, J. F. 1980. A progeny test of (shortleaf × loblolly) × loblolly hybrids to produce rapid growing hybrids resistant to fusiform rust. *Sil. Gen.* **29**(5–6):197–200.

Lester, D. T. 1973. "The Role of Interspecific Hybridization in Forest Tree Breeding." Proc. 14th Mtg. Can. Tree Impr. Assoc., pp. 85–97.

Little, E., and Critchfield, W. B. 1969. "Subdivisions of the genus *Pinus*." U.S. Forest Service Mis. Pub. 1144.

Little, E. L. 1960. Designating hybrid forest trees. *Taxon* **9**:225–231.

Little, E. L., and Righter, F. I. 1965. Botanical description of forty artificial pine hybrids. *Tech. Bull. No. 1345*.

Little, S., and Somes, H. A. 1951. "No Exceptional Vigor Found in Hybrid Pines Tested." Northeast. For. Expt. Sta. Res. Note No. 10.

Little, S., and Trew, I. F. 1976. "Breeding and Testing Pitch × Loblolly Pine Hybrids for the Northeast." Proc. 23rd Northeast. For. Tree Impr. Conf., pp. 71–85.

Marien, J. N., and Thibout, H. 1978. Hybridization naturelle d'eucalyptus plantés dans le Sud de la France [Natural cross pollination of *Eucalyptus* planted in Southern France]. *AFOCEL* **1**:89–112.

Martínez, M. 1948. *Los Pinos Mexicanos.* Ediciones Botas, Mexico City.

Matthews, F. R., and Bramlett, D. L. 1981. Cyclone pollinator improves loblolly pine seed yields in controlled pollinations. *South. Jour. App. For.* **5**(1):42–46.

McMinn, H. E., Babcock, E. B., and Righter, F. I. 1949. The Chase oak, a new giant hybrid oak from Santa Clara Co., Calif. *Madroño* **10**(2):51–55.

McWilliam, J. R. 1958. "Pollination, Pollen Germination and Interspecific Incompatibility in *Pinus.*" Ph.D. thesis, Yale University.

Mergen, F. 1959. Applicability of the distribution of stomata to verify pine hybrids. *Sil. Gen.* **8**(4):107–109.

Mettler, L. E., and Gregg, T. G. 1969. *Population Genetics and Evolution.* Prentice-Hall, Englewood Cliffs, N.J.

Miller, J. M. 1950. "Resistance of Pine Hybrids to the Pine Reproduction Weevil." For. Res. Note No. 68, Calif. For. and Range Experiment Station.

Miller, J. T., and Thulin, I. J. 1967. "Five-year Survival and Height Compared for European, Japanese and Hybrid Larch in New Zealand." Res. Leaflet No. 17, New Zealand Forest Service.

Mirov, N. T. 1967. *The Genus Pinus.* Ronald Press Co, New York.

Moritz, O. 1957. Serologische Differenzierung von Arten als Voraussetzung der Fruhdiagnose des Hybridcharakters [Serological differentiation of species as a hypothesis for early diagnosis of the hybrid character]. *Der Zuchter* **4**:75–76.

Muller, C. H. 1952. Ecological control of hybridization in *Quercus*: A factor in the mechanism of evolution. *Evolution* **612**:147–161.

Namkoong, G. 1963. "Comparative Analyses of Introgression in Two Pine Species." Ph.D. thesis, School of Forestry, North Carolina State University, Raleigh.

Nikles, D. G. 1981. "Some Successful Hybrid Breeds of Forest trees and Need for Further Development in Australia." Proc. 7th Meet. RWG No. 1—Forest Genetics, Traralgon, Victoria.

Nilsson, B. O. 1963. "Intraspecific Hybridization and Heterosis within *Picea abies.*" 1st World Cons. on For. Gen. and Tree Impr., Stockholm, Sweden.

Palmer, E. J. 1948. Hybrid oaks of North America. *Jour. Arnold Arbor.* **29**:1–48.

Pauley, S. S. 1956. "Natural Hybridization of the Aspens." Minnesota For. Notes 47.

Piatnitsky, S. S. 1960. "Evolving New Forms of Oaks by Hybridization." 5th World For. Cong., Seattle, Vol. 2, pp. 815–818.

Pryor, L. D. 1951. "A genetic analysis of some *Eucalyptus* species. *Proc. Lin. Soc. N. S. W.* **76**(3–4) :140–147.

Pryor, L. D. 1976. *The Biology of Eucalyptus,* Studies in Biology No. 61. Camelot Press Ltd., Southampton, England.

Pryor, L. D. 1978. Reproductive habits of the eycalypts. *Unasylva* **30**(119–120):42–46.

Riemenschneider, D., and Mohn, C. A. 1975. Chromatographic analysis of an open-pollinated Rosendahl spruce progeny. *Can. Jour. For. Res.* **5**(3):414–418.

Righter, F. I. 1955. "Possibilities and Limitations of Hybridization in *Pinus.*" Proc., 3rd South. Conf. For. Tree Breed., New Orleans, La., pp. 54–63.

Santamour, F. S. 1972. Interspecific hybridization in *Liquidambar. For. Sci.* **18**(1):23–26.

Santamour, F. S. 1981. "Flavenoids and Coumarines in *Fraxinus* and Their Potential Utility in Hybrid Verification." Proc. 27th Northeast. For. Tree Imp. Conf., Burlington, Vt., pp. 63–71.

Saylor, L. C., and Smith, B. W. 1966. Meiotic irregularity in species and interspecific hybrids of *Pinus. Am. J. Bot.* **53**:453–468.

Saylor, L. C., and Kang, K. W. 1973. A study of sympatric populations of *Pinus taeda* and *Pinus serotina* in North Carolina. *Jour. Elisha Mitchell Sci. Soc.* **89**(142):101–110.

Saylor, L. C., and Koenig, R. L. 1967. The slash × sand pine hybrid. *Sil. Gen.* **16**(4):134–138.

Scamoni, A. 1950. Uber die weitere Entwicklung kunstlicher Kiefernkreuzungen in Eberswalde [The further development of artificial pine crosses in Eberswalde]. *Der Zuchter* **20**(1–2):39–42.

Schmidtling, R. C., and Scarborough, N. M. 1968. "Graphic Analysis of Erambert's hybrid." U.S. Forest Service Research Note SO-80.

Schmitt, D. M. 1973. "Interspecific Hybridization in Forest Trees: Potential Not Realized." 14th Mtg. Can. Tree Impr. Assoc., Part 2, pp. 57–66.

Schmitt, D., and Snyder, E. B. 1971. Nanism and fusiform rust resistance in slash × shortleaf pine hybrids. *For. Sci.* **17**(3):276–278.

Schreiner, E. J. 1965. "Maximum Genetic Improvement of Forest Trees through Synthetic Multiclonal Hybrid Varieties." Proc. 13th Northeast. For. Tree Impr. Conf., Albany, N.Y., pp. 7–13.

Schütt, P., and Hattemer, H. H. 1959. Die Eignung von Merkmalen des Nadelquerschnitts für die Kiefern Bastarddiagnose [The suitability of characteristics of the transverse section of needles for the analysis of pine hybrids]. *Sil. Gen.* **8**(3):93–99.

Sluder, E. R. 1970. "Shortleaf × Loblolly Pine Hybrids Do Well in Central Georgia." Ga. For. Res. Coun. Res. Paper No. 64.

Smouse, P. E., and Saylor, L. C. 1973. Studies of the *Pinus rigida—serotina* Complex II. Natural hybridization among the *Pinus rigida—serotina complex, P. taeda* and *P. echinata. Ann. Missouri Botanical Gardens* **60**(2):192–203.

Snyder, E. B. 1972. "Glossary for Forest Tree Improvement Workers." Southern Forest Experiment Station, U.S. Forest Service, New Orleans, La.

Stafleu, F. A., and Committee. 1978. "International Code of Botanical Nomenclature." Assoc. for Plant Tax., Vol. 97.

Stebbins, G. L. 1959. The role of hybridization in evolution. *Proc. Am. Phil. Soc.* **103**(2):232–251.

Stebbins, G. L. 1969. The significance of hybridization for plant taxonomy and evolution. *Taxon* **18**:26–35.

Stockwell, P., and Righter, F. I. 1947. Hybrid forest trees. *Yearb. Agr.* **1943–1947**:465–472.

Stone, E. C., and Duffield, J. W. 1950. Hybrids of sugar pine by embryo culture. *Jour. For.* **48**(3):200–203.

Stout, A. B., McKee, R. H., and Schreiner, E. J. 1927. The breeding of forest trees for pulpwood. *Jour. N.Y. Bot. Gar.* **28**:49–63.

Tanaka, Z. 1882. A variation of pine. *Bull. Jap. For. Assoc.* **7**:32.

Tucker, J. M. 1959. A review of hybridization in North American oaks. *Proc. Int. Bot. Cong.* **II**:404 (abstracts).

Venkatesh, C. S., and Sharma, V. K. 1976. Heterosis in the flowering precocity of *Eucalyptus* hybrids. *Sil. Gen.* **25**(1):28–29.

Venkatesh, C. S., and Vakshasya. 1977. "Effects of Selfing, Crossing and Interspecific Hybridization in *Eucalyptus camaldulensis*." 3rd World Cons. For. Tree Breed., Canberra, Australia.

Vabre-Durrieu, A. 1954. L'Hybride *Tsuga-picea hookeriana* et ses parents. Étude des plantules [The hybrid Tsuga-picea hookeriana and its parents. Study of seedlings]. *Toulouse Soc. Hist. Nat. Bul.* **89**:47–54.

van Buijtenen, J. P. 1969. Applications of interspecific hybridization in forest tree breeding. *Sil. Gen.* **18**(5–6):196–200.

Wagner, W. H. 1969. The role and taxonomic treatment of hybrids. *BioScience* **19**(9):785–788.

Wang, C. W. 1971. "The Early Growth of *Larix occidentalis* × *P. leptolepis* Hybrid." University of Idaho, Stat. Note 17.

Whitmore, J. L., and Hinojosa, G. 1977. "Mahogany (*Swietenia*) Hybrids." Research Paper ITF-23, U.S. Forest Service, Puerto Rico.

Williford, M., Brown R., and Zobel, B. J. 1977. "Wide Crosses in the Southern Pines." Proc. 14th South. For. Tree Impr. Conf., Gainesville, Fla., pp. 53–62.

Wright, J. W. 1964. Hybridization between species and races. *Unasylva* **18**(2–3):73–74.

Zobel, B. J. 1951a. The natural hybrid between Coulter and Jeffrey pines. *Evolution* **5**(4):405–413.

Zobel, B. J. 1951b. Oleoresin composition as a determinant of pine hybridity. *Bot. Gaz. (Chicago)* **113**(2):221–227.

Zobel, B. J. 1953. Are there natural loblolly–shortleaf pine hybrids? *Jour. For.* **51**(7):494–495.

CHAPTER 12

Wood and Tree Improvement

Although the primary emphasis of most tree breedings programs is to obtain faster-growing, better-formed, well-adapted, and pest-resistant trees, improved wood properties can also be obtained from the same programs. Research has shown that most wood qualities as well as tree form and growth characteristics that affect wood are inherited strongly enough to obtain rapid economically important gains through genetic manipulation.

The differing wood properties have a significant effect on the quality and yield of pulp and paper products and on strength and utility of solid wood products. Publications by Artuz-Siegel et al. (1968), Higgins et al. (1973), Barker (1974), and Foelkel et al. (1975a) are only a very few of the many publications that relate the effect of wood properties to product quality.

There is often considerable reluctance by some persons to include wood as part of a tree improvement program. Deterrents that are given include difficulties in deciding on the desired wood properties, difficulties of prediction about what type wood will be desired in future years, and the realization that no single type of wood is ideal for every product. Another argument put forth in the early years of tree improvement programs was that wood qualities are so strongly affected by growth and environment that genetic manipulation would not be successful. Some investigators felt that the changes in harvesting and utilization (i.e., lowering rotation ages and using small tops and limbs) would result in the use of wood that was so different from that now harvested that any changes caused through genetics would be relatively minor.

No matter what specific type of wood is desired for the future, improvement in wood characteristics will be of value in almost every program. Wood is notably nonhomogeneous, both within and among trees of a species, as well as among species and geographic sources. Genetic manipulation of wood in a breeding program can result in a higher proportion of desired wood. This is by far the most useful improvement that can be made for wood qualities. The easier and more consistent conversion of uniform raw materials results in cheaper production of a higher-value final product (Zobel, 1983). In general, tree improvement programs that have wood production as their goal should include knowledge of the manipulation of wood qualities.

WOOD QUALITY

The question always arises about which wood properties should be changed. Even though nearly all wood properties that have been studied respond satisfactorily to breeding, each has different economic values and importance. Because any genetic program will achieve the greatest gains from concentration on a few characteristics, it is necessary to determine the most important wood property and not try to include everything.

There is no question that wood specific gravity, or wood density, is by far the most important within-species wood characteristic for nearly all products (Eins-pahr et al., 1969; Barefoot et al., 1970). In some breeding programs, fiber or tracheid length are also included. Both specific gravity and fiber and tracheid length have strong inheritance patterns, and changes in them can have a significant effect on the final product. For certain special products, other wood properties can take on great importance, especially for quality hardwoods in which grain or color may be key characteristics.

The woods of softwoods and hardwoods are varied and different. Breeders attempting to improve wood must be aware of its complexity in the hardwoods and the relative simplicity of the wood of the softwoods. There are numerous cell-type differences within hardwoods that sometimes respond quite differently to genetic and silvicultural manipulation than do the simpler coniferous woods. One obvious example is the difference between ring-porous and diffuse-porous hard-wood species. In ring-porous trees, vessels formed early in the growing season are much larger in diameter than those formed later in the year and greatly influence wood properties. Examples of ring-porous species are the oaks and ashes. In diffuse-porous species such as the poplars, birches, and eucalypts, the vessels are smaller in diameter and are of essentially the same size regardless of the time of formation. The general principles related to wood and breeding strategies are the same for softwoods and hardwoods, but details can be grossly different.

Specific Gravity and Wood Density

It is important to understand the meaning of the terms *specific gravity* and *wood density* thoroughly. *Specific gravity* is the ratio of the weight of a given volume of wood to the weight of an equal volume of water. It is unitless. *Wood density* is the weight of wood expressed per cubic volume, for example, $450 \, kg/m^3$ or $28.0 \, lb/ft^3$.

$$\text{Specific gravity} = \frac{\text{weight of given volume of wood}}{\text{weight of an equal volume of water}}$$

$$\text{Wood density} = \text{weight of wood per unit volume such as } kg/m^3 \text{ or } lb/ft^3$$

Specific gravity and wood density are different ways of expressing how much wood substance is present. Specific gravity will be primarily used in this book. Either specific gravity or density can be calculated by knowing the other. In the metric system, density/1000 = specific gravity. Thus $450 \, kg/m^3$ is equal to a specific gravity of 0.45. In the English system, density (lb/ft^3) is equal to specific gravity $\times$ 62.4 (the weight of 1 lb of water). Thus 62.4×0.45 = approximately 28 lb/ft^3.

Specific gravity *is not a simple wood characteristic but is a combination of characteristics*, each of which has a strong inheritance pattern of its own. Combined, they determine what is called *specific gravity* (van Buijtenen, 1964).

Despite its complexity, specific gravity is considered to be a single property in most breeding programs. Specific gravity is primarily determined by three different wood characteristics, which will be described below and which are illustrated in Figure 12.1

1. **Amount of summerwood** Some trees start formation of thick-walled summerwood (latewood) cells early in the year—others later. Because summerwood has a high specific gravity (see Figure 12.2), this pattern results in an overall high wood specific gravity for the early summerwood producer, no matter where the tree may be growing. Percentages of summerwood can vary by 100% among trees of the same species and age that are growing at the same rate with their roots intertwined.

2. **Cell size** Occasionally, trees that are otherwise similar have essentially the same wall thickness but different-sized cells. When this happens, the tree with small cells will have the highest specific gravity.

3. **Thickness of cell wall** Although summerwood is defined by Mork's definition as *cells that have double wall thickness as great or greater than lumen*

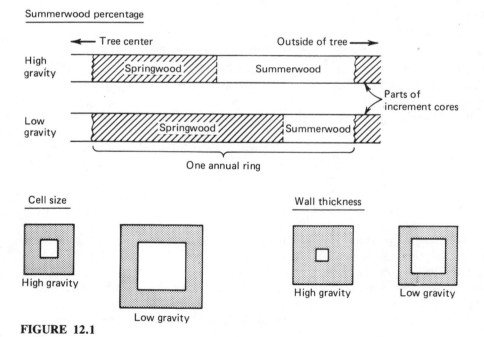

FIGURE 12.1

Specific gravity is not simple and is determined by a number of wood components. Three of these, summerwood percentage, cell size, and wall thickness, are illustrated. Despite its complexity, the combined wood property called specific gravity has a strong inheritance pattern.

diameters (Mork, 1928), the actual wall thickness of summerwood cells varies greatly among trees. Some trees have such thick-walled summerwood that the lumen is very small, resulting in a "rodlike" cell that gives a black or dark summerwood in pines. Other trees have summerwood cell walls that barely fit Mork's definition; in this instance, the summerwood is light brown When two trees have cells of essentially the same size, but one has thicker walls than the other, differences in specific gravity will be considerable.

The differences between springwood and summerwood cells in *P. taeda* are shown in Figure 12.2. In conifers, it is generally the characteristics of the summerwood that determine the differences in wood properties between trees, whereas in hardwoods specific gravity can relate to other things such as the vessel volume or the amount of ray cells (Taylor, 1969). Usually, little importance is given to the effects of springwood (earlywood) cell differences on specific gravity variations among trees, although springwood does have some effect. Springwood cell properties may vary some from tree to tree, but the effect of differing springwood cells is generally small enough so that resulting influences on the overall specific gravity of the tree are not large.

The Importance of Specific Gravity Variations in Forestry   Specific gravity is of key importance to foresters because it has a major effect on both yield and quality of the final product (Barefoot et al., 1970) and because it is strongly inherited (Zobel, 1961; van Buijtenen, 1962; Harris, 1965).

Overall biomass productivity cannot be determined unless wood specific gravity is known. When volume production is assessed by cubic measurements such as a cord, cubic meter, or by green weight, an inaccurate estimate of productivity will result due to the variation in specific gravity and in moisture content (which is negatively related to specific gravity). To illustrate this, green weights are compared to dry weights for a given volume of wood in Table 12.1 for loblolly pine. Note the change in the ratio of green to dry weights as age increases.

Specific gravity determinations permit construction of dry weight yield tables that give a useful prediction of the productivity per unit area of land. Dry weight yields from different age classes permit the determination of the biological productivity potential of stands of trees.

TABLE 12.1
Green and Dry Weight off Wood Varies with Tree Age, as Shown for *P. taeda*

Age of Trees (years)	Green Weight of 100 ft³ (lb)	Dry Weight of 100 ft³ (lb)	Ratio of Green/Dry Weight
18	6230	2696	2.31
30	5880	2759	2.13

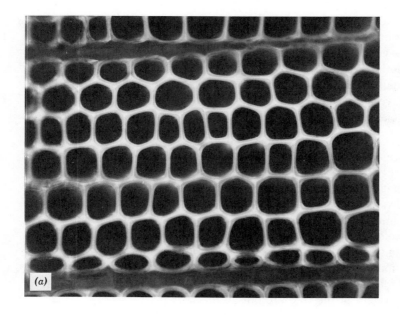

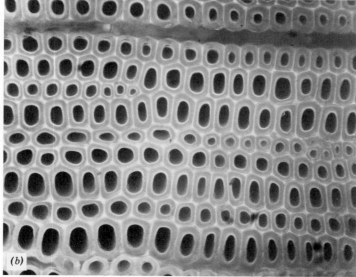

FIGURE 12.2

Within an annual ring springwood (earlywood) and summerwood (latewood), cells are formed that are very different from one another. These are illustrated side by side: (*a*) springwood, (*b*) summerwood. Both were taken from a mature *P. taeda* tree. The summerwood cells have the major effect on wood and product properties.

Much has been written about the effect of specific gravity on the quality of pulp and paper; a few publications summarizing these findings are those of Barefoot et al. (1970), Kirk et al. (1972), Bendtsen (1978), and Zobel (1981). It is clear from these and many other summaries that the importance of specific gravity many times overshadows the importance of other wood properties; this is especially true for the key paper characteristic referred to as *tear strength*. It is so important that in most programs which have pulp and paper as final products specific gravity is the only wood characteristic manipulated. Because of its effect on quality and yield and its high heritability, specific gravity has become of major interest in most tree improvement programs—no matter if the objective is to produce fiber or solid-wood products (Zobel et al., 1978).

Variation Patterns in Wood

It is essential to have a good knowledge of wood variability if its quality and yield are to be manipulated. In addition to the well-known and recognized differences among species, variability in wood also occurs as follows: (1) within a given tree; (2) among trees of the same species; (3) sometimes, between populations of a species growing in a single locality; and (4) frequently, between populations of a species growing in different geographic areas (Zobel et al., 1960a). It is the purpose in this chapter to summarize briefly and to simplify the mass of information relative to the various wood variation patterns. Many examples are from loblolly pine (*P. taeda*), the most completely studied forest tree species with respect to wood properties. A full treatment of wood variation would require several hundred pages; the reader is cautioned, therefore, that a simplified résumé must obviously contain numerous generalizations that are designed to reflect the usual trends and that exceptions will sometimes occur.

Variation in wood is caused by many factors, including tree form, genetic differences, growth variations, differing environments, and evolutionary history. For the latter, Wakely (1969) has emphasized the simplicity of ray and tracheid development of wood of the softwoods through evolutionary processes compared to the much more complex and heterogeneous hardwoods with their fibers, vessels, rays, fiber tracheids, and other cell types (Taylor, 1977). The wood of hardwoods is much more difficult to work with than is that of the softwoods. For example, in the hardwoods, specific gravity is influenced not only by cell wall dimensions but also by the relative amounts of ray and vessel elements (Taylor, 1969).

Variation within Trees—Juvenile and Mature Wood It has been recognized for a very long time that wood properties may vary greatly within a tree, from the pith (or center) outward or from the stump upward. Near the center of the tree, juvenile wood is formed; this is illustrated in Figure 12.3. The concept, qualities, and problems associated with juvenile wood have been covered in many papers and reviews, including an in-depth treatment in the "TAPPI Short Course on Fast-Grown Plantation Wood" in Melbourne, Australia, in 1978. Early authors,

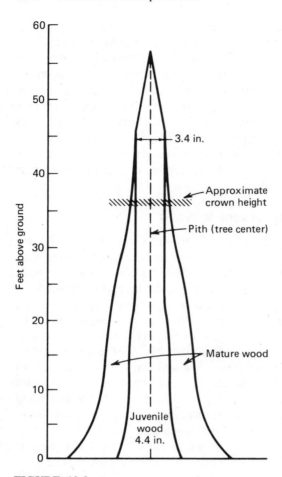

FIGURE 12.3

Juvenile wood exists as a semicylinder within the tree. This is especially evident for the pines as illustrated by the tree cross section representing the average of a number of 17-year-old *P. taeda.*. The trees will produce mostly mature wood at their bases and juvenile wood near their tops. The number of rings from the pith, or tree center, is related to the duration of juvenile wood production.

such as Paul (1957), referred to juvenile wood as "crown-formed" wood. This was explained by Kozlowski (1971) and Larson (1969) as being the result of the relative abundance of growth regulators and carbohydrates in the cambial zone near the crown. The similarity in wood qualities between top wood of older trees and wood near the center of the tree at its base has long been recognized (Marts,

1949). Although juvenile-wood characteristics differ from those of mature wood, it is not necessarily "bad" wood, and it is ideal for certain products. Juvenile-wood characteristics of most pines can be briefly summarized as follows.

1. Juvenile wood is formed near the pith of the tree (Figure 12.4). The number of rings from the tree center during which juvenile wood is formed varies from about 20 in *P. ponderosa* to 10 in *P. taeda*, 7 in *P. elliottii*, and 5 or 6 in *P. caribaea*. The actual age of the tree is not of importance, but the number of rings from the tree center or pith determines whether juvenile wood will be formed. Juvenile- and mature-wood formation apparently is related to the maturity of the cambial cells as influenced by the hormone balance, and juvenile wood is produced near the top of the tree no matter how old the tree is. In some species (*P. elliottii*, *P. caribaea*), the change between juvenile and mature wood can be quite abrupt (Figure 12.5), whereas in others, it is much more gradual (e.g., *P. taeda*, *P. radiata*, *P. oocarpa*) (see Figure 12.4). In no

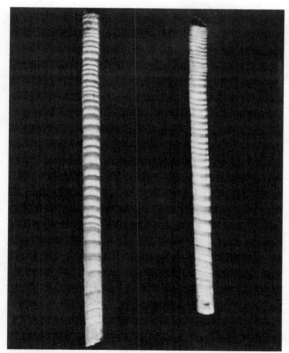

FIGURE 12.4

Juvenile wood has wood qualities that differ greatly from those of mature wood. This can be seen on the two *P. taeda* increment cores. The pith (brown fleck) is at the center of the tree. Note the color and "consistency" of the wood and how it changes out to about the seventh and eighth annual rings where typical mature wood is produced to the bark.

FIGURE 12.5

The transition from juvenile to mature wood is very abrupt in some species. Illustrated is a *P. caribaea* from a tropical area showing the very abrupt transition between the two kinds of wood. Compare it with *P. taeda,* shown in Figure 12.4.

species is there an abrupt shift from juvenile to mature wood during 1 year, and the change from juvenile wood before "typical" mature wood is formed usually is a gradual process occurring over several years (Figure 12.6).

2. Juvenile-wood specific gravity is lower than that of mature wood. The low gravity results primarily from thin cell walls and the low relative amount of summerwood-type cells (see Figure 12.2).

3. Juvenile-wood tracheids are short. Tracheid length is shortest near the center of the tree and increases rapidly toward mature wood, where it stabiizes to some extent. For example, in *P. taeda,*, tracheid length commonly varies from less than 2 mm in the juvenile wood to 3.5 to 5.5 mm in mature wood.

4. Juvenile wood is unstable when dried, because it shrinks longitudinally much more than does mature wood. The instability is the result of relatively flat fibril angles and causes major problems on drying (Meylan, 1968).

5. Juvenile wood produces quite different yields and quality in paper when compared to mature wood (Kirk et al., 1972). In addition to different cell

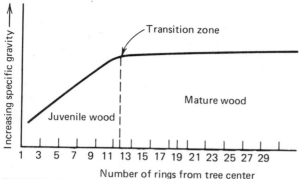

FIGURE 12.6

There usually is a gradual transition in wood qualities from the center of the tree outward. For example, the lowest specific gravity of most softwoods is nearest the tree center; it rises rapidly for a time and then tends to level off. This trend is shown schematically, indicating there is not an abrupt change but a transitional change from juvenile-to-mature wood qualities.

morphology, it has a chemical composition that differs in such things as hemicelluloses, lignins, and resinous constituents. As a result of this and due to poor liquor penetration, it pulps differently than does mature wood.

6. Because of low specific gravity and thin cell walls, juvenile wood is weak when used as a solid-wood product (Pearson and Gilmore, 1980). Nevertheless, it is widely used in the manufacture of structural lumber.

The variation in wood properties associated with height up the tree in pines can perhaps be best visualized if one considers that a core of "juvenile" wood with short tracheids and low specific gravity exists in the form of an inner "cylinder" at the center of the tree bole. This cylinder extends from the base of the bole all the way up to the top of the tree (see Figure 12.3). The result is that top logs consist mainly of juvenile wood, whereas the butt log of the same tree has more mature wood with a higher specific gravity (Stern, 1963; Zobel et al., 1972). Thus, when total tree chips or plywood cores are used, the proportion of juvenile wood is high. Topwood and bolewood differences in several wood properties are shown for 30-year-old loblolly pine trees in Table 12.2. Also shown are values for 11-year-old trees. Compare the topwood values of the 30-year-old trees with those of the 11-year-old trees.

The differences shown in Table 12.2 are of real economic significance, for example, 100 ft³ (2.83 m³) of wood from the basal logs of loblolly pine will yield about 500 lb (227 kg) more dry fiber [equivalent to about 200 to 300 lb (91 to 136 kg) of kraft pulp] than the same volume of the upper logs from the same trees. The

TABLE 12.2
Wood Qualities of Young *P. taeda* (11-Year-Old) and Lower Bole and Top Wood of Mature (30-Year-Old) Trees

		30-Year-Old Trees	
Wood Property	**11-Year-Old Trees**	**Lower Bole**	**Topwood**
Specific gravity	0.42	0.48	0.41
Tracheid length (mm)	2.98	4.28	3.59
Cell wall thickness (μm)	3.88	8.04	6.72
Lumen size (μm)	42.25	32.78	32.47
Cell diameter (μm)	40.01	48.86	45.91

fresh green weights will not be greatly different because differences in specific gravity of the wood within a species are masked by the higher moisture content of lower-gravity wood. Within a species there is a strong negative relationship between specific gravity and the moisture content of green wood, that is, low-gravity green wood has high moisture. Representative values for moisture content, resin content, and density are shown in Table 12.3 for juvenile and mature loblolly pine wood at several locations along the length of the stem.

TABLE 12.3
Wood Properties of 30-Year-Old Loblolly Pines Reported by 5-ft Bolts from Base to Top of Tree, by Juvenile and Mature Trees[a]

5-ft Bolt No.	Wood Density[b] After Resin Extraction (lb/ft³)		Percentage Resin Content		Percentage Moisture Content[b]	
	Juvenile Wood	**Mature Wood**	**Juvenile Wood**	**Mature Wood**	**Juvenile Wood**	**Mature Wood**
Base of tree						
1	27.5	34.3	3.0	2.2	110	74
2	26.8	33.7	2.9	2.0	122	85
3	25.0	31.8	2.8	2.2	133	97
4	25.0	31.2	2.6	2.1	137	102
5	25.0	29.3	2.5	2.4	139	110
6	25.0	29.3	2.5	2.0	145	117
7	24.3	—	2.6	—	151	—
8	24.3	—	2.5	—	153	—
9	23.1	—	2.7	—	163	—
Merchantable top[c]						

[a]Data are based on an average of 63 trees that were felled, divided into 5-ft bolts to a 4-in. top and into juvenile (first 10 rings from tree center) and mature wood.

[b]Expressed as a percentage of dry weight. For example, 163% moisture content means there are 1.63 lb of water for every pound of dry wood.

[c]4 in. (10.1 cm).

Importance of within-Tree Variation   Compared with material from older stands, wood from young pine plantations will have low-cellulose and high-hemicellulose yields when pulped. As an example, in loblolly pine, yields of paper were as much as 3% lower per unit of dry weight of wood from 12-year-old trees, compared with 30-year-old trees (Kirk et al., 1972). The thinner-walled cells associated with a high proportion of low-gravity juvenile wood produce kraft paper with low tear strength. Because the thinner-walled cells collapse more during manufacture, paper produced from juvenile wood has greater tensile strength, and generally the burst strength is good.

Chemical requirements and overall costs of pulping are greater for wood from young plantations. A 5% increase has been estimated in chemical costs for pulping 12-year-old versus 30-year-old loblolly pine (Kirk et al., 1972). In one study, low-specific-gravity wood (0.37) produced only 90% as much pulp as did wood of normal specifiic gravity (0.44) (Table 12.4).

A knowledge of within-tree variation can help answer questions about whether *volume* or *dry weight* of wood should be optimized in a forestry operation. If decisions are based solely on gross volume but wood weight is desired, major errors may result unless the effects of within-tree variation can be assessed. For example, if one can grow as much volume on an area with two 15-year rotations as is possible with one 30-year rotation, what will be the difference in yield of pulp? In loblolly pine, considerably more weight of usable wood fibers would be obtained from the single 30-year rotation than from the two 15-year rotations, although the volumes produced are the same. The green weight of the young stand would be high but only because of high moisture content (Table 12.5). Older stands continue to add considerable wood weight, even as growth modifies, because of the higher specific gravity of the greater amount of mature wood produced.

A number of studies have been made showing the importance and effects of tree age in forestry operations. One of the best of these was by the Hammermill Paper Company in Alabama (Kirk et al., 1972). The differences in mill yields and quality of paper between old and young pine trees were large and reflects the differing amounts of juvenile wood. Even more graphic was a study by the Federal Paper Board Company (Semke and Corbi, 1974) that showed the effect of age and within tree its location of wood used. They found that slabs gave the highest specific gravity and longest tracheids; following in order were roundwood, top

TABLE 12.4

Pulp Yields from Three Specific Gravity Categories of Wood from Young Loblolly Pine Trees

Specific Gravity	0.37	0.42	0.48
Pulp yield (% dry wood)	44	46	47
Kg pulp/m³ green wood	160	191	224
Mill production/% of 30-year-old[a]	76	90	107

[a]Average gravity of 0.44.

TABLE 12.5

Generalized Yields from 100 Solid ft³ (2.83 m³) of Green, Debarked Loblolly Pine Wood of Different Ages

Stand Age (year)	Dry Clear Wood		Water		Resin Extractives		Other[a]	Total
	lb	%	lb	%	lb	%		lb
25	2700	43	3450	55	100	1.5	?	6440
30	2950	47	3200	51	120	1.8	?	6420
35	3030	48	3100	50	140	2.2	?	6440

[a]Include knots, resin associated with knots, "includes" bark, and so forth. It appears this material constitutes between 3 to 7% of woods-run logs.

wood, 15-year-old trees and 10-year-old trees. As one example, they found the average wall thickness in slab wood to be nearly twice than that from 10-year-old trees.

Variation Patterns among Trees   Of great importance to tree breeders is the variation among trees of the same age and of the same species that are growing on the same site (Figure 12.7). Some foresters have the idea that the wood of most trees of any given species will be similar—that *Eucalyptus* wood of a given species grown in one environment will not vary much from one tree to the next. Such uniformity in wood quality among trees from seed does not exist. For all wood characteristics that have been adequately studied to to date, variation among trees of the same age growing on the same site has always been found to be large (van Buijtenen et al., 1961; Thorbjornsen, 1961; Webb, 1964; Skolmen, 1972). For example, regardless of locality, if 50 loblolly pine trees of the *same age, same crown class,* and growing on the *same site* are sampled at breast height, the difference in specific gravity of the mature wood between the highest- and lowest–gravity tree will be about 0.20. This difference between the lightest and heaviest trees is equivalent to approximately 700 to 1000 lb (317 to 454 kg) dry weight of wood per 100 ft³ (2.83 m³).

There are hundreds of references on tree-to-tree variation in wood quality. The one sure thing in forestry is that wood specific gravity as well as other wood qualities will vary greatly from tree to tree, regardless of the species or where the trees are grown. Since heritability of wood characteristics is also usually high, the two ingredients for good gains from a tree improvement program are present.

Wood Variation among Sites and Geographic Areas   Wood characteristics are the result of varying growth processes, and any factor that affects the growth pattern of a tree may also affect its wood properties. Whether trees grow on sandy or clay soils, under short or long growing seasons, or are subjected to major and differing environmental variations, some effect of the environment on wood quality is to be expected. In a number of studies involving several species,

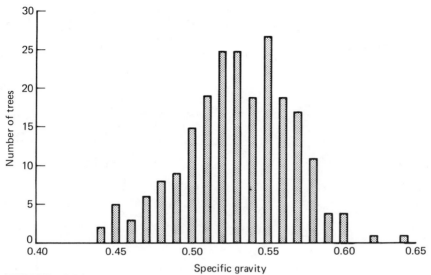

FIGURE 12.7

Within a stand of trees, there is a great variation in specific gravity. Illustrated are the gravities for a large number of *P. taeda* of the same age that are growing on similar sites and that are showing the huge differences that exist. Normally, a forest stand with trees of the same age will contain trees that vary from one another in specific gravity about 0.15 to 0.20, as is illustrated. This magnitude of variation in addition to a strong inheritance pattern enables the tree breeder to change wood specific gravity rather easily in the desired direction.

differences in specific gravity from different geographic areas have been found (Howe, 1974; Talbert and Jett, 1981). Yet it must be emphasized that although geographic differences have been observed, large individual tree-to-tree variation has been maintained in each instance. It is significant that only small differences in mean specific gravity occur among stands within a geographic area that may be growing on environments that are only moderately different.

Reports on trends of variation of wood specific gravity among natural stands have a long history. One trend often observed is that specific gravity within a species range is lower when it is inland from the coast or toward the higher latitudes or higher elevations. These trends hold for many pine species as well as for other softwoods and hardwoods. The magnitude of this trend for loblolly pine in the southern United States is shown in Figure 12.8. Note how specific gravity drops from south to north and from coast to inland; the latter differences are less than those related to latitude. These geographic differences in wood specific gravity may be relatively large and are important to wood-using organizations. Such differences are generally environmentally induced and are not highly heritable. For example, loblolly pines grown from seed from the high-wood-specific-gravity southern coastal areas do not produce higher specific gravity than

FIGURE 12.8

An illustration of variation in average specific gravity and tracheid length of loblolly pine with geographic locations is shown for the Southeast in the United States. The tendency is for lower average specific gravity and shorter tracheids in the north of the species range. Values shown are averages for plots of 23 trees each. The underlined values are for specific gravity and the values in parentheses are tracheid lengths in millimeters.

that of the local trees when grown in the inland areas or in the northern latitudes. Major errors have been made by making the assumption that progeny from trees in high-specific-gravity areas will grow high-gravity wood when planted in other geographic areas. This usually does not happen.

There are numerous instances of extreme changes in wood specific gravity when trees are grown in exotic environments. One of the most outstanding examples is in the coastal region of southern Africa. There *P. caribaea* produces exceptionally low-specific-gravity wood, whereas *P. elliottii* under almost identical environments produces unusually high-specific-gravity wood. One of the greatest dangers when growing exotics is to move a species into its new environment without a previous determination of the kind of wood that will be produced (Howe, 1974). Huge acreages have been planted with no thought given about the kind of wood that would grow, and there have been some very large losses when the wood of the exotic has proven to be subpar and has not produced wood similar to that produced in its indigenous environment.

Methods of Sampling for Wood Properties

A knowledge of the within-tree pattern of variation is of key importance to any studies related to wood qualities or inheritance patterns in wood. Many errors have been made by not knowing or by ignoring this pattern. The key is this: *Never compare wood of different ages* from the pith. If tree that are to be sampled are of different ages, then only the mature (or juvenile) woods can be compared. Even then, the comparisons are not completely valid because there is some change in specific gravity with age. For example, the breast-height juvenile-wood specific gravity of loblolly pine appears to increase with the age of the tree (Talbert and Jett, 1981). Because of its stability, it is best to use mature wood of trees for comparative purposes when such wood is available (Echols, 1959; Zobel et al., 1960b; Klem, 1966).

For many softwoods, the sampling height is of key importance. Since it is easier to sample from the ground, the breast-height level (4.5 ft or 1.4 m) is most commonly used. To be able to estimate whole tree values from such a single sampling location, a regression of breast height to total tree values must be made. Normally, about 40 trees need to be sampled to construct a regression equation suitable to predict total tree values from breast-height values (Figure 12.9). For most hardwoods, the location of the sample is not as important as it is in the softwoods because the variation from the center of the tree outward or from the base upward is generally much less than that of the softwoods.

It takes some skill to recognize and separate juvenile from mature wood, because there is no definite line between the two but only a period of general transition (see Figure 12.6). Often, both the juvenile and transition wood are included in the juvenile sample; therefore, the comparisons made to judge the wood quality among trees are only from known mature wood.

A proper determination of the wood characteristics of a species, race, or progeny must take into account the magnitude of the variability that is present. For trees of unknown parentage, usually a minimum of 30 trees should be sampled before a meaningful average value can be obtained. It does not require much imagination to recognize the futility of an effort to determine the specific gravity of a group of trees by sampling only one or two of them. The results of such limited sampling are often grossly misleading, as might happen when trees on the extremes of the variation pattern were those that were chosen.

Unfortunately, inadequate sampling to determine average wood values has been the rule rather than the exception. In one striking but typical example, the

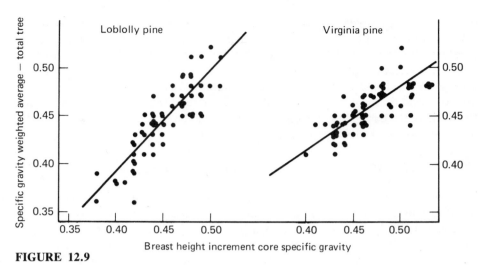

FIGURE 12.9

If samples are to be taken at any easy location, such as breast height (4.5 ft or 1.4 m), a good correlation, such as those shown for two species of southern pines, is necessary. the correlations are usually quite high; it normally takes 40 or more trees on a given site to develop a useful regression of breast height to total tree values.

owner of a large tract of land supporting a number of different species needed to select which species should be favored in a forest management program. The wood property evaluations were made on only *one tree* of each species, and *on the basis of this one sample* each species was retained or rejected for future management. When suitable tests were made by sampling 30 trees of each species, it was found that five of the eight species rated on single-tree samples of their specific gravities were not representative of the species' average specific gravity. Two of the very best species would have had to be discarded and one of the poorest kept, if the final choice of species had been based upon the single-tree sample. Such disregard of the basic nature and magnitude of variation among trees within a species would appear to be inexcusable, but it is common, nevertheless. Large sums of money are at stake, and the decisions based on inadequate data from too few trees often give results so misleading that the forestry enterprise will fail. This has happened a number of times, especially in instances in which exotic trees have been involved.

Variation among trees must, therefore, always be kept fully in mind in all situations when the woods of forest trees are sampled, regardless of whether the information is to be used for research, genetic development, or for operations. For example, if one is to assess the effects of fertilizer, site, soil, or spacing on wood properties, enough trees must be examined for each treatment to permit evaluation of individual-tree responses over and above the inherent variability of the trees. Disturbing as this may seem, there is no such thing as the *tree of average wood quality for any one stand of timber*. Often the wood from a tree of average height, diameter, basal area, or growth rate is sampled as having wood representative of a stand, but this is totally incorrect because all of these characteristics are not directly related to wood properties and environmental conditions can be important (van Buijtenen, 1969). Thus, the "average" tree might represent one of the extreme individuals for a particular wood property (see Figure 12.7 as shown).

In sampling trees for wood qualities, it is essential that a random selection be made if the mean value and the associated error terms are to be measured at some specified confidence level. Sampling can be from the whole population or it can be stratified into a desired portion of the population. For example, often only the dominant and codominant trees are sampled; the selection of trees within this group must be random. The specified confidence level to get "meaningful estimates" depends upon the needs and desires of the forester, but the general standard used is the 95% confidence level.

CONTROLLING WOOD QUALITY

There are a number of ways that wood qualities can be controlled in addition to choosing desirable species and provenances. As discussed previously, the age of harvest is a major tool because of its effects on the percentage of juvenile wood—as the stand becomes older, the proportion of juvenile wood decreases rapidly, as is shown in Table 12.6. The most effective way to control or change wood qualities in softwoods is to change rotation age. Similarly, plantation spacing will have a marked effect upon the proportion of juvenile wood.

Manipulation of tree form, whether through forest genetics or forest management, is a most powerful tool to improve wood qualities. Actual genetic manipulation of wood has proven to be very successful with high inheritance and good gains resulting from selection. Anything that alters growth or growth patterns, such as fertilizers, may change wood properties; there is a special section later in this chapter that is relevant to the effect of a growth rate on wood qualities.

For simplification, each of the factors mentioned later will be discussed primarily with respect to how they relate to specific gravity and, occasionally, to tracheid length. It is of importance to reemphasize that specific gravity is not a simple trait, but is a complex of wood properties involving cell wall thickness, cell size, summerwood percentage and other factors.

TABLE 12.6
The Relative Amount of Juvenile Wood and Mature Wood in the Boles of *P. taeda* Trees of Different Ages

Age of Tree (years)	Percentage Juvenile Wood	
	Dry Weight	Volume
15	76	85
25	50	55
45	15	19

Tree Form

The value of improving wood through improvement of tree form is very often overlooked. Manipulation of tree form is one of the easiest and quickest ways to improve wood, because it can be done both genetically and silviculturally and because gains can be considerable and rapid.

The easiest way to improve wood quality is to develop straighter trees that also have smaller limbs that grow at right angles to the tree bole. The main effect of these improvements is to reduce the percentage of reaction wood that accompanies trees that grow out of the vertical and with large or acute-angled limbs (von Wedel et al., 1968).

Whenever a tree leans, a kind of wood different from the normal is formed whose function is to help straighten the tree. This wood is collectively called *reaction wood* (Scurfield, 1973). When a softwood leans from the vertical, a kind of reaction wood called *compression wood* is formed (Low, 1964). Such wood, which develops on the underside of the bole of a leaning tree, has abnormal longitudinal shrinkage when dried, short tracheids, "fissures" in the thickened cell walls, and a higher than normal lignin content. In hardwoods, *tension wood* is formed on the upper side of the leaning tree. It has an unusually low lignin content and short fibers and often has gelatinous fibers that form planes of weakness in boards containing it. Compression and tension wood never occur in the same tree—the former is found only in softwoods and the latter in hardwoods. Because of its major effects on the morphology and chemistry of the wood produced, reaction wood is of great importance in the manufacture of both solid-wood products and for the use of wood as fibers, energy, or a source of chemicals. It is possible for over 50% of the merchantable volume to consist of compression wood in crooked loblolly pine trees (Zobel and Haught, 1962); about 50% of the volume of straight trees is compression wood.

Branch size has a major effect on the volume of wood in knots and associated abnormal wood around knots. It has an obvious effect on the quality and size of knots as they affect the strength of sawn boards and plywood. Wood in and around knots sometimes has high resin content and low cellulose content; in some ways it is similar to reaction wood. Pulp yields and quality are low, but the wood has a high energy content. In one study, 7% of the merchantable volume of small, 12-year-old normal loblolly pine was knots and associated abnormal wood; large-limbed trees had 14% of such wood (Von Wedel et al., 1968).

Since tree straightness is moderately inherited, it is possible to improve wood quality by breeding for this characteristic (Shelbourne et al., 1969). Good forest management techniques such as control of stocking, thinning, and pruning, are silvicultural tools that are also available to improve tree form. Breeding for straightness and small limbs will be beneficial for improving wood qualities for fiber products, and selection for these traits is essential in an improvement program aimed at production of high-quality solid-wood products. Value improvement from straighter trees has been shown for both yield and quality of lumber and of plywood. One example of the effect of tree straightness and limb size has been reported by Blair et al. (1974). They found that straightness improved both the yield and quality of pulp produced, whereas the greatest effect of limb size was on tear factor, a key quality in many kinds of paper.

Genetics of Wood

One effective way of changing wood is to breed strains of trees with the desired properties. Most wood properties are from moderately to strongly inherited, enabling a rapid change in the desired direction. Some selected summary publications about inheritance of wood in varied species are listed in Table 12.7.

TABLE 12.7

A List Of Some Publications Indicating Inheritance of Wood Qualities for Several Forest Tree Species

Author	Date	Publication	Contents
Akachuku	1983	*For. Sci.*	Genetic control of wood in *Gmelina*
Armstrong and Funk	1979	*Wood and Fiber* **12**(2):112–120	Genetic variation in wood of *Fraxinus americana*
Bendtsen	1978	*For. Prod. Jour.* **28**(10):61–72	General, on improved wood
Burdon and Harris	1973	*N.Z. Jour. For. Sci.* **3**(3):286–303	Wood density in four clones of *P. radiata*
Chudnoff and Geary	1973	*Turrialba* **23**(3):359–362	Heritability of wood density in *Swietenia macrophylla*
Dadswell and Wardrop	1959	*Appita* **12**(4):129–136	Growing trees with wood desirable for paper
Dyson	1965	EAAFRO; For. Tech. Note 16.	Wood quality and tree breeding in East Africa
Goggans	1962	Technical Report 14, North Carolina State University.	Inheritance of wood properties in loblolly pine
Harris	1965	Proc. Conf. of Sec. 41, IUFRO, Melbourne,-Australia, pp. 1–20	Heritability of wood density
Keller	1973	*Ann. Sci. Forest.* **30**(1):31–62	Heritability of wood of *P. pinaster*
Kennedy	1966	*Tappi* **46**(7):292–295	Heritability of several wood characteristics in clonal Norway spruce
Nicholls	1967	*Sil. Gen.* **16**(1):21–28	Wood qualities for tree breeding
van Buijtenen	1962	*Tappi* **45**(7):602–605	Heritability estimates in wood density of loblolly pine
Zobel	1964	*Unasylva* **18**:89–103	Breeding for wood properties in forest trees

Actually, a whole book could be written on the importance of inheritance and variation in wood properties and their potential inclusion in a tree improvement program.

A large inheritance pattern that is useful has been found for nearly every wood property, but the emphasis has been upon specific gravity. Breeding for wood improvement is usually not a major objective; it is supplementary to breeding for growth, form, pest resistance, and adaptability. The inheritance pattern is strong enough to obtain good gains by using this approach. Wood improvement, in a sense, can be likened to "cream on the milk." The main breeding program is usually to improve the amount of "milk," and wood improvement is added to that—just as cream adds to the value of milk.

Wood Specific Gravity   Throughout this chapter the strong inheritance pattern for wood specific gravity has been emphasized. This does not need to be developed further here, other than to emphasize that the characteristic specific gravity combines a high heritability with a large variation pattern, enabling good success with a breeding program.

Wood specific gravity comes close to being the ideal characteristic to manipulate genetically because of the large tree-to-tree variation, the strong heritability, its low genotype × environment interaction, and its major effects on yield and quality. For both softwoods and hardwoods, heritability of specific gravity is in the range of $h^2 = 0.5$ to 0.7 (Stonecypher and Zobel, 1966; Einspahr et al., 1967; McKinney and Nicholas, 1971; Polge, 1971; Nicholls et al., 1980; Land and Lee, 1981). Both of the ingredients for gain are present: good heritability and good selection differential. For example, one comapny found that moderately intensive selection for specific gravity in pine has produced a gain of 300 to 500 lb (140 to 230 kg) dry weight/100 ft^3 (2.83 m^3) of wood.

Fiber and Tracheid Length[1]   Another wood characteristic that has great variability and also a strong inheritance is cell size (Wheeler et al., 1965; Smith, 1967; Ujvari and Szönyi, 1973). Although its effect on the final product is usually much less than is specific gravity (Barefoot et al., 1970), cell length can have important effects on paper properties. This is especially true for short-fibered hardwoods as well as for the juvenile wood of some conifers, whose tracheid lengths are equal to, or are smaller than, the fibers of some hardwoods.

Tree-to-tree variations in average fiber or tracheid length are similar to specific gravity. For example, from a sample of over 300 loblolly pines of the same age growing on fairly similar sites, one tree was found with an average tracheid length of only 2.6 mm for the thirtieth ring at breast height, whereas another tree from the same area has tracheids 6.1 mm long from the thirtieth ring. Such huge

---

[1]Technically, conifers do not have fibers; they only have tracheids and ray cells. However, industrial personnel in most countries traditionally refer to both tracheids and fibers as fibers. In this book, *fibers* and *tracheids* will be referred to separately. Readers of the literature on wood properties should be aware that the terms are often used interchangeably.

differences in tracheid lengths among trees are not unusual, and to the forest geneticist they provide the variability needed in selection to change cell size. A variation pattern up the tree, ranging from shortest at the base, longest at the center, and shorter near the top, has been demonstrated by France and Mexal (1980) for *Picea engelmanii* and *Pinus contorta*. Just as for specific gravity, tracheid length drops for trees grown in the higher latitudes. Differences are as much as 1-mm average tracheid length for southern and northern stands of loblolly pine in the southeastern United States, with the shortest tracheids in the North.

Other Wood Properties   There are numerous other wood properties that might be used in a genetics program because they have reasonably strong inheritance patterns. If maximum gains are to be achieved in a breeding program, however, as few characteristics as possible should be included. Therefore, wood characteristics in addition to specific gravity and tracheid length are only included when there are special circumstances or needs.

Nearly all wood characteristics have an effect on pulp-and-paper properties. These characteristics include such things as cell wall thickness (which is closely related to specific gravity), cell lumen size, and length–width ratio of the cells. Flexibility, tensile strength, tear, burst, printability, and bendability are all important paper properties that are affected by fiber or tracheid properties that can be changed through breeding. However, most pulp-and-paper quality characteristics are so strongly controlled by wood specific gravity, with a lesser effect caused by fiber and tracheid length, that other wood characteristics are seldom used in breeding programs (Barefoot et al., 1970).

An area of wood quality breeding that has been largely ignored is the possibility of developing high-quality woods for special purposes, such as for furniture or finished cabinets. Enough has been done in this area to know that good gains can be made for quality. For example, selection for curly birch (*Betula*) has been successful (Heikinheimo, 1952). Similar gains are possible for wood such as walnut (*Juglans*) (Walters, 1951). Specialty breeding of high-quality hardwoods will likely become more important in the future, especially with tropical hardwoods and high-quality woods from the temperate zones. The anatomy of the tropical hardwoods can be very complex, and it will not be easy to develop breeding programs to improve them (Teles, 1980).

Inheritance of chemical properties of wood has been less well studied, but all indications are that the patterns may be useful. However, studies made on cellulose yield found it to be inherited in a nonadditive manner (Zobel et al., 1966; Jett et al., 1977), making a standard selection program ineffectual.

One kind of inheritance related to wood is the ability of a tree to compartmentalize off diseased wood in the bole. Early studies have shown this ability to be rather strongly inherited, and if used, it will result in much less serious losses due to rot (Garrett et al., 1979; Lowerts and Kellison, 1981). Many other wood qualities, like spiral grain, are found to have from mild to strong inheritance patterns (Champion, 1929; Whyte et al., 1980).

Although less work has been done on hardwoods when compared to soft-woods, considerable information about the genetics of the woods of hardwoods is available (Zobel, 1965). Inheritance patterns for studies done are reasonably strong, but due to the complexity of wood, the results are less predictable. The feasibility of improvement of the wood of tropical species by genetic manipulation is much less well known.

Genetic Relationships among Wood Properties   Many of the different important wood qualities are genetically independent one from another; thus, one can have thick-walled tracheids and high-specific-gravity trees that are either short or long fibered. This is illustrated for different species of Mexican pines in Figure 12.10, which shows the independence of these two characteristics. Species are arranged in a decreasing order of specific gravity but show little relationship to tracheid lengths, thus indicating the independence of specific gravity and tracheid length among species. Similar results have been shown for individual trees within other species.

Some wood qualities are interdependent, such as specific gravity and wall thickness. These are often correlated, sometimes strongly. This is true of many of the morphological characteristics of cells, such as size, wall thickness, lumen size, and other factors such as the chemical characteristics of cell morphology. Thus, when one of these is changed, the other wood properties will also be affected. A prime example is compression or tension woods that are closely associated with variations in cell size, structure, and chemistry.

Because of the general independent inheritance of factors that affect the major wood properties, it is possible to "tailor make" the kind of wood desired. Thus, programs have been developed with *P. taeda* in the southern United States to produce kinds of woods that are best for newsprint, paper board, bags and boxes, writing paper, tissue paper, and other wood products. The first result from a wood improvement program will be to obtain greater amounts of wood with the desired properties that will be most useful for the desired product.

It is possible to breed strains of pine with a reduced core of low-gravity juvenile wood. This can become critical when the percentage of juvenile wood becomes more thn 20% of the furnish used in the mill such as when very short rotations are used or when a high proportion of trees are used from thinning operations in young stands. Zobel et al. (1978) were able to increase the specific gravity of juvenile wood significantly in one generation of selection by using only the very highest-gravity trees from the original 1000 parents. When the 10 best families were used, at age 10 the gains in dry wood were 22.4 kg/m^3.

FIGURE 12.10

Shown are specific gravities (left) and tracheid length (right) of a group of Mexican pines. This illustrates the relative genetic independence of tracheid length and specific gravity among species.

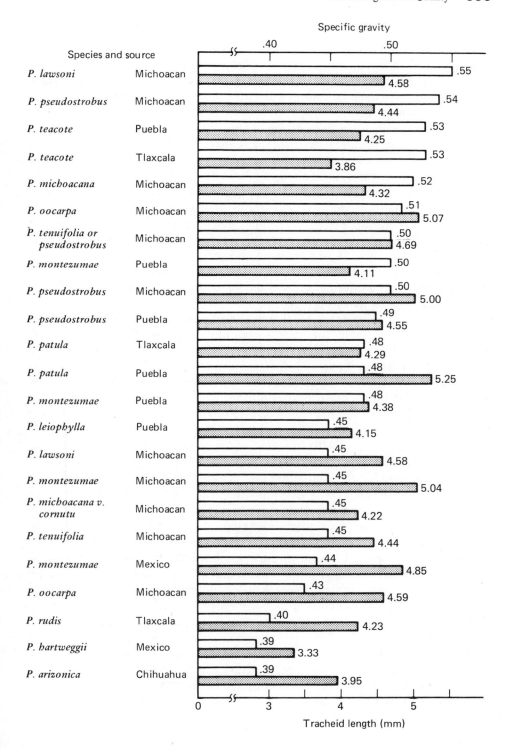

Specific gravity

Species and source

Tracheid length (mm)

Effect of Growth Rate on Wood Properties

It was mentioned earlier that growth rate and wood specific gravity are by and large geneticlly independent, at least for some pine species. Others, like *P. radiata* in New Zealand, have a negative relationship between growth rate and specific gravity. Even when the relationship is negative, it is not strong enough to preclude the development of fast-growing high-specific-gravity trees for boards, bags or boxes or low-specific-gravity trees for tissues, quality writing papers, or newsprint. This relative genetic independence is also evident between tree form and wood qualities, and one can have straight and high-specific-gravity or straight and low-specific-gravity trees, as desired.

The relationship of growth rate to wood qualities is very important, it has been much studied, and it is confused, as is shown by the many contradictory results illustrated in the literature. It is very complicated because of the many factors that affect both wood and tree growth. As Larson (1962) stresses, anything that affects the physiology and growth of a tree can also influence the kind of wood that is formed. The literature in this area is voluminous for the temperate and exotic tree species. Only limited information is available on the relation of growth rate and wood in the tropical hardwoods (Howe, 1974).

Many foresters believe that a fast growth rate causes low specific gravity. This seems to be true generally for some genera like *Abies* and *Picea* (Stairs, 1969; Ollesen, 1976), but it is less so for many pine species in which growth rate and specific gravity are not correlated (Goggans, 1961; deGuth, 1980). Similar controversy, but on a lesser scale, exists for the hardwoods. In *Poplar,* Mutibaric (1967) found a slight decrease in wood specific gravity with increased ring width, whereas for black cherry (*Prunus serotina*), Koch (1967) found no relationship between growth and wood specific gravity. The same finding seems to be true for *Eucalyptus* (Brasil et al., 1979). Because of the confusion, it is difficult to make definitive statements about the relationship of wood to growth rate.

A major reason for the contention that growth rate is strongly and inversely correlated with specific gravity evolved from a failure to recognize within-tree variation. The wood of young wide-ringed trees has been compared frequently with the narrow-ringed wood from older trees, or the wide-ringed wood at the center of the tree has been compared with the narrow-ringed wood at some distance from the pith. Because juvenile wood usually has wide rings and low gravity, the erroneous conclusion was made that growth rate (ring width) caused the gravity differences. In fact, however, it does not matter whether rings are wide or narrow in most softwood juvenile woods; the gravity will be low. Mature wood will have higher gravity. The key point is that *if two pine trees are growing under the same environmental conditions but exhibit widely different growth rates, the faster-growing tree may have either higher or lower specific gravity* than does the slow grower. Attempts to assess specific gravity on the basis of ring width alone will lead to completely erroneous conclusions. In one study, the specific gravities of over 1000 of the very fastest-growing loblolly pines used as parents in seed orchards were compared with those of unselected trees with "average" or slower growth rates. It was found that their specific gravities were similar. The tree improver must be very critical whenever he or she is assessing the effects of growth rate on wood properties. For many of the hard pines, the pattern of little or no relationship between growth rate and wood specific gravity is well documented. This is illustrated for loblolly pine (see Figures 12.11 and 12.12). Usually, correlations between growth rate and specific gravity are very low, ranging from slightly negative to slightly positive. The lack of a strong growth rate–specific gravity correlation means that it is not necessary to sacrifice wood substance per unit volume when striving for rapid-volume production by breeding for growth and wood properties at the same time.

Results have been obtained from enough wood studies on pine so that the lack of a relationship can be accepted as a fact; that is, it is possible to have fast-growing trees with either high or low specific gravity. The forest manager has freedom to handle his or her forest to promote growth without substantially altering the specific gravity of the trees produced. In fact, a number of publications, such as those by Lowery and Schmidt (1967) on western larch or by Parker et al. (1973) on Douglas fir, show that the increased growth following thinning results in normal-specific-gravity or even increased-specific-gravity wood. One major exception is when heavy nitrogen fertilization is used to accelerate growth. Thus, both management factors and genetic factors to improve the growth rate or tree form of many conifers are independent enough from those for specific gravity that they

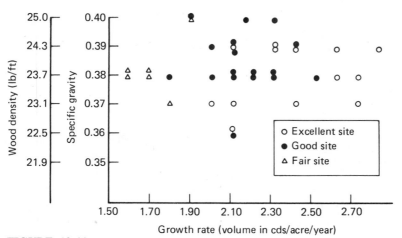

FIGURE 12.11

Shown in the relationship between growth rate and specific gravity for families growing on different sites. Each mark on the map is the average of 40 trees grown and measured for each family. Note the independence of growth rate and specific gravity.

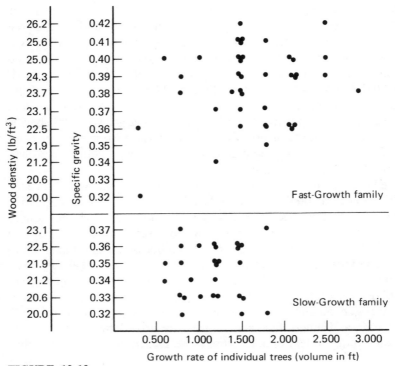

FIGURE 12.12

Growth rates and specific gravities are shown for individual trees from the fastest- and slowest-grown families in Figure 12.11. There is essentially no correlation between growth rate and specific gravity in trees, either in the fast- or slow-growth families.

give the tree improver a powerful tool to tailor-make trees for various products (Zobel, 1981).

Growth and wood-quality relationships are very complex in the hardwoods, in which a pattern is found that is directly opposite to the one frequently quoted for conifers; that is, the faster-growing trees have higher specific gravities than do slow-growing trees. This appears to be true for some of the ring-porous hardwood such as ash (*Fraxinus*) and oak (*Quercus*) but is not general for the numerous species of diffuse-porous hardwoods. In the ring-porous trees, it appears that an approximately equal volume of vessels is produced each year, regardless of the total growth during the year. Therefore, the slow-growing tree will have a greater proportion of vessels per unit volume of the annual ring compared to the denser fibers and tracheids and will have a low-specific-gravity wood. A fast-growing tree continues to produce the denser fibers outside the band of vessels; therefore, the wood will have a higher specific gravity. In diffuse-porous hardwoods the number of vessels formed in an annual ring is closely related to the width of the ring, and growth rate has little direct effect on wood specific gravity.

It has been found that if a pine tree is caused to grow faster because of release by thinning or by fertilization, the tracheids produced during the period of rapid growth will be somewhat shorter than those formed during a period of normal growth. This response is to a sudden or artificial environmental stimulus and usually tapers off within a few years. Within any stand, tracheid lengths are essentially uncorrelated with the inherent growth rates of individual trees, thus making it possible to have short or long tracheids, irrespective of whether the trees are genetically fast growing or slow growing. It must be stressed that for most pine species and Douglas fir, increased growth rate from environmental manipulation results in shorter tracheids, but length is independent of genetic potential for growth rate.

Sometimes the pattern is reversed for hardwoods in which the faster-growing trees have the longest fibers. Such a relationship has been shown for *Populus* by Kennedy (1957), Einspahr and Benson (1967), and several others. In actuality, the relationship of growth rate to fiber length has not been well studied for most hardwood species.

Fertilizers and Wood Qualities

As the use of supplemental nutrients becomes more widespread, there is an increasing concern about the effect that fertilization will have on wood qualities. One general reaction that has been observed and is documented for the hard pines and Douglas fir is that heavy nitrogen fertilization results in a lowering of specific gravity for about a period of 5 years (Posey, 1964) (Figure 12.13). Much more needs to be done to permit more precise evaluation of the effect of sudden and artificial changes in the nutrient environment upon wood when the growth rate has been markedly increased. Sometimes phosphorous fertilization will reduce the high-specific-gravity values that are common to trees grown under strong deficiencies of this element. The lowering of specific gravity by P reduces it to values of wood under normal growing conditions where no P deficiency exists.

One of the most desired benefits from fertilization is to make the wood of trees more uniform than when grown under normal conditions. This improved uniformity can be quite marked. In *P. taeda*, Posey (1964) found that high nitrogen fertilization reduces the gravity of inherently low-specific-gravity trees only slightly, whereas the gravity of high-density trees is greatly reduced. This is of special importance to the tree breeder because the improvement gained by breeding for high specific gravity can be partially nullified if a heavy nitrogen fertilization is used.

It appears that any environmental treatment that makes a softwood tree grow faster will result in shorter cells (Bannan, 1967). This has been explained by the rapidity of transverse divisions of the cambial initial cells that prevents develop-

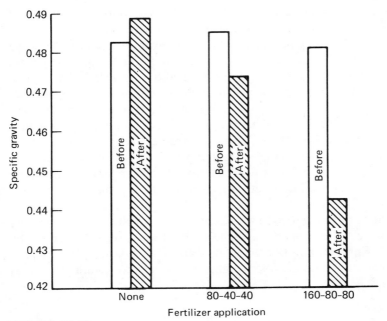

FIGURE 12.13

Wood qualities can be affected by forest management techniques. Shown are specific gravities for a stand of pine fertilized at age 16; *before* indicates the 7 years prior to thinning; *after* indicates the 7 years after fertilization. The high-N fertilizer was found to reduce specific gravity. It reduces individual high-gravity trees more than low-gravity ones, thus making for more uniform wood within the tree.

ment to full cell length before another division occurs. Cambial initials of slower-growing trees have sufficient time to achieve their length capabilities.

WOOD QUALITIES OF EXOTICS

Although general aspects of wood qualities have been thoroughly covered, it is essential also to discuss the wood properties of very fast-grown trees that are so common to exotic plantations in the tropical and subtropical regions. Wood qualities of exotics are often quite different from the same species in their indigenous ranges, especially in tropical plantations where young trees are harvested that contain a high proportion of juvenile wood (Zobel, 1981). In general, the wood qualities of fast-grown exotic hardwoods are acceptable, although sometimes the wood is undesirable for the product that is wanted.

Exotic Softwoods

Much of the coniferous wood produced in the future will be from fast-grown plantations of exotic species. Although the wood may be different from that from natural stands, it is not necessarily inferior; its utility is dependent upon the final product that is desired. Products such as writing papers or some tissue and newsprint can be made efficiently from the wood from young conifer plantations. For products that require good tear strength, a high proportion of juvenile wood is not desirable; therefore, wood from young exotic softwood plantations is inferior. Often tree form is very poor, resulting in a high proportion of reaction wood and large knots. When the young plantations are thinned, the combination of juvenile wood, reaction wood, large knots, and thick bark results in especially poor-quality wood, and their combined effects are that paper made from the young trees sometimes does not meet the standards for tear strength that are necessary for the world market (Dadswell and Wardrop, 1959). However, paper made from predominantly juvenile wood is often used for consumption within the country where it is grown. The strength and finishing properties of solid-wood products made from young exotic conifers with much juvenile wood often are poor (Pearson and Gilmore, 1980).

There is considerable variation among pines in their response to different tropical environments, as expressed in wood quality. Because of different responses to varied growing conditions, species such as *P. caribaea* and *P. kesiya* may have wood with essentially no summerwood when they are grown in certain environments or, in other environments, they will develop an extreme juvenile-wood core at the tree center, with very dense wood in the adjacent mature-wood zone (see Figure 12.5).

There have been a number of studies about the environmental effects on wood of tropical softwoods when they are grown as exotics; only a few can be mentioned here. For example, the wood of young *P. caribaea* was found suitable for dissolving pulps, and a series of papers by Foelkel (Foelkel et al., 1975a, for example) dealt with the value of woods of different fast-grown exotic tropical pines for sulfate pulping. Generally, these reports conclude that wood from these species is quite usable, although it is somewhat low in yield and tear strength.

Wood of young conifers is especially suitable for groundwood and thermomechanical pulping. Both processes require a heavy energy input, but the treatment of juvenile wood requires less energy usage than does the thick-walled mature wood. In the tropics some young wood, especially from thinnings, has been whole-tree-chipped. A limited amount of this kind of wood apparently can be tolerated in the mill furnish with no adverse effects, but problems sometimes result when more than 15 to 20% of the furnish is made up of whole-tree chips. Young trees have a high proportion of leaves and branches that when pulped occupy a disproportionate amount of digester space and require a heavy chemical usage although they contribute relatively little to fiber production.

Exotic Hardwoods

The undisputed leaders in fast-grown exotic hardwood plantations are various species of *Eucalyptus*. Despite the numerous trials being made and the several species planted on an operational scale, the *E. grandis–saligna* complex and *E. globulus* currently are clearly the most important. In good environments with proper care and improved genetic stock, the eucalypts can grow very rapidly and produce a most desirable wood.

There are many species and races of eucalypts that have widely diverse wood qualities (Foekel et al., 1975b). Some major eucalypt species (*E. deglupta,* for example) have wood specific gravities on the low side, whereas others, such as *E. tereticornis, E. citriodora,* and *E. cloeziana,* have high specific gravities that produce strong, dense wood that is especially suitable for charcoal. The two characteristics most affecting pulp qualities of the different eucalypts are specific gravity and extractives (Ferreira, 1968). Older trees frequently develop problems with deposition of phenolic substances in their wood, but young trees are reasonably free of adverse chemicals that can be very important in some species (Baklein, 1960). Eucalypt wood is often considered to be uniform wherever it is grown, but sometimes the environment in different plantations can produce somewhat different wood, and this must be watched closely (Hans and Burley, 1972; Taylor, 1973).

Although there is variability among species, it is of the utmost importance that the species of *Eucalyptus* planted most extensively (*E. grandis, E. saligna, E. regnans, E. globulus E. viminalis*) have wood in the midrange of specific gravity, and that they are suitable for many products. The wood and product characteristics of this group of eucalypts are similar to the soft hardwoods in the southeastern United States, such as *Liquidambar, Platanus,* and *Acer,* and they have wide utility.

The wood qualities of the eucalypts often vary considerably among individual trees within a species. The opportunity to change wood qualities in the desired direction through genetic manipulation is good (Rudman et al., 1969; Davidson, 1972; Doran, 1974). Wood from the eucalypts can be manipulated quite effectively in the desired direction by changes in environment through silvicultural treatment combined with breeding.

A complete treatment of wood from fast-grown exotic plantations could include numerous other hardwoods, but only a few will be mentioned here. One species with the greatest potential for tropical plantations is *Gmelina arborea;* this species grows very rapidly and is used in plantations in several tropical areas, most notably in the Amazon Basin in Brazil. Although its wood and pulping qualities have been extensively studied by many investigators, little wood-quality data have been published (Palmer, 1973). The wood of *Gmelina* is very good for most pulping operations and final products, and fast growth does not seem to have an adverse effect. Many companies have test pulped it during the past 5 years, and reports say that it is a good wood, easy to work with, and is suitable for a number of products. *Gmelina* needs improvement in uniformity of growth and form, but it is easy to manipulate and can be handled using vegetative propagation.

Although some other fast-grown hardwoods other than *Eucalyptus* and *Gmelina* are planted as exotics, none are grown on a large enough scale to be of major importance on the world market yet. In the subtropical and temperate regions, short-rotation hardwoods are becoming more important and, although much information is now available about wood from these species, they cannot be considered as fast-grown when compared to the more tropical species (Jett and Zobel, 1974).

The current trend that will affect the usage of trees from exotic hardwood plantations is the move toward more utility of hardwoods for energy and chemical products (Goldstein, 1980). Currently, energy usage is receiving intense interest, along with the use of wood for chemicals. It appears that these two uses will become more important in the future. The ultimate effect of using wood for other than standard fiber and solid-wood products cannot be predicted, but if it occurs to any great extent, it will have a major impact on fast-grown exotic plantation culture and on tree improvement techniques.

Firewood accounts for about one half the timber consumed on a worldwide basis, and because many of the indigenous forests have been depleted, an increasing plantation culture of fast-grown exotics is being developed specifically for use as firewood. Much of the current emphasis on planting fast-grown exotic hardwoods in the tropical and subtropical areas is related to energy usage. There is an increasing interest in developing trees that are specially adapted to grow on areas close to habitations and that have wood that is especially desirable for firewood. On a worldwide basis, this generally means to breed for resistance to drought and eroded soils and for high specific gravity.

There will be a greatly increased need for genetic manipulation of wood in the tropics. Recently, methods have been developed to use the mixed tropical hardwoods as a source of pulp (Gomez and Mondragon, 1974). As a result, increased areas of tropical hardwoods will be cleared to be planted with exotics or indigenous species. Wood qualities and wood information are poorly known for the latter and must be included in tree improvement programs.

LITERATURE CITED

Artuz-Siegel, E. A., Wangaard, F. F., and Tamalong, F. N. 1968. Relationships between fiber characteristics and pulp-sheet properties in Philippine hardwoods. *Tappi* **51**(6):261–267.

Baklein, A. 1960. The effect of extractives on black liquor from eucalypt pulping. *Appita* **14**(1):5–15.

Bannan, M. W. 1967. Anticlinal divisions and cell length in conifer cambium. *For. Prod. Jour.* **17**(6):63–69.

Barefoot, A. C., Hitchings, R. G., Ellwood, E. L., and Wilson, E. 1970. "The Relationship between Loblolly Pine Fiber Morphology and Kraft Paper Properties," Tech. Bull. 202, North Carolina Agricultural Experiment Station, North Carolina State University, Raleigh.

Barker, R. G. 1974. Papermaking properties of young hardwoods. *Tappi* **57**(8):107–111.

Bendtsen, B. A. 1978. Properties of wood from improved and intensively managed trees. *For. Prod. Jour.* **28**(10):61–72.

Blair, R. L., Zobel, B. J., Franklin, E. C., Djerf, A. C., and Mendel, J. M. 1974. The effect of tree form and rust infection on wood and pulp properties of loblolly pine. *Tappi* **57**(7):46–50.

Brasil, M. A., Veiga, R. A., and Millo, H. 1979. Densidade básica de madeira de *Eucalyptus grandis* aos 3 años de idade. *IPEF* **19**:63–76.

Champion, H. G. 1929. More about spiral grain in conifers. *Indian Forester* **55**(2):57–58.

Dadswell, H. E., and Wardrop, A. B. 1959. Growing trees with wood properties desirable for paper manufacture. *Appita* **12**(4):129–136.

Davidson, J. 1972. "Natural Variation in *Eucalyptus deglupta* and Its Effect on Choice of Criteria for Selection in a Tree Improvement Program." Proc. 3rd Meet., Res. Comm. of Aust. For. Council, Mt. Gambier, Australia, pp. 22–22.2.

de Guth, E. B. 1980. "Relationship between Wood Density and Tree Diameter in *Pinus elliottii* of Missiones, Argentina." Div. 5, IUFRO Meeting, Oxford, England.

Doran, J. C. 1974. "Genetic Variation in Wood Density of *Eucalyptus regnans.*" 4th Meet., Res. Working Group, Aust. For. Council, Melbourne, Australia, pp. 99–101.

Echols, R. M. 1959. Estimation of pulp yield and quality of living trees from paired-core samples. *Tappi* **42**(1):875–877.

Einspahr, D. W., and Benson, M. K. 1967. Geographic variation of quaking aspen in Wisconsin and upper Michigan. *Sil. Gen.* **16**(3):89–120.

Einspahr, D. W., Benson, M. K., and Peckham, J. R. 1967. "Variation and Heritability of Wood and Growth Characteristics of Five-Year-Old Quaking Aspen," Inst. Paper Chem. Notes No. 1.

Einspahr, D. W., van Buijtenen, J. P., and Peckham, J. R. 1969. Pulping characteristics of ten-year loblolly pine selected for extreme wood specific gravity. *Sil. Gen.* **18**(3):57–61.

Ferreira, M. 1970. Estudo da variacão da densidade basica da madeira de *Eucalyptus alba* e *Eucalyptus saligna* Smith. Instituto de Pesquisas e Estudos Flosestas (Piracicaba, Brazil) Report No. 1, pp. 83–96.

Foelkel, C. E., Barrichelo, L. E., do Amaral, A. C. B., and do Valle, C. F. 1975a.

Variation in wood characteristics and sulphate pulp properties from *P. oocarpa* with aging of forest stands. *IPEF* **10**:81–87.

Foelkel, C. E. B., Barrichelo, L. E. G., and Milaney, A. F. 1975b. Study of the *Eucalyptus* sp. wood characteristics and their unbleached sulphate pulps. *IPEF* **10**:17–37.

France, R. F., and Mexal, J. G. 1980. Morphological variation in tracheids in the bolewood of mature *Picea engelmannii* and *Pinus contorta. Can. Jour. For. Res.* **10**(4):573–578.

Garrett, P. W., Randell, W. K., Shigo, A. L., and Shortle, W. C. 1979. "Inheritance of Compartmentalization of Wounds in Sweetgum (*Liquidambar styraciflua*) and Eastern Cottonwood (*Populus deltoides*)," Forest Service Research Paper. NE No. 443, Northeastern Forest Experiment Station, Upper Darby, Pa.

Goggans, J. F. 1961. "The Interplay of Environment and Heredity as Factors Controlling Wood Properties in Conifers with Special Emphasis on their Effects on Specific Gravity," Technical Report No. 11, School of Forestry, North Carolina State University, Raleigh.

Goldstein, I. S. 1980. "Chemicals from Biomass: Present Status. Alternate Feedstocks for Petrochemicals." Proc. American Chemical Society, San Francisco.

Gomez, C. H., and Mondragon, I. 1974. The pulping of Colombian hardwoods for linerboard. *Tappi* **57**(5):140–142.

Hans, A. S., and Burley, J. 1972. Wood quality of eight *Eucalyptus* species in Zambia. *Sep. Exp.* **29**:1378–1380.

Harris, J. M. 1965. "The Heritability of Wood Density," IUFRO Section 41, Melbourne, Australia.

Heikinheimo, O. 1952. Kokemuksia visakoevun kasvatuksesta [Experiments in growing curly birch]. *Comm. Inst. For. Fenn.* **39**(5):26.

Higgins, H. G., Young, J., Balodis, V., Phillips, F. H., and Colley, J. 1973. The density and structure of hardwoods in relation to paper surface characteristics and other properties. *Tappi* **56**(8):127–131.

Howe, J. P. 1974. Relationship of climate to the specific gravity of four Costa Rican hardwoods. *Wood Fiber* **5**(4):347–352.

Jett, J. B., Weir, R. J., and Barker, J. A. 1977. "The Inheritance of Cellulose in Loblolly pine," TAPPI For. Biol. Comm. Meet., Madison, Wisc.

Jett, J. B., and Zobel, B. J. 1974. Wood and pulping properties of young hardwoods. *Tappi* **58**(1):92–96.

Kennedy, R. W. 1957. Fibre length of fast- and slow-grown black cottonwood. *For. Chron.* **33**:46–50.

Kirk, D. B., Breeman, L. G., and Zobel, B. J. 1972. A pulping evaluation of loblolly pine wood. *Tappi* **55**(11):1600–1604.

Klem, G. S. 1966. Increment cores as a basis for determining a number of properties of *Picea abies*. *Norsk Skogler* **12**(11/12):448–449.

Koch, C. B. 1967. Specific gravity as affected by rate of growth within sprout clumps of black cherry. *Jour. For.* **65**(3):200–202.

Kozlowski, T. T. 1971. *Growth and Development of Trees*, Vol. II. Academic Press, New York.

Land, S. B., and Lee, J. C. 1981. Variation in sycamore wood specific gravity. *Wood Sci.* **13**(3):166–170.

Larson, P. R. 1962. A biological approach to wood quality. *Tappi* **45**(6):443–448.

Larson, P. R. 1969. "Wood Formation and the Concept of Wood Quality," Bull. 74, Yale University School of Forestry, New Haven.

Low, A. J. 1964. Compression wood in conifers: A review of the literature. *For. Abs.* **25**(3,4):1–13.

Lowerts, G. A., and Kellison, R. C. 1981. "Genetically Controlled Resistance to Discoloration and Decay in Wounded Trees of Yellow-Poplar." M.S. thesis, School of Forestry Research, North Carolina State University, Raleigh.

Lowery, D. P., and Schmidt, W. C. 1967. "Effect of Thinning on the Specific Gravity of Western Larch Crop Trees." U.S. Forest Service Research Paper INT-70.

Marts, R. O. 1949. Effect of crown reduction on taper and density in longleaf pine. *South. Lumberman* **179**:206–209.

McKinney, M. D., and Nicholas, D. D. 1971. Genetic differences in wood traits among half-century-old families of Douglas-fir. *Wood Fiber* **2**(4):347–355.

Meylan, B. A. 1968. Cause of high longitudinal shrinkage in wood. *For. Prod. Jour.* **18**(4):75–78.

Mork, E. 1928. Die Qualität des Fichtenholzes unter besonderer Rucksichtnahme auf Schlief -und Papierholz. *Papierfabrikant* **26**:741–747.

Mutibaric, J. 1967. Correlation between ring width and wood density in Euramerican Poplars. *Sumarstro* **20**(112) :39–46.

Nicholls, J. W. P., Morris, J. D., and Pederick, L. A. 1980. Heritability estimates of density characteristics in juvenile *Pinus radiata* wood. *Sil. Gen.* **29**(2):54–61.

Ollesen, P. O. 1976. The interrelation between basic density and ring width of Norway spruce. *Det Forstlige Forsgsvaesen Danmark* No. 281, **34**(4):341–359.

Palmer, E. R. 1973. *Gmelina arborea* as a potential source of hardwood pulp. *Trop. Sci.* **15**(3):243–260.

Parker, M. L., Hunt, K., Warren, W. G., and Kennedy, R. W. 1973. "Effect of Thinning and Fertilization on Intra-ring Characteristics and Kraft Pulp Yields of Douglas-Fir." 8th Cell. Conf., Syracuse, N.Y.

Paul, B. H. 1957. "Juvenile Wood in Conifers," Report No. 2094, U.S. Forest Service, For. Prod. Lab., Madison, Wisc.

Pearson, R. G., and Gilmore, R. C. 1980. Effect of fast growth rate on the mechanical properties of loblolly pine. *For. Prod. Jour.* **30**(5):47–54.

Polge, H. 1971. Inheritance of specific gravity in four-year-old seedlings of silver fir. *Ann. Sci. Forest.* **28**(2):185–194.

Posey, C. E. 1964. "The Effects of Fertilization upon Wood Properties of Loblolly Pine (*Pinus taeda*). Proc. 8th South. Conf. For. Tree Impr., Savannah, Ga., pp. 126–130.

Rudman, P., Higgs, M., Davidson, J., and Malajczuk, N. 1969. "Breeding Eucalypts for Wood Properties." 2nd World Consul. on For. Tree Breed., Washington, D.C.

Scurfield, G. 1973. Reaction wood: Its structure and function. *Science* **179**:637–656.

Semke, L. K., and Corbi, J. C. 1974. Sources of less-coarse pine fiber for southern bleached printing papers. *Tappi* **57**(11):113–117.

Shelbourne, C. J. A., Zobel, B. J., and Stonecypher, R. W. 1969. The inheritance of compression wood and its genetic and phenotypic correlations with six other traits in five-year-old loblolly pine. *Sil. Gen.* **18**:43–47.

Skolmen, R. G. 1972. "Specific Gravity Variation in Robusta *Eucalyptus* grown in Hawaii," U.S. For. Service Research Paper PSW No. 78.

Smith, W. J. 1967. The heritability of fibre characteristics and its application to wood quality improvement in forest trees. *Sil. Gen.* **16**(2):41–50.

Stairs, G. R. 1969. "Seed Source and Growth Rate Effects on Wood Quality in Norway Spruce." Proc. 11th Comm. For. Tree Breed. in Canada, Ottawa, pp. 231–236.

Stern, K. 1963. Einfluss der Höhe am Stamm Verteilung der Raumdechte des Holzes in Fichtenbeständen [Influence of height of stem on the distribution of wood density in spruce stands]. *Holzforschung* **17**(1):6–12.

Stonecypher, R. W., and Zobel, B. J. 1966. Inheritance of specific gravity in five-year-old seedlings of loblolly pine. *Tappi* **49**(7):303–305.

Talbert, J. T., and Jett, J. B. 1981. Regional specific gravity values for plantation grown loblolly pine in the southeastern United States. *For. Sci.* **27**(4):801–807.

Taylor, F. W. 1969. The effect of ray tissue on the specific gravity of wood. *Wood Fiber* **1**(2):142–145.

Taylor, F. W. 1973. Variations in the anatomical properties of South African grown *Eucalyptus grandis*. *Appita* **27**(3):171–178.

Taylor, F. W. 1977. Variation in specific gravity and fiber length of selected hardwoods. *For. Sci.* **23**(2):190–194.

Teles, A. A. 1980. Sen Aprovertamento para Polpa a Papel Estudo de Madeiras da Amazonia Visaudo [Anatomical study of the woods of *Virola sebifera* and *Pseudobombax tomentosum* with a view to their use for pulp and paper]. *Bras. Flor.* **42**:25–34.

Thorbjornsen, E. 1961. Variation in density and fiber length in wood of yellow poplar. *Tappi* **44**(3):192–195.

Ujvari, E., and Szönyi, L. 1973. Expectable gain breeding long fibre Norway spruce. *Kulonlenyomat* **69**(2):93–99.

van Buijtenen, J. P. 1962. Heritability estimates of wood density in loblolly pine. *Tappi* **45**(7):602–605.

van Buijtenen, J. P. 1964. Anatomical factors influencing wood specific gravity of slash pines and the implications for the development of a high quality pulpwood. *Tappi* **47**(7):401–404.

van Buijtenen, J. P. 1969. The impact of state–industry cooperative programs on tree planting. *For. Farmer* **29**(2):14, 20, 22.

van Buijtenen, J. P., Zobel, B. J., and Joranson, P. N. 1961. Variation of some wood and pulp properties in an even-aged loblolly pine stand. *Tappi* **44**(2):141–143.

von Wedel, K. W., Zobel, B. J., and Shelbourne, C. J. A. 1968. Prevalence and effects of knots in young loblolly pine. *For. Prod. Jour.* **18**(9):97–103.

Wakeley, P. C. 1969. Effects of evolution on southern pine wood. *For. Prod. Jour.* **19**(2):16–20.

Walters, C. S. 1951. Figured walnut propagated by grafting. *Jour. For.* **49**(12):917.

Webb, C. D. 1964. "Natural Variation in Specific Gravity, Fiber Length and Interlocked Grain of Sweetgum (*Liquidambar styraciflua*) within Trees, among Trees and among Geographic Areas in the South Atlantic States." Ph.D. thesis, North Carolina State University, Raleigh.

Wheeler, E. Y., Zobel, B. J., and Weeks, D. L. 1965. Tracheid length and diameter variation in the bole of loblolly pine. *Tappi* **49**(11):484–490.

Whyte, A. G. D., Wiggins, P. C., and Wong, T. W. 1980. "A Survey of Spiral Grain in *P. caribaea* v. *hondurensis* in Fiji and its effects," IUFRO, Div. 5., Conf., Oxford, England.

Zobel, B. J. 1961. Inheritance of wood properties in conifers. *Sil. Gen.* **10**(3):65–70.

Zobel, B. J. 1965. "Inheritance of Fiber Characteristics and Specific Gravity in Hardwoods—A Review," IUFRO Meet. in Melbourne, Australia.

Zobel, B. J. 1981. Wood quality from fast-grown plantations. *Tappi* **64**(1):71–74.

Zobel, B. J., Campinos, E., Jr., and Ikemori, Y. K. 1983. Selecting and breeding for desirable wood. *Tappi* **66**:70–73.

Zobel, B. J., and Haught, A. 1962. "Effect of Bole Straightness on Compression Wood of Loblolly Pine," Technical Report No. 15, North Carolina State University, Raleigh.

Zobel, B. J., Thorbjornsen, E., and Henson, F. 1960a. Geographic, site and individual tree variation in wood properties of loblolly pine. *Sil. Gen.* **9**(6):149–158.

Zobel, B. J., Henson, F., and Webb, C. 1960b. Estimation of certain wood properties of loblolly and slash pine trees from breast height sampling. *For. Sci.* **6**(2):155–162.

Zobel, B. J., Stonecypher, R., Brown, C., and Kellison, R. C. 1966. Variation and inheritance of cellulose in the southern pines. *Tappi* **49**(9):383–387.

Zobel, B. J., Kellison, R. C., Mathias, M. F., and Hatcher, A. V. 1972. "Wood Density of Southern Pines," North Carolina Agricultural Experiment Station Tech. Bull. No. 208.

Zobel, B. J., Jett, J. B., and Hutto, R. 1978. Improving wood density of short rotation southern pine. *Tappi* **61**(3):41–44.

CHAPTER 13

Advanced Generations and Continued Improvement

In many tree improvement programs throughout the world, gains from first-generation activities are now being realized as seed orchards reach maturity or through the use of vegetative propagation of genetically proven trees. Gains from advanced-generation tree improvement are potentially and considerably greater than those that are achievable in first-generation programs. In agriculture, numerous generations of breeding have resulted in improved varieties that have been altered genetically to such a degree that they bear only a faint resemblance to their ancestral relatives. Annual crop breeders have an advantage over tree breeders in that generations can be turned over at the rate of one or more per year, and many crops have been subjected to selection and genetic improvement for thousands of years both by trained and untrained breeders. The size and longevity of forest trees make them subject to breeding constraints, especially those involving time and space, which are not encountered with annual crops. Nevertheless, opportunities do exist to manage the genetic resources of important forest tree species over several generations in a way to alter their genetic potential significantly to meet the needs and desires of people.

The main objective of advanced-generation tree improvement is to maximize the gain per unit of time. To accomplish this goal, improved tree populations must be managed *from the outset* so that gains can be achieved each generation, while at the same time maintaining sufficient genetic variability to ensure continued long-term progress. Critical decisions in advanced-generation breeding include the choice of mating design and selection method, the intensity of selection applied, and proper management of inbreeding.

Breeders make genetic progress through many generations by recurrent selection (the relevant concepts were introduced in Chaper 4). Recurrent selection involves the choice of the best progeny from selected parents over successive generations. Several types of recurrent selection systems have been devised by plant and animal breeders, some of which are aimed at exploiting differences among trees in general combining ability, whereas others have been devised to utilize specific combining ability or to use both types of genetic effects. This chapter will be primarily concerned with improvement programs in which recurrent selection is used to improve general combining ability, although many of the methods discussed are applicable to any type of selection system. Many of the concepts covered in this chapter have been discussed elsewhere in the book, but they are mentioned together here because of their relevance to advanced-generation tree improvement.

BASE, BREEDING, AND PRODUCTION POPULATIONS

The most important concept related to advanced-generation tree improvement is a separation of populations with different functions. At any given time, three types of populations should be maintained in a breeding program, as are shown diagrammatically in Figure 13.1.

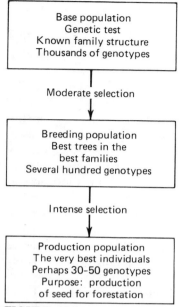

FIGURE 13.1

In most large-scale advanced-generation tree improvement programs, three different types of populations are usually maintained at a given point in time. These populations differ greatly in size and purpose as is indicated by the diagram.

The *base population* of a given generation consists of the trees from which the tree improver chooses to make selections for the next generation of breeding. In the first generation of tree improvement, the base population usually consists of trees growing in natural stands or unimproved plantations. In advanced generations, the base poulation is most often a genetic test consisting of the progeny of selected parent trees from the previous generation. The identity of at least one, and usually both, parents of all progeny growing in the genetic test is known. The base poulation most often contains hundreds to many thousands of genotypes.

The *breeding population* consists of a subset of individuals from the base population that is selected for their desirable qualities to serve as parents for the next generation of breeding. Increments of gain that result from proceeding to the next generation of improvement result from selection efforts for the breeding population. A compromise must be made between increasing the selection differential, which gives greater genetic gain but a smaller breeding population, and the need to maintain a breeding population large enough so that genetic variation is kept at a level that allows continued genetic progress in future generations. In practice, a moderate selection intensity is usually employed on individuals for the breeding population. Usually 200 or more selected trees are included in the breeding population each generation.

The third type of population in most ongoing tree improvement programs is the *production population,* which is used strictly to produce seeds or vegetative propagules for operational reforestation programs. In some instances, the production population may consist of the same set of genotypes as the breeding population, but usually the production population is a highly selected subset of the breeding population. As few as 20 to 30 genotypes may be included in the production population. These individuals represent the very best individuals in the breeding population and are the best selections that can be obtained for any given generation. They are chosen to maximize genetic gain in operational forest plantations. A small, intensively selected production population is a dead end from a breeding standpoint because of a very reduced base that would decrease progress from improvement efforts and very quickly lead to high levels of inbreeding.

Breeding and production populations are usually established in separate orchards. Design criteria for the two types of orchards generally are completely different because of their different functions. Breeding orchards are managed to expedite completion of the matings required in a generation and should be so designed. For example, if the mating design calls for control pollinations, all ramets of a single clone can be grafted next to each other to facilitate movement of the breeder among ramets. Radical cultural treatments may be applied to trees in a breeding orchard to promote the flowering required to complete the mating scheme, even if the long-term health of the trees in the orchard is affected in an adverse way. From a breeding standpoint, once the required matings are completed for a clone, the trees are no longer needed.

In contrast to management criteria and cultural treatments that are applied in breeding orchards, production orchards must be managed for long-term maximum production of genetically superior seed. A discussion of proper management techniques for production seed orchards is in Chapter 6.

The contribution of the breeding and production populations to the genetic gain that is realized in operational plantations is depicted in the hypothetical example in Figure 13.2. Percentage gain figures are not meant to represent those obtainable in any specific program or for any specific trait, but they do serve to illustrate the means by which tree improvement programs can make significant amounts of gain in both the short and long term. In Figure 13.2, gains on the order of 10% are shown to occur with each cycle of selection and breeding in the breeding population. An additional 15% gain is made by further selection each generation within the breeding population for the production population. Therefore, in the first generation, combined total gain is on the order of 25%. It is important to understand, however, that only the 10% gain through selection for the breeding population is accumulated from generation to generation. For example, the total amount of gain achieved through two generations of selection in the breeding population is 20%. The additional 15% gain that comes from establishment of an intensively selected production population is a gain that may be obtained each generation, but it is not passed to the next generation of improvement. Therefore, the total gain in second-generation production seed orchards is 35% in the theoretical example. As stated previously and as shown in Figure 13.2, the production population is a dead end for long-term improvement purposes and is used only for operational production of improved propagules.

In some tree improvement programs, the breeding and production functions may be served by the same populations (Namkoong, 1979). This situation usually results because of cost restraints that make it impossible to maintain both types of populations in one program. Although costs are less in such situations, gains in either the short term, long term, or both, may be severely compromised. When many hundreds of genotypes are included in both populations, prospects for

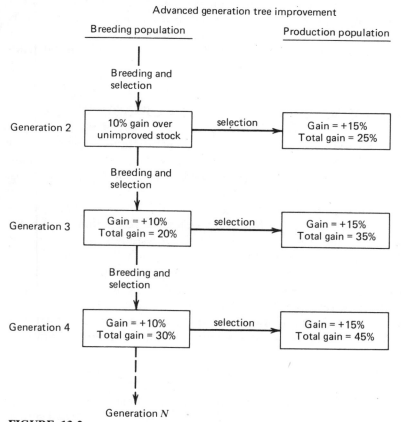

FIGURE 13.2

Genetic gain from tree improvement in a given generation arises from selection for the breeding population and further selection in this group of genotypes for the production population. The extra gain achieved by selection for the production population is not passed along to the next generation.

excellent long-term gains exist, but gains in the short term from operational production of propagules will be reduced because of a small selection differential. Alternatively, if the breeder uses a large selection differential and reduces the breeding and production population to a restricted number of genotypes, gains in the short term will be maximized, but gains in the long term will be limited by a reduced genetic base. For these reasons, breeding and production populations are kept separate in most lage-scale, long-term breeding programs.

The number of individuals that should be included in the breeding population depends upon the objectives of the program and the genetic structure of the population (Burley and Namkoong, 1980). Most tree improvement workers recommend that 200 or more trees be included in breeding populations (Libby, 1973; Schoenike, 1975; Talbert, 1979; van Buijtenen and Lowe, 1979). It has been recommended that up to 10,000 individuals should be saved if the purpose is gene pool conservation (Toda, 1965). Although it is beyond the scope of this book, it is possible to calculate the number of trees that need to be saved in order to assure a high probability of conserving alleles at various gene frequencies (Burley and Namkoong, 1980).

AVOIDANCE VERSUS MANAGEMENT OF INBREEDING

Inbreeding and its possible effect on tree improvement programs has been a major source of concern for tree breeders since tree improvement efforts were begun. Aspects of inbreeding and related matings were covered in Chapter 2. Most inbreeding studies have dealt with selfing, and in general they have shown substantial depression in growth and also in seed yield (Orr-Ewing, 1965; Franklin, 1970; Andersson et al., 1974). There have been few investigations concerning depression at inbreeding levels less than selfing. One study with slash pine in which the effects of matings between half sibs, full sibs, and selfs were investigated showed that significant and predictable amounts of growth depression could be expected with increasing levels of inbreeding in this species (Gansel, 1971). Although many more research data dealing with low levels of inbreeding are needed, it is obvious from the selfing studies that have been conducted that tree improvers must be concerned with the potential buildup of inbreeding in their improved populations.

Inbreeding becomes a complex problem as tree improvement programs move into advanced generations. In first-generation tree improvement programs in which each parent tree has been selected from a different natural stand, or when trees have been selected from plantations established from a very broad genetic base, the chance that selected trees are related to one another is small. In the case of first-generation clonal seed orchards, all that must be done to avoid significant amounts of selfing is to separate the ramets of a clone at a sufficient distance in the seed orchard so that they do not pollinate each other. No related matings will occur in a breeding program involving control pollination unless selfs are made. In advanced generations, however, possibilities arise for matings of half sibs, full sibs, parents and offspring, or perhaps even more distant kinds of relatives. Avoidance of related matings in clonal production seed orchards becomes more difficult when several forms of relatives are included in the select population.

Related matings will eventually occur in a closed breeding population regardless of the mating design used. Even the most extensive crossing scheme available to breeders will result in the number of unrelated families being reduced by one half in each generation (see Chapter 8). The number of unrelated families is further reduced by family selection, which is used to some extent in almost all advanced-generation tree improvement programs. In some instances, opportunities may exist to delay the onset of inbreeding in the population by the infusion of new unrelated selections into the breeding program when relatedness threatens to become a problem. However, as programs proceed through several generations and genetic gains increase, it is unlikely that any new genotypes in unimproved populations will be found that could be introduced into the breeding population without reducing the amount of gain that has been achieved. It might be possible to introduce improved but unrelated material from programs in other regions, but eventually even these sources of new unrelated material will be depleted. Therefore, it is a fact that inbreeding cannot be avoided in the long term in an advanced-generation tree improvement program. As a result, the tree improver must manage the population in such a way so as to minimize deleterious effects of inbreeding or to benefit from its occurrence.

Several strategies are available to manage inbreeding in tree improvement programs. One alternative is to allow inbreeding to build up slowly in breeding and production populations. Results of a long-term experiment with corn, involving over 70 generations of selection and breeding, have shown that substantial gains have been made and are still possible at inbreeding levels that are much higher than those obtained with one generation of selfing (Dudley, 1977). Inbreeding occurred slowly in the corn population, and the effects of selection and repeated recombination of alleles through breeding served to overcome, at least to an extent, the potentially deleterious effects of inbreeding. Whether this would hold true with forest trees is not yet proven, but in advanced generations the potential does exist to select and breed relatives that are only distantly related and to allow a slow buildup of inbreeding. If high levels of inbreeding are approached slowly, rather than quickly as with selfing, inbreeding depression may be less of a problem than selfing studies would indicate.

Another strategy receiving considerable attention as tree improvement programs proceed to advanced generations is that of multiple breeding populations, which were mentioned in Chapter 8. With this procedure, a large breeding population, usually consisting of several hundred individuals, is broken into a number of much smaller populations or breeding groups. The breeding strategy calls for matings to occur only between individuals who belong to the same breeding group. Because breeding groups consist of a small number of individuals, perhaps on the order of 25 or less, relatedness and subsequent inbreeding resulting from related matings will occur quickly within breeding groups. However, if only the best individual in each breeding group was chosen for use in a production seed orchard, parents in the orchard would be unrelated to one another and seed produced would be totally outcrossed. Use of multiple breeding populations to avoid inbreeding in production seed orchards has become known as *sublining*.

Multiple population breeding has been proposed in forest tree breeding for reasons other than avoidance of inbreeding in production seed orchards, including gene conservation (see Chapter 15), and for situations in which uncertainties exist regarding the desired goals of the tree improvement program (Namkoong, 1979; Burley and Namkoong, 1980). In the latter instance, the breeder could plan for each of the small populations to have somewhat different breeding goals and could perhaps have improved material available to meet whatever new future demands the market might present. In forest tree improvement, the current major operational use of multiple breeding populations has been for the purpose of inbreeding avoidance in production seed orchards (van Buijtenen and Lowe, 1979; McKeand and Beineke, 1980; van Buijtenen, 1981).

It is clear that inbreeding is a phenomenon that must be managed but cannot be avoided in long-term tree improvement programs. Whereas the appropriate strategy to use to manage inbreeding will vary with species, region, and program, it should be recognized from the outset of a program that inbreeding will eventually become a problem and that a strategy must be developed to cope with this complexity.

MATING AND TESTING

One of the first jobs of the tree breeder who is involved in a long-term tree improvement program is to choose a mating design. Once trees are mated and seed are produced, progeny must be established in field tests in a way that they will provide the breeder with the information needed to manage the tree improvement program precisely and accurately. As stated in Chapter 8, there may be several objectives to breeding and testing. In advanced-generation breeding programs, the two most important of these are nearly always an estimation of parental breeding value (or general combining ability), along with the establishment of a base population for the next generation of selection. If methods are available to utilize specific combining ability, as with vegetative propagation or the mass production of specific crosses, then determination of specific combining abilities will also be a major objective.

The most appropriate type of mating design depends upon several factors; these include the objectives of testing, types of gene actions, the urgency of time, and the financial resources that are available to the breeder. The mating design that is chosen should ideally be one that can be repeated efficiently generation after generation, that leads to a slow rate of inbreeding, and that can be completed in a timely manner.

If the program is not well funded or is secondary in importance, simple mating designs such as open-pollinated schemes or polymix matings may be employed.

Such designs have a severe limitation because male parentage is unknown, and selection from tests will lead to unknown amounts of relatedness. However, these designs have been used in agricultural crops with reasonable success. If this type of system is used, the breeder should make an effort to include a large number of parents in the program so that the rate of inbreeding can be kept at a low level.

In more sophisticated, large-scale programs, mating designs such as some form of diallel or factorial design are usually employed. Because estimation of the general combining ability of parents is a common objective, designs that require several crosses per parent are normally preferred. Such designs as small disconnected diallels or disconnected factorials, which can be completed in a short period of time, and groups of crosses planted in the field together are being favored in many advanced-generation programs (Talbert, 1979; Goddard, 1980; van Buijtenen, 1981). These designs allow estimation of general combining abilities as well as specific combining abilities for the crosses made and serve well in maintaining genetic diversity in the progeny population. Tester mating designs that use only a few parents that are mated to every other member of the population may give excellent estimates of general combining abilities. However, they are generally not favored in advanced-generation programs because genetic diversity among progeny is restricted by the number of parents used as testers.

Mating designs and field-testing designs cannot be considered separate in a tree improvement program. There must be a "marriage" of mating designs and field-testing designs if maximum information is to be obtained from the breeding program. Therefore, the field-testing design that should be used in advanced-generation testing depends to an extent on the type of mating design that is employed. If the mating design calls for small 4×4 factorials, resulting in 16 crosses per factorial, then all 16 crosses should be planted together in the field if maximum genetic information is to be obtained. Tests would therefore consist of some multiple of 16 seedlots in addition to check lots. Information gathered from first-generation testing programs should be considered in designing an advanced-generation field-testing plan. For example, knowledge about the extent of genotype $\times$ environment interaction in first-generation tests-can be used to determine the appropriate number of environments in which each set of advanced-generation crosses should be tested. If sufficient data are available, it may be possible to define "optimal" test environments that best describe genotypic performance throughout a breeding region, and therefore reduce the number of environments needed for testing (Allen et al., 1978). The considerations for types and distribution of plots, which were discussed in Chapter 8, apply in advanced-generation as well as in first-generation tests.

ADVANCED-GENERATION SELECTION

Selection is the means by which genetic gain is made in a breeding program. A number of different selection procedures or methods are available to tree breeders, the choice of which will influence the gain obtained both in the short and long terms. A summary of different selection methods was given in Chapter 4, and general discussion of them will not be repeated here. This section will concentrate on aspects of selection that are specific to advanced-generation tree improvement.

Selection in advanced-generation programs differs from that in most first-generation programs in several ways. In the first generation, the base population from which selections are made is most often a series of mature, natural stands, or unimproved plantations in which the parentage of the trees is unknown. As a result, breeders are usually limited to using individual or mass selection as a selection method. This is not always the case; in some situations, the initial group of parent trees may be chosen essentially at random (no selection) and their offspring established in genetic tests. Following this, clonal orchards may be established using the genetically best parents based on progeny performance, or seedling or clonal orchards may be established using the best progeny in the best families. If genetically improved planting stock is needed immediately, however, the usual procedure is to use individual selection and to establish the selected genotypes in a clonal seed orchard or in an area that is managed for production of vegetative propagules.

In advanced generations, selections are nearly always made from genetic tests. However, this may not always be the case; in programs with limited finances the only alternative may be to practice individual selection in production plantations from seed orchard stock. This type of selection method in advanced generations is usually not practiced because of fears that some selections will be related through common seed orchard parentage, which would cause inbreeding to proceed at unacceptably rapid rates. However, individual selection can result in gain for heritable characteristics; this is indicated by the achievements of primitive corn breeders who for many hundreds of years collected seeds for the next year's crop from the phenotypically superior plants in their fields. If selections are to be made in production plantations from seed orchard seed, Namkoong (1979) suggests that stands be planted separately by mother trees so that some control of ancestry can be maintained.

Most programs that proceed to advanced-generation selection and breeding will establish genetic tests from selected parents. This is much preferred, because of the greater genetic gain that can be achieved by utilizing some form of family selection and because the breeder can maintain more complete control of ancestry. The discussions that follow will be about selection in genetic tests, and how it differs from that of first-generation selection in stands of unknown parentage.

Selection in a Finite Population

An important aspect of selection in genetic tests is that the base population is finite in size with a limit to the number of individuals that can be screened. This differs from the situation that is often encountered in first-generation programs in which extensive areas of natural stands or plantations can be searched and in which a very large population exists from which to choose selections. Finite population size can have a real impact on the number of traits used as criteria for selection and the selection intensity that the breeder can apply for each trait. If a very large population exists, the breeder can select for many traits and use a high-selection intensity for each trait. This is the case, because if enough acres of natural stands or plantations are searched, a suitable number of trees will be found that meet the minimum criteria. In a finite population like a genetic test, there are only a certain number of individuals that can be screened to find selections, and it may be impossible to find suitable numbers of select trees that meet very intense selection criteria for a large number of traits. For example, it might be desired to select 200 individuals as parents for the next generation from a genetic test base population of 10,000 trees. If height was the only criterion for selection, then the breeder would select the 200 best trees, perhaps using a family and within-family selection method for height. If high wood specific gravity was added as a criterion for selection and given equal weight as height, then 200 trees would still be chosen. However, unless wood specific gravity was perfectly correlated with height (which it is not), the 200 best trees for height would not be the same as the 200 best trees for wood specific gravity. Therefore, the breeder would choose the 200 trees with the best *combinations* of wood specific gravities and heights. This means a lower selection intensity must be used for both height and wood specific gravity than would be the case if selection was practiced on either trait alone. When more traits are added as selection criteria, selection intensity for any one trait will decrease even more. The preceding situation makes it of the utmost importance that the breeder decide carefully and critically which set of traits should be used as selection criteria and that traits of minimal importance be given little or no consideration in the selection scheme. Additions of more traits will result in less gain in any individual trait anytime that a certain number of individuals must be selected from a finite genetic-test population.

Early or Juvenile Selection

The importance of time in the developmental aspects of tree improvement has been emphasized many times in this book. Due to the long rotations of forest tree crops and the extended period before most tree species reach reproductive maturity, generation intervals in forest trees are usually measured in decades rather than in growing seasons. As a result of the importance of time, tree breeders are constantly searching for ways to reduce the number of years required for a generation of selection and breeding. The goal of an advanced-generation tree breeding program is to maximize gain achieved per unit of time (van Buijtenen, 1981). This means that anything that can be done to reduce the generation interval without severely reducing genetic gain per generation can result in a more efficient improvement program.

One way to reduce the generation interval in advanced-generation tree improvement is to make selections in genetic tests long before trees have reached rotation age. Selections can be made most efficiently in young tests if performance of trees in the test at rotation age can be accurately predicted from their performance at younger ages. Phrased another way, there must be a high genetic correlation between rotation age and a younger age if early selection is to be successful. These correlations are known as juvenile–mature correlations. This most important relationship has already been mentioned several times in this book. It will be covered again here because of its extreme importance in advanced-generation breeding.

Unfortunately, juvenile–mature correlations in forest trees are nearly always less than 1. This has been demonstrated for growth in coniferous species such as loblolly pine (Wakeley, 1971; LaFarge, 1972), ponderosa pine (Steinhoff, 1974; Namkoong and Conkle, 1976), Douglas fir (Namkoong et al., 1972), western white pine (Steinhoff, 1974), slash pine (Squillace and Gansel, 1974), and various hardwood species such as hybrid poplars (Wilkinson, 1973) and black walnut (McKeand et al., 1979). As might be expected, correlations of growth performance at very young ages, say age 3 or less, with performance at mature ages are very poor, but correlations improve progressively as the assessment time becomes closer to the mature age.

Because of imperfect juvenile–mature correlations, tree breeders are faced with the dilemma of deciding how much gain per generation should be sacrificed in the hope of improving gain per unit time by selecting at a juvenile age and thereby shortening the generation interval. Selection at a young age in the hope of improving performance at rotation age is a form of indirect selection or selecting for one characteristic (performance at a juvenile age) to improve another trait (performance at a mature age). Genetic formulas are available to calculate the gain that can be expected from indirect selection (Falconer, 1981).

In Chapter 4 it was shown that gain from mass selection can be expressed as

$$G = ih^2\sigma_p$$

where

$$G = \text{gain}$$
$$i = \text{selection}$$
$$h^2 = \text{heritability}$$
$$\sigma_p = \text{phenotypic standard deviation}$$

Gain from early selection, or correlated gain (CG), may be calculated in a similar manner:

$$CG = ih_J h_m r_G \sigma_{p_m}$$

where

$$CG = \text{correlated gain}$$
$$i = \text{selection intensity}$$
$$h_j = \text{square root of the heritability of the juvenile trait}$$
$$h_m = \text{square root of the heritability of the mature trait}$$

r_G = genetic correlation between the juvenile and mature trait

σ_{p_m} = phenotypic standard deviation of the mature trait

Gain per unit time that is achieved by early selection can be calculated simply as

$$G_T = \frac{ih_j h_m r_G \sigma_{p_m}}{T}$$

where

G_T = gain per unit time

T = generation interval

and other symbols are as defined previously. The appropriate age to select would be the one that maximizes gain per unit time.

The optimum age at which to select is currently a topic of considerable debate among tree breeders. The debate revolves mainly around the magnitude of the various components in the gain per unit time formula illustrated previously. For example, the degree to which heritabilities may change with age is somewhat uncertain. There is some evidence from several conifers that heritability for growth may increase as genetic-test plantations increase with age and that heritability may culminate at about the midlife of the stand (Namkoong et al., 1972; Namkoong and Conkle, 1976; Franklin, 1979). An increasing heritability with time would increase optimum rotation age because of the appearance of the square roots of juvenile and mature heritabilities (h_j, h_m) in the numerator of the gain per unit time formula. Likewise, there is debate about the magnitude of genetic correlations (r_G) between the performance at juvenile ages and at maturity (Franklin, 1979; Lambeth, 1980).

Despite the many uncertainties, most tree-breeding organizations feel that selections should be made at relatively young ages in genetic tests. For example, utilizing growth data from numerous species in the family Pinaceae, Lambeth (1980) used a formula similar to the gain per unit time formula given previously to calculate that optimum rotation age was between 6 and 8 years for rotation ages of 20 to 40 years. This is approximately the age at which second-generation selections are currently being made in southern pine improvement programs. A 6-year-old second-generation loblolly pine selection is shown in Figure 13.3.

Anytime juvenile–mature genetic correlations are less than 1, selection at a juvenile age will result in a group of select trees that is *not* the best group of select trees at rotation age, even though they were the best group at the optimal selection age. It is important that the tree improver realize that just because the select group of trees deteriorates somewhat in quality with time, selection efforts have not failed. The deterioration is simply an aspect of imperfect juvenile–mature correlations and is to be expected when trees are selected before rotation age.

FIGURE 13.3

Selections for the next generation of improvement are
often made at young ages from genetic tests, well before
rotation age. Shown is a 6-year-old second-generation
loblolly pine selection. Note its superiority. Selection at
young ages decreases the generation interval and offsets
imperfect juvenile–mature correlations, thus maximizing genetic gain per unit time.

Selection Methods

Nearly all advanced-generation tree improvement programs use some form of
family and individual within-family selection system to rank trees as candidates
for selection. This selection method results in a greater expected genetic gain,
especially for lowly heritable traits (Falconer, 1981), and it makes maximum use
of information derived from genetic tests. For traits that are highly inherited, such
as wood specific gravity, individual or mass selection can result in nearly as much
gain as selection on family and individual values. Traits with lower heritabilities,
such as growth rate, greatly benefit from family and within-family selection. Mass
selection is never more efficient in making genetic progress than combined family
and within-family selection. Use of high-speed computers to rank individuals

based upon their family and individual scores greatly facilitates use of this method.

Although use of family and individual information to rank phenotypes for characteristics of interest allows the breeder to make excellent genetic gain, it also makes it mandatory that care be taken to maintain a sufficient genetic base for long-term improvement. As mentioned in Chapter 4, family selection involves exclusion of entire families from the breeding population and can result in rapid rates of inbreeding in the improved population. Ultimately, there is a trade-off that involves greater short-term genetic gain that can be achieved by only using individuals in the very best families and restrictions in long-term genetic gain that result from a much reduced genetic base. Intensive selection in family performance can result in loss of desirable alleles from individuals in poorer families; this can also hamper long-term progress from selection. In the very long run, selection on phenotypic (individual) values alone may result in greater genetic gain because of the reduced genetic variation that results from selection on family values (Sirkkomaa and Lingstrom, 1981). However, selection systems that include selection on family performance do result in greater short-term gain and are almost always used in tree improvement because adequate levels of genetic gain are needed in each cycle to make tree improvement programs profitable. A viable alternative may be to restrict the number of individuals selected per family so that more families can be included in the program (Roberds et al., 1980). Regardless of the selection method used, very intensive selection in finite populations can reduce long-term gains that can be achieved because of a reduced genetic base, and the breeder must maintain a sufficient number of individuals in the selected population to ensure continued progress.

Advanced-generation tree improvement programs almost always involve selection for several traits simultaneously. Although the selection index approach that was first mentioned in Chapter 4 has been used only sparingly in forestry, it is receiving increasing emphasis in advanced-generation programs. The selection index system combines information on all traits of interest into a single index that enables the breeder to assign a total score to each individual. It involves attaching economic weights to all traits under consideration. In its simplest form, the selection index may combine a set of individual (phenotypic) values that is weighted by relative economic values to produce a single number for each individual. The most complex index combines family and individual information on all traits into one index. Multiple-regression techniques are used to derive appropriate coefficients for family and individual values, with the coefficients depending on economic weights, the heritabilities of each trait, and the correlations between traits. The major restriction on use of selection indexes in forest tree improvement has been the determination of the appropriate economic weights, that is, the value of a unit improvement in one trait relative to a unit improvement in other traits. Inappropriate economic weights can seriously reduce the efficiency of selection indexes.

Despite these complications, selection indexes have been proposed for use in several tree species. Selection indexes were proposed for roguing seed orchards of undesirable parents by Namkoong (1965). Other examples of the use of the index selection system are with aspen (van Buijtenen and van Horn, 1969), maritime pine (Baradat et al., 1970), and loblolly pine (Bridgwater and Stonecypher, 1979). The use of selection indexes will increase in the future as more data become available on the relative economic values of important traits to product yield and quality.

ACCELERATED BREEDING

There are essentially two ways that the generation interval can be shortened in tree improvement programs. One way is through early or juvenile selection, which has been discussed previously. The other is through *accelerated breeding,* or reducing the time required to mate parent trees and collect seed from them once they are selected. The extended period of time before trees reach reproductive maturity is a serious difficulty in tree improvement because it increases generation intervals and therefore decreases gain per unit of time. The time required to complete breeding, once selections have been made, has absolutely no impact on the gain achieved per generation of improvement, but the steps taken to decrease the time required to breed selected trees will increase gain per unit of time. As a result, much effort is being directed in tree improvement research toward enhancing flowering in young trees. These techniques are included under the general rubric *accelerated breeding.*

The impact of accelerated breeding on the generation interval in a tree improvement program can be seen in the hypothetical example in Figure 13.4. The program on the left is one employing traditional breeding methods, whereas the one on the right utilizes accelerated breeding techniques. In both programs, selections are made at 8 years of age in genetic tests and are grafted into breeding orchards. In the traditional program, however, 8 years elapse before grafts begin to produce flowers. In the accelerated program, flowering is stimulated to begin 4 years after grafting by establishing the breeding orchard in a greenhouse in which the environment can be controlled precisely. In both instances, it is assumed that 4 years elapse following the initiation of flowering before breeding is completed and seed are collected for the next generation of testing. The total number of years required to complete one generation of selection and breeding in the traditional program is $8 + 8 + 4 = 20$ years, whereas only $8 + 4 + 4 = 16$ years are required in the accelerated program, a time saving of 4 years. Percentage-wise, the generation interval has been reduced by 20%. Because selections were made at 8 years of age in both programs, the 20% reduction in the generation interval translates directly into a 25% increase in genetic gain per unit time in the tree improvement program.

Much of the research related to accelerated breeding has been involved with increasing understanding about the basic physiological processes involved with

Time Savings with Accelerated Breeding

Year	Traditional breeding	Accelerated breeding
1	Plant test	Plant test
	(8 years)	(8 years)
8	Select, graft outdoors	Select, graft indoors
		(4 years)
12	(8 years)	Breed, collect seed
		(4 years)
16	Breed, collect seed	Next cycle
	(4 years)	Generation interval = 16 years
20	Next cycle	Time savings = 4 years = 25%
	Generation interval = 20 years	

FIGURE 13.4

Accelerated breeding techniques can substantially reduce generation intervals and thereby increase genetic gain per unit time. In the hypothetical example shown, an accelerated breeding program has reduced generation interval from 20 to 16 years, or 20%, which translates directly into an extra 20% gain per unit time.

maturation and in reproduction in trees and how these processes can be manipulated to promote flowering. Two excellent review articles pertaining to reproduction in conifers are those by Puritch (1971) and Lee (1979). Several factors, including drought stress and fertilization during the period of the year when reproduction structures are initiated, have been shown to increase female flowering in pines. Similar results with fertilization have been found for Douglas fir (Ebell, 1972) and the true firs (Eis, 1970). The plant hormone *gibberellic acid* has been found to promote flowering in conifers if it is applied at appropriate times of the year (Greenwood, 1981; Brix and Portlock, 1982).

Because of the greater environmental control possible, breeding seed orchards are increasingly being established in containers indoors in greenhouses, where environmental factors such as moisture, temperature, day length, and fertility can be readily manipulated to promote flowering (Figure 13.5). For example, one

FIGURE 13.5

Generation intervals can often by reduced by establishing breeding orchards indoors in greenhouses. The loblolly pine breeding orchard shown will reduce generation interval by several years. Use of greenhouses to reduce generation interval is successful because of the precise control possible for environmental factors that promote flowering.

prerequisite for production of strobili in loblolly pine appears to be a resting bud (not elongating) during midsummer, the time of the year that flower primordia are initiated in this species (Greenwood, 1978, 1980). Outdoors, very young loblolly pine grafts tend to grow through the summer and not form a resting bud. As a result, flowering is minimal. In the greenhouse, a resting bud can be induced by midsummer, and flowering on young grafts indoors has been good (Greenwood, 1978). Prescriptions for management of a containerized indoor loblolly pine-breeding orchard have been given by Greenwood et al. (1979).

One aspect of an aggressive breeding program that fits into any accelerated breeding scheme is *proper management of outdoor conventional breeding orchards*. Several years can be gained each generation simply by taking care to establish breeding orchards on the proper site, at the proper spacing, and to subject the young, growing trees to intensive, proper management that will promote flowering. Such things as proper pollination techniques and care in seed insect control will also be of tremendous benefit to an early completion of the breeding of selected trees. "Tending to business" in conventional breeding orchards can not be overemphasized as being a vital part of any ongoing tree improvement program.

LITERATURE CITED

Allen, F. L., Comstock, R. E., and Rasmussen, D. C. 1978. Optimal environments for yield testing. *Crop Sci.* **18**:747–751.

Andersson, F., Jansson, R., and Lindgren, D. 1974. Some results of second-generation crosses involving inbreeding in Norway spruce (*Picea abies*). *Sil. Gen.* **23**:34–42.

Baradat, P., Illey, G., Mauge, J. P., and Mendibourne, P. 1970. *Selection pour plosieurs charactieres sur indice.* Programmes de calcul, AFOCEL-Compte-rendo d'activite, pp. 46–70.

Bridgwater, F. E., and Stonecypher, R. W. 1979. "Index Selection for Volume and Straightness in a Loblolly Pine Population." Proc. 15th Sou. For. Tree Impr. Conf., Starkville, Miss., pp. 132–139.

Brix, H., and Portlock, F. T. 1982. Flowering response of western hemlock seedlings to gibberellin and water stress treatments. *Can. Jour. For. Res.* **12**:76–82.

Burley, J., and Namkoong, G. 1980. "Conservation of Forest Genetic Resources." 11th Commonwealth Forestry Conference, Trinidad.

Dudley, J. W. 1977. "Seventy-Six Generations of Selection for Oil and Protein Percentage in Maize." In Proc. Int. Conf. Quant. Gen. (E. Pollak, O. Kempthorne, and T. B. Bailey, Jr., eds.), pp. 459–473. Iowa State University Press, Ames.

Ebell, L. F. 1972. Cone production and stem-growth response of Douglas fir to rate and frequency of nitrogen fertilization. *Can. Jour. For. Res.* **2**:327–338.

Eis, J. 1970. Reproduction and reproductive irregularities of *Abies lasiocarpa* and *Abies grandis*. *Can. Jour. Bot.* **48**:141–143.

Falconer, D. S. 1981. *Introduction to Quantitative Genetics.* Longman, Inc., New York.

Franklin, E. C. 1970. "Survey of Mutant Forms and Inbreeding Depression in Species of the Family Pinaceae," Forest Service Research Paper SE-61, Southeastern Forest Experiment Station.

Franklin, E. C. 1979. Model relating levels of genetic variance to stand development of four North American conifers. *Sil. Gen.* **28**:207–212.

Gansel, C. R. 1971. "Effects of Several Levels of Inbreeding on Growth and Oleoresin Yield in Slash Pine." Proc. 11th Sou. For. Tree Impr. Conf., Atlanta, Ga., pp. 173–177.

Goddard, R. E. 1980. The University of Florida Cooperative Forest Genetics Research Program. In *Research Needs in Tree Breeding* (R. P. Guries and H. C. Kang, eds.), Proc. 15th N. Am. Quant. For. Gen. Group Workshop, Coeur D'Alene, Idaho, pp. 31–42.

Greenwood, M. S. 1978. Flowering induced on your loblolly pine grafts by out-of-phase dormancy. *Science* **201**:443–444.

Greenwood, M. S. 1980. Reproductive development in loblolly pine. I. The early development of male and female strobili in relation to the long shoot growth behavior. *Am. Jour. Bot.* **67**:1414–1422.

Greenwood, M. S. 1981. Reproductive development of loblolly pine. II. The effect of age, gibberellin plus water stress and out-of-phase dormancy on long shoot growth behavior. *Am. Jour. Bot.* **68**:1184–1190.

Greenwood, M. S., O'Gwynn, C. H., and Wallace, P. G. 1979. "Management of an Indoor Potted Loblolly Pine Breeding Orchard." Proc. 15th Sou. For. Tree Impr. Conf., Starkville, Miss., pp. 94–98.

LaFarge, T. 1972. "Relationships among Third, Fifth, and Fifteenth-Year Measurements in a Study of Stand Variation of Loblolly Pine in Georgia." Proc. IUFRO Working Party on Progeny Testing, Macon, Ga., pp. 7–16.

Lambeth, C. C. 1980. Juvenile-mature correlations in Pinaceae, and their implications of early selection. *For. Sci.* **26**:571–580.

Lee, K. J. 1979. "Factors Affecting Cone Initiation in Pines: A Review," Research Report 15, Inst. of For. Gen., Off. of For., Sowan, Korea.

Libby, W. J. 1973. Domestication strategies for forest trees. *Can. Jour. For. Res.* **3**:265–276.

McKeand, S. E., and Beineke, W. F. 1980. Sublining for half-sib breeding populations of forest trees. *Sil. Gen.* **29**:14–17.

McKeand, S. E., Beineke, W. K., and Todhunter, M. N. 1979. "Selection Age for Black Walnut Progeny Tests." Proc. 1st Cent. States Tree Imp. Conf., Madison, Wisc., pp. 68–73.

Namkoong, G. 1965. "Family Indices for Seed Orchard Selection." Proc. Second Gen. Workshop, SAF and Lake States For. Tree Impr. Conf., Madison, Wisc., pp. 7–12.

Namkoong, G. 1979. "Introduction to Quantitative Genetics in Forestry," USDA, U.S. Forest Service Tech. Bull. No. 1588, Washington, D.C.

Namkoong, G., and Conkle, M. T. 1976. Time trends in genetic control of height growth in ponderosa pine. *For. Sci.* **22**:2–12.

Namkoong, G., Usanis, R. A., and Silen, R. R. 1972. Age-related variation in genetic control of height growth in Douglas-fir. *Theor. Appl. Genet.* **42**:151–159.

Orr-Ewing, A. L. 1965. Inbreeding and single-crossing in Douglas-fir. *For. Sci.* **11**:279–290.

Puritoh, G. S. 1972. "Cone Production in Conifers: A Review of the Literature and Evaluation of Research Needs," Pacific For. Res. Center Inf. Report BC-X-5, Canadian Forestry Service, Victoria, British Columbia.

Roberds, J. H., Namkoong, G., and Kang, H. 1980. Family losses following truncation selection in populations of half-sib families. *Sil. Gen.* **29**:104–107.

Schoenike, R. E. 1975. Tree improvement and the conservation of gene resouces. In *Forest Tree Improvement: The Third Decade* (B.A. Thielges, ed.), 24th Ann. For. Symp., Louisiana State University, Baton Rouge, La., pp. 119–139.

Sirkkomaa, S., and Lingstrom, V. B. 1981. Simulation of response to selection for body weight in rainbow trout. *Acta Agric. Scand.* **31**:426–431.

Squillace, A. E., and Gansel, G. R. 1974. Juvenile-mature correlations in slash pine. *For. Sci.* **20**:225–229.

Steinhoff, R. J. 1974. "Juvenile-Mature Correlations in Ponderosa and Western White Pines." IUFRO Joint Meet. of Working Parties on Population and Ecological Genetics, Breeding Theory, and Progeny Testing, pp. 243–250. Royal College Forestry, Stockholm, Sweden.

Talbert, J. T. 1979. An advanced-generation breeding plan for the North Carolina State University–Industry Pine Tree Improvement Cooperative. *Sil. Gen.* **28**:72–75.

Toda, R. 1965. "Preservation of Gene Pool in Forest Tree Populations." Proc. IUFRO Sect. 22 Special Meeting, Zagreb, Yugoslavia.

van Buijtenen, J. P. 1981. "Advanced-Generation Seed Orchards," 18th Can. For. Tree Imp. Assoc. Meeting.

van Buijtenen, J. P., and Lowe, W. J. 1979. "The Use of Breeding Groups in Advanced-Generation Breeding." Proc. 15th Sou. For. Tree Impr. Conf., Starkville, Miss., pp. 59–65.

van Buijtenen, J. P., and van Horn, W. M. 1969. "A Selection Index for Aspen Based upon Genetic Principles," Inst. Paper Chem. Prog. Report 6, Lake States Aspen Genetics and Tree Improvement Group.

Wakeley, P. C. 1971. Relation of thirtieth year to earlier dimensions of southern pines. *For. Sci.* **17**:200–209.

Wilkinson, R. C. 1973. "Inheritance and Correlation of Growth Characteristics in Hybrid Poplar Clones." Proc. 20th Northeast. For. Tree Imp. Conf., Durham, N.H., pp. 121–130.

CHAPTER 14

Gain and Economics
of Tree Improvement

There is great need to make forestland more productive. Increased productivity is especially important for the tropical forest regions where there could be a catastrophe by A.D. 2000 if action if not taken to reverse the trend of reduced forest production (Holden, 1980). The urgency for action in the tropics and the need to capture the timber production potential with desired quality products from tropical forest lands have been stressed by Johnson (1976). Dozens of recent publications have dealt with the needs and methods to increase productivity, for example, the one by Anderson (1978), who feels that production in the southern United States can be doubled if all aspects of forest management (he recognizes that tree improvement is an important component) are used. Anderson makes an additional point about the need for wood-quality improvement. The concepts of how changing forestry activities will affect wood quality has been emphasized by Baskerville (1977).

It is now generally recognized that one major way to increase yield and quality from forestland is through tree improvement. However, if this aspect of silviculture is to be fully utilized, gains and improvements must be quantified and subjected to benefit–cost analyses. Tree improvement efforts become academic unless their use will enhance the value of the forest and its products. Tree improvement benefits may take several forms, such as greater adaptability, increased volume production, better quality of the wood produced, and other forms that will result in an improved final product. Shortening the optimal rotation age to obtain the desired product and developing greater uniformity in the trees produced are major potential benefits. It is clear that these are all interrelated and cannot be assessed independently.

An economic analysis of tree improvement is complex. There are so many variables, such as time, species, location, costs, inflation rates, interest rates, markets, and the like that it may appear to be nearly impossible to make comparative cost estimates. Yet, economic analyses must be attempted in order to justify the maintenance or expansion of tree improvement activities. To do this, a number of assumptions must be made that are based upon experience, opinion, and often judgment about unknown costs and returns. The difficulty is compounded by the major factor of forestry—TIME. It is most difficult to predict values, costs, and economic parameters for the future. Therefore, most economic analyses that have been made are general in nature or are developed to allow options of choosing among several levels of the unknown factors, such as costs, interest rates, or inflation rates. Although imprecise, these generalized results serve a useful purpose.

It is noteworthy that all well-designed analyses have shown that tree improvement is an economically worthwhile endeavor. This general result was stated clearly by Carlisle and Teich (1970a) with their summary sentence. "Even when subjected to this type of objective, rigorous scrutiny, tree improvement is shown not only to be economically beneficial but to be the best of a number of options."

Determination of gain is somewhat simpler than is a full-fledged economic analysis. There are difficulties with test designs and age that make gains from the use of genetics difficult to assess accurately. However, good "ball-park" figures have been obtained that are most useful as a guide. Gain estimates have often been made that are highly unreliable because they are based on immature stands of trees. Estimates made on data from young trees, especially those expressing percentages of improvement, are not only poor but they can be misleading. There are several reasons for this. The most important one is that, as the trees grow in size, the base on which the percentages are calculated changes; therefore, the percentage usually decreases with age.

A cataloging of specific economic returns or gain values in this book would serve little purpose. Only broad general trends will be mentioned, with an occasional specific reference for illustration.

GAIN

General

The question always arises about how much gain is necessary to justify continued intensification of tree improvement operations.

Increments of improvement and the costs of achieving each increment are not usually related in a linear way. Initial gains are generally obtained relatively easily, but additional gains become more difficult and more expensive to attain. The fact is that *optimum* gains are usually sought, rather than *maximum* gains. The former is the gain that is possible before the additional cost for each extra unit of improvement rises beyond the value of the improvement that could be obtained. The concept that optimum gains should be the objective of intensive management and that maximum gains are not usually economically attractive is often overlooked in forestry. It is seldom optimum to produce the maximum, according to Gruenfeld (1975). This is true for genetic gain just as it is for economics, and breeding programs should be governed by this concept.

Assessment of genetic gain is filled with numerous pitfalls. The time when the gain is assessed is all-important as are methodology, species, and location. In addition, gains are restricted by the "rule of limiting factors." For example, regardless of the genetic quality that has been developed, certain factors in the environment, such as moisture or nutrients, may be in short supply, so that the genetic improvement cannot be fully expressed.

As mentioned in earlier chapters, gain in a selection program is a function of selection differential and heritability. This appears to be simple and straightforward when it is applied only to a single characteristic. However, in a breeding program, a number of characteristics are involved simultaneously, each of which has differing heritabilities and selection differentials. In tree improvement, the interest is in the total gain from all characteristics. To express this, it becomes necessary to use some type of index to weigh the gains and importance of each characteristic as part of an overall assessment. Too often a program of multiple-trait improvement is used, but gains are expressed in terms of only one trait. To be correct, total gain should be the total value determined by the gain in each trait, weighted by its economic value. As described in Chapter 13, less gain will be obtained for any one single trait as additional traits are included in the tree improvement effort, but the optimum for all traits combined is what is being sought.

The time necessary to achieve the gain is of prime importance economically. As we expressed in earlier chapters, "time is money," and one of the greatest benefits from a tree improvement program is to reduce the time it takes to grow a desired product. Often, gains from tree improvement are expressed as total gains, but as was stressed in Chapter 13, the real economic standard should be *gain per unit time*.

How genetic gains should best be expressed is a real puzzle. Any measure that is used can be wrong or misleading; this applies to both percentage and to unit values. The safest measure of gain is a monetary one; that is, what value in currency does the gain represent? Although this is the best, it still has multiple pitfalls because the monetary value of a unit of gain, or the cost to obtain it, often is not known. For example, how much value is represented by a reduction of disease infection by 15%, or what is the value of trees that are straightened enough so that three times the number are in a straightness category that could be used for the highest-value products? When specific gravity is increased from 0.48 to 0.50, what is the monetary effect on the forestry and manufacturing operations? An estimate of the value from increased volume or from producing more dry-wood weight per unit area can be obtained reasonably accurately, but such value determinations are most difficult for most tree quality factors.

Assessment of Gains from Juvenile Measurements

Great care is needed in assessing and predicting genetic gains. The data are always needed immediately, and great pressures are sometimes placed upon tree breeders and orchard managers to make predictions and projections, even though data are incomplete or the tests are not sufficiently mature. The mature performance of some characteristics cannot be readily assessed from young trees; for example, it was stated earlier that because of differences in growth curves, growth characteristics usually cannot be reliably determined in much less than half-rotation age. Yet, because of the urgent need for guiding information, gains are often calculated and large programs initiated that are based only on the performance of young trees. Much of the genetic-gain data in the literature is totally unreliable because it is based upon an assessment that was made too early. On the other hand, some characteristics can be assessed at an early date with considerable accuracy. For example, those that are related to survival can be assessed at a young age unless growing conditions were especially favorable in the early life of the stand. Wood specific gravity of older trees can usually be estimated rather well from young trees. In contrast, the trees must be considerably older before tracheid length can be predicted with reasonable accuracy. Another important characteristic that can be assessed early is straightness of tree bole.

The importance of juvenile–mature correlations and the reliability of prediction of later performance from early assessment vary by species and characteristics. Most characteristics related to growth require extended periods to obtain reasonably accurate information, although early predictions may be somewhat more accurate on families compared to those for individual trees. The predictability from young ages is often better for provenances; for example, usually a high-elevation provenance is slower growing than one from lower elevations, no matter what its age. The concept of predicting performance at older ages from young ages always has been important but is much more so now with the advent of more use of vegetative propagation in which juvenile material is needed for easy rooting. A number of so-called "superseedling" studies have been established in which outstanding nursery seedlings were selected for possible increased yield at rotation age. Results have been inconclusive. For example, Sweet and Wareing (1966) have reported that selected large seedlings of radiata pine did not grow faster, and Brown et al. (1961) found the same situation for loblolly pine. However, Hatchell et al. (1972) found greater growth of selected loblolly pine seedlings after 10 years and strongly recommended the method, as did Nienstaedt (1981), for "super" spruce. For spruce, Barneoud et al. (1979) also found a drop-off and warned that care was needed in the use of the superseedling method. Robinson and van Buijtenen (1979) concluded that, despite a drop in growth, meaningful gains were still evident in 15-year-old loblolly pine. Several researchers have emphasized that the crown and bole form of the selected superseedlings were rough, that is, they were similar in many ways to classical "wolf trees."

All the studies made on the relation of juvenile-to-mature growth cannot be cited, but many tests indicate that the first year, or nursery performance, is not a good predictor of later growth. This was even true for fast-growing willow on a 4-year rotation. Barrett and Alberti (1972) stated that "it is concluded that the evaluation or selection based on growth performance during the first year is ineffective." On the other hand, Mohn and Randall (1971) obtained gains on fast-growing poplar by predicting third- and fourth-year height based upon short-term assessments. The authors have observed situations in which early selection of *Populus* has led to some erroneous conclusions about growth potential as early as the third year. The uncertainty was summarized by Wilkinson (1974) who mentioned that for hybrid poplars, 1- to 15-year correlations may be low enough so that selection intensities may need to be reduced to preserve the best clones at year 15. It is clear that a widespread, wholesale use of superseedlings as a major base for selection should be done only with the greatest caution and after complete testing has indicated the juvenile–mature relationships.

Another problem involving age is related to tree size and change of percentage superiority as the tests become older. For example, it is not acceptable to predict commercial volume growth based on volumes of trees that are 2.5 to 5.0 cm in diameter. Such predictions are frequently made, and the predicted volume gains can be worse than useless. Tables for small-tree volumes are often inaccurate. Tree form and relative bark percentage often change greatly with tree age. What is most serious is that a small difference in volume of small trees will translate into a large percentage value that is not at all representative of differences that will be found for the mature trees. For example, it is easy to find families of trees that are 1 m tall at 1 year of age, whereas other families in the same test are only 0.5 m in

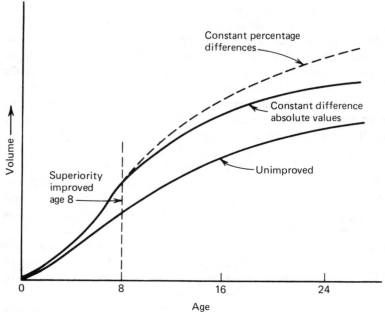

FIGURE 14.1

Improvement projections are quite different, depending on whether absolute gain values or percentage gain values are used. Shown is a hypothetical volume improvement projection from measurement of year 8, showing the kinds of differences in projected volumes whether based on absolute differences or percentage differences at year 8.

height. Thus, the best families are 100% superior to the others. Yet at age 20, one family might be 20 m tall, whereas the other is 15 m tall. The 100% superiority has dropped to 33% superiority, even though the family differences are still very outstanding (Figure 14.1). Percentage differences based on the performance at a young age should never be extrapolated to older trees because the base upon which the percentage is calculated becomes larger, and thus the percentage tends to drop. Obviously, any genetic gains reported as percentage values must be viewed with some caution, and the age at which the percentages were calculated must be taken into account.

The Importance of Plot and Test Design

Data from research plots should not be used to predict production under operational forest conditions. Most forest genetics research plots are designed to show only comparative performances among sources or families. Usually a commercial check is included to give some indication of the relative performance of the test material in relation to what was being planted operationally prior to genetic improvement. Such information is good and useful, but great care must be taken in transferring absolute-growth data from tests to operational plantations and making economic projections therefrom. Growth rate data from row plots designed to test parents in a seed orchard cannot be transferred directly to unit area growth in a plantation. It is not unusual to have a 10 to 15% reduction between the growth rates from the test planting compared to the planting made under operational conditions.

There are many reasons for not using test data for predictions in operations. A primary problem relates to differential competition. In row or pure family block plots, competition effects will be different than those in plantations from mixed seed from a seed orchard. The clones within a seed orchard do not produce equal amounts of seed; yet progeny tests use data from equal numbers per family. Often the test results include inferior clones that will be rogued from the seed orchard following testing. Another problem is that frequently the clonal mix is not equal in the seed orchard; this always occurs following roguing. Frequently, the test site may not be representative of operational planting sites. Also, the care in planting and management of genetic tests is better than that given to operational plantings. Sometimes the check lots are not representative of the unimproved planting. Whan all these difficulties are considered, some of which will lead to an overestimate and others to an underestimate of genetic gain when the improved trees are used in commercial plantings, it behooves the tree improver to be very careful in making production predictions. Certainly the comparison figures from genetic tests are needed and valuable, but extrapolations from them to operational planting normally should not be done.

The only true test of the gain from seed orchards over commercial stock is to collect seed directly from the seed orchard after it has reached full productivity and to test the improved stock against the unimproved in paired plantings that are designed to minimize environmental effects but still be handled in an operational manner. If realized gains from rogued seed orchards are desired, then the tree improver must test after the orchard has been fully rogued. This means that many years must elapse before tests of gains from seed orchards can be started. In their eagerness, many seed orchard managers use their first commercial seed and establish tests of gains from seed orchards with it. In a young orchard, only a few clones produce pollen or seed; a "rule of thumb" used by many pine orchard managers is that in young orchards 80% of the seed is produced by 20% of the clones. If one or two of the heaviest producers are especially good or especially bad, the assessment of orchard gains can be very wrong. Unequal genetic contribution to the seed crop can be as extreme as that found by Bergman (1969), who determined that over half the genetic makeup of the seed in one seed orchard was from one clone. This is an extreme case for a very young orchard; the balance improves as the orchards approach maturity. Furthermore, the chief source of pollen within young orchards may be from nearby unimproved stands.

A special situation exists when seed are collected and planted by mother tree or clone. In that case, testing should be by family blocks and if done correctly, quite accurate predictions can be made of the orchard stock performance. It is especially difficult to make yield projections when survival is not accurately assessed.

Large errors can occcur if an assumption of full survival is made so that yield is calculated on the basis of individual tree performance multipled by an assumed number of trees representing full stocking. Choice of site and silvicultural treatments, such as site preparation or competition control, are most important if meaningful results are to be obtained.

Realized Gain

Measurement of genetic gains through tests planted in an operational manner allows the breeder to calculate actual or realized gains. In Chapter 4, it was shown that anticipated genetic gain from mass selection could be calculated as the product of the selection differential (S) times the narrow-sense heritability (h^2). Symbolically, gain = $h^2 S$. Narrow-sense heritability was defined as a ratio of the-additive genetic variance in a population to total phenotypic variance ($h^2 = \sigma_A^2 / \sigma_p^2$). However, the gain predicted by the formula is only an estimate of the anticipated gain, and often is not the same as what will actually be obtained. Establishment and measurement of studies designed specifically to estimate the realized gain will allow the tree improver to show what has actually been achieved through selection and breeding.

Methods to Obtain Gain

Although there are exceptions, gains from tree improvement can actually be put into three broad categories. Generally these are based upon genetic testing and breeding, which will enable continued progress over time and later generations. The basic categories, all of which were mentioned in earlier chapters, are the following.

1. **Mass selection followed by testing**   Most of tree improvement to date has relied on the selection of desired trees, testing these to determine the best genotypes, and on open pollination among these to produce seed for operational planting. Gains from one generation of selection using this method have been remarkably good, especially for those characteristics having reasonably high heritabilities (i.e., they are under considerable additive genetic control), and where the total variation and thus selection differentials are suitably large. Because of segregation and recombination that takes place when sexual propagation is used, the progeny will not be exactly the same as, or as good as, the parents if there is substantial nonadditive genetic variance. Nonetheless, the gains will represent a movement of the population average in the desired direction.

2. **Phenotypic selection followed by vegetative propagation and testing**   The use of vegetative propagation is becoming increasingly important in forestry. When it is suitable, gains are good because individuals with good additive and nonadditive genetic values are reproduced intact. In characteristics with a large proportion of nonadditive variance, vegetative propagation is particularly important because one can capture all this portion of the genetic quality

of the donor parent in the propagule. The one action in tree improvement that will increase genetic gain more than any other is to learn how to use vegetative propagation more widely and effectively.

3. **Making special crosses** When characteristics are primarily controlled by nonadditive genetics, special crossing designs can be used to capture the desired characteristics by exploiting specific combinations of parents. When tests indicate that two parents produce outstanding offspring, this information can be used by making the required specific crosses to produce the desired seedlots in quantities that are sufficient for reforestation. This must be done by control crosses or by some system of controlled mass pollination. Male sterile plants, or those that do not produce selfs, could be effectively used in the special crossing programs involving two-clone seed orchards. Gains from this approach can be great if there is substantial nonadditive genetic variance; it is a method that will become more widely used to develop trees for problem areas or for special needs in those species in which vegetative propagation is not economically feasible. Currently, production of mass quantities of seeds by special crossing is difficult and expensive, but as technologies develop, more control-pollinated progenies will be used.

Magnitude of Gains

It is of value to mention various categories of characteristics and their responses to genetic manipulation. Genetic improvement can be obtained by choosing among populations or among individual trees within populations. As discussed in detail earlier, characteristics related to adaptability are often more strongly associated with populations, as compared to most other economic characteristics that are more closely related to individual-tree inheritance. It is of the utmost importance that for most species, many of the important tree characteristics are not strongly related genetically; therefore, it is possible work toward "tailor-making" a population containing a package of the desired characteristics.

Gains that have been achieved for several categories of characteristics obtained by manipulation of individual trees are listed next. Large lists of references could be given for each, but only a couple representative studies will be cited.

1. **Growth characteristics** Genetic manipulation of growth characteristics generally will achieve only modest gain through seed regeneration, although the gains certainly are worthwhile. Most growth assessments have been based on height, but when volume growth has actually been determined, gains have been increased (Jeffers, 1969; Talbert, 1982). In a summary of gains from tree improvement, Nikles (1970) reported a net economic yield of 30% on 15-year-old plantations based upon growth of *Pinus elliottii* and *P. radiata* in Australia. A 43% volume gain from the best 10% of longleaf pine families studied was found by Snyder (1973). The genetics of growth is complex and usually has a strong nonadditive and environmental component in addition to an additive component. Also, there is often a strong genotype × environment interaction for growth that restricts the gains possible

when one population is destined for use over wide areas. Thus, gains in growth using a seed orchard program will be modest but economically worthwhile. Gains in growth can be considerably greater when special-breeding or vegetative-propagation methods are used.

2. **Tree straightness and limb-quality characteristics** Straightness is fairly strongly inherited and responds well to either a sexual or vegetative propagation system. Because of the strength of its inheritance, it is often possible to make enough gain in straightness in the first generation of intensive selection so that selection for this trait can be relaxed in subsequent generations (Goddard and Strickland, 1964; Campbell, 1965; Ehrenberg, 1970). Limb characteristics are much more strongly influenced by the environment than is straightness, but there is enough genetic control to improve limb qualities. Gains will usually be less than for straightness (Shelbourne and Stonecypher, 1971). Because of the effect on the final product and its inheritance pattern, emphasis in a tree improvement program should generally be made on bole straightness, but limb qualities should not be ignored. They have a major effect on some products, and gains can be made even though they may be modest.

3. **Wood qualities** Although there are some exceptions, most wood properties are under a strong additive genetic control, and gain using a seed orchard program is good. Although many wood qualities show a reasonably strong inheritance, the two that are most studied (specific gravity and fiber length) show great gain from genetic manipulation (see Chapter 12). It now appears that the chemical property of cellulose yield per unit dry wood is also under some degree of genetic control, but because of its large nonadditive component genetic gains will only be obtained if vegetative-propagation or special-breeding systems are used. The encouraging thing is that the inheritance of a wood property such as specific gravity is so strong that gains can be made even within the framework of desired growth and form qualities.

   Genetic manipulation of wood yields good results; this has been attested to by numerous authors. In a recent report, Jett and Talbert (1982) determined for 12-year-old loblolly pine trees that with only one generation of light selection in which one in two individuals were saved for higher wood specific gravity, improvement in dry-wood weight was increased about 10 kg/m^3 of wood.

   Numerous calculations have been made on gains in wood qualities, particularly for specific gravity (Dadswell et al., 1961; Zobel et al., 1972). In an intensive analysis of the value of including wood in a tree improvement program, van Buijtenen et al. (1975) reported that breeding for wood specific gravity was almost always desirable for making linerboard paper. There is no doubt about the value of gains from including wood in a breeding program.

4. **Pest resistance** Sometimes, huge gains can be made from breeding for pest resistance, and other times the gains achieved are little or none. Results depend upon the genetic variation of the host as well as of the pathogen and

their interactions with the environment. Gains in pest resistance from the use of genetics can sometimes be so spectacular that they make forests profitable out of an otherwise nonprofitable situation. Although pest resistance breeding sometimes does not work, overall genetic gains from this breeding activity have been one of the brightest spots in tree improvement. The complexities, successes, and failures of breeding for pest resistance were reported in Chapter 9.

5. **Adverse environments**   Although much of the genetic variability related to adaptability to adverse environments is a function of a provenance or population, there still is considerable tree-to-tree variability that can be exploited. For example, occasional trees from warm areas are cold hardy, or those from moist areas are drought hardy. Using the individual trees in developing a desired tolerant strain can be difficult and time consuming, but sometims there is no other satisfactory way to get the job done. For example, none of the sources of cold-hardy eucalypts have proper growth and form for the Gulf Coast area of the southern United States. Therefore, vigorous high-quality trees from large cold-susceptible sources are being selected and propagated to develop the needed cold-tolerant strain (Hunt and Zobel, 1978). The gain that is possible from using individuals who are especially tolerant to adverse environmental conditions has not been sufficiently exploited. Good gains not obtainable by other means are possible if the proper effort is expended.

6. **Miscellaneous**   There are many additional aspects of tree improvement in which useful and sometimes large genetic gains can be made. Things such as fruitfulness show huge differences among clones, as do graft incompatibility and rooting ability. These strongly inherited differences will be exploited more often as tree improvement activities become more sophisticated. Many other physiological characteristics, such as resin production, show moderate to strong inheritance patterns. For example, tall oil production from pines has been doubled by using the genetically high yielders as parents (Franklin et al., 1970). Growth patterns and response to light and other environmental factors have been extensively studied (Ekberg et al., 1976; Eriksson et al., 1978).

The genetic gains from forest tree breeding have been larger and easier to obtain than most forest geneticists originally expected. The large variability in forest trees and considerable additive variance have made the easy mass selection schemes used in first-generation programs very successful. Of the many studies reporting specific gain values, only one example is listed to give the reader some idea of the magnitude of gains that have been achieved.

In a recent summary paper of the gains from one generation of tree improvement for loblolly pine using the comparison tree selection system in natural stands, Talbert (1982) made a number of volume gain calculations based upon data from genetic tests up to 12 years of age; much of this was projected through growth and yield models to age 25. As an example, the following percentage improvements were predicted for age 25 for seed orchard seed over commercial check seed.

	Stand Volume (%)	Stand Value (%)[a]
Unrogued seed orchard	6.4	18.0
Rogued seed orchard	12.7	32.0

[a]Includes added value resulting from increased tree size.

Talbert (1982) especially warns about the change in percentage improvement with age in unthinned stands and states the following: "One of the reasons for decreasing percentage gains in volume with increasing age is an increasing volume figure on which the percentage is based. Another reason is increased mortality in stands planted with seed orchard stock because of more intense tree-to-tree competition resulting from more rapid stand development." It would seem apparent that the situation would be helped by a thinning at the correct time.

There is no longer any doubt that substantial gains can be made in most desired characteristics in forest trees in one generation of selection. Changes in the genetic composition of forest stands are of such a magnitude that there will be a large impact on forest management strategies (Zobel, 1979). It is important that the tree breeder and forest manager realize that gain figures for volume, stem straightness, or any other characteristic must be interpreted in relation to their effects on stand development and associated management activities. Gains for any trait, expressed in biological or economic terms, can and will change dramatically during the life of the stand and with different forest management and silvicultural practices.

Summary of Gains

Where do all of the many facets and intricacies of gain leave the tree improver and how does one use the available information? Some especially important considerations related to gain can be summarized as follows.

1. The first consideration is the warning to use care to interpret all reports in light of the product requirements, tree ages, test conditions, species, and areas involved. Do not blindly apply gain figures that may be available for other species, other areas, or other-aged forests because the result is often similar to comparing apples with oranges. This most important warning can be summarized as follows: Be critical and analytical of any gains that are reported and that are being considered for use.

2. Do not make estimates of gains for older operational forests based on those from very young tests. This is especially true for growth characteristics in which growth patterns change with age. Some quality, pest resistance, and adaptive characteristics can be assessed with confidence at young ages, but

even these should be interpreted with caution. The literature is filled with data that are misleading or plainly wrong because they have been based upon small, young, or otherwise unsatisfactory studies and applied to operational programs.

3. Try to convert all gains to monetary units. Be cautious of gains reported on a percentage basis; this caution needs to be exercised also when actual unit values of volume, quality, or adaptability are available.

4. Adaptability assessments are difficult to make. It is the extreme situation or sequence, the 1 day in 1 year or the 1 day in 10 years that can cause trouble. It is necessary that the material being tested is sufficiently exposed to the extremes of environments and unusual environmental sequences that might occur so that one can have confidence in their performance.

5. Unit values of gain for growth characteristics are easy to determine, but those for some quality characteristics are most difficult to quantify. Despite this difficulty, the value of quality improvements is often obvious; an example is producing trees with straighter stems than those found in unimproved populations.

6. A calculation of total gain from a tree improvement program is most complex and ultimately should be based on some form of an aggregate economic index.

7. Be realistic in the types of gain being sought. The objective is usually to make optimal gains rather than maximal gains. Much harm has been done to tree improvement efforts by promising gains larger than can be realistically obtained. No one gets upset when gains are achieved that are greater than a modest gain prediction, but the converse can be fatal to a tree improvement program.

8. Use the best possible methods to capture genetic variability. More refined and precise techniques are becoming available, and these should not be ignored. For example, enough information is now available to use special seed production methods like two-clone orchards or mass pollination. Vegetative propagation methods are rapidly emerging that take advantage of both the additive and nonadditive genetic variance, thus enabling larger gains to be obtained in a shorter period of time. Special developmental breeding programs are needed to reap the optimum benefit from vegetative propagation.

ECONOMICS OF TREE IMPROVEMENT

The ultimate value of tree improvement depends on how much it helps forest management; put more directly, how greatly does tree improvement increase the returns from the forestry operation? Despite the great complexities of assessing the true value of a series of complex actions and investments that often do not give a return for a number of years, numerous studies about the economic value of tree improvement activities have been conducted. At first, these assessments were concerned with costs and predicted or hoped-for gains. Recently, more realistic figures are becoming available that can be used to develop meaningful economic analyses.

As is common for all aspects of tree improvement, *time* is the most formidable hurdle in making suitable economic analyses. Even after realistic costs and genetic gains are known, there is always the uncertainty of interest rates, future markets, inflation, and general economic conditions. For most forest products, added uncertainties relate to competition from materials that can be used to replace wood products; for example, the fear that plastic might replace paper products was once prevalent, and it actually has occurred to some extent with large milk containers and grocery bags. Not many years ago, foresters were told that aluminum, steel, and concrete would greatly reduce the use of wood products in the building industry. This happened to some extent but has slowed because of the high cost of energy needed to manufacture the alternative materials.

A major deterrent to tree improvement programs and their ultimate use is product uncertainty. A rarely recognized but important aspect of this is the consideration of fashion, especially in solid-wood products for use under highly aesthetic situations, such as room finish or furniture. Fashions in wood products can vary just as they do for clothes. One example is curly birch in Europe; this unique type of wood is inherited strongly enough to make good genetic gains relatively rapidly (Johnsson, 1950). Curly birch was for many years a very rare, high-value product. As more trees with this type of wood are produced, it will become more common, and the price of this specialty product will decrease. A change in wood value occurred in the furniture industry in the United States with black cherry (*Prunus serotina*). This species was a favorite for furniture for a number of years, but after it became scarce, fashion shifted to other woods such as ash and white pecan, and black cherry was no longer in vogue. Because of this change, there have been questions recently about the wisdom of pursuing cherry-breeding projects that had been started earlier.

Future product needs and values are critical to any economic assessment of the value of tree improvement. Because they are so difficult to predict, all economic studies that have been made or will be can be challenged. Despite these imperfections, the studies already made have indicated a clear and repetitive picture of the economic worth of tree improvement. In one of the earliest studies on the economics of tree improvement, Davis (1967a) ended his assessment with the following cautious but optimistic statement.

Recognizing the many assumptions used in making the cost and required yield increases that are given, it is still fairly clear that investments in seed from commercial seed orchards are sufficiently low that the minimum expectation of increased yield will justify them. In short, from the stumpage grower's point of view, it certainly appears that current investments in loblolly pine seed orchards are well within the "ball park" with respect to financial justification. If the upper expectations of gains materialize, they should prove to be excellent investments.

This summary, based on some initial costs and very tenuous returns, sounds very similar to the one made by Carlisle and Teich (1970b) later, when more reliable data were available.

It is understandable that, because of the lack of information, many of the early economic analyses as well as some current ones refer to the economics of tree improvement only in general terms. However, some studies do deal with specific situations. One of the earliest was by Perry and Wang (1958) who calculated the added value that would accrue to the forest enterprise when seed with different degrees of genetic improvement was used for planting. Actual costs and genetic gains were not vailable at that time, but the calculations presented enabled one to obtain a good idea about the intensity of genetic effort needed to justify certain costs. Part of the analysis related to the amount of money that could be spent in producing a kilogram of seed that would yield a desired amount of gain. A more recent and in-depth report by Weir (1975) related to the financial problems that would result from the loss of improved growth in operational plantations if insects destroyed the developing seed in the seed orchard. His calculations indicated that loss of seed from seed orchard insects would have a larger impact on the forest economy than the current losses from the southern pine beetle that is considered to be one of the most destructive pests in that region. His article clearly touched on a fact that is often overlooked, that is, "invisible" losses are occurring in forestry because improved seedlings are not being used in plantation establishment.

Economic Value of Tree Improvement

Many economists like to base their assessment on how much genetic gain is needed to justify a given program. This is a relatively easy way to illustrate economic aspects of tree improvement, and one can relate it to the genetic gains actually being achieved. One example is Davis (1976b) who calculated that a 2.5 to 4.0% volume gain over the stock currently used for planting would be necessary to justify a tree improvement program. He emphasized the difficulty of including quality improvement in such a calculation in addition to the more easily assessed volume gains. Based on Canadian experiences, Carlisle and Teich (1970b) came to a similar conclusion, stating that an increase in yield from 2 to 5% would offset the added costs of a tree improvement program. They added that if quality characteristics, such as wood, were considered and that if tree improvement and silviculture were properly coordinated, mill profitability would be profoundly affected. The interesting point about the 2 to 5% required to obtain an economic return reported by the aforementioned authors is that these percentage values are very small when they are compared with the 6 to 12% volume gains that Talbert (1982) reported, or the 12 to 14% volume gains, 5% improvement in wood specific gravity, and 10% in rust resistance that Porterfield et al. (1975) reported. In some recent work on the tropical pines, for which very little economic information has been available, Ledig and Whitmore (1981) show volume gains of 12 to 21%, depending upon the selection intensity used. However, these gains have not been translated to economic values.

A number of other studies have reported various aspects of the economics of tree improvement. Many, like the one by Lundgren and King (1966), involving *Pinus banksiana*, concluded that tree improvement is a good investment. Another study by Reilly and Nikles (1977) who based their analyses on actual costs and returns for improved volume and tree straightness, found a 14% internal rate of return from an unrogued seed orchard. This increased to 19% after roguing. Similarly, Row and Dutrow (1975) showed a 12.4% rate of return on tree improvement, whereas Carlisle and Rauter (1978) indicated an internal rate of return that varied from 6 to 21%, depending on which variables were used. Some authors are very enthusiastic about the potentials of genetic improvement. As an example, Carlisle and Teich (1970a) have stated that "it would be difficult to find a cheaper way of increasing yield" for white spruce. This was determined even though the model they used was weighted toward minimal benefits.

For fusiform rust, Holley and Vale (1977) showed that 18 to 28 million dollars are lost annually due to poorer yields and lower wood quality resulting from fusiform rust infection on southern pines. From this, it is evident that large economic gains will be achieved if reasonable rust resistance can be obtained. There have been numerous studies on gains from improving wood characteristics (e.g., Dadswell et al., 1961; van Buijtenen, 1973; Zobel, 1975; Jett and Talbert, 1982). Space does not permit citing more of the numerous studies and tree characteristics that have been assessed. Overall, it is quite evident that the greatest returns are obtained by working on a few rather than on many characteristics at one time.

Tree improvement is more economically successful with some species than with others. Dutrow (1974) emphasized this point, indicating that much larger genetic gains are required from oak than from birch in order to obtain a reasonable return on tree improvement because of the limitations in seed production. Similar comments about the relative profitability of oak and birch have been made by Marquis (1973).

In addition to the specific studies, a number of general reports indicate both the suitability and good financial returns from tree improvement. Examples of the more general types of published papers are those by Zobel (1966), Dutrow and Row (1976), Porterfield (1977), and Stonecypher (1982). Good profitability is predicted and special emphasis is indicated to the effect that initially large expenditures that are often required can be economically justified in the long run.

Most studies have been based on the shorter-rotation, faster-growing conifers. For hardwoods, Marquis (1973) suggested that tree improvement programs will be most profitable for species that are heavy seed producers, have rapid growth, and high-value products. The economic situation is less clear-cut under other conditions. For example, Ledig and Porterfield (1981) have emphasized that discount rate and length of rotation are particularly crucial variables in determining the economic worth of tree improvement. They reported on the gains needed to justify genetic application in slow-growing species with long rotations. With rotation ages up to 50 years, a volume improvement as low as 6.3% will yield an 8% return on the tree improvement investment. However, Ledig and Porterfield have emphasized that it is very difficult to show profitable gains from tree improvement when rotations from 80 to 120 years are used.

Great differences in profitability are also present, depending on the techniques and methods used. For example, van Buijtenen and Saitta (1972) have reported that mass selection is more cost-effective than progeny testing for the establishment of first-generation orchards and that the latter should be used primarily as a · basis for selection for advanced generations. Most authors emphasize, as do Teich and Carlisle (1977), that much more genetic and economic information is needed and that the strategies chosen are critical. Often the mistake is made of underestimating the side benefits of the tree improvement program on tree quality or wood quality or on the cost of harvest or manufacture (Nantiyal, 1970). Predicting future markets, costs, interest rates, inflation, and the like is especially difficult. It appears that the best approach in the future is to use some linear programming technique, as Teich and Carlisle (1977) suggested, or a systems analysis approach like the one van Buijtenen and Saitta (1972) used.

The information necessary to make economic analyses of tree improvement and the methodology to do it best are badly needed. Unfortunately, use of suitable economic techniques and the required input data will likely continue to lag behind the need for results to justify another operation or more intensification of tree improvement. It is essential that the tree improver forms a team with the economist to develop the most effective program and methods of analysis.

Reporting Economic Gains

It is essential that the value of tree improvement is presented in a realistic and meaninful manner. This also requires teamwork between an economist who is knowledgeable about tree improvement and a tree improver who can appreciate and understand simple economic analyses. Of the many ways to present the value of a tree improvement program that have been attempted, one of the best is to calculate the added value that a given amount of genetically improved seed will contribute to the forestry organization. A number of organizations have used this method successfully; it is illustrated in Table 14.1. One can obtain from Table 14.1 an indication of the *present* value of added income in the future that would be obtained at the time of harvest for two contrasting cases with case 1 representing a good situation; case 2 is less favorable.

However, the values in Table 14.1 alone are quite meaningless without a comparison of the present value of a pound of improved seed with the cost of producing that seed. It can be shown by the following ratio.

$$\frac{\text{Present value of improved seed}}{\text{Present value of the cost of producing a pound of seed}} \qquad \frac{B}{C}$$

If the B/C ratio is greater than 1.0, then (because 8% interest was used in Table 14.1) the return will be greater than 8%. As an example, take the $48/lb in the

TABLE 14.1
Present Value of Additional Wood Obtained from 1 lb of Seed Orchard Seed for Several Stumpage Values, Two Growth Rates, and Two Combinations of Nursery Production, Genetic Gain, and Plantation Stocking

Case 1	Case 2
1. 1 lb of seed produces 9000 plantable seedlings	1. 1 lb of seed produces 7000 plantable seedlings
2. 500 seedlings are planted per acre (1 lb of seed plants 18 acres)	2. 800 seedlings are planted per acre (1 lb of seed plants 8.8 acres)
3. Rotation age = 25 years	3. Rotation age = 25 years
4. Genetic gain = 15%	4. Genetic gain = 10%
5. Interest rate = 8%	5. Interest rate = 8%

Stumpage Value ($/cord at time of harvest)	Base Growth (cords/acre/ year)		Stumpage Value ($/cord at time of harvest)	Base Growth (cords/acre/ year)	
	1.5	2.0		1.5	2.0
10	127	197	10	48	64
15	221	296	15	72	96
24	354	473	24	115	153
30	443	591	30	144	192
40	591	788	40	192	255

table in case 2. If it costs $50/lb to grow the seed, it is not attractive as an economic investment and will not return 8%. If it costs $15/lb, then it is a very attractive economic investment for the organization concerned.

Making Economic Assessments

With all the uncertainties and unknowns, it would appear on the surface that it is not possible to make economic analyses of tree improvement. But this is not so— one uses all available data, uses the best estimates when facts are lacking, and then proceeds. The answer will certainly provide information that would not be available if the analyses had not been done. The key to such an analysis is flexibility. The methodology must be sound and general, enabling the use of new or updated data when they become available. This is the pattern followed by most organizations.

There is no value in this chapter to suggest any particular method to be followed because each organization has its own format and objectives. There are a few general points, however, that should be kept in mind when making an economic assessment of tree improvement.

1. Bring all returns and costs to a common time. The usual method is to convert everything to present value.

2. Costs are relatively easy to determine with considerable accuracy. Care is needed to use realistic costs that will be in effect after a program is operational. Costs based on research or small plots can be very misleading.

3. Results and gains are very difficult to determine accurately, and frequently they must be based on projections and common sense. But one must be careful taking yields based on research and applying them to large operations Almost always, the research results are more optimistic than can actually be obtained operationally. Frequently, research results are based on young trees that cannot give an indication of what the situation would be at rotation age.

4. Keep the system simple and understandable. The personnel that make administrative decisions demand straightforward and simple answers. Results couched in excessive statistical jargon are often ineffective. Results that are tentative because of an excessive use of qualifiers (*about, maybe, perhaps, sometimes*) are often totally ignored or rejected.

5. The results should be conservative. No one is upset if gains are greater than those that were projected. However, do not be so conservative and choose the "worst case" so that an incorrect impression is given about the economic potential of tree improvement.

6. Foresters often become "paralyzed" into taking no action because all the facts are not known. This is not acceptable, and estimations must be made to enable determination of the economic suitability of a program.

LITERATURE CITED

Anderson, G. A. 1978. Effects of intensive pine plantation mangement on southern wood supply and quality. *Tappi* **61**(2):37–46.

Barneoud, C., Brunet, A. M., and Dubois, J. M. 1979. Behavior of the highest plants in a young spruce plantation. Association Forêt-Cellulose (AFOCEL): Annales de Recherches Sylvicoles, Paris, France, pp. 383–400.

Barrett, W. H., and Alberti, F. R. 1972. Value of early selection in progeny of willows [Valor de la seliccion temprana en progenies de sauces]. *IDIA,* Supp. For. No. 7, pp. 3–8.

Baskerville, G. 1977. "Let's Call the Whole Thing Off." Proc. Symp. Inten. Cult. Northern For. Types. U.S. Forest Service Technical Report NE-29, pp. 25–30.

Bergman, A. 1969. "Evaluation of Costs and Benefits of Tree Improvement Programs." 2nd World Cons. For. Tree Breed., Washington, D.C.

Brown, C. L., Goddard R. E., and Klein, J. 1961. Selection of pine seedlings in nursery beds for certain crown characteristics. *Jour. For.* **59**(10):770–771.

Campbell, R. K. 1965. Phenotypic variation and repeatability of stem sinousity in Douglas fir. *Northwest Sci.* **39**(2):47–59.

Carlisle, A., and Teich, A. H. 1970a. "The Costs and Benefits of Tree Improvement Programs." Petawawa Forest Experiment Station, Chalk River, Ontario, Canada, Info. Report PS-X-20.

Carlisle, A., and Teich, A. H. 1970b. "Cost and Benefit Analysis of White Spruce (*Picea glauca*) Improvement." Proc. 12th Meet. Comm. For. Tree Breed. in Canada, pp. 227–230.

Carlisle, A., and Rauter, M. 1978. "The Economics of Tree Improvement in Ontario," Tree Improvement Symp., Ontario Min. Nat. Res. OP-7, Ontario, Canada.

Dadswell, H. E., Fielding, J. M., Nichols, J. W. P., and Brown, A. J. 1961. Tree to tree variations and the gross heritability of wood characteristics of *Pinus radiata*. *Tappi* **44**:174–179.

Davis, L. S. 1967a. "Cost-Return Relationships of Tree Improvement Programs." Proc. 9th South. Conf. For. Tree Impr., Knoxville, Tenn., pp. 20–26.

Davis, L. S. 1967b. Investment in loblolly pine clonal seed orchards. *Jour. For.* **65**:882–887.

Dutrow, G. F. 1974. "Economic Analysis of Tree Improvement: A Status Report." U.S. Forest Service Technical Report 50-6.

Dutrow, G., and Row, C. 1976. "Measuring Financial Gains from Genetically Superior Trees. U.S. Forest Service Research Paper, 50-132.

Ehrenberg, C. 1970. Breeding for stem quality. *Unasylva.* **24**(23):23–31.

Ekberg, I., Dormling, I., Eriksson, G., and von Wettstein, D. 1976. Inheritance of the photoperiodic response in forest trees. In *Tree Physiology and Yield Improvement* (M. G. R. Cannel and F. T. Last, eds.), pp. 207–221. Academic Press, New York.

Eriksson, G., Ekberg, I., Dormling, I., and Matern, B. 1978. Inheritance of bud-flushing in *Picea abies*. *Theor. Appl. Gen.* **52**:3–19.

Franklin, E. C., Taras, M. A., and Volkman, D. A. 1970. Genetic gains in yields of oleoresin, wood extractives and tall oil. *Tappi* **53**(12):2302–2304.

Goddard, R. E., and Strickland, R. K. 1964. Crooked stem form in loblolly pine. *Sil. Gen.* **13**(5):155–157.

Gruenfeld, J. 1975. "Leaning Flagpoles." Workshop South. For. Econ. Workers, Biloxi, Miss.

Hatchell, G. E., Dorman, K. W., and Langdon, O. G. 1972. Performance of loblolly and slash pine nursery selections. *For. Sci.* **18**(4):308–313.

Holden, C. 1980. Rain forests vanishing. *Science* **208**:378.

Holley, D. L., and Veal, M. A. 1977. "Economic Impact of Fusiform Rust." Proc. Fusiform Rust Conf., Gainesville, Fla., pp. 39–50.

Hunt, R., and Zobel, B. 1978. Frost-hardy *Eucalyptus* grow well in the Southeast. *South. Jour. Appl. For.* **1**(1):6–10.

Jeffers, R. M. 1969. "Parent-Progeny Growth Correlations in White Spruce." Proc. 11th Meet. Comm. on For. Tree Breed. in Canada, Ottawa, pp. 213–221.

Jett, J. B., and Talbert, J. T. 1982. "The Place of Wood Specific Gravity in the Development of Advanced Generation Seed Orchards." *South. Jour. Appl. For.* **6**:177–180.

Johnson, N. E. 1976. Biological opportunities and risks associated with fast-growing plantations in the tropics. *Jour. For.* **74**(4):206–211.

Johnsson, H. 1950. Ankommor av masurbjörk [Offspring of curly burch]. Årsberätt. Fören. Växtföräd. *Skogstrad,* pp. 18–29.

Ledig, T. F., and Porterfield, R. L. 1981. "West Coast Tree Improvement Programs: A Break-Even Cost-Benefit Analysis." U.S. Forest Service Research Paper PSW-156.

Ledig, F. T., and Whitmore, J. L. 1981. "The Calculation of Selection Differential and Selection Intensity to Predict Gain in a Tree Improvement Program for Plantation Grown Honduras Pine in Puerto Rico," Southern Forest Experiment Station Research Paper SO-170.

Lundren, A. L., and King, J. P. 1966. Estimating financial returns from forest tree improvement programs. *Jour. For.* **28**(1):37–38.

Marquis, D. A. 1973. Factors affecting financial returns from hardwood tree improvement. *Jour. For.* **71**(2):79–83.

Mohn, C. A., and Randall, W. K. 1971. Inheritance and correlations of growth characteristics in *Populus deltoides. Sil. Gen.* **20**(5–6):182–183.

Nantiyal, J. C. 1970. "Economic Considerations in Tree Breeding." Proc. 12th Meet. Comm. For. Tree Breed. in Canada, pp. 222–223.

Nienstaedt, H. 1981. "Super spruce seedlings continue superior growth for 18 years," North Central Forest Experiment Station Research Note NC-265.

Nikles, D. G. 1970. Breeding for growth and yield. *Unasylva* **24**(2–3):9–22.

Perry, T. O. and Wang, C. W. 1958. The value of genetically superior seed. *Jour. For.* **56**:843–845.

Porterfield, R. L., Zobel, B. J., and Ledig, F. T. 1975. Evaluating the efficiency of tree improvement programs. *Sil. Gen.* **24**(2–3):33–34.

Porterfield, R. L. 1977. "Economic Evaluation of Tree Improvement Programs." 3rd World Cons. of For. Tree Breed., Canberra, Australia.

Reilly, J. J., and Nikles, D. G. 1977. "Analysing Benefits and Costs of Tree Improvement: *Pinus caribaea.*" Proc. 3rd World Cons. For. Tree Breed., Canberra, Australia, pp. 1099–1024.

Robinson, J. F., and van Buijtenen, J. P. 1979. Correlation of seed weight and nursery bed traits with 5-, 10-, and 15-year volumes in a loblolly pine progeny test. *For. Sci.* **25**(4):591–596.

Row, C., and Dutrow, G. 1975. "Measuring Genetic Gains by Projected Increases in Financial Return." Proc. 13th South. For. Tree Imp. Conf., Raleigh, N.C., pp. 17–26.

Shelbourne, C. J. A., and Stonecypher, R. W. 1971. The inheritance of bole straightness in young loblolly pine. *Sil. Gen.* **20**(5–6):151–156.

Snyder, E. B. 1973. "15-Year Gains from Parental and Early Family Selection in Longleaf Pine." Proc. 12th South. For. Tree Impr. Conf., pp. 46–49.

Stonecypher, R. W. 1982. "Potential Gain through Tree Improvement. Increasing Forest Productivity." Proc. 1981 Society of American Forestry Convention.

Sweet, G. B., and Wareing, P. F. 1966. "The Relative Growth Rates of Large and Small Seedlings in Forest Tree Species," New Zealand Forest Service Report No. 210.

Talbert, J. T. 1982. "One Generation of Loblolly Pine Tree Improvement: Results and Challenges." Proc. 18th Can. Tree Imp. Assoc. Meet., Duncan, British Columbia.

Teich, A. H., and Carlisle, A. 1977. "Analysing Benefits and Costs of Tree Breeding Programs." 3rd World Cons. For. Tree Breed., Canberra, Australia.

van Buijtenen, J. P. 1973. Innovation by systems analysis: Southern pine kraft linerboard from breeding to boxcar. *Tappi* **56**(1):121–122.

van Buijtenen, J. P., Alexander, S. D., Einspahr, D. W., Ferrie, A. E., Hart, T., Kellogg, R. M., Porterfield, R. L., and Zobel, B. J. 1975. How will tree improvement and intensive forestry affect pulp manufacture? *Tappi* **58**(9):129–134.

van Buijtenen, J. P., and Saitta, W. W. 1972. Linear programming applied to the economic analysis of forest tree improvement. *Jour. For.* **70**:164–167.

Weir, R. J. 1975. "Cone and Seed Insects—Southern Pine Beetle: A Contrasting Impact on Forest Productivity." 13th South. For. Tree Impr. Conf., Raleigh, N.C., pp. 182–192.

Wilkinson, R. C. 1974. "Realized and Estimated Efficiency of Early Selection in Hybrid Poplar Clonal Tests." Proc. 21st Northeast. For. Tree Impr. Conf., Fredericton, New Brunswick, Canada, pp. 26–35.

Zobel, B.J. 1966. "Tree Improvement and Economics: A Neglected Interrelationship." 6th World For. Conf., Madrid, Spain.

Zobel, B. J. 1975. "Our Changing Wood Resource—Its Effects on the Pulp Industry." 8th Cellulose Conf., Syracuse, N.Y., pp. 5–7.

Zobel, B. J. "Trends in Forest Management as Influenced by Tree Improvement." Proc. 15th Sou. For. Tree Imp. Conf., Starkville, Miss., p. 73–77.

Zobel, B. J., Kellison, R. C., Matthias, M. F., and Hatcher, A. V. 1972. "Wood Density of the Southern Pines," N.C. Agricultural Experiment Station Tech. Bull. No. 208.

CHAPTER 15

The Genetic Base and Gene Conservation

In the short term, the major objective of the tree improver is to manipulate the variability present in a forest tree population to produce more trees with desirable growth, form, or adaptability characteristics. In so doing, the genetic base will usually be maintained or narrowed for economically important characteristics, and the base will be maintained or broadened for those characteristics that affect adaptability. Any tree improvement program carried over many generations will eventually reach a plateau beyond which further meaningful progress is not possible unless steps are taken that ensure maintenance and enhancement of sufficient genetic variability. Therefore, for successful long-term tree improvement, it is essential to begin with *a broad genetic base* and to use a breeding program that will *conserve genetic potential* that is already in the population.

It is vital to recognize that one can breed for a narrowing of the genetic base for certain important economic characteristics such as straightness of tree bole and at the same time develop trees that have wide adaptability that is expressed through sustained good growth and good pest resistance and adaptability to adverse environments. This is possible because in most species there is considerable genetic independence between different economic characteristics and those for adaptability. Desired objectives can be achieved either by using a provenance with the needed adaptability within which selection is practiced for desired economic characteristics, or conversely, by intensively selecting for desired economic characteristics and then choosing individuals within the selected population with the desired adaptability.

Which approach one should follow depends on the needs and desires of the organization concerned and the species of interest. What is basic to both approaches is that the breeding program must be designed to conserve genes and gene complexes of value in order to maximize long-term gains in economically important traits and in adaptabiliy. Therefore, provision must be made so that potential gains in the program are not constrained by a reduction in the genetic base or by the effects of inbreeding depression that result from related matings. It is obvious that no single method of gene or gene complex conservation can be used in all circumstances. The best procedure would be to utilize all methods available for gene conservation, but cost and space limitations usually prohibit this. How soon serious problems will occur using current breeding methods depends on the intensity of selection being used, population size, and the number of generations the program has been in operation.

It was stressed in earlier chapters that all successful tree improvement programs must have an operational, or use, phase and a developmental, or research, phase. Most of this book has dealt with the operational aspects of tree improvement. This chapter will emphasize the gene conservation activities necessary to ensure a successful and ongoing long-term operational tree improvement phase.

Gene conservation as applied to the progress and efficiency of a tree breeding program is somewhat different from the objective of saving genes for some general but undefined future purpose. This chapter will be primarily concerned with gene conservation for an applied forest tree improvement program, although the more conventional gene conservation approach will also be covered.

WHAT IS GENE CONSERVATION?

It is difficult to discuss gene conservation in an orderly and rational way because the subject sometimes becomes very emotionally charged. Many persons equate gene conservation with the necessity to prevent the extinction of a species or a provenance of a species. Sometimes wild and unsubstantiated claims are made (see Zobel and Davey, 1977). Although there are rare exceptions, the problem usually faced is not the extinction of a species but rather the reduction of a species, or a part thereof, to such an extent that it reduces its genetic potential. For the plant breeder, this concern strongly relates to saving those genes and gene complexes that have current or possibly future economic value and to adaptability characteristics (Zobel, 1971, 1978). The problem is large and real, because as Kemp et al. (1976) have stated, the general objectives with which the conservationist is concerned can often only be surmised and not positively identified. The tree breeder must be cautious and conservative because once a gene pool or gene complex has been lost, it is gone forever.

When a species is truly endangered to the extent that it is facing extinction, nearly everyone agrees that all efforts should be made to save as much of it as possible and as quickly as possible. For example, Keiding (1977) has mentioned that three pine and one teak species are in danger of being lost; certainly they are being seriously threatened by depletion of genetic resources and by contamination from related species. But the usual situation is that only a portion of a species is endangered, because its gene pool is in danger of being so reduced that some genes or gene complexes will be lost (Kleinschmitt, 1979). One example of such a situation was reported for *Eucalyptus* by Turnbull (1977) who stated that not one of the 450 species that exists in the genus is in danger of extinction, but a few are definitely faced with extreme genetic impoverishment. Another example is in Central America, where a few species are truly endangered and a number of species have provenances that are being seriously depleted genetically (Figure 15.1). Genetic material from this area is a primary source for planting in South America and other tropical regions. Therefore, genetic impoverishment in Central America will have very great economic as well as biological importance. In fact, concern was so great for the Central American conifers that the international cooperative CAMCORE[1] was formed (Gallegos et al., 1980; Dvorak, 1981), including companies and governments from eight nations to help conserve the gene resources of the endangered trees.

Gene conservation therefore relates to activities directed at saving gene pools for use to prevent loss of genes, gene complexes, and genotypes and, in extreme instances, to prevent extinction of whole taxonomic categories of trees. For ease of reference and accuracy, the term *gene conservation* will be used in this book rather than the term *gene preservation*. It is of importance, however, to recognize that some authors and groups use the two terms synonymously and interchangeably.

---

[1]CAMCORE stands for Central America and Mexico Coniferous Resources Cooperative.

FIGURE 15.1

There are numerous reasons why sources within species, and even some species, are in danger of losing genetic material in Central America. Shown is a woodcutter with a load of wood. Forests are being overutilized for fuel in the drier areas, especially those close to habitations.

CONSERVATION OF GENES AND GENE COMPLEXES

The literature usually refers to *gene conservation,* but this can be somewhat misleading. Almost all economically important tree characteristics are controlled by the alleles of several gene loci. There are a few instances in which an important characteristic in forest trees is under single-gene control, such as certain disease-resistance characteristics, but these are the exception. In reality, then, efforts to conserve genes usually involve conservation of whole gene complexes that make a tree economically desirable and adapted to pests and other aspects of its environment (Zobel, 1978). In this sense, the gene complex *does not* equate to the genotype of the individual; it relates to the gene action or actions for specific traits. Conservation, control, combination, and use of gene complexes is a key concept in tree improvement.

Despite the controversies associated with gene or gene complex conservation, there is one fact on which all parties agree—conservation of genetic material is of critical importance in tree improvement if maximum long-term gains are to be achieved (Burley and Namkoong, 1980). But there are great differences of opinion about what complexes should be conserved and how this can be best achieved. One major difference exists between those foresters who define gene conservation as *saving all possible genes or gene complexes within species or race* and those who espouse *saving those genes or gene complexes that will be most helpful in a long-term breeding program.* A major argument raised by the former group is, Who knows when any given gene or gene complex might become desirable? The most cautious persons will thus insist that all possible genetic materials within the population are saved, an ideal action but one that is deterred by the fact that conservation of *all* genes and gene complexes within a species is highly impractical because of space, time, and cost limitations. In fact, in a breeding program, gain is made by changing gene frequencies; the objective is to increase the gene frequencies of desirable characteristics and to reduce those that are undesirable.

A decision must therefore be made about which genes or gene complexes are desirable, and these should have the highest priority in being conserved. This is difficult indeed, especially when one takes into consideration what might be useful or needed in future generations. Sometimes conservationists deal with saving genes that are related primarily to adaptability. These are vital, but often they are not the characteristics that are endangered. When bad logging is done, which often occurs in poorly executed selective logging systems, the characteristics in danger of loss are those of economic importance, such as straightness of tree bole, small limb size, desired wood qualities, or some other factor (Figure 15.2). When

FIGURE 15.2

A type of gene loss often not recognized can result from differential, or selective, logging. Often, all the good trees of the good species are removed, and the stand is left to grow as is. The stand in the illustration is totally degraded and is almost at the point of not growing because of a series of selective loggings, even though it is on an excellent site. Two types of genetic losses occur: (1) loss of desired species and (2) loss of the best genotypes of the trees of the desired species that are left.

endangered, these characteristics are just as vital to conserve as are those that are usually emphasized and that are related to adaptability to pests and adverse environments.

The concept that every possible gene or gene complex should be saved leads to suggestions that wild stands be preserved. The method is effective but results in trying up very large areas, which is a most inefficient approach if the same gene complexes can be conserved for later use when they are incorporated by breeding into a limited number of individuals in a clone bank or holding area. Essentially every individual tree or genotype within a population is genetically different, although many share certain genes or gene complexes. The objective of a gene conservation program should be to conserve genes and gene complexes, not necessarily genotypes.

CONSERVING GENETIC RESOURCES

The need for conservation of genetic material in forest trees is evident and not arguable (Burley, 1976). The reasons for the need are sometimes debated, and the conservation methods to be followed elicit heated discussions. However, the need for saving genetic material for use and adaptation for future unseen needs is critical.

Reasons for Loss of Genetic Resources

There are numerous reasons why the need for the preservation of forest gene resources is so important and is becoming so critical so rapidly. Any action that destroys forests or destroys one part of a forest can lead to a dangerous situation. The destructive agents are many; for example, insects, diseases, cutting for fuel, logging, clearing for agriculture, urban expansion, fire, storms, and other natural disasters all take their toll. There is no single culprit. The practice of removing the indigenous forests in the southeastern United States and replacig them with pines is sometimes believed to reduce the genetic base of the hardwoods to the endangered-species level; this contention has, however, been challenged by Popovich (1980) who cites the small amount of monoculture in the South and the fact that hardwoods are always a part of conifer plantations.

The most dangerous situations occur in the forest tree populations with restricted ranges or where there are disjunct populations. This can occur for unusual ecotypes on restricted sites, or sometimes for entire, restricted endemic species. In these circumstances, not only genes or gene complexes are endangered, but whole unique populations and species can be totally eradicated. Some forest tree species or provenances have been reduced to a few hundred survivors.

The problem of conservation has become especially critical in the dry tropical areas where the only economically acceptable source of energy is firewood. Wood cutters systematically take the closest trees and move out from their villages, leaving no forests behind (see Figure 15.1). Because these areas are usually hot and dry, forest regeneration is not good. An attempt is often made to farm the denuded areas, which destroys any regeneration. If farming is not done, grazing, usually along with fire, is almost always used, and these two factors wipe out any new trees that might become established. Goats and sheep can be among the worst enemies that forests have. They frequently prevent reestablishment of trees in cutover areas, and thus they create a real problem in gene conservation (Zobel, 1967).

Another problem, which is locally recognized but often not considered, is the destruction of forests by shifting agriculture. Especially in the tropical regions, whenever roads are built through the forests, an army of settlers usually follows. The forests are cut, farmed for a short time, and then are abandoned when the residual nutrients in the soil are gone or after erosion has removed the topsoil. Loss to shifting agriculture is serious indeed in many tropical areas and is considered a most important reason for forest destruction.

Any type of large-scale destruction, such as fires, insects, diseases, or storms, sometimes causes great concern about gene loss. However, the key to the seriousness of this concern is what happens after the disaster. If a new forest becomes established, there is little danger of gene loss, but if the destruction is so great that trees do not become reestablished, severe gene loss can occur (Figure 15.3). For example, Zobel has seen fires in Central America so large (up to 200,000 ha) and so severe that little natural tree regeneration could become established. This type of wholesale destruction is most common in more droughty areas and is a major cause of loss of genetic resources.

Examples of losses large enough to threaten loss of genetic potential due to insects or disease are numerous. Perhaps the most notable case is the loss of the American chestnut (*Castanea dentata*) from eastern North American hardwood forests due to the chestnut blight that was caused by the introduced fungus *Endothia prasitica*. Once a widespread and extremely important species economically, the American chestnut has been almost totally lost except for occasional sprouts that are usually killed before reaching productive maturity or a very rare tree that grows outside the species range. The gene complement of this species has been reduced to such a dangerous degree that, for all practical purposes, it has been lost.

Another example is the current plight of Fraser fir (*Abies balsamea*). Fraser fir is a species that is restricted naturally to a few mountaintops in the southern Appalachian Mountains in the eastern United States. It has considerable economic importance as a high-quality Christmas tree. Natural stands of Fraser fir are currently being threatened by the balsam woolly aphid (*Adelges piceae*). Often, entire natural stands of mature fir are destroyed by this introduced pest. Reproduction by seed is abundant, but if these stands are attacked and destroyed before reaching reproductive maturity, the genetic resources of the stand could be lost. This would be severe from biological, economic, and aesthetic standpoints.

The logging activities of human beings for lumber or pulp can be destructive to the gene base. If all trees are removed, and this action is followed by frequent fires or grazing that prevents regeneration, gene loss can be severe (see Figure 15.3). Another less recognized loss is by selective logging when only a few high-value

FIGURE 15.3

Many species of pines planted in the tropics have their origin in Central America. Loss of gene complexes from this area has special significance for tropical forestry. Shown is an aerial view of a logging operation that totally removed all *P. caribaea*. After logging, regeneration was good, but a subsequent fire killed all the young trees. No further seed source is available. Shown are the roads and skid trails.

species, which occur only sparsely on each hectare, are removed (see Figure 15.2). Regeneration is restricted and severe genetic losses result, even though the forest appears to be intact. The lack of regeneration results partially from a lack of a suitable seedbed for the desired species and from competition from less desired species that prevents the reestablishment of the species that had been selectively logged. There are a few temperate as well as numerous tropical species in which gene complex loss resulting from so-called selective logging has, or will soon, become critical.

Methodology of Conservation

There is a great diversity of opinion about which is the best method to use to preserve forest gene resources. Broadly speaking, conservation efforts follow one or two general approaches: *in situ,* which means preservation of trees and stands in natural populations, and *ex situ,* which refers to saving the genes or gene complexes under artificial conditions, or at least not in their native stands.

In situ **Conservation**   *In situ* conservation appears to be very popular; it certainly has the greatest appeal and is best understood by persons not involved in land management. *In situ* conservation is applied by setting aside and preserving stands of the desired species or complexes to prevent further losses, usually from the activities of humans. One of its major benefits is the conservation of ecosystems. There is no other effective method to achieve conservation of ecosystems than through the "*in situ* approach."

The philosophy of a complete "hands off" strategy with respect to the stand that is to be conserved has great appeal but will fall short of the desired objective of maintaining the genetic structure of the current stand because of the dynamic changes that take place in all forest stands. If natural stands are left solely "to nature" and are not managed, the species content and gene complex distribution will change while the stands pass through one stage of succession to another. For example, many pine forest types have been established as the result of some past, usually dramatic environmental change caused by fires, tornadoes, hurricanes, or clearing for farming. If the current pine stands in the southeastern United States are left to grow and are not managed, the subclimax pine forests are often gradually replaced by hardwoods, and over time the pine component will disappear or be greatly reduced. Thus, if it is desired to preserve and maintain the genes and gene complexes already present in the pine stands, they must be managed to halt the natural succession to a high hardwood component. A *major need for in situ conservation of genetic resources,* which is either not understood generally or is ignored, *is to manage the preserved stand in order to maintain the desired genetic composition.*

One of the least understood aspects of managing stands for *in situ* conservation is the size needed. The general attitude seems to be that "if a few trees are good, a lot of trees are better," and most *in situ* conservation areas are larger than needed. Large-sized *in situ* conservation stands are not harmful from the genetic standpoint, but they impose an excessive strain and drain on the economics of the organization underwriting the conservation effort and often on society in general, because potentially useful forest products are less available. It is not necessary to conserve hundreds of thousands of individuals that contain the same desired gene complexes; at most, a few thousand such trees are usually sufficient. If these individuals are conserved and managed so that they can regenerate themselves, there is no need to set aside many thousands of hectares for gene conservation.

The public as well as some foresters has become confused between *conservation of forests for ecological and aesthetic reasons* and those for *gene conservation.* The former usually requires large acreages, but this should not be interpreted as the need for equally large areas for gene conservation per se. For example, there are moves at the present time to save huge sections of the tropical forests in the Amazon as a "gene conservation measure." The large areas may be desired for ecological conservation but are not needed for gene conservation; a few well-chosen forest stands of moderate size will serve the gene conservation purpose well. It is amazing how many people who want to preserve forests for one reason or another incorrectly use gene conservation as the reason why this should be done. This practice hinders the true gene conservation efforts and often causes unwarranted anatagonism against the gene conservation effort. It usually is not necessary to set aside huge areas of natural forests to achieve the gene conservation objective.

One common problem with *in situ* conservation is that often the wrong forest populations are saved. Instead of conserving the truly endangered populations, stands are often chosen that are growing at high elevations or on other unique poor-site types, because they are less expensive, easier to obtain, or are the desired size. In so doing, the objective of conserving the populations occurring on more typical sites is defeated. Great care must be used in the selection of stands for *in situ* conservation.

One conservation difficulty in some areas arises from contamination of the desired genetic material from related sources that are planted near the area to be conserved. As plantation forestry becomes more common, the danger from such contamination increases. It has been said, for example, that in several countries in western Europe, there are no truly indigenous Scots pines because of a complete mixture between the indigenous and imported sources of this species. Sometimes it is desired to save thinned stands of exotics to preserve their genetic composition as desirable land races. This is most difficult because other undesired sources of exotics planted nearby may affect the stand that is to be saved.

From the botanical standpoint of preserving pure races, gene mixing from contamination of geographic sources is undesirable. For a breeder interested in producing the best yields in the given environment, it can be of minor concern and can represent an unusual type of land race; if the newly created genotypes are superior in the environment of interest, they should be used by the breeder. For an operational program, there is no particular virtue in purity of the local source as such, so long as the new genotypes have the combination of gene complexes that make them superior for the growth and products desired. The "new" trees may have good gene complexes, but the breeder will often need to stabilize them before they can be used in an operational program.

***Ex situ* Conservation**   There are many ways to save desired genes or gene complexes that either contain genetic material that is the same as natural populations or for specific uses. The most common of these is through reproduction by the conventional vegetative propagation techniques of grafting, rooting cuttings, or air layering (Longman, 1976). Foresters have a special opportunity, in that given genotypes (or gene complexes) can essentially be conserved "forever" through vegetative means. Rather than savings hundreds or thousands of acres of trees, a few vegetative propagules of the desired trees can be established, maintained, and crossed when and as desired. Although the objective is gene conservation for special uses, seed orchards effectively maintain and increase the frequency of desired genetic characteristics (Zobel, 1971).

As breeding programs develop, it becomes possible to incorporate many genetic qualities into a few individuals through control pollinations. Saving of the gene base can thus be accomplished through selection and breeding of a limited number of individuals, and new combinations can be obtained by crossing among them. This method of packaging, saving by propagation, and outcrossing of genes and gene complexes is actually what is accomplished by clone banks in applied tree improvement programs. As pressures for forestland use and contamination of natural stands of trees become more widespread, the packaging method will undoubtedly become more important as a method of gene conservation.

Many other *ex situ* methods are available. For example, seed storage methods are very good for some species, and preservation of genotypes, genes, and gene complexes can be done in this way. Ultimately, the seed will lose viability and will need to be replaced. Seed of some species can be kept under proper storage conditions for very many years, but for other species that have transient viability, gene conservation by seed will not work. One danger with seed storage is that mutations may occur in the stored seed so that trees grown from the stored seed will have a genetic component that is a little different from the original population. Similarly, pollen can be stored for a long period of time. But pollen represents only half the desired material, and suitable females need to be available upon which the pollen of the conserved genes can be used.

Some of the more recent methodologies, such as tissue culture, have great potential for *ex situ* gene conservation. As this method becomes more operational, it will be possible to "store" the genetic potential of large numbers of genotypes in a very small area. This is a hope for the future.

Because of the difficulties and costs of *in situ* gene conservation, it is likely that *ex situ* methods, especially those related to packaging the desired genes, preserving by vegetative propagation, or seed and pollen storage followed by multiplying by crossing, will be the most widely used methods of gene conservation in forest trees in the future.

CONSERVATION OF PROVENANCES WITHIN A SPECIES

Too often, discussions about gene conservation leave the impression that the only need is to conserve genes within a single gene pool. However, most important forest tree species have one to several geographic races or provenances that possess rather large and important genetic characteristics that are unique to each. Therefore, the first major job of gene complex conservation for the plant breeder is to save the unique characteristics of geographic races (Zobel et al., 1976). Differences among provenances are primarily caused by a few major, differing gene complexes that give the source a unique advantage for growth and survival in a special environment. Other gene complexes may be common to most or all races within the species.

An important decision relative to gene conservation is immediately faced for species with a wide distribution—does one conserve the characteristics of the outlier provenances, each of which has undergone natural selection in extreme and different environments, or should there be a concentration on populations within the center of the species range? The latter contain a broad group of gene complexes that can be used widely throughout most of the species range but that are not especially adapted for the environmentally extreme fringe areas. Usually, some adaptability to the fringe areas is found in individuals from the center of the species range, but such trees usually occur in low frequencies. It would be ideal to conserve key complexes of all provenances, including the fringe ones, but this is not feasible with species that have a wide geographic distribution and many geographic sources, unless there is well-coordinated and outstanding cooperation among a number of organizations.

Although geographic differences have been widely studied in some species, there often is a considerable lack of knowledge about the gene complex differences that exist among provenances within a species. It is important to recognize that the best sources of genetic material for a breeding program, emphasizing characteristics related to adaptability, come from existing gene complexes that are relatively common to entire populations or provenances, rather than from occasional individuals within a population that may have a desired genetic structure. Conserving gene complexes for adaptability by saving poulations requires a different approach than that for conserving characteristics that are unique to individuals within a population.

A decision to conserve the gene complexes of different provenances raises some interesting questions. Should the trees within the provenance that are to be conserved be obtained randomly, or should they be selected to save only the phenotypes that have the most desirable growth and form for a breeding program? The fact is that there is little indication or reason to believe that the best-formed trees within a provenance will not have the same adaptability as others that typify the provenance. This is true because the lack of genetic correlation between adaptability and morphological chracteristics appears to be the rule rather than the exception. A too common misconception is that because a tree is a scrawny, poorly formed individual, it will magically carry alleles for pest resistance or other types of adaptabilities that are not carried by better-formed, faster-growing trees. Intensive studies have shown few close genetic relationships between adaptability and tree form in forest trees. There are, of course, notable exceptions to this statement, such as prostrate tree form in areas of continuous wind, or foliage characteristics that enable a tree to withstand drought stress better.

The number of trees required to minimize losses of alleles has been debated, and methodology has been developed. Although the mathematics involved is beyond the scope of this book, it has been developed in the article by Namkoong et al. (1980). They propose that a sample of 50 individuals would provide security against gene loses and would preserve genetic variances. They also state that losses and potentials for future breeding would be greatly reduced in populations in which 20 or fewer individuals are used.

From a tree-breeding standpoint, it becomes clear that if funds and land resources are limiting (as they usually are), only trees with the most desirable phenotypes should be used as sources of seed when collecting for conservation of gene complexes among geographic races. If possible, several hundred trees (200 to 400) should be used as the basic number for the collection base, and individuals that are to be conserved should preferably be from separate areas to avoid relatedness. If so many races exist that 200 to 400 trees cannot be represented from each, then fewer individuals should be saved from the races of lesser value or importance. This method will preserve the most outstanding gene complexes that make different provenances of special value.

The initial reaction to conservation of the adaptive characteristics of different geographic races is that it is an impossible job. But the stakes are high, and the need to save and utilize the material in breeding programs is great. It is difficult to set an upper limit on the number of geographic races and trees within races that should be saved, because tree breeding will always be working on the lower limit of the ideal.

CONSERVATION OF CHARACTERISTICS OF INDIVIDUAL TREES

To many people, gene conservation encompasses the preservation of as many indivdiual genotypes as possible. A quesion that is often raised is whether to save trees with currently undesired economic characteristics, such as those with crooked boles, pest infection, slow growth, or undesired wood. It would appear logical to assume that trees with currently unwanted characteristics will not carry any greater potential for combating future pest or other adaptability problems that might arise than will those trees possessing good form and growth.

However, there can be a danger in rejecting all trees having inferior characteristics. The definition of what constitutes desirable or undesirable characteristics is determined by current usage and economic standards. Market requirements change, and what is the *despised* today can become the *wanted* of tomorrow. A good example of such a reversal was the acceptance of knotty-pine lumber. For many years, boards with multiple knots had low value, but then the market desires changed, and knotty pine came into considerable demand as a specialty finish in houses. Another real-life example of this reversal has occurred for wood specific gravity of pines for use in paper manufacture. When the tree improvement program in the southern United States began 30 years ago, the major paper products from southern pines were kraft bags and corrugated boxes, and all emphasis was on trees with high-specific-gravity wood that gave good yields and made paper with good tear strength. The seed orchards established usually contained only high-specific-gravity-wood parents. Fortunately, the select trees meeting all grading criteria but which had lower wood specific gravities (amounting to 40 to 60% of the trees graded) were not destroyed but were preserved (as gene complexes) in clone banks. When tissue, newsprint, and quality printing papers suddenly became of major importance from southern pine wood, it was possible to develop a seed supply immediately, using parents that would produce progeny with low-gravity wood that was highly desired for these end products.

It is essential to look into the future as much as possible and to be careful not to make a judgment about what should be preserved that is based solely on the currently high economic worth. It might even be justifiably argued that the currently increasing pressures toward urban and amenity forests would dictate saving deformed and slow-growing phenotypes for their ornamental or protective value.

Obviously, then, a concern of any plant breeder involved in a long-term improvement program is the fate of genes that are currently neutral, or are of no economic consequence, but that may become important in the future. A prime example would be genes that confer resistance to an insect or pathogen that is unknown or that currently poses no threat but that could become a major pest in later generations. A prime example of a new pest is the pine woolly aphid (*Pineus pini*), which was introduced into Rhodesia (Zimbabwe) in 1962 and spread rapidly, attacking nearly all the hard pines. Great variation among individual trees in resistance to this pest was found (Barnes et al., 1976). Trees under stress were the most susceptible. The authors stated that "these provenance trials illustrate the principle of adaptation to plantation and local climatic conditions as insurance against possible catastrophe when a new injurious organism is introduced."

These "neutral" genes are usually not selected against in breeding efforts, but they can become lost in the improved population due to chance occurrences of genetic drift resulting from small population size. Obviously, miaintenance of a large breeding population will increase the chance that so-called neutral genes will be present when needed. An alternative strategy, which uses genetic drift to *increase* the frequency of neutral genes, is the multiple small-population concept of van Buijtenen and Lowe (1979), Burley and Namkoong (1980), and other researchers. When a large breeding population of several hundred genotypes is divided into numerous smaller groups, perhaps of 20 genotypes or less, the effects of genetic drift will be different for each group. In some groups, neutral alleles will be totally lost by chance, because of the small population size. In other groups, however, drift may operate to increase the frequency of the neutral allele, so that if it ever does become of economic importance, plant material may be immediately available that contains that allele in high frequencies.

In a tree breeding program, *a decision has to be made* about what is, or may be, the most important genotype to conserve. Every genotype cannot be saved. Trees selected should be those having characteristics known or foreseen to be of major importance in a breeding program (Figure 15.4). Each group of trees conserved will represent a small population sample containing desired or potentially desirable gene complexes that, when combined with other groups, will ensure conserving the bulk of the gene complexes that are essential to an ongoing tree improvement program.

THE SPECIAL SITUATION FOR TROPICAL REGIONS

Although gene conservation is vital to all tree improvement programs, it is especially critical when exotic forestry is being practiced (Brazier et al., 1976; Brune and Melchior, 1976; Kemp et al., 1976). Both variation among prove-

FIGURE 15.4

When possible, trees with the best qualities for a breeding program should be saved, such as this beautiful *Pinus tecunumanii* from Guatemala. This species is under great stress and is rapidly disappearing. To conserve this species is a major goal of the CAMCORE Cooperative. (Photo courtesy W. Mittak, Germany.)

nances and conservation of genetic variability within provenances are involved; this must all be combined with the land race concept (Brune and Zobel, 1981). Recognition of the importance of maintaining a proper genetic base and preserving the best for a given environment in exotic plantations has been delayed too long, although there has been a recent upsurge of interest, especially in tropical species. Roche (1979) states that the most pressing conservation problems are in the humid tropics. He makes a plea to expand conservation efforts also to those species that are of value for usage other than for standard forest products of boards or fiber. For example, the book by Burley and Styles (1976) is devoted to various aspects of gene conservation and breeding of tropical forest trees.

In some ways, the most pressing need in the tropics is for gene conservation in the indigenous forests (Myers, 1976; Roche, 1979). This was emphasized by King (1979) who reported that 65% of the land in the tropical areas of the world supports fragile ecosystems; people who live in these regions total 630 million, or 35% of the total population of the developing countries. The need for food and fuel has led to land utilization practices that in turn cause degradation of the fragile ecosystems with a resultant depletion of gene pools. The situation is aggravated because many of the species in the tropical forests are very sensitive to ecological changes. Further, only a limited amount of work has been done on some species; their biology, reproduction, and silvicultural care are poorly understood. Add to this the large numbers of species per hectare in some tropical hardwood forests, and one sees that the job of gene conservation becomes most formidable. A number of authors, such as Wood (1976), feel that one of the best ways to preserve the tropical forests is to remove pressures for their use by growing the (usually) much more productive and uniform exotic forest trees on suitable areas and leaving the rest of the tropical forestlands without intense pressures to manage them. Wood called such plantations of exotics *compensatory plantations.*

Thus, the tropical areas need strong conservation measures to assure that the species used as exotics are not impoverished (Davidson, 1977) or that the indigenous species are not lost or seriously reduced genetically by changing land use patterns. The problems are awesome but must be attacked—and soon—if the biological structures of tropical forest species are to be preserved and if forestry in the tropics is to remain productive.

Concern about gene conservation is evident for species growing in both tropical and temperate regions. Publications dealing with gene conservation date back many years, such as the one by Kanehira (1918) who stressed the need for forest conservation in Taiwan. The Committee on Exploration, Utilization and Conservation of Plant Gene Resources of the Food and Agricultural Organization of the United Nations (FAO) has been active for many years. FAO publishes a newsletter and annual report entitled *Plant Genetic Resources* that contain some excellent information related to gene conservation. Of paticular value are the forestry occasional papers entitled *Forest Genetic Resources,* which are published by FAO and which carry excellent summaries of work in progress related to forest gene pool conservation.

THE POLITICS OF CONSERVATION

As population pressures grow and as the standard of living increases, forest utilization will become greater, and with it comes the potential of increased genetic loss. Gene conservation is one of the most pressing aspects of forestry, one that demands action.

Because of the nature of the problem, which often crosses national boundaries, the long-term payout, and the obvious social implications, gene conservation must necessarily be strongly and governmentally financed and directed. Although gene loss may be of specific importance to a local area, it usually has widespread implications. It is frequently international in scope, thus making the problem difficult to attack. To add to the difficulty, the areas most needing conservation activities often are in the developing countries that have neither the resources nor the leadership to undertake the preservation effort. Frequently, although the loss will occur in one country, the major use of the forest species is in other countries; examples are the pines of Central America that are used in many of the plantation programs in South America. Therefore, international organizations are the primary candidates to take the leadership. This is now being done; organizations such as FAO of the United Nations are playing a major role in the conservation effort. Other organizations, like the Commonwealth Forestry Institute in Oxford, England[2] and the Queensland Forest Service in Austrtalia, are sponsored by one nation, but they work on an international basis; they are spearheading and organizing conservation efforts. These organizations are very active and have been most successful, especially in relation to the exotic species planted in the tropical areas. But much more is needed, particularly for the tropical hardwoods. No one really knows how severe the genetic loss is in tropical forests that often contain economically specialized and relatively unknown species. It is feared that loss of genes may be great, especially when selective logging of a few species is practiced.

All tree improvers must place gene conservation high on their list of needs and activities. Private organizations must become more involved. A good example is the CAMCORE Cooperative (Central America and Mexico Coniferous Resources Cooperative) that combines private companies and governments of a number of nations in a joint conservation effort (Gallegos et al., 1980; Dvorak, 1981). If tree breeders do not do their part to conserve and broaden the gene base in forest trees, continued long-term gains in tree improvement will not be possible.

LITERATURE CITED

Barnes, R. D., Jarvis, R. F., Schweppenhauser, M. A., and Mullin, L. J. 1976. Introduction, spread and control of the pine wooly aphid *Pineus pini* in Rhodesia. *S. Afr. For. Jour. No. 96:1–11.*

Brazier, J. D., Hughes, J. F., and Tabb, C. B. 1976. Exploitation of natural tropical resources and the need for genetic and ecological conservation. *Tropical Trees,* No. 2:1–10.

Brune, A., and Melchior, G. H. 1976. Ecological and genetical factors affecting exploitation and conservation of forests in Brazil and Venezuela. *Tropical Trees,* No. 2:203–215.

---

[2]The CFI is sponsored by a consortium of 20 Commonwealth companies in addition to FAO. It is an international organization and has supplied genetic material to over 50 countries in the tropics.

Brune, A., and Zobel, B. J. 1981. Genetic base populations, gene pools and breeding populations for *Eucalyptus* in Brazil. *Sil. Gen.* **30**(4–5):146–191.

Burley, J. 1976. Genetic systems and genetic conservation of tropical pines. *Tropical Trees*, No. 2:85–100.

Burley, J., and Styles, B. T. 1976. *Tropical Trees—Variation, Breeding and Conservation.* Academic Press, London.

Burley, J., and Namkoong, G. 1980. "Conservation of Forest Genetic Resources." 11th Commonwealth For. Conf., Trinidad.

Davidson, J. 1977. "Exploration, Collection, Evaluation, Conservation and Utilization of the Gene Resources of Tropical *Eucalyptus deglupta.*" 3rd World Consul. For. Tree Breed., Canberra, Australia, pp. 75–102.

Dvorak, W. S. 1981. CAMCORE is the industry's answer to coniferous preservation in Central America and Mexico. *For. Prod. Jour.* **31**(11):10–11.

Gallegos, C. M., Zobel, B. J., and Dvorak, W. S. 1980. "The Combined Industry–University–Government Efforts to Form the Central America and Mexico Coniferous Resources Cooperative." Symp. on Fast Growth Plantations, São Pedro, São Paulo, Brazil.

Kanehira, R. 1918. The necessity of natural forest conservation. *Jour. Nat. Hist. Soc. Taiwan* **8**(36):56–66.

Keiding, H. 1977. "Exploration, Collection and Investigation of Gene Resources: Tropical Pines and Teak." 3rd World Consul. For. Tree Breed., Canberra, Australia, pp. 13–31.

Kemp, R. H., Roche, L., and Willan, R. L. 1976. Current activities and problems in the exploration and conservation of tropical forest gene resources. *Tropical Trees*, No. 2: 223–233.

King, K. F. 1979. Agroforestry and utilization of fragile ecosystems. *For. Ecol. Mgt.* **2**(3):161–168.

Kleinschmitt, J. 1979. Limitations for restriction of genetic variation. *Sil. Gen.* **28**(2–3):61–67.

Longman, K. A. 1976. Conservation and multiplication of gene resources by vegetative multiplication of tropical trees. *Tropical Trees*, No. 2:19–24.

Myers, N. 1976. An expanded approach to the problem of disappearing species. *Science* **193**:198–202.

Namkoong, G., Barnes, R. D., and Burley, J. 1980. "A Philosophy of Breeding Strategy for Tropical Forest Trees," Tropical Forestry Papers No. 16, Commonwealth For. Inst., Oxford, England.

Popovich, L. 1980. Monoculture—A bugaboo revisited. *Jour. For.* **78**(8):487–489.

Roche, L. 1979. Forestry and conservation of plants and animals in the tropics. *For. Ecol. Mgt.* **2**(2):103–122.

Turnbull, J. W. 1977. "Exploration and Conservation of Eucalypt Gene Resources." 3rd World Cons. For. Tree Breed., Canberra, Australia, Vol. 1, pp. 33–44.

van Buijtenen, J. P., and Lowe, W. J. 1979. "The Use of Breeding Groups in Advanced-Generation Breeding." 15th South. For. Tree Impr. Conf., Starkville, Miss., pp. 59–66.

Wood, P. J. 1976. The development of tropical plantations and the need for seed and genetic conservation. *Tropical Trees,* No. 2:11–18.

Zobel, B. J. 1967. Mexican Pines. In *Genetic Resources in Plants—Their Exploration and Conservation* (O. H. Frankel and E. Bennett, eds.), FAO Tech. Conference on Exploration, Utilization and Conservation of Plant Gene Resources, Section 6(IX), pp. 367–373, FAO, Rome.

Zobel, B. J. 1971. "Gene Preservation by Means of a Tree Improvement Program." Proc. 13th Mgt. Comm. on For. Tree Breed. in Canada, Prince George, British Columbia, pp. 13–17.

Zobel, B. J. 1978. Gene conservation—As viewed by a forest tree breeder. *For. Ecol. Mangt.* **1**:339–344.

Zobel, B. J., and Davey, C. B. 1977. A conservation miracle. *Alabama For. Prod.* **20**(5):5–6.

Zobel, D. B., McKee, A., Hoek, G. M., and Dryness, C. T. 1976. Relationship of environment to composition, structure and diversity of forest communities of the central-western Cascades of Oregon. *Ecol. Mono.* **46**:135–156.

CHAPTER 16

Developing Tree Improvement Programs

STARTING A TREE IMPROVEMENT PROGRAM

METHODS TO BE USED

IMPORTANT GENERAL CONCEPTS

THE COOPERATIVE APPROACH

THE COMMITMENT

LITERATURE CITED

Forestry is playing an ever more important role in the world's society and economy. Forests have become widely recognized as a most valuable renewable natural resource. The heavy emphasis in past years on development of food production in preference to fiber is changing somewhat, although food production still has priority (Zobel, 1978a; Brown, 1980).

Forests must be managed for all types of products, including recreation and conservation, and the contributions to society from forests are rapidly changing. There is an urgent need to make forestland fully productive (Armson, 1980). This need is indicated by the predicted timber shortfall by A.D. 2000 and the accelerated reduction of forestland productivity by fuelwood cutting, farming, use of forestlands for other purposes, and the poor harvesting and regeneration programs that are still being used in a number of areas (Keays, 1975; Zobel, 1980). The increasing need for greater forest production can only be met if more intensive forest management is practiced. Per capita use of forest products is one of the best barometers to gauge societal development. Many developing countries are arriving at an explosive stage of utilization because of the increasing needs for forest products.

More intensive forest management requires the application of tree improvement. Use of wood for fuel and for energy generation and for the production of organic chemicals is revolutionizing forestry operations (Goldstein, 1980; Parde, 1980; Lin, 1981). Trees with different kinds of wood and growth patterns are needed to produce the desired biomass; genetic manipulation can be used as a primary method to achieve this. For example, *Eucalyptus* trees that are to be used for charcoal production should have high-specific-gravity wood, and should grow so that they can be harvested on short rotations.

It is becoming widely recognized that it costs little more to plant improved rather than ordinary trees and that any successful forestry operation will become better by the inclusion of a tree improvement program. But good programs do not just happen; they need much planning and an investment in time and money. Time is critical because trees are long-lived organisms, and it takes time to change quality or to increase production (Zobel, 1978b).

The returns that will be obtained from tree improvement relate to the ultimate use that is made from the information obtained and whether the program has been sufficiently founded to enable continued long-term progress. Research or information about forest management is of limited value unless it is put to use in operational forestry programs. It is now generally accepted in forestry that planting requires better trees and that the only way to obtain optimal gains is to combine good silviculture with improved planting stock. Thus, the stage is set to take full advantage of tree improvement. If maximum benefits are to be obtained from tree improvement, careful planning is needed to assure the greatest efficiency, both in the short and long terms. This chapter is a summary of how to use some of the most important information discussed in the preceding chapters to establish new programs.

STARTING A TREE IMPROVEMENT PROGRAM

In Chapter 1, a greatly simplified way of viewing tree improvement was outlined, which consisted of determining variation patterns, assessing the intensity and cause of variation, packaging the variation into desirable trees, and mass-producing the improved individuals. This can only be accomplished if the species is well known to the researcher and if one has an in-depth knowledge of the species. Within this broad approach there are numerous specific decisions and actions that must be taken.

The basic requirement for starting a tree improvement program is to determine whether or not one is really needed. When programs are initiated with only vague ideas and poorly defined objectives, they are doomed to mediocrity or failure. Planning requires projection into the future as well as an estimation of current needs. In addition to the biological factors, assessments of the need for a potential tree improvement program require estimates of future markets, economic climates, utilization practices, and political conditions.

The following basic principles must be incorporated if a tree improvement program is to be successful.

1. *What is the objective*? The products needed and the urgency to produce them must be determined. Will solid-wood products be a major part of the forest production or are fiber products the primary end goal? Will forest uses such as energy or chemicals from wood be of primary concern? Answers to these questions will determine the species or seed sources as well as the emphasis and methodology best suited for the program. The most serious error made in starting a tree improvement program is to organize and to become committed to specific goals before the objectives of the program have been determined.

2. *What basic biological facts are needed*? The biology of certain species is so poorly known that intensive studies are required before a program can proceed (Figure 16.1). Such simple things as how to collect and store seed and pollen, how to grow seedlings in the nursery, and how to outplant the trees and care for the plantations must sometimes be determined. This need is especially critical for the lesser known tropical species. Foresters in the tropics often choose to work with pines and eucalypts because they know the silviculture of those species, whereas such information is often lacking for the indigenous species. Very large programs have proven to be unsuccessful because the basic information about how to grow seedlings in the nursery or how best to establish and care for plantations was not known; therefore, all the potential advantages from a tree improvement program could not be realized. When an applied tree improvement program is developed *it must be accompanied by parallel efforts to solve forest management needs.*

FIGURE 16.1

Before a tree improvement program can be successful, many basic biological facts must be known. Although well understood at present, in the past the biology of the developmental stages of pine reproductive structures had to be worked out; an early stage of conelet development is shown. Such information is missing for many tropical hardwood species.

3.   *What species, or seed sources within species, should be used?* Choosing the correct species and seed sources is essential for the success of a tree improvement program. This important step is often given inadequate consideration because of the time required to make meaningful tests. Pressures sometimes dictate using results of studies from trees assessed at very young ages, and sometimes decisions on species or seed source are based upon such relatively unimportant items as cost of seed. When working with indigenous species, the initial decision should be to use the local material unless (or until) later tests show that something else is better. The problem of determining the proper species or sources is more complex when exotics, rather than indigenous species, are used. Although the steps that should be taken in deciding which exotic species or seed sources should be used were described earlier, they are summarized here.

Evaluate any existing plantations in the area for tree growth, form, and wood quality. Because of the potential change of wood quality when trees are grown in differing environments (see Chapters 3 and 12), it is especially essential to determine wood quality in the specific environment where the exotic will be planted. If there are suitable stands of exotics, and if the trees are producing seed, collections from the best trees can be used as immediate seed sources for planting. If plantations are extensive, with a broad enough genetic base, selections of the most outstanding trees can be made and a land race developed as a future source of seed.

When there is no indication about which species or source to use, rely on the judgment of people with extensive experience and consult the available literature. The importance of this preliminary step cannot be overemphasized. Species or source decisions are made too often upon a whim or upon the advice of someone with limited experience. The fate of whole programs and millions of dollars depends on such "nondecisions." When political or economic pressures require immediate planting, the best known source can be used with the understanding that land race development and further source testing will be started as soon as it is feasible to possibly replace the initial source that was used.

Regardless of whether the situation exists as described in the two preceding paragraphs, tests of the potentially best species and sources need to be started immediately. These tests should be carefully chosen; a common error is to waste energy and resources on material that has little or no potential for the environments under consideration. Once indications of good species and sources are evident, they should be planted on a scale that is large enough to allow for selections that will ultimately be used for the development of land races.

Tests should be made of sources that have proven their worth in other regions. Often, improved stock has already been developed in exotic environments and is usually available for most of the species that are used widely as exotics. If tests show that these are well adapted to the new environment, good gains may be quickly achieved by obtaining plant material from the original improved plantations for local use. It is important not to use improved stock from other regions on a large scale until the utility of the improved material in the new environment has been well determined.

4. *Always have at least one secondary species or source along with the primary one.* The secondary species or sources should be sufficiently tested so they can be used in the event that something unforeseen happens to the primary species and source. At least some commercial plantings should be made with secondary species or sources to provide the necessary experience about how to grow them and the opportunity to develop the needed land races if catastrophe should strike the primary species.

5. *Establish the necessary seed production capacity* (or facilities for vegetative propagation) in seed orchards or clonal "nurseries." Selecting and breeding the genetically improved material is only a first step; it must be possible to produce the improved trees in mass quantities at a reasonable cost.

6. *Do the testing necessary for the determination of the genetic worth of the selected trees and to form a base for long-term, advanced-generation improvement.* Tests should be made in an area and under conditions that are typical of

those used for commercial planting; there should be progeny tests to determine the value of the parents and genetic tests to develop populations that can be used for advanced-generation breeding. Accomplishing both objectives simultaneously is possible only with considerable planning.

7. *The tree improvement program must have both an operational (applied) and developmental (research) function.* For a successful tree improvement program, the operational phases must be associated with the equally important developmental phases (see Chapter 1), so that long-term as well as short-term objectives are required if a program is to be successful (Figure 16.2). It is easy to become so involved in the day-to-day chores of conducting an operational tree improvement program that new ideas are not pursued or that a reassessment is not made of the current operational program. New possibilities and technologies need to be explored.

8. *Make certain there is sufficient commitment to support and finance the project over the long term, with capable people to carry on the program so that its*

FIGURE 16.2

Testing newly developed strains of trees takes much time and effort. Shown is a 6-year-old test planting of especially wet-site-tolerant loblolly pine. These trees grew well on a site on which standard loblolly pine is ill adapted.

objectives can be fulfilled. Too often, programs are initiated, get started well, and then lose support because of a lack of knowledge about how much it costs to maintain a proper program over many years. The assurance of proper and adequate support is especially critical in the developing nations where the economic situation may change rapidly, or governmental agencies may alter their goals following changes in governmental leadership.

9. *Combine breeding for improved economic characteristics with breeding for a broad genetic base for adaptability and to develop* trees suitable for new products (Figure 16.3). Because most economically important traits are usually genetically independent, it is possible to develop them simultaneously. One of the greatest needs in forestry is to have trees that will grow on marginal sites. The genetic base that is necessary to develop trees for shorter rotations and wood for nonconventional products such as energy or chemicals must also be maintained.

FIGURE 16.3

Broadening the genetic base is a necessary part of a tree improvement program. One way to do this is to make wide crosses within a species. Shown are 3-year-old tests of wide crosses of loblolly pine; crosses are North Carolina × Texas and Louisiana × South Carolina.

METHODS TO BE USED

Advice is plentiful, varied, and often contradictory about the best approach is organizing new tree improvement program. Each person has knowledge about a special set of circumstances related to past experience, and he or she will tend to recommend what has worked best under those conditions. Advice is often positive and dogmatic about why a certain method is the only (or best) one to use in setting up the program. However, each species and each situation must be approached differently (Zobel, 1977; Nikles, 1979).

It is of the utmost importance to recognize that there is no single "correct" way to organize a tree improvement program. An intelligent decision requires a sorting among the options and acceptance of the methods that are the most correct for the set of circumstances involved. After the objectives have been set and available funding, facilities, and personnel are known, the following questions must be asked and other factors must be considered before the methodology of a program is set.

1. "Has it been tried before?" If it has, making a decision is simple. Existing programs should be studied and analyzed, always with the question in mind, "Will it work for us?" The tendency to copy ongoing successful programs without analyzing the parts can result in costly failures. A small tree improvement program cannot operate in the same way as a large one; therefore, methodologies must often be altered. In large programs, such as one established through a cooperative, partial results can be obtained by each member and pooled for the benefit of all. An organization with a small program has to be more self-sufficient and have a broader testing and crossing program than does each individual member of a cooperative.

2. "What are the advantages and problems of the proposed program?" Some program approaches should be automatically rejected as being too expensive or too difficult for the objectives and resources available. A program must be suitable biologically, or it will not result in optimal returns. No program is perfect, but the pros and cons must be considered before a decision is made. The decision with respect to the best program must take into consideration both the long-term and short-term criteria. Shortcut analyses of program alternatives can be dangerous and misleading. In the final analysis, the program must be viewed with respect to what is essential, and the other factors should be given a lower priority or deleted.

3. "Should a new method be used?" New and sometimes quite different ideas are constantly being proposed for development of tree improvement programs (Figure 16.4). Those that sound promising in theory must be evaluated for operational conditions. New methods sometimes are based on the concept of quick returns combined with minimal costs; they may even be a version of get-rich-quick schemes. New ideas should never be rejected until well-designed and well-executed studies have shown their true worth. How-

FIGURE 16.4

Many innovations must be tried in tree improvement; these are much more possible with a cooperative approach. Shown is the vacuum seed harvester developed through the combined efforts of members of the North Carolina State–Industry Tree Improvement Cooperative. Such development would not have been done by individual members.

ever, a full-fledged program should never be developed on theoretical or unproven methods. Always make the intended program flexible enough so that new ideas can be incorporated into it with no interruption of the ongoing work.

4. Accelerated breeding plans should be incorporated into all tree improvement programs. A quick turnover of generations is very important in obtaining genetic gain through a breeding program (Zobel, 1978b). The objective is not to see how much total gain can be obtained per generation but *how much gain can be achieved per unit* of time (Weir and Zobel, 1975). Although the total gain from the conventional and accelerated programs may be the same, obtaining the gain several years earlier results in planting improved trees that would not have been available otherwise during the interim period while a conventional program was being developed.

5. One must estimate future methodologies, such as vegetative propagation, and include the ability to incorporate new methods into the program so that advantage can be taken of advancements. In addition, the following must all

be considered: changes related to nonconventional forest products, how much uniformity will be needed, how much will quality needs change with improved technology, and how important will coppice regeneration become (Berger et al., 1974; Ceancio, 1977).

IMPORTANT GENERAL CONCEPTS

In addition to the previous lists of specific actions needed to start a tree improvement program, certain other important factors need to be considered. The first of these is the time required to complete the various steps of the program (Zobel, 1978b). How urgent is the need for use of the material developed in the tree improvement program? As discussed previously, time is of key importance in any economic assessment because profitability is tied to the length of time an investment is to be carried. Thus, if one can reduce rotation age for a desired product by a few years through tree improvement, returns on the planting investment will be greatly increased.

Underlying all decisions in determining the type of tree improvement program is whether the gain is worth the *risk*. The more intensive the selection program, the greater will be the gain; however, a greater reduction in the genetic base will result. A balance must be maintained between gain and an acceptable amount of risk. A determination of this balance takes great skill and experience and is often ignored during planning, or it is not seriously considered. Usually the financially oriented foresters want to maximize gain, whereas those with other orientations place priority on risk reduction. It is necessary that people with the two viewpoints work closely together to achieve a suitable compromise to develop a well-balanced tree improvement program.

The general understanding is that improved seed, and thus benefits from tree improvement, will not be available until after seed orchard seed are available. However, modest gains, especially in tree quality, adaptability, and pest resistance, can be obtained in the interim before the seed orchard comes into production. Seed can be collected from good individual trees in the forest, or seed production areas can be established. Such seed sources are particularly valuable in exotic forestry programs in which adaptability is such a highly important characteristic. Some genetic improvement is even possible by means of the proper manipulation of natural regeneration and through control of harvesting practices or by application of precommercial thinning.

Often, tree improvement programs are begun with the only objective being to obtain short-term gains in operational planting programs. When this is done, tree improvement is viewed as consisting only of selecting good trees, establishing them in seed orchards, and collecting the seed. This method will eventually lead to problems, due to the fact that the true genetic value of the parents is unknown because there are no progeny tests and there will be no possibility for advanced-generation breeding. Tree improvement programs are continuously developing, and constant effort is required to obtain additional increments of improvement. To achieve this best, the developmental phase should be started at about the same time as the operational phase, so that the results can be available to supplement and perhaps even replace the initial operational phase. As tree improvement becomes more sophisticated and moves into advanced generations, plant material must be available to take advantage of advanced-generation improvements. For example, a program using vegetative propagation will result in only limited gains unless an accompanying breeding program has been especially designed to produce material that can be used in the vegetative propagation program.

THE COOPERATIVE APPROACH

Tree improvement requires a large expenditure of effort and money, trained people, and suitable facilities. Because of this, it is usually not economical to undertake tree improvement on a small scale. It is an activity that is best suited for large corporations and governments to undertake, especially in situations where the forestland base is extensive enough to obtain a good payback (van Buijtenen, 1969). This restriction does not mean that smaller organizations cannot share in its benefits. The way to obtain more general application of tree improvement is to establish cooperatives. Tree improvement is well suited to a cooperative effort in which the members share costs and returns as well as exchange equipment, plant material, and information.

A cooperative effort becomes especially valuable when advanced generations are developed (Weir and Zobel, 1975). A few trained professionals with proper technical support can direct a very large program. Each member cannot afford its own specialists, but it can share them by means of a cooperative. The success and efficiency of the cooperative approach have been well proven, and many cooperatives have been started throughout the world. Most of them have been successful and have made great contributions. Much of the information and many of the ideas expressed in this book are based upon experiences with cooperatives. There are many rules and methods necessary to make a cooperative successful; these could fill a small book. A few of the more important ones have been outlined by Zobel (1981).

1. Enthusiasm is needed. The supporters must be sold on the need and value of a tree improvement program. Halfhearted support will doom a cooperative.

2. All members must make a full commitment. Nothing will ruin a cooperative quicker than having a member or members who fail to give their share fully. This includes not only financial support but also technical support and action in field operations. A minimum contribution of time and action is expected from each member. Also, every member must make a contribution that is of value to the other members.

3. Development and tests of improved materials should be on the lands of the cooperators. Contributions of money are not enough. Each member must feel that "this is my program." There must be pride in what the cooperative achieves, both for the overall membership and for each member. Without such pride, a cooperative will not be effective nor will it survive.

4. Information and ideas must be fully exchanged among members; a proprietary attitude cannot prevail. Exchanges should take place in written reports but also in meetings within the cooperative in which members can compare ideas and see what others are doing. In forest biology, it is not the obtaining of information that will give an organization an economic advantage; rather, it is the using of available knowledge that enables one organization to forge ahead of another.

5. The membership usually has common objectives for all members, although there may be specific ones for individual members. For example, developing seed orchards is a common objective, whereas developing a strain of trees that is especially adaptable to an unusual adverse environment may be of interest to only one or to a few of the members.

6. Strong leadership is needed to bring the members together and to keep them all headed in the same direction. This need cannot be overemphasized. A cooperative will fail unless it has at its head a person who is respected by the members, one they will follow to get the job done, and one who has the authority to get necessary action. Such a director needs to have rather broad decision-making powers. There should be responsibility to a group, such as an advisory committee composed of the cooperative's membership, but the director is the one who has the authority over the operation of the cooperative and who directs actions to achieve its objectives. Occasionally, cooperatives have been administered by committee, but this system often is less than successful.

7. It is always best to have the cooperative headquarters located at a neutral location or neutral site. Often, universities are selected; if the cooperative has its headquarters at one industry or in one governmental unit, jealousies soon appear among the members. The advantage of being located at a university is the backup available in the technical fields. Of special importance is the fact that graduate students can efficiently undertake phases of the necessary research.

8. Each member should have equal authority and responsibility and receive equal benefits. Cooperatives in which the larger organizations pay more and thus also have more influence frequently develop political problems. The cooperative must be large enough to justify its activities economically; this is also true for the operations of each member. It is important that each potential new member be carefully assessed to determine his or her sincere interest, commitment, and ability to make the needed contribution to the cooperative before he or she is accepted into it.

9. Both short- and long-term objectives are needed. No matter what the attitude is at the beginning of a program, there always comes a time within a few years when the question will be asked, "What are we getting for our money?" The program must be so designed that a continuous feedback of results to the program supporters is possible so that they can see the worth of the effort. Some short-term projects serve this purpose well.

10. Good communication is necessary. This is achieved by using the "language" that the program supporters understand. Highly scientific or complex reporting of results to cooperative administrators is self-defeating. One cannot teach the supporters a new "language"; the cooperative staff and associated scientists must learn the method of expression that is best understood by the administrators and present results in such a way that they are understandable to the administrators. This is particularly necessary with respect to the people who control finances.

11. The terms *basic* or *fundamental research* are often viewed unfavorably by forestry administrators. Yet, both types of studies are needed if programs are to be efficient and continue to make progress. Use of the word *supportive* research rather than *basic* research has been most successful in enabling the administrators to appreciate the need for basic studies and to accept them in the applied program.

The success of the cooperatives that are already established in several countries on several continents has been outstanding. Most applied tree improvement programs would just now be in the establishment phases if cooperatives had not been organized and functioning at the time when the need for tree improvement was recognized.

THE COMMITMENT

A tree improvement program must have continuity. It is a long-term program and costly. All too often a program is started, only to falter because the people involved are transferred within or out of the organization. This results in a program that flounders and loses its initiative. The first part to be lost is the developmental or research aspect. Once nonfunctional, it cannot be easily regained, and time will always be lost. Lack of continuity from fluctuating leadership or nonregular support caused by lack of commitment means loss of potential income to the organization involved. The authors feel so strongly about this that their advice to those considering starting a tree improvement program is EITHER CONDUCT THE PROGRAM CORRECTLY, WITH TOTAL SUPPORT IN MANPOWER, FACILITIES, AND EQUIPMENT, OR DO NOT DO IT AT ALL. Tree improvement does not come free; it is expensive. Without tree improvement, forestry can never come close to reaching the goal of optimum productivity.

LITERATURE CITED

Armson, K. A. 1980. "Productive Forest Land—The Factory Base." The Forest Imperative. Proc. Can. For. Cong., Toronto, pp. 41–42.

Berger, R., Simoes, J. W., and Leite, N. B. 1974. Method for economic evaluation of the improvement of *Eucalyptus* stands reserved for cutting. *IPEF,* No. 8:55–62.

Brown, L. R. 1980. Food or fuel: New competition for the world's cropland. *Interciencia* 5(6):365–372.

Ceancio, A. 1977. Il metodo dell' invecchiamento nella conversione der cedui di faggio [On the coppicing period and productivity of *Eucalyptus camaldulensis* and *E. globulus* stands at Prozzo Armerma]. *Ann. Ist. Sper. Selvi.* 8:17–96.

Goldstein, I. S. 1980. New technology for new uses of wood. *Tappi* 63(2):105–108.

Keays, J. L. 1975. Projection of world demand and supply for wood fiber to the year 2000. *Tappi* 58(1):90–95.

Lin, Feng-Bor. 1981. Economic desirability of using wood as a fuel for steam production. *For. Prod. Jour.* 31(1):31–36.

Nikles, D. G. 1979. "Forest Plantations: The Shape of the Future. The Means to Excellence—Through Genetics." Proc. Science Symp., Weyerhaeuser Co. Tech. Cent., Tacoma, Wash., pp. 87–118.

Parde, J. 1980. Forest biomass. *Comm. For. Bur.* 41(8):343–362.

van Buijtenen, J. P. 1969. The impact of state–industry cooperative programs on tree planting. *For. Farmer* 29(2):14, 20, 28.

Weir, R. J., and Zobel, B. J. 1975. "Managing Genetic Resources for the Future, a Plan for the N.C. State–Industry Cooperative Tree Improvement Program." Proc. 13th Sou. For. Tree Impr. Conf., Raleigh, N.C., pp. 73–82.

Zobel, B. J. 1977. Increasing southern pine timber production through tree improvement. *South. Jour. App. For.* 1(1):3–10.

Zobel, B. J. 1978a. The good life or subsistence—Some benefits of tree breeding. *Unasylva* 30(119/120):5–9.

Zobel, B. J. 1978b. "Progress in Breeding Forest Trees—The Problem of Time." Proc. 27th Annual Session, Nat. Poultry Breeders Roundtable, Kansas City, Mo., pp. 18–29.

Zobel, B. J. 1981. Imbalance in the world's conifer timber supply. *Tappi* 63(2):95–98.

Zobel, B. J. 1981. "Research Needs in Tree Breeding—To Make a Cooperative Work." Proc. 15th N. Amer. Quant. For. Gen. Group Workshop, Coeur D'Alene, Idaho, pp. 130–132.

Species Index

Scientific Name	Common Name	Reference Pages
Abies sp.	fir	199, 226, 289, 368, 400, 411, 431, 433
Abies fraseri	fraser fir	340, 465
Abies grandis	grand fir	433
Abies lasiocarpa	alpine fir	433
Acer sp.	maple	221, 406
Acer rubrum	red maple	145, 324
Acer saccharum	sugar maple	229, 297, 302, 327, 339
Aesculus sp.	buckeye	350, 368
Albizzia sp.	mimosa	281, 306
Alnus sp.	alder	56, 71
Alnus glutinosa	European black alder	72
Betula sp.	birch	56, 226, 397, 409, 450, 452, 457
Betula alleghaniensis	yellow birch	163, 229, 306, 357, 367
Betula papyrifera	paper birch	43, 301, 357, 367
Betula pendula	European white birch	368
Betula pubescens	white birch	368
Carya sp.	hickory	291, 450
Castanea dentata	chestnut	283, 302, 465
Celtis occidentalis	hackberry	224
Chamaecyparis nootkata-tensis	Alaska yellow cedar	361, 368–369
Cryptomeria japonica	Japanese cedar	207, 210, 218, 310, 325, 335, 340, 342
Cupressus leylandi	Leyland cypress	369
Cupressus lusitanica	Mexican cypress	90, 104
Cupressus macrocarpa	Monterey cypress	361, 369
Eucalyptus sp.	eucalypts	18, 43, 79, 80, 97, 100–102, 104, 106, 108, 113, 171, 181, 187–188, 203, 278, 293, 298, 302, 310, 315, 319–320, 325–328, 338–340, 346, 349, 352, 355, 357–360, 366–371, 400, 406–407, 409, 411, 447, 456, 461, 476, 480, 492

Scientific Name	Common Name	Reference Pages
Picea sp.	spruce	325, 337, 342, 346, 349, 361, 363, 369, 372, 400, 441, 455
Picea abies	Norway spruce	61, 71, 79, 97, 113–114, 162, 210, 230, 300, 304, 340, 342, 368, 370, 395, 410–412, 433, 456
Picea engelmanii	Engelman spruce	397, 409
Picea glauca	white spruce	82, 289, 452, 456–457
Picea mariana	black spruce	181, 289
Picea sitchensis	Sitka spruce	79, 97, 300, 342
Pinus armandii	armand pine	358
Pinus attenuradiata	—	364
Pinus banksiana	jack pine	55, 58, 73–74, 87, 190, 212, 261, 266, 282, 298, 302, 452
Pinus caribaea	Carib pine	58, 71–72, 79, 87, 90–92, 97, 100–101, 105, 108, 112, 115, 164, 172, 211, 214, 263, 278, 291, 320, 342, 360, 383–384, 390, 403, 412, 457, 466
Pinus clausa	sand pine	360
Pinus contorta	lodgepole pine	97–98, 114, 303, 397, 409
Pinus coulteri	Coulter pine	69, 347, 350, 356, 363, 373
Pinus densiflora	Japanese red pine	213
Pinus echinata	shortleaf pine	209, 299, 343, 355–356, 369, 371, 373
Pinus elliottii	slash pine	73–74, 101, 106, 114, 130, 139–140, 152, 163, 200, 209–211, 213–215, 227, 230, 261–263, 265–266, 272, 275, 290, 300, 302–303, 305–306, 340, 343, 356, 360, 371, 383, 391, 408, 412–413, 426, 433, 435, 445, 456
Pinus grifithii	Himalayan white pine	165
Pinus jeffreyi	Jeffrey pine	69, 112, 347, 350, 354, 356, 363, 373
Pinus kesiya	Benguet pine	209, 403
Pinus lambertiana	sugar pine	118, 140, 358, 372

Scientific Name	Common Name	Reference Pages
		209–213, 215, 227, 229, 243, 262–263, 265–267, 271–272, 274–275, 286–287, 290, 292, 298, 302–304, 306, 315, 325, 336–338, 341–343, 351, 353, 355, 358, 361, 363, 369–371, 373, 379–395, 401, 403, 408–413, 426, 428, 430, 432–434, 441, 446–447, 456–458, 484–485
Pinus tecunumanii	Tecun uman pine	473
Pinus thunbergii	Japanese black pine	290, 340
Pinus virginiana	Virginia pine	58, 115, 338, 392
Platanus sp.	sycamore	71, 101, 209, 358
Platanus occidentalis	sycamore	43, 172, 187–188, 230, 282, 292, 299, 303, 341, 406, 410
Pupulus sp.	poplar	54, 71, 73–74, 79, 97, 99, 101, 162, 164, 220, 282–283, 287, 291, 299–300, 303–305, 310, 325, 335, 355, 357–358, 370, 400, 410, 426, 430, 435, 441
Populus deltoides	Eastern cottonwood	409, 457
Populus tremuloides	trembling aspen	87, 154, 408, 435
Populus trichocarpa	black cottonwood	292, 409
Prunus serotina	black cherry	112, 327, 339, 400, 410, 450
Pseudobombax tomen-tosum	—	411
Pseudotsuga menziesii	Douglas fir	43, 71, 73, 79, 87–88, 97, 108, 130, 139, 141, 180, 190, 196, 209–211, 214, 282, 290–291, 300, 303–305, 337–338, 341, 343, 368, 401, 410, 426, 431, 434, 455
Quercus sp.	oak	325, 339, 351, 358, 367–368, 370, 372, 401
Quercus alba	white oak	230, 339

Subject Index

Adaptability (adapted, adaptation):
to adverse environments, *see*
  Resistance
to air pollution and acid rain, *see*
  Resistance
definition, 80, 270
gains from, 21, 270–271, 440, 446–447
to marginal sites, 12–14, 270, 484
to pests, *see* Resistance
selection and breeding for, 218, 270,
  463
Air layers, 319–320
Allelopathy, 293

Breeding, tree:
accelerated, 430–431, 487
advanced generation, 416–417, 419–
  422, 428, 445, 483, 489
development, 8
general, 2–3, 5–6, 445
history, 5
intuitive, 10–11
methods, general, 5, 445, 472
objectives, 20
population, 417–418
production, 416–419
for several characteristics simultaneously, 22
systems, *see* Mating (breeding systems)

Cells:
chromosomes:
  composition of, 42, 45
  definition, 42
  numbers of, 42–44
components of, 41–42
Cline:
definition, 83–85
examples, 84
general, 81
Clone:
degradation, 331–332
deployment, 328–331
general, 314, 316, 318–319, 328–329,
  331–332
number, to use, 328–329
Competition, 443

Correlations among characteristics:
genetic, 22
juvenile-mature, 23, 330, 426–427,
  440–441
Cyclophysis, 323

Ecotype:
definition, 84–85
general, 84–85
Environment:
definition, 25
limiting factors, 13–14
manipulation of, 20
Environments, adverse:
cold, 297, 447
definition, 296
gains, from breeding for, 296, 447
moisture extremes, 297
resistance to, 296–298
see also Resistance
Exotics:
definition, 80
general, 93–94, 482
gene resources, 472–475
land races, use of, *see* Land race
pests of, 99, 101, 103–104, 277–278
problems with, 83, 94, 98–101, 111,
  278
rules for movement, 107–111
soils, importance of, 95–96
use and value of, 97–99
when, where, why to use, 88, 93–97,
  483
where to obtain, 88–89, 99, 104–108
why wrong sources are used, 102–103
Experimental designs:
general, 245–246
plot-definition, 244–245
plot-designs, 245–247

Family, definition, 26
Forest genetics:
applied, 2
definition, 6
history, 2–3, 5
see also Forest tree improvement

499